THE OXFORD HANDBOOK OF CRIMINOLOGY

Fourth Edition

EDITED BY

MIKE MAGUIRE

ROD MORGAN

AND

ROBERT REINER

OXFORD
UNIVERSITY PRESS

OXFORD
UNIVERSITY PRESS

Great Clarendon Street, Oxford OX2 6DP

Oxford University Press is a department of the University of Oxford.
It furthers the University's objective of excellence in research, scholarship,
and education by publishing worldwide in

Oxford New York

Auckland Cape Town Dar es Salaam Hong Kong Karachi
Kuala Lumpur Madrid Melbourne Mexico City Nairobi
New Delhi Shanghai Taipei Toronto

With offices in

Argentina Austria Brazil Chile Czech Republic France Greece
Guatemala Hungary Italy Japan Poland Portugal Singapore
South Korea Switzerland Thailand Turkey Ukraine Vietnam

Oxford is a registered trade mark of Oxford University Press
in the UK and in certain other countries

Published in the United States
by Oxford University Press Inc., New York

British Library Cataloguing in Publication Data

Data available

Library of Congress Cataloging in Publication Data

Data available

Typeset by Newgen Imaging Systems (P) Ltd., Chennai, India
Printed in Great Britain
on acid-free paper by
CPI Bath

ISBN 978–0–19–920543–1 (pbk)
ISBN 978–0–19–920544–8 (hbk)

10 9 8 7 6 5 4 3 2 1

THE OXFORD HANDBOOK
OF CRIMINOLOGY

OUTLINE CONTENTS

PART I   CRIMINOLOGY: HISTORY AND THEORY

PART II   THE SOCIAL CONSTRUCTION OF CRIME AND CRIME CONTROL

PART III DIMENSIONS OF CRIME

DETAILED CONTENTS

PART I CRIMINOLOGY: HISTORY AND THEORY

PART II   THE SOCIAL CONSTRUCTION OF CRIME AND CRIME CONTROL

PART III DIMENSIONS OF CRIME

PART IV   FORMS OF CRIME

PART V REACTIONS TO CRIME

NOTES ON CONTRIBUTORS

ANDREW ASHWORTH is Vinerian Professor of English Law and a member of the Centre for Criminology, University of Oxford.

ANTHONY BOTTOMS is Emeritus Wolfson Professor of Criminology at the University of Cambridge and Professorial Fellow in Criminology at the University of Sheffield.

BEN BOWLING is Professor of Criminology and Criminal Justice, School of Law, King's College London.

FIONA BROOKMAN is a Principal Lecturer in Criminology and Deputy Director of the Centre for Criminology at the University of Glamorgan.

ADAM CRAWFORD is Professor of Criminology and Criminal Justice and Director of the Centre for Criminal Justice Studies at the University of Leeds.

DAVID DOWNES is Professor Emeritus of Social Administration at the London School of Economics.

CLIVE EMSLEY is Professor of History at the Open University.

DAVID P. FARRINGTON is Professor of Psychological Criminology at the University of Cambridge.

LORAINE GELSTHORPE is Reader in Criminology and Criminal Justice in the Institute of Criminology, University of Cambridge, and a Fellow of Pembroke College, Cambridge.

KEITH HAYWARD is Senior Lecturer in Criminology and Sociology at the University of Kent.

FRANCES HEIDENSOHN is Visiting Professor, Dept of Sociology, London School of Economics and Emeritus Professor of Social Policy, University of London.

CLIVE R. HOLLIN is Professor of Criminological Psychology, School of Psychology, University of Leicester.

CAROLYN HOYLE is Reader in Criminology in the Law Faculty, University of Oxford, and a Fellow of Green College, Oxford.

BARBARA HUDSON is Professor of Law, Lancashire Law School, University of Central Lancashire.

TREVOR JONES is Senior Lecturer in Criminology and Criminal Justice at the School of Social Sciences, Cardiff University.

NICOLA LACEY is Professor of Criminal Law and Legal Theory at the London School of Economics and Adjunct Professor of Social and Political Theory, Research School of Social Sciences, Australian National University.

MICHAEL LEVI is Professor of Criminology at the School of Social Sciences, Cardiff University.

ALISON LIEBLING is a Professor of Criminology and Criminal Justice at the University of Cambridge and Director of the Cambridge Institute of Criminology's Prisons Research Centre.

IAN LOADER is Professor of Criminology and Director of the Centre for Criminology at the University of Oxford.

MIKE MAGUIRE is a Professor of Criminology, now working part-time at both Cardiff University and the University of Glamorgan.

ROD MORGAN is Chairman of the Youth Justice Board for England and Wales and Professor Emeritus at the University of Bristol.

DAVID NELKEN is Distinguished Professor of Legal Institutions and Social Change, University of Macerata, Italy, and Distinguished Research Professor of Law at the University of Wales, Cardiff, and Visiting Professor of Law at the LSE.

TIM NEWBURN is Professor of Criminology and Social Policy, and Director of the Mannheim Centre for Criminology, London School of Economics and Political Science.

JILL PEAY is a Professor of Law, in the Department of Law, London School of Economics and Political Science.

CORETTA PHILLIPS is Lecturer in the Department of Social Policy, London School of Economics and Political Science.

PETER RAYNOR is Professor of Criminology and Criminal Justice in the Department of Applied Social Sciences, University of Wales, Swansea.

ROBERT REINER is Professor of Criminology in the Law Department, London School of Economics and Political Science.

PAUL ROCK is Professor of Social Institutions in the Department of Sociology, London School of Economics, and occasional Visiting Professor at the Department of Criminology, University of Pennsylvania.

ANDREW SANDERS is Professor of Criminal Law and Criminology at the University of Manchester.

DAVID J. SMITH is Honorary Professor of Criminology at the University of Edinburgh and Visiting Professor at the London School of Economics.

NIGEL SOUTH is Professor in the Department of Sociology and Pro-Vice Chancellor (Academic and Regional Development), University of Essex.

RICHARD SPARKS is Professor of Criminology at the University of Edinburgh. He is also a co-director of the Scottish Centre for Crime and Justice Research.

JOCK YOUNG is Distinguished Professor of Sociology at the University of Kent and Distinguished Professor of Criminal Justice Graduate Center, John Jay College, City University of New York.

RICHARD YOUNG is Professor of Law and Policy Research, School of Law, University of Bristol.

LUCIA ZEDNER is Professor of Criminal Justice in the Law Faculty, University of Oxford, and a Fellow of Corpus Christi College, Oxford.

INTRODUCTION TO THE FOURTH EDITION

Mike Maguire, Rod Morgan, and Robert Reiner

This is the fourth edition of *The Oxford Handbook of Criminology*. The first edition was prepared in 1992–3 and published in 1994. The second edition, which had a much shorter gestation, was prepared in 1996 and appeared in 1997. The third was written during the summer and autumn of 2001 and published in 2002. The chapters for this fourth edition were written between late 2005 and August 2006—as usual some chapters were real cliffhangers, only produced at or just after the very last minute. We would like to thank all our contributors for producing chapters of such a high standard while meeting such a demanding schedule.

In 1994 we said that we hoped the *Handbook* would meet a research as well as a teaching need. We intended to commission state-of-the-art surveys of all the key issues in criminology, very broadly defined. The essays were intended to offer a one-stop shop to academics, practitioners, and students seeking a quick yet comprehensive and reliable analysis of each particular topic. The *Handbook* is now widely acknowledged as the leading British text in its field and we conclude that our editorial rationale, explained in the Introduction to the first edition, has been vindicated. We therefore see no need to change our basic strategy. However, for this new edition we have not only ensured that all material has been thoroughly updated, but also added some new chapters and made substantial changes in the coverage of others. This has entailed some changes in authorship (including bringing in some 'new blood'), but the great majority of the current contributors have been with us from the beginning. Sadly, one change of authorship was forced upon us by the untimely death of Ian Taylor before he could complete his chapter on Political Economy for the third edition, which did not have a chapter on this topic. (For this fourth edition Robert Reiner has written a new chapter on Political Economy.) We greatly miss Ian, and we remain very grateful for the high-quality contributions he made to the first two editions.

We came to this venture in the early 1990s as three long-serving members of British universities with a wide variety of teaching and research experience in the broad area of criminology and criminal justice. The initial stimulus came from our strong feeling that there was no single comprehensive textbook covering sufficient ground in enough depth to build a general criminology course around it. There were (and are still) many excellent texts on most *specific* areas of crime and criminal justice, such as the criminal justice process, the penal system, policing, victims, gender, and race. There were also a number of well-established and stimulating texts on the theoretical development of criminology. However, reading lists for courses intending to cover theoretical and substantive issues had to use a variety of different references (books and articles) for each topic. Reading lists had become dauntingly elephantine, and increasingly unfriendly to students with limited resources in time and money. This is the gap we originally set out to fill, and do so again with the fourth edition. The *Handbook* aims to provide students with authoritative overviews of the major issues that most criminology courses cover, whether taught in schools of law or social science, to undergraduates, postgraduates, or practitioners.

As described at some length in the Introductions to the previous editions, criminology is a field that has experienced a huge and continuing expansion, as well as a major 'fragmentation' (Ericson and Carriere 1994) in terms of substantive areas of specialization and epistemological, methodological, and political orientations. It is no longer possible, as once it was, for individuals to keep abreast of all this activity and output. Scores of research monographs and general texts of a criminological nature are published each year. At least a dozen British publishing houses carry a substantial list of criminology titles, and many university centres have in-house monograph series. The *British Journal of Criminology* and the *Howard Journal* now compete with several other British-based academic journals in more specialized areas of criminology—*Theoretical Criminology, Punishment and Society* and *Criminology and Criminal Justice* are among those that have recently joined the pack—and with journals on substantive areas like policing, victimology, and aspects of penal policy. In addition, most of the general social science and law journals regularly publish articles of a criminological character.

We set out to assemble a collection of state-of-the-art reviews by leading academics covering, as nearly as possible, the full range of issues addressed by criminology, and representing the diverse array of viewpoints in criminological discourse. To make this already highly ambitious task more manageable, we have since the beginning maintained a fairly strong focus on issues and material of particular interest to British criminologists and their students, but this does not by any means exclude reference to major international developments and literature. For this fourth edition, we commissioned thirty-five British scholars to provide reviews of thirty-two major topics, most as single but some as joint authors. We asked them to refer to relevant theory and recent research, to point to policy developments, and to highlight those aspects of current debate of which students, teachers, and practitioners should be aware. We also asked them to provide a short guide to further reading and include comprehensive bibliographies so that students can follow up topics in greater detail. All the feedback we have received on the previous editions suggests that these bibliographical resources are a valuable feature of the *Handbook* for students and teachers alike.

We have for each edition selected contributors recognized for their research and scholarship, usually, though not always, in the topic areas about which we asked them to write. However, we have never stipulated the theoretical approach they should adopt, and have deliberately approached scholars representing different perspectives. The *Handbook* remains unashamedly a collection of different voices.

The result will not please everyone. We recognize that our commitment to non-dogmatic inclusiveness carries with it the pitfall that a way of seeing is also always a way of not seeing (Burke 1989). Editorial inclusion, however wide-ranging and non-partisan, always entails exclusion, and our claims to be non-dogmatic are to some extent necessarily disingenuous. A few of the chapters in this collection are contributed by fairly obvious authors who could not easily be replaced. But most topics could have been covered by equally worthy others. Our choice of collaborators has inevitably been shaped by our circles of acquaintanceship, our disciplinary origins and affiliations, and our theoretical orientations.

CHANGES TO THE FOURTH EDITION

As in the past, we have tried to ensure that all the principal topics ordinarily included in criminology and criminology-related courses are covered. Clearly, criminology is a rapidly changing field, which responds to new ideas in other academic fields as well as to developments in crime policy and politics. Since the last edition, there have been some important shifts in direction, and the changes we have made to the structure of the book reflect these to some extent.

In addition to updating—itself a major exercise—the principal changes in this fourth edition are intended to rectify gaps and weaknesses evident to us from our own discussions and the feedback provided by colleagues and collected by Oxford University Press. We think that the coverage of substantive topics achieved in the first three editions was broadly adequate, and the enhanced discussion of contemporary theoretical developments achieved in the second and third editions a great improvement compared to the first. We have sought further to strengthen the place of contemporary theory in the collection, by including new pieces on the important areas of cultural criminology, the governance of security, and diversity, crime, and criminal justice. In shuffling the structure of the book and the topic coverage of individual chapters, we have had to make some difficult decisions about authorship. On the one hand, we are very pleased to welcome five new contributors, who will not only bring fresh ideas and approaches, but between them bring down the average age of the *Handbook* authors: Adam Crawford, Keith Hayward, Trevor Jones, Carolyn Hoyle, Fiona Brookman, and Alison Liebling. We were very sorry not to be able to include David Garland this time, whose chapter on the development of criminology in Britain was a jewel of all three earlier editions. Because of other commitments David was unable to update the chapter for this edition, but we hope we will be able to include him again next time. His important chapter will still be available electronically on the website to the *Handbook*, as it appeared in the third edition. So also will some extracts from previous versions of chapters that are again included, extracts providing detail to which we think some readers will wish to refer, but which, for want of space needed for updating, we had no room in the fourth edition. Crime and criminal justice are such rapidly changing fields now that we are painfully aware of how our chapters become out of date as soon as they have been completed. No doubt this will be the stimulus for further, future editions. We hope we have provided as comprehensive and up-to-date a guide for students, teachers, researchers, and practitioners as it is possible to do.

■ REFERENCES

BURKE, K. (1989), *On Symbols and Society*, Chicago, Ill.: Chicago University Press.

ERICSON, R., and CARRIERE, K. (1994), 'The Fragmentation of Criminology', in D. Nelken (ed.), *The Futures of Criminology*, 89–109, London: Sage.

GUIDED TOUR OF THE ONLINE RESOURCE CENTRE

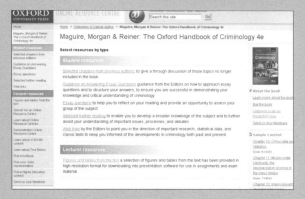

www.oxfordtextbooks.co.uk/orc/maguire4e/

The Online Resource Centre that accompanies this book provides students and lecturers with ready-to-use teaching and learning materials. These resources are free of charge and are designed to maximize the learning experience.

STUDENT RESOURCES

SELECTED CHAPTERS FROM PREVIOUS EDITIONS

In-depth material on topics, including the development of criminology as a discipline, and key issues such as punishment and control, and crime reduction, have been taken from the previous two editions of this text and provided in electronic format for those interested in a more thorough discussion of these topics.

This resource is password protected. The login details to enter this part of the Online Resource Centre are:

Username: maguire4e
Password: chapters

WEB LINKS

A selection of annotated web links, chosen by the Editors, has been provided to point you in the direction of important research, statistical data, and classic texts to keep you informed of the developments in criminology both past and present.

SELECTED FURTHER READING

Each chapter contains a list of selected further reading to enable you to develop a broader knowledge of the subject and to assist further your understanding of important issues, processes, and debates.

ESSAY QUESTIONS

To encourage you to fully consider they key criminological issues, the Editors have written essay questions to accompany each chapter. These essay questions will help you to reflect on your reading and provide an opportunity to assess your understanding of the subject.

ADVICE ON ANSWERING ESSAY QUESTIONS

Advice from the Editors on how to approach essay questions and to structure your answers to ensure you are successful in demonstrating your knowledge and critical understanding of criminology.

LECTURER RESOURCES

FIGURES AND TABLES FROM THE TEXT

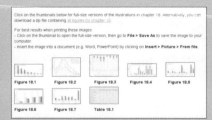

A selection of figures and tables from the text has been provided in high resolution format for downloading into presentation software for use in assignments and exam material.

PART I

CRIMINOLOGY: HISTORY AND THEORY

1

SOCIOLOGICAL THEORIES OF CRIME

Paul Rock

INTRODUCTION: THE DEVELOPMENT OF CRIMINOLOGY IN BRITAIN

Criminology emerged so fitfully and indecisively in Britain that its history does not lend itself easily to a coherent narrative. Although it is now some forty years old, Hermann Mannheim's account of its loosely connected stages remains as serviceable as any (1965: Vol. 1, 79). First, he said, there were private individuals working alone, and he cited as examples John Howard and Jeremy Bentham. Piers Beirne and others would call them part of an Enlightenment phase of thinking about crime and control (1994: xii) (although Garland (2002) would demur a little). One might also add that Howard, Bentham, and others were men working in a newly established tradition of social, juridical, and political improvement, often lawyers by training and Nonconformists or utilitarians by inclination, who believed in the possibility of reform through the application of reason to a welter of confusing and apparently illogical laws, institutions, and practices that composed an English and Welsh *ancien régime*. They were tenuously united at the end of the eighteenth and the beginning of the nineteenth centuries by a copious correspondence; an independence of thought; an independence of wealth; the holding of pivotal positions as magistrates, sheriffs, and Members of Parliament; and a common membership of philanthropic societies and religious organizations (see Whitten 2002). They learned at first or second hand about conditions in Britain and elsewhere, and they cultivated in their turn the beginnings of a comparative, investigative stance towards problems of crime, policing, and punishment. John Howard's *The State of the Prisons* of 1784, Colquhoun's *A Treatise on the Police of the Metropolis* of 1797, and Samuel Romilly's *Observations on the Criminal Law of England* of 1811 are prime examples of their method. But, being independent individuals, they did not lay much of a foundation for an enduring tradition of research and teaching.

Second and third in Mannheim's chronology was what he described as the work of public officials acting first in a private and then in a public capacity, and he cited as examples A. M. Guerry and Cesare Lombroso (Beirne and others would call that the Positivist phase). One might again add that that second era was marked by the activity of embryonic criminologists who made use of the copious data and institutions that the newly reformed, expanding, interventionist, and increasingly wealthy state of the nineteenth century—the state that the Enlightenment reformers had built—furnished in the service of public administration. The very word 'statistic' refers to a fact bearing on the condition of the state, and it first came into use in the late 1780s, to be joined by the word 'statistician' in 1825, and they heralded the arrival of a new kind of blue book knowledge. The first population census in Britain was conducted in 1801; the new police, judicial, and penal authorities began to produce their own statistical returns after the 1830s; and a great mass of numerical data began to flood into the public realm. Chevalier remarked of that period in France that there was 'a determination to obtain figures for everything, to measure everything, to know everything, but to know it by numbers, [it was an] encyclopedic hunger' (1973: 43). The new statistics were eagerly explored by those who sought to discover patterns, commonalities, and trends in the social world: Fletcher (1850), Guerry (1864) and Quetelet (1848), above all, sought to devise a new social physics that could reveal law-like regularities of behaviour in space and time. One of the three, the Belgian, Quetelet, boldly claimed in 1846, for instance, that 'we can count in advance how many individuals will soil their hands with the blood of their fellows, how many will be swindlers, how many poisoners, almost as we can number in advance the births and deaths that will take place' (in Radzinowicz and Hood 1990: 51).

A second concomitant of the emergence of the new penitentiaries, police forces, and asylums (see Scull 1979) was the creation of a new stratum of penal administrators who managed, diagnosed, and ministered to their inmates, and claimed new mandates and fostered new intellectual disciplines to shore up their infant and somewhat fragile professional authority. There was W. D. Morrison, a prison chaplain and pioneering criminologist, the author of *Crime and its Causes*, published in 1891, and *Juvenile Offenders*, published in 1896, and the editor of the criminology series in which Lombroso's *The Criminal Woman* first appeared in English translation in 1895. There was S. A. Strahan, a doctor and lawyer, a physician at the Northampton County Asylum, and author of writings on 'instinctive criminality', criminal insanity, suicide, and morphine habituation. There was Henry Maudsley, the co-founder of the eponymous hospital, who wrote about homicidal insanity, insanity, and criminal responsibility, and other matters in the first stirrings of the new science (1888). These men established new professional associations to promote and defend their expertise—for instance, the Association of Medical Officers of Asylums and Hospitals for the Insane that was founded in 1841; and the Medico-Legal Association that was founded in 1901. And the new associations founded new journals and new stocks of knowledge. The very word 'professional' appeared for the first time in 1848, to be followed by 'professionalism' eight years later, and these words signify the emergence of a new kind of expert. The new disciplines of criminal anthropology, criminal psychiatry, criminology, and medico-legal science gave them a capacity to control and speak about new problems, and it conferred a tenuous legitimacy, but they had few examples to follow, and it was to be medicine, the science of bodily pathology, that became the principal template for their fledgling science of social pathology. British criminology took much of its form at that time, remaining for a long while a statistically driven, administratively bent form of knowledge copying the forms of applied medicine, practised in the service of the state (see Sim 1990: 9) and adopting the language of diagnosis, prognosis, epidemiology, treatment, and rehabilitation. And, Garland would argue, it was a project that came to embody ensuing contradictions which have yet fully to be resolved: the quest, on the one hand, for a criminology as the science of the causes of crime and, on the other, for a discipline subordinate to the practical administrative demands of the state (2002).

The penultimate phase was identified by Mannheim as work undertaken by university departments or individual teachers (and by Beirne, rather parochially one might think, as the growth of criminology in the United States). By the end of the nineteenth century, enough had been accomplished by the pioneers to invite people to view a newly born criminology as a discrete perspective that could be detached from its anchorage in the applied, working practices of state institutions to be pursued as an intellectual object in its own right. The word 'criminology' was devised first in the 1850s and came into more general currency in the 1890s when it began to be taught in universities in Italy, Austria, Germany, and France.It was to be associated with a cluster of European thinkers, and particularly, and not always usefully, with Lombroso and his followers. Lombroso tended to be too fanciful, too extravagant in his mannerisms, to warrant serious consideration by the largely pragmatic and empirical scholars of the United Kingdom. His theories, said Kenny, which had been 'disseminated so quickly amongst the younger jurists of the Latin lands, did not find equally rapid acceptance in the countries of Teutonic speech. ... in the cooler latitudes of Leipzig or London or Boston, there is less reluctance to test the brilliant Italian theories by the results of old experience, and to discount their sweeping generalisations by patient analysis' (1910: 220). British criminology is not and never has been significantly Lombrosian in its affections, and when criminology did come eventually and tentatively to establish itself in Britain in the early 1920s, it was not as an offshoot of the new criminal anthropology. A university post in the discipline was created first at Birmingham University for Maurice Hamblin Smith, and he was a Freudian-leaning psychologist (see Garland 1988: 8; Valiér 1995).

What came in time decisively to spur its growth was the flight of intellectuals from Nazi Europe in the 1930s (see Morris 1988: 24–6). Three legally trained *emigré* criminologists implanted the discipline in three universities: Leon Radzinowicz at the University of Cambrige in 1941; Max Grünhut, first at the London School of Economics in 1934, and thence in the University of Oxford in 1940, where he was appointed to the university's first lectureship in 1947; and Hermann Mannheim at the London School of Economics in 1935—and it was in that year of 1935, said Garland, that criminology was instituted as a professional academic discipline in Britain (1988: 1). Injected into English universities, virtually at a stroke, was the criminology which had been maturing apart in the universities of western Europe, but neither did it receive a ready acceptance (see Hood 2004) nor was it injected into an intellectual framework that yielded easily.

Mannheim's course on the Principles of Criminology at the LSE in the 1930s is indicative of what then passed as criminology. It was eclectic, comprehensive and multi-disciplinary, embracing:

> I. The use of Criminal Statistics. History and present character of crime in England and abroad. II. The criminal types and the causes of crime: (1) Physical factors. The anthropological theory (Lombroso). The biological theory. The significance of physical defects. (2) Psychological and pathological factors: The intelligence of the criminal. Insanity and mental deficiency. The psychoanalytical explanation ... (3) Alcoholism. Climate. Race and Religion. (4) The age factor ... (5) The sex factor: Female delinquency and prostitution. (6) Social and economic factors: Family, broken homes, housing, delinquency areas ... The gang. Profession and unemployment. Poverty. Economic and political crises.

What followed showed the same stamp. Thus the editorial of the first issue of the new *British Journal of Delinquency*, published in July 1950, about to become the chief vehicle of the newly institutionalized discipline, and later to be re-baptized the *British Journal of Criminology*, proclaimed:

> it is perhaps unnecessary to add that the *British Journal of Delinquency* is not in the customary sense a clinical journal. Clinical contributions will of course receive special consideration, but it is hoped to publish articles, both theoretical and practical, from trained workers in the various departments of criminology; namely, medical psychology, psychiatry, psychoanalysis, organic medicine, educational psychology, sociology, economics, anthropology, psycho-biology and statistics; also from social workers, probation officers, prison and other institutional personnel, and from forensic specialists whose work brings them into intimate contact with problems of delinquency.

That was the vein in which British criminology long remained: catholic, multi-causal, averse to a reliance on single theories and disciplines; grounded in medicine and medical metaphor; reformist, applied, and tied to the penal politics of the day. But its very eclecticism brought it about that successive generations of students were able routinely to receive instruction and conduct research across a very broad terrain. Sociologists like Terence Morris and Roger Hood could study under Hermann Mannheim or Leon Radzinowicz, and their students, like Bridget Hutter, David Downes, Stan Cohen, Paul Wiles, and Jock Young, and their students' students, like Dick Hobbs, Nigel Fielding, Ken Plummer, and Ian Taylor, could advance, refine, extend, widen, and revise criminology along a great chain of begats—and there were other centres and other lineages besides. When the great wave of university expansion was launched in England and Wales in the 1960s, when the number of universities grew from 30 to 52 in twenty years, the number of students from 130,000 to 600,000, and the number of academic staff from 19,000 to 46,000, criminology could come freely into its own, blossoming with the rest of the academy, and colonizing departments of psychology, law, social policy, and, above all, sociology. The 1970s were especially propitious: a survey conducted in 1986 revealed that nearly 60 per cent of the criminologists teaching in British universities had been appointed in that decade, and 30 per cent in the years between 1973 and 1976 alone (Rock 1988). In that take-off phase, egged on by publishers, made discontinuous with the past by a thrusting generation of newly appointed young Turks, criminology became striving, expansive, quarrelsome, factious, and open, its practitioners jostling with one another for a place in the sun (see Taylor, Walton, and Young 1973). Some established the National Deviancy Symposium in 1968 in open confrontation with what was conceived to be the old orthodoxies represented by the Institute of Criminology at the University of Cambridge and the Home Office Research Unit (S. Cohen 1971; Downes 1988). They splintered along the theoretical and political faultlines of sociology proper, refracting the larger arguments of Marxist and post-Marxist theory then in vogue, the new phenomenologies of social life, and feminism. And then, after a while and inevitably—in the 1980s and beyond—most, but not all (see Hillyard *et al.* 2004; Sumner 1994, 2004) were to become progressively reconciled to one another as new facts became available through instruments such as crime surveys, battle fatigue set in, scholars mellowed with age, and the pragmatics of having to work together continually in departments, committees, and journals began to supersede the earlier, heady pleasures of intellectual struggle. Yet what the young Turks had succeeded in constructing was an inchoate, exciting, and ambitious discipline that bore all the marks of its diverse origins, earlier quarrels, and competing aspirations, a discipline memorably described by David Downes as a 'rendezvous' subject that was shaped by the confluence of many ideas and schools around an empirical area rather than a single orthodoxy.

SOCIOLOGICAL CRIMINOLOGY

The Oxford English Dictionary defined sociology as 'the study of social organization and institutions and of collective behaviour and interaction, including the individual's relationship to the group'. That is a catholic definition which encompasses almost every situation in which individuals or groups can influence one another. Sociological theories of crime are themselves correspondingly wide-reaching: they extend, for example, from an examination of the smallest detail of street encounters between adolescents and the police to comparative analyses of very large movements in nations' aggregate rates of crime over centuries, and it is sometimes difficult to determine where their boundaries should be drawn. Two of the sociological criminologists most influential in the development of the discipline once defined it in the most catholic terms as 'the body of knowledge regarding crime as a social phenomenon. It includes within its scope the processes of making laws, of breaking laws, and of reacting towards the breaking of laws' (Sutherland and Cressey 1955: 3).

There is no one, royal way to lay out the sociology of crime. In an empirically driven subdiscipline where formally different theories often contend with the same problems in very much the same way, as useful a procedure as any is to identify and describe a number of broad families of theories that share some big idea or ideas in common. The organization of the remainder of this chapter will therefore dwell on a group of intellectual themes which convey some part of the present preoccupations and environment of sociological criminology.

I shall, in particular, attend to the key issues of control, signification, and order. Crime, after all, is centrally bound up with the state's attempts to impose its will through law; with the meanings of those attempts to lawbreaker, law-enforcer, observer, and victim; and with concomitant patterns of order and disorder. Criminologists differ about the weights and meanings that should be attached to those attributes: some, and control theorists in particular, would wish to be what David Matza once called 'correctionalist', that is, to use knowledge about crime to suppress it. Others would look upon the exercise of control more critically. But they all feed off one another's ideas even if their practices and politics diverge. The themes are visible features of the discipline's landscape, and I shall employ them to steer a more or less straight route through Durkheimian and Mertonian theories of anomie; control theories; rational choice theory; routine activities theory; the work of the 'Chicago School'; studies of the relations between control and space, including Newman's 'defensible space', and more recent ideas of risk and the marshalling of dangerous populations; radical criminology and Left Realism; functionalist criminology; and 'labelling theory' and cultural and subcultural analyses of crime as meaningful behaviour. I shall take it that such a grand tour should encompass most of the major landmarks which criminologists would now consider central to their field.

What this chapter cannot do, of course, is provide substantial context, history, criticism, and detail. That would be impossible in a short piece, although the rest of this *Handbook* may be read as its frame. I can hope at best to select only a few illustrative ideas that are of current or recent interest, as well as discussing some of the older arguments that informed them.

Further, like any scheme of classification, this chapter will inevitably face some problems of anomaly and overlap, not only internally but also with other chapters. If the study of crime cannot be severed from the analysis of control, the state, or gender, there will always be such problems at the margins. But this chapter should both furnish the larger contours of an introductory map of contemporary sociological theories of crime and serve as a complement to those other chapters.

CRIME AND CONTROL

ANOMIE AND THE CONTRADICTIONS OF SOCIAL ORDER

I shall begin by describing anomie theory, one of the most enduring and, for a while, hard-researched of all the ideas of criminological theory, and one that still persists in disguised form.

At heart, many theories take it that crime is a consequence of defective social regulation. People are said to deviate because the disciplines and authority of society are so flawed that they offer few restraints or moral direction. The idea is a very old one, antedating the emergence of sociology itself, but its formal birth into theory is linked indissolubly with anomie and the French sociologist, Émile Durkheim.

Durkheim awarded two rather different meanings to anomie, or normlessness. In *The Division of Labour in Society*, published in 1893, and in *Suicide*, published in 1897, he asserted that French society was in uneasy transition from one state of solidarity or social integration to another. A society without an elaborate division of labour rested on what he called (perhaps misleadingly) the mechanical solidarity of people who not only reacted much alike to problems, but also saw that everyone about them reacted alike to those problems, thereby lending objectivity, scale, unanimity, and solidity to moral response, and bringing a potential for massive disapproval and repression to bear down on the deviant. Such a social order was conceived to lie in the simpler past of a less differentiated pre-industrial society. The future of industrial society would be distinguished by a state of organic solidarity, the solidarity appropriate to a complex division of labour. People would then be allocated by merit and effort to very diverse positions, and they would not only recognize the legitimacy of the manner in which rewards were distributed, but also acknowledge the indispensability of what each did in his or her work for the other and for the common good. Organic solidarity would thus have controls peculiar to itself: 'Sheerly economic regulation is not enough … there should be moral regulation, moral rules which specify the rights and obligations of individuals in a given occupation in relation to those in other occupations' (Giddens 1972: 11). People might no longer think wholly in unison, their moral response might not be substantial and undivided, but they should be able to compose their differences peaceably by means of a system of restitutive justice that made amends for losses suffered.

Durkheim's distinction between the two forms of solidarity and their accompanying modes of control was anthropologically suspect, but it was in his analysis of the liminal state between them that criminologists were most interested. In that transition, where capitalism was thought to impose a 'forced division of labour', people acquiesced neither in the apportionment of rewards nor in the moral authority of the economy or state. They were obliged to work and act in a society that not only enjoyed little legitimacy but also exercised an incomplete control over their desires. In such a setting, it was held, 'man's nature [was to be] eternally dissatisfied, constantly to advance, without relief or rest, towards an indefinite goal' (Durkheim 1952: 256). Moral regulation was relatively deficient and people were correspondingly free to deviate. That is the first meaning Durkheim gave to anomie. His second will be visited below.

Given another, distinctively American, complexion by Robert Merton, anomie became a socially fostered state of discontent and deregulation that generated crime and deviance as part of the routine functioning of a society which promised much to everyone but actually denied them equal access to its attainment (Merton 1938). People might have been motivated to achieve success in the United States, the society on which Merton focused, but they confronted class, race, and other social differences, that manifestly contradicted the myth of openness. It was not easy for a poor, inner-city adolescent to receive sponsorship for jobs, achieve academic awards, or acquire capital. In a society where failure was interpreted as a sign of personal rather than social weakness, where failure tended to lead to guilt rather than to political anger, the pressure to succeed could be so powerful that it impelled people thus disadvantaged to bypass legitimate careers and take to illegitimate careers instead: 'the culture makes incompatible demands ... In this setting, a cardinal American virtue—"ambition"—promotes a cardinal American vice—"deviant behavior" ' (Merton 1957: 145).

Merton's anomie theory was to be modified progressively for some thirty years. In the work of Richard Cloward and Lloyd Ohlin, for example, his model was elaborated to include *illegitimate* routes to success. Their *Delinquency and Opportunity* (1960) described the consequences of young American men (in the 1950s and 1960s the criminological gaze was almost wholly on the doings of young American *men*) not only being pushed into crime by the difficulties of acquiring money and position in conventional ways, but also being pulled by the lure of lucrative and unconventional criminal careers. There would be those who were offered an unorthodox path in professional or organized crime, and they could become thieves, robbers, or racketeers. There would be those for whom no path was available, and they could become members of conflict gangs. And there were those who failed to attain admission to either a law-abiding or a law-violating group, the 'double failures', who would, it was conjectured, give up and become drug-users and hustlers. Each of those modes of adaptation was, in effect, a way of life, supported by a system of meanings or a subculture, and Cloward and Ohlin provided one of the bridges between the structural and the interpretive models of crime which will be discussed towards the end of this chapter.

In the work of Albert Cohen (1957), anomie was to be synthesized with the Freudian idea of 'reaction formation' in an attempt to explain the manifestly expressive and 'non-rational' nature of much delinquency. The prospect of failure was depicted as bringing about a major psychological rejection of what had formerly been sought, so that the once-aspiring working-class adolescent emphatically turned his back on the middle-class world that spurned him and adopted a style of behaviour that was its systematic inversion. The practical and utilitarian in middle-class life was transformed into non-utilitarian delinquency; respectability became malicious negativism; and the deferment of gratification became short-run hedonism. Again, in the work of David Downes, conducted in London in the early 1960s to explore how far beyond America anomie theory might be generalized, the ambitions of English adolescents were found to be so modulated by what was then a stable and legitimated system of social stratification that working-class youth did not seem to undergo a taxing guilt, shame, or frustration in their failure to accomplish middle-class goals. They neither hankered after the middle-class world nor repudiated it. Rather, their response was 'dissociation'. Where they *did* experience a strong dissatisfaction, however, was in their thwarted attempts to enjoy leisure, and their delinquencies were principally hedonistic, focused on drinking, fighting, and malicious damage to property, rather than instrumentally turned towards the accumulation of wealth. And that theme—of the part played by the adolescent 'manufacture of excitement' and the courting of risk—was to be echoed repeatedly in the empirical and theoretical work of criminologists. Making 'something happen' in a world without significant cultural or material resources could easily bring about a drift into delinquency (see Matza 1964; Corrigan 1979; Cusson 1983; Katz 1988; Presdee 2000).

The current incarnation of anomie theory is to be found in muted form in 'Left Realism', where the idea of structural tension is integrated with that of the social meanings of the act to produce a conception of delinquency as a motivated response to the inequalities of capitalism. 'The Mertonian notion of contradiction between culture and structure', wrote Jock Young, 'has run throughout all my work, from *The Drugtakers* onwards' (2004: 553). I shall return to Left Realism below.

ANOMIE AND SOCIAL DISORGANIZATION

The second reading of anomie stemming from Durkheim touched on moral regulation that was not so much flawed as in a critical or chronic state of near collapse. People, he argued, are not endowed at birth with fixed appetites and ambitions. On the contrary, their purposes and aspirations are shaped by the generalized opinions and reactions of others, by a collective conscience, that can appear through social ritual and routine to be externally derived, solid, and objective. When society is disturbed by rapid change or major disorder, however, that semblance of solidity, authority, and objectivity can itself founder, and people may no longer find their ambitions subject to effective social discipline. It is hard to live outside the reassuring structures of social life, and the condition of anomie was experienced as a 'malady of infinite aspiration' that was accompanied by 'weariness', 'disillusionment', 'disturbance, agitation and discontent'. In extreme cases, Lukes observed, 'this condition would lead a man to commit suicide and homicide' (1967: 139).

Durkheim conceived such anomic deregulation to be a matter of crisis, innately unstable and short-lived. Disorganization could not be tolerated for very long before a society collapsed or order of a sort was restored. Indeed, sociologists are generally ill-disposed towards the term, believing that it connotes a want of understanding and perception on the part of the observer (see Anderson 1976; Katz 1997; and Whyte 1942). It is evident that informal control can survive in even the most perverse circumstances (see Walklate and Evans 1999) and, even in Iraq, the Congo, Sierra Leone, or Uganda at their most devastated, people are able to sustain a measure of organization within disorganization. Yet, on both the small and the large scale, there are also clear examples of people living in conditions where informal control and cooperativeness are only vestigial; where formal control is either absent or erratic; where others are, or are seen to be, predatory and dangerous; where life is unpredictable; and where, as cause and consequence, there is little personal safety, much anxiety, and abundant crime. Take William Julius Wilson's description of life in the poorest areas of the American city: 'broken families, antisocial behavior, social networks that do not extend beyond the ghetto environment, and a lack of informal social control over the behavior and activities of children and adults in the neighborhood' (1996: xvi). On some housing estates in Paris, London (see Genn 1988), Nottingham (Davies 1998), and St Louis (Rainwater 1970), social groupings have been portrayed as so lacking in cohesion that they enjoyed no shared trust, neighbour preyed on neighbour, and joint defensive action was virtually impossible.

Rampant anomie has been well documented (see Erikson 1994). Consider Davis's half-prophetic description of MacArthur Park, one of the poorest areas of Los Angeles, as 'feral' and dangerous, 'a free-fire zone where crack dealers and street gangs settle their scores with shotguns and Uzis' (1992a: 6). Consider, too, Turnbull's description of the condition of the Ik of northern Uganda, a tribe that had been moved to a mountainous area after their traditional hunting grounds had been designated a national park. They could no longer live, cooperate, and work as they had done before; familiar patterns of social organization had become obsolete; and the Ik were portrayed as having become beset by 'acrimony, envy and suspicion' (1973: 239), 'excessive individualism, coupled with solitude and boredom' (ibid.: 238), and the victimization of the weak: 'without killing, it is difficult to get closer to disposal than by taking the food out of an old person's mouth, and this was primarily an adjacent-generation occupation, as were tripping and pushing off balance' (ibid.: 252).

A number of criminologists and others are beginning to prophesy a new apocalypse in which anomie will flourish on such a massive scale that entire societies will dissolve into chaos and lawlessness. There are parts of the world whose political structures are so radically disordered that it becomes difficult to talk about legitimate governments operating effectively within secure national boundaries at all (see Bayart, Ellis, and Hibou 1999). So it was that Kaplan wrote graphically about the road-warrior culture of Somalia, the anarchic implosion of criminal violence in the Ivory Coast, and Sierra Leone, which he depicted at the time as a lawless state that had lost control over its cities at night, whose national army was a 'rabble', and which was reverting to tribalism. The future for many, he luridly predicted, would be a 'rundown, crowded planet of skinhead Cossacks and *juju* warriors, influenced by the worst refuse of Western pop culture and ancient tribal hatreds, and battling over scraps of overused earth in guerilla conflicts' (1994: 62–3). So, too, Martin van Creveld analysed what he called the ubiquitous growth of 'low-intensity conflict' waged by guerrillas and terrorists who threatened the state's conventional monopoly of violence: 'Should present trends continue, then the kind of war that is based on the division between government, army, and people, seems to be on its way out. . . . A degree of violent activity that even as late as the 1960s would have been considered outrageous is now accepted as an inevitable hazard of modern life' (1991: 192, 194). If Kaplan and van Creveld are even partially gifted with foresight (and much of their argument is quite stark), the trends they foretell will be of major consequence to criminology. Without a viable state legislature, laws, and law enforcement, without adequate state control over the distribution of violence, how can one manage to write intelligently about a discrete realm of crime at all? Crime, after all, is contingent on a state's ability clearly to define, ratify, and execute the law. When the police of a state are massively and routinely corrupt (as they appear to be in Mexico);

when, for example, the Colombian president's aeroplane was found to be carrying large quantities of cocaine in September 1996 (see the *New York Times*, 22 September 1996); and when a President of Liberia was accused of cannibalism (*The Times*, 2 November 1999); it is not difficult to recognize what Aldana-Pindell somewhat paradoxically called 'institutional *anomie*' (2002). Neither is it difficult to acknowledge the disarray to which Stan Cohen pointed when he asked whether it was possible any longer to distinguish firmly between crime and politics. There has been, S. Cohen asserted, a widespread decline of the myth that the sovereign state can provide security, law, and order; a decline in the legitimacy of the state through corruption scandals; a growth of international crime and a rise of criminal states such as Chechnya; and, in Africa particularly, the emergence of barbarism, horror, and atrocity. In some settings, he remarked, 'lawlessness and crime have so destroyed the social fabric that the state itself has withdrawn' (1996: 9).

CONTROL THEORY

A second, large, and linked cluster of theories centres loosely around the contention that people seek to commit crime because it is profitable, useful, or enjoyable for them to do so, and that they will almost certainly break the law if they can. Even if that contention, with its covert imagery of feral man (and woman), is not strictly 'correct', control theorists would argue that it certainly directs enquiry in a helpful direction. They profess to be interested less in the fidelity of description than in its yield for policy intervention and prediction in concrete situations. Theirs is a theory of practical rather than of empirical truths, and the practical is thought to suggest that more will be learned by exploring a few, uncomplicated factors that seem to *prevent* people from offending than by investigating all the complicated motives, meanings, and antecedents of their actions. Travis Hirschi put the issue baldly: 'The question "Why do they do it?" is simply not the question the theory is designed to answer. The question is, "Why don't we do it?" ' (1969: 34). Such a doctrine is a recognizably close neighbour of anomie theories in its focus on the regulation of potentially unbridled appetites; and, indeed, it is occasionally very difficult to distinguish one set of ideas from the other. Earlier variants of control theory, compiled in the 1960s and 1970s, proceeded by drafting lists of the constraints which could check the would-be offender, an offender who, it was assumed for analytic purposes, could be much like you, me, or anyone. Thus, arguing against subcultural theory, and grounded in a Freudian conception of human impulses that required taming, Hirschi claimed that 'delinquent acts result when the individual's bond to society is weak or broken' (1969: 16).

Four chief elements were held by Hirschi to induce people to comply with rules: attachment, commitment, involvement, and belief. Attachment reflected a person's sensitivity to the opinions of others; commitment flowed from an investment of time, energy, and reputation in conformity; involvement stemmed from engrossment in conventional activity; and belief mirrored a person's conviction that he or she should obey legal rules. There is tautology and repetition in that formulation, but he nevertheless usefully directed the criminological mind towards answering his one big question, 'Why *don't* we do it?'

Later, with Gottfredson, Hirschi developed control theory by turning to self-control and impulsivity. Crime, they claimed, flows from low self-control: it provides a direct and simple gratification of desires that is attractive to those who cannot or will not postpone pleasure. In the main, it requires little skill or planning. It can be intrinsically enjoyable because it involves the exercise of cunning, agility, deception, or power. It requires a lack of sympathy for the victim. But it does not provide medium- or long-term benefits equivalent to those that can flow from more orthodox careers. In short, it is, they say, likely to be committed by those who are 'impulsive, insensitive, physical ... Risk-taking, short-sighted, and non-verbal' (1990: 90).

David Matza almost certainly would not have called himself a control theorist, but in *Delinquency and Drift* (1964) he did effectively straddle theories of control, anomie, and signification, and he did portray delinquents and delinquency in a manner that control theorists would find apposite. Delinquents are not very different from us, he argued. Most of the time they are conventional enough in belief and conduct, and it is difficult to predict who will conform and who will not. But there are occasions when the grip of control loosens, adolescents fatalistically experience themselves as if they were object and effect rather than as subject and cause, as if they were no longer morally responsible for their actions, and they will then find themselves released to drift in and out of delinquency. What eases that process of disengagement are widely-circulating accounts or 'techniques of neutralization' (a massively influential idea that he had developed earlier with Gresham Sykes (Sykes and Matza 1957)) which enable people methodically to counter the guilt and offset the censure they might experience when offending. Matza claimed that delinquents could be fortified in their resolve by their ability to condemn their condemners (by asserting that police and judges were themselves corrupt and invalid critics, for instance); to deny injury (by asserting that no significant harm was done); to deny the victim (by asserting that the victim was of no consequence, or deserved what happened); or to appeal to higher loyalties (a noble motive could be cited for an ignoble deed).

Steven Box attempted to take analysis yet further by reconciling Hirschi's emphasis on social bonds with Matza's conception of drift. He compiled his own new alliterative list of variables that were held to affect control: secrecy (the delinquent's chances of concealment); skills (a mastery of knowledge and techniques needed for the deviant act); supply (access to appropriate equipment); social support (the endorsement offered by peers and others); and symbolic support (the endorsement offered by accounts available in the wider culture) (1971: 150). The greater the access to requisite skills, secrecy, supplies, and social and symbolic support, the greater would be the likelihood of offending.

Perhaps one of the most telling and economical contributions to control theory was supplied by Harriet Wilson. Examining 'socially deprived' families in Birmingham, England, she was to conclude that what most sharply differentiated families with delinquent children from those with none was simply what she called the exercise of 'chaperonage' (1980). Parents who acted as chaperons effectively prevented their children from offending: they were so convinced that the neighbourhood in which they lived was dangerous and contaminating that they sought to protect their children by keeping them indoors or under close supervision, escorting them to school, and prohibiting them from playing with others defined as undesirable.

Control theory has also been applied with effect to the problem of gender differences in offending. Apart from age, no other demographic feature at present so powerfully discriminates between offenders and non-offenders. At one time, however, scant criminological attention was paid to female crime because there was so very little of it (see Innes 2003: 54). As Lemert once said, like Custer's men, criminologists rode to the sound of the guns, and there were few female guns indeed firing. By contrast, what made male offending appear so interesting was its sheer seriousness and scale.

Feminist criminologists and others adopting a control perspective retorted that that was precisely what made women so important analytically, and they began to ask Travis Hirschi's central question (without actually citing Hirschi himself) about why women did *not* offend. There was the new and intriguing riddle of the conforming woman, and the riddle was answered, in part, by reference to the effects of differentials in control. John Hagan and his colleagues put it that deviation as a form of fun and excitement in public space was more commonly open to males than to females because daughters are more frequently risk-averse and more frequently subject to intense, continual, and diffuse family control in the private, domestic sphere. That control, by extension, not only removed girls from the purview of agents of formal social control, the criminal justice system, and the possibility of public identification as criminal; it also worked more effectively because it rested on the manipulation of emotional sanctions rather than the imposition of physical or custodial controls. Shaming strategies and the withdrawal of affection are seemingly more potent than fines, probation, or prison. It followed that the more firmly structured and hierarchical the family, the sharper the distinction drawn between male and female roles, the more women were confined to private space, the greater would be the disparity between rates of male and female offending (see Hagan *et al.* 1979, 1985, and 1988). Pat Carlen gave that analysis yet another twist by reflecting that female criminals were most likely to emerge when domestic family controls were eroded or removed altogether, when what she called the 'gender deal' was broken, young women left home or were taken into the care of the state, and were thereby exposed to controls characteristically experienced by men (1988). The answer to the 'crime problem', Frances Heidensohn once concluded, would have to lie in the feminization of control.

Control theory is now greatly in vogue, particularly in the United States, where it is linked with the work of authors such as Sampson and Laub, whose *Crime in the Making* of 1993 was to be succeeded by Laub and Sampson's *Shared Beginnings, Divergent Lives* of 2003. Both works explored the genesis of, and desistance from, delinquency in the lives of men studied over decades: and they devoted especial attention to the manner in which the social bonds of family, friends, employment, and military service work as controls that filter influences emanating from the wider social structure. Marriage, the onset of work, and military service, they argue, may act as critical turning points which induce discontinuities in a life history; create new sets of social relations, dependencies, and responsibilities; introduce new disciplines into social life; and invite stock-taking and reflection. Conversely, involvement with the criminal justice system and imprisonment may interrupt or undermine participation in stabilizing social environments; stigmatize the offender and prevent re-entry into the 'straight' world; encourage cynicism about criminal justice through a close acquaintance with its game-like and seedier features; and introduce the offender to other lawbreakers who help to amplify deviance through differential association. And, throughout, and following Matza, Katz, and others, Laub and Sampson portray the process not as a grim and ineluctable progression into criminality, but as a sequence of events and actions which is influenced always by the capacity of people to interpret and *choose* how they will respond. The part played by human agency and contingency is repeatedly underscored, leading them to observe how impossible it is to predict future criminality from present circumstances.

RATIONAL CHOICE THEORY

An increasingly important, but not indispensable, foundation for control theories is 'rational choice theory', a resuscitation of old utilitarian theories that preceded sociology and were once linked with Adam Smith, Jeremy Bentham, Cesare Beccaria, and James Mill. Rational choice theory has been reintroduced to criminology through the medium of a revived economics of crime, and it brings with it the convenient fiction of economic man (see Becker 1968), a fiction which has an immediate affinity with the criminal man (or woman) of control theory. Economic man, deemed to be continually looking about him for opportunities, making amoral and asocial choices to maximize his personal utility, may not be an empirically grounded or well-authenticated entity, but, it is argued, he does help to simplify model-making, strip away what rational choice theorists conceive to be unessential theoretical and descriptive clutter, and aim directly at what are conceived to be practically useful policy questions (see Clarke and Cornish 1985). Economic man in his (or her) criminal guise does not have a past, complex motives, rich social life, or, indeed, a recognizable social identity (a 'disposition' is how Ron Clarke would put it (1992)). He or she does not need to have any of those attributes. Indeed, he or she may not be perfectly rational, muddling through, as we all do, on the basis of imperfect information and the presence of risks and uncertainty. He or she is very much like any one of us or, better still, like some Everyman who stands abstractly and plainly for all of us. He or she needs no such complexity, because what weighs in control theory is the piecemeal theoretical analysis of discrete instances of disembodied offending behaviour conducted by people making decisions around the issues of risk, effort, and reward (Clarke and Cornish 2000: 7) in the settings in which they may take place (see introduction to Clarke and Felson 1993).

In Ron Clarke's particularly influential formulation, the rate of crime was held to vary in response to three broad configurations of factors. The first grouping revolved around increasing the effort Everyman would have to expend in committing a crime, and that entailed what was called 'target hardening' (by defending objects and people by shields and other devices); 'access control' (and that involved making it difficult for predators to approach targets); deflecting offenders (by encouraging them, for example, to act in a legitimate rather than an illegitimate manner through the provision of graffiti boards, litter bins, and spittoons); and 'controlling facilitators' (through gun control or checks on the sales of spray cans, for instance). The second revolved around increasing the risks of offending through the screening of people (by means of border searches, for example); formal surveillance by police, security guards, and others; surveillance by employees such as bus conductors, train guards, concierges, and janitors; and 'natural surveillance' (aided by lowering or removing obstacles such as hedges and shrubs around private dwellings, installing closed circuit television cameras, lighting the interiors of stores, and enhanced street lighting). The final grouping was 'reducing the rewards' of crime, itself composed of 'target removal' (using electronic transactions to reduce the number of cash payments, and thus the accumulation of cash in single places, for instance); property identification; removal of inducements (by the rapid cleaning of graffiti or repair of vandalized property); and rule-setting (through income tax returns, customs declarations, and the like) (taken from Clarke 1992: 13). A pursuit of those common-sense, sometimes indistinguishable, but nevertheless practical ideas allowed research officers at the Home Office in the 1970s and early 1980s to undertake a succession of illustrative studies, discovering, for example, that compact, old school buildings on small urban sites were a third as likely to be burgled as large, sprawling, modern buildings with their many points of access and weak possibilities of surveillance (see Hope 1982); or that there was some twenty times as much malicious damage on the upper than on the lower decks of 'one man', double-decker buses whose drivers' powers of surveillance were confined to one level only (Mayhew *et al.* 1976: 26).

None of those variables touched on conventional sociological questions about who offenders might be, how they reason, and how they act (and for that rational choice theorists have been criticized (see Wright and Decker 1997; Fukuyama 2004; and Haggerty, who remarked a little astringently that control theorists are more akin to 'Wal-Mart security consultants than research criminologists' (2004: 218)). Control theorists concentrated instead on the imagined impact of different forms of control on Everyman or Everywoman abroad in space, and from that it was but a short step to extend control theory to an analysis of the disciplines that are built into everyday social practices, on the one hand, and into the social uses of space, on the other.

ROUTINE ACTIVITIES THEORY

Ron Clarke, the situational control theorist, and Marcus Felson, the theorist of crime and routine activities, agreed that they shared ideas in common (see Clarke and Felson 1993) as well as ideas apart (thus situational control theory is microscopic, routine activities theory largely macroscopic in its application (Clarke and Cornish undated: 25)). Clarke and his colleagues had asked what prevented specific criminal incidents from occurring in specific situations. Felson asked how such incidents originate or are checked in the routine activities of mundane social life (1994). Just as Clarke and others had emphasized how, for explanatory purposes, it was convenient to assume that offenders were little different from anyone else, so Felson and his colleagues argued that most criminals are unremarkable, unskilled, petty, and non-violent people much like us. Just as control theorists made use of a tacit version of original sin, so routine activities theory adopted a series of presuppositions about basic human frailty, the importance of temptation and provocation, and the part played by idleness ('We are all born weak, but . . . we are taught self-control', Felson claimed (1994: 20)).

The routine activities criminologist would argue that the analysis of predatory crime does not necessarily require weighty causes. Neither does it demand that the theorist commit the 'like-causes-like' fallacy which covertly insists that a 'pathological' phenomenon such as crime must be explained by a pathological condition such as alienation, poverty, family dysfunction, or class or racial oppression. Crime was taken to be inscribed in the very architecture of everyday life. More precisely, it was to be found in the convergence in space and time of what were called motivated offenders, suitable targets, and capable guardians (see Cohen and Felson 1979): being affected by such matters as the weight, value, incidence, and distribution of stealable goods (the growth in the quantity of portable, high-cost goods such as video-recorders and mobile (or 'cell') telephones will encourage more theft, for instance); the impact of motor cars (they aid rapid flight, permit the discreet transportation of objects, and give rise to a geographical dispersal of the population which dilutes surveillance); habits of leisure (adolescents now have larger swathes of empty time than did their predecessors, time in which they can get up to mischief); habits of work (when all members of a household are in employment, there will be no capable guardians to protect a home); habits of residence (single people are less effective guardians of property than are larger households); the growth of technology (telephones, for instance, amplify the public's ability to report crime); and so on. It is an uncomplicated enough theory but again, like its near neighbour, control theory, it does ask empirically productive questions.

CRIME, CONTROL, AND SPACE

THE CHICAGO SCHOOL

Routine activities theory and control theory both talk about convergence in space, and space has always been analytically to the fore in criminology. Indeed, one of the earliest and most productive of the research traditions laid down in criminology was the social ecology and urban mapping practised by the sociology department of the University of Chicago in the 1920s and beyond (see Park 1925; Thrasher 1927; and Landesco 1968).

As cities grow, it was held, so there would be a progressive and largely spontaneous differentiation of space, population, and function that concentrated different groupings in different areas. The main organizing structure was the *zone*, and the Chicago sociologists discerned five principal concentric zones shaping the city: the central business district at the very core; the 'zone in transition' about that centre; an area of stable working-class housing; middle-class housing; and the outer suburbia.

The zone in transition was marked by the greatest volatility of its residents. It was an area of comparatively cheap rents, weak social control, internal social differentiation, and rapid physical change. It was to the zone in transition that new immigrant groupings most frequently came, and it was there that they settled into what were called 'natural areas', small communal enclaves that were said to be relatively homogeneous in composition and culture. Chicago sociologists plotted the incidence of social problems on to census maps of the city, and it was the zone in transition that was found repeatedly to house the largest proportions of the poor, the illegitimate, the illiterate, the mentally ill (see Faris and Dunham 1939), juvenile delinquents (Shaw and McKay 1942), and prostitutes (Reckless 1933). The zone in transition was virtually coextensive with what was then described as social pathology. Not only were formal social controls held to be at their weakest there (the zone in transition was, as it were, socially dislocated from the formal institutions and main body of American society (see Whyte 1942)); but informal social controls were eroded by moral and social diversity, rapid population movement, and a lack of strong and pervasive local institutions: 'contacts are extended, heterogeneous groups mingle, neighborhoods disappear, and people, deprived of local and family ties, are forced to live under . . . loose, transient and impersonal relations' (Wirth 1964: 236).

A number of the early Chicago sociologists united social ecology, the study of the patterns formed by groups living together in the same space, with the fieldwork methods of social anthropology, to explore the traditions, customs, and practices of the residents of natural areas. They found that, while there may well have been a measure of social and moral dislocation between the zone in transition and the wider society, as well as within the zone in transition itself, those natural areas could also manifest a remarkable inner coherence and persistence of culture and behaviour that were reproduced from generation to generation and from immigrant group to immigrant group within the same terrain over time. Delinquency was, in effect, not disorganized at all, but a stable attribute of social life, an example of continuity in change: 'to a very great extent . . . traditions of delinquency are preserved and transmitted through the medium of social contact with the unsupervised play group and the more highly organized delinquent and criminal gangs' (Shaw and McKay 1971: 260). Cultural transmission was to be the focus of the work pursued by a small group of second-generation Chicago sociologists. Under the name of 'differential association', it was studied as a normal process of learning motives, skills, and meanings in the company of others who bore criminal traditions (see Sutherland and Cressey 1955).

That urban research was to prepare a diverse legacy for criminology: the spatial analysis of crime; the study of subcultures (which I shall touch on below); the epidemiology of crime; crime as an interpretive practice (which I shall also touch on); and much else. Let me turn first to some examples of spatial analysis.

CONTROL AND SPACE: BEYOND THE CHICAGO SCHOOL

The Chicago sociologists' preoccupation with the cultural and symbolic correlates of spatial congregations of people was to be steadily elaborated by criminologists. For instance, Wiles, Bottoms, and their colleagues, originally working at (and later returned to) the University of Sheffield, added two important observations. They argued first that, in a then more tightly regulated Britain, social segregation did not emerge, as it were, organically with unplanned city growth (although Chicago itself was never quite as unplanned as some of the early social ecologists had alleged (see Suttles 1972)), but with the intended and unintended consequences of policy decisions taken by local government departments responsible for housing a large proportion of the population in municipal accommodation. Housing allocation was an indirect and sometimes unintended reflection of moral judgements about tenants that resulted, or were assumed to result, in the concentration of criminal populations (see Bottoms *et al.* 1989). Further, and partly in accord with that argument, the reputations of natural areas themselves became a criminological issue: how was it, criminologists asked, that the moral meanings attached to space by residents and outsiders affected people's reputations, choices, and action? One's very address could become a constraining moral fact that affected not only how one would be treated by others in and about the criminal justice system (see Damer 1974), but also how one would come to rate oneself as a potential deviant or conformist (see Gill 1977).

Secondly, Bottoms and his colleagues argued, while the Chicago sociologists may have examined the geographical distribution of offenders, it was instructive also to scrutinize how *offending* itself could be plotted, because the two measures need not correspond (Baldwin and Bottoms 1976). Offending has its maps. Indeed, it appears to be densely concentrated, clustered around offenders' homes, areas of work and recreation, and the pathways in between (Brantingham and Brantingham 1981–2). So it was that, pursuing routine activities theory, Sherman and his colleagues surveyed all calls made to the police in Minneapolis in one year; and they discovered that a few 'hot spots' had exceptional densities of crime: only 3 per cent of all places produced 50 per cent of the calls; all robberies took place in only 2.2 per cent of places, all rapes in 1.2 per cent of places, and all car thefts in 2.7 per cent of places (Sherman *et al.* 1989; see also Roncek and Maier 1991).

DEFENSIBLE SPACE

If offending has its maps, so does social control; and criminologists and others have become ever more interested in the fashion in which space, conduct, and control intersect. One forerunner was Jane Jacobs, who speculated about the relations between city landscapes and informal controls, arguing, for example, that dense, busy thoroughfares with their *habitués* have many more 'eyes on the street' and opportunities for witness reporting and bystander intervention, than sterile pedestrian zones, 'confused' mixed space or streets without stores and other lures (Jacobs 1965).

The idea of 'defensible space', in particular, has been borrowed from anthropology and architecture, coupled with the concept of surveillance, and put to work in analysing formal and informal responses to different kinds of terrain. 'Defensible space' itself leans on the psychological notion of 'territoriality', the sense of attachment and symbolic investment that people can acquire in space. Territoriality is held by some to be a human universal, an imperative that leads people to wish to guard what is their own. Those who have a stake in a physical area, it is argued, will care for it, police it, and report strangers and others who have no apparent good purpose to be there.

What is quite critical is how space is marked out and bounded. The prime author of this formulation of the idea of defensible space, Oscar Newman (1972), claimed that, other things being equal, what induces territorial sentiments is a clear demarcation between private and public areas, even if the demarcations are only token. The private will be protected in ways that the public is not, and the fault of many domestic and institutional buildings is that separations and segregations are not clearly enough inscribed in design. The geographer, Alice Coleman, and others took it that improvements to the physical structures of built space could then achieve a significant impact on crime: above all, she insisted on restricting access to sites; reducing the interconnections between buildings; and emphasizing the distinction between public and private space and minimizing what Oscar Newman called 'confused space', the space that was neither one nor the other (Coleman 1985, 1986). She has been roundly faulted, both methodologically and analytically, for her neglect of dimensions other than the physical, but she and Newman have succeeded in introducing an analytic focus on the interrelations between space and informal control that was largely absent before. Only rarely have criminologists such as Campbell (1993), Duneier (2001), Power (1997) and Shapland and Vagg (1988) enquired into the informal controlling practices of people as they observe, interpret, and respond to the ambiguous, deviant, and non-deviant conduct in the spaces around them. It was Shapland and Vagg's contention, for instance, that there is a continuous, active, and often informed process of surveillance transacted by people on the ground; a process which is so discreet that it has escaped much formal notice, and which meshes only haphazardly with the work of the police. And very similarly Duneier laid bare the complex webs of informal control practised by homeless entrepreneurs selling books and magazines from stalls on New York's streets. Far from being a problem of deregulation, they acted as palpable but subtle agents of order, looking after and protecting one another, and preserving public stability.

CRIME, POWER, AND SPACE

Surveillance has not always been construed as neutral or benign, and there are current debates about what its newer forms might portend. Even its sponsors in government departments and criminal justice agencies have spoken informally and privately about their anxiety that people are being encouraged to become unduly fearful of crime and to retreat into private fastnesses. It began to be argued, especially by those who followed Michel Foucault, that a 'punitive city' was in the making, that, in Stan Cohen's words, there was 'a deeper penetration of social control into the social body' (1979a: 356) (and, Cohen would add privately, sociologists do not in the main look on social control with a favourable eye).

Some came to claim not only that there has been a move progressively to differentiate and elaborate the distribution of controls in space, but also that there has been a proliferating surveillance of dangerous areas, often conducted obliquely and with an increasingly advanced technology. Michel Foucault's (1977) dramatic simile of Jeremy Bentham's model prison, the Panopticon, was to be put to massive use in criminology. Just as the Panopticon, or inspection house, was supposed to have permitted the unobserved observation of many inmates around the bright, illuminated rim of a circular prison by the few guards in its obscured centre, just as the uncertainty of unobserved observation worked to make the controlled control themselves, so, Foucault and those who followed him wished to argue, modern society is coming to exemplify the perfection of the automatic exercise of power through generalized surveillance. The carceral society was a machine in which everyone was supposed to be caught (even, it seems, the police, who may survey one another as well as the wider population (see *The Times*, 4 November 1999): it relied on diffuse control through unseen monitoring and the individualization and 'interiorization' of control (Gordon 1972)). Public space, it has been said, was becoming exposed to ever more perfunctory, distant, and technologically driven policing by formal state agencies; while control in private and semi-private space (the space of the shopping malls, university campus, and theme park) was itself becoming more dense, privatized, and widespread, placed in the private hands of security guards and store detectives, and reliant on a new electronic surveillance (Davis 1992b: 233; but see Welsh and Farrington 2002 which concluded that the introduction of CCTV appears to affect only the commission of motor thefts. All other forms of crime are untouched).

A paradigmatic case study of oblique regulation has been provided by Shearing and Stenning's ethnography of Disney World as a 'private, quasi-feudal domain of control' (Shearing and Stenning 1985: 347) that was comprehensively, discreetly, and adeptly controlled by employees, extensive surveillance, the encouragement of self-discipline, and the very configuration of physical space. The nature of crime and deviance itself can undergo change in such a transformed environment: they are no longer always and everywhere so markedly affronts to deep values but are, instead, very often breaches of what appear to be impersonal, morally neutral, technical controls (see Lianos and Douglas 2000: 270–1).

What also underlies much of that vision is a new, companion stress on the sociology of risk, a focus linked importantly with the work of Ulrich Beck (although he has not himself written about crime (1992)). It has been argued that people and groups are becoming significantly stratified by their exposure to risk and their power to neutralize harm. The rich can afford private protection, the poor cannot, and a new ecology emerges (Simon 1987). Phrased only slightly differently, and merged with the newly burgeoning ideas about the pervasiveness of surveillance by machine and person (Gordon 1986–7 and Lyon 1994), those theories of risk suggest that controls are being

applied by state and private organizations, not on the basis of some moralistic conception of individual wrongdoing, but on a foundation of the identification, classification,
and management of groups categorized by their perceived dangerousness (Feeley and
Simon 1992; Simon and Feeley 1995). Groups are becoming ever more rigidly segregated in space: some (members of the new dangerous classes or underclass) being confined to prison, semi-freedom under surveillance, or parole in the community; others
(the more affluent) retreating into their locked and gated communities, secure zones,
and private spaces. There are new bifurcations of city space into a relatively uncontrolled 'badlands' occupied by the poor and highly controlled 'security bubbles' inhabited by the rich. Geographical and social exclusion thereby conspires to corral together
populations of the unprotected, victimized, and victimizing—the mentally disordered,
the young, and the homeless—reinforcing both their vulnerability and their
propensities to offend (Carlen 1996; Hagan and McCarthy 1998).

RADICAL CRIMINOLOGY

So far, control has been treated without much direct allusion to the power, politics, and
inequalities that are its bedfellows. There was to be a relatively short-lived but active
challenge to such quiescence from the radical, new, or critical criminologies of the late
1960s and 1970s, criminologies that claimed their mandate in Marxism (Taylor,
Walton, and Young 1973), libertarianism (Douglas 1971), anarchism (Kittrie 1971;
Cohen 1985), or American populism (Quinney 1970), and whose ambitions pointed to
the need for political activism or praxis (Mathiesen 1974).

Crime control was said to be an oppressive and mystifying process that worked
through legislation, law-enforcement, and ideological stereotyping to preserve unequal
class relations (Chambliss 1976; Box 1983). The radical political economy of crime
sought chiefly to expose the hegemonic ideologies that masked the 'real' nature of crime
and repression in capitalist society. Most mundane offending, it was argued, was
actually less politically or socially consequential than other social evils such as alienation, exploitation, or racism (Scraton 1987). Much proletarian crime should actually
be redefined as a form of redistributive class justice, or as a sign of the possessive
individualism which resided in the core values of capitalist society. Criminal justice
itself was engineered to create visible crowds of working-class and black scapegoats
who could attract the public gaze away from the more serious delicts of the rich and the
more serious ills of a capitalism that was usually said to be in terminal crisis. If the
working class reacted in hostile fashion to the crime in their midst then they were, in
effect, little more than the victims of a false consciousness which turned proletarian
against proletarian, black against black, inflated the importance of petty problems, and
concealed the true nature of bourgeois society. So construed, signification, the act of
giving meaning, was either manipulative or misconceived, a matter of giving and

receiving incorrect and deformed interpretations of reality. Indeed, it was in the very nature of subordination in a capitalist society that most people must be politically unenlightened about crime, control, and much else, and the task of the radical criminologist was to expose, denounce, and demystify.

It was concluded variously that crime was not a problem which the poor and their allies should actually address (there were more important matters for Marxists to think about: Hirst 1975); that the crime which *should* be analysed was the wrongdoing of the powerful (the wrong crimes and criminals were being observed: Chapman 1967; Reiman 1990; Pearce and Tombs 1998); or that crime and its problems would shrivel into insignificance as a criminogenic capitalism gave way to the tolerant diversity of socialism (Taylor, Walton, and Young 1973). The crime and criminals that chiefly warranted attention were the crimes of the powerful (Slapper and Tombs 1999) or those exceptional examples of law-breaking that seemed to represent an incipient revolt against the state, and they demanded cultivation as subjects of study, understanding, and possible politicization. Black prisoners, in particular, were sometimes depicted, and depicted themselves, as prisoners of class or race wars (Cleaver 1969). Prisons were the point of greatest state repression, and prison riots a possible spearhead of revolution (Fitzgerald 1977).

In its early guise, radical criminology withered somewhat under a quadruple-barrelled assault. In some places, and in America especially (where it had never been firmly implanted), it ran foul of university politics, and some criminology departments, such as that of the University of California at Berkeley, were actually closed down. More often, radical criminology did not lend itself to the government-funded, policy-driven, 'soft money', empiricist research that began to dominate schools of criminology in North America in the 1970s and 1980s.

Second was the effect of the publication of mass victim surveys in the 1970s and 1980s (Hough and Mayhew 1983) which disclosed both the extent of working-class victimization and the manner in which it revolved around intra-class, rather than inter-class, criminality. It was evident that crime *was* a manifest problem for the poor, adding immeasurably to their burdens, and difficult to dismiss as an ideological distraction (David Downes called it a regressive tax on the poor). Two prominent radical criminologists came frankly to concede that they had believed that 'property offences [were] directed solely against the bourgeoisie and that violence against the person [was] carried out by amateur Robin Hoods in the course of their righteous attempts to redistribute wealth. All of this [was], alas, untrue' (Lea and Young 1984: 262).

Third was the critique launched from within the left by a new generation of feminist scholars, who asserted that the victimization of women was no slight affair or ideological diversion, and that rape, sexual assault, child abuse, and domestic violence should be taken very seriously indeed (Smart 1977). Not only had the female criminal been neglected, they said, but so had the female victim, and it would not do to wait until the revolution for matters to be put right. Once more, a number of radical criminologists gave ground. There had been, Jones, Maclean, and Young observed, 'a general tendency in radical thought to idealize their historical subject (in this case the working class) and to play down intra-group conflict, blemishes and social disorganization. But the power of the feminist case resulted in a sort of cognitive schizophrenia amongst radicals' (Jones *et al.* 1986: 3). The revitalized criminology of women is one of the subjects of Chapter 13, the chapter that deals with gender and crime, in this book.

Fourthly, there was a critique launched belatedly from non-feminist criminologists who resisted the imperious claims of radical criminology to be *the* sole fully social theory of crime (Downes and Rock 1979; Inciardi 1980). Marxist and radical theories of crime, it was argued, lacked a comparative emphasis: they neglected crime in 'non-capitalist' and 'pre-capitalist' societies and crime in 'socialist' societies. There was a naivety about the expectation that crime would wither away as the state itself disappeared after the revolution. There was a trust in socialist justice which could actually be very repressive indeed (socialist legality, Stan Cohen mused, tends to mean a 'model of social control in which offenders wearing sandwich-boards listing their crimes before a crowd which shouts "Down with the counter-revolutionaries!" and are then led away to be publicly shot' (1979b: 44)). And there was an irresponsibility about radical arguments that 'reformism' would only strengthen the grip of the capitalist system.

'Left Realism' was to be the outcome, and it was represented by Jock Young, one of its revisionist parents, as a novel fusion of analyses of crime in the vein of anomie theory and symbolic interactionist analyses of the reactions which crime evokes (Young 1997: 484). It was 'realist' because, refusing to accept the so-called 'left idealists'' dismissal of crime as an ideological trick, it acknowledged the practical force of crime in society and its especially heavy impact on the poor, minority ethnic people, and women. It was 'left' because it focused descriptively and politically on the structural inequalities of class, race, and gender. Its project was to examine patterns of crime and control as they emerged out of what Young came to call the 'square of crime', a field of forces dominated by the state, the victim, the offender, and the public.

Left Realism was to follow the earlier radical criminologists' injunction to act, but action was now as much in the service of more effective and practical policing and crime reduction strategies as in the cause of radical social change (if not more so). Left Realists joined the formerly disparaged 'administrative criminologists' working in and for the state to work on situationally based projects to prevent crime and the fear of crime (see Matthews and Young 1992). They designed new and confusing configurations of streets to make it more difficult for 'kerb-crawlers' to cruise in search of prostitutes. They explored the impact of improved street lighting on the fear of crime. They assisted in the rehabilitation of dilapidated housing estates. Were it not for their theoretical preambles, it was at times difficult to distinguish between the programmes of the Home Office or other state criminal justice ministries, on the one hand, and of Left Realism, on the other.

If Left Realism was radical criminology's *praxis*, its more scholarly current continued to evolve, and it evolved in diverse directions. A number of criminologists began to turn away from analyses of causation towards studies of current (Cohen 1985; Simon 1993) and historical forms of social control (see Scull 1979), originally under the influence of E. P. Thompson and Eric Hobsbawm and latterly under that of Michel Foucault,

Anthony Giddens, and Ulrich Beck. Others responded to the wider theories that began to dominate sociology proper in the 1980s and 1990s, incorporating them to write about crime, postmodernism (or late modernity), and globalization, and producing what were, in effect, examples of the 'fully social theory' promised by the new criminologists back in 1973. Above all, that promise was fulfilled by books published in 1999 by two of the original troika of new criminologists: Ian Taylor's *Crime in Context* and Jock Young's *The Exclusive Society.*

Crime in Context catalogues a series of crises flowing from transitions in the political and economic structures of society, and the manner in which they impinge upon poverty, class, gender, race, and the family to affect the national and transnational environments of crime and control. *The Exclusive Society* is subtitled 'Social Exclusion, Crime and Difference in Late Modernity', and its focus is more narrow but nevertheless effective, concentrating upon the social and political consequences of what then seemed to be the inexorable and vast increases in crime in the West. Crime is held by Young to be no longer regarded as abnormal, the property of a pathological few who can be restored therapeutically to the security of a moral community at one with itself, but *normal*, the actions of a significant, obdurate minority of Others who are impatiently excluded and demonized in a world newly insecure, fractured, and preoccupied with problems of risk and danger.

In other hands, what had once been a politically radical criminology became yoked to the analysis of what is called postmodernity, and it began to lose its connection to an analysis of the brute facts of power, structure, and stratification, becoming instead an epistemologically radical approach that concentrated on the consequences of a babble of contending interpretations (see Henry and Milovanovic 1996). Arrigo and Bernard came to declare of such a postmodern criminology that it now 'identifies the conflict over which various segments of society struggles to be about languaging [*sic*] reality/existence through multiple voices and ways of knowing' (2002: 8).

FUNCTIONALIST CRIMINOLOGY

Another, apparently dissimilar but substantially complementary, theory presented deviance and control as forces that worked discreetly to maintain social order. Functionalism was a theory of social systems or wholes, developed at the beginning of the twentieth century within a social anthropology grown tired of speculative accounts of the origins and evolution of societies which lacked the written history to support them, and dedicated to what was seen to be the scientific pursuit of intellectual problems. It was argued that the business of a social science necessitated moving enquiry beyond the reach of common sense or lay knowledge to an examination of the unintended, objective consequences of action that were visible only to the trained eye.

There were three clear implications. First, what ordinary people thought they were doing could be very different from what they actually achieved. The functionalist was preoccupied only with what were thought to be objective outcomes, and people's own accounts of action held little interest. Secondly, the functionalist looked at the impact made by institution upon institution, structure upon structure, in societies that were remarkable for their capacity to persist over time. Thirdly, those consequences, viewed as a totality, constituted a system in which, it was thought, not only did the parts affect one another and the whole, but also, the whole affected them in return. To be sure, some institutions were relatively detached, but functionalists would have argued that the alternative proposition—that social phenomena lack all influence upon one another, that there was no functional reciprocity between them—was conceptually insupportable. Systemic interrelations were an analytic *a priori*, a matter of self-evidence so compelling that Kingsley Davis could argue at one point that 'we are all functionalists now' (Davis 1959).

There have been very few dedicated functionalist criminologists (see Gottfredson and Hirschi 1990: 78). Functionalists tend to deal with the properties of whole systems rather than with empirical fragments. But crime and deviance did supply a particularly intriguing laboratory for thought-experiments about social order. It was easy enough to contend that religion or education shaped social cohesion, but how much harder it would be to show that *crime* succeeded in doing so. After all, 'everyone knew' that crime undermined social structures. It followed that functionalists occasionally found it tempting to try to confound that lay knowledge by showing that, to the contrary, the seemingly recalcitrant case of crime could be shown scientifically to contribute to the working of the social system. From time to time, therefore, they wrote about crime to demonstrate the potency of their theory. Only one functionalist, its grand master, Talcott Parsons, ever made the obvious, and therefore intellectually unsatisfying, point that crime could be what was called 'dysfunctional' or injurious to the social system as it was then constituted (Parsons 1951). Everyone else asserted that crime actually worked mysteriously to support it.

The outcome was a somewhat heterogeneous collection of papers documenting the multiple functions of deviance: Kingsley Davis showed that prostitution bolstered monogamy by providing an unemotional, impersonal, and unthreatening release for the sexual energy of the promiscuous married male (Davis 1937) (Mary McIntosh once wondered what the promiscuous married female was supposed to do about *her* sexual energy); Ned Polsky made much the same claim for pornography (Polsky 1967); Daniel Bell showed that racketeering provided 'queer ladders of success' and political and social stability in the New York dockside (1960); Émile Durkheim (1964) and George Herbert Mead (1918) contended that the formal rituals of trial and punishment enhanced social solidarity and consolidated moral boundaries; and, more complexly, Mary Douglas (1966), Kai Erikson (1966), Robert Scott (1972), and others argued that deviance offered social systems a dialectical or educational tool for the clarification and management of threats, ambiguities, and anomalies in classification systems. The list could be extended, but all the arguments tended to one end: what appeared, on the surface, to undermine social order accomplished the very reverse. A sociological counterpart of the invisible hand transmuted deviance into a force for cohesion.

Functionalism was to be discarded by many criminologists in time: it smacked too much of teleology (the doctrine that effects can work retrospectively to act as the causes of events); it defied rigorous empirical investigation (see Cotterrell 1999: 75); and, for some, more politically driven criminologists, it represented a form of Panglossian conservatism that championed the status quo. But its ghost lingers on. Any who would argue that, contrary to appearances, crime and deviance buttress social order; any who argue for the study of seamless systems; any who argue that the sociologist should mistrust people's own accounts of their actions; any who insist that social science is the study of unintended consequences; must share something of the functionalist's standpoint. Anomie theories that represented crime as the system-stabilizing, unintended consequence of strains in the social order are one quite explicit example (see Merton 1995): deviance in that guise becomes the patterned adjustments that defuse an otherwise disruptive conflict and reconcile people to disadvantage (although, as I have argued, the theories can also envisage conditions in which crime becomes 'system-threatening'). And anomie theories were the direct offspring of functionalism, Merton himself being Parson's heir. But, less explicitly, some versions of radical criminology provide another example. More than one criminologist has argued that crime, deviance, and control were necessary for the survival of capitalism (Stinchcombe 1968). Again, although they did not talk explicitly of '*function*', the neo-Marxists, Hall *et al.* (1978), Pearce (1976), and Reiman (1990), *were* recognizably functionalist in their treatment of the criminal justice system's production of visible and scapegoated roles for the proletarian criminal, roles that attracted public anxiety and outrage, diverted anger away from the state, emasculated political opposition, and preserved capitalism (Pearce and Tombs 1998). Consider, for example, Ferrell and Sanders's observation that 'the simplistic criminogenic models at the core of ... constructed moral panics ... deflect attention from larger and more complex political problems like economic and ethnic inequality, and the alienation of young people and creative workers from confining institutions' (1995: 10). What could be more transparently functionalist than that?

SIGNIFICATION

LABELLING THEORY

Perhaps the only other outstanding big idea is signification, the interpretive practice that orders social life. There has been an enduring strain of analysis, linked most particularly to symbolic interactionism and phenomenology, which insists that people do not, and cannot, respond immediately, uncritically, and passively to the world 'as it is'. Rather they necessarily respond to their *ideas* of the world, and the business of

sociology is to capture, understand, and reproduce those ideas; examine their interaction with one another; and analyse the processes and structures that generated them.
Sociology becomes the study of people, relations, and practices as symbolic and
symbolizing processes.

Central to that idea is reflectivity, the capacity of consciousness to translate itself into
its own object. People are able to think about themselves, define themselves in various
ways, toy with different identities, and project themselves imaginatively into any manner of contrived situation. They can view themselves vicariously by inferring the
reactions of 'significant others', and, in so 'taking the role of the other', move symbolically to a distance outside themselves to inspect how they might appear. Elaborating
action through 'significant gestures', the symbolic projection of acts and identities, they
can anticipate the likely responses of others, and tailor their own prospective acts to
accommodate them (Mead 1934). In all this, social worlds are compacted symbolically
into the phrasing of action, and the medium that makes that possible is language.

Language is held to objectify, stabilize, and extend meaning. Used conversationally in
the anticipation of an act, it permits people to be both their own subject and object,
speaker and thing spoken about, 'I' and 'me', opening up the mind to reflective action.
Conferring names, it enables people to impart moral and social meanings to their own
and others' motives (Mills 1940; Sykes and Matza 1957; Scott and Lyman 1970), intentions, and identities. It will matter a great deal if someone is defined as eccentric, erratic,
or mad; a drinker, a drunk, or an alcoholic; a lovelorn admirer or a stalker; a freedom
fighter or a terrorist. Consequences will flow from naming, consequences that affect not
only how one regards oneself and one's position in the world, but also how one may be
treated by others. Naming can create a self.

Transposed to the study of crime and deviance, symbolic interactionism and phenomenology gave prominence to the processes by which deviant acts and identities are
constructed, interpreted, judged, and controlled (Katz 1988). A core pair of articles was
Howard Becker's 'Becoming a Marihuana User' and 'Marihuana Use and Social Control',
both reprinted in *Outsiders* (1963), and both describing the patterned sequence of steps
that could shape the experience, moral character, and fate of one who began to smoke
marihuana. Becoming a marihuana user was a tentative process, developing stage by
stage, which required the user satisfactorily to learn, master, and interpret techniques,
neutralize forbidding moral images of use and users, and succeed in disguising signs of
use in the presence of those who might disapprove. It became paradigmatic.

Deviance itself was to become more generally likened to a moral career consisting of
interlocking phases, each of which fed into and shaped the next; each of which presented different existential problems and opportunities; each of which was populated
by different constellations of significant others; and each of which could distinctively
mould the self of the deviant. But the process was not inexorable but contingent. Not
every phase was inevitable or irreversible, and deviants could often choose to change
direction. Luckenbill and Best (1981: 201) provide a graphic description:

> Riding escalators between floors may be an effective metaphor for respectable organiza-
> tional careers, but it fails to capture the character of deviant careers. A more appropriate

image is a walk in the woods. Here, some people take the pathways marked by their predecessors, while others strike out on their own. Some walk slowly, exploring before moving on, but others run, caught up in the action. Some have a destination in mind and proceed purposively; others view the trip and enjoy it for its own sake. Even those intent on reaching a destination may stray from the path; they may try to shortcut or they may lose sight of familiar landmarks, get lost, and find it necessary to backtrack.

What punctuates such a career is acts of naming, the deployment of language to confer and fix the meanings of behaviour, and symbolic interactionism and phenomenology became known within criminology as 'labelling theory'. One of the most frequently cited of all passages in sociological criminology was Becker's dictum that 'deviance is not a quality of the act the person commits, but rather a consequence of the application by others of rules and sanctions to an "offender". The deviant is one to whom that label has successfully been applied; deviant behavior is behavior that people so label' (1963: 9).

Labelling itself is contingent. Many deviant acts are not witnessed and most are not reported. People may well be able to resist or modify deviant designations when attempts *are* made to apply them: after all, we are continually bombarded by attempts to label us and few succeed. But there are special occasions when the ability of the self to resist definition is circumscribed; and most fateful of all may be an encounter with agents of the criminal justice system, because they work with the often irresistible power, force, and authority of the state. In such meetings, criminals and deviants are obliged to confront not only their own and others' possibly defensive, fleeting, and insubstantial reactions to what they have done, their 'primary deviation', but also contend publicly with the formal reactions of others, and their deviation can then become a response to responses, 'secondary deviation': 'When a person begins to employ his deviant behavior or a role based upon it as a means of defense, attack, or adjustment to the overt and covert problems created by the consequent societal reaction to him, his deviation is secondary' (Lemert 1951: 76).

What is significant about secondary deviation is that it may be a symbolic synthesis of more than just the meanings and activities of primary deviation. It may also incorporate the myths, professional knowledge, stereotypes, experience, and working assumptions of lay people, police officers, judges, medical practitioners, prison officers, prisoners, policy-makers, and politicians. Drug-users (see Schur 1963), mental patients (Goffman 1968; Scheff 1966), homosexuals (Hooker 1963), and others may be obliged to organize their significant gestures and character around the public symbols and interpretations of their behaviour. Who they are and what they do may then be explained as much by the symbolic incorporation of a public response as by any set of original conditions, and control will be written into the very fabric of their selves.

What is significant is that secondary deviation may also entail confrontations with new obstacles that foreclose future choice. Thus, Gary Marx listed a number of the ironic consequences that can flow from forms of covert social control such as undercover policing and the work of *agents provocateurs*: they include generating a market for illegal goods; the provision of motives and meanings for illegal action; entrapping

people in offences they might not otherwise have committed; the supply of false or misleading records; retaliatory action against informers, and the like (Marx 1988: 126–7).
Once a person is publicly identified as a deviant, moreover, it becomes difficult for him
or her to slip back into the conventional world, and measures are being taken with
increasing frequency to enlarge the visibility of the rule-breaker. In the United States,
for instance, 'Megan's Law' makes it mandatory in certain jurisdictions for the names of
sex offenders to be publicly advertised, possibly reducing risk to some but certainly
freezing the criminal as a secondary deviant. Sheriffs have been known to shame prisoners by making them wear pink clothing or carry placards in public. Quite deliberately
in response to such dangerously amplified problems of the outlawed deviant is the
increasing adoption by states of strategies of restorative justice, based largely on the
work of Braithwaite (1989), which attempt to unite the informal control of shaming by
significant others with rituals of reintegration that work against the alienating consequences of secondary deviation.

Borrowing its ideas from Durkheim and labelling theory and its procedures from a
number of forms of dispute resolution, but from Maori and Japanese practice in particular, shaming is for Braithwaite at its most effective when it is practised by those
whose opinions matter to the deviant—his or her 'significant others'; and that it would
work only to exclude and estrange the deviant unless it was accompanied by rituals of
reparation and restoration, effected, perhaps, by the tendering and acceptance of a public apology. Reintegrative shaming is currently one of the 'big ideas' underpinning the
ideas (if not always the practice) of criminal justice policy across the Western world, but
also in South Africa and elsewhere, where it is seen to be a return to the procedures of
aboriginal justice. And it sits remarkably well with an interesting study of reoffending
after prison that argues that the critical variable in desistance from crime is the capacity
of a former inmate to construct a new narrative about his or her life which frames a new
self now going 'straight' (Maruna 2001).

CULTURE AND SUBCULTURE

Meanings and motives are not established and confirmed by the self in isolation. They
are a social accomplishment, and criminology has paid sustained attention to signification as a collaborative, subcultural process. Subcultures themselves are taken to be exag-
gerations, accentuations, or editings of cultural themes prevalent in the wider society.
Any social group which has permanence, a common pursuit, and, perhaps, common
problems is likely to engender, inherit, or modify a subculture; but the criminologist's
particular interest is in those subcultures that condone, promote, or otherwise make
possible the commission of delinquent acts. A subculture was not conceived to be utterly
distinct from the beliefs held by people at large. Neither was it necessarily oppositional.
It was a *sub*culture, not a discrete culture or a counterculture, and the analytic stress has
tended to be on dependency rather than conflict or symbolic autonomy.

The materials for subcultural theory are to be found across the broad range of criminology, and they could be combined in various proportions. Anomie theory supplied

the supposition that social inequalities generate problems that may have delinquent solutions, and that those solutions, in their turn, could be shared and transmitted by people thrown together by their common disadvantage. Albert Cohen, the man who invented the phrase 'delinquent subculture', argued: 'The crucial condition for the emergence of new cultural forms is the existence, in effective interaction with one another, of a number of actors with similar problems of adjustment' (1957: 59). The social anthropology of the Chicago School, channelled for a while into differential association theory, supplied an emphasis upon the enduring, intelligible, and locally adapted cultural traditions shared both by professional criminals and by boys living, working, and playing together on the crowded streets of morally differentiated areas. Retaining the idea of a 'subculture of delinquency', David Matza and a number of control theorists pointed to the manner in which moral proscriptions could be neutralized by invoking commonly available and culturally transmitted extenuating accounts. And symbolic interactionism supplied a focus on the negotiated, collective, and processual character of meaning. In all this, an argument ran that young men (it was almost always young men), growing up in the city, banded together in groups or 'near-groups' (Yablonsky 1962) in the crowded public life of the streets, encountering common problems, exposed to common stereotypes and stigmas, subject to similar formal controls, setting themselves against common Others who are used oppositionally to define who they are, are likely to form joint interpretations that are sporadically favourable to delinquency. Subcultural theory and research were to dominate explanations of delinquency until they exhausted themselves for a while in the 1960s, only to be revived in a new guise a decade later.

Subcultural theory lent itself to amalgamation with radical criminology, and particularly that criminology which was preoccupied with the reproduction of class inequalities through the workings of ideology. In Britain, there was to be a renaissance of anomie-derived subcultural theory as a group of sociologists centred around Stuart Hall at the University of Birmingham gave special attention to the existential plight of young working-class men about to enter the labour market. The prototype for that work was Phil Cohen's analysis of proletarian cultures in London: young men responded to the post-war decline of community, loss of class cohesion, and economic insecurity by resurrecting in subcultural form an idealized and exaggerated version of working-class masculinity that 'express[ed] and resolve[d], albeit "magically", the contradictions which remain hidden or unresolved in the parent culture' (1972: 23). Deviance became a form of symbolic resistance to tensions perceived through the mists of false consciousness. It was doomed to disappoint because it did not address the root causes of discontent, but it *did* offer a fleeting release. There was a contradiction within that version of subcultural theory because it was not easy to reconcile a structural Marxism which depicted adolescent culture as illusory with a commitment to understanding meaning (Willis 1977). But it was a spirited and vivid revival of a theory that had gone into the doldrums in the 1960s, and it continues to influence theorizing (see Ferrell 1993). Indeed, interestingly, there are currently strong signs of a *rapprochement* between critical cultural studies, symbolic interactionism (see Becker and McCall

1990) and radical criminology, that has led to the creation of a new theoretical hybrid, cultural criminology (see Ferrell *et al.* 2004), which emphasizes how transgression attains meaning in what is called a fluid, pluralistic, contested, hedonistic, 'edgy', and 'media-saturated world'.

CRIMINOLOGY AS AN ECLECTIC DISCIPLINE

It would be misleading from my description so far to conclude that criminology can easily be laid out as an array of discrete clumps of theory. On the contrary, it has continually borrowed ideas from other disciplines, and has compared, contrasted, amalgamated, reworked, and experimented with them to furnish an eclectic discipline marked by an abundance of theoretical overlaps, syntheses, and confusions.

There are exchanges and combinations of criminological ideas *within* disciplines. For instance, sociological criminologists have been exposed continually to changes in intellectual fashion in their parent discipline, and the result has been that almost every major theory in sociology has been fed in some form into criminology at some time, undergoing adaptation and editing in the process, and occasionally becoming very distant from its roots. Indeed, one of the distinctive properties of that process is that criminology can sometimes so extensively rework imported ideas that they will develop well beyond their original limits in sociology, becoming significant contributions to sociological theory in their own right. Anomie, the symbolic interactionist conception of the self and its others, and feminism are examples of arguments that have grown appreciably in scale and sophistication within the special environment of criminology.

There are exchanges and combinations *between* disciplines. Criminology is defined principally by its attachment to an empirical area: it is the study of *crime* that gives unity and order to the enterprise, not adherence to any particular theory or social science. It is in the examination of *crime* that psychologists, statisticians, lawyers, economists, social anthropologists, sociologists, social policy analysts, and psychiatrists meet and call themselves criminologists, and in that encounter, their attachments to the conventions and boundaries of their parent disciplines may weaken. So it is that sociological criminologists have confronted arguments born and applied in other disciplines and, from time to time, they have domesticated them to cultivate new intellectual hybrids. Stan Cohen (1972) and Jock Young (1971) did so in the early 1970s when they married the symbolic interactionism of Edwin Lemert (1951) and Howard Becker (1963) to the statistical theory of Leslie Wilkins (1964). Wilkins had argued that deviant events fall at the poles of normal distribution curves, that knowledge about those events will be distorted by the ensuing social distance, and that patterns of control and deviant responses are likely to become ever more exaggerated as they are affected by those distortions. That concept of deviance amplification married well with interactionist ideas of secondary deviation.

Thus constituted, the development of sociological criminology over the last few decades is at once marked by discontinuities and continuities. It may be represented as a staggered succession of interchanges with different schools and disciplines which do not always meld well together. It is evident, for instance, that the feminist may entertain a conception of theory and the theorist very unlike that of the functionalist or rational choice theorist. Yet there are also unities of a kind. All competent criminologists may be presumed to have a rough working knowledge of the wide range of theory in their discipline; theory once mastered is seldom forgotten or neglected entirely, and there is a propensity for scholars overtly and covertly to weave disparate ideas together as problems and needs arise. Quite typical was an observation offered in the author's introduction to a work on the lives of urban street criminals in Seattle, Washington: 'I link ... ethnographic data to criminological perspectives as a *bricoleur* seeking numerous sources of interpretation. Had I selected just one criminological perspective to complement these ethnographic data, the value of these firsthand accounts would be constrained' (Fleisher 1995: 5). Scholars thus tend frequently to be more accommodating in practice than in principle, and if there *is* an ensuing gap between a professed purity of theory and an active pragmatism of procedure, it may well be masked by the obliteration of sources or the renaming of ideas. Seemingly distinct sociological theories are open to continual merging and blurring as the practical work of criminology unfolds, and in that process may be found opportunities for theoretical innovation.

PROSPECTS FOR THE FUTURE

What is uncertain, and what has always been uncertain, is how those criminological theories may be expected to evolve in the future. Very few would have predicted the rapid demise of radical criminology, a brand of theorizing that once seemed so strong that it would sweep all before it, at least in large parts of Europe, Canada, and Australasia. Few would have predicted the resurgence of utilitarian theories of rational choice—they seemed to have been superseded forever by a sociology that pointed to the part played by social and moral contexts in the shaping of meaning and action. Yet Marshall felt himself constrained to lament that 'it seems that the hey-days of creative criminological (sociological) theory development in the US are long gone'(2002: 21)).

What may certainly be anticipated is a continuation of the semi-detached relations between criminology and its parent disciplines, and with sociology above all. The half-life of sociological theories is brief, often bound up with the duration of intellectual generations, and sociological theory is itself emergent, a compound of the familiar and the unfamiliar. It is to be assumed that there will always be something new out of sociology, and that criminology will almost always respond and innovate in its turn.

Other matters are also clear. First, criminology remains a substantively defined discipline, and it tends not to detain the intellectual system-builders. Those who would be the sociological Newtons, the men and women who would explain the great clockwork of society, are often impatient with the limitations imposed by analysing the mere parts and fragments of larger totalities. At first or second hand, almost all the grand theorists have made something of a mark on criminology, but they, or their disciples, have rarely stayed long. Their concern is with the wider systemic properties of society, not the surface features of empirical areas. Thus the phenomenologist, Phillipson, long ago remarked that '[we should] turn away from constitutive and arbitrary judgements of public rule breaking as deviance towards the concept of rule itself and the dialectical tension that ruling is, a subject more central to the fundamental practice of sociology' (1974: 5). And Marxists (Bankowski *et al.* 1977) and feminists (Smart 1989) have said much the same about the relations between their theories and the subdiscipline of criminology.

Secondly, criminology will probably persist in challenging economics as a contender for the title of the dismal science. Criminologists are not professionally optimistic. A prolonged exposure to the pain of crime, rates of offending that (until fairly recently at least) had seemed prone inexorably to rise, frequent abuses of authority, misconceived policies, and 'nothing' or very little appearing to work, seems to have fostered a propensity amongst thinkers to infuse their writing with gloom and to argue, in effect, that all is really not for the best in the best of all possible worlds. Stan Cohen once confessed that 'most of us—consciously or not—probably hold a rather bleak view of social change. Things must be getting worse' (1979a: 360). Prophecies of a criminological future will still be tinged at the margins with the iconography of Mad Max, Neuromancer, and Blade Runner.

Thirdly, there is the growing influence of government and government money in shaping criminological work, particularly in North America, and that has shaped the form, mode, and content of the discipline. Formally, policy-makers and politicians have a liking for argument phrased in numbers: it lends itself to an appearance of exactitude and control. One commentator, Bernard, remarked that 'The past 20 years have seen a vast expansion of quantitative research in criminology. Twenty years ago there were fewer journals and they published a greater variety of articles, including quantitative and qualitative research, theoretical and policy arguments, and even polemical pieces. Today, there are more journals and they mainly publish quantitative research' (1990: 325). And, substantively, policies and politics have conspired to make certain kinds of applied reasoning, such as restorative justice and rational choice theory, the criminological anti-theory, particularly attractive to criminal justice agencies. Restorative justice is new, and modest in its reach, and it seems to 'work'. Rational choice and control theories lay out a series of neat, inexpensive, small-scale, practicable, and non-controversial steps that may be taken to 'do something' about crime. Moreover, as theories that are tied to the apron strings of economics, they can borrow something of the powerful intellectual authority that economics wields in the social sciences.

Fourth is the persistence of a feminist influence. Crime is clearly gendered, the intellectual yield of analysing the connections between gender and crime has not yet been fully explored, and women are entering the body of sociological criminology in ever greater numbers (although, to be sure, some feminists, like Carol Smart, have also emigrated and absolute numbers remain small). Criminological feminisms and feminist criminologies (Gelsthorpe and Morris 1988) will undoubtedly sustain work on gender, control, and deviance and, increasingly, on masculinity. After all, if crime is largely a male preserve, criminology must ask what it is about masculinity that seems to have such an affinity with offending. Connell (1987), not himself a criminologist, has sketched the possibilities of an answer in his writing on 'hegemonic masculinity'—the overriding ideology of male power, wealth, and physical strength—that lends itself to exploit, risk-taking, and aggression. Messerschmidt (1997), Bourgois (1995), and Polk (1994) have pursued that model of masculine behaviour into criminology, Bourgois exploring the work done to maintain 'respect' by cocaine-dealing Latin Americans on the streets of New York, and Polk describing how the defence of masculine conceptions of honour and face can precipitate homicide.

A role will continue to be played by the sociological criminology that attaches importance to the ethnographic study of signifying practices. Symbolic interactionism and phenomenology have supplied an enduring reminder of the importance of reflectivity; the symbolically mediated character of all social reality; and the sheer complexity, density, and intricacy of the social world. And, lastly, one would hope that criminology will continue to contribute its own distinct analysis of the wider social world, an analysis that can take it beyond the confines of a tightly defined nexus of relations between criminals, legislators, lawyers, and enforcement agents. A criminology without a wider vision of social process would be deformed. A sociology without a conception of rule-breaking and control would be an odd discipline indeed.

■ SELECTED FURTHER READING

There is no substitute for the original works, some of the more important of which are Howard Becker's *Outsiders* (1963); John Braithwaite's *Crime, Shame and Reintegration* (1989); Richard Cloward and Lloyd Ohlin's *Delinquency and Opportunity* (1960); David Matza's *Delinquency and Drift* (1964); Ian Taylor, Paul Walton, and Jock Young's *The New Criminology* (1973); and Jock Young's *The Exclusive Society* (1999). Among the secondary texts are David Downes and Paul Rock's *Understanding Deviance* (2003 and 2007), and John Tierney's *Criminology: Theory and Context* (1996 and 2005).

■ REFERENCES

AKERLOF, G., and YELLEN, J. (1994), 'Gang Behavior, Law Enforcement, and Community Values', in H. Aaron *et al.* (eds), *Values and Public Policy*, Washington DC: Brookings Institute.

ALDANA-PINDELL, R. (2002), 'In Vindication of Justiciable Victims' Rights to Truth and Justice for State-Sponsored Crimes', *Vanderbilt Journal of Transnational Law*, November, 35: 5.

ANDERSON, E. (1976), *A Place on the Corner*, Chicago: University of Chicago Press.

ARRIGO, B., and BERNARD, T. (2002), 'Postmodern Criminology in Relation to Radical and Conflict

Criminology', in S. Cote (ed.), *Criminological Theories: Bridging the Past to the Future*, Thousand Oaks: Sage.

BALDWIN, J., and BOTTOMS, A. (1976), *The Urban Criminal*, London: Tavistock.

BANKOWSKI, Z., MUNGHAM, G., and YOUNG, P. (1977), 'Radical Criminology or Radical Criminologist?', *Contemporary Crises*, 1(1): 37–51.

BAUMAN, Z. (1989), *Modernity and the Holocaust*, Cambridge: Polity Press.

BAYART, J.-F., ELLIS, S., and HIBOU, B. (1999), *The Criminalization of the State in Africa*, Bloomington: Indiana University Press.

BECK, U. (1992), *Risk Society*, London: Sage.

BECKER, G. (1968), 'Crime and Punishment: An Economic Approach', *The Journal of Political Economy*, 76.

BECKER, H. (1963), *Outsiders*, New York: Free Press.

——and McCALL, M. (eds) (1990), *Symbolic Interaction and Cultural Studies*, Chicago: University of Chicago Press.

BEIRNE, P. (ed.) (1994), introduction to *The Origins and Growth of Criminology*, Aldershot: Dartmouth.

BELL, D. (1960), 'The Racket-Ridden Longshoremen', in *The End of Ideology*, New York: Collier.

BERNARD, T. (1990), 'Twenty Years of Testing Theories', *Journal of Research in Crime and Delinquency*, 27.

BOTTOMS, A. *et al.* (1989), 'A Tale of Two Estates', in D. Downes (ed.), *Crime and the City*, Macmillan: Basingstoke.

——and WILES, P. (1996), 'Crime and Insecurity in the City', in C. Fijnaut *et al.* (eds), *Changes in Society, Crime and Criminal Justice in Europe*, The Hague: Kluwer.

BOURGOIS, P. (1995), *In Search of Respect*, Cambridge: Cambridge University Press.

BOX, S. (1971), *Deviance, Reality and Society*, London: Holt, Rinehart, and Winston.

——(1983), *Power, Crime and Mystification*, London: Tavistock.

BRAITHWAITE, J. (1989), *Crime, Shame and Reintegration*, Cambridge: Cambridge University Press.

BRANTINGHAM, P., and BRANTINGHAM, P. (1981–2), 'Mobility, Notoriety, and Crime', *Journal of Environmental Systems*, 11(1).

CAMPBELL, B. (1993), *Goliath: Britain's Dangerous Places*, London: Methuen.

CARLEN, P. (1988), *Women, Crime and Poverty*, Milton Keynes: Open University Press.

——(1996), *Jigsaw: A Political Criminology of Youth Homelessness*, Buckingham: Open University Press.

CHAMBLISS, W. (1976), 'The State and Criminal Law', in W. Chambliss and M. Mankoff (eds), *Whose Law, What Order?*, New York: Wiley.

CHAPMAN, D. (1967), *Sociology and the Stereotype of the Criminal*, London: Tavistock.

CHEVALIER, L. (1973), *Labouring Classes and Dangerous Classes in Paris During the First Half of the Nineteenth Century*, London: Routledge & Kegan Paul.

CLARKE, R. (1992), *Situational Crime Prevention*, New York: Harrow and Heston.

——(1999), 'Situational Prevention', paper delivered at the Cambridge Workshop on *Situational Crime Prevention—Ethics and Social Context*, 14–16 October.

——and CORNISH, D. (undated), 'Rational Choice', unpublished.

——and——(1985), 'Modeling Offenders' Decisions', in M. Tonry and N. Morris (eds), *Crime and Justice*, 6, Chicago: University of Chicago Press.

——and——(2000), 'Analyzing Organized Crime', unpublished.

——and FELSON, M. (eds) (1993), *Routine Activity and Rational Choice*, New Brunswick: Transaction.

CLEAVER, E. (1969), *Post-Prison Writings and Speeches*, London: Cape.

CLOWARD, R., and OHLIN, L. (1960), *Delinquency and Opportunity*, New York: Free Press.

COHEN, A. (1957), *Delinquent Boys*, Glencoe: Free Press.

COHEN, L., and FELSON, M. (1979), 'Social Change and Crime Rate Trends', *American Sociological Review*, 44.

COHEN, P. (1972), 'Working-Class Youth Cultures in East London', *Working Papers in Cultural Studies*, Birmingham, 2.

COHEN, S. (1971), *Images of Deviance*, London: Penguin.

——(1972), *Folk Devils and Moral Panics*, London: Paladin.

——(1979a), 'The Punitive City: Notes on the Dispersal of Social Control', *Contemporary Crises*, 3.

——(1979b) 'Guilt, Justice and Tolerance', in D. Downes and P. Rock (eds), *Deviant Interpretations*, Oxford: Martin Robertson.

——(1985), *Visions of Social Control*, Cambridge: Polity.

COHEN, S. (1996), 'Crime and Politics: Spot the Difference', *British Journal of Sociology*, 47.

COLEMAN, A. (1985), *Utopia on Trial*, London: Hilary Shipman.

—— (1986), 'Dangerous Dreams', *Landscape Design*, 163.

COLQUHOUN, P. (1797), *A Treatise on the Police of the Metropolis*, London: H. Fry.

CONNELL, R. (1987), *Gender and Power*, Cambridge: Polity.

CORRIGAN, P. (1979), *Schooling the Smash Street Kids*, London: Macmillan.

COTTERRELL, R. (1999), *Émile Durkheim: Law in a Moral Domain*, Stanford: Stanford University Press.

CUSSON, M. (1983), *Why Delinquency?*, Toronto: University of Toronto Press.

DAMER, S. (1974), 'Wine Alley: The Sociology of a Dreadful Enclosure', *Sociological Review*, 22.

DAVIES, N. (1998), *Dark Heart: The Shocking Truth about Hidden Britain*, London: Vintage.

DAVIS, K. (1937), 'The Sociology of Prostitution', *American Sociological Review*, 2.

—— (1959), 'The Myth of Functional Analysis as a Special Method in Sociology and Anthropology', *American Sociological Review*, 24.

DAVIS, M. (1992a), 'Beyond Blade Runner', *Open Magazine Pamphlet*, New Jersey.

—— (1992b), *City of Quartz*, New York: Vintage.

DOUGLAS, J. (1971), *American Social Order*, London: Collier-Macmillan.

DOUGLAS, M. (1966), *Purity and Danger*, London: Pelican.

DOWNES, D. (1966), *The Delinquent Solution*, London: Routledge & Kegan Paul.

—— (1988), 'The Sociology of Crime and Social Control in Britain, 1960–1987', in P. Rock (ed.), *A History of British Criminology*, Oxford: Clarendon Press.

—— and ROCK, P. (eds) (1979), *Deviant Interpretations*, Oxford: Martin Robertson.

—— and —— (2003), *Understanding Deviance*, 4th edn (5th edn 2007, forthcoming) Oxford: Oxford University Press.

DUNEIER, M. (2001), *Sidewalk*, New York: Farrar, Straus and Giroux.

DURKHEIM, É. (1952), *Suicide*, London: Routledge & Kegan Paul.

—— (1964), *The Division of Labour in Society*, New York: Free Press.

ERIKSON, K. (1966), *Wayward Puritans*, New York: Wiley.

—— (1994), *A New Species of Trouble*, New York: Norton.

FARIS, R., and DUNHAM, H. (1939), *Mental Disorders in Urban Areas*, Chicago: University of Chicago Press.

FEELEY, M. (1996), 'The Decline of Women in the Criminal Process', in *Criminal Justice History*, 15, Westport, Ct.: Greenwood Press.

—— and SIMON, J. (1992), 'The New Penology', *Criminology*, 30.

FELSON, M. (1994), *Crime and Everyday Life*, California: Pine Forge.

—— and CLARKE, R. (1998), *Opportunity Makes the Thief*, Police Research Series Paper, London: Home Office.

FERRELL, J. (1993), *Crimes of Style*, Boston, Mass.: Northeastern University Press.

—— and SANDERS, C. (1995), *Cultural Criminology*, Boston, Mass.: Northeastern University Press.

——, HAYWARD, K., MORRISON, W., and PRESDEE, M. (eds) (2004), *Cultural Criminology Unleashed*, London: Glasshouse.

FITZGERALD, M. (1977), *Prisoners in Revolt*, Harmondsworth: Penguin.

FLEISHER, M. (1995), *Beggars and Thieves*, Madison, Wis.: University of Wisconsin Press.

FLETCHER, J. (1850), *Summary of the Moral (and Educational) Statistics of England and Wales*, London: privately printed.

FOUCAULT, M. (1977), *Discipline and Punish*, Harmondsworth: Penguin.

FUKUYAMA, F. (2004), *State Building*, London: Profile Books.

GARLAND, D. (1988), 'British Criminology before 1935', in P. Rock (ed.), *A History of British Criminology*, Oxford: Clarendon Press.

—— (2002), 'Of Crimes and Criminals: The Development of Criminology in Britain', in M. Maguire, R. Morgan, and R. Reiner (eds), *The Oxford Handbook of Criminology*, 3rd edn, Oxford: Oxford University Press.

GELSTHORPE, L., and MORRIS, A. (1988), 'Feminism and Criminology in Britain', *British Journal of Criminology*, 28.

GENN, H. (1988), 'Multiple Victimisation', in M. Maguire and J. Pointing (eds), *Victims of Crime: a New Deal?*, Milton Keynes: Open University Press.

GIDDENS, A. (1972), *Émile Durkheim: Selected Writings*, Cambridge: Cambridge University Press.

——(1991), *Modernity and Self-Identity*, Cambridge: Polity Press.

GILL, O. (1977), *Luke Street: Housing Policy, Conflict and the Creation of the Delinquent Area*, London: Macmillan.

GLUCKMAN, M. (1955), *The Judicial Process Among the Barotse of Northern Rhodesia*, Manchester: Manchester University Press.

GOFFMAN, E. (1968), *Asylums*, Harmondsworth: Penguin.

GORDON, C. (ed.) (1972), *Power/Knowledge*, Brighton: Harvester Press.

GORDON, D. (1986–7), 'The Electronic Panopticon', *Politics and Society*, 15.

GOTTFREDSON, M., and HIRSCHI, T. (1990), *A General Theory of Crime*, Stanford, Cal.: Stanford University Press.

GUERRY, A. (1864), *Statistique morale de l'Angleterre comparée avec la statistique morale de la France*, Paris: J. B. Bailliere et Fils.

HAGAN, J. (1985), 'The Class Structure of Gender and Delinquency: Toward a Power-Control Theory of Common Delinquent Behavior', *American Journal of Sociology*, 90.

——(1988), *Structural Criminology*, Cambridge: Polity Press.

——and McCARTHY, B. (1998), *Mean Streets: Youth Crime and Homelessness*, Cambridge: Cambridge University Press.

——, SIMPSON, J. H., and GILLIS, A. R. (1979), 'The Sexual Stratification of Social Control', *British Journal of Sociology*, 30.

HAGGERTY, K. (2004), 'Displaced Expertise', *Theoretical Criminology*, 8, 2.

HALL, S., CRITCHER, C., JEFFERSON, T., CLARKE, J., and ROBERTS, B. (1978), *Policing the Crisis*, London: Macmillan.

HENRY, S., and MILOVANOVIC, D. (1996), *Constitutive Criminology: Beyond Postmodernism*, London: Sage.

HILLIER, W. (1973), 'In Defence of Space', *RIBA Journal*, November.

——(1986), 'City of Alice's Dreams', *Architecture Journal*, 9.

HILLYARD, P., SIM, J., TOMBS, S., and WHYTE, D. (2004), 'Leaving a "Stain upon the Silence": Contemporary Criminology and the Politics of Dissent', *British Journal of Criminology*, 44: 369–90.

HIRSCHI, T. (1969), *The Causes of Delinquency*, Berkeley, Cal.: University of California Press.

HIRST, P. (1975), 'Marx and Engels on Law, Crime and Morality', in I. Taylor *et al.* (eds), *Critical Criminology*, London: Routledge & Kegan Paul.

HOOD, R. (2004), 'Hermann Mannheim and Max Grünhut: Criminological Pioneers in London and Oxford', *British Journal of Criminology*, July, 44(4): 469–95.

HOOKER, E. (1963), 'Male Homosexuality', in N. Farberow (ed.), *Taboo Topics*, New York: Prentice-Hall.

HOPE, T. (1982), *Burglary in Schools*, London: Home Office.

HOUGH, M., and MAYHEW, P. (1983), *The British Crime Survey*, London: HMSO.

HOWARD, J. (1784), *The State of the Prisons*, London: Cadell, Johnson, and Dilly.

INCIARDI, J. (ed.) (1980), *Radical Criminology: the Coming Crises*, Beverly Hills, Cal.: Sage.

INNES, M. (2003), *Understanding Social Control: Deviance, Crime And Social Order*, Maidenhead: Open University Press.

JACOBS, J. (1965), *The Death and Life of Great American Cities*, Harmondsworth: Penguin.

JONES, T., MACLEAN, B., and YOUNG, J. (1986), *The Islington Crime Survey*, Aldershot: Gower.

KAPLAN, R. (1994), 'The Coming Anarchy', *The Atlantic Monthly*, February.

KATZ, J. (1988), *Seductions of Crime*, New York: Basic Books.

——(1997), 'Ethnography's Warrants', *Sociological Methods and Research*, 25: 4.

KENNY, C. (1910), untitled piece in *Journal of the Society of Comparative Legislation*, 10: 2.

KITTRIE, N. (1971), *The Right to be Different*, Baltimore, Md.: Johns Hopkins Press.

KORNHAUSER, R. (1978), *Social Sources of Delinquency: An Appraisal of Analytic Models*, Chicago: University of Chicago Press.

KUMAR, R. (1993), *The History of Doing*, New Delhi: Kali for Women.

LANDESCO, J. (rep. 1968), *Organized Crime in Chicago*, Chicago: University of Chicago Press.

LAUB, J., and SAMPSON, R. (2003), *Shared Beginnings: Divergent Lives: Delinquent Boys to Age 70*, Cambridge, Mass.: Harvard University Press.

LEA, J., and YOUNG, J. (1984), *What is to be Done about Law and Order?*, London: Penguin Books.

LEMERT, E. (1951), *Social Pathology*, New York: McGraw-Hill.

LIANOS, M., with DOUGLAS, M. (2000), 'Dangerisation and the End of Deviance: The Institutional Environment', *British Journal of Criminology*, Spring, 40: 2.

LLEWELLYN, K., and HOEBEL, A. (1941), *The Cheyenne Way: Conflict and Case Law in Primitive Jurisprudence*, Norman, Okla.: University of Oklahoma Press.

LOMBROSO, C. (1895), *The Female Offender*, London: T. Fisher Unwin.

LUCKENBILL, D., and BEST, J. (1981), 'Careers in Deviance and Respectability', *Social Problems*, 29.

LUKES, S. (1967), 'Alienation and Anomie', in P. Laslett and W. Runciman (eds), *Philosophy, Politics and Society*, Oxford: Blackwell.

LYON, D. (1994), *The Electronic Eye*, Cambridge: Polity Press.

McROBBIE, A., and GARBER, J. (1976), 'Girls and Subcultures', in S. Hall and T. Jefferson (eds), *Resistance through Ritual*, London: Hutchinson.

MANNHEIM, H. (1965), *Comparative Criminology*, London: Routledge & Kegan Paul.

MARSHALL, I. (2002), 'The Criminological Enterprise in Europe and America', in S. Cote (ed.), *Criminological Theories: Bridging the Past to the Future*, Thousand Oaks, Cal.: Sage.

MARTINSON, R. (1974), 'What Works? Questions and Answers about Penal Reform', *Public Interest*, 35.

MARUNA, S. (2001), *Making Good: How Ex-Convicts Reform and Rebuild their Lives*, Washington DC: American Psychological Association.

MARX, G. (1988), *Under Cover*, Berkeley, Cal.: University of California Press.

MATHIESEN, T. (1974), *The Politics of Abolition*, London: Martin Robertson.

MATTHEWS, R., and YOUNG, J. (eds) (1992), *Rethinking Criminology: The Realist Debate*, London: Sage.

MATZA, D. (1964), *Delinquency and Drift*, New York: Wiley.

——(1969), *Becoming Deviant*, New Jersey: Prentice-Hall.

MAUDSLEY, H. (1888), 'Remarks on Crime and Criminals,' *Journal of Mental Science*, July.

MAYHEW, P., CLARKE, R. V. G., SHURMAN, A., and HOUGH, J . M. (1976), *Crime as Opportunity*, Home Office Research Study No. 34, London: Home Office.

MEAD, G. (1918), 'The Psychology of Punitive Justice', *American Journal of Sociology*, 23.

——(1934), *Mind Self and Society*, Chicago: University of Chicago Press.

MERTON, R. (1938), 'Social Structure and Anomie', *American Sociological Review*, 3.

——(1957), *Social Theory and Social Structure*, Glencoe, Ill.: Free Press.

——(1995), 'Opportunity Structure: The Emergence, Diffusion and Differentiation of a Sociological Concept, 1930s–1950s', in F. Adler and W. Laufer (eds), *The Legacy of Anomie Theory*, New Brunswick: Transaction.

MESSERSCHMIDT, J. (1997), *Crime as Structured Action: Gender, Race, Class, and Crime in the Making*, Thousand Oaks, Cal.: Sage.

MILLS, C. (1940), 'Situated Actions and Vocabularies of Motive', *American Sociological Review*, 5.

MORRIS, T. (1958), *The Criminal Area*, London: Routledge & Kegan Paul.

——(1988), 'British Criminology: 1935–48', in P. Rock (ed.), *A History of British Criminology*, Oxford: Clarendon Press.

MORRISON, W. (1891), *Crime and its Causes*, London: Swan Sonnenschein.

——(1896), *Juvenile Offenders*, London: Swan Sonnenschein.

NEWBURN, T., and STANKO, E. (eds) (1994), *Just Boys Doing Business: Masculinity and Crime*, London: Routledge.

NEWMAN, O. (1972), *Defensible Space: People and Design in the Violent City*, London: Architectural Press.

NORRIS, C., and ARMSTRONG, G. (1999), *The Maximum Surveillance Society*, Oxford: Berg.

O'MALLEY, P. (1992), 'Risk, Power and Crime Prevention', *Economy and Society*, August, 21.

PARK, R. (1915), 'The City: Suggestions for the Investigation of Human Behavior in the City Environment', *American Journal of Sociology*, 20.

——(1925), 'Community Organization and Juvenile Delinquency', in R. Park and R. Burgess (eds), *The City*, Chicago: University of Chicago Press.

PARSONS, T. (1951), *The Social System*, London: Routledge & Kegan Paul.

PEARCE, F. (1976), *Crimes of the Powerful*, London: Pluto.

——and TOMBS, S. (1998), *Toxic Capitalism: Corporate Crime and the Chemical Industry*, Aldershot: Dartmouth.

PHILLIPSON, M. (1974), 'Thinking Out of Deviance', unpublished paper.

POLK, K. (1994), *When Men Kill*, Cambridge: Cambridge University Press.

POLSKY, N. (1967), *Hustlers, Beats and Others*, Chicago: Aldine.

POWER, A. (1997), *Estates on the Edge: The Social Consequences of Mass Housing in Northern Europe*, New York: St. Martin's Press.

PRESDEE, M. (2000), *Cultural Criminology and the Carnival of Crime*, London: Routledge.

QUETELET, L. (1848), *Du système social et des lois qui le régissent*, Paris: np.

QUINNEY, R. (1970), *The Social Reality of Crime*, Boston, Mass.: Little Brown.

RADZINOWICZ, L., and HOOD, R. (1990), *The Emergence of Penal Policy in Victorian and Edwardian England*, Oxford: Clarendon Press.

RAINWATER, L. (1970), *Behind Ghetto Walls*, Chicago: Aldine.

RECKLESS, W. (1933), *Vice in Chicago*, Chicago: University of Chicago Press.

—— et al. (1957), 'The Good Boy in a High Delinquency Area', *Journal of Criminal Law, Criminology, and Police Science*, 48.

REIMAN, J. (1990), *The Rich Get Richer and the Poor Get Prison*, New York: Macmillan.

ROCK, P. (1988), 'The Present State of British Criminology', in P. Rock (ed.), *A History of British Criminology*, Oxford: Clarendon Press.

ROMILLY, S. (1811), *Observations on the Criminal Law of England*, London.

RONCEK, D., and MAIER, P. (1991), 'Bars, Blocks, and Crimes Revisited: Linking the Theory of Routine Activities to the Empiricism of "Hot Spots" ', *Criminology*, 29.

RORTY, R. (1991), *Objectivity, Relativism, and Truth*, Cambridge: Cambridge University Press.

SAMPSON, R., and LAUB, J. (1993), *Crime in the Making: Pathways and Turning Points Through Life*, Cambridge, Mass.: Harvard University Press.

SCHEFF, T. (1966), *Being Mentally Ill*, London: Weidenfeld & Nicolson.

SCHUR, E. (1963), *Narcotic Addiction in Britain and America*, London: Tavistock.

SCOTT, M., and LYMAN, S. (1970), 'Accounts, Deviance and Social Order', in J. Douglas (ed.), *Deviance and Respectability*, New York: Basic Books.

SCOTT, R. (1972), 'A Proposed Framework for Analyzing Deviance as a Property of Social Order', in R. Scott and J. Douglas (eds), *Theoretical Perspectives on Deviance*, New York: Basic Books.

SCOTTISH CENTRAL RESEARCH UNIT (1999), 'The Effect of Closed Circuit Television on Recorded Crime Rates and Public Concern about Crime in Glasgow', Edinburgh: The Scottish Office.

SCRATON, P. (ed.) (1987), *Law, Order, and the Authoritarian State: Readings in Critical Criminology*, Milton Keynes: Open University Press.

SCULL, A. (1979), *Museums of Madness: The Social Organization of Insanity in Nineteenth-Century England*, New York: Allen Lane.

SEMPLE, J. (1993), *Bentham's Prison: A Study of the Panopticon Penitentiary*, Oxford: Clarendon Press.

SHAPLAND, J., and VAGG, J. (1988), *Policing by the Public*, Oxford: Clarendon Press.

SHAW, C. (1971), 'Male Juvenile Delinquency and Group Behavior', in J. Short (ed.), *The Social Fabric of the Metropolis*, Chicago: University of Chicago Press.

—— and MCKAY, H. (1942), *Juvenile Delinquency and Urban Areas*, Chicago: University of Chicago Press.

SHEARING, C., and STENNING, P. (1985), 'From the Panopticon to Disney World: The Development of Discipline', in A. Doob and E. Greenspan (eds), *Perspectives in Criminal Law*, Aurora: Canada Law Book.

SHERMAN, L., GARTIN, P., and BUERGER, M. (1989), 'Hot Spots of Predatory Crime: Routine Activities and the Criminology of Place', *Criminology*, 27.

SHORT, E., and DITTON, J. (1998), 'Seen and Now Heard: Talking to the Targets of Open Street CCTV', *British Journal of Criminology*, 38: 3.

SHORT, J., and STRODBECK, F. (1967), *Group Process and Gang Delinquency*, Chicago: University of Chicago Press.

SIM, J. (1990), *Medical Power in Prisons: The Prison Medical Service in England 1774–1989*, Milton Keynes: Open University Press.

SIMON, J. (1987), 'The Emergence of a Risk Society', *Socialist Review*.

—— (1993), *Poor Discipline: Parole and the Social Control of the Underclass*, Chicago: University of Chicago Press.

—— and FEELEY, M. (1995), 'True Crime: The New Penology and Public Discourse on Crime', in T. Blomberg and S. Cohen (eds), *Punishment and Social Control*, New York: Aldine de Gruyter.

SLAPPER, G., and TOMBS, S. (1999), *Corporate Crime*, London: Longman.

SMART, C. (1977), *Women, Crime and Criminology*, London: Routledge & Kegan Paul.

SMART, C. (1989), *Feminism and the Power of Law*, London: Routledge.

SMITH, D. (2000), 'Changing Situations and Changing People', in A. von Hirsh, D. Garland, and A. Wakefield (eds), *Ethical and Social Perspectives on Situational Crime Prevention*, 147–74, Oxford: Hart Publishing.

STEPHENS, J. (1976), *Loners, Losers and Lovers*, Seattle: University of Washington Press.

STINCHCOMBE, A. (1968), *Constructing Social Theories*, New York: Harcourt Brace and World.

SUMNER, C. (1994), *The Sociology of Deviance: An Obituary*, Buckingham: Open University Press.

—— (ed.) (2004), Introduction to *The Blackwell Companion to Criminology*, Oxford: Blackwell.

SUTHERLAND, E., and CRESSEY, D. (1955), *Principles of Criminology*, Chicago: Lippincott.

SUTTLES, G. (1972), *The Social Construction of Communities*, Chicago: University of Chicago Press.

SYKES, G., and MATZA, D. (1957), 'Techniques of Neutralization', *American Sociological Review*, 22.

TAYLOR, I. (1999), *Crime in Context: A Critical Criminology of Market Societies*, Cambridge: Polity Press.

TAYLOR, I., WALTON, P., and YOUNG, J. (1973), *The New Criminology*, London: Routledge & Kegan Paul.

THRASHER, F. (1927), *The Gang*, Chicago: University of Chicago Press.

TIERNEY, J. (1996), *Criminology: Theory and Context*, 2nd edn 2005, London: Prentice-Hall.

TURNBULL, C. (1973), *The Mountain People*, London: Paladin.

VALIÉR, C. (1995), 'Psychoanalysis and crime in Britain During the Inter-War Years', The British Criminology Conferences: *Selected Proceedings. Volume 1: Emerging Themes in Criminology. Papers from the British Criminology Conference*, Loughborough University, 18–21 July.

VAN CREVELD, M. (1991), *The Transformation of War*, New York: Free Press.

WALKLATE, S., and EVANS, K. (1999), Zero Tolerance or Community Tolerance, Aldershot: Ashgate.

WELSH, B., and FARRINGTON, D. (2002), *Crime Prevention Effects of Closed Circuit Television: A Systematic Review*, London: Home Office.

WHITTEN, M. (2002), 'Protection, Prevention, Reformation: A History of the Philanthropic Society', PhD dissertation, London School of Economics.

WHYTE, W. (1942), *Street Corner Society*, Chicago: University of Chicago Press.

WILKINS, L. (1964), *Social Deviance*, London: Tavistock.

WILLIS, P. (1977), *Learning to Labour*, Farnborough, Hants: Gower.

WILSON, H. (1980), 'Parental Supervision: A Neglected Aspect of Delinquency', *British Journal of Criminology*, 20.

WILSON, W. (1996), *When Work Disappears: The World of the New Urban Poor*, New York: Alfred Knopf.

WIRTH, L. (1964), 'Culture Conflict and Misconduct', in *On Cities and Social Life*, Chicago: University of Chicago Press.

WRIGHT, R., and DECKER, S. (1997), *Armed Robbers in Action: Stickups and Street Culture*, Boston: Northeastern University Press.

YABLONSKY, L. (1962), *The Violent Gang*, London: Pelican.

YOUNG, J. (1971), *The Drugtakers*, London: Paladin.

—— (1997), 'Left Realist Criminology', in M. Maguire, R. Morgan, and R. Reiner (eds), *The Oxford Handbook of Criminology*, 2nd edn, Oxford: Oxford University Press.

—— (1998), 'From Inclusive to Exclusive Society: Nightmares in the European Dream', in V. Ruggiero, N. South, and I. Taylor (eds), *The New European Criminology*, London: Routledge.

—— (1999), *The Exclusive Society*, London: Sage.

—— (2004), 'Crime and the Dialectics of Inclusion/ Exclusion', *British Journal of Criminology*, July, 44: 44.

2

CRIMINOLOGICAL PSYCHOLOGY

Clive R. Hollin

INTRODUCTION

The current vogue in psychology in Britain is to use the term 'forensic psychology' when referring to any topic even remotely connected with crime. Blackburn has commented on this etymological inaccuracy, noting of the word 'forensic' that 'Its established English meaning is hence "pertaining to or used in courts of law", and that is how it has been understood by the public in general and lawyers in particular' (1996: 4). Indeed, this sense of psychology applied to legal decision-making is the way in which forensic psychology is properly understood elsewhere (Hess 2006). It is difficult, however, to arrive at a straightforward term that accurately describes the application of psychological theory and research to antisocial conduct, criminal behaviour, and law. For many years The British Psychological Society (the professional body for psychologists in Britain) used the term 'Criminological and Legal Psychology' rather than 'Forensic Psychology' to describe this specialist area of psychological knowledge and practice. The British Psychological Society maintains this terminology in the title of its academic journal, *Legal and Criminological Psychology*.

The topic of legal psychology, the application of psychological knowledge and methods to the process of law, has become a speciality in its own right (e.g., Bartol and Bartol 1994; Bull and Carson 1995; Gudjonsson and Hayward 1998; Weiner and Hess 2006; Kapardis 2003; O'Donohue and Levensky 2004; Roesch, Corrado, and Dempster 2001). However, the focus of this chapter is on *criminological* psychology: that is, the application of psychological theory and investigation to understanding (and attempting to change) criminal behaviour. It is important at the outset to emphasize the point that criminological psychology is concerned with the use of psychology to help explain criminal behaviour. It follows, therefore, that criminological psychology represents a meeting of psychology and criminology. The juxtaposition of psychology and criminology has been a constant issue for both disciplines. One way to understand the interplay between the disciplines, and hence the aetiology and changing emphases of criminological psychology, is to consider the historical highs and lows of this cross-discipline relationship. Adopting a historical perspective allows a picture to emerge of the theoretical points of contact and departure of the two disciplines. As this chapter is concerned with psychology, the perspective here is from a psychological viewpoint; based on this approach Hayward (2005) offers a criminologist's perspective of psychology.

THE GROWTH OF PSYCHOLOGY

Criminological psychology is a specialist branch of what might be called mainstream psychology, that is the assembly of knowledge and theory about human functioning. To understand the evolution of criminological psychology it is helpful to set this against the development of psychology as an academic discipline and a profession.

PSYCHOLOGY AS AN ACADEMIC DISCIPLINE

It is generally taken that the founding of the first psychological laboratory at Leipzig in 1879 by Wilhelm Wundt (1832–1920) signalled the beginning of psychology as a scientific, experimental discipline. (Another school of thought gives that particular credit to William James (1842–1940) at Harvard.) After the 1870s, the spread of experimental psychology (with the attendant growth in sophisticated statistical techniques) to universities in Britain and the United States quickly followed. Thus, by the early 1900s, psychology had become an established academic discipline in its own right across the university system (Richards 1996). The empirical, scientific approach adopted by the early experimental psychologists was in marked contrast to the strong continental European style of psychology heavily influenced by philosophy and intellectual analysis, as seen for example in psychoanalysis and Gestalt Psychology.

The subject matter of these two approaches (Anglo-American versus European) to psychology also differed markedly. Early British psychology, heavily influenced by the theories of Charles Darwin (1809–82) and by intellectual figures of the time such as Sir Francis Galton (1822–1911), looked primarily to the study of individual differences. The empirical search by psychologists for individual differences in psychological constructs, such as intelligence, incorporated biological as well as psychological variables.

Early American psychology, as seen most clearly in the writings of John B. Watson (1878–1958), eschewed the inner world and focused on overt behaviour as the proper subject matter for psychological investigation. Indeed, Watson's 1913 paper, 'Psychology as the Behaviourist Views it', has been called a 'manifesto paper' (Richards 1996: 47) for the later development of behavioural psychology. Two trademarks of this emergent behavioural approach were an implicit assumption of the link between behaviour and biological structures; and a belief in the scientific legitimacy of the use of animals in experimental research. In both instances the influence of the major physiologists of the time, such as the Nobel Prizewinner Ivan Pavlov (1849–1936), is clearly discernible.

THE BEHAVIOURAL TRADITION

From the 1930s onwards, the growth of an empirical literature with a specific focus on behaviour saw a profusion of theoretical concepts and associated theoretical positions under the general theme of 'behavioural' (O'Donohue and Kitchener 1999). The work of B. F. Skinner (1904–90) is undoubtedly the most influential within the behavioural tradition (Skinner 1938, 1974). Briefly, Skinner was concerned to show empirically the nature of the relationship between behaviour and its environmental setting and consequences. Over time, a body of experimental evidence accrued to show that the environment provides settings for particular behaviours to occur that are likely to produce predictable environmental effects. Thus, the environment is said to *operate* on the individual to increase or decrease the frequency of a given behaviour. Thus, the concept of *operant* learning was developed, with a growing understanding of how behaviour is acquired and maintained through the force of the environment.

In brief, behaviour that produces consequences that the individual finds rewarding is likely to be repeated, a process termed *positive reinforcement*; behaviour that produces the consequence of avoiding an outcome that the individual finds aversive is, similarly, likely to be repeated, which is termed *negative reinforcement*. On the other hand, behaviour that produces directly aversive consequences is likely to decrease in frequency, termed *positive punishment*; while behaviour with the consequence of losing something of value is similarly likely to decrease in frequency, termed *negative punishment*. (In operant theory the term 'punishment' is used in a technical sense: behaviour that is decreasing in frequency is said to be punished. Punishment in this technical sense is not value-laden, nor specifically about physical chastisement; the term simply refers to the nature of the relationship between a behaviour and its consequences.) This deceptively straightforward theory is underpinned by complex and controversial philosophical arguments about the very substance of human nature (Nye 1992).

The behavioural approach, with its emphasis on the role of the environment, challenged the widespread orthodoxy that the origins of behaviour are to be found inside the person. There is a long history of theorizing, both within and outwith psychology, that sees inner forces as the causes of an individual's behaviour. Such inner forces have at various times been portrayed as spiritual, or biological, or, as most notably articulated by Sigmund Freud (1859–1939) in the European tradition, psychic in origin. In the history of psychology, Freud's work is of huge importance in its critical influence on generations of theorists (Brown 1961).

As psychological theories grew in sophistication so, inevitably, they were applied to offer explanations of a range of human conditions. One application of psychological theories was to attempt to provide an explanation for criminal behaviour.

PSYCHOLOGY AND CRIMINOLOGY: EARLY ACCORD

THEORY AND CRIME

With their concern focused on the individual, the first psychological theories of criminal behaviour variously applied what was known of genetics, intelligence, and psychic functioning. It is difficult, however, to distinguish the concerns of some of the early schools of psychology and those of the similarly emergent discipline of criminology. For example, the study of genetics and individual differences was of interest to psychologists, as seen in the first empirical studies of intelligence (e.g. Spearman 1927). In early criminology there are similar interests to be found. Famously, Cesare Lombroso (1835–1909) advanced theories of criminal behaviour based primarily on the hereditability of criminogenic traits (Lombroso 1876). Charles Goring (1870–1919) studied large numbers of prisoners, using anthropological methods and measures, and arrived at the view that criminals were characterized by defects in intelligence (Goring 1913). This concern with the interplay between genetic influences and physical and psychological conditions in explaining criminal behaviour occupied notable criminologists such as Raffaele Garofalo (1852–1934) and Enrico Ferri (1856–1929), as well as eminent psychologists such as Sir Cyril Burt (1883–1971). Garland (2002) provides further discussion of the development of criminology in Britain.

In a parallel stream of theorizing, Freud's psychodynamic ideas were also being used to explain criminal behaviour. Freud himself had remarkably little to say about criminal behaviour, but the concepts drawn from his theory were steadily applied to criminal behaviour by several of the post-Freudians. For example, Aichhorn (1925/1955) developed a view of delinquency that saw juvenile crime as a consequence of a psychological disposition which was called 'latent delinquency'. Based on the Freudian notion of a 'pleasure principle'—the supposed hedonistic basis of behaviour—Aichhorn took the view that a failure of socialization and emotional development allowed the latent delinquency to become overt behaviour. There are other examples to be found, such as Healy and Bronner's (1936) application of the psychoanalytic concept of *sublimation* (the channelling of unsatisfied psychological impulses into action, typically linked with emotional ties with a parent) as an explanation for antisocial behaviour.

Within the study of delinquency, perhaps the most influential of the psychodynamic theories was developed by John Bowlby (1907–90). As explained in a string of texts (e.g. Bowlby 1944, 1951; Bowlby and Salter-Ainsworth 1965), the 'maternal deprivation' thesis was developed on the basis of clinical study. This influential theory holds that the emotional impact on the child of separation from and rejection by his or her mother can provide a means by which to explain problems during childhood, including persistent delinquency, and later development.

APPLYING THEORY

As theory develops, so its applications to real world issues will be explored. As practitioners, the early applied psychologists followed theory and so naturally gravitated towards arenas in which the focus was on the individual. Thus, the emerging areas of professional psychological practice became the selection of personnel, including military personnel during wartime (Capshew 1999), and an alignment with the psychiatric profession in the treatment of individual distress and dysfunction. Consequently, many of the early practitioners applying psychological theory approached the task of working with offenders with an implicit understanding of criminal behaviour as a result of an individual failing or dysfunction. As early psychological theories, perhaps particularly the psychodynamic theories, were concerned with abnormal development, so explanations for criminal behaviour were couched in terms of defect and disorder. Indeed, given the historical association between mental illness and crime (Long and Midgely 1992), it would have been in keeping with the times to account for criminal behaviour in terms of psychopathology.

The solution for criminal behaviour favoured by practitioners, naturally, was to 'put right' the dysfunction 'causing' the criminal behaviour by the application of psychological methods of bringing about change. The methods employed to bring about such change were steeped in a quasi-medical, clinical tradition as seen with psychotherapy, counselling, group therapy, and so on. The thesis underpinning this approach is straightforward: criminal behaviour is a consequence of individual dysfunction; correct the dysfunction and the individual will no longer be criminal. Thus the treatment ideal was born.

The notion of treating offenders found its place alongside the liberal reforms of the early twentieth century when the broader notion of rehabilitation of offenders had taken hold. The rehabilitative movement held that a range of measures, encompassing social welfare and educational improvements, was required in order to reduce crime.

Thus, in the beginning, the association between criminology and psychology was evident: as Tierney (1996: 55) notes: 'By the late 1930s, mainstream criminology was linking criminal behaviour to a range of psychological and social factors, against the backdrop of a continuing debate about the relative importance of genetic endowment'. Similarly, Tierney comments that 'by the time we reach World War Two psychology was clearly in pole position within criminological discourses' (ibid.). The focus of this discourse was the interplay between heredity and environment, in the sense of criminal behaviour as the product of a predisposition to crime interacting with inadequate social conditions.

These early attempts both to understand and to treat criminal behaviour, as Jeffery (1960) notes, implicitly hold the three assumptions of *determinism*, *differentiation*, and *pathology*. Deterministic in holding that factors outside the individual's control—such factors might be biological, psychological, social, or some combination of these three—directly cause criminal behaviour. Following determinism is the assumption of differentiation: that criminals are in some way (biologically, psychologically, or socially) different to non-criminals. Lastly, the difference between criminals and non-criminals (whatever it may be) is manifest in a pathology evinced by criminal behaviour: this pathology, with clear medical overtones, necessitates treatment.

It is clear that these early assumptions form the basis of some contemporary criminological criticisms of psychological theory. For example, Siegal (1986: 175–6) comments: 'Psychological theories are useful as explanations of the behaviour of deeply disturbed, impulsive, or destructive people. However, they are limited as general explanations of criminality. For one thing, the phenomenon of crime and delinquency is so widespread that to claim that all criminals are psychologically disturbed is to make that claim against a vast majority of people.' Hopkins Burke (2001: 94–5) voices similar sentiments in commenting that the implication of psychological theories 'is that there is such a thing as the criminal mind or personality ... the causes are dysfunctional, abnormal emotional adjustment or deviant personality traits formed in early socialisation and childhood development'.

The accuracy of these statements from a contemporary perspective will be discussed in due course; however, as we move through the 1930s and beyond so tensions begin to appear in the relationship between psychology and criminology.

PSYCHOLOGY AND CRIMINOLOGY: THE PARTING OF THE WAYS

THE CHICAGO SCHOOL

The beginnings of the split between criminology and psychology are often traced back to the influence of the Chicago School of Criminology, particularly reflected in the work of Ernest Burgess, Clifford Shaw, and Henry McKay (see Rock, in Chapter 1, this volume). Briefly, the force of the Chicago School's research was to shift the focus of the study of crime away from the individual (i.e., psychology) and towards social structure (i.e., sociology). The theoretical impact of the Chicago School was to instigate a movement away from the notion that the study of criminal behaviour entailed the study of the individual. Rather, it was argued, a richer understanding of criminal behaviour could be found in the study of the social structures that shaped, influenced, and defined the social ecology. Lilly, Cullen, and Ball (1995: 39) capture the essence of the force of the Chicago School in saying, 'It was only a short leap for them to believe that growing up in the city, particularly the slums, made a difference in people's lives. In this context crime could not be seen simply as an individual pathology, but made more sense when viewed as a social problem.'

In a series of seminal studies, Shaw and McKay illustrated how the development and persistence of delinquent behaviour is associated with social deprivation, disorganization, and disadvantage (e.g. Shaw and McKay 1942). Further, Shaw and McKay ventured that the process by which delinquency was transmitted across generations was via the loosening of social controls. If the social and institutional forces that bind society—the church, the family, the educational system—are starved of resources then their influence weakens, leaving young people free to act in a delinquent way. Further, if weak social bonds create the conditions for delinquency, then ready association with delinquent peers provides the stimulus for persistent offending.

It follows that if social conditions create the setting for crime then environmental not individual change is required to reduce crime. Social policies to alleviate poverty and disadvantage were the way ahead, a message with a ready audience during the Progressive era of American political thought.

DIFFERENTIAL ASSOCIATION THEORY

The environmental focus evident in criminology (particularly in America) during the 1930s and 1940s is most clearly seen in the formulation of differential association theory by the American criminologist Edwin H. Sutherland (1853–1950). Influenced by the work of the Chicago group, of which he was briefly a member, Sutherland placed a sociological emphasis on the forces that define crime and the types of environment in which crime occurs most frequently. In formulating the principles of differential learning theory, Sutherland advanced nine propositions (Sutherland 1947). The key principles, in which Sutherland demonstrated a keen anticipation of contemporary behavioural research, were hinged around the proposition that against a social backdrop, criminal behaviour is a *learned* behaviour. This explanatory stance immediately raises a number of questions. First, how does learning occur: what are the processes by which behaviour is acquired? Secondly, what exactly is learned? Thirdly, what is the substance of learned behaviour? Sutherland's answers to these questions, bounded by the knowledge of his time, speculated that learning occurs in close social groups (not necessarily delinquent groups), and hence behaviour is acquired through such contacts. The product of learning is not only the skills needed to commit a crime, but also the attitudes that outweigh conformist attitudes and so are conducive to breaking the law. While not articulating the exact mechanisms by which behaviour is acquired, Sutherland made the critical statement that as a learned behaviour, criminal behaviour is no different in nature to any other learned behaviour.

From a psychological perspective there is nothing at all startling about the ideas expressed by the Chicago School. Indeed, as American psychology was setting itself for the paradigm shift of behaviourism, in which the clear focus would be the power of the environment in shaping behaviour, a parallel steam of theorizing in another discipline might well be seen as a stimulus for collaboration. Ironically, Sutherland's theory failed to attract any substantial attention from psychologists, particularly behavioural psychologists, interested in explanations of crime. Psychological research maintained a focus on the individual offender, with studies of the relationship between physical physique and crime becoming particularly popular (Sheldon, Hartl, and McDermott 1949). Thus, at a key point psychology failed to connect with criminology and the opportunity for a genuine academic alliance slipped away.

Criminology continued along the line of moving away from the study of the individual and increasingly focusing on the environment, particularly in terms of social process and social structure. Nonetheless, it is possible to see instances where there are obvious points of contact between the two disciplines and where fruitful connections could be made. For example, the concept of drift draws on cognitive processes ('techniques of neutralization' such as denial of harm or responsibility) and suggests that in daring to become delinquent the individual has *learned* to play a social role (Matza 1964, 1969).

DIFFERENTIAL REINFORCEMENT THEORY

The most overtly psychological theory of criminal behaviour of the period, again formulated by a criminologist, that clearly draws on the theoretical advances in behavioural psychology is to be found in differential reinforcement theory (Jeffery 1965). As with Sutherland's differential association theory, Jeffery also suggested that learning plays a fundamental part in understanding criminal behaviour. Thus, Jeffery (ibid.) refined the principles inherent in differential association theory by incorporating theoretical constructs from operant learning theory. Jeffery suggested, following Sutherland's criminological lead and Skinner's behavioural research, that criminal behaviour is operant behaviour: in other words, criminal behaviour is a function of the consequences it produces for the individual concerned. It follows, therefore, that an understanding of criminal behaviour relies on a comprehension of the consequences of the act for the individual concerned. For example, a substantial number of crimes produce material and financial gain; such gains are, in learning theory terms, positively reinforcing the offending. Alternatively, if the gains from theft help to avoid the effects of poverty then (again in learning theory terms) the criminal behaviour would be negatively reinforced. Of course, the rewards from crime can be social as well as material, as with gains in social approval and status following offending. The aversive consequences of criminal behaviour—including prison, a probation order, family problems—can have a punishing effect (in the sense of decreasing the frequency of the behaviour). As Jeffery (ibid.: 295) notes:

> The theory of differential reinforcement states that a criminal act occurs in an environment in which in the past the actor has been reinforced for behaving in this manner, and the aversive consequences attached to the behaviour have been of such a nature that they do not control or prevent the response.

Thus, from this theoretical perspective, the individual's history of reinforcement and punishment can be used to explain his or her criminal behaviour. The defining characteristic of this approach, as with behavioural theory in general, is that each person *must* be considered as an individual: depending on their social environment, some individuals will have gained rewards for criminal behaviour, others will have suffered aversive consequences. Thus, patterns of reinforcement and punishment are unlikely to be constant either between individuals, or for the same person over time. Within even similar social and cultural groups, differences in experience across individuals will exist in terms of peer group interactions, family functioning, education, and so on. It is axiomatic to this approach that for individuals living within comparable environments there will be some people who become criminal while others do not. Individuals will have complex learning histories, leading to intricate theoretical accounts of the development and maintenance of criminal behaviour (Gresswell and Hollin 1992).

Thus, as we move through the 1950s and into the 1960s, behaviourism continued to be the main paradigm influencing mainstream psychological research. The advances in learning theory were utilized by criminologists, but criminological psychology failed to make the connection. Nonetheless, there was potential for a fruitful association between criminology and psychology; but any common ground slipped away as the next phase of development unfolded in the aetiology of the two disciplines.

PSYCHOLOGY AND CRIMINOLOGY: LITTLE COMMON GROUND

PERSONALITY AND CRIME

The study of personality has a long tradition in psychology, but the use of increasingly sophisticated methodological and statistical techniques gave a new impetus to its scientific study (Cattell 1965). Drawing on his own theory of personality, Hans Eysenck (1916–90) began to develop during the 1960s what is perhaps to date the most complete *psychological* theory of crime (Eysenck 1964). Drawing on theoretical developments and empirical research, Eysenck continued to refine his theory of crime over the next decade (Eysenck 1970, 1977, 1984, 1987, 1996; Eysenck and Gudjonsson 1989). As Eysenck's theory is a widely cited example of what psychological theory has to offer in explaining crime, with a substantial associated research literature, it is worth considering in some detail. However, its reception by the most influential criminology text of the time provides a perfect example of disciplines that have moved so far apart as to have little to say to each other.

Eysenck's theory is expansive in that it seeks to offer an explanation of crime based on an interaction of biological, social, and individual factors. The foundation of the theory lies in the proposition that through genetic inheritance there are individual differences in the functioning of the cortical and autonomic nervous systems. These physiological differences are associated with individual differences in the ability to learn from, or more properly to *condition* to, environmental stimuli.

In his early research, Eysenck (1959) defined two dimensions of personality, *extraversion* (E) and *neuroticism* (N). In later research (Eysenck and Eysenck 1968) a third personality dimension, *psychoticism* (P), was described. Eysenck conceives these three personality dimensions (E, N, and P) in terms of a continuum: most people fall at the

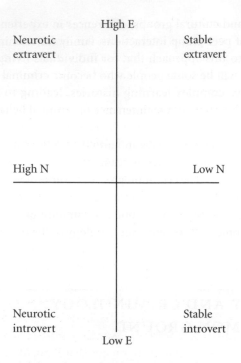

Fig. 2.1 Representation of the relationship between E and N

centre of the continuum with, it follows, fewer individuals at the extremes. Extraversion runs from high (extravert) to low (introvert); similarly, neuroticism runs from high (neurotic) to low (stable); as also does psychoticism.

The interrelationship between extraversion and neuroticism is shown in Figure 2.1. It can be seen that there are four combinations of the two personality dimensions (it can be understood that P adds another dimension across all the quadrants), and the physiological differences between those at the extreme corners of quadrants begins to form the basis of Eysenck's theory.

In terms of physiological functioning, Eysenck describes the extravert as cortically *under*-aroused, therefore seeking stimulation to increase cortical arousal to an optimal level. Thus, the extravert personality is characterized by impulsivity, risk-taking, and thrill-seeking. On the other hand, the introvert is cortically *over*-aroused and so avoids stimulation to hold arousal at a comfortable, optimal level. The introvert personality is characterized by a quiet, reserved demeanour, avoiding excitement and high levels of stimulation. In terms of conditioning, that is learning by Pavlovian conditioning or association (i.e., classical conditioning rather than operant learning), Eysenck's theory maintains that extraverts condition less efficiently than introverts.

Neuroticism, or emotionality, is held to be related to the functioning of the autonomic nervous system (ANS). Individuals at the high end of the N continuum are characterized by a highly labile ANS, giving strong reactions to any unpleasant or painful stimuli: High N individuals are characterized by irritable, anxious behaviour.

Conversely, those at the lower end of the neuroticism continuum have a highly stable ANS, showing calm, even-tempered behaviour even when under stress. As with E, N is also related to conditionability: High N is associated with poor conditioning because of the disruptive effects of anxiety; Low N leads to efficient conditioning. As condition-ability is related to levels of *both* E and N (see Figure 2.1 for the four combinations), it is further suggested that stable introverts (Low N–Low E) will condition best; stable extraverts (Low N–High E) and neurotic introverts (High N–Low E) will be at some mid-level; while neurotic extraverts (High N–High E) will condition least well.

These individual differences in conditionability lead to varying levels of socializa-tion. An individual's stable pattern of behaviour, influenced by both biological and social factors, thus flows from that person's *personality*. Through the development of psychometric tests such as the Eysenck Personality Inventory, Eysenck was able to pro-vide a simple and straightforward means by which to assess and measure personality. These standard psychometric tests typically give each individual a score on both E and N. These scores can therefore be used in research, say to look at the relationship between personality and some other form of behaviour.

The third personality dimension, psychoticism (P), is not so well formulated as E and N and its biological basis has not been described in detail (Eysenck and Eysenck 1976). Initially intended to differentiate the personality traits underlying psychosis, as opposed to neurosis, the proposal was later made that P might better denote psychop-athy rather than psychoticism (Eysenck and Eysenck 1972). The P scale is concerned with aspects of behaviour such as a preference for solitude, a lack of feeling for others, the need for sensation-seeking, toughmindedness, and levels of aggression (Eysenck, Eysenck, and Barrett 1985).

The application of Eysenck's theory of personality to explaining criminal behaviour incorporates the key proposition that as they grow older so children learn to control their antisocial behaviour as they develop a 'conscience'. The conscience, Eysenck main-tains, is a set of conditioned emotional responses to the environmental events associ-ated with an occurrence of antisocial behaviour. For example, if a child misbehaves and is reprimanded by his or her parents, the unpleasantness of the reprimand is associated with the antisocial behaviour: over time this process of conditioning determines the child's level of socialization which, in turn, mainly depends upon personality. Now, as the High E–High N combination produces poor conditionability, so individuals with this particular combination of personality traits will have weak control over their behaviour and therefore, the theory predicts, will be over-represented in offender populations. Conversely, the Low E–Low N personality configuration leads to effective socialization, so that this type of individual would be predicted to be under-represented among offender groups. The remaining two combinations, High E–Low N and Low E–High N, would be at a mid-level and would be found in both offender and non-offender groups. Psychoticism (P) is also seen to be related to criminal behaviour, particularly with regard to offences that involve aggression.

In summary, Eysenck (1977: 58) suggests that 'in general terms, we would expect persons with strong antisocial inclinations to have high P, high E, and high N scores'.

TESTING EYSENCK'S THEORY

Given the possibility of measurement of personality and the testability of the predictions, Eysenck's theory of crime has generated a substantial body of empirical research. The reviews of the literature up to 1980 (e.g. Bartol 1980; Feldman 1977) suggest that there is strong support for the prediction that offenders will score highly on P and on N. However, the findings are varied for E: some studies support the theory (i.e., high E scores in offenders); other studies report no difference in the E scores of offender and non-offender samples; while a small number of studies report *lower* E scores in offender groups. The general pattern for P, E, and N is similar with both young and adult offender groups.

To explain the variation in findings for E, Eysenck and Eysenck (1971) suggested that E might be divided into two components, sociability and impulsiveness, with only the latter related to criminal behaviour. A study by Eysenck and McGurk (1980) provided evidence in support of this hypothesis, showing that an offender sample scored higher than a non-offender sample only on impulsiveness but not sociability.

One of the criticisms of the pre-1980 studies is that they looked at the personality traits singly, rather than in combination as originally suggested by the theory. A study by McGurk and McDougall (1981) used cluster analysis to look at the patterns of P, E, and N scores in delinquent and non-delinquent samples. McGurk and McDougall reported that there were four personality clusters in each sample: both samples contained the Low E–High N and High E–Low N combinations, but the combinations predicted to be related to criminal behaviour—High E–High N and High P–High E–High N—were found only in the delinquent sample. The highly socialized Low E–Low N combination was, as predicted, found only in the non-delinquent group. Several subsequent studies attempted to replicate the McGurk and McDougall study, with varying degrees of exactness of match with the original theory (McEwan 1983; McEwan and Knowles 1984). It is the case that contemporary research still produces findings testing Eysenck's theory (e.g. Kirkcaldy and Brown 2000); however, it is also true to say that as personality theory has waned generally in mainstream psychology, so has research testing Eysenck's theory.

Overall, there is empirical evidence in favour of Eysenck's theory, leading one influential criminological psychologist to state that the 'Eysenckian personality dimensions are likely to make a useful contribution to the explanation of criminal behaviour' (Feldman 1977: 161). Nonetheless, there are reservations, as Eysenck acknowledges, such as the need firmly to establish the relationship between classical conditioning and socialization. Further, Eysenck's theory is specifically a trait theory of personality, an approach that is not without its critics in mainstream psychology (Mischel 1968). However, these points are mere quibbles when set against the criticism delivered by the new criminologists.

NEW CRIMINOLOGY AND PERSONALITY

The key text that heralded a sea change in thought in criminology, certainly in Britain, was *The New Criminology* by Taylor, Walton, and Young (1973). Tierney (1996: 157) suggests that this text represented 'an ambitious attempt to develop a Marxist theory of deviance ... Whatever the merits of *The New Criminology*, it stands as a supreme example of criminological work nurtured by the twin influences of the New Left and the counter culture.'

Eysenck is heavily cited in the first part of the text and there is a concerted criticism of his theory. The criticisms delivered by Taylor *et al.* clearly reject Eysenck's approach to understanding criminal behaviour. To appreciate the differences between Taylor *et al.* and Eysenck is to see how that at that time there could be no point of contact between the new criminology and mainstream psychology (of which Eysenck was a leading figure).

The first point of departure is to be seen in Taylor *et al.*'s analysis of positivism which, they suggest, characterizes Eysenck's work (as well as other researchers, including some criminologists). The key attribute of positivism 'is its insistence on the unity of scientific method' (Taylor *et al.* 1973: 11). (Certainly this is one characterization of positivism, although Halfpenny (1982/1992) identifies no fewer than twelve positivisms, not all of which would concord with the centrality of the scientific method.) Thus, Taylor *et al.* continue, to promote a positivistic approach is implicitly to seek to measure and quantify behaviour, to proclaim the objectivity of the scientist, and to see human action as determinate and law governed. A positivistic approach is to be found in the work of the early criminologists, but it is Eysenck as a *biological* positivist who is placed in the critical spotlight.

Eysenck is clear in his understanding of human nature: through conditioning, influenced by biological factors (and hence personality), we become socialized in the sense that we learn to control our impulses and actions. Taylor *et al.* (1973: 49) are forthright in their views on Eysenck's model of human functioning:

> Therefore man's voluntary, rational activity comes to be seen as being solely concerned with the satisfaction of his individual and pre-social ideas ... The model of learning is Darwinian in its mindlessness ... The conscience is a passive reflex which unthinkingly checks those hedonistic impulses by virtue of autonomic distress.

Thus, on the one hand there is the basic philosophical stance, exemplified by Eysenck, of a world in which behaviour is rule governed and determinate. It follows that once the basic science has been completed and the rules properly understood, the intellectual problem will be solved (and practical solutions might well follow). On the other hand, Taylor *et al.* express an altogether different perspective. They do not seek to deny the role of biological factors in understanding human behaviour: 'The central and autonomic nervous systems are undoubtedly involved in the learning process—to deny this would be to deny that man has a body' (ibid.: 51). However, Taylor *et al.* view the interaction between the biological individual and society not as something which is fixed and measurable, but as a dynamic, shifting process: 'His definitions of himself evolve not as a determinate result of the addition of social factors on to a biological substratum but rather as a *praxis*, as the meaningful attempt by the actor to construct and develop his own self-conception' (ibid.: 56).

Taylor *et al.* repeatedly make a point regarding the centrality of meaning in their understanding of human nature. Thus, the reactions of society to criminal behaviour are not an automatic delivery of positive or negative consequences, but 'are meaningful attempts of the powerful to maintain and justify the status quo' (ibid.: 52). Again, the different behaviour of extraverts and introverts is not a product of poor conditionability and socialization, but represents 'meaningful behaviour by individuals which is judged by others, in this case the psychological testers, to be undesirable' (ibid.: 56). Yet further, Taylor *et al.* note that even if it were true that behaviour was biologically driven, this would not explain deviant behaviour: 'To explain social phenomena demands social analysis involving the meaning that behaviour has to the actor' (ibid.: 60).

The point being made by Taylor *et al.* with regard to meaning is fundamental and, in truth, is a basic philosophical issue: is human behaviour determined (by whatever means), or are we active, rational agents shaping and interpretating our own destiny? This is an issue that has been played out in debate within the recent history of criminology, as seen in the discussion generated by classical criminology (Roshier 1989), and in psychology around the notion of consciousness (Dennett 1991). On an altogether grander historical stage, the issue of free will versus determinism has been pondered by philosophers through the ages (Honderich 1993; Russell 1961). Despite attempts to square the circle (e.g. Alper 1998), it is a solid academic wager that the issue is not about to be resolved.

Taylor *et al.* turn next to the matter of the scientist as the objective recorder of human behaviour. The matter they raise is not one of technicalities, of the finer points of Eysenck's use of psychometrics and statistics (although others have criticized Eysenck in this regard). Rather they ask a bigger question: if Eysenck sees all behaviour as the product of mindless learning, how can understanding of the process of learning be put to work for the common good?

> But who, then, are to be the far-seeing, 'unnatural' men who are able to transcend utilitarian natures and act rationally for society in general? Presumably the psychologists—but, if this is true, it would demand that Eysenck's paradigm of behaviour does not apply to all men [Taylor *et al.* 1973: 54].

The point is well made by Taylor *et al.*: in the human sciences, can the scientist ever be objective and detached? The issue being raised here hinges around ideas of measurement, another of the basic issues Taylor *et al.* raised regarding this style of psychological research and theory. Is it possible to measure intangible constructs such as personality in a way that is value free and valid? As Richards (1996: 110) notes: 'For Psychology, quantifying the phenomena that it studies has been a perennial problem. For many thinkers, like Kant, it was the apparent impossibility of doing so that excluded Psychology from natural science.' It is probably true to say that many contemporary psychologists would have sympathy with the view that it is difficult to separate the research from the researcher (or vice versa).

Taylor *et al.* move on to perform a similar critical analysis of the work of Gordon Trasler, whose theories are perhaps more all-encompassing than Eysenck's in terms of an inclusion of a wide range of psychological and social factors (e.g. Trasler 1962). However, the line was drawn and there could be no point of contact between the criminologist and the psychologist because 'the positivist conception of science as exemplified in the work of Eysenck, is a conception of science which denies any meaning to the action taken outside the consensus and thereby the established social order itself' (Taylor *et al.* 1973: 61).

PSYCHOLOGY AND CRIMINOLOGY: NOT ON SPEAKING TERMS

It is fair comment to suggest that Eysenck's research is a reasonably representative example of mainstream academic psychology during the 1960s, 1970s, and into the 1980s. This is not to say that all psychological research was of this nature, but the predominant approach was empirical and experimental. There were a minority of psychologists engaged in research on criminal behaviour who were working in a style which would have meshed with Taylor *et al.*, but this work was the exception rather than the norm. In particular, the early work of Kevin Howells, influenced by Kelly's (1955) personal construct theory, sought to understand criminal acts in terms of the meaning they held for the individual (Howells 1978, 1979). Within the field of psychology and crime there are examples to be found of work that directly continues in this tradition (e.g. Houston 1998), and those which seek to ask similar questions (e.g. Elmer and Reicher 1995); although it is also the case that biological research continues apace (Ciba Foundation 1996).

As we move out of the 1970s and into the 1980s, mainstream criminology developed further its political ideas with the advent of Left Realism (Young 1997) and became increasingly occupied with a feminist critique (Heidensohn and Gelsthorpe, Chapter 13, this volume). Critical criminology offered an alternative political stance, while postmodernism made an impact (Hopkins Burke 2001). However, as mainstream psychology began to enter its next theoretical phase, the focus did not follow criminology in moving outwards to look for social accounts for behaviour, but rather turned inwards to search for cognitive explanations for human action. It thereby became increasingly difficult to find any point of contact between psychology and criminology.

COGNITION AND CRIME

As reflected in the title of Baars's (1986) text, *The Cognitive Revolution in Psychology*, the shift from a behavioural to a cognitive perspective in mainstream psychology seemed to happen almost overnight. It is true, of course, that psychologists had always been interested in cognition: for example, there is a long history of psychological research into aspects of cognition such as intelligence, mathematical problem-solving, and the strategies used by high-level chess players. The cognitive revolution saw a resurgence of interest not only in these traditional topics, but also in what came to be called social cognition. Ross and Fabiano (1985) have helpfully drawn the distinction between *im*personal cognition, such as solving mathematical puzzles, and *inter*personal cognition that is concerned with the style and content of our thinking about ourselves and our relationships with other people. During the 1980s and into the 1990s, a clutch of studies appeared which were concerned with various aspects of cognition, but primarily interpersonal cognition, in offender groups. The contribution that came to be made by this cognitive slant was to reframe some existing theoretical concepts in cognitive terms and to introduce some fresh ideas. Some examples drawn from the cognitive literature are given below.

A lack of *self-control*, at times leading to impulsive behaviour, has a long history in explanations of crime (Wilson and Herrnstein 1985), and figures in at least one major theory of crime (Gottfredson and Hirschi 1990). Brownfield and Sorenson (1993) have suggested several different ways by which low levels of self-control may be related to criminal behaviour, including inability to defer gratification, a lack of concern about other people, and impulsivity. In keeping with the mood of the times, Ross and Fabiano (1985: 37) offered a cognitive perspective on impulsivity, which they viewed 'as a failure to insert between impulse and action a stage of reflection, a cognitive analysis of the situation'.

The notion of *locus of control* refers to the degree to which an individual believes that his or her behaviour is under his or her personal control. Individuals high on *internal* control believe that what happens to them is under their own control; while individuals high on *external* control believe that forces such as luck or authority figures influence their behaviour (Rotter 1966). A number of studies have found that offenders tend to external control: that is, they explain their behaviour as controlled by outside influences beyond their personal control (e.g., Hollin and Wheeler 1982; Kumchy and Sayer 1980).

As we mature as individuals we develop the ability, variously termed *empathy*, or *perspective-taking*, or *role-taking*, to 'see things from the other person's point of view'. The cognitive processes underpinning empathy probably have two related components: first, the thinking skills that allow comprehension of the other person's situation; secondly, an emotional capacity to 'feel for' the other person. As empathy develops across the life-span, so we learn to adjust our own behaviour to account for how we judge our actions will affect others. Several studies have suggested that some offenders tend to view life principally from their own perspective, not taking the other person into account, as seen in low scores by offenders as compared to non-offenders on measures of empathy and perspective-taking ability (e.g. Ellis 1982; Feshbach 1984; Kaplan and Arbuthnot 1985).

Moral reasoning is another aspect of social cognition associated with criminal behaviour (Palmer 2003). The process of socialization is related to moral development in the theories of both Piaget (1932) and Kohlberg (1964, 1978). Kohlberg, like Piaget, takes the view that as the individual attains maturity so moral reasoning develops in a sequential manner. Kohlberg describes three levels of moral development, with two

Box 2.1 LEVELS AND STAGES OF MORAL JUDGEMENT IN KOHLBERG'S THEORY

Level 1: Pre-morality

Stage 1. Punishment and obedience: moral behaviour is concerned with deferring to authority and avoiding punishment.

Stage 2. Hedonism: the concern is with one's own needs irrespective of others' concerns.

Level 2: Conventional conformity

Stage 3. Interpersonal concordance: moral reasoning concerned with general conformity and gaining social approval.

Stage 4. Law and order: commitment to social order for its own sake, and hence deference to social and religious authorities.

Level 3: Autonomous principles

Stage 5. Social contract: acknowledgement of individual rights and the role of the democratic process in deriving laws.

Stage 6. Universal ethical principles: moral judgement determined by justice, respect, and trust, and may transcend legal dictates.

stages at each level. As shown in Box 2.1, at the lower stages moral reasoning is concrete in orientation, becoming more abstract as the stages progress to involve abstract ideas such as 'justice', 'rights', and 'principles'.

Offending, Kohlberg argues, is associated with a delay in the development of moral reasoning: when the opportunity for offending presents itself, the individual does not have the reasoning that would allow him or her to control and resist temptation. A number of reviews have examined this basic premise with respect to the empirical evidence, and the generally accepted position is that offenders are typically more likely to show levels of reasoning commensurate with Kohlberg's immature stages (1 and 2) than non-offenders (e.g. Blasi 1980; Nelson, Smith, and Dodd 1990).

Social problem-solving skills are the complex cognitions we all use to deal effectively with the interpersonal struggles that are part of life, including those circumstances that are associated with offending (McMurran and McGuire 2005). In everyday functioning, social problem-solving skills require the ability first to understand the situation, then to envisage potential courses of action, then to consider and evaluate the outcomes that might follow the various actions, and finally to decide on a course of action and plan its execution to achieve a desired outcome. A number of studies have shown that offenders, both male and female, give responses to social problems that are seen to be less socially competent than those of non-offenders (e.g. Antonowicz and Ross 2005; Higgins and Thies 1981; Palmer and Hollin 1996).

Cognitive connections?

There are two points that arise from this body of research: first, how, if at all, do the various aspects of cognition connect to each other?; secondly, what is the overall model that explains the dynamics of cognition?

The search for an answer to the first point brings us to more recent concerns in psychological research. For example, the evidence suggests an association between anti-social behaviour and moral development as seen in immature, hedonistic, self-centred, moral judgements. However, as Gibbs (1993) notes, moral reasoning does not function in a vacuum: Gibbs argues that the relationship between moral development and cognitive distortions provides a more complete theoretical picture (ibid.; Goldstein, Glick, and Gibbs 1998). In this context, the term 'cognitive distortions' is used to mean 'nonveridical attitudes or beliefs pertaining to the self or one's social behaviour' (Gibbs 1993: 165).

Gibbs suggests that cognitive distortions can function directly to support the attitudes consistent with sociomoral developmental delay, and can also act to reduce any dissonance. An example of self-centred moral reasoning is seen in the view that 'if I want it, I take it': Gibbs terms this type of reasoning a *primary distortion*. The distorted secondary cognitions associated with such a primary distortion will serve to rationalize or mislabel the behaviour. To follow the example, the primary cognitive distortion evident in the reasoning 'I want it, I take it' might be rationalized (secondary cognitive distortion) by blaming other people: thus, if car owners leave their cars unlocked then they 'deserve to have them stolen'; or victims of physical assault got what they deserved because 'they were asking for it'. Similarly, the secondary cognitive distortion seen in mislabelling is evident in a biased view of one's behaviour: for example, car theft is 'just a laugh', or 'nothing serious'; victims of assault 'could have had it worse' and 'no real damage was done' (Gibbs 1996). This style of distorted thinking is seen as both socially supported and reinforced by the offender's peer group. Some of the recent work in this area attempts to look for complex relationships between aspects of cognition such as sociomoral reasoning, perception of own parenting, and attribution of intent (Palmer and Hollin 2000, 2001); and the interplay between moral and social reasoning with social information processing (Harvey 2005).

Social information processing

While appreciation of the content of some aspects of cognition may provide some understanding of offending, an overall model of cognitive functioning is clearly required. In this regard, criminological psychologists have borrowed the notion of *social information processing* from mainstream cognitive psychology. There are several models of social information processing, but one of the most influential in criminological psychology has been developed by Nicki Crick and Kenneth Dodge (e.g. Crick and Dodge 1994, 1996). As shown in Box 2.2, the model of social information processing proposed by Crick and Dodge has six related stages. It should be noted that this is not a model of abnormal or deviant behaviour, but a general model of human functioning.

The first two stages are concerned with the encoding and interpretation of social cues: the focus here lies in the way the individual is actively perceiving and attending to the words and actions of other people, and seeking to make sense of a given social interaction within a given situational context. At the third stage the person attempts to set or select a goal or some desired end point for the situation. At the fourth stage the

Box 2.2 SIX STAGES OF SOCIAL INFORMATION PROCESSING

1. Encoding of Social Cues.
2. Interpretation of Social Cues.
3. Clarification of Goals.
4. Response Access or Construction.
5. Response Decision.
6. Behavioural Enactment.

individual judges how best to respond to the situation, in the main by relying on previous experience, although novel situations may necessitate a new way of acting. The fifth stage, response decision, requires a range of cognitive skills and abilities, including generating a range of alternative responses, considering the consequences of different courses of action, and planning what needs to be done to achieve the different outcomes. This type of cognitive activity obviously overlaps most closely with social problem-solving. Lastly, the individual needs the physical social skills, both verbal and non-verbal, to perform the actions he or she has decided are best suited to gaining the outcome he or she wants in that social situation.

In summary, the model proposed by Crick and Dodge encompasses three fundamental questions central to human psychology: (1) How do we perceive and make sense of our social world?; (2) How do we effectively solve the problems our social world sets for us? (3) What social skills do we need to respond to social situations and achieve the goals we value? These are basic psychological questions, but the specific query within criminological psychology is whether there is anything characteristic about the social information-processing of offenders. The main weight of research in this respect has been devoted to aggressive and violent offenders, particularly young offenders. A brief overview of this research shows how the model can be applied to generate more comprehensive models of offending.

Applying the model

The first part of the cognitive sequence involves the individual in perceiving and interpreting situational cues. There is some research evidence to suggest that aggressive individuals search for and perceive fewer social cues than non-violent people (e.g. Dodge and Newman 1981). It also appears to be the case that violent people are more likely to interpret cues in a hostile fashion (Slaby and Guerra 1988). This hostile interpretation of social cues may be a fundamental component in a general understanding of some forms of violent behaviour.

In the next part of the model, social problem-solving, the aggressive person will make decisions on how best to respond to the situation as he or she sees matters. Thus, given a restricted perception of the situation and a hostile interpretation of events, the individual must judge what outcome he or she wants and what action he or she needs to take to gain this outcome. There is some evidence to suggest that violent people generate fewer solutions to interpersonal conflicts—remembering that the violent person may be perceiving hostility when others may not—and hence consider fewer consequences of their actions (Slaby and Guerra 1988).

Finally, the individual must act to respond to the situation. There are two issues to consider with regard to violent acts. The first point is that the violent individual may see his or her violent behaviour as an acceptable form of conduct, a legitimate response in a hostile world (Slaby and Guerra 1988). The second point is that the violent person may not have learned the social, interpersonal skills to behave in a less aggressive manner. There is research evidence to suggest that some violent people may be characterized by inappropriate assertive skills, so that they resort to violence to solve interpersonal problems (Howells 1986).

As mainstream psychology concentrated its efforts on events inside the skin, so to speak, so the topic of emotion once more returned to the attention of researchers and theorists. For example, in understanding violence, the relationship between emotional arousal and cognitions such as perception, attribution, and problem-solving may be important.

The role of emotion

The work of the social psychologist Raymond Novaco has shown that there can be reciprocal relationships between environmental events, both physical and social, cognitive processes, and the emotion of anger (e.g. Novaco 1975, 1994; Novaco and Welsh 1989). In his model of violence, Novaco suggests that situational events can trigger angry thoughts; these angry thoughts heighten emotional (including physiological) arousal, in turn intensifying the hostile, angry thoughts. This reciprocity between cognition and emotional arousal may then increase the likelihood of the individual acting in a violent manner. This model has much in common with Crick and Dodge in that, for example, Novaco and Welsh (1989) identified several information-processing biases in individuals prone to anger: these biases are all concerned with the cognitive encoding of external and internal cues, and the interpretation and cognitive representation of those cues. For example, Novaco and Welsh (ibid.) explain that the process of *attentional cueing* refers to the tendency of individuals who are prone to anger to see hostility and provocation in the words and actions of other people (cf. Dodge *et al.* 1990).

As the cognitive revolution gathered momentum, so the associated research base grew and the theoretical models became increasingly complex. Could there ultimately be a cognitive model of criminal behaviour? With regard to this question, Andrews and Bonta (1998: 190) are clear where they stand:

> Moral reasoning, egocentrism and empathy are just some of the cognitive factors that play a role in the development of delinquency. They are, however, not necessary factors: simply being unempathic, self-centered and functioning at Stage 2 of moral reasoning does not automatically result in antisocial behaviour. Sometimes other personal

characteristics such as sensation-seeking and negative family socialization experiences are needed. Nevertheless, these cognitive abilities appear to be mild risk factors for delinquency.

The important point here is that psychologists are beginning to move to complex models which, while seeing a role for psychological variables, seek to locate these in a broader social context. For example, Nietzel, Hasemann, and Lynam (1999) have provided a model of violence based on four sequential stages across the life span. First, there are distal antecedents to violence: Nietzel *et al.* suggest that these are *biological precursors*, including genetic transmission and ANS lability; psychological predispositions, including impulsivity and deficient problem-solving; and environmental factors, such as family functioning and the social fabric of the neighbourhood. Secondly, there are early indicators of violence in childhood, including features of childhood such as conduct disorder and poor emotional regulation. Thirdly, as the child matures through adolescence so developmental processes associated with the escalation of violent behaviour are evident: these processes include school failure, association with delinquent peers, and substance abuse. Finally, as the adolescent moves into adulthood, there is a stage at which maintenance variables come into force. These maintaining variables include continued reinforcement for violent conduct, association with criminal peers, and social conditions.

In summary, the cognitive revolution that swept through mainstream psychology also shifted the focus of psychological research into criminal behaviour. Nonetheless, there was always an awareness that cognitive factors were not, in and of themselves, going to offer a full explanation for offending (cf. Andrews and Bonta 1998). However, before moving to the current concerns in criminological psychology, it is worth taking a detour to another development in the cognition and crime literature.

THE REASONING CRIMINAL

In terms of style of explanation, it is evident that most psychological (and some criminological) research takes a 'dispositional' approach to criminal behaviour. Thus, with varying degrees of emphasis, criminal behaviour is seen as the consequence of an interaction between individual, social, cultural, and legal variables which act to dispose the person towards an offence. A contrary approach, with overtones of classical theory (Roshier 1989), took shape during the 1970s and 1980s.

The beginnings of this new approach are seen in research concerned with the environmental conditions in those parts of cities that seem to attract crime. The link between specific environmental conditions and patterns of crime was seen, for example, in the rise in frequency of burglary and more empty houses as increasing numbers of family members leave to go to work, or a greater incidence of street violence in poorly lit areas of towns and cities. Cohen and Felson's (1979) routine activities theory drew this research together, suggesting that a crime will occur when three elements combine: these three elements are a specific situation (i.e., a time and a place), a target, and the absence of effective guardians (Crawford, Chapter 26, this volume). The combination of these elements gives the *opportunity* for successful offending, and the idea of 'crime as opportunity' took hold. Thus, a crime occurs when the environmental circumstances present the opportunity; the criminal is the individual who seizes the chance. While one line of work looked more closely at aspects of this approach such as the distinctiveness of a target (Bottoms, Chapter 17, this volume; Pease 2002), another line focused on the individual.

Closer to economic rather than psychological theory, the view was advanced that, motivated by self-interest, the basis of human action lies in the 'expected utility' from a criminal act. Van Den Haag (1982: 1026–7) provides an example of this approach:

> I do not see any relevant difference between dentistry and prostitution or car theft, except that the latter do not require a license ... The frequency of rape, or of mugging, is essentially determined by the expected comparative net advantage, just as is the rate of dentistry and burglary. The comparative net advantage consists in the satisfaction (produced by the money or by the violative act itself) expected from the crime, less the expected cost of achieving it, compared to the net satisfaction expected from other activities in which the offender has the opportunity to engage. Cost in the main equals the expected penalty divided by the risk of suffering it.

Thus, like an accountant with a balance sheet, the individual reckons his or her likely net gains and losses and enters the criminal marketplace intending to make a profit. Lilly *et al.* (1995) have dryly described this approach as offering a model of the criminal as a calculator. However, implicit within this approach was the notion that the offender does not act in a random or in a disorganized manner. Rather, the individual makes rational choices about whether to obey or break the law: the offender is a rational decision-maker, a 'reasoning criminal'.

A key text in the further development of this approach was *The Reasoning Criminal: Rational Choice Perspectives on Offending*, edited by Cornish and Clarke (1986). The thesis underpinning this approach, as articulated by Cornish and Clarke, is that personal benefit is the prime motivation for crime. In pursuit of personal gain, individuals make decisions and choices that, to a greater or lesser degree, are rational in nature. Social factors, including family and peer group, play a background role in an individual's development in growing up with an association with crime. However, the rational 'event decision' at the point of committing the offence is predominant. For example, circumstances such as the presence of an entrance hidden from view, an open window, or sight of expensive goods will all influence the offender's thinking with respect to committing a burglary. Similarly, the rational choice model has been applied to other offences including shoplifting, robbery, and drug use (Clarke 1992; Cornish and Clarke 1986).

Akers (1990) argues that it is questionable whether development of the idea of rational choice is a radical new development in criminology. Nonetheless, the point was made that the frequency of crime is associated with increased opportunity: further, when confronted with opportunity, offenders do make rational choices about their behaviour.

PSYCHOLOGY AND CRIMINOLOGY: RETURN TO CORDIALITY?

As the 1980s became the 1990s, and into the new millennium, criminological psychologists became sufficiently confident in their subject to begin to produce a string of textbooks on the topic of psychology and crime (e.g. Ainsworth 2000; Andrews and Bonta 1994; Bartol and Bartol 2005; Blackburn 1993; Hollin 1989, 1992). As part of this growing confidence, some psychologists challenged directly what they perceived to be a criminological bias against psychology. For example, Andrews (1990) chastised the report of the Canadian Sentencing Commission for the criminological bias that led to its failure to utilize psychological research in setting its policies. Andrews and Wormith (1989) coined the term 'knowledge destruction' to describe what they saw as the fraudulent and spurious dismissal of psychological research and theory by criminologists. This theme of knowledge destruction was expounded by Andrews (1989) in his paper on the spurious tactics used by critics to destroy evidence on the effectiveness of correctional treatment.

However, as Lilly *et al.* (2002) suggest, during the 1990s criminology itself was revisiting theories of crime with a focus on the individual offender.

CRIMINOLOGY REDISCOVERS THE INDIVIDUAL

Lilly *et al.* (2002) suggest several strands of thinking, and a supporting weight of psychological research (including Eysenck's research), within American conservative criminology that have led criminologists to resurrect the study of the individual offender. The first reason Lilly *et al.* raise is the return to popularity of biological theories, fuelled partly by technological developments that allowed much better observation and measurement, and partly by a growing weight of empirical data (some psychological). Secondly, there is the popularity of texts such as *Crime and Human Nature* (Wilson and Herrnstein 1985) which seek to explain crime primarily by recourse to constitutional and other biosocial factors. Thirdly, a cluster of developments place the individual at centre stage: these include a return by criminologists to the primacy of psychological factors such as intelligence (Herrnstein and Murray 1994); the spate of publications around the notion of a 'criminal mind' (Samenow 1984); the growth of research around the notion of the 'reasoning criminal' (see above); and the formulation of explanations for crime framed in terms of the offender's 'moral poverty' (Bennett *et al.* 1996).

While there is some overlap between American and British developments, it is possible to see another two lines of research which have led to increased harmony between criminologists and psychologists in Britain. The first unifying theme stems from the accumulation of research focused on Developmental Criminology (see Farrington, Chapter 19, this volume) and the associated Life-Course Criminology (Moffitt 1993; Smith, Chapter 20, this volume). The force of this work is to show empirically that complex models of behaviour, involving a wide range of individual and social factors, must be developed to have any degree of explanatory power.

The second area of research to stimulate discussion between criminologists and psychologists comes from the research on the effect of treatment on offenders. This particular line of enquiry will be considered in detail.

'WHAT'S WORKING'?

As documented in a string of publications (e.g. Gendreau 1996; Gendreau and Andrews 1990; Hollin 1993, 1994; Lipsey 1995; Lösel 1996), a reasonable consensus has developed in the literature regarding the components of interventions that are effective in reducing offending. In Britain this treatment initiative has coalesced around the theme of 'What Works' (McGuire 1995), a phrase borrowed from the title of Martinson's (1974) paper which is generally taken as implying that 'nothing works'. The broader details of the What Works initiative and offender treatment are discussed elsewhere in this text (Raynor, Chapter 31, this volume), but the theoretical issues it raises are germane to the current discussion.

The 'What Works' literature has looked at interventions in terms of their effects on offending and has presented issues of treatment management, treatment focus, and the types of treatment that characterize effective treatment. Treatment management and focus have been discussed elsewhere (Hollin *et al.* 1995), but there are points to be made about theory. The research suggests that effective interventions will address the offender's behaviour but will also include a cognitive component to address the 'attitudes, values, and beliefs that support anti-social behaviour' (Gendreau and Andrews 1990: 182). The interweaving of behaviour and cognition in interventions can be traced directly to cognitive-behavioural treatment and, indeed, it is this particular approach to treatment that has been identified by the meta-analyses as having the greatest likelihood of success (see also Lipsey *et al.* 2001).

COGNITIVE-BEHAVIOURAL THEORY

This focus on the effectiveness of cognitive-behavioural treatment has, naturally, led to an upsurge in interest in cognitive-behavioural explanations for criminal behaviour. At face value cognitive-behavioural theory provides a ready meeting point for criminology and psychology. Within criminology there is a history of theories that include learning, behaviour, and cognition (e.g. differential association theory and differential reinforcement theory), and these concepts are central to behavioural learning theories (e.g. operant theory) and cognitive theories (e.g. social information-processing). However, a theoretical difficulty comes about when we look for a common understanding of the term 'cognitive-behavioural theory'.

In its traditional form, as exemplified by the work of Skinner (see above), behavioural theory concentrated on the relationship between the environment and observable behaviour. However, within mainstream psychological theory the significant development was in terms of social learning theory which, while maintaining its behavioural origins, incorporated cognition and emotion into a theoretical account of human behaviour (Bandura 1977, 1986). As social learning theory precipitated interest in the role of cognition within an overarching behavioural framework, the term cognitive-behavioural slipped into popular usage. In particular, the term became increasingly used by practitioners, and cognitive-behavioural treatment became popular for a range of groups, including offenders (Hollin 1990). However, with its varied background, from the standpoint of both research and practice, it is difficult to give a sound definition of cognitive-behavioural theory and practice.

Kendall and Bacon (1988) have previously commented on the problems in attempting to define cognitive-behaviour therapy and to indicate precisely how it relates to traditional theory. Indeed, they suggest that it is preferable to see a cognitive-behavioural approach to practice as a general perspective rather than as a single unified theory. Thus, McGuire (2000) is able to show with clarity the strands in the evolution of cognitive-behavioural therapies, but can be far less certain about an agreed definition of cognitive-behavioural theory.

Consequently, rather than the purist sequence of a theory leading to the design of an intervention, so producing outcome evidence by which to amend theory and practice, 'What Works' has started from a quite different position. The research, employing meta-analytic techniques, brought together a disparate batch of treatment outcome studies and distilled their effective components into 'What Works' (McGuire 1995). In an about-turn, the position has been arrived at whereby positive treatment outcome data have outstripped theory. As noted elsewhere (Hollin 1999), one of the tasks following the 'What Works' data on effective treatment is to make theoretical sense of *why* treatment works. To date this theoretical clarity is sorely missing in the literature.

It might, briefly, be interesting to speculate what such theory might look like and how it might offer a bridge for psychological and criminological research. It seems likely that a cogent account of criminal behaviour would seek to blend cognitive, behavioural, and environmental factors, probably drawing on basic principles of learning. This is a complex task, requiring genuine cross-disciplinary collaboration, but the basic theoretical structures are probably available. One might venture that social learning theory—which in itself has crossed the divide between psychology and criminology (Akers 1985, 1999)—has the potential to be the springboard for such an ambitious journey into theory.

In this light it is interesting that psychologists and criminologists are making essentially the same points regarding theory and practice in light of 'What Works'. Hollin (1999: 369) makes the following observation:

> It is important that 'what works' develops as practice evolves, as the research base increases, and as other complementary models of effective practice unfold. Clearly, treatment will never eliminate crime, but if effective work with offenders can reduce the human and financial costs of victimization then the effort is surely worthwhile.

While from a criminological perspective, Crow (2001: 78–9) writes as follows:

> Programmes for the individual offender need to be seen as part of a broader attack on the
> conditions that give rise to crime. Programmes for offenders rightly take many forms and
> include economic and social provision, including education, training, jobs and housing.
> However, unless programmes take place in circumstances which favour good educational,
> training and job prospects their impact may be no greater than that of Sispyhus rolling a
> rock uphill.

The points made in the above two quotations are similar in emphasis. First, there are
no grandiose claims for the benefits of treatment; secondly, that the 'What Works' style
of treatment needs to be connected to other styles of effective practice (see Hollin
2001); thirdly, this must all be set against a backdrop that includes victims, financial
costs, and social conditions.

As the studies evaluating the effects of offending behaviour programmes appear, it is
evident that when offenders *complete* a programme there is a demonstrable and consistent effect on reoffending (Hanson and Bussière 1998; Hollin, forthcoming; Hollin
et al. 2004; Van Voorhis *et al.* 2004). Cann *et al.* (2003) reported no treatment effect on
reconviction following cognitive skills programmes in prisons when all offenders allocated to treatment were compared to a matched no-treatment control group. However,
when disaggregating the programme starters into completers and dropouts, the completers had a significantly lower reconviction rate at one year than their matched controls (17 per cent vs 19.5 per cent); conversely the dropouts had a significantly higher
rate than their controls (28.7 per cent vs 23.8 per cent). Hollin *et al.* (2004) reported a
similar pattern of findings with an evaluation of community-based cognitive skills programmes, with completers having a lower reconviction rate that the controls (54.5
per cent vs 57.9 per cent), and dropouts a higher rate than the controls (77.6 per cent vs
57.92 per cent). Statistical control across a range of variables showed that these
differences were significant.

In seeking to account for this 'completion effect' Debidin and Lovbakke (2005) assert
that completion 'Simply served to sort those who would do well anyway from those
who would not, regardless of the treatment' (p. 47); and that 'Completion rates are
strongly linked to motivation' (p. 50): implying that any effects of treatment are explicable by an offender's motivation to change behaviour and stop offending. In other
words, as Merrington and Stanley (2004) also suggest, those offenders who enter and
complete a programme are strongly motivated before they enter a programme to
change their behaviour in order to stop offending; any effects observed after treatment
can be accounted for by the powers of motivation. Given the evidence that completion
of a treatment programme is associated with reduced reoffending, can this 'treatment'
effect be explained away by the offender's motivation? The evidence for this view is
limited and sometimes contrary (Hanson and Bussière 1998; Wormith and Olver 2002),
suggesting that the 'completion effect' may not be so easily explained by recourse to
motivation as an explanation. Nonetheless, the concept of motivation is one that is
increasingly seen elsewhere in the criminological literature. For example, in commenting

on offenders giving up crime, Farrall (2004) suggests that 'Having the motivation to avoid further offending is perhaps one of the key factors in explaining desistance' (p. 195). Similarly, there are popular techniques, such as motivational interviewing (Mann, Ginsburg, and Weekes 2002), that are used with offenders.

Thus, the concept of motivation is used in two ways within the criminological literature: first as an explanation for why an intervention may have worked (regardless of the intervention itself); secondly, as a vehicle by which positive changes in behaviour may be brought about. There is a long history of psychological research on motivation with current advances that clearly impact on its use within a criminological context.

MOTIVATION: MODELS AND PROBLEMS

Across a range of areas, from stopping smoking to dieting, there is interest in peoples' motivation to change and how this influences their engagement with interventions intended to bring about behavioural change. The Transtheoretical Model (TTM; Prochaska and DiClemente 1984) is a widely cited motivational model, used to inform attempts to change a range of behaviours, including offending (e.g. Tierney and McCabe 2001). The TTM suggests that motivation to change behaviour moves through six discrete stages beginning with pre-contemplation, moving through various phases of action, and culminating in complete behaviour change. Casey, Day, and Howells (2005) have considered the application of the TTM to offender populations. Casey *et al.* suggest there are two particular problems with TTM: first, there is a critical theoretical debate about the validity of stage models of motivation; secondly, for offender populations the process of behaviour change is particularly difficult to understand. Following the second point, offending has a relatively low frequency, compared say to problem drinking or smoking, and so changes are difficult to measure. There are also many pressures on offenders, such as eligibility for parole, to demonstrate behavioural change which have little to do with motivation. Casey *et al.* reach the view that, 'The conclusion to be drawn from this review of application of the TTM to offenders and offending is that the stages of change construct is, by itself, unlikely to adequately explain the process by which offenders desist from offending' (p. 167).

In a similar vein, Drieschner, Lammers, and Staak (2004) review the literature and suggest that the widespread interest in the idea of treatment motivation 'Sharply contrasts with the almost chronic ambiguity of the concept' (p. 1116). This conceptual vagueness and lack of precision in meaning has led to several attempts to refine the notion of motivation (e.g. Viets, Walker, and Miller 2002), and to the development of alternative conceptualizations of motivation such as 'readiness for change' (Howells and Day 2003). The notion of readiness to change is interesting as it includes intrinsic motivation alongside other individual and situational factors that can influence engagement in behaviour-change programmes (Howells and Day 2003). As Ward *et al.* (2004) note, readiness for change encompasses the person's motivation or willingness to change, their ability to respond appropriately, whether they find the process relevant and meaningful, and that they have the capacities to enter a programme.

The idea of readiness for change may offer an explanation of the supposed selection effect regarding programme entry and completion (Debidin and Lovbakke 2005). Some offenders who enter programmes are ready to change, in the sense that they are ready to *try* to stop offending: their completion of the programme and reduced offending therefore flows from both their readiness to change *and* the effects of the programme. Clarke, Simmonds, and Wydall (2004) note that the desisting programme completers in their sample emphasized that readiness for change was critical in their completing and benefiting from a programme. Thus, it can be argued that the 'selection' effect is in fact a naturally occurring fallout in practice between offenders ready to seize the opportunity to change and those who reject the opportunity. The treatment programme, rather than some abstract notion of 'motivation', is therefore the vehicle by which readiness for change translates into real changes in behaviour.

A major problem with the use of psychological terms such as motivation is the implication that the force for change is *within* the offender. An alternative, which again speaks to explaining programme completion, is to consider the *interaction* between the individual and the treatment environment, in other words, as Wormith and Olver (2002) suggest, to consider *responsivity* in terms of situational and individual factors. It is plain that situational factors are strongly associated with programme completion rates, and hence treatment effects. Van Voorhis *et al.* (2004) noted an overall completion rate of 60 per cent for the *Reasoning and Rehabilitation* programme with parolees in 16 parole districts (see also Farrington, Chapter 19, this volume). However, the programme completion rates varied considerably across parole districts, from a low of 42 per cent completion to a high of 80 per cent. Similarly, across 20 prisons, Pelissier, Camp, and Motivans (2003) showed that both individual- and treatment-level variables predicted treatment non-completion among prisoners participating in drug treatment.

Understanding more about readiness to change, programme completion and dropout, and desistance from offending is a pressing issue both theoretically and practically.

CONCLUDING COMMENT

Finally, it is time to put to rest the question of pathology, that psychological theories are only fit for explanation of abnormal states. Of course, there are mentally disordered offenders, and a substantial theoretical and practical literature has accumulated in this specialist field (e.g. Blumenthal and Lavender 2000; Howells and Hollin 1993; Peay, Chapter 16, this volume). (It is interesting, though, that a meta-analysis of prediction of recidivism in mentally disordered offenders (Bonta *et al.* 1998) suggested that 'criminological predictors' such as offence history outperformed 'mental disorder' predictors such as diagnosis.) However, psychological theories, such as operant learning, social information-processing, and social learning theory, have been developed in mainstream psychology to generate theories of human behaviour in general, not abnormal or pathological behaviour. These psychological theories may be applied to abnormal states, but are not restricted to that context. (For discussion in relation to violent crime, see Levi, Maguire, and Brookman, Chapter 21, this volume.) If that point is taken and a connection can be made between criminological theory and psychological theory then, with informed collaboration, significant theoretical advances will be possible. A strong criminology-psychology theory that provides a solid platform for a coordinated multi-component crime prevention programme would be progress of the highest order.

■ SELECTED FURTHER READING

The texts listed below have been selected as giving reviews and informed commentary across the broad field of psychology and criminal behaviour. Inevitably, some stray into legal psychology, although it is useful to see the two topics together to appreciate their similarities and differences.

Curt and Anne Bartol's text, *Criminal Behaviour: A Psychosocial Approach* (Upper Saddle River, NJ: Prentice-Hall, 2005) is now in its 7th edition and offers a considered view of the field. Dennis Howitt combines legal and criminological concerns in *Forensic & Criminal Psychology* (London: Prentice Hall, 2002), as does Curt and Anne Bartol's *Introduction to Forensic Psychology* (Thousand Oaks, Cal.: Sage, 2004). A more assertive view of the role of psychology in explaining crime can be found in the 3rd edition of *The Psychology of Criminal Conduct* (Cincinnati, OH: Anderson Publishing, 2003) by Don Andrews and James Bonta. Clive Hollin's books *Psychology and Crime: An Introduction to Criminological Psychology* (London: Routledge, 1989) and *Criminal Behaviour: A Psychological Approach to Explanation and Prevention* (London: Falmer Press, 1992) were written primarily for an undergraduate audience; Ron Blackburn's text *The Psychology of Criminal Conduct: Theory, Research and Practice* (Chichester: Wiley, 1993) reaches a more advanced readership. For a detailed exposition of personality theories, *The Causes and Cures of Criminality* (New York: Plenum Press, 1989) by Hans Eysenck and Gisli Gudjonsson is available. James McGuire provides an excellent text with *Understanding Psychology and Crime: Perspectives on Theory and Action* (Berkshire: Open University Press, 2004); while *Behaviour, Crime and Legal Processes: A Guide for Forensic Practitioners* (Chichester: John Wiley, 2000), edited by James McGuire, Tom Mason, and Aisling O'Kane, cuts across criminological psychology, legal psychology, and practice. A comprehensive recent overview of theory and practice with regard to treatment issues can be found in Clive Hollin's edited book, *Handbook of Offender Assessment and Treatment* (Chichester: John Wiley, 2001), or the more concise *Essential Handbook of Offender Assessment and Treatment* (Chichester: John Wiley, 2004).

■ REFERENCES

AICHHORN, A. (1955), *Wayward Youth* (trans.), New York: Meridian Books. Original work published 1925.

AINSWORTH, P. B (2000), *Psychology and Crime: Myths and Reality*, London: Longman

AKERS, R. L. (1985), *Deviant Behavior: A Social Learning Approach*, 3rd edn, Belmont, Cal.: Wadsworth.

—— (1990), 'Rational Choice, Deterrence, and Social Learning Theory in Criminology: The Path Not Taken', *Journal of Criminal Law and Criminology*, 81: 653–76.

—— (1999), *Social Learning and Social Structure: A General Theory of Crime and Deviance*, Boston, Mass.: Northeastern University Press.

ALPER, J. S. (1998), 'Genes, Free Will, and Criminal Behavior', *Society, Science, and Medicine*, 46: 1599–1611.

ANDREWS, D. A. (1989), 'Recidivism is Predictable and Can Be Influenced: Using Risk Assessments to Reduce Recidivism', *Forum on Corrections Research*, 1: 11–18.

—— (1990), 'Some Criminological Sources of Anti-Rehabilitation Bias in the Report of The Canadian Sentencing Commission', *Canadian Journal of Criminology*, 32: 511–24.

—— and BONTA, J. (1994), *The Psychology of Criminal Conduct*, Cincinnati, OH: Anderson Publishing.

—— and —— (1998), *The Psychology of Criminal Conduct*, 2nd edn, Cincinnati, OH: Anderson Publishing.

—— and WORMITH, J. S. (1989), 'Personality and Crime: Knowledge Destruction and Construction in Criminology', *Justice Quarterly*, 6: 289–309.

ANTONOWICZ, D. H., and ROSS, R. R. (2005), 'Social Problem-Solving Deficits in Offenders', in M. McMurran and J. McGuire (eds), *Social Problem Solving and Offending: Evidence, Evaluation and Evolution*, 91–102, Chichester: John Wiley.

BAARS, B. J. (1986), *The Cognitive Revolution in Psychology*, New York: Guilford Press.

BANDURA, A. (1977), *Social Learning Theory*, Englewood Cliffs, NJ: Prentice-Hall.

—— (1986), *Social Foundations of Thought and Action: A Social-Cognitive Theory*, Englewood Cliffs, NJ: Prentice-Hall.

BARTOL, C. R. (1980), *Criminal Behavior: A Psychosocial Approach*, Englewood Cliffs, NJ: Prentice-Hall.

—— and BARTOL, A. (2005), *Criminal Behavior: A Psychosocial Approach*, 7th edn, Upper Saddle River, NJ: Prentice-Hall.

—— and BARTOL, A. M. (1994), *Psychology and Law*, 2nd edn, Pacific Grove, Cal.: Brooks/Cole.

BENNETT, W. J., DILULIO, J. J. Jr, and WALTERS, J. P. (1996), *Body Count: Moral Poverty and How to Win America's War Against Crime and Drugs*, New York: Simon and Schuster.

BLACKBURN, R. (1993), *The Psychology of Criminal Conduct: Theory, Research and Practice*, Chichester: Wiley.

—— (1996), 'What *is* Forensic Psychology?', *Legal and Criminological Psychology*, 1: 3–16.

BLASI, A. (1980), 'Bridging Moral Cognition and Moral Action: A Critical Review', *Psychological Bulletin*, 88: 1–45.

BLUMENTHAL, S., and LAVENDER, T. (2000), *Violence and Mental Disorder: A Critical Aid to the Assessment and Management of Risk*, London: Jessica Kingsley Publishers.

BONTA, J., LAW, M., and HANSON, R. K. (1998), 'The Prediction of Criminal and Violent Recidivism Among Mentally Disordered Offenders: A Meta-analysis', *Psychological Bulletin*, 123: 123–42.

BOWLBY, J. (1944), 'Forty-Four Juvenile Thieves', *International Journal of Psychoanalysis*, 25: 1–57.

—— (1951), *Maternal Care and Mental Health*, Geneva: World Health Organisation.

—— and SALTER-AINSWORTH, M. D. (1965), *Child Care and the Growth of Love*, Harmondsworth: Penguin.

BROWN, W. C. (1961), *Freud and the Post-Freudians*, Harmondsworth: Penguin.

BROWNFIELD, D., and SORENSON, A. M. (1993), 'Self-Control and Juvenile Delinquency: Theoretical Issues and an Empirical Assessment of Selected Elements of a General Theory of Crime', *Deviant Behavior*, 14: 243–64.

BULL, R., and CARSON, D. (eds) (1995), *Handbook of Psychology in Legal Contexts*, Chichester: Wiley.

CANN, J., FALSHAW, L., NUGENT, F., and FRIENDSHIP, C. (2003), *Understanding What Works: Accredited Cognitive Skills Programmes for Adult Men and Young Offenders*, Home Office Research Findings No. 226, London: Home Office.

CAPSHEW, J. H. (1999), *Psychologists on the March: Science, Practice, and Professional Identity in America 1929–1969*, Cambridge: Cambridge University Press.

CASEY, S., DAY, A., and HOWELLS, K. (2005), 'The Application of the Transtheoretical Model to Offender Populations: Some Critical Issues', *Legal and Criminological Psychology*, 10: 157–71.

CATTELL, R. B. (1965), *The Scientific Analysis of Personality*, Harmondsworth: Penguin.

CIBA FOUNDATION (1996), *Ciba Foundation Symposium 194. Genetics of Criminal and Antisocial Behaviour*, Chichester: Wiley.

CLARKE, A., SIMMONDS, R., and WYDALL, S. (2004), *Delivering Cognitive Skills Programmes in Prison:*

A Qualitative Study, Home Office Online Report 27/04. London: Home Office.

CLARKE, R. V. (ed.) (1992), *Situational Crime Prevention: Successful Case Studies*, New York: Harrow and Heston.

COHEN, L. E., and FELSON, M. (1979), 'Social Change and Crime Rate Trends: A Routine Activities Approach', *American Sociological Review*, 44: 588–608.

CORNISH, D. B., and CLARKE, R. V. G. (eds) (1986), *The Reasoning Criminal: Rational Choice Perspectives on Offending*, New York: Springer-Verlag.

CRICK, N. R., and DODGE, K. A. (1994), 'A Review and Reformulation of Social Information-processing Mechanisms in Children's Social Adjustment', *Psychological Bulletin*, 115: 74–101.

—— and —— (1996), 'Social Information-Processing Mechanisms in Reactive and Proactive Aggression', *Child Development*, 67: 993–1002.

CROW, I. (2001), *The Treatment and Rehabilitation of Offenders*, London: Sage Publications.

DEBIDIN, M., and LOVBAKKE, J. (2005), 'Offending Behaviour Programmes in Prison and Probation', in G. Harper and C. Chitty (eds), *The Impact of Corrections on Re-Offending: A Review of 'What Works'*, 31–55. Home Office Research Study 291, 2nd edn, London: Home Office.

DENNETT, D. C. (1991), *Consciousness Explained*, London: Allen Lane.

DODGE, K. A., and NEWMAN, J. P. (1981), 'Biased Decision-Making Processes in Aggressive Boys', *Journal of Abnormal Psychology*, 90: 375–9.

——, PRICE, J. M., BACHOROWSKI, J.-A., and NEWMAN, J. P. (1990), 'Hostile Attributional Biases in Severely Aggressive Adolescents', *Journal of Abnormal Psychology*, 99: 385–92.

DRIESCHNER, K. H., LAMMERS, S. M. M., and STAAK, C. P. F. VAN DER (2004), 'Treatment Motivation: An Attempt for Clarification of an Ambiguous Concept' *Clinical Psychology Review*: 23: 1115–37.

ELLIS, P. L. (1982), 'Empathy: A Factor in Antisocial Behavior', *Journal of Abnormal Child Psychology*, 2: 123–33.

ELMER, N., and REICHER, S. (1995), *Adolescence and Delinquency: The Collective Management of Reputation*, Oxford: Blackwell.

EYSENCK, H. J. (1959), *Manual of the Maudsley Personality Inventory*, London: University of London Press.

—— (1964), *Crime and Personality*, London: Routledge & Kegan Paul.

—— (1970), *Crime and Personality*, 2nd edn, London: Granada Press.

—— (1977), *Crime and Personality*, 3rd edn, London: Routledge & Kegan Paul.

—— (1984), 'Crime and Personality', in D. J. Muller, D. E. Blackman, and A. J. Chapman (eds), *Psychology and Law*, Chichester: Wiley.

—— (1987), 'Personality Theory and the Problems of Criminality', in B. J. McGurk, D. M. Thornton, and M. Williams (eds), *Applying Psychology to Imprisonment: Theory & Practice*, 29–58, London: HMSO.

—— (1996), 'Personality and Crime: Where Do We Stand?', *Psychology Crime & Law*, 2: 143–52.

—— and EYSENCK, S. B. G. (1968), 'A Factorial Study of Psychoticism as a Dimension of Personality', Special issue of *Multivariate Behavioural Research*: 15–31.

—— and —— (1976), *Psychoticism as a Dimension of Personality*, London: Hodder & Stoughton.

—— and GUDJONSSON, G. H. (1989), *The Causes and Cures of Criminality*, New York: Plenum Press.

EYSENCK, S. B. G., and EYSENCK, H. J. (1971), 'Crime and Personality: Item Analysis of Questionnaire Responses', *British Journal of Criminology*, 11: 49–62.

—— and —— (1972), 'The Questionnaire Measurement of Psychoticism', *Psychological Medicine*, 2: 50–55.

——, —— and BARRETT, P. (1985), 'A Revised Version of the Psychoticism Scale', *Personality and Individual Differences*, 6: 21–29.

—— and McGURK, B. J. (1980), 'Impulsiveness and Venturesomeness in a Detention Centre Population', *Psychological Reports*, 47: 1299–1306.

FARRALL, S. (2004), 'Supervision, Motivation and Social Context: What Matters Most When Probationers Desist?', in G. Mair (ed.), *What Matters in Probation*, 187–209, Cullompton, Devon: Willan.

FELDMAN, M. P. (1977), *Criminal Behaviour: A Psychological Analysis*, Chichester: Wiley.

FESHBACH, N. D. (1984), 'Empathy, Empathy Training and the Regulation of Aggression in Elementary School Children', in R. M. Kaplan, V. J. Konecni, and R. W. Novaco (eds), *Aggression in Children and Youth*, 192–208, The Hague: Martinus Nijhoff.

GARLAND, D. (2002), 'Of Crimes and Criminals: The Development of Criminology in Britain', in M. Maguire, R. Morgan, and R. Reiner (eds), *The Oxford Handbook of Criminology*, 3rd edn, 9–50, Oxford: Oxford University Press.

GENDREAU, P. (1996), 'Offender Rehabilitation: What We Know and What Needs to be Done', *Criminal Justice and Behavior*, 23: 144–61.

—— and ANDREWS, D. A. (1990), 'What the Meta-Analyses of the Offender Treatment Literature Tells Us About "What Works" ', *Canadian Journal of Criminology*, 32: 173–84.

GIBBS, J. C. (1993), 'Moral-Cognitive Interventions', in A. P. Goldstein and C. R. Huff (eds), *The Gang Intervention Handbook*, 159–85, Champaign, Ill.: Research Press.

—— (1996), 'Sociomoral Group Treatment for Young Offenders', in C. R. Hollin and K. Howells (eds), *Clinical Approaches to Working with Young Offenders*, 129–149, Chichester: Wiley.

GOLDSTEIN, A. P., GLICK, B., and GIBBS, J. C. (1998), *Aggression Replacement Training* (rev. edn), Champaign, Ill.: Research Press.

GORING, C. (1913), *The English Convict*, London: Methuen.

GOTTFREDSON, M. R., and HIRSCHI, T. (1990), *A General Theory of Crime*, Paulo Alto, Cal.: Stanford University Press.

GRESSWELL, D. M., and HOLLIN, C. R. (1992), 'Towards a New Methodology for Making Sense of Case Material: An Illustrative Case Involving Attempted Multiple Murder', *Criminal Behaviour and Mental Health*, 2: 329–41.

GUDJONSSON, G. H., and HAYWARD, L. R. C. (1998), *Forensic Psychology: A Guide to Practice*, London: Routledge.

HALFPENNY, P. (1982/1992), *Positivism and Sociology: Explaining Social Life*, London: George Allen & Unwin/Aldershot, Hants: Gregg Revivals.

HANSON, R. K., and BUSSIÈRE, M. T. (1998), 'Predicting Relapse: A Meta-Analysis of Sexual Offender Recidivism Studies', *Journal of Consulting and Clinical Psychology*, 66: 348–62.

HARVEY, R. (2005), 'Moral Reasoning', in M. McMurran and J. McGuire (eds), *Social Problem Solving and Offending: Evidence, Evaluation and Evolution*, 265–95, Chichester: John Wiley.

HAYWARD, K. (2005), 'Psychology and Crime: Understanding the Interface', in C. Hale, K. Hayward, A. Wahidin, and E. Wincup (eds), *Criminology*, 109–37, Oxford: Oxford University Press.

HEALY, W., and BRONNER, A. F. (1936), *New Light on Delinquency and its Treatment*, New Haven, Conn.: Yale University Press.

HERRNSTEIN, R. J., and MURRAY, C. (1994), *The Bell Curve: Intelligence and Class Structure in American Life*, New York: Free Press.

HESS, A. K. (2006), 'Defining Forensic Psychology', in I. B. Weiner and A. K. Hess (eds), *The Handbook of Forensic Psychology*, 3rd edn, 28–58, New York: Wiley.

—— and WEINER, I. B. (eds) (1999), *The Handbook of Forensic Psychology*, New York: Wiley.

HIGGINS, J. P., and THIES, A. P. (1981), 'Social Effectiveness and Problem-Solving Thinking of Reformatory Inmates', *Journal of Offender Counselling Services and Rehabilitation*, 5: 93–8.

HOLLIN, C. R. (1989), *Psychology and Crime: An Introduction to Criminological Psychology*, London: Routledge.

—— (1990), *Cognitive-Behavioral Interventions with Young Offenders*, Elmsford, NY: Pergamon Press.

—— (1992), *Criminal Behaviour: A Psychological Approach to Explanation and Prevention*, London: Falmer Press.

—— (1993), 'Advances in the Psychological Treatment of Criminal Behaviour', *Criminal Behaviour and Mental Health*, 3: 42–57.

—— (1994), 'Designing Effective Rehabilitation Programmes for Young Offenders', *Psychology, Crime, & Law*, 1: 193–9.

—— (1999), 'Treatment Programmes for Offenders: Meta-Analysis, "What Works", and Beyond', *International Journal of Law and Psychiatry*, 22: 361–72.

—— (ed.) (2001), *Handbook of Offender Assessment and Treatment*, Chichester: Wiley.

—— (forthcoming), 'Offending Behaviour Programmes and Contention: Evidence-based Practice, Manuals, and Programme Evaluation', in C. R. Hollin and E. J. Palmer (eds), *Offending Behaviour Programmes: Development, Application, and Controversies*, Chichester: John Wiley & Sons.

——, EPPS, K., and KENDRICK, D. (1995), *Managing Behavioural Treatment: Policy and Practice With Delinquent Adolescents*, London: Routledge.

——, PALMER, E. J., McGUIRE, J., HOUNSOME, J., HATCHER, R., BILBY, C., and CLARK, C. (2004). *Pathfinder Programmes in the Probation Service: A Retrospective Analysis*. Home Office Online Report 66/04. London: Home Office.

—— and WHEELER, H. M. (1982), 'The Violent Young Offender: A Small Group Study of a Borstal Population', *Journal of Adolescence*, 5: 247–57.

HONDERICH, T. (1993), *How Free Are You? The Determinism Problem*, Oxford: Oxford University Press.

HOPKINS BURKE, R. (2001), *An Introduction to Criminological Theory*, Cullompton, Devon: Willan.

HOUSTON, J. (1998), *Making Sense with Offenders: Personal Constructs, Therapy and Change*, Chichester: Wiley.

HOWELLS, K. (1978), 'The Meaning of Poisoning to a Person Diagnosed as a Psychopath', *Medicine, Science and the Law*, 18: 179–84.

—— (1979), 'Some Meanings of Children for Pedophiles', in M. Cook and G. Wilson (eds), *Love and Attraction*, Oxford: Pergamon Press.

—— (1986), 'Social Skills Training and Criminal and Antisocial Behaviour in Adults', in C. R. Hollin and P. Trower (eds), *Handbook of Social Skills Training, Volume 1: Applications Across the Life Span*, 185–210, Oxford: Pergamon Press.

—— and DAY, A. (2003), 'Readiness for Anger Management: Clinical and Theoretical Issues', *Clinical Psychology Review*, 23: 319–37.

—— and HOLLIN, C. R. (eds) (1993), *Clinical Approaches to the Mentally Disordered Offender*, Chichester: Wiley.

JEFFERY, C. R. (1960), 'The Historical Development of Criminology', in H. Mannheim (ed.), *Pioneers in Criminology*, 364–94, London: Stevens.

—— (1965), 'Criminal Behavior and Learning Theory', *Journal of Criminal Law, Criminology and Police Science*, 56: 294–300.

KAPARDIS, A. (2003), *Psychology and Law: A Critical Introduction*, 2nd edn, Cambridge: Cambridge University Press.

KAPLAN, P. J., and ARBUTHNOT, J. (1985), 'Affective Empathy and Cognitive Role-taking in Delinquent and Non-delinquent Youth', *Adolescence*, 20: 323–33.

KELLY, G. A. (1955), *The Psychology of Personal Constructs*, New York: Norton.

KENDALL, P. C., and BACON, S. F. (1988), 'Cognitive Behavior Therapy', in D. B. Fishman, F. Rotgers, and C. M. Franks (eds), *Paradigms in Behavior Therapy: Present and Promise*, 141–67, New York: Springer.

KIRKCALDY, B. D., and BROWN, J. M. (2000), 'Personality, Socioeconomics and Crime: An International Comparison', *Psychology, Crime, & Law*, 6: 113–25.

KOHLBERG, L. (1964), 'Development of Moral Character and Moral Ideology', in M. Hoffman and L. Hoffman (eds), *Review of Child Development Research*, Vol. 1, 383–431, New York: Russell Sage Foundation.

—— (1978), 'Revisions in the Theory and Practice of Mental Development', in W. Damon (ed.), *New Directions in Child Development: Moral Development*, 83–97, San Francisco, Cal.: Jossey-Bass.

KUMCHY, C., and SAYER, L. A. (1980), 'Locus of Control and Delinquent Adolescent Populations', *Psychological Reports*, 46: 1307–10.

LILLY, J. R., CULLEN, F. T., and BALL, R. A. (1995), *Criminological Theory: Context and Consequences*, 2nd edn, Thousand Oaks, Cal.: Sage.

——, —— and —— (2002), *Criminological Theory: Context and Consequences*, 3rd edn, Thousand Oaks, Cal.: Sage.

LIPSEY, M. W. (1995), 'What do we Learn from 400 Studies on the Effectiveness of Treatment with Juvenile Delinquents?', in J. McGuire (ed.), *What Works: Reducing Reoffending*, 63–78, Chichester: Wiley.

——, CHAPMAN, G. L., and LANDENBERGER, N. A. (2001), 'Cognitive-Behavioral Programs for Offenders', *Annals of The American Academy of Political and Social Science*, 578: 144–57.

LOMBROSO, C. (1876), *L'Uomo Delinquente*, 5th edn, Turin: Bocca. First pub. Milan: Hoepli.

LONG, C. G., and MIDGELY, M. (1992), 'On the Closeness of the Concepts of the Criminal and the Mentally Ill in the Nineteenth Century: Yesterday's Professional and Public Opinions Reflected Today', *Journal of Forensic Psychiatry*, 3: 63–79.

LÖSEL, F. (1996), 'Working with Young Offenders: The Impact of the Meta-Analyses', in C. R. Hollin and K. Howells (eds), *Clinical Approaches to Working With Young Offenders*, 57–82, Chichester: Wiley.

MCEWAN, A. W. (1983), 'Eysenck's Theory of Criminality and the Personality Types and Offences of Young Delinquents', *Personality and Individual Differences*, 4: 201–4.

—— and KNOWLES, C. (1984), 'Delinquent Personality Types and the Situational Contexts of Their Crimes', *Personality and Individual Differences*, 5: 339–44.

MCGUIRE, J. (ed.) (1995), *What Works: Reducing Reoffending*, Chichester: Wiley.

—— (2000), *Cognitive-Behavioural Approaches: An Introduction to Theory and Research*, London: Home Office.

——, MASON, T., and O'KANE, A. (eds) (2000), *Behaviour, Crime and Legal Processes: A Guide for Forensic Practitioners*, Chichester: John Wiley.

McGurk, B. J., and McDougall, C. (1981), 'A New Approach to Eysenck's Theory of Criminality', *Personality and Individual Differences*, 2: 338–40.

McMurran, M., and McGuire, J. (eds) (2005), *Social Problem Solving and Offending: Evidence, Evaluation and Evolution*, Chichester: John Wiley.

Mann, R. E., Ginsburg, J. I. D., and Weekes, J. R. (2002), 'Motivational Interviewing with Offenders', in M. McMurran (ed.), *Motivating Offenders to Change: A Guide to Enhancing Engagement in Therapy*, 87–102, Chichester: John Wiley.

Martinson, R. (1974), 'What Works? Questions and Answers About Prison Reform', *The Public Interest*, 35: 22–54.

Matza, D. (1964), *Delinquency and Drift*, New York: Wiley.

—— (1969), *Becoming Deviant*, Englewood Cliffs, NJ: Prentice-Hall.

Merrington, S., and Stanley, S. (2004), ' "What Works?": Revisiting the Evidence in England and Wales', *Probation Journal*, 2: 7–20.

Mischel, W. (1968), *Personality and Assessment*, New York: Wiley.

Moffitt, T. E. (1993), 'Adolescence-Limited and Life-Course-Persistent Antisocial Behavior: A Developmental Taxonomy', *Psychological Review*, 100: 674–701.

Nelson, J. R., Smith, D. J., and Dodd, J. (1990), 'The Moral Reasoning of Juvenile Delinquents: A Meta-analysis', *Journal of Abnormal Child Psychology*, 18: 709–27.

Nietzel, M. T., Hasemann, D. M., and Lynam, D. R. (1999), 'Behavioral Perspective on Violent Behavior', in V. B. Van Hasselt and M. Hersen (eds), *Handbook of Psychological Approaches with Violent Offenders: Contemporary Strategies and Issues*, 39–66, New York: Kluwer Academic/Plenum.

Novaco, R. W. (1975), *Anger Control: The Development and Evaluation of an Experimental Treatment*, Lexington, Mass.: D.C. Heath.

—— (1994), 'Anger as a Risk Factor for Violence Among the Mentally Disordered', in J. Monahan and H. Steadman (eds), *Violence and Mental Disorder: Developments in Risk Assessment*, 21–59, Chicago, Ill.: University of Chicago Press.

—— and Welsh, W. N. (1989), 'Anger Disturbances: Cognitive Mediation and Clinical Prescriptions', in K. Howells and C. R. Hollin (eds), *Clinical Approaches to Violence*, 39–60, Chichester: Wiley.

Nye, R. D. (1992), *The Legacy of B.F. Skinner: Concepts and Perspectives, Controversies and Misunderstandings*, Pacific Grove, Cal.: Brooks/Cole Publishing Company.

O'Donohue, W., and Kitchener, R. (eds) (1999), *Handbook of Behaviorism*, San Diego, Cal.: Academic Press.

—— and Levensky, E. (eds) (2004), *Handbook of Forensic Psychology*, San Diego, Cal.: Elsevier Press.

Palmer, E. J. (2003), *Offending Behaviour: Moral Reasoning, Criminal Conduct and the Rehabilitation of Offenders*, Cullompton, Devon: Willan.

—— and Hollin, C. R. (1996), 'Assessing Adolescent Problems: An Overview of the Adolescent Problems Inventory', *Journal of Adolescence*, 19: 347–54.

—— and —— (2000), 'The Interrelations of Socio-moral Reasoning, Perceptions of Own Parenting and Attributions of Intent with Self-reported Delinquency', *Legal and Criminological Psychology*, 5: 201–18.

—— and —— (2001), 'Sociomoral Reasoning, Perceptions of Parenting and Self-reported Delinquency in Adolescents', *Applied Cognitive Psychology*, 15: 85–100.

Pease, K. (2002), 'Crime Reduction', Ch. 26 in M. Maguire, R. Morgan, and R. Reiner (eds), *The Oxford Handbook of Criminology*, 3rd edn, Oxford: Oxford University Press.

Pelissier, B., Camp, S. D., and Motivans, M. (2003), 'Staying in Treatment: How much Difference is there from Prison to Prison?', *Psychology of Addictive Behaviors*, 17: 134–41.

Piaget, J. (1932), *The Moral Judgement of the Child*, London: Kegan Paul.

Prochaska, J. O., and Diclemente, C. C. (1984), *The Transtheoretical Approach: Crossing Traditional Boundaries of Therapy*, Homewood, Ill.: Dow Jones-Irwin.

Richards, G. (1996), *Putting Psychology in its Place: An Introduction from a Critical Historical Perspective*, London: Routledge.

Roesch, R., Corrado, R. R., and Dempster, R. (eds) (2001), *Psychology in the Courts: International Advances in Knowledge*, London: Routledge.

Roshier, B. (1989), *Controlling Crime: The Classical Perspective in Criminology*, Milton Keynes: Open University Press.

Ross, R. R., and Fabiano, E. A. (1985), *Time to Think: A Cognitive Model of Delinquency Prevention and Offender Rehabilitation*, Johnson City, Tenn.: Institute of Social Sciences and Arts.

ROTTER, J. B. (1966), 'Generalized Expectancies for Internal Versus External Control of Reinforcement', *Psychological Monographs*, 80 (Whole No. 609).

RUSSELL, B. (1961), *A History of Western Philosophy*, 2nd edn, London: George Allen & Unwin.

SAMENOW, S. E. (1984), *Inside the Criminal Mind*, New York: Times Books.

SHAW, C. R., and McKAY, H. D. (1942), *Juvenile Delinquency in Urban Areas*, Chicago, Ill.: Chicago University Press.

SHELDON, W. H., HARTL, E. M., and McDERMOTT, E. (1949), *Varieties of Delinquent Youth: An Introduction to Constitutional Psychiatry*, New York: Harper.

SIEGAL, L. J. (1986), *Criminology*, 2nd edn, St Paul, Minn.: West Publishing.

SKINNER, B. F. (1938), *The Behavior of Organisms: An Experimental Analysis*, New York: Appleton-Century-Crofts.

—— (1974), *About Behaviorism*, London: Jonathan Cape.

SLABY, R.G., and GUERRA, N.G. (1988), 'Cognitive Mediators of Aggression in Adolescent Offenders: 1. Assessment', *Developmental Psychology*, 24: 580–8.

SPEARMAN, C. (1927), *The Nature of Intelligence and the Principles of Cognition*, London: Macmillan.

SUTHERLAND, E.H. (1947), *Principles of Criminology*, 4th edn, Philadelphia, Pa.: Lippincott.

TAYLOR, I., WALTON, P., and YOUNG, J. (1973), *The New Criminology: For a Social Theory of Deviancy*, London: Routledge & Kegan Paul.

TIERNEY, D. W., and McCABE, M. P. (2001), 'The Validity of the Transtheoretical Model of Behaviour Change to Investigate Motivation to Change among Offenders', *Clinical Psychology and Psychotherapy*, 8: 176–90.

TIERNEY, J. (1996), *Criminology: Theory & Context*, London: Prentice Hall.

TRASLER, G. (1962), *The Explanation of Criminality*, London: Routledge & Kegan Paul.

VAN DEN HAAG, E. (1982), 'Could Successful Rehabilitation Reduce the Crime Rate?', *Journal of Criminal Law and Criminology*, 73: 1022–35.

VAN VOORHIS, P., SPRUANCE, L. M., RITCHEY, P. N., LISTWAN, S. J., and SEABROOK, R. (2004), 'The Georgia Cognitive Skills Experiment: A Replication of Reasoning and Rehabilitation, *Criminal Justice and Behavior*, 31: 282–305.

VIETS, V. L., WALKER, D. D., and MILLER, W. R. (2002), 'What is Motivation to Change? A Scientific Analysis' in M. McMurran (ed.), *Motivating Offenders to Change: A Guide to Enhancing Engagement in Therapy*, 15–30, Chichester: John Wiley.

WARD, T., DAY, A., HOWELLS, K., and BIRGDEN, A. (2004), 'The Multifactor Offender Readiness Model', *Aggression and Violent Behavior*, 9: 645–73.

WATSON, J. B. (1913), 'Psychology as the Behaviourist Views It', *Psychological Review*, 20: 158–77.

WEINER, L. B., and HESS, A. K. (eds) (2006), *The Handbook of Forensic Psychology*, 3rd edn, New York: Wiley.

WILSON, J. Q., and HERRNSTEIN, R. J. (1985), *Crime and Human Nature*, New York: Simon & Schuster.

WORMITH, J. S., and OLVER, M. E. (2002), 'Offender Treatment Attrition and its Relationship with Risk, Responsivity, and Recidivism', *Criminal Justice and Behavior*, 29: 447–71.

YOUNG, J. (1997), 'Left Realist Criminology: Radical in its Analysis, Realist in its Policy', in M. Maguire, R. Morgan, and R. Reiner (eds), *The Oxford Handbook of Criminology*, 2nd edn, 473–98, Oxford: Oxford University Press.

3

CONTEMPORARY LANDSCAPES OF CRIME, ORDER, AND CONTROL: GOVERNANCE, RISK, AND GLOBALIZATION

Ian Loader and Richard Sparks

INTRODUCTION

Our aim in this chapter is to outline certain challenges and prospects for criminological thinking in seeking to address in timely and relevant fashion the world it confronts in the early years of the twenty-first century. This review is necessarily partial and personal in its choice of topics and sketchy in its coverage of any of them. It also consciously leaves many large and important issues to others. We seek simply to raise for discussion a number of sightings on the changing landscape of crime, order, and control that seem to us to require (and in many cases to be beginning to receive) some response from criminological theory and research.

In summary form our argument is that as the landscape of crime, order, and control shifts and changes so the shape of criminology as a field of study cannot but be revised. Our sense of which topics command the most serious attention, of which theoretical resources and empirical materials best advance contemporary analysis, of how to contribute most pertinently to public debates about crime and its control; these need, or so we contend, to be fully attuned to the changing contours of the world we inhabit. Among the features of that world which strike us as significant, and that we pursue here are: contemporary shifts in the character of the governance of crime; the changing postures and capacities of the state; the intensity of public sensibilities towards criminal justice matters; the shifting boundaries between the public and private realms in providing 'security'; the social consequences of risk and the place of crime and social order in public culture. What in our view connects up these various topics is a series of questions to do with the contemporary reconfiguration—and possible futures—of the nation-state: can the modern sovereign state—considered for some two centuries to be pivotal to the production of social order—any longer remain the sole or even pre-eminent guarantor of civil peace and public tranquillity? What effects are current transformations of the state—perhaps even its displacement from a once pivotal place in the field of crime control—likely to have on the politics of in/security?

With this in mind, we organize the discussion that follows under the three sub-headings that figure in our title and which seem to us to summarize some of the main points of intersection between criminological work and the wider domains of social and political inquiry: governance, risk, and globalization. We conclude with some thoughts on how criminological research and reflection might best orient itself to inform discussion and intervention under the altered conditions we set out.

GOVERNANCE

The field of crime control was—until the 1970s—characterized by what seemed an entrenched matrix of institutions and ideas. It was, most fundamentally, dominated by a set of state institutions (police, courts, prisons, and so on) that had since the advent of modernity come to assume a pivotal place in the production of order and security. These institutions, in turn, had over the early and middle decades of the twentieth century become progressively infused with, and shaped by, some specific ways of thinking and act-ing in relation to crime and its control (Loader 2006). The resultant complex of institu-tional sites, dispositions, and practices—what Garland (2001a: ch. 2) has termed 'the penal-welfare state'—was orchestrated around the following mutually reinforcing axioms:

1. *A conception of crime as conceptually unproblematic ('we know what it is') and geographically and socially delimited ('we know where it happens and the kinds of people who do it')*. The attendant official focus was on identifying and re-assimilating the indi-vidual 'delinquent'; a task that seemed relatively 'obvious, clear cut and uncontested' (Young 1999: 4).

2. *A causal theory that understood crime as a presenting symptom of more deep-seated social problems*. The ensuing policy focus here was on welfarist measures (public hous-ing, social security, family support, etc.) aimed at tackling the 'roots' of offending, coupled with 'correctionalist' treatment programmes oriented to returning individual offenders to the fold of social democratic citizenship. This, in turn, formed part of a strategy of government oriented to securing a range of basic citizen needs (education, work, home, health, etc.), one underpinned by 'a civic narrative of inclusion' (Garland 2001a: 46; see generally, Hobsbawm 1994: ch. 9; Hay 1996: chs 2–4).

3. *An attachment to the idea of crime control policy as the province of 'experts' and 'expert knowledge'*—a sphere of government in which a coterie of civil servants and

senior practitioners could (and should) determine the direction of policy, with relatively little direct input from politicians, and at some remove from the interest or supervision of citizens (Windlesham 1987). It was a style of policy formation in which criminological research (especially that conducted in the Home Office Research and Planning Unit and the Cambridge Institute of Criminology) came to occupy a prominent and influential place (see Lodge 1974; Radzinowicz 1999: chs 8–9).

Since the 1970s, this field of control institutions and mentalities has been profoundly called into question and transformed—undone by a combination of at least the following three factors. First a massive escalation in recorded crime rates between the 1950s and the mid-1990s (see Maguire, Chapter 10, this volume), one that saw criminal victimization move from the margins of social life to 'become a routine part of modern consciousness, a standing possibility that is constantly to be "kept in mind" ' (Garland 2001a: 106). This, according to Jock Young (1999: 35), represents 'the central motor of change' in post-war criminal justice and crime control—something that has exposed the limitations of simple social democratic accounts of crime causation (wherein better social conditions should mean less crime); seen the 'discovery' of hitherto hidden offences and unknown victims (domestic violence, sexual and physical abuse of children, stalking, environmental pollution, and so on); and given the crime question (and crime imagery) a prominent, noisy, and hotly disputed place in everyday life and political discourse (Hope and Sparks 2000; Garland 2001a: ch. 6).

Secondly, there have been some significant shifts in the pattern of economic, social, and cultural relations—transitions profound enough for social theorists and criminologists to speak of the advent of 'late' (Giddens 1990; Young 1999; Garland 2001a) or 'post' (Harvey 1989; Bauman 1992; Reiner 1992) modernity. These include: (i) transformations in capitalist production and exchange (e.g. the creation of core, secondary, and peripheral labour markets, the rise of consumerism); (ii) changes in family structure (e.g. the proliferation of dual-career households, rising divorce rates) and the ecology of cities (e.g. suburbanization); (iii) the proliferation of electronic mass media; and (iv) a 'democratization' of everyday life—as witnessed in altered relations between men and women, parents and children, etc., and a marked decline in unthinking adherence towards authority. Each of these can plausibly be said to have contributed to new opportunities and motivations for crime, to intensified demands for 'something to be done' about it, and to heightened levels of popular scrutiny of criminal justice agencies (Taylor 1999; Young 1999; Garland 2001a).

Thirdly, and more contingently, have been the effects of the New Right governments that ruled in Britain, the USA, Australia, and New Zealand throughout much of the 1980s and 1990s. These administrations strove explicitly to break with the economic and social consensus of the post-war decades. They thus embarked on a sustained assault on the institutions and 'social insurance' logics of the welfare state and public provision; seeking to replace 'dependence' on the state with private enterprise and individual responsibility ('standing on one's own two feet'). The resultant formation of 'market *societies*' in which social solidarity atrophied and inequalities deepened (Taylor 1999) has had profound ramifications, not only on levels of, and responses to, crime and dis-order (Currie 1997), but also in fuelling an overt politicization of questions of crime and punishment (Tonry 2003; Downes and Morgan, Chapter 9, this volume).

We cannot in this chapter consider these transformations and their effects in any depth. Nor can we hope to determine the weight that ought properly to be accorded to each of the aforementioned explanations (cf. Loader and Sparks 2004). What can be claimed with some warrant, however, is that these factors, taken together, have served to make 'crime-related' anxieties and public demands for order pervasive—if differen-tially felt and articulated—features of late modern societies. This has not merely ren-dered untenable the liberal-elitist crime management that held sway until the 1970s (Loader 2006); but also, more profoundly, called into doubt—even undermined—the sovereign state's claim to be able to offer security to its citizens (Garland 2001a: ch. 5). But what effects are these mutations and realizations having? What institutions and styles of control are emerging in their wake?

The landscape here is volatile, uneven, and contradictory. On the one hand, there exists ample evidence of governments seeking to re/assert their sovereign authority over the terrain of crime, policing, and punishment—to, in Jonathon Simon's (2006) nice phrase, 'govern through crime'. In Britain and the USA especially, the last decade or so have seen the emergence of emotionally charged and (ostensibly) punitive lay sensibilities and media discourses towards crime, and of governments that aim, not to temper and tame such sentiments, but to give voice and effect to them (Windlesham 1996, 1998, 2001). Record levels of imprisonment (Garland 2001b); 'boot camps' (Simon 1995); 'Three Strikes' sentencing (Zimring et al. 2001); new controls on sex offenders (Simon 2001; Matravers 2003); antisocial behaviour orders and summary controls on teenage disorder (Squires and Stephen 2005) and—post 9/11—a raft of new powers against terrorism (Zedner 2005) all attest to this. So too do the rhetorics of condemnation—what Garland (2001a: 184–6) terms a 'criminology of the other'—that now routinely surround such measures. However we are to understand these phenom-ena—as 'the flexing of the muscles of the displaced state' (Bauman 1999: 50), or as manifestations of an antique conservatism within the neo-liberal project (O'Malley 1999)—they clearly represent significant structuring properties of the contemporary crime control field.

This, however, is not the only game in town. We can also discern in the present signs of some quieter, less prominent, but also more conceptually novel, shifts in the archi-tecture and technologies of control, figurations that may turn out to be far-reaching in their effects. It is in this context that criminologists and social theorists have began to speak of, and analyse, a shift from *government* to *governance* (see Jones, Chapter 25, this volume). Two main strands of enquiry are relevant here. For some—taking their cue from Foucault's (1991) essay on 'governmentality'—investigation has centred on the *multiplicity* of strategies, techniques, and rationalities that are today deployed to govern 'economic activity, social life and individual conduct' (Rose and Miller 1992: 174; see also Garland 1997; Rose 2000). Others, working more straightforwardly within polit-ical science, emphasize the emergence of a 'differentiated polity' (Rhodes 1997: 3), wherein government institutions become—in Osborne and Gaebler's (1992) terms—less concerned with 'rowing' (delivering actual services on the ground) and oriented more towards 'steering' (establishing overall policy frameworks), and one sees the formation—in policy domains once dominated by the unitary state—of inter-organizational *networks* of public, commercial, and voluntary agencies (Kooiman 2003).

There are some important differences between these two bodies of work. But they share in common a concern with the fragmentation and diffusion of power, the emergence of new sites of social authority, the deployment of new rationalities and technologies of rule, and the advent of new professional actors and expert knowledges. With this in mind, let us try to discern the broad contours of what we might call the *new governance of crime* and, in so doing, offer some brief remarks on its likely implications and effects.

The first significant aspect of these shifts has been a relocation of responsibility for crime prevention into the hands of individual citizens—figures who have in recent years been re-imagined, not as mere recipients of state policing and criminal justice, but as self-calculating, risk-monitoring actors with important parts to play in the 'co-production' of order and security. This, in general terms, has taken the form of encouraging individuals, communities, and organizations to think about their everyday and/or working lives in terms of crime prevention and to act accordingly, whether by participating in anti-crime activity, forming preventative habits and routines, or deploying their judgement and resources as consumers in order to secure in the marketplace the kinds of protection of person and property they find desirable—a process increasingly fuelled by the inducements and stipulations of the insurance industry (Ericson *et al.* 2003). There is, of course, much in these 'responsibilization strategies' (O'Malley 1992; Garland 2001a: 124–7) that makes good sociological sense—order and security ultimately depend, not on formal agencies of criminal justice, but on informal social controls exercised within civil society. There may, in addition, be sound normative reasons why democratic societies should seek to enhance citizen participation in crime control. In their current form, however, these trajectories—which amount to a form of 'privatized prudentialism' (O'Malley 1992: 261)—possess a number of potentially troubling elements. In terms of democracy, they introduce some subtle but important shifts in the meanings of 'responsibility' and 'accountability', these terms coming to denote within governmental discourse either the *responsibility* of individuals and organizations to manage their own crime risks (and to assume a proportion of the blame should they fail so to do), and/or the *responsiveness of* commercial security providers to their *paying* consumers—a form of contractual (rather than political) accountability that tends to efface a number of wider, public-interest considerations. In terms of equity, the encouragement of market-based and citizen-initiated prevention tends to effect a reallocation of policing services and security hardware in favour of the (already) advantaged at the expense of the disadvantaged. It serves, in particular, to harden divisions between those consumers and communities who are well placed to become active risk-managers and those (generally more 'at risk' groups) who lack the economic and social capital required to provide for their own individual and collective safety (Crawford 2006).

A second dimension of this shift in responsibility for security from state to citizen has been the significant expansion of commercial involvement in the provision of policing services and security technology (Jones and Newburn 1998: chs 3–4; Jones, Chapter 25, this volume). The key developments here can be categorized thus: first is the commercial supply of guarding and patrol services, something that has included deployment by government organizations and corporations of either 'in-house' or 'contracted-in' security; the use of private security in shopping malls, office complexes, and other sites of 'mass private property' (Shearing and Stenning 1983; Wakefield 2004), and citizens clubbing together to employ commercial patrols to keep watch over their neighbour-hood—a development more pervasive in the USA (Blakely and Snyder 1997), though not unknown in Britain (Crawford and Lister 2005). Second are the burgeoning markets in the supply of security hardware and technology. This includes locks, bars, grilles, gates, and alarms—things that have become an increasingly visible (and audible) feature of the urban landscape in Britain in recent years. But it also encompasses the installation and running of CCTV and cognate security systems, as well as more 'sophisticated' monitoring, surveillance, and data-processing technologies—technologies that have received a significant boost since the events of 9/11 (Lyon 2003). Third is the increasingly rapid entry of commercial security into the policing of 'new social spaces' (Manning 2000), such as cyberspace, industrial espionage, the protection of multinational corporations, and military conflict (Avant 2005; Johnston 2006). Policing and security has, in short, become a fragmented, plural, and commodified phenomenon, the distribution of which is being increasingly determined by people's capacity and willingness to pay.

The fragmentation and commodification of policing and security is thus having at least two effects that demand further empirical and analytic attention. It creates, first of all, commercial and residential spaces in which an exclusive, particularistic order comes to be defined and enforced. The sanitized, consumer-friendly realms offered by shop-ping malls represent important instances of the former. In respect of the latter, walled, gated, privately guarded enclaves serve cognately as a means of physical protection, mark of 'distinction', and vehicle for upholding the value of economic assets (Loader 1999). But what new forms of solidarity, identification, and affiliation are being forged in such places? Is the commodification of policing and security operating to cement (sometimes literally) and deepen social and spatial inequalities generated elsewhere? Are we witnessing the formation of a tribalized, 'neo-feudal' world of private orders in which social cohesion and common citizenship are strained to the point of collapse?

We appear, secondly, to be witnessing the advent of new modes of 'private govern-ment' (Shearing 2006). Policing, it seems, is being de-coupled from the state and relocated in diverse networks of agents and agencies that are coming to perform what has for some two centuries been regarded as a constitutive task of government—the production of order. It is not merely—against this backdrop—that the state is ceasing to 'row' when it comes to policing. There are also increasingly good grounds for think-ing that it lacks the effective capacity to 'steer', so that we can longer assume—under conditions of what Johnston and Shearing (2003) call 'nodal governance'—that the state is or should be the pre-eminent supplier of security. Indeed, some of the liveliest debate in contemporary criminology centres on this very question of how in a pluralized environment one can realize security as a public or collective good, and the role that the state can or should legitimately play in that endeavour (cf. Wood and Dupont 2006; Wood and Shearing 2006; Loader and Walker 2007).

RISK

In the responses of criminologists and other social observers to the stew of developments sketched above one term seems to recur with increasing insistence and frequency (and hence, arguably, with less and less dependability as to the consistency and precision of its uses): risk. In our attempts to grasp the peculiar features of the present, whether on the levels of states' actions in choosing to 'govern through crime'; or that of private corporations selling 'security'; or of local criminal justice agencies engaging in 'partnerships' to *audit* and *manage* losses and threats to individuals, households, and businesses; or indeed of people's everyday practices and decisions about housing, consumption, and leisure, this protean and seemingly limitlessly adaptable notion presses itself on our attention.

In the last twenty years or so risk has moved from the periphery to the core of criminological theorizing and crime control practice. Until relatively recently it held a relatively specialized and limited, though respectable, place somewhere on the margins of criminological research and policy discussion. For those who explicitly used the term at all it arose in the context of certain determinate and particular questions—Could early intervention reduce the chances of 'at-risk' youth embarking on criminal careers? Was the extended incarceration of some individuals on grounds of 'dangerousness' justified? Were parole boards good enough at predicting future behaviour? Did deterrence have any measurable bearing on crime rates?

In some cases of its use the increasing centrality of 'risk' just means in essence that such discussions have become more intensive and more technically sophisticated. In that process long-standing professional concerns with judgements about ways of anticipating and forestalling future harms (concerns that have their origin in nineteenth-century preoccupations with 'moral statistics' and twentieth-century innovations in preventive detention amongst other places) have evolved and extended to incorporate new methods, statistical models, and the availability of previously unimagined computational power. Such extensions of technology and technique, however, arguably change the character of the crime-control apparatus in more pronounced ways than might at first appear. Far from merely furnishing better data about and more advanced and exhaustive analyses of the same topics and questions (whilst leaving its basic purposes unchanged) the refocusing of the theory and practice of crime control in terms of risk actually serves to reconfigure its objects of attention and intervention, its intellectual and institutional connections with other domains and its cultural and political salience and sensitivity in potentially fundamental fashion. The intrusion of risk into criminal justice thus carries a certain inherent irony in that the enhanced role attributed to anticipation and prevention restructures the field in unanticipated (and apparently un-preventable) ways. Here we can do no more than sketch some of the key aspects of this restructuring and, in particular, point to certain connections between the growth of risk-based practices and techniques and the larger contours of change which is our main concern in this chapter.

It is important to note that in criminal justice as in other domains (industrial safety, pollution and environmental policy, food hygiene, fire prevention, medicines management—this list could go on, and on) attention to risk assessment and risk management does not arise arbitrarily. The ascendancy of risk-based reasoning derives in large measure from the fact that probabalistic models based on large data samples do provide more efficient and pragmatic guides to intervention in many spheres of activity than previous methods did. Just as we no longer expect the licensing of, for example, new pharmaceuticals to proceed without rigorous testing, numerous contemporary fields of criminological enquiry (such as, classically, criminal careers research and attempts to scale the probability of reconviction after release from prison but also, especially latterly, attempts to estimate the risks of victimization experienced by given categories of people or those living in particular localities) are increasingly unimaginable without reference to such methods.

Yet this is very far from being the whole story. On one hand, the fact that risk management in crime control bears such close technical similarity to other fields and practices of governance poses the question of how far specifically *criminological* varieties of expertise can remain immune from colonization by new cadres of versatile technician-managers for whom crime is just one species of manipulable risk among others. In this respect the stage is set for various as yet unresolved struggles for predominance between risk-based reasoning and other resources of knowledge, influence, and prestige (for example, between judicial wisdom and actuarial prediction in sentencing; between clinical judgement and algorithmic scaling in parole decisions; and between 'personalist' social-work values and 'craft' skills versus numericized risk inventories in probation). In other words 'risk' may be seen as a 'cognitive habit' (Brown and Pratt 2000: 3) whose origins lie outwith the criminological field as such but which gradually infiltrates its every nook and cranny. The expression 'actuarial justice' famously coined by Feeley and Simon (1992) in their account of the rise of the 'new penology' nicely and deliberately expresses some of the internal tensions that result.

On the other hand, the very fact that every one of the fields that 'actuarial' thinking enters is already occupied by existing practitioners and their associated specialist discourses conversely suggests that we should not expect 'risk' always to emerge pristine and unadulterated from the encounter. Rather we should expect to see new hybrid or compromise formations ('effort-bargains' as they are sometimes called) between 'actuarial' reasoning properly so called and other priorities and commitments. In this respect 'risk' may be the paradigm case of rational decision-making or resource allocation *de nos jours* but it is remarkable how commonly actual practices depart from their prototypical models (see further O'Malley 2000; Sparks 2000; Kemshall and Maguire 2001; Robinson 2002).

Moreover, and of more pressing concern for us here, the term risk cannot feasibly be restricted only to what happens in specialist, technical arenas (even if one of its chief properties is precisely that of bringing into being many new arenas of quasi-technical intervention). Rather risk 'seeps out' from such protected spaces to become part of the very idiom of our contemporary moral and political conversations. Increasingly, and undoubtedly at much cost in terms of precision as to when it is or is not being used appositely, risk is part of the common currency of cultural exchange (creeping into the language of everything from weather forecasting to the control of avian influenza). For this reason Mary Douglas wonders at the 'innocence' of those professional risk analysts who evince surprise when the increasing sophistication of their collective wisdom fails to put an end to public controversy over nuclear power, or biotechnology, or indeed crime, policing, and public safety. Quite the reverse: when we speak now of risk in relation to crime we are plumb in the middle of our topic in this chapter, namely how theory and research speak to the moral aspects of the governance of our contemporary insecurities. A risk, Douglas observes, is not a 'thing' but a way of thinking—not just the probability of an event 'but also the probable magnitude of its outcome, and everything depends on the value that is set on the outcome' (1992: 31). Douglas's 'cultural theory of risk' thus brings into special focus the way in which the identification of particular sources of threat and danger (and by extension whom we blame for them) refracts a given community's dispositions towards order and authority.

The presentiment of risk, therefore, is inherently political: it galvanizes action and prompts discourse. But studying the connections between risk, fear, and blame can never be solely an activity of quantitatively cataloguing dangers and assorting responses to risk into boxes marked 'rational' and 'irrational' (Sparks 1991).

In principle this suggests a daunting and exciting research agenda for criminologists, one that is today being pursued quite vigorously especially in relation to the vexed issue of the 'fear of crime' (Sparks 1992; Walklate 1998; Girling *et al.* 2000; Hope and Sparks 2000; Jackson 2004). Such an agenda would draw attention to the weight that attaches to the dangers of crime, and to some crimes rather than others, in the social and political conversations that go on in particular times and places—the social construction of their differential visibility. It also gives a clue to why amidst the proliferation of technical means of risk assessment in the administrative culture of modern societies (the generic 'probabilization' of which Hacking speaks (1991)) the social discourse of crime and punishment still 'falls into antique mode' (Douglas, 1992: 26) and refuses to shed 'its ancient moral freight' (ibid.: 35).

Douglas here nails a point that in some degree clarifies a number of the diverse developments already noted in this chapter. Crime and punishment have consequences both for the very texture of personal life and for some embedded features of social organization. And they are janus-faced phenomena—they have both novel and archaic dimensions (cf. Garland 1990). A number of social theorists have concluded that the identification and management of risks have become structuring principles of contemporary organizational and political life. Once they have been named and identified, risks demand responses from the responsible bodies even though it may exceed their powers substantially to control, let alone to abolish them. Thus for Beck (1992) as for Giddens (1990, 1991) thinking about danger *in terms of risk* is a pervasive feature of contemporary life. For Giddens we live in a world of 'manufactured uncertainty', and it is characteristic of such a 'risk-climate' that its institutions become *reflexive*—endlessly monitoring, adjusting, and calculating their behaviour in the face of insatiable demands for information and pressures for accountability. For Beck (1992: 21):

> Risk may be defined as a systematic way of dealing with hazards and insecurities induced and introduced by modernization itself. Risks, as opposed to older dangers, are consequences which relate to the threatening force of modernization and to its globalization of doubt.

In Beck's view the 'risk society' is characterized by ambivalence: between faith in progress and nostalgia (or what Giddens elsewhere terms 'reactive traditionalism'); between demands for technical information and suspicion of experts and hence between authority and withdrawal of legitimacy; between local particularism and the utopic image of a world society; between indifference and hysteria. Nor does he doubt that such a society has authoritarian potentialities, arising in part from the accumulation of expert knowledge in the hands of elites (1992: 80) and partly on the formation of solidarities based in fear and given to scapegoating (1992: 75).

In this respect the term 'risk' increasingly does not just denote what happens within specialized expert-systems designed to anticipate and manage harm or loss (or the tendency for the familiar institutions of criminal justice to be reconfigured into risk-managing agencies of this kind). Rather it also concerns the often fevered politics that swirl around questions of risk and the battles that determine which risks are selected for particular attention, which categories of person and which places come to be regarded as bearers or containers of intolerable levels of risk, and so on. At the same time the problem of risk is critical to the restructuring of the criminal justice state that we have sketched above. It does appear that in certain senses the state has latterly tended to lose some of its former centrality and authority and that power leeches out and passes to other actors. Yet in other respects this very process engenders a refocusing on certain 'core' activities and a more heated politics of crime and punishment, precisely because the state's capacity to deliver 'security' is so much in question. To this extent there is a narrowing of the grounds on which the state can claim legitimacy and every failure of propriety or competence in risk management is potentially a scandal. Two primary consequences result. First, risk is never the dry, technocratic matter that it initially appears. Instead each system of risk management creates as its counterpart a *blaming* system (see further Sparks 2000, 2001; Garland 2001a). Secondly, the 'minimal' state' of neo-liberalism—the state which is, as we shall shortly see, in some degree 'hollowed out' by globalization—is also a *penal* state in ways that are often more intense and more politically central than was the case for its predecessor 'state regimes' of the post-war period (Hay 1996; Young 1999; Wacquant 2006).

GLOBALIZATION

The advent of 'global figuration' is, according to Zygmunt Bauman (2001: 11), 'by far the most prominent and seminal feature of our times'. Globalization has, as such, come to the forefront of analysis across the social sciences, as well as assuming a visible and sharply contested place within media and political discourse. A term barely known beyond academia but a decade or so ago is today a staple of public conversation—its existence, benefits, and costs routinely tussled over by politicians, commentators, corporate executives, and social movements. But what—beyond some commonly uttered platitudes concerning the planetary reach of Starbucks, or the dramatic rise of Google—is signified by the idea of 'globalization'? How is this process—or, better, processes—most adequately understood? And what interest or relevance does it have for those concerned with the social analysis of crime, order, and the institutions of 'sovereign' crime control?

Let us start with some attempts at definition. For Beck (2000: 11) globalization refers to 'the processes through which sovereign national states are criss-crossed and undermined by transnational actors with varying prospects of power, orientations, identities and networks'. In a similar spirit, Giddens (1990: 64) suggests that 'globalization can thus be defined as the intensification of worldwide social relations which link distant localities in such a way that local happenings are shaped by events occurring many miles away and vice versa'. While, in a recent synthesis, David Held and his colleagues conceptualize globalization in the following terms:

> A process (or set of processes) which embodies a transformation in the spatial organization of social relations and transactions—assessed in terms of their extensity, intensity, velocity and impact—generating transcontinental or interregional flows and networks of activity, interaction, and the exercise of power [Held *et al.* 1999: 16].

A number of helpful pointers can be distilled from these formulations, four of which we wish to pursue further. They suggest, first, that relations between states and societies (and the economic and political systems within which they are embedded) have altered in ways that rob analyses of 'societies' as distinct entities with clear boundaries of much of their purchase, and bring to the fore the issue of *networks* and *flows*—movements of capital, goods, people, symbols, and information across formerly separate national contexts (Castells 1996). Secondly, they indicate that *local* social relations, and the fate of particular *places*, are being reconfigured in ways that contemporary social—and criminological—enquiry is only beginning to get to grips with (Girling *et al.* 2000; Savage *et al.* 2004). Thirdly, they alert us to the possibility (should that be fact?) that *sovereign authority* is no longer merely territorial, the sole prerogative of nation-states, but has instead escaped national enclosures in a fashion that creates new sites of power beyond the state and calls radically into doubt some entrenched theories of accountability, legitimacy, and democracy (Held 1995; Held and McGrew 2002a). Finally, in respect of each of these overlapping domains, they draw attention both to some emergent social *cleavages, insecurities, and inequalities* (of affluence and destitution, access and exclusion, mobility and fixity) sparked by globalization, and to the *contradictory political responses* (old fundamentalisms and violent protectionism on the one hand, new international social movements and cosmopolitan possibilities on the other) that globality has ushered forth (Giddens 1990; Bauman 1998; Beck 2006). Let us elaborate a little on each of these themes, paying particular attention to three important elements of their intersections with questions of crime, security, and control.

One 'type of anxiety' (Nelken 1997: 253) found in contemporary accounts of the globalization of crime centres upon how globalizing processes are creating new opportunities for transnational corporate and organized crime—opportunities that territorially bound state criminal justice agencies are poorly placed to stem (Edwards and Gill 2003). The category 'transnational organized crime' generally includes the cross-border smuggling of drugs, weapons, radioactive materials, information, art, cars, and other stolen goods; trafficking in illegal immigrants, women and children (often to work in the sex industry), and body parts; counterfeiting, international fraud, and other financial crime; and espionage, terrorism, extortion, and kidnapping (Castells 1998: 168–80)—modes of illicit action that depend crucially upon 'money laundering by the hundreds of billions (maybe trillions) of dollars' (ibid.: 167; see Levi, Chapter 23, this volume). These activities are, moreover, taken to be the work of criminal groups and networks that effectively couple (pre-modern) local identities and kinship affiliations with (postmodern) entrepreneurial organization and know-how (Karstedt 2000) and, though often embedded in specific localities and regions, today strive to 'transplant' themselves—successfully and unsuccessfully—to territories elsewhere (e.g. Varese 2006). The most extensively researched and analysed of such groups include the Sicilian Mafia (Gambetta 1993), the Russian Mafia (Varese 2001), and the Japanese Yakuza (Hill 2003).

All this, Castells (1998: 166) contends, 'is a new phenomenon that profoundly affects international and national economies, politics, security, and, ultimately, societies at large'. It does so in several ways. Illegal activity—generally pursued in close combination with forms of legitimate enterprise—contributes in significant (if difficult to estimate) measure to the size and functioning of the global economy (Nordstrom 2000: 37–8). Criminal networks operate ruthless protection and enforcement systems that challenge directly 'an essential component of state sovereignty *and legitimacy*: its ability to impose law and order' (Castells 1998: 203; emphasis in original). Such networks become appealing cultural idols for many dispossessed young males who see no other obvious route out of poverty, as well as having more diffuse effects at the level of popular culture. And, in many states across the world (Colombia, Bolivia, Russia, Afghanistan, large swathes of Africa), 'shadow' enterprises deploy some variant of bribery, extortion, political funding, assassination, or armed combat as means to undermine the governing capacities and political authority of 'weak' or 'failed' states (Goldsmith 2003). Such networks have, in short, assumed a key role in setting the basic terms of existence across many parts of the globe; something that calls into question many received—criminological—wisdoms about the locus of effective, sovereign crime control.

A second 'type of anxiety' (Nelken 1997: 253) one encounters in the criminological literature on globalization concerns the slow, halting, but nonetheless discernible advent of networks and institutions of crime control at the transnational level. The concern here is that, far from rebuilding the capacity of states to deal in effective *and* accountable ways with transnational organized crime, the fears of such crime are, instead, being 'exploited with a view to cutting normative corners and eroding civil rights' (Ruggiero 2000: 195). More of such concerns in a moment. First let us briefly sketch the contours of this unfolding landscape.

The most extensive developments in this field lie in the realm of policing (Sheptycki 2000; Walker 2003). These reach back to the formation of Interpol, originally in 1923, in its current guise in 1949 (Deflem 2003). While still a significant actor in international policing, Interpol has, however, been eclipsed of late; first, by US efforts to extend and coordinate law enforcement beyond its borders (Nadelman 1993)—activities that the 'war on terror' conducted since September 2001 has only served to deepen; and, secondly, by the building of an enhanced police and criminal justice capacity within the European Union (Anderson *et al.* 1995; Walker 2003). These latter developments have included: first, the extension—in the years since the creation under the 1992 Maastricht Treaty of a Third Pillar of EU competence in 'justice and home affairs'—of forms of intergovernmental activity and supranational policy-making in areas of police cooperation, efforts to tackle organized crime, and measures concerning immigration, asylum policy, and other matters pertaining to the 'free movement of persons' (Lavenex and Wallace 2005; Huysman 2006). Today these are brought together under the rubric of a European Commission Directorate tasked with developing the EU into an area of 'Freedom, Justice and Security'. Secondly, there is the onset of institutions, networks, and training programmes aimed at furthering the exchange of information and know-how among Europe's police officers, prosecutors, and judges (e.g. Europol, Eurojust, the Operational Task Force of European Police Chiefs, a European Police College); and, thirdly, there are new modes of ground-level cooperation between national police forces, whether through the auspices of Europol liaison officers; under programmes 'twinning' EU forces with their counterparts in eastern Europe; or in respect of new security 'hotspots' such as the Channel Tunnel and the post-Schengen French-German 'border zone' (Sheptycki 1996; Bigo 2000a; Nogala 2001).

The future direction of these developments is hard to anticipate. It is certainly true that some obstinate professional interests and entrenched national sentiments litter the path towards further transnationalization; not least because policing and criminal justice stand as powerful icons of sovereign statehood (Walker 2002). Yet under conditions of globalization events and processes seem likely to exert a continuing pressure to thicken and extend forms of cross-border crime control and to speed up the travel across the borders of what were once more nationally insulated penal practices and rhetorics (Newburn and Sparks 2004). To this one must add the politics and practices of security that have emerged since the attack on the Twin Towers and the Pentagon in September 2001 and subsequent bombings in Madrid, Bali, and London. The response to these transnational crimes has appeared to involve both—somewhat *contra* the discussion of governance above—the reassertion and extension of state power and authority in the name of 'national security' (think of the Department of Homeland Security in the USA, or the Serious and Organized Crime Agency in the UK) *and* the further development and thickening of bilateral, multi-national, and transnational security cooperation—developments that critical security studies (Krause and Williams 1997), and to a lesser extent criminology, have begun to track and analyse using, most prominently, the concepts of 'securitization' (Buzan, 1991; Buzan *et al.* 1998), and 'exception' (Agamben 2005; Bigo 2006).

In this context a whole series of questions and concerns arise about the consequences (for effective policing, for human rights, for democratic accountability) of these emergent developments. Given the uncertain state of the field, and the limits of our present knowledge, they are best posed—and left hanging—in the shape of questions: Are we witnessing the radical erosion of some once hard-and-fast modern distinctions between 'external' and 'internal' security, 'war' and 'crime', and the 'police' and 'military' (Bigo 2000b; Kaldor 2006)? Is inter- and trans-national cooperation between governmental and criminal justice elites unfolding in ways that are inimical to democratic rights and practices, which remain 'stuck' at the level of the nation-state (Loader and Walker 2006)? Or is it possible to discern the emergence of a new international consciousness around, for example, environmental crimes and human rights, and with it the emergence of innovative legal norms and accountable institutions of global policing and transnational criminal justice (Henham and Findlay 2006)? These issues seem likely to form an increasingly significant part of the crime control landscape, and of the explanatory and normative agenda of criminological enquiry, in the coming period.

Yet in addressing them, it is important to remain mindful of the fact that globalization is not merely an 'out-there' phenomenon, a process impacting only on distant occurrences and relations between states, and leading our enquiries towards some 'big' questions of international relations and world politics. Its effects, Giddens (1991) reminds us, are also experienced *by* and felt *within* localities that can no longer insulate themselves from events and processes happening elsewhere. Global flows of capital and culture today powerfully shape the texture of local social relations and the fate of particular neighbourhoods, towns, and cities, altering people's sense of what it means to live 'here' as against there, of who 'we' are, and where we feel 'at home' (Savage *et al.* 2004). None of this means that 'place' ceases to matter—although global trends appear in some respects to be eroding the distinctiveness of particular places. Rather, it is to point to a process of 'divergent modernization' that produces not 'sameness' but new 'particularities' and 'hybridizations' (Robertson 1995). It thus, in a global economy, makes a fatal difference to one's life chances *who* one is (in terms of one's skills and 'social capital') and *where one lives* (a 'sunrise zone' or 'rust-belt city', a 'gentrifying suburb', or an 'impacted ghetto'). In these respects, the notoriously widening income-dispersions in many major economies, and the creation of structurally widening sub-populations within them, are the key properties of capitalist globalization.

This could hardly be of greater import to criminology. In part this has to do with the fact that the forms of transnational crime just alluded to are themselves global and local, registering their effects (unevenly) on social relations in Medellin and Palermo *and* in the Bronx and Birkenhead. But this is far from all. Criminologists interested in the ecology of urban crime have also done much of late to flesh out empirically the social impact of current macroeconomic transformations. They have, in the first place, indicated how the differential 'urban fortunes' (Logan and Molotch 1987) of late modernity are profoundly interlaced with both the distribution and effects of victimization risks and the contemporary forms and meanings of urban crime and violence. In respect of the former, such concerns have given rise not just to a microscopically detailed 'criminology of place' (Sherman *et al.* 1989; Eck and Weisburd 1995), but also to a criminological concern with the spatial dynamics of inequality in the contemporary city, especially in the forms of 'white flight', 'ghettoization', 'disrepute', and so on (Taub *et al.* 1984; Skogan 1990; Hagan and Petersen 1995; Hope 2001). In terms of the latter, one can point to a clutch of powerfully observed ethnographies describing the—often violent, criminal—street cultures formed in urban localities washed up on the tide of global capitalism, and making sense of these formations in ways that make explicit their englobement within transnational circuits of capital and culture (Sullivan 1988; Nightingale 1993; Bourgois 1995).

Secondly, mention can be made of certain 'local' lay responses to crime and the closely connected topic of the renewed politicization of order and penality (Beckett 1997; Tonry 2003). These appear—under global conditions—to be deeply entangled with the inability of individuals to protect established identities from a 'generalized risk climate' (Giddens 1991: 126) and with the erosion of state sovereignty. Bauman (1998: 117) has written provocatively in this regard of how the economic precariousness and existential insecurity attendant upon globalization generates 'withdrawal into the safe haven of territoriality' and condensed anxieties about—and social demands for—safety. Supporting warrants for such a proposition appear to abound. We have for instance (in collaboration with Evi Girling) striven to make sense of the demands for order found among residents of one—relatively prosperous, low-crime—town in 'Middle England' very much in these terms (Girling *et al.* 2000). The aforementioned mushrooming of private security patrols, gating, and related measures designed to create 'bubbles of security' (whether in Los Angeles (Davis 1990), São Paulo (Caldeira 2000), or elsewhere) is at least partly explicable in such ways. So too, arguably, are the fears stirred up in many states of western Europe by real and imagined migrants—fears that in some places (Britain and Germany, for instance) have given rise to racialized violence directed by young, dispossessed males towards asylum-seekers and guest-workers. Bauman (1998: 120) notes further how state governments (in their now diminished role as administrators of what he terms 'over-sized police precincts') eagerly concur with and encourage the translation of citizen insecurities into the question of 'law and order'; not least because it enables them—to often great electoral advantage—to practically and rhetorically deploy those levers over which they appear to retain some control—to wit, the punishment of lawbreakers. An adequate account of the febrile politics of order that obtains today across many liberal democracies (notably the USA and the UK) cannot but make some reference to such considerations.

Yet we must also take care not to read the emerging—global—landscape too flatly. For while the prospects of particular places (towns, cities, regions, nations) and their citizens *are* today structured by events and processes happening quite elsewhere, we ought not to disregard the ways in which the levels and meanings of crime, and public and official responses to it, remain constituted—at least in part—within the national political cultures and local 'structures of feeling' of different societies. This—or, to be more precise, the demands, refusals, and resistances that attend the reception of CCTV, commercial security, and the like into one particular place—we took to be an abiding lesson of our researches in Macclesfield (Girling *et al.* 2000: ch. 8). It is also something that recent comparative enquiry in criminology has nicely and importantly documented (Nelken 2000; Karstedt and Bussmann 2000: Part III; Sparks 2001; Whitman 2003; Barker 2006). These findings raise, for us, some thorny problems pertaining to crime's place within contemporary culture, and it is to these issues that, by way of conclusion, we now turn.

CONCLUSION: CRIMINOLOGY, CULTURE, AND PUBLIC LIFE

One might be forgiven for concluding that the import of the social transformations we have surveyed in this chapter is that criminology should henceforth concern itself primarily with things that are big—the global, the geo-political, the transnational. In fact this is by no means our thesis. We have indeed suggested—it has been our central, organizing claim—that questions of security and order (and regimes of governance and the position of the state) are currently being rapidly and radically altered in some fairly fundamental ways and towards no very certain destination. In order to speak to these conditions in a properly contemporary and relevant fashion criminology certainly does need to think anew about its relations with social theory (and, increasingly, security studies and international relations) and really cannot rest content only with doing the old work in the old way (cf. Garland and Sparks 2001). Equally, however, criminology's topics and themes always have been caught up irredeemably in the grander movements of social and political change. This is not in itself new, even if at times it has appeared possible to conduct research (somewhat in the way that Kuhn calls 'normal science') as if this could be bracketed off. Yet, in common with all the other social sciences, criminology itself is originally a child of another era of massive upheavals, namely the industrial and scientific revolutions of the nineteenth century. And equally it always has been possible to look at criminology's involvements with social, political, and technological change from either end of the telescope; from afar off or from up close. As C. Wright Mills (1959) wrote long ago, the sociological imagination addresses 'the place where history and biography meet'.

A concern with the implications of macrolevel developments for criminological theory and research, therefore, is not now (any more than at any other time) simply a licence for preferring the novel, the fashionable, and the sweeping over the grounded, the empirical, and the local, nor for disengaging from intricate and detailed problems of policy and politics wherever we happen to encounter them. One can readily make these points in respect of each one of the issues that we have sketched above. We may need to remind ourselves more sharply than we often do that new structures and regimes of *governance* are not just models dreamed up by management consultants (though they often *are* this); they also introduce significant changes to the conditions and pressures under which people work, or the ways in which they receive (as 'customers') the services that organizations deliver. When we speak of changes in the delivery and consumption of 'security', in respect, for example, of the electronic surveillance of public space, we are dealing with developments that alter the mundane experiences of shopping, travelling, working, and 'going out' in important respects, and indeed that are generally *designed* to do so. Surveillance techniques, therefore, are in no sense abstract matters; rather, they form part of the infrastructure of the environment in which they operate and hence of the everyday habitat of the people using those spaces. But we cannot know just how this infiltrates our subjective worlds or affects our daily routines and with what consequences for the participation of some and the exclusion of others unless we study these matters *in situ* and in detail.

Similarly when we speak of *risk* we are not generally alluding only to the calculation of probabilities *stricto sensu*. We are talking also about ways of *representing* risky topics, people, and places and this generally suggests an active and often impassioned disposition towards them. We select the risks that we want to calculate and manage in large measure because of the ways in which they alarm and disconcert us. For these reasons the ways in which we perceive, depict, magnify, displace, deny, or indeed seek out risky things are inherent to what they are for us. Finally, *globalization*, as we have been at pains to point out here and elsewhere, is not some 'out-there' phenomenon that strips 'place' and 'locality' of all contemporary significance. Far from it. Rather, it continues to matter greatly—to one's opportunities, access to resources, chances of becoming a crime victim, and so forth—*where* one happens to reside, and criminological research has much to contribute to public understanding of these spatial inequalities and their effects. It is also precisely under globalizing conditions that people's *sense of place*—and of *differences* between 'here/there', 'inside/outside', 'us/them'—takes on renewed force as a structuring feature of social relations and culture; questions of crime, danger, safety, and order often today figure pivotally in how the social life of particular neighbourhoods, towns, cities, and nations is experienced, imagined and defended.

We can see then that—in the midst some potentially far-reaching transformations in the world we inhabit—there remains much to be said for research strategies that continue to attend to such things as experience, beliefs, values, sensibilities, and feeling, and, furthermore, that there is much to be gained from seeking to grasp aspects of global social and political change *microscopically*—through ethnography, and observation, and talking to people about the lived texture of their everyday lives. Those dimensions of social life denoted by the idea of 'culture' continue, in short, to matter and ought properly to command criminological attention.

They matter because macrolevel social change of the kind we have been concerned with here filters into the lives, experiences, and dispositions of individuals and social groups (become, as it were, features of *mundane culture*) in ways that are uneven and never entirely predictable, and which cannot simply be 'read off' from the texts and tenets of social theory—they stand, in other words, in need of patient empirical investigation. In part, this points to the renewed significance of that rich body of enquiry concerned with how crime, order, justice, and punishment are represented through print and an increasingly bewildering and diverse array of electronic media; this being one of the principal routes through which the profane meanings of notions such as security, risk, and danger are encoded and passed into cultural circulation. The criminological gaze might also fruitfully turn (further) here towards the ways in which crime and social order figure in the lived, and always in some part local, social relations of differently situated citizens—towards what it *means*, in the altered conditions of the present, to be a jobless teenager, or parent, or asylum-seeker, or to have property to protect or a neighbourhood to defend, or to be a computer-hacker, or community safety practitioner, or Europol liaison officer. One might suggest, in addition, that this is unlikely to be fully accomplished without due attention being afforded to the *feelings* and *passions* that continue to animate the politics of crime, policing, and punishment; something that requires human emotion—anger, fear, shame, resentment, pleasure, and so on—to be located somewhere near to the heart of contemporary criminological enquiry (Karstedt *et al.* 2007). And it signals, finally, the importance of paying close *comparative* attention, not merely to variation in the ways in which the crime question is represented and acted upon in different locations across the globe, but also to the intersections that exist between the often affectively charged demands of citizens for security and the volatile dynamics and popular-punitive tone of much contemporary 'law and order' politics and governmental practice.

This brings us, in turn, to a bundle of questions pertaining to aspects of *political culture*, and, in particular, to the ways in which criminological research and reflection might (or should?) strive to connect with wider forms of cultural and political disputation concerning 'its' subject matter (Garland and Sparks 2001). Criminology has since its inception been for the most part a consciously 'applied' undertaking (both in its 'official' and in various 'radical' guises), concerned to participate in, and make effective contributions to, the realm of politics and practical affairs. Throughout much of the twentieth century it seemed relatively clear what this entailed and how it might be effected (even if 'success' was never guaranteed). For some, it meant presenting to government and policy-makers scientifically legitimate knowledge that could inform rational policy-making—a stance that, among others, Alfred Blumstein (1993) and Roger Hood (2002) have sought to defend and rehabilitate. For others, of more 'radical' political persuasions, the appropriate stance of the 'criminologist' was never the pursuit of 'relevance' (as defined by the policy audience) but, rather, that of sceptic and problem-raiser, someone whose knowledge and skills were to be placed—if anywhere at all—at the service of pressure groups and new social movements (Cohen 1988; Walters 2003). The implication of our argument in this chapter is that things have, in ways that disturb the coherence of both of these outlooks, become murky, distinctly less clear-cut, and in need of thinking about anew. When the criminal justice state has become but one node within a diverse network of security actors; when crime and crime control whirl above our heads at the transnational level; when policing and punishment seem shaped less by hard-won knowledge and reasoned deliberation than by punitive passions and short-term political calculation; when judgements concerning crime 'risks' are no longer the province of a cosy coterie of 'experts'—what under these conditions does it mean for criminological knowledge to make effective, intelligible contributions in the public sphere? And within what settings, by what means, and to what ends, might such contributions plausibly be made?

These are pressing questions for which there are no instant, off-the-shelf answers. Suffice it then, by way of conclusion, to suggest that it is timely to revisit and revise the ways in which we approach the social analysis of crime, order, and control and seek to acquire some purchase over how crime problems are represented culturally and treated politically. Such reconsideration has begun to surface elsewhere in the social sciences—notably in the debates about 'public sociology' prompted by the interventions of Michael Burawoy in the USA and subsequently the UK (Burawoy 2004, 2005). We see little worth in seeking to translate unthinkingly into the subfield of criminology Burawoy's typology of 'professional', 'policy', 'critical', and 'public' sociology, or in adopting uncritically his advocacy of the latter. But it may well be –this, at any rate, is the hunch guiding our current work on this topic (Loader and Sparks forthcoming)—that the idea of a public criminology offers an analytically rich space within which to forge an intellectually serious and worldly approach towards the study of crime and society in the twenty-first century. Such criminology needs, in our view, to address and strive to apprehend—theoretically, empirically, and normatively—the emergent landscapes of crime, order, and control we have started to sketch here. In so doing, it must develop a sociologically informed grasp of the mundane and political cultures in which questions of crime and social order have come to assume a prominent, emotively charged place, and remain fully alive to the fact that this is at least in part the case because crime and justice are ineluctably entangled with the properly political question of what—today—would constitute the 'good society'.

■ SELECTED FURTHER READING

Extended treatments of the broad themes we have surveyed in this chapter can be found in David Garland's (2001) *The Culture of Control* (Garland 2001a) and Jonathan Simon's (2006) *Governing Through Crime*—both key reference points in this discussion. Two edited collections—Kevin Stenson and Robert Sullivan's (2001) *Crime, Risk and Justice* and Tim Hope and Richard Sparks's (2000) *Crime, Risk and Insecurity*—bring together many of the key authors in the field and provide useful 'ways in' to current debates.

Readers may, in addition, usefully refer to the several texts dealing in more depth with particular aspects of the three themes we have addressed. Johnston and Shearing's (2003) *Governing Security* is an innovative treatment of the pluralization of security and offers a powerful case against state-centric approaches to the subject. Their approach is variously defended and criticized by the contributors to Jennifer Wood and Benoit Dupont's (2006) collection on *Democracy, Society and the Governance of Security*. Our take on globalization was originally much inspired by Zygmunt Bauman's (1988) great little polemic, *Globalization: The Human Consequences*, a text that also has some important things to say about safety and security.

In general, the best advice to anyone who wishes to keep abreast of current thinking remains to keep their eye on the journals. The best of these include those that were around on the last occasion we considered this chapter's themes—*The British Journal of Criminology, Punishment and Society, Theoretical Criminology*, and *Social and Legal Studies*—to which can now be added several others, including *Crime Media Culture, Criminology and Criminal Justice, The European Journal of Criminology*, and *Global Crime*.

■ REFERENCES

AGAMBEN, G. (2005), *State of Exception*, Chicago: University of Chicago Press.

ANDERSON, M., BOER, M. DEN, CULLEN, P., GILMORE, W., RAAB, C., and WALKER, N. (1995), *Policing the European Union: Theory, Law and Practice*, Oxford: Clarendon.

AVANT, D. (2005), *The Market for Force*, Cambridge: Cambridge University Press.

BARKER, V. (2006), 'The Politics of Punishing: Building a State Governance Theory of American Imprisonment Variation', *Punishment & Society*, 8(1): 5–32.

BAUMAN, Z. (1992), *Intimations of Postmodernity*, London: Routledge.

—— (1998), *Globalization: The Human Consequences*, Cambridge: Polity.

—— (1999), *In Search of Politics*, Cambridge: Polity.

—— (2001), 'Wars of the Globalization Era', *European Journal of Social Theory*, 4(1): 11–28.

BECK, U. (1992), *Risk Society*, London: Sage.

—— (2000), *What is Globalization?*, Cambridge: Polity.

—— (2006), *Cosmopolitan Vision*, Cambridge: Polity.

BECKETT, K. (1997), *Making Crime Pay: Law and Order in Contemporary American Politics*, Oxford: Oxford University Press.

BIGO, D. (2000a), 'Liaison Officers in Europe: New Officers in the European Security Field', in J. Sheptycki (ed.), *Issues in Transnational Policing*, London: Routledge.

—— (2000b), 'When Two Become One: Internal and External Securitisations in Europe', in M. Kelstrup and M. Williams (eds), *International Relations Theory and the Politics of European Integration: Power, Security and Community*, London: Routledge.

—— (ed.) (2006), *Illiberal Practices in Liberal Regimes*, Paris: L'Harmattan.

BLAKELY, E., and SNYDER, M. (1997), *Fortress America: Gated Communities in the United States*, Washington DC: Brookings Institution Press.

BLUMSTEIN, A. (1993), 'Making Rationality Relevant', *Criminology*, 31(1): 1–16.

BOURGOIS, P. (1995), *In Search of Respect: Selling Crack in El Barrio*, Cambridge: Cambridge University Press.

BROWN, M., and PRATT, J. (2000), 'Introduction', in M. Brown and J. Pratt (eds), *Dangerous Offenders: Punishment and Social Order*, London: Routledge.

BURAWOY, M. (2004), 'Public Sociologies: Contradictions, Dilemmas and Possibilities', *Social Forces*, 82(4): 1603–18.

—— (2005), 'For Public Sociology', *British Journal of Sociology*, 56(2): 259–94.

BUZAN, B. (1991), *People, States and Fear*, 2nd edn, Brighton: Harvester.

——, WÆVER, O., and de WILDE, J. (1998), *Security: A New Framework for Analysis*, London: Lynne Reinner.

CALDEIRA, T. (2000), *City of Walls: Crime, Segregation and Citizenship in São Paulo*, Berkeley, Cal.: University of California Press.

CASTELLS, M. (1996), *The Information Age: Economy, Society and Culture: Vol. I, The Rise of the Network Society*, Oxford: Basil Blackwell.

—— (1998), *The Information Age: Economy, Society and Culture: Vol. III, End of Millennium*, Oxford: Basil Blackwell.

COHEN, S. (1988), *Against Criminology*, New Brunswick, N.J.: Transaction Books.

CRAWFORD, A. (2006), 'Policing and Security as "Club Goods": The New Enclosures', in J. WOOD and B. DUPONT (eds), *Democracy, Society and the Governance of Security*, Cambridge: Cambridge University Press.

—— and LISTER, S. (2005), *The Extended Police Family: Visible Patrols in Residential Areas*, Bristol: Policy Press.

CURRIE, E. (1997), 'Market, Crime and Community', *Theoretical Criminology*, 1(2): 47–72.

DAVIS, M. (1990), *City of Quartz: Excavating the future in Los Angeles*, London: Vintage.

DEFLEM, M. (2003), *Policing World Society*, Oxford: Oxford University Press.

DOUGLAS, M. (1992), *Risk and Cultural Theory*, London: Routledge.

ECK, J., and WEISBURD, D. (eds) (1995), *Crime and Place*, Monsey, New York: Criminal Justice Press.

EDWARDS, A., and GILL, P. (eds) (2003), *Transnational Organized Crime: Perspectives on Global Security*, London: Routledge.

ERICSON, R., DOYLE, A., and BARRY, D. (2003), *Insurance as Governance*, Toronto: University of Toronto Press.

FEELEY, M., and SIMON, J. (1992), The New Penology', *Criminology*, 30(4): 449–74.

FOUCAULT, M. (1991), 'Governmentality' in G. Burchell *et al.* (eds), *The Foucault Effect Studies in Governmentality*, Hemel Hempstead: Harvester Wheatsheaf.

GAMBETTA, D. (1993), *The Sicilian Mafia: The Business of Private Protection*, Camb., Mass.: Harvard University Press.

GARLAND, D. (1990), *Punishment and Modern Society: A Study in Social Theory*, Oxford: Clarendon.

—— (1997), 'Governmentality and the Problem of Crime: Foucault, Criminology, Sociology', *Theoretical Criminology*, 1(2): 173–214.

—— (2001a), *The Culture of Control: Crime and Social Order in Contemporary Society*, Oxford: Clarendon.

—— (ed.) (2001b), *Mass Imprisonment: Social Causes and Consequences*, London: Sage.

—— and SPARKS, R. (2001), 'Criminology, Social Theory and the Challenge of Our Times', in D. Garland and R. Sparks, (eds), *Criminology and Social Theory*, Oxford: Clarendon.

GIDDENS, A. (1990), *The Consequences of Modernity*, Cambridge: Polity.

—— (1991), *Modernity and Self-Identity: Self and Society in the Late Modern Age*, Cambridge: Polity.

GIRLING, E., LOADER, I., and SPARKS, R. (2000), *Crime and Social Change in Middle England: Questions of Order in an English Town*, London: Routledge.

GOLDSMITH, A. (2003), 'Policing Weak States: Citizen Safety and State Responsibility, *Policing and Society*, 13: 3–21.

HACKING, I. (1991), *The Taming of Chance*, Cambridge: Cambridge University Press.

HAGAN, J., and PETERSEN, R. (eds) (1995), *Crime and Inequality*, Stanford, Cal.: Stanford University Press.

HARVEY, D. (1989), *The Condition of Postmodernity*, Oxford: Basil Blackwell.

HAY, C. (1996), *Re-Stating Social and Political Change*, Buckingham: Open University Press.

HELD, D. (1995), *Democracy and the Global Order: From the Modern State to Cosmopolitan Governance*, Cambridge: Polity.

—— and MCGREW, A. (eds) (2002a), *Governing Globalization: Power, Authority and Global Governance*, Cambridge: Polity.

—— and —— (2002b), *Globalization/Anti-Globalization*, Cambridge: Polity.

——, ——, GOLDBLATT, D., and PERRATON, J. (1999), *Global Transformations: Politics, Economics and Culture*, Cambridge: Polity.

HENHAM, R., and FINDLAY, M. (2006), *Transforming International Criminal Justice: Retributive and Restorative Justice in the Trial Process*, Cullompton, Devon: Willan.

HILL, P. (2003), *The Japanese Mafia: Yakuza, Law, and the State*, Oxford: Oxford University Press.

HOBSBAWM, E. (1994), *The Age of Extremes: The Short Twentieth Century 1914–1991*, London: Michael Joseph.

HOOD, R. (2002), 'Criminology and Penal Policy: The Vital Role of Empirical Research' in A. Bottoms and

M. Tonry (eds), *Ideology, Crime and Criminal Justice*, Cullompton, Devon: Willan.

HOPE. T. (2001), 'Crime Victimisation and Inequality in Risk Society', in R. Matthews and J. Pitts (eds), *Crime, Disorder and Community Safety*, London: Routledge.

—— and SPARKS, R. (eds) (2000), *Crime, Risk and Insecurity: Law and Order in Political Discourse and Everyday Life*, London: Routledge.

HUYSMAN, J. (2006), *'The Politics of Insecurity. Fear, Migration and Asylum in the EU*, London: Routledge.

JACKSON, J. (2004), 'Experience and Expression: Social and Cultural Significance in the Fear of Crime', *British Journal of Criminology*, 44: 946–66.

JOHNSTON, L. (2006), 'Transnational Security Governance', in J. Wood and B. Dupont (eds), *Democracy, Society and the Governance of Security*, Cambridge: Cambridge University Press.

—— and SHEARING, C. (2003), *Governing Security*, London: Routledge.

JONES, T., and NEWBURN, T. (1998), *Private Security and Public Policing*, Oxford: Clarendon.

KALDOR, M. (2006), *New and Old Wars: Organized Violence in a Global Age*, 2nd edn, Cambridge: Polity.

KARSTEDT, S. (2000), 'Knights of Crime: The Success of "Pre-Modern" Structures in the Illegal Economy', in S. Karstedt and K.-D. Bussmann (eds), *Social Dynamics of Crime and Control: New Theories for a World in Transition*, Oxford: Hart.

—— and BUSSMANN, K.-D. (eds) (2000), *Social Dynamics of Crime and Control: New Theories for a World in Transition*, Oxford: Hart.

——, LOADER. I., and STRANG, H. (eds) (2007), *Emotions, Crime and Justice*, Oxford: Hart.

KEMSHALL, H., and MAGUIRE, M. (2001), 'Public Protection, Partnership and Risk Penality: The Multi-Agency Management of Sex and Violent Offenders', *Punishment and Society*, 3(2): 237–64.

KOOIMAN, J. (2003), *Governing as Governance*, London: Sage.

KRAUSE, K., and WILLIAMS, K. (eds) (1997), *Critical Security Studies*, London: University College London Press.

LAVENEX, S., and WALLACE, W. (2005), 'Justice and Home Affairs', in H. Wallace, W. Wallace, and M. Pollack (eds), *Policy-Making in the European Union*, 5th edn, Oxford: Oxford University Press.

LOADER, I. (1999), 'Consumer Culture and the Commodification of Policing and Security', *Sociology*, 33(2): 373–92.

—— (2006), 'Fall of the "Platonic Guardians": Liberalism, Criminology and Political Responses to Crime in England and Wales', *British Journal of Criminology*, 46(4) (forthcoming).

—— and SPARKS, R. (2004), For an Historical Sociology of Crime Policy in England and Wales since 1968', *Critical Review of International Social and Political Philosophy*, 7(2): 5 32.

—— and —— (forthcoming), *Public Criminology?: Studying Crime and Society in the Twenty-First Century*, London: Routledge.

—— and WALKER, N. (2006), 'Locating the Public Interest in Transnational Policing', in A. Goldsmith and J. Sheptycki (eds), *Crafting Global Policing*, Oxford: Hart

—— and —— (2007), *Civilizing Security*, Cambridge: Cambridge University Press.

LODGE, T. (1974), 'The Founding of the Home Office Research Unit', in. R. Hood (ed.), *Crime, Criminology and Public Policy*, London: Heinemann.

LOGAN, J., and MOLOTCH, H. (1987), *Urban Fortunes: The Political Economy of Place*, Berkeley, Cal.: University of California Press.

LYON, D. (2003), *Surveillance After September 11*, Cambridge: Polity.

MANNING, P. (2000), 'Policing New Social Spaces', in J. Sheptycki (ed.), *Issues in Transnational Policing*, London: Routledge.

MATRAVERS, A., (ed.) (2003), *Sex Offenders in the Community*, Cullompton, Devon: Willan.

NADELMAN, E. (1993), *Cops Across Borders: The Internationalization of US Criminal Law Enforcement*, Philadelphia: Pennsylvania State University Press.

NELKEN, D. (1997), 'The Globalization of Crime and Criminal Justice: Prospects and Problems', *Current Legal Problems*, 50: 251–77.

—— (ed.) (2000), *Contrasting Criminal Justice: Getting from Here to There*, Aldershot: Dartmouth.

NEWBURN, T., and SPARKS, R. (2004), *Criminal Justice and Political Cultures*, Cullompton, Devon: Willan.

NIGHTINGALE, C. (1993), *On the Edge*, New York: Basic Books.

NOGALA, D. (2001), 'Policing Across a Dimorphous Border: Challenge and Innovation at the French-German Border', *European Journal of Crime, Criminal Law and Criminal Justice*, 9(2): 130–43.

NORDSTROM, C. (2000), 'Shadows and Sovereigns', *Theory, Culture and Society*, 17(4): 35–54.

O'MALLEY, P. (1992), 'Risk, Power and Crime Prevention', *Economy and Society*, 21(3): 251–68.

O'MALLEY, P. (1999), 'Volatile and Contradictory Punishment', *Theoretical Criminology*, 3(2): 175–96.

——(2000), 'Risk Societies and the Government of Crime', in M. Brown and J. Pratt (eds), *Dangerous Offenders: Punishment and Social Order*, London: Routledge.

——(2001), 'Policing Crime Risks in the Neo-Liberal Era', in K. Stenson and R. Sullivan (eds), *Crime, Risk and Justice: The Politics of Crime Control in Liberal Democracies*, Cullompton, Devon: Willan.

OSBORNE, D., and GAEBLER, T. (1992), *Re-Thinking Government*, Harmondsworth: Penguin.

RADZINÒWICZ, L. (1999), *Adventures in Criminology*, London: Routledge.

REINER, R. (1992), 'Policing a Postmodern Society', *Modern Law Review*, 55(6): 761–82.

RHODES, R. (1997), *Understanding Governance: Policy Networks, Governance, Reflexivity and Accountability*, Buckingham: Open University Press.

ROBERTSON, R. (1995), 'Glocalization: Time-Space and Homogeneity-Heterogeneity', in M. Featherstone, S. Lash, and R. Robertson (eds), *Global Modernities*, London: Sage.

ROBINSON, G. (2002), 'Exploring Risk Management in Probation Practice: Contemporary Developments in England and Wales', *Punishment and Society*, 4(1): 5–25.

ROSE, N. (2000), 'Government and Control', in D. Garland and R. Sparks (eds), *Criminology and Social Theory*, Oxford: Clarendon.

——and MILLER, P. (1992), 'Political Power Beyond the State: Problematics of Government', *British Journal of Sociology*, 43(2): 173–205.

RUGGIERO, V. (2000), 'Transnational Crime: Official and Alternative Fears', *International Journal of the Sociology of Law*, 28: 187–99.

SAVAGE, M., BAGNALL, G., and LONGHURST, B. (2004), *Globalization and Belonging*, London: Sage.

SHEARING, C. (1996), 'Reinventing Policing: Policing as Governance', in O. Marenin (ed.), *Changing Police: Policing Change*, New York: Garland.

——(2006), 'Reflections on the Refusal to Acknowledge Private Government', in J. Wood and B. Dupont (eds), *Democracy, Society and the Governance of Security*, Cambridge: Cambridge University Press.

——and STENNING, P. (1983), 'Private Security: Implications for Social Control', *Social Problems*, 30(5): 493–506.

SHEPTYCKI, J. (1996), 'Police Co-operation in the English Channel Region 1968–1996', *European Journal of Crime, Criminal Law and Criminal Justice*, 6(3): 216–35.

——(ed.) (2000), *Issues in Transnational Policing*, London: Routledge.

SHERMAN, L., GARTIN, P., and BUERGER, M. (1989), 'Hot Spots of Predatory Crime: Routine Activities and the Criminology of Place', *Criminology*, 27(1): 27–55.

SIMON, J. (1995), 'They Died With Their Boots on: The Boot Camp and the Limits of Modern Penality', *Social Justice*, 22(2): 25–48.

——(2001), 'Megan's Law: Crime and Democracy in Late Modern America', *Law and Social Enquiry*, 25(4): 1111–50.

——(2006), *Governing Through Crime*, New York: Oxford University Press.

SKOGAN, W. (1990), *Disorder and Decline: The Spiral of Decay in American Neighborhoods*, New York: Oxford University Press.

SPARKS, R. (1991), 'Reason and Unreason in Left Realism: Some Problems in the Constitution of the Fear of Crime', in R. Matthews and J. Young (eds), *Issues in Realist Criminology*, London: Sage.

——(1992), *Television and the Drama of Crime: Moral Tales and the Place of Crime in Public Life*, Buckingham: Open University Press.

——(2000), 'Risk and Blame in Criminal Justice Controversies: British Press Coverage and Official Discourse on Prison Security (1993–6)', in M. Brown and J. Pratt (eds), *Dangerous Offenders: Punishment and Social Order*, London: Routledge.

——(2001), 'Degrees of Estrangement: The Cultural Theory of Risk and Comparative Penology', *Theoretical Criminology*, 5(2): 159–76.

SQUIRES, P., and STEPHEN, D. (2005), *Rougher Justice: Anti-Social Behaviour and Young People*, Cullompton, Devon: Willan.

STENSON, K., and SULLIVAN, R. (eds) (2001), *Crime, Risk and Justice: The Politics of Crime Control in Liberal Democracies*, Cullompton, Devon: Willan.

SULLIVAN, M. (1988), *Getting Paid: Youth, Crime and Work in the Inner City*, Ithica, NY: Cornell University Press.

TAUB, R., TAYLOR, D., and DUNHAM, J. (1984), *Paths of Neighborhood Change*, Chicago: University of Chicago Press.

TAYLOR, I. (ed.) (1999), *Crime in Context: A Critical Criminology of Market Societies*, Cambridge: Polity.

TONRY, M. (2003), *Punishment and Politics*, Cullompton, Devon: Willan.

VARESE, F. (2001), *The Russian Mafia: Private Protection in a New Market Economy*, Oxford: Oxford University Press.

—— (2006), 'How Mafias Migrate: The Case of the 'Ndrangheta in Northern Italy', *Law and Society Review*, 40(2): 411–44.

WACQUANT, L. (2006), *Prisons of Poverty*, Minneapolis: University of Minnesota Press.

WAKEFIELD, A. (2004), *Selling Security*, Cullompton, Devon: Willan.

WALKER, N. (2002), 'Policing and the Supranational', *Policing and Society*, 12(4): 307–22.

—— (2003), 'The Pattern of Transnational Policing', in T. Newburn (ed.), *Handbook of Policing*, Cullompton, Devon: Willan.

WALKLATE, S. (1998), 'Excavating the Fear of Crime: Fear, Anxiety or Trust?', *Theoretical Criminology*, 2(4): 403–18.

WALTERS, R. (2003), *Deviant Knowledge: Criminology, Politics and Policy*, Cullompton, Devon: Willan.

WHITMAN, J. Q. (2003), *Harsh Justice: Criminal Punishment and the Widening Divide Between America and Europe*, Oxford: Oxford University Press.

WINDLESHAM, L. (1987), *Responses to Crime—Volume 1: Ministering to a Gentler Age*, Oxford: Clarendon.

—— (1996), *Responses to Crime—Volume 3: Legislating with the Tide*, Oxford: Clarendon.

—— (1998), *Politics, Punishment and Populism*, Oxford: Oxford University Press.

—— (2001) *Responses to Crime—Volume 4: Dispensing Justice*, Oxford: Clarendon.

WOOD, J., and DUPONT, B. (eds) (2006), *Democracy, Society and the Governance of Security*, Cambridge: Cambridge University Press.

—— and SHEARING, C. (2006), *Imagining Security*, Cullompton, Devon: Willan.

WRIGHT MILLS, C. (1959), *The Sociological Imagination*, Harmondsworth: Penguin.

YOUNG, J. (1999), *The Exclusive Society: Social Exclusion, Crime and Difference in Late Modernity*, London: Sage.

ZEDNER, L. (2005), 'Securing Liberty in the Face of Terror: Reflections from Criminal Justice', *Journal of Law and Society*, 32(4): 507–33.

ZIMRING, F. E., HAWKINS, G., and KAMIN, S. (2001) *Punishment and Democracy: Three Strikes and You're Out in California*, Oxford: Oxford University Press.

4

CULTURAL CRIMINOLOGY

Keith Hayward and Jock Young

INTRODUCTION

The complex interrelationships and homologies that link crime and culture have long been a source of inspiration for criminologists. Over the years, interest in this relational dynamic has inspired many of the foundational works of the discipline, from investigations into the symbolic and magical interactions of sub-cultural milieu to critical analyses of the culture and power relations associated with state institutions. Yet, for all this scholarly endeavour, the story of the 'cultural focus' within criminology has remained one of ebb and flow. This situation endures today, as those engaged in the exploration of the crime-culture nexus jostle for position in a 'rendezvous discipline' constituted from an array of competing theoretical and ideological paradigms. The last decade or so, however, has seen a revivification of the cultural tradition, with the emergence of a more consistent flow of studies in the area—not least a clustering of analyses that have coalesced around the emergent intellectual movement known as *cultural criminology* (e.g. Ferrell and Sanders 1995; Ferrell 1999; Banks 2000; Presdee 2000; Hayward and Young 2004; Ferrell *et al.* 2004).[1]

What, then, is cultural criminology? Above all else, it is the placing of crime and its control in the context of culture; that is, viewing both crime and the agencies of control as cultural products—as creative constructs. As such they must be read in terms of the meanings they carry. Furthermore, cultural criminology seeks to highlight the interaction between two key elements: the relationship and the interaction between constructions upwards and constructions downwards. Its focus is always upon the continuous generation of meaning around interaction; rules created, rules broken, a constant interplay of moral entrepreneurship, moral innovation, and transgression.

Such complex foci require the utilization of a wide-ranging set of analytical tools. No surprise, then, that cultural criminology is stridently interdisciplinary, interfacing not just with criminology, sociology, and criminal justice studies, but with perspectives and methodologies drawn from inter alia cultural, media and urban studies, philosophy,

[1] We wish to acknowledge the scholarship of the many criminologists who have contributed to this recent flow of studies on culture and crime. While these scholars often do not self-define themselves as 'cultural criminologists', their work has greatly contributed to this critical mass.

postmodern critical theory, cultural and human geography, anthropology, social movement studies, and other 'action' research approaches. In other words, cultural criminology's remit is to keep 'turning the kaleidoscope' on the way we think about crime, and importantly, the legal and societal responses to rule-breaking.

Whilst this body of work has made great strides in (re)directing the criminological 'imagination' towards the study of culture, it remains the case that, despite many positive developments, the trajectories and methods of cultural criminology have yet to be firmly established. We would argue that this is as much a strength as a weakness. Certainly, one of cultural criminology's stated aims is to be 'less a definitive paradigm than an emergent array of perspectives' (Ferrell 1999: 396). In this sense it self-consciously eludes any attempt at static definition; something already in evidence in the movement's albeit brief history. For example, in its original manifestation (as an operationalizing rubric) in the United States, cultural criminology was primarily focused on the role of 'image, meaning, and representation in the interplay of crime and crime control'; especially in relation to the 'stylised frameworks and experiential dynamics of illicit subcultures; the symbolic criminalisation of popular cultural forms; the mediated construction of crime and crime control issues . . .; and the links between crime, crime control, and cultural space, and the collectively embodied emotions that shape the meaning of crime (ibid.: 395). However, as cultural criminology gathered traction in the UK, British criminologists were keen to 'inject a more materialist spine into cultural criminology's theoretical body' (O'Brien 2005: 605). This 'British augmentation' sought firmly to embed within the movement the rich tradition of critical British criminology, and, in particular, a critique of the hegemonic discourses associated with late modern market culture (e.g. Hayward 2003, 2004; Young 2003; Hall and Winlow 2006). Such theoretical fluidity clearly mitigates against making any all-encompassing or enduring claims about cultural criminology as a universalizing theoretical imperative. Rather we see cultural criminology as an ongoing adventure; a journey that provides new vantage points from which to view the landscape of contemporary culture—in all its conflicting manifestations. However, at the same time because of its increasing momentum, there is a need to signpost some of the more general aims and themes that cross-cut the diverse strands and methodological approaches that under-gird cultural criminology. What follows is our attempt to point the way forward.

FOR A SOCIOLOGICALLY INSPIRED CRIMINOLOGY

Most fundamentally, cultural criminology seeks to *bring back sociological theory to criminology*; that is to continue to (re)integrate the role of culture, social construction, human meaning, creativity, class, and power relations into the criminological project. No doubt for some, this aim will seem redundant in that such key foci have always featured on the landscape of theoretical criminology (e.g. Downes 2005: 320; relatedly Rock 2005). Yet, whilst this is undoubtedly the case, we would argue that what is important about the theories that constitute and animate cultural criminology—from media analyses to critiques of oppressive structures, from critical theory to phenomenological exegeses—is the way they strive to reflect the peculiarities and particularities of the late modern socio-cultural milieu. But what especially makes cultural criminology late modern? We suggest it is (at least) a twofold process.

First, there is the extraordinary emphasis on creativity, individualism, and generation of lifestyle in the present period, coupled with mass media which have expanded and proliferated so as to transform human subjectivity. From this perspective, the virtual community becomes as real as the community outside one's door—reference groups, vocabularies of motive, and identities become global in their demesne. Cultural criminology offers a powerful theoretical framework for analysing the relationship between these conditions and crime. With its mix of intellectual influences, it sets out to develop theories of crime that merge a 'phenomenology of transgression' (Katz 1988; Lyng 1990; Henry and Milovanovic 1996; Van Hoorebeeck 1997) with a sociological analysis of late modern culture to create what O'Malley and Mugford (1994) refer to as a 'historically contextualized phenomenology' (of which more later). In this reconstruction of aetiology, cultural criminology, arguably, returns to the original concerns of mainstream criminology. However, for us, it returns with fresh eyes, offering new and exciting ways in which to reinvigorate the study of crime and deviance through an ongoing engagement with debates on the transition into postmodernity.

Secondly, the antecedents of cultural criminology emerged at the beginning of the late modern period. We refer to the intellectual energy that occurred in the sociology of deviance, which, lest we forget, was inherently cultural in its focus and postmodern in its seriability. As Stan Cohen famously put it: 'After the mid 1960's—well before Foucault made these subjects intellectually respectable and a long way from the Left Bank—our little corner of the human sciences was seized by a deconstructionist impulse' (1997: 101). In Britain, there were two major influences on this process of deconstruction: phenomenology and subcultural theory. The radical phenomenological tradition of Becker, Kitsuse, and Lemert, supplemented by the social constructionist work of writers such as Peter Berger and Thomas Luckmann, was extraordinarily influential, particularly in so far as it involved a stress upon the existential freedoms of those 'curtailed' and 'oppressed' by the labels and essentialism(s) of the powerful. This was never truer than in David Matza's book, *Becoming Deviant* (1969), with its concepts of 'naturalism', 'drift', pluralism, ambiguity, and irony, on the one hand, and crime as transgression on the other. The synthesis of such an approach with subcultural theory commenced in the late 1960s at the London School of Economics with David Downes's book *The Delinquent Solution* (1966). Here an emphasis on both subcultures as 'problem solvers' and the expressive rather than the instrumental nature of much juvenile delinquency began to neutralize the more wooden American subcultural theory of the Mertonian tradition. Culture was not a thing out there to be learned and enacted, rather, lifestyles were something which constantly evolved. This line of inquiry was further developed in the work of PhD students at the LSE, including Mike Brake (1980), Stan Cohen (1972), and Jock Young (1971), all of whom focused on how deviant subcultures were both created by the actors involved and mediated and constructed by the impact of the mass media and the interventions of the powerful. It gathered further theoretical traction at the National Deviancy Conference; the work of Phil Cohen, Ian Taylor, and Geoff Pearson all stressing the need for a humanistic sociology of deviance that had at its core a sensitive ethnographic method. Finally, it came of age at the Birmingham Centre for Contemporary Cultural Studies, most notably in the various analyses of youth culture undertaken by Stuart Hall, John Clarke, Dick Hebdige, Tony Jefferson, Angela McRobbie, and Paul Willis. In this body of work, youth culture is seen as a hive of creativity, an arena of magical solutions where symbols are bricollaged into lifestyles, a place of identity and discovery, and, above all, a site of resistance.

This re-working of American sociology replaced a narrow subcultural theorization with notions of expressivity and style, relocating transgression as a source of meaning and 'leisure'. It evoked a rich narrative of symbolism and an awareness of mediated reality. By the mid-1980s such a humanistic sociology, buttressed by strong critiques of positivistic methods, was a major force within criminology. Since then, however, there was been a palpable lurch back to positivism. It is in this context that cultural criminology seeks to retrace its roots and move on into the twenty-first century.

THIS IS 'WHAT IS CULTURAL' ABOUT CULTURAL CRIMINOLOGY

Crucial to the understanding of cultural criminology is its interpretation of the 'cultural', itself a subject of controversy and contest. First of all, it is not positivism in the sense that it does not see culture as a function of material situations or structural positions. Culture is *not* a dependent variable of structure. Yet, and here we have differences with the 'new American cultural sociology' (see Smith 1998; Alexander and Smith 2002), it does not see culture as an independent variable: it certainly is not autonomous of the patterns of inequality and power or the material predicaments of the actors. Witness, for example, the Gramscian concern with class and power in the work of the Birmingham School (e.g. Hall and Jefferson 1975; Hall *et al.* 1978; Willis 1977) which, incidentally, the cultural sociologists dismiss as a 'presuppositional commitment to a power-based frame of analysis' which is 'unduly restrictive' (Smith 1998; Sherwood *et al.* 1993). Of course, both the cultural hegemony of the powerful and the subcultures of acquiescence and resistance of the less powerful are scarcely independent of class and power. And as for the immediate material predicament of social actors, the very early subcultural work on 'the pains of imprisonment' demonstrated the dialectical relationship between conditions and culture. Namely, although all inmates experienced 'the pains of imprisonment', the extent and the nature of these pains are dependent on the culture they bring to the prison (e.g. in terms of class and gender) just as the pains in turn shape the particular inmate culture that arises in the attempt to surmount the privations of prison life (Young 1999: 89–90).

Secondly, and related to the first, cultural criminology is not a cultural positivism where crime or deviance is ascribed to the simple acting out of the static culture of a group. Thus it would take issue with the tradition of cultural conflict theory commencing with the work of Thorsten Sellin (1938) and highlighted in the well-known subcultural formulation of Walter Miller (1958), where crime is simply the enactment of lower-working-class values. Such a position originally formulated by Sellin in terms of the justification for vengeance and vendetta amongst Sicilian immigrants, which in turn led inevitably to conflicts with wider American values, has clear echoes today in the supposition that multiculturalism generates a sense of ineluctable collisions of norms, most particularly that between Muslim and Western values. Cultures are not static, they are not an essence waiting to be enacted, rather they are heterogeneous, they blur, cross boundaries, and hybridize. To talk, for example, of ahistorical and context free proclivities to crime in relationship to ethnic cultures—say Jewish or Jamaican—is a pointless essentialism, stereotypical in its notion of fixity and stasis and of no explanatory value.

In *Culture as Praxis*, Zygmunt Bauman distinguishes two discourses about culture, long-standing and seemingly diametrically opposed. The first conceptualizes 'culture as the activity of the free roaming spirit, the site of creativity, invention, self-critique and self-transcendence', suggesting 'the courage to break well-drawn horizons, to step beyond closely-guarded boundaries'. The second sees culture as 'a tool of routinization and continuity—a handmaiden of social order', here 'culture' stood for regularity and pattern—with freedom cast under the rubric of 'norm-breaking' and 'deviation' (1999: xvi–xvii).

Culture of the second sort is the province of orthodox social anthropology, of Parsonian Functionalism, of post-Parsonian cultural sociology. Culture is the stuff of cohesion, the glue of society, the preservative of predictability, the *soi-disant* support of social structure. Culture of the first sort fits much more readily within the subcultural tradition; it is culture as praxis, the culture of transgression, of resistance, of human creativity. And if for this first discourse, transgression signals creativity, with culture of the second sort, transgression signifies the very opposite: the absence of culture. Yet the two discourses are not irreconcilable, they both suggest an ongoing and contested negotiation of meaning and identity. Of course, the notion of culture as somehow outside of human creation, as an unreflexive prop of social structure, as a mysterious functional creation of the social organism, is preposterous. But the *belief* in tradition, the embracing of stasis and conformity, the mobilization of rigid stereotype and fundamental values is, of course, a fact in itself and a fact of considerable impact and reality.

Thus a sociology which foregrounds human creativity does not entail the ignoring of those cultures and actions which involve its renunciation. Human beings, as Matza (1969) famously pointed out, have always the feasibility, the capacity to transcend even the most dire circumstances but they have also the possibility of acting 'as if' they were a cultural puppet or an inanimate artifice. Thus, if we are, in Dwight Conquergood's (1991) wonderful phrase, to view culture as a verb rather than as a noun, then we must remember that this verb is cast both in a passive and an active tense. Culture may well be a performance, but it can be as much an act of acquiescence as of rebellion.

Criminology and the sociology of deviance by the very nature of their subject matter occupy a privileged cultural vantage point in sociology. Their focus is at precisely that point where norms are imposed and threatened, enacted and broken. They are borderline subjects which foreground the processes of cultural generation and are, of course intrinsically dyadic, that is, they involve the social constructions 'downwards' of the agencies of social control (the culture of control) and 'upwards' of the deviant individuals and groups (the culture of deviance). Here two of the various traditions which prefigure cultural criminology, labelling and subcultural theory, contribute immensely. The notion of a 'label' carries the stereotype of deviance (very frequently, of course, carrying implications of a lack of socialization and culture), whilst 'subculture' carries the motivations and justifications for deviance: both contribute to a narrative which involves creativity, negotiation, and change on behalf of both controllers and controlled. For control and deviance are cultural products, products of human creativity, an interplay of constructions which necessitate that the sociology of crime and the sociology of punishment frequently constituted as separate discourses come together within the rubric of cultural criminology.

In all these ways, then, cultural criminology seeks to develop a criminology which incorporates a notion of culture which is constantly in flux, which has always the potentiality for creativity and transcendence. And, of course, although such an analysis has always applied to the human condition, it is (as we stated earlier) all the more transparently applicable today. For in late modernity the insistent stress on expressivity and personal development, in a world where the narratives of work, family, and community no longer provide a constancy of identity, places a high emphasis on cultural change and personal reinvention. Couple this with an ever-present pluralism of values presented in terms of mass immigration and tourism and the vast plethora of factual and fictional cultural referents carried by the media as part of the process of globalization, and the role of cultural negotiation becomes dramatically heightened. In terms of criminality, the reference points which give rise to relative deprivation and discontent, the vocabularies of motives and techniques of neutralization available off the peg, so to speak, to justify crime, the *modus operandus* of the criminal act itself are manifold, plural, and global. And precisely the same is true of the other aspects of crime: the experience of victimization, images and justifications for punitiveness, modes of policing, political responses to crime are all heavily mediated and widely available. Yet although the moorings of social action are loosened in time and in space, this is not to suggest that vocabularies of motive circulate outside of the political economy of daily life, or without reference to material setting and applicability. Culture may no longer be so fixed in space and time, but the very act of creating culture, of making action meaningful, necessitates an appropriate fit between culture and predicament.

INSIDE THE 'HALL OF MIRRORS': MEDIA, REPRESENTATION, MEANING

As the editors of *Cultural Criminology Unleashed* recently made clear, 'under contemporary conditions a remarkable inversion is all but complete. Images of crime and crime control have now become as "real" as crime and criminal justice itself—if by "real" we denote those dimensions of social life that produce consequences; shape attitudes and policy; define the effects of crime and criminal justice; generate fear, avoidance and pleasure, and alter the lives of those involved' (Ferrell *et al.* 2004: 4). It is one of the primary goals of cultural criminology, then, to attempt to understand the ways in which mediated processes of cultural reproduction and exchange 'constitute' the experience of crime, self, and society under conditions of late modernity (see Kidd-Hewitt and Osborne 1995; Manning 1999; Banks 2005). In a world in which media images of crime and deviance proliferate, where every facet of offending is reflected in a vast hall of mirrors, cultural criminology sets out to make sense of the increasingly blurred line between the real and the virtual. To dismiss this focus on style, representation, and situated meaning simply as a decorative or 'aesthetic' criminology—as some critics have attempted—is to mistake method for meaning. In a world where power is increasingly exercised through mediated representation and symbolic production, battles over image, style, and cultural representation emerge as essential moments in the contested negotiation of late modern reality.

A core methodological component of cultural criminology is therefore the scholarly reading of the numerous mediated texts and images that circulate and promulgate the 'story' of crime and crime control within society (Barak 1994; Anderson and Howard 1998; Bailey and Hale 1998; Potter and Kappeler 1998). Here, everything from the analysis of televisual and filmic depictions of crime and criminality (Fishman and Cavender 1998; Cheatwood 1998; Schofield 2004) to representations of crime and power in comic books (Nyberg 1998; Williams 1998), from the interpretative analysis of crime and punishment in artwork (Valier 2000; A. Young 2004) to examinations of news media imagery (Chermak 1995; Barak 1996; Chermak *et al.* 2003; Valier and Lippens 2005) are grist to the cultural criminologist's mill. The various mix of descriptive readings, counter-readings, and other modes of media/textual deconstructions utilized in these imaginative case studies defy simple description. Instead, by way of introduction to this facet of cultural criminology, we offer a few select examples of the ongoing process by which the mass media continue to commodify crime and transgression.

It is a notable irony that, the more the British government attempts to control the youth crime problem by imposing a series of dominant and seemingly logical controls—including everything from curfews to exclusion orders, from benefit reform to Public Disorder Acts—the more it engenders within young people not compliant rationality, but rather heightened emotionality. Hence a sort of mutating double helix in which the 'irrational responses' of young people provoke ever-more punitive measures from the state (Presdee 2000). Youth culture thus becomes at once the site of excitement and social contestation, of experimentation and dissonance. That this is the case is not surprising. The transgressive nature of youth (sub)cultural practices has long provoked indignation among politicians keen to curry favour with the 'moral majority' by vilifying the perceived 'immorality of contemporary youth'. Whether lowering the level of imprisonment for children or siding with schools that ban snowball fights, the government is turning the screw on the young, subjecting not only their 'oppositional forms of popular and personal pleasure', but also their legitimate cultural practices and even, in many instances, their everyday round to increasing political arbitration and state agency sanction. However, rather than dwell on the obvious (Foucauldian) point about repression/control proliferating rather than suppressing its object of alteration, we are here interested in how that other great agent of social reaction—the market—is reacting and contributing to this social dynamic.

Today, moral panics unfold in a far more complex series of loops and spirals than was the case when Stan Cohen first articulated the concept some four decades ago. Now, for many young people, a decent dose of moral outrage remains the only acid test of a truly oppositional, and therefore, worthwhile cultural practice. As McRobbie and Thornton (1995) make clear, even this response has become, literally, incorporated, as corporations actively use moral panics (in the form of 'a bit of controversy—the threat of censorship, the suggestion of sexual scandal or subversive activity') for their own profitable ends. Images of crime and deviance are now prime marketing tools for selling products in the youth market.

At one level, there is nothing inherently new about this. The compelling and sometimes salacious nature of certain criminal acts ensures a ready audience for crime and it has remained an enduring theme in popular culture throughout the twentieth century. What has changed, however, is both the force and range of the message and the speed at which it loops and reverberates. 'Crime has been seized upon: it is being packaged and marketed to young people as a romantic, exciting, cool, and fashionable cultural symbol. It is in this cultural context that transgression becomes a desirable consumer choice' (Fenwick and Hayward 2000: 44). Within consumer culture, crime is aestheticized and stylized, presented in the mass media on a par with a fashion aesthetic. This is not to suggest any simple deterministic link between images of violence and crime in consumer culture and contemporary youth crime; it is simply to suggest that the distinction between representations of criminality and the pursuit of excitement, especially in the area of youth culture, is becoming extremely blurred.

For example, the most obvious 're-branding' of crime is perhaps the way in which 'gangsta' rap combines images of criminality with street gang iconography and urban transgression to create a product that is immediately seductive to youth audiences (Miller 1995; Kubrin 2005). However, it is no longer simply a question of identifying whether gangsta rap imagery and styling are affecting 'the code of the street' or vice versa. Now, the market has decided to plug into the rap scene and use the aural backdrop of urban hip hop to peddle luxury products to young people desperate for some ontological stability within social environments often stripped of traditional avenues of advancement and self-expression. While brands have always been an intrinsic element of rap culture, in recent years the stakes have increased. In the late 1980s and early 1990s hardcore rappers like Ice.T or Tim Dogg rapped about $60 Nike trainers or 40-oz bottles of Colt 45 malt liquor, today, the giants of corporate hip hop like P.Diddy, 50 Cent, or Jay-Z extol the virtues of (and gratuitously product place) Louis Vuitton luggage, Cristal champagne, or the new Porsche Cayenne sports utility vehicle. The ethos behind these overt displays of consumer products is simple: in a world of frustration and exclusion, commodities such as jewellery, sportswear, designer watches, and mobile phones act as symbolic messages of power and status. Identity and self-worth are reduced to simple symbolic codes, as interpretable as a Nike 'swoosh' or a Gucci monogram (Hayward 2004: 181). But the market's exploitation of rap music does not stop there. The porn industry is also keen to take advantage of hip hop's edgy youthful appeal. Cross-marketed simultaneous music and porn releases, co-hosted by major artists such as 50 Cent, Lil' John, and most notably Snoop Dogg, whose recent association with porn baron Larry Flint resulted in the biggest grossing porn film ever, have greatly contributed to hardcore pornography's entry into the mainstream.

The commodification of crime is not constrained by genre; rather it is now mainstream entertainment. While stylized and glamourized images of crime have always featured as televisual and filmic staples, today they transcend straightforward 'culture wars' over censorship in films such as *Trainspotting*, *Reservoir Dogs*, or *Natural Born Killers* (all of which now look decidedly tame when compared to the examples below). Today, popular 'reality TV' police shows such as *C.O.P.S*, *Protect and Serve*, *Justice Files*, *Police, Camera, Action*, and *America's Wildest Police Chases* turn 'cops and robbers' into prime-time performers, and police chases and traffic stops into violent vignettes for network television. While this trend has been much commented on, what is less discussed is the rise of so-called 'extreme television'. With its compelling mix of nihilistic-hedonism, the popular US show (and now major feature film series), *Jackass*, illustrates how certain forms of extreme behaviour (including such ill-advised activities as shooting oneself in the face with pepper spray and scuba diving in municipal sewage plants!) are crossing over into mainstream entertainment (see also the highly derivative MTV spin-off shows *Dirty Sanchez* and *The New Tom Green Show* as well as Channel 4's tawdry game show *Distraction*). Yet this is only the leading edge of this trend. Bubbling under the mainstream are widely available 'underground fight videos' such as *Beatdowns*, *Felony Fights*, and *Urban Warfare: Gangs Caught on Tape*, all of which feature brutal 'uncensored', 'caught on camcorder' street fights and schoolyard beatings, both spontaneous and pre-organized. Meanwhile the proliferation of cable networks and broadband downloads offers entry into a whole new world of lightly censored, global 'extreme TV'. These include such explicit crime 'documentaries' as Bolivia's hyper-violent *Telepolicial* and the Russian crime-driven, prime-time offerings, *Criminal Russia* and *Interception*—the former based around graphic crime scene photographs of infamous serial killings, the latter a game show in which 'contestants' are required to steal a car live on air. If they successfully avoid the police for the duration of the show they win the game and a series of prizes.

More banal, but perhaps more socially corrosive, images of crime and transgression are now prominent themes in major advertising campaigns. For example, in-car entertainment manufacturers Kenwood—the car stereo of choice for any discerning 'boy racer'—recently used the strap-line, 'We want to be free to do what we want to do', underneath a photograph of the poll tax riots, an image clearly designed to tap into the subjectivities associated with transgressive driving and the *sub rosa* worlds of 'hotting' and car 'cruising'. Likewise major car manufacturers promote new models using similar cultural rubrics. Nissan promoted their *Shogun* model with the strap-line 'Joyriding' (somewhat ironic given that throughout the 1990s this model was a popular choice for 'ram raiding' and 'hoisting' firms!). Audi meanwhile tapped into this transgressive sensibility in a commercial for their *A3* model. Against the backdrop of trance music, a young man sets light to a pyre in the desert and then burns family mementos and other such trappings of domesticity, before speeding off into the desert night and a new life of unencumbered excitement (Hayward 2004: 171).

While the state responds to the reconfigurations and transformations associated with the late modern condition by imposing what it believes to be more 'rational' forms of control and authority, the market takes a very different approach. Rather than attempt to curtail the excitement and emotionality that, for many individuals, is the preferred antidote to ontological precariousness, the market chooses instead to exacerbate, celebrate, and, very importantly, commodify these same sensations. Whether experiencing the vicarious thrill of the violent visual imagery associated with crime environment 'shoot-em-up' video games such us *Grand Theft Auto III* or *True Crime: Streets of LA*, or the 'Gothic' pleasure derived from membership of one of the many serial killer 'fan club' websites, looped and spiralled images of criminality now circulate through the production of youth culture, becoming inscribed in numerous forms of related entertainment and performance.

TRANSGRESSIVE SUBJECTS: UNCOVERING THE MEANINGS AND EMOTIONS OF CRIME

Crime is an act of rule-breaking. It involves an attitude to rules, an assessment of their justness and appropriateness, and a motivation to break them whether by outright transgression or by neutralization. It is not, as in positivism, a situation where the actor is mechanistically propelled towards desiderata and on the way happens to cross the rules; it is not, as in rational choice theory, a scenario where the actor merely seeks the holes in the net of social control and ducks and dives his or her way through them. Rather, in cultural criminology, the act of transgression itself has attractions—it is through rule-breaking that subcultural problems attempt solution.

Cultural criminology strives to re-energize aetiological questions of crime by replacing the current bias toward rational choice and sociological determinism with an emphasis on—as suggested above—the 'lived experience' of everyday life and existential parameters of choice within a 'winner-loser' consumer society (see de Haan and Vos 2003; Hayward 2007). Its aim is to introduce notions of passion, anger, joy, and amusement as well as tedium, boredom, repression, and elective conformity to the overly cognitive account of human action and rationality. Put simply, cultural criminology seeks to emphasize the emotional and interpretative qualities of crime and deviance. Important here is the stress placed by cultural criminology on the foreground of experience and the existential psychodynamics of the actor, rather than on the background factors of traditional positivism (e.g. unemployment, poverty, poor neighbourhoods, lack of education, etc.). In this sense cultural criminology can be seen as following the framework set out by Jack Katz (1988) but, at the same moment, it is also critical of his position for the way it dismisses any focus on social background as irretrievably positivistic or as a mistaken materialism. Thus Jeff Ferrell, in his review of Katz's *Seductions of Crime*, where he writes that, despite Katz's critique, 'the disjunctions between Katz's criminology and certain aspects of left criminology are not insurmountable'. Understanding 'social and economic inequality to be a cause, or at least a primary context, for crime, we can also understand that this inequality is mediated and expressed through the situational dynamics, the symbolism and style, of criminal events'. And so, 'while we cannot make sense of crime without analyzing structures of inequality, we cannot make sense of crime by *only* analyzing these structures, either. The aesthetics of criminal events interlocks with the political economy of criminality' (Ferrell 1992: 118–19; see also Young 2003; Hayward 2004: 152–7). By melding Katz's ideas with the cultural tradition within criminology, a cultural criminology has emerged that seeks to reinterpret criminal behaviour (in terms of meaning) as a technique for resolving certain psychic conflicts—conflicts that in many instances are indelibly linked with various features of contemporary life/culture.

For example, cultural criminology would point to the way poverty is perceived in an affluent society as an act of exclusion—the ultimate humiliation in a consumer society. It is an *intense* experience, not merely of material deprivation, but of a sense of injustice and of ontological insecurity. But to go even further than this, that late modernity, as described earlier, represents a *shift in consciousness*, so that individualism, expressivity, and identity become paramount and material deprivation, however important, is powerfully supplemented by a widespread sense of ontological deprivation. In other words, what we are witnessing today is a *crisis of being* in a society where self-fulfilment, expression, and immediacy are paramount values, yet the possibilities of realizing such dreams are strictly curtailed by the increasing bureaucratization of work (its so-called McDonaldization) and the commodification of leisure. Crime and transgression in this new context can be seen as the breaking through of restraints, a realization of immediacy, and a reassertion of identity and ontology. In this sense, identity becomes woven into rule-breaking.

An extraordinary example of this line of thinking within cultural criminology is the work of Stephen Lyng (1990) and his associates on edgework. Here cultural criminologists study the way in which individuals engaging in acts of extreme risk-taking (base-jumping, joyriding, sky-diving, motorbike racing, etc.), push themselves to the edge of danger in search of both excitement and certainty. Like a metaphor for reality, they lose control only to take control.

At this point it is essential to stress that cultural criminology's focus on the dynamic nature of experience takes many forms. It is not, as certain critics have erroneously suggested (O'Brien 2005: 610; Ruggiero 2005: 499; Howe 2003: 279), simply a criminology of 'thrills and risks'. Many cultural criminologists have been drawn to the 'pursuit of passions' and the exciting and violent feelings which crime often induces both in offenders and victims, producing—*àla* Katz—a series of phenomenologically inspired accounts of various forms of expressive criminality. It is wrong to suggest, though, that cultural criminology's analytical framework is blind to the more mundane aspects of criminality (see, for example, Ferrell 2004; Yar 2005). Cultural criminology's focus on meaning, representation, and subcultural milieu ensures that it is equally at home explaining the monotonous tasks and dull rhythms associated with DVD piracy or the illegal trade in counterfeit 'grey' automotive components, as it is unravelling the *sub rosa* world of illegal graffiti artists. Moreover, it is obvious that the formal components of an adequate criminological analysis must be covered, namely the actor, the control agencies—both informal and formal—and the victim. Here, we urge the continued development of a cultural criminology of the state (e.g. Wender 2001; Hamm 2004). Thus there would be no contradiction with the realist 'square of crime': rather, that realism, by being overly and simplistically rationalistic in its conception of agency, is not realistic enough. The substantive requirements of a fully social theory of crime and deviance must incorporate a notion of agency which involves energy, tension, and alternative rationalities.

DANGEROUS KNOWLEDGE

In his remarkable *Geographies of Exclusion*, David Sibley talks not only of spatial and social exclusion—the exclusion of the dangerous classes—but the exclusion of *dangerous knowledge*, in that knowledge is:

> conditioned by power relations which determine the boundaries of 'knowledge' and exclude dangerous or threatening ideas and authors. It follows that any prescriptions for a better integrated and more egalitarian society must also include proposals for change in the way academic knowledge is produced [Sibley 1995: xvi].

In fact the traditional positivism of sociologists and psychologists, or the private applications associated with 'crime science', have exceptional interest in *maintaining* rigid definitions and demarcations between science and non-science, between crime and 'normality', between the expert and the criminal, between criminology and more humanistic academic disciplines—and even between the individuals studied themselves as isolated atoms incapable of collective activity. It is the nature of cultural criminology that it questions all these distinctions and is thus an anathema to the project of criminology as a 'science' of crime. It seeks not to add to the 'state-serving' noise that Foucault famously dismissed as the 'garrulous discourse' of criminological knowledge, but actively to identify and challenge the external, material forces that are transforming criminology. Two (closely interrelated) current tendencies are perhaps most notable, both of which bring with them their own corrosive set of methodological, theoretical, ideological, and substantive constraints.

First, the rapid growth of punitive criminal justice systems in the United States, and the ongoing roll-out of neo-liberal forms of governance and control and associated culture(s) of risk and resource management in the United Kingdom, are increasingly bringing about the replacement of a critically inspired sociological criminology with 'administrative' forms of 'criminal justice management'. This seemingly unchecked development involves massive expenditure on prisons, police, and a growing array of dubious, unsubstantiated treatment regimes and crime prevention devices, from CCTV to electronic 'tagging'. It is a process accompanied and augmented by the 'war' against drugs and, more recently, 'the war against terrorism'. Such developments have ensured, of course, that the demand for consultancy and evaluative research has rocketed. These transformations are clearly reflected in the way criminology is now taught and delivered in western universities, as departments respond to new demands to train criminal justice personnel, both practitioners and researchers. Indeed, the exponential growth in criminal justice studies has ensured that this subdiscipline is now the largest sector of social science teaching. In the United States, for example, students, who once would have studied social policy and administration, now routinely study criminal justice—a clear consequence of the movement from welfare to 'justice system' interventions as the leading edge of social policy. Further, the restricted funding available for higher education has led to considerable pressure on faculties to bring in external funding from research (see Robinson 2001; Walters 2003; Hillyard *et al.* 2004). The crime control industry has, therefore, come to exert a hegemonic influence upon academic criminology. The subsequent 'wars' against crime, drugs, terrorism, and now 'antisocial behaviour', demand facts, numbers, quantitative incomes, and outcomes (of which, more later)—they do *not* demand debates as to the very nature of these battles. Nor for that matter do they want to question definition, rather they want 'hard' facts and 'concrete' evidence; disciplinary imperatives that ensure the social basis for positivism is firmly established.

The response in the academy has been substantial and far-reaching. Research has begun to be dominated by statistical testing, theory has been downplayed, and 'soft' data eschewed (Ferrell 2004; Young 2004). It takes little reflection to realize that the now dominant journal format—ill-developed theory, regression analysis, usually followed by rather inconclusive results—is, in fact, a relatively recent genre. Data that are in fact technically weak (because of the well-known difficulties inherent in the collection of statistics whether by the police, victimization studies, or self-report studies) and, by their very nature, contested, blurred, ambiguous, and unsuited for quantification, are mindlessly churned through personal computers.[2] The journals and the articles become myriad yet their conclusions and pontifications become more and more obscure—lost in a mess of figures, techno-speak, and methodological obfuscation (see relatedly, Waters 2004). Meanwhile the ramifications within the academy involve a form of quasi-professionalization or bureaucratization. This is most blatantly apparent in current PhD programmes. Here, induction into quantitative methodological techniques becomes a central part of academic training. Qualitative methods, meanwhile, take a more lowly position—and even here bizarre attempts are made to produce software that will enable the researcher to quantify the qualitative. The distance between the world out there—the place, you will remember, where Robert Park famously admonished his students to: stop 'grubbing in the library' and to go get the 'seat of your pants dirty in real research' (Park quoted in McKinney 1966: 71)—and the academy becomes wider and wider, fenced in by numbers and sanitized by computer printouts. On top of this, the bureaucratization of the research process by overseeing academic committees has stultified the possible range and type of research. As Patricia and Peter Adler put it, with the proliferation of institutional review boards, codes of ethics, and subject benchmarks, we risk losing

> any ethnographic research involving a covert role for the investigator (thus removing hidden populations further from view), any ethnographic research on minors that does not obtain parental consent (obviously problematic for youth involved in deviance or crime or who are victims of parental abuse), and any ethnographic research on vulnerable populations or sensitive (including criminal) issues without signed consent forms that explicitly indicate the researchers' inability to protect subjects' confidentiality. This approach puts governmental and institutional bureaucratic mandates ahead of the research bargains and confidences previously forged by fieldworkers, denigrating the impact of critical dimensions of fieldwork techniques such as reciprocity, trust, evolving relationships, depth, shifting roles, and the relative weighting of research loyalty (subjects versus society) [1998: xiv–xv].

Between the iron cage of the institutional review board and the gentle pulling and pushing of government funding, the discipline inevitably changes its form, its critical edge, and its direction.

The second point stems directly from the ascendance of neo-liberal thinking in the economic and political spheres, and the inexorable rise of the 'market society' wherein corporate values and consumerist subjectivities are now the dominant ethos. One of the baselines within cultural criminology has been a fundamental concern with cultural conditions of late capitalism and the ways in which global economies now run on the endless creation of hyper-consumptive panic, on the symbolic construction of insatiable wants and desires. Cultural criminology's assault on consumerism continues, but it must now be extended to include the impact of the market on intellectual and university life, for developments in this area are directly affecting criminology's long-term ability to function as a sociologically and critically inspired discipline.

[2] On this point see Nils Christie's (1997) notion of 'the compelling archive'.

In 1961 the Robbins Committee on British higher education declared that 'the essential function of the institutions of higher education' should be the 'search for truth'. However, the policies of successive UK governments have severely compromised this edict. The belief that universities are institutions where ideas are fostered and critical thinking (in all its various forms) is encouraged is fast being replaced by the view that seats of learning must now be 'relevant' and 'in tune' with 'the perceived needs of commerce and industry'; *pace* the following quotation from New Labour MP, Ian Pearson:

> Britain's universities have the potential to contribute significantly to the government's objectives of increasing growth and prosperity. By building stronger links with business, and through becoming more entrepreneurial and competitive, they have the ability to transform themselves into genuine universities for industry [Pearson 2002].

At the level of education provision, this will only exacerbate the situation documented by Hall and Winlow who found that, for most young people, 'education is [now] simply another site of atomized instrumental competition over the acquisition of the symbolic and cultural capital necessary for favourable selection in the labour market and upgraded participation in social life loosely structured by various modes of conspicuous consumption' (2006: 314; and Hayes and Wynward 2002).[3] More worrying, however, is the way this commercial ethos pushes open the door to what Reece Walters (2003) describes as 'market-led criminology'. Under this rubric, the increasing commercialization of the university sector within neo-liberal political and economic discourses 'continues to colonise research agendas with critical voices demarcated to an increasingly marginalised periphery'—all the time ensuring that academics are forced to act as 'service providers to paying clients' (often signing away their entitlements to publish in the process) (ibid.: 146–8). Walters illustrates how this tendency has become manifest within criminology in a passage worth citing in full:

> Many academics are entering a growing industry or market where their knowledge and expertise has considerable commercial value. There is growing evidence of some academics ... opening their own consultancy businesses or alternatively operating their own private research companies while maintaining their academic posts. The primary motivation for engaging in these commercial arrangements is not the production of new knowledges or to influence policy and practice, but to make money ... This is insidious in both an ideological and ethical sense as the academic responsibility to develop new knowledges and to act as critic and conscience of society is jettisoned in favour of individual profit where academic credentials give credence to the policies of security firms that aim to maximize margins while (often) adopting a range of strategies that serve to marginalize and regulate the already seriously marginalized groups in society [Walters 2004].

---

[3] One could also point to the intensified regulation and standardization of higher education facilitated by the practices introduced in the name of 'quality assurance'. As Beckmann and Cooper (2004) suggest, these 'centrally-defined statements introduce prescription, instrumentalism, uniformity and compliance within nationally-determined objectives', resulting in the increasing production of 'raw material' or 'uncritical thinkers, compliant to the needs of the market'.

It is against this backdrop that cultural criminology seeks to re-create a sociologically inspired criminology that is more critical, not less—a criminology capable of understanding the full implications of this fundamental shift to the 'consumer society' and which is thus fully equipped with the analytic tools that can unpick (and thereby expose) the representations and structures through which market discourses and subsequent power relations are exercised. Simply stated, then, the aim of cultural criminology is to confront the posturing of neutrality (in terms of both values and politics) within much contemporary criminology with a critical emphasis on the ideological commitments of the terms by which we frame problems of crime, inequality, and criminal justice.

CONCLUSION

Cultural criminology seeks to reconnect to the roots of sociological criminology, to its origins in phenomenological sociology and in subcultural theory, to critically appraise these earlier positions, and to develop a theory which can fully comprehend the conditions of late modernity in which we now find ourselves. It has its basis in the discourse on culture which stresses the potentiality of human reflexivity and transcendence, but which is only too fully aware that much cultural activity is ritualistic and essentialist, seeking to escape the privations and tribulations of modern life. It spans the compass from acquiescence to rebellion, although it stresses that resistance and resilience are frequently found in groups which are conventionally scorned and pathologized (Brotherton and Barrios 2004). It is concerned with the phenomenology both of excitement and of tedium, it is a sociology neither solely of thrills nor of thrall. Culture is placed at the centre of the analysis but it is a culture rooted in the material predicament of the actors concerned. It eschews both a social positivism of material conditions and a cultural positivism of stasis and of essence. In contrast cultural criminology puts great stress on fluidity and change: a loosening of moorings, particularly in this period of cultural globalization and manifest pluralism of values. And lastly, in terms of method, it must seek to rescue the human actors who form the focus of our subject, whether offenders, victims, police officers, or members of the public, from the condescension both of inappropriate quantification and of deterministic methods which diminish and obfuscate the underlying creativity of social action.

■ SELECTED FURTHER READING

Many of the ideas and themes covered in this chapter will be explored in greater detail in the forthcoming text *Cultural Criminology*, co-authored by Jeff Ferrell, Keith Hayward, and Jock Young (2007, London: Sage).

The first book to announce cultural criminology as a specific theoretical variant was Jeff Ferrell and Clinton Sanders' *Cultural Criminology* (1995, Boston: Northeastern University Press), an edited collection of essays on crime and culture that included chapters on criminal subcultures, media representations of crime, and various criminalized forms of music and style. Ferrell has done as much as anyone to promote cultural criminology, both in a series of important statement articles (see Ferrell 1999, 2004, and his entry in *The Blackwell Encyclopaedia of Sociology* (2006, Oxford: Blackwell), and in a number of thoughtful cultural criminological case-study monographs (e.g. *Crimes of Style* (1996, Boston: Northeastern University Press) on graffiti subcultures; *Tearing Down the Streets: Adventures in Urban Anarchy* (2001, New York: Palgrave) on corporate urban redevelopment and the demise of public space; and *Empire of Scrounge* (2006, New York: New York University Press) on the illicit worlds of street scrounging and dumpster diving. For a student-friendly introduction to the crime-culture relationship, see Ferrell's chapter, 'Crime and Culture', in the Oxford University Press textbook *Criminology* (2005, edited by C. Hale, K. Hayward, A. Wahidin, and E. Wincup).

Another useful introduction to cultural criminology that includes research into crime and culture across a variety of local, regional, and national settings is the stimulating collection of essays gathered together by Ferrell, Hayward, Morrison, and Presdee in *Cultural Criminology Unleashed* (2004, London: Glasshouse Press); as is the 2004 Special Edition of the international journal *Theoretical Criminology* (8(3)), edited by Hayward and Young.

Mike Presdee's monograph *Cultural Criminology and the Carnival of Crime* (2000) did much to promote cultural criminology in the United Kingdom, as did Hayward's cultural analysis of the changing nature of urban space/crime in *City Limits: Crime, Consumerism and the Urban Experience* (2004)—both texts focusing on the commodification of crime and the visceral, emotive thrill of certain forms of expressive criminality (see, relatedly, the work of Stephen Lyng (1990); and, of course, most famously Jack Katz's (1988) seminal text, *Seductions of Crime*).

For an insight into some of the ethnographic approaches associated with cultural criminology see Ferrell and Hamm's *Ethnography at the Edge* (1998, Boston: Northeastern University Press), Stephanie Kane's article, 'The unconventional methods in cultural criminology', in the aforementioned Special Edition of *Theoretical Criminology*, and a number of the chapters in Cyndi Banks' edited book, *Developing Cultural Criminology: Theory and Practice in Papua New Guinea* (2000). For examples of cultural criminological research on crime and the media see Peter Manning's chapter, 'Media loops', in Bailey and Hale (1998), Gregg Barak's writing on 'newsmaking criminology' (e.g. 1994), the chapters in Part 3 of Ferrell *et al.*, *Cultural Criminology Unleashed*, and the new journal *Crime, Media, Culture* (London: Sage), a periodical dedicated to exploring the relationships between crime, criminal justice, and the media.

For further examples of cultural criminological research, readers are advised to explore the references listed in the present chapter. Finally, to access a number of key papers and to keep up to date with news about conferences and publications in the area of cultural criminology log on to www.culturalcriminology.org.

■ REFERENCES

ADLER, P., and ADLER, P. (1998), 'Moving Backwards', in J. Ferrell and M. Hamm (eds), *Ethnography on the Edge,*. Boston: Northeastern University Press.

ALEXANDER, J., and SMITH, P. (2002), 'The Strong Program in Cultural Theory', in J. Turner (ed.), *Handbook of Sociological Theory*, New York: Plenum.

ANDERSON, S., and HOWARD, G. (1998), *Interrogating Popular Culture*, Guilderland, NY: Harrow and Heston.

BAILEY, F., and HALE, D. (1998), *Popular Culture, Crime and Justice*, Belmont, Cal.: Wadsworth.

BANKS, C. (2000), *Developing Cultural Criminology: Theory and Practice in Papua New Guinea*, Sydney: University of Sydney Press.

BANKS, M. (2005), 'Spaces of (in)security: media and fear of crime in a local context', *Crime, Media, Culture*, 1(2): 169–87.

BARAK, G. (1994), *Media Processes and the Social Construction of Crime*, New York: Garland.

——(1996), *Representing O.J.: Murder, Criminal Justice and Mass Culture*, Guilderland, NY: Harrow and Heston.

BAUMAN, Z. (1998), *Consumerism, Work and the New Poor*, Buckingham: Open University Press.

——(1999), *Culture as Praxis*, London: Sage.

BECKMANN, A., and COOPER, C. (2004), '"Globalisation", the new managerialism and education: rethinking the purpose of education in Britain', *Journal for Critical Education Policy Studies*, 2: 2.

BRAKE, M. (1980), *The Sociology of Youth Culture*, London: Routledge & Kegan Paul.

BROTHERTON, D., and BARRIOS, L. (2004), *The Almighty Latin King and Queen Nation*, New York: Columbia University Press.

CHEATWOOD, D. (1998), 'Prison movies: films about adult, male, civilian prisons: 1929–1995', in F. Bailey, and D. Hale (eds), *Popular Culture, Crime and Justice*, Belmont, Cal.: Wadsworth.

CHERMAK, S. (1995), *Victims in the News*, Boulder, Cal.: Westview.

——, BAILEY, F., and BROWN, M. (2003), *Media Images of September 11th*, Newport: Praeger.

CHRISTIE, N. (1997), 'Four blocks against insight: notes on the oversocialization of criminologists', *Theoretical Criminology*, 1(1): 3–23.

COHEN, S. (1972), *Folk Devils and Moral Panics*, London: McGibbon and Kee.

——(1997), 'Intellectual Scepticism and Political Commitment', in P. Walton and J. Young (eds), *The New Criminology Revisited*, London: Macmillan.

CONQUERGOOD, D. (1991), 'On Rethinking Ethnography', *Communications Monographs*, 58: 335–59.

DE HAAN, W., and VOS, J. (2003), 'A crying shame: the over-rationalized conception of man in the rational choice perspective', *Theoretical Criminology*, 7(1): 29–54.

DOWNES, D. (1966), *The Delinquent Solution*, London: Routledge & Kegan Paul.

——(2005), 'Book Review: *City Limits, Crime, Consumerism and the Urban Experience*', *Criminal Justice*, 5(3): 319–21.

FENWICK, M., and HAYWARD, K. J. (2000), 'Youth Crime, Excitement and Consumer Culture: The Reconstruction of Aetiology in Contemporary Theoretical Criminology: in J. Pickford (ed.), *Youth Justice: Theory and Practice*. London: Cavendish.

FERRELL, J. (1992), 'Making Sense of Crime: Review Essay on Jack Katz's *Seductions of Crime*', *Social Justice*, 19(3): 111–23.

——(1999), 'Cultural Criminology', *Annual Review of Sociology*, 25: 395–418.

——(2004), 'Boredom, crime and criminology', *Theoretical Criminology*, 8(3): 287–302.

——and Sanders, C. (eds) (1995), *Cultural Criminology*, Boston: Northeastern University Press.

——, HAYWARD, K., MORRISON, W., and PRESDEE, M. (2004), *Cultural Criminology Unleashed*, London: Glasshouse.

FISHMAN, M., and CAVENDER, G. (1998), *Entering Crime: Television Reality Programmes*, New York: Aldine de Gruyter.

Guardian, The (2003), 'Hodge stands firm over research funding', 30 April.

HALL, S., and JEFFERSON, T. (eds) (1975), *Resistance Through Ritual*, London: Hutchinson.

——, and WINLOW, S. (2006), *Violent Night*, Oxford: Berg.

——, CRITCHER, C., JEFFERSON, T., CLARKE, J., and ROBERTS, B. (eds) (1978), *Policing the Crisis: Mugging, the State and Law 'n' Order*, London: Macmillan.

HAMM, M. (2004), 'The US Patriot Act and the politics of fear', in J. Ferrell, K. Hayward, W. Morrison, and M. Presdee, (2004), *Cultural Criminology, Unleashed*. London: Glasshouse.

HAYES, D., and WYNWARD, R. (2002), *The McDonaldization of Higher Education*, Westport, Conn.: Greenwood Press.

HAYWARD, K. J. (2003), 'Consumer Culture and Crime in late Modernity', in C. Sumner (ed.), *The Blackwell Companion to Criminology*, Oxford: Blackwell.

—— (2004), *City Limits: Crime, Consumer Culture and the Urban Experience*,. London: Glasshouse Press.

—— (2007), 'Situational crime prevention and its discontents: rational choice theory versus the "culture of now" ', *Social Policy and Administration*, (forthcoming).

—— and YOUNG, J. (eds) (2004), Special Edition on Cultural Criminology, *Theoretical Criminology*, 8(3).

HENRY, S, and MILOVANOVIC, D. (1996), *Constitutive Criminology: Beyond Postmodernism*, London: Sage.

HILLYARD, P., SIM, J., TOMBS, S., and WHYTE, D. (2004), 'Leaving "a stain upon the silence" ': contemporary criminology and the politics of dissent', *British Journal of Criminology*, 44(3): 369–90.

HOWE, A. (2003), 'Managing men's violence in the criminological arena', in C. Sumner (ed.), *The Blackwell Companion to Criminology*, Oxford: Blackwell.

KIDD-HEWITT, D., and OSBORNE, R. (1995), *Crime and the Media: the Postmodern Spectacle*, London: Pluto.

KATZ, J. (1988), *Seductions of Crime*, New York: Basic Books.

KUBRIN, C. (2005), 'Gangstas, Thugs and Hustlas: identity and the code of the street in Rap music', *Social Problems*, 52(3): 360–78.

LYNG, S. (1990), 'Edgework: A Social Psychological Analysis of Voluntary Risk-Taking', *American Journal of Sociology*, 95(4): 876–921.

MCKINNEY, J. C. (1966), *Constructive Typology and Social Theory*, New York: Appleton-Century-Crofts.

MCROBBIE, A., and THORNTON, S. (1995), 'Rethinking "moral panic" for multi-mediated social worlds', *British Journal of Sociology*, 46(4): 245–59.

MANNING, P. (1999), 'Reflections: the visual as a mode of social control', in J. Ferrell and N. Websdale (1999), *Making Trouble: Cultural Constructions of Crime, Deviance, and Control*, Hawthorne,: NY: Aldine de Gruyter.

MATZA, D. (1969), *Becoming Deviant*, Englewood Cliffs, NJ: Prentice Hall.

MILLER, J. (1995), 'Struggles over the symbolic: gang style and the meanings of social control', in J. Ferrell and C. R. Sanders (eds), *Cultural Criminology*, Boston: Northeastern University Press.

MILLER, W. (1958), 'Lower Class Culture as a Generating Milieu of Gang Delinquency', *Journal of Social Issues*, 14: 5–19.

NYBERG, A. (1998), 'Comic books and juvenile delinquency: a historical perspective', in F. Bailey and D. Hale, (eds), *Popular Culture, Crime and Justice*, Belmont, Cal.: Wadsworth.

O'BRIEN, M. (2005), 'What is *cultural* about cultural criminology?', *British Journal of Criminology*, 45(5): 599–612.

O'MALLEY, P., and MUGFORD, S. (1994), 'Crime, excitement and modernity', in G. Barak (ed.), *Varieties of Criminology*, Westport, Conn.: Praeger.

PEARSON, I. (2002), *Universities and Innovation: Meeting the Challenge*, London: Social Market Foundation, March.

POTTER, G., and KAPPELER, E. (1998), *Constructing Crime: Perspectives on Making News and Social Problems*, Prospect Height, Ill.: Waveland.

PRESDEE, M. (2000), *Cultural Criminology and the Carnival of Crime*, London: Routledge.

ROBINSON, M. (2001), 'Whither Criminal Justice?', *Critical Criminology*, 10(2): 97–106.

ROCK, P. (2005), 'Chronocentrism and British criminology', *British Journal of Sociology*, 56(3): 473–91.

RUGGIERO, V. (2005), 'Review: *City Limits: Crime, Consumer Culture and the Urban Experience*', *Theoretical Criminology*, 9(4): 497–9.

SCHOFIELD, K. (2004), 'Collisions of culture and crime: media commodification of child sex abuse', in J. Ferrell, K. J. Hayward, W. Morrison, and M. Presdee (eds), *Cultural Criminology Unleashed*, London: Glasshouse Press.

SELLIN, T. (1938), *Culture Conflict and Crime*, New York: Social Science Research Council.

SHERWOOD, S., SMITH, P., and ALEXANDER, J. (1993), 'The British are Coming . . . Again! The Hidden Agenda of Cultural Studies', *Contemporary Sociology*, 22(2): 370–5.

SIBLEY, D. (1995), *Geographies of Exclusion*, London: Routledge.

SMITH, P. (1998), 'Introduction', in P. Smith (ed.), *The New American Cultural Sociology*, Cambridge: Cambridge University Press.

VALIER, C. (2000), 'Looking daggers: a psychoanalytical reading of the scene of punishment', *Punishment and Society*, 2(4): 379–94.

——and LIPPENS, R. (2005), 'Moving images, ethics and justice', *Punishment and Society*, 6(3): 319–33.

VAN HOOREBEECK, B. (1997), 'Prospects of reconstructing aetiology', *Theoretical Criminology*, 1(4): 501–18.

WALTERS, R. (2003), *Deviant Knowledge*, Cullompton, Devon: Willan.

——(2004), 'Deviant Knowledge: reclaiming the critical voice' posted at www.theorynetwork.org.

WATERS, L. (2004), *Enemies of Promise: Publishing, Perishing, and the Eclipse of Scholarship*, Chicago: Prickly Paradigm Press.

WENDER, J. (2001), 'The eye of the painter and the eye of the police: what criminology and law enforcement can learn from Manet', Paper presented at the Annual Conference of the American Society of Criminology, Atlanta.

WILLIAMS, J. (1998), 'Comic books: a tool of subversion?', in S. Anderson and G. Howard (eds), *Interrogating Popular Culture*, Guilderland, NY: Harrow and Heston.

WILLIS, P. (1977), *Learning to Labour*, Aldershot: Gower.

YAR, M. (2005), 'The Global "Epidemic" of Movie "Piracy": Crime-Wave or Social Construction?', *Media, Culture & Society*, 27(5): 677–96.

YOUNG, A. (2004), *Judging the Image: Art, Value, Law*, London: Routledge.

YOUNG, J. (1971), *The Drugtakers*, London: Paladin.

——(1999), *The Exclusive Society*, London: Sage.

——(2003), 'Merton with Energy, Katz with Structure', *Theoretical Criminology*, 7(3): 389–414.

——(2004), 'Voodoo criminology and the numbers game', in J. Ferrell, K. Hayward, W. Morrison, and M. Presdee (eds), *Cultural Criminology Unleashed*, London: Glasshouse.

5

HISTORICAL PERSPECTIVES ON CRIME

Clive Emsley

INTRODUCTION

The questions on the agendas of historians working on crime, policing, and penal policy invariably have similar origins to those on the agendas of more conventional criminologists and even of practitioners and policy-makers. The current academic interest in the history of crime dates largely from the late 1960s and early 1970s. This interest has a variety of origins, but among them can be counted what David Garland has described as the breakdown of the system of penal welfare and the increasing centrality of crime as an issue in political and media debate (Garland 2001). The historian's exploration of crime does not necessarily depend on the study of new sets of data, though these can sometimes be found or are newly released, and contemporary criminological research can underscore the value of material previously thought unworthy of investigation. More often, however, this kind of research requires posing new questions of material that has been known and examined with other matters in mind. Also, it is in the nature of the historian's craft that he or she may examine a topic over a period of much greater length than other researchers so as to assess the extent of change through time.

The aim of this chapter is to highlight some of the issues raised by historical research particularly with respect to long-term trends, methodology, and various kinds of data. In so doing it seeks also to underline the contribution that a historical perspective can provide for an understanding of contemporary crime and criminal justice. Most of the discussion here centres on work done on the British experience; given the nature of the research to date, this essentially means the English experience. Comparisons are made with other countries where this appears either central or helpful. The range of this work has recently been assessed in two detailed bibliographical essays (Emsley 2005b; Wood 2005).

THEORY

The tradition of empirical research among historians in the United Kingdom has led some to decry theoretical perspectives and to stress the primary importance of archival sources. In a sense they are right. Historical research depends on the careful analysis of primary source material, usually, but by no means always written archives. Nevertheless, it is rarely possible to venture into an archive without some notion of the questions to be asked of the evidence. Posing questions of historical evidence generally means that the researcher has some hypothesis to test. Much of the work on the history of crime that has explored key questions about the pattern of crime over a long period has drawn, directly or indirectly, on the explanatory power of a few broad metahistorical theories.

The Whig interpretation of history was never formally presented by one of its exponents as a way of understanding the past. Rather it was first outlined by Herbert Butterfield in the early 1930s as the way in which much British political and constitutional history had been understood, though not articulated, over the preceding hundred years (Butterfield 1931). Essentially the Whig interpretation is based on a notion of progress in history and takes the present as its point of reference. As far as crime and criminal justice is concerned Whig historians have taken their contemporary police and penal institutions as models. They have then traced the formation of these institutions singling out for praise the reformers who could be considered as contributing to the progression to the present and criticizing those who had opposed the reformers. This has usually meant taking at face value the criticisms that the so-called reformers levelled at any institutions that they sought to change.

The history of police and policing in Britain was dominated by a Whig interpretation both before and long after Butterfield first published his small book. The view was that, while the modern institution of police in Britain might need some tinkering to iron out minor problems, it was ideally suited to its designated tasks. Though these historians might not have expressed it in such clear terms, they largely went along with the assertion made at the end of the nineteenth century and in the first half of the twentieth century, that the police in Britain were 'the best in the world'. The origins of the police were found in a group of eighteenth- and early nineteenth-century reformers, most notably Henry and Sir John Fielding and Patrick Colquhoun. Sir Robert Peel who, as home secretary, established London's Metropolitan Police (now widely known as 'the Met') in 1829 was equally celebrated, as were the first two commissioners of the Met who gave Peel's concept a practical form. Reformers and moral entrepreneurs, most significantly Edwin Chadwick who wrote much of the 1839 Report of the Royal Commission on a Rural Constabulary, claimed that the Metropolitan Police was a considerable improvement over everything that had preceded it. The Whig historians accepted the claim. They charted various milestones from 1829 onwards to their present, praising as far-sighted those who introduced the legislation and the other reforms that constituted those milestones, and criticizing as reactionary and even foolish those who opposed reforms. British police history had a succession of articulate and forceful exponents of the Whig perspective well into the final third of the twentieth century and the interpretation remains significant within the police institution itself.

A similar Whig interpretation can be found in the older histories of the development of punishment and penal institutions. Again there are a succession of milestones—such as the abolition of the various physical punishments inflicted on an offender's body—and a succession of great reformers—Sir Samuel Romilly, Sir James Mackintosh, Elizabeth Fry, and so on. Here, perhaps, a humanitarian perspective reinforces the Whig view given that execution, mutilation, and public shaming, all significant elements of punishment until at least the beginning of the nineteenth century, are offensive to many in the contemporary western world. Moreover until very recently, a wide range of texts by international scholars focusing on the development of punishment and penal institutions in different national contexts were infused with Whig assumptions.

Marxist theory was amongst the first theoretical perspectives to be used by academics to challenge broadly Whig interpretations. Karl Marx himself had relatively little to say in detail about crime, policing, and penal policy. His criticism of the debates on wood theft in the Rhenish Assembly in 1842 and his support for the peasantry's claim to their customary rights of collecting fallen wood from the forests constitute his most sustained discussion of activities defined in law as crimes. Marx's engagement with the issues here was also significant for his own intellectual development, particularly with reference to his understanding of socio-economic relationships (Lascoumes and Zander 1984; McLellan 1972: 126–31). During the interwar years, however, his concept of the importance of the means of production prompted Georg Rusche and Otto Kirchheimer to embark on a major rethinking of the development of punishment. Rusche and Kirchheimer linked the changes over time in punishment to changes in the means of production and to the dominance of different social groups with different priorities (Rusche and Kirchheimer 1968). First published in 1939 the book did not achieve a significant impact until a generation after the end of the Second World War, when others began to use broadly Marxist perspectives to explore changes in crime, policing, and penal policy. Whereas the Whig interpretation had thought in terms of a society in which there was a broad consensus the new approaches conceived of societies in which conflict, and specifically class conflict, was a defining element. Thus hypotheses were presented that theft was a form of protest against and resistance to developing capitalist systems, while the factory and the police became understood as means of controlling and domesticating the new industrial workforce.

Norbert Elias's account of the 'civilizing process' is another theory that has been very influential in the thinking of historians interested in criminal justice and penal policy. It is also another work which, although first published in 1939, did not gain significant currency until after the Second World War (Elias 2000). Elias, a German sociologist, was interested in exploring shifts in human behaviour and specifically how, in the early modern period, a warlike caste of knights was transformed into a courtly society. He described the complex interaction of growing social interdependence, of peer pressure, and emulation. His work has been especially influential in underpinning some of the work on changes in punishment. According to Elias, elite groups became increasingly sensitized to certain aspects of life, such as bodily functions, sex, suffering, and death, and sought to banish them from public life. Similarly, according to the analysis of Pieter Spierenburg, they also began to reject public physical punishment (Spierenburg 1984 and 1991).

The English translation of Elias's title has encouraged an assumption among many in the Anglo-Saxon world that Elias was taking a neo-Whig line. But in German *Prozess* can also mean 'trial' and, with his own parents falling victim to the Holocaust, Elias was always aware of the fragility of civilization and the way in which the contents of its attributes might shift. He never conceived of it moving in a progressive, linear direction. Instead, Elias saw the individual psyche being moulded by its surroundings and patterns of behaviour being regulated by the network of social interactions. Thus, in some historical circumstances, the psychological apparatus of self-control could become weaker rather than stronger.

The thinker who, since the mid-1970s, probably has had the most influence on the history of crime and penal changes, however, is the French philosopher-historian Michel Foucault. Foucault's bleak vision was a direct challenge to notions of the emergence of a more liberal humanitarian world since the Enlightenment and hence, by extension, to the unspoken Whig assumptions about the evolution of penal policy and practice. His best-known text in this area charted a shift from the public infliction of harsh physical punishment on the body of an offender under the old regime, to the regimentation, surveillance, and disciplining, in private, of the offender under a new bourgeois order. The prison, for Foucault, was the apex of a carceral archipelago that, in modern society, spread downwards encompassing orphanages, charitable societies, and a wide variety of other organizations and institutions employing disciplinary and surveillance mechanisms (Foucault 1977). This perception of a shift from the scaffold to the penitentiary in penal policy was not new nor was it particularly contentious. Moreover Foucault unquestionably slid over some of the complexities in this broad change. Nevertheless, the academic debates about the theories that, since the Enlightenment, drove the ideas behind punishment and about the structure of power within the developing penal system have been significantly progressed by Foucault's work and the controversies resulting from it (Garland 1990; Spierenburg 2004).

FROM VIOLENCE TO THEFT?

As a working hypothesis the idea of a long-term shift in the pattern of crime from a preponderance of violence in the medieval and early modern periods to a greater emphasis on property crime in the modern world has much to recommend it. Such a trend fits well with the kind of metahistorical perspectives derived from the work of both Karl Marx and Norbert Elias. But, more importantly, it appears to fit well with the general impression that can be gleaned from the evidence of crime patterns since the Middle Ages.

There are, of course, no reliable statistics for the measurement of property and interpersonal crime much earlier than the nineteenth century. But from a variety of sources it is possible to get some idea of the patterns of homicide in different countries. While in some countries, notably England and the Netherlands, the homicide rate appears to have started out at a rather lower level than that in many other countries, what is particularly noticeable in these different figures is the overall decline that appears to start from around the fourteenth century and to continue until the mid-twentieth century (Eisner 2001 and 2003).

Theft patterns cannot be measured in such a way. There were no official statistics for different countries until the early nineteenth century. For earlier periods historians have had to construct their own statistics usually out of the records left by the courts. For England and Wales the initial work focused on the major courts of assizes and quarter sessions. From the early modern period it would appear that property crime predominated in the courts. But recent research has emphasized, first, the process required before a case went before one of these courts, and secondly, how, at numerous moments during the proceedings, the matter might be dropped, usually at the discretion of the prosecutor (King 2000). Sometimes the prosecutor, who was commonly the victim, might decide that the threat of legal action and the beginning of the process was sufficient to punish the offender. Sometimes, moreover, a magistrate was fully prepared to allow or even to pressurize parties to 'make up' a criminal offence by coming to an agreement. In such a situation the victim of the offence, or an individual proven to have been wrongly or maliciously accused, would receive a monetary payment from the accuser or a public apology in a newspaper, and sometimes both (Andrew 2002; King 2004; Sullivan 2005). Nor were the British Isles alone in this. Infra-judicial resolution, sometimes involving minor judges, magistrates, local priests, or other men of some social standing within a community, appears to have been common in many parts of Europe well into the nineteenth century (Garnot 2000b).

It has been suggested that 'if the forces governing the selection of cases to be tried worked roughly the same way from year to year, or at least did not change randomly and wildly, then changes in the number of indictments might be expected to derive from changes in the number of offences' (Beattie 1981: 138). Constructing the pattern of crime from indictments—even those dropped through prosecutorial discretion— might therefore give some notion of the pattern of crime. The problem is that random and wild changes may have occurred when, for example, victims of theft feared a greater incidence of the offence and, in consequence, were determined to make examples as a warning to others. There were fears of rising crime when soldiers and sailors were discharged at the end of the eighteenth century's regular wars. There were fears that, in times of high grain prices and food shortages, the poor might resort to theft. Peter King has attempted a victim survey based on eighteenth-century diaries and this led him to the very tentative conclusion that possibly only one in ten out of the crimes committed during the period was prosecuted. A 5 per cent increase in the number of *decisions* to prosecute as a result of one of the post-war panics or food shortages could thus result in a 50 per cent increase in the number of *indictments* available for the historian's personal count (King 2000: ch. 5). Even the increasing availability of expenses for prosecutors and the advent of the new police did not immediately encourage victims to come forward and prosecute sometimes quite major thefts (Emsley 2004: 190–5).

In sum then, it appears impossible to prove a broad shift from violent crime to property crime over an extended period. It is true that, by the eighteenth century at the latest, across the European world the principal courts were dealing with many more thefts than murders, rapes, and assaults. But, in the English summary courts and possibly also in the lower courts and the smaller seignerieual courts on continental Europe, small-scale assaults, whether verbal or physical, outnumbered cases of petty theft (King 2004). Furthermore, it would appear that by the late eighteenth and early nineteenth centuries the new, respectable bourgeois society was discovering violence as a social problem. The English experience has been best analysed. Here it seems that the new middle class was idealizing practices of rationality and self-restrained refinement in contrast to traditional, customary practices that still existed within plebeian society and legitimated direct physical confrontation and equated honour with a preparedness to fight (Wood 2004). In the courts violent crime, especially that perpetrated by men against women, began to be punished more harshly. Judges and magistrates often took the lead, confronting juries who remained more inclined to lenience (Wiener 2004). Violence was commonly described as un-English, as something common among foreigners, among children—especially boys who had to be disciplined into social behaviour—and among the brutal 'residuum', the lowest strata of the working class. Un-English violence was set against the model of the English gentleman who never struck the first blow but always came to the defence of the weak, most obviously women and children. This ideal type was exalted by a variety of commentators; its disappearance and a greater acknowledgement of the potential for violence among all social classes was accelerated within the more egalitarian context that emerged in the aftermath of the Second World War (Emsley 2005a).

Even if a shift from violence to theft could be proven, there is little doubt that it was violent crime which commonly characterized people's perceptions of crime. And it was violent crime that worried people even if the English, at least, liked to think that they did not commit it. Few people experience crime on a regular, day-to-day basis and their perceptions of criminality would appear to depend largely on what they read or see. Violence figured significantly in the reporting of crime and in the representation of crime that people gained through the media. The growth of the press and of a reading public during the nineteenth century encouraged editors to look for eye-catching and thrilling stories that would sell their products. Petty theft did not sell newspapers; 'orrible murder did. Moreover, as the nineteenth century progressed, the experts who wrote about crime switched from a focus on offenders who were understood to be members of the criminal classes to a focus on the criminal as biologically degenerate.

An assessment of the texts published in Germany during the nineteenth century has described a significant increase in the number of studies concerned with murderers and violent sexual assailants after 1850 (Becker 2002). This shift would appear to have been echoed elsewhere and was picked up in the emphases present in the newspapers. The murders of Jack the Ripper enabled the British press significantly to extend the frontiers of what might be described legitimately and respectably in terms of a woman's body and injuries inflicted (Curtis 2001).

The cinema appeared with, and grew during the twentieth century. Like the newspaper editors and publishers before them, film producers knew that thrills attracted audiences. In Britain particularly the cinema was rapidly condemned by many as a school for all kinds of offender, providing visual training in how best to carry out robberies. It was also feared that films particularly encouraged the impressionable young to copy the violence portrayed on the screen. Early in 1917 an examiner for the British Film Censors explained to a Commission of Enquiry that:

> In dealing with 'crime' subjects, the examiners had had to discriminate between such stories as were calculated, in their judgement, to familiarize young people with theft, robberies and crimes of violence, and stories which dealt with 'costume' crime—that is, cowboy shootings, 'feather and rapier' stabbings, bandits, and Mexican robberies, etc. The latter were regarded by the young as simply dramatic and thrilling adventures, having no connexion with their own lives or possible experiences. When the same crimes were committed by people in ordinary dress and home surroundings, the examiners aimed at eliminating details which made them too realistic, and entirely forbade any scenes which depicted the actual method of committing theft. They also drew a distinction between subjects in which a theft, or burglary, or murder was simply the dramatic motive round which the story with other interests turned, and those in which the crime was the sole and entire interest [*The Times*, 6 February 1917, p. 5].

This kind of paternalist thinking persisted for the first two-thirds of the twentieth century, together with an insistence that cinematic portrayals of any and all elements within the British criminal justice system had to be both respectable and uncritical. The extent to which this had any impact on criminal behaviour remains an open and probably unanswerable question.

STATISTICAL DATA

However hard they try, historians of crime have difficulty in separating themselves entirely from the statistics of crime. In part this is because any assessment of change in crime over time invariably requires some kind of statistical assessment. Perhaps more important, people in the past have commonly spoken of increasing or, probably less commonly, decreasing crime, and since the early nineteenth century there have been official statistics available to support or challenge the arguments.

Social commentators of the early nineteenth century put considerable faith in statistics. In England and Wales criminal statistics began to be collected in 1810. The first set of figures amassed went back to 1805 but, initially, they only listed commitments for trial. By the mid-1830s they were organized into six main types of offence, a classification that has remained more or less unchanged ever since. These were:

1. Offences against the person;
2. Offences against property involving violence;
3. Offences against property not involving violence;
4. Malicious offences against property;
5. Offences against the currency;
6. Miscellaneous offences.

Following an appendage to the County and Borough Police Act of 1856 a further division was added, distinguishing between:

1. Indictable offences notified to the police but not necessarily resulting in an arrest or solved;
2. Committals for trial on both indictment and before summary jurisdiction;
3. The number of individuals convicted and imprisoned.

A rather more sophisticated system was developed in France from the mid-1820s. The *Compte générale de l'administration de la justice criminelle* gave details of individuals accused of crimes by age, sex, place of birth, residence, occupation, and level of education. The form and content were praised and emulated in other parts of Europe. By the 1830s there appeared to be sufficient statistical information around to enable early sociologists to start drawing conclusions about crime and criminals. Among the first was the Belgian Adolphe Quetelet and many of his conclusions about the youth and male sex of most offenders would not seem out of place today. Quetelet also noted the problem of the dark figure, the number of crimes never reported and, in consequence, that never appeared on the statistical tables. A generation after Quetelet the Bavarian statistician, Georg von Mayr, set the crime figures for Bavaria alongside figures for the cost of grain and drew conclusions about the impact of poverty, food shortages, and high prices on the pattern of offending. Moving on another twenty years, Wilhelm Starke, a leading figure in the Prussian Justice Ministry, provided a statistical underpinning to the long-held beliefs about war leading to reductions in crime by removing young men from their native environment. Starke deployed crime figures from France and Prussia over twenty years spanning the Franco-Prussian War. He also posed questions about how far war might brutalize the young men who fought in it with potential repercussions for peacetime society.

Historians have not been unaware of the problems with the official crime statistics. There have been three broad approaches to their use that can be labelled the 'positivist', the 'interactive', and the 'pessimist'. These suggest, respectively, that the statistics can reveal something about the state and pattern of crime, that they are most valuable for the information that they provide about the way the criminal justice system functioned, and that they are so unreliable that, at best, they can only provide a rough guide to the image of crime. The most detailed and profound analysis of the statistics for England and Wales has been that of V. A. C. Gatrell. Situated essentially within the positivist outlook, Gatrell charted an overall decline in theft and violence from the mid-nineteenth century until the beginning of the twentieth. He stressed also that, by and large, contemporaries perceived this trend and congratulated each other on it. They believed that the state was making significant inroads against criminal disorder and they expected that it would continue so to do. Gatrell himself considered the overall pattern to be real enough to be worth investigation. Amongst other things, he explored three potential influences on the crime pattern: the assault on juvenile crime; the increasing deterrence of the new police and the courts; and broad economic variables, most notably a downward diffusion of a degree of prosperity (Gatrell 1980).

The most significant of the 'interactionist' studies is that by Chris A. Williams which sets out to replace 'crime' with 'arrest' as a basic starting point for investigation of the Victorian criminal justice system. Focusing on the returns of the Sheffield City Police between 1845 and 1862 Williams charts an astonishing degree of police intervention in the lives of young working-class males. The arrests were overwhelmingly for summary offences and appear to have led to a fifth of the total male population of Sheffield having some sort of police record by the 1860s (Williams 2000). Williams has developed these statistics in another direction to suggest that the returns were also used to develop the image of an efficient, incorruptible police force that was effectively securing the safety of the city from a criminal threat that came primarily from outside its confines (Williams 2003).

The most interesting and challenging contribution to the 'pessimist' line has been that made by Howard Taylor. In a series of articles Taylor argued that the crime statistics were generated neither by crimes reported nor by arrests made but, first, by financial considerations emanating from within the Treasury and, secondly, by police discretion exercised with a view to bolstering or maintaining police manpower and funding. Taylor describes a system from the mid-nineteenth to the mid-twentieth century in which distant bureaucrats based in Whitehall acted in a mechanical fashion applying the 'usual averages'. It was a system, moreover, that rejected the pursuit of every offender, which would be extremely expensive, in preference to a policy of deterrence through the exemplary imprisonment of a few offenders (Taylor 1998a). The police, in contrast, became more proactive during the first half of the twentieth century. Recognizing that the Exchequer had replaced local authorities as their principal paymaster, Taylor argues, they restructured their activities towards a greater focus on things that were of concern to central government (Taylor 1998b and 1999). A powerful counterblast has come from a historian who was formerly a senior administrator in the Home Office. Robert M. Morris insists that there is no evidence, and certainly none provided by Taylor, that central government, first, ever sought to control expenditure in the manner described and, secondly, ever used any powers to suppress prosecution rates. Moreover, it would appear that there were plenty of alternative explanations for the increase in motor vehicle accidents in the interwar period, for example, that appear rather more credible than supply-side theories and police self-interest. Morris's riposte to Taylor has, unfortunately, gone unanswered. Morris acknowledges the importance of Taylor's challenge to the value of the criminal statistics and does not, himself, champion their value in either a 'positivist' or 'interactionist' sense (Morris 2001).

CULTURAL HISTORY

Culture is a word with many meanings and probably all of the uses of the term thus far employed by historians in the analysis of crime and criminal justice have at least some claim to validity. Nevertheless in recent years 'cultural' history has tended to compete with, and even to displace 'social' history as the area in which many, and perhaps most historians of crime consider as their home. Culture in the context of modern cultural history is seen primarily as a product—or even producer—of social practice and focuses much more on representations than on processes or structures.

Historians have always recognized the need to study their sources closely and to look for the unwitting testimony. The new cultural history puts an even greater emphasis on the close reading of the text and draws much of its intellectual impetus from literary theory. It stresses, moreover, that crimes and criminals were and always have been social constructions, and that both primary source texts—ballads, novels, police reports, legal papers, the accounts of trials, as well as visual representations from the wood-cut to the feature film—and the historical accounts that historians build on them, depend to some degree on the creation of a narrative of crimes and criminal events (Srebnick 2005). Such historical narratives have taken a traditional, long-view perspective exploring how, for example, images of the offender, the space and setting for domestic violence, or the understanding of child sexuality and the abuse of children have changed over time (Wiener 1990; D'Cruze 1998; Jackson 2000; Brown and Barrett 2002). But they have also made a point of using the close analysis of texts narrating specific moments and specific crimes as a way into the assessment of the relationships between different genders and different classes. In the latter examples of the history of crime the focus is less on crime rates and criminology, and more on individual crimes, criminals, police officers or the moments of punishment and what can be drawn from them as a means of understanding elements of a past society (D'Cruze 2000; Srebnick and Lévy 2005).

The cultural perspective to historical work has also highlighted the texts themselves, not simply as narratives to be contested, but also as significant players in certain events and in certain forms of a criminal justice process. The way in which the press used the murders of Jack the Ripper to push back the frontiers of what it was permissible to report has already been noted. In the eighteenth and early nineteenth centuries, when the press was a forum in which an apology could be made to escape a formal prosecution, sometimes with the prompting of a magistrate, then newspapers themselves and the texts that they contain become the subject as well as the source of investigation. And the 'cultural turn' in history can also examine the inter-relationship between fictional characters, flesh and blood characters, and the popular understanding of both in terms of the criminal, the police officer, and others involved in the criminal justice system (Sydney-Smith 2002).

HUMAN AGENCY

Historians have always emphasized the role of individuals in creating and enforcing the criminal law and in establishing the institutions of the criminal justice system. The Whigs stressed the far-sightedness and humanitarianism of reformers. The first cluster of social historians to focus on crime in the 1970s emphasized the class nature of law. It argued, in particular, that during the eighteenth century the ruling class constructed a criminal justice system which boasted equality but maintained a massively unequal division of property and enforced that division with the gallows (Hay 1975). Such arguments provoked a lively response in which, for instance, the value of rooting out instances of ruling-class domination was denied, not least because members of this class were never prominent among the ranks of prosecutors (Langbein 1983). The latter point has been emphasized in more detail elsewhere (King 2000). There were others who looked at the passage of laws through Parliament and concluded there was no evidence of an undifferentiated ruling class legislating in its own interest. Indeed, while there is a scarcity of documentation available for assessing the preparation of criminal legislation during the Hanoverian period, it appears that Members of Parliament engaged in detailed arguments about legal principles and about the use of the death penalty (Innes and Styles 1993).

Many of the individuals tried and convicted for offences involving theft or interpersonal violence in Hanoverian England were prosecuted under legislation that went back at least to the Tudor period. But eighteenth-century England experienced a growth in business, commerce, and, towards the end of the eighteenth century there were significant developments in industrialization. All of this interrelated with changes in the nature of finance and an increasing dependence on trust. While the notion of the Hanoverian legal code being extended and shaped to enforce class domination remains problematic, there are examples of the law being extended and fiercely enforced to protect the production of wealth and the use of paper credit in the changing economic environment. Forgery became a capital offence in 1729. A variety of offenders fell within the remit of the new law including, for example, sailors who sought to obtain prize money with forged documents. But whereas a respectable offender might have received a pardon or a reprieve for another crime, the executive and the judiciary were merciless in cases of forgery (McGowen 1999).

Embezzlement provided a similar, but rather more complex problem. For much of the eighteenth century the word was used to denote either the fraudulent theft of public funds by trusted officials or the misappropriation of materials from, or left over from, a production process. Sometimes the 'waste' in such a process was regarded as a trade perquisite by those involved: carpenters collected 'chips', tailors collected 'cabbage', weavers, perhaps most notoriously as far as the merchants who handed wool to out-workers were concerned, collected 'thrums'. In these instances 'embezzlement' commonly defined acts of appropriation where the ordinary law of theft appeared inapplicable. Attempts were made to tighten up the law most notably in 1799, but the use of 'clerk' and 'servant' in the legislation created confusions and problematic techni-calities when employers sought to prosecute their agents or others for embezzlement. The problems continued well into the nineteenth century and many offences that are now categorized as 'white collar crimes' were not prosecuted because of the complica-tions or because of the stigma that might attach to the business that had been the victim. Historians are now seeking to unpick the scale of the problem at the level of both the big-business entrepreneur and financier and the humble railway clerk selling tickets (Robb 1992; Locker 2004 and 2005).

It is one thing to make a law; enforcing it is something very different. The history of the police, like the history of crime and criminal justice in general, was rarely a subject for serious academic debate before the last quarter of the twentieth century. The new, more critical history continues to force reappraisals of the effectiveness and the distinctiveness of police institutions. It is increasingly clear, for example, that the locally based structures of parish constables and watchmen that pre-dated the 'new police' of the nineteenth century, were by no means as ineffective and outmoded as the trad-itional, largely Whig histories allowed. Watchmen were often relatively young and fit; they commonly patrolled their beats conscientiously and made arrests courageously (Reynolds 1998). Across the country it would appear that, as the eighteenth century wore on, there were increasing numbers of men serving as parish constables who, not seeing the job as periodic imposition, pursued it as a trade. Several of the constables in London, and most notably those working out of the Bow Street office, made considerable reputations as thief-takers within and outside the metropolis (Beattie 2006). The structure of the new policing established in England, moreover, rather than being something distinctly 'English', can be seen as fitting with a broader typology that can be detected across Europe. Thus the Metropolitan Police of London, a centralized body directly responsible to central government, was similar in structure and chain of authority to the state-civilian police institutions to be found elsewhere across the Continent. Similarly the county and borough forces, responsible to local government in the form, respectively, of standing joint committees and watch committees, were similar to the municipal police to be found across Europe. What the English went out of their way to avoid, because of their sensitivity to liberty and hostility to things French, was a state-military police like the gendarmeries. But what was prohibited by political culture for England was established in Ireland and across many parts of the British Empire (Emsley 1999a and 1999b). Moreover, some of the changes considered as developing in the closing years of the twentieth century, notably privately funded policing, have a long pedigree within English system and practice (Williams 2005).

It is often assumed that the law is made in Parliament and enforced by various practitioners outside. Some of the recent historical research, however, has shown that actors outside the legislature occasionally reshaped the criminal law, particularly with reference to punishments. Statutory authority for private whipping came in 1779, but orders from the bench by judges and magistrates had pre-dated this, particularly with reference to women (Cockburn 1994). Similarly, in the late eighteenth and early nineteenth centuries, and again without statutory authority, magistrates in London began experimenting with informal sentencing practices that put juvenile offenders in an institution—the London Refuge for the Destitute—specifically because it possessed a reformatory regime (King 2006).

In the nineteenth century the courts became much more formal and so too did the legal process. The old practices of 'making up' were increasingly frowned upon, though they could still be found even in counties close to London where a greater degree of formality might be supposed (Conley 1991). Judges and sometimes magistrates might seek to impose new standards from the bench, particularly in cases of assault and domestic violence. As a result there could be tensions between the judges and magistrates hearing a case and the jurors called upon to bring in a verdict (Wiener 2004).

Throughout the nineteenth and twentieth centuries Britain claimed to be a liberal society different from both the states of continental Europe where, it was claimed, the state enforced its control over its citizens, and the United States, where, it was suggested, unfettered democracy bred licence. Yet Britain clung to both capital and corporal punishment long after some of the more authoritarian regimes of Europe and several of the constituent states of the USA had rejected them.

CONTINUITIES, DISCONTINUITIES, AND CONNECTIONS

Historians commonly deal with much longer time frames than criminologists. One of the most significant contributions of historical research to the study of crime is the extent to which it shows continuities in the apprehension or development of problems. The treatment of crime by the media is an obvious example and has already been discussed. From the ballad and the chapbook to the tabloids and the television news, the focus has always been on the most sensational and often the most violent. But there are other examples.

The comparison of eighteenth-century and nineteenth-century crime waves with modern examples has suggested considerable similarities in the development and life cycles of moral panics over violent street crime. The role of the media, and a symbiotic relationship between the media and the police appears central, often relegating offenders to mere walk-on parts. At the same time, these panics seem not to be the result of any general crises or serious contradictions in social relations, but much more rooted in institutional and entrepreneurial needs and aims of the moment (King 2003).

Finally, historians might be criticized for not having followed their colleagues in criminology fast enough in two particular areas. First, they have been slow to pick up on the growth of victim research in modern criminology, though there have been moves in this direction, particularly in the study of women and children as victims (e.g. D'Cruze 1998; Jackson 2000; and, more generally, Garnot 2000a). Secondly, and perhaps more seriously, historians have been slow to take a more critical approach to the paradigm of crime being the result of deprivation. The reason is probably that this notion still provides a useful explanation for the patterns of crime exposed by statistics in the eighteenth and nineteenth centuries. It still seems to make sense to explain the apparent levelling out of crime in the second half of the nineteenth century—the so-called 'English miracle'—at least in part by an overall improvement in living standards. An interesting corollary here is that, as yet, no historian has made a detailed assessment of crime in the interwar period. The overall statistics here suggest a steady, but not particularly alarming, increase in crime, at a time when old industries from the Victorian heyday were dying but when smaller development was fuelling the origins of the consumer boom that followed the austerity of the Second World War and its immediate aftermath. Hermann Mannheim addressed the problem of the interwar depression and crime rates in a study published at the beginning of the Second World War. He concluded that unemployment contributed to crime, but that there were wide fluctuations and considerable regional differences that could be explained in a variety of ways such as the pride of former labour aristocrats and staunch Nonconformist religious commitment (Mannheim 1940). This is surely a neglected area that awaits a historian of crime.

■ SELECTED FURTHER READING

The issues raised in this chapter are taken up and explored a greater length in Clive Emsley, *Crime, Police and Penal Policy: European Experiences 1750–1940* (Oxford: Oxford University Press, forthcoming). The book is a synthesis of recent work providing a broad sweep of the changing understanding of crime and the criminal, and of the resulting developments in police and penal policy across Europe. For a more theoretical critique of some of the theories deployed in assessing penal policy, however, see David Garland, *Punishment and Modern Society: A Study in Social History* (Oxford: Clarendon Press, 1991).

Recent developments in the history of crime, violence, policing, and penal policy can be drawn out of the two bibliographical essays: Clive Emsley (2005), 'Filling In, Adding Up, Moving On: Criminal Justice History in Contemporary Britain,' *Crime, Histoire et Sociétés/Crime, History and Societies*, 9(1): 117–38; and John Carter Wood (2005), 'Criminal Violence in Modern Britain', *History Compass*, 3 BI 200: 1–14, www.history-compass.com/viewpoint.asp?section=5&ref=176. The latter's *Violence and Crime in Nineteenth-Century England: The Shadow of Our Refinement* (London: Routledge, 2004) also provides a stimulating introduction to the 'discovery' of violence in England that is usefully informed by theoretical perspectives, and the conclusions of which almost certainly have resonances beyond the English experience. For the patterns of murder, generally perceived as a significant measure of violence within a society, see the analyses of Manuel Eisner, especially 'Long-term Historical Trends in Violent Crime', in M. Tonry (ed.), *Crime and Justice: A Review of Research*, 30 (Chicago and London: University of Chicago Press, 2003). Debates on the value of the historical statistics of crime are best initially approached through the contrasting arguments of Howard Taylor and Robert Morris: for the former, see 'Rationing Crime: The Political Economy of Criminal Statistics Since the 1850s', *Economic History Review* (1998), 51(3): 569–90 and 'The Politics of the Rising Crime Statistics of England and Wales, 1914–1960', *Crime, Histoire et Sociétés/Crime, History and Societies* (1998), 2(1): 5–28; for the latter see ' "Lies, Damned Lies and Criminal Statistics": Reinterpreting the Criminal Statistics in England and Wales', *Crime, Histoire et Sociétés/Crime, History and Societies* (2001), 5(1): 111–27.

Most criminology journals and most history journals concerned with cultural, legal, and social topics regularly carry articles on crime, policing and punishment, and the theoretical perspectives used in such work. But it is also worth noting the specialist bilingual (English and French) journal *Crime, Histoire et Sociétés/Crime, History and Societies* which is essential for keeping abreast of the subject.

■ REFERENCES

ANDREW, D. (2002), 'The Press and Public Apologies in Eighteenth-Century London', in N. Landau (ed.), *Law, Crime and Society, 1660–1830*, Cambridge: Cambridge University Press.

BEATTIE, J. M. (1981), 'Judicial Records and the Measurment of Crime in Eighteenth-Century England', in L. A. Knafla (ed.), *Crime and Criminal Justice in Europe and Canada*, Waterloo, Ont.: Wilfred Laurier University Press.

—— (2006), 'Early Detection: The Bow Street Runners in late Eighteenth-Century London', in C. Emsley and H. Shpayer-Makov (eds), *Police Detectives in History, 1750–1950*, Aldershot: Ashgate.

BECKER, P. (2002), *Verderbnis und Entartung: eine Geschichte der Kriminologie des 19. Jahrhunderts als Diskurs und Praxis*, Göttingen: Vandenhoeck und Ruprecht.

BROWN, A., and BARRETT, D. (2002), *Knowledge of Evil: Child Prostitution and Child Sexual Abuse in Twentieth-Century England*, Cullompton, Devon: Willan.

BUTTERFIELD, H. (1931), *The Whig Interpretation of History*, London: G. Bell and Sons.

COCKBURN, J. S. (1994), 'Punishment and Brutalization in the English Enlightenment', *Law and History Review*, 12(1): 155–79.

CONLEY, C. A. (1991), *The Unwritten Law: Criminal Justice in Victorian Kent*, Oxford: Oxford University Press.

CURTIS, L. P. Jnr (2001), *Jack the Ripper and the London Press*, New Haven and London: Yale University Press.

D'CRUZE, S. (1998), *Crimes of Outrage: Sex, Violence and Victorian Working Women*, London: UCL Press.

—— (ed.) (2000), *Everyday Violence in Britain, 1850–1950*, London: Routledge.

EISNER, M. (2001), 'Modernization, Self-Control and Lethal Violence: The Long-term Dynamics of European Homicide Rates in Theoretical Perspective', *British Journal of Criminology*, 41: 618–38.

—— (2003), 'Long-term Historical Trends in Violent Crime', in M. Tonry (ed.), *Crime and Justice: A Review of Research*, 30, Chicago and London: University of Chicago Press.

ELIAS, N. (2000), *The Civilizing Process: Sociogenetic and Psychogenetic Investigations*, revised edn, Oxford: Blackwell.

EMSLEY, C. (1999a), 'A Typology of Nineteenth-Century Police', *Crime, Histoire et Sociétés/Crime, History and Societies*, 3(1): 29–44.

—— (1999b), *Gendarmes and the State in Nineteenth-Century Europe*, Oxford: Oxford University Press.

—— (2004), *Crime and Society in England 1750–1900*, 3rd edn, London: Longman.

—— (2005a), *Hard Men: Violence in England since 1750*, London: Hambledon.

—— (2005b), 'Filling In, Adding Up, Moving On: Criminal Justice History in Contemporary Britain,' *Crime, Histoire et Sociétés/Crime, History and Societies*, 9(1): 117–38.

FOUCAULT, M. (1977), *Discipline and Punish: The Birth of the Prison*, London: Allen Lane.

GARLAND, D. (1990), *Punishment and Modern Society*, Oxford: Clarendon Press.

—— (2001), *The Culture of Control: Crime and Social Order in Contemporary Society*, Oxford: Oxford University Press.

GARNOT, B. (ed.) (2000a), *Les victimes, des oubliées de l'histoire*, Rennes: Presses Universitaires de Rennes.

—— (2000b), 'Justice, infrajustice, parajustice et extrajustice dans la France d'ancien régime', *Crime, Histoire et Sociétés/Crime, History and Societies*, 4(1): 103–20.

GATRELL, V. A. C. (1980), 'The Decline of Theft and Violence in Victorian and Edwardian England', in V. A. C. Gatrell, B. Lenman, and G. Parker (eds), *Crime and the Law: The Social History of Crime in Western Europe since 1500*, London: Europa.

HAY, D. (1975), 'Property, Authority and the Criminal Law', in D. Hay, P. Linebaugh, E. P. Thompson, J. G. Rule, and C. Window, *Albion's Fatal Tree: Crime and Society in Eighteenth-Century England*, 17–63, London: Allen Lane.

INNES, J., and STYLES, J. (1993), 'The Crime Wave: Recent Writing on Crime and Criminal Justice in Eighteenth-Century England', in A. Wilson (ed.), *Rethinking Social History: English Society 1570–1920 and its Interpretation*, Manchester: Manchester University Press.

JACKSON, L. A. (2000), *Child Sexual Abuse in Victorian England*, London: Routledge.

KING, P. (2000), *Crime, Justice and Discretion in England 1740–1820*, Cambridge: Cambridge University Press.

—— (2003), 'Moral Panics and Violent Street Crime 1750–2000: A Comparative Perspective', in B. S. Godfrey, C. Emsley, and G. Dunstall (eds), *Comparative Histories of Crime*, Cullompton, Devon: Willan.

—— (2004), 'The Summary Courts and Social Relations in Eighteenth-Century England, *Past and Present*, 183: 125–72.

—— (2006), *Remaking Justice from the Margins: The Courts, the Law and Patterns of Lawbreaking, 1750–1840*, Cambridge: Cambridge University Press.

LANGBEIN, J. H. (1983), 'Albion's Fatal Flaws', *Past and Present*, 98: 96–120.

LASCOUMES, P., and ZANDER, H. (1984), *Marx: du 'vol du bois' à la critique du droit*, Paris: Presses Universitaires de France.

LOCKER, J. P. (2004), ' "This Most Pernicious Species of Crime": Embezzlement in its Public and Private Dimensions, *c*.1850–1930', PhD Thesis, Keele University.

—— (2005), ' "Quiet Thieves, Quiet Punishment": Private Responses to the "Respectable" Offender, *c*.1850–1930', *Crime, Histoire et Sociétés/Crime, History and Societies*, 9(1): 9–31.

McGOWEN, R. (1999), 'From Pillory to Gallows: The Punishment of Forgery in the Age of the Financial Revolution', *Past and Present*, 165: 107–40.

McLELLAN, D. (1972), *Marx before Marxism*, Harmondsworth: Penguin.

MANNHEIM, H. (1940), *Social Aspects of Crime in England Between the Wars*, London: Allen and Unwin.

MORRIS, R. M. (2001), ' "Lies, Damned Lies and Criminal Statistics": Reinterpreting the Criminal Statistics in England and Wales', *Crime, Histoire et Sociétés/Crime, History and Societies*, 5(1): 111–27.

REYNOLDS, E. A. (1998), *Before the Bobbies: The Night Watch and Police Reform in Metropolitan London, 1720–1830*, London: Macmillan.

ROBB, G. (1992), *White-Collar Crime in Modern England: Financial Fraud and Business Morality, 1845–1929*, Cambridge: Cambridge University Press.

RUSCHE, G., and KIRCHHEIMER, O. (1968), *Punishment and Social Structure*, New York: Russell and Russell.

SPIERENBURG, P. (1984), *The Spectacle of Suffering: Executions and the Evolution of Repression: From a Preindustrial Metropolis to the European Experience*, Cambridge: Cambridge University Press.

—— (1991), *The Prison Experience: Disciplinary Institutions and their Inmates in Early Modern Europe*, New Brunswick, NJ: Rutgers University Press.

SPIERENBURG, P. (2004), 'Punishment, Power and History: Foucault and Elias', *Social Science History*, 28(4): 607–36.

SREBNICK, A. G. (2005), 'Does the Representation Fit the Crime? Some Thoughts on Writing Crime History as Cultural Text', in Srebnick and Lévy (eds).

——and LÉVY, R. (eds) (2005), *Crime and Culture: An Historical Perspective*, Aldershot: Ashgate.

SULLIVAN, S. (2005), 'A Just Method of Justice: Informal Ordering in Kent, 1770–1830', PhD Thesis, Canterbury Christ Church University College.

SYDNEY-SMITH, S. (2002), *Beyond Dixon of Dock Green: Early British Police Series*, London: I.B. Tauris.

TAYLOR, H. (1998a), 'Rationing Crime: The Political Economy of Criminal Statistics Since the 1850s', *Economic History Review*, 51(3): 569–90.

——(1998b), 'The Politics of the Rising Crime Statistics of England and Wales, 1914–1960', *Crime, Histoire et Sociétés/Crime, History and Societies*, 2(1): 5–28.

——(1999), 'Forging the Job: A Crisis of "Modernization" or Redundancy for the Police in England and Wales, 1900–1939', *British Journal of Criminology*, 39(1): 113–33.

WIENER, M. J. (1990), *Reconstructing the Criminal: Culture, Law and Policy in England, 1830–1914*, Cambridge: Cambridge University Press.

——(2004), *Men of Blood: Violence, Manliness, and Criminal Justice in Victorian England*, Cambridge: Cambridge University Press.

WILLIAMS, C. A. (2000), 'Counting Crimes or Counting People: Some Implications of Mid-Nineteenth-Century British Police Returns', *Crime, Histoire et Sociétés/Crime, History and Societies*, 4(2): 77–93.

——(2003), 'Catégorisation et stigmatisation policières à Sheffield, au milieu du XIXe siècle', *Revue d'Histoire Moderne et Contemporaine*, 50(1): 104–25.

——(2005), 'Constables for Hire: The Long and Significant History of Private and "Public" Policing in the UK', unpublished paper.

WOOD, J. C. (2004), *Violence and Crime in Nineteenth-Century England: The Shadow of Our Refinement*, London: Routledge.

——(2005), 'Criminal Violence in Modern Britain', *History Compass*, 3 BI 200: 1–14, www.history-compass.com/viewpoint.asp?section=5&ref=176.

6

COMPARING CRIMINAL JUSTICE

David Nelken

Even the best of current English-language theorizing about crime and crime control takes much of its sense and point from background assumptions and developments which are most at home in 'Anglo-American' legal culture. This can make it difficult to recognize that there are other ways of constructing or rebuilding social order, and can produce a 'globalizing criminology' for export that mistakes local treatments for universal panaceas (Newman 1999; Nelken 2003). Textbooks on comparative criminal justice are slowly improving by becoming less tied to descriptions of different jurisdictions and more issue oriented (Pakes 2004). But there is still uncertainty over the best way for this type of research to fulfil its potential (P. Roberts 2002). The options range from, on the one hand, seeking comparative evidence so as to ensure that criminological hypotheses have cross-cultural validity to, on the other, trying to use such research in order to undermine any such pretensions. This chapter discusses issues of rationale, method, and approach in addressing the following questions: Why should we study criminal justice comparatively? What methods can we use to gather our data? What types of theoretical approaches should we draw on in comparing criminal justice systems?

WHY STUDY CRIMINAL JUSTICE COMPARATIVELY?

Interest in learning more about different systems of criminal justice can be shaped by a variety of goals of explanation, understanding, and reform. For many scholars the major contribution of comparative work lies in the way it could advance the agenda of a scientific criminology aimed at identifying the correlates of crime as antisocial behaviour. These writers use cross-national data so as to test claims about the link between crime and age, crime and social structure, crime and modernization, and so on. Much the same could be done in constructing arguments about variations between types of crime and social reaction (Black 1997).

By contrast, evidence of differences in the relationship between crime and criminal justice may be sought in order to excavate the positivist worm at the core of criminology. When 'crime' is treated as a social construct, a product of contrasting social and political censures, criminology is obliged to open out to larger debates in moral philosophy and the humanities as well as in the social sciences themselves. By posing fundamental problems of understanding the 'other' it challenges scholars to overcome ethnocentrism without denying difference or resorting to stereotypes. Engaging in comparative criminology thus has the potential to make criminologists become more reflexive (Nelken 1994a), for example learning to avoid the common error of treating the modern Anglo-American type of 'pragmatic instrumental' approach to law as if it were universal. Setting out to describe other countries' systems of criminal justice in fact often leads to rival accounts proposed by criminologists of the countries concerned (see, for example, Downes 1988, 1990; Franke 1990; Clinard 1978; Balvig 1988; Killias 1989). The debates that follow, painful and replete with misunderstanding as they sometimes tend to be, are fundamentally healthy for limiting the pretensions of a discipline that too often studies the powerless.

One result of studying the way crime is defined and handled in different jurisdictions by legislatures, criminal justice agencies, and the media (and others) is to discover—yet again—the crucial need to relate the study of crime to that of criminal justice. But it also demonstrates the difficulty of distinguishing criminal justice from social control more broadly. The exceptionally low crime rates in Switzerland and Japan, for example, can only be understood in terms of such interrelationships. Likewise, if Italian courts send to prison only one-fifth of the youngsters who end up there in England and Wales this may in part be explained by differences in the type and level of offences carried out by young people. But it will also have to do with the way Italian juvenile court judges and social workers feel they can (and should) defer to family social controls—given that children generally live at home at least until their late twenties, and often rely on family help to find work. On the other hand, cross-national data may on occasion also show that criminal behaviour is relatively uninfluenced by legal and social responses. There is evidence that even when different nation states change their drug laws at different times and in different directions, the patterns of national drug use (and drug overdose) seem to be less affected by this than by international developments in supply and demand.

But we should not limit our interest in comparative criminal justice only to its effects on levels of crime. We can also study it in its own right. This sort of comparative enquiry has as one of its chief concerns the effort to identify the way a country's types of crime control resonate with other aspects of its culture. Why is it that countries like the UK and Denmark, who complain most about the imposition of European Union law, also maintain the best records of implementation? What does this tell us about the centrality of enforcement as an aspect of law in different societies? Why, in the United States and the UK, does it often take a sex scandal to create official interest in doing something about corruption, whereas in Latin countries it takes a major corruption scandal to excite interest in marital unfaithfulness? What does this suggest about the way culture conditions the boundaries of law and the way criminal law helps shape those self-same boundaries?

It can be important to investigate how far particular methods of crime control are conditioned by these sorts of cultural factors. Much British writing on the police, for example, takes it for granted that nothing could be more ill-advised than for the police to risk losing touch with the public by relying too much on military, technological, or other impersonal methods of crime control. The results of this, it is claimed, could only be a spiral of alienation that would spell the end of 'policing by consent'. In Italy, however, two of the main police forces are still part of the military, and this insulation from the pressures of local people is actually what inspires public confidence. Britain, like most English-speaking countries, adopts a preventive style of responding to many white-collar offences which is sufficiently different to be characterized as a system of 'compliance' as compared to 'punishment' (Nelken, Chapter 22, this volume). This is often justified as the only logical way of proceeding given the nature of the crimes and offenders involved. But in Italy such a contrast is much less noticeable. Enforcement is guided by the judiciary, who do their best to combat pollution, the neglect of safety at work, etc. using the normal techniques of criminal law and punishment.

As these examples illustrate, the interest in how criminal justice is organized elsewhere is often (some would say predominantly) guided by practical and policy goals. Perceived differences, such as the continued use of the death penalty in the United States, as well as its relatively high rate of imprisonment, may be used to reassure us about the superiority of our own institutions. But, more commonly, scholars cite evidence from abroad in an attempt to challenge and improve the way we do things at home. The concern for reform is manifest for example in the long-standing search by Anglo-American authors to see whether anything can be learned from Continental European countries about better ways of controlling police discretion (Frase 1990; Hodgson 2005). Many descriptive or explanatory cross-cultural exercises are often shaped by a more or less hidden normative agenda, or finish by making policy recommendations. Even cross-national victim surveys can be deployed as much as a tool for change as in a search for understanding variability (Van Dyke 2000).

The search for patterned differences in law and practice also raises the question of what it could mean to affirm (either as a sociological or a normative claim) that a country has the system it 'requires'. What price might a society have to pay to introduce 'reintegrative shaming'? What are the costs of pursuing 'zero tolerance'? If the Italian criminal process can effectively decriminalize most cases involving juvenile delinquency (with the important exceptions of cases involving young immigrants or Gypsies), could we and should we do the same (Nelken 2006)? If prosecutors in Japan succeed in keeping down the level of cases sent to court, could we and should we follow their example (Johnson 2000)? Policy-led research can itself produce interesting descriptive and explanatory findings. But cultural variability in ideas and values means that it can also be tricky. Is it safe, for example, to assume that 'all criminal justice systems have to handle the "built-in-conflict" of how to maximise convictions of the guilty at the same time as maximising the acquittal of the innocent' (Feest and Murayama 2000)? What would it mean to shift our focus from 'taking or leaving' single elements of other systems in favour of a broader effort to rethink practices as a whole in the light of how things are done elsewhere (Hodgson 2000)?

The search to find convincing, plausible interpretations of systems of criminal justice at the level of the nation state, as in accounts of 'Japanese criminal justice' or descriptions of 'French criminal procedure', continues to be an ambition of comparative researchers. But, in an era of globalization, there is increasing recognition of the difficulties of drawing boundaries between systems of criminal justice. Many current changes in political systems and boundaries, such as those following the implosion of the ex-Soviet Union, or the menace posed by terrorist groups in some Islamic countries, are producing a different focus for research. Attempts to deal with a host of perceived international or transnational threats such as (amongst others) organized crime, terrorism, corruption, illegal dumping of waste, computer crime, money-laundering, and tax evasion raise the problem of how far it is possible or advisable to harmonize different systems of criminal justice (Sheptycki and Wardak 2005). The weakness of current national and international efforts to combat transnational crimes is no secret. Cultural differences, practical difficulties, and political factors (including turning a blind eye, or even colluding with crime) inhibit collaboration between states (Nelken 2002d).

Globalization is a name for complex and contradictory developments. It should not be reduced simply to the opportunities it opens up for organized crime or for terrorism (Nelken 1997b). It also leads to greater borrowing of models of criminal justice, as well as to processes of ideological homogenization that help produce more world-wide fear of 'ordinary crimes' such as mugging or burglary. Neither should we underestimate the significance of the International Courts dealing with war crimes (with their mixed civil and common law criminal procedures), nor the way the line between crime and war has likewise been blurred by recent terrorist attacks and the response to them. It should be remembered, though, that even before the climactic events of September 2001, countries in the European Union, individually and collectively, had already developed a 'fortress' mentality, intent on finding ways to prevent an influx of immigrants from less economically favoured countries. In sum, students of comparative criminal justice need to be concerned not only with the growth of transnational crimes, but also with the implications of transnational policing (Nelken 1997b; Sheptycki 1995).

In the realm of criminal justice, moreover, many of the phenomena allegedly connected to globalization have a long history. It is enough to think of the spread of Beccaria's ideas about punishment, or the flurry of international exchange visits in the nineteenth century to compare styles of prison-building. Thus an important issue for policy in many societies involves deciding when and how to borrow foreign ideas and practices in criminal justice, which ones are likely to be most appropriate and in what sense punishment practices are 'embedded' in a given context (Newburn and

Sparks 2004). It is tempting to judge the likely success of such legal 'transplants' or transfers in terms of their 'fit' to existing features of society and culture. But it should not be forgotten that in many cases legal transfers are as much about changing as about preserving existing patterns of society and culture. Some societies hope to transform their political and economic conditions through borrowing legal institutions from other societies, even if this aspiration may often have something 'magical' about it (Nelken 2001a, 2001b, 2002a; Nelken and Feest 2001). Conversely, economically more developed societies can and do borrow ideas about criminal justice institutions, such as mediation and other forms of dispute processing, from less economically developed societies.

ON METHODS OF COMPARATIVE RESEARCH

In the past, a common but unsatisfactory way of trying to reach out to the experience of other systems was by what can be called 'comparison by juxtaposition'. The resulting texts, whether produced by one hand or many hands, often had the merits of offering careful accounts of different systems of criminal justice in their legal, historical, and political settings. But merely juxtaposing descriptions of various aspects of the criminal process in different cultures does little to advance the goal of explanation or understanding, and provides an unsound basis for policy-making. It even begs too many questions simply to assume that the Anglo-American idea of 'criminal justice', conceived as a series of interconnected decisions by decision-makers, exists as such in other cultures. Our guiding problem must be: how can we be sure that we are comparing 'like with like', both in terms of the distinctive elements of the criminal process and in terms of its place in the larger culture?

Many US textbooks aimed at undergraduates set out to provide summary descriptions of a large variety of national systems. But these accounts are too often out of date, and are usually much less well informed about the 'law in action' than about the 'law in books'. Even in the better texts the urge to classify, as in so much work by comparative lawyers, often stands in for a concern to explain or understand. The organizing typologies chosen, framed in terms of alternatives such as justice or welfare, or crime control versus due process, can too easily present American dilemmas as if they were cultural universals (Reichel 2002). The American literature is also patchy, revealing deeper knowledge of Japanese criminal justice practices than of those in Europe (or elsewhere). But increasingly, English language writing about criminal justice, crime prevention, and criminology in European Union countries and elsewhere is slowly becoming available (see, for example, Crawford 1998: ch. 7; Downes 1988; Harding et al. 1995; Findlay and Zvekic 1993; Fionda 1995; Heidensohn and Farrell 1991; King 1989; Muncie and Sparks 1991; Ruggiero et al. 1995; Ruggiero et al. 1998; Vagg 1994; Van Swaaningen 1998, 1999). Historically informed comparisons of criminal justice systems offer important background knowledge (Mawby 1990). International self-report or victim surveys (e.g. Junger-Tas 1994; Van Dyke 2000) provide information about those on the receiving end of criminal justice agencies. There are even valuable attempts to pool knowledge from all the above sources, as well as to relate to it the challenges posed by transnational crimes (Newman 1999). Collections in other languages (e.g. Robert and Van Outrive 1993) should not be overlooked, and where possible studies in the local language of the culture concerned should always be consulted.

With rare exceptions, however, most texts about comparative criminal justice contain relatively little about the actual process of doing cross-cultural research in criminal justice. At best this question is addressed by the editors rather than by the contributors themselves (e.g. Cole *et al.* 1987; Fields and Moore 1996; Heiland, Shelley, and Katoh 1992). There is never only one ideal research method, and choice of method is inseparably linked to the objectives being pursued. But the questions posed in comparative work are often more ambitious than the methodologies which comparative lawyers usually adopt. For example, Fennell *et al.* ask, 'could there be a relationship between the mildness or severity of a penal climate and an inquisitorial or an accusatorial system of justice?' (Fennell *et al.* 1995: xvi). But they then add immediately afterwards, 'or is the question absurd?' Methodological issues loom still larger when comparative enquiries seek to tackle fundamental problems such as, 'how do different societies conceive "disorder"?', how do 'differences in social, political, and legal culture inform perceptions of crime and the role of criminal agencies in responding to it?', or 'what factors underlie the salience of law and order as a political issue?' (Zedner 1996). Only long and intimate familiarity with a society could even begin to unravel such complex puzzles.

How, then, are we to acquire sufficient knowledge of another culture for such purposes? Either we can rely mainly on cooperation with foreign experts, or we can go abroad to interview legal officials and others, or we can draw on our direct experience of living and working in the country concerned. These three possible strategies I have elsewhere dubbed as 'virtually there', 'researching there', or 'living there' (Nelken 2000a).

The first of these methods allows for a variety of focused forms of international collaboration in comparative research. Feest and Murayama, for example, describe the result of a 'thought experiment' which starts from a careful description of the actual case of an American student arrested and tried in Spain on a false charge of participating in an illegal squatting demonstration. The authors then discuss what would have been the likely outcome given the same sequence of events in Germany and Japan, the countries whose criminal justice systems they know best (Feest and Murayama 2000). Other scholars set out to explain past and possible future trajectories in various aspects of the work of police, courts, or prisons. Thus Brants and Field ask how different jurisdictions have responded to the rise of covert and proactive policing—and why (Brants and Field 2000). These authors are constantly worried about the dangers of not comparing like with like, and they draw attention to the continuing difficulties of reaching shared meanings between experts in different legal cultures even after long experience of cooperation. Such collaboration, they say, requires a high degree of mutual trust and involves 'negotiating' mutually acceptable descriptions of legal practice in each of their home countries. The lesson they seek to drive home is that correct interpretation of even the smallest detail of criminal justice organization requires sensitivity to 'broader institutional and ideological contexts'.

Given these difficulties it is not surprising to find that many scholars advocate going to the research site in person. Immersion in another social context gives the researcher invaluable opportunities to become more directly involved in the experience of cultural translation. On the basis of his regular visits to France, Crawford, for example, offers a sophisticated reading of the contrasting meanings of mediation in two different settings (Crawford 2000). In France the move to introduce mediation can be seen as part of a project of 'bringing law to the people' both by making the criminal justice response more immediate in time and also by subtly transforming its referent. But it is not about involving the 'community' in the actual delivery of criminal justice. For this conception of the 'community' has a meaning and appeal which is strongly tied to the Anglo-American type of political and social order. In France it has historically been the role of the state to represent the larger community, and its social institutions have it as their fundamental task to lead those who are not yet part of the *polis* into becoming bona fide French citizens. 'Researching there' also provides the chance for 'open-ended' enquiry that can lead to the discovery of new questions and new findings about the 'law in action'. Some things are never written down because they belong to 'craft rules of thumb'. Other matters are considered secrets that should not be written down, for example, because theory and practice do not coincide, and so on (Hodgson 2000).

Short research visits, however, usually involve considerable reliance on local experts and practitioners. Indeed obtaining their views is very often the whole point of the exercise. But care must be taken in drawing on such insiders as the direct or indirect source of claims about other cultures. Who count as experts, and how do *they* know? What are the similarities and differences between academics and practitioners? If experts and practitioners are in agreement, could this be because experts themselves get their information from practitioners? In all cultures descriptions of social and legal ideas carry political implications, in some cases even issuing directly from particular political or social philosophies. When we think of experts in our own culture we will normally, without much difficulty, be able to associate them with 'standing' for given political or policy positions. But what about this factor when we rely on experts from abroad? In much of the comparative criminal justice literature there seems to be little recognition, and less discussion, of the extent to which those describing the aims or results of local legal practices or reforms are themselves *part* of the context they are describing, in the sense of being partial to one position rather than another. In France some commentators are strongly against importing ideas from the common law world, others are less antagonistic; in Italy, some academics are notoriously pro-judges, others are anti-judges. It can be misleading to rely on the opinions or work of members of different camps without making allowance for this fact.

Moreover, cultural variability means that the problem faced here is not always the same. There are some cultures (Italy and Latin America, for example) where many consider it quite appropriate for academics—and even for judges and prosecutors—to identify and to be identified as members of a faction. In playing the role of what Gramsci called an 'organic intellectual', your prime duty is understood, both by your allies and by your opponents, to be the furtherance of a specific group ideal. In consequence, in such societies the question of social and political affiliation is one of the first questions raised (even if not always openly) in considering the point and validity of academic criticisms of current practices and of corresponding proposals for reform. In other cultures, however, the approved practice is to do one's best to avoid such identification. In some cases this just makes the process of establishing affiliation more elusive. Alternatively, the extent of political consensus, or of admiration for allegedly neutral criteria based on 'results' or 'efficiency', may be such that academics are indeed less pressed to take sides. Or intellectuals may simply count for less politically! The point again is that without knowledge about their affiliations, and an understanding of the role responsibilities in the culture under investigation, it can be hard to know what credit to give to the arguments of any expert about criminal justice.

Even if we assume that our sources are not 'partial' (or, better still, if we try to make proper allowance for this) there still remains the problem that experts and practitioners are undoubtedly part of their own culture. This is after all why we consult them. But this also means that they do not necessarily ask or answer questions based on where the researcher is 'coming from' (and may not even have the basis for understanding such questions). In a multitude of ways both their descriptions and their criticisms will also belong to their culture. In Italy, local commentators regularly attack a principled but inefficient system on grounds of principle; in England and Wales, a system highly influenced by managerial considerations, sometimes at the expense of principle, will tend be criticized for its remaining inefficiencies.

Longer-term involvement in another culture offers, amongst other advantages, a better route to grasping the intellectual and political affiliations of insiders. Through everyday experience of another culture, 'observant participation' (Nelken 2000a), rather than merely 'participation observation' in a given research site, the researcher can begin to fill in the 'taken-for-granted' background to natives' views and actions. Direct experience and involvement with what is being studied can also help give the researcher's accounts the credibility that comes from 'being there' (Nelken 2004). But actually moving to a research site—for shorter or longer periods—does not mean that the researcher necessarily comes to see things as a native. Our 'starting points' (Nelken 2000b) play a vital role in what we set out to discover. Our own cultural assumptions continue to shape the questions we ask or the answers we find convincing. Much of the voluminous American research on the specificity of Japanese criminal justice, for example, can be criticized for seeking to explain what is distinctive about Japanese legal culture in contrast to familiar American models without recognizing how much it derived from the civil law systems of Continental Europe from which Japan borrowed.

Similarities and differences come to life for an observer when they are exemplified by 'significant absences' in relation to past experience. A good example is provided by Lacey and Zedner's discussion of the lack of any reference to 'community' in discourse about crime prevention in Germany (Lacey and Zedner 1995, 1998). But the vital question of starting points is often left begging, especially in research based on short visits, because of the implicit collusion between the writer and his or her audience which *privileges what the audience wants to know as if it is what it should want to know*. The long-stay researcher, by contrast, is engaged in a process of being slowly re-socialized. He or she will increasingly want to re-formulate the questions others back home wish to address to the foreign setting. As important, he or she may even begin to doubt whether they ever really understood their own culture of origin. The comparative researcher, like Simmels' 'stranger', is thus *obliged* to move between worlds, never entirely 'at home' in either (cf. S. Roberts 1998). Sometimes the researcher will try to see things like a native insider, at other times he or she will try to do 'better' than the natives. The ability to look at a culture with new eyes is, after all, the great strength of any outsider.

This said, the heavy investment required by 'observant participation', or by sustained ethnography, may not always be necessary or feasible. The choice to follow any particular approach to data-gathering is linked to the many considerations which influence the feasibility of a given research project; not least the time available, whether one is able to visit the country concerned, and with what sort of commitment. Depending on its purposes, collaboration with experts or a limited period of interviewing abroad may even have some advantages as compared with living and working in a country. There are the usual trade-offs amongst methodologies. It is possible to cover a large number of cases with questionnaires or interviews only by dispensing with in-depth observation. And the short-termer can also pretend to a useful naivety that the long-term researcher must abandon, since that is part of what it means to become an insider/ outsider. In practice, even the insider/outsider or 'observant participant' cannot possibly experience everything at first hand. So all three approaches have to face, to some extent, similar problems in knowing who to trust, and then conveying credibility. However findings are (re)presented, they are always in large part the result of interviews and consultation of experts and practitioners, and the resident scholar may often obtain these in ways which are less systematic than those followed by the other approaches. The main advantage of 'full immersion' in another society for this purpose is that enquiry becomes more fruitful when you have enough cultural background to identify the right questions to ask. But there may be more than one way of acquiring such background.

APPROACHES TO COMPARISON

Within the social sciences, some argue that *all* sociological research is inherently comparative: the aim is always the same: the explanation of 'variation' (Feeley 1997). But explicitly comparative work does have to face special difficulties. These range from the technical, conceptual, and linguistic problems posed by the unreliability of statistics, lack of appropriate data, meaning of foreign terms, etc., to the complications of understanding the differences in other languages, practices, and world views which make it difficult to know whether we are comparing like with like. Indeed often it is that which becomes the research task. Others claim that for these and other reasons comparative work is near impossible. Legrand, for example, argues that what he calls 'legal epistemes' are incommensurable and certainly never the same matter for those who have been socialized in the culture being studied and those who are merely researching into it (Legrand 2001; but see Nelken 2002b). Cain, who prefers a form of active collaboration with the subjects of her research, insists that comparison faces the allegedly unavoidable dangers of 'occidentalism'—thinking that other societies are necessarily like ours—or 'orientalism'—assuming that they are inherently different from us. Her advice is to 'avoid comparison, for it implies a lurking occidentalist standard and user, and focuses on static and dyadic rather than dynamic and complex relations' (Cain 2000: 258).

These reservations about comparison are given added point by the current processes of globalization. In a globalized world there is no Archimedean point of comparison from which to understand distinct nations or traditions. Within anthropology the process of producing accounts of other cultures has become increasingly contested (Clifford and Marcus 1986). The very idea of 'culture' becomes highly problematic, no more than a label to be manipulated by elements within the culture concerned or by outside observers (Kuper 1999). Cultures are influenced by global flows and trends; the purported uniformity, coherence, or stability of given national cultures will often be no more than ideological projection or rhetorical device. The links between societies and individuals have been so extended and transformed that it makes little sense to look for independent legal cultures. Hence 'all totalising accounts of society, tradition and culture are exclusionary and enact a social violence by suppressing contingent and continually emergent differences' (Coombe 2000). For all this, however, at any given time there continue to be important and systematic differences in criminal justice, whether this be regarding the relationship between law and politics, the role of legal and lay actors, levels of leniency, degrees of delay, and so on (Nelken 2002b).

In exploring such differences some studies set out:

1. to test and validate explanatory theories of crime or social control (which we may, at some risk of oversimplification, call the approach of 'behavioural science' or 'positivist sociology');

2. to show how the meaning of crime and criminal justice is embedded within changing, local and international, historical and cultural contexts (an approach which we will call 'interpretivist');

3. to classify and learn from the rules, ideals, and practice of criminal justice in other jurisdictions (which we can call the approach followed by 'legal comparativists' and 'policy researchers').

In the rest of this chapter I shall say something more about each of these approaches so as to show, as against much scholarly opinion, that their strengths can and should be combined.

The behavioural science approach itself includes a wide range of different points of view about the role of comparative work. For some writers, taking the model of science seriously means that comparative work must show that cultural variability is as *irrelevant* to social laws as it is to physical laws. Gottfredson and Hirschi argue that failure to recognize this has meant that up until now 'cross national research has literally not known what it was looking for and its contributions have rightfully been more or less ignored' (Gottfredson and Hirschi 1990: 179). Some of the most influential American explanations of crime, such as Merton's anomie theory and Cohen's subcultural theory of delinquency, on the other hand, seem almost deliberately ethnocentric in the sense that the explanation is designed to fit variables found in American society. Yet anomie theory was first developed in France, and only afterwards was it reworked in the United States with particular reference to the American dream of egalitarianism and the cultural emphasis on success as measured in money. It has since been applied with advantage in very different cultural contexts; for example, in Italy to explain the growth of political corruption in the 1980s (Magatti 1996), and in Japan to account for the relative lack of crime there (Miyazawa 1997). Is the same theory being employed? How and why does this matter?

Gottfredson and Hirschi argue that Cohen's account of the frustrations of American lower-class children is hardly likely to be applicable to the genesis of delinquency in an African or Indian slum, and this spells its doom. Rather than assume that every culture will have its own crime with its own unique causes, which need to be sought in all their specificity, the object of criminological theorizing must be to transcend cultural diversity in order to arrive at genuine scientific statements (Gottfredson and Hirschi 1990: 172–3). In this search for a universal criminology Gottfredson and Hirschi define crimes as 'acts of force or fraud undertaken in pursuit of self interest'. For them, different cultural settings cannot influence the causes of crime except by affecting the opportunities and the ease with which crimes can occur. They are therefore comforted by apparent cross-cultural consistency in correlations between crime involvement and age and sex differences, urban–rural differences, and indices of family stability. A similar approach is—or could be—followed by those scholars who seek to establish general laws about judicial institutions. Shapiro's classic study of appeal courts sets out to demonstrate that higher courts always function primarily as agents of social control, whatever other political and legal differences may characterize the systems in which they are found, and whatever other legitimating ideologies they may themselves employ (Shapiro 1981). Gottfredson and Hirschi, however, just *assume* that the agencies that apply the criminal law have the universal task of reminding people both of their own long-term interests and of those of other people.

Most behavioural scientists are less concerned than Gottfredson and Hirschi with finding cultural universals. What matters is the *implicit* generalizability of the variables, not whether they actually do apply universally. For theories which link crime and industrialization, for example, it is strategically important to investigate apparent counter-instances such as Switzerland (Clinard 1978) or Japan (Miyazawa 1997), both so as to test existing hypotheses and so as to uncover new ones. Similarly, we can ask about variations in the patterns of policing, courts, or prisons in terms of the patterns found in different cultures or historical periods. If the Dutch prison rate could, at least until recently, be kept so much lower than that of other countries in Europe, this is important not only because it shows that there is no inevitable connection between crime rates and prison rates but also because it challenges us to look for the particular variables that explain the Dutch case (Downes 1988).

On the other hand, many scholars of comparative criminal justice are more fascinated by difference than by similarity. Yet the point of compiling differences, apart from its value as description or in correcting ethnocentrism, is not always made as clear as it might be. Certainly, the assumption that all economically advanced countries would be expected to have exactly similar ideas and practices for dealing with crime seems far-fetched. Why study difference? The interpretivist approach seeks to uncover the inner meaning of the facts that positivist social scientists take as the starting or finishing points of their comparisons. Even the technical definition of crime varies between legal systems, so that in Japan, for example, assaults that result in death are classified as assault, not murder; and in Greece the definition of 'rape' includes lewdness, sodomy, seduction of a child, incest, prostitution, and procuring (Kalish 1988). Less obviously, there is considerable variation in the importance that legislatures, justice agencies, or the media put on responding to different sorts of behaviour as crime. Until very recently, in Germany or Italy the police and the mass media kept a remarkably low profile regarding most street crime or burglary, at least by British or American standards (Zedner 1995; Nelken 2000b).

The prosecution or prison statistics that constitute the data of behavioural science explanations are here treated as cultural products. But it would be wrong to take too extreme a stand on the idea of crime as a cultural construction. This could lead to a relativism by which comparative criminology would become implausible (Beirne 1983), and this could be simply countered by the argument that if understanding 'the other' was really so difficult then even social science research into different social worlds at home would be impossible (Leavitt 1990). As noted, criminal justice cultures are in any case less and less sealed off from each other for them not to have some common language in which to express their concerns. Far from being either cognitively or morally relativist, the interpretivist approach in fact actually presupposes the possibility of producing and learning from cross-cultural comparisons, even if it does seek to display difference more than demonstrate similarity. It may be used, for example, to compare different societies in terms of their levels of 'punitiveness' (Nelken 2005) or 'tolerance' (Nelken 2006a), taking care to distinguish the external observers' judgement from the way such practices are experienced by members of the societies concerned. It is unfortunate that some scholars continue to insist that the interpretativist approach is necessarily relativist and non-evaluative (Pakes 2004, 13 ff.).

The search for difference only really becomes interesting when the attempt is made to show how differences in the punitiveness or any other aspect of criminal justice are linked to other differences (e.g. in types of political culture). If the positivist approach operationalizes 'culture' (or deliberately simplified aspects of it) to explain variation in levels and types of crime and social control, this second approach tends more to use crime and criminal justice as themselves an 'index' of culture. Grasping the 'other' requires the willingness to put our assumptions in question: the more so the greater the cultural distance. Some of the most exciting current work in comparative criminal justice sets out to interpret what is distinctive in the practice and discourse of a given system of criminal justice by drawing an explicit or implicit contrast with another system, usually that of the scholar's culture of origin (e.g. Crawford 1996; Zedner 1995). In an important study, Whitman seeks to explain the relative harshness of the treatment of criminals in the USA in comparison to that reserved for them in the countries of Continental Europe. His argument is that whereas France and Germany 'levelled up' their treatment of criminals, on the basis of long-standing more respectful treatment for higher-status prisoners, in America criminals suffered from a general levelling-down process that presupposed status equality (Whitman 2003; Nelken 2006b).

This said, interpretative approaches do face their own problems (Nelken 1995a). One difficulty is that of knowing who or what can speak for the culture (especially when matters are controversial). Very different results will be obtained by analysing texts and documents, testing public attitudes, or relying on selected informants such as criminologists or public officials: the drawbacks of exclusive reliance on these last sources have already been discussed. Because the interpretative approach is so labour intensive it does not allow for large-scale, cross-cultural comparison. Much therefore depends on which other system is taken as the yardstick of comparison—and how this is to be justified. Taking criminal justice discourse in England as our starting point may reveal that France works with one model of 'mediation' whereas we have several (Crawford 2000). If we compare England with Germany, on the other hand, we may find that Germany seems to have several ideas of 'community' where we have just one (Lacey and Zedner 1995, 1998). But what exactly is the significance of such findings?

Care also needs to be taken in assuming that a given feature of the practice or discourse of criminal justice necessarily indexes, or 'resonates' with, the rest of a culture. Specific ideals and values of criminal justice may not always be widely diffused in the culture. In many societies there is a wide gulf between legal and general culture, as where the criminal law purports to maintain principles of impersonal equality before the law in polities where clientilistic and other particularistic practices are widespread. It is also not easy to get the balance right between identifying relatively enduring features as compared to contingent aspects of other cultures. Relying on ideas of national character would make it difficult to reconcile the defiance of law in Weimar Germany as compared to the over-deference to law of the Fascist period. What are taken to be entrenched cultural practices in the sphere of criminal justice can be overturned with remarkable rapidity. The Dutch penal system was rightly celebrated for its 'tolerance', from the 1960s on, keeping its proportionate prison population well below that of its European neighbours (Downes 1988). But shortly after gaining such praise, the criminal justice elite who pioneered the 'Utrecht' approach was sidelined by the pressures of gaining popular political consensus in the face of Holland's growing drug problem (Downes 1996). Holland engaged in a massive programme of prison-building that took it back towards the levels of the 1950s, a period when its relative level of incarceration was comparable to the rest of Europe.

The third approach, followed by comparative lawyers, is particularly sensitive to the fact that criminal justice and procedure will often not 'mirror' wider features of social structure and culture. This is explained as the consequence of the extent to which they have been shaped by processes of borrowing, imitation, or imposition from elsewhere. Another advantages lies in the way its language and concerns connect directly to those used by many of the legal actors themselves whose behaviour is being interpreted (Nelken 1995b). It must be relevant to pay attention to rules and ideals to which actors are obliged at least to pay lip-service but which they may well take as guides for much of the time. The evolution of the discourse used by criminal justice actors may also be better understood, even for sociological purposes, when related to its own forms rather than simply translated into sociological language.

Research carried out by comparative lawyers is sufficiently different from comparative social science for both to have something to gain from the other's approach. Although comparative lawyers rely mainly on historical, philosophical, and juridical analyses they are well aware that legal and other rules are not always applied in practice, and that legal outcomes do not necessarily turn out as planned. But the sociological significance of such evidence is usually ignored in favour of processing it normatively, as an example of deviance or 'failure', to which the solution is typically a (further) change in the law. The weaknesses of this approach, which are the converse of its strengths, thus come from its tendency to share rather than understand or criticize the self-understanding of the legal perspective. Because the terms it uses are legal and normative it will not capture many of the organizational or personal sources of action which shape what actors are trying to do, still less the influences of which actors are not aware.

Social scientists, on the other hand, are more interested in what does happen than in what should happen, looking beyond written rules and documents to the structures which shape the repeated patterns of everyday action. Their approach has the opposite drawbacks. The determination to take practice more seriously than protestations of ideals can sometimes lead to an underestimation of the role law plays in many cultures as a representation of values, including 'counterfactual' values (Van Swaaningen 1998, 1999) which are all the more important for not being tied to existing practice. And the importance given to the present, rather than to the past or future of law, can block an appreciation of law's character as a bearer of tradition that makes 'the past live in the present'.

Each of these three approaches to comparison tends to be associated, in its pure form, with a distinctive epistemology, respectively (predictive) explanation, 'understanding by translation', and categorization-evaluation. The standard way of deciding which approach to choose is to ask: are we trying to contribute to the development of explanatory social science, or to improve existing penal practice? Combining such different enterprises, it is said, will only produce confusion (Feeley 1997). But, on the other hand, social scientists cannot afford to lose touch with those nuances of legal culture that bring the comparative exercise to life. Effective comparison is as much a matter of good translation as of successful explanation. We may need, for example, to understand how and why 'diversion' from criminal justice is treated as intrinsic to the criminal process in Holland, but as somehow extrinsic to it in the UK (Brants and Field 2000). And this will require considerable historical, juridical, and linguistic analysis.

In practice these three approaches are rarely found in their pure form. Sociologists—especially those interested in legal culture and ideology—need to know about law and legal procedures (and sometimes get it wrong); comparative lawyers often make sociologically questionable assumptions about what a system is trying to do and how it actually operates. Debates within, as well as between, comparative law and sociological criminology turn on mixed questions of explanation and evaluation, so that it is not the choice of one or other of these aims which guarantees either insight or confusion. Within the field of comparative law, Goldstein and Marcus, who reported that there was little America could learn from Europe in order to reform its pre-trial procedures, used sociological-type arguments based on the attempt to see how the rules actually worked in practice (Goldstein and Marcus 1977). But those who claimed that this understanding of Continental procedure was superficial were able to show how the very desire for generalizable explanation reinforced American ethnocentrism (Langbein and Weinreb 1978). On the other hand, Downes's sociological study of the role of prosecutors in keeping down prison rates in Holland clearly had a practical purpose aimed at changing the situation in Britain, but it was not (or at least not for that reason) unsuccessful in illuminating the Dutch situation.

Key conceptual building blocks for comparing criminal justice, such as the term 'legal culture' (Nelken 1997a), figure in each of the three approaches even if they are often employed with competing meanings. Another heuristic idea, used both by social scientists and by comparative lawyers, is that of 'functional equivalence'. One comparative law textbook tells us to assume that other societies will often meet a given legal 'problem' by using unfamiliar types of law and legal techniques (Zweigert and Kotz 1987). Likewise, Feest and Murayama, in their study of criminal justice in Spain, Germany, and Japan, demonstrate that each jurisdiction has some (but not necessarily the same) crucial pre-trial and post-trial filters to distinguish the innocent from the guilty, while others are more formalistic and typically presuppose that the required critical attention has or will be given at another stage. They come close to suggesting that there are 'functional equivalents' in each system for legitimizing even unsound cases of police arrests, and that systems 'self-correct' to reach rather similar outcomes (Feest and Murayama 2000).

But assumptions of functional equivalence can also be misleading. At a minimum we shall also need to extend our analysis to the role of non-legal institutions, alternatives to law, and competing professional expertises as well as to other groupings within civil society such as the family or patron-client networks. Moreover, in some cultures, some problems may simply find no 'solution'—especially, but not only, if the 'problem' is not perceived as such. Cultures have the power to produce relatively circular definitions of what is worth fighting for and against, and their institutions and practices can express genuinely different histories and distinct priorities (Nelken 1996c). Often matters are 'problematized' only when a society is exposed to the definition used elsewhere. In the 1980s, for example, the appearance of league tables of relative levels of incarceration induced Finland to move towards the norm by reducing its prison population—and were used in Holland to justify doing the opposite!

■ SELECTED FURTHER READING

The student of comparative criminal justice will need to sample literatures that touch on many different disciplines. For example, a lot of the running in anything to do with judges is made by political scientists. Likewise, works inspired by the positivist, interpretative, and comparative law approaches do not communicate much, though this is slowly beginning to change. Many textbooks on comparative law and comparative criminal justice are little more than guides to classification. But Damaska's typology of hierarchical and coordinate forms of justice is still an important starting point for the attempt to theorize differences in criminal justice in civil law and common law countries (M. Damaska, *The Faces of Justice and State Authority*, New Haven: Yale University Press, 1986). The best way to get deeper into the subject is to read monographs and articles about one or two specific societies, for example David Downes, *Contrasts in Tolerance* (1988) or David Johnson's *The Japanese Way of Justice* (2001). Renee Van Swaaningen's *Critical Criminology in Europe* (1998) is good on different national styles of criminology. Jim Sheptycki and Ali Wardak's (2005) *Transnational and Comparative Criminology* is one of the best recent edited collections on the topic.

■ REFERENCES

BALVIG, F. (1988), *The Snow White Image: The Hidden Reality of Crime in Switzerland*, Scandinavian Studies in Criminology 17, Oslo: Norwegian University Press, Scandinavian Research Council for Criminology.

BEIRNE, P. (1983), 'Cultural Relativism and Comparative Criminology', *Contemporary Crises*, 7: 371–91.

BLACK, D. (1997), *The Social Structure of Right and Wrong*, New York: Academic Press.

BLANKENBURG, E., and BRUINSMA, F. (1994), *Dutch Legal Culture*, 2nd edn, Amsterdam: Kluwer.

BRAITHWAITE, J. (1989), *Crime, Shame and Integration*, Cambridge: Cambridge University Press.

BRANTS, C., and FIELD, S. (2000), 'Legal Culture, Political Cultures and Procedural Traditions: Towards a Comparative Interpretation of Covert and Proactive Policing in England and Wales and the Netherlands', in D. Nelken (ed.), *Contrasting Criminal Justice*, 77–116, Aldershot: Dartmouth.

CAIN, M. (2000), 'Orientalism, Occidentalism and the Sociology of Crime', *British Journal of Criminology*, 40: 239–60.

CLIFFORD, J., and MARCUS, G. (1986), *Writing Culture: The Poetics and Politics of Ethnography*, Berkeley, Cal.: University of California Press.

CLINARD, M. B. (1978), *Cities with Little Crime*, Cambridge: Cambridge University Press.

COLE, G. F., FRANKOWSKI, S. J., and GERTZ, M. G. (eds) (1987), *Major Criminal Justice Systems: A Comparative Survey*, 2nd edn, Beverly Hills, Cal.: Sage.

COOMBE, R. J. (2000), 'Contingent Articulations: Critical Studies of Law', in A. Sarat and T. Kearns (eds), *Law in the Domains of Culture*, Ann Arbor: University of Michigan Press.

CRAWFORD, A. (1998), *Crime Prevention and Community Safety*, Harlow: Longman.

——(2000), 'Contrasts in Victim/Offender Mediation and Appeals to Community in Comparative

Cultural Contexts: France and England and Wales', in D. Nelken (ed.), *Contrasting Criminal Justice*, 205–29, Aldershot: Dartmouth.

DOWNES, D. (1988), *Contrasts in Tolerance*, Oxford: Clarendon Press.

——(1990), 'Response to H. Franke', *British Journal of Criminology*, 30(1): 94–6.

——(1996), 'The Buckling of the Shields: Dutch Penal Policy 1985–1995', unpublished paper presented at the Onati Workshop on Comparing Legal Cultures, April.

FAVELL, A. (1998), *Philosophies of Integration, Immigration and the Idea of Citizenship in France and England*, Basingstoke: Macmillan.

FEELEY, M. (1997), 'Comparative Law for Criminologists: Comparing for what?', in D. Nelken (ed.), *Comparing Legal Cultures*, 93–105, Aldershot: Dartmouth.

FEEST, J., and MURAYAMA, M. (2000), 'Protecting the Innocent through Criminal Justice: A Case Study from Spain, Virtually compared to Germany and Japan', in D. Nelken (ed.), *Contrasting Criminal Justice*, 205–29, Aldershot: Dartmouth.

FENNELL, P., SWART, B., JORG, N., and HARDING, A. (1995), 'Introduction', in C. Harding, P. Fennell, N. Jorg, and B. Swart (eds), *Criminal Justice in Europe: A Comparative Study*, xv–xix, Oxford: Clarendon Press.

FIELDS, C. B., and MOORE, R. H. (eds) (1996), *Comparative Criminal Justice*, Prospect Heights, Ill.: Waveland Press.

FINDLAY, M., and ZVEKIC, U. (eds) (1993), *Alternative Policing Styles*, Deventer: Kluwer.

FIONDA, J. (1995), *Public Prosecutors and Discretion: A Comparative Study*, Oxford: Clarendon Press.

FRANKE, H. (1990), 'Dutch Tolerance: Facts and Fallacies', *British Journal of Criminology*, 30(1): 81–93.

FRASE, R. S. (1990), 'Comparative Criminal Justice as a Guide to American Law Reform', 79, *California Law Review*: 539.

GOLDSTEIN, A., and MARCUS, M. (1977), 'The Myth of Judicial Supervision in Three Inquisitorial Systems: France, Italy and Germany', *Yale Law Journal*, 87: 240.

GOTTFREDSON, M., and HIRSCHI, T. (1990), *A General Theory of Crime*, Stanford, Cal.: Stanford University Press.

HARDING, C., FENNELL, P., JORG, N., and SWART, B. (eds) (1995), *Criminal Justice in Europe: A Comparative Study*, Oxford: Clarendon Press.

HEIDENSOHN, F., and FARRELL, M. (1991), *Crime in Europe*, London: Routledge.

HEILAND, H. G., SHELLEY, L. I., and KATOH, H. (eds) (1992), *Crime and Control in Comparative Perspectives*, Berlin: de Gruyter.

HODGSON, J. (2000), 'Comparing Legal Cultures: The Comparativist as Participant Observer', in D. Nelken (ed.), *Contrasting Criminal Justice*, 139–56, Aldershot: Dartmouth.

——(2005), *French Criminal Justice*, Oxford: Hart.

JOHNSON, D. (2000), 'Prosecutor Culture in Japan and USA', in D. Nelken (ed.), *Contrasting Criminal Justice*, 157–204, Aldershot: Dartmouth.

——(2001), *The Japanese Way of Justice*, Oxford: Oxford University Press.

JUNGER-TAS, J. (1994), *Delinquent Behaviour among Young People in the Western World*, Amsterdam: Kugler.

KALISH, C. (1988), *International Crime Rates*, Washington DC: Bureau of Justice Statistics, US Department of Justice.

KILLIAS, M. (1989), book review (of Balvig), *British Journal of Criminology*, 29: 300–5.

KING, M. (1989), 'Social Crime Prevention à la Thatcher', in D. Nelken (ed.), *Criminal Justice on the Margin*, special issue of *Howard Journal of Criminal Justice*: 291–312.

KUPER, A. (1999), *Culture: The Anthropologist's Account*, Cambridge, Mass.: Harvard University Press.

LACEY, N., and ZEDNER, L. (1995), 'Discourses of Community in Criminal Justice', *Journal of Law and Society*, 22(1): 301–20.

——and——(1998), 'Community in German Criminal Justice: A Significant Absence?', 7, *Social and Legal Studies*: 7–25.

LANGBEIN, J., and WEINREB, L. (1978), 'Continental Criminal Procedure: Myth and Reality', *Yale Law Journal*, 87: 1549.

LEAVITT, G. (1990), 'Relativism and Cross-Cultural Criminology', *Journal of Crime and Delinquency*, 27(1): 5–29.

LEGRAND, P. (2001), 'What "Legal Transplants?"', in D. Nelken and J. Feest (eds), *Adapting Legal Cultures*, 1–55, Oxford: Hart.

MAGATTI, M. (1996), *Corruzione Politica e Società Italiana*, Bologna: Il Mulino.

MAWBY, R. (1990), *Comparative Policing Issues*, London: Unwin Hyman.

MIYAZAWA, S. (1997), 'The Enigma of Japan as a Testing Ground for Cross Cultural Criminological Studies', in D. Nelken (ed.), *Comparing Legal Cultures*, 195–215, Aldershot: Dartmouth.

MUNCIE, J., and SPARKS, R. (1991), *Imprisonment: European Perspectives*, Milton Keynes: Open University Press.

NELKEN, D. (1994a), 'Reflexive criminology', in D. Nelken (ed.), *The Futures of Criminology*, 7–43, London: Sage.

—— (1994b), 'Whom can you trust? The future of comparative criminology', in D. Nelken (ed.), *The Futures of Criminology*, 220–44, London: Sage.

—— (1995a), 'Disclosing/Invoking Legal Culture', in D. Nelken (ed.), *Legal Culture, Diversity and Globalization*, special issue of *Social and Legal Studies*, 4(4): 435–52.

—— (1995b), 'Can there be a sociology of legal meaning?', in D. Nelken (ed.), *Law as Communication*, 107–29, Aldershot: Dartmouth.

—— (1996c), 'Law without Order: A letter from Italy', in V. Gessner, A. Hoeland, and C. Varga (eds), *European Legal Cultures*, 355–58, Aldershot: Dartmouth.

—— (ed.) (1997a), *Comparing Legal Cultures*, Aldershot: Dartmouth.

—— (1997b), 'The Globalisation of Crime and Criminal Justice: Prospects and Problems', in M. Freeman (ed.), *Law at the Turn of the Century*, 251–79, Oxford: Oxford University Press.

—— (ed.) (2000a), *Contrasting Criminal Justice*, Aldershot: Dartmouth.

—— (2000b), 'Telling Difference: Of Crime and Criminal Justice in Italy', in D. Nelken (ed.), *Contrasting Criminal Justice*, 233–64, Aldershot: Dartmouth.

—— (2001a), 'Towards a Sociology of Legal Adaptation', in D. Nelken and J. Feest (eds), *Adapting Legal Cultures*, 1–55, Oxford: Hart.

—— (2001b), 'Beyond the Metaphor of Legal Transplants?: Consequences of Autopoietic Theory for the Study of Cross-Cultural Legal Adaptation', in J. Priban and D. Nelken (eds), *Law's New Boundaries: The Consequences of Legal Autopoiesis*, 265–302, Aldershot: Dartmouth.

—— (2002a), 'Changing Legal Cultures', in M. B. Likosky (ed.), *Transnational Legal Processes*, London, Butterworth.

—— (2002b), 'Comparative Sociology of Law', in M. Travers and R. Benakar (eds), *Introduction to Law and Social Theory*, Oxford: Hart.

—— (2002c), 'Comparatists and Delocalisation', in P. Legrand and R. Munday (eds), *Comparative Legal Studies: Traditions and Transitions*, Cambridge: Cambridge University Press.

—— (2002d), 'Corruption in the European Union', in M. Bull and J. Newell (eds), *Corruption and Scandal in Contemporary Politics*, London: Macmillan.

—— (2003), 'Crime's Changing Boundaries', in P. Cane and M. Tushnet (eds), *The Oxford Handbook of Legal Studies*, Oxford: Oxford University Press.

—— (2004), 'Being there', in L. Chao and J. Winterdyk (eds), *Lessons from International/Comparative Criminology*, 83–92, Toronto: De Sitter publications.

—— (2005), 'When is a Society non-punitive? A case study of Italy', in J. Pratt, D. Brown, S. Hallsworth, M. Brown, and W. Morrison, (eds), *The New Punitiveness: Current Trends, Theories, Perspectives*, 218–38 Cullompton, Devon: Willan.

—— (2006a), 'Italy: A lesson in tolerance?', in J. Muncie and B. Goldson (eds), *Comparative Youth Justice: Critical Issues*, London: Sage.

—— (2006b), 'Patterns of Punishment', *Modern Law Review*, 69: 262–77.

—— and FEEST, J. (eds) (2001), *Adapting Legal Cultures*, Oxford: Hart.

NEWBURN, T., and SPARKS, R. (eds) (2004), *Criminal Justice and Political Cultures: National and International Dimensions of Crime Control*, Cullompton, Devon: Willan.

NEWMAN, G. (ed.) (1999), *Global Report on Crime and Justice*, Oxford: Oxford University Press.

PAKES, F. (2004), *Comparative Criminal Justice*, Cullompton, Devon: Willan.

REICHEL, P. L. (2002), *Comparative Criminal Justice Systems: A Topical Approach*, 3rd edn, Englewood Cliffs, NJ: Prentice Hall.

ROBERTS, P. (2002), 'On Method: The Ascent of Comparative Criminal Justice', *Oxford Journal of Legal Studies*, 22: 517–38.

—— and VAN OUTRIVE, L. (eds) (1993), *Crime et Justice en Europe*, Paris: L'Harmattan.

ROBERTS, S. (1998), 'Against Legal Pluralism: Some Reflections on the Contemporary Enlargement of the Legal Domain', *Journal of Legal Pluralism*, 42: 95–106.

RUGGIERO, V. (1996), *White Collar and Organised Crime*, Aldershot: Dartmouth.

——, RYAN, M., and SIM, J. (eds) (1995), *Western European Penal Systems*, London: Sage.

——, Soᴜᴛʜ, N., and Tᴀʏʟᴏʀ, I. (1998), *The New European Criminology*, London: Routledge.

Sʜᴀᴘɪʀᴏ, M. (1981), *Courts*, Chicago: Chicago University Press.

Sʜᴇᴘᴛʏᴄᴋɪ, J. (1995), 'Transnational Policing and the Makings of a Postmodern State', *British Journal of Criminology*, 35: 613.

——and Wᴀʀᴅᴀᴋ, A. (2005), *Transnational and Comparative Criminology*, London: Glasshouse Press.

Vᴀɢɢ, J. (1994), *Prison Systems*, Oxford: Oxford University Press.

Vᴀɴ Dʏᴋᴇ, J. (2000), 'Implications of the International Crime Victims survey for a victim perspective', in A. Crawford and J. Goodey (eds), *Integrating a Victim Perspective within Criminal Justice: International Debates*, 97–124, Aldershot: Dartmouth.

Vᴀɴ Sᴡᴀᴀɴɪɴɢᴇɴ, R. (1998), *Critical Criminology in Europe*, London: Sage.

——(1999), 'Reclaiming Critical Criminology: Social Justice and the European Tradition', *Theoretical Criminology*, 3(1): 5–29.

Wʜɪᴛᴍᴀɴ, J. (2003), *Harsh Justice*, Oxford: Oxford University Press

Zᴇᴅɴᴇʀ, L. (1995), 'In Pursuit of the Vernacular: Comparing Law and Order Discourse in Britain and Germany', in *Social and Legal Studies*, 4(4): 517–35.

——(1996), 'German Criminal Justice Culture', unpublished paper presented at the Onati Workshop on Changing Legal Cultures, 13–14 July.

Zᴡᴇɪɢᴇʀᴛ, K., and Kᴏᴛᴢ, H. (1987), *An Introduction to Comparative Law*, Oxford: Oxford University Press.

7

DIVERSITY, CRIME, AND CRIMINAL JUSTICE

Barbara Hudson

INTRODUCTION: FROM DIFFERENCE TO DIVERSITY

This chapter examines criminology's engagement with *diversity*. By diversity I mean the range of identities to be found within any population (local, national, global), such as young, old, male, female, indigenous, immigrant, foreign, Christian, Muslim, rich, poor, homosexual, heterosexual, and so on. These elements of identity combine together in various ways: we all have an age, a gender, a sexuality, a financial status, a nationality, a religion or none; some of these elements of identity change over time, but others are fixed, or at least long-standing, producing diverse populations within and between social groups. Some elements of diverse identities—gender, race, religion—come to have particular salience at particular times and places.

Diversity is not a characteristic of populations that is either new or pathological: it is simply a matter of fact about groups of humans. Large complex groupings (nations, continents, the global community) are obviously more diverse than smaller, simpler groupings. Even small groups, however, contain diversities: families, for example, contain diversities of age and gender, and as children grow into adulthood they may come to contain diversity of economic status, of sexuality and religion, maybe of nationality. Smaller groups often contain fewer elements of diversity, and some groups try to exclude diversity—gated housing estates whose residents may try to preclude non-white or non-affluent people moving in; other housing developments may be defined as 'retirement homes', excluding age diversity. Larger groups may try to manage or reduce diversity—states implement policies which restrict immigration, and may try to make migrants assimilate to the dominant culture. Whatever efforts there may be made to reduce the extent of diversity and eliminate some forms of it, however, diversity is inevitable; it is an inherent quality of social groupings.

The word that naturally seems to follow 'diversity' is *of*, whereas the word that naturally seems to follow 'difference' is *from*. Diversity suggests a range of options from which to choose, a spectrum of lifestyles and attributes to enjoy and appreciate. Difference, on the other hand, suggests difference from the standard case, and implies not only dichotomy, but also hierarchy, that one of the qualities is superior to that which differs from it. While diversity has a positive or neutral connotation, difference has a negative connotation. Differentiation of these two terms has significance for crime and criminal justice policy, and for criminology. If we look at new criminalizations, some are predicated on diversity, others on difference. For example, the creation of a new category of 'hate crime', increased penalties for racially motivated crime, efforts to recruit more minority police and magistrates, seem to demonstrate moves towards better protection and representation of our diverse population. On the other hand, increasing criminalization of asylum and immigration offences, parts of the anti-terrorist legislation, increased stopping and searching of Muslim Asians, indicate preoccupation with difference. A very important task for criminology is, therefore, to expose and critique the politics and policies of criminalization and crime control which are grounded on an ideology of difference, rather than on an acknowledgement of diversity.

The chapter is organized into three parts. The first part looks at crime and diversity, the second part looks at criminal justice and diversity, although inevitably this division will not be entirely clear-cut. Each of these two parts will begin by looking at the 'adding in' of concern with difference and diversity to the established criminological agenda of crime and criminal justice: normal crimes and established justice processes. They will then look at theories and perspectives which are developing to examine 'new' crimes and new models of justice which are predicated on difference and diversity: terrorism, immigration and asylum offences, and new models of justice proposed as being more adequate than existing modes to deal with diverse and divided societies. A concluding part of the chapter will look at the relationship between community—a very strong theme in contemporary criminology and crime/justice policy—and diversity.

There is necessarily some overlap between the themes of this chapter and those of others in the history and theory part of this book. Chapters elsewhere in the volume deal comprehensively with particular dimensions of difference and diversity (chapters by Heidensohn and Gelsthorpe; Newburn; Phillips and Bowling, and Peay, for example), and these chapters are recommended to accompany reading of the present chapter.

DIVERSITY AND CRIME

As elements of difference and diversity have been added to the criminological mix, there has been a similar pattern of development. First of all comes critique of neglect of a component of identity by 'mainstream' criminology, next comes a volume of literature on one pole of the factor in question, and then attention shifts to the other pole. For example, much of the early sociological criminology was concerned with juvenile behaviour. Adolescence was turned over and over under the criminological microscope, but it is only now that a criminology of the elderly is emerging. The elderly appear in fear of crime literature and as victims of abuse by families and carers (Brogden and Nijar 2000), but make few appearances as offenders. Where they do, this is usually in discussion of the needs and problems of an ageing prison population as sentences get longer and parole rules become stiffer, or in articles regretting the lack of community penalties appropriate for elderly offenders (Codd and Bramhall 2002; Howse 2003; Wahidin 2004). Criminal justice discussion of elders is dominated by attention to elders as sex offenders (Bramhall 2004; Sampson 1994), with elderly perpetrators of other kinds of offences neglected.

Gender and race have followed similar routes: first criticism of lack of attention, and then attention to one pole. Just as 'age' meant 'youth', so 'gender' meant female offending. When feminist criminology emerged there was critique of male-dominated criminology for its failure either to consider why females committed relatively few crimes compared to men, or to produce adequate theories to account for the crimes of those women who did commit them (Smart 1976). Once feminist attention was turned to offending by females, a key question that arose was *generalizability*, the question of whether theories developed to explain the behaviour of males (even if the maleness of the subjects was not examined) could be generalized to explain the behaviour of females as well (Heidensohn 2002), or whether female crime patterns were so different that they required a separate criminology.

It took criminology longer to recognize masculinity—the other pole of gender—as needing exploration. From being 'the great unspoken' (Campbell 1993), masculinity became one of the hot topics of the 1990s (Jefferson 1997; Messerschmidt 1997; Newburn and Stanko 1994). The social construction of masculinity in modern western societies, and a crisis of masculinity brought about by the disappearance of traditionally male semi-skilled and unskilled employments, were the two main explanations put forward for the 'maleness' of crime. Criminologies of masculinity produced a series of criminal identities which were wild or exotic, depictions of masculinity that while they may fascinate, denote males who are intellectually inferior, socially malfunctional, uncivilized, and barbarous (Walklate 1995). They are, as one critic has argued, the imaginings of the white, male criminologist; they are 'his stories of class, of "dangerous" boys and underworld villains, his accounts of resistances, rituals and struggles' (Collier 1998: 52). What masculinities criminologies have ignored is the crime of the 'normal' male, with the result that studies and theories of routine crimes continue to overlook the maleness of most perpetrators.

Masculinity work exemplifies the way in which criminology produces a sequence of criminal characters; the deviant masculinities depicted by writers such as Messerschmidt (2000) demonstrate the grounding of criminology in *difference* rather than *diversity*. Criminologists writing about masculinity have often incorporated Connell's work on 'hegemonic' and 'subordinated' masculinities and their work therefore produces a series of subordinated masculinities—usually lower-class, often black—who use crime as a resource for achieving and demonstrating their male identity (Connell 1987). 'Hegemonic' or idealized dominant masculinity is white, heterosexual, financially comfortable, professionally established; the thirty-something with attractive wife, young children, a detached house with a lavishly fitted kitchen and a new family saloon car in the drive. Although Connell's work is a powerful sociological analysis of the relationship between power and gender identities, when translated into criminology it inevitably produces these criminological identities which cast those who are different from the hegemonic ideal as deviant from a norm, and as criminal or potentially criminal.

Attention to race by criminologists has produced its own criminal masculinities: the mugger in the UK; the gang member and the drive-by shooter in the USA. As well as these characters who populate the criminology texts and the television screen, whole groups have been portrayed as 'suspect'. The African-Caribbean in the UK; the African-American; the East Indian in the Netherlands; the North African in France; and the Turkish worker in Germany have been the subject of attention by officials and by academic criminologists; they have been surveyed, observed, and speculated about endlessly. Whether minority race/ethnic groups really have higher crime rates than majority groups, or whether apparently high minority crime rates are a product of criminal justice and law enforcement has long been a matter of dispute between Realist and critical criminologists (Hudson 1993; Phillips and Bowling, Chapter 14, this volume). What is beyond dispute is that the young, black male living in the economically deprived areas of towns and cities of modern industrial societies is the criminal identity that emerges from most strands of criminology, from subculture and high-crime area theories to Realisms of left and right and to contemporary masculinity theories (Hudson 2000).

In the UK, until recently the group that has been criminalized by popular and criminological discourse is the African-Caribbean males of major towns and cities. How entrenched and unthinking stereotypes of the African-Caribbean as criminal rather than victim have become, was made glaringly clear by the police reaction to the death of Stephen Lawrence in South London on 22 April 1993. The initial police assumption was that the A-level student was part of the trouble rather than an entirely innocent victim, which meant that his friend Duwayne Brooks was not immediately treated as an eye-witness. This revealed a depressing continuity of attitudes to African-Caribbeans as crime-prone and non-cooperative with authority as whole communities not just particular individuals or families, attitudes exposed and critiqued by Gilroy in the early 1980s (Gilroy 1982, 1987).

During the 1980s and 1990s, criminalization was most noticeable and strident in relation to African-Caribbeans; Asians, for the most part, were seen as more likely to be victims than offenders. Although, as Jefferson (1993) explains, South Asians, especially Pakistani Muslims, were seen as the most 'other' of others, the discourse of Asianness was not a criminalizing discourse. They were seen as different and strange in their style of dress, their music, and above all by the strength of their ties to family, community, and religion. These strong ties were seen as explanations for Asian Muslims' comparative lack of crime, both through the provision of employment and support by Asian communities for their young people, and by young people's respect for *izzat*, family honour, so that they would not wish to tarnish their families' good name by committing crimes (Mawby and Batta 1980).

Jefferson had warned that the discourse of Asianness was not a criminalizing discourse 'for now', and as the 1990s progressed a new discourse emerged which saw Muslim Asian young men as less likely to be passive victims of white racism and more likely to defend their territory against inroads by white racist youth. These young men were termed *resisters*: resisting white racism and resisting family and cultural constraints on criminality (Desai 1999). The economic/structural constraints on criminality were eroded during the 1980s and 1990s. With the decline of the traditional employments (especially the textile industry in the Midlands and the North of England) which had attracted large numbers of Pakistani immigrants, came the rise of local economies, with small-scale businesses—typically the corner convenience store and taxi firm—masking some of the effects of large-scale unemployment by providing income and occupation for family members. Progressive impoverishment of these areas of industrial decline, however, made these businesses less sustainable, and the alternative economy has become less able to provide jobs for the younger generation of Pakistani males. As one commentator has said, 'If a racial underclass exists in Britain, here it is' (Modood 1992: 261). The behaviour of young 'resisters' defending their ground against encroachment by white gangs means that they are acting more as white young men in these areas of deprivation act (Webster 1997). Media responses to the eruptions of violence between white and Asian young men in Burnley, Bradford, and Oldham in June 2001 generally portrayed the Asian 'resisters' and the white racist gangs who had entered their neighbourhoods as more or less as bad as each other; there was little attempt to give an account of attack provoking defence. Inquiries into the events revealed a degree of separation between Pakistani and other communities that heightened the discourse of otherness, while undermining the perception of Muslim Asians as victims and strengthening the image of violent criminality.

There has been a hardening of attitudes against Islam since the Salman Rushdie affair in 1989 when the author's publication of his novel *The Satanic Verses* was said to be blasphemous, and a *fatwa*, a death threat, was proclaimed by Ayatollah Khomeini, then ruler of Iran. Since then, the emergence of al-Qaeda with the attacks on the USA on 11 September 2001, subsequent attacks in Madrid, and then the London transport system bombings and attempted bombings in July 2005, have led to the view that allegiance to Islam indicates potential terrorism rather than moral virtue.[1] This racial and religious criminalization of South Asian Muslims has also been fuelled by recognition and publicity given to forced marriages and to atrocities such as 'honour killings', so that the very factors which were formerly regarded as constraints on criminality—family, community and religion—are now more often viewed as causes and justifications of criminality.

---

[1] In early 2006, European attitudes to Muslims were further inflamed by hostile and in some cases violent reactions to the publication of cartoons depicting the prophet Mohammed in newspapers in several European countries, starting with Denmark.

Criminalizing of the discourse of Muslim Asianness has had concrete consequences. Ideas that appeared in the tabloid press in the late 1990s are now to be found in criminal justice and political discourses (Hudson and Bramhall 2005). The Home Office classification 'South Asian' aggregates and hides different criminal justice fates of Indians, Bangladeshis, and Pakistanis (Phillips and Bowling, Chapter 14, this volume). While Indians and Bangladeshis are under-represented in prison populations in comparison with other ethnic groups including whites, the imprisonment rate of Pakistanis is much higher than whites and double that of other South Asians. Moreover, between 1993 and 2002 there was a higher than average growth of Muslim prisoners (161 per cent), but an average increase of Hindus (69 per cent) (Home Office 2003). Whether there is really an increase in Muslim Asian crime is, of course, very difficult to know, but there is certainly a rise in police stop-and-search, more imprisonment, more suspicion, more division, and a criminalization which displays many of the features of the earlier criminalization of African-Caribbeans. The Muslim Asian is now well established as an 'enemy within'; in the light of recent events, perhaps as *the* enemy within.

Another criminal identity which has emerged in popular and political discourse is that of the immigrant involved in transnational crime. Immigrants have long been viewed with hostility and suspicion as burdens on the state, importers of drugs and diseases, and aliens who will dilute traditional cultures, and this general antipathy has intensified as recent waves of immigration are associated with push factors of wars, persecution, and impoverishment in the source nations, rather than with pull factors of the need for labour in destination nations (Marshall 1997). Migratory movements and modernization of societies go together (Melossi 2003), and 'the stranger' has always been an object of suspicion (Bauman 1991). The current discourse, however, constructs a range of immigrant criminal types who are seen as especially reprehensible and as presenting very serious threats to the security and integrity of the societies which they enter. Prominent among these types are those involved with terrorism—the bomber, the trainer, the recruiter, and the inciter—and the professional criminal—the trafficker in drugs or humans, the so-called new mafias. The various groups it is said, either migrate in order to commit crimes, or else become involved in crime because of the act of migration, for example women who are forced into prostitution to repay their costs of travel and accommodation. The public/political feeling that something should be done about these crimes and criminals is matched by the feeling among criminologists that something should be done to expose and explain these new criminalities. With terrorists, the criminalizing discourse of migration melds with that of religion and ethnicity directed towards Muslims, South Asians, and Arabs. Organized criminals and traffickers are characterized as not 'genuine' migrants (whether seeking a more prosperous life or fleeing persecution) but as predators who use established migration patterns and routes for their own criminal ends (Schmid and Savona 1996).

These new, or newly noticed, criminalities pose difficult questions for criminologists. There is an ethical question—how can criminologists study these behaviours without feeding or recirculating the criminalizing discourses of migration? In approaching terrorism and the crimes of migration, criminologists tend to adopt one of two strategies. The first strategy is that of documentation and description: who are the terrorists, how many are there, how are they recruited, how do they operate? This approach has most often been used in the study of 'home-grown' groups, particularly groups such as white supremacists (Hamm 2002; Ross 2002; White 2003). With terrorism by marginalized, dispossessed, or oppressed groups such as the Palestinians, or some south and central Americans, radical and critical criminologists who have sympathy with the terrorists' grievances, if not their methods, stress the social relationships of exclusion and oppression that nurture resistance and generate fundamentalism and terrorism (Hamm 2005). Similarly with crimes linked with migration, radical sociologists say that all modernizing societies produce varieties of 'human waste', which means that there are always and everywhere groups of the dispossessed roaming the earth (Bauman 2004). Critical criminologists stress the social relationships of power and exclusion which produce moral panics and inflated crime rates which reflect criminalization of acts of movement (such as 'false' asylum claims, overstaying, and illegal immigration) as much as or more than they reflect involvement of migrants in acts that would be criminal whoever did them (Melossi 2003; Young 2003).

Another solution to the ethical dilemma of analysing these kinds of crime without reinforcing criminalizing discourses of the outsider is to concentrate the criminological gaze on victims (Goodey 2003). Sex-trafficking, slave-like labour conditions, child labour, extortions, robberies, and assaults have victims, and criminology needs to be analysing victimization and also contributing to the development of policies to rescue and protect victims. Goodey argues that the victimization of illegal immigrants by EU and non-EU citizens is not at the heart of EU justice policy, which is predominantly concerned with prosecution, deportation, and security. Focusing on victims raises methodological difficulties: victims may be unable (because of captivity and coercion) or afraid (because of fear of deportation) to report crimes, or they may lack the ability to speak the language of the host society. Police interest in trafficked and coerced victims is primarily in them as potential witnesses, and where prosecution is unlikely, little may be done or recorded. Although the problem appears to be being taken more seriously now, there are still few law-enforcement operations which have provided data on the extent of the problem, and on the profiles and stories of the victims. Criminologists are not, therefore, able to place much reliance on official statistics, and must find new sources of data, working with community groups, women's refuges and the like. Ethnographic and case history research is needed, which is likely to be slow and painstaking, and to pose considerable ethical dilemmas and personal safety risks to researchers.

The tableau of criminal identities which criminology has produced, has, because of its anchoring in ideas of difference from a norm, obscured analytic focus on the criminality of 'normal' men and women. From theorizing within a set of assumptions about crime being disproportionately prevalent among certain social groups, and that new arrivals bring new crimes, the normal citizen is presumed to be non-criminal, not criminal to a problematic degree, or at least not criminologically interesting. Crimes of 'normal' citizens have been raised by feminists engaging with male violence (Stanko 1990), and by criminologists concerned with corporate and white collar crime (Nelken, Chapter 22, this volume). More recently, new criminologies of state crime have emphasized the 'normality' of war crimes, including rape and torture, concentrating not on the individual monsters leading wars and dictatorships, but on the ordinary soldiers who may participate in massacres and other violations, and on the state officials who may torture and abuse captives during the course of their days' work (Jamieson 1998; Cohen 2000; Green and Ward 2004; *British Journal of Criminology* 2005).

State crime is hard to define. 'Violence perpetrated by states' is both over-inclusive and under-inclusive. Some forms of violence (war, punishment) may be deplorable but not illegal, making the definition over-inclusive. Because the definition does not include non-violent forms of crime, such as misappropriation of state finances, or corruption, it is also under-inclusive. Green and Ward offer the definition of state crime as 'state organisational deviance involving the violation of human rights' (2004: 2). This begs some questions, for example, what is the state, what do we mean by organizational, what is to be included in rights? But it has the advantage of calling upon a normative, internationally agreed standard to decide what is to be counted as state crime, rather than leaving states to define for themselves what they may legitimately do.

Understanding crime as part of the routine of 'normal' persons—whether members of corporations or governments, soldiers or functionaries—takes criminology beyond its normal disciplinary boundaries. Turning to organizational theory, political science and psychology have generated interesting mixes of perspective, taking criminological ideas beyond their normal applications. Anomie theory has been added into organizational science, for example, to contribute to understanding of corporate crime (Passas 1990). Sykes and Matza's (1957) 'techniques of neutralization' have been expanded to illuminate the denial of the victim in torture, when dehumanization of victims is routine ('they're not like us, they don't feel pain', 'they're animals, they don't have human feelings'), and are joined to psychoanalytic concepts such as 'splitting' to show how people can do terrible things and then go home and behave ordinarily with their families (Cohen 2000). Milgram's famous psychological experiment which demonstrated the willingness of college students to deliver electric shocks to others when told to do so by the experimenters is much drawn on to illustrate the way in which 'normal' people can do 'abnormal' things (Milgram 1963).[2] Philosopher Hannah Arendt's work on the atrocities perpetrated by the Nazi regime in Germany against the Jewish people is widely drawn on to demonstrate the way that monstrous acts can be perpetrated by people doing their jobs, trying to gain favour with their superiors, and failing to question orders and ideologies promulgated by governments (Arendt 1965, 1973).

---

[2] Students were asked to deliver electric shocks to persons sitting behind a screen, when ordered to do so. The people on the other side were actors, but the students had no way of knowing that the screams were not real screams resulting from real electric shocks. Also illustrating the capability of normal people to inflict pain on others, a few years ago a television programme, versions of which were screened in the UK and the USA, randomly assigned participants to play prisoners or prison guards. The show had to be abandoned because the 'guards' indulged in excessive brutality against the 'inmates'.

This emerging criminology of corporate and state crime is extremely important in moving criminology from preoccupation with difference to examining diversity. Only by engaging with the crimes of 'normal' people can criminology move away from its production of a range of deviant characters, and show that people of all statuses and in all social groups carry out a range of acts, some of which are good, some of which are bad; some of which may be legal, others of which may be illegal, some of which may be legal but wrong. Diversity of populations will engender diversity of criminal as well as non-criminal acts, with crimes being the outcome of circumstances, social and economic relationships that structure opportunities, motivations, proclivities, and resistances to criminality.

DIFFERENCE, DIVERSITY, AND JUSTICE

Race, gender, and other biographical elements have been added in to studies of punishment and justice, as well as to work on crime. Again, they have usually been treated as separate topics, so that 'different' identities—females, minority offenders—are generally measured against the white, male, 'normal' subject of punishment. This approach produced contradictory findings, and also rendered groups such as black women invisible, by comparing 'women' as an undifferentiated group with men, and comparing 'blacks' as an undifferentiated group with whites.

Gender and race have prompted different questions on penal treatment. Sentencing patterns for women offenders have been compared with those for male offenders and the question asked has been whether women are treated more leniently or more severely than men; with minorities, sentencing of black and Asian offenders has been compared to that of white offenders and the question asked has been whether there is any difference solely attributable to race/ethnicity or not.[3] Findings in response to these questions have been contradictory. Statistics can be produced to show that women are treated more severely or more leniently than men; equally, there is research which demonstrates that there is no difference in sentencing attributable to race (rather than to factors such as criminal record, employment status) or that there is. The research questions produce mirror-opposite positions in relation to race and gender. With gender, there is consensus that females are treated differently to males, but lack of consensus on whether the difference is in the direction of leniency or severity; with race, there is no consensus about different treatment but consensus that where there is difference, it is in the direction of greater severity (Hudson 1998).

Looking at difference and diversity throws some light on one important current debate: whether there is such a phenomenon as 'new punitiveness'. It has been argued that western societies have become much more punitive in recent years. The evidence

---

[3] In the context of criminal justice, minority largely means 'black', African-Caribbeans and Black Americans in the UK and the USA, black Aboriginals and other black minorities elsewhere.

given is higher imprisonment rates, harsher prison regimes, tougher community sentences, more use of the death penalty in the USA, and hardening public and political attitudes to offenders. In a recent volume a group of authors associated with the idea of new punitiveness attempt to define it, demonstrate it, speculate about the causes of it, and question why some countries appear to have resisted the punitive trend (*The New Punitiveness*, Pratt *et al.* 2005). New punitiveness is defined as a form of penality which redefines the relationship between the punished and the state. Instead of being someone subject to a temporary suspension of some rights (such as the right to liberty), the person being punished in new punitiveness mode becomes a non-citizen, an example of 'human waste' (Bauman 2004) fit only for exclusion from the law-abiding community. Scandinavia, Canada, and Italy are put forward as examples of countries that have not taken the new punitiveness turn. These states are proposed as exceptions to an established trend, not as evidence that the trend does not exist; the question that is asked about them is, 'what is different', or 'why not here'?

Elsewhere, however, new punitiveness is dismissed as a myth, rather than a demonstrable penal strategy (Matthews 2005). Matthews argues that proponents of the new punitiveness thesis look only at rising imprisonment rates and increased austerity of regimes, ignoring developments such as the resurgence of rehabilitative programmes, or diversionary projects such as 'therapeutic justice', where offenders whose crimes are drug related are 'sentenced to treatment' in specialist courts (O'Malley 2006). He points out that punitive responses to crime have always co-existed with more welfare-oriented sanctions, not only disputing the dominance of punitiveness in contemporary penal strategies, but also asking, 'what's new?'

While there is a real disagreement between Matthews and the proponents of 'new punitiveness', if we consider at whom these punitive strategies are targeted, we clear up some apparent contradictions. Tonry (1995) and Mauer (2001) have highlighted the way in which the 'war on crime' in the USA has been largely directed at African-Americans. Garland (2001b) defines the 'mass imprisonment' that he argues is a feature of penality in the USA, by two features: (1) that the rate of imprisonment and the size of the prison population is markedly above the historical and comparative norm for societies of the same type; (2) that the excessive imprisonment is concentrated on certain groups among the population. Other contributors to the volume also point to the race-targeting of the tactics of mass imprisonment. Wacquant (2001) argues that the prison and the ghetto have merged; in the rundown areas of 'rust-belt' cities (Detroit, for example) where heavy manufacturing jobs have gone for ever, policing and other means of control are brutal to the degree that life in the neighbourhood comes to resemble life in prison, while within the prisons inmates group themselves into ethnic 'communities'. In the same volume, Simon (2001) argues that new punitiveness strategies of imprisoning people for long terms with little hope of release in the most basic of prison regimes—'life-trashing' sentences as he terms them—are directed at people whom white, respectable, Americans 'fear and loathe'.

In *The New Punitiveness*, the point is again made that this strategy is directed mainly at poor, black males. Two chapters are particularly interesting in this respect. Nelken

(2005) looks at juvenile justice in Italy, and says that the punitive trend has been resisted there, but notes that migrants and other 'visible minority' youth are being dealt with more punitively. Mark Brown (2005) analyses new punitiveness in Australia within the framework of colonialism. He says that colonial subjects have traditionally been dealt with as non-citizens, and that the changed relationship to the state, the exclusion from citizenship that is said to be the nature of new punitiveness, but which has never disappeared from the penal treatment of indigenous groups in Australia and elsewhere, has become more absolute and more vengeful.

Criminal justice innovations in response to difference have been repressive and regrettable. As well as new punitiveness, the detention of migrants and asylum-seekers (Malloch and Stanley 2005), suspension of due process rights in anti-terrorism legislation, 'rendition' of suspects to states where they may well be tortured, and other discriminatory law-enforcement practices, suggest penalization as well as criminalization of difference. We are seeing an escalating repression of non-white persons and of non-western religions, and we have also seen an escalating repression of poverty. Wacquant (2005) identifies expansion in the repression of the poor through criminal justice as a major trend, and indeed poverty is the common factor in the selection of groups for excessive penalization.

There are, however, criminal justice developments which seek to respond to the demands of diversity, rather than indulge in repression of difference. As well as seeking to recruit more police and criminal justice professionals from minority groups, criminal justice agencies such as probation and prisons have taken steps to recognize and respond to diversity in their policies and practices. For example, efforts have been made to ensure that the language and content of the cognitive behavioural programmes that are delivered to prison inmates and to those under supervision in the community to help reduce the risks of their reoffending, is meaningful for offenders from different ethnic backgrounds. Resettlement programmes also pay increased attention to the needs of offenders of different ethnicities in re-entering the community after imprisonment, and there is increased emphasis within prisons and in probation centres on respect for different religions, accommodating dietary rules and other cultural traditions and requirements (see the chapters by Raynor on community penalties (Chapter 31) and Morgan and Leibling (Chapter 32) on imprisonment, in this volume).

Diversity has been a concern for prison and probation managers and staff for several years, but was given added impetus by the implementation of the Human Rights Act 1998. Compliance with the HRA is a requirement for any new legislation, and care has been taken to ensure that policies and practices, as well as legislation itself, do not provoke challenges under the HRA. The Macpherson Report investigating the Stephen Lawrence killing has influenced attempts not only to recruit more minority police officers but also to alter training, policies, and practices to improve the response to diversity (Macpherson 1999; see also the chapter by Newburn and Reiner on policing, Chapter 27, this volume). Although the Macpherson Report is primarily concerned with policing, it has prompted all the criminal justice agencies to examine their own practices, looking for any evidence of 'institutional racism' within themselves.

These developments reflect genuine commitment to diversity on the part of criminal justice agencies, but there is still a long way to go before criminal justice in the UK demonstrates adequate understanding of the effects of its processes on offenders of different identities. Risk assessment, for example, is presumed to accommodate diversity, but has been shown to produce different outcomes for white and Muslim Asian offenders convicted of similar crimes (Hudson and Bramhall 2005). A report by the Chief Inspector of Prisons not only comments on low levels of understanding of cultural differences within prisons, identifying as indicators lack of choice of food and general disrespect for different religions, but also reports that Muslims feel unsafe in prisons (HMIP 2005). The UK lags behind comparable jurisdictions in its response to diversity in other respects. For example, the UK government is only just beginning to consider using a wider range of expert witnesses in rape cases, so that feminist understandings of the trauma suffered by victims can be heard; in Canada and some other western European countries they have been used for some time.

More radical criminal justice responses to diversity are the various forms of 'peace-making' justice. Criminal justice as peace-making takes several forms: models of community justice oriented towards conflict resolution between individuals (victims and offenders), or between social/ethnic groups (Catholics and Protestants in North Ireland, Hutu and Tutsi in Rwanda, Serbs and Bosnians in former Yugoslavia, for example), or between governments and peoples (new governments following military dictatorships in Latin America and former communist regimes in Eastern Europe). Community justice initiatives include restorative justice, which in several countries may incorporate recognition of forms of indigenous justice, and transitional justice processes such as truth and reconciliation commissions.

Restorative justice is the best-known 'new justice' model in England and Wales, and is a form of justice that has proliferated around the world in recent years. Restorative justice is usually concerned with individual offences, and aims to bring together offenders, victims, and community representatives; among its aims is that of seeking understanding of their different perspectives on the criminal event that has occasioned the intervention. There is great variety in restorative approaches. Some—such as the restorative justice based 'referral orders' introduced in the UK youth justice system under the 1999 Crime and Disorder Act (Crawford and Newburn 2003)—are incorporated into formal criminal justice processes, while elsewhere they exist outside the main system and indeed they are sometimes advocated as a 'replacement discourse', to replace rather than augment existing systems (Hudson 2003a). From the beginning, restorative justice has been responsive to diversity in that it admits a greater range of participants than does traditional criminal justice, and most important, victims and offenders can offer their accounts in their own terms rather than having to give them within the confines of legal discourse.

As the scope and number of restorative justice projects has expanded, more specific attention has been paid to its capacity to provide justice for traditionally marginalized groups such as minority and indigenous women (*Theoretical Criminology* 2006). There remains considerable debate about whether, for example, offences such as partner violence should be dealt with by mainstream systems, or by restorative processes within offenders' and victims' own communities. This is an urgent and important issue for Muslim Asian women in the UK, and for aboriginal women in Australia, Canada, and elsewhere (Cameron 2006; Hudson 2006a; Nancarrow 2006). Powerless groups, such as minority women who are victims of partner violence, may want acknowledgement by the most powerful institutions of state—the judgement and punishments of the formal criminal justice system—or they may think that restorative justice conferences and meetings, with participation by representatives of their own community, rather than formal processes, offer more hope of actually getting something done, and of influencing their community towards greater condemnation of offences such as gendered violence.

It is not axiomatic that indigenous or community justice schemes represent an embracing of diversity. At a society level, it may be that supporting indigenous and/or community schemes is an acknowledgement of and an accommodation to diversity, but there is always concern about whether in fact such schemes are reflections of lack of concern by the dominant group for the wrongs suffered by subordinated or marginalized groups. This long-standing concern with 'informal justice'—that it may be second-class justice for those deemed second-class citizens—has resurfaced as indigenous and community justice projects have proliferated in western nations (McEvoy and Mika 2002). Another difficulty with indigenous justice is whether practices of which the legal values of the dominant society would disapprove can be allowed. Some processes may involve what to liberal western subjectivities seems to be excessive shaming, degradation, or punitiveness. The compromise is usually to support community/minority processes, but to disallow sanctions that go beyond what is legally available in the society as a whole.

Another form of justice that has emerged in response to diversity is 'transitional justice'. This appears in post-conflict situations, typically when the formal justice system has been used as an instrument of repression by one social group against another. Sometimes, restorative justice can be used as a post-conflict transitional model, with the aim of replacing undesirable patterns of community justice. In Northern Ireland, for example, restorative justice is being developed with Catholic and Protestant communities to displace the rough justice of the paramilitaries, while it is acknowledged that communities remain mistrustful of state justice (McEvoy and Ellison 2003).

Perhaps the best-known transitional justice innovation is the Truth and Reconciliation Commission, introduced in South Africa after the demise of apartheid. Truth and Reconciliation processes are valuable for re-establishing the rule of law and re-democratizing a state so that all citizens can feel they have a stake in the new society and that as well as past wrongs being acknowledged, they will have the protection of the law in future. Truth Commissions usually offer an amnesty or a reduced liability to punishment for those who admit to wrongs committed under the previous regime. This means that the Commission can seem an empty process, relieving guilt and absolving the oppressors and violators from punishment, without providing the victims with anything other than acknowledgement of the truth of their complaints and the fact of their sufferings.

Truth Commissions can seem entirely offender orientated, leaving the victim no role other than that of witness. Although bearing witness is important for the future integration and smooth running of the society, and may offer important validation to the victim, it also makes demands, and it may offer little to improve the situation of the victim in the new society. With some models, the main demand made of the victim is acceptance that the offender can be forgiven. The way that the commission model works can mean that the state assumes the role of forgiver, whereas only the actual person harmed can rightfully forgive the harmer. Victims may not necessarily want vengeance, but their forgiveness should not be demanded or taken for granted (Minow 1998). Truth and Reconciliation processes need to offer empowerment within and beyond the proceedings themselves; they need to be accompanied by tangible forms of compensation, and by resources to enable the formerly oppressed to achieve parity of citizenship (Stanley 2005).

COMMUNITY, DIVERSITY, AND HUMAN RIGHTS

Nation states and the international community are unavoidably sites of diversity, and inevitably contain within them groups and individuals with whom the majority feel no sense of belonging to the same community. There are, moreover, people who move between communities, and people who appear to belong to no community at all. Within states, there are some whose behaviour is incomprehensible: young people who commit unconscionable amounts of violence for what seem like small amounts of money, for example. In today's divided, individualistic societies, such people are treated as aliens or 'animals' (Melossi 2000; Young 1999). Citizens are also faced with migrants who may turn out to be terrorists or people-traffickers, or they may be law-abiding persons fleeing persecution and destitution; judges and politicians are faced with demands for extradition, and judges may be called upon to participate in international criminal courts and tribunals.

Questions of what rights are due to some, most, or all human beings are therefore important, and much debated (Hudson 2003b). Contemporary communitarianism has been influential with UK and US politicians, insisting that rights are only due to those who accept the responsibilities of good citizenship. Theorists of human rights have argued that some rights are due to all humans simply in virtue of being human, while other rights are civil or political rights which derive from persons' status as citizens of particular societies. Fundamental human rights, such as the right to life and to freedom from torture, are absolute and should never be suspended for any reason, including national security, while civil rights may be suspended in times of emergency, but only temporarily, and only in proportion to necessity and reasonable judgement of effectiveness (Ashworth 2002). Other theorists, who have been known as defenders of absolute human rights, now say that some fundamental human rights can be suspended to prevent acts of terrorism or other great evil (Ignatieff 2004).

Feminist political theorist Seyla Benhabib (2004) has addressed the question of the rights due to strangers who are outside of community, and argues that 'the right to have rights' must be uncoupled from citizenship of a state. Like many other writers, she sees the way forward in a philosophy of 'cosmopolitanism', which demands a right of strangers to be received without violence, and which insists that though protection against demonstrable probable danger is permissible, any limitation of basic human rights (including a right of shelter) on grounds related to difference is impermissible. Moreover, she argues that 'danger' must be serious physical danger, and not any perceived threat to standards of living of the destination society, such as by migrants drawing welfare benefits, or using health and education resources. Ideas such as cosmopolitanism, and the acceptance that although we may not recognize others as having characteristics in common with ourselves, we nevertheless recognize that we share human frailty and the unpredictability of life on a crowded, volatile planet, are advocated as the only way to secure justice for difference and diversity. Recognition of a duty to uphold the fundamental rights of others because of our common human predicament, rather than because of any shared qualities and values as in traditional liberal philosophy, is the only way that we can do justice to diversity in an age when encounters with strangers are unavoidable (Hudson 2006b).

■ SELECTED FURTHER READING

A good critical review of 'masculinities' criminology is given by Collier (1998) *Masculinities, Crime and Criminology*. Spalek (2002), *Islam, Crime and Justice*, covers a range of issues concerning the involvement of Muslim Asians in the UK in crime as offenders and as victims, and their experiences of criminal justice. Marshall (1997), *Minorities, Migrants and Crime*, provides a review of research, statistics, and policy issues on minorities, migrants, crime, and criminal justice in the USA and several European countries, including the UK. On state crime, Green and Ward (2004), *State Crime: Governments, Violence and Corruption*, offers innovative theory, drawing on a range of disciplines and on case studies from several countries, while Cohen (2000) *States of Denial*, draws on criminology, sociology, and psychology to examine ways in which ordinary people can deny knowledge of, and feel comfortable with their participation in, gross human rights violations. Literature on terrorism has proliferated since 11 September 2001: Martin (2003), *Understanding Terrorism: Challenges, Perspectives and Issues*, and White (2003), *Terrorism: An Introduction*, provide good introductions and overviews.

Garland (2001), *Mass Imprisonment: Social Causes and Consequences*, and Pratt *et al.* (2005), *The New Punitiveness: Trends, theories, perspectives*, contain excellent essays which demonstrate the entrenchment of punitive strategies to control groups defined as 'different'. There is now a large body of literature on restorative justice. For the topics dealt with in this chapter, two useful volumes are Weitekamp and Kerner (2002), *Restorative Justice: Theoretical Foundations*, and Elliott and Gordon (2005), *New Directions in Restorative Justice*. On truth commissions, see Hayner (2001), *Unspeakable Truths: Confronting State Terror and Atrocity* and on transitional justice generally, Teitel (2000), *Transitional Justice*.

■ REFERENCES

ARENDT, H. (1965), *Eichmann in Jerusalem*, revised edn, Harmondsworth: Penguin.

—— (1973), *The Origins of Totalitarianism*, New York: Harcourt Brace Jovanovich.

ASHWORTH, A. (2002), *Human Rights, Serious Crime and Criminal Procedure*, The Hamlyn Lectures, London: Sweet & Maxwell.

BAUMAN, Z. (1991), *Modernity and Ambivalence*, Cambridge: Polity.

—— (2004), *Wasted Lives: Modernity and its Outcasts*, Cambridge: Polity.

BENHABIB, S. (2004), *The Rights of Others: Aliens, Residents and Citizens*, Cambridge: Cambridge University Press.

BRAMHALL, G. (2004), 'Older Offenders and Community Penalties', paper presented to the Ageing, Crime and Society Conference, British Society of Criminology and Better Government for Older People, March, London.

British Journal of Criminology (2005), special issue on State Crime, 45(4), whole issue.

BROGDEN, M., and NIJHAR, P. (2000), *Crime, Abuse and the Elderly*, Cullompton, Devon: Willan.

BROWN, M. (2005), 'Liberal Exclusions and the New Punitiveness', in J. Pratt *et al.* (eds), *The New Punitiveness: Trends, Theories, Perspectives*, London: Sage.

CAMERON, A. (2006), 'Stopping the Violence: Canadian Feminist Debates on Restorative Justice and Intimate Violence: *Theoretical Criminology*, 10(1): 49–66.

CAMPBELL, B. (1993), *Goliath: Britain's Dangerous Places*, London: Methuen.

CODD, H., and BRAMHALL, G. (2002), 'Older Offenders and Probation: A Challenge for the Future?', *Probation Journal*, 49(1): 27–34.

COHEN, S. (2000), *States of Denial: Knowing about Atrocities and Suffering*, Cambridge: Polity.

COLLIER, R. (1998), *Masculinities, Crime and Criminology*, London: Sage.

CONNELL, R. (1987), *Gender and Power*, Cambridge: Polity.

CRAWFORD, A., and NEWBURN, T. (2003), *Youth Offending and Restorative Justice*, Cullompton, Devon: Willan.

DESAI, P. (1999), 'Spaces of Identity; Cultures of Conflict: The Development of New British Asian Identities', PhD Thesis, University of London, Goldsmiths College.

ELLIOTT, E., and GORDON, R. (eds) (2005), *New Directions in Restorative Justice*, Cullompton, Devon: Willan.

GARLAND, D. (2001a), *The Culture of Control: Crime and Social Order in Contemporary Society*, Oxford: Oxford University Press.

—— (ed) (2001b), *Mass Imprisonment: Social Causes and Consequences*, London: Sage.

GILROY, P. (1982), 'Police and Thieves', in Centre for Contemporary Cultural Studies (ed.), *The Empire Strikes Back*, London: Hutchinson.

—— (1987), 'The Myth of Black Criminality', in P. Scraton (ed.), *Law, Order and the Authoritarian State*, Milton Keynes: Open University Press.

GOODEY, J. (2003), 'Migration, Crime and Victimhood: Responses to Sex Trafficking in the EU', *Theoretical Criminology*, 5(4): 415–32.

GREEN, P., and WARD, T. (2004), *State Crime: Governments, Violence and Corruption*, London: Pluto.

HAMM, M. (2002), *In Bad Company: America's Terrorist Underground*, Boston, Mass.: Northeastern University Press.

—— (2005), 'After September 11: Terrorism Research and the Crisis in Criminology', *Theoretical Criminology*, 9(2): 237–50.

HAYNER, P. (2001), *Unspeakable Truths: Confronting State Terror and Atrocity*, London: Routledge.

HEIDENSOHN, F. (2002), 'Gender and Crime', in M. Maguire, R. Morgan, and R. Reiner (eds), *The Oxford Handbook of Criminology*, 3rd edn, 491–530, Oxford: Oxford University Press.

HER MAJESTY'S INSPECTORATE OF PRISONS (HMIP) (2005), *Parallel Worlds: A Thematic Review of Race Relations in Prisons*, London: Home Office.

HOME OFFICE (2003), *Prison Statistics for England and Wales, 2002*, London: Home Office.

HOWSE, G. (2003), *Growing Old In Prison: A Scoping Study on Older Prisoners*, London: Prison Reform Trust.

HUDSON, B. (1993), 'Racism and Criminology: concepts and controversies', in D. Cook and B. Hudson (eds), *Racism and Criminology*, London: Sage.

—— (1998), 'Doing Justice to Difference', in A. Ashworth and M. Wasik (eds), *Fundamentals of Sentencing Theory*, Oxford: Clarendon.

HUDSON, B. (2000), 'Criminology, Difference and Justice: Issues for Critical Criminology', *Australian and New Zealand Journal of Criminology*, 33(2): 168–82.

——(2003a), *Understanding Justice: An Introduction to Ideas, Perspectives and Controversies in Modern Penal Theory*, 2nd edn, Buckingham: Open University Press.

——(2003b), *Justice in the Risk Society: Challenging and Re-affirming Justice in Late Modernity*, London: Sage.

——(2006a), 'Beyond White Man's Justice: Race, Gender and Justice in Late Modernity', *Theoretical Criminology*, 10(1): 29–47.

——(2006b, forthcoming), 'Punishing Monsters, Judging Aliens: Justice at the Borders of Community', *Australian and New Zealand Journal of Criminology*.

——and BRAMHALL, G. (2005), 'Assessing the "Other": Constructions of "Asianness" in Risk Assessments by Probation Officers', *British Journal of Criminology*, 45(5): 721–40.

IGNATIEFF, M. (2004), *The Lesser Evil: Political Ethics in an Age of Terror*, Edinburgh: Edinburgh University Press.

JAMIESON, R. (1998), 'Towards a Criminology of War in Europe', in V. Ruggiero, N. South, and I. Taylor (eds), *The New European Criminology*, London: Routledge.

JEFFERSON, T. (1993), 'The Racism of Criminalization: Policing and the Reproduction of the Criminal Other', in L. R. Gelsthorpe (ed.), *Minority Ethnic Groups in the Criminal Justice System*, Cambridge: Institute of Criminology.

——(1997), 'Masculinities and Crime', in M. Maguire, R. Morgan, and R. Reiner (eds), *The Oxford Handbook of Criminology*, 2nd edn, 535–58, Oxford: Oxford University Press.

McEVOY, K., and ELLISON, G. (2003), 'Criminological Discourses in N. Ireland: Conflict and Conflict Resolution', in K. McEvoy and T. Newburn (eds), *Criminology, Conflict Resolution and Restorative Justice*, London: Palgrave.

——and MIKA, H. (2002), 'Restorative Justice and the Critique of informalism in Northern Ireland', *British Journal of Criminology*, 42(3): 534–62.

MACPHERSON, W. (1999), *The Stephen Lawrence Inquiry*, Report of an Inquiry by Sir William Macpherson of Cluny, advised by Tom Cook, The Right Reverend Dr John Sentamu and Dr Richard Stone, Cmnd 4262-1, London: The Stationery Office.

MALLOCH, M. S., and STANLEY, E. (2005), 'The Detention of Asylum Seekers in the UK: Representing Risk, Managing Dangerousness', *Punishment and Society*, 7(1): 53–72.

MARSHALL, I. H. (1997), 'Minorities and Crime in Europe and the United States: More Similar than Different!', in I. H. Marshall (ed.), *Minorities, Migrants and Crime*, London: Sage.

MARTIN, G. (2003), *Understanding Terrorism: Challenges, Perspectives and Issues*, Thousand Oaks, Cal.: Sage.

MATTHEWS, R. (2005), 'The Myth of Punitiveness', *Theoretical Criminology*, 9(2): 175–202.

MAUER, M. (2001), 'The Causes and Consequences of Prison Growth in the USA', in D. Garland (ed.), *Mass Imprisonment: Social Causes and Consequences*, London: Sage.

MAWBY, B. I., and BATTA, I. D. (1980), 'Asians and Crime: The Bradford Experience', Middlesex: Scope Communication.

MELOSSI, D. (2000), 'Social Theory and Changing Representations of the Criminal', *British Journal of Criminology*, 40(2): 296–320.

——(2003), 'In a Peaceful Life: Migration and the Crime of Modernity in Europe/Italy', *Theoretical Criminology*, 371–98.

MESSERSCHMIDT, J. (1997), *Crime as Structured Action: Gender, Race, Class and Crime in the Making*, Thousand Oaks, Cal.: Sage.

——(2000), *Nine Lives: Adolescent Masculinities, the Body and Violence*, Boulder, Col.: Westview Press.

MILGRAM, S. (1963), 'Behavioural Study of Obedience to Authority', *Journal of Abnormal Social Psychology*, 67(4): 277–85.

MINOW, M. (1998), *Between Vengeance and Forgiveness: Facing History after Genocide and Mass Violence*, Boston, Mass.: Beacon Press.

MODOOD, T. (1992), 'British Asian Muslims and the Rushdie Affair', in J. Donald and A. Rattansi (eds), *Race, Culture and 'Difference'*, London: Sage.

NANCARROW, H. (2006), 'In Search of Justice for Domestic and Family Violence: Indigenous and Non-Indigenous Australian Women's Perspectives', *Theoretical Criminology*, 10(1): 87–106.

NELKEN, D. (2005), 'When is a Society Non-Punitive? The Italian Case', in J. Pratt *et al.* (eds), *The New Punitiveness: Trends, Theories, Perspectives*, Cullompton, Devon: Willan.

NEWBURN, T., and STANKO, E. (eds) (1994), *Just Boys Doing Business? Men, Masculinities and Crime*, London: Routledge.

O'MALLEY, P. (2006), 'Risk and Restorative Justice: Governing Through the Democratic Minimization of Harms', in I. Aertsen, T. Daems, and L. Robert (eds), *Institutionalizing Restorative Justice*, Cullompton, Devon: Willan.

PASSAS, N. (1990), 'Anomie and Corporate Deviance', *Contemporary Crises*, 14: 157–78.

PRATT, J., BROWN, D., BROWN, M., HALLSWORTH, S., and MORRISON, W. (eds) (2005), *The New Punitiveness: Trends, Theories, Perspectives*, Cullompton, Devon: Willan.

ROSS, J. I. (2002), *The Dynamics of Political Crime*, Thousand Oaks, Cal.: Sage.

SAMPSON, A. (1994) *Acts of Abuse: Sex Offenders and the Criminal Justice System*, London: Routledge.

SCHMID, A. P., and SAVONA, E. U. (1996), 'Migration and Crime: A Framework for Discussion', in A. P. Schmid (ed.), *Migration and Crime*, Milan: International Scientific and Professional Advisory Council of the United Nations Crime Prevention and Criminal Justice Program.

SIMON, J. (2001), 'Fear and Loathing in Late Modernity', in D. Garland (ed.), *Mass Imprisonment: Social Causes and Consequences*, London: Sage.

SMART, C. (1976), *Women, Crime and Criminology*, London: Routledge & Kegan Paul.

SPALEK, B. (ed.) (2002), *Islam, Crime and Criminal Justice*, Cullompton, Devon: Willan.

STANKO, E. (1990), *Everyday Violence*, London: Unwin Hyman.

STANLEY, E. (2005), 'Truth Commissions and the Recognition of State Crime', *British Journal of Criminology*, 45(4): 582–97.

SYKES, G., and MATZA, D. (1957), 'Techniques of Neutralization', *American Sociological Review*, 22.

TEITEL, R. (2000), *Transitional Justice*, Oxford: Oxford University Press.

Theoretical Criminology (2006), 10(1), whole issue on restorative justice and indigenous women.

TONRY, M. (1995), *Malign Neglect: Race, Crime and Punishment in America*, New York: Oxford University Press.

WACQUANT, L. (2001), 'Deadly Symbiosis: When Ghetto and Prison Meet and Merge', in D. Garland (ed.), *Mass Imprisonment: Social Causes and Consequences*, London: Sage.

—— (2005), 'The Great Penal Leap Backward: Incarceration in America from Nixon to Clinton', in J. Pratt *et al.* (eds), *The New Punitiveness: Trends, Theories, Perspectives*, Cullompton, Devon: Willan.

WAHIDIN, A. (2004), *Older Women in the Criminal Justice System: Running Out of Time*, London: Jessica Kingsley.

WALKLATE, S. (1995), *Gender and Crime: An Introduction*, Hemel Hempstead: Prentice Hall/Harvester Wheatsheaf.

WEBSTER, C. (1997), 'The Construction of British "Asian" Criminality', *International Journal of the Sociology of Law*, 25: 65–86.

WEITEKAMP, E. G. M. and KERNER, H-J. (eds) (2002), *Restorative Justice: Theoretical Foundations*, Cullompton, Devon: Willan.

WHITE, J. R. (2003), *Terrorism: An Introduction*, Belmont, Cal.: Wadsworth.

YOUNG, J. (1999), *The Exclusive Society*, London: Sage.

—— (2003), 'To these Wet and Windy Shores: Recent Immigration Policy in the UK', *Theoretical Criminology*, 5(4): 449–62.

PART II

THE SOCIAL CONSTRUCTION OF CRIME AND CRIME CONTROL

8

LEGAL CONSTRUCTIONS
OF CRIME

*Nicola Lacey**

The concept of crime is so familiar that it is taken for granted: by lawyers, by criminal justice practitioners and scholars, and by the general public. Yet when we try to subject it to analysis, it tends to slip away from us, defying any neat characterization. It seems natural to turn to criminal law for help here: criminal law, surely, supplies the answer to how we can identify crime. The idea that the intellectual concerns of criminology are intimately connected in this way with those of criminal law seems obvious. Yet within the institutional construction of disciplines, such common sense is often effaced by the development of theoretical frameworks which illuminate particular aspects of a practical terrain whilst obscuring their links with others. This (in some ways productive) blindness is one to which lawyers are probably more prone than criminologists. Both the professional autonomy of legal practice and the technical nature of legal argumentation have lent themselves to the construction of relatively rigid disciplinary boundaries. By contrast, the status of criminology as a discrete discipline has always been contested, and criminological research is inevitably informed by the methods and insights of the social sciences in general—insights which continue to have a rather fragile position within legal scholarship (Lacey 2006a; Nelken 1987b; Sumner 1994; Tamanaha 2001). It is nonetheless almost as rare to find a criminology text which concerns itself with the scope and nature of criminal law as it is to find a criminal law text which addresses criminological questions about the idea of crime (Lacey, Wells, and Quick 2003; Bronitt and McSherry 2005).

In this chaper, I shall examine the relationship between legal constructions of crime (criminal law) on the one hand and social constructions of crime and criminality (the subject matter of criminology and criminal justice studies) on the other. Focusing initially on criminal law, I shall consider two aspects of the contemporary legal construction of crime: its conceptual form and its substantive scope. I shall then set this analysis in social and historical perspective, illustrating the links between legal and social constructions of crime—and hence between criminal legal and criminological/

* I should like to thank Arlie Loughnan and Robert Reiner for helpful comments on a draft of this chapter.

criminal justice enquiry. On the basis of this preliminary analysis, the latter part of the chapter will consider two further issues. First, what can students of criminal law learn from the study of criminal justice? What questions might a degree of criminological insight prompt a criminal lawyer to ask? Secondly, what do criminologists need to know about criminal law? And what might they learn from criminal law scholarship?

My argument will be that an adequate grasp of the two fields may best be attained by conceptualizing them as interlocking spaces within a broader conceptual frame: that of 'criminalization' (Lacey 1995, 2001a, 2004). The framework of criminalization keeps the close relationship of the criminal legal and criminological/criminal justice practices in view, whilst avoiding a synthesis which would lose sight of their specificity. Such a framework is, moreover, implicit in some of the most intellectually persuasive recent contributions to criminal law scholarship (Bronitt and McSherry 2005; Farmer 1996a, 1996b; Loveland 1995; Norrie 2001; Wells 2001). In what follows, I shall assume that the reader is a student of criminology or criminal justice who may not have studied criminal law.

THE RELATIONSHIP BETWEEN CRIMINAL LAW, CRIMINOLOGY, AND CRIMINAL JUSTICE STUDIES

Within the academy in the United Kingdom, the study of the various social practices associated with 'criminal justice' is currently divided into two main blocks. These blocks are themselves marked by a combination of disciplinary tools and institutional objects. Let us call these two blocks the legal and social construction of crime (though 'legal' and 'extra-legal' might be more accurate, given that legal constructions of crime are, evidently, themselves social phenomena). Study of the social construction of crime itself divides into two broad fields—criminology and criminal justice—brought together in this particular volume. Criminology concerns itself with social and individual antecedents of crime and with the nature of crime as a social phenomenon: its disciplinary resources come mainly from sociology, social theory, psychology, history, and, though more rarely, economics and political science. Criminologists raise a variety of questions about patterns of criminality and its social construction, along with their historical, economic, political, and social conditions of existence. While the dynamic social construction of crime gives reason for scepticism about criminology's discreteness as a discipline, it continues to hold a distinctive institutional position in the academy. Criminal justice studies, which have a variety of legal, historical, sociological, and other interests, deal with the specifically institutional aspects of the social construction of crime: with criminal processes such as policing, prosecution, plea bargaining (McConville and Mirsky 2005), trial procedure (Duff *et al.* 2004), sentencing (Ashworth 2005), and punishment, and with normative questions about the principles around which a criminal justice system worth the name ought to be organized (Ashworth and Redmayne 2005; Lacey 2006b; Zedner 2004).

Criminal law, by contrast, concerns itself with the formally established norms according to which individuals or groups are adjudged guilty or innocent. These norms are of several kinds, arguably mapping on to the core functions of criminal law. For criminal law encompasses not only substantive rules of conduct addressed to citizens but also rules determining how liability should be attributed and how breaches of criminal norms should be graded—rules which are arguably more plausibly seen as addressed to officials than to potential offenders (Robinson 1997). Contemporary criminal lawyers tend to be concerned not so much with the historical development or changing scope of these norms—matters which would be of obvious interest to the criminologist—as with their conceptual structure and judicial interpretation in particular cases or sets of cases. Criminal lawyers are therefore also concerned with the doctrinal framework of 'general principles' within which interpretive legal practice and—though more tenuously—legislative development purportedly proceed (Ashworth 2003; Clarkson and Keating 2003; Williams 1983). The rules of evidence and procedure, which have an important bearing on the application and historical development of criminal law, tend to find only a small place in criminal law studies in the UK, and are often dealt with in specialist, optional courses or relegated to interstitial treatment in criminal justice or legal methods courses. Within degree courses in law in England and Wales, only criminal law is regarded as a 'core' part of the curriculum.

Whilst the organization of research conforms less rigidly to this division, it nonetheless bears a close relationship to the different areas of expertise claimed by scholars within the field. This partitioning of the intellectual terrain is, it should be noted, both historically and culturally specific. To Continental European eyes, the Anglo-American separation of criminal law and criminal procedure, and indeed of criminal law and sentencing, appears extraordinary (Cole *et al.* 1987; Fletcher 1978). And although a superficially similar division has characterized the British approach for much of the last century, the rationale underlying the three branches of 'criminal science' of the 1920s and 1930s was rather different from that underlying today's division (Radzinowicz and Turner 1945; Kenny 1952: ch. 1, Pt II).

What is the significance of the contemporary partition between the study of legal and of social constructions of crime; between criminal law on the one hand and criminology and criminal justice on the other? Is it not merely a common-sense division of labour based both on distinctive expertise and on the distinctive roles of legal and social factors in the construction of crime? While there is some truth in this, I would argue that the prevailing division obscures our view of certain crucially important issues. For example, criminological insights about patterns of 'deviance' pose important questions about the working of criminal justice institutions such as police and courts. The practice of legal interpretation takes place within a particular social context and in relation to criminal laws which are themselves the product of a political process which is relevant to their application and enforcement. Practices of punishment take place against the background of prevailing concerns about patterns of criminality (Reiner 2006), of attitudes to the vitality of social norms thought to be embodied in criminal law, and of beliefs about the legitimacy of state power. The problems of legitimation and coordination faced by systems of criminal law vary according to both the institutional frameworks within which criminal law is enforced—policing, prosecution, trials, penal practices—and the shifting range of social tasks which the criminal law is expected to fulfil. Furthermore, the very edifice of criminalization as a relatively discrete object of enquiry is porous, given that criminal justice practices exist alongside and relate in an intimate albeit complex way to a variety of other—political, economic, moral, psychiatric, religious, educational, familial—normative, labelling, and sanctioning practices (Lacey, Wells, and Quick 2003: ch. 1).

Whilst it would clearly be impossible to address all criminal justice concerns within a single research project or course, there is a real risk that questions which transcend the prevailing boundaries marking off the three areas may be lost from view. For example, the relevance of the political context or of particular features of the criminal process to the development of legal doctrine in a series of appeal cases may be excluded from a criminal law course, whilst criminal justice or criminology courses may ignore the bearing of legal developments upon practices of prosecution and punishment. In short, a legitimate focus on the issues raised both within particular disciplines and in relation to particular institutional practices may serve to obscure broader questions about the assumptions on which those disciplines and practices are based. What are lawyers' implicit ideas about the nature of crime and of offenders? What assumptions do criminologists make about the nature of criminal law? And who, within the prevailing division of intellectual labour, is to study these important matters?

CRIMINAL LAW

As I have already suggested, a certain discreteness of both subject matter and disciplinary framework is much more firmly established in relation to criminal law than in relation to the extra-legal processes contributing to the construction of crime which form the object of criminological and criminal justice enquiry. In this section, I shall focus specifically on the distinguishing features of criminal law—substantive and formal—so as to examine the degree to which these pretensions to disciplinary autonomy are justified. Of course, many criminal law scholars have concerned themselves with sociology and history and with questions about the criminal process: indeed, this socio-legal leaning has probably been more marked in criminal law than in other fields of legal scholarship over the last half century (Hall 1960; Packer 1969). The objection to socio-legal approaches to criminal law has been, however, that they underestimate or obscure the specificity of legal techniques and legal argumentation, reducing legal regulation to the exercise of political or economic power, and assuming legal decision-making to be explicable in terms of some crude set of personal, economic, or political causes. Furthermore, it has been argued that socio-legal scholars often ask the wrong kinds of questions about criminal law—questions which assume that law is to be judged in terms of its instrumental functions rather than its symbolic dimensions or its discrete logic. These problems are probably best exemplified by American Legal Realism and Chicago-style law and economics, reductive approaches in which legal decision-making is explained, respectively, in terms of judicial actors' policy preferences and their concern to maximize economic efficiency (Farmer 1995, 1996a; Nelken 1987b). In the context of this debate about the proper balance between autonomy and openness in criminal law scholarship, the development over the last fifteen years of 'critical' and historical approaches is worthy of particular attention (for a general review, see Nelken 1987a; Norrie 1992). For, as I shall try to show, they combine a focus on legal specificity without obscuring broader questions about the historical, political, and social conditions under which the apparently discrete and technical practices of modern criminal law flourish.

THE SUBSTANCE AND SCOPE OF CRIMINAL LAW: CONCEIVING 'CRIME'

One obvious reason why criminologists and criminal justice scholars might be interested in studies of criminal law would be to get a picture of the extent and shape of the formally articulated rules which in some sense provide the jumping-off point for all other criminal justice practices—crime prevention, reporting, investigation, prosecution, punishment. More than this, the criminal justice scholar might expect criminal lawyers to deliver some overall and coherent conception of the aims and functions of criminal law (Feinberg 1984–8): a conception which would explain or rationalize why the legal order deals with certain kinds of conduct as a criminal rather than a civil or private matter; as calling for state prosecution and punishment rather than privately initiated resolution. Why are some social harms dealt with by criminal law while others—equally costly or damaging—are not (Hillyard *et al.* 2004)? The social scientist would also be interested in the shifting boundaries of this overall conception, and in what it can tell us about the relationship between legal and popular conceptions of crime: she would attend to the changing contours of criminal law over time and space, the changing balance between different kinds of legal regulation and between legal and informal, social modes of governance, and the implications of these changes for our understanding of how societies are organized.

In pursuing these questions, the criminal justice scholar would not be entirely disappointed in criminal law commentaries. In almost all of them, she would be greeted with a discussion of the aims and functions of criminal law and of the rationale of punishment. From her understanding of criminal justice more generally, she would already be familiar with the way in which two rather different visions of the rationale of criminal law compete for dominance in most accounts (Lacey 2004). On the one hand, criminal law is understood—as distinct from civil law—as being concerned with *wrongdoing* in a quasi-moral sense. On this view, crime is conduct judged to be a sufficiently seriously violation of core social or individual interests or shared values that it is appropriate for the state to proscribe and punish its commission. This is a view which sits naturally with a retributive approach to punishment and with a strong emphasis on the symbolic, expressive dimensions of criminal justice. On the other hand, criminal law is understood in more neutrally instrumental terms as a regulatory system: as attaching costs, through sanctions, to certain kinds of conduct which it is in the overall public interest to reduce. This second view sits naturally with a deterrent or otherwise utilitarian view of punishment. The obvious question arises as to how these competing views are to be reconciled as rationalizations of contemporary criminal law.

Two attempted resolutions are of interest in this context. At a philosophical level, H. L. A. Hart's account, which builds on the liberal utilitarianism of J. S. Mill (Hart 1963, 1968; Mill 1859), argues that, while the general justifying aim of criminal law is a utilitarian one of crime reduction through deterrence, the state is only justified in invoking its coercive criminalizing power as against conduct for which an individual is responsible and which is harmful to others or (in Hart's modified, social-democratic version of Mill's 'harm principle), under certain conditions, to oneself. This account provides a less moralistic version of the nature of crime than is characteristic of the quasi-moral, retributive conception already discussed, while nonetheless providing an account of why criminal law is of special moral significance. It has difficulty, however, in generating an adequately specified concept of harm: does, for example the offence felt by people who disapprove of certain kinds of behaviour such as homosexual conduct or public displays of nudity count as 'harm'? Furthermore, this approach fails to ask an obvious—and crucially important—question for any social scientist: if the concept of 'harm' is neither fixed nor analytically robust, how are sociocultural notions of 'harm' constructed, and how do they influence criminal/legal constructions of harm (Harcourt 1999; Hillyard *et al.* 2004)?

In legal scholarship, the most common approach to reconciling the different aspects of criminalization consists in a division of the terrain of criminal law between the 'moral core' of 'real crime'—theft, homicide, assault, rape, and so on—and the 'quasi-criminal' 'regulatory offences'—licensing offences, driving offences, tax offences, pollution offences, and so on. In other words, it is accepted that criminal law has not one, but two rationales; and their coexistence is enabled by a functional differentiation between offences. This functional differentiation is then, so the argument goes, mapped on to legal doctrine. Again, however, this pragmatic reconciliation leaves many questions of interest to the social scientist unaddressed. How is the division between 'quasi-moral' and 'regulatory' crimes defined, and is the boundary a clear one? How does it change over time? Under what kinds of social, political, and institutional conditions does such a criminal law system emerge, and what broader governmental or ordering roles, if any, does it pursue? These are questions, however, in which contemporary criminal lawyers are relatively uninterested: as we shall see in the next section, their rationalization of criminal law moves on quickly from the sketchy substantive conceptions mentioned above to a more elaborated, technical account of the specific form which criminal liability must take.

The reason for this lack of focus on a substantive account of criminalization (Katz 2002) is relatively clear. In a system in which criminal law is regarded as a regulatory tool of government and in which (as in the UK) there are very weak constitutional constraints on what kinds of conduct can be criminally proscribed—a world in which everything from terrorism through dumping litter to licensing infractions and 'raves' can be criminalized—there is little that can be said by way of substantive rationalization of the nature of criminal law. This, however, is a contingent matter. If we look back to the legal commentaries of the mid-eighteenth century (Blackstone 1765–9) or even the late nineteenth century (Stephen 1883), we will find a richer and more confident assertion of a substantive rationale for criminal law: of the interests and values which criminal law sets out to express and protect. In Blackstone's Commentaries, the account is organized around groups of offences threatening these interests—offences against God and religion; offences against the state; offences against the person; offences against property. This works well enough for a very circumscribed system of criminal law. But over the last two hundred and fifty years the scope and functions of criminal law have increased dramatically. The expansion of criminal law's scope has entailed a fragmentation of its rationale and, as we shall see in the next section, has gone along with an intensification of focus, among legal commentaries, on the formal conditions of criminal liability. This change in the way in which criminal law is organized and thought about is of enormous significance to criminal justice scholars, because it gives us a real clue to the way in which criminal law resolves the changing legitimation and coordination problems thrown up by its environment (Lacey 2001a, 2001b).

THE CONCEPTUAL FRAMEWORK OF CRIMINAL LAW

Contemporary codes and commentaries on criminal law in both the common law and the civilian traditions tend to be organized around a core framework which sets out the general conditions under which liability may be established. This core framework is often known as the 'general part' or 'general principles' of criminal law—in other words, the set of rules and doctrines which apply across the whole terrain of criminal law rather than to specific offences. In the UK, this framework consists in four main elements: capacity, conduct, responsibility, and (absence of) defence.

1. *Capacity*: only those who share certain basic cognitive and volitional capacities are regarded as genuine subjects of criminal law. One might regard defences such as insanity as defining certain kinds of people as simply outwith the system of communication embodied by criminal law. Since law operates in terms of general standards, the line between criminal capacity and criminal incapacity is a relatively crude one from the point of view of other disciplines. For example, almost every criminal law system exempts from criminal liability people under a certain age, whatever their actual capacities.

2. *Conduct*: criminal conviction is founded, secondly, in a certain kind of conduct specified in the offence definition: appropriating another person's property in the case of theft; causing a person's death in the case of homicide; having sexual intercourse with a person without their consent in the case of rape; driving with a certain level of alcohol

in one's blood in the case of driving while intoxicated. Though there are exceptions in the UK's criminal law doctrine, it is generally asserted that mere thoughts, being of a certain status rather than doing an act, and, in the absence of a specific duty to act, omitting to do something rather than acting positively, are insufficient to found criminal liability.

3. *Responsibility/fault*: criminal liability is generally said to depend, thirdly, on the capable subject being in some sense responsible for or at fault in committing the conduct specified in the offence definition: we do not hold people liable, to put it crudely, for accidents. Responsibility or fault conditions generally consist of mental states or attitudes such as intention, recklessness, knowledge, belief, dishonesty, or negligence. To revert to the examples above, the relevant conditions consist in a dishonest intention permanently to deprive in the case of theft; an intention to kill or cause some less serious kind of harm or gross negligence in relation to these results in the case of homicide; recklessness or negligence as to the victim's lack of consent in the case of rape. The fourth example—driving while intoxicated—provides an exception to what is generally represented as the general principle that a discrete responsibility element must be proven by the prosecution: only the driving and the blood alcohol level need be established by the prosecution. Notwithstanding their 'exceptional' status, however, these offences of so-called 'strict' liability are in fact empirically dominant in English criminal law today. This division between offences of 'strict' liability and offences requiring proof of fault is the way in which the division between the 'quasi-moral' and 'instrumental/regulatory' terrains of criminal law is purportedly mapped on to legal doctrine. However, as the example of driving while intoxicated—an offence which thirty years ago was regarded as a quintessentially regulatory offence, yet which today carries a marked moral stigma—illustrates, this line is in fact far from clear.

4. *Defences*: Even where a capable subject has committed the relevant conduct with the requisite degree of fault, a range of defences may operate to preclude or mitigate his or her liability. For example, if the defendant has committed a theft while under a threat of violence, she may plead a defence of duress; if a person kills, intentionally, in order to defend himself against an immediate attack, he may plead self-defence; and if she kills under provocation, she may be convicted of a lesser degree of homicide. 'General defences' apply not only to crimes which require proof of responsibility but also to those of strict liability. Hence, for example, a person who drives while intoxicated because of duress, whether in the form of a threat or in the form of highly compelling circumstances, may be able to escape liability. Defences are often thought to fall into three main groups—*exemptions, justifications*, and *excuses*—each relating to the other three components of liability already mentioned. The defence of insanity, for example, arguably operates to recognize that the defendant's *incapacity exempts* him or her from the communications of criminal law; the defence of self-defence may be seen as amounting to a claim that the *conduct* in question was, in the circumstances, *justified*

and hence not the sort of *conduct* which criminal law sets out to proscribe; the defence of duress may be viewed as *excusing* the defendant on the basis that the conditions under which she formed the relevant *fault* condition—in cases of duress, this would generally be intention—are such that the usual inference of *responsibility* is blocked. The defences may be seen as fine-tuning, along contextualized and morally sensitive lines, the presumptive inferences of liability produced by the first three elements.

At one level, this conceptual framework is analytic: it simply provides a set of building blocks out of which legislators and lawyers construct criminal liability. On the other hand—as the description of the framework as a set of 'general principles' suggests—it contains an implicit set of assumptions about what makes the imposition of criminal liability legitimate. The ideas, for example, that there should be no punishment for mere thoughts, or that a defendant should not be convicted unless she was in some sense responsible for her conduct, or under circumstances in which some internal capacity or external circumstance deprived her of a fair opportunity to conform to the law, express a normative view of criminal law as not merely an institutionalized system of coercion but, rather, a system which is structured around certain principles of justice or morality. This normative aspect of the 'general part' of criminal law becomes yet clearer in the light of two broad procedural standards which characterize most modern systems. The first of these is the *principle of legality*: criminal law must be announced clearly to citizens in advance of its imposition. Only those who know the law in advance can be seen as having a fair opportunity to conform to it. Principles such as clarity and non-retroactivity are therefore central tenets of the liberal ideal of the rule of law. The second procedural doctrine is the *presumption of innocence*: a crime must be proven by the prosecution (generally the state, and hence far more powerful than the individual defendant) to a very high standard. Criminal law is therefore implicitly justified not only in terms of its role in proscribing, condemning, and, perhaps, reducing conduct which causes or risks a variety of harms, but also in treating its subjects with respect, as moral agents whose conduct must be assessed in terms of attitudes and intentions and not merely in terms of effects. And underlying this normative framework is a further set of assumptions about the nature of human conduct: about voluntariness, will, agency, capacity as the basis for genuine human personhood and hence responsibility (Hart 1968).

The various assumptions underlying the conceptual framework within which criminal liability is constructed should be of great interest to criminological and criminal justice scholars. For they give us insight into the processes of interpretation in the courtroom—one key site in the process of criminalization. They also provide some interesting points of both contrast and similarity when compared with the assumptions on the basis of which other practices within the criminal process are founded. Are the assumptions of responsible subjecthood which constitute the core of criminal law thinking the same as, or even consistent with, those which underpin the development of policing strategy, sentencing decision-making, probation practice, or prison regimes? If not, does it matter? And what does it signify?

'GENERAL PRINCIPLES' OF CRIMINAL LAW: A CRITICAL ASSESSMENT

The need to bring criminal justice and criminal law analyses into relation with one another is therefore clear. However, it is equally clear that criminal justice scholars ought to be wary of taking the 'general principles' of criminal law on lawyers' terms. For the fact is that the 'general principles of criminal law' are honoured, in many systems and certainly in the UK, as much in the breach as in the observance. The preponderance of criminal offences in fact derogates from these principles in some way: by imposing 'strict' liability without fault; by requiring proof of responsibility in relation only to certain components of the offence; or by modifying the prosecution's burden of proof by imposing evidential or, occasionally, legal burdens on the defence (Ashworth and Blake 1996; Tadros and Tierney 2004) The fact that a substantial number of these derogations occur in serious offences such as sexual, financial, and drug-related crime suggests that the 'general principles' are as much an ideological as an actual feature of criminal law's operations. In this respect, the criminal justice scholar will gain some enlightenment from the more critical genre of criminal law scholarship which has subjected the 'general principles' of criminal law to a searching examination.

Conventional criminal law scholars, as we have seen, generally provide a brief résumé of the moral/retributive, regulatory/deterrent aspects of criminal justice. They go on to give a terse statement of the competing concerns of fairness and social protection, due process, and crime control which are taken to inform the development and implementation of criminal law in liberal societies. From this point on, they take the idea of 'crimes' as given by acts of law-creation. In this way both political and criminological issues are quietly removed from the legal agenda. In contrast, critical criminal lawyers assume that the power and meaning of criminal laws depend on a more complex set of processes and underlying factors than the mere positing of prohibitory norms to be enforced according to a particular procedure. Most obviously, they assume that the influences of political and economic power permeate not only the statutory construction of crime but also the practice of doctrinal interpretation. Yet their view is not the reductive, instrumental one of Realism or the Chicago School. Rather, critical criminal lawyers argue that judicial practice is shaped by tensions between competing values whose power infuses all social practices, and which cannot be reconciled by either legislative reform or feats of rationalizing interpretation. From this perspective, further links between the legal and social construction of crime appear. For it seems, a priori, likely that the evaluative and pragmatic tensions which shape the development of criminal law will also manifest themselves, albeit to different degrees and in different ways, in other criminal justice practices.

The primary aim of early critical criminal law scholarship was to develop an internal or 'immanent' critique of the doctrinal framework within which different areas of law have been taken to be organized. Taking a close interest in the way in which criminal liability is constructed within legal discourse, critical scholars took as their focus the structure of 'general principles' which are usually taken to underpin criminal law in liberal societies. These included not only the liberal ideals about the fair terms under which criminal punishment may be imposed upon an individual agent, which we considered above, but also the aspirations of neutrality, objectivity, and determinacy of legal method which are associated with the rule of law (Norrie 2001). For example, Kelman's work scrutinized the basis of the responsibility/fault doctrine which purports to structure and justify the attribution of criminal responsibility to the free individual via the employment of standards of fault such as intent and recklessness. He showed that fault requirements veer in an unprincipled way between 'subjective' standards in which attributions of responsibility depend on what the defendant actually intended or contemplated and 'objective' standards such as negligence which impute to the defendant the state of mind of the 'reasonable man'. Following from this, Kelman emphasized the fact that criminal law doctrine evinces no consistent commitment to either a free-will or a determinist model of human behaviour (Kelman 1981).

Furthermore, Kelman and others demonstrated the manipulability of the generally accepted doctrinal framework according to which criminal liability is constructed in terms of the four elements discussed above; capacity, conduct, responsibility or fault, and absence of defence. For example, the issue of mistake could be conceptualized as a matter pertaining to the existence of the conduct or fault elements of a crime or to the existence of a defence (Lacey, Wells, and Quick 2003: ch. 1). A person who assaults another person in the mistaken belief that that other person is in the process of committing an assault on a third party could, in other words, be regarded as having a defence (of mistaken-self defence), or as lacking the conduct (no 'unlawful' act), or (in certain circumstances) fault/responsibility (no relevant intention) elements of a crime. Since these conceptualizations sometimes affect the outcome of the legal analysis, this entails that doctrinal rules are not as determinate as the conventional theory of legal reasoning assumes. Moreover, the outcome of legal reasoning is contingent upon factors such as the time frame within which the alleged offence was set. For example, whether or not a person is regarded as negligent, in the sense of having failed to reach a reasonable standard of care or awareness, may depend on what range of conduct the court is able to examine. What appears an unreasonable lapse judged in itself may look more reasonable if evidence about its history can be admitted. This broadening of the time frame or context is precisely what the defences often effect. Yet the influence of the framing process is not acknowledged within the doctrinal structure, which accordingly fails to regulate judicial interpretation in the way which is generally supposed.

The critical enterprise here is to hold criminal law up to scrutiny in terms of the standards which it professes to instantiate, and, in doing so, to reveal that, far from consisting in a clear, determinate set of norms, based on a coherent set of 'general principles', it rather exemplifies a contradictory and conflicting set of approaches which are obscured by the superficial coherence and determinacy of legal reasoning. By scrutinizing carefully the form which criminal legal reasoning takes, it becomes possible to reveal that practice as having important ideological dimensions, rationalizing and legitimating a system which serves a variety of powerful interests by representing criminal law as a technical and apolitical sphere of judgement (Norrie 2001).

An important part of this process is the (re)reading of cases not merely as exercises in formal legal analysis but also as texts whose rhetorical structure is at least as important as their superficial legal content (Goodrich 1986). In this kind of reading, critical scholars emphasize the significant symbolic aspect of the power of criminal law, along with the implicit yet powerful images of wrongdoing and rightful conduct, normal and abnormal subjects, guilt and innocence which legal discourse draws upon and produces (Lacey 1993).

RELATING FORM TO SUBSTANCE: PERSPECTIVES FROM HISTORY AND THE SOCIAL SCIENCES

The early critical focus on the intricacies of doctrinal rationalization and the exposure of conflicts which such rationalization obscures has, however, gradually been supplemented by a further set of questions suggested by the process of immanent critique. If critical criminal law was not to remain a set of observations about the apparent irrationality of legal doctrine, the question of the deeper logics underpinning legal discourse had to be addressed (Norrie 2001). Hence questions about the broad socio-political conditions under which a particular doctrinal framework arises and 'works', about the historical conditions of existence of particular doctrinal systems of classification (taken as 'given' within conventional scholarship), and about the relationship between criminal law's form and its substantive regulatory project, have begun to claim the attention of criminal law scholars (Norrie 1992; Lacey 1998a, 2001a, 2001b). This development, which might be conceptualized as 'external' critique, illuminates some important links between criminal law scholarship and socio-legal and sociological work on the criminal process. For as critical scholars have sought to understand the deeper political and historical dynamics underpinning the logical defects of criminal law doctrine, new issues began to force themselves on to the research agenda. These include questions about the ways in which a focus on certain portions of substantive criminal law, and a lack of attention to others—notably the so-called 'regulatory' offences—serves to perpetuate the myth of coherent 'general principles', and about the ways in which this selectivity relates to prevailing understandings of what constitutes 'real crime', the imperatives of 'law and order' politics, and the deeper factors underpinning the governmental and judicial need to represent criminal law as just and as politically 'neutral' (Reiner 2006). They also include questions about the way in which a certain model of criminal procedure—that of trial by jury—plays a legitimating role which can only be maintained by diverting attention away from the exceptional nature of jury trials and the prevalence of lay justice, diversion from the criminal process, and practices such as plea-bargaining (McConville and Mirsky 2005).

Whilst earlier examples of critical criminal law scholarship were primarily concerned with the form of criminal reasoning, later examples have begun to examine the substantive patterns of criminal legislation and judicial interpretation, and the relationship between shifts in these frontiers of criminality and the broader social meaning of the practice of criminal justice (Loveland 1995). Striking examples include the development of criminal law in the area of serious fraud (Weait 1995) and the debate about homicide doctrine following a number of unsuccessful 'corporate manslaughter' prosecutions consequent upon incidents which would until recently have been regarded as fatal 'accidents' (Tombs and Hillyard 2004; Wells 1995, 2001). Similarly, socio-legal work on patterns of enforcement in the so-called 'regulatory' offences have revealed that, in the context of limited resources, specialist regulatory enforcement agencies often fall back on criminal law-like notions of fault such as negligence or recklessness in selecting cases for prosecution—hence disrupting the doctrinal distinction between regulatory and fault-based offences, between 'real' crime and 'quasi'-crime discussed above (Richardson 1987).

Further insight can be achieved by taking a longer-term, historical perspective on the substantive development of criminal law and of the institutional framework within which it is interpreted and enforced. As we noted above, two hundred years ago, English criminal law was far less extensive than it is today, and was more readily rationalized in terms of a set of core interests and values. Of course, this does not mean that there was no social or value conflict, or that criminal law was not already being used for what today we would think of as 'regulatory' purposes. But with rapid urbanization and industrialization in the early nineteenth century, and with the growth of the nation state's governmental capacities and ambitions, the conditions under which criminal law operated changed markedly (Lacey 2001a). Social mobility and fragmentation also had direct implications for the environment which shaped the extent of social reliance on criminal law, as opposed to informal or private dispute resolution. The first institutional responses to these developments were the reforms of the policing, prosecution, trial, and penal processes of the nineteenth century (Langbein 2003; Lacey 2001b), with a professionalization of enforcement and legal practice and a regularization of penal practice consonant with an emerging, rationalist, modernist, and, potentially, liberal conception of the rationale of criminal law (Dubber 2005). In the UK, the obvious counterpart in the substantive law—full-scale codification—never materialized. But the successive attempts at codification, along with the changing conditions under which criminal trials went forward—a developed set of rules of evidence, legal representation of defendants, the slow emergence of an appellate system—conduced to the judicial and scholarly articulation of more general principles of criminal law (Smith 1998). Such general principles were important not only in rationalizing criminal law power in the context of an increase in democratic sentiments and hence within an emerging liberal understanding of the legitimation problems of the system, but also—crucially—in focusing the legitimation narrative on the *form* of criminal law rather than its *substance*, hence managing the substantive fragmentation and diversification of criminal law occasioned by its rapid expansion. Furthermore, these doctrinal developments spoke to the resolution of the changing problems of gathering and validating knowledge—the facts on the basis of which a criminal conviction is arrived at via the application of legal norms—in an increasingly centralized system in which reliance on the local knowledge of jurors and justices of the peace, characteristic of the early modern criminal law, was no longer feasible.

One striking feature which illustrates further connections between criminal law developments and broader social and intellectual developments here is the gradual formalization of principles of criminal responsibility around mental concepts such as intention, knowledge, belief, and recklessness, as opposed to the overtly evaluative concepts such as malice and wilfulness which had characterized the common law for centuries (Binder 2002; Horder 1997). This development played a crucial role in criminal law's legitimation, because it shifted the focus of justified liability from an overt evaluation (malice) to a factual, psychological state (intention), hence (apparently) distancing controversial moral and political judgements from the courtroom. This shift from older ideas of 'fault' to a more empirically based conception of 'responsibility' was made possible by the growth of what we would now call psychology, itself premised on a certain understanding of the mind-body distinction and of the idea of the mental as a discrete object of social knowledge. But the legal development could not have occurred had it not been for the further belief that the factual question of what is going on in someone's mind when he or she is acting can be an object of investigation and indeed proof in a criminal court (Smith 1981). This in turn depended on institutional developments in the trial process, and particularly in the law of evidence (Lacey 2001b).

These brief examples suggest that the full implications of legal critique can only be realized in the context of a broader set of historical, political, and social questions about the conditions of existence and efficacy of particular doctrinal arrangements. These questions are not legal questions, nor do they detract from the importance of a specifically legal critique. What they do is to give that critique a greater significance than it would otherwise have, both by relating it to a wider set of social-theoretic questions and by suggesting links with normative thinking about the conditions under which the criminal process might operate in less unjust, undemocratic, and oppressive ways. In this sense criminal law scholarship has begun to open up a new agenda for cross-institutional and interdisciplinary study.

CONTEXTUALIZING CRIMINAL LAW: CRIMINOLOGICAL PERSPECTIVES

It follows from what has been said in the last section that criminological thinking, broadly understood, brings important insights to the study of criminal law. Since the specific practices of both legislation and legal interpretation take place within the context of broader social processes which shape not only the range and definition of criminal laws but also the particular subjects in relation to which the courts apply their legal techniques, that context is an important factor in understanding the dynamics of legal interpretation. Ideas and principles which are central to criminal law doctrine and its broader accompanying framework, the ideal of the rule of law, begin to take on a different colour once we appreciate, as criminology helps us to do, the partiality and selectivity of their enforcement.

As an overtly coercive state practice within societies which think of themselves as liberal—as composed of self-determining individuals whose rights and freedoms must be respected—criminal law confronts a serious challenge of legitimation. The challenge is accentuated by the increasing scope and diversifying functions which characterize the development of criminal law since the early nineteenth century, and by the value pluralism and social conflict which characterize late modern societies (Garland 2001; Young 1999). Criminal law seeks to meet this challenge by making a number of normative claims which relate both to the substance of legal norms and to the process through which they are enforced. In relation to the former, criminal law legitimates itself in two main ways. First, it does so by appealing to the normative, purportedly 'objective' status of the standards which it applies. Yet, as we have seen, this poses problems of reconciliation with both the vast range of actual criminal laws and the political manipulation of the frontiers of criminality by legislative changes and executive decisions which criminalize hitherto lawful activities or remove criminal sanctions from formerly prohibited conduct. Secondly, criminal law legitimates itself by appealing to the basis of its standards in common, shared understandings or commitments. This is difficult to reconcile with pervasive social conflict in relation to the existence or interpretation of particular criminal norms. Instructive contemporary examples include not only obvious disagreements about the propriety of criminalizing certain forms of sexual behaviour and commercial conduct but even dissensus about the proper standard of fault to be applied in the key offence of homicide (Lacey 1993; Lacey, Wells, and Quick 2003: ch. 6).

In relation to procedure and enforcement, criminal law legitimates itself as the fair and even-handed application of rules to subjects conceptualized in terms of their formal capacities for understanding and self-control. Yet how is this claim to be reconciled with the statistics on disparate patterns of enforcement along lines of race or ethnicity, gender, socio-economic status, age, place of residence? Criminal law claims legitimacy by appealing to the detached and even-handed application of its standards to all who come before it. How is this claim to be reconciled with the pervasiveness of practices such as plea-bargaining, which are driven by the relative power relations of particular actors within the process and by managerialist concerns about the cost-efficient disposal of cases? Criminal law prides itself on its application of a standard of proof beyond reasonable doubt and on its tailoring of liability requirements to the particular individual before the court. How is this to be reconciled with extensive plea-bargaining, with the indeterminacy of fault/responsibility standards, or with reverse burdens of proof? Evidently, these legitimating strategies are heavily dependent on criminal law's capacity to sustain the aura of its separateness from the politics and practicalities of the criminal process. Many principles which are central to the 'common sense' of doctrinal criminal law come to look somewhat fragile as that separateness is eroded by a little knowledge of criminal justice.

THE DOCTRINAL STRUCTURE OF CRIMINAL LAW: QUESTIONS FOR THE SOCIAL SCIENCES

The idea that criminological insight can sharpen the perspective of criminal lawyers will probably be accepted by anyone who has chosen to study criminology. The converse idea that criminologists or students of criminal justice ought to concern themselves with criminal law may be less intellectually digestible. For some students of criminology this has to do with a (not entirely unjustified) scepticism about the relative importance of law in shaping social practices of labelling and punishment. Yet criminal law has a discrete significance as an interpretive practice which plays a central role in the legitimation of the state's penal power. I shall suggest, therefore, that much is to be gained from examining the specificities of criminal law from a socio-legal or regulatory point of view.

First, the critical criminal lawyer's focus on shifting boundaries of criminal law provides one important part of the broader criminal justice jigsaw. Whilst changes in the legislative content of criminal law are themselves highly significant as both political and legal events, the subsequent process of judicial interpretation is what shapes both the meaning and (to some degree) the social efficacy of new criminal laws. Judicial interpretations which, for example, render criminal laws very difficult to enforce will have both knock-on effects for future prosecution policy and implications for the symbolic meaning of the relevant law. An excellent example is the law on incitement to racial hatred, the strict interpretation of which has arguably rendered it virtually unenforceable and which is regarded by some as a de facto legitimation of racial abuse (Fitzpatrick 1987). Furthermore, long-standing aspects of the doctrinal framework of criminal law may facilitate or inhibit the movement of the boundaries of criminality in directions aspired to by political institutions and other groupings. One good example here is the inchoate move towards imposing criminal liability on corporations—a development which continues to be inhibited by the association of the 'mens rea' framework with the mental states of individual human agents (Wells 2001).

Secondly, the critical criminal lawyer's focus on the specificities of legal reasoning sheds light on the ways in which power at one stage of the criminal process is exercised and legitimated. Notwithstanding their relative infrequency, trial by jury and criminal appeals play a central role in the legitimation of the entire criminal process (Duff *et al.* 2004). A close appreciation of how these stages work is therefore of central importance to any integrated understanding of criminal justice. Critical scholarship has generated important insights into the ways in which the power of law depends on the capacity of legal discourse to construct itself as generating 'truths' which are impervious to critical scrutiny from other perspectives (Smart 1989). This in turn sheds light on processes by which other knowledges introduced as evidence in criminal trials—sociological or psychological knowledges, for example—are subtly invalidated or modified in the course of 'translation' into the terms of legal discourse. A good example here is the slow and partial legal recognition of evidence about the effects of long-term violence in 'domestic' homicide cases. Whilst recent cases have begun to accept such evidence as relevant, its force was initially limited by the need to shape it to fit the conceptual straitjackets of legal defences such as provocation, self-defence, and diminished responsibility (Lacey 1998b: ch. 7; Lacey, Wells, and Quick 2003: ch. 6). For instance, the legal requirement that, to qualify as provocation or self-defence, a violent response must follow immediately upon provocative or threatening conduct posed difficulties in several cases in which defendants (most of them women) who have been subject to 'domestic' violence kill their abusers, yet in which there was no immediate relation between the ultimate killing and a particular attack (Nicolson and Bibbings 2000: Pt II; Renteln 2004). The result is that defence lawyers were forced to reconstruct the relevant evidence in psychiatric terms so as to invoke a diminished responsibility defence which misrepresented the defendant's position. Such transformations of non-legal knowledges in the legal process have generally been invisible to conventional legal analysis and until recently received only partial recognition and understanding in socio-legal scholarship.

This is not to imply a reductive, sociological reading of the criminal trial or the criminal appeal: nor is it, conversely, to deny the importance of interpretive questions about the meaning of the rituals and architecture of the trial as a public event. It is rather to assert that the images of subject and society, of guilt and innocence, of responsibility and non-responsibility, of the autonomy and independence of legal power and of the objectivity and political neutrality of judgement which are produced within legal reasoning are discrete objects of criminal justice knowledge. Whilst the ultimate direction of my argument is that these legal specificities have meanings which are systematically obscured by the structure of legal doctrine, these meanings cannot be grasped without a close analysis of the practices of legal argumentation themselves, along with their historical development and place within particular professional institutions. Hence the critical criminal lawyer's approach of taking the doctrinal framework seriously, but of simultaneously reading it as a clue to broader sociopolitical factors, sheds light on matters of central concern to the criminologist.

Thirdly, historical shifts in the patterns of 'general principles' which purportedly structure legal doctrine, and indeed in the degree of insistence on any such structure, are themselves significant from a criminological point of view. Let us take the fact that today's focus on fault/responsibility as the central doctrinal problem in legitimizing criminal liability emerged only during the nineteenth century and reached its current predominance only in the second half of the twentieth century (Lacey 1998a). Before this, the organizing framework for doctrine was focused on the types of conduct proscribed rather than the basis on which individuals could fairly be held responsible for that conduct. This shift relates to a number of social developments of direct relevance to criminalization: a changing conception of the subject as an individual and of his or her relation to the polity and to government (Wiener 1990); a shifting view of the legitimation problems posed by the criminal justice system occasioned by, among other things, the diffusion of liberal-democratic expectations (Lacey 2001a, 2001b); a changing view of the role of criminal law as one form of social ordering among others, the latter driven by significant transformations in the shape and variety of criminal procedure over the last one hundred and fifty years (Farmer 1996b: ch. 3). Whilst these developments have been central to the social history of crime, and relate directly to the shift from substance to form in the rationalization of criminal law (Norrie 2001), their significance and its relationship with changes in the organizing framework of criminal law doctrine have largely been ignored. Hence a promising avenue of enquiry into the developing nature of crime and criminal justice has been closed off by the current organization of disciplines.

Finally, critical criminal law scholarship generates a finely tuned analysis of the shape of particular criminal laws and their interpretation over time. From a criminological or criminal justice point of view, it is all too easy to take 'criminal law' as a unitary, undifferentiated body of norms which are straightforwardly applied by the courts. Yet a close reading of cases and statutes reveals an enormous diversity among criminal laws: in terms of the style of their drafting; their scope; their construction of their subjects and objects; their assumptions about responsibility; their procedural requirements. Careful microlevel analysis of legal discourse illuminates assumptions about human nature, and about the status of various kinds of conduct, which structure legal reasoning yet which may not appear on the face of legal arrangements. Good examples are the close feminist readings of criminal laws dealing with sexual offences, and with rape in particular (Temkin 1987, 2000; Lacey, Wells, and Quick 2003: ch. 5; Lacey 1998b: ch. 4; Duncan 1996; Zedner 1995), which reveal a troubling set of assumptions about male and female sexuality and about the reliability of female witnesses. Similarly, the readings of criminal law's construction of homosexuality within queer legal theory (Moran 1996; Stychin 1995) reveal a situation which is substantially at odds with the (relatively) liberal approach which appears on the surface of criminal laws. And critical readings of the property offences have generated a wealth of insights about their assumptions about honesty and propriety, their construction of the fragile lines between 'enterprise' and 'dishonesty', and the ways in which this construction shifts as between different kinds of property offence (Lacey, Wells, and Quick 2003: ch. 4; Hall 1952). Such analysis of individual criminal laws or areas of criminal law generates an enormous amount of material which can illuminate the broad social meaning of criminalization. It also reveals a multidirectional process in which both legislature and courts are involved in reflecting, interpreting, and shaping the social attitudes and norms upon which the efficacy and legitimacy of criminal justice depends.

FROM CRITICAL CRIMINAL LAW TO CRIMINALIZATION

My suggestion, then, is that criminology, broadly understood, and criminal law scholarship of a critical temper are complementary albeit distinctive tasks within the intellectual enterprise of working towards an understanding of the diverse social practices associated with criminal justice. I have argued that the term 'criminalization' constitutes an appropriate conceptual framework within which to gather together the constellation of social practices which form the subject matter of criminal law on the one hand and criminal justice and criminological studies on the other (Lacey 2004; Farmer 1996a). Escaping the notion of crimes as 'given', the idea of criminalization captures the dynamic nature of the field as a set of interlocking practices in which the moments of 'defining' and 'responding to' crime can rarely be completely distinguished and in which legal and social (extra-legal) constructions of crime constantly interact. It accommodates the full range of institutions within which those practices take shape and the disciplines which might be brought to bear upon their analysis; it allows the instrumental and symbolic aspects of the field to be addressed, as well as encompassing empirical, interpretive, and normative projects. It embraces questions about offenders and victims, individuals and collectivities, state and society.

Within the framework of criminalization, we may accommodate the relevant practices of a variety of social actors and institutions: citizens, the media, the police, prosecution agencies, courts, judges and lawyers, social workers, probation officers, and those working in the penal and mental health systems, legislators, and members of the executive. We can also acknowledge the relevance of a wide variety of disciplines to the analysis of these institutions: sociology, psychology, political science, economics, legal studies, moral and political philosophy, and anthropology, to name only the most obvious. This we can do without collapsing the study of criminalization into a chaotic mass which escapes rigorous analysis, and without falling prey to fantasies about the possibility of a unitary synthesis of different approaches. Doubtless the study of criminalization is less intellectually tidy than the all-encompassing 'theories of criminal justice' which have been academically fashionable since the 1960s (Hall 1960; Packer 1968; Gross 1979). This seems an eminently worthwhile sacrifice if it enables us to define a field of scholarship which is sufficiently open to identify the intersecting issues which, as I argued earlier, are all too often lost from view in the prevailing division of labour within the field.

■ SELECTED FURTHER READING

Readers interested in the debate about 'critical criminal law' should consult the important early papers by Mark Kelman, 'Interpretive Construction in the Substantive Criminal Law', *Stanford Law Review* 33(4): 591–673 (1981) and David Nelken, 'Critical Criminal Law', *Journal of Law and Society*, 14(1): 105–17 (1987). Alan Norrie's *Crime, Reason and History*, 2nd edn, London: Butterworths, 2001, provides an extended application of critical method to criminal law, and pushes the critical approach forward by exploring the historical context in which criminal law doctrine has developed (see in particular ch. 1) and the relationship between criminal law doctrine and sentencing practice (see ch. 10). An assessment of the relationship between developments in political culture, criminal justice institutions, and criminal law doctrine is attempted in Nicola Lacey's 'In Search of the Responsible Subject', *Modern Law Review*,

64(3): 350–71 (2001) and 'Responsibility and Modernity in Criminal Law,' *Journal of Political Philosophy* 9(3): 249–77 (2001).

The relationship between questions of criminal law and those of criminal justice is explored in greater detail in Nicola Lacey, Celia Wells, and Oliver Quick (2003), *Reconstructing Criminal Law*, 3rd edn, Cambridge: Cambridge University Press, ch. 1; Simon Bronitt and Bernadette McSherry (2005), *Principles of Criminal Law*, 2nd edn, Pyrmont, N.S.W.: Law Book Company; Nicola Lacey, 'Criminalisation as Regulation', in C. Parker, C. Scott, N. Lacey, and J. Braithwaite (eds) (2004), *Regulating Law*, Oxford: Oxford University Press, 144–67; and Donald Nicolson and Lois Bibbings (eds) (2000), *Feminist Perspectives on Criminal Law*, London: Cavendish. Lindsay Farmer's *Criminal Law, Tradition and Legal Order*, Cambridge: Cambridge University Press, 1996, provides another useful exposition of critical method in the criminal law field, and a fascinating case study of the interaction between national politics, criminal law and criminal procedure in nineteenth-century Scotland: see in particular chs 1 and 3.

■ REFERENCES

ASHWORTH, A (2003), *Principles of Criminal Law*, 4th edn, Oxford: Clarendon Press.

—— (2005), *Sentencing and Criminal Justice*, 4th edn Cambridge: Cambridge University Press.

—— and BLAKE, M. (1996), 'The Presumption of Innocence in English Criminal Law', *Criminal Law Review*, 306–17.

—— and REDMAYNE, M. (2005), *The Criminal Process: An Evaluative Study*, 3rd edn, Oxford: Oxford University Press.

BLACKSTONE, W. (1765–9), *Commentaries on the Laws of England*, Chicago: University of Chicago Press, 1979.

BINDER, G. (2002), 'The Rhetoric of Motive and Intent', *Buffalo Criminal Law Review*, 1–96.

BRONITT, S., and MCSHERRY, B. (1995), *Principles of Criminal Law*, Oxford: Clarendon Press.

—— and —— (2005), *Principles of Criminal Law*, 2nd edn, Pyrmont, N.S.W.: Law Book Company.

CLARKSON, C., and KEATING, H. (2003), *Criminal Law: Text and Materials*, 5th edn, London: Sweet & Maxwell.

COLE, G. F., FRANKOWSKI, S. J., and GERTZ, M. G. (eds) (1987), *Criminal Justice Systems: A Comparative Survey*, 2nd edn, London: Sage.

DUBBER, M. D. (2005), *The Police Power*, New York: Columbia University Press.

DUFF, A., FARMER, L., MARSHALL, S., and TADROS, V. (eds) (2004), *The Trial on Trial: Truth and Due Process*, Oxford: Hart Publishing.

DUNCAN, S., UNCAN, S. (1996), 'The Mirror Tells its Tale: Constructions of Gender in Criminal Law', in A. Bottomley (ed.), *Feminist Perspectives on the Foundational Subjects of Law*, 73, London: Cavendish, 73.

FARMER, L. (1995), 'Bringing Cinderella to the Ball: Teaching Criminal Law in Context', *Modern Law Review*, 58(5): 756–66.

—— (1996a), 'The Obsession with Definition', *Social and Legal Studies* 5:57.

—— (1996b), *Criminal Law, Tradition and Legal Order*, Cambridge: Cambridge University Press.

FEINBERG, J. (1984–8), *The Moral Limits of the Criminal Law*, Oxford and New York: Oxford University Press.

FITZPATRICK, P. (1987), 'Racism and the Innocence of Law', *Journal of Law and Society*, 14(1): 119–32.

FLETCHER, G. (1978), *Rethinking Criminal Law*, Boston and Toronto: Little, Brown & Co.

GARLAND, D. (2001), *The Culture of Control*, Oxford: Oxford University Press.

GOODRICH, P. (1986), *Reading the Law*, Oxford: Blackwell.

GROSS, H. (1979), *A Theory of Criminal Justice*, Oxford: Oxford University Press.

HALL, J. (1952), *Theft, Law and Society*, New York: Bobbs-Merrill.

—— (1960), *General Principles of Criminal Law*, 2nd edn, Indianapolis and New York: Bobbs-Merrill.

HARCOURT, B. (1999), 'The Collapse of the Harm Principle', *Journal of Criminal Law and Criminology*, 90: 109–94.

HART, H. L. A. (1963), *Law, Liberty and Morality*, Oxford: Oxford University Press.

—— (1968), *Punishment and Responsibility*, Oxford: Clarendon Press.

HILLYARD, P., PANTAZIS, C., TOMBS S., and GORDON, D. (eds) (2004), *Beyond Criminology: Taking Harm Seriously*, London: Pluto Press.

HORDER, J. (1997), 'Two Histories and Four Hidden Principles of Mens Rea', *Law Quarterly Review* 113: 95–119.

KATZ, L. (2002), 'Villainy and Felony: A Problem Concerning Criminalization', *Buffalo Criminal Law Review*, 6: 451.

KELMAN, M. (1981), 'Interpretive Construction in the Substantive Criminal Law', *Stanford Law Review* 33(4): 591–673.

KENNY, C. S. (1952), *Outlines of Criminal Law*, 16th edn, ed. J. W. C. Turner, Cambridge: Cambridge University Press.

LACEY, N. (1993), 'A Clear Concept of Intention: Elusive or Illusory', *Modern Law Review*, 58(5): 692–5.

—— (1995), 'Contingency and Criminalisation', in I. Loveland (ed.), *Frontiers of Criminality*, Ch. 1.

—— (1998a), 'Contingency, Coherence and Conceptualism: Reflections on the Encounter between 'Critique' and 'Philosophy of the Criminal Law', in A. Duff (ed.), *Philosophy and the Criminal Law*, Cambridge: Cambridge University Press.

—— (1998b), *Unspeakable Subjects: Feminist Essays in Legal and Social Theory*, Oxford: Hart.

—— (2001a), 'In Search of the Responsible Subject', *Modern Law Review*, 64(3): 350–71.

—— (2001b), 'Responsibility and Modernity in Criminal Law', *Journal of Political Philosophy* 9(3): 249–77.

—— (2004), 'Criminalisation as Regulation: The Role of Criminal Law', in C. Parker, C. Scott, N. Lacey, and J. Braithwaite (eds), *Regulating Law*, 144–67, Oxford: Oxford University Press.

—— (2006a), 'Analytical Jurisprudence versus Descriptive Sociology Revisited', *University of Texas Law Review*, 84(4): 945–82.

—— (2006b), 'Criminal Justice', in R. E. Goodin, P. Pettit, and T. Pogge (eds), *Companion to Contemporary Political Philosophy*, Oxford: Blackwell.

—— WELLS, C. and QUICK, O. (2003), *Reconstructing Criminal Law: Critical Perspectives on Crime and the Criminal Process*, 3rd edn, Cambridge: Cambridge University Press.

LANGBEIN, J. (2003), *The Origins of Adversary Criminal Trial*, Oxford: Oxford University Press.

LOVELAND, I. (ed.), (1995), *Frontiers of Criminality*, London: Sweet & Maxwell.

MCCONVILLE, M., and MIRSKY, C. L. (2005), *Jury Trials and Plea-Bargaining: A True History*, Oxford: Hart.

MILL, J. S. (1859), *On Liberty*, Harmondsworth, Penguin, 1974.

MORAN, L. (1996), *The Homosexual(ity) of Law*, London: Routledge.

NELKEN, D. (1987a), 'Critical Criminal Law', *Journal of Law and Society*, 14(1): 105–17.

—— (1987b), 'Criminal Law and Criminal Justice: Some notes on their irrelation', in I. Dennis (ed.), 139 *Criminal Law and Justice*, London: Sweet & Maxwell.

NICOLSON, D., and BIBBINGS L. (eds), (2000), *Feminist Perspectives on Criminal Law*, London: Cavendish.

NORRIE, A. (1992), 'Criminal Law', in I. Griggs Spall and P. Ireland (eds), *The Critical Lawyer's Handbook*, 76, London: Pluto Press.

—— (2001), *Crime, Reason and History*, 2nd edn, London: Butterworths.

PACKER, H. (1969), *The Limits of the Criminal Sanction*, Stanford, Cal.: Stanford University Press.

RADZINOWICZ, L., and TURNER, J. W. C. (1945), 'The Meaning and Scope of Criminal Science', in Radzinowicz and Turner (eds), *The Modern Approach to Criminal Law*, Cambridge: Cambridge University Press.

REINER, R. (2006), 'Beyond Risk: A Lament for a Social Democratic Criminology', in T. Newburn and P. Rock (eds), *The Politics of Crime Control*, Oxford: Clarendon Press.

RENTELN, A. D. (2004), *The Cultural Defence*, New York: Oxford University Press.

RICHARDSON, G. (1987), 'Strict Liability for Regulatory Crime: the Empirical Research', *Criminal Law Review*, 295–306.

ROBINSON, P. H. (1997), *Structure and Function in Criminal Law*, Oxford: Clarendon Press.

SMART, C. (1989), *Feminism and the Power of Law*, London: Routledge.

—— (1995), *Law, Crime and Sexuality*, London: Sage.

SMITH, K. J. M. (1998), *Lawyers, Legislators and Theorists*, Oxford: Clarendon Press.

SMITH, R. (1981), *Trial by Medicine*, Edinburgh: Edinburgh University Press.

STEPHEN, J. F. (1883), *A History of the Criminal Law of England*, London: Macmillan.

STYCHIN, C. (1995), *Law's Desire*, London and New York: Routledge.

SUMNER, C. (1994), *The Sociology of Deviance: An Obituary*, Buckingham: Open University Press.

TADROS, V., and TIERNEY, S. (2004), 'The Presumption of Innocence and the Human Rights Act', *Modern Law Review*, 67(3): 402–34.

TAMANAHA, B. (2001), *A General Jurisprudence of Law and Society*, Oxford: Clarendon Press.

TEMKIN, J. (1987), *Rape and the Legal Process*, London: Sweet & Maxwell.

—— (2000), 'Prosecuting and Defending Rape: Perspectives from the Bar', *Journal of Law and Society*, 27(2): 219–48.

TOMBS, S., and HILLYARD, P. (2004), 'Towards a political economy of harm: states, corporations and the production of inequality', in Hillyard *et al.* (eds), *Beyond Criminality*, 30–54.

WEAIT, M. (1995), 'The Serious Fraud Office: Nightmares (and Pipe Dreams) on Elm Street', in Loveland (ed.), *Frontiers of Criminality*, ch. 4.

WELLS, C. (1995), 'Cry in the Dark: Corporate Manslaughter and Cultural Meaning', in Loveland (ed.), *Frontiers of Criminality*, ch. 5.

—— (2001), *Corporations and Criminal Responsibility*, 2nd edn, Oxford: Clarendon Press.

WIENER, M. (1990), *Reconstructing the Criminal: Culture, Law and Policy in England, 1830–1914*, Cambridge: Cambridge University Press.

WILLIAMS, G. (1983), *A Textbook of Criminal Law*, 2nd edn, London: Stevens.

YOUNG, J. (1999), *The Exclusive Society*, London: Sage.

ZEDNER, L. (1995), 'Regulating Sexual Offences within the Home', in Loveland (ed.), *Frontiers of Criminality*, Ch. 8.

—— (2004), *Criminal Justice*, Oxford: Oxford University Press.

9

NO TURNING BACK: THE POLITICS OF LAW AND ORDER INTO THE MILLENNIUM

David Downes and Rod Morgan

INTRODUCTION

This chapter concerns the public contestation of crime and disorder—debates about which phenomena should be defined as such, how crime and disorder events are interpreted, and, above all, how they are reacted to. The key players are: the major political parties, in particular home secretaries and their ministerial and Opposition teams; senior civil servants who, despite their non-political role, bear crucial advisory responsibilities; criminal justice pressure and interest groups, and the mass media. The private, off-stage processes of discussion, negotiation, and exchange, which provide the ingredients of public utterance and action, remain implicit. Further, by such terms as 'Conservative Party' we do not mean to propagate the fallacy of misplaced concreteness: these terms are necessary abbreviations for the welter of actions of many thousands of individuals. Nor, in quoting the words of ministers or other politicians, do we assume that perfect comprehension can be achieved—if it ever can be—without much more detail about timing, context, and much else. Our purpose is limited—to demonstrate a point rather than to convey some total reality.

Compared with the contested party politics of the economy, foreign affairs, health, education, etc., those of 'law and order' are of remarkably recent origin: they emerged in the mid-1960s, and came decisively to the fore in the 1979 election. This absence from party political discourse seems now to be surprising. At the beginning of the twenty-first century we think of law and order as emotive, fundamentally political issues: we have got used to the fact that they arouse passionate political debate. But it was not always so. That law and order were relatively insulated from the realm of party politics for so long testifies perhaps to the strength of the belief that crime, like the weather, is beyond political influence; and that the operation of the law and criminal justice should be above it. This is not to deny that criminal law reform has long been regarded as the prerogative of Parliament. But once laws are enacted, the liberal doctrine of the separation of powers holds that their enforcement is the preserve of the police and the judiciary. Hence, bipartisanship regarding criminal justice issues was the rule rather than the exception in the twentieth century. Even at the fringes of political life, few challenges were made to this profound consensus. This bipartisan approach was largely abandoned in the 1970s and 1980s though we have since begun to witness a return to some underlying agreement. Party political squabbles today are largely about relative levels of expenditure on law and order services, police numbers, and the like. Moreover, contemporary campaigns typically involve one or more competitively expressive gestures about what should be done with some particular group of deviants—predatory psychopaths or prolific young offenders, for example, recently the high-profile subject of outrage or scandal. But closer analysis of party statements reveals that this sound and fury masks substantial agreement that the incidence of volume crime—common property crime and public disorder—is not easily reduced by legislation or the manner in which the law is applied, and that responsibility for reasserting control must be more widely dispersed.

The reasons for the change from a broadly bipartisan, to a sharply contested, and now a more twin-track, politics of law and order, are central to our concerns. The prelude to the change was significant because the nature of the bipartisanship was both complex and far from apolitical. But this was a politics more of nuance and inflection than of explicit difference. The politics of law-breaking are not necessarily those of order-defiance (Elder 1984), and the latter has a far more developed history, particularly in the realm of industrial conflict (Dixon and Fishwick 1984). Friction over public order legislation and its enforcement has throughout the period been far more evident than that concerning straightforward criminality. It was the achievement of 'Thatcherism' to blur the difference between the two and even to fuse them symbolically to political effect. And the consequences of the change have been more than a simple matter of the major parties taking up starkly opposing stances across the range of relevant issues. Despite new, overt differences, a species of second-order consensus has emerged to replace former orthodoxies. Moreover, the politics of law and order are not confined to the party sphere. Extra-parliamentary processes have often been more vigorous than those at Westminster, and developments at local government level, or formulations by pressure groups and lobbies, have frequently been the stimulus for national attention. Finally, the eruption of particular scandals and concerns, via a rapidly changing media framework, have consistently proved catalysts for changing policies. We shall address these topics in turn.

BRITISH GENERAL ELECTIONS AND 'LAW AND ORDER', 1945–2005

Earlier versions of this chapter (Downes and Morgan 1994, 1997, 2002) examined in some detail how law and order issues figured in the 16 General Elections from 1945 to 1992 inclusive. Those of our readers interested in that detail should refer to those earlier versions. For present purposes it is necessary only to summarize what those analyses demonstrated as a prelude to a close examination of the 2005 election when New Labour, as it likes to style itself, won an historic 'third term'.

FROM ATTLEE TO THATCHER TO BLAIR: THE POST-WAR MANIFESTOS AND CAMPAIGNS

In 1945 the huge task of post-war reconstruction led the three main political parties to contend overwhelmingly about the priorities of rebuilding the economy and constructing the 'welfare state'. A form of consensus prevailed, usually known as 'Butskellism', which limited political conflict. Full employment, core entitlements to receive mainstream public services, a mixed economy, and economic growth based on Keynesian assumptions, were broadly accepted as shared goals. Issues relating to crime, policing, and criminal justice were minor, taken-for-granted aspects of this consensus and did not significantly figure in the five post-war elections from 1945 to 1959. During the 1960s 'law and order' issues began to creep into manifesto statements. Recorded crime rates had begun to rise steeply and all three parties began to indicate how they would pursue policies more effectively to combat crime. But they did not suggest that crime was attributable to the policies of the party in government.

All that changed in the 1970s. The Conservatives began to argue, in restrained terms, that Labour in government was responsible for aspects of the worsening crime figures: 'the Labour government cannot entirely shrug off responsibility for the present situation' (Conservative Party Manifesto 1970). By 1979, the incoming Thatcher Government claimed a much stronger connection, both during their victorious 1979 election campaign and subsequently, between crime, protest, and the industrial disputes during the time of the preceding Labour administration. This set the tone for the 1980s and the following 18 years of continuous Conservative rule. The Conservatives fused the issues of law-breaking and order-defiance. They attacked not just the policies but the integrity of Labour. They refashioned their traditional claim to be the natural party of government, representing the order of established authority (Honderich 1990). They successfully pinned to Labour responsibility for the alleged 'ungovernability' of Britain. They capitalized on widespread public fears about: national decline; loss of economic competitiveness and bad industrial relations; the growth of permissiveness and declining public morals; fear of crime, inner city decay, and the extravagances of youth fashion and street protests. They made restoring the 'rule of law', which they claimed Labour had undermined, one of their five major tasks. They undertook to do so by implementing a whole raft of specific law and order policies and spending more on law and order services (police, courts, and prisons) while economising elsewhere (Conservative Party 1979). They dispelled the last vestiges of the bipartisan consensus on law and order.

Neither Labour nor the Liberals initially made much of a response to the gradually raised law and order stakes. But they abandoned their self-restraint in 1979. They also began to devote space to these issues in their manifestos and campaigns. But Labour stuck to its traditional objective of creating 'one nation' by attacking 'the social deprivation which allows crime to flourish' and continued to put its faith in the welfare state. Most of Labour's law and order policy was implicitly to be found elsewhere in its manifesto, in its social and economic policies.

The evidence suggests that the stance developed by the Conservatives during the 1970s was greatly to the detriment of Labour. Opinion polls showed that 'maintaining law and order' grew in importance and in 1979 *no* policy placed the Conservatives so far ahead of Labour. One-third of Labour voters and almost half of Liberal voters expressing a clear preference on the issue thought that the Tories had a better 'law and order' policy than their own parties (Butler and Kavanagh 1980: 163).

The Conservatives' tough stance in the early 1980s was a bravura stance given that the decade witnessed a continued rise in recorded crime, a rash of ferocious inner-city disorders, and the bitter, year-long Miners' Strike of 1984–5. Labour initially stuck to their 'one nation' position, focusing on 'healing the wounds' brought about by unemployment and the Conservative cuts in public expenditure. They also promised to repeal some of the police powers granted by the Police and Criminal Evidence Act 1984. By contrast the Liberals (and subsequently the Liberal Democrats) took a more radically reformist position, arguing for incorporation into domestic law of the European Convention on Human Rights, the creation of a Ministry of Justice, and local authority crime prevention units. In the 1987 and 1992 elections, however, all the main parties began to adjust their positions, displaying more realism and restraint. The Conservatives no longer claimed that their policies would straightforwardly reduce the incidence of crime: crime prevention was now a task for everyone because the origins of crime lie 'deep in society'. Meanwhile Labour abandoned its opposition to the new police powers and assured voters, vis-à-vis the governance of the police, that they would not tamper with police responsibility for operational matters. Labour also began playing the Conservatives at their own law and order game. In the 1987 election they attributed to Conservative policies the continued steep rise in recorded crime and in 1992 called for greater police numbers. But they failed to press home this attack, and made nothing of the continued rise in crime despite additional spending on law and order services. The Conservatives accused them of being 'soft and flabby on crime' and unveiled a poster depicting a policeman with one hand tied behind his back. The opinion poll evidence suggested that the Conservatives still inspired greater confidence on this issue.

By the early 1990s law and order issues were less prominent than they had been a decade earlier. A new second-order consensus had emerged. No party could any longer afford to cede the law and order ground to the opposition: all parties felt obliged to address it in some way. They all asserted their support for the police and the need to increase their effectiveness; agreed that crime prevention and victim support were priorities; and accepted the logic of 'bifurcation' (Bottoms 1974), according to which longer custodial sentences for serious, repeat, and dangerous offenders, but an enhanced range of non-custodial measures for minor, occasional offenders, were considered appropriate. Following the 1992 election, however, Labour began systematically to fashion a more resolutely critical law and order stance, skilfully summarized in Tony Blair's borrowed American slogan, 'tough on crime, tough on the causes of crime'.

THE 1997, 2001, AND 2005 ELECTIONS: THE ASCENDANCE AND CONSOLIDATION OF NEW LABOUR

Law and order issues were not prominent in the election campaigns of 1997, 2001, or 2005. In their manifestos all three major political parties devoted what has in recent years become the required high proportion of space to community safety, policing, and criminal justice issues. In 2001, and even more so in 2005, coverage of immigration and political asylum questions was added to this mix. However, these were not the issues that flared during the campaigns. In all three elections it was: the management of the economy; the future shape of taxation; Britain's place in Europe; constitutional issues (devolution in 1997 and the political consequences of possible British entry to the euro-zone in both 1997 and 2001); and the general quality of public services given the major parties' particular taxation commitments; which assumed the greatest importance (Butler and Kavanagh 1997). The latter topic encompassed law and order, particularly in relation to police numbers. Further, the charges and counter-charges made during the campaigns were remarkably similar.

In 1997 New Labour castigated the Conservative Government for presiding over unprecedented rises in recorded crime and failing to provide promised additional police officers, both of which trends they undertook to reverse (Labour Party 1997: 22–3). In their defence the Conservatives asserted that since 1992 recorded crime had fallen by 10 per cent—the biggest fall since records began—and police spending substantially increased (Conservative Party 1997: 34). In 2001 both the Conservatives and the Liberal Democrats attacked Labour for their broken promises on police numbers, an accusation which Labour attempted to rebut with recent evidence of police recruitment. In 2005 the Conservatives brought together what they maintained to be the increase in violent crime and antisocial behaviour and the stubbornly low clear-up rate. 'Criminals', they claimed, 'have a better chance of getting away with breaking the law than at any time in the last 25 years' (Conservative Party 2005). In response Labour proudly proclaimed in 2001 that crime had fallen under their stewardship, a claim that they made more insistently in 2005. Crime, as measured by the British Crime Survey, was now down by 30 per cent and 'today, there is less chance of being a victim of crime then for more than 20 years' (Labour Party 2005: 43). In both 2001 and 2005 all three parties engaged in auctions regarding the additional police officers they would ensure were in future provided. By 2005 Labour reported that there were now record police numbers, 13,000 more than in 1997 supported by 4,600 Community Support Officers (CSOs). Moreover, they promised much more. They would raise CSO numbers to 24,000, thereby freeing up 12,000 police officers for 'front-line duties'. Their pledge was 'a neighbourhood policing team for every community' (ibid.: 43–4). The Conservatives promised to recruit an additional 5,000 police officers, and the Liberal Democrats an additional 10,000 (Liberal Democratic Party 2005: 9). Both the major opposition parties undertook to release the police from the bureaucratic burdens they accused Labour of having placed on them. The implication of these police auctions was that the incidence of crime is directly related to police numbers, which, of course, it is not (Reiner 2000: 77–8).

The party manifestos for all three elections were not short on law and order attacks and defences of the government's record, or detailed undertakings about what each party would deliver if elected. On the contrary, such material was provided in abundance, though there was a striking contrast between the detailed 112-page document produced by Labour in 2005 and the unusually brief manifestos of both their principal opponents. But there were striking similarities in the policies the parties promised to pursue. In 1997, for example, all three major parties undertook to get tough with persistent young offenders, including those engaged in petty crime and disorder: all said that they would ensure that the parents of offending children were made to face up to their parental responsibilities; and all promised to do more for the victims of crime. The latter refrain, geared up now to give victims greater voice in court proceedings and more rights to information, appeared again in 2001. In 2005 combating antisocial behaviour was a common refrain. Labour trumpeted the number of antisocial behaviour orders (ASBOs) and Penalty Notices for Disorder (PNDs) that had been issued and claimed that their new Licensing Act would make it easier for the police and councils to act against pubs and clubs generating disorder. The Liberal Democrats promised a crackdown on licensees and under-age drinking, to which end they would employ acceptable behaviour contracts (ABCs) and, where necessary ASBOs, a device that in 1997 they had opposed. The Conservatives promised real action, maintaining 'that too many of Mr Blair's responses'—'like marching yobs to cash machines' (a proposal made by the Prime Minister, but subsequently dropped as untenable)—'have been gimmicks' (Conservative Party 2005).

This is not to say that there were no differences between the parties. In 2001, for example, the Conservatives accused the Labour Government of having, through the Home Detention Curfew Scheme (an early release programme for short and medium-term prisoners), permitted crimes to be committed which would otherwise have been prevented (for a detailed evaluation, see Dodgson *et al.* 2001). The Conservatives claimed that more such crimes would be prevented if, as they proposed, there were 'honesty in sentencing so that the sentence handed down in court is the one served by the criminal' (Conservative Party 2001: 12). This stance was taken again in 2005, this time with the promise of an additional 20,000 prison places (Conservative Party 2005), a policy which, were it enacted, would represent imprisonment in Britain to a hitherto unprecedented extent: at 200 prisoners per 100,000 population, the foothills of mass imprisonment would rapidly be scaled. The fact that this proposal made no impact on the campaign is an index of how inured the media and politicians have in general become to penal expansion. By contrast, the challenges offered by the Liberal Democrats served to emphasize what they saw as the common ground between their principal opponents. The Liberal Democrats bewailed the fact that Labour in 1997–2001, echoing the Tory record from 1992–7, had unduly concentrated resources on prison-building rather than primary crime prevention: they believed there was 'more scope for the use of community sentences which are proven to work' (Liberal Democrats 2001: 7) and in 2005 they promised greater investment in prison education (Liberal Democrats 2005: 9).

Moreover in 2005 both the Liberal Democrats and the Conservatives promised more effective control of Britain's borders, a sensitive issue given heightened concerns about international terrorism and growth in the numbers of asylum seekers and illegal immigrants. The Conservatives would appoint a Minister for Homeland Security, the Liberal Democrats a Border Police Force. But as in the 1970s the Liberal Democrats expressed concerns about civil liberties. They would repeal the Prevention of Terrorism Act and argued that though successive governments 'keep talking tough . . . everyone knows it isn't working' (ibid.), whereas the Conservatives took every opportunity still to out-tough Labour. They would reverse the Government's reclassification of cannabis and provide an extra 25,000 residential places for drug treatment (Conservative Party 2005).

Labour, meanwhile, displayed their laurels, but were careful not to rest on them. Like the Tories in their 1997 manifesto, they were not complacent about law and order: much remained to be done. But their 1997 manifesto commitment on crime—'We will be tough on crime and tough on the causes of crime'—a slogan first enunciated by Tony Blair in 1993—'and halve the time it takes persistent juvenile crime to come to court' (Labour Party 1997), had, they proclaimed, been delivered:

> The British Crime Survey shows that overall crime fell by 10 per cent from 1997 to 1999. Investment is now rising. The time from arrest to sentence for persistent young offenders is down from 142 days to 89 days—on track to halve the time within the five years promised in 1997 [Labour Party 2001: 44].

None of these detailed messages attracted much press comment or inspired high-profile inter-party argument during the campaigns, however. Even the Conservatives' attempt to label Labour as soft on 'bogus' asylum seekers, thereby stimulating a flood of them to enter the country—a flood that the Conservatives would stem by detaining all asylum seekers in specially created institutions—failed to capture the imagination of either the media or the electorate. It was 'the economy, stupid' and everything else—including the effective management of crime—appeared derivative. As a result of the September 1993 debacle of Black Wednesday and British withdrawal from the exchange rate mechanism, bitter Party in-fighting over British membership of the European Community and entry to the eurozone, and the moral failings of significant Party figures—represented by their opponents as 'sleaze'—the Conservatives had by 1997 lost their reputation for governmental competence and party discipline. By contrast Labour had, during the final years of their long period in the political wilderness, rebranded themselves. Through an assiduous programme of modernization, New Labour had established themselves as a credible party to take up the reins of government and, during their first administration, proved that they could run the economy to the satisfaction of the majority of the electorate—particularly their new voters occupying the prosperous middle ground. Labour was now:

> a broad-based movement for progress and justice . . . in strong communities . . . but we have liberated those values from outdated dogma or doctrine . . . On crime, we believe in personal responsibility and in punishing crime . . . different from the Labour approach of the past [Labour Party 1997: 2–3].

That is, Labour claimed now to be the party of 'law and order'. By their failure to criticize Conservative proposals while in opposition, and by their legislation and other initiatives while in government, it was the 'tough on crime' part of their slogan that they emphasized. It was not that they were unable in 2001 to point to policy initiatives which addressed the 'causes of crime' and diminished 'social exclusion', but the latter policies were noticeably less hard-hitting than the ones being pursued against criminals. After four years in office Labour was convincingly able to claim to be managing crime. The Conservatives fired their best shots but were unable effectively to resurrect the old adage that Labour was 'soft': it was manifestly not the case.

FROM OLD TO NEW LABOUR

It used to be argued that the principal strength of the Conservative Party was its claim to oneness with traditional British sovereignty: the monarchy and aristocracy, property, the City of London, the armed forces, the ancient universities, and, not least, the law (Parkin 1967; Honderich 1990). The Labour Party, it used to be said, offered a countervailing force, as representative of the working-class labour movement and the trade unions. Yet this constituency was always deviant with respect to the core values and most cherished allegiances of British traditionalism. The Labour Party could flourish only in its industrial heartland and one-class urban areas. Against the Tories' keystone value of what Macpherson (1962) termed 'possessive individualism', the Labour Party rested on an appeal to the alternative morality of redistributive social justice and community.

These ideological differences translated readily into quite distinct post-1945 policy choices. In housing the Conservative preference was for owner occupation compared to Labour's emphasis on large-scale, estate-based, municipal, rented accommodation. On taxation, Labour supported the steeply progressive direct taxation of income and wealth; the Conservatives favoured lower direct and more indirect, regressive taxation on spending. On education, Labour came to back comprehensive, neighbourhood schooling; the Conservatives more selective, specialist education with a large private sector. On the other hand Labour's development of the National Health Service commanded far more widespread support than the system of private medicine it largely replaced. Enough overlap and compromise prevailed for it plausibly to be said that there was an underlying consensus. Not until the mid-1970s did sharper conflicts emerge with the rise of New Right policies, designed to challenge the growing dominance of the trade unions and to undercut Labour's hold on the skilled working class vote. So successful was the Thatcherite strategy that Labour lost four successive elections in 1979, 1983, 1987 and 1992. The shift to New Labour in the post-1992 period was the most decisive realignment of the past two decades.

This shift needs to be explained in the context of the unique character of post-war political developments in Britain. From 1945 to 1951, the Labour Government under Clement Attlee constructed the 'Welfare State' in conditions of post-war hardship and economic crisis, an outstanding achievement recaptured in Peter Hennessey's *Never Again* (1992), a title which dramatically registers the determined seizure of a historic and never-to-be-repeated opportunity. But the Labour Party, unlike all other left-wing parties in Europe, was unable to capitalize on the era of rapidly growing post-war prosperity that, in the 1950s, succeeded austerity and severe constraint. Forced in part by British involvement in the Korean War of 1949–51 to postpone the end of rationing, Labour lost office to the Conservatives in 1951, whose succeeding 13 years in government coincided with the post-war boom that Harold Macmillan, Prime Minister from 1957 to 1963, termed the 'Never Had It So Good' era. As a result, the association of Conservative government and affluence became cemented to the point where their aura was that of the 'natural' party of government. No other right-wing party in Europe was so fortunately enabled to evade the negative associations of post-war austerity and to capitalize on the positive associations of post-war prosperity. As a result, even when Labour regained office, their tenure seemed provisional and counter-intuitive. Thus was created the Labour bogey which the 2001 election exorcized.

It was this aura of 'Old Labour' as the party of austerity rather than affluence, of economic crisis rather than stability, that Tony Blair and Gordon Brown sought to dispel with the creation of 'New Labour', assisted by two key aspects of 'Thatcherism'. First, the rigours of marketization weakened the Conservatives' hold over some of their key constituencies—Oxford University, for example, famously refused Mrs Thatcher an honorary degree in 1984 because of resentments regarding higher education controls—and gave rise to sapping, bitter conflicts which often seemed too high a price for change. Secondly, the Tories became increasingly schizoid about European Union terms of membership and policy, just as Labour came to realize that far from the Union being simply a rich man's club, the trend of Union policy was mainly Social Democratic.

Forged in the mid-1990s, 'New Labour' capitalized on these disjunctions and tensions and their re-election in 2001 and 2005 represents a political achievement of real magnitude. They may not have reversed the tables, but there cannot any longer be said to be a 'natural' party of government. The right to govern is now genuinely contested. The question, however, is at what cost has this political reconfiguration been purchased? Labour has arguably morphed into a party of the Centre Right rather than the Centre Left, and is implementing 'Thatcherism' by other means—a cooler, managerialist version. The willingness of the electorate to vote at all has seriously declined as the major parties have stolen each other's clothes and sought to outmanoeuvre each other in marketing them.

New Labour have embraced policies and principles associated with neo-liberal rather than social democracy, of the Right rather than the Left. They have eschewed increases in direct taxation, even on incomes over £100,000 p.a., preferring instead to juggle regressive taxes on spending. They have pursued public-private partnerships in the capital renewal and management of public services from public transport to schools and hospitals. They have elevated individual, consumer choice to a defining criterion for the organization of almost everything. They have made competition, or what in order to embrace the voluntary sector they prefer to term 'contestability', the ideological model for their programme of public service reform, or 'modernization'. Moreover, by imposing strict limits on public expenditure in their first two years of office, 1997–9, they ended their first term with lower rather than raised spending on public services as a proportion of GDP, which remained almost the lowest in Europe (see, for example, Elliott 2001). Since 2001, however, spending on education and health rose substantially, with the aim of making good two decades of comparative underspending on those services compared with other countries in western Europe, to the point where in 2010, for example, health spending would attain the EU average. Does this signify a 'back on track' phase to traditional Labour priorities? Far from it: all the indications are that Tony Blair sees his final period as Prime Minister as the decisive break with the 'Old Labour' past.

NO TURNING BACK: NEW LABOUR'S THIRD TERM

The term 'no turning back', a phrase adopted by a small group of Conservative ministers in 1985 to signify their dedicated opposition to further UK integration into the European Union (a policy which arguably helped to divide the Tories to permanent and electorally disastrous effect), refers in this context to the apparent determination of New Labour to embark on a truly decisive phase of government that not only *adds to* its panoply of legal and institutional reforms but renders those changes *irreversible*. The institutional landscape is to be so transformed that no future government can feasibly unpack the results to return to the past and cast aside its legacy. This would be the Blairite equivalent to such Thatcherite policies as the privatization of the state-owned utilities, the severe curtailment of local government powers in relation to public housing by the freezing of assets flowing from tenants' 'Right to Buy' council property, and the abolition of the Greater London Council. Far from reversing, even in part, these changes which Labour vehemently rejected when in opposition, New Labour in office have if anything reinforced them, with the exception of its re-creation of the GLC, with much reduced powers.

Despite internal party opposition, New Labour have embarked on a comparable transformation of the two remaining bastions of post-war welfare state provision: health and education. Pursuing its innovations of the 1997–2005 period, the Government plans to open up the heartlands of NHS services to private provision. In education it intends giving schools effective rights to pursue selection policies without strict regard to the previous 'balanced intake' guidelines to ensure comprehensive schooling remains a possibility. Non-binding guidelines are offered as the only barrier to selection by ability (HM Government 2005). The logical effect of these measures could well be to return secondary education to the state of affairs analysed by Floud, Halsey, and Martin (1956), who documented the extent to which teacher choice favoured middle-class over working-class children substantially more than even the 11-plus competitive examination.

In other respects too, New Labour seem set on breaking with long-established policies. The principle of 'unstimulated demand' was for over three decades a genuine compromise between prohibition and laissez-faire market provision of alcohol and gambling. In both cases, New Labour have abandoned that principle. Current concerns about drink-fuelled disorder are focused on recent legislation permitting 24-hour opening times. In fact the most significant change in relation to recreational drinking had already happened:

> A profound transformation has recently occurred in the way in which magistrates consider new liquor licensing applications. Following publication of the Justices' Clerks Society's *Good Practice Guide* (1999), justices have been issued with new guidelines recommending the abolition of need/demand as a criterion relevant to the granting of licences . . . The recent abandonment of the 'need' criterion . . . has played a key role in facilitating the recent growth of city centre drinking circuits [Hobbs *et al.* 2003: 248–9; see also Light 2005].

In short, the key move towards opening up the new night-time frontier to a licensing free-for-all had already taken place well in advance of the furore over round-the-clock opening of pubs and clubs. Driven by the need, in the wake of de-industrialization, to find new sources of revenue once supplied by productive industry, local authorities have turned to the night-time economy of recreational consumption to replace the depleted fruits of the day-time economy. The problems of policing tens of thousands of so-called 'binge drinkers' have swamped 'the police' and have been met mainly by the deployment of a growing army of privately recruited bouncers. The key fact, however, is that 'in the night-time economy, locations that are "bad" for crime and disorder are invariably "good" for business' (Hobbs *et al.* 2003: 247–8).

These developments signify the abandonment of the need/demand criterion in other forms of service provision. In the case of gambling, the key principle for policy from the legalization of off-course betting in 1961 until the introduction of the National Lottery in 1994 was that of 'unstimulated demand'. This principle, anathema to the 'spirit of capitalism', was a compromise evolved historically to meet the opposition to legalized gambling. It entailed a ban on gambling premises offering more than the opportunity to place bets and watch races off-course. It also prescribed a 24-hour waiting period before individuals could engage in casino gaming. This approach worked to end the prohibition of gambling (of the sort still current in most US states, to the benefit of organized crime) but prevented outright commercialization. The arrival of the National Lottery, however, rode rough-shod over the constraints against advertising and other gambling providers saw their opportunity to press for further change. This is now in train with the Gambling Act 2005, which inter alia, will permit the establishment of at least one new regional casino, up to eight new large casinos, and up to eight new small casinos, each of which will be able to offer a greater number of gaming machines with increased levels of stake and prize money. It follows that there are 17 new casino licences to be competed for. Comparable developments can be predicted for off-course betting and bingo. In short, attempts to hold the line against commercial inducements to gamble over and above the need and/or desire to do so have now been jettisoned.

The principle of 'unstimulated demand' was a genuine 'Third Way' between prohibition and full-blown commercialism (it is therefore not to be confused with New Labour's self-styled 'Third Way' (Giddens 1998), a term which denotes a transcending of both Old Labour and New Right ideologies). It operated in one crucial respect in the drugs field, with heroin being supplied to registered users on a 'need' basis until, in the mid-1970s, the treatment centres rejected that course, substituting the supply of oral methadone to addicts (see Spear 2002 for a meticulous account of how the 'British system' came to be effectively dismantled). Since that policy change, heroin addiction (and other forms of drug use) has become vastly more prevalent; drug-related crime has been boosted to an unknowable extent; and profits from the trade help finance organized crime networks: something of a catastrophe in policy terms, yet one about which most governments around the world, including our own, are in a state of denial. Instead of responding to drug dependence as a public health matter, the government regards its criminalization as the *sine qua non* of responsible policy-making.

In sum, the demise of the 'unstimulated demand' (or proven 'need') principle in relation to heroin, alcohol, and gambling has driven policy and practice towards a bifurcation of 'deregulated marketization' and commercialization in the case of alcohol and gambling, or towards prohibition, in the case of heroin. In all three cases, the outcomes have either been, or are likely to prove, distinctly criminogenic.

There have, of course, been counterbalancing initiatives to these developments. The level of unemployment is the lowest for two decades. New Labour have introduced the minimum wage, the New Deal for the unemployed, and SureStart for children in deprived areas. They have achieved reductions in family and child poverty by means of the Working Families Tax Credit, raised child benefit, and embarked on a substantial programme of increased spending on public services. But, on balance, Labour's policies have more in common with recent Conservative than with past Labour governments. How far do their specific policies on 'law and order' fit that pattern?

THE NEW CONSENSUS ON LAW AND ORDER

The character of Conservative policy on law and order from the mid-1980s until 1993 was in key respects a remarkably liberal departure from Tory orthodoxy. The 1979 election, which marked the beginning of 18 years in government, was won on the most radically tough law and order ticket the Conservatives had ever produced. They would restore the 'rule of law' which the Labour Government had 'undermined'. They would spend more money on law and order services while 'we economize elsewhere'. There would be more police, and more powers for them to use. There would be 'short, sharp shock' sentences for young 'hooligans' and 'tough sentences . . . for violent criminals and thugs' (Conservative Party 1979). By the late 1980s the Conservative tone had changed, however. Their 1987 election manifesto maintained that fighting crime was a task for 'all of us'. The worsening crime rate was a problem 'not just in Britain but in most other societies too'. Its origins lay 'deep in society' (Conservative Party 1987). Further, David Faulkner, a senior Home Office administrator, was given an unusually free hand to develop criminal justice and penal policy afresh (Rutherford 1996: 86–7). Drawing on the work of penal reform pressure groups, academic criminology, and in-house research, he fashioned a programme for decarceration which, over several years, was widely canvassed and to some extent 'sold' to the judiciary, partly on the basis of successful developments in community alternatives to custody for young offenders from the early 1980s (Cavadino and Dignan 1997: ch. 9). Perhaps the most striking index of its success was the fall in the prison population from 50,000 in 1987–8 to 42,500 in 1991. This was done in parallel with the passage of the Criminal Justice Act 1991, which sought, among other things, to adopt a minimalist 'just deserts' basis for sentencing—a measure aimed at diverting from custody those petty, persistent offenders jailed more for their persistence than the seriousness of their crimes (see Ashworth, Chapter 29, this volume).

The fateful twist to this ambitious but well-formulated programme lay in the character of the 1987 election victory of the Conservatives, which was fuelled by a pre-election consumer boom engineered by the then Chancellor, Nigel Lawson. When boom turned to bust after the election, with soaring inflation and unemployment reaching three million by 1992, the crime rate soared with it, by some 50 per cent between 1989 and 1992. Despite these monumental failures, the Conservatives under a new Prime Minister, John Major, still managed to win the 1992 election, only to have their image as the party of economic good management finally destroyed by the forced devaluation of 'Black Wednesday' in October 1992. By this point, the new Shadow Home Secretary, Tony Blair, had begun decisively to change the grounds of opposition to Conservative policy on crime. Labour would press home criticism of the costs in crime terms of economic mismanagement leading to high unemployment. They would also attack the key provision of the 1991 Criminal Justice Act, the emphasis on just deserts for the current offence rather than for previous convictions. Labour's long-standing but largely ineffective project to nail the weakness of the Conservative position—the refusal to link crime with social and economic policies they themselves had promoted—was now to be renewed, and linked *implicitly* with undue leniency in sentencing.

In his celebrated phrase summarizing Labour's 'law and order' policy— 'tough on crime, tough on the causes of crime'—Blair resonated with public fear of, and anger about, rising crime in several respects. Having hit on this phrase, thereby illustrating the immense potency of symbolic language in politics, Labour were now positioned to extract maximum advantage from the fact that the Tories had presided over four years of steeply rising crime from 1989 to 1993. Alarmed by their deteriorating position in public opinion polls, both in general and on crime, the Conservatives rapidly cast their previous, and long germinated, penal policy to the winds and sought to reoccupy lost terrain. First Kenneth Clarke, then Michael Howard, as the new Conservative Home Secretaries after 1992, quickly dropped the key reforming clauses of the 1991 Act: unit fines (which linked the level of fines to disposable incomes) and the need normally to disregard previous convictions in sentencing. Michael Howard's notorious 'Prison Works' speech to the Tory Party Conference in 1993 was the climax to this somewhat panic-stricken shift. However much it might appal the liberal reformers in his own party, Howard was determined to deal with the Labour challenge by re-creating their image as a party 'soft on crime'. By 1997 the prison population had risen to 65,000, some 50 per cent higher than it had been less than a decade earlier.

But if Howard thought he could shake off Labour's new-found embrace of 'tough' penal policies, he was badly mistaken. This was no longer the Labour Party of the 1970s and early 1980s when, in response to Conservative assaults on their law and order record and the Conservative fusion of law-breaking and order-defiance (notably in relation to labour disputes), Labour initially failed to respond and later maintained an almost passive 'one nation' response. First Blair, then Straw, not only dogged Howard's heels: they became his doppelgänger, even his caricature. They beat him to the punch on several fronts. They trumpeted their admiration for the 'zero tolerance' policing in New York, the need to crack down on 'incivilities', 'squeegee merchants', and beggars (Jones and Newburn 2004, 2006; Morgan 2006). The punitive measures in the 1994 Criminal Justice and Public Order Bill went unopposed by Labour, as did proposals for mandatory sentencing. Labour reneged on their pre-1992 support for the reforms of the 1991 Act, criticizing the Conservatives for their promotion of lenient sentencing. For the first time since law and order became a partisan issue in the 1970s, an effective bipartisanship in 'toughness' now prevailed in the contest for leadership (Dunbar and Langdon 1998). A major irony was that the forced devaluation of sterling in 1992 inaugurated an economic recovery which steadily reduced unemployment levels and, at least in part, the rate of crime. Yet the Conservatives were ideologically unable to link crime reduction with economic factors: that would be to render their previous responsibility for soaring crime admissible. But nor were Labour prepared to give the Conservatives credit for having reduced crime by better economic management. Both locked themselves in to the position of defining undue leniency as the prime cause of high crime rates. The politics of law and order had now become inherently and increasingly punitive. They were to shape the character of New Labour's policies after 1997, as well as the remnant of Conservative rule until that point. Looking back, it is more accurate to see Clarke and Howard as the prisoners of Blair and Straw's agenda, rather than—as is conventionally assumed—the reverse (Downes 1998). And both were heavily influenced by the example of the United States rather than Europe, with New Labour gurus in particular regarding Clinton's success in the 1992 presidential election as a blueprint for their own strategy. 'Policy transfers' in the cases of prison privatization, minimum mandatory sentencing, and 'zero tolerance' policing may not have been replicas of the American (see especially Jones and Newburn 2006) but they would hardly have been gestated but for the association with electoral success.

THE REDISCOVERY OF THE CRIMINAL

Labour's mantra—'Tough on crime, tough on the causes of crime'—was notable for more than contriving to get the word 'tough' twice into a single phrase (Newburn 2000). It cloaked implications and difficulties none too apparent at the point of utterance. First, the agenda for being 'tough on crime' was immediate, that for tackling the 'causes of crime' much more long term (Downes 1998). The scope for tensions and goal displacement in this dual agenda was soon to surface. Secondly, whilst liberal reformers had interpreted 'tough on crime' to mean target-hardening and other forms of situational crime prevention, and 'tough on the causes of crime' to mean tackling poverty, unemployment, and inequality, in reality it largely meant being tough on the *criminal*. A string of largely punitive measures, announced in discussion papers in Opposition and mostly enacted in office, in the Crime and Disorder Act 1998 and other statutes, were designed to meet the 'tough on crime' agenda. These included Anti-Social Behaviour Orders (ASBOs), a new device to curtail 'neighbours from hell' (see Morgan and Newburn, Chapter 30, this volume), the activation of minimum mandatory sentencing for repeat burglary, drug-trafficking, violence, and sexual offending; curfews for juveniles; electronic monitoring of offenders on early release; ending *doli incapax*, a measure in effect reducing the age of full criminal responsibility from 14 to 10, alongside Parenting Orders—a form of double jeopardy for families; extending grounds for the disclosure of offending histories to employers to virtually all offences (see Commission on Families 2005); and depriving offenders in breach of community penalties of benefits: all measures that would hardly have been countenanced by Labour before 1992. The political effect of these policies was to neutralize any claim by the Conservatives that New Labour was 'soft on crime'.

Yet Labour hegemony on law and order was not translated, in the 2001 and 2005 elections, into policies that sought to retrieve what *had been* their position in the 1980s and early 1990s. With volume crime rates initially down initially by one-fifth and then one-third (see Maguire, Chapter 10, this volume), and with prisons bulging and criminal justice practitioners under strain, this could have been the ideal time to signal the resumption of decarceration. Instead, their first new term in office was heralded by announcements that the first year would contain yet more 'tough on crime' legislation: the confiscation of criminal assets (again using civil rather than criminal evidential bases); stepping up penalties for persistent offenders, however petty their crimes; and targeting the 100,000 offenders allegedly responsible for committing 50 per cent of crime. The pattern was repeated in 2005. The campaign began with Blair proclaiming 'the end of the 1960s liberal consensus on law and order' (Morgan 2006), and victory was followed with undertakings to give the drive against antisocial behaviour, crime, and terrorism even greater priority. Headteachers were to be empowered to seek Parenting Orders. Terrorist suspects were to be detained without charge for up to 90 days, a proposition amounting to internment regarded as excessive and likely to be counterproductive by critics, and which was rejected by the House of Commons in the first parliamentary defeat Blair was to suffer.

Predictions seemed to be borne out that, once in the grip of 'populist punitiveness' (Bottoms 1995), once addicted to the rhetoric of 'zero tolerance' (Jones and Newburn 2006), once bought into the logic of 'prison works' (Downes 2001), there is every prospect of self-confirming penal expansionism at the expense of due process and civil liberties. The constant raising of the emotional temperature about the need for emergency measures, special powers, and the like—calls given added urgency by the events of 11 september 2001 and 7 July 2005, the destruction of the World Trade Center, Manhattan, and the four near-simultaneous London suicide bombings—which the media as well as the major parties promote, can thereby accompany falls as well as rises in the crime rate.

There are some compensating measures to weigh against the above, in particular: the incorporation into domestic law of the European Convention on Human Rights in the Human Rights Act 1998; the Macpherson Report (1999) on the Stephen Lawrence case, which has led to a tightening of procedures for policing racist violence, and, more contentiously, to proposals to remove the double jeopardy obstacle in cases of murder; the creation of Youth Offending Teams (Yots) to deliver preventive and other programmes, including restorative justice, for young offenders in the community; and the noble purposes set out in *Every Child Matters* (HM Treasury) and the Childrens Act 2003 for better joined-up child-related services. However, it remains to be seen how far these services will be adequately resourced, whether restorative justice will extend beyond the margins of criminal justice practice, and whether the reformed youth justice system will achieve any reduction in the substantial number of children and young people in custody (see Morgan and Newburn, Chapter 30, this volume). On balance the overall impact of this welter of legislative innovation tends so far to be at the punitive end of the scale.

THE SKELETONS IN THE CUPBOARD

In our previous analyses of why Labour challenges to the Tories on law and order were either muted or unsuccessful, despite Labour's record being their equal or even superior on that front, we argued that Labour had suffered from their traditional links with three key constituencies. These were: trade unionism and the labour movement; the most deprived working-class communities and the ethnic minorities; and supporters of civil disobedience and libertarian causes. For over two decades, from the late 1960s until the early 1990s, these associations were a source of vulnerability to Tory claims that Labour were 'soft on crime and weak in upholding the Rule of Law'. After 1992, however, New Labour moved swiftly to dump these 'hostages to fortune': by distancing the Party from the militant wing of trade unionism; by a sequence of policy papers heralding a crack-down on incivilities, hooliganism, and crime in general; by not opposing the 1994 Act legislating against travellers, hunt saboteurs, and 'ravers'; and by forbidding any discussion by shadow ministers of changes to the drugs laws, even to the point of reprimanding those who sought to reopen discussion on decriminalizing cannabis.

Since the 1997 election, the 'hostages to fortune' have been even more decisively dumped, to the point where they can more accurately be termed 'the skeletons in the cupboard'. Indeed so confident is New Labour about the distance placed between itself and its legacy that it opened its Manifesto by proclaiming that its (old Labour) 'demons' had been exorcized (Labour Party 2005: Preface). How was this achieved?

First, moderate unionism has been granted its primary demands: the minimum wage; the right of workers at GCHQ (the MI5 'factory') to regain union membership; and UK signature of the Social Charter of the European Union (not accepting that the Charter had been John Major's compromise to keep the Tory Party from open hostility over the terms of continued EU membership). The trades unions were thus kept 'on board' despite wishing for stronger rights regarding such questions as company stake-holding. The guarantee of union rights within the EU enabled New Labour surgically to remove any hint of association with militant trade unionism and its municipal socialist bases. Ken Livingstone's candidacy for the new mayoralty of London was openly and vehemently opposed by Blair and Brown in person, and Livingstone was expelled from the Party for standing as an Independent following his failure to be selected as the official Labour Party candidate. Livingstone's resounding victory embar-rassed the New Labour leadership, but they had taken the precaution of denying the new mayoralty any substantial powers or funding. However, Livingstone's success as Mayor, in particular in relation to the 2012 Olympics bid and congestion charging, has led to a rapprochement with Blair, and the Labour leadership are now more inclined to woo rather than spurn him. Though the signs are that even moderate unions will strongly resist further extending privatization of the core public sector services of health and education, Labour is now set on driving them through. The 'social model' of the EU is increasingly defined as uncompetitive in the context of globalized trade, a critique which devalues the fact that Germany remains the world's leading exporter and other partners, particularly the Scandinavian countries, are widely regarded as economic success stories. Yet the Government now lobbies the CBI rather than the reverse, adulating the 'wealth creation' of the City of London whilst denigrating the failures of the major public sector services.

Secondly, on the issue of crime, delinquency, and disorder, especially on the worst-hit housing estates, Labour have repositioned the Party from regarding such problems as largely symptomatic of underlying social and economic distress, and therefore remediable by social and economic programmes. A more condemnatory and morally censorious view has been adopted. *No More Excuses* (Home Office 1997) was the telling title of a White Paper aiming, in David Garland's (1996, 2001) phrase, for the 'responsi-bilization' of delinquents and their parents. A great deal was made of the inefficiencies of the youth justice system, especially following the Audit Commission (1996) report on *Misspent Youth*, which concluded that swifter and more efficient justice could be delivered by 'final warnings' replacing second or more cautions and other procedural reforms to youth justice. The Audit Commission's reports have themselves been audited, and found seriously flawed in both their data and their reasoning (Jones 2001), but they nonetheless proved a basis for much of New Labour's thinking on youth crime. More recent initiatives involve the tracking of 2,500 persistent young offenders and the targeting of the 100,000 most persistent offenders who allegedly commit half of all crime (Labour Party 2001: 32). The skewed character of offending has long been known (see, e.g., Shaw 1931; Wolfgang, Figlio, and Sellin 1972) and provides many clues to the underlying causes of crime. But to regard the skew as an identifiable and fixed popula-tion of constant offenders is to mistake the nature of the problem, and risks joined-up labelling of a small minority as innately criminal.

If *zero tolerance* is the basis for tackling the criminal, *social exclusion* is New Labour's definition of the main underlying problem. The New Deals, the Social Exclusion Unit at 10 Downing Street, and British versions of Welfare to Work have emerged as key policies to address it, but on terms which preclude the need to address inequality in income and wealth (Levitas 1998). New Labour has thereby fashioned a strategy for crime reduction which shifts the need for intervention and control from structural to community and family levels. In this respect, the party has converged with the trend of Conservative policies (Crawford 1997). Labour has alleviated poverty more than the Conservatives would have done, lifting one million children out of poverty (Piachaud and Sutherland 2001; Hills 2004: 228 and 234). But, by refusing to impose extra taxation even on the very rich, Labour has allowed income and wealth inequalities to proliferate even more than under the Conservatives. An array of tax and benefit reforms has made a significant impact in closing the gap between the lowest and middle income groups. But inequality as measured by the gap between the highest and lowest incomes is now greater than that prevailing before 1939. 'Since 1979, we have seen a reversal [in the declining share of top incomes], with shares of the top income groups returning to their position of fifty years earlier. The equalisation of the post-war period has been lost' (Atkinson 2002: 38).

From the mid-1980s to the mid-1990s, income inequality in the UK grew to be second only to that of the USA among Western democracies. And it is this fount of polarization in inequality which classical social theories of crime see as far more criminogenic than absolute deprivation. Indeed the inequalities are arguably more potent sources of influence today because modern mass media have made them so much more 'in your face'. Nor is there any clear overriding rationale for the gulf of inequality in income and wealth. It is a 'veritable chaos of reward' (Young 1999: 152), a recipe for anomie which helps account for the persistently high rates of 'fear of crime' despite falling property crime rates. What people arguably perceive is that crime is falling not because its causes have been effectively tackled but because its most accessible targets have been massively 'hardened'.

Yet instead of tackling this 'cause of crime' at the roots, Labour prefer the politically more popular course of what Robert Reiner (2000: 220) conveys as policing the symptoms. A three-pronged approach has been developed by New Labour to extend *formal social controls* as surrogates for the *informal social constraints* which are seen as critically weakened by rapid social and economic changes. The extent to which the depletion of social cohesion and social capital is the outcome of successive government policies is not acknowledged: instead, responsibility is emphatically placed on the perpetrators of crime and disorder. First, a shadow or secondary form of criminal justice is formed as an extension to the primary system. 'Antisocial' as well as criminal behaviour is targeted by the 1998 Crime and Disorder Act, and subsequently a succession of Acts, whereby ASBOs can be imposed on adults and children as young as 10. ASBOs are civil orders, but any breach of the often myriad prohibitions in an order is a criminal offence punishable by up to five years' imprisonment. Despite substantial criticism that ASBOs unduly infringe civil liberties, weaken due process, displace existing criminal laws, and 'widen the net' of those subject to criminal sanctions, New Labour has through a calculated Home Office campaign successfully encouraged their use (Morgan 2006). The Government has also introduced, through the Anti-Social Behaviour Act 2003 and other Acts, further powers available to local authorities. Curfew powers over all children under 16 can now be applied requiring that they be 'off the streets', usually by 9.00 p.m., unless accompanied by an adult, even if they are not committing an offence or disturbing the peace. That is, the 'freedom of the streets' can at a stroke be withdrawn on a generational basis.

Secondly, the 'responsibilization' strategy (Muncie 1999; Garland 2001) is to be developed further through a third-term 'Respect' agenda. It is not yet clear what this will comprise. But early indications are that headteachers are to be drawn into the extending 'policing family' so they can better discipline students and, if necessary, their parents. Parents of offending youths, including those who repeatedly fail to attend school, can be required under a Parenting Order to attend parenting classes, some of which may be residential. This measure logically implies co-responsibility for the delinquencies of young offenders—themselves over the age of criminal responsibility—and their parents. This development is at odds with the foundational meaning of criminal responsibility, unless some element of *mens rea* can be invoked (Commission on Families 2005: 29–37). The 'Respect' agenda is also to encompass renewed schemes and summary penalties against graffiti, vandalism, and the kind of 'rough presence' (Willis 1977: 36) that could be seen as 'threatening' in local neighbourhoods. Groups of 'hoodies' will be dispersed under pain of prosecution should they refuse to move on. The criminal law already embodies penalties against such behaviour accompanied by safeguards to forestall their misuse: the 'Respect' agenda suggests that some of these may now be overridden.

These innovations signify a reversal in key respects of Labour's traditional approach to law and order issues in high-crime working-class neighbourhoods. There are continuities between Old and New Labour in the welfare-based Sure Start and community regeneration schemes which have been implemented since 1997, and which have clear relevance to long-term measures against the 'causes of crime'. But the net-widening, coercive, and co-responsibility prongs of the ASB and 'Respect' agendas signify a punitive, exclusionary approach which bears down most heavily on the already stigmatized and marginalized groups in society.

Thirdly, New Labour is more removed from the world of civil disobedience than at any point in party history. To capture the 'centre' ground, Labour has distanced itself from the ruck of street demonstrations, marches, and unticketed public meetings. Smooth corporate management is the New Labour style rather than noisy public assemblies. This fits the global trend, with management at all levels far more at home in air-conditioned, smoke-free pods than the sweaty, smoke-filled rooms of yore, of which the younger generation of elite politicians have no direct experience. The 'centre' also occupies ground on which scope for the genuine contestation of issues is narrowed to a small segment of the spectrum of acceptable opinion. Hence, the proliferation of single-issue pressure groups, who feel themselves unrepresented in the party political process, and the rise of what might be termed the super-issue networks, concerned with globalization, genetic engineering, and global warming, immense problems which governments are slowly wheeling round to confront. This stalemate produces a sense of disenfranchisement combined with disengagement from formal political processes. It generates the street politics of Seattle, Prague, and Gothenberg, where world trade and finance conferences were disrupted by concerted protest groups. The forces of economic globalization, largely driven by vast corporate capitalist interests, are as yet unregulated by any Wellsian form of world governance. Nation states are far from ceding their sovereignty to supra-national bodies, but defer to the power of corporate capital to shift their investments around the globe to seek maximum profit (Held 2001). International institutions are seen as either unable to cope (the United Nations and its myriad agencies), or cloaking and reinforcing the problems (the World Bank, the World Trade Organization, etc.).

This matrix is suffused with conflicts of interest which will inevitably explode into future direct action. The danger is that governments will simply insulate themselves by tighter security against the unsightly disturbances that might challenge the 'business as usual' atmosphere of high-level conferencing. In the wake of the protests against the invasion of Iraq, the Government introduced a ban on street demonstrations within a mile of Parliament. A single protester was recently arrested for placing a list of the names of British soldiers killed in Iraq on the Cenotaph in Whitehall. Symbolic of the New Labour stance on civil disobedience and public criticism of its policies was the ejection of a long-term Party member, Walter Wolfgang, an 82-year-old former refugee from Nazi Germany, from the 2005 Labour Party Conference for shouting 'Nonsense' during a speech by Jack Straw, the Foreign Secretary, justifying the Iraq invasion. It would be difficult to conceive a more telling example of the sea change in

Labour's approach to civil disobedience, from its qualified acceptance in matters of cardinal principle to exorcizing the ghost of its deviant past by a species of hyperactive control.

Fourthly, in relation to civil liberties, New Labour has adopted a markedly progressive approach to the civil liberties of minority groups, such as gays and ethnic minorities, which can be advanced without any hint that they connote being 'soft on crime'. Thus, the enactment of 'civil partnership' that falls short of formal marriage but enhances key legal entitlements such as property rights, and adoption, has been created for homosexual couples (though that status remains withheld from cohabiting heterosexual couples). A Bill to outlaw the incitement to religious hatred has been debated, on the grounds that 'religion' is now a surrogate for 'race' in extremist discourse. That Bill is, however, opposed by those who argue it is an infringement of freedom of expression in matters relating to belief as distinct from ethnicity.

By contrast, in matters relating to crime, antisocial behaviour, and terrorism, New Labour has pursued policies which in several respects erode civil liberties. In his speech to the 2005 Labour Party Conference Tony Blair proudly claimed to have subjected the criminal justice system to a 'battering' over several years to force it into the twenty-first century. He went on: 'The whole of our system starts from the proposition that its duty is to protect the innocent from being wrongly convicted . . . . But surely our *primary* duty should be to allow law-abiding people to live in safety' (emphasis added). Between the two clauses was the *caveat* that the first 'must be the duty of any criminal justice system', and following this passage he asserted that his approach did not mean 'abandoning human rights'. But this was not the Government's 'primary duty': the interests of law-abiding people came first (Blair 2005).

Blair's rhetoric stems from the Government's need constantly to renew its crime-fighting credentials. This approach has seemingly overridden its earlier incorporation of European human rights provisions into English law. For example, the Criminal Justice Act 2003 and other measures have abandoned traditional safeguards against wrongful conviction. 'The Act eliminates the double-jeopardy rule, greatly narrows the scope of the hearsay rule, permits introduction of evidence of offenders' prior crimes, and narrows jury trial rights. All of these changes diminish procedural protections and civil liberties in England and Wales and most will increase the prevalence of convictions of innocent people' (Tonry 2003: 21). The establishment of the Criminal Records Bureau in 1998 had extended the scope for virtually all employers, as well as restricted occupations, to compel disclosure of previous convictions. The much larger numbers in custody for longer sentences will mean far more ex-prisoners lose exemption from disclosure for longer periods, thus weakening safeguards against discrimination against ex-offenders in the labour market. As argued above, curfews, ASBOs, powers to disperse groups of two or more in designated zones, and on-the-spot penalties for public disorder, all diminish previously accepted canons of due process and freedom of movement.

Such measures are distinguished by the Government from those it argues are essential for the fight against terrorism: control orders amounting to indefinite house arrest;

proposals for ID cards; and the compromise 28-day detention without charge which Parliament, objecting to the Government's 90-day proposal, eventually accepted (and which is still the longest such period available in any jurisdiction in western Europe). All these measures, however strong their justification, are frontal assaults on civil liberties. However, when pressed, the Government includes the war against crime as an argument for ID cards, and acknowledges that none of these measures would have prevented the London suicide bombings of 7 July 2005. New Labour's stance arguably has as much to do with exorcizing its 1960s 'permissive' past as with formulating sound policy.

PRESSURE-GROUP AND INTEREST-GROUP POLITICS

Prior to the first party political stirrings of the law and order pot in the 1970s, the business of generating policy was largely left to permanent or temporary expert bodies with memberships broadly representative of the key criminal justice decision-making agencies. It was government on the 'inner circle', by the 'great and good', exercised to a substantial extent behind the scenes. If the principal political parties did not promise in their manifestos to adopt new approaches to such issues as policing or sentencing, neither did they come to government with a programme ready to implement. The Labour Party's 1964 statement, *Crime, A Challenge To Us All*, was the exception that proved the rule. New criminal justice statutes were introduced seldom and their formulation and gestation were mostly left to non-political processes and specialists. The Advisory Council on the Treatment of Offenders (ACTO) (1944–64), shadowed within the Home Office by the Departmental Committee on the Treatment of Offenders, was the acme of this tradition. It comprised judges, magistrates, academics, and prominent reformers. During its life it considered everything from corporal punishment to prisoner after-care. It was replaced by the other favoured policy-making forum, the Royal Commission, a mechanism which in 1960–2 was also used to formulate the arrangements, adopted in the Police Act 1964, for the governance of the police. In retrospect the ill-fated Royal Commission on the Penal System (1964–6) might be considered a foretaste of the controversies to come: it was disbanded, the only Royal Commission ever not to report, because its members could not agree on fundamental aspects of their task. However, such was the strength of the traditional reliance on policy-making by professionals, that the government response was to revert to the *modus quo ante*: an Advisory Council on the Penal System (ACPS) was created which, until killed off by Margaret Thatcher's so-called Quango axe of 1980, produced a series of reports on, inter alia, detention centres, prison regimes, reparation by offenders, and sentences of imprisonment.

The final years of the ACPS coincided with the rise of the interest or pressure groups, an emerging phenomenon across the whole range of British politics, but given momentum in the law and order field by the apparently inexorable rise of the crime rate from the mid-1950s onwards, despite growing prosperity and the creation of a fairly comprehensive welfare safety net. Policy formation and electoral behaviour were more capable of being altered by short-term single issues which could 'only with difficulty be forced within the straitjacket of the old, class-based, two-party system' (Gamble 1990: 353).

Within the criminal justice field, moreover, the reformists were dismayed by the manner in which the Conservatives were dominating the policy agenda with Labour showing little inclination to formulate a systematic one of its own. Further, the most influential lobbies within the law and order arena, the staff unions—the Police Federation and Prison Officers' Association, for example—and the professional associations—the Magistrates' Association, the Law Society, and so on—were usually less than progressive and often downright reactionary. In this particular sphere there was no close alliance between Old Labour and the trade unions, quite the contrary.

THE PENAL PRESSURE GROUPS AND CONSORTIA

It is perhaps because law and order issues and personnel never easily fitted the left–right straitjacket, that the criminal justice pressure groups have very different pedigrees, some of them much older than the Thatcher decade. The oldest, the Howard League for Penal Reform, emerged in 1921 from the amalgamation of the original Howard Association, founded in 1866, and the more militant Penal Reform League, formed in the wake of the suffragette movement in 1907 (see Ryan 1978). It has counterparts in many Commonwealth countries. Until the foundation of the National Association for the Care and Resettlement of Offenders (NACRO) in 1966, it had no real contenders in the field of penal reform. From the late 1960s, however, new pressure groups flourished: Radical Alternatives to Prison (RAP) in 1969; the Legal Action Group (LAG) in 1971; and, within the Labour Party, the Labour Campaign for Criminal Justice in 1978. JUSTICE had, however, preceded even NACRO: founded by Tom Sargent, it was a remarkably successful pressure group in its highly focused pursuit of legal reform. On occasion, alliances between two or more of these groups enhanced their effectiveness, as with the battle of the Howard League, JUSTICE, and NACRO to expunge certain classes of ex-offender records in the Rehabilitation of Offenders Act 1974 (ibid.: 60–3). Inquest (founded 1981) and the Prison Reform Trust (founded 1982) were more clearly the reactive product of Thatcher's tough-talking policing and penal agenda of 1979.

It was the illiberal penal policy climate of the early 1980s, combined with the proliferation of criminal justice pressure groups, which led to the concept of the campaigning consortium. This was successfully adopted between 1978 and 1983 when *New Approaches to Juvenile Crime*—a grouping of NACRO and the principal social work and probation practitioner organizations—did much to foster the views leading to the dramatic decline in the use of custody for juvenile offenders in the 1980s. The group used all the informational techniques which in the 1980s and early 1990s made NACRO a force to be reckoned with: briefing papers and press releases were regularly produced; deputations to ministers arranged; meetings with magistrates held; and regular parliamentary briefings organized. It was Lady Faithful, the group's organizer, who, against government wishes, introduced amendments to the Bill which became the custody criteria for young offenders in the Criminal Justice Act 1982, section 1: this measure led to greatly reduced use of custody. Though cause and effect can never precisely be established, *New Approaches* did much to counter the tough political rhetoric of the early 1980s (see Morgan and Newburn, Chapter 30, this volume).

A more recent pressure grouping is the Penal Affairs Consortium, a lobbying collective which comprised 13 organizations when it was formed in 1989 and now comprises 48, ranging from the Prison Governors' and the Prison Officers' Associations to NACRO, the Prison Reform Trust, the Howard League, and Liberty—a previously unthinkable combination. By contrast, some single-issue pressure groups, such as the National Campaign for the Abolition of the Death Penalty (1955), rise and fall as the issue around which they are built waxes and wanes. It remains to be seen what course will be charted by 'asboconcern', a group formed in 2004–5 to campaign against the current use of ASBOs, comprising more than 30 organizations including the National Association of Probation Officers, the British Association of Social Workers, and the Childrens' Rights Alliance.

The extent and breadth of contemporary pressure group activity can be gauged from the list of such groups which gave evidence to the 1990 Woolf Inquiry into the prison disturbances of April that year. They included 65 groups in all, as well as professional associations, public service unions and ministries, and agencies of central and local government (Woolf Report 1991). More recently, the Home Office review of the sentencing framework, *Making Punishments Work* (the Halliday Report), deliberated with the assistance of an 'External Reference Group' with a membership of more than 40, including the Directors or Chairs of JUSTICE, the Penal Affairs Consortium, the Federation of Prisoners' Families Support Group, Drugscope, Payback, the Prison Reform Trust, DIVERT, and Victim Support. Combining these pressure-group activists with representatives of the major government departments and agencies and criminal justice professionals represented an attempt at corporate consensus-building with regard to an aspect of policy, sentencing, notoriously prone to founder (Home Office 2001: Appendix 1).

The sheer proliferation of pressure groups in the law and order field is striking, but less salient than the impressive professionalization of the larger organizations. A good many do not merely campaign, they provide extensive services and undertake evaluative research. This makes them a formidable counter to Home Office senior advisors, who increasingly, as we have seen, seek representation from them when it comes to undertaking major stocktakes. Their challenge, if the Government pursues policies of which they disapprove, can be high profile: some of their leading spokespersons gather as much media attention, and are as widely known, as junior Home Office ministers. NACRO's Paul Cavadino, for example, achieved such prominence, and became such a bête noire for Conservative Home Secretary Michael Howard in the mid-1990s, that NACRO decided it was politic to give him a backroom role for a while. In autumn 2005 Liberty's General Secretary, Shami Chakrabarti, became the foremost media spokesperson of the victorious civil libertarian forces ranged against the Government's proposal to introduce up to 90 days' detention without charge and, in effect, allow use of evidence possibly extracted under torture abroad. These examples illustrate a trend.

Before 1970, the date assigned by Bailey (1987) to the final break-up of the post-war consensus on delinquency, pressure-group activity metaphorically sought to influence policy by a well-informed word in the ministerial ear. From that date, reformers increasingly began to beat on the ministerial door in a far more public, confrontational way, albeit one which was, if anything, even more highly informed. Douglas Hurd, Home Secretary from 1984 to 1988, remarked that such clamour was counterproductive. However, this metaphor should not be allowed to obscure the growth, from the 1980s onwards, of myriad links between the Home Office and the pressure groups. This was partly because some groups, of which NACRO and Crime Concern are prime examples (their websites claim that they employ hundreds of staff and volunteers providing services to thousands of (mostly offender) beneficiaries each year), had developed a network of local contacts, services, and experience which matched that available to senior civil service policy-makers. In conferences, media debates, seminars, and the regular call for expert evidence on penal matters in particular, opportunities abounded for pressure groups to inform penal policy-making processes. None of these processes, either singly or in total, however, equalled the kind of unforced insider access that the Howard League enjoyed in its heyday of close informal as well as formal contact with the Home Office, or the strong role for criminological expertise, which in the early days was thin on the ground, provided by the ACTO and ACPS before 1980 (see Ryan 1978, 2003).

That inside track carried the danger that research might uphold punitive measures, and inhibit challenge to government policy, as in the example of Max Grunhut's long gestation of a project which eventually reported in favour of detention centres, to the detriment of the Howard League's stance on the issue (Ryan 1978: 83–4). Further, in its final years, the ACPS produced more and more lengthy reports—on *Young Adult Offenders* in 1974 and *Sentences of Imprisonment* in 1978, for example—which attracted critical academic judgement as well as ministerial impatience (see Morgan 1979). In the 1980s the government largely replaced advice from Royal Commissions and standing advisory bodies with official inquiries set up whenever a need was perceived.

It was partly this decline in government reliance on grand, officially organized advice that stimulated the emergence of more professional pressure groups, most of them, even when beneficiaries of government funding—as NACRO has always been—more or less critical of government policy. The pressure groups have generally favoured: explanations of crime which stress economic inequality, social exclusion, and individual vulnerability; use of social policy in general rather than criminal justice policy in particular, to prevent or control crime; scepticism as to the value of police powers and punitive methods (particularly imprisonment) as crime control measures—indeed, they generally stress the discriminatory and unjust consequences of such methods for repressing already oppressed minorities (Ryan 1978, 1983, 2003). Thus though there are substantial differences between these groups regarding their ideological commitments, constitutional form, access to policy-makers, and credibility with government, they have a good deal in common. They are generally perceived as left of centre, generally have allegiances with Liberal or Labour rather than Conservative politicians (though NACRO and the Prison Reform Trust are always careful to involve politicians of all parties on their councils), and tend, in spite of the consortia arrangements referred to above, also to have fragile relationships with the practitioner sectional groups, such as the Prison Officers' Association, the Police Federation, the Association of Chief Police Officers (ACPO), and the Magistrates' Association. The latter tend to adopt policies emphasizing the 'thin blue line' and the importance of their members' powers to safeguard the community from crime.

Given these dissonances, it is notable how much interchange occurred between the groups and the government from the 1980s on. In other fields of social policy, such as education, where pressure groups of comparable expertise are largely lacking, ideologically driven changes since 1979 arguably met with less resistance, despite strong interest-group and practitioner unease or hostility. Given the immense imbalance of power between the groups and the Home Office, the latter could be said to have little to lose and much to gain from such contacts. The pressure groups provide positive feedback services for governments in furnishing early warnings of probable trouble, in canvassing feasible reforms, and in heightening the legitimacy of the governmental process itself. In a complex society, pressure-group and interest-group activities are the major avenues for active citizen participation in democratic decision-making. In the 1980s, pressure groups also fitted the ideological predispositions of the Thatcher administrations to accord client-based and consumerist agencies a better hearing, albeit at the expense of local government (which still harboured socialist residues) and the trade unions. Quangos and Royal Commissions were seen as stifling government and citizen initiative. The Woolf Inquiry of 1990 was a model of democratic participation by an informed citizenry (by comparison with, say, the average Royal Commission), holding seminars at which the views and evidence of different groups were debated rather than simply presented seriatim—though the views of prisoners were separately canvassed and, to that extent, somewhat devalued (Morgan 1991; Sim 1993). This consultative model was subsequently adopted by the *Committee of Inquiry into Complaints about Ashworth Hospital* in 1991–2, with similarly radical impact (Blom-Cooper Report 1992; see also Richardson 1993) and is now regarded as almost standard procedure (both the Halliday review of sentencing (Home Office 2001) and the Auld review of the criminal courts (Auld Report 2001) employed a range of consultative arrangements—posting ideas on websites, employing advisory groups, and holding consultative seminars).

Even so, the huge imbalance of power remains a political reality. When 'pressured', the Home Office can brush aside any protest, as exemplified by the prisons privatization programme, a policy vehemently opposed by both the penal pressure groups and the prison staff associations. Both Conservative and New Labour governments in their drive to cut the cost of public services and expose them to the allegedly beneficial rigours of market competition have increasingly viewed the practitioner-representative organizations as little more than vested interests resisting any challenge to the inefficient monopolistic services within which they shelter. Thus the consultative style adopted by senior judges, like Woolf and Auld, asked to undertake official inquiries, has seldom characterized ministerial policy initiatives. Changes in the rank structure and proposals radically to alter the basis of police pay—changes recommended by a 1992 inquiry (Sheehy Report 1993)—and major amendments to the constitutional framework for the governance of the police—amendments first set out in the 1991 White Paper on *Police Reform* and implemented in the Police and Magistrates' Courts Act 1994—were taken speedily and in spite of the views of practitioners, local government associations, and the overwhelming majority of informed commentators. Likewise, current plans effectively to dismember the Prison and Probation Services, under the direction of the newly created commissioning body, the National Offender Management Service (NOMS), was announced without consultation within days of a No 10-inspired, in-house review undertaken by Patrick Carter (see Raynor, Chapter 31, this volume).

In the same vein both Conservative and Labour administrations have resisted change widely called for. It was successive governments' refusal to institute a review of the drugs laws which led the Police Foundation, a small interest group founded in 1979 to promote police-related research, to set up in 1997 an independent inquiry under Lady Runciman, the next best thing to a Royal Commission. The exercise was funded by the Prince's Trust and the membership of the inquiry, which included two chief constables and senior academic experts, was not dissimilar to that which might have been expected of a Royal Commission, whose methods and typical timescale were also adopted. The resulting report (Police Foundation 2000) was authoritative, measured, and far from radical, but the Government, to the increasingly public irritation of Lady Runciman, took almost a year to respond to the recommendations, and then only to say that it was not inclined to make the legislative changes proposed. This particular stone wall cracked, however, when some leading Conservatives, following their disastrous defeat in June 2001, suggested that it might be time to reconsider current drugs legislation. In the following autumn, the new Labour Home Secretary, David Blunkett, announced that there were to be changes in the use of police discretion, which virtually decriminalized possession of small amounts of cannabis.

THE THINK TANKS

This last example illustrates a new trend. Successive governments' drives to effect certain changes in law and order services despite practitioner and pressure group opposition have prompted them selectively to nurture sympathetic practitioner organizations and distance themselves from the pressure groups whose liberal credentials and 'soft' image have themselves become hostages to fortune in the struggle for the political middle ground. Pressure groups have not recently enjoyed the direct contacts and influence with the world either of Whitehall or of Westminster which they achieved in the 1980s. They have to some extent been displaced, particularly with New Labour, by the think tanks.

It was the free marketeers who first established think tanks. Their function was to promote a political and economic philosophy. The Institute of Economic Affairs (IEA), founded in 1955, and the Adam Smith Institute, founded in 1977, were the precursors of the Thatcherite revolution, advocating deregulation, privatization, and, as part of that exercise, trade union reform. Keen advocates of privatization of prisons and private security provision on the grounds that state monopolistic provision is inefficent and has failed to deliver, they have seen their core ideas to a substantial extent incorporated in New Labour's mixed economy programme which is now advocated by the Institute for Political and Policy Research (IPPR), founded in 1988, and Demos, founded in 1993. What the IEA and the Adam Smith Institute did for the Conservatives in the years preceding 1979, the IPPR and Demos did for New Labour in the run-up to their electoral victory in 1997. They defined New Labour's 'modernizing government' agenda. This agenda, a mixed economy of provision, private finance partnerships, and, within the state services, an emphasis on managerial techniques developed in the private sector, encompasses SMART objectives and planning processes combined with measurable outputs and outcomes and regular reviews of achievement.

The ascendancy of New Labour and its landslide victory in June 2001 have currently put the IEA (and Civitas, a successor organization) and the Adam Smith Institute very much in the shade. But the IPPR and Demos have in many observers' eyes become extensions of the Cabinet Office, flying kites for ministers to see how the wind of public or elite opinion blows. Law and order issues figure relatively prominently in this arrangement.

THE MASS MEDIA, THE CIVIL SERVICE, AND THE POLICY-MAKING PROCESS

The pressure groups are finding it more of a struggle to get their views across, and their voices heard, in a media world increasingly dominated by the think tanks and governmental public relations spin. In response to being held more at arm's length, they have subdued their critical stance and 'kept their powder dry' for a support role in backing up such heavyweight, retired players as Lord Woolf, formerly Lord Chief Justice, and Lord Ramsbotham, formerly Chief Inspector of Prisons, both outspoken critics of aspects of Home Office policy. Otherwise, especially where they depend substantially on governmental funding, they tend to be scripted, if not incorporated, into Home Office scenarios. The IPPR is more likely to host seminars attended by NACRO than the reverse. Professional groups have become more constrained by central directives and reorganization, better coordinated but less autonomous professionally, though some individual voices retain their critical force. NAPO's Harry Fletcher spoke out knowledgeably against the 'naming and shaming' of former 'paedophile' offenders and is today voicing objections to the development of NOMS, as are key members of the Probation Boards Association. Current plans to amalgamate police forces are likewise encountering opposition from the police authorities and some chief constables.

Overall, however, the media skills which made NACRO and other pressure groups such a force to be reckoned with in the 1980s and early 1990s have now been upstaged by governmental strategists. Moreover, the resort to comparative European examples, once so telling for its placing of the UK at or near the top of the prison population league table, has to some extent been displaced by the apparent success of the USA in reducing crime rates. That may come under increasing challenge as the full (not just financial) costs of mass imprisonment in the USA gains wider currency (see, especially, Garland 2001); and as links between the character of a society's political economy and its resort to imprisonment are more fully analysed on a comparative basis (see especially Cavadino and Dignan 2006). However, public perception of 'the facts' and their interpretation are increasingly drawn from media reportage and snapshot polls in which the tabloid rather than the broadsheet press hold sway. 'Metropolitan elites' no longer make the running in criminal justice policy terms (Ryan 2003), though the extent to which they did so even in their heyday is easily exaggerated. How to engage more fully and innovatively in public policy debate on crime and punishment increasingly preoccupies penal analysts (Ryan 2003; Green 2005) via such methods as deliberative polling, in which representatives of diverse public, professional, and academic groups engage in more extended, informed, and, therefore, democratic debate.

The micro-politics of law and order are intimately bound up with the processes whereby the goals and agendas set by ministers are translated into policies and specific directives by civil servants. They are also creatively authored in key respects by senior civil servants, whose briefings and policy formulations have a distinct part to play in formal policy-making. As Rock (1995) has shown, policy formation within the Home Office is typically a matter of written argument developing 'crescively'. For example, the 1991 Criminal Justice Act was the outcome of a decade-long process of casting about for the most appropriate means of reducing the level of the prison population without either eroding judicial independence or offending the more reactionary wing of the Conservative Party (see Rutherford 1996 for his analysis of the leading role played by David Faulkner in that process). By their creation of a 'symbolic environment' (Edelman 1971) and by their active refinement of issues and arguments culled from such diverse gatherings as international conferences and informal discussion groups, it is possible for senior civil servants such as Faulkner and, in an earlier period, Morrell (in connection with the Children and Young Persons Act 1970)), to energize the field (see also Rock 1986; Bottoms 1974; King and McDermott 1995: ch. 1). They are far from being passive bureaucrats, though the most prominent example currently, Louise Casey, formerly head of the Home Office's Anti-Social Behaviour Unit and now director of the 'Respect Unit' directly accountable to the Prime Minister, arguably represents a very different phenomenon, the rise of the activist, celebrity civil servant taking the Prime Minister's message to the country (Morgan 2006).

Other relevant processes can be found in the Select Committee stages of drafting legislation, which can be the site for its profound amendment or effective termination by delay. For example, the Police and Criminal Evidence Act 1984 was a vastly different affair from the 1983 Bill which lapsed on the calling of the 1983 General Election (Ryan

1983). Such major transformations due to detailed parliamentary scrutiny are, however, increasingly the exception rather than the rule. Within four months of the implementation of the 1991 Criminal Justice Act, the then Home Secretary, Kenneth Clarke, conceded, in the face of criticisms from the judiciary and the media, and polls showing a new-found public preference for Labour over the Conservatives on 'law and order', that some key clauses required amendment. Two in particular, on unit fines and the constraints on basing sentences in part on previous convictions, were scrapped. Critics argued that a policy of decarceration that had taken a decade to construct was despatched with indecent haste, partly because of shoddy drafting and too little parliamentary scrutiny. More recently, the reconstituted House of Lords threw out or amended for re-scrutiny in the Commons a record number of Bills on criminal justice, again in part due to over-hasty drafting and the over-use of three-line whips to bulldoze controversial laws through despite a huge majority. For example, private prisons have now survived two U-turns: the first under Douglas Hurd in 1987, the second by Jack Straw in 1998. Both Home Secretaries accepted in practice what they had previously denounced in principle. Another example was the repeated attempts by Labour in 2000–1 to bludgeon the Lords into accepting the restricted right to jury trial by defendants in 'triable either-way' cases. In sum, despite the occasional instance of parliamentary scrutiny bearing innovatory discussion on criminal justice and penal policy, many important policy developments are preceded by virtually no public debate, parliamentary or otherwise (see Richardson 1993).

Despite the exceptional landmark Police and Criminal Evidence Act 1984, the history of policing is redolent with major changes effected without parliamentary debate. Policing policy underwent a sea change in the late 1970s and early 1980s, with the creation of Special Patrol Groups whose activities involved the killing of Blair Peach in Southall 1978 and sparked the major riot in Brixton 1981 (Hall *et al.* 1978; Scarman 1981); the increased reliance on mutual aid between forces, sometimes under the direction of the National Reporting Centre (Spencer 1985); the deployment of new paramilitary equipment and techniques (Jefferson 1990; Waddington 1991); and the adoption of neighbourhood crime prevention strategies (Bennett 1990; Rosenbaum 1988), all without the benefit of research, or public or parliamentary debate. Whether in early 2006 government plans to reduce 43 police forces to around a third of that number—plans drawn up with scarcely any parliamentary or public debate—will get through unscathed, remains to be seen.

It is because so much policy is made and implemented without adequate public debate on its implications that many analysts of criminal justice and penal policy insist that statutes should, in future, state more precisely what objectives agencies should pursue and what specific powers decision-makers should have, and provide for procedural rights for those citizens—suspects, prisoners, and mental hospital patients—caught up in the system (Richardson 1993). Ideally, accountability should begin with Parliament and end with the day-to-day answerability of practitioners. And yet, despite the endless evaluations and managerial reorganizations of the 'Audit Society' (Power 1997), the exigencies of the politics of law and order increasingly mean that 'the buck', to adapt Harry Truman's phrase, no longer 'stops here', or indeed anywhere, but is endlessly recycled.

MATTERS OF SCANDAL AND CONCERN

The remaining variable is the unpredictable realm of scandal and concern. Both parliamentary and extra-parliamentary groupings can be utterly outpaced by events which explode in such a way that unusual responses are called for by 'public opinion'—a phenomenon for which media attention is often taken as proxy. In the law and order realm, four types of event seemingly dwarf all others in their dramatic impact on politics and policy: prison escapes; high-profile crimes; miscarriages of justice; and riotous assemblies. Examples are legion, and in previous editions of this handbook we have singled out:

- prison escapes in 1965–6 and 1994–5, and the prison occupations in 1990 (see Morgan and Leibling, Chapter 32, this volume);

- the murder of James Bulger in 1993 (see both Ashworth and Morgan and Newburn, Chapters 29 and 30 respectively, this volume; also Green 2005, for responses to a comparable case in Norway);

- the paedophile murder of Sarah Payne by Roy Whiting in 2000;

- the murder of Stephen Lawrence in 1993, the bungled police response, the campaign for a re-trial by his parents, and the subsequent inquiry and report chaired by Lord Macpherson, with its key conclusion on 'institutional racism';

- the murder of Zahid Mubarek in Feltham Young Offenders Institution in 2000;

- the miasma of debate surrounding immigration, both legal and illegal; refugees and asylum-seeking; migrant labour; host/migrant community tensions; and majority/ethnic minority tensions, erupting in several towns and cities into riotous conflicts (e.g. Bradford 2001, Birmingham 2005);

- the release of the Guildford Four, the Birmingham Six, and the Maguire Seven, all Irish suspects convicted of multiple homicides by verdicts declared 'unsafe' as long as 15–17 years later.

Responses to such 'events' are highly variable. Governments at times act promptly and decisively, as with the establishment of the Mountbatten Inquiry into the prison escapes of the mid-1960s, and the Woolf Inquiry into the occupation of Strangeways Prison and other prison disturbances in 1990. Their recommendations are at times followed, at times not; sometimes they are acted on initially and then abandoned, or the reverse. There is no clear tariff of response or policy process. This variability is exemplified in two sets of phenomena which have flared most dramatically in the past four years: terrorism, and the exploitation of migrant labour.

FROM IRELAND TO IRAQ: CONTRASTS IN RESPONSES TO TERRORISM

The context for the notorious miscarriages of justice referred to above is of course the political quagmire of Northern Ireland and its ramifications for the control of terrorism in Britain. Some 3,000 fatalities in Northern Ireland and approximately 200 in Great Britain and elsewhere may seem relatively small over three decades since the 'troubles' reignited in 1969. 'However, scale matters . . . Comparatively speaking, the death-toll in Northern Ireland alone made the UK absolutely the most violent liberal democracy' (O'Leary and McGarry 1993: 4). The costs in law-enforcement measures have been huge, as have the negative effects on public trust in British political institutions. To combat what would now be termed the 'insurgency', strong emergency powers overrode traditional safeguards against wrongful arrest and conviction. There seemed no possible resolution to the incompatible demands of the Republicans for the unification of Ireland and the Unionists (still the majority, albeit a declining one) for the continuing Union with Great Britain.

Nevertheless, Northern Ireland has proved the site for 'the most surprising co-achievement of the New Labour government' (O'Leary 2001: 449): the 1998 Belfast Agreement, more widely known as the 'Good Friday Agreement'. While Blair has been the legatee of the foundations laid by others, Northern Ireland is arguably his own best legacy. He gave the peace process momentum, setting in motion such highly charged measures as the prisoner release scheme, the full-blown, costly and as yet incomplete Inquiry into the events of 'Bloody Sunday' in 1972, and the Patten Report on the Royal Ulster Constabulary, leading to its partial remodelling in 2001 as the new Police Service of Northern Ireland. While the peace process flourished under the late Mo Mowlam, stalled under Mandelson, and has been constrained throughout by the formidable nature of the entrenched interests of the various groups and parties to the Agreement, Blair has committed an immense amount of personal time, energy, and political capital into steering the participants towards a workable settlement and a renewed form of power-sharing, taking care throughout to work with Bertie Ahern, the Irish Premier. While falling short of any resemblance to a 'Truth and Reconciliation' basis for a stable future, it has been a lengthy and constructive engagement with a lethally complex set of problems, albeit one which could still unravel if the infinite possibilities for hugely symbolic false moves are not avoided.

By contrast with his genuine statesmanship in this realm, Blair's co-achievement with President George W. Bush of the invasion of Iraq has been somewhat more destructive of both international law and domestic civil liberties. It is as if, having partially bought into American policies on crime control (Jones and Newburn 2006), Blair moved seamlessly to doing so in tow to a foreign policy embracing war: 'policy transfer' on a truly awesome scale. Following the attack by al-Qaeda on the 'twin towers' in New York on 11 September 2001, Bush could claim some military and moral grounds for regime change in Afghanistan, one of its key bases. No such justification could be made for the invasion of Iraq. Blair's now discredited claim was that Iraq had weapons of mass destruction capable of being launched within 45 minutes. 'Even more breathtaking was his subsequent admission that he had never bothered to enquire what sort of weapons—battlefield or mega-death? The reason can only have been his desperate search for justification for action to which he was committed because he knew the Americans were committed' (Toynbee and Walker 2005: 180). Had Blair been Prime Minister instead of Harold Wilson in the years 1964–70, Britain would doubtless have been directly engaged in the Vietnam War.

It is all too likely that, despite denials, the British involvement in the invasion and occupation of Iraq inspired four British Muslims to launch their lethal sequence of suicide bombings in London on 7 July 2005. Even before that attack, but following 9/11, the UK had suspended those clauses of the European Convention on Human Rights prohibiting detention without trial. Thirteen foreign nationals suspected of links with terrorism were detained for three years in Belmarsh Prison, until the Law Lords' ruling on the unconstitutionality of the detention released them to indefinite house arrest. After 7/7, and the Prime Minister's statement on 5 August 2005 that 'the rules of the game are changing', the Government tried to extend the time limit for detention without charge, for terrorism suspects, from 14 to 90 days. Cross-party opposition, including a sizeable number of Labour MPs, reduced that to 28 days. Critics argued that not only was the extension wrong in principle, but it would be counterproductive, reinforcing sources of disaffection and alienation among ethnic minorities, especially those of Muslim faith. Other clauses in the current Terrorism Bill, such as those criminalizing the 'encouragement' and 'glorification' of terrorism, invite the same objections, and are said to fail the 'Mandela test': would these clauses have been used against opponents of apartheid who refused to renounce violence? The Northern Ireland test is perhaps more germane: would they be used against those supporting the IRA or the Protestant equivalents? The lessons of Northern Ireland—the hardening of resistance in response to demonization, the ease with which martyrdom can flow from disproportionate armed force—have not been applied to Iraq.

CRIME AT A DISTANCE: THE EXPLOITATION OF MIGRANT LABOUR

'After 9/11, right through Labour's second term, defence/foreign affairs/international terrorism topped people's list of concerns when they answered polls. Second came race relations/immigration/immigrants. Crime combined with law and order plus vandalism was third' (Toynbee and Walker 2005: 196). Under New Labour, the screw has been increasingly tightened even on those claiming refugee status, a key priority being to differentiate them from the even more stigmatized groups now termed 'economic migrants'. These are regarded as little short of predators, unless they happen to fill key vacancies in such fields as teaching, nursing, or medicine. Yet throughout the economy, increasing prosperity hinges on their contribution, mainly in jobs which are hyper-exploitative. 'Pity for migrants only showed when they were safely dead. Some 58 young Chinese had suffocated in a lorry coming through Dover; 19 Chinese cockle-pickers drowned in Morecambe Bay, illegals working under tyrannical gangmasters. Labour moved to regulate such gangs' (ibid.: 213) by the Gangmasters (Licensing) Act 2004, which focused on workers in agriculture and fishing. But the real villain of the piece is the food industry, especially the supermarkets, which wield immense corporate power and control the food chain so adeptly that the legality of their operations is fire-walled. All they do is set the scene and call the shots for crimes committed at a safe distance from their shelves.

An unexpected source of criminological expertise has emerged in the past decade in the nutrition columns of the broadsheets. In her study of the food industry, *Not On The Label*, Felicity Lawrence (2004: 43–5) documents the new division of labour down on the farm as driven by the voracious demands of the supermarkets for suppliers to meet tight specifications with

> complete flexibility . . . Labourers are often needed at very short notice and for long and unsocial hours . . . Farmers are both required to take the loss on any surplus and to meet any shortfall at their own expense . . . The work is hard, as agricultural labour has always been, often in freezing conditions in refrigerated plants. Industrial injuries are common. The pay is unattractive and never guaranteed. Small wonder that the need for labour is no longer met by the indigenous population. Instead, large numbers of migrants have filled the gap.

Yet the product is often no cheaper and less nutritious than that offered in the past by the local greengrocers now driven out of business by the appeal of the supermarkets' long opening hours and convenience packaging.

Moreover, 'the scale of migrant labour in the food industry is much larger than anyone is prepared to acknowledge, and a very substantial proportion of that labour is being employed illegally', one estimate being as high as approaching two million (ibid.: 36–7). The migrant workers brought in by 'mafia-style' networks lead lives of near-slavery, in conditions with parallels in the sex trade. To our shame, 'we have allowed a structure to emerge that enables our shops to be resupplied at short notice by casual labourers picked up from the roadside whatever the hour in the Costa del Sol, or collected from their Dickensian housing in rural England' (ibid.: 76)—though the term 'Dickensian' fails to convey the range of rancid and dilapidated caravans and porta-kabins to which they are consigned. Moreover, while the relevant inspectorates remain so under-manned and under-resourced, no amount of legislation could make much difference to any aspect of this late-modern food chain.

CONCLUSIONS

The politics of law and order since 1945 have been shaped by the perceived need to respond to the almost continuous rise in recorded crime, the reduced potency of certain informal controls, the growth of illicit drug-taking, and the threat of politically inspired terrorism. Three phases can be discerned in the party political sphere. First, until 1970 a consensus prevailed whose terms, heavily influenced by 'liberal progressive' ideology, implicitly rested on the non-partisan character of crime and on the merit of adopting more community-based, rehabilitative policies for its control. This consensus was not universal. The judiciary continued to adhere to broadly retributive and deterrent principles of sentencing, except in relation to juveniles and a small minority of clinically diagnosed mentally ill offenders. Governments of both left and right shared a strong reluctance to intrude into the judicial realm and in any case imprisonment was proportionately less relied on by sentencers.

The 1970 election was a watershed, and that of 1979 virtually swept away the last vestiges of non-partisanship. Thereafter, in a second phase, there was sharp, growing contention between the parties for the increasingly important 'law and order' terrain. In the late 1980s and early 1990s the Conservatives in power emerged relatively unscathed from Labour's tentative attempts to link rising crime with the social and economic effects of growing inequality and unemployment. Labour's traditional attachments to the trade unions and to libertarian causes proved to be hostages to fortune. They led Labour leaders to seek to neutralize, rather than sharply contest, Conservative hegemony on this issue.

After the 1992 election a third phase began. Rebranding itself in opposition, New Labour distanced itself from the trade unions, libertarian causes, and the civil liberty and penal pressure groups. Meanwhile the Conservatives, bent on further restructuring public services to achieve cuts in public expenditure whilst simultaneously pursuing tough populist penal measures, prejudiced their traditional support base with the police, probation and prison personnel, and the judiciary. In the run-up to the 1997 election, the tables now being reversed, New Labour was coy about opposing Conservative 'law and order' legislation, on several occasions sought to out-tough Conservative legislative proposals, and, following its electoral victory, implemented Conservative measures that its members would have anathematized a decade earlier.

Since that time New Labour has consolidated its hold on government, though in the first year of its third term its tenure looks somewhat less secure. New Labour's accumulated strength lies principally in its perceived competence in economic management, but is in part due to its shedding the unwarranted image of being 'soft on crime'. New Labour's new-found and more justified image, that it is 'tough on crime', has been bought at considerable cost in terms of civil liberties and the humane and just penal policies that the party espoused in the 1980s. There is now a new, uneasy, 'second-order consensus' which is challenged, fitfully, only by the Liberal Democrats.

The major political parties are agreed, for example, that: victims must be given more information about proceedings against 'their' offenders, and greater voice; an 'active community', or 'civil society', must be reconstructed; prolific and dangerous offenders should be targeted and more effectively controlled or incapacitated; the parents of juvenile offenders should be held more accountable; restorative justice is a good thing; communitarian crime-reduction initiatives should be pursued; and there should be a mixed economy in the provision of policing and penal services, i.e., there is considerable scope for privatizing, voluntarizing, or civialianizing them. They do not always agree about the means for achieving these objectives. The Labour Party, for example, has always placed greater emphasis on the role of local authorities as the linchpin of crime prevention. The Conservatives have preferred alternative self-help and agency frameworks—Neighbourhood Watch and Crime Concern, the catalyst organization that they created and funded in the early 1990s. But Crime Concern continues and is now the principal national advisor of local authority crime prevention partnerships into most of which Neighbourhood Watch groups are now woven. Moreover, Crime Concern, together with other large-scale voluntary providers, is gearing up to bid for the provision of probation services in a mixed probation economy which the creation of NOMS is designed to promote. There is arguably more fusion than faction.

The establishment of this second-order consensus means that there is constant jockeying for party political advantage to both left and right of the agreed central ground. In 2001 and 2005, in the wake of the 9/11 and 7/7 terrorist attacks, for example, the Conservatives opposed the Government's anti-terrorist legislative proposals on the grounds that they threatened civil liberties (the Liberal Democrats opposed more consistently). Meanwhile the Government ducks and dives. In 2001 Home Secretary, David Blunkett, cut through the increasingly discredited log-jam created by his predecessor, Jack Straw, by virtually decriminalizing the small-scale possession and personal use of cannabis. In 2006, however, David Blunkett's successor, Charles Clarke, has let it be known that he is thinking of reversing the measure. Clarke has already abandoned the cap of 80,000 on the prison population adopted by his predecessor. Yet, he proposes introducing the 'community prisons' recommended by Lord Justice Woolf in 1991, a policy which would operationally be feasible only were the prison population significantly reduced.

We can confidently predict that in the months and years ahead that Government and Opposition will battle for the high ground as to who best promotes public order, community safety, effective policing, and law enforcement. They will argue that different managerial structures and service provider mixes will deliver outcomes which the public want or which serve their long-term interests. In reaction the various law and order practitioner associations will seek to secure party political support for their vested interests, or what they will claim to be the public interest or human rights. The pressure groups and think tanks will do much the same. How far the traditional liberal bastions, now paradoxically embodied in certain core members of the judiciary, the House of Lords, and the pressure groups, can hold the line against the ever-tightening 'culture of control' (Garland 2001) remains to be seen. Much will depend on how far the New Labour approach to law and order will prove to be a specifically Blairite agenda, which in turn will hinge on when, how, and to whom the premiership is handed on.

■ SELECTED FURTHER READING

There have been few studies of the part played by 'law and order' in British political life. Philip Norton's *Law and Order and British Politics* (Gower, 1984) and Mike Brake and Chris Hale's *Public Order and Private Lives: the Politics of Law and Order* (Routledge, 1992), the latter a highly critical account of the Thatcher years, are exceptions. David Downes's edited collection, *Unravelling Criminal Justice* (Macmillan, 1992), contains relevant essays, particularly those by Bottoms and Stevenson on the extent and difficulties of the liberal consensus, and McBarnet on the burgeoning field of tax avoidance and evasion. Roger Hood's collection, *Crime, Criminology and Public Policy: Essays in Honour of Leon Radzinowicz* (Heinemann, 1974), provides detailed scrutiny of the public policy issues of the mid-period, and Terence Morris's *Crime and Criminal Justice in Britain since 1945* (Blackwell, 1989) covers the entire period with shrewd political insight. The criminal justice record in government of New Labour since 1997 is the subject of critical scrutiny by Michael Tonry in *Confronting Crime* (Willan, 2003). The collections of essays edited by Kevin Stenson and Richard Sullivan, *Crime, Risk and Justice: The politics of crime control in liberal democracies* (Willan, 2001) and Tim Newburn and Richard Sparks, *Criminal Justice and Political Cultures—National and international dimensions of crime control* (Willan, 2004), together with Trevor Jones and Tim Newburn's monograph, *Policy Transfer and Criminal Justice* (Open University Press, 2006), place British developments in a broader, international, comparative dimension, in particular tracing American influence. Michael Cavadino and James Dignan's *Penal Systems: A Comparative Approach* (Sage, 2006) does the same specifically for penal policy. Finally, Mick Ryan (*Penal Policy and Political Culture in England and Wales* (Waterside, 2003)) is a political scientist in criminology who over many years has documented the micro-politics of penal reform in the wider political economy of Britain.

■ REFERENCES

ATKINSON, T. (2002), *Top Incomes in the UK over the Twentieth Century* (Discussion Paper in Economic and Social History No. 43), Oxford: University of Oxford.

AUDIT COMMISSION (1996), *Misspent Youth*, London: Audit Commission.

AULD REPORT (2001), *Review of the Criminal Courts of England and Wales*, London: Stationery Office.

BAILEY, V. (1987), *Delinquency and Citizenship: Reclaiming the Young Offender 1914–1948*, Oxford: Clarendon Press.

BENNETT, T. (1990), *Evaluating Neighbourhood Watch*, Farnborough: Gower.

BLAIR, T. (2005), Speech in Hertfordshire to launch a Respect and Parenting Order Task Force, 2 September.

BLOM-COOPER REPORT (1992), *Report of the Committee of Inquiry into Complaints About Ashworth Hospital*, Cm 2028, London: HMSO.

BOTTOMS, A. E. (1974), 'Reflections on the Renaissance of Dangerousness', *Howard Journal*, 16: 70–96.

—— (1995), 'The Philosophy and Politics of Punishment and Sentencing', in C. Clarkson and R. Morgan (eds), *The Politics of Sentencing Reform*, Oxford: Clarendon Press.

BUTLER, D., and KAVANAGH, D. (1980), *The British General Election 1979*, Basingstoke: Macmillan.

—— and —— (1997), *The British General Election 1997*, Basingstoke: Macmillan.

CAVADINO, M., and DIGNAN, J. (1997), *The Penal System: An Introduction*, 2nd edn, London: Sage.

—— and —— (2006), *Penal Systems: A Comparative Approach*, London: Sage.

COMMISSION ON FAMILIES AND THE WELLBEING OF CHILDREN (2005), *Families and the State: Two-way support and responsibilities—An inquiry into the relationship between the state and the family in the upbringing of children*, Bristol: Policy Press.

CONSERVATIVE PARTY (1979), *The Conservative Manifesto*, London: Conservative Party.

—— (1987), *Our First Eight Years: The Next Moves Forward*, London: Conservative Party.

—— (1997), *You Can Only Be Sure with the Conservatives*, London: Conservative Party.

—— (2001), *Time for Common Sense,* London: Conservative Party.

—— (2005), *Are you thinking what we're thinking? It's time for Action: Conservative Election Manifesto 2005*, London: Conservative Party.

CRAWFORD, A. (1997), *The Governance of Crime*, Oxford: Clarendon Press.

DIXON, D., and FISHWICK, E. (1984), 'The Law and Order Debate in Historical Perspective', in P. Norton (ed.), *Law and Order and British Politics*, Aldershot: Gower.

DODGSON, K., GOODWIN, P., HOWARD, P., LLEWELLYN-THOMAS, S., MORTIMER, E., RUSSELL, N., and WEINER, M. (2001), *Electronic monitoring of released prisoners: an evaluation of the Home Detention Curfew scheme*, Home Office Research Study No. 222, London: Home Office.

DOWNES, D. (1998), 'Toughing It Out: From Labour Opposition to Labour Government', *Policy Studies*, 19, (3–4), 191–8.

—— (2001), 'The macho penal economy', *Punishment and Society*, 3(1), 61–80.

—— and MORGAN, R. (1994), ' "Hostages to Fortune"?: The Politics of Law and Order in Post-War Britain', in M. Maguire, R. Morgan, and R. Reiner (eds), *The Oxford Handbook of Criminology*, 1st edn, Oxford: Oxford University Press.

—— and —— (1997), 'Dumping the "Hostages to Fortune"?: The Politics of Law and Order in Post-War Britain', in M. Maguire, R. Morgan, and R. Reiner (eds), *The Oxford Handbook of Criminology*, 2nd edn, Oxford: Oxford University Press.

—— and —— (2002), 'The Skeletons in the Cupboard. The Politics of Law and Order at the Turn of the Millennium', in M. Maguire, R. Morgan, and R. Reiner (eds), *The Oxford Handbook of Criminology*, 3rd edn, Oxford: Oxford University Press.

DUNBAR, I., and LANGDON, A. (1998), *Tough Justice: Sentencing and Penal Policies in the 1990s*, London: Blackstone.

EDELMAN, M. (1971), *Politics as Symbolic Action*, Chicago, Ill.: Markham.

ELDER, N. C. M. (1984), 'Conclusion', in P. Norton (ed.), *Law and Order and British Politics*, Aldershot: Gower.

ELLIOTT, L. (2001), 'Labour underspends Tories', *Guardian*, 24 April.

FLOUD, J., HALSEY, A. H., and MARTIN, F. M. (1956), *Social Class and Educational Opportunity*, London: Heinemann.

GAMBLE, A. (1990), 'The Thatcher Decade in Perspective', in P. Dunleavy, A. Gamble, and G. Peele (eds), *Developments in British Politics*, London: Macmillan.

GARLAND, D. (1996), 'The Limits of the Sovereign State: Strategies of Crime Control in Contemporary Society', *British Journal of Criminology*, 64(4): 445–71.

—— (2001), *The Culture of Control: Crime and Social Order in Contemporary Society*, Oxford: Oxford University Press.

GIDDENS, A. (1998), *The Third Way*, Cambridge: Polity.

GREEN, D. (2005), The Politics of Tragedy: Child-on-Child Homicide and Political Culture', PhD thesis, unpubl., Cambridge: Institute of Criminology.

HALL, S., CRITCHER, S., JEFFERSON, T., CLARKE, J., and ROBERTS, B. (1978), *Policing the Crisis: Mugging, the State and Law and Order*, London: Macmillan.

HELD, D. (2001), 'Regulating Globalisation? The Reinvention of Politics', in A. Giddens (ed.), *The Global Third Way Debate*, Cambridge: Polity.

HENNESSEY, P. (1992), *Never Again*, London: Cape.

HM GOVERNMENT (2005), *Higher Standards, Better Schools for All: More choice for parents and pupils*, Cm 6677, London: DfES.

HM TREASURY (2003), *Every Child Matters*, London: TSO.

HILLS, J. (2004), *Inequality and the State*, Oxford: Oxford University Press.

HOBBS, D., HADFIELD, P., LISTER, S., and WINLOW, S. (2003), *Bouncers: Violence and Governance in the Night-time Economy*, Oxford: Oxford University Press.

HOME OFFICE (1997), *No More Excuses* (White Paper), London: Home Office.

—— (2001), *Making Punishments Work: Report of a Review of the Sentencing Framework for England and Wales* (The Halliday Report), London: Home Office.

HONDERICH, T. (1990), *Conservatism*, London: Hamish Hamilton.

JEFFERSON, T. (1990), *The Case Against ParaMilitary Policing*, Milton Keynes: Open University Press.

JONES, D. (2001), '"Misjudged Youth": A Critique of the Audit Commission's Reports on Youth

Justice', *British Journal of Criminology*, 41(2): 362–80.

JONES, T., and NEWBURN, T. (2004), 'The Convergence of US and UK Crime Control Policy: Exploring Substance and Process', in T. Newburn and R. Sparks (eds), *Criminal Justice and Political Cultures: National and international dimensions of crime control*, Cullompton, Devon: Willan.

—— and —— (2006), *Policy Transfer and Criminal Justice*, Open University Press.

JUSTICES' CLERKS SOCIETY (1999), *Good Practice Guide*, Liverpool: JCS.

KING, R. D., and McDERMOTT, C. (1995), *The State of Our Prisons*, Oxford: Clarendon Press.

LABOUR PARTY (1964), *Crime: A Challenge to us All* (Longford Report), London: Labour Party.

—— (1997), *New Labour—Because Britain Deserves Better*, London: Labour Party.

—— (2001), *Ambitions for Britain: Labour's Manifesto 2001*, London: Labour Party.

—— (2005), *Britain—forward not back: the Labour Party Manifesto 2005*, London: Labour Party.

LAWRENCE, F. (2004), *Not On The Label: What Really Goes into the Food on your Plate*, London: Penguin.

LEVITAS, R. (1998), *The Inclusive Society? Social Exclusion and New Labour*, Basingstoke: Macmillan.

LIBERAL DEMOCRATIC PARTY (2001), *Freedom, Justice, Honesty: Manifesto for a Liberal and Democratic Britain—General Election 2001*, London: Liberal Democrat Party.

—— (2005), *Liberal Democrats—The Real Alternative*, London: Liberal Democratic Party.

LIGHT, R. (2005), 'The Licensing Act 2003: Liberal Constraint?', *Modern Law Review*, 68: 268–85.

MACPHERSON, C. B. (1962), *The Political Theory of Possessive Individualism*, Oxford: Oxford University Press.

MACPHERSON REPORT (1999), *The Stephen Lawrence Inquiry: Report of an Inquiry by Sir William Macpherson of Cluny*, Cm 4262-I, London: Stationery Office.

MORGAN, R. (1979), *Formulating Penal Policy: The Future of the Advisory Council on the Penal System*, London: NACRO.

—— (1991), 'Woolf: In Retrospect and Prospect', *Modern Law Review*, 54: 713–25.

—— (2006), 'With Respect to Order, the Rules of the Game Have Changed: New Labour's Dominance of the "Law and Order" Agenda', in T. Newburn

and P. Rock (eds), *The Politics of Crime Control: Essays in Honour of David Downes*, Oxford: Clarendon.

MUNCIE, J. (1999), *Youth and Crime: A Critical Introduction*, London: Sage.

NEWBURN, T. (2000), 'Atlantic Crossings: Crime Control in America and Britain', Inaugural Lecture, London: Goldsmiths College.

O'LEARY, B. (2001), 'The Belfast Agreement and the Labour Government', in A. Seldon (ed.), *The Blair Effect: The Blair Government 1997–2001*, London: Little, Brown, ch. 21.

—— and McGARRY, J. (1993), *The Politics of Antagonism: Understanding Northern Ireland*, London: Athlone.

PARKIN, F. (1967), 'Working-Class Conservatives: A Theory of Political Deviance', *British Journal of Sociology*, 18(3): 278–90.

PIACHAUD, D., and SUTHERLAND, H. (2001), 'Child poverty—aims, achievements and prospects for the future', *New Economy*, 8(2): 71–6.

POLICE FOUNDATION (2000), *Drugs and the Law* (Runciman Report), London: Police Foundation.

POWER, M. (1997), *The Audit Explosion*, Oxford: Oxford University Press.

REINER, R. (2000), *The Politics of the Police*, 3rd edn, Oxford: Oxford University Press.

RICHARDSON, (1993), *Law, Process and Custody: Prisoners and Patients*, London: Weidenfeld & Nicolson.

ROCK, P. (1986), *A View From the Shadows: The Ministry of the Solicitor General of Canada and the Justice for Victims of Crime Initiative*, Oxford: Clarendon Press.

—— (1995), 'The Opening Stages of Criminal Justice Policy Making', *British Journal of Criminology*, 35: 1–6.

ROSENBAUM, D. (1988), 'A Critical Eye on Neighbourhood Watch: Does it Reduce Crime and Fear?', in T. Hope and M. Shaw (eds), *Communities and Crime Reduction*, London: HMSO.

RUTHERFORD, A. (1996), *Transforming Criminal Policy*, Winchester: Waterside.

RYAN, M. (1978), *The Acceptable Pressure Group—Inequality in the Penal Lobby: A Case Study of the Howard League and PAP*, Farnborough: Saxon House.

—— (1983), *The Politics of Penal Reform*, London: Longman.

RYAN, M. (2003), *Penal Policy and Political Culture in England and Wales*, Winchester: Waterside Press.

SCARMAN, REPORT (1981), *The Brixton Disorders 10–12 April 1981*, London: HMSO.

SHAW, C. (1931), *The Natural History of a Delinquent Career*, Chicago: University of Chicago Press.

SHEEHY REPORT (1993), *Report of the Inquiry into Police Responsibilities and Rewards*, Cm 2281, London: HMSO.

SIM, J. (1993), 'Reforming the Penal Wasteland?: A Critical Review of the Woolf Report', in E. Player and M. Jenkins (eds), *Prisons After Woolf: Reform Through Riot*, London: Routledge.

SPEAR, H. B. (2002), *Heroin Addiction Care and Control: the British System 1916–1984*, London: DrugScope.

SPENCER, S. (1985), *Called To Account*, London: National Council for Civil Liberties.

TAYLOR, I. (1999), 'Respectable, Rural and English: the Lobby Against the Regulation of Firearms in Great Britain', in P. Carlen and R. Morgan (eds), *Crime Unlimited: Questions for the 21st* Century, Basingstoke: Macmillan.

TONRY, M. (2003), *Confronting Crime: Crime control policy under New Labour*, Cullompton, Devon: Willan.

TOYNBEE, P., and WALKER, D. (2001), *Did Things Get Better? An Audit of Labour's Successes and Failures*, Harmondsworth: Penguin.

—— and —— (2005), *Better or Worse? Has Labour Delivered?* London: Bloomsbury.

WADDINGTON, P. A. J. (1991), *The Strong Arm of the Law*, Oxford: Oxford University Press.

WILLIS, P. (1977), *Learning to Labour*, Farnborough: Gower.

WOLFGANG, M. E., FIGLIO, R. M., and SELLIN, T. (1972), *Delinquency in a Birth Cohort*, Chicago: University of Chicago Press.

WOOLF REPORT (1991), *Prison Disturbances April 1991: Report of an Inquiry by the Rt. Hon. Lord Justice Woolf (Parts I and II) and His Honour Judge Stephen Tumin (Part II)*, Cm 1456, London: HMSO.

WOOTTON COMMITTEE (1968), *Cannabis: Report by the Advisory Committee on Drug Dependence*, London: HMSO.

YOUNG, J. (1999), *The Exclusive Society: Social Exclusion, Crime and Difference in Late Modernity*, London: Sage.

10

CRIME DATA AND STATISTICS

Mike Maguire

> Let me be quite clear about this. Statistics is not tables or numbers, sets of techniques, lists of formulae, but is an approach to understanding the world about us. However, that world is very complex and there is no quick and easy way of gaining such understanding . . . If everything appears simple and crystal clear probably you have misunderstood the issue you are considering.
>
> (W. M. Harper, *Statistics.*)

INTRODUCTION

This chapter explores a number of interrelated questions about 'crime levels', 'crime patterns', and 'crime trends' and how they are measured. These range from what may sound like (but are not) straightforward empirical and methodological questions, such as 'how much crime is there?', 'how is it changing?' and 'how do we know?', to more sociological and political questions about the relationships between, on the one hand, the kinds of crime data which are collected and published and, on the other, changing perceptions of the nature of 'the crime problem' and developments in criminal justice policy and the politics of crime control. The chapter is divided into four main sections. Two of these (the first and the fourth) relate mainly to the latter kinds of questions, while the second and third discuss the main sources of data that are available and the various pictures of crime that they portray.

The first section provides a broad historical overview of changing approaches to the 'measurement' of crime in England and Wales. Here it is argued that, from Victorian times until the 1970s, the field was dominated by what came to be known as the 'official statistics', a series of annual compilations by the Home Office of offences recorded by the police, whose broad efficacy as a national 'barometer' of crime was rarely challenged. However, since then, crime has risen up the political agenda and a whole new industry has developed around the goal of reducing and 'managing' it, both at local and national (and, increasingly, international) level. Greater attention has also been paid to relatively 'hidden' forms of crime that take place in the privacy of the home or the workplace, as well as to new kinds of cross-border and Internet crime, none of which are adequately reflected in the official statistics. These changes have fuelled an explosive growth in the collection, analysis, and publication of crime data from many new sources, in which many more organizations and individuals have become involved. At the same time, the value of the recorded crime figures has been increasingly questioned. They are widely regarded as 'unfit for purpose' in terms of new data needs, and the general picture they paint of the scale and changing contours of the 'crime problem' has been challenged as seriously misleading. The Home Office has responded to some of these criticisms and demands, not only by developing several major new sources of crime data of its own (mainly through large-scale surveys), but also by the fairly radical step of publishing the annual recorded crime figures alongside results from the British Crime Survey(BCS) (Walker *et al.* 2006). This has in effect elevated the latter to the status of a second set of 'official statistics'.

The second section looks more closely at what these two principal 'official' sources of data appear to tell us about the overall scale of crime and trends over time, and examines their main problems and limitations in this respect. Comparisons are also made between the two, especially in relation to areas in which they have appeared to give contradictory messages. A key message throughout is that this is an area of shifting sands, and that any assertion about crime numbers or trends should be based on a thorough understanding of how the figures were produced.

The third section looks at pictures of crime which have emerged from alternative sources of data, beginning with the challenge that was mounted in the 1980s to both police and BCS figures by local crime surveys in inner city areas. Brief accounts are also given of recent developments in (and problems of) data-gathering in relation to types of crime that are especially difficult to 'count' and/or do not often come to police notice. These include domestic violence, child abuse, crimes within closed institutions, crimes against business, corporate fraud, cross-border and organized crime, and crimes by governments. Finally, attention is drawn to the recent rekindling of interest in data on *offenders* (as opposed to offences), particularly through a revival of self-report studies.

The fourth section returns to questions about the relationship between crime data and developments in the policy and political realms. Recent significant changes in the Home Office approach to the collection and presentation of crime data, it is argued, have taken place mainly in response to new data demands from policy-makers and practitioners. These demands are driven both by new *operational* needs (to support local and national crime-reduction initiatives, 'evidence-based policy', partnership working, and so on) and by the strong government focus on *performance management* of the police and criminal justice agencies. They have been addressed, on the one hand, by gathering and disseminating more comprehensive information about crime; and on the other, by introducing more checks on the integrity of crime recording (such as the National Crime Recording Standard). While welcome to policy-makers, these developments have had the unintended consequences of confusing the public and politicians about trends in crime, and contributing to a general decline in trust in government statistics. These issues will be discussed in the light of a new Statistic Commission review, which concludes that the governance of 'official statistics' should be placed into independent hands.

Two general points should be noted before beginning. First, most of the 'official' data and statistics discussed refer to England and Wales: these are complicated enough, and to attempt to delve into similar data elsewhere would have been over-ambitious. Nevertheless, international literature is referred to, and many of the points made have general application. Secondly, the terms 'data' and 'statistics' tend to be used very loosely in the field of criminology, as well as by government departments. Strictly speaking, the simple frequency tables that are often published under the name of 'criminal statistics' are not 'statistics' in the sense understood by mathematicians (which implies analysis and interpretation). However, we shall not break ranks, and will use the term as it is used in everyday language, to describe any set of data analysed or presented in a systematic fashion. Similarly, the term 'data' will be used very broadly to refer to any kind of information collected in a quantifiable form.

HISTORICAL OVERVIEW: THE RISE AND FALL OF OFFICIAL STATISTICS

The idea of 'measuring' crime in a systematic way—for example, attempting to count the numbers of offences committed, or to determine where and when they most often occur—first came to prominence in France in the early nineteenth century, where it was promoted by the so-called 'moral statisticians', Quetelet and Guerry, as part of a scientific vision of discovering laws and regularities in the social world akin to those that had been identified in the natural world (see, for example, Beirne 1993). However, the idea was also highly compatible with the aims and practices of the centralized bureaucracies that were expanding across Europe in support of the emerging nation states. As theorists such as Foucault (1977) have argued, the compilation of detailed information about many aspects of social life was a crucial factor in the development of modernity, and closely tied up with the consolidation of governments' control over their populations. It was unsurprising, therefore, that the collection and analysis of crime data soon became predominantly the province of government employees, rather than academic scientists.

Of course, there are many different kinds of crime-related information that can be collected by or on behalf of governments, and it can be used for a variety of purposes (benign or otherwise), which may also change over time. At one extreme, detailed information about individuals can be gathered and stored in centralized file systems and databases. This usually has more to do with direct surveillance and control than with 'measurement': for example, at around the same time as Quetelet and Guerry were writing, Eugene-François Vidocq, the first head of the Paris Sûreté, was operating on behalf of the French government the most sophisticated system of surveillance yet devised, using an innovative card index system of intelligence files on hundreds of people designated as criminals or enemies of the state (Morton 2005).[1] At the other extreme, the information collected may consist of regular anonymized statistical returns from local courts or police forces, which have little immediate operational value, but may have a number of broader functions (as discussed below). In between are many other kinds of data collected on a one-off basis to inform policy or practice at national or local level, including the results of inquiries or research into specific types of crime.

In England and Wales, particular value came to be attached from the middle of the nineteenth century onwards to regular statistical series based on data sent to the Home Office from every local area. The first set of these national crime statistics was compiled in 1857, and similar tables continued to be published annually in government Command Papers—latterly under the title *Criminal Statistics, England and Wales*—for nearly one hundred and fifty years. Widely known as the 'official statistics', the tables were based on annual returns from the police and the courts which were checked and aggregated by government statisticians. Although the terminology and coverage changed in minor ways over time, the basic format remained remarkably similar for many years. The publication was divided into two main sections, one covering offences recorded by the police and the other 'offenders cautioned or found guilty'. Most of the tables on recorded crime (the main object of our interest here) consisted of counts of specific types of offence, classified by legal categories and broken down by, for example, police force area. They also showed trends in the various totals over both the long and short term. The offender-based tables were mainly concerned with the types and lengths of sentence given for different categories of offence, broken down variously by age, sex, and area. Innovation in presentation or analysis was rare, as the statisticians (who over time became to some extent distanced from the policy-making world) were driven more by the aim of producing consistent statistical series rather than that of producing data or analysis geared to immediate practical needs.

The production of annual criminal statistics of these kinds has a number of potential purposes and uses, the prominence and value of which can change considerably over time. Their introduction in England and Wales initially provided an important new window for central administrators on to what was going on in different areas of the country, and the statistics were increasingly used to assist them in allocating resources and monitoring court and police activities (including, for example, sentencing trends and police detection rates). At a more abstract level, they came to be seen as providing something akin to an official barometer of the 'moral health of the nation', paralleling

---

[1] However, modern databases which hold information about individuals, such as the new central IT system which will store all 'e-OASys' risk/needs assessments undertaken on convicted offenders in England and Wales can also be used to provide statistical information—for example, to measure the extent of drug problems among the convicted offender population.

the use of mortality statistics to assess its physical health. To some extent, too, they were taken as a measure of the success or failure of government policies in protecting the public from crime. However, until the 1960s official crime rates generally remained low and there were few rapid upward trends or dramatic year-on-year increases to generate serious concern. There was also something of a tacit agreement among politicians that the power of governments to influence crime rates over the short term is limited, and it was not until much later that crime began to be regarded as a major issue in general elections. Thus while the publication of the annual volume of *Criminal Statistics* usually attracted some political debate and media attention, this was usually fairly muted and short-lived. Again, although (a) the police, as sole providers of crime data, and (b) the Home Office, as the agency which specified the form in which they should be recorded and presented, occupied what was almost a duopolistic position in terms of determining how the shape and scale of the 'crime problem' was portrayed to the country, surprisingly few challenges were mounted against the validity of the data or the 'truth' of the overall picture they painted.

In terms of crime data other than the regular statistical returns from criminal justice agencies, the cupboard remained bare—or, at least, stocked with a very limited range of products—for many years. In line with the predominant emphasis in crime prevention policy then accorded to the rehabilitation of offenders, most of the more detailed studies and inquiries carried out or commissioned by government in the early and mid-twentieth century focused upon analysis of the backgrounds and characteristics of imprisoned offenders. By contrast, little attention was paid to the physical circumstances or geographical distribution of offences. This applied not just to policy-makers, but to academic criminologists, who were small in number and came mainly from psychological or psychiatric backgrounds. Few looked beyond samples of offenders identified through police and criminal justice processes, and field-based studies of how and where particular kinds of crime were committed were rare. Broadly speaking, then, until well into the second half of the twentieth century, the collection, analysis, and presentation of data about crime was based on limited sources and carried out mainly in a mechanical fashion within a narrow frame of reference. It had a fairly low public profile and was largely left to government statisticians, occasionally assisted by academics who rarely looked beyond the official figures or questioned the assumptions behind their production.

However, since the early 1970s significant changes have taken place. Crime has become a major focus of public concern and a critical issue in party politics (Downes and Morgan, Chapter 9, this volume). Governments have increasingly set out to 'manage' crime problems, and the crime prevention and control industry, in the broadest sense of the term, has expanded rapidly. Rather than relying solely on traditional criminal justice responses such as deterrent sentences or rehabilitative interventions, this has involved efforts to manipulate the environment in order to reduce opportunities for offending, as well as the encouragement of proactive and problem-oriented forms of policing (Maguire 2000; Bullock and Tilley 2003). In addition, concerns have extended beyond the 'conventional' forms of crime (such as theft, vandalism, and burglary) which make up the bulk of recorded offences, to many kinds of criminal behaviour (such as domestic violence and child sexual abuse) that previously remained largely hidden from official view, as well as to the growth of new and more organized forms of crime with international dimensions (such as computer fraud, people-trafficking, and money-laundering) made possible by rapid technological change and globalization (Loader and Sparks; Levi, Chapters 3 and 23, respectively, this volume). Such changes have created a need for new kinds of information about crime at local, national, and international level, including detailed analysis of patterns in particular types of offence that can directly inform policy-making and operational practice, and data that can be processed and disseminated much more quickly than in the past.

In response, the numbers of people engaged in data collection and research, and the sources of information available to them, have increased dramatically and numerous new fields of enquiry have been opened up, producing a veritable 'data explosion' in the field. This has been evident in the Home Office itself, whose research unit (now called Research Development and Statistics Directorate, or 'RDS') has grown much larger than that of any other government department, and has played a significant part in the development of new ways of measuring crime (notably the BCS). At the same time, criminology in universities has grown from a minor subject taught only as part of other degrees, to a flourishing specialist discipline employing several hundred academics, many of them engaged in empirical research. Many other organizations in the public, private, and voluntary sectors also now employ their own researchers to analyse agency records or conduct surveys to produce new data (at national, regional, or local level) about specific types of crime. In essence, we have moved from a situation in which there was only one 'official picture' of crime, to one in which (a) the Home Office's own official statistics are now based on more than one kind of data (as will be discussed towards the end of the chapter, the Command Paper *Criminal Statistics* has been replaced by a series of statistical bulletins, headed by an annual publication in which crime survey and police figures are presented jointly—see Walker *et al.* 2006); and (b) data from many other respected (and less well respected) organizations provide a kaleidoscope of different, overlapping, and in some cases competing, pictures. Parallel changes have been occurring in many other countries, encouraging a growth of comparative information, as well as a search for more reliable information about the nature and scale of cross-border crime.

To illustrate the scale of these changes, a brief comparison of the current situation with the 1970s shows that important new sources of knowledge have been developed in all the following areas. They will be discussed in more detail later in the chapter.

1. *Unreported and unrecorded offences.* Before the 1980s, very little data had been systematically collected in England and Wales on offences not reported to, or recorded by, the police. The first BCS was not carried out until 1982 (Hough and Mayhew 1983). It has now become an annual survey of over 40,000 people, and has been complemented by a variety of local surveys, as well as special surveys of under-reported

offences such as those against businesses (Shury *et al.* 2005). In addition, the possibility has been explored of measuring some crime trends through data from agencies outside the criminal justice system (for example, tracking violence via records of assault victims attending hospital Accident and Emergency departments: see Shepherd *et al.* 2000; Simmons 2000: 31–2; Estrada 2006).

2. *Locations and circumstances of offences.* Much more detailed information is now collected (in the BCS, from police records, and elsewhere) on, for example, where, when, and how offences take place, how far offenders travel to offend, and what kinds of loss or damage victims suffer. The spatial aspects of this kind of information have attracted particular attention, which has led to the growth of a flourishing new branch of the subject, usually referred to as 'environmental criminology' (see Bottoms, Chapter 17, this volume), and to the development of new ways of analysing and representing relevant data. These include 'mapping' based on the geo-coding of offences by the police, mainly through the use of postcodes, which allows visual representations to be made of crime 'hot-spots' (Hirschfield and Bowers 1998).

3. *Specificity.* Criminologists have become much more aware of the diversity of criminal behaviour. Rather than perceiving and analysing 'crime' in terms of a few broad legal categories, they now tend to focus on highly specific forms of behaviour (the variety of which, moreover, grows as offenders devise new ways of stealing property, or as the police or media discover a new 'crime threat'). For example, it would be unusual nowadays to find an analysis of 'robbery': researchers are more likely to examine a more specific problem such as 'street robbery' (as opposed to, say, bank or building society robbery, or security van robbery), or even something as narrow as the forcible theft of mobile phones (Harrington and Mayhew 2001).

4. *Hidden types of crime.* More and more kinds of 'private' criminal activity which formerly lay largely hidden from public view—and which remain even now greatly under-represented in recorded crime figures—not only have become familiar subjects in television programmes and newspaper articles, but have been studied in systematic fashion. Prominent among these are some intra-household offences such as domestic violence and child sex abuse; 'white collar' and corporate offences; and crimes involving consenting parties—sometimes called 'victimless' or 'consensual' crimes—such as supplying or possessing drugs.

5. *Victim perspectives and public opinion.* Much more information is also now available—mainly from crime surveys, interview studies, and analysis of police incident records—about crime from the perspective of the victim or potential victim. This includes detailed knowledge about the emotional and financial impact of different kinds of offence (Shapland *et al.* 1985; Maguire and Corbett 1987); calculations of the relative risks among different social groups of falling victim to particular kinds of crime (see Hoyle and Zedner, Chapter 15, this volume); public and victim attitudes towards offenders and the criminal justice system (Mattinson and Mirrlees-Black 2000; Roberts and Hough 2002); ratings of the seriousness of different types of crime

(Pease 1988); and regular measures of 'fear of crime' (Farrall *et al.* 1997; Semmens 2001).

6. *Comparative and cross-national data.* There has been a considerable investment since the mid-1990s in international surveys of both victimization and offending. These ask similar questions to samples of residents from several countries and the results are analysed singly and together (Graham and Bowling 1995; Van Kesteren *et al.* 2000). Some attempts have also been made to explore the nature and scale of organized cross-border crime, but these are relatively underdeveloped as yet.

Of course, the collection, storage, and analysis of data has been greatly encouraged and facilitated by the development of information technology. There are now several massive electronic data sets in existence, including the results of large-scale victim surveys (notably the BCS) and national databases of offenders (e.g. the Offenders Index, the Police National Computer, and latterly the *e*-OASys database, which will eventually contain detailed risk-needs assessments of virtually all convicted offenders in England and Wales). To these can be added national databases of specific types of offence (e.g. the Homicide Index and 'Catchem')[2] and a host of local record systems maintained by the police, courts, prisons, probation service and other statutory and voluntary agencies. Other large data sets—many of them accessible for secondary analysis through the ESRC data archive at Essex University—have been produced by major funded research projects, including longitudinal 'cohort' studies, local crime surveys, and self-report surveys. There have also been significant advances in the analytical tools available, such as computer packages for multivariate analysis and statistical modelling (Hair *et al.* 1998).

However, as already intimated, in trying to make sense of this 'data explosion', it is important to look not just at advances in technology, but at changes in ways of thinking about and responding to crime. These stand in a dynamic relationship with the production of crime data, both driving demands for new kinds of information and in turn being influenced by the new knowledge they generate. The following can be identified as key factors which have contributed to this process over the last thirty years.

ACADEMIC CRITIQUES OF RECORDED CRIME STATISTICS

Although many academic criminologists in the 1970s were (deliberately) remote from government policy-making circles, the fertile developments in academic theory and research during this period had a considerable indirect influence over the longer term on how crime is measured. The so-called 'deviancy theorists', who pioneered a sea

---

[2] The Catchem (Centralised Analytical Team Collating Homicide Expertise and Management) database was set up 1986 and now holds details on forty years of homicide cases involving younger victims of homicide, especially sexually motivated child homicides. For discussions of the Homicide Index, see Brookman (2005) and Levi *et al.*, Chapter 21, this volume.

change in the previously narrow discipline of criminology, were strongly influenced by the American 'labelling' perspective and its emphasis on the role of legal, institutional, and social processes in 'creating' crime (see Rock, Chapter 1, this volume). Police and court records, they argued, are not the product of a neutral fact-collecting process, but of activities geared first and foremost to organizational aims and needs. Thus the statistics that are derived from them tell us more about the organization than about the 'real' extent of crime (a concept which anyway has no useful meaning): in the words of Kitsuse and Cicourel (1963), they are simply 'indices of organisational processes'. This 'institutionalist', as opposed to 'realist', approach was broadly the starting position adopted by Bottomley and Coleman (1981) in an important study of crime-recording processes in police stations which revealed the importance of police practices and attitudes in shaping the official statistics. While some criminologists took these ideas in directions that most policy-makers found unconvincing—including arguments that all rises in crime were illusory and in some cases deliberately manufactured by the police, government and/or media (e.g. Hall *et al.* 1978)—the basic message that changes in recorded crime figures did not necessarily reflect changes in criminal behaviour began to be widely accepted.

In addition to their sustained critique of official crime figures, the deviancy theorists and their immediate successors left an important legacy in terms of opening up research into types of criminal behaviour that had hitherto remained largely hidden from official view. To do so, they broke away from the use of institutionally produced data, preferring to generate their own by means of qualitative methods such as participant observation, interviews based on 'snowball' samples (rather than samples of, say, convicted offenders), analysis of newspaper stories, and so on. In doing so, they tapped rich new sources of knowledge and produced revealing new insights into activities about which little was known and which rarely in those days appeared in police records, such as drug-taking, workplace 'fiddles', and business fraud (examples being, respectively, Young 1971; Ditton 1977; Levi 1981). It should be noted that some of these behaviours, though readily understood as types of illegal activity, could not easily be mapped on to specific offence categories that appear in criminal statistics. It was partly to get away from the traditional focus on legally defined categories of behaviour as the main objects of research, and encourage instead a focus on socially defined categories of unacceptable behaviour, that some academics chose to name their field of study as 'deviance' rather than 'crime' (see Downes and Rock 2007).

It is emphasized that most of these writers contributed little in terms of developing new sources of *statistical* data about crime, nor were they interested in measuring the frequency of particular kinds of incident. On the contrary, they were largely responsible for a period in British criminology when the climate in the discipline was generally *anti*-statistical and quantitative data were neglected. Nevertheless, they undoubtedly played an important part in steering criminologists—and eventually also government researchers—away from reliance on traditional ways of measuring crime towards new and more creative approaches, whether qualitative or quantitative.

PRESSURE GROUPS AND CAMPAIGNING

The search for more systematic information about the nature and extent of 'hidden' crimes has also been strongly influenced by the persistence of groups campaigning or lobbying to get particular forms of behaviour taken more seriously by the police and criminal justice system. Most notably, the pioneering work of feminist writers and campaigners in the 1970s stimulated a growing body of empirical research on both domestic violence and sexual assault, including surveys of women which demonstrated that the incidence of both was several times greater than suggested by official records (Dobash and Dobash 1979; Hanmer and Saunders 1984). Such research further showed that domestic violence was not heavily concentrated in lower-class households, but found across a wide social spectrum. Almost certainly, by pressing police to arrest perpetrators rather than simply give advice, this campaigning work also had the effect of creating more official records of its incidence. A similar pattern of events—with similar results—was evident some years later following campaigns demanding more government and police action in relation to another largely hidden form of criminal behaviour, child sexual abuse (in particular, by 'Childline', set up in the UK in 1986).

THE PERSPECTIVE FROM THE VICTIM

A broader influence on the kinds of data that came to be collected in the 1980s and beyond was a general growth in attention to the experiences and needs of crime victims. This perspective, which had already been prominent for over ten years in the USA, rapidly began to affect the thinking of British criminologists and policy-makers, informing debates about, inter alia, the relative rights of victims and offenders, policing policy, crime prevention, court processes, racial harassment, and oppression of women (for overviews, see Hoyle and Zedner, Chapter 15, this volume; Maguire and Pointing 1988; Walklate 1989; Heidensohn 1985; Maguire 1991; Davis et al. 1997). More important for our purposes here, it had the general effect of directing attention much more at the *offence* than the *offender*, including the production of large amounts of detailed information about where, when, how, and against whom different types of crime are (or are likely to be) committed. The most obvious example of this is the BCS. Another is the body of academic work on residential burglary that emerged in the UK and North America in the late 1970s and early 1980s. This provided detailed analyses of the circumstances under which burglary is committed, the motives and behaviour of those committing it, and the experiences of victims (see, for example, Reppetto 1974; Waller and Okihiro 1978; Brantingham and Brantingham 1975; Maguire and Bennett 1982; Winchester and Jackson 1982; Bennett and Wright 1984). The patterns of burglary identified began to be explained in terms of interactions between, on the one hand, variations in the attractiveness of targets and in the risks and opportunities they offered and, on the other, the behaviour patterns of different types of offender. This work contributed to a more general and growing theoretical interest in crime patterns as, for example, the product of 'opportunity' (Mayhew et al. 1976; Clarke 1988) or as a by-product of 'routine activities' (Cohen and Felson 1979). It also helped to inform new approaches to crime prevention (see below).

SITUATIONAL CRIME PREVENTION

Another factor in the shift of focus towards the offence, rather than the offender—and hence in the production of new forms of knowledge about crime—was a growing disillusionment among influential policy-makers with the idea that crime can be controlled solely, or even principally, through the traditional activities of the police and criminal justice system (cf. Brody 1976; Clarke and Hough 1984). Faced with the apparent failure of such activities to stem rising crime rates or reduce reoffending—reflected in the then current mantra, 'nothing works' (Martinson 1974)—the director of the Home Office Research Unit, Ronald Clarke, took a decision in the late 1970s to curtail work on the rehabilitation of offenders and to concentrate research efforts on more direct ('primary') forms of crime prevention. This led to the formation of the Home Office Crime Prevention Unit, whose distinctive contribution was the development of 'situational crime prevention' (Clarke 1980). Its researchers set out to use detailed crime pattern analysis to pinpoint areas of the environment which could be altered in such a way as to make it less easy or less attractive for potential offenders to commit particular types of crime. This might entail extra physical security, new design of buildings or vehicles, increased surveillance, or the marking of property (for overviews and examples, see Clarke and Mayhew 1980; Heal and Laycock 1986; Crawford, Chapter 26, this volume). This 'targeting' approach necessitated detailed knowledge about the prevalence, geographical and temporal patterning, and typical modus operandi, of particular offences, thus stimulating the Home Office to fund much more empirical research in these areas. More recent developments in this general direction include the growth of interest in the 'mapping' of offences, as mentioned earlier.

'CRIME MANAGEMENT' AND MULTI-AGENCY PARTNERSHIP

Situational crime prevention forged the path for a much broader shift in crime control policy that has taken place in the last decade or so, revolving around the concept of 'crime management'. This can be seen in many aspects of policing, where 'intelligence-led' and 'problem-oriented' approaches have become commonplace, and 'crime management units' are found in most divisions. The general thrust—encapsulated in the National Intelligence Model, which has been implemented by all forces since 2005—is towards identifying and prioritizing existing or emerging crime problems (which may concern specific types of crime, groups of known offenders, or locations), and then deploying resources to deal with the problem (see, for example, Maguire 2000; Maguire and John 2006). This has led to the employment by police forces of many more analysts, and the development of increasingly sophisticated ways of collecting, analysing, and presenting local data for operational use.

Importantly, too, these ideas have spread beyond the police, and have stimulated a major growth in 'partnership' approaches to crime control, notably the development of Crime and Disorder Partnerships (CDRPs, known in Wales as Community Safety Partnerships). These are statutory partnerships of local agencies (among the key players being local councils, police, probation, social services, and health authorities) set up under the Criminal Justice Act 1998 in every local authority area in England and Wales. They each have a duty to prepare detailed 'crime audits' of their area (soon to be replaced by 'strategic assessments', to make them compatible with the National Intelligence Model) and to publish plans to tackle jointly the main problems which emerge (see Hough and Tilley 1998; Crawford, Chapter 26, this volume). Latterly, they have also been given crime-reduction targets by the Home Office in relation to 'volume crime'. These requirements have also given a major boost to data collection and analysis at a local level, including increased data-sharing between agencies and the integration and overlaying of police and criminal justice data with that from other fields (Corcoran and Bowen 2003). This allows connections to be established between, for example, patterns of truancy and patterns and of shoplifting, and encourages multi-agency initiatives to tackle the 'roots of the problem' rather than simply arresting offenders.

In terms of the production of new kinds of knowledge about crime, and their translation into new kinds of crime policy, the cumulative impact of such developments over the next few years could be considerable. A key aspect of their impact has been the expansion of crime data analysis at *local level*, where it can be of direct use in operational decision-making.

'EVIDENCE-BASED POLICY' AND 'WHAT WORKS'

Closely linked to the notion of crime management is that of 'evidence-based policy', which became a mantra of the New Labour Government at the turn of the century and underpinned the growth of the 'What Works' movement and the implementation of the 'Crime Reduction Programme' (CRP), an unprecedented £400 million programme of experimental interventions aimed at reducing either crime rates or reconviction rates (see Bullock and Tilley 2003; Hough 2004; Maguire 2004). A key element of the CRP was the evaluation of interventions (to determine whether they had 'worked'). This led to efforts by the Home Office to improve the quality and consistency of data used for this purpose, including conviction data held on the Offenders Index and Police National Computer, as well as the development of new databases to record, for example, psychometric measures of offenders attending cognitive-behavioural programmes (see Raynor; Hollin, Chapters 31 and 2, respectively, this volume). It also led researchers to seek new ways of measuring changes in the levels of highly specific types of criminal behaviour such as 'alcohol-related violence', at local level (Maguire and Hopkins 2003; Maguire and Nettleton 2003).

MANAGERIALISM AND THE RISE OF THE PERFORMANCE CULTURE

Since the early 1980s, when the then Government introduced the concept of the 'three E's' (efficiency, economy, and effectiveness) as a guiding principle for the public services, criminal justice agencies have become increasingly subject to inspection, audit, evaluation, and other means of testing their 'performance' against defined criteria (Pollitt 1993). This has grown in intensity over the past few years, as the present Labour Government has seen one of its greatest priorities as the 'modernization' of the public services, and the distribution of resources has come to depend increasingly on local agencies' performance in relation to 'targets' (Hough 2004). Reliable data with which to measure performance have become a prime requisite of these processes, and this has generated serious efforts to control the quality, consistency, and integrity of recording practices. Where crime data are concerned, an important development has been the introduction and enforcement of the National Crime Recording Standard (NCRS), which aims to reduce the gap between the numbers of incidents reported to the police as crimes and those actually recorded as such (some of its consequences for recorded crime totals will be discussed later). Equally important, the need for rapidly produced data to monitor the relative 'performance' of every Basic Command Unit (BCU) in the country, has led to the development of an Internet-based analysis tool (i-Quanta) which allows the production of monthly crime figures, in a standard format and with little delay, for every BCU in England and Wales.[3]

THE POLITICIZATION OF CRIME AND DECLINING TRUST IN STATISTICS

Finally, many of the advances in data collection and research would not have occurred without major increases in government funding. These in turn would not have been sanctioned without the emergence of crime (as evidenced in opinion polls and elsewhere) as one of the areas of greatest public concern and as a key issue on the national political agenda. While crime has always attracted considerable attention, its prominence and degree of 'politicization' over the last decade or so is probably unprecedented (Downes and Morgan, Chapter 9, this volume). Explanation of this phenomenon is beyond the scope of this chapter, but it is clear that growing intolerance and fear of crime among the public, sensationalist media reporting, and exploitation of the subject by politicians have all combined to produce a general perception that—whatever the official statistics may say—crime is 'getting out of control'. At a deeper level, this has been fuelled by the general sense of insecurity and heightened awareness of risk associated with life in the globalized economies of 'late modernity' (Bottoms 1995; Garland 2001; Loader and Sparks, Chapter 3, this volume).

The general politicization of crime has also extended to crime statistics, in that doubts are quite frequently expressed about the reliability and integrity of figures released by the government. For example, the BCS was recently dismissed by an opposition MP as an 'opinion poll', in support of his argument that it gave a false picture of falling crime rates and that recorded crime figures (which showed a recent rise in violence) were much more reliable. Opinion polls also suggest that the general public is increasingly mistrustful of all government statistics, and a significant minority of respondents to the BCS continues to believe that crime has been generally rising over

[3] http://police.homeoffice.gov.uk/performance-and-measurement/iquanta/.

the past ten years when both the BCS and police records (the latter after adjustments) suggest the opposite (Walker *et al.* 2006). As will be discussed later, this is seen by the Statistics Commission (2005) as potentially a serious enough problem to warrant the transfer of responsibility for producing official crime statistics to an independent body.

To sum up this section, a much more pluralistic situation has developed over the past thirty years in terms of the sources of data that are used to 'measure' crime, the owner-ship and control of the processes of collecting and analysing such data, and the messages about the shape of the 'crime problem' that are conveyed to the outside world through publication of the results. The counting of offences officially recorded by the police has thereby been relegated to only one of a variety of alternative ways of exploring the nature and scale of crime, and the somewhat static, monochrome picture it produces has been challenged by a shifting kaleidoscope of new pictures produced by a wide range of individuals and organizations. This is not to deny the continuing importance of the traditional recorded crime figures, especially at the level of symbolic politics: on the contrary, the salience of crime in current political and media discourse ensures that even a small percentage rise in one category of recorded offences can set off tabloid headlines and heated political debates. However, they no longer have even the field of 'official crime statistics' entirely to themselves. As will be discussed later, since 2001/2 recorded crime figures have been published alongside, and to some extent contrasted with, results from the BCS, in a new statistical bulletin entitled *Crime in England and Wales* (Walker *et al.* 2006)—a move which amounts to a highly visible acknowledgement of the limitations of police data. Similarly, while the Home Office remains the major player in the field, it no longer has anything like a 'monopoly on truth' where statements about the extent of crime are concerned. Crime figures now occupy a contested—and increasingly politicized—area, in which knowledge claims are often challenged, public and media mistrust of 'official statistics' has grown, and the achievement of legitimacy is becoming as important as the quality of the data.

INTERPRETING THE STATISTICS

It is now time to explore in more detail what the available statistics appear to tell us about crime, as well as the main questions, considerations, and potential pitfalls that should be borne in mind when interpreting them. We begin with crimes recorded by the police which, despite all the changes referred to above, remain an important source of evidence for criminologists as well as others. We shall then examine what has become the most comprehensive alternative source of information, the British Crime Survey (BCS), looking in particular at ways in which its findings complement, support, or undermine the main messages that emerge from the recorded crime figures. Finally, comments will be made on the contribution of a variety of 'unofficial' sources of data.

Although the statistics discussed can be used to tackle all kinds of questions about crime, the focus here will be on what they tell us about the basic 'contours' of crime, and in particular the pictures they paint of (a) the overall scale of crime, (b) the relative incidence of different kinds of offence, (c) trends in crime over time, and (d) its geographical distribution.

RECORDED CRIME

Let us begin by looking at what the traditional 'official statistics', based on crimes recorded by the police, would appear to tell us if we were to take them entirely at face value. These figures, it should first be noted, are misleadingly precise. The latest statistics available at the time of writing indicate that the total number of crimes recorded by the police in England and Wales in the financial year 2005/6[4] was 5,556,513 (Thorpe and Roff 2006:30). As the equivalent total in the previous year had been 5,640,573, there was an apparent reduction over the period of about 1 per cent.

As the records date back over a very long period, it is also possible to look at long-term trends in such figures. Figure 10.1 presents a graphical representation of the raw 'official totals' for the whole of the 130-year period between 1876 and 2006. The result is a striking pattern, consisting of little change until the 1930s, a modest rise up to and through the Second World War, small falls in the early 1950s, then a sharp and sustained increase from the mid-1950s until the early 1990s, since when the totals have appeared to undulate. This recent change in the pattern, however (reasons for which will be discussed later), should not obscure the central 'message' that during the second half of the twentieth century, there was a dramatic and unprecedented increase in recorded crime in England and Wales—a message, it is important to note, similar to that which emerges from the official crime statistics in most other Western democracies.[5]

In addition to overall totals, the official crime statistics break recorded crimes down into separate offence groups. Table 10.1 shows in simplified form the contributions of the main such groups to the total number of offences recorded in 2005/6. The picture of the current 'crime problem' that emerges is one in which, as one might expect, the theft of property looms quite large: theft and handling offences together with burglaries constitute close to half of the total. However, the relative sizes of the different offence groups have changed markedly over time, and despite increasing in absolute numbers, thefts and burglaries now make up a smaller proportion of the total than they used to. By contrast, two offence groups in particular—criminal damage and violence against the person—have become increasingly prominent. In comparison with the 1950s, for example, the most striking difference concerns criminal damage. Then an almost negligible category, criminal damage has risen to the extent that the number of such offences recorded is now over 230 times higher, and makes up more than a fifth of the

[4] Before 1997, criminal statistics were presented on the basis of calendar years, but have since moved to accord with the financial year (April to March).

[5] An interesting exception was Switzerland, which produced such low crime rates that a distinguished American criminologist (Clinard 1978) wrote a book attempting to explain why.

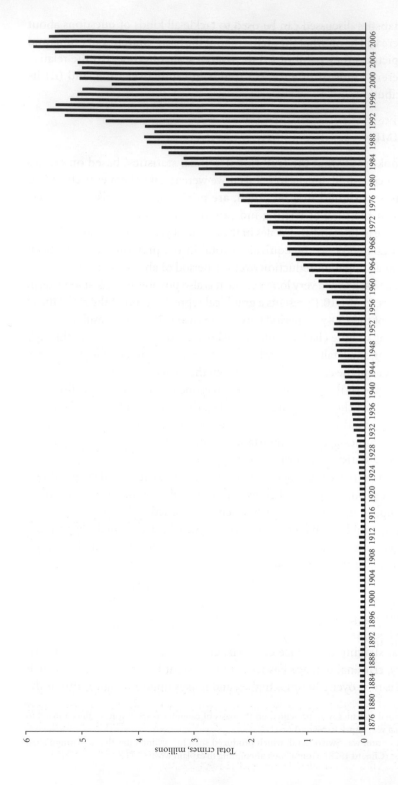

Fig. 10.1 Total offences recorded by the police, 1876–2006.

Notes: 1. From 1997/8 onwards the totals apply to financial years (i.e. April–March) rather than calendar years.

2. New counting rules were introduced in 1998/9 which included several new categories of offence, thus 'artificially' raising the totals in comparison with previous years. The figures from 2002/3 onwards are also affected by the introduction of the National Crime Recording Standard (see discussion in text).

Source: Criminal Statistics, England and Wales (various years) and Crime and England and Wales 2005/06 (Walker et al. 2006).

Table 10.1 Offences recorded by the police, 2005/6

Offence group	Number (to the nearest 1,000)	Per cent
Theft/handling	1,298,000	23
Criminal damage	1,184,000	21
Violence against the person	1,060,000	19
Theft of/from vehicles	721,000	13
Burglary	645,000	12
Drugs/other offences	254,000	5
Fraud and forgery	233,000	4
Robbery	98,000	2
Sexual offences	62,000	1
Total	5,557,000	100

Source: Adapted from A. Walker *et al.* (2006), *Crime in England and Wales 2005/06*, London: Home Office.

overall crime total.[6] Indeed, the total of criminal damage offences recorded in 2005/6 was over twice the total of *all* offences recorded in 1955! Likewise, the raw numbers of recorded offences of violence against the person are more than 140 times higher than in the early 1950s, rising from under 7,000 to over one million, and now make up 19 per cent of all recorded crime compared with 2 per cent then.

Of course, none of these figures can be taken at face value. If they are to be used to say anything sensible about trends in crime or the prevalence of particular kinds of offence, they have to be carefully interpreted. This necessitates close consideration of the possibility that some, or even all, of a particular change in offence totals does not reflect a change in criminal behaviour, but is a result of changes in the processes by which the statistics are produced—a comment, as we shall see, particularly pertinent to the period between 1998 and 2006. In order to make judgements about this, it is important to have a good understanding of these processes, as well as to be aware of a range of key factors that might have an impact on the figures. Confidence in such judgements will also be enhanced if the statistics are examined in the light of evidence from other sources which may support or contradict particular conclusions. Box 10.1 outlines three of the most problematic factors, which should always be taken into account. These will be discussed briefly in turn.

Legislative change and formal recording rules

From time to time, legislation creates new criminal offences and redefines others, which can cause considerable problems for the measurement of trends. One of the most important examples occurred in 1968, when the Theft Act redefined several key

---

[6] Between 1950 and 1954, the average annual recorded total of 'malicious injuries to property' was just over 5,000; in 2005/6, recorded offences of criminal damage totalled over 1,180,000.

Box 10.1 KEY FACTORS WHICH SHAPE RECORDED CRIME FIGURES

1. Legislation and formal recording rules

Legislation may create new offences or legalize behaviour that was previously defined as criminal; definitions of offences may also be significantly changed.

The Home Office decides which categories of offence will be included in the official total of recorded crimes; the categories to be included are sometimes changed.

The Home Office's 'counting rules' also provide guidance on how many individual offences should be recorded when, for example, an offender repeats the same type of criminal behaviour many times within a short period; these, too, are subject to change.

2. Police recording behaviour

Despite rules to limit it, the police inevitably retain considerable discretion as to which of the incidents observed by or reported to them are deemed to be crimes and recorded as such. How this discretion is exercised or constrained can be influenced by a wide variety of social, political, and institutional factors, and may change over time.

3. The reporting behaviour of the public

The propensity of the public to report crimes to the police may be affected by a range of factors, including views of the seriousness of particular forms of behaviour, faith in the police, and more pragmatic considerations such as the need to report offences to support insurance claims; again, such factors can change over time.

property offences and introduced other new ones. For example, the definition of burglary, which had previously been restricted to 'breaking and entering' at night, was extended to include 'entering as a trespasser with intent' at any time, while offences such as 'housebreaking' and 'shopbreaking' disappeared (Maguire and Bennett 1982: 8–9). This necessitated several changes to the offence categories shown in *Criminal Statistics*, making it difficult to make meaningful comparisons pre- and post-1968 across a broad range of property crime. More recently, the Public Order Act 1986 created several new offences such as 'violent disorder'.

Equally important, the recorded crime statistics do not include all categories of offence. Recorded crimes are largely, though not fully, co-terminous with 'indictable' offences—i.e. those which may be tried in a Crown Court (Home Office 2001: 244).[7] This means that a large number of summary offences (i.e. those triable only in Magistrates' Courts) do not appear in the figures. No records are kept of the totals of such offences, although statistics are available on the numbers of people officially sanctioned for them. For example, in 2004, around 1,330,000 people were convicted or formally cautioned for summary (mostly motoring) offences: a total, it is worth noting,

---

[7] 'Indictable' is used here as shorthand for offences which are either 'triable only on indictment' (i.e. in Crown Court) or 'triable either way' (i.e. in either Crown or Magistrates' Court) under the 1977 Criminal Law Act.

well over double that of people convicted or cautioned for indictable offences (Home Office 2005a). In addition, the official recorded crime statistics do not include numerous cases of tax and benefit fraud known to HM Revenue & Customs and the Benefits Agency, which have investigative and prosecution powers but which deal with the great majority of cases by using their administrative powers to impose financial penalties (Levi 1993). Again, such agencies keep internal records of the numbers of people dealt with in these ways, or of the total amounts of revenue saved, but not of the total numbers of 'offences' coming to their notice—a task which, given that a single offender may repeat the same kinds of fraud numerous times over a period, would require complex counting rules.

Debates about the logic of including or omitting particular kinds of offence from the recorded crime totals have periodically led the Home Office to change its instructions to police forces. These changes have had a significant impact on apparent trends in the total amount of crime. To the Home Office's credit, in most cases the changes have been in the direction of including more rather than fewer offence categories and hence artificially increasing rather than decreasing the official totals (this is in contrast to the measurement of unemployment, for example, where it often used to be said that changes in counting rules had had the effect of painting a 'rosier' picture). The most important recent example of this occurred in 1998/9, when a number of summary offences were newly included in the published totals of recorded offences. The most significant of these numerically were common assault, harassment, and assault on a constable, which between them immediately added over 250,000 extra offences of 'violence against the person' to the total. This created the impression, among those unaware of the technical issues, of a major 'rise in violent crime'—interestingly, during a period when, as will be discussed later, the BCS indicated that incidents of violence had been generally falling in number.

In addition to the issue of which categories of offence are included, there are important questions to ask about how individual crimes are *counted*. Some kinds of offence tend to be repeated many times within a short period, to the extent that, though there may be several separate actions or people involved, they could be considered to form part of one concerted criminal incident. For example, a thief may go through twenty trouser pockets in a changing-room, or try the doors of a row of cars, or steal a cheque card and use it many times to obtain goods or cash. Equally, a large affray—for example, at a demonstration, football match, or nightclub—may involve numerous assaults by many people on many others; or a man may assault his partner virtually every night for a period of months or years.

Prior to 1968, little attention was paid to discrepancies between police forces in the numbers of offences recorded in these kinds of situations. However, following the recommendations of the Perks Committee in 1967, clearer 'counting rules' were established (Home Office 1971), which tidied up some of the discrepancies, but at the same time appeared arbitrary and inconsistent in some respects and clearly understated the relative frequency of some offences. These rules were revised again in 1980 and in 1998, in the latter case partly to align them more closely with the counting rules used in the BCS. The basic rule is now that, wherever possible, the statistics should reflect the *number of victims*, rather than the number of criminal acts. This principle was previously applied in relation to violent offences, but was new for property offences. In the above examples, then, the changing-room thief and the cheque fraudster, who might previously have produced only one offence each, would now produce several (depending upon how many victims can be identified). The spouse abuser, as in the past, is likely to be credited with only one offence, while the affray (again, as before the changes) may produce quite a large number of offences. Overall, it has been estimated that the joint impact of the inclusion of more summary offences and the changes in counting rules was to elevate the total number of recorded offences between 1997/8 and 1998/9 by about 14 per cent (Home Office 2001: 28).

Police recording practice

Of course, Home Office rules provide only the formal framework for the recording of crime. Within this framework there remains ample room for police discretion, which is inevitable in a world in which it is often unclear whether a report from a member of the public is truthful or whether, for example, a 'stolen' bag has in fact been mislaid. While decisions not to record a crime in such circumstances are often fully justified, discretion can also be misused in order to 'manipulate' figures. Over the years, some of the main doubts raised about the validity of recorded crime statistics have revolved around suspicions of this kind. Researchers have identified examples of, on the one hand, the 'cuffing' (hiding) of offences for reasons ranging from work avoidance to a wish to improve the overall clear-up rate (Bottomley and Coleman 1981; Young 1991)[8] and on the other, the recording (amounting to the 'creation') of large numbers of minor offences in order to elevate the crime rate, for example with a view to supporting a case for more resources.[9] More recently, as increasing importance has been attached to police 'performance' in meeting crime-reduction targets, bodies such as HM Inspectorate of Police and the Audit Commission have taken a closer interest in individual forces' levels of adherence to recording rules, and have found numerous cases of breaches, mainly in respect of under-recording (Loveday 2000; Audit Commission 2004), though the picture is now said to be improving (Audit Commission 2006). In 2002, detailed national crime-recording standards (NCRS) were introduced in an attempt to improve the overall integrity of police recording practices,

---

[8] The more 'hopeless' cases, in terms of their potential for detection, that are omitted from the figures, the higher the proportion detected (the clear-up rate) is likely to be. If a division's or force's clear-up rate is exceptionally low, officers (especially those in the CID) can expect criticism from management as well as, in some cases, the media. There is thus some incentive to 'massage' local crime statistics to avoid such criticism (for a first-hand account of police behaviour in this respect, see Young 1991).

[9] One particularly strong critic in this regard, Hal Pepinsky, showed how significant increases in crime could be created simply by assiduously recording every trivial offence that comes to light: for example, in a small unpublished study in one subdivision of a British city he claimed that almost half the year's 'increase in crime' had been produced by the police recording every admission by a single offender who frequently stole milk bottles from doorsteps. On a wider scale, Selke and Pepinsky (1984) claimed that rises (and occasional falls) over time in crime figures in Indiana could be shown to coincide closely with shifts in the political needs of the party in power (see also Pepinsky 1976).

as well as to produce more consistency between forces. These standards were consciously designed to increase recording rates—in particular, to bring about a closer correspondence between the numbers of 'crime incidents' logged and the number of 'crimes' recorded. They stipulate a basic assumption that an incident log containing an allegation of a crime—most commonly, the result of a telephone call from a member of the public—should be automatically recorded as a crime and only removed from the crime records, with a supervisor's agreement, if there is clear evidence to suggest that no offence was involved (this is known as the prima facie principle—see later). As demonstrated by Simmons *et al.* (2003) there is little doubt that the NCRS has had an impact on both police behaviour and recorded crime levels, as calculations from BCS data indicate that the recording rate (i.e. the percentage of personal and household 'crimes' reported to the police that end up as recorded offences) rose from 62 per cent in 2000/1 to 75 per cent in 2003/4 (though it has recently fallen back to 70 per cent: see Allen and Ruparel 2006: Table 4.04). Nevertheless, there is a limit to how far discretion can be constrained, and how closely practices can be monitored.

Finally, offences 'discovered' by the police themselves—either in the course of patrols or observation, or through admissions by arrested offenders—have a significant impact on the overall numbers of recorded crimes. Not only is the scope for individual officers' discretion to make or not to make official reports on incidents much greater than in the case of calls from the public, but the chances of arrests are affected by changes in policing policy and operational priorities, the extent and nature of patrolling, or pressures from the public or media to 'do something' about particular kinds of behaviour. At local level, planned operations or 'crackdowns' will often result in an increase in arrests and the recording of many new offences; for example, strong policing of a pop festival is almost guaranteed to generate a boost in an area's recorded drug offences, while current concern about alcohol-related violence has led to greater police presence and more arrests around city centre pubs and clubs. Conversely, numbers may fall owing to reduced police interest in a particular type of crime, as in the early 1960s when, anticipating legislation to legalize homosexuality, most forces turned a blind eye to 'indecency between males' and the recorded total of such offences declined to half the previous level (Walker 1971). It may be that recent messages from the government that simple possession of cannabis does not necessarily require a police response will have a similar effect on recorded drug offences.[10]

The reporting behaviour of the public

Despite the importance of offences which come to light solely through police activity, the bulk of recorded crimes first come to official notice through reports from members of the public.[11] For this reason, changes in the 'reporting behaviour' of the public can have an even greater impact on recorded crime trends. Decisions on whether or not to report possible offences to the police are influenced by a huge variety of factors, including views

[10] In 2005/6, there were 178,502 recorded drug offences, 119,922 (67%) of which were possession of cannabis.

[11] McCabe and Sutcliffe (1978) calculated this from samples of records at about 85%.

about the police and expectations of their response, the ease with which reports can be made (to which, for example, the spread of mobile telephones has made a difference), the number of victims with insurance policies (reporting being necessary to support a claim), and levels of public tolerance of particular kinds of behaviour. Over the longer term, too, major social changes such as the gradual erosion of traditional communities and the increasing anonymity of life in urban areas may have made people more inclined to call in the police rather than 'sort the problem out' by themselves or with neighbours: this applies particularly to minor criminal behaviour by local children.

A specific example that has been cited by researchers of reporting behaviour being affected by views about the police, concerns a rising trend in recorded offences of rape which was evident in the late 1980s. This may have been partly or even fully explained by improvements in the treatment of victims such as the introduction of 'rape suites' into police stations and a greater willingness on the part of police officers to believe their accounts (Blair 1984). These developments may have encouraged more victims to go to the police, as well as raising police recording rates.

Re-examining recent 'trends'

In the light of the above discussions, the 'trends' in crime apparent in Figure 10.1 need to be looked at with a rather more critical eye. While it may be implausible that the steeply rising figures during the 1960s, 1970s, and 1980s were largely 'artificially' created by factors such as changes in counting rules or in reporting and recording rates, particularly careful consideration has to be given to the influence of such factors on the figures since 1998. To reiterate:

1. In 1998/9, (alongside other changes in the counting rules) offences of common assault, harassment, and assault on a constable were counted in the totals for the first time.

2. In 2002, the National Crime Recording Standard was introduced, instructing police to adopt a prima facie (and hence more 'liberal') approach to the recording of crime.

These two changes alone have been responsible for a sizeable 'artificial' increase in total recorded crime—indeed, enough to make a downward trend into an upward one. As will be discussed later, Home Office statisticians make adjustments in their analysis of trends to take account of the effects of these and other factors, but (a) such adjustments are based on estimates, not certainties, and (b) explaining what has in recent years entailed an unusually complex set of adjustments to sceptical politicians, the media, and the general public presents a considerable challenge.

COMPARISON BETWEEN AREAS: THE STRANGE CASE OF NOTTINGHAMSHIRE

One of the most interesting examples of how official crime rates can be interpreted and explained through criminological investigation is to be found in relation to their geographical distribution. Generally speaking, on the basis of a great deal of criminological theory and research, one would expect police forces covering areas with high-density metropolitan or urban populations to have the highest crime rates (obvious factors include the presence of large areas of deprivation in close proximity to wealthy areas, the anonymity of city life, and so on). Indeed, a simple comparison of recorded crime rates between police forces indicates that this is broadly borne out by the official statistics. Table 10.2 shows those forces with the highest and the lowest recorded crime rates per 1,000 population in 2005/6.[12] It is clear that most of those with the highest rates include major metropolitan areas within their boundaries, while those with the lowest rates are predominantly rural in character.

However, there appears to be a strong anomaly in the case of Nottinghamshire, a county force whose per capita recorded crime rate topped that of all the major

Table 10.2 Recorded offences per 1,000 population: selected police force areas, 2005/6

	Offences per 1,000 population
1. *Forces with rates above 120 per 1,000 population*	
Nottinghamshire	134
MPS (London)	133
Humberside	131
Cleveland	130
Greater Manchester	129
South Yorkshire	127
Merseyside	126
West Yorkshire	123
2. *Forces with rates below 80 per 1,000 population*	
Norfolk	79
Devon & Cornwall	77
Suffolk	77
North Yorkshire	77
North Wales	75
West Mercia	72
Wiltshire	67
Surrey	65
Dyfed-Powys	60

Source: Adapted from A. Walker *et al.*, Table 2.07, *Crime in England and Wales 2005/06*. London: Home Office.

[12] Of course, some forces are much larger than others, so a straightforward comparison of raw totals of crimes would be meaningless. In order to afford a more equitable means of comparison, crime rates are often expressed in terms of numbers of recorded offences per 1,000 population (long-term changes over time are similarly adjusted in some of the national statistical tables to take into account changes in the population).

metropolitan areas, including London. The force has been at or near the top of the table for many years, a situation that has long been an object of curiosity and that has been held up as a prime example of the potentially misleading nature of official statistics. Farrington and Dowds (1985) published a detailed study of police recording practices in the county, from which they concluded that its apparently huge crime rate relative to its neighbouring counties of Leicestershire and Staffordshire (which are socially not dissimilar to Nottinghamshire) was a function of: (a) a much greater number and proportion of recorded crimes originating directly from offenders' admissions to the police (25 per cent, compared to 4 and 8 per cent in the other forces), (b) a greater number and proportion of recorded crimes involving property of little value (48 per cent valued at £10 or under, compared with 29 and 36 per cent), and (c) a somewhat higher 'true' crime rate (or, more accurately, a higher crime rate as measured by public surveys). The researchers stated:

> It is reasonable to conclude that between two-thirds and three-quarters of the difference in crime rates . . . reflected differences in police reactions to crime, while the remaining one-third reflected differences in criminal behaviour . . .
>
> The research shows once again the difficulties of interpreting official statistics. Almost certainly, Nottinghamshire has never been the most criminal area in the country (Farrington and Dowds 1985: 70–1).

Interestingly, Nottinghamshire fell from its top place in the national table in 1981 to fifth place in 1982, a change which, Farrington and Dowds (*op cit.*) claimed,

> is almost certainly attributable to changes in police policies for recording offences, which may have been caused partly by this research project.

The foregoing discussion provides us with two messages about the value of the official statistics as a means of comparing crime rates between areas. On the one hand, some confidence can be drawn from the fact that the broad pattern they indicate— i.e. of higher crimes in more densely populated parts of the country, and particularly the metropolitan areas—is consistent with the differences one would expect according to most sociological theories of crime causation, as well as from ordinary experience. On the other hand, as the Nottinghamshire example shows, variations in recording practices can have such a great effect on the totals produced as to render 'face value' comparisons almost meaningless. This underlines once again the necessity to treat all police figures with caution, as well as the point that they can nevertheless yield valuable insights when one probes closely into the practices which generate them.

OTHER CONSIDERATIONS AND POTENTIAL PITFALLS

In addition to the above fundamental issues, there are a number of other potential problems and pitfalls to bear in mind when interpreting recorded crime statistics. These can be very briefly outlined and illustrated as follows.

Short-term 'trends'

Although graphic references to the frequency of offences (e.g. 'A burglary every 20 seconds') are not uncommon, the kinds of statistic most likely to feature in newspaper headlines are those referring to apparent *trends* in crime (e.g. 'Burglary up 20 per cent'). In many cases, figures wrongly presented as 'trends' refer only to a rise or fall relative to the previous year, paying no attention to earlier years. Sometimes, too—a practice which, if used deliberately, is simply dishonest—commentators refer to a percentage fall or increase since a particular year, selecting as their baseline year one in which the official total had deviated significantly from the underlying trend. To take a concrete example, if one had stated at the end of 1992 that, 'Recorded burglaries have risen by 65 per cent since 1988', this would have been factually correct, but it would be misleading not to point out that 1988 had produced one of the lowest recorded totals of burglary for many years and that, for example, the figure had risen by only 45 per cent since 1986. To represent trends properly, then, it is necessary at the very least to use figures produced at regular intervals over a sufficient period of time.

Frequency and seriousness

An obvious, but often overlooked, point is that the relationship between frequency and seriousness is not straightforward. For example, fraud and forgery appear in recorded crime figures in relatively small numbers. However, if one were to measure the importance of property offences in terms of the value stolen, rather than the number of incidents, fraud would come out as of greater significance than other categories with many times the number of recorded offences. For example, Levi (1993) points out that the minimum criterion for cases to be accepted for investigation by the Serious Fraud Office is a fraud of £5 million and that in April 1992, the Frauds Divisions of the Crown Prosecution Service were supervising cases involving nearly £4 billion. By contrast, the combined costs of the prolific offences of 'autocrime' and burglary for 1990 were estimated by the Association of British Insurers at under £1.3 billion. (Levi also points out that the alleged fraud in any one of several major cases—Barlow Clowes, Guinness, Maxwell, BCCI, Polly Peck—alone exceeded the total amount stolen in thefts and burglaries recorded by the police.)

Is it the same behaviour?

Even when the categories of crime appear to be the same as, or similar to, those included in past counts, the behaviour they refer to may be very different. For example, the current offence groups of 'theft and handling stolen goods', 'burglary', and 'fraud and forgery' may be broadly equivalent to the 1950s groups of 'larceny', 'receiving', 'breaking and entering', and 'frauds and false pretences', but they refer to a world in which computers, cheque cards, and mass ownership of cars are taken for granted and where to commit a 'theft' or a 'fraud', for example, often involves actions which were simply not possible in the 1950s.

Populations and property 'at risk'

It is important when comparing crime figures over time, or between areas, to consider differences in the size and composition of the populations. For example, the population of a town may double over twenty years, creating many more potential victims and offenders. As noted above, to allow for such differences (especially when looking at long-term trends or comparing police force areas) statisticians often express recorded crime rates in the form of 'offences per 1,000 population'. However, this is not the end of the story, as the social characteristics of the population (e.g. the proportion of young or old people, or the average income level) may be more important than its overall size, in determining of people 'at risk'.[13] Similarly, a major increase in, say, the numbers of cars on the road, or of people using cheque cards or Internet banking, means more potential targets for thieves and fraudsters, but it cannot be assumed that they are all equally at risk. Importantly, too, an area (e.g. the City of London) can have few residents but many visitors. Dealing with such issues is critical to any attempt to make sense of differences in crime figures over time and space.

Context

Finally, it is important not to jump to conclusions about what kinds of event an increase in a particular legal offence category refers to. A long-standing criticism of the recorded crime figures (see, for example, McLintock and Avison 1968) has been that they do not give a clear picture of the social or situational context of crimes. For example, 'robbery' includes actions as diverse as an organized bank raid, the theft at knifepoint of the contents of a shopkeeper's till, and a drunken attempt to snatch a handbag in the street. Knowing that 98,204 robberies were recorded in 2005/6, or that this represented an increase of 8 per cent over the previous year, does not tell us whether specific styles of robbery are declining or becoming more prevalent. Increases in recorded robbery in the late 1990s and early 2000s led to considerable political argument (at one point the term 'national emergency' being used) and the setting up at short notice of the high-profile Street Crime Initiative, directed from central government and involving the deployment of 2,000 officers across ten cities in England and Wales. However, it emerged later that much of the increase—and much of the subsequent reduction—in recorded robberies was accounted for by young people taking mobile phones from other young people, particularly in London (Curran et al. 2005). While this is undoubtedly a problem that should be taken seriously, whether it warranted such a dramatic, government-coordinated response is highly debatable.

---

[13] As Bottomley and Pease (1986: 11–12) long ago pointed out in relation to changes in one area over time: 'We should beware of easily reaching the conclusion that "people commit crime, therefore more people can be expected to commit more crime" so that if the ratio between crime and population is unchanged then there can be nothing which requires an explanation. It can be seen at once that underlying such an assumption is an emergent theory about rates of offending, and possibly about rates of victimization, which leaves itself wide open to a series of supplementary questions such as whether all members of a population are equally "at risk" of offending . . . what significance should be attached to the gender composition of the population . . . [and] given the change in the pattern of criminal opportunities, should one adjust for social changes like the number of cars registered.'

The old *Criminal Statistics* provided contextual information, of a limited kind, only in relation to homicide and offences involving firearms. It used data from the Homicide Index—which contains more detail from police records than is collected for other offences—to show, for example, rates of victimization by age group (children under one year usually emerging with the highest rate) and victim-offender relationships by gender (e.g. 42 per cent of female victims in 2000/1 were killed by a current or former spouse, cohabitant, or lover: Home Office 2001: 75–7).[14] For firearms it presented tables on the type of offence involved (violence against the person, robbery, burglary, or criminal damage), type of weapon used (air weapons, handguns, shotguns, and rifles/other weapons), whether or not the weapon was discharged, and the degree of injury caused.

To conclude this section, it should be clear from the discussion throughout that the use of police-generated crime statistics to try to say virtually anything definite about crime— including its overall incidence, patterns, and trends—is a pursuit fraught with pitfalls. Such data are collected by busy people for a variety of purposes, not by researchers setting out to answer specific questions in a systematic way. Over the last few years, especially, they have been subject to major changes in recording rules. Importantly, too, they simply do not contain some of the most important kinds of information that are now in strong demand by criminologists, researchers, policy-makers, crime analysts, members of crime and disorder partnerships, and others: notably, information about the 'context' of events that result in crime, and about the distribution of risks of victimization among different social groups. In the next section, we look at the main alternative 'official' source of knowledge, the British Crime Survey (BCS).

THE BRITISH CRIME SURVEY

As with the recorded crime statistics, in order to comment sensibly on the status of knowledge about crime derived from the BCS, it is first necessary to know something about the purposes of the survey and how its data are collected and compiled.

First conducted in 1982 and repeated at intervals thereafter, it has been since 2001 an annual survey with an interview sample of over 40,000 households—large enough to allow analysis at police force as well as national level. The main rationale for the survey—and, particularly, for its regular repetition—is that, by asking samples of the public to describe crimes committed against them within the past 12 months, the vagaries of crime-reporting behaviour and police-recording behaviour are neatly avoided, and the responses can be 'grossed' up to produce a 'fuller' (and arguably more reliable) picture than the recorded crime statistics of the extent of, and trends in, certain types of offence (Mayhew and Hough 1988).

The complex sampling techniques used[15] are aimed at producing representative cross-sections of: (a) all private households in England and Wales; and (b) all individuals

[14] For a comprehensive academic analysis of data from the Homicide Index, see Brookman 2005.

[15] For the first three surveys, the households were selected from the Electoral Register, but since 1992 the Postcode Address File (PAF) has been used as the sampling frame, it being argued that this produces a better representation of the population: the Electoral Register may significantly under-represent young people, the

aged 16 and over living in them. The basic format of the questionnaire, and the framework for presenting the results, were established in the 1982 survey and have changed surprisingly little since. The interviews (which last on average around 50 minutes) are designed first to establish whether the respondents, or anyone else in their household, have been the victim of any of a list of specified crimes (described to them in ordinary language) within the past 12 months.[16] If any positive answers are received, interviewers complete a detailed 'Victim Form' for each incident.[17] The results are analysed and grossed up to produce estimated national totals of both 'household offences' (such as burglary) and 'personal offences' (such as assaults), based on calculations using, respectively, the total number of households and the total adult population of England and Wales.[18]

In addition to being asked about offences to which they have fallen victim, respondents answer questions from a variety of 'Follow Up Modules', which elicit their views or attitudes on a range of topics. They are also asked to complete 'self-interviewing questionnaires' directly on to a computer screen (which is not seen by the interviewers) on sensitive topics which have included at different times their own knowledge and use of illicit drugs, and their experiences of domestic violence, sexual attacks, or 'stalking'. However, the results of these exercises do not form part of the core measurement of crime numbers and trends.

COMPARISONS BETWEEN POLICE AND BCS DATA

The offence categories which are included in the annual estimates of crime numbers produced by the BCS (known as 'BCS crime') are shown in the first two sections of Table 10.3. The first point to emphasize (again) is that BCS crime does not cover all kinds of crime recorded by the police. As its designers pointed out at the outset (see, for example, Hough and Mayhew 1985: ch. 1), the BCS is more suited to gleaning information about some types of incident than others. Those it does not attempt to 'count' as part of the above totals include all crimes against commercial or corporate victims, fraudulent offences, sexual offences, and so-called 'victimless' crimes such as the possession of or dealing in drugs. BCS crime also does not include offences committed against children below the age of 16 (though, as with several other areas not included in

unemployed, ethnic minorities, and those living in rented accommodation (Mayhew *et al.* 1993: 149–51; Grant *et al.* 2006).

[16] In order to facilitate comparison with the previous year's official crime figures, the survey used to be conducted between January and April, people being asked to recall incidents within the previous calendar year. However, now that the police-generated figures cover the financial year (April to March), the need for this has disappeared and the BCS has moved to a 'rolling' programme of interviews in which people are asked simply about incidents occurring during the past 12 months.

[17] Up to a maximum of six separate incidents. However, if the respondent reports a number of similar events involving the same offender, these may treated as one 'series incident'.

[18] As the total interview sample deliberately includes an over-representation of households from denser urban areas (to maximize the chances of finding 'victims' to interview), the calculated victimization rates are weighted to take account of this (see Kershaw *et al.* 2001: 89. For the latest technical report on the BCS as a whole, see Grant *et al.* 2006).

the annual counts, the Home Office has recently attempted to collect data on these through other survey methods: see Wood 2005). Equally important, the survey gathers information on large numbers of (overwhelmingly minor) personal and household thefts which do not map sufficiently well on to police categories of crime for direct comparisons to be made between the two sets of figures.

In other words, 'BCS crime', like 'recorded crime', is to some extent an arbitrarily constructed aggregation of disparate types of offence: both include some offences in the 'count', and omit others. It is therefore a serious misunderstanding to regard the BCS as offering a full picture (let alone 'the true picture') of 'crime in England and Wales'. Indeed, it does not necessarily present a fuller picture than that provided by the recorded crime statistics: it is 'fuller' than the latter in some respects (notably the inclusion of unrecorded and unreported offences), but 'narrower' in others (notably the exclusion of 'victimless' crimes, crimes against organizations, and crimes against children under 16).

Consequently, it makes more sense to discuss offence categories separately than as an aggregated group. While the somewhat arbitrary overall totals of 'BCS crime' and 'recorded crime' do not relate directly to any commonly understood category of behaviour, subgroups such as 'bicycle theft' or 'vandalism' have a much clearer social meaning. Importantly, too, while the overall BCS and police figures cannot be directly compared, there are several offence categories where it is generally agreed that meaningful comparisons are possible, once some statistical adjustments have been made.[19] These are known as the *comparable subset* (see Patterson and Thorpe 2006: 49): altogether they contain around three-quarters of all BCS crimes and just under half of all police-recorded offences. The relevant offence categories, and the estimated totals in each in 2005/6, can be seen in the top section of Table 10.3. (The other two sections show the remaining BCS and police-recorded offences that cannot be directly compared.)

In 1983, the authors of the initial BCS summarized the results of a similar comparison as follows:

> Only for one category—thefts from motor vehicles—were the figures similar. For instance, the survey indicated twice as many burglaries as were recorded by the police; nearly five times as much wounding; twelve times as much theft from the person; and thirteen times as much vandalism (or criminal damage) . . . The overall ratio for incidents which had been compared was one in four [Hough and Mayhew 1983: 10, emphasis added].

It will be seen from Table 10.4 that, though the proportions have changed somewhat, the general thrust of this statement also holds for the results of the 2005/6 survey. In 2005/6, the total number of offences recorded by the police in categories covered by the BCS was around two and a half million, whereas the BCS evidence suggests that about eight and a half million offences of these kinds were experienced by victims in the same period—i.e. about three and a half times the police total. The only really striking

---

[19] These mainly entail removing from the police figures estimated numbers of offences committed against young people or against corporate victims (see Patterson and Thorpe 2006: 49).

Table 10.3 Estimated totals of offences in England and Wales, 2005/6, as derived from the British Crime Survey and offences recorded by the police

	BCS		Police[1]		
	N	(% of comparable offences)	N	(% of comparable offences)	(% of all recorded offences)
Comparable offences					
Theft of/from vehicles	1,731,000	(20)	714,000	(28)	(13)
Vandalism private property	2,731,000	(33)	587,000	(23)	(11)
Burglary dwelling	733,000	(9)	307,000	(12)	(6)
Assault/wounding	2,038,000	(24)	652,000	(26)	(12)
Robbery	311,000	(4)	66,000	(3)	(1)
Theft from person	576,000	(7)	114,000	(4)	(2)
Bicycle theft	439,000	(5)	111,000	(4)	(2)
Subtotals	**8,558,000**	**(100)**	**2,551,000**	**(100)**	**(46)**
BCS offences not comparable with police data					
Other household theft	1,158,000	(11)	***		
Other personal theft	1,196,000	(11)	***		
Subtotals	**2,354,000**	**(22)**	***		

Police-recorded offences not covered by/comparable with BCS

Other theft	***	1,080,000	(19)	
Other vandalism	***	1,597,000	(11)	
Non-residential burglary	***	338,000	(6)	
Fraud and forgery	***	233,000	(4)	
Other violence/robbery[2]	***	439,000	(8)	
Sexual offences	***	62,000	(1)	
Drug offences	***	179,000	(3)	
Other	***	76,000	(1)	
Subtotals	***	3,004,000	(54)	
Totals	10,912,000 (100)	5,556,000	(100)	

Source: Adapted from Thorpe and Roft (2006: Table 2.4) and Allen and Ruparel (2006: Table 4.01). All figures are rounded to the nearest 1,000. Percentage columns may not add to 100 due to rounding.

Notes: 1. The figures shown in this column refer to offences recorded by the police in the financial year 2005/6. The totals of 'comparable' police-recorded offences reflect adjustments outlined by Walker *et al.* (2006: 49) which make reductions to allow for cases where the victim was either an organization or institution, or was under 16 years old (i.e. types of offence not measured by the BCS).
2. Mainly assaults and robberies where the victim was under 16.

Table 10.4 Ratios of recorded offences to BCS totals, comparable subset 2005/6

	Offence totals		
	BCS estimate	*Police recorded*	*Ratio Police : BCS*
Comparable offences			
Theft of vehicles	185,000	157,000	1 : 1.2
Attempted vehicle theft	425,000	191,000	1 : 2.2
Theft from vehicles	1,121,000	366,000	1 : 3.1
Vandalism private property	2,731,000	587,000	1 : 4.7
Burglary dwelling with loss	315,000	227,000	1 : 1.4
Burglary dwelling no loss	418,000	80,000	1 : 5.2
Common assault	919,000	175,000	1 : 5.3
Wounding	1,119,000	477,000	1 : 2.3
Robbery	311,000	66,000	1 : 4.7
Theft from person	576,000	114,000	1 : 5.1
Bicycle theft	439,000	111,000	1 : 4.0
Totals	**8,558,000**	**2,551,000**	**1 : 3.4**

differences from 1983 concern vandalism and theft from the person, where it appears that much higher proportions of such offences are now being reported to and recorded by the police.

There is a strong temptation to interpret the overall figures as showing that there is 'three to four times as much crime' as the official records suggest: a trap into which many people have duly fallen. The problem lies in the wide variations between offences in terms of their reporting and (to a lesser extent) recording rates. For example, as Table 10.4 indicates, whereas 157,000 (85 per cent) out of an estimated 185,000 vehicle thefts that were known to victims ended up in the official crime statistics, this was the case for only 175,000 (19 per cent) of an estimated 919,000 'common assaults'. Such variations mean that the choice of offence groups to include in any comparison can significantly affect the overall ratio between the police figures and the survey figures. Indeed, if the comparison included survey data covering some of the offences in the final section of Table 10.3—let us say, estimates of instances of shoplifting or pilfering from work or cheque frauds, derived from surveys of employers or shopkeepers or bank employees (where the proportions which end up in police records are known to be tiny),[20] this ratio would emerge as much lower. In this context, it is worth noting that the overall 'dark figure' estimated by Sparks *et al.* (1977) in their pioneering victim survey was one of *eleven* times the police figure, unlike the 'three to four times' estimate that has emerged from the BCS over the years. This is partly explained by differences in the

[20] See, for example, Martin (1962) and Levi (1993).

nature of the geographical areas surveyed and in the methodologies used, but also by the different spread of offences covered. These remarks are highly pertinent to differences that are often found between the 'image' of crime presented by national surveys such as the BCS and that presented by *local* surveys, which will be discussed later.

Contradictory trends?

For much of the 1980s and 1990s, the basic shapes of the trends displayed by both BCS and official crime statistics were fairly similar. Between 1982 and 1997, both showed an increase to a peak in the early to mid-1990s, followed by the beginnings of a downward trend. Indeed, a statistical analysis by Farrington and Langan (1998) of the relationship between the two sets of data from 1981 to 1996 found that they were closely correlated in relation to all four categories of crime examined (vehicle theft, burglary, robbery, and assault).[21] The main difference was that, as with surveys in the USA, the rise in BCS crime was less steep than police figures suggested. Between 1981 and 1991 recorded crime rose by 78 per cent, while the BCS estimated totals rose by 37 per cent. In addition, while recorded crime peaked in 1992, the BCS totals peaked in 1995.

However, the picture has subsequently become much less clear, and apparent differences in trends have become the subject of both academic and political debate. Since peaking in 1995, estimated BCS crime totals have fallen significantly, showing a reduction of 44 per cent between then and 2005/6 (from over 19 million to under 11 million offences—the latter figure being lower than that calculated from the very first BCS in 1982). By contrast, over the same period, the raw recorded crime totals have *increased* (by 9 per cent). As has already been made clear, this is an artificial increase, all of it (and more) being accounted for by additions to the types of offence counted, other changes in counting rules, and the introduction of the National Crime Recording Standard. Nevertheless, even with these qualifications, there remain some divergences to explain.

The arguments have centred mainly around violent crime, which has fallen according to the BCS since 1995 (by 43 per cent), but has risen substantially according to the recorded crime statistics. Clearly, the counting rule changes have been particularly important here, the inclusion of common assault and harassment in the recorded crime totals from 1998/9 having had a major effect (see Table 10.5). However, even after their effect is factored out, Home Office researchers calculate that recorded offences of violence still increased by 94 per cent between 1996 and 2005/6 (Allen and Ruparel 2006: 66). They explain a quarter of this increase as due to the introduction of the National Crime Recording Standard in 2002, arguing further that 'it is likely that the remainder of the recorded increase was largely due to extraneous factors: increased reporting of violent crime by the public, increased police activity and other improvements in recording by the police in previous years' (op. cit.). This may well be the case with relatively minor incidents, but it is perhaps less plausible with the most *serious* offences

---

[21] By contrast, however, a similar analysis of American data found much weaker correlations and, where assault was concerned, no systematic relationship at all between official and survey figures.

Table 10.5 Trends in recorded and BCS violent offences, 1995–2005/6

	Recorded Crime Totals[1]		BCS Crime Totals	
	More serious violence[2]	*All violence against the person*	*'Wounding'*[2]	*Common assault*
	000s	*000s*	*000s*	*000s*
1995	19	213	914	2923
1996	22	239		
1997	24	251	804	2455
1997/8	24	256		
1998/9	27 ⎤ 27	231 ⎤ 503		
1999/00	30	581		
2000/1	32	601		
2001/2	32	650	648	1724
2002/3	40	845	709	1702
2003/4	45	967	656	1557
2004/5	46	1048	577	1488
2005/6	40	1060	547	1490

Notes: 1. The breaks in police figures in 1998/9 and 2002/3 are due to, respectively, changes in counting rules and the introduction of the National Crime Recording Standard, both of which mean that recorded crime figures are not directly comparable before and after those years.

2. BCS 'woundings' are not directly comparable with 'more serious violence' recorded by the police. There are not enough serious woundings reported to the BCS to allow estimates to be made of their overall numbers.

of violence (principally serious woundings), which were relatively unaffected by the changes in counting rules and continued to increase each year even before the introduction of the NCRS (Table 10.5).

This is the nub of the argument, which has become sharpened by the decision to present and discuss BCS and recorded crime figures together in a new, high-profile annual research bulletin, *Crime in England and Wales*: the Home Office view appears to be that the BCS provides a more reliable picture of trends in crime and therefore that the whole of the increase in police-recorded violence must be explicable by reporting and recording changes (though the evidence for this is unclear, especially in relation to serious violence), while opponents argue that it cannot be so simply 'explained away' (for further discussion see Levi, Maguire, and Brookman, Chapter 21, this volume; Hough *et al*. 2005). Moreover, some concerns have been expressed that the vigour with which the case is put in the new bulletin is very different to the 'neutral' tone that typified the old *Criminal Statistics* (where commentary and interpretation were kept to a minimum) and smacks somewhat of defensive politics. As will be discussed later, this has led to suggestions that the task of presenting crime figures should pass to an independent body.

Conclusions

How, then, can we summarize the similarities and differences between the pictures of crime that have emerged from the BCS and the recorded crime figures? First, the central message sent out by the authors of the BCS during the initial passage of its results into the public domain was, in essence: the bad news is that there is a lot more crime than we thought, the good news is that most of it is not very serious. Their remark about 'the petty nature of most law-breaking' (Hough and Mayhew 1983: 33) was designed to deflect a possible moral panic in reaction to the huge amount of 'new' crime revealed by the survey, but it also reflected the key finding—supported by all surveys conducted since—that unreported crimes generally involve much lower levels of financial loss, damage, and injury than those reported to the police.

Secondly, aside from the much larger totals of offences, the BCS produces a basic picture of crime not wildly dissimilar to that projected by police records: for example, 'autocrime' (theft of or from vehicles) is prominent in both sets of figures, and property crime is more frequent than violence. BCS crime, even more than the police figures, is dominated above all by offences committed by *strangers*: it has been much less successful in identifying 'serial' offences such as frequent sexual or physical assaults by people known to the victim. Most incidents reported to the survey consist of discrete incidents in which individuals suddenly and unexpectedly suffer an assault, the theft of or damage to a piece of their property, or an illegal entry into their house. Crime in this mode takes on an appearance in many ways akin to an accident, or an 'act of God'—an almost random event which can strike anyone at any time, but which is relatively rare in the life of any individual.

Finally, the overall shape of trends in crime between the early 1980s and the late 1990s emerges as similar in each case, although the BCS suggests a less steep rise. The two sets of data also give similar messages about significant falls in certain offences over the last ten years (notably burglary). However, not only are the overall falls in crime since 1995 less sharp in the recorded crime figures (even after adjustments for the changes in counting rules and the introduction of the NCRS), but in the case of violence there appear to be contradictory trends, the police statistics suggesting considerable rises (again after adjustments) and the BCS considerable falls.

Despite these recent doubts, the BCS has gained the respect of most criminologists as a useful tool for measuring trends in certain types of crime—notably the clear-cut 'stranger to stranger' incidents referred to above. One of its impacts has been that few still take the extreme line that the steady increases in crime indicated by official statistics between the late 1950s and early 1990s were entirely an artificial creation of data-collection processes. Most now agree, at least, that the incidence of visible predatory crimes such as burglary and vehicle theft did increase over this period. This may not seem a surprise now, but it was a major step for many radical criminologists to take, and writers such as Jock Young, who with others developed the 'Left Realist' movement in the 1980s, had to fight polemical battles with academics he dubbed 'Left Idealists' to establish his view that long-term increases in these kinds of crime not only were real, but had created a serious social problem (Matthews and Young 1986; Young 1988a;

Rock, Chapter 1, this volume). Indeed, as we shall see in the next section, his argument with the BCS was that it did not reveal the exceptional extent and range of crime suffered by *particular kinds of victims*, principally vulnerable people living in socially deprived areas.

ALTERNATIVES AND CHALLENGES TO THE OFFICIAL PICTURE

As noted earlier, the last twenty to thirty years have seen the development of many new sources of crime data other than the British Crime Survey. In this section we examine some of the most important of these. First, we discuss the contribution of some local crime surveys that were conducted in the 1980s with the particular purpose of gathering information about the victimization of certain social groups which, their designers believed, were grossly under-represented in recorded crime figures *and* in the BCS. These surveys provided important evidence in criminological debates about Left Realism, and also encouraged some new approaches by the Home Office researchers responsible for the BCS. We then look at other efforts, by a variety of researchers for a variety of purposes, to find out more about types of offending which tend to be almost invisible in recorded crime statistics and are not readily susceptible to measurement through conventional crime surveys. These include domestic violence, child abuse, crimes by and against businesses, crime in institutions like schools and prisons, and organized and cross-border crime.

THE CHALLENGE FROM LOCAL SURVEYS

While the BCS has achieved widespread respect among academics, as well as policy-makers, it has also attracted criticism on the grounds that it gives a distorted picture of patterns of victimization. In the 1980s, especially, those writing from a Left Realist and/or a feminist perspective argued that it did not sufficiently reflect the experiences either of women or of the very poor (see, for example, Matthews and Young 1986; Young 1988a; Stanko 1988; Genn 1988; Dobash and Dobash 1992). It was pointed out that a large proportion of assaults on women are likely to be committed by people known to them, including their partners, and that they are unlikely to report these in response to brief questions from an interviewer on the doorstep. Moreover, many members of marginalized groups—the homeless, the mentally ill, those who drift from bed-sitter to bed-sitter, and so on—are unlikely to have contact with interviewers in a survey based on samples of householders; such people may also be subject to exceptionally high levels of victimization.

To right this balance, some academics conducted rather different kinds of crime survey. These were local surveys, funded mainly by left-leaning local authorities in inner city areas,[22] which aimed to uncover areas of criminal behaviour not seriously touched by the BCS and, equally important, to examine the extent to which victimization is unequally distributed among the population (see, for example, Kinsey 1984; Jones *et al.* 1986, 1987; Crawford *et al.* 1990). By focusing chiefly upon inner city areas, such crime surveys brought out much more vividly than the BCS the extent to which crime is concentrated in some small areas—predominantly those blighted by poverty. For example, the first Islington Crime Survey (Jones *et al.* 1986) indicated that a third of local households had been touched by burglary, robbery, or assault within the previous 12 months: a situation quite different from that of the notional 'statistically average' person referred to in the first BCS.[23]

In addition, particular efforts were made to find ways of obtaining more information about sexual and other assaults on women. These included less restrictive wording of questions and emphasis on sensitive approaches to these topics in the training and selection of interviewers. Again, the results stand in considerable contrast to the BCS findings: in the Islington survey, significantly higher levels of sexual assault were found, while over one-fifth of reported assaults were classified as 'domestic'—more than twice the BCS proportion. Moreover, questions were asked about incidents which would not necessarily be classified by the police as 'crime', but may be experienced as serious by victims, namely sexual and racial 'harassment'. It was found, for example, that over two-thirds of women under the age of 24 had been 'upset by harassment' in the previous 12 months.

One of the most important general insights that emerged from the local surveys was that, while there are differences in risks of victimization between broad social groups (male and female, old and young, etc.), such differences can be massive when one looks at very specific subgroups. A particularly striking finding in the Islington survey, for example, was that young, black females in the area were 29 times more likely to be assaulted than white females over 45. As Young (1988b: 171) observed, such findings illustrate 'the fallacy of talking of the problem of women as a whole, or of men, blacks, whites, youths, etc.' . Rather, he insisted, criminological analysis should 'start from the actual subgroups in which people live their lives'.

A graphic illustration of this point is the early exploration by Hazel Genn (1988) of the problem of 'multiple victimization'. Genn, who had been involved in a major pilot survey in some deprived areas of London (Sparks *et al.* 1977) later revisited (and temporarily lived with) some of the female respondents who had claimed to have been

---

[22] Since then, however, local surveys crime have been carried out, for a variety of other purposes, in many different kinds of environment, including rural areas (Koffman 1996).

[23] In the first BCS report, it was calculated that a 'statistically average' person aged 16 or over could expect to fall victim to:

- a robbery once every five centuries (excluding attempts);
- an assault resulting in injury (even if slight) once every century;
- a family car stolen or taken by joyriders once every 60 years;
- a burglary in the home once every 40 years.

The authors added that 'These risks can be compared with the likelihood of encountering other sorts of mishaps: the chances of burglary are slightly less than the chances . . . of a fire in the home; the chances a household runs of car theft are smaller than the chances . . . of having one of its members injured in a car accident' (Hough and Mayhew 1983: 15).

victimized many times. She gives an eye-opening account of the way that the lives of these women were blighted by frequent sexual and physical assaults, thefts, burglaries, and other forms of mistreatment, many of them from people with whom they had some sort of continuing relationship. Yet this kind of crime, she notes, is lost from view in most surveys, partly because they tend to impose artificial limits upon the number of crimes that can be counted for any one victim, and partly because such victims may be less likely than others to respond to the survey or to admit their victimization to interviewers. At the same time, Genn raises fundamental questions, touched on earlier in this chapter, about how meaningful it is to 'count' certain crimes at all. She writes:

> In asking respondents about their experiences of crime, victim surveys have tended to use an approach which Skogan has termed 'the events orientation': that which conceptualizes crime as *discrete incidents*. This . . . can be traced back to one of the original primary objectives of victim surveys: the estimation of the 'dark figure' of unrecorded crime for direct comparison with police statistics. In order to accomplish this, . . . information obtained from victims had to be accommodated within a rigid 'counting' frame of reference. *Although isolated incidents of burglary, car theft or stranger attacks may present few measurement problems, for certain categories of violent crime and for certain types of crime victim, the 'counting' procedure leads to difficulties. It is clear that violent victimization may often be better conceptualized as a process rather than as a series of discrete events.* This is most evident in cases of prolonged and habitual domestic violence, but there are also other situations in which violence, abuse and petty theft are an integral part of victims' day-to-day existence [Genn 1988: 91, emphasis added].

Many researchers have since come to similar conclusions and, generally speaking, the findings of quantitative studies of 'serial' criminal behaviour such as domestic violence and sexual abuse have been expressed in terms of the *prevalence*, rather than the *incidence*, of the behaviour—that is, the proportion of a given population that has experienced it, rather than the numbers of individual 'offences' committed.

Finally, an important related point, also emphasized by Young, is that while it is informative to examine differential risks of victimization between social groups, this should be complemented with an understanding of the differential *impact* of crime on these groups. A debate about this arose from the prominence given in the first BCS reports to findings that younger males, and people who frequently went out drinking, faced the highest risks of being assaulted. From these findings the Home Office authors concluded that the fears of street violence expressed by both women and the elderly (which were greater than those of young men) were to some extent 'irrational' (Hough and Mayhew 1983). Young (1988b: 173–5) responded that such a conclusion, like their argument that fears are exaggerated because much crime is 'trivial' in terms of loss or injury, obscures the fact that what are 'objectively' similar events can have enormously different meanings and consequences for different people:

> People differ greatly in their ability to withstand crime . . . The 'same' punch can mean totally different things in different circumstances . . . Violence, like all kinds of crime, is a social relationship. It is rarely random: it inevitably involves particular social meanings and occurs in particular hierarchies of power. Its impact, likewise, is predicated on the

relationship within which it occurs . . . The relatively powerless situation of women—economically, socially and physically—makes them more unequal victims than men.

Later BCS 'sweeps' and reports have benefited to some extent from the above kinds of criticism, and more attention has since been paid to differential patterns of victimization. For example, 'booster' samples have been interviewed to explore the victimization of ethnic minorities (e.g. Mayhew *et al.* 1989; Clancy *et al.* 2001) and separate analysis has been undertaken of crime against older people (Chivite-Matthews and Maggs 2002). Computer-aided self-interviewing systems—whereby the interviewer does not see what the respondent keys in—have been used to explore sensitive topics such as sexual assaults on women and 'stalking' (Percy and Mayhew 1997; Mirrlees-Black 1999; Budd and Mattinson 2000; Walby and Allen 2004), although these are not counted as part of the 'BCS crime' totals. And as discussed later, data have also been collected from other Home Office surveys on crime against children aged 10–15 (Wood 2005).

OTHER SOURCES OF DATA ON 'HIDDEN' AND 'DIFFICULT TO MEASURE' CRIME

In addition to the local surveys referred to above, other sources of information have been used by academics, as well as by a variety of public, private, and voluntary agencies, to find out more about the scale and shape of types of offending not readily measured by recorded crime figures or national crime surveys. These tend to cover relatively 'private' spheres of activity, notably crimes that occur in domestic, commercial, or institutional contexts: a few examples are given below, together with some comments on the problems of obtaining reliable data.

Domestic violence

Domestic violence against adult women was one of the types of criminal behaviour afforded particular attention in the 1980s local crime surveys discussed above. Such behaviour was also explored in a variety of special surveys of women, mainly conducted by feminist researchers. For example, Hanmer and Saunders (1984) found that 59 per cent of 129 women surveyed in Leeds had suffered some form of threat, violence, or sexual harassment within the previous year, and Hall (1985) and Radford (1987) produced even more startling figures. Among the most challenging of all was a survey by Painter (1991), based on a representative sample of over 1,000 married women, which suggested that 14 per cent had been raped by their husbands at some time during their marriage—over 40 per cent of them perceiving the incident as 'rape' at the time.[24] Other work has since been carried out to investigate the extent of domestic violence against men (Grady 2002; Dobash and Dobash 2004; see also Saunders 2002) and between same-sex partners (Ristock 2002).

[24] The question used was, 'Have you ever had sex with your present husband (or previous husband) against your will, when you had clearly insisted that you did not want to and refused your consent?' This is a legal definition of rape, though despite court decisions which mean that a man can be convicted of raping his wife, it is unlikely that many police officers would arrest on allegations of refused consent by a wife living with her husband, without evidence of violence.

However, research into all these issues comes up against major methodological problems, and the results vary widely depending upon the kind of population sampled, the wording of the questions, and the situation in which they are put. Where interviewers are used, the degree of empathy established between them and the respondents is also a major factor (Dobash and Dobash 2004). Several such surveys have been based on imprecisely defined 'samples' and have lacked rigour in defining the period covered: clearly, it makes a considerable difference whether one asks if the respondent has been the victim of *x* within the past year, past few years, or 'ever'.

Child abuse

An even more 'hidden' form of criminal behaviour, a high proportion of which appears to occur within the domestic sphere (or at least within circles of family or acquaintances), is abuse of children. While it is feasible to ask women in surveys about recent physical or even sexual violence against them, this presents major ethical difficulties in relation to children. Some evidence of physical violence and neglect of children can be gleaned from hospital data on 'non-accidental injuries', although what is recorded of course depends on whether children are seriously enough injured to go to hospital and whether hospital staff recognize their injuries as being the result of violence. Particularly where child sexual abuse is concerned, most evidence has come from samples of adults who are asked to recall events from their own childhoods. However, this has major methodological problems, and has resulted in a wide variety of results (see Straus, Gelles, and Steinmetz 1980; Baker and Duncan 1985; Finkelhor and Araji 1986; Morgan and Zedner 1992; Hoyle and Zedner, Chapter 15, this volume).

As with domestic violence against adults, it makes little sense to attempt to count the numbers of 'offences' that have been committed. Normally, results are expressed in terms of the prevalence of victimization among samples of the population. However, this too can be very misleading: a person who has been victimized in a minor way only once counts the same as someone who has been seriously abused for years. Thus, for example, a major US study in the 1970s claimed that 30 per cent of all children in the USA had been victims of 'child mistreatment', but it was later pointed out that a different definition of mistreatment would reduce this proportion to only 1 per cent (see Levi *et al.*, Chapter 21, this volume).

Crime within institutions

Another important 'difficult to research' area which is still largely neglected concerns crime within institutions to which outsiders have relatively little access. These include prisons, army barracks, mental institutions, children's homes, old people's homes, and schools (particularly boarding schools), which are quite often reluctant to involve the police in any criminal behaviour that comes to light. Cultures can also be created in which victims of bullying, sexual abuse, or other violent behaviour find it difficult to get the managers of the institution to take action to stop it. Collection of data about the nature and scale of such abuses, even in official investigations, can be extremely difficult. Some surveys have been conducted of prison inmates (e.g. Edgar and

O'Donnell 1998), but this is an area that may be better researched through a variety of qualitative methodologies (such as in-depth interviews with ex-residents, or participant observation) than through standard survey approaches. A valuable edited collection of papers about innovative work on bullying among prisoners has recently been published by Ireland (2005). There is also some work on bullying in schools, mainly based on interviews and questionnaires, but again the proportions of students found to have been bullied varies widely, depending on the definitions and time frames used and the way the questions are put (Junger-Tas and Van Kesteren 1999). Even so, most studies have found the behaviour to be widespread. A fairly recent example is a study commissioned by Childline of 1,000 British schoolchildren, which found that more than half of primary school and a quarter of secondary school pupils said they had been bullied in the present school term; over half also believed bullying to be 'a big problem' or 'quite a problem' in their schools (Oliver and Candappa 2003). Research on the other institutions mentioned is less well developed, despite recent high-profile cases involving deaths in army barracks and maltreatment of old people.

Crimes against businesses

Crimes against businesses may be committed by members of the public (for example, through shoplifting or cheque frauds), by employees (though workplace theft or embezzlement) or by other businesses (for example, through 'long firm fraud'—see Levi 1981). Such crimes all pose considerable difficulties for measurement. First of all, in many cases they never come to light: for example, losses through low-level employee theft may be not be distinguishable from legitimate forms of 'shrinkage' (such as goods being damaged at warehouses), and embezzlement by people responsible for preparing the firm's accounts can be very difficult to detect. Secondly, it may not be clear when losses through theft are detected (often a considerable time after they have occurred) whether they have been committed by, say, shoplifters or counter staff. Thirdly, it may be unclear whether losses are the result of a small number of sizeable crimes by relatively few people or a large number of minor thefts by a large number of people (or indeed, repeated minor thefts over a long period by the same person). Finally, definitions of 'fraud', in particular, are fraught with difficulties, not least because legal definitions—many of which date back many years—are often out of date in relation to the myriad of new forms of criminal activity that have evolved to exploit opportunities created by changes in technology and the business environment (though see the Fraud Act 2006 for an updated approach). This means, again, that attempting to 'count crimes' is often an unproductive approach in this field. The scale of such crime therefore tends to be represented in terms of the prevalence of victimization (i.e. the proportion of a given population experiencing it), or as estimates(or guesstimates) of the total amount stolen in various ways over defined periods.

The *Fraud Review* (Attorney General's Office 2006) provides an overview of the limitations of existing sources in depicting the shape and scale of fraud in England and Wales, and outlines plans to develop more accurate and comprehensive measures (though these are still at an early stage). It notes, for example, that although recorded crime statistics show reductions in cheque and credit card fraud since 2000, only an estimated 5 per cent of fraudulent credit card transactions are reported to the police, so one can have little confidence in such figures.[25] It welcomes Home Office plans that, in future publications of statistics on this topic, police records will be supplemented with data from the Association for Payment Clearing Services (APACS), which reflect all cases known to the industry (for further discussion, see Wilson *et al.* 2006).

A useful new source of information about both theft and fraud against business is the *Commercial Victimisation Survey* (Shury *et al.* 2005), which surveyed retailers and manufacturers in England and Wales in 2002. This found that 74 per cent of retailers, and 53 per cent of manufacturers, had experienced some form of crime during the year. Where retailers were concerned, as one might expect, theft by customers (mentioned by 43 per cent of respondents), by staff (10 per cent), and 'by persons unknown' (20 per cent) were prominent. In addition, 18 per cent were aware of falling victim to 'fraud by outsiders'. One assumes that these results refer mainly to shoplifting and cheque card fraud. Among manufacturers, the most commonly mentioned crime was burglary (22 per cent); only 8 per cent recalled incidents involving fraud.

There are also some important private surveys of losses to major companies, such as those by Ernst and Young (2003) and Pricewaterhouse Coopers (2005), which look at fraud on a global as well as a UK basis. However, as Levi (2001) points out, these often neglect issues such as whether international frauds occurred 'in', for example, England and Wales, or whether they should be counted also (or instead) in another country. In addition, most public sector organizations make estimates of losses from fraud, some of them using quite different methodologies to that of simply analysing detected cases. For example, the Department of Work and Pensions and the National Health Service take a sample of transactions in a given area of spend (e.g. income support, or patients' prescriptions claims) and assess them to determine whether the claim was genuine. Where not, the amount of loss is calculated, and the results are grossed up to produce national estimates of loss (Attorney General's Office 2006: 31).

Despite all this activity, however, the overall picture remains very unclear, and many of the estimates of losses to organizations through theft and fraud remain highly speculative. There is little consistency in the definitions or methodologies used, and the quality of the data collected is often poor. While it is certainly worthwhile attempting to produce better quantitative measures—of the prevalence of victimization, of the scale of financial loss, and of other kinds of harm caused (e.g. bankruptcies)—it is also worth pointing out that information of this kind is much more valuable if supported by qualitative research of the kind undertaken many years ago by Ditton (1977) and Mars (1982), who spent time with people working in, for example, warehouses and docks, and came to understand the informal cultural rules among employees by which pilfering was simultaneously accepted as normal but restricted in scale.

[25] While the BCS does not regularly count frauds against individuals, it has recently included some relevant questions, the results of which are reported in Wilson *et al.* (2006). These indicate, for example, that only 3% of card users were victims of credit card fraud (to their knowledge, of course) in 2003/4. On the other hand, around half worried about it, especially in relation to Internet use.

Corporate crime

Crime *by* organizations is a somewhat difficult kettle of fish, and much of it is not subject to measurement by conventional criminological methods. It may include crimes against an organization's own employees (such as neglect of health and safety rules leading to death or injury—see Levi *et al.*, this volume), crimes against other organizations (including failures to pay for orders, and the operation of illegal cartels), or crimes against customers or the general public (ranging from the sale of sub-standard or stolen goods, through deliberate frauds and 'scams' to, for example, pollution of the environment). There is no space to consider these here (they are discussed by both Nelken; and Levi in this volume, Chapters 22 and 23, respectively; see also Slapper and Tombs 1999; Croall 2001; Simpson 2002), but it is worth making the basic point that most insights into the nature and scale of such offences emerge only when they come to light through a bankruptcy, a police investigation, or a 'whistle-blower', and events can be reconstructed through analysis of investigation files, court records, or newspaper stories (see, for example, Clinard and Yeager 1980; Levi 1985; Passas and Groskin 2001; Passas and Nelken 1993; Punch 1996). Of course, 'participant observation' is much harder for academics to do in relation to elite corporate crime than for crimes further down the ladder. There have been some attempts to gather data on corporate criminal behaviour that has not yet come to light, for example by investigative journalists, or to explore the problem in more general ways through interviews with business people or auditors, but systematic studies are rare and the overall level of knowledge (and indeed criminological interest) in the field remains low. This is regrettable given the fact that the scale of corporate offending can be immense: as noted earlier, international fraud cases such as BCCI, Enron, and the Maxwell pension fund each involved many hundreds of millions of pounds and affected huge numbers of individuals and businesses.

International, organized, and cross-border crime

The growing need for crime data on an international scale has been recognized through the development of major surveys which collect information in a consistent way across several different countries at once. Most notable among these are the International Crime Victim Survey (Van Kesteren *et al.* 2000) and the International Crime Business Survey (Alvazzi Del Frate 2005).[26] Both suffer from methodological problems and shortages of resources (Barclay 2000), but offer rich sets of data for analysis. By contrast, there is very little strong evidence available about the scale of crime that crosses international borders (such as EU subsidy fraud, money-laundering, smuggling, and drug- or people-trafficking), and especially about crime of this kind committed by highly organized groups. This represents a major challenge owing to the rapidly changing and well-concealed nature of the activities, and is an area in which conventional methods of gathering data are plainly inadequate (see Levi, this volume).

---

[26] The 'Eurobarometer', a regular survey of public opinion in Europe has also asked some crime-related questions. See http://ec.europa.eu/public_opinion/index_en.htm.

At present, among the most systematic attempts to summarize what is known about changing patterns of organized crime, inasmuch as it impacts on the UK and Europe, are the regular 'threat assessments' produced by the National Criminal Intelligence Service and Europol. These are based on a wide variety of data from both 'closed' and 'open' sources, and are published in a sanitized form (see SOCA 2006; Europol 2006). Otherwise, much of the available information is based on newspaper reports, court cases, police or secret service agencies' investigation files, and interviews with convicted organized criminals: getting closer to the 'field' clearly entails considerable dangers to researchers and informants. Generally speaking, empirical investigations have tended to focus on charting the numbers, size, and ethnic connections of organized criminal groups, rather than attempting to measure the scale of 'organized crime' in terms of offences committed. The latter, indeed, comes up against the problem that some kinds of offence are committed as much by individuals as by 'organized' criminal groups (see Levi, this volume, and Levi and Maguire 2004, for further discussion).

Crimes by governments and in war

Finally, both Levi *et al.* and Hoyle and Zedner (this volume) draw attention to a whole raft of horrific state-sanctioned crimes, including crimes against humanity, that have to a large extent remained off the radar of most criminological work (see also Cohen 2001). Unsurprisingly, figures on war crimes, torture, or killings sanctioned by governments are not usually gathered or published by state officials, but by external bodies such as Amnesty International and Human Rights Watch. Such data are gradually being used in analysis by small numbers of criminologists (for good examples, see the Special Issue of the *British Journal of Criminology* edited by Green and Ward 2005) but are still too rarely thought of as 'criminal statistics'—which, of course, they are.

NEW DATA ON OFFENDERS

Most of the new developments in data collection that took place in the 1980s and 1990s were offence and victim focused rather than offender focused. However, more recently there has been something of a revival in interest in data about offenders, which merits brief discussion here.

Just as the annual statistics compiled from police records produce an 'official' account of the extent of crime, so statistics compiled from court and Crown Prosecution Service records, together with police records of cautions, produce a picture of all those officially held responsible for recorded offences. And just as crime surveys tell us more about unrecorded crime, so 'self-report' surveys tell us more about people who have committed crimes without being caught and convicted. Let us begin with a few comments on the numbers and characteristics of convicted offenders and then look at some data from other sources, including important recent self-report studies.

Adjudicated offenders

Until 2001, statistics on offenders who had been convicted or cautioned were published alongside recorded crime figures in the annual Command Paper, *Criminal Statistics*

England and Wales. The crime figures were then removed to a separate statistical bulletin (*Crime in England and Wales*). The offender data continued to appear for a few years in publications under the old name, but recently these have been replaced by, on the one hand, a Statistical Bulletin entitled *Offender Management Caseload Statistics* (RDS NOMS 2006) and on the other, a detailed breakdown of sentencing outcomes in a separate publication entitled *Sentencing Statistics* (Home Office 2005b).

In looking at the people officially held responsible for criminal offences in any given year, the first point to note is that they are much lower in number than the offences recorded. In 2004, about 318,000 people were sentenced in court for indictable offences and a further 156,000 were cautioned—small figures compared with the recorded crime total of over five and a half million offences. (Many more were convicted or cautioned for summary offences—around 1,330,000 in 2004, of which most were motoring related—but as explained earlier, these do not form part of the recorded crime statistics.) Even taking into account the fact that some offenders are convicted of more than one offence, this means that the great majority of crimes recorded by the police (over 90 per cent) do not result in a conviction or caution, and nothing is 'officially' known about who committed them—though the police may have suspicions about many more. (Indeed, if one uses BCS results to bring into the picture crimes not reported to the police, the 'attrition rate' becomes even more striking: for example, based on data from 1997, it was estimated by Barclay and Tavares (1999: 29) that only about 3 in 100 crimes against individuals or their property had led to an offender being convicted or cautioned for the offence.) This so-called 'justice gap' has received considerable attention in recent years, and the present Government has set targets for the police to 'narrow' it by arresting and charging a higher proportion of offenders.[27] However, we are more interested here in the implications for our knowledge about offenders. Obviously, with such a large 'unknown', it cannot simply be assumed that the characteristics of 'offenders' as a whole can be inferred from those of adjudicated offenders—a key point which we shall return to in a moment. First, though, let us look briefly at those who passed through the criminal justice system.

Among the 474,000 offenders convicted or cautioned for indictable offences in 2004, 80 per cent were male, and 38 per cent were under 21. The peak age of offending—that is, the age at which people had the highest risk of acquiring a conviction or caution— stood at 17 for males and 15 for females. The highest proportion (36 per cent) were held responsible for theft or handling offences, and 17 per cent for violent or sexual offences (for further details, see Home Office 2005a; for 2005 data, see RDS NOMS 2006).

Another, more detailed, picture of adjudicated offenders—in this case, the subgroup thought to have offended seriously enough to warrant a custodial sentence—is provided by analysis of information held in prison records. The most obvious characteristic of the prison population is its 'maleness': despite rapid increases in the numbers of women imprisoned in the 1990s, they still make up only 6 per cent of the average daily prison population (see Morgan and Liebling, Chapter 32, this volume). The most

[27] http://www.cps.gov.uk/publications/docs/justicegap.pdf.

detailed breakdown of the social characteristics of the custodial population was provided by the 1991 National Prison Survey (Walmsley *et al.* 1992), which analysed a large sample of records of prisoners over the age of 17 in England and Wales. The prison population was shown to be predominantly young: 62 per cent of inmates were aged below 30, compared with 25 per cent of the general population. Disproportionate numbers of prisoners were also found to come from ethnic minorities: 15 per cent of male, and as many as 23 per cent of female, prisoners described themselves as black or Asian. Where social class was concerned, 41 per cent of males had had unskilled or partly skilled jobs, compared with 18 per cent of the general population.

Other striking findings included the revelation that over a quarter of prisoners had at some time been in local authority care (compared with an estimated 2 per cent of the general population); 40 per cent of male prisoners had left school before the age of 16 (compared with 11 per cent of all British males); and 13 per cent had been 'of no fixed abode' before coming into prison (for further details, see Morgan and Liebling, Chapter 32, this volume).

A more recent—and potentially the richest yet—source of data on convicted offenders is the 'OASys' (Offender Assessment System). This is a standardized tool which is used (mainly by probation officers) to assess the risk of harm and risk of reconviction, as well as to identify the 'criminogenic needs' of offenders prior to sentence and afterwards (National Probation Service 2003). It has now been computerized (as 'e-OASys') and a new centralized IT system already holds assessments on thousands of offenders. This can be analysed to provide detailed statistical information on a wide range of issues, including for example levels of drug use, educational deficits, or unemployment among the convicted offender population (National Probation Service 2005: 13). Early unpublished results suggest that high proportions of offenders suffer from major problems in all these areas, while a study by Clancy *et al.* (2006) found particularly high OASys scores among a sample of short-term prisoners.

Overall, the above data clearly illustrate that the social characteristics of people who are arrested and processed by the criminal justice system—and particularly those who are sent to prison—present a very different pattern from that found in the general population. There are many more males, young people, black people, poor people, poorly educated people, people with disturbed childhoods, and people with severe substance-misuse problems, than one would find in a random sample.

Self-report studies

Of course, if only about 3 per cent of known crimes end in a conviction or caution, it is important to ask whether the other 97 per cent are likely to have been committed by a similarly skewed section of the population (or, indeed, by the very same people). This is the province of self-report studies—the technique by which samples of the population are asked in confidence whether they have committed crimes for which they have not been caught. Many such surveys were carried out in the 1960s and 1970s, but there was a hiatus until quite recently, when some sizeable self-report studies were commissioned by government. These include an international survey of young people (see Graham and Bowling 1995); the *Youth Lifestyles Survey*, which covered many areas in addition to criminal behaviour (Flood-Page *et al.* 2000); and the Home Office's *Offending, Crime and Justice Survey*, or OCJS (Budd *et al.* 2005).

Depending upon the age, sex, and other social characteristics of those questioned, as well as upon the wording of the questions, self-report studies have generally found that between 40 and almost 100 per cent will admit to having committed at least one criminal offence during their lifetime. Most such studies have used samples of young males, often schoolchildren or students. For example, in one of the best early studies, Elmhorn (1965) found that 92 per cent of a random sample of teenage schoolboys in Stockholm admitted to at least one offence, while 53 per cent admitted to at least one 'serious' offence (roughly the equivalent of an indictable crime in Britain), principally theft. More recently, the first international self-report survey indicated that consistently high proportions of young people across a range of developed countries had committed at least one criminal offence (Junger-Tas *et al.* 1994). The British version of this survey found that nearly a third of 22–25 year old males (though only 4 per cent of females) admitted to committing a criminal offence within the previous year (Graham and Bowling 1995: 25). Moreover, these figures exclude drug offences, which would have increased them considerably.

At the same time, most self-report studies have found that much smaller proportions of respondents admit to frequent or serious offending. Thus, for example, Graham and Bowling (1995) found that over a quarter of all offences admitted by 14–25 year olds were committed by just 3 per cent of the 'offenders', and that only 7 per cent of the sample admitted to the most serious offences on the list (see also Christie *et al.* 1965; Farrington 1973; Huizinga and Elliott 1986). In short, as Hood and Sparks (1970: 51) put it many years ago:

> While it may be correct to say that to commit one or two delinquent acts is 'normal behaviour' for boys, to be involved in frequent criminal acts is apparently relatively rare.

Other important issues explored through the early self-report studies included the extent to which (as suggested by the court and prison data discussed above) crime is committed disproportionately by males and by people from lower social classes. Where class is concerned, there were some fierce debates when different methodological approaches (e.g. using interviews or self-completion questionnaires) produced contradictory results. However, in the end the general consensus seemed to be, as Braithwaite (1979) put it after reviewing 41 self-report studies:

1. Lower-class adults commit *those types of crime which are handled by the police* at a higher rate than middle-class adults.

2. Adults living in lower-class areas commit *those types of crime which are handled by the police* at a higher rate than adults who live in middle-class areas.

3. Lower-class juveniles commit crime at a higher rate than middle-class juveniles.

4. Juveniles living in lower-class areas commit crime at a higher rate than juveniles living in middle-class areas [Braithwaite 1979: 62, emphasis added].

The use of the phrase *those types of crime which are handled by the police* is telling here. This underlines the point that the offences covered in most such studies are chiefly the common and visible predatory street offences like burglary and car crime—almost by definition the 'crimes of the poor'—which occupy a high proportion of police atten- tion, rather than the more hidden kinds of crime which happen within the private spheres of the commercial world or within the household. It is surely unsurprising that surveys reveal them to be committed more often by poorer people!

Equally important questions have been raised in relation to both race and gender. These are highly complex and there is no space to do them justice here (though relevant discussions can be found in Phillips and Bowling, and in Heidensohn and Gelsthorpe, Chapters 14 and 13 respectively, in this volume; see also Smith 1997). Where race is concerned, it will simply be noted that one of the most significant findings is that, despite the relatively high proportions of black people who are prosecuted and impris- oned, there tend to be few differences between black and white respondents in terms of offences admitted to self-report studies. Indeed, in some surveys, white respondents report higher offending rates than black respondents: this was apparent in recent find- ings from the OCJS (see Sharp and Budd 2005). To what extent these kinds of findings reflect 'reality' (and hence biases in the police and criminal justice system—see Hood 1992) and to what extent they arise from the unreliability of the self-report method— and/or differences in trust in the confidentiality of surveys and hence in willingness to admit offences—remains unclear. However, one area in which the pictures painted by both court data and self-report studies are in close agreement is that of low offending rates on the part of people with an Asian background.

Where gender is concerned, by contrast, self-report studies have generally reflected the picture that emerges from data on adjudicated offenders—i.e. that males are greatly over-represented among 'offenders'. For example, Graham and Bowling (1995: 13) found that males were, respectively, eight, six, and four times more likely than females to admit to having committed burglary, car theft, and theft from vehicles. As Heidensohn (1989: 87) once put it: 'There is little or no evidence of a vast shadowy underworld of female deviance hidden in our midst like the sewers below the city streets.' At the other extreme, as women are still greatly under-represented in the high- level positions in business from which markets can be manipulated or major frauds perpetrated, it is probably safe to assume that corporate crime, too, is overwhelmingly a male province.

The OCJS

The most important recent self-report study is the Home Office's *Offending, Crime and Justice Survey* (OCJS). This was first conducted in 2003 with a sample of 12,000 people aged 10–65 living in private households in England and Wales (Budd *et al.* 2005). Its main aim is to explore the extent of offending, 'antisocial behaviour', and drug use, particularly among children and young people. In addition to many of the BCS offences such as burglary and assault, the survey covers self-reported shoplifting, fraud, and technology offences. It also helps to fill a gap in the BCS coverage by asking children from the age of 10 questions about their experiences as victims of crime. Finally, it has so far contained a longitudinal element, re-interviewing some individuals at intervals to glean more information about changes over time and 'pathways' into and out of criminal and antisocial behaviour.

In addition to general findings on self-reported offending, more specialized reports have been published on, inter alia, underage drinking (Matthews *et al.* 2006), 'binge drinking' (Matthews and Richardson 2005), drug-taking (Becker and Roe 2005), and fraud and technology crimes (Wilson *et al.* 2006). The survey is also interesting in that it attempts to quantify the prevalence of 'antisocial' as well as criminal behaviour. In this it is to some extent following in the footsteps of early self-report studies, many of which blurred the distinction between crime and 'delinquency': thus questions to young people about stealing were quite often interspersed with questions about behaviour such as 'smoking' or 'defying parents' authority' and in some cases the responses were included with criminal behaviour in global estimates of the prevalence of 'delinquency'. OCJS reports do make a distinction: for example, Hayward and Sharp (2005: 1) found that 'about 17% of young people had committed antisocial behaviour but no more serious offence. 12% had committed both antisocial behaviour and offences.' However, this does not resolve questions about the definition of 'antisocial behaviour', which not only appears to have no clear rationale, but includes 'joyriding' and 'racial harassment', both of which are likely to entail criminal behaviour.

Concluding comments

In the light of results from self-report studies, there now appears to be relatively little dispute about the broad validity of the general picture, as reflected in the official statistics, of the relative 'contributions' as offenders of males and females, but there is much more argument about other major social groups, particularly around social class and ethnicity.

Where the persistent commission of common predatory street offences is concerned, it is true, both 'official' and 'self-reported' offenders emerge with a not too dissimilar profile (young, male, and poor)—partly, one may presume, because few persistent burglars or car thieves succeed in escaping conviction entirely. However, this does not alter the vital point that, just as victim surveys are vastly more effective in revealing 'hidden' instances of some kinds of crime than of others, so the perpetrators of different kinds of offence are not equally well 'revealed' through the medium of self-report studies. Thus, while respondents tend to be asked in great detail about the kinds of antisocial activity which are associated with the arrests or court appearances of adolescents, they are not often asked whether they have assaulted their partners or sexually abused their children, nor whether they have perpetrated a significant financial fraud. If it were possible to overcome the ethical problems of expanding self-report studies into such sensitive areas, the results might well support the indications from some (also methodologically problematic) victim surveys, that the perpetrators of intra-family violence and abuse are much more evenly distributed throughout the population (see Morgan 1988; Morgan and Zedner 1992; Dobash and Dobash 1992;

though for scepticism on this point, see Levi *et al.*, this volume). And without doubt, if they were expanded into the commercial sphere, they would confirm that the social-class distribution of people involved in business fraud is skewed in a different direction to that of burglary and street robbery.

RECENT DEVELOPMENTS AND EMERGING ISSUES

We return in this last section to some of the broader questions that were raised at the beginning of the chapter about the relationship between crime data and changing attitudes and approaches to crime and its control. We focus on developments in the early 2000s, particularly on changes in Home Office approaches to the collection and presentation of criminal statistics. These changes have been driven to a large extent by new data demands from policy-makers and practitioners. On the one hand the demands relate to *new operational needs*, and on the other to the high priority attached by government to *performance monitoring and management* of the police, criminal justice agencies, and local partnerships.

As discussed earlier, the rhetoric—and to a lesser extent the practice—of crime control has moved increasingly in recent years in the direction of 'evidence-based' and 'problem-oriented' approaches, in which the nature and scale of crime or disorder problems are identified through analysis of a variety of data sources and (ideally) responded to in a planned fashion. Much of this activity now takes place at local level and is undertaken by local partnerships (especially Crime and Disorder Reduction Partnerships—see Crawford, Chapter 26, this volume), although the Home Office plays a major part in terms of disseminating 'good practice' and monitoring the results. The National Intelligence Model, too, is increasingly being used as a framework to guide the process of collecting and analysing data, planning and implementing interventions, and monitoring the results (John and Maguire 2003; Maguire and John 2006). Such approaches and systems require a great deal of data: for example, detailed information about offences which allows analysts to identify crime patterns; data that can be used to monitor interventions; and data that can supply reliable evidence of any changes that these have produced. To be of real use, practitioners argue, such data must be:

- comprehensive (to give as complete a picture of the problem as possible);
- reliable (to avoid misunderstanding it);
- timely (data a year out of date are of little use operationally);
- context rich (to allow greater understanding of the problem);
- local (national or even police force-level data provide only 'background').

At the same time, the passion for target-setting and performance-monitoring in the Home Office has created a parallel demand for data produced both with *integrity* and in a *consistent* and standardized fashion. This applies particularly to police crime records, which are used as the main measure of performance at Basic Command Unit level (BCS data can only be used at force level and above), and have come under increasingly close scrutiny by bodies such as the Audit Commission (2004, 2006).

THE SIMMONS REPORT AND ITS AFTERMATH

In 2000, the Home Office published a far-reaching report entitled *Review of Crime Statistics*, which put forward plans to respond to many of the above challenges. The report set out a vision of a 'modernization' process, '[a revision of] the philosophy underlying the production of statistics', in which 'nineteenth-century' aims and practices would be replaced by

> a more flexible view of information—one where we first define the problems requiring solution and then develop the information needed to better understand those problems, . . . rather than rely on the routine statistics supplied in summary form by the police [Simmons 2000: ii].

The recommendations included the replacement of the traditional *Criminal Statistics* with an annual 'Picture of Crime in England and Wales' incorporating data from a range of sources including police crime and incident data, the British Crime Survey, research studies, and information from other agencies and institutions. The central focus on legally defined offences would also be weakened, more attention being given to social definitions of crime and to non-crime events which cause concern to the public. In addition, more detailed and more comprehensive data would be recorded on crime and disorder, including postcodes or grid references of the locations of incidents, which can be used to 'map' crimes to identify 'hotspots'; more information about the immediate context and modus operandi of offences; and victims' views of offenders' motives and of the seriousness of incidents. Indeed, the author looked forward to systems of data collection in which a common incident record format is used by every police force, and part-records of individual cases (as opposed to simply counts of offence types) can be transferred electronically to the Home Office, hence allowing more analysis to be undertaken centrally. If such information was to be useful, it was argued, it had to be as comprehensive as possible. Police officers should therefore be directed both to record more detail on serious offences, and to

> ensure that *every* incident relating to crimes, allegations of crimes and also disorder that is brought to their attention is recorded as an incident (or 'call for service') [Simmons 2000: 19, emphasis in original].

The Simmons report provides a good illustration of the theme explored in the early part of this chapter, that decisions about how to collect and present crime data do not occur in a vacuum: they respond to the changing demands of the 'consumers' of the information and to the dominant preoccupations of the day. It argues, in essence, that there is no longer any strong demand for a crude general 'barometer' of the level of crime, constructed from simple counts of recorded offences. Instead, the demand now tends to be for more malleable and contextualized forms of information with which to assess and respond quickly to the new and highly specific 'problems' and 'risks' which emerge at frequent intervals to preoccupy the public, politicians, and the media.

A number of important changes followed the publication of the report, not all of them in line with Simmons's recommendations. It is argued that these have cumulatively produced some significant improvements from the viewpoint of policy-makers and practitioners, not least some detailed and informative statistical bulletins on specific kinds of offence, based on deeper analysis of police records, supplemented by information from other sources including the BCS (see, for example, the enhanced analyses of homicide and gun crime in Coleman *et al.* 2006). At the same time, these gains have come at the price of some problematic unintended consequences in terms of reactions from the public, the media, and politicians. The focus here will be on two of the most important changes in this respect: (a) the introduction of the National Crime Recording Standard (NCRS), based on a 'prima facie' approach to crime recording, and (b) the publication and discussion of BCS results and recorded crime figures in the same bulletin.

The NCRS and 'crime inflation'

The National Crime Recording Standard was instituted in April 2002 in order to introduce more integrity and consistency into police recording. Its most important feature in terms of impact on recorded crime was the adoption of the prima facie (as opposed to 'evidential') principle. In its most extreme form, this means that a member of the public's claim to have been the victim of a particular crime should be taken at face value and a crime report made reflecting their account, rather than allowing the police to discount it immediately as mischievous or mistaken (Burrows *et al.* 2000).[28] Simmons had recommended that this principle should be applied to *incident* data, but not to recorded crime, but the view of the police service and HM Inspectorate of Constabulary prevailed and it was applied (though not to this extreme degree) to crime records.[29] As noted earlier, this had a substantial inflationary effect on recorded crime levels, and has made the identification of recent trends very difficult. Moreover, this is only one of a number of recent developments around reporting and recording which have had a similar effect. These include the changes to the counting rules in 1998/9 (particularly the addition of common assault and harassment to the crime categories counted). More recently, plans are in place for the introduction of a 'single non-emergency number' (SNEN), which will make it easier for people to report low-level crime and disorder (see http://snen.homeoffice.gov.uk/), as well as for the introduction of a national incident recording standard, which will encourage the police to record

---

[28] This principle of 'believing the victim' had previously been applied to allegations of rape, and later (through police instructions issued following the Stephen Lawrence case) to allegations that an offence was racially motivated.

[29] Crimes can be removed from the records with the agreement of supervisors if there is evidence that the report was mischievous or mistaken.

reports of this kind more consistently than in the past. It is likely that both these developments, which reflect a more general tendency for the borderline between crime and 'antisocial behaviour' to becoming blurred, will further increase crime reporting and recording of crime, and hence contribute to further inflation of the crime figures.

This 'inflation' is not necessarily a problem for practitioners or policy-makers: on the contrary, the standardization of recording practices should eventually assist those concerned with performance-monitoring, while more comprehensive reporting and recording of offences should be of assistance to those concerned with analysing crime problems and planning responses. On the other hand, it can have some less welcome consequences. First of all, it makes analysis of both national and local trends, in the short term at least, a complex and problematic task. Secondly, to the untutored eye (and to political opponents looking for an angle of attack on the government) it gives a strong impression that 'crime is rising', when most of the available evidence, if carefully analysed, does not support this as a general conclusion. As crime has become a highly charged political issue, media treatments of the release of statistics tend to look no further than the raw figures, and show little interest in 'technical' arguments that there have 'actually' been falls, not rises. Indeed, they are likely to regard the latter as simply 'spin' (see below).

Joint analysis of BCS and recorded crime: the problem of trust

As noted earlier, from 2001/2, the traditional annual publication *Criminal Statistics England and Wales* was replaced by a new annual bulletin with named authors, entitled *Crime in England and Wales* (see for example, Walker *et al.* 2006). The new bulletin not only presents BCS results alongside recorded crime figures, but has added a great deal more analysis, interpretation, and discussion than was previously included. Indeed, it now has more the appearance and style of a research report than of a statistical publication—not least in that the ratio of text and analysis to tables has significantly increased.

While this move has been generally welcomed by specialists, including academics, as a more useful and informative approach, once again it has come at a price in terms of communication with the public. The publication in one high-profile 'official' bulletin of two sets of statistics which at first glance appear to be moving in different directions, inevitably creates a certain amount of public confusion. More than this, to the growing numbers of people already inclined to treat government statistics with suspicion (see, for example Duffy *et al.* 2005), it may be seen as another example of the government 'spinning' bad news.

Perhaps of more concern, the presentation of complex statistical analysis on a controversial subject in a highly charged political climate places considerable pressures on the civil servants charged with this task. These pressures include fears that the media will deliberately misinterpret the data and look only for negative news, and perhaps concern about upsetting political masters. The old *Criminal Statistics* contained relatively little analysis as such, and consisted mainly of tables, but the new statistical bulletins encourage analysis and interpretation and are as such a 'different animal'.

There is undoubtedly a risk that pressures of the above kind will lead the analysts, consciously or unconsciously, to focus on what appear to be the more positive conclusions that emerge from the statistics: in other words, indeed to engage in something approaching 'spin'. Arguably, there are some signs of 'defensive' interpretations of the data in the most recent bulletin. As described in the last section, the discussion of trends in violent crime could be seen in this light (Walker *et al.* 2006: 66), while the use of language such as 'settling down' (p.4) and 'stabilising' (p.13) to describe trends, could be interpreted as part of an attempt to sound reassuring. Of course, in an era when 'spin' itself is a high-profile political issue, any hint of such defensiveness—whether intentional or not—will be quickly identified and criticized, adding to the general sense of mistrust of government statistics that already exists. The Statistics Commission (2005: 4) puts a similar point rather more strongly:

> [O]ur impression is that, faced with a sceptical and at times antagonistic press, the Home Office and other official bodies have sought to contain the flow of statistical messages—prescribing the frequency and form in which statistics are released, and making sure that policy responses are issued at the earliest possible moment, sometimes ahead of the figures themselves. Whilst there is inevitably an element of conjecture in this 'outsider's analysis', we believe that any such control is almost always counterproductive in terms of public confidence. It creates an environment in which the media and public assume that they are receiving a filtered, government friendly, version of the truth—even though the statistical message may not be either of those things.

In its final report of the review from which the above quotation is taken, the Statistics Commission (2006: 6) recommended that, in the light of these problems of trust, (1) 'Responsibility for the composition and publication of crime statistics should be located at arm's length from Home Office policy functions and with clear accountability within the evolving framework of the government statistical service'; and (2) 'Treasury and Home Office Ministers should consider together a fully developed business case for moving responsibility for the British Crime Survey to the Office for National Statistics'. The basic idea of distancing the production of official crime statistics from the Home Office had also been endorsed earlier by the Chancellor of the Exchequer (Statistics Commission 2005: 3).[30] Of course, whether this in itself would be sufficient to allay public and media cynicism and distrust is by no means certain.

CONCLUDING COMMENTS

In the spirit of the above discussion, if there are two key 'messages' to take from this chapter, they are probably the following:

1. Crime statistics are not simple reflections of 'facts', but one of many possible tools for gaining a better understanding of the highly complex and rapidly changing forms of

---

[30] Another recent report, Adrian Smith's *Crime Statistics: An Independent Review* (2006) recognized similar problems, but recommended the less radical solution of greater separation between statistical and policy functions within the Home Office, combined with clearer communication with the public at both national and local levels.

behaviour that can be described as 'crime'. A 'rise (or fall) in crime' indicated by police records or survey results should be regarded as an important piece of evidence about, rather than conclusive proof of, changes in the scale and patterns of such behaviours.

2. Crime statistics are not immune from political and social change, and the ways in which data about crime are collected, analysed, and presented (and the importance and resources attached to them) are both influenced by, and influence, changes in thinking about the nature and importance of the 'crime problem' and how to respond to it.

■ SELECTED FURTHER READING

Although already out of date in some respects, *Understanding Crime Data*, by Clive Coleman and Jenny Moynihan (Open University Press, 1996) is still one of the best recent British text-books on the subject, and covers in more depth several of the main issues discussed in this chapter. It has the added advantage of accessibility and a light and humorous touch. Despite their much greater age, both *Understanding Crime Rates*, by Keith Bottomley and Clive Coleman (Saxon House, 1981) and *Crime and Punishment: Interpreting the Data*, by Bottomley and Ken Pease (Open University Press, 1986) are both theoretically informed and illuminating books of high quality. *Interpreting Crime Statistics*, edited by Monica Walker (Oxford University Press, 1995) contains some useful chapters on specialized topics such as prison statistics and homicide data.

The traditional Command Paper which presented the 'official crime statistics' annually since 1857 (*Criminal Statistics, England and Wales*) has recently been replaced by a series of more specialized statistical bulletins published by the Home Office. The most important of these is *Crime in England and Wales* (Walker *et al.* 2006), which provides an annual overview of crime totals and trends based on both police records and the results of the British Crime Survey; others cover offenders convicted or cautioned, and sentencing decisions and trends. The thinking behind these new ways of presenting data is outlined in a key paper by Jon Simmons (2000), the *Review of Criminal Statistics: A Discussion Document*.

The above documents can be downloaded from the Home Office website, which should be the first port of call for anyone wishing to explore the subject. It contains other detailed statistics relating to policing, the courts, prisons, and probation, as well as numerous studies and reports based on both internal and external research. Many of these are based on results from major surveys, including the British Crime Survey, the Offending Crime and Justice Survey (Budd *et al.* 2005), the Youth Lifestyles Survey (Flood-Page *et al.* 2000), and the Commercial Victimisation Survey (Shury *et al.* 2005). Interesting recent examples include findings on self-reported drug-taking (Becker and Roe 2005), the victimization of young people (Wood 2005), and domestic violence and stalking (Walby and Allen 2004).

There are also several compilations of data and statistics providing international comparisons of crime patterns and criminal justice responses. Among the most comprehensive are *Cross-National Studies in Crime and Justice* (Farrington *et al.*, Washington DC: U.S. Department of Justice, 2004) and the *European Sourcebook of Crime and Criminal Statistics*, 3rd edn (Killias, The Hague: WODC 2006). Specific international surveys include the International Crime Victim Survey (Van Kesteren *et al.* 2000), the International Crime Business Survey (Alvazzi Del Frate 2005), and the International Self-Report Delinquency Study (Junger-Tas *et al.* 1994).

Finally, two important reviews of the current state of criminal statistics in England and Wales, with recommendations for significant changes, were published in 2006: the Statistics Commission's report on *User Perspectives*, and Adrian Smith's *Crime Statistics: An Independent Review*.

■ REFERENCES

ALLEN, J., and RUPAREL, C (2006), 'Reporting and Recording Crime', in A. Walker, C. Kershaw, and S. Nicholas (2006). *Crime in England and Wales 2005/06*. London: Home Office.

ALVAZZI DEL FRATE, A. (2005), 'The International Crime Business Survey: Findings from Nine Central–Eastern European Cities', *European Journal on Criminal Policy and Research*, 10(2–3): 137–61.

ATTORNEY GENERAL'S OFFICE (2006), *Fraud Review: Final Report*, London: Attorney General's Office.

AUDIT COMMISSION (2004), *Improving the Quality of Crime Records in Police Authorities and Forces in England and Wales*, London: Audit Commission.

——AND THE WALES AUDIT OFFICE (2006), *Crime Recording 2005: Improving the Quality of Crime Records in Police Authorities and Forces in England and Wales*, London: Audit Commission.

BAKER, A., and DUNCAN, S. (1985), 'Child Sexual Abuse: A Study of Prevalence in Great Britain', *Child Abuse and Neglect*, 9: 457–67.

BARCLAY, G. (2000), 'The comparability of data on convictions and sanctions: are international comparisons possible?', *European Journal of Criminal Policy and Research*, 8: 13–26.

——and TAVARES, C. (1999), *Digest—Information on the Criminal Justice System in England and Wales,*. London: Home Office.

BECKER, H. S. (1963), *Outsiders: Studies in the Sociology of Deviance*, London: Macmillan.

BECKER, J., and ROE, S. (2005), *Drug Use among Vulnerable Groups of Young People: Findings from the 2003 Crime and Justice Survey,*. Findings 254, London: Home Office.

BEIRNE, P. (1993), *Inventing Criminology: Essays on the Rise of 'Homo Criminalis'*, Albany, NY: State University of New York Press.

BENNETT, T., and WRIGHT, R. (1984), *Burglars on Burglary*, Aldershot: Gower.

BLAIR, I. (1984), *Investigating Rape: A New Approach for the Police*. London: Croom Helm.

BOTTOMLEY, A., K., and COLEMAN, C. A. (1981), *Understanding Crime Rates*, Farnborough: Saxon House.

——and PEASE, K. (1986), *Crime and Punishment: Interpreting the Data*, Milton Keynes: Open University Press.

BOTTOMS, A. E. (1995), 'The Philosophy and Politics of Punishment and Sentencing', in C. Clarkson and R. Morgan (eds), *The Politics of Sentencing Reform*, Oxford: Clarendon Press.

BRAITHWAITE, J. (1979), *Inequality, Crime and Public Policy*, London: Routledge & Kegan Paul.

BRANTINGHAM, P. J., and BRANTINGHAM, P. L. (1975), 'The spatial patterning of burglary', *Howard Journal*, 14(2): 11–23.

BRODY, S. (1976), *The Effectiveness of Sentencing*, Home Office Research Study No 35, London: HMSO.

BROOKMAN, F. (2005), *Understanding Homicide*, London: Sage.

——and MAGUIRE, M. (2005), 'Reducing Homicide in the UK: A Review of the Possibilities', *Crime, Law and Social Change*, 42: 1–79.

BUDD, T., and MATTINSON, J. (2000), *The Extent and Nature of Stalking: Finding from the 1998 British Crime Survey*, Research Study No. 210, London: Home Office.

——, SHARP, C., and MAYHEW, P. (2005), *Offending in England and Wales: First Results from the 2003 Crime and Justice Survey*, Research Study No. 275, London: Home Office.

BULLOCK, K., and TILLEY, N. (eds) (2003), *Crime Reduction and Problem-oriented Policing*, Cullompton Devon: Willan.

BURROWS, J., TARLING, R., MACKIE, A., LEWIS, R., and TAYLOR, G. (2000), *Review of Police Forces' Crime Recording Practices*, Home Office Research Study 204, London: Home Office

CHIVITE-MATTHEWS, N., and MAGGS, P. (2002), *Crime, Policing and Justice: The Experience of Older People. Findings from the British Crime Survey, England and Wales*, Online Report 08/02, London: Home Office.

CHRISTIE, N., ANDENAES, J., and SKIRBEKK, S. (1965), 'A Study of Self-reported Crime', in K. O. Christiansen (ed.), *Scandinavian Studies in Criminology*, London: Tavistock.

CLANCY, A., HOUGH, M., AUST, R., and KERSHAW, C. (2001), *Crime, Policing and Justice: The Experience of Ethnic Minorities. Findings from the 2000 British Crime Survey*, Home Office Research Study No. 223, London: Home Office.

——, HUDSON, K., MAGUIRE, M., PEAKE, R., RAYNOR, P., VANSTONE, M., and KYNCH, J. (2006), *Getting Out and Staying Out: Results of the Prisoner Resettlement Pathfinders*, Bristol: Policy Press.

CLARKE, R. V. G. (1980), 'Situational Crime Prevention: Theory and Practice', *British Journal of Criminology*, 20: 136–47.

—— (1988), 'The British gas suicide story and its criminological implications', in N. Morris and M. Tonry (eds), *Crime and Justice*, Vol 10, Chicago: University of Chicago Press.

—— and HOUGH, M. (1984), *Crime and Police Effectiveness*, Home Office Research Study No 79, London: HMSO.

—— and MAYHEW, P. (eds) (1980), *Designing Out Crime*, London: HMSO.

CLINARD, M. (1978), *Cities with Little Crime*, Cambridge: Cambridge University Press.

—— and YEAGER, P. (1980), *Corporate Crime*, New York: Free Press.

COHEN, L. E., and FELSON, M. (1979), 'Social Change and Crime Rate Trends: a Routine Activity Approach', *American Sociological Review*, 44: 588–608.

COHEN, S. (2001) *States of Denial: Knowing about Atrocities and Suffering*, Cambridge: Polity Press.

COLEMAN, C., and MOYNIHAN, J. (1996), *Understanding Crime Data*, Buckingham and Philadelphia, Penn.: Open University Press.

COLEMAN, K., HIRD, C., and POVEY, D. (2006), *Violent Crime Overview, Homicide and Gun Crime, 2004/5*, Statistical Bulletin 02/06, London: Home Office.

CORCORAN, C., and BOWEN, B. (2003), 'New Insights into Community Safety: An Application of the Hascade Model', *British Journal of Community Justice*, (2)1: 37–50.

CRAWFORD, A., JONES, T., WOODHOUSE, T., and YOUNG, J. (1990), *Second Islington Crime Survey*, London: Middlesex Polytechnic.

CROALL, H. (2001), *Understanding White Collar Crime*, Milton Keynes: Open University Press.

CURRAN, C., DALE, M., EDMUNDS, M., HOUGH, M., MILLIE, A., and WAGSTAFF, M. (2005), 'Street Crime in London: Deterrence, Disruption and Displacement', London: Government Office for London.

DAVIS, R., LURIGIO, A., and SKOGAN, W. (eds) (1997), *Victims of Crime*, New York: Sage.

DITTON, J. (1977), *Part-time Crime*, London: Macmillan.

DOBASH, R. E., and DOBASH, R. P. (1979), *Violence against Wives*, London: Tavistock.

—— and —— (1992), *Women, Violence and Social Change*, London: Routledge.

—— and —— (2004), 'Women's Violence to Men in Intimate Relationships', *British Journal of Criminology*, 44(3): 324–49.

DOWNES, D., and ROCK, P. (2007), *Understanding Deviance*, 5th edn, Oxford: Oxford University Press.

DUFFY, B., HALL, S., and WILLIAMS, M. (2005), *Who do you Believe? Trust in Government Information*, London: MORI

EDGAR, K., and O'DONNELL, I. (1998), 'Assault in Prison: The 'Victim's' Contribution', *British Journal of Criminology*, 38(4): 635–50.

ELMHORN, K. (1965), 'Study in Self-reported Delinquency Among School Children in Stockholm', in K. O. Christiansen. (ed.), *Scandinavian Studies in Criminology*, London: Tavistock.

ERNST & YOUNG (2003), *Fraud—The unmanaged Risk*, 8th Global Survey, www.ey.com.

ESTRADA F. (2006), 'Violence in Scandinavia According to Different Indicators: An Exemplification of the Value of Swedish Hospital Data', *British Journal of Criminology*, 46(3): 486–504.

Europol (2006), *EU Organised Crime Threat Assessment 2006*, The Hague: Europol.

FARRALL, S. *et al.* (1997), 'Measuring Crime and the Fear of Crime: Findings from a Methodological Study', *British Journal of Criminology*, 37(4): 657–78.

FARRINGTON, D. P. (1973), 'Self-reports of Deviant Behaviour: Predictive and Stable?', *Journal of Criminal Law and Criminology*, 64: 99–110.

—— and DOWDS, E. A. (1985), 'Disentangling Criminal Behaviour and Police Reaction', in D. P. Farrington and J. Gunn (eds), *Reaction to Crime: The Public, The Police, Courts and Prisons*, Chichester: John Wiley.

—— and LANGAN, P. (1998), *Crime and Justice in the United States and in England and Wales 1981–96*, Washington DC: Bureau of Justice.

FARRINGTON, D. P., LANGAN, P., and TONRY, M. (2004), *Cross-National Studies in Crime and Justice*, Washington, DC: US Department of Justice.

FINKELHOR, D., and ARAJI, S. (1986), *A Sourcebook on Child Sexual Abuse*, Newbury Park: Sage.

FLOOD-PAGE, C., CAMPBELL, S., HARRINGTON, V., and MILLER, J. (2000), *Youth Crime: Findings from the 1998 Youth Lifestyles Study*, Home Office Research Study No. 209, London: Home Office.

FOUCAULT, M. (1977), *Discipline and Punish: The Birth of the Prison*, London: Allen Lane.

GARLAND, D. (2001), *Punishment and Control*, Oxford: Oxford University Press.

GENN, H. (1988), 'Multiple Victimization', in M. Maguire and J. Pointing (eds), *Victims of Crime: A New Deal?*, Milton Keynes: Open University Press.

GRADY, A. (2002), 'Female-on-Male Domestic Abuse: Uncommon or Ignored?', in C. Hoyle and R. Young (eds), *New Visions of Crime Victims*, Oxford: Hart Publishing.

GRAHAM, J. G., and BOWLING, B. (1995), *Young People and Crime*, Home Office Research Study No. 145, London: HMSO.

GRANT, C., HARVEY, A., BOLLING, K., and CLEMENS, S. (2006), *2004–5 British Crime Survey Technical Report*, London: Home Office.

GREEN, P., and WARD, T. (2005), 'Introduction', Special Issue, *British Journal of Criminology*, 45(4): 431–33.

HAIR, J. ANDERSON, R., TATHAM, R., and BLACK, W. (1998), *Multivariate Data Analysis*, New York: Prentice Hall.

HALL, R. (1985), *Ask Any Woman: A London Enquiry into Rape and Sexual Assault*, Bristol: Falling Wall Press.

HALL, S., CUTCHER, C., JEFFERSON, T., and ROBERTS, B. (1978), *Policing the Crisis*, London: Macmillan.

HANMER, J., and SAUNDERS, S. (1984), *Well-founded Fear*, London: Hutchinson.

HARPER, W. M. (1991), *Statistics*, 6th edn, London: Pitman.

HARRINGTON, V., and MAYHEW, P. (2001), *Mobile Phone Theft*, Home Office Research Study No. 235, London: Home Office.

HAYWARD, R., and SHARP, C. (2005), *Young people, Crime and Antisocial Behaviour: Findings from the 2003 Crime and Justice Survey*, Findings 245, London: Home Office.

HEAL, K., and LAYCOCK, G.(eds) (1986), *Situational Crime Prevention: From Theory into Practice*, London: HMSO.

HEIDENSOHN, F. M. (1985), *Women and Crime*, London: Macmillan.

——(1989), *Crime and Society*, London: Macmillan.

HIRSCHFIELD, A., and BOWERS, K. (1998), 'Monitoring, Measuring and Mapping Community Safety', in A. Marlow and J. Pitts (eds), *Planning Safer Communities*, London: Russell House Publishing.

HOME OFFICE (1971), *Instructions for the Preparation of Statistics Relating to Crime*, London: HMSO.

——(2001), *Criminal Statistics, England and Wales 2000*. Cm. 5312, London: Home Office.

——(2005a), *Criminal Statistics, England and Wales 2004*, RDS Office of Criminal Justice Reform, London: Home Office.

——(2005b), *Sentencing Statistics 2004, England and Wales*, RDS National Offender Management Service, London: Home Office.

HOOD, R. (1992), *Race and Sentencing: A Study in the Crown Court*, Oxford: Clarendon Press.

——and Sparks, R. (1970), *Key Issues in Criminology*, London: Weidenfeld & Nicolson.

HOUGH, M. (ed.) (2004), *Evaluating the Crime Reduction Programme*, Special Issue of *Criminal Justice*, 3(3): 211–325.

——and MAYHEW, P. (1983), *The British Crime Survey*, Home Office Research Study No. 76, London: HMSO.

——and —— (1985), *Taking Account of Crime: Key Findings from the Second British Crime Survey*, Home Office Research Study No. 85, London: HMSO.

——and TILLEY, N. (1998), *Auditing Disorder: Guidance for Local Partnerships*, Crime Detection and Prevention Series No. 91, London: Home Office.

——, MIRRLEES-BLACK, C., and DALE, M. (2005), *Trends in Violent Crimes Since 1999/2000*, London: Institute for Criminal Policy Research. Available at: www.kcl.ac.uk/depsta/law/research/icpr/publications/ViolenceReport.pdf

HUIZINGA, D., and ELLIOTT, D. S. (1986), 'Reassessing the Reliability and Validity of Self-report Measures', *Journal of Quantitative Criminology*, 2: 293–327.

IRELAND, J. (ed.) (2005), *Bullying Among Prisoners: Innovations in Research and Theory*, Cullompton, Devon: Willan.

JOHN, T., and MAGUIRE, M. (2003), 'Rolling out the National Intelligence Model: Key challenges', in

K. Bullock and N. Tilley (eds), *Crime Reduction and Problem-oriented Policing*, Cullompton, Devon: Willan.

JONES, T., MACLEAN, B., and YOUNG, J. (1986), *The Islington Crime Survey: Crime, Victimization and Policing in Inner City London*, Aldershot: Gower.

——, LEA, J., and YOUNG, J. (1987), *Saving the Inner City: The First Report of the Broadwater Farm Survey*, London: Middlesex Polytechnic.

JUNGER-TAS, J., TERLOUW, G., and KLEIN, M. (1994), *Delinquent Behaviour Among Young People in the Western World: First Results of the International Self-Report Delinquency Study*, Amsterdam: Kugler.

——and van KESTEREN, J. (1999), *Bullying and Delinquency in a Dutch School Population*, The Hague: Kugler Publications.

KERSHAW, C., CHIVITE-MATTHEWS, N., THOMAS, C., and AUST, R. (2001), *The 2001 British Crime Survey*, Home Office Statistical Bulletin 18/01, London: Home Office.

KILLIAS, M. (chair) (2006), *European Sourcebook of Crime and Criminal Statistics*, 3rd edn, The Hague: Boom Jurische Vitgevers. See: www.wodc.nl/eng/Onderzoeken/Onderzoek_416.aop

KINSEY, R. (1984), *Merseyside Crime Survey: First Report*, Liverpool: Merseyside Metropolitan Council.

KITSUSE. J. I., and CICOUREL, A. V. (1963), 'A Note on the Uses of Official Statistics', *Social Problems* 11: 131–9.

KOFFMAN, L. (1996), *Crime Surveys and Victims of Crime*, Cardiff: University of Wales Press.

LEVI, M. (1981), *The Phantom Capitalists: The Organization and Control of Long-Firm Fraud*, London: Heinemann.

—— (1985), 'A Criminological and Sociological Approach to Theories of and Research into Economic Crime', in D. Magnuson (ed.), *Economic Crime—Programs for Future Research*, Report No. 18: 32–72, Stockholm: National Council for Crime Prevention, Sweden.

—— (1993), *The Investigation, Prosecution and Trial of Serious Fraud*, Research Report No. 14, London: Royal Commission on Criminal Justice.

—— (2001), 'The costs of transnational and other financial crime: making sense of worldwide data', *International Journal of Comparative Criminology*, 1(2): 8–26.

—— and MAGUIRE, M. (2004), 'Reducing and preventing organised crime: An evidence-based critique', *Crime, Law and Social Change*, 41(5), 397–469.

LOVEDAY, B. (2000), 'Managing Crime: Police Use of Crime Data as an Indicator of Effectiveness', *International Journal of the Sociology of Law*, 28 (3): 215–37.

MCCABE, S., and SUTCLIFFE, F. (1978), *Defining Crime: A Study of Police Decisions*, Oxford: Blackwell.

MCLINTOCK, F., and AVISON, N. H. (1968), *Crime in England and Wales*, London: Heinemann.

MAGUIRE, M. (1991), 'The Needs and Rights of Victims of Crime', in M. Tonry (ed.), *Crime and Justice: a Review of Research*, 14: 363–433, Chicago, Ill.: University of Chicago Press.

—— (2000), 'Policing by risks and targets: Some dimensions and implications of intelligence-led crime control', *Policing and Society*, 9: 1–22.

—— (2004), 'The Crime Reduction Programme in England and Wales: Reflections on the Vision and the Reality', *Criminal Justice*, 3(3): 213–38.

—— in collaboration with BENNETT, T. (1982), *Burglary in a Dwelling: The Offence, the Offender and the Victim*, London: Heinemann Educational Books.

—— and CORBETT, C. (1987), *The Effects of Crime and the Work of Victims Support Schemes*, Aldershot: Gower.

—— and HOPKINS, M. (2003), 'Data and analysis for problem-solving: alcohol-related crime in pubs, clubs and the street', in K. Bullock and N. Tilley (eds), *Crime Reduction and Problem-oriented Policing*, Cullompton, Devon: Willan.

—— and JOHN, T. (2006), 'Intelligence Led Policing, Managerialism and Community Engagement: Competing Priorities and the Role of the National Intelligence Model in the UK', *Policing and Society*, 16(1): 67–85.

—— and NETTLETON, H. (2003), *Reducing Alcohol Related Violence and Disorder: An Evaluation of the TASC Project*, Home Office Research Study No. 265, London: Home Office.

—— and POINTING, J. (eds) (1988), *Victims of Crime: A New Deal?*, Milton Keynes: Open University Press.

MARS, G. (1982), *Cheats at Work*, London: Allen and Unwin.

MARTIN, J. P. (1962), *Offenders as Employees*, London: Macmillan.

MARTINSON, R. (1974), 'What Works? Questions and Answers about Prison Reform'. *The Public Interest*, 35, 22–54.

MATTHEWS, R., and YOUNG, J. (eds) (1986), *Confronting Crime*, London: Sage.

MATTHEWS, S., and RICHARDSON, A. (2005), *Findings from the 2003 Offending, Crime and Justice Survey: Alcohol-related Crime and Disorder*, Findings 261, London: Home Office.

——, BRASNETT, L., and SMITH, J. (2006), *Underage Drinking: Findings from the 2004 Offending, Crime and Justice Survey*, Findings 277, London: Home Office.

MATTINSON, J., and MIRRLEES-BLACK, J. (2000), *Attitudes to Crime and Justice: Findings from the 1998 British Crime Survey*, Home Office Research Study No. 200, London: Home Office.

MAYHEW, P. and HOUGH, J. M. (1988), 'The British Crime Survey: Origins and Impact', in M. Maguire and J. Pointing (eds), *Victims of Crime: A New Deal?*, Milton Keynes: Open University Press.

——, and MIRRLEES-BLACK, C. (1993), *The 1992 British Crime Survey*, Home Office Research Study No. 132, London: HMSO.

——ELLIOTT, D., and DOWDS, L. (1989), *The 1988 British Crime Survey*, Home Office Research Study No. 111, London: HMSO.

——, CLARKE, R. V. G., STURMAN, A., and HOUGH, J. M. (1976), *Crime as Opportunity*, Home Office Research Study No. 34, London: HMSO.

MIRRLEES-BLACK, C. (1999), *Domestic Violence: Findings from a new British Crime Survey Self-Completion Questionnaire*, Home Office Research Study No. 191, London: Home Office.

MORGAN, J. (1988), 'Children as Victims', in M. Maguire and J. Pointing, (eds), *Victims of Crime: A New Deal?*, Milton Keynes: Open University Press.

——and ZEDNER, L. (1992), *Child Victims: Crime, Impact and Criminal Justice*, Oxford: Oxford University Press.

MORTON, J. (2005), *The First Detective: The Life And Revolutionary Times Of Eugene-François Vidocq, Criminal, Spy and Private Eye*, London: Trafalgar Square.

NATIONAL PROBATION SERVICE (2003), *OASys: The New Offender Assessment System*, London: National Probation Service.

——(2005), *Annual Report 2004–5*, London: National Probation Service.

OLIVER, C., and CANDAPPA, M. (2003), *Tackling Bullying: Listening to the Views of Children and Young People*, DfES Research Report RR400, London: Department for Education and Skills.

PAINTER, K. (1991), *Wife Rape, Marriage and the Law: Survey Report*, Manchester: Faculty of Economic and Social Science, University of Manchester.

PASSAS, N., and GROSKIN, R. (2001), 'Overseeing and overlooking: The US federal authorities' response to money laundering and other misconduct at BCCI', *Crime Law and Social Change*, 35(1–2): 141–75

——and NELKEN, D. (1993), 'The thin line between legitimate and criminal enterprises: subsidy frauds in the European Community', *Crime, Law and Social Change*, 3: 223–44.

PATTERSON, A., and THORPE, K. (2006), 'Public Perceptions', in A. Walker, C. Kershaw, and S. Nicholas, *Crime in England and Wales 2005/06*, London: Home Office.

PEASE, K. (1988), *Judgements of Offence Seriousness: Evidence from the 1984 British Crime Survey*, Research and Planning Unit Paper No. 44, London: Home Office.

PEPINSKY, H. (1976), 'Police patrolmen's offence reporting behaviour', *Journal of Research in Crime and Delinquency*, 13: 33–47.

PERCY, A., and MAYHEW, P. (1997), 'Estimating sexual victimisationin a national crime survey: a new approach', *Studies in Crime and Crime Prevention*, 6(2): 125–50.

POLLITT, C. (1993), *Managerialism and the Public Services*, Oxford: Blackwell.

PRICEWATERHOUSE COOPERS (2005), '*Global Economic Crime Survey 2005*', http://www.econcrime. uni-halle.de, http://www.pwcglobal.com.

PUNCH, M. (1996), *Dirty Business: Exploring Corporate Misconduct*, London; Sage.

RADFORD, J. (1987), 'Policing Male Violence', in J. Hanmer and M. Maynard, (eds), *Women, Violence and Social Control*, London: Macmillan.

RDS NOMS (2006), *Offender Management Caseload Statistics 2005*, Statistical Bulletin 18/06, London: Home Office.

REPPETTO, T. (1974), *Residential Crime*, Cambridge Mass.: Ballinger.

RISTOCK, J. (2002), *No More Secrets: Violence in Lesbian Relationships*, New York: Routledge.

ROBERTS, J., and HOUGH, M. (eds) (2002) *Changing Attitudes to Punishment: Public Opinion around the Globe*, Cullompton, Devon: Willan.

SAUNDERS, D. (2002), 'Are Physical Assaults by Wives and Girlfriends a Major Social Problem? A Review of the Literature', *Violence Against Women*, 8(12): 1424–48.

SELKE, W., and PEPINSKY, H. (1984), 'The Politics of Police Reporting in Indianapolis 1948–78', in W. J. Chambliss (ed.), *Criminal Law in Action*, New York: Wiley.

SEMMENS, N. (2001), 'The Relationship between accuracy and confidence in survey-based research: Findings from a pilot study on the fear of crime', *International Journal of Research Methodology*, 4(3): 173–82.

SHAPLAND, J., WILLMORE, J., and DUFF, P. (1985), *Victims in the Criminal Justice System*, Aldershot: Gower.

SHARP, C., and BUDD, T. (2005), *Minority Ethnic Groups and Crime: Findings from the 2003 Offending, Crime and Justice Survey*, Online Report 33/05, London: Home Office.

SHEPHERD, J., SIVARAJASINGAM, V., and RIVARA, F. (2000), 'Using injury data for violence prevention', *British Medical Journal*, 16(321): 1481–2.

SHURY, J., SPEED, M., VIVIAN, D., KUECHEL, A., and NICHOLAS, S. (2005), *Crime against retail and manufacturing premises: Findings from the 2002 Commercial Victimisation Survey*, Online report 37/0,. London: Home Office.

SIMMONS, J. (2000), *Review of Crime Statistics: A Discussion Document*, London: Home Office.

—— LEGG, C., and Hosking, R. (2003), *National Crime Recording Standards (NCRS): An Analysis of the Impact on Recorded Crime*. RDS Online Report 31/03, London: Home Office.

SIMPSON, S. (2002), *Corporate Crime, Law and Social Control*, Cambridge: Cambridge University Press. 1

SLAPPER, G., and TOMBS, S. (1999), *Corporate Crime*, Harlow: Longman.

SMITH, A. (2006), *Crime Statistics: An Independent Review*. London: Home Office.

SMITH, D. (1997), 'Ethnic origins, crime and criminal justice', in M. Maguire, R. Morgan, and R. Reiner (eds), *The Oxford Handbook of Criminology*, 2nd edn, Oxford: Oxford University Press.

SOCA (2006), *Organised Crime Threat Assessment 2006–7*, London: Serious Organised Crime Agency.

SPARKS, R. (1992), *Television and the Drama of Crime*, Buckingham: Open University Press.

——, GENN, H., and DODD, D. (1977), *Surveying Victims*, Chichester: John Wiley.

STANKO, E. (1988), 'Hidden Violence against Women', in M. Maguire and J. Pointing, (eds), *Victims of Crime: A New Deal?*, Milton Keynes: Open University Press.

STATISTICS COMMISSION (2005), *Crime Statistics: User Perspectives: Interim Report*, London: Statistics Commission.

—— (2006), *Crime Statistics: User Perspectives*, Report No. 30, London, Statistics Commission.

STRAUS, M., GELLES, R., and STEINMETZ, S. (1980), *Behind Closed Doors*, New York: Anchor Press.

THORPE, K., and ROBB, P. (2006), 'Extent and Trends', in A. Walker, C. Kershaw, and S. Nicholas, *Crime in England and Wales 2005/06*, London: Home Office.

van KESTEREN, J., MAYHEW, P., and NIEUWBEERTA, P. (2000), *Criminal Victimisation in Seventeen Industrialised Countries*, The Hague: WODC.

WALBY, S., and ALLEN, J. (2004), *Domestic Violence, Sexual Assault and Stalking: Findings from the British Crime Survey*, London: Home Office.

WALKER, A., KERSHAW, C., and NICHOLAS, S. (2006), *Crime in England and Wales 2005/06*, London: Home Office.

WALKER, M. (ed.) (1995), *Interpreting Crime Statistics*, Oxford: Oxford University Press.

WALKER, N. D. (1971), *Crimes, Courts and Figures: An Introduction to Criminal Statistics*, Harmondsworth: Penguin.

WALKLATE, S. (1989), *Victimology: The Victim and the Criminal Justice System*, London: Unwin Hyman.

WALLER, I., and OKIHIRO, N. (1978), *Burglary: the Victim and the Public*, Toronto: University of Toronto Press.

WALMSLEY, R., HOWARD, L., and WHITE, S. (1992), *The National Prison Survey 1991: Main Findings*, Home Office Research Study No. 128, London: HMSO.

WILSON, D., PATTERSON, A., POWELL, G., and HEMBURY, R. (2006), *Fraud and Technology Crimes: Findings from the 2003/04 British Crime Survey, the 2004 Offending, Crime and Justice Survey and Administrative Sources*, Online Report 09/06, London: Home Office.

WINCHESTER, S., and JACKSON, H. (1982), *Residential Burglary*, Home Office Research Study No. 74, London: HMSO.

WOOD, M. (2005), *The Victimisation of Young People: Findings from the 2003 Crime and Justice Survey*, Findings 246, London: Home Office.

YOUNG, J. (1971), *The Drugtakers*, London: Paladin.

—— (1988a), 'Radical Criminology in Britain: The Emergence of a Competing Paradigm', *British Journal of Criminology*, 28(2): 289–313.

—— (1988b), 'Risk of Crime and Fear of Crime: a Realist Critique of Survey-based Assumptions', in M. Maguire and J. Pointing, (eds) *Victims of Crime: A New Deal?*, Milton Keynes: Open University Press.

YOUNG, M. (1991), *An Inside Job*, Oxford: Clarendon Press.

11

MEDIA-MADE CRIMINALITY: THE REPRESENTATION OF CRIME IN THE MASS MEDIA

Robert Reiner

CRIME IN THE MEDIA: SUBVERSION, SOCIAL CONTROL, OR MENTAL CHEWING GUM?

'In contemporary Britain, the average three- or four-year old now watches a screen for around five hours each day, and more than 50 per cent of three-year-olds have a TV set in their bedrooms . . . . Is there really hard scientific evidence that watching television affects how children communicate? Well yes—and the evidence grows steadily' (Winston 2004). In this *Guardian* article, and an accompanying TV documentary, Lord Winston summarized what he claimed was an experiment that 'finally proves' that children imitate violent images. The experiment was a re-creation of the classic social psychological effects research that is summarized later in this chapter.

Lord Winston's article illustrates a long-standing concern about mass media representations of crime, deviance, and disorder. It has long been feared that the media are a significant cause of offending, and are fundamentally subversive. This has been a constantly recurring aspect of the 'history of respectable fears' that Geoffrey Pearson has traced back through the last few centuries (Pearson 1983).

A contrasting concern about media representations of crime has worried liberals and radicals (Wykes 2001). To them the media are the cause not of crime itself but of exaggerated public alarm about law and order, generating support for repressive solutions (Gerbner 1970, 1995). In their ideal-typical form these perspectives are polar opposites, sharing in common only their demonization of the media. Each has generated huge research industries conducting empirical studies of media content, production, and effects (Carrabine *et al.* 2002: ch. 5, 2004: ch. 18; Brown 2003; Jewkes 2004; Greer 2005).

The difficulties in rigorously establishing straightforward causal relationships between images and effects have evoked the canard that media researchers are blinkered by libertarian prejudices. For example, Melanie Phillips has claimed that 'for years, media academics have pooh-poohed any link between violence on screen and in real life', because 'media images . . . merely provide "chewing gum for the eyes" '(Phillips 1996). This is a caricature of the media research on effects. A more sophisticated criticism of the effects research is that 'repeated failures to find anything much out would . . . suggest that the wrong question was being asked' (Brown 2003: 28). But as the Winston article cited above demonstrates, 'the effects debate refuses to go away' (ibid.).

This chapter reviews the broad contours of empirical research, theorization, and policy debates about crime and the media. It is organized in terms of three interrelated issues that have been the primary foci of research: the *content*, *consequences*, and *causes* of media representations of crime. These are phases of an intertwined process that can only be separated artificially: texts, audiences, and authors are interdependent, and their separation is only a presentational device.

THE CONTENT OF MEDIA IMAGES OF CRIME

PROBLEMS OF CONTENT ANALYSIS

As defined by one leading practitioner, 'content analysis is a method of studying and analyzing communications in a systematic, objective, and quantitative manner for the purpose of measuring certain message variables, . . . free of the subjective bias of the reviewer' (Dominick 1978: 106–7). Dominick concedes that 'inferences about the effects of content on the audience are, strictly speaking, not possible when using only this methodology. More importantly, the findings of a particular content analysis are directly related to the definitions of the various content categories developed by the researcher' (ibid.).

There are major problems with the claim that traditional content analysis is 'object-ive'. While the categories used to quantify 'certain message attributes' may be free of 'subjective bias' they are not randomly plucked out of thin air, nor do they miraculously reflect a structure of meaning objectively inherent in the texts analysed. They always embody theoretical presuppositions by the researcher about criteria of significance. Moreover, while content analysis indeed cannot justify 'inferences about the effects of content on the audience', the categories selected for quantification usually presuppose some theory about likely consequences. Meticulously counting units of 'violence' is not a form of train-spotting for sadists but motivated by concern that exposure to these images carries risks such as desensitization, or heightened anxiety. Thus the 'objectivity' of traditional content analysis lies in the precision of the statistical manipulation of data, but the categories used necessarily presuppose some theory of meaning, usually about likely consequences (Sparks 1992: 79–80).

There is a further fundamental problem with traditional content analyses. What the researcher codifies as instances of the 'same' image may have very different meanings within particular narrative genres and contexts of reception. How viewers interpret images of 'violence', for example, is not just a function of the amount of blood seen or number of screams heard. The same physical behaviour, for instance a shooting, means different things in different genres, say a Western, a war film, a contemporary cop show, or news bulletins. It will be interpreted differently if the violence is perpetrated on or by a character constructed in the narrative as sympathetic. How audiences construe violence will vary according to how they see their own position vis-à-vis the narrative characters, quite apart from any preferred reading intended by the creators or supposedly inscribed in the narrative (Livingstone *et al.* 2001). For example, to black audiences, Rodney King, whose beating by Los Angeles police officers was captured on an amateur videotape, was a victim of police racism, while to many white police officers he appeared to be a threatening deviant who invited the beating (Lawrence 2000: 70–3).

These problems do not mean that quantification can or should be avoided, but they refute the claims of positivist content analysis to quantify a supposed objective structure in texts. Counting features of texts should be self-consciously seen as based on the observer's frame of reference, according to explicit criteria. Results must be interpreted reflexively and tentatively as one possible reading. As such, they can yield valuable insights and questions about the significance of trends and patterns.

CONTENT ANALYSIS: A REVIEW OF RESULTS

Crime and criminal justice have long been sources of popular spectacle and entertainment, even before the rise of the mass media. This is illustrated by the genre of criminal biography and pre-execution confessions and apologias, of various degrees of authenticity, which flourished in the seventeenth and eighteenth centuries (Faller 1987; Rawlings 1992; Durston 1997). Similar accounts continue to the present day, filling the 'true crime' shelves of bookshops (Rawlings 1998; Peay 1998; Wilson 2000: ch. 4; Biressi 2001), and they have been joined by the many volumes retelling the exploits of legendary cops as if they were fictional sleuths (e.g. Fabian 1950, 1954). In overtly fictional crime narratives, ultra-realism (often a quasi-documentary style of presentation) has been the predominant style.

The fact/fiction distinction has become ever more fluid, with the emergence of what is usually referred to as 'reality' television or 'infotainment' (Fishman and Cavender 1998; Surette 1998: 70–80; Beckett and Sasson 2000: 111–16; Leishman and Mason 2002: ch. 7). There has been the growth of programming such as *Crimewatch UK* that re-creates current cases, often with an avowed purpose of solving them (Dobash *et al.* 1998; Jewkes 2004: ch.6). Fly-on-the-wall footage of actual incidents has proliferated in documentaries like Roger Graef's pioneering 1982 Thames Valley Police series (Gregory and Lees 1999), and entertainment programming based on real cops in action, for example *Cops* (Doyle 1998; Kooistra *et al.* 1998). Live newscasts of particular occurrences are increasingly common, such as the O. J. Simpson car chase and subsequent trial (Brown 2003: 56–60). Film footage of criminal events in process is frequently used in news broadcasts, like the amateur video capturing the beating by

Los Angeles police of Rodney King (Lawrence 2000), or the CCTV shots of Jamie Bulger being led away by his killers (Jewkes 2004: 56–7). The police in turn resort to the media as a part of criminal investigations (Innes 1999, 2001, 2003), as well as to cultivate support more generally (Mawby 1998, 1999, 2001, 2002, 2003). The media and criminal justice systems are penetrating each other increasingly, making a distinction between 'factual' and 'fictional' programming ever more tenuous (Manning 1998; Ferrell 1998; Tunnell 1998; Brown 2003). The implications will be explored further in the conclusions, but I will turn next to a consideration of the results of content analyses.

Deviant news

Crime narratives and representations are, and have always been, a prominent part of the content of all mass media. The proportion of media content that is constituted by crime items clearly will depend on the definitions of 'crime' used. Richard Ericson and his colleagues adopted an exceptionally broad definition of deviance for their penetrating study of newsmaking in Toronto (Ericson *et al.* 1987, 1989, 1991): 'the behaviour of a thing or person that strays from the normal . . . not only . . . criminal acts, but also . . . straying from organisational procedures and violations of common-sense knowledge' (Ericson *et al.* 1987: 4). When defined so widely deviance is the essence of news, '*the* defining characteristic of what journalists regard as newsworthy' (ibid.). Stories about crime in the narrower sense of violations of criminal law are a more limited proportion of news, varying according to medium (e.g. radio, television, or print journalism) and market (e.g. 'quality' or 'popular' journalism).

Unsurprisingly, given their broad definition, Ericson *et al.* found that a high proportion of news was about 'deviance and control', ranging from 45.3 per cent in a quality newspaper to 71.5 per cent on a quality radio station (Ericson *et al.* 1991: 239–42). Contrary to most other studies, they found that 'quality' broadcasting outlets had *more* deviance stories, because of 'their particular emphasis on deviance and control in public bureaucracies' (ibid.).

Ericson *et al.* also used a broad concept of 'violence', in which ' "state violence" and "state terrorism" were conceptualised in the same way as various acts of violence by individual citizens' (ibid.: 244). They included stories, for example, about 'harms to health and safety such as impaired driving, unsafe working environments, and unsafe living environments' (ibid.). This covered concerns that are more characteristic of 'quality' than 'popular' news outlets, but nonetheless Ericson *et al.* found that in each medium more attention was paid to violence by popular than by quality journalism. Broadcast news gave more prominence to stories of violence than print (ibid.: 244–7).

Ericson *et al.* adopted an equally wide-ranging concept of 'economic' deviance, including 'questionable business practices . . . legal conflict over property . . . and social problems related to economic matters' (ibid.: 247). 'The reporting of economic *crimes* was rare in all news outlets . . . Much more common in all news outlets were reports of violation of trust, with or without criminal aspects or criminal charges being laid' (ibid.). The reporting of white-collar crime tends to be concentrated in 'quality' newspapers and is often restricted to specialist financial pages, sections, or newspapers

(Stephenson-Burton 1995: 137–44), framed in ways that mark it off from 'real' crime unless they are sensational celebrity-style stories that are treated as a form of 'infotainment' (Tombs and Whyte 2001; Levi 2001, 2006).

Overall, Ericson *et al.* found that whilst the pattern of reporting varied in complex ways according to media and markets, stories about deviance and control in a broad sense were the staple, defining feature of newsworthiness.

The extent of crime in the news

Most analyses of the content of media representations of crime have focused more narrowly on the legally defined category, not the broad sociological concept of deviance. Some studies only consider stories about specific criminal incidents, but others include reports, articles, or editorials about the state of crime generally, about criminal justice, and about criminal law violations related to political and social conflict, such as terrorism. 'Because of this variability, estimates of the proportion of total news that is devoted to crime coverage range from 5 to 25%' (Sacco 1995: 142).

The lower estimates tend to come from earlier research (such as Harris 1932; Swanson 1955; Deutschmann 1959). More recent American studies have found higher proportions of crime-related items. Graber found that crime and justice topics accounted for 22 to 28 per cent of stories in the newspapers she studied, 20 per cent on local television news, and 12 to 13 per cent on network television news (Graber 1980: 24). A literature review of 36 American content analyses of crime news conducted between 1960 and 1980 found considerable variation in the proportion of crime: from 1.61 per cent to 33.5 per cent (Marsh 1991: 73).

The first study of crime news in Britain looked at crime news reporting in September 1938, 1955, and 1967 (Roshier 1973). In September 1967 the percentage of crime news was 5.6 per cent in the *Daily Mirror*, 4.4 per cent in the *Daily Express*, 2.4 per cent in the *Daily Telegraph* (and 2 per cent in the *Newcastle Journal*). The *News of the World* gave crime much more prominence: 11 per cent of news space. There was no clear trend over time. In the dailies the proportion of crime news in 1967 was virtually the same as in 1938, but it had been higher in 1955 in the *Daily Mirror* and *Daily Express*. The *News of the World* showed a similar U-shaped pattern: crime was 17.8 per cent of news in 1938, 29.1 per cent in 1955, and 11 per cent in 1967 (ibid.: 45).

In Britain, more recent studies find higher proportions of crime news than Roshier's average of 4 per cent for 1938–67. For example, a study of six Scottish newspapers in 1981 found that an average of 6.5 per cent of space was given to crime news (Ditton and Duffy 1983: 161; see also Smith 1984; Schlesinger *et al.* 1991: 411–15). This rise was confirmed by a later study comparing coverage of crime in 10 national daily newspapers for four weeks from 19 June 1989 (Williams and Dickinson 1993). 'On average, 12.7% of event-oriented news reports were about crime' (ibid.: 40). The proportion of space devoted to crime was greater the more 'downmarket' the newspaper. The smallest proportion of crime news was 5.1 per cent in the *Guardian*; the largest was 30.4 per cent in the *Sun* (ibid.: 41).

Broadcast news generally devotes more attention to crime reports than newspapers (Cumberbatch *et al.* 1995: 5–8). There are also variations in the proportion of crime news items between different markets. Commercial radio and television broadcast a higher proportion of crime news stories overall than the BBC, although the latter carried more reports about crime in general and criminal justice. Crime news is more frequent than any other category for every medium at each market level (ibid.: 7).

Given that different studies work with different concepts of crime, and have ranged over many different newspapers and places, it is not possible to conclude from a literature review whether there is a trend for an increasing proportion of news to be about crime. Although later studies predominantly find higher proportions of crime stories than earlier ones, they have also adopted broader concepts of crime, so the increase may well be a result of the measurement procedures used rather than a reflection of change in the media.

A historical study examined a random sample of issues of *The Times* and the *Mirror* for each year between 1945 and 1991 (Reiner *et al.* 2000, 2001, 2003; Reiner 2001). It found a generally upward (albeit fluctuating) trend in the proportion of stories focused on crime in both newspapers (from under 10 per cent in the 1940s to over 20 per cent in the 1990s). The sharpest increase occurred during the late 1960s, when the average annual proportion of crime stories almost doubled, from around 10 per cent to around 20 per cent in both papers. In both papers the proportion of stories about the criminal justice system, as distinct from the commission of criminal offences, has clearly increased since the Second World War. Criminal justice stories were on average 2 per cent of all stories in the *Mirror* between 1945 and 1951, and 3 per cent in *The Times*. By 1985–91 the average had increased to 6 per cent in the *Mirror*, and 9 per cent in *The Times*.

In conclusion, deviance and control in a broad sense are the very stuff of news. However, stories about the commission of particular offences are more common in 'popular' news outlets (although for official or corporate crime the reverse is true). The proportion of news devoted to crime and criminal justice has increased over the last half-century.

The pattern of crime news

Crime news exhibits remarkably similar patterns in studies conducted at many different times and places. From the earliest studies (e.g. Harris 1932) onwards, analyses of news reports have found that crimes of violence are featured disproportionately compared to their incidence in official crime statistics. Indeed a general finding has been the lack of relationship between patterns and trends in crime news and crime statistics (Davis 1952; Beckett 1997).

Marsh reviewed 36 content analyses of crime news in the USA published between 1960 and 1988, and 20 studies in 14 other countries between 1965 and 1987. These all found an over-representation of violent and interpersonal crime, compared to official statistics, and an under-reporting of property offences (Marsh 1991). In America 'the ratio of violent-to-property crime stories appearing in the surveyed newspapers was 8 to 2; however, official statistics reflected a property-to-violent crime ratio of more than 9 to 1 during the survey period' (ibid.: 73). A similar pattern is found in the content analyses reviewed for other countries (ibid.: 74–6).

A historical study of two British newspapers since the Second World War found that homicide was by far the most common type of crime reported, accounting for about one-third of all crime news stories throughout the period. Other violent crimes were the next most common. However, there were significant shifts in the proportion of stories featuring other sorts of crime. In particular there was a marked decline in the proportion of stories featuring 'volume' property crimes such as burglary in which no violence occurred (these are of course the overwhelming majority of crimes according to official statistics and crime surveys, cf. Maguire, Chapter 10, this volume). During the 1940s and 1950s property crimes featured frequently in news stories, but after the mid-1960s they were hardly ever reported unless there was some celebrity angle. On the other hand, some offences began to feature prominently in news stories only after the mid-1960s, notably drug offences, which by the 1990s accounted for about 10 per cent of all crime stories (Reiner *et al.* 2000 and 2001, 2003; Reiner 2001).

Recent studies confirm the pattern of increasing over-representation of violent and interpersonal (especially sex) crimes (Chiricos *et al.* 1997; Beckett and Sasson 2000: ch. 5; Greer 2003). Between 1951 and 1985 the number of rape trials in Britain increased nearly four times, from 119 to 450. In the same period, the number of rape cases reported in the press increased more than five times, from 28 to 154. The percentage of rape cases reported jumped from 23.5 per cent in 1951 to 34.2 per cent in 1985 (Soothill and Walby 1991: 20–22). In Northern Ireland press reporting of sex cases tripled (Greer 2003).

The proportion of news devoted to crime of different types, and the prominence with which it is presented, varies according to market and medium. In one month of 1989, 64.5 per cent of British newspaper crime stories featured violence, while the British Crime Survey found that only 6 per cent of crimes reported by victims were violent (Williams and Dickinson 1993: 40). The percentage of stories dealing with crimes involving personal violence, and the salience they were given, was considerably greater in more downmarket newspapers (ibid.: 40–3).

The pattern of offences reported varies according to medium as well as market. In Britain, the proportion of violent crimes reported in television news broadcasts is closer to the tabloid figure than the quality press, especially for local rather than national bulletins. A study in January–March 1987 found that the proportion of crime stories reporting non-sexual violence against the person in 'quality', 'mid-market', and 'tabloid' newspapers respectively was 24.7 per cent, 38.8 per cent, and 45.9 per cent. On national news bulletins it was 40 per cent; on local bulletins violent crime stories were 63.2 per cent of all crime news. There was no significant difference between ITV (43.5 per cent) and BBC1 (42.3 per cent), but Channel 4 was more like the quality press (18.2 per cent; Schlesinger *et al.* 1991: 412–15). There were some 'market' differences between broadcast news channels, but on the whole the proportion of different offences portrayed on television news is closer to tabloid than broadsheet print journalism.

Violent crimes in general figure disproportionately in British broadcast news, although there are substantial variations according to medium and market. In one study, over 40 per cent of crime news items concerned death and murder on nearly all BBC Radio stations. On television, murder and death accounted for 53 per cent of all crime stories on Sky News, 42 per cent on ITN, and 38 per cent on BBC1 (Cumberbatch *et al.* 1995: 25).

Homicide in general is the most prominent crime in news stories, but the likelihood of particular cases being reported varies systematically. An important recent study analysed the reporting of homicide in three British newspapers between 1993 and 1997 (Peelo *et al.* 2004). Of the 2,685 police-recorded homicides in this period, just under 40 per cent were reported in at least one of the papers studied (ibid.: 261). 'Sexual homicides were most likely to be reported in all three newspapers, as were homicides where there was a clear motive for monetary gain, or a jealousy or revenge motive' (ibid.: 272). Least likely to be reported were the most common homicides, those arising out of 'rage or quarrel' (ibid.: 269). Victim characteristics were also important determinants of the likelihood of reporting. Homicides where the victim was a child (but not an infant), female, or of higher status were more likely to be reported (ibid.: 262–7).

An indirect consequence of the pattern of offences reported by news stories is an exaggeration of police success in clearing-up crime, 'because the police are more successful in solving violent crimes than property crimes' (Marsh 1991: 73). A historical study of British crime news stories found, however, that whilst the majority report crimes that are cleared up by the police, this is declining. The clear-up rate in news stories fell from 73 per cent in 1945–64 to 51 per cent in 1981–91 (Reiner *et al.* 2003: 23).

There is a clear pattern to news media portrayal of offenders and victims. Most studies find that offenders featuring in news reports are typically older and of higher status than those officially processed by the criminal justice system (Roshier 1973: 45–6; Graber 1980; Reiner *et al.* 2003: 19–21). But the officially recorded profile of offenders is likely to be biased misleadingly towards lower-status groups— 'the rich get richer and the poor get prison' (Reiman 2003). In this respect the socio-economic characteristics of offenders in media stories may actually be closer to the—ultimately unknowable— 'real' pattern than official statistics based on the small proportion of offenders who are the losers of the criminal justice lottery (see Maguire, Chapter 10, in this volume).

There is contradictory evidence about whether news reports disproportionately feature ethnic minority offenders (Graber 1980; Garofalo 1981: 324; Marsh 1991: 74; Sacco 1995: 143; Barlow 1998). Crime reports in local newspapers or broadcasting clearly focus more on ethnic minority and lower-status group suspects (Dussuyer 1979; Garofalo 1981: 324; Beckett and Sasson 2000: 79). 'Reality' television programmes also present a marked variation to national news reports in terms of the demography of the offenders portrayed, concentrating on stories with young, ethnic minority suspects (Oliver and Armstrong 1998; Kooistra *et al.* 1998). The one demographic characteristic of offenders which is overwhelmingly congruent in news stories and in all other data sources on crime is their gender: 'both crime statistics and crime news portray offending as predominantly a male activity' (Sacco 1995: 143).

Studies assessing the profile of victims in news stories are fewer in number than analyses of the representation of offenders. There is a clear trend for victims to become the pivotal focus of news stories in the last three decades (Reiner *et al.* 2003), paralleling the increasing centrality of victims in criminal justice and criminology (see Hoyle and Zedner, Chapter 15 in this volume) and crime fiction (Reiner *et al.* 2000 and 2001). News stories exaggerate the crime risks faced by higher-status white people, as well as disproportionately representing women, children, or older people as victims (Graber 1980; Garofalo 1981: 324; Mawby and Brown 1983; Chermak 1995; Chiricos *et al.* 1997; Beckett and Sasson 2000: 79–80; Greer 2003: 70–2; Reiner *et al.* 2003: 21–2; Peelo *et al.* 2004: 262–7).

Another consistent finding is the predominance of stories about criminal incidents, rather than analyses of crime patterns or the possible causes of crime (Garofalo 1981: 325; see also Marsh 1991: 76; Sasson 1995; Barlow 1998; Beckett and Sasson 2000: 80–1; Greer 2003: 66–70). Although an aspect of the more general event-orientation that is part of the 'eternal recurrence' of news (Rock 1973), the 'mass media provide citizens with a public awareness of crime . . . based upon an information-rich and knowledge-poor foundation' (Sherizen 1978: 204). An important example is the reporting of rape and other sex crimes, where issues of power and gender disappear in the fascination with the demonization of individual offenders or victims (Soothill and Walby 1991; Lees 1995; Gregory and Lees 1999; Greer 2003). Stories with child homicide victims and/or perpetrators are particularly likely to be featured so prominently that they become long-running stories with a familiar cast of characters, regularly invoked as symbols of wider issues or the state of the nation, illustrated by the Moors murders, and the Jamie Bulger and Soham cases.

The tendency to exclude analysis of broader structural processes or explanations is also evident in stories about political disorder (Halloran *et al.* 1970; Hall 1973: 232–43; Sumner 1982; Tumber 1982; Cottle 1993). The portrayal of political conflict such as riot or terrorism is often in terms of sheer criminality (Clarke and Taylor 1980; Hillyard 1982; Iyengar 1991: 24–46). This has been evident again in the overall media coverage of the events of 11 September 2001 or 7 July 2005. However, the pattern varies according to different phases in the reporting of such conflicts (Wren-Lewis 1981/2). After the initial reporting of events such as the 1981 Brixton riots, which tends to be in terms of criminality, there is often a later phase of analysis of possible causes (Murdock 1982).

There are also variations between different media and markets. Print journalism, especially 'quality' newspapers and editorial pages, will often have more analysis than broadcast news (Ericson *et al.* 1991; Cumberbatch *et al.* 1995: 7). Newspapers and quality broadcasting channels are more likely to carry points of view critical of the authorities. There is a tendency in recent years for critical and campaigning groups to have more access to the media, partly because of the increasing politicization of law and order (Schlesinger and Tumber 1994; Lawrence 2000; Downes and Morgan, Chapter 9, this volume).

Although critical stories exposing malpractice by the police or other criminal justice officials are regularly published, this 'watchdog' function does not necessarily undermine the legitimacy of criminal justice institutions. Corruption and other police deviance stories have traditionally been set within the 'one bad apple' framework, whereby the exposure of individual wrongdoing is interpreted as a testimony to the integrity of the system which dealt with it (Chibnall 1977: ch. 5). As the volume of police deviance stories has increased in recent years (Reiner *et al.* 2003: 22–4), the 'one bad apple' story becomes harder to recycle. An alternative damage-limitation narrative is to present scandals as stories of institutional reform. This acknowledges previous malpractice, but safeguards the legitimacy of the institution as it is portrayed as putting things right (Schlesinger and Tumber 1994: ch. 7).

THE CONTENT OF CRIME FICTION

Some social scientists have conducted quantitative content analyses of film and television crime fiction.[1] More commonly, however, crime fiction—in print, the cinema, or on television—has been analysed using a variety of qualitative techniques and theoretical perspectives drawn from literary, film, and social theory.[2] The pattern of representation of crime in fictional stories, in all media, resembles the content analyses of crime news.

The frequency of crime fiction

Crime and detection have always been staples of modern literature, as Defoe, Fielding, Poe, and Dickens illustrate (Ousby 1976; Durston 1996). Some authors have sought to trace the ancient ancestry of the detective story. 'We find sporadic examples of it in Oriental folk-tales, in the Apocryphal Books of the Old Testament, in the play-scene in *Hamlet*; while Aristotle in his *Poetics* puts forward observations about dramatic plot-construction which are applicable today to the construction of a detective mystery' (Sayers 1936: vii). This was clearly an attempt to emphasize the 'snobbery' rather than the 'violence' of the classic ratiocinative detective story (Watson 1971). The dominant style of crime fiction has varied from the classic puzzle mystery exemplified by Sayers and Agatha Christie, to the tougher private eye stories pioneered by Dashiell Hammett and Raymond Chandler, and the police procedurals of Ed McBain, Joseph Wambaugh, and others (Symons 1972; Binyon 1989; Ousby 1997).

One estimate suggests that 'between a quarter and a third of total paperback output could probably be put into the category of "thriller" of one kind or another . . . since

---

[1] Gerbner 1970; Pandiani 1978; Carlson 1985; Lichter *et al.* 1994; Powers *et al.* 1996; Surette 1998: ch. 2; Allen *et al.* 1998.

[2] McArthur 1972; Shadoian 1977; Rosow 1978; McCarty 1993; Clarens 1997; Hardy 1997, 1998; Rubin 1999; Chibnall and Murphy 1999; and Rafter 2000 are just a few of the many studies of gangster and crime movies. Haycraft 1941; Watson 1971; Cawelti 1976; Palmer 1978; Knight 1980; Porter 1981; Mandel 1984; Bell and Daldry 1990; Thompson 1993; and Clarke 2001 are some of the numerous texts on literary detective stories. Everson 1972; Tuska 1978; and Meyers 1981, 1989 offer histories of detective films and television shows. Reiner 1978, 1981, 1994, 2000a and 2000b, 2003; Park 1978; Hurd 1979; Kerr 1981; Clarke 1983, 1986, 1992; Dove 1982; Dove and Bargainnier 1986; Inciardi and Dee 1987; Buxton 1990; Laing 1991; Winston and Mellerski 1992; Sparks 1992: ch. 6, 1993; Eaton 1996; Hale 1998; King 1999; Wilson 2000; Gitlin 2000: ch. 11–14; Leishman and Mason 2002 examine police stories. Nellis and Hale 1982; Mason 1996, 2003a, 2003b are studies of prison films.

1945, at least 10,000 million copies of crime stories have been sold world-wide' (Mandel 1984: 66–7).

Crime stories have also been a prominent genre in the cinema, the dominant mass medium of the first half of the twentieth century (Rafter 2000). As with its successors, television and video, the cinema has been haunted by respectable fears about its portrayal of crime and violence (Barker 1984a; Mathews 1994; Miller 1994; Barker and Petley 2001). The proportion of films about crime has fluctuated cyclically since the Second World War, but there is no long-term increase or decrease (Allen *et al.* 1997). In most years, around 20 per cent of all films are crime movies, and around half of all films have significant crime content.

Radio was the main broadcasting medium of the first half of the twentieth century. Stories about crime and law enforcement were a popular part of radio drama, in Britain and North America, although never as dominant as they subsequently became on television (Dominick 1978: 112–13; Shale 1996). Stories about crime and law enforcement have been prominent on television ever since it became the leading broadcasting medium in the 1950s. By 1959 over one-third of American prime-time television was crime shows. Since then at least 20 per cent of prime-time has been crime shows (Dominick 1978: 114). Crime shows are just as much a staple of British television. Since 1955 around 25 per cent of the most popular television shows in Britain in most years have been crime or police series. While there are sharp cyclical fluctuations, there is no long-term trend (Reiner *et al.* 2000 and 2001), but there have been changes in *how* crime and criminal justice are represented.

The pattern of crime in fiction

The pattern of fictional representations of crime is similar to that in news stories—and shows similar discrepancies from the picture conveyed by official crime statistics. Murder and other violent crimes feature vastly more frequently than the property offences that predominate in official statistics. A historical analysis of the crime films that have done best at the British box office since the Second World War (Allen *et al.* 1998; Reiner *et al.* 2000 and 2001) found that murder was the primary crime (the McGuffin of the plot, in Hitchcock's terminology) in the overwhelming majority of films throughout the period. However, property offences provided the McGuffin in a significant minority of films up to the late 1960s, though seldom thereafter. Sex and drug offences began to appear as central aspects of narratives only after the late 1960s. Up to the mid-1960s, most films did not feature any crimes that were not directly related to the McGuffin. From then films portray a world full of contextual crimes, unrelated to the central crime animating the narrative (to the point where characters like the eponymous Dirty Harry cannot go for a hamburger without coming across a bank robbery in progress). Crime is represented as an all-pervasive threat, not an abnormal, one-off intrusion into a stable order. Linked to this is the increasing prevalence in films of police heroes, signifying that crime has become sufficiently routine to provide employment for a large bureaucracy, not just a diversion for enthusiastic amateurs at country house weekends (Reiner 1978, 2000b, 2003; Allen *et al.* 1998: 67–8; King 1999; Rafter 2000: ch. 3; Wilson 2000; Leishman and Mason 2002).

The representation of violence has become increasingly graphic throughout the period since the Second World War. Up to the early 1970s hardly any films showed more than a minor degree of pain or suffering by victims—even if they were murdered! (Reiner *et al.* 2001: 184). Since then an increasing proportion of films depict victims in severe torment (ibid.; Powers *et al.* 1996: 104–6).

On television too, fictional narratives have always featured violent crimes most prominently, but are focusing on them even more. Studies of American television suggest that about two-thirds of crime on prime-time shows consists of murder, assault, or armed robbery (Garofalo 1981: 326; Sparks 1992: 140; Lichter *et al.* 1994; Beckett and Sasson 2000: ch. 6).

A content analysis of 620 randomly selected prime-time television shows broadcast between 1955 and 1986 found that 'television violence has far outstripped reality since the 1950s . . . During the second decade of our study, covering 1965 to 1975 . . . The FBI-calculated rate for violent crimes . . . doubled to 3 incidents per 1,000 inhabitants. The TV rate for violent crimes, at 114 incidents per 1,000 characters, was more than 30 times greater' (Lichter *et al.* 1994: 275–6).

In the third decade covered by Lichter *et al.*'s historical content analysis, television and the world of statistically recorded crime converged slightly, 'but television continues to present far more violent crimes than occur in real life' (ibid.: 278). There was also increasing representation of serious crimes that hitherto had hardly featured in genre crime fiction: prostitution and other organized vice such as pornography, and drug-related offences. On American television there was a fifteenfold increase in prostitution offences and a tenfold rise in drug-related crime between 1975 and 1985 (ibid.: 285).

Ironically, in relation to property crime risks television has become safer than the world presented in official statistics. Between 1955 and 1984, the average annual rate for serious property offences in the USA increased from 10 to 50 incidents per 1,000 people according to the FBI data. However, on television 'the rate for serious property crimes has remained steady at 20 incidents per 1,000 characters over the thirty years of our study' (ibid.: 284). Thus between 1955 and 1964 the television property crime rate exceeded the official statistics, but since then it has fallen far behind them. There is also a trend for the cinema (and newspapers) to understate the risks of property crime increasingly (Allen *et al.* 1998: 65; Reiner *et al.* 2003: 18–19).

The *qualitative* character of crimes depicted in fiction is also vastly different from the officially recorded pattern. While most 'real' murders are extensions of brawls between young men (Dorling 2004), or domestic disputes, in fiction murder is usually motivated by greed and calculation (Garofalo 1981: 326–7; Lichter *et al.* 1994: 279; Allen *et al.* 1998: 69). Rape and other sex crimes are also presented in opposite ways in fiction (or news) and criminal justice statistics (Greer 2003: ch. 7; Jewkes 2004: 48–9). Most rapes are perpetrated by intimates or acquaintances (Barclay and Tavares 1999: 16). On television and in other fiction (and in news stories), rape is usually committed by psychopathic strangers and involves extreme brutality, often torture and murder ('5% of the murders on TV result from rape', Lichter *et al.* 1994: 279–80).

While crime fiction presents property crime less frequently than the reality suggested by crime statistics, the crimes it portrays are far more serious than most recorded offences. Official statistics and victim surveys concur in calculating that the overwhelming majority of property crimes involve little or no loss or damage, and no physical threat or harm to the victim—indeed, there is usually no contact at all with the perpetrator. In fiction, however, most property crimes involve tightly planned, high-value, project thefts, and are frequently accompanied by violence (Garofalo 1981: 326; Lichter *et al.* 1994: 284).

Related to the disproportionate emphasis on the most serious end of the crime spectrum is the portrayal of the demographic characteristics of offenders and victims. Offenders in fiction are primarily higher-status, white, middle-aged males (Pandiani 1978: 442–7; Garofalo 1981: 326; Lichter *et al.* 1994: 290–5; Reiner *et al.* 2000 and 2001). Interestingly, the new genre of 'reality' infotainment cop shows such as *Cops* differs from this pattern, primarily presenting offenders as non-white, underclass youth (Fishman and Cavender 1998; Beckett and Sasson 2000: 113). The social characteristics of fictional victims are similar, but a higher proportion are female. The demographic profile of offenders and victims in fiction is the polar opposite of criminal justice statistics, apart from the maleness of most offenders (Surette 1998: 47 calls this 'the law of opposites'. Sparks 1992: 140–5 offers a qualitative analysis.)

A final important feature of fictional crime is the high clear-up rate. In fiction cops usually get their man (Garofalo 1981: 327; Lichter *et al.* 1994: ch. 9; Powers *et al.* 1996: ch. 5). In Allen *et al.*'s sample of movies since 1945, there was no film before 1952 in which criminals escaped capture, and hardly any up to the early 1970s. Thereafter, offenders get away with their crimes in an increasing number of films, albeit still a minority (Allen *et al.* 1998: 185; Reiner *et al.* 2000 and 2001). Trends on television are similar, with the overwhelming majority of crimes cleared up by the police, but an increasing minority where they fail (Lichter *et al.* 1994: ch. 9.).

The police and the criminal justice system are thus overwhelmingly portrayed in a positive light in popular fiction, as the successful protectors of victims against serious harm and violence. This continues to be so, although with increasing questioning of police success and integrity (Reiner 2000b, 2003). Although the majority of police characters in films and television shows are represented as sympathetic, honest, and just, there is an increasing portrayal of police deviance. Corrupt, brutal, and discriminatory police officers have become more common since the mid-1960s in films (Powers *et al.* 1996: 113–16; Allen *et al.* 1998: 185–6) and television (Lichter *et al.* 1994: ch. 9), as has acceptance of routine police violation of due process legal restraints (Dominick 1978: 117; Garofalo 1981: 327; Sparks 1992: ch. 6).

Victims have moved from a shadowy and purely functional role in crime narratives to a pivotal position. Film and television stories focus increasingly on the plight of victims, whose suffering is portrayed more graphically and often constitutes the driving force of the story (Allen *et al.* 1998; Reiner *et al.* 2000 and 2001). Support for law enforcement and criminal justice is increasingly constructed in narratives by presenting them as defenders or avengers of victims with whose suffering the audience is invited to identify.

THE MEDIA REPRESENTATION OF CRIME: A SUMMARY

1. News and fiction stories about crime are prominent in all media. While there is evidence of increasing attention to crime in some parts of the media, overall this fascination has been constant throughout media history.

2. News and fiction concentrate overwhelmingly on serious violent crimes against individuals, albeit with some variation according to medium and market. The proportion of different crimes represented is the inverse of official statistics.

3. The demographic profile of offenders and victims in the media is older and higher status than those processed by the criminal justice system. Child victims and perpetrators are also represented disproportionately.

4. The risks of crime as portrayed by the media are both quantitatively and qualitatively more serious than the official statistically recorded picture, although the media underplay the current probabilities of victimization by property crimes.

5. The media generally present a very positive image of the success and integrity of the police, and criminal justice more generally. However, in both news and fiction there is a clear trend to criticism of law enforcement, in terms of both its effectiveness and its justice and honesty. While in the past the unbroken media picture was that *Crime Does Not Pay* (the title of a series of short films produced by MGM between 1935 and 1947), this is increasingly called into question in contemporary news and fiction.

6. Individual victims and their suffering increasingly provide the motive force of crime stories.

The next section will discuss the possible implications of this pattern of representation.

THE CONSEQUENCES OF MEDIA IMAGES OF CRIME

This section offers an analysis of the vast research literature assessing the impact of media images of crime. Much of the inspiration (and dollars) for empirical evaluations of media effects derives from the broader, apocalyptic concerns of subversion or hegemony. However, in practice most research has sought to measure two possible consequences of media representations (which are not mutually exclusive): criminal behaviour (especially violence); and fear of crime (for a detailed critical survey see Howitt 1998: chs 1, 5–8, 10–11).

THE MEDIA AND CRIMINOLOGICAL THEORY

For a crime to occur there are several logically necessary preconditions: labelling; motive; means; opportunity; and the absence of controls. The media potentially play a part in each of these.

Labelling

For an act to be 'criminal' (as distinct from harmful, immoral, antisocial, etc.) it has to be labelled as such. This involves the creation of a legal category. A recorded crime also requires the labelling of the act as criminal by citizens and/or law-enforcement officers. The media are an important factor shaping the conceptual boundaries and recorded volume of crime.

The role of the media in developing new (and eroding old) categories of crime has been emphasized in most of the classic studies of the emergence of criminal law within the 'labelling' tradition. Becker's seminal *Outsiders* analysed the 1937 passage of the US Marijuana Tax Act, showing the use of the media as a tool of the Federal Bureau of Narcotics' moral entrepreneurship (Becker 1963: ch. 7). Jock Young analysed how media representations amplified the deviance of drug-takers (Young 1971). Stan Cohen coined the influential concept of 'moral panic' in his study of how the media together with the police developed a spiral of respectable fear about 'mods' and 'rockers' (Cohen 1972). Hall *et al.*'s analysis of the 1973 moral panic about a supposedly new type of robbery, 'mugging', emphasized the crucial part played by the media. Newspapers stimulated public anxiety, producing changes in policing and criminal justice that became a self-fulfilling spiral of deviancy amplification (Hall *et al.* 1978).

Many subsequent studies have illustrated the role of the media in shaping the boundaries of criminality by creating new categories of offence, or by changing perceptions and sensitivities, leading to fluctuations in apparent crime. For example, Roger Graef's celebrated 1982 fly-on-the-wall documentary about the Thames Valley Police was a key impetus to reform of police treatment of rape victims (Gregory and Lees 1999; 'TV that changed the world', *Radio Times*, 24–30 November 2001). This also contributed, however, to a rise in the proportion of victims reporting rape, and thus an increase in the recorded rate. Many other studies document media-amplified 'crime waves' and 'moral panics' about law and order.[3] Thus increases and decreases in recorded crime levels may be due in part to the deviance construction and amplifying activities of the media (Barak 1994; Ferrell and Sanders 1995; Jewkes 2004: ch. 3).

Motive

A crime will not occur unless someone is tempted, driven, or otherwise motivated to carry out the 'labelled' act. The media feature in many of the most commonly offered social and psychological theories of the formation of criminal dispositions. Probably the most influential sociologial theory of how criminal motives are formed is Merton's

---

[3] e.g. Fishman 1981; Christensen *et al.* 1982; Altheide 1993; Lees 1995; Brownstein 1995; Beckett and Sasson 2000: chs 4, 5, 7; Critcher 2003.

version of anomie theory (Merton 1938; Messner and Rosenfeld 2000; Rock, Chapter 1 in this volume). The media are pivotal in presenting for universal emulation images of affluent lifestyles and a consumerist culture, accentuating relative deprivation and generating pressures to acquire ever higher levels of material success regardless of the legitimacy of the means used. Psychological theories of the formation of motives to commit offences also often feature media effects as part of the process. It has been claimed that the images of crime and violence presented by the media are a form of social learning, and may encourage crime by imitation or arousal effects (Bailey 1993; Carey 1993; Wartella 1995: 309–11; Livingstone 1996: 308).

Means

It has often been alleged that the media act as an open university of crime, spreading knowledge of criminal techniques. This is often claimed in relation to particular *causes célèbres* or horrific crimes, for example during the 1950s' campaign against crime and horror comics (Barker 1984b; Nyberg 1998). A notorious case was the allegation that the murderers of Jamie Bulger had been influenced by the video *Child's Play 3* in the manner in which they killed the unfortunate toddler (Jewkes 2004: 12). A related line of argument is the 'copycat' theory of crime and rioting (Tumber 1982; Howitt 1998: 75–84; Surette 1998: 137–52). Video games such as *Grand Theft Auto* have been accused of being an especially potent source of learning about crime, as the player is placed in the subject position of a criminal (Hayward 2004: 172–3, 193–4). Despite much discussion, the evidence that these are major sources of crime is weak (Young 2004; Hargrave and Livingstone 2006).

New forms of media have sometimes been seen as creating new means to commit crime. This concern has been particularly stimulated by the Internet, which is feared as facilitating all sorts of offences, from fraud, identity theft, child pornography and grooming children for sex, to organizing transnational crime and terrorism (Wall 2001; Jewkes 2003; Brown 2003: ch. 5; Hargrave and Livingstone 2006).

Opportunity

The media may increase opportunities to commit offences by contributing to the development of a consumerist ethos, in which the availability of tempting targets of theft proliferates (Hayward 2004; Hallsworth 2005: 62–3, ch. 7). They can also alter 'routine activities', especially in relation to the use of leisure time, which structure opportunities for offending (Cohen and Felson 1979). The domestic hardware and software of mass media use—TVs, videos, radios, CDs, personal computers, mobile phones—are the common currency of routine property crime, and their proliferation has been an important aspect of the spread of criminal opportunities.

Absence of controls

Motivated potential offenders, with the means and opportunities to commit offences, may still not carry out these crimes if effective social controls are in place. These might be *external*—the deterrent threat of sanctions represented in the first place by the police—or *internal*—the still, small voice of conscience—what Eysenck has called the 'inner policeman'.

A regularly recurring theme of respectable anxieties about the criminogenic consequences of media images of crime is that they erode the efficacy of both external and internal controls. They may undermine external controls by derogatory representations of criminal justice, for example ridiculing its agents, a key complaint at least since the days of Dogberry, resuscitated more recently by the popularity of comic images of the police, from the Keystone Cops onwards. Serious representations of criminal justice might undermine its legitimacy by becoming more critical, questioning the integrity and fairness, or the efficiency and effectiveness of the police. Negative representations of criminal justice could lessen public cooperation with the system, or potential offenders' perception of the probability of sanctions, with the consequence of increasing crime.

Probably the most frequently suggested line of causation between media representations and criminal behaviour is the allegation that the media undermine internalized controls, by regularly presenting sympathetic or glamorous images of offending. In academic form this is found in the psychological theories about disinhibition and desensitization (Wartella 1995: 309–12; Surette 1998: 119–30 are succinct evaluations).

CRIMINOGENIC MEDIA? THE RESEARCH EVIDENCE

In a comprehensive review of the research literature, Sonia Livingstone noted that 'since the 1920s thousands of studies of mass media effects have been conducted' (Livingstone 1996: 306). She added that even listing the references to research in the previous decade would exhaust the space allocated to her article (some twenty pages). Reviews of the literature regularly recycle the apotheosis of agnosticism represented by the conclusion of one major study from the 1960s: 'for some children, under some conditions, some television is harmful. For some children under the same conditions, or for the same children under other conditions, it may be beneficial. For most children, under most conditions, most television is probably neither particularly harmful nor particularly beneficial' (Schramm *et al.* 1961: 11).

This meagre conclusion from the expenditure of countless research hours and dollars is primarily a testimony to the limitations and difficulties of empirical social science. The armoury of possible research techniques for assessing directly the effects of media images on crime is sparse, and suffers from evident and long-recognized limitations.

The archetypal technique has been some version of the classic experiment: a group of subjects are exposed to a media stimulus—say a film—and the response is measured, by comparing behaviour or attitudes before and after. In a characteristic example, children of four to five were shown a five-minute film in the researcher's office, and then taken to a room with toys and observed for 20 minutes through a one-way mirror (Bandura *et al.* 1961, 1963). The children were randomly assigned to watch one of three films, enacting scenarios in which a boy who attacked another boy and some toys was depicted as being rewarded, or punished, or neither. The children (especially the boys) who saw the film about the boy rewarded for his attack by getting all the toys, were observed to carry out twice as much imitative aggression as the other groups, but no more non-imitative aggression.

This example shows all the problems of inferring conclusions about links between media and violence from laboratory-style experiments. Are the results a Hawthorn effect arising from the experimental situation itself? For instance, were the more aggressive children who saw a film in which aggression was rewarded influenced by their perception that the experimenter approved of such behaviour? How far can results from one context of viewing be extrapolated to others? Do experimental results exaggerate the links in the everyday world by picking up short-term effects of media exposure that rapidly evaporate? Or do they underestimate the long-term cumulative effects of regular, repeated exposures by measuring only one-off results? To some the artificiality of such experiments fatally compromises them (Surette 1998: 122–3). Others point out that 'laboratories' (or more typically researchers' offices or other convenient campus locations) are social situations 'whose particular dynamics and meanings must be considered . . . and generalisability depends on how far these same factors may occur or not in everyday life' (Livingstone 1996: 310).

Given the huge number of such experimental studies (using different forms of stimuli and different types of measures of response, for different sorts of subjects, at many different times and places) it is hardly surprising that there are variations in the extent of effect shown, if any. However, most studies do show *some* effect, and the few that conducted follow-ups over time found that while effects diminished by about 25 per cent over the fortnight or so after an experiment, they do not disappear (Livingstone 1996: 309–10). There are many suggestions in the experimental literature about what determines the degree of effect caused by media exposures. These include the perceived realism of the representation, whether violence or deviance was seen as justified, punished, or rewarded, whether the viewers identified with the perpetrator, the variable vulnerability or susceptibility of the viewer, and so on (ibid.).

Typically, however, the effects of exposure to media stimuli in experimental situations are small. Interestingly, most of the research has looked at supposed negative effects of media, such as violence. The few studies that have examined the effects of 'prosocial' images suggest that these are much larger. One meta-analysis of 230 studies of media effects estimated that overall they showed that a single exposure to violent or stereotyped content was followed by about an extra 20 per cent of 'antisocial' responses, compared to an extra 50 per cent of 'prosocial' responses after viewing positive images (Hearold 1986; Livingstone 1996: 309).

Given the limitations of laboratory experiments, some studies have tried to assess the effects of media exposure in 'natural' everyday situations. One method has been by looking at the introduction of some form of medium (usually television) in an area where it did not exist before. This was most frequently done in the 1950s, when the spread of television ownership, first in the USA, then in the UK, provided the opportunity of a once-and-for-all natural experiment. One study of matched sets of 34

US cities in the early 1950s found that larceny increased by about 5 per cent in those cities where television was introduced for the first time, compared to cities without TV or those that had been receiving it for some time (Hennigan *et al.* 1982). However, British research in the same period does not find similar effects on deviance (Himmelweit *et al.* 1958; Livingstone 1996: 312–13). Since the virtually universal availability of television, such natural experiments are seldom possible. One recent example found that children's verbal and physical aggression increased in a Northern Canadian town after television was introduced, compared to two towns with established television (Williams 1986). While such natural experiments do not suffer from the artificiality of their laboratory counterparts, they are of course less completely controlled: the possibility can never be ruled out that differences between areas (even if roughly matched) were due to factors other than television.

Several studies have compared the viewing patterns of known offenders and (supposed) non-offenders. Some have concluded that more exposure to television is related to greater aggressiveness (see Belson 1978, and the other examples in Wartella 1995: 307–9); others that the viewing preferences of delinquents are remarkably similar to the general pattern for their age (Hagell and Newburn 1994). Neither conclusion is free from the possibility of other, unmeasured factors explaining either the association or the lack of it.

There is also evidence that abuses of power by police and other criminal justice agents may be affected by media representations. A study of 'reality' television programmes such as *Cops* suggested that the police may adopt forms of entrapment or illicit punishment of offenders to ensure good video footage for such shows (Doyle 1998: 110–12, 2003).

The big fix: the media-crime connection

Reviews of the research literature generally 'conclude that there is a correlation between violence viewing and aggressive behaviour, a relationship that holds even when a variety of controls are imposed' (Wartella 1995: 306). However, the overall negative effects of media exposure seem to be small compared to other features in the social experience of offenders. Thus 'the question that remains is not whether media violence has an effect, but rather how important that effect has been, in comparison with other factors, in bringing about major social changes such as the post-war rise in crime' (ibid.: 312).

One problem with most of the effects debate and research is that it has often been directed at a rather implausible notion (Brown 2003: 27–9). What has been at issue is the will-o'-the-wisp of a 'pure' media effect. The implicit model was of the media as hypodermic syringe, injecting ideas and values into a passive public of cultural dopes. Audiences are not passive recipients, however, but active interpreters, in a complex process of interaction with other cultural and social practices (Livingstone *et al.* 2001; Carrabine *et al.* 2002: 129–34). Changes in media representations do not come fully formed from another planet and affect behaviour patterns *ex nihilo*, but reflect ongoing changes in social perceptions and practices. Changing media images are interpreted by different audiences in various ways, which may reinforce or alter emerging social patterns. The relationship between developments in the media and in the wider society is a dialectical one. While this makes the isolation and measurement of pure media effects chimerical, it certainly does not imply that media representations have no significant consequences.

As Sonia Livingstone concluded:

> Most media researchers believe that the media have significant effects, even though they are hard to demonstrate, and most would agree that the media make a significant contribution to the social construction of reality. The problem is to move beyond this platitude . . . The study of enculturation processes, which work over long time periods, and which are integral to rather than separate from other forms of social determination, would not ask how the media make us act or think, but rather how the media contribute to making us who we are [Livingstone 1996: 31–2].

A further limitation of the effects literature is that it has been almost exclusively concerned with the consequences of violent and other representations of deviance. The theoretical connections examined earlier suggest that media representations of non-law-breaking behaviour, for example advertising and other images of consumerist lifestyles, may increase anomie and hence offending. The most plausible criminogenic implications of media representations concern how they impact on material aspirations and conceptions of legitimate means of achievement, not how they depict crime or violence directly.

THE MEDIA AND FEAR OF CRIME

In recent years policy debates have identified fear of crime as an issue potentially as serious as crime itself (Ditton and Farrell 2000; Hope and Sparks 2000; Jackson 2004; Ditton *et al.* 2004; Chadee and Ditton 2005). Concern is not just about the unnecessary pain of excessive anxiety, nor even the damage done to trust and social relations by fear and the prevention strategies it encourages. In the 'cultivation analysis' tradition which Gerbner and his associates have been developing for thirty years, media images of crime and violence are a threat to democracy (Gerbner 1970, 1995).

Fearful people are more dependent, more easily manipulated and controlled, more susceptible to deceptively simple, strong, tough measures and hard-line postures—both political and religious. They may accept and even welcome repression if it promises to relieve their insecurities and other anxieties (Signorielli 1990: 102). When reel-world violence is compared to real-world crime as measured by official statistics, it appears that the media images exaggerate the probability and severity of danger. This is said to 'cultivate' a misleading view of the world based on unnecessary anxiety about levels of risk from violent crime (ibid.: 96–102).

There has been extensive criticism of the empirical and theoretical validity of these claims (Howitt 1998: ch. 4; Ditton *et al.* 2004). How much of the association between measures of exposure to the media and of fearfulness survives the introduction of other control variables such as class, race, gender, place of residence, and actual experience of crime (Doob and MacDonald 1979; Chadee 2001; Roberts 2001)? Could any association between viewing and fearfulness result from the opposite causal process, that is, do more fearful viewers watch more television rather than vice versa? More generally, it appears that 'cultivation' does not export well. British attempts to replicate the Gerbner findings have failed to do so (Wober 1978; Gunter 1985).

Although the debate about the empirical validity of the cultivation hypothesis continues, there is only limited evidence from other studies to confirm the plausible idea that exposure to media images is associated with fear of crime. An extensive multivariate analysis concluded that there was a significant relationship between reading newspapers with more emphasis on violent crime and measures of fearfulness expressed in a survey (Williams and Dickinson 1993). This association survived control by a number of demographic variables, such as socio-economic status, gender, and age. However, this association was not found with behavioural concomitants of fear, such as going out after dark. Neither could the study rule out the possibility that fear led to heavier readership of newspapers with more crime, rather than vice versa. On the empirical issue, while it remains a reasonable hypothesis that much public fear of crime is created or accentuated by media exposure, the research evidence remains equivocal about the strength, or even existence, of such a causal relationship (Sacco 1995: 151; Jewkes 2004: ch. 6; Greer 2005: 171–3; Ditton *et al.* 2004; Chadee and Ditton 2005). Most studies have not examined how frequently people experience fear, as opposed to their responses to particular surveys (Farrall and Gadd 2004).

Much of this inconclusiveness is rooted in the theoretical limitations of positivist content analysis (Sparks 1992: ch. 4). Items of violence are collated according to operational definitions used by observers, without reference to the narrative contexts within which they are embedded. Most stories have conclusions concurring with Miss Prism's celebrated definition of fiction: 'The good ended happily, and the bad unhappily' (Oscar Wilde, *The Importance of Being Earnest*, Act II). Although there is a trend towards greater ambivalence and ambiguity, most crime stories still have an underlying emphasis on just resolutions of conflict and violence (Zillman and Wakshlag 1987; Reiner *et al.* 2000 and 2001). It is not obvious that exposure to high degrees of violence en route to a happy ending has a fear-enhancing effect. 'When suspenseful drama featuring victimisation is known to contain a satisfying resolution, apprehensive individuals should anticipate pleasure and enjoyment' (Wakshlag *et al.* 1983: 238).

Quantitative assessments of the relationship between 'objectively' measured units of media content and survey responses cannot begin to understand the complex and dynamic interdependence of the differential experiences of crime, violence, and risk of different social groups and their subjective interpretations of the meaning of texts. The subtle intertwinings of differential social positions and life experiences with the reception of media texts is only beginning to be addressed by studies of content and interpretation. These use qualitative methods and ways of reading that seek to be sensitive to the complexities of analysing meaning (Sparks 1992, 2000, 2001; Schlesinger *et al.* 1992; Livingstone *et al.* 2001; Ditton *et al.* 2004). As with the issue of the effects of media images on criminality, so too with fear, the issue is not whether media representations have consequences. Hardly anyone would deny this. The agenda is the unravelling of the complex interrelationship of media content and other dimensions of social structure and experience in shaping offending behaviour, fear of crime, and the politics of law and order (Sasson 1995; Beckett 1997; Girling *et al.* 2000; Stenson and Sullivan 2000; Hope and Sparks 2000; Garland 2001; Greve 2004; Cavender 2004).

THE CAUSES OF MEDIA REPRESENTATIONS OF CRIME

What processes and priorities produce the pattern of representation of crime? Until recently, accounts of the production of crime news were primarily based on inferences drawn from content analyses and the political economy of the media (e.g. Hall *et al.* 1978; Sherizen 1978; Tunnell 1998; Green 2001). There is now a body of empirical research on the production process, based on interviews with reporters and other creative personnel, or the police (e.g. Chibnall 1977; Fishman 1981; Ross 1998; Mawby 1998, 1999, 2001, 2002; Innes 1999, 2001; Greer 2003), and/or observation (Ericson *et al.* 1987, 1989, 1991; Schlesinger *et al.* 1991; Schlesinger and Tumber 1992, 1993, 1994; Chermak 1995, 1998; Skidmore 1996; Doyle 1998, 2003).

CRIME NEWS AS HEGEMONY IN ACTION

Most of the earlier studies supported a version of the dominant ideology model. The immediate source of news content was the ideology of the reporter, personal and professional. However, a variety of organizational and professional imperatives exerted pressure for the production of news with the characteristics identified by content analyses. The sources of news production were seen as threefold:

1. The political ideology of the press.
2. The elements of 'newsworthiness'.
3. Structural determinants of news-making.

The political ideology of the press

The majority of newspapers have a more or less overtly C/conservative political ideology, and individual reporters are aware of this whatever their personal leanings. The broadcasting media, especially the BBC, are characterized by an ethic of political neutrality and professional objectivity in performing a public service of providing news information. In practice, however, this becomes a viewpoint which takes for granted certain broad beliefs and values, those of moderate, middle-of-the-road majority opinion—what Stuart Hall succinctly called a 'world at one with itself' (Hall 1970). The master concepts of this worldview include such notions as the 'national interest', the 'British way of life', and the 'democratic process' as epitomized by Westminster. In political or industrial conflict situations these are seen as threatened by 'mindless militants' manipulated by extremist minorities seeking 'anarchy' and subversion, with only the 'thin blue line' to save the day for law and order (Chibnall 1977: 21). Political conflict is assimilated to routine crime: both are portrayed as pathological conditions unrelated to wider social structures (Clarke and Taylor 1980; Hillyard 1982; Iyengar 1991; Beckett 1997: 38; Lawrence 2000: 57–60).

Traditional crime reporters explicitly saw it as their responsibility to present the police and the criminal justice system in as favourable a light as possible. As one put it: 'If I've got to come down on one side or the other, either the goodies or the baddies, then obviously I'd come down on the side of the goodies, in the interests of law and order' (Chibnall 1977: 145). This of course did not mean that even the most pro-police crime reporter would not pursue stories of police malpractice as assiduously as possible. But it generated a tendency to present these within a 'one bad apple' framework (ibid.: ch. 5). However, the characteristics of crime reporting were more immediately the product of a professional sense of news values rather than any explicitly political ideology.

The elements of 'newsworthiness'

News content is generated and filtered primarily through reporters' sense of 'newsworthiness', what makes a good story that their audience wants to know about, rather than any overtly ideological considerations. The core elements of this include immediacy, dramatization, personalization, titillation, and novelty (Chibnall 1977: 22–45; Jewkes 2004: ch. 2 offers an elaborated set). The primacy of these news values explains the predominant emphasis on violent and sex offences, and the concentration on higher-status offenders and victims, especially celebrities. It also accounts for the tendency to avoid stories about crime trends and patterns.

These news values also encourage the presentation of political violence or disorder in terms of individual pathology rather than ideological opposition; as discrete criminal events, not manifestations of structural conflict (Halloran *et al.* 1970; Hall 1973; Lawrence 2000: ch. 3).

Structural determinants of news-making

A variety of concrete organizational pressures underlying news production have unintended consequences, bolstering the law and order stance of most crime reporting. For example, concentrating personnel at institutional settings like courts, where newsworthy events can be expected to recur regularly, is an economic use of reporting resources. But it has the unintended consequence of concentrating on cleared-up cases, creating a misleading sense of police effectiveness.

The need to produce reports to fit the time schedules of news production contributes to their event orientation, the concentration on specific crimes at the expense of analysis of causal processes or policies (Rock 1973: 76–9; Lawrence 2000: ch. 8).

Considerations of personal safety and convenience lead cameramen covering riots typically to film from behind police lines, which unintentionally structures an image of the police as vulnerable 'us' threatened by menacing 'them' (Murdock 1982: 108–9).

The police and the criminal justice system control much of the information on which crime reporters rely, and this gives them a degree of power as essential accredited sources. Crime reporters tend to develop a symbiotic relationship with the contacts and organizations they use regularly, especially the police (Chibnall 1977: chs 3 and 6). Institutional sources on which reporters structurally depend, notably the police, become the 'primary definers' of crime news, which tends to be filtered through their perspective (Hall *et al.* 1978: 58; Lawrence 2000: ch. 3).

In recent years the production of crime news (like news in general) has been transformed by a decline in the use of specialist reporters, including court and crime correspondents. This is due to the increasing news emphasis on celebrities, and the increasingly commercial orientation of the multimedia conglomerates that own most news outlets, which has restricted editorial budgets severely. Many crime and criminal justice stories, cases, and issues now fail to get aired prominently or perhaps at all, even in the sensationalist manner that used to be a core news staple (Davies 1999). Crime news increasingly shares in the increasingly dominant celebrity culture. Stories with famous victims or perpetrators are the acme of news value, as illustrated by the impact of the murder of Jill Dando.

In sum, the hegemonic model sees news content as the largely unintended but determined consequence of the structure and political economy of news production. 'Journalists are not *necessarily* biased towards the powerful—but their bureaucratic organisation and cultural assumptions make them conduits of that power' (McNair 1993: 48).

CRIME NEWS AS CULTURAL CONFLICT

Empirical studies of the crime news production process suggest that the deterministic implications of the hegemonic model require qualification (Ericson *et al.* 1987, 1989, 1991; Schlesinger *et al.* 1991; Schlesinger and Tumber 1992, 1993, 1994; Greer 2003). They do not overthrow its fundamental implications, however, but confirm earlier accounts of the structuring of news-gathering and presentation around a sense of news values, criteria leading to the selection of particular types of stories and perspectives. These constitute a 'vocabulary of precedents': not hard and fast rules, but 'what previous exemplars tell them should be done in the present instance' (Ericson *et al.* 1987: 348). There is scope for flexibility and judgement; the newsroom is not characterized by normative consensus but by negotiation and conflict between reporters, editors, and sources. News stories vary in character. Many are routine fillers, where a clearly established paradigm is followed, albeit with new names, dates, and details each time. What usually makes a story newsworthy at all is some departure from expected norms, an element of freakishness or an opportunity to explore everyday moral dilemmas (Katz 1987). But the big stories are ones where novelty and other news values are high, and there is proximity to the intended audience so the events have particular salience for them (Greer 2003: ch. 3; Jewkes 2004: ch. 2).

There is always a tension between two contradictory pressures. The highest journalistic accolade is the 'scoop', reporting a high-news-value story that has not yet been reported. This exerts pressure to be ahead of the pack, to seek out sources that no rivals have yet found. However, the worst possible scenario is to miss important information that everybody else has. This generates a tendency to hunt with the pack, mining the same sources as rivals. The fear of failure usually prevails over the lure of the scoop, on minimax principles, which is why front pages tend to be so similar.

There are also systematic variations between news stories in different media and markets. This is partly because they have different variants of political and professional journalistic ideology according to patterns of ownership (state versus private, for example) and perceived audience (business or policy elites, other opinion leaders, liberal professionals, or a mass public seeking entertainment; local or national). These are interconnected with differences in technological resources, budgetary limitations, and the different 'grammars' of written and spoken language, still and moving pictures.

Observation also alerts analysts to the ever-present role of contingency and cock-ups (Ericson *et al.* 1991: 93–4). 'We know that at the level of production news is more procedure-related than content-related' (ibid.), and procedures can be disrupted for all sorts of random reasons.

Detailed study reveals that there is more diversity, negotiation, and contingency than the hegemony model implies, not only within news organizations, but also in the sources used. These now range far beyond the accredited agencies of the formal criminal justice institutions (Schlesinger and Tumber 1994; Lawrence 2000; Greer 2003: 32–3). Groups critical of the establishment (such as penal reform or civil liberties groups) *are* given a voice, depending in part on their organizational and presentational skills, their hold on interesting knowledge, and on medium and market differences.

Empirical analyses of news production in action do emphasize its contingency and fluidity, but they do not fundamentally challenge the hegemonic model. While news may be a competitive arena of conflicting viewpoints, it is culturally and structurally loaded. For all the fluidity and contingency observed in the process of production, in the final analysis 'the news media are as much an agency of *policing* as the law-enforcement agencies whose activities and classifications are reported on' (Ericson *et al.* 1991: 74). They reproduce order in the process of representing it.

Although there have been many studies of the production of crime news, there has been no comparable research on fiction. All we have is memoirs of writers, directors, and other creators of crime fiction, and fan-oriented biographies or accounts of the making of particular films or programmes. The sole exception is an interview study of Hollywood writers, directors, and producers of television shows and cinema films (Lichter *et al.* 1994: Part IV; Powers *et al.* 1996: ch. 3). This depicts them as former 1960s radicals on a 'long march' through the institutions. Their ideology combines acceptance of the economic and political institutions of America, to which they owe their status and privileges, with a libertarian stance on issues of personal and sexual morality that they have carried since their youth. They feel a mission to put as much of this into their work as is compatible with the overriding priority of keeping the audience ratings high and the networks happy. How this expressed ideology translates into actual creative and production practices has not been studied, however, in any research analogous to that on crime news.

OBSERVERS OR PLAYERS? THE MEDIA AND CRIME IN POSTMODERNITY

In the introduction to this chapter two competing concerns about media representations of crime were outlined: the 'respectable fear' that they were subversive and desubordinating; and the radical anxiety that they were a means of social control and discipline. The review of research suggests that there is a complex interplay between media representations of crime, criminal behaviour, and criminal justice.

With variations according to medium and market, mass media news and entertainment are saturated with stories about crime. These disproportionately feature the most serious and violent crimes, but strip them from any analytic framework. The emphasis is on crime as the product of individual choice and free-floating evil, diverting attention from any links to social structure or culture (Sasson 1995). There is strong evidence that media images *can* influence criminal behaviour, but overall their direct effect is small relative to other factors. This is largely because people vary in their interpretation of representations according to demographic, generational, and other life-course factors. There is a variety of ways theoretically in which media representations could influence crime rates and patterns. For example, the overall volume of property crime is likely to be affected by media portrayals of material success as the acme of the good life in a context of structural inequalities of opportunity, as Mertonian strain theories suggest. It is unlikely to be an accident that the remorseless rise of volume property crime after the mid-1950s in Britain coincided with the advent of commercial television. Research on media effects has mainly assessed the consequences of representations of crime, using rather inadequate models and methods, not the theoretically more plausible criminogenic implications of other aspects of the media, for example the celebration of consumerism.

The disciplinary role of media stories about crime, reproducing as well as representing order, is supported more clearly by the research. This is partly because media representations exaggerate the threat of crime and promote policing and punishment as the antidote. Because of organizational exigencies as for much as ideological reasons, the media present viewpoints on crime and criminal justice policy which—though not monolithic—are loaded towards official definitions. They tend to frame crime issues increasingly in a 'law and order' perspective so other approaches become marginalized (Sasson 1995; Beckett 1997; Altheide 2002; Cavender 2004).

The present trends indicate a growing symbiosis between media images, criminality, and criminal justice. In Simon Lee's words, 'The media are no longer, if they ever were, observers of the scene, they are players in the game' (cited in Peay 1998: 8). This accentuates past patterns to an extent amounting to a qualitatively new stage. The insecure borderline between purportedly factual and fictional narratives is eroding. A growing variety of criminal justice lobbies and pressure groups seek to influence, if not construct, the news. At the same time technological developments interact with cultural changes to produce more 'reality' broadcasting (Fishman and Cavender 1998).

The current stage of development reflects the impact of the more general features of 'postmodernity' on the relationship between media, crime, and criminal justice (Brown 2003). The space–time distanciation between criminal cases and their reporting in the media, and the reciprocal feedback of images on practice, are eroding rapidly (Giddens 1984; Thompson 1995). Increasing numbers of criminal justice events, such as the 1992 Los Angeles riots or the O. J. Simpson case, are broadcast around the world literally as they are happening. An ever-wider range of participants in the criminal justice process are not only seeking to influence representations but are creating events specifically for the media. 'We live in a dramatised world' (Ericson 1991: 235), where the media are participants in the processes they represent. Criminal justice agencies tailor their activities to public relations, how their activities will play on the news. Police investigate (sometimes instigate) all the crimes fit to print. Crimes and legal processes are not only reflected in reporting with greater rapidity, they may be created for news stories. Offences have been incited by law-enforcement agencies in order to have the successful investigation televised (as in the Azscam entrapment case analysed by Altheide 1993). Since the 1960s, protesters and police act with self-conscious awareness that 'the whole world is watching' (Gitlin 1980). The tragedy of 11 September 2001 is simply the most vivid and dramatic example of these developments to date, when thousands of people were murdered in front of the eyes of television audiences around the globe, in a way calculated to achieve the maximum possible media impact.

The mass media are important not only because of their ideological significance. Media technology plays an increasingly direct role in social control, above all through the growth of CCTV and other forms of surveillance (Norris and Armstrong 1999; McCahill 2003; Jewkes 2004: ch. 7). Media technology can also be used to control the controllers, to make authorities more accountable, as the use of CCTV and other recording devices in police stations shows (Newburn and Hayman 2001). The proliferation of cheap, portable cameras contributes to this too, as the Rodney King case indicated (Lawrence 2000). Mass media technologies make the model of contemporary social control a Synopticon (Mathiesen 1997): they provide the means for the many to see the few, offsetting the Benthamite paradigm of the few observing the many. However, this reciprocal process of surveillance between elites and masses is highly unbalanced. The greater vulnerability of the powerful to exposure and scandal does not fundamentally change structures of power and advantage. Indeed Mathiesen argues plausibly that the illusion of intimacy with elites, provided by contemporary media surveillance of their activities, gives people a misleading sense of empowerment which acts as a more complex process of discipline than traditional forms of legitimation. It is possible, he argues, 'that the control and discipline of the "soul", that is, the creation of human beings who control themselves through self-control and thus fit neatly into a so-called democratic capitalist society, is a task which is actually fulfilled by a modern Synopticon' (Mathiesen 1997: 215).

The growing interdependence of media representation and social 'reality' raises the spectre of 'a media spiral in which the representations of crime and the fear of crime precisely constitute . . . the hyperreal' (Osborne 1996: 36). Certainly these developments vastly complicate the vexed question of how images and narratives that are felt to be undesirable can be regulated or influenced. Perhaps hope lies precisely in the greater openness of the media to a diversity of inputs and influences. Past experience, however, suggests the more pessimistic prediction that although contemporary mass communications present 'an appreciably open terrain for struggles for justice' (Ericson 1991: 242), the dice are loaded in favour of dominant interests—even if they have to struggle harder for their hegemony.

■ SELECTED FURTHER READING

Richard Sparks's *Television and the Drama of Crime* (Buckingham: Open University Press, 1992) is a theoretically sophisticated critique of content analyses of crime fiction, and their relationship to fear of crime. Illuminating recent studies of the production of crime news are the trilogy by R. Ericson, P. Baranek, and J. Chan, *Visualising Deviance*, *Negotiating Control*, and *Representing Order* (Milton Keynes: Open University Press, 1987, 1989, 1991 respectively); P. Schlesinger and H. Tumber's *Reporting Crime* (Oxford: Oxford University Press, 1994); and C.Greer, *Sex Crime and the Media* (Cullompton, Devon: Willan, 2004). Useful reviews of the research on media effects can be found in: S. Livingstone, 'On the Continuing Problem of Media Effects', in J. Curran and M. Gurevitch (eds), *Mass Media and Society* (London: Arnold, 1996); D. Howitt, *Crime, The Media and the Law* (London: Wiley, 1998); and from a fundamentally critical perspective, M. Barker and J. Petley (eds), *Ill Effects*, 2nd edn, (London: Routledge, 2001). Excellent recent texts on crime and media are S. Brown, *Crime and Law in Media Culture* (Buckingham: Open University Press, 2003) and Y. Jewkes, *Media and Crime* (London: Sage, 2004). Chapters offering excellent brief reviews of the literature are: K. Beckett and T. Sasson, *The Politics of Injustice* (Thousand Oaks, Cal.: Pine Forge, 2000), chs 5, 6; E. Carrabine, P. Iganski, M. Lee, K. Plummer, and N. South, *Criminology* (London: Routledge, 2004), ch. 18; C. Greer 'Crime and Media' in C. Hale, K. Hayward, A. Wahidin, and E. Wincup (eds), *Criminology* (Oxford: Oxford University Press, 2005). Useful edited volumes offering a rich diversity of research papers on media and crime are: R. Ericson (ed.), *Crime and the Media* (Aldershot: Dartmouth, 1995); D. Kidd-Hewitt and R. Osborne (eds), *Crime and the Media: The Post-Modern Spectacle* (London: Pluto, 1996); P. Mason (ed.), *Criminal Visions* (Cullompton, Devon: Willan, 2003). Valuable specialist journals are *Crime, Media, Culture* (London: Sage) and *Journal of Crime, Conflict and Media Culture* (www.jc2m.co.uk).

■ REFERENCES

ALLEN, J., LIVINGSTONE, S., and REINER, R. (1997), 'The Changing Generic Location of Crime in Film', *Journal of Communication*, 47(4): 1–13.

——, ——, and —— (1998), 'True Lies: Changing Images of Crime in British Postwar Cinema', *European Journal of Communication*, 13(1): 53–75.

ALTHEIDE, D. (1993), 'Electronic Media and State Control: The Case of Azscam', *The Sociological Quarterly*, 34(1): 53–69.

—— (2002) *Creating Fear: News and the Construction of Crisis*, New York: Aldine de Gruyter.

BAILEY, F., and HALE, D. (eds) (1998), *Popular Culture, Crime and Justice*, Belmont, Cal.: Wadsworth.

BAILEY, S. (1993), 'Fast Forward to Violence: Violent Visual Imaging and Serious Juvenile Crime', *Criminal Justice Matters*, 11 (Spring): 6–7.

BANDURA, A., ROSS, D., and ROS, S.A. (1961), 'Transmission of Aggression Through Imitation of Aggressive Models', *Journal of Abnormal and Social Psychology*, 63(3): 575–82.

BARAK, G. (ed.) (1994), *Media, Process, and the Social Construction of Crime*, New York: Garland.

BARCLAY, G., and TAVARES, C. (1999), *Information on the Criminal Justice System in England and Wales: Digest 4*, London: Home Office.

BARKER, M. (1984a), *A Haunt of Fears*, London: Pluto.

—— (1984b), *The Video Nasties: Freedom and Censorship in the Media*, London: Pluto.

—— and PETLEY, J. (eds) (2001), *Ill Effects: The Media/Violence Debate*, 2nd edn, London: Routledge.

BARLOW, M. H. (1998), 'Race and the Problem of Crime in Time and Newsweek Cover Stories, 1946–1995', *Social Justice*, 25: 149–83.

BECKER, H. (1963), *Outsiders*, New York: Free Press.

BECKETT, K. (1997), *Making Crime Pay*, New York: Oxford University Press.

—— and SASSON, T. (2000), *The Politics of Injustice*, Thousand Oaks, Cal.: Pine Forge Press.

BELL, I. A., and DALDRY, G. (eds) (1990), *Watching the Detectives*, London: Macmillan.

BELSON, W. (1978), *Television Violence and the Adolescent Boy*, Westmead: Saxon House.

BINYON, T. J. (1989), *Murder Will Out: The Detective in Fiction*, Oxford: Oxford University Press.

BIRESSI, A. (2001), *Crime, Fear and the Law in True Crime Stories*, London: Palgrave.

BROWN, S. (2003), *Crime and Law in Media Culture*, Buckingham: Open University Press.

BROWNSTEIN, H. (1995), 'The Media and the Construction of Random Drug Violence', in J. Ferrell and C.R. Sanders (eds), *Cultural Criminology*, 45–65, Boston, Mass.: Northeastern University Press.

BUXTON, D. (1990), *From The Avengers to Miami Vice: Form and Ideology in Television Series*, Manchester: Manchester University Press.

CAREY, S. (1993), 'Mass Media Violence and Aggressive Behaviour', *Criminal Justice Matters*, 11 (Spring): 8–9.

CARLSON, J. M. (1985), *Prime-Time Law Enforcement: Crime Show Viewing and Attitudes to the Criminal Justice System*, New York: Praeger.

CARRABINE, E., COX, P., LEE, M., and SOUTH, N. (eds) (2002), *Crime in Modern Britain*, Oxford: Oxford University Press.

——, IGANSKI, P., LEE, M., PLUMME R, K., and SOUTH, M. (2004), *Criminology*, London: Routledge.

CAVENDER, G. (2004), 'Media and Crime Policy', *Punishment and Society*, 6(3): 335–348.

CAWELTI, J. G. (1976), *Adventure, Mystery and Romance*, Chicago: Chicago University Press.

CHADEE, D. (2001), 'Fear of Crime and the Media: From Perceptions to Reality', *Criminal Justice Matters*, 43: 10–11.

—— and DITTON, J. (2005), 'Fear of Crime and the Media: Assessing the Lack of Relationship', *Crime, Media, Culture*, 1(3): 322–32.

CHERMAK, S. M. (1995), *Victims in the News: Crime in American News Media*, Boulder Cal.: Westview.

—— (1998), 'Police, Courts, and Corrections in the Media', in F. Bailey and D. Hale (eds), *Popular Culture, Crime and Justice*, 87–99, Belmont, Cal.: Wadsworth.

CHIBNALL, S. (1977), *Law-and-Order News*, London: Tavistock.

—— and MURPHY, R. (eds) (1999), *British Crime Cinema*, London: Routledge.

CHIRICOS, T., ESCHHOLZ, S., and GERTZ, M. (1997), 'Crime, News and Fear of Crime', *Social Problems*, 44(3): 342–57.

CHRISTENSEN, J., SCHMIDT, J., and HENDERSON, J. (1982). 'The Selling of the Police: Media Ideology and Crime Control', *Contemporary Crises*, 6(3): 227–39.

CLARENS, C. (1997), *Crime Movies*, New York: Da Capo.

CLARKE, A. (1982), *Television Police Series and Law and Order* (Popular Culture Course Unit 22), Milton Keynes: Open University.

—— (1983), 'Holding the Blue Lamp: Television and the Police in Britain', *Crime and Social Justice*, 19: 44–51.

—— (1986), 'This is Not the Boy Scouts: Television Police Series and Definitions of Law and Order', in T. Bennett, C. Mercer, and J. Woollacott (eds), *Popular Culture and Social Relations*, 219–32, Milton Keynes: Open University Press.

—— (1992), '"You're Nicked!" Television Police Series and the Fictional Representation of Law and Order', in D. Strinati and S. Wagg (eds), *Come On Down? Popular Media Culture in Post-War Britain*, 232–53, London: Routledge.

—— and TAYLOR, I. (1980), 'Vandals, Pickets and Muggers: Television Coverage of Law and Order in the 1979 Election', *Screen Education*, 36: 99–112.

CLARKE, J. (2001), 'The Pleasures of Crime: Interrogating the Detective Story', in J. Muncie and E. McLaughlin (eds), *The Problem of Crime*, 2nd edn, 71–106, London: Sage.

COHEN, L., and FELSON, S. (1979), 'Social Change and Crime Rate Trends: A Routine Activities Approach', *American Sociological Review*, 44: 588–608.

COHEN, S. (1972), *Folk Devils and Moral Panics*, London: Paladin.

—— and YOUNG, J. (eds) (1973), *The Manufacture of News*, London: Constable.

COTTLE, S. (1993), *TV News, Urban Conflict and the Inner City*, Leicester: Leicester University Press.

CRITCHER, C. (2003), *Moral Panics and the Media*, Buckingham: Open University Press.

CUMBERBATCH, G. (1989), *A Measure of Uncertainty: The Effects of Mass Media*, Broadcasting Standards Council Research Monograph 1, London: John Libbey.

——, WOODS, S., and MAGUIRE, A. (1995), *Crime in the News: Television, Radio and Newspapers: A Report for BBC Broadcasting Research*, Birmingham: Aston University, Communications Research Group.

DAHLGREN, P. (1988), 'Crime News: The Fascination of the Mundane', *European Journal of Communication*, 3(1): 189–206.

DAVIES, N. (1999), 'Getting away with murder', *The Guardian* (*Media Section*): 4–5,11 January.

DAVIS, J. (1952), 'Crime News in Colorado Newspapers', *American Journal of Sociology*, 57: 325–30.

DEUTSCHMANN, P. (1959), *News Page Content of Twelve Metropolitan Dailies*, Cincinnati, Ohio: Scripps-Howard Research Centre.

DITTON, J., and DUFFY, J. (1983), 'Bias in the Newspaper Reporting of Crime News', *British Journal of Criminology*, 23(2): 159–65.

—— and FARRALL, S. (eds) (2000), *The Fear of Crime*, Aldershot: Dartmouth.

——, CHADEE, D., FARRALL, S., GILCHRIST, E. and BANNISTER, J. (2004), 'From Imitation to Intimidation: A Note on the Curious and Changing Relationship Between the Media, Crime and Fear of Crime', *British Journal of Criminology*, 44(4): 595–610.

DOBASH, R. E., SCHLESINGER, P., DOBASH, R., and WEAVER, C. K. (1998), ' "Crimewatch UK": Women's Interpretation of Televised Violence', in M. Fishman and G. Cavender (eds), *Entertaining Crime*, 37–58, New York: Aldine De Gruyter.

DOMINICK, J. (1978), 'Crime and Law Enforcement in the Mass Media', in C. Winick (ed.), *Deviance and Mass Media*, 105–28, Beverly Hills, Cal.: Sage.

DOOB, A., and MACDONALD, G. (1979), 'Television Viewing and the Fear of Victimisation: Is the Relationship Causal?', *Journal of Personality and Social Psychology*, 37(1): 170–9.

DORLING, D. (2004), 'Prime Suspect: Murder in Britain', in P. Hillyard, C. Pantazis, S. Tombs, and D. Gordon (eds), *Beyond Criminology*, 178–91, London: Pluto.

DOVE, G. (1982), *The Police Procedural*, Bowling Green, Ohio: Bowling Green Popular Press.

—— and BARGAINNIER, E. (eds) (1986), *Cops and Constables: American and British Fictional Policemen*, Bowling Green, Ohio: Bowling Green Popular Press.

DOYLE, A. (1998), ' "Cops": Television Policing As Policing Reality', in M. Fishman and G. Cavender (eds), *Entertaining Crime*, 95–116, New York: Aldine De Gruyter.

—— (2003), *Arresting Images*, Toronto: University of Toronto Press.

DURSTON, G. (1997), *Moll Flanders: Analysis of 18th Century Criminal Biography*, Chichester: Barry Rose.

DUSSUYER, I. (1979), *Crime News: A Study of 40 Toronto Newspapers*, Toronto: University of Toronto Centre of Criminology.

EATON, M. (1996), 'A Fair Cop? Viewing the Effects of the Canteen Culture in *Prime Suspect* and *Between the Lines*', in D. Kidd-Hewitt and R. Osborne (eds), *Crime and the Media: The Post-Modern Spectacle*, London: Pluto.

ELTON, B. (1996), *Popcorn*, London: Simon & Schuster.

ERICSON, R. (1991), 'Mass Media, Crime, Law, and Justice', *British Journal of Criminology*, 31(3): 219–49.

—— (ed.) (1995), *Crime and the Media*, Aldershot: Dartmouth.

——, BARANEK, P., and CHAN, J. (1987), *Visualising Deviance*, Milton Keynes: Open University Press.

——, ——, and —— (1989), *Negotiating Control*, Milton Keynes: Open University Press.

——, ——, and —— (1991), *Representing Order*, Milton Keynes: Open University Press.

EVERSON, W. (1972), *The Detective in Film*, New York: Citadel.

FABIAN, R. (1950), *Fabian of the Yard*, London: Naldrett.

—— (1954), *London After Dark*, London: Naldrett.

FALLER, L. (1987), *Turned to Account: The Forms and Functions of Criminal Biography in Late Seventeenth and Early Eighteenth Century England*, Cambridge: Cambridge University Press.

FARRALL, S., and GADD, D. (2004), 'The Frequency of the Fear of Crime', *British Journal of Criminology*, 44(1): 127–32.

FERRELL, J. (1998), 'Criminalising Popular Culture', in F. Bailey and D. Hale (eds), *Popular Culture, Crime and Justice*, 71–84, Belmont, Cal.: Wadsworth.

—— and SANDERS, C. R. (eds) (1995), *Cultural Criminology*, Boston, Mass.: Northeastern University Press.

FISHMAN, M. (1981), 'Police News: Constructing An Image of Crime', *Urban Life*, 9(4): 371–94.

—— and CAVENDER, G. (eds) (1998), *Entertaining Crime: Television Reality Programs*, New York: Aldine De Gruyter.

GARLAND, D. (2001), *The Culture of Control*, Oxford: Oxford University Press.

GAROFALO, J. (1981), 'Crime and the Mass Media: A Selective Review of Research', *Journal of Research in Crime and Delinquency*, 18(2): 319–50.

GERBNER, G. (1970), 'Cultural Indicators: The Case of Violence in Television Drama', *Annals of the American Academy of Political and Social Science*, 338(1): 69–81.

—— (1995), 'Television Violence: The Power and the Peril', in G. Dines and J. Humez (eds), *Gender, Race and Class in the Media*, 547–57, Thousand Oaks, Cal.: Sage.

—— and GROSS, L. (1976), 'Living With Television: The Violence Profile', *Journal of Communication*, 26(1): 173–99.

GIDDENS, A. (1984), *The Constitution of Society*, Cambridge: Polity Press.

GIRLING, E., LOADER, I., and SPARKS, R. (2000), *Crime and Social Change in Middle England*, London: Routledge.

GITLIN, T. (1980), *The Whole World Is Watching*, Berkeley, Cal.: University of California Press.

—— (2000), *Inside Prime Time*, revised edn, Berkeley, Cal.: University of California Press.

GRABER, D. (1980), *Crime News and the Public*, New York: Praeger.

GREEN, P. (2000), 'American Television, Crime and the Risk Society', in K. Stenson and R. Sullivan (eds), *Crime, Risk and Justice*, 214–27, Cullompton, Devon: Willan.

GREER, C. (2003), *Sex Crime and the Media*, Cullompton, Devon: Willan.

—— (2005), 'Crime and Media', in C. Hale, K. Hayward, A. Wahidin, and E. Wincup (eds), *Criminology*, 157–82, Oxford: Oxford University Press.

GREGORY, J., and LEES, S. (1999), *Policing Sexual Assault*, London: Routledge.

GREVE, W. (2004), 'Fear of Crime Among Older and Younger Adults: Paradoxes and Misconceptions', in H.-J. Albrecht, T. Serassis, and H. Kania (eds), *Images of Crime II*, 167–86, Freiburg: Max Planck Institute.

GUNTER, B. (1981), 'Measuring Television Violence: A Review and Suggestions for a New Analytic Perspective', *Current Psychological Research*, 1(1): 91–112.

—— (1985), *Dimensions of Television Violence*, Aldershot: Gower.

HAGELL, A., and NEWBURN, T. (1994), *Young Offenders and the Media*, London: Policy Studies Institute.

HALE, D. C. (1998), 'Keeping Women in their Place: An Analysis of Policewomen in Videos, 1972–1996', in F. Bailey and D. Hale (eds), *Popular Culture, Crime and Justice*, 159–79, Belmont, Cal.: Wadsworth.

HALL, S. (1970), 'A World At One With Itself', *New Society*, 18 June: 1056–8.

—— (1973), 'The Determination of News Photographs', in S. Cohen and J. Young (eds),

The Manufacture of News, 226–43, London: Constable.

—— (1979), *Drifting Into A Law and Order Society*, London: Cobden Trust.

——, CRITCHLEY, C., JEFFERSON, T., CLARKE, J., and ROBERTS, B. (1978), *Policing the Crisis*, London: Macmillan.

HALLORAN, J., ELLIOTT, L., and MURDOCK, G. (1970), *Demonstrations and Communication*, London: Penguin.

HALLSWORTH, S. (2005), *Street Crime*, Cullompton, Devon: Willan.

HARDY, P. (1997), *The BFI Companion to Crime*, London: Cassell.

—— (1998), *Gangsters*, London: Aurum.

HARGRAVE, A. M., and LIVINGSTONE, S. (2006), *Harm and Offence in Media Content: A Review of the Evidence*, Bristol: Intellect.

HARRIS, F. (1932), *Presentation of Crime in Newspapers*, Minneapolis, Minn.: Minneapolis Sociological Press.

HAYCRAFT, H. (1941), *Murder For Pleasure*, New York: Appleton Century.

HAYWARD, K. (2004), *City Limits*, London: Glasshouse.

HEAROLD, S. (1986), 'A Synthesis of 1043 Effects of Television on Social Behaviour', in G. Comstock (ed.), *Public Communications and Behaviour Vol. 1*, 65–133, New York: Academic Press.

HENNIGAN, K. M., DELROSARIO, M. L., HEATH, L., COOK, J. D., and CALDER, B. J. (1982), 'Impact of the Introduction of Television Crime in the United States: Empirical Findings and Theoretical Implications', *Journal of Personality and Social Psychology*, 42(3): 461–77.

HILLYARD, P. (1982), 'The Media Coverage of Crime and Justice in Northern Ireland', in C. Sumner (ed.), *Crime, Justice and the Mass Media*, 36–54 (Cropwood Papers 14), Cambridge: Institute of Criminology.

HIMMELWEIT, H., OPPENHEIM, A. N., and VINCE, P. (1958), *Television and the Child*, London: Oxford University Press.

HOPE, T., and SPARKS, R. (eds) (2000), *Crime, Risk and Insecurity*, London: Routledge.

HOWITT, D. (1998), *Crime, The Media and The Law*, London: Wiley.

HURD, G. (1979), 'The Television Presentation of the Police', in S. Holdaway (ed.), *The British Police*, London: Edward Arnold.

INCIARDI, J., and DEE, J. L. (1987), 'From the Keystone Cops to Miami Vice: Images of Policing in American Popular Culture', *Journal of Popular Culture*, 21(2): 84–102.

INNES, M. (1999), 'The Media as an Investigative Resource in Murder Enquiries', *British Journal of Criminology*, 39(2): 268–85.

—— (2001), ' "Crimewatching": Homicide Investigations in the Age of Information', *Criminal Justice Matters*, 43: 42–3.

—— (2003), ' "Signal Crimes": Detective Work, Mass Media and Constructing Collective Memory', in P. Mason (ed.), *Criminal Visions*, 51–69, Cullompton, Devon: Willan.

IYENGAR, S. (1991), *Is Anyone Responsible? How Television Frames Political Issues*, Chicago, Ill.: Chicago University Press.

JACKSON, J. (2004), 'An Analysis of a Construct and Debate: The Fear of Crime', in H-J. Albrecht, T. Serassis and H. Kania (eds), *Images of Crime II*, 35–64, Freiburg: Max Planck Institute.

JEWKES, Y. (ed.) (2003), *Dot.Cons: Crime, Deviance and Identity on the Internet*, Cullompton, Devon: Willan.

—— (2004), *Media and Crime*, London: Sage.

KATZ, J. (1987), 'What Makes Crime "News"?', *Media, Culture and Society*, 9(1): 47–75.

KERR, P. (1981), 'Watching the Detectives: American Television Crime Series 1949–81', *Prime-Time*, 1(1): 2–6.

KIDD-HEWITT, D., and OSBORNE, R. (eds) (1996), *Crime and the Media: The Post-modern Spectacle*, London: Pluto.

KING, N. (1999), *Heroes in Hard Times: Cop Action Movies in the US*, Philadelphia: Temple University Press.

KNIGHT, S. (1980), *Form and Ideology in Crime Fiction*, London: Macmillan.

KOOISTRA, P. G., MAHONEY, J. S., and WESTERVELT, S. D. (1998), 'The World of Crime According to "Cops" ', in M. Fishman and G. Cavender (eds), *Entertaining Crime*, 141–58, New York: Aldine De Gruyter.

LAING, S. (1991), 'Banging in Some Reality: The Original "Z-Cars" ', in J. Corner (ed.), *Popular Television in Britain: Studies in Cultural History*, 125–43, London: British Film Institute.

LAWRENCE, R. G. (2000), *The Politics of Force: Media and the Construction of Police Brutality*, Berkeley, Cal.: University of California Press.

LEES, S. (1995), 'Media Reporting of Rape: The 1993 British "Date Rape" Controversy', in D. Kidd-Hewitt and R. Osborne (eds), *Crime and the Media*, 107–30, London: Pluto.

LEISHMAN, F., and MASON, P. (2002), *Policing and the Media: Facts, Fictions and Factions*, Cullompton, Devon: Willan.

LEVI, M. (2001), 'White-Collar Crime in the News', *Criminal Justice Matters*, 43: 24–5.

—— (2006), 'The Media Construction of Financial and White-Collar Crimes', *British Journal of Criminology* (forthcoming).

LICHTER, S. R., LICHTER, L. S., and ROTHMAN, S. (1994), *Prime Time: How TV Portrays American Culture*, Washington: Regnery.

LIVINGSTONE, S. (1996), 'On the Continuing Problem of Media Effects', in J. Curran and M. Gurevitch (eds), *Mass Media and Society*, 305–24, London: Arnold.

——, ALLEN, J., and REINER, R. (2001), 'Audiences for Crime Media 1946–91: A Historical Approach to Reception Studies', *Communication Review*, 4(2): 165–92.

MCARTHUR, C. (1972), *Underworld USA*, London: Secker and Warburg.

MCCAHILL, M. (2003), 'Media Representations of Visual Surveillance', in P. Mason (ed.), *Criminal Visions*, 192–213, Cullompton, Devon: Willan.

MCCARTY, J. (1993), *Hollywood Gangland*, New York: St Martin's Press.

MCNAIR, B. (1993), *News And Journalism in the UK*, London: Routledge.

MANDEL, E. (1984), *Delightful Murder: A Social History of the Crime Story*, London: Pluto.

MANNING, P. (1998), 'Media Loops', in F. Bailey and D. Hale (eds), *Popular Culture, Crime and Justice*, 25–39, Belmont, Cal.: Wadsworth.

MARSH, H. L. (1991), 'A Comparative Analysis of Crime Coverage in Newspapers in the United States and Other Countries From 1960–1989: A Review of the Literature', *Journal of Criminal Justice*, 19(1): 67–80.

MASON, P. (1996), 'Prime Time Punishment: The British Prison and Television', in D. Kidd-Hewitt and R. Osborne (eds), *Crime and the Media*, 185–205, London: Pluto.

—— (2003a) 'The Screen Machine; Cinematic Representations of Prison', in P. Mason (ed.), *Criminal Visions*, 278–97, Cullompton, Devon: Willan.

—— (ed.) (2003b), *Criminal Visions*, Cullompton, Devon: Willan.

MATHEWS, T. D. (1994), *Censored*, London: Chatto and Windus.

MATHIESEN, T. (1997), 'The Viewer Society: Michel Foucault's "Panopticon" Revisited', *Theoretical Criminology*, 1(2): 215–34.

MAWBY, R. C. (1998), 'The Changing Image of Policing in Television Drama 1956–96', *Journal of the Police History Society*, 13: 39–44.

—— (1999), 'Visibility, Transparency, and Police-Media Relations', *Policing and Society*, 9(3): 263–86.

—— (2001), 'Promoting the Police? The Rise of Police Image Work', *Criminal Justice Matters*, 43: 44–5.

—— (2002), *Policing Images: Policing, Communication and Legitimacy*, Cullompton, Devon: Willan.

—— (2003) 'Completing the "Half-formed Picture"? Media Images of Policing', in P. Mason (ed.), *Criminal Visions*, 214–37, Cullompton, Devon: Willan.

MAWBY, R. I., and BROWN, J. (1983), 'Newspaper Images of the Victim', *Victimology*, 9(1): 82–94.

MEDVED, M. (1992), *Hollywood vs. America*, London: HarperCollins.

MERTON, R. (1938/1957), 'Social Structure and Anomie', *American Sociological Review*, 3: 672–82. Reprinted in R. Merton, *Social Theory and Social Structure*, Glencoe, Ill.: Free Press, 1957; revised edn, 1963.

MESSNER, S. F., and ROSENFELD, R. (2000), *Crime and the American Dream*, 3rd edn, Belmont, Cal.: Wadsworth.

MEYERS, R. (1981), *TV Detectives*, San Diego, Cal.: Barnes.

—— (1989), *Murder on the Air*, New York: The Mysterious Press.

MILLER, F. (1994), *Censored Hollywood: Sex, Sin and Violence on Screen*, Atlanta, Ga.: Turner.

MURDOCK, G. (1982), 'Disorderly Images', in C. Sumner (ed.), *Crime, Justice and the Mass Media*, 104–23 (Cropwood Papers 14), Cambridge: Institute of Criminology.

NELLIS, M., and HALE, C. (1982), *The Prison Film*, London: Radical Alternatives to Prison.

NEWBURN, T., and HAYMAN, S. (2001), *Policing, CCTV and Social Control*, Cullompton, Devon: Willan.

NORRIS, C., and ARMSTRONG, G. (1999), *The Maximum Surveillance Society: The Rise of CCTV*, Sussex: Berg.

NYBERG, A. K. (1998), 'Comic Books and Juvenile Delinquence: A Historical Perspective', in F. Bailey and D. Hale (eds), *Popular Culture, Crime and Justice*, 61–70, Belmont, Cal.: Wadsworth.

OLIVER, M. B., and ARMSTRONG, G. B. (1998), 'The Color of Crime: Perceptions of Caucasians' and African-Americans' Involvement in Crime', in M. Fishman and G. Cavender (eds), *Entertaining Crime*, 19–36, New York: Aldine De Gruyter.

OSBORNE, R. (1996), 'Crime and the Media: From Media Studies to Post-modernism', in D. Kidd-Hewitt and R. Osborne (eds), *Crime and the Media*, 25–48, London: Pluto.

OUSBY, I. (1976), *Bloodhounds of Heaven: The Detective in English Fiction From Godwin to Doyle*, Cambridge, Mass.: Harvard University Press.

—— (1997), *The Crime and Mystery Book*, London: Thames & Hudson.

PALMER, J. (1978), *Thrillers*, London: Edward Arnold.

PANDIANI, J. (1978), 'Crime Time TV: If All We Knew Is What We Saw . . .', *Contemporary Crises*, 2: 437–58.

PARK, W. (1978), 'The Police State', *Journal of Popular Film*, 6(3): 229–38.

PEARSON, G. (1983), *Hooligan: A History of Respectable Fears*, London: Macmillan.

PEAY, J. (1998), 'The Power of the Popular', in T. Newburn and J. Vagg (eds), *Emerging Themes in Criminology*, Loughborough: British Society of Criminology.

PEELO, M., FRANCIS, B., SOOTHILL, K., PEARSON, J., and ACKERLEY, E. (2004), 'Newspaper Reporting and the Public Construction of Homicide', *British Journal of Criminology* 44(2): 256–75.

PHILLIPS, M. (1996), *The Observer Review*, 8 December: 2.

PORTER, B. (1981), *The Pursuit of Crime*, New Haven, Conn.: Yale University Press.

POWERS, S. P., ROTHMAN, D. J., and ROTHMAN, S. (1996), *Hollywood's America: Social and Political Themes in Motion Pictures*, Boulder, Col.: Westview.

RAFTER, N. (2000), *Shots in the Mirror: Crime Films and Society*, New York: Oxford University Press.

RAWLINGS, P. (1992), *Drunks, Whores, and Idle Apprentices: Criminal Biographies of the Eighteenth Century*, London: Routledge.

—— (1998), 'Crime Writers: Non-Fiction Crime Books', in T. Newburn and J. Vagg (eds), *Emerging Themes in Criminology*, Loughborough: British Society of Criminology.

REINER, R. (1978), 'The New Blue Films', *New Society*, 43(808): 706–708.

—— (1981), 'Keystone to Kojak: The Hollywood Cop', in P. Davies and B. Neve (eds), *Politics, Society and Cinema in America*, 195–220, Manchester: Manchester University Press.

—— (1994), 'The Dialectics of Dixon: The Changing Image of the TV Cop', in S. Becker and M. Stephens (eds), *Police Force, Police Service*, 11–32, London: Macmillan.

—— (2000a), *The Politics of the Police*, 3rd edn, Oxford: Oxford University Press.

—— (2000b), 'Romantic Realism: Policing and the Media', in F. Leishman, B. Loveday, and S. Savage (eds), *Core Issues in Policing*, 52–66, London: Longman.

—— (2000c), 'Crime and Control in Britain', *Sociology*, 34(1): 71–94.

—— (2001), 'The Rise of Virtual Vigilantism: Crime Reporting Since World War II', *Criminal Justice Matters*, 43: 4–5.

—— (2003), 'Policing and the Media' in T. Newburn (ed.), *Handbook of Policing*, 259–82, Cullompton, Devon: Willan.

——, LIVINGSTONE, S., and ALLEN, J. (2000), 'No More Happy Endings? The Media and Popular Concern About Crime Since the Second World War', in T. Hope and R. Sparks (eds), *Crime, Risk and Insecurity*, 107–25, London: Routledge.

——, ——, and —— (2001), 'Casino Culture: Media and Crime in a Winner-Loser Society', in K. Stenson and R. Sullivan (eds), *Crime, Risk and Justice*, 175–93, Cullompton, Devon: Willan.

——, ——, and —— (2003), 'From Law and Order to Lynch Mobs: Crime News Since the Second World War', in P. Mason (ed.), *Criminal Visions*, 13–32, Cullompton: Willan.

ROBERTS, J. V., and STALANS, L. J. (2000), *Public Opinion, Crime and Criminal Justice*, Boulder, Col.: Westwood.

ROBERTS, M. (2001), 'Just Noise? Newspaper Crime Reporting and Fear of Crime', *Criminal Justice Matters*, 43: 10–11.

ROCK, P. (1973), 'News As Eternal Recurrence', in S. Cohen and J. Young (eds), *The Manufacture of News*, 64–70, London: Constable.

ROSHIER, B. (1973), 'The Selection of Crime News By the Press', in S. Cohen and J. Young (eds), *The Manufacture of News*, 40–51, London: Constable.

ROSOW, E. (1978), *Born to Lose*, New York: Oxford University Press.

ROSS, J. I. (1998), 'The Role of the Media in the Creation of Public Police Violence', in F. Bailey and D. Hale (eds), *Popular Culture, Crime and Justice*, 100–10, Belmont, Cal.: Wadsworth.

RUBIN, M. (1999), *Thrillers*, Cambridge: Cambridge University Press.

SACCO, V. F. (1995), 'Media Constructions of Crime', *The Annals of the American Academy of Political and Social Science*, 539: 141–54.

SASSON, T. (1995), *Crime Talk: How Citizens Construct A Social Problem*, New York: Aldine De Gruyter.

SAYERS, D. (ed.) (1936), *Tales of Detection*, London: Dent.

SCHLESINGER, P., and TUMBER, H. (1992), 'Crime and Criminal Justice in the Media', in D. Downes (ed.), *Unravelling Criminal Justice*, 184–203, London: Macmillan.

—— and —— (1993), 'Fighting the War Against Crime: Television, Police and Audience', *British Journal of Criminology*, 33(1): 19–32.

—— and —— (1994), *Reporting Crime*, Oxford: Oxford University Press.

——, DOBASH, R., and MURDOCK, G. (1991), 'The Media Politics of Crime and Criminal Justice', *British Journal of Sociology*, 42(3): 397–420.

——, ——, DOBASH, R., and WEAVER, C. (1992), *Women Viewing Violence*, London: British Film Institute.

SCHRAMM, W., LYLE, J., and PARKER, E. B. (1961), *Television in the Lives of Our Children*, Stanford, Cal.: Stanford University Press.

SHADOIAN, J. (1977), *Dreams and Dead Ends*, Cambridge, Mass.: MIT Press.

SHALE, S. (1996), 'Listening to the Law: Famous Trials on BBC Radio 1934–69', *Modern Law Review*, 59(6): 813–44.

SHERIZEN, S. (1978), 'Social Creation of Crime News: All the News Fitted to Print', in C. Winick (ed.), *Deviance and Mass Media*, 203–24, Beverly Hills, Cal.: Sage.

SIGNORIELLI, N. (1990), 'Television's Mean and Dangerous World: A Continuation of the Cultural Indicators Perspective', in N. Signorielli and M. Morgan (eds), *Cultivation Analysis: New Directions in Media Effects Research*, 85–106, Newbury Park: Sage.

SKIDMORE, P. (1996), 'Telling Tales; Media Power, Ideology, and the Reporting of Child Sexual Abuse in Britain', in D. Kidd-Hewitt and R. Osborne (eds), *Crime and the Media*, 78–106, London: Pluto.

SKLAR, R. (1975), *Movie-Made America*, New York: Vintage.

SMITH, S. (1984), 'Crime in the News', *British Journal of Criminology*, 24(3): 289–95.

SOLOMONS, S. (1976), *Beyond Formula: American Film Genres*, New York: Harcourt, Brace, Jovanovich.

SOOTHILL, K., and WALBY, S. (1991), *Sex Crime in the News*, London: Routledge.

SPARKS, R. (1992), *Television and the Drama of Crime*, Buckingham: Open University Press.

—— (1993), 'Inspector Morse', in G. Brandt (ed.), *British Television Drama in the 1980s*, Cambridge: Cambridge University Press.

—— (2000), ' "Bringin' It All Back Home": Populism, Media Coverage, and the Dynamics of Locality and Globality in the Politics of Crime Control', in K. Stenson and R. Sullivan (eds), *Crime, Risk and Justice*, 194–213, Cullompton, Devon: Willan.

—— (2001), 'The Media, Populism, Public Opinion and Crime', *Criminal Justice Matters*, 43: 6–7.

STENSON, K., and SULLIVAN, R. (eds) (2000), *Crime, Risk and Justice: The Politics of Crime Control in Liberal Democracies*, Cullompton, Devon: Willan.

STEPHENSON-BURTON, A. (1995), 'Through the Looking-Glass: Public Images of White Collar Crime', in D. Kidd-Hewitt and R. Osborne (eds), *Crime and the Media*, 131–63, London: Pluto.

SUMNER, C. (1982), ' "Political Hooliganism" and "Rampaging Mobs": The National Press Coverage of the Toxteth "Riots" ', in C. Sumner (ed.), *Crime, Justice and the Mass Media*, 25–35, Cropwood Papers 14, Cambridge: Institute of Criminology.

SURETTE, R. (1998), *Media, Crime and Criminal Justice: Images and Realities*, 2nd edn, Belmont, Cal.: Wadsworth.

SWANSON, C. (1955), 'What They Read in 130 Daily Newspapers', *Journalism Quarterly*, 32(4): 411–21.

SYMONS, J. (1972), *Bloody Murder*, London: Penguin.

THOMPSON, J. (1993), *Fiction, Crime and Empire: Clues to Modernity and Postmodernity*, Urbana, Ill.: University of Illinois Press.

THOMPSON, J. B. (1995), *The Media and Modernity: A Social Theory of the Media*, Cambridge: Polity Press.

Tombs, S., and Whyte, D. (2001), 'Reporting Corporate Crime Out of Existence', *Criminal Justice Matters*, 43: 22–23.

Tumber, H. (1982), *Television and the Riots*, London: British Film Institute.

Tunnell, K. D. (1998), 'Reflections on Crime, Criminals, and Control in Newsmagazine Television Programs', in F. Bailey and D. Hale (eds), *Popular Culture, Crime and Justice*, 111–22, Belmont, Cal.: Wadsworth.

Tuska, J. (1978), *The Detective in Hollywood*, New York: Doubleday.

Wakshlag, J., Vial, V., and Tamborini, R. (1983), 'Selecting Crime Drama and Apprehension About Crime', *Human Communication Research*, 10(2): 227–42.

Wall, D. (ed.) (2001), *Crime and the Internet*, London: Routledge.

Wartella, E. (1995), 'Media and Problem Behaviours in Young People', in M. Rutter and D. Smith (eds), *Psychological Disorders in Young People*, 296–323, London: Wiley.

Watson, C. (1971), *Snobbery With Violence: English Crime Stories and Their Audience*, London: Eyre Methuen.

Williams, P., and Dickinson, J. (1993), 'Fear of Crime: Read All About It? The Relationship Between Newspaper Crime Reporting and Fear of Crime', *British Journal of Criminology*, 33(1): 33–56.

Williams, T. M. (ed.) (1986), *The Impact of Television: A Natural Experiment in Three Communities*, New York: Academic Press.

Wilson, C. P. (2000), *Cop Knowledge: Police Power and Cultural Narrative in Twentieth Century America*, Chicago: University of Chicago Press.

Winston, R. (2004), 'Seeing is Believing', *Guardian G2*, 7 January.

Winston, R., and Mellersi, N. (1992), *The Public Eye: Ideology and the Police Procedural*, London: Macmillan.

Wober, M. (1978), 'Televised Violence and Paranoid Perception: The View From Great Britain', *Public Opinion Quarterly*, 42(3): 315–21.

Wren-Lewis, J. (1981/2), 'TV Coverage of the Riots', *Screen Education*, 40: 15–33.

Wykes, M. (2001), *News, Crime and Culture*, London: Pluto.

Young, J. (1971), *The Drug-Takers*, London: Paladin.

—— (1999), *The Exclusive Society*, London: Sage.

—— (2004), 'Constructing the Paradigm of Violence: Mass Media, Violence and Youth', in H.-J. Albrecht, T. Serassis and H. Kania (eds), *Images of Crime II*, 187–98, Freiburg: Max Planck Institute.

Zillman, D., and Wakshlag, J. (1987), 'Fear of Victimisation and the Appeal of Crime Drama', in D. Zillman and J. Bryant (eds), *Selective Exposure to Communication*, Hillsdale, NJ: Erlbaum.

PART III

DIMENSIONS OF CRIME

12

POLITICAL ECONOMY, CRIME, AND CRIMINAL JUSTICE

Robert Reiner

INTRODUCTION: POLITICAL ECONOMY AND CRIME: A ONE-SIDED ACCENTUATION?

The notion that there exists some sort of connection between crime and economic circumstances, especially deprivation, is age-old, as the etymology of the terms 'villain' and 'rogue' indicate for example.[1] The exploration of such links has been a prominent activity within criminology. Much of this has been within an implicit (or sometimes explicit) economic determinist model, 'the proposition that economic life is fundamental and therefore the determining influence upon which all social and cultural arrangements are made' (Taylor 1997: 266).[2] The literature on the role of economic factors in crime and criminal justice will be reviewed in this chapter, but the title 'political economy' is intended to signify a broader and more complex approach than simply spotlighting the significance of the economic, let alone economic determinism.

There has in the last couple of decades been a tendency to downplay political economy in criminology. Tony Blair made this explicit in a recent article, when he claimed that 'the left, by the 1980s . . . had come to be associated with the belief that the causes of crime are entirely structural . . . we had eliminated individual responsibility

---

[1] The Oxford English Dictionary states that 'villain' derives from the medieval French for peasant, and 'rogue' from the Latin for beggar. By contrast 'propriety' and 'property' share a common root, indicating a connection between economic class and conceptions of 'good' behaviour (Neocleous 2000: 39).

[2] The late Ian Taylor wrote the chapter on 'The Political Economy of Crime' for the first two editions of *The Oxford Handbook of Criminology*. Sadly he died before completing a revised version for the third edition. He brought a breadth of knowledge, penetrating insight, and profound moral and political commitment to his analysis that are impossible to emulate. My survey in this edition necessarily owes much to his definitive earlier versions.

from the account' ('Our Citizens Should Not Live in Fear', *The Observer*, 11 December 2005: 30).[3]

This chapter focuses on the economic aspects of crime and criminal justice, precisely the position from which Tony Blair sought to distance himself. It will seek to demonstrate the significance of the economic for the understanding of crime and criminal justice. *Pace* Mr Blair, however, this does not mean that 'the causes of crime are entirely structural' nor that 'individual responsibility' should be 'eliminated . . . from the account'. The economic must be seen as part of a complex set of interdependencies with individual, moral, cultural, and other social dimensions. It is this dialectical interplay of levels of analysis that the label 'political economy' is intended to convey.[4]

WHAT IS POLITICAL ECONOMY?

The term 'political economy' is used nowadays in contradictory ways. Although it most frequently signifies a perspective that is distinct from 'economics', it is also sometimes treated as synonymous with it. *The Journal of Political Economy*, for instance, is the title of the house journal of the Chicago School, most famously associated with Milton Friedman and other exponents of neo-classical economics. It was *The Journal of Political Economy* that initiated the application of neo-classical economics to crime with seminal articles by Gary Becker and Isaac Ehrlich in the late 1960s and early 1970s (Becker 1968; Ehrlich 1973), as well as the broader 'law and economics' movement (Posner 1998). The journal's title is explicable because economics as a discipline emerged out of classical political economy in the late nineteenth century, but the neo-classical perspective that the Chicago School espouses is frequently seen as diametrically opposed to 'political economy'.

What is now practised and taught as 'economics' is very different from the 'political economy' that was its origin. The most famous work of eighteenth-century political economy, Adam Smith's *The Wealth of Nations*, 'was part of a much broader inquiry into the foundations of society. It was inseparable from moral philosophy' (Backhouse 2002: 132). Over time it fed into what is now referred to as 'classical political economy', the leading exponents of which were Malthus, Ricardo, James Mill, and his son John Stuart Mill (ibid.: ch. 7). Marx saw himself as heir to this tradition, synthesizing it with the dialectical philosophy of Hegel and with French St Simonian socialism, and indeed 'political economy' is sometimes used as virtually a synonym for Marxism.

---

[3] Tony Blair has emphasized this theme consistently from his celebrated early interventions as Shadow Home Secretary in 1993 (e.g. Blair 1993). As David Downes and Rod Morgan have shown in their chapter on the politics of law and order (Chapter 9, this volume), he had identified an emphasis on economic structural causes of crime as one of the electoral 'hostages to fortune' offered by 'Old Labour'.

[4] I would echo in reverse the qualifying warning by Max Weber in his account of the role of religious and ethical factors in the rise of capitalism. He stressed that he was accentuating 'only one side of the causal chain' in his emphasis on the idealist sources of economic change. He acknowledged 'the fundamental importance of the economic factor . . . But at the same time the opposite correlation must not be left out of consideration' (Weber 1903/1992: 26–7). Similarly in this chapter the concentration on the economic is not intended to downplay the significance of other dimensions.

'Economics' grew out of political economy in the late nineteenth century as a distinct discipline focusing on the economic in abstraction from these wider dimensions.[5] There was a parallel emergence of other social science disciplines out of the broad discourses of political economy and philosophy: political science, sociology, psychology— and indeed criminology. This was interrelated with the growing separation between what came to be seen as different social and institutional fields. Liberal capitalism was characterized by ideal and to some extent actual distinctions between the spheres of the 'private' and 'public'; 'civil society' and 'the state'; 'the economy' and 'the polity'; 'criminal' and 'civil' law, each constituted and studied by an autonomous discipline (Neocleous 2000: 13–14; Lea 2002: chs. 1–3).

POLITICAL ECONOMY AS 'FULLY SOCIAL THEORY'

The most explicit exposition in criminology of the formal elements of a perspective rooted in political economy is the sketch of 'a fully social theory of deviance' in *The New Criminology* (Taylor, Walton, and Young 1973: 268–80). This was explicitly intended as 'a political economy of criminal action, and of the reaction it excites', together with 'a politically informed social psychology of these ongoing social dynamics' (ibid.: 279). It was an attempt 'to move criminology out of its imprisonment in artificially segregated specifics . . . to bring the parts together again in order to form the whole' (ibid.). Specifically it postulated that a 'fully social theory' must satisfy seven formal requirements. It must include analysis of:

> 1) The wider origins of the deviant act . . . what might be called *a political economy of crime* . . . 2) Immediate origins of the deviant act . . . a *social psychology of crime* . . . 3) The actual act . . . 4) Immediate origins of social reaction . . . a *social psychology of social reaction* . . . 5) Wider origins of social reaction . . . a *political economy of social reaction* . . . 6) The outcome of the social reaction on deviant's further action . . . 7) The nature of the deviant process as a whole [ibid.: 270–8].

Probably the closest attempt to incorporate all these elements into the study of one specific phenomenon was the magisterial study of mugging and the reaction to it by Stuart Hall and his associates, *Policing the Crisis* (Hall *et al.* 1978).[6] Starting from a particular robbery in Birmingham, and the sentencing of its perpetrators the book analysed the mass media construction of a 'moral panic' about 'mugging', and police responses to this. It then proceeded to a wide-ranging account of British economic, political, social, and cultural history since the Second World War to explain the deeper concerns that 'mugging' condensed. The later chapters offered an account of the impact of transformations in the political economy on black young men in particular, and how

---

[5] The label 'economics' now refers primarily to a supposedly apolitical, value-free, 'scientific' enterprise, analysing the 'economic' using primarily mathematical models based on particular axioms about human motivation, decision-making processes, and forms of social organization of a highly abstract and simplified kind.

[6] This has been acknowledged recently by one of the authors of *Policing the Crisis* (Jefferson 2004: 30–1).

this structured the formation of specific subcultures in which robbery was more likely to be perpetrated. Altogether, *Policing the Crisis* remains a uniquely ambitious attempt to synthesize macro-, middle-range and micro-analysis of a particular offence and the reaction to it, embodying all the facets of political economy as 'fully social theory'.

Most research studies inevitably focus on a narrower range of phenomena or policy issues, using more limited methodological tools and explanatory variables. But the value of the checklist of elements for a 'fully social theory' is to be a constant reminder of the wider contexts in which particular aspects of deviance and control are embedded, and their mediations and interrelationships. Even so the framework can be criticized for not including enough. Despite its emphasis on the need for social psychology as well as political economy, it has been argued that it remains a fundamentally structuralist perspective, precluding adequate exploration of the psychodynamics of crime and control (Jefferson 2004: 31). Despite recognizing the need to incorporate analysis of the dynamics of deviant acts themselves, it brackets off the existentialist appreciation of 'the seductions of crime' from the perspective of offenders (Katz 1988; Ruggiero 2000; Ferrell *et al.* 2004), and more generally downplays cultural, interpretive, and symbolic dimensions (Nelken 1994).[7] Furthermore, it does not explicitly relate to crime control policy issues, the basis of the subsequent 'Left Realist' auto-critique (Taylor 1981; Lea and Young 1984).

These critiques, however, have now in turn produced an unjustifiable neglect of structural and macro-social dimensions of crime and control. The pincer pressures of the Realist and the interpretive turns have squeezed out recognition of the significance of the political economy as a key to understanding crime and control (Currie 1997: 147–51; Hall and Winlow 2003, 2004). Re-emphasizing the importance of the economic, as this chapter does, is not intended to encourage a reverse one-sided accentuation. But it is intended to show that without the holistic sensibility that political economy connotes it is impossible to explain patterns and trends in crime and control.

The next part of the chapter will review the fluctuating influence of political economy on criminological theorizing. The third section examines the empirical, primarily econometric, literature on the role of economic factors in explaining crime and criminal justice. As argued earlier, whilst not neglecting these variables, political economy sees them within a wider political, social, and cultural context. How do different kinds of political economy in their routine as opposed to pathological functioning impact on crime and criminal justice? This will be considered in the fourth section of this chapter, which will show how different types of political economy are related to comparative and historical variations in crime and criminal justice across space and time. Finally, the conclusion will assess the significance of political economy for understanding crime and control.

---

[7] It is precisely this combination of the structural and the cultural that one of the authors of *The New Criminology* called for in the pithy title of a recent article, 'Merton With Energy, Katz With Structure' (Young 2003b).

POLITICAL ECONOMY AND CRIMINOLOGICAL THEORY

This section will review the influence of political economy in the history of criminological theory. Whilst there have been key stages in which political economy played a major role in attempts to theorize crime and criminal justice, there have also been long periods when its role has been denied or marginalized.

THE SCIENCE OF POLICE AND THE DAWN OF CRIMINOLOGY

The standard account of the history of criminology sees its origins in the 'classical' perspective associated with Beccaria's 1764 book *Dei Delitti e Delle Pene*, and its profound influence, via Blackstone, Bentham, and others, on the Enlightenment movements for reform of criminal law and punishment (Mannheim 1960; Taylor, Walton, and Young 1973: ch.1; Vold *et al.* 1998: ch. 2). This picture has been questioned by recent historical research on the intellectual history of criminology (See Rock, Chapter 1, in this volume), and David Garland has called the application of the label 'criminology' to these eighteenth-century thinkers 'altogether misleading' (Garland 1985: 14–15, 2002: 7–25). Apart from anachronistic terminology—the word 'criminology' was only coined in the late nineteenth century—it is argued that the 'classical' perspective did not concern itself much with aetiological questions, presuming a voluntaristic, rational, economic actor model of offenders. Beirne has shown that this was not true of Beccaria, who was strongly influenced by the emerging 'science of man' in the discussions of the philosophers and political economists of the Scottish Enlightenment, notably Hume, Adam Ferguson, and Adam Smith (Beirne 1991). This was a deterministic discourse concerned with explaining the causes of human conduct and society. Nonetheless, the primary focus of the classical school was not on the causation of crime but on its control by criminal law and justice.

Textbook histories of criminology usually neglect the relationship between political economy and Enlightenment discussions of crime and criminal justice and political economy, reflected partly in the work of Beccaria.[8] Political economy was intertwined particularly with the 'science of police' that flourished in the eighteenth and early nineteenth centuries, but has been overlooked by criminologists until recently.[9] It is well known that the term 'police' originally had a much broader meaning, essentially

---

[8] Beccaria himself was appointed to a Chair of 'Political Economy and Science of Police' at Milan in 1768, where he delivered lectures on the 'Elements of Political Economy' (Pasquino 1978: 45).

[9] The main exception is Radzinowicz, who discussed it extensively in the third volume of his *History of the English Criminal Law* (Radzinowicz 1956). Originally rediscovered by Foucault and some of his followers in the late 1970s (Foucault 1977; Pasquino 1978), it has been increasingly influential in recent years, above all in Foucaultian discussions of 'governmentality' (Smart 1983; Burchell *et al.* 1991; Garland 1997; McMullen 1998) but more generally in attempts to reconnect criminology with broader issues of the state and political economy (Reiner 1988; Neocleous 2000; Garland 2001: 31–4; Dubber 2005; Zedner 2006a; Dubber and Valverde 2006).

coterminous with the internal policies of governments (Neocleous 2000: ch.1). What is less acknowledged is the intimate intertwining of 'police' and political economy. In his 1763 *Lectures on Justice, Police, Revenue and Arms* Adam Smith defined 'police' as 'the second general division of jurisprudence. The name is French, and is originally derived from the Greek "politeia" which properly signified the policy of civil government, but now it only means the regulation of the inferior parts of government, viz: cleanliness, security and cheapness of plenty' (cited in Radzinowicz 1956: 421).

The eighteenth-century 'science of police' was a vast body of work that flourished across Europe.[10] Its remit was correspondingly capacious, as summed up in the title of a 1760 treatise by von Justi, *Foundations of the Power and Happiness of States, or an Exhaustive Presentation of the Science of Public Police* (cited in Pasquino 1978: 44). Gradually this all-encompassing 'science' of happiness or 'police'came to be separated out into an array of distinct fields and disciplines, as liberalism sought to delimit the appropriate role of the state (Neocleous 2000: chs 2 and 3).

In England the leading exponent of the 'science of police' was the magistrate Patrick Colquhoun. Colquhoun is most commonly remembered as a precursor of the modern British police in the narrow post-1829 sense. However he wrote extensively on political economy, crime, and criminal justice,[11] and his work can be seen as a precursor of a 'fully social' criminology. Unlike the radical 1970s version of this, however, Colquhoun was a staunch conservative, both in his practice as a magistrate and as a political economist.

'Colquhoun's starting point is the insecurity of property' (Neocleous 2000: 49). Wealth depended on labour, but the maintenance of incentives to labour required that the working class remained poor, creating a perennial problem of order (Colquhoun 1806: 7–8). The task of police 'is to prevent the poverty-stricken class from becoming a criminalized and pauperised rabble' (ibid.). To achieve this police (in the widest sense) had to be both tough and smart on crime, *and* on the (multi-layered) causes of crime.

To Colquhoun crime and criminal justice were not independent phenomena that could be considered in isolation from broader issues of social and economic structure. Colquhoun was engaged not in criminology or economics as autonomous disciplines, but political economy and the 'science of police', which embraced the totality of social and cultural relations. His proposals for the prevention and control of crime were rooted in empirical investigation of crime patterns. Colquhoun's analysis located the ultimate causes of crime in the overall structure of economy and society, but he was concerned to trace down the social and cultural mediations generating criminality and conformity. Crime was 'the constant and never-failing attendant on the accumulation of wealth', providing the opportunities and temptations for misappropriation (*Treatise*

[10] Pasquino cites a bibliography that lists 'for German-speaking lands alone and within the period from the start of the 17th century to the end of the 18th, no fewer than 3,215 titles under the heading "Science of police in the strict sense"' (Pasquino 1978: 48). More recently it has been claimed that there are around 14,000 tracts emanating from the associated school of 'cameralism' (Neocleous 2000: 12).

[11] His main books were *A Treatise on the Police of the Metropolis* (1796) and *A Treatise on Indigence* (1806), both of which went through several editions, as well as numerous other works on police and political economy.

on the Commerce and Police of the River Thames, 1800: 155–6). Crime (mainly theft) was attributable to the poor, but not all the poor. Colquhoun saw a crucial distinction between poverty and indigence (Neocleous 2000: 49–56). Poverty did not determine crime, and was inevitable and indeed beneficial (as the crucial incentive for labour). The 'evil' was indigence—the inability or unwillingness to labour in order to relieve poverty (Colquhoun 1806: 7–8).

The task of analysis and control or 'police' was to minimize indigence. Indigence arose for both structural and cultural reasons. Structural factors included variations in the opportunities for training available to different ethnic groups (such as Ashkenazi as distinct from Sephardi Jews, according to Colquhoun, cf. Radzinowicz 1956: 273–4), and downturns in the economic cycle. But cultural and informal moral controls (such as religion and the promotion of uplifting rather than 'bawdy' forms of popular pastimes) were also important to encourage 'manners' that were 'virtuous' rather than 'depraved'.

The reform of formal policing arrangements for which Colquhoun is best known was only a relatively minor aspect of the policies required to prevent crime. Effective deterrence by regular police patrol was important, and certainly more effective than harsh punishment.[12] Even the operation of formal policing was primarily important in symbolic and cultural rather than instrumental, utilitarian terms. The beneficial effects of police patrol were more to encourage moral discipline than to deter or catch perpetrators. Its terrain was to be 'upon the broad scale of General Prevention—mild in its operations—effective in its results; having justice and humanity for its basis, and the general security of the State and Individuals for its ultimate object' (Colquhoun 1800: 38).

Overall the analysis of security, order, crime, and policing advanced by Colquhoun and the 'science of police' were more sensitive to the interplay of politics, law, and justice with criminality than the later nineteenth-century 'science of the criminal'. As with the contemporaneous displacement of political economy by economics, the apparent gain in 'scientific' rigour was bought at a high price in terms of the obscuring of the political, economic, and ethical dimensions of crime and welfare.

POLITICAL ECONOMY AND POSITIVIST CRIMINOLOGY

The term 'positivism' in histories of criminological theory is used to refer to the project of seeking causal explanations of crime on the methodological and logical model attributed to the natural sciences. As a specific and self-conscious movement,

---

[12] In emphasizing certainty rather than severity of punishment as crucial, Colquhoun was of course following in the footsteps of Beccaria, but his original contribution was the prioritization of policing. As he put it, 'security does not proceed from *severe punishments* .... It is to be attributed to a more correct and energetic system of Police, joined to an early attention to the education and morals of the lower orders of the people; aided by a system of industry and sobriety' (Colquhoun 1796: 94–5). In short, crime control required appropriate management of the political economy, informal social controls, and preventive policing, with criminal justice operating only to deal with the failures of these policies.

positivism is associated with Lombroso and his influence in the last quarter of the nineteenth century, but the broad quest to analyse crime causally had already existed for some time in a diversity of forms (Garland 1985, 2002). The Lombrosian school primarily emphasized individual constitutional factors, although social and economic aspects were also considered, above all by Ferri (Taylor 1997: 272–3). But the most significant pioneers of the exploration of economic dimensions of crime were the 'moral statisticians' of the early nineteenth century (Morris 1957: ch. 3; Rock, Chapter 1, this volume).

The moral statisticians

The acknowledged pioneers of sociological criminology were Andre-Michel Guerry and Adolphe Quetelet, who took advantage of the development of national crime statistics in France in the 1820s to explore the contours of criminality. They anticipated many of the patterns and complexities subsequently found in the later econometric studies that will be reviewed in the next section. Guerry found, for example, that contrary to the common belief that poverty was associated with crime, there were higher rates of property crime (but not violence) in wealthier regions of France. He attributed this to an opportunity effect—there was more to steal in richer areas by the poor within them.

This was confirmed by Quetelet's later more detailed analysis of the new crime statistics (Vold *et al.* 1998: 30). He showed that the young, male, poor, unemployed, and uneducated were more likely to commit offences—but in places where there were more wealthy people to steal from. In his analysis crime was a function both of social pressures stemming from inequality *and* of the distribution of targets and temptations.

The most fundamental discovery made by Quetelet was the relative constancy of the rates and patterns of crime (and many other social phenomena) over substantial periods of time. Quetelet has been widely attacked for his supposed ultra-rigid determinism. Certainly he made remarks that invited such criticism. Perhaps the best known was his claim to be 'able to enumerate in advance how many individuals will stain their hands with the blood of their fellow creatures, how many will be forgers, how many poisoners' (cited in Beirne 1993: 90–1). But he intended only to offer descriptions of social patterns that were probabilistically, not inevitably, related to individual actions.[13] He regarded crime as fundamentally a function of morality, but social factors such as lack of education or poverty made immoral decisions more likely, because they increased temptations and impeded the development of a prudent character. Overall the explorations of the 'moral statisticians' paved the way for the much more elaborate analyses of subsequent positivist sociological criminology, above all the theory of anomie as developed by Merton.

---

[13] As Jock Young has noted recently, Quetelet was also well aware of the problem of the 'dark figure' of unrecorded crime, although he was unjustifiably confident that it was a constant ratio to the recorded figure (Young 2004: 17–18).

Anomie theory

Merton's anomie theory is the most influential and cogent formulation of a political economy of crime outside the Marxist tradition (for a fuller account of its sources and influence see, Rock, Chapter 1, this volume). Merton adopted the concept of anomic from Durkheim's 1897 book *Suicide*. Durkheim suggested that healthy societies require effective cultural definition and regulation of people's aspirations (which are otherwise potentially insatiable). Rapid social change dislocated such controls, producing anomie, characterized by restlessness, dissatisfaction, agitation, and other maladies conducive to suicide and other deviance. Amongst the key sources of this, argued Durkheim, was the economic cycle. Both economic downturns *and* upturns can disrupt the regulation of aspirations and produce anomie.

Merton's theory picked up on this analysis in a brief but seminal article, originally published in 1938, offering a framework for explaining variations in deviance between and within societies (Merton 1957). Despite the huge secondary literature it has generated, and the ritual slaying of Merton's analysis (arguably misrepresented, cf. Reiner 1984) in countless textbooks and exam answers over the decades, Merton remains the (often unacknowledged) paradigm for a structural social theory of crime (Lea and Young 1984: 218–25; Messner and Rosenfeld 2001; Young 2003b; Downes and Rock 2003: ch. 5).

Most accounts of Merton's analysis of anomie represent it as 'strain' theory. They focus on one aspect of his paper: the argument that a society combining *cultural* encouragement of common material aspirations by a mythology of meritocracy, and a *structural* reality of unequal opportunities, generates anomic pressures, leading to a variety of deviant reactions. Contemporary American versions frequently reduce Merton's structural political economy to a social psychology of deviance, attributing it to a psychic gap between individual aspirations and achievement (Agnew 1992; Walsh 2000). Merton's analysis was only partly directed at explaining the individual or even subcultural pattern of deviance within a society, although his typology of possible reactions to societal anomic pressure is probably the most frequently reproduced section of his paper (Merton 1957: 140). This aspect was also most influential in policy terms, leading—via Cloward and Ohlin's development of the concept of opportunity structures—to some of the 'Great Society' programmes of the early 1960s (Cloward and Ohlin 1960; Taylor 1997: 276–8).

Merton's analysis of anomie as an explanation of intra-societal variations in crime was only part of a broader account aimed at understanding differences between societies. Anomie arose not only from a strain between culturally prescribed goals and structurally limited legitimate means to fulfil them. Anomie was also a consequence of the nature of the goals encouraged by particular cultures. A highly materialistic culture—especially one that defines success almost exclusively in monetary terms[14] (like the USA)—is prone to anomie, and hence to crime at *all* levels, not just among the

[14] Money as a definer of success is 'indefinite and relative' (Merton 1957: 136), and hence ipso facto liable to generate anomie.

relatively deprived lower classes. This is especially so if the goals of material attainment are extolled at the expense of consideration of the legitimacy of the means used to attain them.

Merton is a paradigm for a political economy of crime, suggesting links between a materialistic culture and overall problems of moral regulation. He also sketches how different tendencies to deviance can arise within a society in relation to the distribution of legitimate opportunities. But it is not an economically determinist account. It is not inequality or deprivation per se that generate anomie and deviance. The cultural significance these material factors have in different social settings is crucial to how they are experienced. The brief typology of possible reactions also points to many other factors mediating between structural pressure and human reaction. The informal moral controls in particular cultures are significant, for example, as shown in Merton's account of 'ritualism'.

For all its strengths, however, Merton's theory has been rather out of fashion in recent decades. Its social democratic critique of unbridled capitalism made him too 'cautious' a rebel for the radical criminology of the 1960s/1970s (Taylor, Walton, and Young 1973: 101), and too radical for post-1980s neo-liberal triumphalism.[15]

Political economy and realism

Since the mid-1970s mainstream criminology, especially in the USA, has been increasingly dominated by administrative realism, concerned with 'what works?' in terms of immediately practicable policies. This was initially predicated on an explicit rejection of 'root cause' theories such as Merton's that sought to explain crime by macro-social causes (Wilson 1975: xv). Causal explanation was not eschewed altogether, but it has been pursued at individual[16] (Wilson and Herrnstein 1985), situational, or community levels. These are more amenable to policy interventions that do not raise questions of wider social justice or reform. Whilst realism has largely ousted political economy, paradoxically it has been associated with a resurgence of studies of the economics of crime, starting with the influential work of Becker and Ehrlich mentioned earlier. There has also been a broader revival of neo-classical perspectives based on an 'economic man' model of the offender, such as rational choice theory (Zedner 2006b; Rock, Chapter 1, this volume).

POLITICAL ECONOMY AND RADICAL CRIMINOLOGY

Marx, crime, and law

Until the flowering of radical criminology in the 1960s and 1970s little systematic attention was given by Marxists or others on the Left to crime or criminal justice. Marx and Engels themselves wrote little specifically on crime (Taylor, Walton, and Young 1973: ch. 7).

---

[15] His analysis is also too structuralist for postmodernists or Foucaultians!

[16] Wright and Miller (1998) documents the increasing eclipse of social by individualist explanations in criminology journal articles during the late 1980s and 1990s.

Attempts to reconstruct their views on crime are based on collecting scattered remarks from Marx's early works or journalistic writings (ibid.). Critics have dismissed Marx's analysis as simple economic determinism, mainly by extrapolation from (mis?)interpretations of his general theoretical framework (ibid.: fn. 3).[17] This has been countered by arguments that stressed Marx's humanism (mainly from his early work), and the attention he gave to ideology and to the autonomy of human action within structured limits (ibid.: 216–21). It is of course possible to construct several alternative readings of Marx's voluminous corpus of work, and, given its political significance, all interpretations are highly contested (Reiner 2002: 239–52).

It is widely stated that in his mature theoretical work Marx did not systematically address issues of law, crime, or criminal justice. Chapter 10 of *Capital*, however, is a lengthy historical analysis of the emergence of the Factory Acts in early nineteenth-century England (Marx 1867/1976: ch. 10). It constitutes a pioneering case study of criminalization and of what would nowadays be called corporate crime[18] (see Nelken, Chapter 22, this volume). It is an early example of a political economy of a particular kind of crime, adopting many elements of a 'fully social' theory. Marx's account is very far from the economic determinism attributed to him, and gives weight to both structure and action, in complex interaction (for a fuller analysis see Reiner 2002: 240–6).

The emergence of the Factory Acts presented something of a puzzle to Marx (as did the Welfare State more generally for later generations of Marxists). How could legislation that restricts the autonomy of manufacturers be passed by a state that was not only rhetorically 'a committee for managing the common affairs of the whole bourgeoisie', as the 1848 *Communist Manifesto* had claimed (Marx and Engels 1848/1998: 37), but also some decades away from even the beginning of working-class enfranchisement? Marx starts his explanation with structuralist factors. Without external regulation competitive pressures constrained factory-owners to increase the hours and intensity of work by their employees, to a point that was beginning to threaten the long-term viability of the system of production as a whole. However benign or enlightened they might be individual capitalists could not introduce more humane conditions unilaterally, so legislation compelling them to do so on an equal footing was necessary for the social order.

The introduction of legislation also required effective human action. Marx shows the role of progressive factory-owners, workers themselves, and (once they were established) the Factory Inspectors in the formulation and enforcement of the new laws. At first legislation was symbolic rather than effective. Marx says of the Acts preceding the 1833 Factory Act that 'Parliament . . . was shrewd enough not to vote a penny for their compulsory implementation' (Marx 1867/1976: 390). He documented the subsequent

[17] Support for attributing to Marx an economic determinist theory of crime is also adduced from a newspaper article in which he cited approvingly the work of Quetelet as establishing a correlation between criminality and economic conditions (Taylor, Walton, and Young 1973: 215–17).

[18] Its specific subject matter, the creation and violation of laws regulating safety and other conditions of work, has of course been the basis for many important criminological studies more recently, notably Carson 1970, 1981; Slapper 1999; Wells 2001; Gobert and Punch 2003; Tombs 2004; Tombs and Whyte 2006).

ebb and flow of struggle by the Factory Inspectors to enforce the new 'law in the books' and ensure it became the 'law in action'. There was a continuous struggle between the Inspectors and deviant owners over avoidance devices introduced by the latter, stretching and testing the limits of the law. Marx traced this conflict up to the 1860s, showing how the extent of law-breaking, and the fluctuations in the strictness of case law and new legislation, were shaped by a complex interplay of shifting balances of economic and political forces (for example the split between the agricultural and manufacturing capitalists) and the success of human strategies within these changing structural pressures and opportunities.

Human actors operated within constraints that were shaped by histories and wider circumstances beyond their control, but could and did act in ways that could not be simply read off from an analysis of their structural position. Marx gave due credit, for example, to the efforts of more philanthropic capitalists, and to the 'bourgeois' Factory Inspectors (on whose Reports he heavily relied). Altogether, this long chapter is a significant but neglected early example of a political economy of crime and control.

Early twentieth-century radical criminology

Willem Bonger, a Dutch professor, made the first attempt to develop a systematic Marxist analysis of crime (Bonger 1916/1969). Bonger was in many ways an ethically inspiring figure, who pioneered many themes of subsequent radical (and indeed liberal) criminology (Cohen 1998), but whose work has usually been treated harshly, not least by later radical criminologists (Taylor, Walton, and Young 1973: 222–36 for example). This fails to give Bonger his due as a pioneer of the political economy of crime and control.

In Bonger's analysis the structure of capitalism generates particular criminogenic pressures and conflicts. In common with Marxism in general he has been accused of economic determinism, but his attempt to spell out the mediating links between structural roots and criminal acts is complex, and allowed scope for individual autonomy and moral responsibility. To Bonger the main way in which capitalism was related to crime was through the stimulation of a moral climate of egoism, at all levels of society. This enhanced the material aspirations of workers and the poor, and weakened their internal controls against predation in times of hardship.

In terms that anticipated Merton's analysis of anomie, Bonger talked of the stimulation of material desires by modern marketing and retail methods, so that 'the cupidity of the crowd is highly excited' (Bonger 1916/1969: 108). This explained not only proletarian crime but also crimes of the powerful. The egoism engendered by capitalism was particularly virulent higher up the social scale, so that 'although cupidity is a strong motive with all classes of our present society, it is especially so among the bourgeoisie, as a consequence of their position in the economic life' (ibid.: 138).

Bonger recognized a complex multiplicity of linkages between the structural conflicts of capitalism, with its general egoism, and particular forms of crime. He acknowledged for example the need to analyse internalized controls as a factor preventing offending in the face of motives for crime generated by the egoistic culture

(Bonger 1916/1969: 401). He also saw the problem of understanding the immediate situation and process of criminal action, not just its antecedent precipitating factors (ibid.). Determinism was probabilistic rather than absolute. The wider or immediate causes of crime in the larger immorality and injustices of capitalism did not remove the moral accountability of offenders (Bonger 1935: 23). Individual psychology as well as contingent factors such as suddenly occurring temptations had also to be considered (Bonger 1916/1969: 36). For recognizing the complexity of causal webs and relations leading to crime Bonger has been accused of 'eclecticism' (Taylor, Walton, and Young 1973: 227–8). However, it is difficult to see how to draw a principled line between 'eclecticism' and the checklist of elements of a 'fully social' theory of deviance, most of which Bonger seems to have been aware of.

Bonger introduced many ideas that were explored much further in later criminology, especially its more critical variants. He recognized that legal conceptions of crime reflected disproportionately the interests of the powerful, anticipating subsequent labelling theory.[19] But whilst acknowledging that class and power influenced the content and operation of the legal system, he nonetheless saw that it contributed to the maintenance of order in general, which benefited all classes. Whilst some aspects of law were controversial, and its enforcement might sometimes be seen as biased, most criminal law had the moral approval of the population. For accepting the moral condemnation of the harms inflicted by much crime Bonger was castigated by later 'Left idealist' radical criminologists, paradoxically for 'idealist' (i.e. morally based) socialism (Taylor, Walton, and Young 1973: 232, 235). They attribute to him (as to Marx and Engels) a 'correctionalist' bourgeois distaste for disorder, and a failure to 'appreciate' crime as diversity (ibid.: 232–3). In many ways, however, Bonger anticipated the arguments of the subsequent auto-critique by these writers when they espoused 'Left Realism' in the 1980s (Cohen 1998: 125–6). Not only did he acknowledge the harm done by much conventional crime, he also saw it as particularly inflicting pain on the least powerful.[20]

The other significant contribution to political economy by early twentieth-century radical criminology was Rusche and Kirchheimer's historical study of punishment (Rusche and Kirchheimer 1939). Two of the Frankfurt School refugees from Nazism who came to the USA in the late 1930s, Rusche and Kirchheimer published *Punishment and Social Structure* in 1939. The book was largely neglected for some thirty years. Republished in 1968, in an era of efflorescence for critical criminology, it 'formed the inspiration for a growing literature on economics, crime, and punishment'[21] (Garland 1990: 106). The book was a long-term historical analysis of trends in punishment since the early medieval period. It attempted to demonstrate that the development of penal measures was shaped above all by changes in the mode of production, in particular fluctuations in the supply of and demand for labour power. The general model of

---

[19] 'Penal law has been principally constituted according to the will of the [ruling class]' (Bonger 1916/1969: 24).

[20] For his recognition of the oppression of women see Bonger 1916/1969: 58–60. He was also sensitive to the prevalent persecution of gay people and ethnic minorities, cf. Bemmelen 1960.

[21] Examples include Platt and Takagi 1980, and Melossi and Pavarini 1981.

applying Marxist political economy to the explanation of crime and criminal justice was hugely influential, especially in the 1970s and 1980s.

Subsequent scholars, whether working within this broad tradition or critical of it, have qualified Rusche and Kirchheimer's account in two main ways. Empirically their history has been subject to detailed critique and qualification. Theoretically it has been attacked for excessive economic determinism. Although Rusche and Kirchheimer recognized the role of cultural, political, and other factors, it was left to later studies to spell these out in much more elaborate detail, considerably qualifying the economism of their account.[22]

Political economy and critical criminology

Political economy had a central but fluctuating place in the critical criminologies that began to flourish in the 1960s.[23] The labelling theory that developed in the early 1960s owed much more to symbolic interactionism and other micro-sociologies than to political economy (Downes and Rock 2007: ch. 7; Rock, Chapter 1, this volume). But labelling theorists did explore how the structurally patterned play of power and advantage shaped the emergence and enforcement of criminal law and other definitions of deviance (Becker 1963; Stinchcombe 1963; Piliavin and Briar 1964; Chapman 1968).

Political economy assumed a central position with the Marxist-influenced radical criminologies that became prominent in the early 1970s, above all the 1973 book *The New Criminology*, with its conception of a 'fully social' theory of crime as discussed above (Taylor, Walton, and Young, op. cit.). The 'Left Realist' auto-critique that some of these radical criminologists offered in the 1980s explicitly distanced itself from straightforward economic analyses of crime (Lea and Young 1984: ch. 3). These economic models were associated with a supposed 'aetiological crisis' of radical criminology, as the reductions in poverty and unemployment associated with the post-war Keynesian Welfare State failed to stop crime from rising (Young 1986). The Left Realist emphasis was on the need for and possibility of immediate steps to control crime in the shape of more effective policing and criminal justice, not the 'root causes' approach attributed to earlier 'left idealism'.

Nonetheless, in so far as Left Realists concerned themselves with crime causation, this was largely by incorporating into their analyses earlier political economy perspectives such as relative deprivation and anomie, even if the origin of these ideas was scarcely acknowledged (e.g. Lea and Young 1984: ch. 6). In the 1990s the erstwhile 'Left Realists' moved back to more macro-analyses of the relationship between crime, criminal justice, and late modernity or market society (Young 1999; Taylor 1999), in combination with cultural analysis (see Hayward and Young on cultural criminology, Chapter 4, this volume). These and other attempts to develop a political economy of contemporary trends in crime and control will be considered in the fourth section of

---

[22] A comprehensive but judicious exposition and critique of Rusche and Kirchheimer can be found in Garland 1990: ch. 4. Examples of later research that qualifies their heavily economistic Marxism are Thompson 1975; Hay *et al.* 1975; Ignatieff 1978; Cohen and Scull 1983.

[23] For historical accounts see Cohen 1988; Young 1988; Downes and Rock 2007: ch.10.

this chapter . First, however, the next section will review the empirical evidence about the role of economic factors in explaining crime.

ECONOMIC FACTORS AND CRIME: WHAT IS THE EMPIRICAL EVIDENCE?

CRIME AND ECONOMY: A COMPLEX CONNECTION

As the above review showed, the idea of an association between economic conditions and crime is embedded deeply in our culture and also in the history of criminology more specifically. At a straightforward empirical level it is amply indicated by official statistics and surveys on patterns of formally labelled offending and victimisation (see chapters by Maguire on official statistics, and Hoyle and Zedner on victims, Chapters 10 and 15, respectively, in this volume). As Braithwaite's 1979 review of the self-report studies concluded, 'lower-class adults commit those types of crime which are handled by the police at a higher rate than middle-class adults', and the same applies to juveniles[24] (Braithwaite 1979: 62). This is true a fortiori of those who are processed by the criminal justice system as offenders, as summed up sharply in the title of Jeffrey Reiman's critical text—*The Rich Get Richer and the Poor Get Prison* (Reiman 2004).

However, in recent decades it has become fashionable to play down the role of the political economy in explaining crime. The dominant trend, on the political left and the right, in the worlds of criminological research and in policy and politics, has been 'Realism'— what works? 'What is to be done?' is Realism's key question (a faintly ironic echo of Lenin surviving in the political discourse of market societies). Left Realists emphasize the value (or at any rate, potential) of criminal justice and policing in delivering security *now*, whilst not denying altogether the significance of the political economy. Realists of the Right sought to banish political economy from discussion of crime policy. Throughout the 1980s Margaret Thatcher's government vehemently denied Labour allegations that their neo-liberal economic policies stoked the pressures generating crime, above all attacking the view that crime was due to unemployment (Downes and Morgan, Chapter 9, this volume). If there was no such thing as society, it certainly could not be an explanation of crime. The paradox is that this turn away from political economy coincided with the emergence of the strongest evidence of precisely such connections.

As the earlier discussion of the nineteenth-century 'moral statisticians' indicated, there is a long history of attempts to test empirically the notions that economic

---

[24] Braithwaite's caveat is of course vitally important. By definition this pattern of greater 'lower-class' crime or punishment is not true of corporate or state crime, but these 'crimes of the powerful' are notoriously unrecorded and unsanctioned by the criminal justice system (Slapper and Tombs 1999; Green and Ward 2004; Gobert and Punch 2003, 2006; Hillyard *et al.* 2004; Nelken, Chapter 22, this volume). The differential treatment accorded to tax and social security fraud is a prime example, cf. Cook 1989, 2006.

variables are related to crime. Theoretically there are many ways in which economic factors might be expected to impact on crime. However the empirical literature has been far from conclusive in its attempts to test these.

A priori, economic factors might be expected to impact on crime in a variety of ways, as the review of the history of theoretical perspectives implied. For a crime to occur there are several logically necessary preconditions, which can be identified as: labelling, motive, means, opportunity, and the absence of control (Reiner 2000: 79–80). Economic factors are potentially relevant to all of these.

1. *Labelling.* As 'labelling theory' re-emphasized in the 1960s, acts and actors that might be regarded as harmful, immoral, or antisocial are not necessarily seen as deviant or criminal. To become part of the apparent problem of crime requires a process of 'labelling'. Labelling processes are contingent and fluctuating. Legal categories of crime change and evolve: acts are criminalized and de-criminalized. Only a small and unrepresentative sample of all acts or actors that could be treated as criminal end up being recorded as such in any type of criminal statistics or subject to criminal justice processing of any sort.

Economic factors shape these labelling processes at all levels. Studies of the emergence of criminal law have accorded significant weight to changes in the political economy (e.g. Marx's (1867/1976), and Carson's (1981), analyses of the Factory Acts cited earlier; the studies collected in Chambliss 1969; Chambliss and Mankoff 1975). Fluctuations in the propensity of victims to report crimes, and/or the police to record them, are also influenced by economic factors, such as the proliferation of high-value stealable consumer goods and insurance cover for them, or the impact of managerial performance management in policing (Reiner 1996). The application of criminal labels to individuals is patterned by police deployment strategies and enforcement decisions. In turn these are influenced by perceptions of particular (usually poorer) areas as high crime hotspots, or stereotypes of particular groups (usually low in power and advantage) as likely offenders—'police property' (Stinchcombe 1963; Chapman 1968; Lee 1983). The official labelling of crimes and criminals which underpins the apparent problem of crime is thus shaped in part by political economy.

2. *Motive.* A crime will not occur unless there is someone motivated to commit it. Most criminological theories have been directed at uncovering the sources of motivations tempting, seducing, or driving people to commit crimes, whether within the individual offender or their social position. Economic factors have been emphasized by most sociological and social psychological analyses of criminal motivation. Anomie theory, discussed earlier, is probably the most influential sociological attempt to explain the sources of criminal motivation, and centres on the significance of economic aspirations and strains. Developmental theories also identify economic variables such as poverty, unemployment, and relative deprivation as risk factors precipitating individuals towards criminal motivations, in conjunction with other aspects of family context and socialization (Farrington, Chapter 19, this volume).

Although in the 1980s neo-liberals such as Mrs Thatcher denied a link between economic conditions and crime, it is a straightforward inference of neo-classical economic theory that economic fluctuations affect the perceived costs and benefits of legitimate as compared with illegitimate actions (Becker 1968; Fielding, Clarke, and Witt 2000: 1–14 and Part I). An unemployed person dependent on benefits, for example, will[25] find the relative rewards of illegitimate activity higher than someone earning legitimate wages, and, especially when legitimate work opportunities are restricted by recession, will find the costs of acquiring a criminal record lower. From the point of view of conventional economic analysis, a utility-maximizing rational economic actor will commit crimes if the reward is higher than available legitimate wages, so crime should fluctuate with the buoyancy of labour markets (Grogger 2000: 268–73). Although in economic theory (as in classical 'criminology') offenders are not presumed to have different motivations from the law-abiding, it is their changing economic circumstances that determine whether people will be motivated to commit crimes or not.

3. *Means.* The capacity to commit crimes of various types will be affected by economic developments. The availability of illegal markets for stolen goods, and the shifting attractiveness of different goods on them, will structure changes in crime patterns (Sutton 1998; Sutton *et al.* 2001; Fitzgerald *et al.* 2003; Hallsworth 2005: 112). Changes in the labour market also affect the capacity to commit offences. Unemployment may affect crime in various ways, but one is the time and idle pair of hands it provides for the Devil, as conveyed by the old adage. Conversely, different types of employment offer varying means for the commission of crimes at work. Prosperity increases the means to purchase and consume socially the intoxicating drink and drugs that fuel fights (Field 1990).

4. *Opportunity.* The availability of targets for crime is affected by economic development. The proliferation of valuable and easily stolen consumer goods—cars, videos, mobile phones, etc.—since the mid-1950s has often been seen as a key factor in the growth of crime. Field for example has shown that 'thefts and burglaries are both linked to the stock of crime opportunities, represented by the sum of real consumer expenditure . . . For every 1 per cent increase in this stock, burglary and theft have increased by about 2%' (Field 1999: 7). Economic development also changes the 'routine activities' of different groups, shifting their vulnerability to victimization (Felson 1994). For example, 'when people have money, they tend to spend more time away from their homes earning and spending, increasing the vulnerability of persons and property to crime' (Field 1999: 3). In these and other ways it is true in part that 'opportunity makes the thief' (Felson and Clarke 1998).

5. *Absence of controls.* A motivated offender with the means and opportunity to commit a labelled crime may still desist or be deterred because of internalized or

---

[25] One should add the conventional disclaimer in the economics literature, *ceteris paribus*. All other things are of course never equal, and different people faced with similar cost–benefit calculations about the rewards of offending will react differently for many reasons including an irreducible element of human autonomy.

informal controls, or external prospects of sanctioning. The occurrence of a crime requires the absence of effective controls, whether the 'inner police' of conscience (Eysenck 1965: 261, discussed by Hollin, Chapter 2, this volume), or the threat of external policing and punishment.

Economic factors affect the functioning of both informal and formal controls. Employment is amongst other things a direct and indirect form of discipline. Directly it limits the opportunity and temptation to commit offences (although it may also provide workplace opportunities). Indirectly it facilitates the possibility of effective education and of marriage, which are also important control factors (Willis 1977; Currie 1985, 1998a, 1998b; Campbell 1991). The availability, resourcing, deployment, and management of the formal controls of policing and punishment are also heavily influenced by economic factors, such as changes in the politics of public expenditure (McLaughlin *et al.* 2001).

CRIME AND ECONOMY: THE EMPIRICAL LITERATURE

In 1987 the late Steven Box published a seminal analysis of the relationships between 'recession, crime and punishment' (Box 1987). This was 14 years after the slump triggered by the 1973 oil crisis, and eight years on from Margaret Thatcher's enthusiastic espousal of monetarism, which produced huge increases in unemployment, inequality, and poverty, reversing the gains of the post-war decades (Box op. cit.: ch. 1).

Box provided a comprehensive review of econometric studies published up to the mid-1980s[26] that had sought to measure the impact of economic variables on crime (Box op. cit.: ch. 3). His literature search found 50 studies testing for relationships between unemployment and crime levels.[27] Simply taking all these studies at face value, there were 32 which found that higher unemployment was associated with more crime, while 18 found the opposite. This was the result that would be predicted by anomie theory, radical criminology, and neo-classical economics.

Unemployment increases the pressures and incentives motivating crime, in particular the property crimes that constitute the bulk of the officially recorded figures. But the scoreline was far from overwhelming! Those espousing theoretical perspectives making the opposite prediction, that recession reduces crime by decreasing the available targets of crime and increasing the number of unemployed 'guardians' staying at home (e.g. situational crime prevention and routine activities theories), could take some comfort from the fact that nearly half the studies went their way.

Box also highlights the methodological weaknesses of many of the studies. In particular several use measures of crime such as arrest or conviction rates that are even more problematic than the officially recorded crime rates with all their well-known

---

[26] The studies he reviews were published between 1963 and 1985.

[27] 18 were time-series analyses, looking at the relationship between measures of crime and unemployment over a number of years; 32 were cross-sectional studies, assessing whether there are associations between crime and unemployment levels in different places at a given time.

limitations[28]. There were also important conceptual and methodological issues concerning which variables should be controlled for in order to try and isolate the relationship between unemployment and crime, and what measures of unemployment were used (Box op. cit.: 90 2). Box further underlined the rather small relationship between unemployment and crime uncovered in most of the studies, in either direction, meaning that whilst on balance they provided some support for the hypothesis of a link, it was a weak one.[29] Box cited with approval the conclusion of a slightly earlier literature review by an American economist: 'despite differences and weaknesses among the studies, a general finding emerges: namely that rises in unemployment ... are connected with rises in the crime rate, but the effect tends to be modest and insufficient to explain the general upward trend of crime in the period studied' (Freeman 1983: 96).

Box also reviewed econometric studies probing links between income inequality[30] and crime levels (Box op. cit.: 86–90). Theoretically it would be expected that these variables were closely associated, because inequality would be likely to produce a sense of relative deprivation, motivating property crime in particular. Of the 17 studies[31] reviewed by Box, 12 reported a positive relationship between inequality and crime and five did not (Box op. cit.: 87). The five exceptions were all studies of homicide. There was unanimous support for the view that greater inequality was associated with more property crime.

Box also looked at one American longitudinal study of a cohort of boys born in 1945 (Thornberry and Christensen 1984). This found a clear link between periods of unemployment and greater levels of arrest for the boys. However, Box pointed out that this could be because the police were more likely to arrest them when they were unemployed. The boys' own self-reported offending was not clearly related to unemployment (Box op. cit.: 93–5). This was a disappointing finding, because cohort studies offer the potential for overcoming some of the problems of either time-series or cross-sectional aggregate studies: self-reported offending does not suffer from the reporting and recording issues bedevilling official statistics (though it has its own problems), and there is no need to control for other socio-economic variables that could affect both crime and unemployment as the same people are being studied throughout. It is thus important to note that a study based on the British Cambridge Study of Delinquent Development was published shortly before Box's book, but too late for its inclusion (Farrington et al. 1986). This showed that the boys in the sample did admit to committing more offences whilst unemployed, providing support for the standard hypothesis.

[28] Box op. cit.: 69–74. Only one of the 18 time-series studies used victimization data (Box op. cit.: 77–8).

[29] This is also the conclusion of another literature review published in an American journal in the same year as Box's book: Chiricos 1987.

[30] In econometric studies inequality is usually measured by the 'Gini coefficient'. This is based on calculating the proportion of total income earned by particular percentages of earners. Equality is defined as the situation where each percentage of income receivers gets the corresponding percentage of income, which on a diagram would be represented by a straight diagonal line. The Gini coefficient measures the deviation of the actual distribution from this.

[31] All but one of these were cross-sectional studies.

There are crucial limitations of all econometric studies from a criminological perspective that must be borne in mind in assessing their results. One is that the variables measured by econometricians have at best a rough and ready correspondence to the concepts in the criminological theories being tested. Unemployment or inequality rates, for example, may be related to anomie, but they are not direct measures of it. The social and psychological meaning of economic variables such as employment or income will vary according to different social, cultural, and individual circumstances and interpretations. At best econometrics can establish correlations between economic indicators and official crime measures (with all the pitfalls of these statistical indices), not causal relationships. Interpreting such associations as causal explanations requires assumptions about the direction of causality. More fundamentally, the relationships have to be 'adequate at the level of meaning' as Weber put it (Weber 1947/1964: 99–100). There have to be plausible narratives linking the variables as sequences of comprehensible human action.

It is important to note that the studies reviewed by Box were all carried out before the mid-1980s. The social character, meaning, and impact of such variables as unemployment and inequality changed fundamentally in the years immediately before Box's book, indeed that was what prompted him to write it (Box 1987: Preface). This means that the data for the studies he reviewed were gathered mainly in the post-Second World War decades of virtual full employment, during which unemployment would have been mainly transitional and voluntary. Theoretically there would be little reason to expect such unemployment to be associated with crime.

After 1973, however, the recession and the advent of monetarism resulted in long-term, sometimes permanent, exclusion from legitimate livelihoods of growing numbers of young men. The social impact and meaning of this, especially in an increasingly consumerist culture, is quite different from what unemployment represented in earlier decades. It signified a fatal combination of enhanced anomie and an erosion of the controls represented by legitimate work, and indeed marriage and family responsibilities (Campbell 1993; Currie 1998a, 1998b; Davies 1998). The changed meaning of unemployment after the mid-1970s would be expected to produce a closer association between unemployment and crime levels than in earlier decades.

This is confirmed by reviews of econometric research carried out more recently than Box's 1987 book (Marris 2000; Witt *et al.* 1999; Field 1999: Pt II; Kleck and Chiricos 2002; Deadman and Macdonald 2002; Hale 2005). Although most studies conducted since the 1980s *do* find positive relationships between higher unemployment and higher crime rates (especially property crime), the strength of the association remains fairly modest. In part this may be because measures of total unemployment continue to include both voluntary and involuntary unemployment. Robin Marris has tried to estimate the significance of this, by assuming that unemployment rates below 4 per cent mainly involve transitional, voluntary unemployment and only levels above 4 per cent signify involuntary unemployment. He demonstrates that there were very strong associations during the 1980s and early 1990s between burglary and *involuntary* unemployment (estimated by including only levels over 4 per cent: Marris 2000: 73–4).

Furthermore, unemployment statistics have become an *increasingly* problematic measure of levels of prosperity or economic hardship. Partly this is because official statistics on unemployment were considerably revised during the 1980s, as a result of the increasingly controversial increases in unemployment due to the Thatcher government's neo-liberal economic policies (Hale 2005: 332).

It has also been argued that unemployment fluctuations lag behind changes in economic conditions. In a recession, for example, earnings will begin to fall before employment statistics do, because of wage-cuts, reduced overtime, and greater resort to part-time work. These cuts in conditions will generate stronger incentives for property offending *before* unemployment begins to rise, dampening the apparent effect of subsequent rises in the unemployment statistics (Pyle and Deadman 1994).

Wider transformations in the structure of the labour market, associated with the change from Keynesian economic management to neo-liberalism, have also made unemployment statistics a less crucial measure of economic exclusion and relative deprivation. Chris Hale has demonstrated the criminogenic significance of the emergence of a 'dual labour market' since the 1970s (Hale 1999, 2005: 333–4). There is an increasing contrast between a *primary* or core sector of skilled workers, enjoying relative security, and buoyant earnings, benefits, and employment rights, and a *secondary*, peripheral sector—mainly in service industries—lacking these advantages. Employment in the peripheral sector is low skilled, unstable, insecure, poorly paid, and without employment rights and benefits. These 'McJobs' are much less likely to reduce crime in the way that work in the primary sector traditionally did. De-industrialization in the wake of neo-liberalism during the 1980s enormously increased the peripheral relative to the primary sector. This was associated with increasing crime rates, especially in economic downturns when earnings in the secondary sector are squeezed even more (Grogger 1998, 2000). Machin and Meghir have shown that declining wages for unskilled workers were associated with increasing property crime (Machin and Meghir 2003). Conversely, the introduction of the minimum wage in 1999 was followed by greater decreases in crime in areas with disproportionately high numbers of workers previously earning less than the minimum, who thus gained most from the new policy (Hansen and Machin 2003). Whilst the changing structure of the labour market explains much of the growth and fluctuations in crime, it also means that the division between unemployment and marginal employment in the secondary sector becomes less clear-cut and significant.

Another factor complicating the crime-unemployment relationship is the contradiction between the motivational and opportunity effects of economic prosperity or hardship (Cantor and Land 1985; Kleck and Chiricos 2002). Simon Field's work for the Home Office has shown that both are important, but in different ways (Field 1990, 1999; Dhiri *et al.* 1999). Analysing data between the Second World War and the late 1990s, Field found that the short term cyclical effects of economic change must be distinguished from the long-term consequences of economic growth. In the short run there is an inverse relationship between economic fluctuations[32] and property crime,[33] and hence recorded crime overall. In the long term, however, crime has increased as affluence has grown. This discrepancy was accounted for by the contradictory short- and long-run effects of prosperity. In the short term economic upturns reduce *motivations* for property crime. But the long-run result of affluence is the expansion of criminal opportunities (due to the proliferation of goods to steal and routine activity effects, such as fewer homes guarded during working hours or leisure time. Cf. Field 1999: 2–3).

It was noted earlier that Box's 1987 study already showed overwhelmingly strong evidence that greater inequality was related to more property and violent crime, but not homicide (Box 1987: 87). Since then there has continued to be a sharp increase in economic inequality, with the partial exception of the last few years in Britain as New Labour's measures targeted at the alleviation of child poverty have begun to take effect (Hills 2004; Hills and Stewart 2005). More recent studies, in Britain and the USA, have continued to confirm the strong association between inequality and crime (Hale 2005: 334–6).

A significant change, however, is that homicide is no longer an apparent exception. Studies in several countries show strong associations between greater inequality and more homicide (Beckett and Sasson 2000: 32–5; Dorling 2004; Wilkinson 2005: 47–51, ch. 5). The difference from the earlier period studied by Box is probably due to increases in the proportion of homicides involving poor young men as victims and perpetrators (Dorling 2004).

The clear conclusion indicated by a review of the econometric evidence is that there is a plethora of material confirming that crime of all kinds is linked to inequality, relative deprivation, and unemployment (especially if it is an index of long-term social exclusion).[34] The downplaying of economic 'strain' factors in criminal justice policy discourse since the 1970s was due to shifts in dominant political and intellectual perspectives, not evidence that there are no significant economic correlates—arguably 'root causes'(*pace* Wilson 1975)—of crime. Examination of the seminal work of Ehrlich, for example, shows this. In his 1970s papers that pioneered the revival of interest in the economics of crime, Ehrlich's data clearly showed strong associations between poverty, inequality, unemployment, and crime levels (Ehrlich 1973, 1975: 409–13).

---

[32] Field used the level of consumption expenditure as the main indicator of the business cycle. He found that unemployment was not associated with crime if consumption was taken into account (Field 1990: 7). This does not mean it was not associated with crime fluctuations, but that on his analysis it was only related to crime through its effects on consumption. Subsequent analyses of the time-series relationship between crime trends since the Second World War and economic variables, using different modelling techniques and assumptions, confirmed the link with consumption levels, but also found associations between crime and Gross Domestic Product and unemployment (Pyle and Deadman 1994; Hale 1998). Altogether this is a powerful body of evidence confirming the negative relationship between fluctuations in prosperity and property (and overall) crime levels.

[33] Field found a positive cyclical relationship between consumption and *violent* crime. He accounted for this by suggesting that in times of prosperity there is more socializing and alcohol consumption, leading to more fights between young men in pubs, etc. (the association with beer consumption in particular indicated this).

[34] This is also the conclusion reached in other recent overviews (Downes 2004; Garside 2004a; Hale 2005).

The emphasis on the significance of deterrence variables (probability and severity of sanctions) by Ehrlich himself and his primary audience of neo-liberals was because policing and punishment were seen as desirable and available policy levers, whilst the economic factors either could not or should not be reversed by government action.

POLITICAL ECONOMIES, CRIME, AND CRIMINAL JUSTICE: COMPARATIVE AND HISTORICAL PERSPECTIVES

The econometric evidence reviewed above focuses on the relationships between economic factors and crime within particular social orders. Ian Taylor pointed out in his chapter on 'Political Economy' in the first and second editions of *The Oxford Handbook of Criminology* that the econometric literature was primarily concerned with 'the causal relations between "economic crisis", "the business cycle", or other *departures from normal economic conditions or circumstances* and the outgrowth of crime. There is often very little curiosity, in this pragmatic "political economy" tradition, about the ways in which the routine functioning of economies organised around the capital-labour relation or around individual self-interest may in itself be a factor in crime' (Taylor 1997: 266. See also Currie 1997: 148–50). This has, of course, been a concern of the macro-social theories examined earlier. The econometric studies *do* demonstrate that economic factors—inequality, unemployment, poor pay, and insecure conditions—are significantly related to crime fluctuations, especially in contemporary political economies. In this section comparative and historical evidence will be reviewed, showing that the overall character of different political economies is also related to variations in their patterns of crime and violence, and the style of criminal justice they develop.

CRIME AND JUSTICE: CONTEMPORARY COMPARISONS

A major recent book by Michael Cavadino and James Dignan provides a cogent analysis of systematic differences in penal systems in the contemporary world (Cavadino and Dignan 2006). The book reports on a comparative study of 12 industrial, liberal-democratic countries,[35] seeking to relate variations in their penality to differences in their political economies. The material on particular countries was provided by expert criminologists in each one, responding to detailed questions from the volume's authors, with the final versions written by Cavadino and Dignan themselves (op. cit.: x–xi). This was intended to achieve a combination of 'theoretical depth with a degree of overall coherence which could easily be lost in a book with several authorial voices' (op. cit.).

---

[35] The countries analysed are the USA, England and Wales, Australia, New Zealand, South Africa, Germany, France, Italy, the Netherlands, Sweden, Finland, Japan.

The book is explicitly set within the context of globalization (op. cit.: 10–12), in the sense of massively heightened flows of information, global commodity and financial markets, with increasing economic and cultural domination by the USA and its neo-liberal economic strategy. In the criminal justice realm, Cavadino and Dignan note that US models such as 'zero tolerance' spread with unprecedented rapidity in the discourse and policies of practitioners and governments around the world, leading to talk of penal convergence.[36] But whilst there may be common international pressures and trends, and increasing American cultural domination, this does not entail homogenization.[37]

There have been many attempts in the last 15 years to characterize the 'varieties of capitalism' (Hall and Soskice 2003) that may still be distinguished in the contemporary world. Despite a shared trajectory of globalization and 'disorganised capitalism' (Lash and Urry (1987) under neo-liberal, 'Washington consensus' auspices, there remain significantly different models and 'real worlds' of welfare capitalism and corporatism.[38] Developing these analyses (especially the seminal typology formulated by Esping-Anderson 1990), Cavadino and Dignan suggest a distinction between four ideal-type, contemporary political economies. These are:

1. *Neo-liberalism*—minimal welfare state, extreme income and wealth differences, formal status egalitarianism, individualism with limited social rights, increasing social exclusion, right-wing political dominance.

2. *Conservative corporatism*—status-related welfare state, pronounced but not extreme income differentials, moderately hierarchical status rankings, moderate social rights, some social exclusion, centrist politics.

3. *Social democratic corporatism*—universalistic, generous welfare state, limited income differentials, egalitarian status system, relatively unconditional generous social rights, limited social exclusion, left political dominance.

4. *Oriental corporatism*—private sector based paternalistic welfare, limited income differentials, traditional status hierarchy, quasi-feudal corporatist duties, little social exclusion but alienation of 'outsiders', centre-right politics (Cavadino and Dignan 2006: 15).[39]

---

[36] Wacquant has dubbed this 'the new "made-in-USA" security vulgate' (Wacquant 2005: 109). For detailed analysis of criminal justice policy transfers see Jones and Newburn (2002); Newburn (2002); Newburn and Sparks (2004).

[37] This has been a major point of criticism of some of the celebrated and influential attempts to offer a comprehensive analysis of current penal trends such as Garland (2001), cf. Nelken (2000), and his chapter on comparative criminology in this volume (Chapter 6); Zedner (2002); Lacey (2006).

[38] Esping-Anderson (1990); Goodin *et al.* (1999); Mishra (1999); Macewan (1999); Glyn (1999); Hall and Soskice (2003).

[39] The closest exemplars of the types are the USA (neo-liberal); Germany (conservative corporatist); Sweden (social democratic); Japan (oriental corporatist). Other states placed in each type fit the model less closely, though they still approximate it. England and Wales for example are placed in the neo-liberal group, but retain more vestiges of social democracy and corporatism than the USA, albeit far less than Sweden. Political shifts make some but not a fundamental difference (for an analysis of the real but limited impact of New Labour on inequality in Britain, for example, see Hills 2004: Pt III; Hills and Stewart 2005).

The nub of Cavadino and Dignan's analysis is the demonstration that this typology of political economies corresponds to clear differences in the punitiveness of both penal policy and culture. The chapters on individual countries, and on particular aspects of policy (privatization, youth justice), show the complexity and internal variations that any summary must ignore or over-simplify. Nonetheless the four types of political economy appear to differ qualitatively in penal practice and culture— although not in a linear way. In terms of punitiveness of *policy* as measured by the (admittedly crude and problematic)[40] data on official imprisonment rates, four fundamentally different groups can be discerned[41] (Cavadino and Dignan 2006: 29–32): neo-liberal countries are the most punitive (rates ranging from 701 per 100,000 population in the USA to 115 in Australia); conservative corporatist next (imprisonment rates varying from 93 to 100 per 100,000); social democracies considerably lower (70–73 per 100,000); with the oriental corporatism of Japan having the lowest imprisonment rate (53). In terms of punitiveness of popular attitudes, as measured by the International Crime Victim Survey (Mayhew and van Kesteren (2002), Japan appears more punitive than all the social democracies or conservative countries and even some of the neo-liberal ones. There are also overlaps between the groupings, although South Africa, the USA, and England and Wales (the majority of the neo-liberal group) score the highest by a long way.

These differences correspond also to variations in styles of penal policy. Neo-liberal regimes are much more receptive than social democracies to prison privatization, for example. They also differ in their modes of punishment, with social democracies and Japan more inclined to inclusionary rather than exclusionary methods. The penal ideologies of these regimes differ fundamentally (Cavadino and Dignan 2006: 15). Neo-liberalism is associated with a dominant politics of 'law and order', whilst conservative corporatism emphasizes rehabilitation, and social democracies[42] a rights-based approach.[43]

Cavadino and Dignan's important analysis demonstrates the variations in criminal justice policy between different types of political economy in the contemporary world,[44] even though all are subject to similar pressures and tendencies resulting

[40] Cavadino and Dignan 2006: 4–5.

[41] Although the groupings show considerable variation between the countries comprising them, there is no overlap between the types in terms of imprisonment rates.

[42] The significance of differences in political economy, but also their tenuousness in the face of the common globalizing forces all are subject to, albeit with differing degrees of resistance, is illustrated by detailed comparison of the UK and Scandinavian social democracies, notably Sweden. The stronger survival of a social democratic welfare state in Scandinavian countries seems to have mitigated the rise both in crime and in punitive penal policy, but threats to both are becoming apparent (Tham 1998; Bondeson 2005).

[43] Japan's penal ideology is described as an 'apology-based rehabilitative' philosophy (Cavadino and Dignan 2006: 15).

[44] Beckett and Western found similar patterns in their analysis of variations between different states in the USA (Beckett and Western 2001). States with relatively higher spending on welfare tended to have lower rates of imprisonment, whether analysed over time or cross-sectionally. Downes and Hansen have shown that the same applies cross-nationally: countries with lower welfare expenditure are more punitive, and vice versa (Downes and Hansen 2006).

from globalization. It is important to emphasize that the explanatory variable they are looking at is *political economy*, not economics. Their theoretical model explicitly rejects economic determinism. It is a pluralist framework that gives weight to the interaction between material and cultural dimensions, as well as to political conflicts and the practices of individual actors and groups (op. cit.: 12–14).

Cavadino and Dignan offer a compelling demonstration of relationships between the political economy of different states and their penal systems. They explicitly disavow a similar relationship with crime patterns (op. cit.: 37). Certainly many studies have demonstrated an absence of any close correspondence between fluctuations in crime rates and penal policy. Beckett's study of the growth of law and order politics in the USA, for example, showed that there was no immediate correspondence between trends in recorded crime and public concern about crime (as registered in polls), media crime coverage, or state anti-crime policy initiatives (Beckett 1997: ch. 2). This is not to say, of course, that there was no fundamental relationship between the long-term growth in recorded crime from the late 1950s to the mid-1990s in most industrial countries, and the emergence of law and order politics. But the relationship is complex and highly influenced by the way that the media and politicians frame the issue of crime.[45]

There is no systematic comparative study of the relationship between crime and political economy, analogous to Cavadino and Dignan on penal policy. An obvious issue is that the problems of comparison between recorded crime rates in different jurisdictions are vastly greater than the acknowledged difficulties in comparing penal severity (see the discussion of the severe problems of comparative criminology in Nelken, Chapter 6, this volume). The well-known hazards of interpreting national crime statistics are amplified into another dimension altogether by the huge variations in legal definitions, police practices, and cultural conceptions of crime, order, and morality affecting public perceptions and reporting.[46]

Since 1989 a group of criminologists in different countries have mounted several sweeps of the 'International Crime Victims Survey' (ICVS) seeking to overcome some of these issues (van Kesteren *et al.* 2000 reports on the third sweep and a fourth is in progress). They have attracted particular media attention in the UK because they show England and Wales as highest (with Australia) of the 17 countries surveyed in overall incidence of reported victimization, as well as in the top three for every specific offence category[47] (op. cit.: ch. 2). The USA, often assumed to be the world's crime capital, comes eleventh.

[45] Apart from the evidence of Beckett's study, the failure of public or political concern about crime to respond to the sustained fall in recorded crime and victimization since the mid-1990s—itself a focus of policy discussion under the label, the 'reassurance gap' (Hough 2003)—demonstrates the lack of congruity between crime and penal policy trends, and public perceptions, cf. Roberts and Hough (2005).

[46] For these reasons the regular Home Office publication of comparative official crime statistics only reports league tables showing rates of change for each society, not absolute or even per capita levels of recorded crime (Barclay and Tavares 2003: 3–4), for all offences except homicide where they believe the problems of comparison to be fundamentally less.

[47] The survey covers all the main volume property crimes and offences against the person, apart from homicide (an omission for obvious reasons).

The survey is scrupulously rigorous in its methodology, and open about its possible limitations (such as the use of telephone interviewing). It is clearly an ambitious and interesting undertaking, representing a state-of-the-art attempt to provide data on comparative crime patterns and trends. For all that, the results obtained seem bizarre from the point of view of analysis in terms of political economy or indeed any other theoretical framework, and defy any attempt at interpretation or explanation (Young 2003a, 2004). The authors themselves do not offer any account of the pattern of differences, beyond noting its consistency across the sweeps, although they offer some plausible suggestions about the possible sources of decline in overall victimization shown by their data (van Kesteren *et al.* op. cit.: 91–2, 98–9).

The ordering of the countries by the ICVS bears no relationship to the types of political economy distinguished by Cavadino and Dignan, nor to the rankings of punitiveness. It is thus equally mysterious to liberals, political economists, or deterrence theorists. When crimes are weighted by their seriousness, as judged by the public in the surveys, the pattern approximates more closely to the political economy typology (van Kesteren *et al.* op. cit.: 48). The top three countries are the neo-liberal ones (England and Wales and Australia as in the unweighted tables, but with the USA jumping to third place), and the bottom three are social democratic Denmark and Finland, and 'oriental corporatist' Japan. But before rushing to judgement, it remains puzzling to note that the archetypal social democracy, Sweden, is in fourth place, not far off the neo-liberals, with the Netherlands next.

It is difficult to avoid endorsing Jock Young's acerbic dismissal of the surveys as 'maverick results' (Young 2003a: 36–7), owing more to cross-cultural vicissitudes in perceptions of order and indeed official interviewers than to crime patterns. As Young suggests, the league tables of different societies run so counter to expectation that it is plausible that higher-ranked societies may be ones paradoxically where the relative *absence* of serious violence makes respondents more sensitive to low-level incivility, and thus more likely to report incidents to interviewers, boosting the survey rate! (Young op. cit.: 37).

There are fewer problems of international comparison of homicide statistics, because there is less diversity in legal definitions and recording practices. The international pattern of homicide rates does correspond systematically to variations in political economies—indeed it fits the typology developed by Cavadino and Dignan as closely as their analysis of penal systems. The Home Office volume on international criminal justice statistics regularly publishes a table offering comparative recorded homicide rates for 39 countries (Barclay and Tavares 2003: 10). The figures for the 12 countries studied by Cavadino and Dignan show that the variations in their homicide rates correspond to the types of political economy they distinguish (with the sole exception of Finland). The neo-liberal countries have the highest rates. South Africa is by far the highest at 55.86 per 100,000 population. The USA is next at 5.56 (for all the celebrations of the sharp decline in American murder rates since the early 1990s). New Zealand, England and Wales, and Australia are somewhat lower (with 2.5, 1.6, and 1.87 respectively). The anomaly is social-democratic Finland, with a homicide rate of 2.86, placing it just above New Zealand. The 'conservative corporatist' countries, Italy, Germany, the Netherlands, and France, are next: rates respectively of 1.5, 1.15, 1.51, and 1.73—all lower than any of the 'neo-liberal' group. Social-democratic Sweden is lower still: 1.1. As the other two Nordic social democracies, Denmark and Norway, are comparably low (respectively, 1.02 and 0.95), it seems that Finland is for some reason an anomaly to the general pattern of much higher homicide rates in neo-liberal than social-democratic countries.[48] Japan is the lowest of the Cavadino and Dignan set of 12 countries at 1.05, although this is higher than social-democratic Denmark and Norway. The overall conclusion is clear: rates of lethal violence are highest in neo-liberal political economies, and lowest in social democracies.

Many recent studies have offered cogent analyses of why serious violent crime rates could be expected to be much higher in neo-liberal than social democratic political economies (Currie 1985, 1997, 1998a, and 1998b; James 1995; Hall 1997; Davies 1998; Hall and Winlow 2003; Hallsworth 2005; Hall and McLean 2005; Dorling 2004). The earlier review of econometric studies showed considerable evidence that inequality, relative deprivation, and involuntary, exclusionary unemployment are linked to more property crime and serious violence. Neo-liberalism is associated with much greater inequality, long-term unemployment, and social exclusion (Taylor 1999; Young 1999). In addition to economic inequality and deprivation, Currie has spelled out several other mediating links between political economy and greater pressures towards violent crime (Currie 1997: 154–66). These include 'the withdrawal of public services and supports, especially for women and children; the erosion of informal and communal networks of mutual support, supervision, and care; the spread of a materialistic, neglectful, and "hard" culture; the unregulated marketing of the technology of violence; and ... the weakening of social and political alternatives' (op. cit.: 154). This link between neo-liberal political economies and higher propensities towards serious crime is supported by historical evidence about long-term trends in crime and disorder in many societies.

CRIME, JUSTICE AND POLITICAL ECONOMY:
HISTORICAL DIMENSIONS

The post-Enlightenment incorporation of the mass of the population in industrial capitalist, liberal democracies into a common status of citizenship was associated with a secular decline in violence and disorder. Manuel Eisner has recently synthesized and updated the results of numerous historical studies exploring long-term trends in homicide in Europe (Eisner 2001). Eisner builds on the seminal work of Ted Robert Gurr and colleagues, which had earlier estimated long-term trends in violence in a number of European countries, as well as the USA and Australia (Gurr et al. 1977; Gurr 1981).

---

[48] Examination of the table for the capital cities of these 39 countries adds a further complication. The homicide rate in Helsinki is lower than for Finland as a whole, unlike the general pattern for capitals to have higher rates than the rest of the country (Barclay and Tavares 2003: 11).

The long-term trajectory from the medieval period can be summarized roughly as a J-curve (Eisner 2001: 629). Homicide rates fall sharply up to the late eighteenth century. There is then a period of increase up to the middle of the nineteenth century, but much smaller than the earlier fall, taking the level back only to that of a century earlier. After the middle of the nineteenth century the decline resumes, until the last quarter of the twentieth century, when there is a return to the levels of the mid-Victorian period. Focusing on the trend since the early nineteenth century in greater detail suggests a U-shape pattern in homicide and other serious crime over this period. Gurr shows this for the USA, Britain, Australia, and some European countries. Crime rates increased between the late eighteenth and mid-nineteenth century, declined in the later nineteenth century, and were fairly stable until the later twentieth century, when there was a return to rising crime[49] (Gurr 1981: 325). Gatrell's detailed analysis of the trends in theft and violence in England during the nineteenth and early twentieth centuries supported this picture of decline in the later nineteenth century, followed by rough stability for the first quarter of the twentieth[50] (Gatrell 1980).

There have also been a number of historical studies showing a similar U-shaped pattern for the extent of violence in political and industrial disorders: secular decline from the mid-nineteenth to the last quarter of the twentieth century, with an increase thereafter (Geary 1985; della Porte and den Boer 1998). This has gone hand in hand with a similar trend in the militarism of policing tactics (Reiner 1998; Waddington 2004).

Attempts to explain these long-term trends must involve a complex mix of inter-dependent considerations. Eisner and Gurr themselves primarily invoke Norbert Elias's analysis of a broader 'civilising process' (Elias 1939/1994). This depicted a secular cultural, social, and psychic tendency of greater sensitization towards control and display of bodily processes generally, including violence, during modernization (Garland 1990: ch. 10). Whilst the emphasis in Elias's analysis is on cultural and psychic sensibilities, these are seen as interlocked with developments in state formation, as well as discip-linary and stabilization processes associated with the emergence of markets and factories (Fletcher 1997: 36, 64). The state came to monopolize the means of violence, as part of a process of pacification of social and economic life,[51] with the police emerging as the insti-tutional locus for this (Silver 1967; Bittner 1970). The changes in cultural sensibilities

---

[49] Gurr's 1981 study does not of course take into account the fall in US homicide and other crime rates after the early 1990s.

[50] The validity of the English statistics on which these analyses rely has been called into question by Howard Taylor, in a series of papers attempting to demonstrate that even the homicide figures are essentially driven by 'supply-side' factors, the shifting exigencies and strategies of the authorities responsible for producing the data, primarily the Home Office and police forces (Taylor 1998a and 1998b, 1999). Taylor's evidence and arguments certainly offer a sharp and salutary reminder of the need for caution in interpreting all criminal statistics (they have been challenged in turn by other historians, notably Morris 2001. For a review of the arguments see Emsley, Chapter 5, this volume).

[51] This is obviously similar to Weber's analysis of the state, but Elias placed much less emphasis on the *legitimacy* of state monopolization of violence, seeing this as an ambiguous and problematic notion (Elias 1939/1994: 450; Fletcher 1997: ch. 3).

analysed in Elias's account of the civilizing process were bound up with broad shifts in the political economy. A sharpening of social conflicts, crime, and disorder in the early stages of industrial capitalism during the late eighteenth and early nineteenth centuries was succeeded by a long-term process of inclusion of the majority of the population in legal, political, and (to a lesser extent) economic and social citizenship (Marshall 1950). This was the precondition for the mix of mass seduction and discipline represented by 'penal welfarism' during the first three-quarters of the twentieth century (Garland 1985, 2001: ch. 2).

The sharp upturns in crime and violence experienced throughout the Western world in the last third of the twentieth century (with somewhat different periodicity in terms of onset) were largely associated with the displacement of Keynesian welfarist social management by the increasingly triumphant neo-liberalism of the 'Washington consensus' that has come to dominate the globalized political economy. Of course the profound changes in social order, crime, and control over the last three decades have complex, multiple, interacting sources, but the shift in political economy plays a pivotal role.

The only challenge to this view is the conservative account that places the primary if not sole explanatory weight on 'permissiveness', the undermining of social controls by liberalism.[52] As Currie has argued most cogently, this either/or approach

> begins to get in the way of understanding both the multiplicity and the interconnectedness of the forces that operate to increase the risks of violent crime in specific, real world social circumstances. When we examine patterns of youth violence in, say, South Chicago or South London, we don't see evidence of 'strain' and *not* disorganisation, for example, and *not* a weakening of 'parental' controls. We are likely to see great structural inequalities *and* community fragmentation and weakened ability of parents to monitor and supervise their children—and a great many other things, all going on at once, all entwined with each other, and all affecting the crime rate—with the combination having an impact that is much greater than the sum of its parts [Currie 1997: 150].

It is precisely this holistic analysis that is represented by political economy, as argued earlier.

The emergence of the globalized neo-liberal political economy has been associated with social and cultural changes that are likely to aggravate crime, and to displace all frameworks for crime control policy apart from 'law and order'. The spread of consumerist culture, especially when coupled with increasing social inequality and exclusion, involves a heightening of what Merton called anomie, to a degree that Jock Young has aptly characterized as social 'bulimia' (Young 1999; Lea 2002; Hayward 2004).[53] At the same time the egoistic culture of a 'market society', with its zero-sum, 'winner–loser', survival of the fittest ethos, erodes conceptions of ethical means of

---

[52] Tony Blair has of course espoused this conservative analysis in recent years (as in his 2004 speech launching the Government's five-year strategy on crime ('Blair Urges New Era in Crime Fight', BBC website, 19 July 2004). For an academic version see Wilson and Herrnstein 1985: or Dennis and Erdos 2005).

[53] For empirical demonstration of the role of consumerist culture and heightened expectations in generating 'anomic' pressures see the interviews with street robbers in Fitzgerald *et al.* 2003; Hallsworth 2005).

success being preferable, or of concern for others limiting ruthlessness, and ushers in a 'new barbarism' (Hall and Winlow 2004: 277; see also James 1995; Currie 1997: 163–4; Taylor 1999).[54] Informal social controls, the inculcation of a 'stake in conformity', through family, education, and work, become forlorn dreams (Currie 1985, 1998a, 1998b; Taylor 1999; Ruggiero 2000). The eclipse of social democratic hopes shuts off prospects of alleviating deprivation (absolute or relative) by legitimate collective industrial or political action, leaving the 'responsibilized' individual to sink or swim (Currie 1997: 165–6; Hall and Winlow 2003). Sometimes, as neo-classical economics would predict, offending is the 'rational choice' in adverse labour market conditions (Grogger 2000). The reversal of the 'solidarity project' (Garland 2001: 199), the long-term incorporation of the mass of the population into a common status of citizenship, which underpinned the 'civilizing process' of declining violence and crime, has formed the dark couple of rising crime and harsher control efforts.

In the 1990s recorded crime figures and victimization survey rates began to fall, first in the USA, but then in most Western countries, including the UK (Blumstein and Wallman 2000; Young 2003b). The dramatic fall in New York City, formerly seen as a world crime capital, attracted particular media attention. This has caused a reverse 'aetiological crisis' to that associated with the 1950s crime rise (Young 2004: 24–5). No 'grand narrative' seems satisfactory. Neo-liberalism, the Left's prime suspect, retains its global economic hegemony. But conversely there has not been any reversal of 'permissiveness', the Right's dominating bête noire. The favourite criminal justice accounts all have some plausibility, but not as complete explanations.

The zero-tolerance policing explanation, celebrated by many promoters of the supposed New York miracle,[55] has been demolished definitively by close analyses. The precise timing of the crime changes in New York does not fit the zero-tolerance account, and many US cities showed similar falls in crime without the same policing changes (Bowling 1999; Karmen 2000; Eck and Maguire 2000; Dixon and Maher 2005). In so far as policing changes contributed to the fall, it was the 'smart' rather than the 'tough' aspects of the NYPD reforms that were crucial—the managerial and intelligence-analysing reforms referred to as 'Compstat' (Weisburd *et al.* 2003; Moore 2003).

Nor has the enormous expansion of punitiveness, above all the staggering and gross levels of imprisonment, contributed more than marginally (Spelman 2000). More mundane improvements in the effectiveness of crime prevention, referred to by Garland as the 'criminologies of everyday life' (Garland 2001: 127–31), have played an important part in the reduction of 'volume crimes' such as burglary and car theft.

Within the array of explanations, economic factors are certainly significant, if peculiarly unheralded by governments wishing to appear 'tough on crime' (Downes 2004). But they cannot provide more than part of the explanation. Unemployment has

---

[54] The insecurities and pressures engendered by neo-liberalism and consumerism affect all levels of society, as indicated by Karstedt and Farrall's study of 'The Moral Maze of the Middle Class'. This charts the growth of fraud and unethical business practices in the UK and Germany, and the techniques of neutralization facilitating it (Karstedt and Farrall 2004).

[55] 'Crime is down in New York City, blame the police', as former NYPD Chief Bratton put it (Bratton 1998).

certainly been at much lower levels than during the crime explosion of the 1980s. This has been achieved, however, largely by the expansion of secondary labour market jobs. In the USA there has been no reduction in poverty or inequality. In the UK, New Labour has succeeded in reducing child poverty substantially. As shown earlier, the minimum wage had a significant crime reduction effect in some areas. But overall there has not been any significant change in the extreme level of economic inequality and insecurity that New Labour inherited, despite welcome improvements in crucial aspects of poverty (Hills 2004; Hills and Stewart 2005). The crime drop remains something of a mystery, defying any simple account.[56] But economic factors are an important part of the explanation.

CONCLUSION: MARKETS, MEANINGS, MORALS

Political economy and other primarily structural perspectives have been sidelined in the last thirty years, by a number of 'turns' in intellectual, cultural, and political life.[57] They have been caught in a pincer movement from right and left, denying the reality of 'society', or at any rate structural causes and grand narratives. In criminology specifically, political economy perspectives were first attacked by the right-wing 'Realist' critique advanced most noisily in the mid-1970s by James Q. Wilson's polemic against 'root cause' perspectives (Wilson 1975: xv). Subsequently 'Left Realism' pointed to a supposed 'aetiological crisis' of earlier Left criminology (Young 1986), and argued for the necessity and possibility of short-term crime-control strategies (Lea and Young 1984). More recently, 'cultural criminologists' have claimed that political economy and structural perspectives are over-deterministic and simplistic, and fail to be true to the subjective meanings and seductions of deviance and crime (Ferrell *et al.* 2004; Hayward

---

[56] One obvious temptation is to deny its reality, a line that has been taken particularly by some conservative commentators in Britain (Dennis and Erdos 2005; Green *et al.* 2005). The recorded crime figures in Britain have indeed increased in most years since 1998, but this is primarily due to major changes in the Home Office count-ing rules (see Maguire, Chapter 10, this volume). The main reason most criminologists do not question the downward trend is because it is indicated by the British Crime Survey and similar victimization surveys else-where. Whilst these are not subject to the same well-known problems as the police-recorded figures, they are certainly not beyond dispute (Garside 2004b; Young 2004: 17–22). It could be that trends in the nature of crime make the BCS increasingly unable to uncover the crimes it used to record, thus producing a spurious decline in victimization levels. For example several studies have suggested that one consequence of better domestic and car security is that potential thieves switch to robbery (Fitzgerald *et al.* 2003; Hallsworth 2005), in particular of young people. As the BCS only samples people over 16, if there is a trend towards disproportionate victimization of younger people it could produce an increasing underestimate of crime. It would be as premature to conclude that the apparent trend towards falling crime is spurious as to suggest that any of the array of possible contributing factors is *the* one 'whodunnit'. But it may be that at any rate a partial solution to the mystery of the falling crime rate is that it didn't happen.

[57] For recent critical histories of the cultural 'turns' more generally see Sanbonmatsu (2004, 2005) and Brennan (2006). Harvey (2005) and Glyn (2006) offer cogent critical accounts of the rise of their economic parallel, neo-liberalism.

and Young, Chapter 4, this volume). All these critiques have been buttressed by a belief that the econometric evidence itself called into question any postulated relationships between crime and economic factors.

This chapter has sought to rehabilitate political economy approaches from these various critiques, and restate their importance for understanding patterns and trends in crime and criminal justice. As argued earlier political economy stands for a holistic approach, but one that recognizes the dialectical complexity of mediations and inter-actions between macro-structures and individual actions. As Weber put it long ago, explanation has to be both 'causally adequate' and 'adequate at the level of meaning' (Weber 1947/1964: 99–100). *Verstehen* and structural pressures are each necessary elements of explanation, complementary not contradictory. Nor (again following Weber's venerable lead) are understanding or explanation incompatible with ethical judgements or policies. Contrary to the critiques of 'Realists' of the Left, Right or centre, recognition of the existence of 'root causes' does not mean that it is unnecessary or undesirable to explore also all possible avenues of immediate crime reduction, victim support, or penal reform. What this chapter has tried to demonstrate is the theoretical viability of political economy perspectives, and that there is empirical evidence both of the importance of economic factors in crime, and of variations between types of political economy and patterns of crime and punishment. Specifically it has shown that neo-liberal as distinct from social-democratic political economies tend to have a 'dark heart' (Davies 1998) of both serious crime and cruel punishment. Short-term pain and symptom relief are helpful and ethical, but only provided they do not become a futile struggle to hold down the lid[58] on what remain 'root causes'.

■ SELECTED FURTHER READING

The classic attempt to develop a Marxist-inspired political economy of crime is Bonger, W. (1916/1969), *Criminality and Economic Conditions*, Bloomington: Indiana University Press. Two important analyses from the heyday of 1970s critical criminology are Taylor, I., Walton, P., and Young, J. (1973), *The New Criminology*, London: Routledge; and Hall, S., Critcher, C., Jefferson, T., Clarke, J., and Roberts, B. (1978), *Policing the Crisis*, London: Macmillan. For analyses of recent crime and criminal justice trends incorporating political economy see Currie, E. (1998b), *Crime and Punishment in America*, New York: Holt; Taylor, I. (1999), *Crime in Context*, Cambridge: Polity; Young, J. (1999), *The Exclusive Society*, London: Sage; and Garland, D. (2001), *The Culture of Control*, Oxford: Oxford University Press. Two important attempts to analyse the US crime drop are Karmen, A. (2000), *New York Murder Mystery*, New York: New York University Press; and Blumstein, A., and Wallman, J. (eds) (2000), *The Crime Drop in America*, Cambridge: Cambridge University Press. A stimulating analysis of recent British homicide trends is Dorling, D. (2004), 'Prime Suspect: Murder in Britain', in P. Hillyard, C. Pantazis, S. Tombs, and D. Gordon (eds), *Beyond Criminology*, London: Pluto. A useful

---

[58] In the context of the 'war on terror', Paul Rogers has coined the neat term 'liddism' to refer to such Canute-like attacks on symptoms not causes (Rogers 2002).

review of the economic literature is Hale, C. (2005), 'Economic Marginalization and Social Exclusion', in C. Hale, K. Hayward, A. Wahidin, and E. Wincup (eds), *Criminology*, Oxford: Oxford University Press. A valuable collection of readings is Fielding, N., Clarke, A., and Witt, R. (eds) (2000), *The Economic Dimensions of Crime*, London: Palgrave. Zedner, L. (2006b), 'Opportunity Makes the Thief-Taker: the Influence of Economic Analysis on Crime Control', in T. Newburn and P. Rock (eds), *The Politics of Crime Control*, Oxford: Oxford University Press (forthcoming) is a cogent critique of the impact of neo-classical economic models. Cavadino, M., and Dignan, J. (2006), *Penal Systems: A Comparative Approach*, London: Sage is a major pioneering attempt at a comparative analysis of the political economy of penal systems.

■ REFERENCES

AGNEW, R. (1992), 'Foundations for a General Strain Theory of Crime and Delinquency', *Criminology*, 30: 47–87.

BACKHOUSE, R. (2002), *The Penguin History of Economics*, London: Penguin.

BARCLAY, G., and TAVARES, C. (2003), *International Comparisons of Criminal Justice Statistics 2001*, London: Home Office.

BECKER, G. (1968), 'Crime and Punishment: An Economic Approach', *Journal of Political Economy*, 76: 175–209.

BECKER, H. (1963), *Outsiders*, New York: Free Press.

——(1967), 'Whose Side are We On?', *Social Problems*, 14: 32–40.

BECKETT, K. (1997), *Making Crime Pay*, New York: Oxford University Press.

——and SASSON, T. (2000), *The Politics of Injustice*, Thousand Oaks, Cal.: Pine Forge.

——and WESTERN, B. (2001), 'Governing Social Marginality: Welfare, Incarceration and the Transformation of State Policy', *Punishment and Society*, 3: 43–59.

BEIRNE, P. (1991), 'Inventing Criminology: The "Science of Man" in Cesare Beccaria's *Dei delitti e delle penne*', *Criminology*, 29: 777–820.

——(1993), *Inventing Criminology*, Albany, NY: State University of New York Press.

BEMMELEN, J. M. (1960), 'Willem Adrian Bonger', in H. Mannheim (ed.), *Pioneers in Criminology*, London: Stevens.

BITTNER, E. (1970), *The Functions of the Police in Modern Society*, Maryland: National Institute of Mental Health.

BLAIR, T. (1993), 'Why Crime Is A Socialist Issue', *New Statesman* 29(12): 27–8.

BLUMSTEIN, A., and WALLMAN, J. (eds) (2000), *The Crime Drop in America*, Cambridge: Cambridge University Press.

BONDESON, U. (2005), 'Levels of Punitiveness in Scandinavia: description and explanations', in J. Pratt, D. Brown, M. Brown, S. Hallsworth, and W. Morrison (eds), *The New Punitiveness* Cullompton, Devon: Willan.

BONGER, W. (1916/1969), *Criminality and Economic Conditions*, Bloomington: Indiana University Press.

——(1935), *An Introduction to Criminology*, London: Methuen.

BOWLING, B. (1999), 'The Rise and Fall of New York Murder', *British Journal of Criminology*, 39: 531–54.

BOX, S. (1987), *Recession, Crime and Punishment*, London: Macmillan.

BRAITHWAITE, J. (1979), *Inequality, Crime and Public Policy*, London: Routledge.

BRATTON, W. (1998), 'Crime is Down: Blame the Police', in N. Dennis (ed.), *Zero Tolerance: Policing A Free Society*, 2nd edn, London: Institute of Economic Affairs.

BRENNAN, T. (2006), *Wars of Position: The Cultural Politics of Left and Right*, New York: Columbia University Press.

BURCHELL, G., GORDON, C., and MILLER, P. (eds) (1991), *The Foucault Effect: Studies in Governmentality*, London: Wheatsheaf.

CAMPBELL, B. (1993), *Goliath: Britain's Dangerous Places*, London: Methuen.

CANTOR, D., and LAND, K. C. (1985), 'Unemployment and Crime Rates in Post World War II United States: A Theoretical and Empirical Analysis', *American Sociological Review*, 50: 317–32.

CARSON, W. G. (1970), 'White-collar Crime and the Enforcement of Factory Legislation', *British Journal of Criminology*, 10: 383–98.

—— (1981), *The Other Price of Britain's Oil*, Oxford: Martin Robertson.

CAVADINO, M., and DIGNAN, J. (2006), *Penal Systems: A Comparative Approach*, London: Sage.

CHAMBLISS, W. (ed.) (1969), *Crime and the Legal Process*, New York: McGraw Hill.

—— and MANKOFF, M. (eds) (1975), *Whose Law, What Order?*, New York: Wiley.

CHAPMAN, D. (1968), *Sociology and the Stereotype of the Criminal*, London: Tavistock.

CHIRICOS, T. G. (1987), 'Rates of Crime and Unemployment', *Social Problems*, 34: 187–211.

CLOWARD, R., and OHLIN, L. (1960), *Delinquency and Opportunity*, New York: Free Press.

COHEN, S. (1988), *Against Criminology*, New Jersey: Transaction Books.

—— (1998), 'Intellectual Scepticism and Political Commitment: The Case of Radical Criminology', in P. Walton and J. Young (eds), *The New Criminology Revisited*, London: Macmillan.

—— and SCULL, A. (eds) (1983) *Social Control and the State*, Oxford: Martin Robertson.

COLQUHOUN, P. (1796), *A Treatise on the Police of the Metropolis*, 2nd edn, London: H. Fry.

—— (1800), *Treatise on the Commerce and Police of the River Thames*, London: J. Mowman.

—— (1806), *Treatise on Indigence*, London: J. Hatchard.

COOK, D. (1989), *Rich Law, Poor Law*, Milton Keynes: Open University Press.

—— (2006), *Criminal and Social Justice*, London: Sage.

CURRIE, E. (1985), *Confronting Crime*, New York: Pantheon.

—— (1997), 'Market, Crime and Community: Toward a Mid-range Theory of Post-industrial Violence', *Theoretical Criminology*, 1: 147–72.

—— (1998a), 'Crime and Market Society: Lessons From the United States', in P. Walton and J. Young (eds), *The New Criminology Revisited*, London: Macmillan.

—— (1998b), *Crime and Punishment in America*, New York: Holt.

DAVIES, N. (1998), *Dark Heart*, London: Verso.

DEADMAN, D., and MACDONALD, Z. (2002), 'Why Has Crime Fallen? An Economic Perspective', *Economic Affairs*, 22: 5–14.

DELLA PORTA, D., and DEN BOER, M. (eds) (1998), *Policing Protest*, Minneapolis: University of Minnesota Press.

—— and REITER, H. (eds) (1998), *Policing Protest*, Minneapolis: University of Minnesota Press.

DENNIS, N., and ERDOS, G. (2005), *Cultures and Crimes: Policing in Four Nations*, London: Civitas.

DHIRI, S., BRAND, S., HARRIES, R., and PRICE, R. (1999), *Modelling and Predicting Property Crime Trends in England and Wales*, London: Home Office.

DIXON, D., and MAHER, L. (2005), 'Policing, Crime and Public Health: Lessons for Australia From the "New York Miracle"', *Criminal Justice*, 5: 115–44.

DORLING, D. (2004), 'Prime Suspect: Murder in Britain', in P. Hillyard, C. Pantazis, S. Tombs, and D. Gordon (eds), *Beyond Criminology*, London: Pluto.

DOWNES, D. (2004), 'New Labour and the Lost Causes of Crime', *Criminal Justice Matters*, 55: 4–5.

—— and HANSEN, K. (2006), 'Welfare and Punishment in Comparative Perspective', in S. Armstrong and L. McAra (eds), *Perspectives on Punishment*, Oxford: Oxford University Press.

—— and ROCK, P. (2003), *Understanding Deviance*, 4th edn, Oxford: Oxford University Press.

DUBBER, M. (2005), *The Police Power*, New York: Columbia University Press.

—— and VALVERDE, M. (eds) (2006), *The New Police Science*, Stanford: Stanford University Press (forthcoming).

ECK, J., and MAGUIRE, E. (2000), 'Have Changes in Policing Reduced Violent Crime?', in A. Bloomstein and J. Wallman (eds), *The Crime Drop in America*, Cambridge: Cambridge University Press.

EHRLICH, I. (1973), 'Participation in Illegal Activities: A Theoretical and Empirical Investigation', *Journal of Political Economy*, 81: 521–63.

—— (1975), 'The Deterrent Effect of Capital Punishment', *American Economic Review*, 65: 397–447.

EISNER, M. (2001), 'Modernisation, Self-control and Lethal Violence: The Long-term Dynamics of European Homicide Rates in Theoretical Perspective', *British Journal of Criminology*, 41: 618–38.

ELIAS, N. (1939/1994), *The Civilising Process*, Oxford: Blackwell.

ESPING-ANDERSON, G. (1990), *The Three Worlds of Welfare Capitalism*, Cambridge: Polity.

EYSENCK, H. (1965), *Fact and Fiction in Psychology*, London: Penguin.

FARRINGTON, D., GALLAGHER, B. MORLEY, L. St. LEDGER, R. J. and WEST, D. J. (1986), 'Unemployment, School Leaving and Crime', *British Journal of Criminology*, 26(4): 335–56.

FELSON, M. (1994), *Crime and Everyday Life*, Thousand Oaks, Cal.: Pine Forge.

——and CLARKE, R. (1998), *Opportunity Makes the Thief*, London: Home Office.

FERRELL, J., HAYWARD, K., MORRISON, W., and PRESDEE, M. (eds) (2004), *Cultural Criminology Unleashed*, London: Glasshouse.

FIELD, S. (1990), *Trends in Crime and Their Interpretation: A Study of recorded Crime in Post-war England and Wales*, London: Home Office.

——(1999), *Trends in Crime Revisited*, London: Home Office.

FIELDING, N., CLARKE, A., and WITT, R. (eds) (2000), *The Economic Dimensions of Crime*, London: Palgrave.

FITZGERALD, M., STOCKDALE, J., and HALE, C. (2003), *Young People and Street Crime*, London: Youth Justice Board.

FLETCHER, J. (1997), *Violence and Civilization*, Cambridge: Polity.

FOUCAULT, M. (1977), *Discipline and Punish*, London: Penguin.

FREEMAN, R. (1983), 'Crime and Unemployment', in J. Q. Wilson (ed.), *Crime and Public Policy*, San Francisco: Institute of Contemporary Studies.

——(1995) 'Crime and the Labour Market', in J. Q. Wilson and J. Petersilia (eds), *Crime*, San Francisco: Institute of Contemporary Studies.

GARLAND, D. (1985), *Punishment and Welfare*, Aldershot: Gower.

——(1990), *Punishment and Modern Society*, Cambridge: Cambridge University Press.

——(1997), ' "Governmentality" and the Problem of Crime: Foucault, Criminology, Sociology', *Theoretical Criminology*, 1: 173–214.

——(2001), *The Culture of Control*, Oxford: Oxford University Press.

——(2002), 'Of Crime and Criminals', in M. Maguire, R. Morgan, and R. Reiner (eds), *The Oxford Handbook of Criminology*, 3rd edn, Oxford: Oxford University Press.

GARSIDE, R. (2004a), 'Is It The Economy?', *Criminal Justice Matters*, 55: 32–3.

——(2004b), *Crime, Persistent Offenders and the Justice Gap*, London: Crime and Society Foundation.

GATRELL, V. (1980), 'The Decline of Theft and Violence in Victorian and Edwardian England', in V. Gatrell, B. Lenman, and G. Parker (eds), *Crime and the Law*, London: Europa.

GEARY, R. (1985), *Policing Industrial Disputes*, Cambridge: Cambridge University Press.

GLYN, A. (ed.) (1999), *Social Democracy in Neo-Liberal Times*, Oxford: Oxford University Press.

——(2006), *Capitalism Unleashed*, Oxford: Oxford University Press.

GOBERT, J., and PUNCH, M. (2003), *Rethinking Corporate Crime*, London: Butterworths.

——and ——(2006), 'Motivations and Intent of White Collar Criminals', in G. Geis and H. Pontell (eds), *International Handbook of White Collar Crime*, Dordrecht: Springer-Verlag (forthcoming).

GOODIN, R., HEADEY, B., MUFFELS, R., and DIRVEN, H. J. (1999), *The Real Worlds of Welfare Capitalism*, Cambridge: Cambridge University Press.

GREEN, D., GROVE, E., and MARTIN, N. (2005), *Crime and Civil Society*, London: Civitas.

GREEN, P., and WARD, T. (2004), *State Crime*, London: Pluto.

GROGGER, J. (1998), 'Market Wages and Youth Crime', *Journal of Labour Economics*, 16: 756–91.

——(2000), 'An Economic Model of Recent Trends in Violence', in A. Bloomstein and J. Wallman (eds), *The Crime Drop in America*, Cambridge: Cambridge University Press.

GURR, T. R. (1981), 'Historical Trends In Violent Crime', in M. Tonry and N. Morris (eds), *Crime and Justice 3*, Chicago: Chicago University Press.

——, GRABOSKY, P., and HULA, R. (1977), *The Politics of Crime and Conflict: A Comparative History of Four Cities*, Beverly Hills, Cal.: Sage.

HALE, C. (1998), 'Crime and the Business Cycle in Post-war Britain Revisited', *British Journal of Criminology*, 38: 681–98.

——(1999), 'The Labour Market and Post-war Crime Trends in England and Wales', in P. Carlen and R. Morgan (eds), *Crime Unlimited*, London: Macmillan.

—— (2005), 'Economic Marginalization and Social Exclusion', in C. Hale, K. Hayward, A. Wahidin, and E. Wincup (eds), *Criminology*, Oxford: Oxford University Press.

HALL, P., and SUSKICE, D. (eds) (2003), *Varieties of Capitalism*, Oxford: Oxford University Press.

HALL, S. (1997), 'Visceral Cultures and Criminal Practices', *Theoretical Criminology*, 1: 453–78.

—— and MCLEAN, C. (2005), 'A Tale of Two Capitalisms: A Preliminary Comparison of Violence Rates in European and Anglo-American Market Societies', unpublished manuscript, University of Northumbria, Division of Sociology and Criminology.

—— and WINLOW, S. (2003), 'Rehabilitating Leviathan: Reflections on the State, Economic Regulation and Violence Reduction', *Theoretical Criminology*, 7: 139–62.

—— and —— (2004), 'Barbarians at the Gates: Crime and Violence in the Breakdown of the Pseudo-pacification Process', in J. Ferrell, K. Hayward, W. Morrison, and M. Presdee (eds), *Cultural Criminology Unleashed*, London: Glasshouse.

——, CRITCHER, C., JEFFERSON, T., CLARKE, J., and ROBERTS, B. (1978), *Policing the Crisis*, London: Macmillan.

HALLSWORTH, S. (2005), *Street Crime*, Cullompton, Devon: Willan.

HANSEN, K., and MACHIN, S. (2003), 'Spatial Crime Patterns and the Introduction of the UK Minimum Wage', *Oxford Bulletin of Economics and Statistics*, 64: 677–97.

HARVEY, D. (2005), *A Brief History of Neoliberalism*, Oxford: Oxford University Press.

HAY, D., LINEBAUGH, P., THOMPSON, E. P., RULE, J. G., and WINSLOW, C. (1975), *Albion's Fatal Tree*, London: Penguin.

HAYWARD, K. (2004), *City Limits*, London:Glasshouse.

HILLS, J. (2004), *Inequality and the State*, Oxford: Oxford University Press.

—— and STEWART, K. (eds) (2005), *A More Equal Society?*, Bristol: Policy Press.

HILLYARD, P., PANTAZIS, C., TOMBS, S., and GORDON, D. (eds) (2004), *Beyond Criminology: Taking Harm Seriously*, London: Pluto.

HOUGH, M. (2003), 'Modernization and Public Opinion: Some Criminal Justice Paradoxes', *Contemporary Politics*, 9: 143–55.

IGNATIEFF, M. (1978), *A Just Measure of Pain*, London: Macmillan.

JAMES, O. (1995), *Juvenile Violence in a Winner-Loser Society*, London: Free Association Books.

JEFFERSON, T. (2004), 'From Cultural Studies to Psychosocial Criminology: An Intellectual Journey', in J. Ferrell, K. Hayward, W. Morrison, and M. Presdee (eds), *Cultural Criminology Unleashed*, London: Glasshouse.

JONES, T., and NEWBURN, T. (2002), 'Policy Convergence and Crime Control in the USA and the UK', *Criminal Justice*, 2: 173–203.

KARMEN, A. (2000), *New York Murder Mystery*, New York: New York University Press.

KARSTEDT, S., and FARRALL, S. (2004), 'The Moral Maze of the Middle Class: The Predatory Society and its Emerging Regulatory Order', in H.-J. Albrecht, T. Serassis, and H. Kania (eds), *Images of Crime II*, Freiburg: Max Planck Institute.

KATZ, J. (1988), *Seductions of Crime*, New York: Basic Books.

KLECK, G., and CHIRICOS, T. (2002), 'Unemployment and Property Crime: A Target-Specific Assessment of Opportunity and Motivation as Mediating Factors', *Criminology*, 40: 649–79.

LACEY, N. (2006), 'Historicising Contrasts in Tolerance', in T. Newburn and P. Rock (eds), *The Politics of Crime Control*, Oxford: Oxford University press (forthcoming).

LASH, S., and URRY, J. (1987), *The End of Organised Capitalism*, Cambridge: Polity.

LEA, J. (2002), *Crime and Modernity*, London: Sage.

—— and YOUNG, J. (1984), *What is to be Done about Law and Order?*, London: Penguin.

LEE, J. (1983), 'Some Structural Aspects of Police Deviance With Minority Groups', in C. Shearing (ed.), *Organisational Police Deviance*, Toronto: Butterworth.

MACEWAN, A. (1999), *Neo-liberalism or Democracy?*, London: Zed Books.

MACHIN, S., and MEGHIR, C. (2004), 'Crime and Economic Incentives', *Journal of Human Resources*, 39: 958–79.

MCLAUGHLIN, E., MUNCIE, J., and HUGHES, G. (2001), 'The Permanent Revolution: New Labour, New Public Management and the Modernization of Criminal Justice', *Criminal Justice*, 1: 301–18.

MCMULLEN, J. (1998), 'Social Surveillance and the Rise of the "Police Machine"', *Theoretical Criminology*, 2: 93–117.

MANNHEIM, H. (ed.) (1960), *Pioneers in Criminology*, London: Stevens.

MARRIS, R. (2000), *Survey of the Research Literature on the Economic and Criminological Factors Influencing Crime Trends*, London: Volterra Consulting.

MARSHALL, T. H. (1950), *Citizenship and Social Class*, Cambridge: Cambridge University Press.

MARX, K. (1867/1976), *Capital Vol.1*, London: Penguin.

——and ENGELS, F. (1848/1998), *The Communist Manifesto*, London: Verso.

MAYHEW, P., and VAN KESTEREN, J. (2002), 'Cross-National Attitudes towards Punishment', in J. Roberts and M. Hough (eds), *Changing Attitudes to Punishment*, Cullompton, Devon: Willan.

MELOSSI, D., and PAVARINI, M. (1981), *The Prison and the Factory*, London: Macmillan.

MERTON, R. (1938),'Social Structure and Anomie', *American Sociological Review* 3: 672–82 (revised in R. Merton (1957), *Social Theory and Social Structure*, London: Free Press).

MESSNER, S., and ROSENFELD, R. (2001), *Crime and the American Dream*, 3rd edn, Belmont, Cal.: Wadsworth.

MISHRA, R. (1999), *Globalization and the Welfare State*, Cheltenham: Edward Elgar.

MOORE, M. (2003), 'Sizing Up Compstat: An Important Administrative Innovation in Policing', *Criminology and Public Policy*, 2: 469–94.

MORRIS, R. (2001), ' "Lies, Damned Lies and Criminal Statistics": Reinterpreting the Criminal Statistics in England and Wales', *Crime, History and Societies*, 5: 111–27.

MORRIS, T. (1957), *The Criminal Area*, London: Routledge.

NELKEN, D. (ed.) (2000), *Contrasting Criminal Justice*, Aldershot: Dartmouth.

NEOCLEOUS, M. (2000), *The Fabrication of Social Order*, London: Pluto.

NEWBURN, T. (2002), 'Atlantic Crossings: Policy Transfer and Crime Control in America and Britain', *Punishment and Society*, 4: 165–94.

——and SPARKS, R. (eds) (2004), *Criminal Justice and Political Cultures*, Cullompton, Devon: Willan.

PASQUINO, P. (1978), 'Theatrum Politicum: The Genealogy of Capital—Police and the State of Prosperity', *Ideology and Consciousness*, 4: 41–54.

PILIAVIN, I., and BRIAR, S. (1964), 'Police Encounters With Juveniles', *American Journal of Sociology*, 70: 206–14.

PLATT, A., and TAKAGI, P. (eds) (1980), *Punishment and Penal Discipline*, Berkeley, Cal.: Center for Research on Criminal Justice.

POSNER, R. (1998), *Economic Analysis of Law*, 5th edn, New York: Aspen.

PYLE, D., and DEADMAN, D. (1994), 'Crime and the Business Cycle in Post-war Britain', *British Journal of Criminology*, 34: 339–57.

RADZINOWICZ, L. (1956), *A History of the English Criminal Law Vol. 3*, London: Stevens.

REIMAN, J. (2004), *The Rich Get Richer and the Poor Get Prison*, 7th edn, Boston: Allyn and Bacon.

REINER, R. (1984), 'Crime, Law and Deviance: The Durkheim Legacy', in S. Fenton, *Durkheim and Modern Sociology*, Cambridge: Cambridge University Press.

——(1988), 'British Criminology and the State', *British Journal of Criminology*, 29(1): 138–58.

——(1996), 'The Case of the Missing Crimes', in R. Levitas and W. Guy (eds), *Interpreting Official Statistics*, London: Routledge.

——(1998), 'Policing, Protest and Disorder in Britain', in D. Della Porta and H. Reiter (eds), *Policing Protest*, Minneapolis: University of Minnesota Press.

——(2000), 'Crime and Control in Britain', *Sociology* 34: 71–94.

——(2002), 'Classical Social Theory and Law', in J. Penner, D. Schiff, and R. Nobles (eds), *Jurisprudence*, London: Butterworths.

——(2006), 'Beyond Risk: A Lament for Social Democratic Criminology', in T. Newburn and P. Rock (eds), *The Politics of Crime Control*, Oxford: Oxford University Press (forthcoming).

ROBERTS, J., and HOUGH, M. (2005), *Understanding Public Attitudes to Criminal Justice*, Maidenhead: Open University Press.

ROGERS, P. (2002), *Losing Control: Global Security in the Twenty-first Century*, London: Pluto.

RUGGIERO, V. (2000), *Crime and Markets*, Oxford: Oxford University Press.

RUSCHE, G., and KIRCHHEIMER, O. (1939/2003), *Punishment and Social Structure*, New Jersey: Transaction.

SANBONMATSU, J. (2004), *The Postmodern Prince*, New York: Monthly Review Press.

—— (2005), 'Postmodernism and the Academic Intelligentsia', in L. Panitch and C. Leys (eds), *Telling the Truth*, London: Merlin.

SILVER, A. (1967), 'The Demand For Order in Civil Society', in D. Bordua (ed.), *The Police*, New York: Wiley.

SLAPPER, G. (1999), *Blood in the Bank*, Aldershot: Ashgate.

—— and Tombs, S. (1999), *Corporate Crime*, London: Longman.

SMART, B. (1983), 'On Discipline and Regulation', in D. Garland and P. Young (eds), *The Power to Punish*, London: Heinemann.

SPELMAN, W. (2000), 'The Limited Importance of Prison Expansion', in A. Blumstein and J. Wallman (eds), *The Crime Drop in America*, Cambridge: Cambridge University Press.

STINCHCOMBE, A. (1963), 'Institutions of Privacy in the Determination of Police Administrative Practice', *American Journal of Sociology*, 69: 150–60.

SUTTON, M. (1998), *Handling Stolen Goods and Theft: A Market Reduction Approach*, London: Home Office.

——, SCHNEIDER, J., and HETHERINGTON, S. (2001), *Tackling Theft With the Market Reduction Approach*, London: Home Office.

TAYLOR, H. (1998a), 'The Politics of the Rising Crime Statistics of England and Wales 1914–60', *Crime, History and Societies*, 2: 5–28.

—— (1998b), 'Rising Crime: The Political Economy of Criminal Statistics Since the 1850s', *Economic History Review*, 51: 569–90.

—— (1999), 'Forging the Job: A Crisis of "Modernisation" or Redundancy for the Police in England and Wales 1900–39', *British Journal of Criminology*, 39: 113–35.

TAYLOR, I. (1981), *Law and Order: Arguments for Socialism*, London: Macmillan.

—— (1997), 'The Political Economy of Crime', in M. Maguire, R. Morgan, and R. Reiner (eds), *The Oxford Handbook of Criminology*, 2nd edn, Oxford: Oxford University Press.

—— (1999), *Crime in Context*, Cambridge: Polity.

——, WALTON, P., and YOUNG, J. (1973), *The New Criminology*, London: Routledge.

THAM, H. (1998), 'Crime and the Welfare State: the Case of the United Kingdom and Sweden', in V. Ruggiero, N. South, and I. Taylor (eds), *The New European Criminology*, London: Routledge.

THOMPSON, E. P. (1975), *Whigs and Hunters*, London: Penguin.

THORNBERRY, T., and CHRISTENSEN, R. (1984), 'Unemployment and Criminal Involvement', *American Sociological Review*, 49: 398–411.

TOMBS, S. (2004), 'Workplace Injury and Death: Social Harm and the Illusions of Law', in P. Hillyard, C. Pantazis, S. Tombs, and D. Gordon (eds), *Beyond Criminology*, London: Pluto.

—— and WHYTE, D. (2006), *Safety Crimes*, Cullompton, Devon: Willan.

VAN KESTEREN, J., MAYHEW, P., and NIEUWBEERTA, P. (2000), *Criminal Victimisation in Seventeen Industrialised Countries: Key Findings From the 2000 International Victims Survey*, The Hague: Ministry of Justice.

VOLD, G., BERNARD, T., and SNIPES, J. (1998), *Theoretical Criminology*, 4th edn, New York: Oxford University Press.

WACQUANT, L. (2005), 'The "Scholarly Myths" of the New Law and Order Doxa', in L. Panitch and C. Leys (eds), *Telling the Truth*, London: Merlin.

WADDINGTON, P. A. J. (2004), 'Policing Public Order and Political Contention', in T. Newburn (ed.), *Handbook of Policing*, Cullompton, Devon: Willan.

WALSH, A. (2000), 'Behaviour Genetics and Anomie/Strain Theory', *Criminology* 38: 1075–1108.

WEBER, M. (1903/1992), *The Protestant Ethic and the Spirit of Capitalism*, London: Routledge.

—— (1947/1964), *The Theory of Social and Economic Organisation*, Glencoe, Ill.: Free Press.

WEISBURD, D., MASTROFSKI, S., MCNALLY, A., GREENSPAN, R., and WILLIS, J. (2003), 'Reforming to Preserve: Compstat and Strategic Problem Solving in American Policing', *Criminology and Public Policy*, 2: 421–56.

WELLS, C. (2001), *Corporations and Criminal Responsibility*, Oxford: Oxford University Press.

WILKINSON, R. (2005), *The Impact of Inequality*, New York: New Press.

WILLIS, P. (1977), *Learning to Labour*, London: Saxon House.

WILSON, J. Q. (1975), *Thinking About Crime*, New York: Vintage.

—— and HERRNSTEIN, R. (1985), *Crime and Human Nature*, New York: Simon and Schuster.

WITT, R., CLARKE, A., and FIELDING, N. (1999), 'Crime and Economic Activity: A Panel Data Approach', *British Journal of Criminology*, 39: 391–400.

WRIGHT, R., and MILLER, J. (1998), 'Taboo Until Today? The Coverage of Biological Arguments in Criminology Textbooks 1961 to 1970 and 1987 to 1996', *Journal of Criminal Justice*, 26: 1–19.

YOUNG, J. (1986), 'The Failure of Criminology: The Need for a Radical Realism' in R. Matthews and J. Young (eds), *Confronting Crime*, London: Sage.

—— (1988), 'Radical Criminology in Britain', *British Journal of Criminology*, 28: 159–83.

YOUNG, J. (1999), *The Exclusive Society*, London: Sage.

—— (2003a), 'Winning the Fight Against Crime? New Labour, Populism and Lost Opportunities', in R. Matthews and J. Young (eds), *The New Politics of Crime and Punishment*, Cullompton, Devon: Willan.

—— (2003b), 'Merton With Energy, Katz With Structure: The Sociology of Vindictiveness and the Criminology of Transgression', *Theoretical Criminology*, 7: 389–414.

—— (2004), 'Voodoo Criminology and the Numbers Game', in J. Ferrell, K. Hayward, W. Morrison, and M. Presdee (eds), *Cultural Criminology Unleashed*, London: Glasshouse.

ZEDNER, L. (2002), 'The Dangers of Dystopias in Penal Theory', *Oxford Journal of Legal Studies*, 22: 341–66.

—— (2006a), 'Policing Before the Police', *British Journal of Criminology*, 46: 78–96.

—— (2006b), 'Opportunity Makes the Thief-Taker: the Influence of Economic Analysis on Crime Control', in T. Newburn and P. Rock (eds), *The Politics of Crime Control*, Oxford: Oxford University Press (forthcoming).

13

GENDER AND CRIME

Frances Heidensohn and Loraine Gelsthorpe

INTRODUCTION

The history of the relationship between feminism and criminology is now rich with critical explorations of the contours of each discipline, epistemology, methods, politics, policy, and praxis. Scholars within this field have set out to question some of the gender-blind assumptions within criminology and not only to create a space for women's voices and experiences, but at a theoretical level to examine constructions of gender. Here, we aim to: (i) outline key precepts and issues which are relevant to an understanding of *feminist contributions to criminology*; (ii) summarize *the early feminist critique of criminology*; (iii) examine *methodological issues and developments*; (iv) review *theoretical work on masculinity*; (v) explore a range of issues relating to *women, men, and crime*, including illumination of key findings from research relating to women and criminal justice; and (vi) focus on *gender, crime, and justice in late modernity* and examine the impact of both feminist perspectives in criminology and feminist-inspired work on gender, crime, and justice more generally.

The chapter offers an overview of the critical insights provided or prompted by feminism which might be said to have transgressed both the theory and politics of research and action in criminology. Associations between gender and crime are profound, persistent, and paradoxical. For as long as observation of offending has been made, it has been noted that men and women differ in their offence rates and patterns, and in their experiences of victimization. Moreover, the considerable body of work flowing from the statement has had major effects on criminological thinking and on criminal justice policies.

FEMINIST CONTRIBUTIONS TO CRIMINOLOGY

It is now an axiomatic principle that we must speak of different feminist perspectives, and of different criminologies. The chapters in this volume provide ample evidence of this. There is thus no one relationship, but a myriad of relationships between feminism and criminology. Moreover, the criminology of the 1970s, which prompted Carol Smart's 1976 critical text *Women, Crime and Criminology*, one of the first openly feminist critiques of criminology in Britain (bearing in mind that there was earlier pre-feminist work by Heidensohn 1968 and 1970, and Bertrand 1969 on the neglect of women in the study of crime), is not the criminology of today. Whether today's criminology is sufficiently diverse or open enough to accommodate some of the critical precepts of feminisms remains a matter for debate. There are those who have made a strong case for abandoning criminology (Smart 1990), or who, because of resistance to a feminist transformation of the discipline of criminology, see fundamental incompatibilities between feminism and criminology (Stanko 1993; A. Young 1994). In a percipient conclusion to her 1976 text Smart commented:

> Criminology and the sociology of deviance must become more than the study of men and crime if it is to play any significant part in the development of our understanding of crime, law and the criminal process and play any role in the transformation of existing social practices [1976: 185].

Her concern was that criminology, even in its more radical form, would be 'unmoved' by feminist critiques. By 1990, she viewed criminology as the 'atavistic man' in intellectual endeavours and wished to abandon it because she could not see what it had to offer feminism. Nevertheless, we think that there are good reasons to pause before pursuing this option, a point to which we return in the final part of the chapter.

There have been several serious explorations of the relationship between feminism and criminology over the years. A key question is whether key substantive and political and epistemological and methodological projects within feminism make engagement with criminology difficult. So, what is it about feminist work that might make links with criminological work untenable?

We should add that when we speak of feminism, of course, we are not speaking of something which is obvious or can be taken for granted (see Gelsthorpe 2002 for a description of different kinds of feminism). Liberal feminism, with its commitment to equality of opportunity and the recognition of women's rights in welfare, health, employment, and education probably has the closest relationship with criminology. Postmodernism—with its opposition to essentialism[1] probably has the most difficult relationship with criminology (Carrington 1998).

There are many sophisticated explorations of the different feminist positions and of the differences within categories (Jackson and Scott 2002). But these different positions collectively illustrate men's material interest in the domination of women and the different ways in which men construct a variety of institutional arrangements to sustain this domination. Feminists argue the case to 'make visible the invisible' by bringing into focus the gender structure of society. Feminists have thus challenged the political, ontological, and epistemological assumptions that underlie patriarchal discourses

---

[1] Essentialism reflects a mode of thinking which relies on some presumed essence or interest rather than the specific conditions of social phenomena.

(put simply, understandings of the world which reflect men's interests) as well as their theoretical contents. They have developed both an anti-sexist stance, and a stance which involves the construction of alternative models, methods, procedures, discourses, and so on. We elaborate some of these challenges below.

THE EARLY FEMINIST CRITIQUE OF CRIMINOLOGY

One of the first tasks in second-wave feminism from the 1960s onwards was to develop a comprehensive critique of the discipline. The early critique has been well rehearsed elsewhere (see, for example, Heidensohn 1996). It has frequently focused on the two main themes of amnesia or neglect and distortion. Women account for a very small proportion of all known offenders, and as a consequence relatively little attention has been given to them. The majority of studies of crime and delinquency prior to the 1980s were of men's crime and delinquency (Leonard 1982; Scraton 1990). A second theme in the critique is that, even when women were recognized, they were depicted in terms of stereotypes based on their supposed biological and psychological nature. Whilst critical criminology challenged the assumptions of positivism in explaining men's crime, it neglected to acknowledge how such assumptions remained most prevalent in academic and popular conceptions of women's crime. Similarly, while analyses of class structure, state control, and the political nature of deviance gained credibility, the study of women's crime remained rooted in notions of biological determinism and an uncritical attitude towards the dominant sexual stereotypes of women as passive, domestic, and maternal (Smart 1976). Tracing the continuance of sexist assumptions from Lombroso to Pollak and beyond, Smart (1976) examined how assumptions of the abnormality of female offenders came to dominate both theory and criminal justice policy—despite evidence of more critical thinking in relation to men and men's crime. Women were ignored, marginalized, or distorted, both in their deviancy and in their conformity. The exposure of criminology as the criminology of men marked the starting point of feminists' attempts to find alternative modes of conceptualizing the social worlds of deviance and conformity, punishment and control.

The focus of this general critique, however, was limited. Some writers assumed that a remedy to criminological and criminal justice deficiencies could be sought by appropriating existing criminological theories and 'inserting' women: for example, by discovering girl gangs (Velimesis 1975) and considering girls in relation to subcultural theory (McRobbie 1980; Shacklady Smith 1978). Rafter and Natalizia (1981) presented the message in a different way, suggesting that 'women only' studies should strive to produce a body of information as extensive as that which existed for men.

In criminal justice practice there were strivings for 'equality' (that is, for women to be treated like men), though this early liberal feminist position gradually came to be challenged by those who questioned the meaning and nature of equality (e.g. MacKinnon 1987a, 1987b; Smart 1990). Some of these feminist claims and assertions now seem somewhat naive, but the significance of the critique as a starting point for reflection and for changes in criminal justice practice should not be underestimated. Moreover, feminist contributions soon moved beyond a critique.

Dominant strands in the development of feminist perspectives in criminology have included empirical illuminations about discriminatory practices as we show later in the chapter. New ways of conceptualizing matters—the different ways in which conformity is produced for instance—were also developed. Heidensohn (1985, 1996) concluded her review of women, crime, and criminal justice by arguing for a return to the sociology of gender and for the use of insights from other studies of women's oppression. Such a redirection helped expose the explicit and informal controls exercised over women—in the home and at work—and, above all, focused on the rather peculiar notion of 'normal behaviour'. A number of writers have made apparent the correspondences between the policing of everyday life and policing through more formal mechanisms of social control (see Heidensohn 2000). A large body of empirical work drew attention to the experiences of female victims of crime and to female victims' and offenders' experiences of criminal justice processes (see, for example, Walklate 2004). Again, as we show later, some of the focus on women and criminal justice developed from important feminist work in this area.

Daly and Chesney-Lind (1988) raise two key questions in relation to criminological theory. First, they ask whether theories generated to describe men's or boys' offending can apply to women and girls (what they call the 'generalisability problem') Secondly, they ask why women commit less crime than men (what they term the 'gender ratio problem') In other words, they express concern about 'gender', the implication being that theories of crime must be able to take account of both men's and women's (criminal) behaviour, and that they must also be able to highlight factors which operate differently on men and women. But more than this, they draw attention to the crucial problematization of gender in different feminist perspectives. This leads to a sophisticated notion of gender relations in which gender is seen not as a natural fact, but as 'a complex, historical, and cultural product . . . related to, but not simply derived from, biological sex difference and reproductive capacities' (1988: 504). Thus complex gender codes are internalized in a myriad of ways to regulate behaviour. In other words, criminologists could learn a great deal from looking at feminist insights in relation to gender. Daly and Chesney-Lind also urge criminologists to read at first hand of women's experiences rather that relying on distorted, received wisdom about women, for these accounts of experience have not only enriched feminist thought, but become a central part of feminist analyses and epistemological reflections. There is also encouragement for criminologists to reflect on the ethnocentricity inherent in mainstream criminological thinking: the fact that the questions posed by criminologists are generally those of white, economically privileged men.

In *Feminist Perspectives in Criminology* (Gelsthorpe and Morris 1990), it was similarly noted that creative feminist contributions to criminology go well beyond critique.

The contributors to this book both illustrated the hegemonic masculinity of most criminological work and clarified the foundations for future gender-conscious work. Smart's (1990) distinctive contribution was to question whether the focus on female lawbreakers is a proper concern for feminism and whether a feminist criminology is theoretically possibly or politically desirable. She contrasted the limited horizons of criminology—stuck in a conventional mode of seeking 'the truth' through scientific empirical endeavours—with some of the major theoretical and political questions which engage feminist scholarship in relation to postmodern reappraisals of knowledge forms and scientific approaches to knowledge.

METHODOLOGICAL ISSUES AND DEVELOPMENTS

Feminist writers have focused on the processes of knowledge production and have reflected on research experiences and research methodologies: engaging with 'the researched', recognizing their subjectivity in a non-hierarchical way, and using sensitive research methods which maximize opportunities to reflect more accurately the experiences of 'the researched'. Whilst feminist research practices have been the focus of much debate in recent years (Ramazanoglu and Holland 2002), myths abound. For example, the oft-quoted phrase from sociologists Stanley and Wise, that feminist research must be 'on, by and for women' (1983: 17), is often misunderstood: they question this dictum. Close reading of feminist discussions (Oakley 1999, and Finch 2004, for example) ultimately reveal no fixed 'absolutes' beyond the need for sensitivity in the research task, for personal reflexivity—to reflect on the subjectivities of all involved—and commitment to make the research relevant to women.

The focus on women's 'experiences' (with democratic insistence that women should be 'allowed to speak for themselves') has been used both to make women visible and to link feminist ontology (beliefs about the nature of the world) with feminist epistemology (beliefs about what counts as appropriate knowledge). From this, appropriate knowledge is that which allows women to speak for themselves, rather than knowledge about men's worlds which so often presumes itself to be about women's worlds too. As Cain puts it, this is not as a corrective to traditional criminology which has excluded or marginalized women, but for 'women's unspeakable "experiences" to be captured, experienced, named and tamed' without using men and their experiences as a yardstick against which women's experiences must be compared (1990: 9). Thus Cain proposes a focus on the construction of gender, on discourses which lie beyond criminology, and on sites which are relevant to women. Cain's claims for serious consideration of gender include men: 'We shall fall into essentialism if we exclude men from our analyses, even if we may wish to exclude them from much of our field research' (1990: 11).

The concern to place women's experiences, viewpoints, and struggles at the centre of projects has led to the development of what Harding (1987) has called 'feminist standpointism': a commitment to try and understand the world from the perspective of the socially subjugated—to see things through women's eyes. Whilst there are debates about the nature of women's 'shared' experience and different experiences, and about assumptions that women's realities are somehow 'more real' or produce 'better know-ledge' than those discerned from traditional methodologies (Cain 1986), there are no fixed views. Indeed, there is increasing recognition of ontological complexities. 'Feminist standpointism' has nevertheless encouraged both theoretical and personal reflexivity in relation to knowledge and the processes of knowledge production through research: this can help overcome some of the problems of conventional methodologies associated with mainstream criminology.

Feminist writers have reflected long and hard on the research methodologies they employ. Early dismissals of anything tainted with positivism (and quantitative methods in particular) have (rightly, in our view) given way to critical reflections on the need to use research methods appropriate to the nature of the task (see Kelly 1990; Finch 2004; Gelsthorpe and Sharpe 2005/6). There is no longer anything to suggest that the ideas of feminist writers in criminology are fundamentally antithetical to those of criminologists. Oakley (2000), for example, argues that divisions between 'quantitative' and 'qualitative' methods are unhelpful in the pursuit of knowledge, and recent large-scale statistical analyses of sentencing trends concerning women (which we describe later) demonstrate this very well (see also Heimer and Kruttschnitt 2006). The UK-based ESRC programme of research on violence also demonstrates this through the wide range of methodologies employed (ESRC 1998). In the wake of feminist concerns to place women's experiences at the centre of research we have witnessed an expansion of interest in the study of lived experience taking place within the social sciences generally.[2] At the same time, it is hard to sustain a claim that some of the challenges to conventional research methodologies are distinctively 'feminist', but certainly feminist writers might lay claim to a concern to do 'good' research which is not automatically and unthinkingly driven by positivist paradigms and processes.

If we characterize the first two main developments in feminist criminology as *feminist empiricism* (as evidenced in the wide-ranging criminological research on women, crime, control, and justice to counterbalance the absence of women from conventional work), and *feminist standpointism* (drawing attention to the need to place women's experience at the centre of knowledge), the third is best described as *feminist deconstructionism* (Naffine 1997) since it draws on postmodern insights relating to the problematizing of language and concepts.

These are foundational feminist contributions to criminology and to methodological thinking. One key feature of feminist contributions to criminology is the push to rec-ognize gender as a social construct and not simply as a statistical 'variable'. Whilst early feminist work focused on the need to incorporate women in all areas of criminological debate, later work introduced a more critical consideration of the concept of gender

[2] See, for example, Hollway and Jefferson (2000) and Goodey (2000) for a detailed account of this interest as well as description of methods. It has to be acknowledged, though, that this new interest takes place against a background of concern that too few social scientists are numerate.

(Daly 1997; Walklate 2004). Feminist criminologists have encouraged theorizations of gender, gender differences, gender relations, gender order, and the meaning of gender as a subjective lived experience rather than merely an ascription, within a context of power relations and patriarchy.[3] There have been some criticisms of the focus on gender to the neglect of other dimensions of lived realities (in relation to race and ethnicity for example), but there have nevertheless been significant steps towards a sophisticated understanding of gender. As Chesney-Lind (2006) has put it:

> Contemporary approaches to gender and crime...tend to avoid the problems of reductionism and determinism that characterize early discussions of gender and gender relations, stressing instead the complexity, tentativeness, and variability with which individuals, particularly youth, negotiate (and resist) gender identity [2006: 8].

Work on masculinity provides illustration of such developments.

THEORETICAL WORK ON MASCULINITY

Although the 'maleness of crime' has traditionally been acknowledged within mainstream criminology in terms of 'males', 'men', or 'boys' dominating the crime scene, it has not often been viewed as a socially constructed concept. But a sociology of masculinity has emerged from feminist work on gender, and from men's involvement in feminism, as well as the growing field of gay and lesbian studies. A vital change came in asking what it is about men as men and 'not as working-class, not as migrants, not as underprivileged individuals but *as men*, that induces them to "commit crime" ' (Grosz 1987). Feminist criminologists such as Cain (1990), for instance, argued that feminist criminology must consider what it was in the social construction of maleness that was so criminogenic. Others writers such as Newburn and Stanko (1994) and Collier (1998) have made significant contributions to recognition of masculinity as critical to an understanding of crime and victimization.

But it is also fair to say that some sociological thinking about gender was prompted by the rather one-dimensional images of men's dominance presented by radical feminist work on gender (for example, the notion that all men are rapists). Further obstacles to an appreciation of masculinity as a social construct can be seen in the failure to address the larger issues of social structure in understanding men's power. ('Power', of course, has been central to feminist concepts of patriarchy and to the social analyses which have flowed from it.)

The literature on masculinity has increased markedly in the last few years (see, for example, Messerschmidt 1993, 1997, 2002). As indicated, a key shift came with the introduction of a gender paradigm based on the idea that gender was socially

---

[3] Literally meaning 'the power of the father', but more generally referring to systems of power, hierarchy, and dominance that oppress women.

constructed and where encultured sex roles were ascribed to bodily difference. Connell (1995) looked at the key concepts of patriarchy, domination, oppression, and exploitation through which men are deemed the powerful (and women the 'other'); he suggested that masculinity is negotiated and practised in varying ways in different contexts. This at once draws together feminist perspectives on the social construction of gender and puts the contestation of power at the centre of an analysis of masculinities.

Over time, the focus on masculinity has been transformed into an understanding of complex and multiple masculinities: 'hegemonic' masculinities (associated with heterosexuality, toughness, power, authority, and competition) or 'subordinated' masculinities (associated with gay men, for example). Part of Connell's (1995) argument is to suggest that the dominant gender structure is always being reproduced and reconstituted. This leads to a more acute appreciation of the situations in which masculinities are learned, how they are learned, and how they are played out in everyday life—whether the school playground, the factory floor or office, in the police station, or in prison.

Connell's (1995) aim to promote a more sophisticated understanding of masculinities, however, has become somewhat clouded by the varying usage of the term 'hegemonic masculinity'. Collier, for instance, has indicated that the term is used 'on the one hand as referring to a certain set of characteristics or traits, which are then meant to signify "the masculine" in particular contexts; and on the other, as explaining, the *cause* of, the crimes of men' (1998:19). Hegemonic masculinity is thus expected to explain a vast array of (almost always negative) male behaviours and criminal activities. The concept then becomes too vague, overused, and potentially tautological. McMahon (1993) suggests that 'masculinity' is an explanatory cliché in many academic and popular accounts of men, in the same way that sex-role theory was in earlier accounts of behaviour. Indeed, we are left with many questions as to how 'masculine' qualities relate to what men do in concrete and material ways. These analyses also leave unanswered questions of the relationship of masculinity to the individual and the 'embodied social selves' of men. Further, they fail to help us understand the dimensions of the unities and differences among men.

Tony Jefferson (2002) adds criticisms of studies of hegemonic masculinity for taking an overly socialized view of masculinity. He argues that psychoanalytical dimensions of behaviour have been underplayed, and that males choose 'admired masculine conduct' at any one time in a way that best suits their psychological purposes—allowing them to ward off feelings of anxiety and powerlessness. Willis (1977) and Archer (2001) provide useful examples of this in practice. In *Learning to Labour*, for example, building on earlier sociological theories about the search for status from peers through delinquent activity, Willis (1977) shows how young men may become criminal to reassert a sense of power and achievement in an otherwise oppressed social position. Archer (2001) gives important attention to young men's use of discourses of hegemonic masculinity in their negotiations between 'Muslim', 'black', and 'Asian' masculinities.

A number of responses can be made to these varied criticisms—beginning with recognition of the changeability of the characteristics of what is considered to be hegemonic masculinity both historically and across the life course, and how this changeability is linked to cultural, political, and economical ideologies and motivations. For example, hegemonic masculinities represent the currently most glorified way of being a 'man' and how this is open to change as older forms of 'being a man' are replaced by newer ones. This has particular resonance since as men get older they may no longer judge their masculinity in terms of 'pints of beer consumed', flash cars driven at speed, and ability to 'pull girls', but rather their ability to provide for their families. This may have ramifications for their involvement in criminal activity.

Connell and Messerschmidt (2005) have addressed some of the criticisms by amplifying how the concept of hegemonic masculinity does not equate to social reproduction, and by recognizing more the social struggles in which subordinated masculinities influence dominant forms. They suggest a reformulation of the concept by introducing a more complex model of gender hierarchy (acknowledging the agency of women more), by giving explicit recognition to the geography of masculinities (acknowledging the interplay between local, regional, and global levels), by giving specific greater attention to embodiment in contexts of privilege and power (acknowledging transgender practices along the way), and by giving stronger emphasis to the dynamics of hegemonic masculinity (through life histories, for example). Certainly this reformulation is more likely than previous formulations to recognize constructions of racialized and gendered identities and to recognize that psychological as well as sociological factors are essential to analysis.

But in revisiting the concept of hegemonic masculinity Connell and Messerschmidt (2005) go further to express regret that the concept of 'emphasized femininity' which acknowledges the asymmetrical position of masculinities and femininities in a patriarchal gender order, has dropped out of focus. As they argue, 'Gender is always relational, and patterns of masculinity are socially defined in contradistinction from some model (real or imaginery) of femininity' (2005: 848). Thus the focus on hegemonic masculinities, without the wider gaze on femininities, clouds vision of the interplay of femininities and masculinities. The authors suggest that focus on the interplay is particularly important in a context of new configurations of women's identity and place. This might have particular significance in the context of crime and justice where young women are emerging as active agents of crime as much as they are seen as 'victims' of abuse. No longer the gangster's moll then perhaps, but then no longer the single image gangster either.

Messerschmidt's (1993) analysis has been the most extensive attempt to apply Connell's framework to the study of crime. He developed the idea of gender as a 'situational accomplishment' and of crime as a means of 'doing gender'. Following Connell, Messerschmidt addresses race and class alongside gender in his theorization of these categories as 'structured action' (1997). The idea is that masculinity can be seen as a crucial point of intersection of different forms or structures of power, stratification, desire, and subjective identity formation. (On the other hand Mac an Ghaill (1994), for instance, makes the criticism that these 'structures' omit age and disability.) Hood-Williams (2001) further questions whether or not it is actually possible to know and accomplish 'class', for example, in any systematic way. Importantly, Jody Miller (2002) has advanced Messerschmidt's analysis by looking at the strengths and limitations of 'doing gender' for understanding street crime, and in particular by challenging gender dualism and focusing on the transformative aspects of social action to capture the dynamic nature of agency as it impacts on 'doing gender' and creating identity (see also Messerschmidt 2002).

Some of the work in this area has attracted criticism for its 'essentializing tendencies' —as did early feminist work (see Hood-Williams 2001; Haywood and Mac an Ghaill 2003; and Walklate 2004, for overviews). Nor is it entirely clear where sophisticated theories about masculinity leave us in terms of comprehending crime. In many respects they make the task infinitely more complex, particularly the new 'puzzles' suggested to us by questions of subjectivity.

Hood-Williams's conclusion is that 'criminology knows about gender, confidently goes out to find it and does indeed discover it' (2001: 54): a clear critique of unthinking positivism. Analytic work, on the other hand, raises the difficult question of just exactly what is to count as masculinity, and lays bare the unresolved difficulties and the relationship between masculinity theory and crime. One of the challenges is in understanding the lived reality of crime. As Hood-Williams puts it, 'the radical question is 'whether the term "masculinities" adds anything to the analysis of criminal events or is it an empty tautology signifying nothing more than (some of) the things men and boys do' (2001: 39).

By focusing on the 'foreground factors' of the experience of crime and its 'moral emotions', Katz (1988) has perhaps brought us closer to understanding the lived reality of crime. His analysis of 'excitement' and 'seduction' is free from any sustained attempt to perceive or analyse these emotions as masculine elements of identity. What such work suggests is that at the moment of desire, pleasure, and risk-seeking, a specifically masculine identity may not be the most important element in engagement in crime. As indicated, Jefferson (1997) has also called for a more sophisticated understanding of agency and individual identity by highlighting the importance of psychoanalytic theory to provide a more contextualized account of individuals and crime; a theme taken up in later work by Gadd (2003), amongst others, in relation to subjectivity and men's violence. Frosh *et al.* (2002) exemplify some of these themes in their contemporary analysis of boys as 'active agents'; their everyday notions of 'macho' behaviour and of 'popular' and 'unpopular' masculinities in terms of what it is legitimate to achieve by way of scholastic attainment and sport, for example, and of how transgressions of gender boundaries are viewed, are shaped by social structures and individual agency. Thus, crucially, we return to feminist precepts regarding reality as 'lived experience'. The foregrounding of agency goes straight to the heart of the feminist enterprise.

Our aim here has been to highlight some of the theoretical reasoning regarding masculinity and masculinities studies promoted, at least in part, by feminist insights into conceptions and practices of gender. There is further work to be done in relation to crime and victimization, and in relation to the need to recognize the state (and the criminal justice system) as a gendered institution. There is also need to identify how and under what circumstances the state acts as a gendered institution (in combination with considerations of race and class). Whilst feminist scholars in criminology have made inroads in this area in relation to women and the criminal justice system, as we show below, there has so far been too little attention to masculinities in criminal justice responses to crime.

WOMEN, MEN, AND CRIME

We now examine issues relating to gender and crime. We should say at the outset that 'gender' is used rather than 'sex' because it covers both aspects of innate and acquired characteristics and the interaction between them and society.

'Women commit far less crime than do men 'was the standard introduction to this topic for a long time; closer examination leads, however, to some qualifications and there are increasing concerns with ideas of convergence of male and female rates. On many comparisons, the differences remain remarkable and robust, and, as we shall see, appear to be valid. The overall female share of recorded crime appears to be fairly stable. In England and Wales, for instance, in 1984, 84 per cent of known offenders were male and in 2004 80 per cent. Of the population born in 1953, 34 per cent of men, but only 9 per cent of women, had a conviction for an indictable or other serious offence by the age of 46 (Home Office 2004b see Burman 2004b for some cross-cultural comparisons in English-speaking countries).

This difference, variously called the 'the gender gap' or the 'sex crime ratio', has become one of the key themes of modern feminist criminology and of the wider field of gender-related studies of crime. A number of established observations about female crime remain valid: women commit fewer and less serious offences, they desist from crime more readily, girls reach their peak age of offending sooner than boys and are much less involved in professional crime. Offences of dishonesty are the most common for which women are cautioned or convicted in England and Wales (57 per cent in 2002); 80 per cent of women have criminal careers lasting less than a year compared with 55 per cent of males; 24 per cent of males, but only 7 per cent of females, have crime careers of 10 years or more. Girls' peak age of offending is 15, boys' is 19 (all references are to Home Office section 95 reports).[4]

These ratios changed very little in the second half of the twentieth century (the longer historical view is considered below). Nevertheless, concerns with shifts in these patterns have come from several sources with growing frequency. Arguments about whether female crime was rising at a faster rate than male, and that thus the female share was going up, have been highly contended criminological issues since the 1970s.

---

[4] All statistics are taken from the annual Home Office reports, *Statistics on Women and the Criminal Justice System*, issued pursuant to section 95 of the Criminal Justice Act 1991, and known as 'Section 95 reports'.

Indeed, this is one of the few topics to do with women and crime to excite widespread attention (Heidensohn 1989). The issue was first raised by Freda Adler (and in a more modified form by Rita Simon) who argued that female crime rates had been rising more rapidly in the late 1960s and early 1970s; that women offenders were changing their patterns of offending to more 'masculine' styles, becoming more aggressive and violent; and that this was due to the growth of the modern women's movement. 'Liberation', in short, 'causes crime' (Adler 1975).

These contentions have been much discussed and analysed. Given what we know of the limitations of such data (see Maguire, in Chapter 10, this volume), great caution is necessary in interpreting crime statistics. Smart, for instance, taking a long time-series for England and Wales, found that female crime rates were already rising at a faster rate than male long before the advent of the modern women's movement (1979; cf. Austin 1981). Nevertheless, well into the twenty-first century, the concept of liberation causing crime is still used by journalists as in the *Chicago Sun–Times* 'Violent Femmes ... is violence the new frontier for girls? Will they catch up with boys? ... now comes greater equality in violence'(15 February 2006). Even a liberal paper like *The Guardian* takes this approach, featuring an international survey, which reported that two-thirds of boys in Scotland and England, but fewer than a third of girls, reported violent behaviour, as 'British Girls among the most violent in the world' (24 January 2006). There have also been some changes in the gender gap, particularly for younger age groups, and notable increases in imprisonment levels of women. A range of studies have explored these developments and suggested reasons for them (see below).

The female share of crime does appear to be increasing, if slightly, in Britain, up from 10 : 1 in the 1950s to 6 : 1 in the 1990s. In the USA there have shifts also, with women representing 13 per cent of arrests in 1975 and 19 per cent in 1995 (NCJRS 1998). In England and Wales, part of the change can be attributed to drugs crimes, and partly to increasing violence amongst women, although there are many myths about this (Gelsthorpe and Morris 2002). For instance, among Adler and Worrall's (2004) findings are that, while there were instances of recorded increases in girls' violent offending in Australia, the UK, and Canada, their convictions were often for the most minor forms of offending not involving weapons, and many of their victims were care workers or police officers, suggesting, that girls' normal resistance to discipline is more readily criminalized and punished today, where once it was treated as a welfare issue. Worrall follows this general view of girls and violence across the English-speaking world with a detailed dissection of recent British policies which, she argues, have resulted in the ' "welfarization" and "soft policing" of young women's behaviour by both formal and informal social control mechanisms having given way to straightforward "criminalization" of that same behaviour, with increasing numbers of young women being incarcerated not on spurious benevolent welfare grounds, but on spuriously equitable "justice" grounds' (Worrall 2004). In short, more bad behaviour by girls is being redefined as criminal, particularly fighting. In related research, Burman (2004a) has explored the meanings of violence to groups of teenage girls in Scotland. The picture she presents is similarly complex: 'a focus on physical violence ... would be misguided, as it obscures and detracts from other forms of intentionally harmful violating behaviour . . . they experience verbally abusive behaviour (threats, name calling, taunting etc.) as more hurtful and damaging' (Burman 2004: 85).

Self-report studies have become important sources of data on gender-gap issues and offer some interesting perspectives on these topics, bearing in mind, of course, the reservations which must apply to them. A study of alcohol, crime, and disorder, which covered young people, did not find any hugely surprising revelations however: 'A substantial minority of young people drank excessively . . . twenty-eight per cent of 18–24-year old men and nineteen per cent of women had drunk more than the weekly recommended amount . . . Males were more likely to binge drink (48 per cent) than females (31 per cent)' (Richardson and Budd 2003: vii).

The same researchers found that 'almost half of the men reported taking an illegal drug compared with just over a third of women' (2003: 27). When disorderly activity was compared: 'young men were significantly more likely to admit offending than young women (33 and 13 per cent). Among young men, violence was the most common offence (15 per cent) compared with 2 per cent' (2003: 36). The researchers note that 'men, and particularly young men, were mentioned as being more likely to react aggressively after drinking. The masculine culture and the need to defend their image in front of friends and girlfriends was thought to be the basis of this' (2003: 48). Another British survey which questioned schoolchildren aged between 10 and 16 on their anti-social and offending behaviour found that 'There was little difference between boys and girls, with 55 per cent of boys and 49 per cent of girls admitting they had committed an offence in the last twelve months' (Armstrong *et al.* 2005). However, while reports of vandalism and truancy showed little variation between the sexes, 'boys . . . were more than twice as likely as girls . . . to say they had attacked someone' (19 compared with 8 per cent) (2005: vii). This study found very significant ethnic and racial differences in the sample, often with links between them, thus black and mixed-race children were more often excluded from school, as were boys, and both groups were bullied more frequently (2005: vii–viii). The research suggests greater gender parity in some kinds of delinquent behaviour, but that the traditional divides persist in others.

The findings of these surveys are given added depth by some of the ethnographies and participant studies of the lives of young people. Hobbs and colleagues have produced accounts of the night-time economies of British cities full of vivid detail and observation of the nuances of modern urban life. They describe how 'the alcohol-fuelled night-time economy also provides an ideal environment for those who regard fighting as an expressive hobby . . . [and] a common thread to the hard case cobblestone fighters of yesteryear' (2003: 38). Most of these fighters are young, working class and male, 'weekend warriors'. Bouncers expressed disbelief at the behaviour of women involved in disturbances: 'Ejecting women from the bar was regarded as one of the most annoying aspects of the job. The prevailing logic seemed to be better to deal with a group of brawling men than a group of irate women' (2003: 136). Similarly, traditional conceptions of bad behaviour are blurred in modern studies of bullying. In a small school-based study, for example, Myers found mixed groups of bullies which represented changes in gender roles: 'the pupils still behaved in masculine and feminine ways but they were not in opposition all of the time and they did not always assume "traditional" gender roles' (2006).

Most self-report surveys examine the lives of young people and many ethnographic and qualitative studies focus on youthful lives too because of their visibility or ease of access. Some studies, most especially on domestic violence and related topics, cover mature adults in a comparative way (e.g. Walby and Allen 2004). Indeed, these have given rise to considerable debate: 'Research findings are contradictory and point in two directions, with some revealing that women are as likely as men to perpetrate violence against an intimate partner (symmetry) and others showing that it is overwhelmingly men who perpetrate violence against women partners (asymmetry)' (Dobash and Dobash 2004: 324).

On a different point of comparison, in the USA major efforts have gone into analysing recorded increases which show that between 1980 and 2003 the female percentage of all arrests increased from one-fifth to one-third for simple assault (Steffensmeier *et al.* 2006). Steffensmeier and his colleagues in two recent articles use alternative data sets from the Uniform Crime Reports of the FBI (from which the figures above come) to test out hypotheses about female violence generally and recent trends in girls' violence (2006 and 2005). For the latter, they compare UCR data with victim surveys and self-report studies. They 'find that the rise in girls' violence as counted in police arrest data is not borne out in unofficial longitudinal sources' (Steffensmeier *et al.* 2005: 395). The rise in girls' violence, they suggest, is due to a variety of factors, some of which may include differential arrest policies and social constructionist penal policies:

> Recent changes in law enforcement practices and the juvenile justice system have apparently escalated the arrest proneness of adolescent females. The rise in girls' arrest for violent crime and the narrowing gender gap have less to do with underlying behavior and more to do, first, with net-widening changes in law and policing toward prosecuting less serious forms of violence . . . in private settings . . . and second, with less biased or more efficient responses to girls' . . . aggression (Steffensmeier *et al.* 2005: 389–90).

In their second study, the same group compare all female and male violent crime rates in the USA over two decades, again using the UCR and the National Crime Victimization Survey (NCVS). This time they test two simpler hypotheses of behaviour change and policy change (Steffensmeier *et al.* 2006). Again their 'key conclusion is that there has been no meaningful or systematic change in women's involvement in crimes of interpersonal violence and in the gender gap in the past couple of decades' (op. cit.: 93). Instead, they find a strong case for the policy change thesis: 'we have changed our laws, police practices, and policies in . . . ways toward enhanced identification and criminalization of violence in general and of women's violence in particular' (op. cit.: 94). In the same journal issue, Chesney Lind argues that one specific policy, that of mandatory arrests for domestic violence, has led to dramatic jumps in rates of female violence (2006: 15). These findings are close to those reported above in Britain and those emerging in Australia (Carrington 2006).

One problem here of course is the assumption that female offending needs to be compared with male, and that the significant issues are what the size of the gender gap is, and whether it is narrowing or may even disappear. From all the studies cited in this section, no firm conclusions can be made. Nevertheless, we can attempt some answers to queries about the persistence of gender differences in crime in the twenty-first century. First, the differences remain striking, but there are concerns that they may be narrowing. Yet research suggests that it is not so much the attitudes and actions of offenders which have shifted, but rather those of policy-makers and law-enforcers, even activists and researchers (Snider 2003), and which require examination. Further, that the context, meaning, and complexity of actions are crucial to their understanding and interpretation, and indeed that variety of research methods is necessary to achieve these. As Downes and Rock put it, this discipline 'can only benefit from addressing more creatively the question of why the oppression of women has not led to rates of crime as high as those of males' (1998: 325). However, much the most interesting work inspired by the recognition of gender as a key aspect of crime can be found in areas where 'women's perspectives within criminology [have] significantly reoriented the field . . . [and] revitalized existing perspectives' (ibid.). In the twenty-first century there is an immense amount of such material to consider; there follow some major examples.

GENDER, CRIME, AND HISTORY

Modern historical work on crime has experienced a renaissance, and studies of women offenders have been one offshoot of this. They enrich, and also complicate, the patterns of crime we are trying to unravel. We have already shown the importance of the gender gap to modern criminological analysis, and it has occupied historians of crime too. In her comprehensive study of seventeenth-century Cheshire court records, Walker urges close analysis of discourses on violence. She found that there was 'little difference in actual methods of fighting by men and by women, (Walker 2003: 270), yet men claimed the privileges of manhood and honour to explain their actions, not an option open to women. Walker presents a fascinating comparison of two gendered sources of reprieve before the courts: benefit of clergy and benefit of belly (pregnancy) and shows that women were not morally equivalent, nor indeed successful; many women gained only temporary reprieve because of their pregnancy and were later executed (op. cit.: 197–201). Writing of Britain in the eighteenth century, McLynn states that 'Only 12 per cent of the accused in the home counties in 1782–7 were female' (1989: 128). Nonetheless, Feeley and Little (1991), taking a sample of Old Bailey cases tried between 1687 and 1912, found that 45 per cent of defendants were women.[5]

However, figures for these, and earlier, periods need to be treated with even more circumspection than those from today. In particular, Zedner notes that: 'Overall there was a considerable decline in those designated as the "criminal classes". Over the period 1860–90 they fell by more than half. The number of women fell at roughly the same rate

---

[5] See Beattie 1975 on women's role in the food riots in the pre-modern period.

as men, remaining at around a fifth of the total in this category over the period' (Zedner 1991: 20). She concludes that this relatively low rate was due to the exclusion of prostitutes, vagrants, and tramps. In terms of convictions, Zedner notes that 'overall, women's crimes made up a steady 17 per cent of all summary convictions' (ibid.: 34), with drunkenness, assault, and larceny the commonest types of offence. In contrast to the steady state in summary jurisdiction, 'over the second half of the nineteenth century, women formed a declining proportion of those proceeded against by indictment '(from 27 per cent of the total in 1867 to only 19 per cent by 1890) (ibid.: 36). Zedner's detailed work on nineteenth-century data confirms on the whole the 'modest share' view of female crime as compared with male. She also notes some reporting of a decline in convictions of women for serious offences by the end of the century (ibid.: 23).

Other historians have asserted that women's share of criminality declined relatively in certain modern periods (see Mannheim 1965; Boritch and Hagan 1990; Jones 1982). Several writers are more cautious or rely on changed practices of recording, controlling, and classifying crime and misdemeanours (Walkowitz 1980), or on 'chivalry' arguments (McLynn 1989), or on views about the changed nature of femininity in Victorian Britain (Zedner 1991), or on combinations of all three.

While gendered, historical accounts of crime and the criminal justice system are important in their own right, it is for the contribution to contemporary discourse that they have most salience for criminology. Wiener's (1998) view of the 'vanishing female' in Victorian crime figures is that this was partly due to the increasing prominence and visibility of the male criminal. In his analysis of male and female workplace appropriation (embezzlement) in mid-nineteenth-century Yorkshire, Godfrey (1999) provides support for modern arguments which attribute female conformity to greater levels of social control and the harsh effects of punishment.

> Women clearly faced many disincentives to appropriate workplace materials, ranging from the physical and the supervisory structures of the factory, to the deterrence of punishments which were particularly severe for women—the loss of children and future employment . . . foremen and employers preferred to use informal punishments [Godfrey 1999: 147].

Following King (1999: 46), who reviews evidence from court records over the period 1791–1822 where he claims that there was an 'apparent continuity of relatively lenient trial outcomes in cases involving females accused for major property crimes from the late sixteenth century to the early nineteenth century' (ibid.: 59), Godfrey (1999) also contributes to the debates on leniency, or chivalry, towards women in the criminal justice system. He found that, although the evidence is mixed, courts were perceived by manufacturers who were their employers to excuse women.

In a study of street violence in the late nineteenth century in Manchester and Salford, Davies describes how 'young working-class women on occasion fought each other, and assaulted men (including police officers) in the streets' (1999: 87). He also found evidence of gender discrimination in sentencing and of the use of informal controls. For instance, he found that 'girls who were occasionally rough were kept out of the clutches of the police' and notes, 'the cycle of repeat offending that seems to have affected young lads' Godfrey (2004: 34). Girls were willing to fight and to take risks, but he argues that the risks they took had more to do with unprotected sex and illegal abortion than with violence. All these examples illustrate the ways in which gendered historical perspectives on crime both illuminate their subject matter and inform current debates.

EXPOSING DOMESTIC 'SECRETS'

Our understanding of other features of the gender ratio has not, in any case, remained static. The subject of victimization, and the contributions of feminists, amongst others, to its 'discovery', are covered elsewhere in this volume (see Hoyle and Zedner, Chapter 15, this volume). It is important to note how the focus on the 'private' harms perpetrated within the home in domestic violence, and physical and sexual abuse of children, alter the gender ratio adversely for men, since they are largely, though not exclusively, the offenders in such crimes. While measures of incidence are shadowy, victim surveys do suggest that there are low reporting rates for such offences and yet a high rate of distress (Stanko 1990b; Griffiths and Hanmer 2005). Serious sexual crimes such as rape also have low reporting rates because of women's fear of shame and of police and court procedures. In a recent Home Office study of women who had been subject since the age of 16 to an act that met the test in the 1994 Act for legally defined rape or attempted rape, the majority (67 per cent) did not define the act as rape (Walby and Allen 2004: viii). In the same study 24 per cent of women and 5 per cent of men had been subject to some form of sexual victimization at least once in their lifetime. This survey also found that 'while some experience of interpersonal violence is quite widespread, a minority is subject to extreme levels of violence, consistent with exceptional degrees of coercive control' (op. cit.: vii). In this group, 89 per cent were women. Most rapists were intimates of the victim, 45 per cent being husbands or partners and 9 per cent former partners; a further 29 per cent were known to the woman and only 17 per cent were strangers (op. cit.: ix). Numerous studies have sought to show the link between female offending and victimization, both physical and sexual. While boys are often the victims of abuse too, it is sexual abuse which females appear to suffer more often (Hale 2005).

GENDER AND POLICING

Women's entry into policing in the UK and the USA, and in some European nations and Australia, was promoted in the late nineteenth and early twentieth centuries precisely to provide protection to female and juvenile offenders and victims which, it was felt, they did not receive from an all-male force (Carrier 1988; Feinman 1986). For more than fifty years, until integration in the 1970s, small numbers of female officers worked in this fashion in all these systems.

A considerable body of recent research has applied gender perspectives to law-enforcement. Studies of police culture have arguably always had masculinity at their core (Reiner 1985) because of the nature of that culture (see also Waddington 1999). But other writers have challenged, the notion that such a cop culture is inevitable or immutable, let alone desirable (Young 1991; Heidensohn 1992; Chan 1996).

Findings from studies with a gender perspective throw light on the role and position of women in law-enforcement, reconstruct the notion of police culture, and form part of the basis for 'modernization' in many agencies around the world. Martin (1980), Jones (1986), and Heidensohn (1992), for example, have respectively looked at the notion of 'defeminized' women who compete directly with their male colleagues and 'deprofessionalized' women who accept subordinate roles and routine tasks in the station house; 'traditional' and 'modern' types of woman officer; and work identitites which revolve around a sense of mission regarding values of law and order and a perception of a duty to keep the peace. Paradoxically, this could lead some women to take, or be perceived as taking, a deviant stand by challenging custom and practice: this could be in cases of alleged police corruption, in bullying, or by exposing their organization to public scrutiny through legal challenges (Heidensohn 1994).

In a later project, Brown and Heidensohn (2000) compared the experiences of an international sample of policewomen and, as with others, found widespread evidence of a macho cop culture, manifested in sexual discrimination and sexual harassment of women officers by their male colleagues. The authors developed a comparative framework for this study, grouping police organizations around the world into four categories of cops, colonials, transitionals, and gendarmeries. They noted the relationship between these models, the impact of police culture on women officers, and the attitudes to the victimization of women. The theme of how 'deviant' and threatening women officers could still seem was apparent. More recent research reflects the growing levels of recruitment of women into policing and their promotion to the highest levels: the first female chief constable was appointed in Britain in 1995 and there have been several since. Westmarland (2001) argues that women may now have a better chance of achieving promotion than men since they specialize in areas such as child protection which are part of a new and vital agenda of policing. However, other evidence suggests a more cautious interpretation. Westmarland herself found an 'antiwomen' atmosphere in police departments with very low numbers of females (ibid.: 85). In a study of senior women officers, Silvestri (2003) found that female officers could not afford to be seen as feminists and focused on 'representation and retention issues rather than changing the culture'.

Women's entry into law-enforcement and their roles, careers, and contributions are the most widely researched of all the gender issues in relation to professionals in the criminal justice system. While these studies are of course significant in their own right, this is not least because 'studies of policing are somewhat distinctive in that the importance of gender had been accepted, albeit in a very different way, almost from the earliest studies of policing' (Heidensohn 2003: 556). Other professionals in the criminal justice system face similar problems (Martin and Jurik 1996; Thomas 2005).

Commitment to diversity in all aspects of criminal justice is slowly changing this situation.

GENDER, JUSTICE, AND SENTENCING

We have already observed that gender has its greatest impact on recorded patterns of offending. With some important exceptions, it is the differences to which this gives rise thet are reflected in sentencing patterns. Most notably, the numbers of women in prison are relatively small compared with the numbers of males at any one time. However, the numbers of women sentenced to immediate imprisonment in England and Wales grew faster than comparable figures for males for much of the 1990s and into the twenty-first century. Between 1992 and 2002 the average female population grew by over 173 per cent, the male by only 50 per cent (Home Office 2005). In an international survey of women in prison, Carlen and Worrall (2004) report that this phenomenon is widespread.

Much modern research on women and crime has been marked by its engagement with debates from the past. One enduring belief is that women offenders are protected from the full rigours of the law; but a series of concepts which modify the notion of chivalry have been advanced and discussed. These include the notions of double deviance and double jeopardy, of stigma, and of the importance of formal and informal controls in the lives of women. We have already discussed a range of projects which address what has been termed the new punitiveness toward offending women. Here, we summarize earlier studies and look at new patterns of treatment of females in the criminal justice system.

CHIVALRY

Several authors have reviewed and/or researched the respective treatment of women and men by the courts although few offer straightforward support for chivalry or leniency towards women unrelated to offence seriousness (see Gelsthorpe 2001 for an overview of early studies). Allen's study (1987) is perhaps exceptional in suggesting that violent women offenders received more sympathetic and individualized justice for serious crimes than men. Most British researchers point to the complexities in sentencing. Eaton (1986), for instance, noted that men and women conforming to conventional roles were better treated than those such as homosexuals or single mothers, who did not. Carlen (1983) also found that Scottish sheriffs distinguished between 'good' and 'bad' mothers and were prepared to sentence them accordingly. Worrall (1990) discerned a still more complex situation in which various agents and agencies contrived to make female offenders in the system invisible.

In the USA, Daly (1989a) found that it was children and the family, rather than women themselves, who were the focus of chivalry, or 'judicial paternalism', as the courts sought to support and conserve the fabric of society. Using a sample of matched pairs, in a study of a New Haven felony court, Daly concluded that men and women were not sentenced differently for like crimes (1994b).

DOUBLE DEVIANCE, DOUBLE JEOPARDY, AND STIGMA

To explore some of the above points further, women's low share of recorded criminality has significant consequences for those women who do offend: they are seen to have transgressed not only social norms but gender norms as well. As a result they may, especially when informal sanctions are taken into account, feel that they are doubly punished. Carlen (1983, 1985) notes the prevalence of informal punishment of women by their partners. Several observers have stressed that concern over the anomalous position of deviant women leads to excessive zeal in their treatment, in remands in custody for reports, and in more medicalized interventions (Heidensohn 1981; Edwards 1984). Steward's (2006) study of remand decisions in London magistrates' courts in the twenty-first century, however, found a more complex and individualized pattern in decision-making. Such approaches are particularly marked towards young girls, whose minor sexual misdemeanours seem consistently to be more harshly handled than those of boys (Webb 1984; Cain 1989; Gelsthorpe and Sharpe 2006; see also Morgan and Newburn, Chapter 30, this volume). Such bias is not, as Gelsthorpe emphasizes (1989), the sole determining factor in the way young people are handled by agencies, however; other variables, such as organizational features, are important as well. Nevertheless, there is accumulated evidence to suggest that women suffer especially from the stigma associated with deviance (Heidensohn 1996). One striking example of the impact of stigma on a (mainly) female group of the families of serious offenders is offered by Condry (2006), who observes that relatives of serious offenders are stigmatized and shamed and this stigma has its roots in ideas about familial blame and contamination.

Much of the sense of injustice felt by women who come before the courts stems from their perceptions of such agencies as male dominated and unsympathetic (Heidensohn 1986). The reactions are by no means consistent. They vary by age, ethnic background, and social class, and whether a woman has herself been a victim (Schlesinger et al. 1992). What research does make clear is the considerable effect victimization can have on women's world views (Stanko 1990a; Walklate 1989, 2004). Such was the concern about public reaction to these issues that the Home Office published a research paper reviewing evidence regarding the claim 'that the criminal justice system in England and Wales routinely discriminates against women', concluding 'that the weight of evidence is against this claim' (Hedderman and Hough 1994: 1). The subsequent Home Office study by Hedderman and Gelsthorpe (1997) on the sentencing of women was part of this same attempt to resolve the issue of whether or not there was discrimination in sentencing, whilst at the same time attempting to achieve some impact on the broader issue of women's trust in the criminal justice system that their needs as 'victims' of society would be met.

The rise in the number of women in prison at the turn of the millennium has prompted a major rethink. In Britain, the women's prison population and the incarceration rate fell to such an extent during the 1960s and 1970s in particular, that the Home Office was able to contemplate ending women's imprisonment by 2000. Yet as the century drew to a close the massive growth of overall rates of imprisonment in both Britain and the USA, despite the decline in recorded crime, led analysts to point to a new penality as part of a wider culture of control (Garland 2001: 14) and to seeming punitiveness towards women, as we have previously indicated.

A Home Office study suggests that the interaction of three factors has led to the rise in the numbers of women in prison:

1. an increase in the number of women appearing before the courts;

2. an increase in the proportion of those women receiving a custodial sentence;

3. an increase in the length of prison sentences being imposed on women.

Its conclusions are that the causes of the rise in women in custody are complex and differ over time. For example, in 1996–7, 95 per cent of the increase was due to more women coming before the courts, whereas earlier 50 per cent of it was due to greater use of custody for women. Convictions for drug offences explain a significant part of the growth since they attract longer sentences (Woodbridge and Frosztega 1998).

In contrast, Carlen (1998) uses a series of interviews with prisoners and staff to illustrate her argument that the increases are due to more women falling into the category of social and economic deprivation—a category traditionally more vulnerable to imprisonment, and to an increased punitiveness by the courts to women. Gelsthorpe and Morris, however, are more cautious in their analysis of the reasons for increased penality towards women. They argue that:

> [t]here is some evidence of increased punitiveness because a greater proportion of women are being sentenced to imprisonment and more women are being received into prison for short periods,...although the 'type' of woman imprisoned remains much the same...However,...there is little evidence of an increased punitiveness solely towards women [2002: 287].

The paradox remains that women's relatively minor offending, and distinctive 'troubled' rather than 'troublesome' status as offenders (Gelsthorpe and Loucks 1997), have led to what is widely seen as a dramatic and extraordinary increase.

It is now common ground between most participants in policy-making and analysis for women offenders that 'the evidence suggests that courts are imposing more severe sentences on women for less serious offences' (Home Office 2004: 3). Hedderman's detailed study of why more women are being sentenced to custody in England and Wales concludes that the changes are not due to changes in offending rates: 'there is little to suggest that female offending...has become more prevalent or more serious' (2004: 86). What has changed, on the other hand, is the custody rate: '40% of the women sentenced in the Crown Court are now being given custodial sentences compared to under a quarter eight years ago...at the magistrates' court...the rate of increase has been higher...custody is now used five times more frequently than in 1992' (op. cit.: 89). The Home Office *Section 95 report* (2003) updates these figures, although evidence from sentencers themselves as to why this may be happening is not presented. Other research suggests that sentencers are imposing longer prison sentences for serious crimes and are more likely to imprison those appearing before the courts today than ten years ago (Hough *et al.* 2003) . But this still does not explain why women, who are generally seen as less threatening, and who commit fewer and less serious crimes, have been so affected by this punitive turn. Thomas (2002) has argued that the decline in the use of the suspended prison sentence accounts for some of the rise, but both Gelsthorpe and Morris (2002) and Carlen and Worrall (2004) surmise that this is only a partial explanation.

Most attention has been given, and continues to be given, to women sentenced to imprisonment, yet the vast majority of offending women are cautioned or given community punishments, fines, discharges, or other non-custodial disposals. In her review of the use of community punishment for women, Rumgay cites several examples of differential treatment of females in the system, due to their low numbers, the problems of providing childcare, and the overall perception of community service as a fit punishment for young men (Rumgay 2004a; see also Gelsthorpe 2001 for an overview of research studies). Player (2005), reviewing major changes following the Criminal Justice Act 2003, suggests that these will lead to even greater levels of custody for women. One of the ironies of the situation, as Player notes, is that the official policy approach to women offenders changed notably in the 1990s, with a new programme, explicitly drawing its rationale from gender equality (Home Office 2003, 2004). The Women's Offending Reduction Programme is directed at reducing women's offending and is regularly reviewed in relation to its extensive objectives and numerous stakeholders (both within and without prison), but offending patterns have not yet changed; more importantly, some commentators are sceptical of this approach, arguing that it results in 'carceral clawback' and further punishment of women (Carlen and Worrall 2004). Strong claims for examples of good practice in England and Wales have been made but often there is more talk of strategy than practice (Scottish Office 1998; Her Majesty's Chief Inspectorate of Prisons (HMCIP) 2000). The impact of 'gender-blind' mandatory sentences and sentencing guidelines in the USA appears to have backfired against women, since the current male-based sentencing model defies any attempt to develop a rational sentencing policy for non-violent female offenders (Raeder 1995: 157).

PRISONS FOR WOMEN

Since the start of incarceration as punishment, women have been subject to broadly the same prison system as men, but with distinctive variations introduced from time to time. Welfare objectives have sometimes been to the fore, especially in the nineteenth century and in relation to women said to be in moral danger. Rafter has catalogued the history of one such institution in the USA and noted how the lofty intentions of its founders led it to becoming additionally repressive of its female inmates who were infantilized by middle-class maternalism (1985). Zedner (1991) describes two schemes in Britain primarily designed for women: diversion from the penal system, care and welfare of offenders, and moral protection. In the first programme from 1898 to 1914, a number of inebriate reformatories for habitual female drunkards were founded, the purpose being 'quite simply, to create of the enfeebled and degraded drunk a model of healthy, domesticated femininity' (ibid.: 237). This initiative was followed by another in which assumptions about female deviance had changed and centred on a switch to 'feeble-mindedness' as a prime cause of female crime and deviance, and, indeed, wider social evils (Simmons 1978). Because of their reproductive role, women were again the especial focus of such policies, their containment being emphasized (Zedner 1991). It was the undermining of its key assumptions which irreparably damaged this approach, although not before many women had been institutionalized. Barton has examined the history of what she terms a 'semi penal institution', one of many, neither formal nor informal, but which 'used ... regulatory methods and disciplinary techniques ... to contain, supervise and control and ... to normalise deviant women back to an acceptable standard of feminine behaviour' (Barton 2005: 3). While her focus is on a church-owned institution, once a refuge for destitute women, latterly a bail hostel for women, she finds continuity with present-day developments and its past history. She found 'a regime that whilst claiming to "empower", actually led to the infantilisation of its residents' (op. cit.: 155).

Such case histories are highly instructive. They show that when women are the subjects of special penal treatment, it frequently results in the development of benevolently repressive regimes which emphasize dependency and traditional femininity and fail to facilitate rehabilitation. Secondly, such programmes tend to be determined by the assumed characteristics and needs of women, rather than well-explored evidence. Such examples are not just historical. The rebuilding of Holloway Prison, London, in the 1970s was based on views about women offenders being physically or mentally sick, or both, and thus needing a therapeutic environment. The case was not proven, and the design of the prison proved unsatisfactory and controversial (RAP 1969; Rock 1996).

Recent accounts of the punishment of women have stressed its growing punitiveness. Several studies of the attempts made in Canada to set up a more woman-centred programme of provision based on the well-intentioned, radical proposals in the Task Force Report on Federally Sentenced Women (1990) describe their failure (Hannah-Moffat 2001, 2002; Hayman 2006). Indeed, Carlen attributes her development of the term 'carceral clawback' (meaning the ideological mechanisms necessary to the existence of the maintenance of prisons) to the inspiration and understanding she gained from this work (Carlen and Worrall 2004: 91). Worrall has argued forcefully that complex political and ideological processes have produced a situation, disastrous and disadvantageous for women, in which

'the search for equivalence', driven by a misunderstood feminist hegemony calling for the empowerment of women by making them accountable for their deeds, has resulted in an inevitable increase in the numbers of women rendered punishable' [2002: 64].

She and many others are particularly concerned about the application of programmes of cognitive skills training, based on male norms and male models, to female prisoners (ibid.; Carlen and Worrall 2004; Hannah-Moffat and Shaw 2000). Since female inmates may be required to complete such programmes despite their lack of fit, they will have poorer outcomes (Hedderman 2004: 241).

WOMEN'S RESPONSES TO IMPRISONMENT

Early women's prison studies reflected dominant themes in relation to studies of men's prisons: the process of prisonization and the existence of inmate subcultures (Morgan and Liebling, Chapter 32, this volume). Certainly much research on prisons for women in the USA has used the now rather dated features of such studies to explore women's reactions—with some interesting findings which point to the salience of sexual and emotional relations in female correctional establishments and the idea that the penal life of women, largely because of their small numbers and restricted provision, was distinctive. Female felons in the USA were said to feel the pains of imprisonment (the loss of family and home) more acutely and therefore set up alternative sexual relationships with one another, or formed 'pseudo families' to replace their missing kin (Ward and Kassebaum 1965; Giallombardo 1966). Several studies found women's commitment to inmate codes to be less than men's (Tittle 1969; Kruttschnitt 1981).

In Scotland, Carlen (1983) found little evidence of inmate solidarity, or indeed the presence of subcultures. One of the paradoxical conclusions of a review of research on female subcultures is that they are weaker and more diffuse than male (Pollock-Byrne 1990) yet, certainly in Britain, women perceive the pains of imprisonment as sharper and react with greater vehemence against them (Heidensohn 1975, 1981; Casale 1989; Mandaraka-Sheppard 1986; Carlen 1985). A higher proportion of women are charged with disciplinary offences, tranquillizers are more frequently prescribed, and there is a significantly greater incidence of self-mutilation (Sim 1990). A new generation of women's prison studies provides both confirmation and challenge to the earlier accounts. Owen's ethnographic study of a Californian women's prison on the whole supports a gendered and importational view of female experiences of imprisonment. She observed three critical areas of life: '(1) negotiating the prison world (2) styles of doing time and [3]involvement in the "mix"' (Owen 1998: 167). The 'mix' comprises a number of problems inside the prison—drugs, homosexuality, fighting. Avoiding trouble meant keeping out of these. Kruttschnitt et al. compared two other women's prisons (CIW and VSP), also in California. While 'how women at CIW talked about their experiences... [had] important similarities, including diverse styles of adapt-ation, the importance placed on primary group relationships, and the absence of serious violence or racial conflict... women's adaptations at VSP—anomic, suspicious and detached' were quite different (2000: 712). They attributed these differences to the quite distinct institutional features of the two institutions. VSP represented the new, harsher penology, and CIW a historic, maternal, therapeutic culture. Their conclusion is that

> women's adaptations to prison may not be as fundamentally structured by gender in many of the ways traditionally assumed... The adaptations described in so many other studies

of women in prison are likely as much or more a product of the nature of women's corrections at a particular time and place as they are a product of the nature of women themselves [ibid.: 713].

Bosworth's (1999) study of power relations in three women's prisons in Britain also found distinctive responses. Her subjects resist the regime imposed on them and construct new identities (see also Barton 2005: 155).

While scholars may differ on how far experience of imprisonment is distinctly gendered, there is a growing policy consensus in Britain that women offenders should be differentially treated. Carlen argues that this is essential because of the nature and the context of female offending: they are already more severely sentenced and subject to a double form of regulation (Carlen 1998: 153). Moreover, building on the findings of an international comparative study of provision for women, Carlen and Worrall (2004) offer a range of examples of how successful, gender-specific policies can be achieved.

A series of reports on women's establishments in Britain by the Chief Inspector of Prisons, including a highly critical Thematic Review (HMCIP 1997), described the shortcomings of the system. On one unannounced visit to Holloway Prison, London, he and his team were so shocked by what they found that they walked out, thus creating a great deal of adverse publicity (HMCIP 2000). In 1998, the Prison Reform Trust (PRT) set up an inquiry, led by Dorothy Wedderburn, on women's imprisonment. The resulting report identified key problems and that 'the criminal justice and prison system is so dominated by the handling of men that it is failing to provide for the particular needs of women' (PRT 2000: xii). They instance four distinctive characteristics of women:

1. their different patterns of offending from men and lower levels of risk to the public;
2. their role as mothers and primary carers and the resulting higher costs of their imprisonment;
3. their histories of psychiatric illness and earlier abuse;
4. the 'Cinderella' factor of small numbers [ibid.].

Among their key recommendations are the formation of a National Women's Justice Board, on the lines of the Youth Justice Board, and a network of local Women's Supervision, Rehabilitation, and Support Centres, linked to small, local, custodial units, to replace the existing women's system.

This sounds close to Carlen's (1983) 'womenwise' model, yet it would be wise to enter a note of caution about creating specific models of penal treatment for women. Zedner's (1991) and Rafter's (1985) accounts of historical examples which failed, or which resulted in benign but oppressive regimes, are apposite. A more recent example is that of Canada where a series of well-intentioned reforms appear not to have been wholly successful (Shaw 1991; Hannah-Moffat 2002). British policy-makers have been convinced by aspects of these arguments and have issued two documents on their approach to women offenders (Home Office 2000, 2001). Their emphasis is on crime reduction, the specific needs of women offenders, and the high costs, individual and social, of their offences. The second report announced the development of the Women's Offending Reduction Programme: 2002–2005 ('WORP') (Home Office 2001) and the WORP statement and its reviews can be found on the Home Office website. Examples of apparently successful gender-specific penal experiments for women involve the Duchas centre in Dublin, which replaced an old outdated unit with a modern building and programme and none of the problems usually linked to such initiatives (Mason 2006) and Centre 218—a community-based resource for women offenders in central Glasgow (Loucks *et al.* 2006).

GENDER, CRIME, AND JUSTICE IN LATE MODERNITY

Criminology is protean: the early twenty-first century sees it being subjected to another series of reviews about its character, its position in conditions of 'late modernity', and its relationships vis-à-vis the 'new' forms of regulation and control in contemporary society (Garland and Sparks 2000; Braithwaite 2000; Garland 2001; J. Young 1999; Heidensohn 2000; and Rock, Chapter 1, this volume). Setting the new themes against a background of risk and ontological insecurity (see Loader and Sparks, Chapter 3, this volume), Garland and Sparks (2000), amongst others, draw attention to new themes of expressive punishment, concern for victims, public protection, exclusion, enhanced control; in another account Garland (2001) has noted that the older social welfare criminology has been replaced by 'the piecemeal development of a network of unobtrusive situational controls, retrofitted to modify existing routines', . . . and 'an excess of control . . . from the outside in the form of legal threats and moral exhortations' (2001: 186). To this picture we can add the growth of the regulatory state and new forms of social control which have also shaped the policy shifts (Braithwaite 2000). Thus there is a striking change in vocabulary, reflecting new key concepts and concerns. Among these new concepts are those of risk, insecurity, responsibility, regulation, exclusion, and control. Defining and using them are complex and contentious tasks.

Whilst gender perspectives and feminist issues have formed part of the cutting edge of criminology in recent years, it is striking that there is still need to press the case for women's experiences not to be forgotten or marginalized, and for men's subjectivities to be recognized. For critiques of the culture of control and managerialism, and stories of responsibilization, must be acknowledged and attention paid to gender. Most of the new 'control' stories and studies present the citizen in a passive, helpless way. Rose's depiction of control is perhaps the most dystopian picture in this gallery: 'Control society is one of constant and never ending *modulation* . . . One is in continuous training, lifelong learning, perpetual assessment . . . Surveillance is "designed in" to the flows of everyday existence' (2000: 235). Jock Young rebuffs this kind of approach in robust manner: 'some theories . . . focus on "social control" as if it were autonomous of what was being controlled . . . nearly all tend to regard social control as, somehow, separate from the public, as if control and social discipline were something unilaterally imposed upon people' (1999: 58).

An important critique of these kinds of stories is also provided by Maureen Cain (2000) in her contribution to a *British Journal of Criminology* special issue on social theory. Her paper stands out because she provides a nuanced account of the politics of gender and social control in the Caribbean, which challenges many of the key assumptions of the new social control: that it is global, irresistible, exportable, or even effective in another context. A number of feminist writers have explored how some of the broad social themes have impacted on the policy shifts which have resulted in more women being sent to prison (Hudson 2002a; Worrall 2002; Gelsthorpe 2005). Their writings show complexity in the 'culture of control' audit trail and the irony that women are actuarially insignificant in the reckoning of serious criminal risk and harm is not lost on these authors. Similarly, Brown and Heidensohn (2000) and Schulz (2000) have noted how generations of women reformers took part in, and sometimes took over, or invented, forms of social control.

We can also draw on a wider range of recent work to illustrate three key themes which are so far missing from accounts and which should be integrated into them: agency, identity, and resistance. Some of the best examples of resistance to control come from recent feminist studies which describe the resourcefulness of some of the most marginal and oppressed subjects, deviant women and girls who are conventionally seen as passive and submissive. Lisa Maher, in a study of gender, race, and resistance in a Brooklyn drug market, describes 'the tactics women use to resist and contest the constraints that shape their occupational lives' (1997: 199). In a different setting, Sharon Pickering provides a perspective on women's resistance in Northern Ireland by focusing on their experience of house raids: she argues that women have become increasingly politicized and organized in their resistance to repeated incursions into the home by security forces and suggests that the coercive agents of the state have played a significant role in both the individual and collective resistance of women. Paradoxically, she says, the security forces have become agents of change (2000: 49). A British study of the meaning girls give to violence in their lives (Burman *et al.* 2001), and Miller's (2001, 2002) account of women's participation in street robbery in the USA, address the question of the agency of women who have few channels of expression yet find their own, and both contribute to nuanced understandings of the creation of identity along the way (see also Laidler and Hunt 2001 on accomplishing femininity among the girls in the gang).

In some respects the new culture of control resembles its predecessors: it lacks gendered dimensions. Feminist scholars are left to build in correctives and nuanced understandings of affairs. Yet the future of criminology and of criminal justice surely lies most securely in inclusiveness, integration, and innovation.

HAS ANYONE BEEN LISTENING?

Our observations on the lack of attention to gendered dimensions of the new penology and its themes of control and risk suggest that any answer to questions about the impact of feminist perspectives and the feminist-inspired focus on gender is necessarily mixed.

There are awakenings in some quarters of criminology and this is reflected in theory, research, teaching, and policy developments. In other quarters, there is 'selective deafness'.

In the third edition of the *Oxford Handbook of Criminology* (2002) in our separate chapters, we thus expressed both pessimism and optimism with regard to the impact of feminist perspectives and the attention to gender more generally. It is certainly the case that, over the past decade, there has been a considerable decline in the mass base of feminist activism, as well as a popular backlash against feminism. It is arguable, moreover, that this backlash has impinged upon the academic world of criminology. At the same time lively feminist debates and intellectual advances in criminology abound in the Women's Division of the American Society of Criminology (the ASC) and in the British Society of Criminology annual conferences in particular. The introduction of a new journal *Feminist Criminology* is telling of intellectual interest and scholarship.

Of course, feminist work in criminology has drawn criticism. Leaving aside the fallacious, but significant, inferences of some criminological writers that feminist work is somehow just ideological reasoning or irrelevant to criminological tasks (Bottomley and Pease 1986; Walker 1987), Marcia Rice (1990) for example, rightly took early feminist writers to task because black women were noticeably absent from their work. Indeed, she argues that feminists have failed to notice that traditional macho-centric criminology was constructed on *racist* and sexist ideologies, and that feminist work is equally ethnocentric.

The criticism of a 'gender-centric' tendency, and the privileging of gender over race and class in feminist approaches, is undoubtedly valid. But writers have acknowledged this tendency in constructive ways (see Daly and Stephenson 1995). Moreover, we have indicated that some of the important theoretical developments regarding 'doing gender' include race and class issues (Jefferson 1997; Miller 2001). Contributors to Daly and Maher's (1998) review of the crossroads and intersections of criminology and feminist work on crime and justice highlight these themes too. Chesney-Lind (2006) and Burgess-Proctor (2006) enjoin others in recognizing that proper treatment of the race, gender, punishment nexus is critical to the development of feminist criminology, especially in a context of backlash (see, for example, Faludi 2001). It is also fair to say that Rafter and Heidensohn (1995) present *International Feminist Perspectives* as a genuine attempt to contribute to our understanding of such issues by offering a multicultural collection of papers.

INTERNATIONAL FEMINIST PERSPECTIVES IN CRIMINOLOGY

One of the first combined attempts to address feminist perspectives regarding criminology on an international basis took place in Quebec in 1991, when Marie-Andrée Bertrand, Kathleen Daly, and Dorie Klein organized an international feminist conference on Women, Law and Social Control. But it is Rafter and Heidensohn's (1995) edited collection of essays, *International Feminist Perspectives* which notably attempted to provide an international picture of developments in feminist thinking in criminology.

The contributors collectively question the extent to which the 'macho criminology' (so characterized by Meda Chesney-Lind) can become 'engendered' and they identify a number of themes which reflect feminist interests which are central to theoretical, methodological, and pedagogical developments and policy in criminology. On the positive side, such themes include a unifying focus on the gendered nature of victim-hood and the authors provide evidence of changes in understandings of rape and the abuse of children in theory, policy, and practice. On the negative side, there are stories of the continued marginalization of feminism, feminist scholars, and female students within the academy, and of an intellectual and political backlash against feminism. Individual authors identify tensions too, where feminist concerns seem marginal to broader political concerns.

ENVISIONING JUSTICE: GENDER AND JUSTICE

Many feminist writers and activists have concluded that conventional legal and judicial systems do not work for women. As Dobash and Dobash, put it: 'it is impossible to use the law and legal apparatus to confront patriarchal domination and oppression when the language and procedures of these social processes and institutions are saturated with patriarchal beliefs and structures' (1992: 147; see also Edwards 1989). Carol Smart has perhaps gone furthest in arguing that 'it is important to think of non-legal strategies and to discourage resort to law as if it holds the key to unlock women's oppression' (1989: 5). She constructs a warning to feminism to 'avoid the siren call of law . . . and to acknowledge the power of feminism to construct an alternative reality to the version which is manifested in legal discourse' (1989: 160).

In terms of constructing alternative realities, there has certainly been no shortage of alternative proposals to deal with women offenders[6] ranging from Heidensohn's (1986) identification of two models of justice: Portia (rational, judicial, and masculine) and Persephone (relational, informal, feminine) which broadly reflect Gilligan's (1982) analysis of gendered morality,[7] to Carlen's (1990) notion of 'a womenwise penology' which aims to ensure that penal policy for women does not increase their oppression as women further and that penal policy for men does not brutalize them to the extent that they become more oppressive to women (see also Daly 1989b).

These studies, combined, amount to a sophisticated critique of the administration of justice and the structures in which it operates. Clearly, there are certain gender-specific forms of discrimination rife within it. However, as Gelsthorpe (1989) points out, it is

---

[6] Victims are largely dealt with in Chapter 15, this volume.

[7] See also Spader's (2002) later work on the morality of justice and the alternative morality of care which similarly draws on Gilligan's work; Spader set out the different conceptions of justice and poses questions about the superiority of the care model, whether it can operate as a separate and equal model or whether elements of the care model might be integrated into the justice model, although she does not come to any clear-cut conclusions. Riley *et al.* (2005) also outline a feminist vision of justice which asserts that interdependence, responsibility, respect for and relationship with the environment, and an ethics of care are the foundation for a more reasoned and reasonable practice of justice, although translating these ideas into practice may be another matter.

impossible to try to demonstrate the existence of a conspiracy behind such practices. It is even more difficult to relate them, aetiologically, to women's crime. As Zedner shows, redefinitions of female deviance can diminish their apparent deviance or increase it (1991). This is not, of course, solely due to the operation of the criminal justice system. On the contrary, many other features of the Zeitgeist contribute: culture, values, changes in medical science. Politics and the media have also played crucial roles in such developments, as A. Young, for example, shows in her analysis of the media reactions to the women protesters at the Greenham Common Airbase in Britain in the 1980s. She argues that the criminal justice system and the media rely on each other's definitions of deviance (1990).

This set of approaches informs much writing on women and crime. It leads us to question some of the most basic assumptions about law, justice, and punishment in our society and to raise queries about unstated 'patriarchal' values which were highlighted in the early critique. However, it is also then essential to question all the other implicit parts of the system, and we need to raise at least as many points about what happens to men, especially if they are young and poor, and come from minorities, as we do about women. One much canvassed alternative to conventional approaches is the use of restorative justice (RJ) (Braithwaite 1989) although there are considerable problems with this approach too; as Alder (2002), amongst others, points out, the notion of 'shaming', which is central to the process, has very major differences of meaning for males than for females; and while Hudson (2002b) argues for RJ in some 'hard cases' (such as gendered violence and sexual assault), she recognizes that the more of these the process deals with, the closer it will come to the conventional criminal justice system. In an important review of feminist engagement with RJ, Daly and Stubbs (2006) urge greater recognition of the complexities, developments, and different meanings and practices within the field of RJ, so that feminist ideals about justice are neither solely shaped nor constrained by RJ ideals.

Alongside the search for alternative conceptions of justice or adaptations of existing models of justice, there is evidence of an impact of feminism on criminological research, policy, and practice (see, for instance, Lacey 2001; ESRC Violence Programme 1998; Prison Reform Trust 2000), at least in the kinds of questions asked, if not in the end result. It is notable that the same questions have to be rehearsed time and time again, but it is also heartening that there is currently a Home Office gender network involving academics as well as policy-makers and practitioners from statutory and voluntary agencies (Fawcett Society 2006). There is also scope to celebrate the Scottish Executive's (2006) innovative Centre 218 (a community-based centre for women offenders at risk of custody) as previously mentioned (Loucks *et al.* 2006), and the Home Office is poised to bring to fruition the two promised pilot studies of Women's Supervision, Rehabilitation, and Support Centres in England and Wales following on from the Wedderburn Report (Prison Reform Trust 2000). Whilst it is recognized that some of the energetic policy-related work might have contributed to the increase in the use of custody for women (with notions of prisons being perceived as 'social services' as a result of improvements prompted by critics), and a need for further work in relation to specificity in the creation and delivery of services is identified (Zaplin 1998; Kendall 2002; Bloom 2003), there is much to suggest positive activism of the sort that Chesney-Lind (2006) amongst others encourages.

BACKLASH AND BEYOND

But feminist perspectives in criminology have to be set against a politics of backlash. It is now thirty years since Carol Smart published *Women, Crime and Criminology* (1976) and a good moment to take stock. Where do we stand? In reviewing the contributions of feminism to the *epistemological and methodological project* in criminology we can see a continuation of epistemological questioning and creative thinking about the production of knowledge and processes of knowledge production. Some difficult issues remain unresolved in this, we do not doubt. For example, whilst borrowed postmodern insights enhance the epistemological and methodological project by challenging and deconstructing the constitution of meaning in criminological discourse, we are not entirely sure that there are useful postmodern insights regarding *concrete practices and knowledges* which could replace current ones. Postmodernists have very little to say about visions of justice, for example, or about the ways in which difference can be accommodated in notions of justice. Yet this is vital to the broad feminist political project (Flax 1992; Hudson 2000).

In thinking about the *gender project* we can see a good deal of important work which focuses on the different ways in which race and class might mediate gender, and ways in which 'doing gender' impact on identity. And in assessing the *political project* we have identified and described (above) a number of important developments and reflections. (Elsewhere in this volume there is discussion of victims and this is yet another area where gender awareness has come to the fore.)

As well as drawing attention to the positive contributions of feminism to criminology, this review of feminist contributions to criminology and outline of the treatment of gender and crime rehearses a number of problems. The range of feminist work is extremely wide—from empirical studies which are undertaken in the name of feminist criminology, to theoretical developments on gender and deconstructionist approaches. Criticisms of feminist work within criminology abound, but it is arguable that neither criticisms of incompatability between feminism (as it develops and engages with postmodern thought) and criminology (Carrington 1998, 2002), nor criticisms of continuing empiricism (Howe 1997), necessarily cast feminists struggling to work within criminology into the intellectual shadows. On the contrary, there is much evidence of a liveliness and spiritedness in these debates. But as contemporary theoretical accounts of the impact of late modernity show (through their neglect of gender as much as anything), there is still work to do to ensure that the issues identified by feminists working within criminology do not remain unheard.

■ SELECTED FURTHER READING

For further coverage on some of the topics in this chapter see S. Walklate (2004) *Gender, Crime and Criminal Justice* (Cullompton, Devon: Willan). See also *The Encyclopedia of Women and Crime* (Phoenix, Ariz.: Onyx Press, 2000) edited by N. H. Rafter (which gives some cross-cultural information for students new to the subject area).

In relation to feminism and criminology, L. Gelsthorpe and A. Morris (eds), *Feminist Perspectives in Criminology* (Buckingham, Open University Press, 1990), and N. H. Rafter and F. M. Heidensohn (eds), *International Feminist Perspectives in Criminology* (Buckingham: Open University Press, 1995) cover the broad feminist critique of criminology and its theoretical parameters. F. Heidensohn (ed), *Gender and Justice* (Cullompton, Devon: Willan, 2006) is a recent collection of essays which reflect research and theory.

On feminist epistemology and methodology, see A. Oakley's *Experiments in Knowing: Gender and Methods in the Social Sciences* (Cambridge: Polity, 2000), and C. Ramazanoglu and J. Holland, *Feminist Methodology. Challenges and Choices* (London: Sage, 2002). The former challenges some of the precepts promoted by feminism in respect of quantitative methods; the latter guides the reader through the terrain of feminist methodology, providing examples of issues in fieldwork practice.

For further details on feminist theory see M. Eagleton's edited *A Concise Companion to Feminist Theory* (Oxford: Blackwell, 2003). For gender theory (especially relating to masculinities), see R. Connell, *Gender* (Cambridge: Polity, 2002), T. Newburn and E. Stanko (eds), *Just Boys Doing Business* (London: Routledge, 1994) and R. Collier, *Masculinities, Crime and Criminology* (London: Sage, 1998).

Useful websites for information about women and criminal justice

The Fawcett Society: www.fawcettsociety.org.uk
The Griffins Society: www.thegriffinssociety.org
Women in Prison: www.womeninprison.org.uk
More generally, the Home Office RDS website will yield results on relevant research: www.homeoffice.gov.uk/rds/

Key online journals

Women and Criminal Justice website:
http://www.haworthpressinc.com/store/product.asp? sku = J012
Feminist Criminology website:
http://www.sagepub.co.uk/journalsProdDesc.nav?prodId = Journal201772

■ REFERENCES

ADLER, F. (1975), *Sisters in Crime*, New York: McGraw Hill.

ALDER, C. (2002), 'Young Women Offenders and the Challenge for Restorative Justice', in H. Strang and J. Braithwaite (eds), *Restorative Justice: Philosophy to Practice*, Aldershot: Ashgate.

——and WORRALL, A. (2004) (eds), *Girls' Violence*, New York: State University of New York Press.

ALLEN, H. (1987), *Justice Unbalanced: Gender, Psychiatry and Judicial Decisions*, Milton Keynes: Open University Press.

ARCHER, L. (2001), ' "Muslim Brothers, Black Lads, Traditional Asians": British Muslim Young Men's Constructions of Race, Religion and Masculinity', *Feminism and Psychology*, 11(1): 79–105.

ARMSTRONG, D., HINE, J., HACKING, S., ARMAOS, R., JONES, R., KLESSINGER, N., and FRANCE, A. (2005), *Children, Risk and Crime: The On Track Youth Lifestyles Surveys*, Home Office Research study 278, London: Home Office.

ARNOT, M., and USBORNE, C. (eds) (1999), *Gender and Crime in Modern Europe*, London: UCL Press.

AUSTIN, R. (1981), 'Liberation and Female Criminality in England and Wales', *British Journal of Criminology*, 21(4): 371–4.

BARTON. A. (2005), *Fragile Moralities and Dangerous Sexualities*, Aldershot: Ashgate.

BEATTIE, J. (1975), 'The Criminality of Women in Eighteenth Century England', *Journal of Social History*, 8: 80–116.

BERTRAND, M. (1969), 'Self-Image and Delinquency: A Contribution to the Study of Female Criminality and Women's Image', *Acta Criminologica*, II: 71–144.

——, DALY, K., and KLEIN, D. (eds) (1992), *Proceedings of the International Feminist Conference on Women, Law, and Social Control*, Mont Gabriel, Quebec, 18–21 July, 1991.

BLOOM, B. (ed) (2003), *Gendered Justice. Addressing Female Offenders*, Carolina, USA: Carolina Academic Press.

BORITCH, H., and HAGAN, J. (1990), 'A Century of Crime in Toronto: Gender, Class and Patterns of Social Control, 1859 to 1955', *Criminology*, 20(4): 567–99.

BOSWORTH, M. (1999), *Engendering Resistance: Agency and Power in Women's Prisons*, Aldershot: Ashgate.

BOTTOMLEY, K., and PEASE, K. (1986), *Crime and Punishment: Interpreting the Data*, Milton Keynes: Open University Press.

BRAITHWAITE, J. (1989), *Crime, Shame and Reintegration*, Cambridge: Cambridge University Press.

—— (2000), 'The New Regulatory State and the Transformation of Criminology', *British Journal of Criminology*, 40(2): 222–38.

BROWN, J., and HEIDENSOHN, F. (2000), *Gender and Policing*, Basingstoke: Macmillan/Palgrave.

BURGESS-PROCTOR, A. (2006), 'Intersections of Race, Class, Gender and Crime', *Feminist Criminology*, 1(1): 27–47.

BURMAN, M. (2004a), 'Turbulent Talk: Girls' Making Sense of Violence', in C. Alder and A. Worrall (eds), *Girls' Violence*, New York: SUNY Press.

—— (2004b), 'Breaking the Mould: Patterns of Female Offending', in G. McIvor (ed), *Women Who Offend*, London: Jessica Kingsley.

——, BATCHELOR, S., and BROWN, J. (2001), 'Researching Girls and Violence: Tracing the Dilemmas of Fieldwork', *British Journal of Criminology*, 41(3): 443–59.

CAIN, M. (1986), 'Realism, Feminism, Methodology, and Law,' *International Journal of the Sociology of Law*, 14(3): 255–67.

—— (1989), *Growing Up Good. Policing the Behaviour of Girls in Europe*, London: Sage.

—— (1990), 'Towards Transgression: New Directions in Feminist Criminology', *International Journal of the Sociology of Law*, 18: 1–18.

—— (2000), 'Orientalism, Occidentalism and the Sociology of Crime', *British Journal of Criminology*, 40(2): 239–60.

CARLEN, P. (1983), *Women's Imprisonment*, London: Routledge & Kegan Paul.

—— (1985), *Criminal Women*, Oxford: Polity Press.

—— (1990), *Alternatives to Women's Imprisonment*, Buckingham: Open University Press.

—— (1998), *Sledgehammer*, Basingstoke: Macmillan/Palgrave.

—— (ed) (2002), *Women and Punishment: The Struggle for Justice*, Cullompton, Devon: Willan.

—— and WORRALL, A. (eds) (2004), *Analysing Women's Imprisonment*, Cullompton, Devon: Willan.

CARRIER, J. (1988), *The Campaign for the Employment of Women as Police Officers*, Aldershot: Gower.

CARRINGTON, K. (1998), 'Postmodernism and Feminist Criminologies: Disconnecting Discourses', in K. Daly and L. Maher (eds), *Criminology at the Crossroads*, New York: Oxford University Press.

—— (2002) 'Feminism and Critical Criminology: Confronting Genealogies', in K. Carrington and R. Hogg (eds), *Critical Criminology: Reflection and Renewal*, Cullompton, Devon: Willan.

—— (2006), 'Does Feminism Spoil Girls? Explanations for Official Rises in Female Delinquency', *The Australian and New Zealand Journal of Criminology*, 39(1):34–53.

CASALE, S. (1989), *Women Inside. The Experience of Women Remand Prisoners in Holloway*, London: Civil Liberties Trust.

CHAN, J. (1996), 'Changing Police Culture', *British Journal of Criminology*, 36: 109–34.

—— (1997), *Changing Police Culture*, Cambridge: Cambridge University Press.

CHESNEY-LLND, M. (2006) 'Patriarchy, Crime, and Justice: Feminist Criminology in an Era of Backlash', *Feminist Criminology*, 1(1): 6–26.

COLLIER, R. (1998), *Masculinities, Crime and Criminology*, London: Sage.

CONDRY, R. (2006), 'Stigmatised Women: Relatives of Serious Offenders and the Broader Impact of Crime', in F. Heidensohn (ed.), *Gender and Justice: New Concepts and Approaches*, Cullompton, Devon: Willan.

CONNELL, R. (1995), *Masculinities*, Cambridge: Polity Press.

—— and MESSERSCHMIDT, J. (2005), 'Hegemonic Masculinity. Rethinking the concept', *Gender and Society*, 19(6): 829–59.

DALY, K. (1989a), 'Rethinking Judicial Paternalism: Gender, Work-Family Relations and Sentencing', *Gender and Society*, 3(1): 9–36.

—— (1989b), 'Criminal Justice Ideologies and Practices in Different Voices: Some Feminist Questions about Justice', *International Journal of the Sociology of Law*, 17: 1–18.

—— (1994a), 'Criminal Law and Justice System Practices as Racist, White and Racialised', *Washington and Lee Law Review*, 15(2): 431–64.

—— (1994b), *Gender, Crime and Punishment*, New Haven: Yale University Press.

—— (1997), 'Different Ways of Conceptualizing Sex/Gender in Feminist Theory and Their Implications for Criminology', *Theoretical Criminology*, 1(1): 25–51.

—— and CHESNEY-LIND, M. (1988), 'Feminism and Criminology', *Justice Quarterly*, 5(4): 498–538.

—— and MAHER, L. (1998), *Criminology at the Crossroads. Feminist Readings in Crime and Justice*, Oxford: Oxford University Press.

—— and STEPHENSON, D. (1995), 'The "Dark Figure" of Criminology: Toward a Black and Multi-Ethnic Feminist Agenda for Theory and Research', in N. Rafter and F. Heidensohn (eds), *International Feminist Perspectives in Criminology*, Buckingham: Open University Press.

—— and STUBBS, J. (2006) 'Feminist Engagement with Restorative Justice', *Theoretical Criminology*, 10(1): 9–28.

DAVIES, A. (1999), '"These Viragoes are No Less Cruel Than the Lads": Young Women, Gangs and Violence in Late Victorian Manchester and Salford', *British Journal of Criminology*, 39(1): 72–89.

DOBASH, R. E., and DOBASH, R. P. (1992), *Women, Violence and Social Change*, London: Routledge.

—— and —— (2004), 'Women's Violence to Men in Intimate Relationships working on a Puzzle', *British Journal of Criminology*, 44(3): 324–49.

DOWNES, D., and ROCK, P. (1998), *Understanding Deviance*, 3rd edn, Oxford: Oxford University Press (5th edn, 2007, forthcoming).

EATON, M. (1986), *Justice for Women?*, Milton Keynes: Open University Press.

Economic and Social Research Council (ESRC) (1998), *Research Programme on Violence*, Swindon: ESRC.

EDWARDS, S. (1984), *Women on Trial*, Manchester: Manchester University Press.

—— (1989), *Policing 'Domestic' Violence*, London: Sage.

FALUDI, S. (1991), *Backlash. The Undeclared War against American Women*, New York: Doubleday.

FAWCETT SOCIETY (2006), *Gender and Justice Policy Network* (minutes of meetings), London: Fawcett Society.

FEELEY, M., and LITTLE, D. (1991), 'The Vanishing Female: The Decline of Women in the Criminal Process, 1687–1912', *Law and Society Review*, 25(4): 719–57.

FEINMAN, C. (1986), *Women in the Criminal Justice System*, New York: Praeger.

FINCH, J. (2004), 'Feminism and Qualitative Research', *International Journal of Social Research Methodology*, 7(1): 61–4.

FLAX, J. (1992), 'Beyond Equality: Gender, Justice and Difference,' in G. Bock and S. James (eds), *Beyond Equality and Difference*, London: Routledge.

FROSH, S., PHOENIX, A., and PATTMAN, R. (2002), *Young Masculinities*, Basingstoke: Palgrave.

GADD, D. (2003), 'Reading between the Lines: Subjectivity & Men's Violence', *Men and Masculinities*, 5(3): 1–22.

GARLAND, D. (2001), *The Culture of Control*, Oxford: Oxford University Press.

—— and SPARKS, R. (2000), 'Criminology, Social Theory and the Challenge of Our Times', *British Journal of Criminology*, 4(2): 189–204.

GELSTHORPE, L. (1989), *Sexism and the Female Offender. An Organizational Analysis*, Aldershot: Gower.

——(1990), 'Feminist Methodologies in Criminology: A New Approach or Old Wine in New Bottles?', in L. Gelsthorpe and A. Morris (eds), *Feminist Perspectives in Criminology*, Buckingham: Open University Press.

——(2001), 'Critical Decisions and Processes in the Criminal Courts', in E. McLaughlin and J. Muncie (eds), *Controlling Crime*, 2nd edn, London: Sage.

——(2002), 'Feminism and Criminology', in M. Maguire, R. Morgan, and R. Reiner (eds), *Oxford Handbook of Criminology*, 3rd edn, Oxford: Oxford University Press.

——(2005), 'Back to Basics in Crime Control: Weaving in Women', in M. Matravers (ed), *Managing Modernity. Politics and the Culture of Control*, London: Routledge.

——and LOUCKS, N. (1997), 'Magistrates' Explanations of Sentencing Decisions', in C. Hedderman and L. Gelsthorpe (eds), *Understanding the Sentencing of Women*, Home Office Research Study 170, London: Home Office.

——and MORRIS, A. (eds) (1990), *Feminist Perspectives in Criminology*, Buckingham: Open University Press.

——and MORRIS, A. (2002), 'Women's Imprisonment in England and Wales in the 1990s: A Penal Paradox', *Criminal Justice*, 2(3): 277–301.

——and SHARPE, G. (2005/6), 'Criminological Research: Typologies versus Hierarchies', *Criminal Justice Matters*, 62: 8–9 and 43.

————(2006), 'Gender, Youth Crime and Justice', in B. Goldson and J. Muncie (eds), *Youth Crime and Justice*, London: Sage.

GIALLOMBARDO, R. (1966), *Society of Women: A Study of a Women's Prison*, New York: Wiley.

GILLIGAN, C. (1982), *In a Different Voice*, Cambridge, Mass.: Harvard University Press.

GODFREY, B. (1999), 'Workplace Appropriation and the Gendering of Factory "Law": West Yorkshire, 1840–80', in M. Arnot and C. Usborne (eds), *Gender and Crime in Modern Europe*, London: UCL Press.

GOODEY, J. (2000), 'Biographical Lessons for Criminology', *Theoretical Criminology*, 4(4): 473–98.

GRIFFITHS, S., and HANMER, J. (2005), 'Feminist Quantitative Methodology: Evaluating Policing of Domestic Violence', in T. Skinner, M. Hester, and E. Malos (eds), *Researching Gender Violence: Feminist Methodology in Action*, Cullompton, Devon: Willan.

GROSZ, E. (1987), 'Feminist Theory and the Challenge to Knowledge', *Women's Studies International Forum*, 10(5): 208–17.

HALE, B. (2005), 'The Sinners and the Sinned Against: Women in the Criminal Justice System', 4th Longford Lecture, London: Prison Reform Trust.

HANNAH-MOFFAT, K. (2001), *Punishment in Disguise. Penal Governance and Federal Imprisonment of Women in Canada*, Toronto: University of Toronto Press.

——(2002), 'Creating Choices? Reflecting on the Choices', in P. Carlen (ed.), *Women and the Struggle for Justice*, Cullompton, Devon: Willan.

——and SHAW, M. (2000), 'Thinking about Cognitive Skills? Think Again!', *Criminal Justice Matters*, 39: 8–9.

HARDING, S. (1987), *Feminism and Methodology*, Milton Keynes: Open University Press.

HAYMAN, S. (2006), 'The Reforming Prison: A Canadian Tale', in F. Heidensohn (ed.), *Gender and Justice: New Perspectives*, Cullompton, Devon: Willan.

HAYWOOD, C., and MAC an GHAILL, M. (2003), *Men and Masculinities*, Buckingham: Open University Press.

HEDDERMAN, C. (2004), 'Why are More Women Being Sentenced to Custody?', in G. McIvor (ed.), *Women Who Offend*, London: Jessica Kingsley.

——and GELSTHORPE (1997), *Understanding the Sentencing of Women*, London: Home Office.

——and HOUGH, M. (1994), *Does the Criminal Justice System Treat Men and Women Differently?*, Home Office Research Findings No. 10, London: Home Office.

HEIDENSOHN, F. (1968), 'The Deviance of Women: A Critique and an Enquiry', in *British Journal of Sociology*, 19(2): 160–75.

——(1970), 'Sex, Crime and Society', (ed.) in G. Harrison, *Biosocial Aspects of Sex*, Oxford: Blackwell.

——(1975), 'The Imprisonment of Females', in S. McConville (ed.), *The Use of Imprisonment*, London: Routledge & Kegan Paul.

——(1981), 'Women and the Penal System', in A. Morris and L. Gelsthorpe (eds), *Women and Crime*, Cambridge: Cropwood Conference Series 13.

——(1985), *Women and Crime*, London: Macmillan.

——(1986), 'Models of Justice: Portia or Persephone? Some Thoughts on Equality, Fairness and Gender in the Field of Criminal Justice', *International Journal of Sociology of Law*, 14: 287–98.

—— (1989), *Crime and Society*, Basingstoke: Macmillan.

—— (1992), *Women in Control? The Role of Women in Law Enforcement*, Oxford: Oxford University Press.

—— (1994), 'From Being to Knowing: Some Reflections on the Study of Gender in Contemporary Society', *Women and Criminal Justice*, 6(1): 13–37.

—— (1996), *Women and Crime*, 2nd edn, Basingstoke: Macmillan.

—— (2000), *Sexual Politics and Social Control*, Buckingham: Open University Press.

—— (2002), 'Gender and Crime', in M. Maguire, R. Morgan, and R. Reiner (eds), Oxford Handbook of Criminology, 3rd edn, Oxford: Clarendon Press.

—— (2003), 'Gender and Policing', in T. Newburn (ed), *Handbook of Policing*, Cullompton, Devon: Willan.

—— (2006) (ed), *Gender and Justice: New Concepts and Approaches*, Cullompton, Devon: Willan.

HEIMER, K., and KRUTTSCHNITT, C. (eds) (2006), *Gender and Crime: Patterns of Victimization and Offending*, New York: New York University.

Her Majesty's Chief Inspectorate of Prisons (HMCIP) (1997), *Women in Prison: A Thematic Review*, London: Home Office.

—— (2000), *An Unannounced Follow-up Inspection of HM Prison Holloway*, London: Home Office.

HOBBS, D., HADFIELD, P., LISTER, S., and WILLOW, S. (2003), *Bouncers*, Oxford: Oxford University Press.

HOLLWAY, W., and JEFFERSON, T. (2000), *Doing Qualitative Research Differently*, London: Sage.

HOME OFFICE (2000), *Statistics on Women and the Criminal Justice System, Section 95 Report*, London: Home Office.

—— (2001), *Women's Offending Reduction Programme: 2002–2005*, London: Home Office.

—— (2003), *Statistics on Women and the Criminal Justice System, Section 95 Report*, London: Home Office.

—— (2004), *Statistics on Women and the Criminal Justice System, Section 95 Report*, London: Home Office.

—— (2005), *Statistics on Women and the Criminal Justice System, Section 95 Report*, London: Home Office.

HOOD-WILLIAMS, J. (2001), 'Gender, Masculinities and Crime: From Structures to Psyches', *Theoretical Criminology*, 5(1): 37–60.

HOUGH, M., JACOBSON, J., and MILLIE, A. (2003), *The Decision to Imprison: Sentencing and the Prison Population*, London: Prison Reform Trust.

HOWE, A. (1997), 'Criminology Meets Postmodern Feminism (and Has a Nice Day)', in B. MacLean and D. Milanovanovic (eds), *Thinking Critically About Crime*, Vancouver: The Collective Press.

HUDSON, B. (2000), 'Criminology, Difference and Justice: Issues for Critical Criminology', *The Australian and New Zealand Journal of Criminology*, 33(2): 168–82.

—— (2002a), 'Gender Issues in Penal Policy and Penal Theory', in P. Carlen (ed.), *Women and Punishment*, Cullompton, Devon: Willan.

—— (2002b), 'Restorative Justice and Gendered Violence: Diversion or Effective Justice?', *British Journal of Criminology*, 42(3): 616–34.

JACKSON, S., and SCOTT, S. (2002), *Gender. A Sociological Reader*, London: Routledge.

JEFFERSON, T. (1997), 'Masculinities and Crimes', in M. Maguire, R. Morgan, and R. Reiner (eds), *Oxford Handbook of Criminology*, 2nd edn Oxford: Clarendon Press.

—— (2002), 'Subordinating Hegemonic Masculinity', *Theoretical Criminology*, 6(1): 63–88.

JONES, D. (1982), *Crime, Protest, Community and Police in Nineteenth Century Britain*, London: Routledge.

JONES, S. (1986), *Policewomen and Equality*, London: Macmillan.

KATZ, J. (1988), *Seductions of Crime: Moral and Sensual Attractions in Doing Evil*, New York: Basic Books.

KELLY, L. (1990), 'Journeying in Reverse: Possibilities and Problems in Feminist Research on Sexual Violence', in L. Gelsthorpe and A. Morris (eds), *Feminist Perspectives in Criminology*, Buckingham: Open University Press.

KENDALL, K. (2002), 'Time to Think Again about Cognitive Behavioural Programmes', in P. Carlen (ed), *Women and Punishment: the struggle for justice*, Cullompton, Devon: Willan.

KING, P. (1999), 'Gender, Crime and Justice in Late Eighteenth Century and Early Nineteenth Century England', in M. Arnot and C. Usborne (eds), *Gender and Crime in Modern Europe*, London: UCL Press.

KRUTTSCHNITT, C. (1981), 'Prison Codes, Inmate Solidarity and Women: A Re-examination', in M. Warren (ed.), *Comparing Female and Male Offenders*, Newbury Park, Cal.: Sage.

——GARTNER, R., and MILLER, A. (2000), 'Doing Her Own Time? Women's Response to Prison in the Context of the Old and the New Penology', *Criminology*, 38(3): 681–717.

LACEY, N. (2001), 'Beset by Boundaries. The Home Office Review of Sex Offences', *Criminal Law Review*, January: 3–14.

LAIDLER, K., and HUNT, G. (2001), 'Accomplishing Femininity Among the Girls in the Gang', *British Journal of Criminology*, 41: 656–78.

LEONARD, E. (1982), *Women, Crime and Society: a Critique of Criminology Theory*, New York: Longman.

LOUCKS, N., MALLOCH, M., MCIVOR, G., and GELSTHORPE, L. (2006), *Evaluation of the 218 Centre*, Edinburgh: Scottish Executive Justice Department.

MAC AN GHAILL, M. (1994), *The Making of Men: Masculinities, Sexualities and Schooling*, Buckingham: Open University Press.

MACKINNON, C. (1987a), *Feminism Unmodified: Discourses on Life and Law*, Cambridge, Mass.: Harvard University Press.

——(1987b), 'Feminism, Marxism, Method and The State: Toward Feminist Jurisprudence', in S. Harding (ed), *Feminism and Methodology*, Milton Keynes: Open University Press.

MCLYNN, F. (1989), *Crime and Punishment in the Eighteenth Century*, Oxford: Oxford University Press.

MCMAHON, A. (1993), 'Male Readings of Feminist Theory: The Psychologisation of Sexual Politics in the Masculinity Literature', *Theory and Society*, 22(5): 675–96.

MCROBBIE, A. (1980), 'Settling Accounts with Subcultures', in S. Hall and T. Jefferson (eds), *Resistance Through Rituals*, London: Hutchinson.

MAGUIRE, M., MORGAN, R., and REINER, R. (eds) (1994; 1997; 2002), *Oxford Handbook of Criminology*, Oxford: Clarendon Press.

MAHER, L. (1997), *Sexed Work*, Oxford: Oxford University Press.

MANDARAKA-SHEPPARD, A. (1986), *The Dynamics of Aggression in Women's Prisons in England*, Aldershot: Gower.

MANNHEIM, H. (1965), *Comparative Criminology*, London: Routledge & Kegan Paul.

MARTIN, S., and JURIK, N. (1996), *Doing Justice, Doing Gender*, Thousand Oaks, Cal.: Sage.

MARTIN, S. E. (1980), *Breaking and Entering*, Berkeley, Cal.: University of California Press.

MASON, B. (2006), 'A Gendered Irish Experiment—grounds for Optimism?', in F. Heidensohn (ed.), *Gender and Justice: New Concepts and Approaches*, Cullompton, Devon: Willan.

MESSERSCHMIDT, J. (1993), *Masculinities and Crime: Critique and Reconceptualisation of Theory*, Lanham, Md.: Rowman and Littlefield.

——(1997), *Crime as Structured Action: Gender, Race, Class and Crime in the Making*, Thousand Oaks, Cal.: Sage.

——(2002), 'On Girl Gangs, Gender and Structured Action Theory: A Reply to Miller', *Theoretical Criminology*, 6(4): 477–80.

MILLER, J. (2001), *One of the Guys. Girls, Gang, and Gender*, New York: Oxford University Press.

——(2002), 'The Strengths and Limits for "Doing Gender" for Understanding Street Crime', *Theoretical Criminology*, 6(4): 433–60.

MORGAN, D. (1992), *Discovering Men*, London: Routledge.

MYERS, C. (2006), 'School Bags at Dawn: The Role of Gender in Incidents of School Bullying', in F. Heidensohn (ed.), *Gender and Justice:: New Concepts and Approaches*, Cullompton, Devon: Willan.

NAFFINE, N. (1997), *Feminism and Criminology*, Cambridge: Polity.

NEWBURN, T., and STANKO, E. (eds), (1994), *Just Boys Doing Business? Men, Masculinities and Crime*, London: Routledge.

NCJRS (1998), *Women in Criminal Justice: A Twenty Year Update*. Canada: National Criminal Justice Reference Service; Maryland: Rockville.

OAKLEY, A. (1999), 'People's Ways on Knowing: Gender and Methodology', in S. Hood, B. Mayall, and S. Oliver (eds), *Critical Issues in Social Research. Power and Prejudice*, Buckingham: Open University Press.

——(2000), *Experiments in Knowing. Gender and Method in the Social Sciences*, Cambridge: Polity.

OWEN, B. (1998), *'In the Mix': Struggle and Survival in a Women's Prison*, Albany: State University of New York Press.

PICKERING, S. (2000), 'Women, the Home and Resistance in Northern Ireland', *Women & Criminal Justice*, 11(3): 49–82.

PLAYER, E. (2005), 'The Reduction of Women's Imprisonment in England and Wales: Will the Reform of Short Prison Sentences Help?', *Punishment and Society*, 7(4): 419–39.

POLLOCK-BYRNE, J. (1990), *Women, Prison and Crime*, Belmont, Cal.: Wadsworth.

PRISON REFORM TRUST (PRT) (2000), *Justice for Women: The Need for Reform*, Report of the Committee on Women's Imprisonment. Chaired by Professor Dorothy Wedderburn, London: Prison Reform Trust.

RAEDER, M. (1995), 'The Forgotten Offender: The Effect of the Sentencing Guidelines and Mandatory Minimums on Women and Their Children', *Federal Sentencing Reporter*, 8(3): 157–62.

RAFTER, N. (1985), 'Chastizing the Unchaste: Social Control Functions of a Women's Reformatory', in S. Cohen and A. Scull (eds), *Social Control and the State*, Oxford: Blackwell.

—— (ed) (2000), *The Encyclopedia of Women and Crime*, Phoenix, Ariz.: Onyx Press.

—— and NATALIZIA, E. (1981), 'Marxist feminism: implications for criminal justice', *Crime and Delinquency*, 27: 81–98.

—— and HEIDENSOHN, F. (eds) (1995), *International Feminist Perspectives in Criminology*, Buckingham: Open University Press.

RAMAZANOGLU, C., and HOLLAND, J. (2002), *Feminist Methodology. Challenges and Choices*, London: Sage.

RAP (1969), *Radical Alternatives to Prison*, London: Christian Action Publications.

REINER, R. (1985), *The Politics of the Police*, Oxford: Oxford University Press.

RICE, M. (1990), 'Challenging Orthodoxies in Feminist Theory: A Black Feminist Critique', in L. Gelsthorpe and A. Morris (eds), *Feminist Perspectives in Criminology*, Buckingham: Open University Press.

RICHARDSON, A., and BUDD, T. (2003), *Alcohol, Crime and Disorder: A Study of Young Adults*, Home Office Research Study 263, London: Home Office.

RILEY, J., TORRENS, K., and KRUMHOLZ, S. (2005), 'Contemporary Feminist Writers: Envisioning a Just World, *Contemporary Justice Review*, 8(1): 91–106.

ROCK, P. (1996), *Reconstructing a Women's Prison*, Oxford: Clarendon Press.

ROSE, N. (2000), 'Government and Control', *British Journal of Criminology*, 40(2): 321–39.

RUMGAY, J. (2004a), 'Living with Paradox: Community Supervision of Women Offenders', in G. McIvor (ed), *Women who Offend*, London: Jessica Kingsley.

—— (2004b), 'Scripts for Safer Survival: Pathways Out of Female Crime', *The Howard Journal*, 43(4): 405–19.

SCHLESINGER, P., DOBASH, R. E., and DOBASH, R. P. (1992), *Women Viewing Violence*, London: British Film Institute.

SCHULZ, D. (2000), 'Review Essay: Maternal Justice', *Women and Criminal Justice*, 11(1): 89–98.

SCOTTISH OFFICE (1998), *Women Offenders—A Safer Way*, Edinburgh: Social Work Services and Prisons Inspectorate for Scotland.

SCRATON, P. (1990), 'Scientific Knowledge or Masculine Discourses? Challenging Patriarchy in Criminology', in L. Gelsthorpe and A. Morris, (eds), *Feminist Perspectives in Criminology*, Buckingham: Open University Press.

SEGAL, L. (1990), *Slow Motion: Changing Masculinities, Changing Men*, London: Virago.

SHACKLADY SMITH, L. (1978), 'Sexist Assumptions and Female Delinquency: An Empirical Investigation', in C. Smart and B. Smart (eds), *Women, Sexuality and Social Control*, London: Routledge & Kegan Paul.

SHAW, M. (1991), *The Federal Female Offender*, Ottawa: Solicitor General of Canada.

—— and HANNAH-MOFFAT, K. (eds) (2000), *An Ideal Prison? Critical Essays on Women's Imprisonment in Canada*, Halifax: Fernwood Publishing.

SILVESTRI, M. (2003), *Women in Charge: Policing, Gender and Leadership*, Cullompton, Devon: Willan.

SIM, J. (1990), *Medical Power in Prisons*, Milton Keynes: Open University Press.

SIMMONS, H. (1978), 'Explaining Social Policy: The English Mental Deficiency Act of 1913', *Journal of Social History*, 11(3).

SIMON, R. (1975), *Women and Crime*, Toronto: Lexington.

SMART, C. (1976), *Women, Crime and Criminology*, London: Routledge & Kegan Paul.

—— (1979), 'The New Female Criminal: Reality or Myth', *British Journal of Criminology*, 19(1): 50–71.

—— (1989), *Feminism and the Power of Law*, London: Routledge.

—— (1990), 'Feminist Approaches to Criminology', in L. Gelsthorpe and A. Morris (eds), *Feminist*

Perspectives in Criminology, Buckingham: Open University Press.

——and SMART, B. (eds) (1978), *Women, Sexuality and Social Control*, London: Routledge & Kegan Paul.

SNIDER, L. (2003), 'Constituting the Punishable Woman: atavistic Man Incarcerates Postmodern Woman', *British Journal of Criminology*, 43(2): 354–78.

SPADER, D. (2002) 'The Morality of Justice and the Morality of Care: Are there Distinct Moral Orientations for Males and Females?', *Criminal Justice Review*, 27(1): 66–88.

STANKO, E. (1990a), *Danger Signals*, London: Pandora.

——(1990b), *Everyday Violence*, London: Pandora.

——(1993), *Feminist Criminology: An Oxymoron?*, Paper presented to the British Criminology Conference, Cardiff (July).

STANLEY, L., and WISE, S. (1983), *Breaking Out: Feminist Consciousness and Feminist Research*, London: Routledge & Kegan Paul.

STEFFENSMEIER, D. J., SCHWARTZ, J., ZHONG, H., and ACKERMAN, J. (2005), 'An Assessment of Recent Trends in Girls' Violence using Diverse Longitudinal Sources: Is the Gender Gap Closing?', *Criminology*, 43(2): 355–405.

——and ZHONG, H., ACKERMAN, J., SCHWARTZ, J., and AGHA, S. (2006), 'Gender Gap Trends for Violent Crimes, 1980 to 2003: A UCR-NCVS Comparison', *Feminist Criminology*, 1(1): 72–98.

STEWARD, K. (2006), 'Gender Considerations in Remand Decision-Making', in F. Heidensohn (ed.), *Gender and Justice: New Concepts and Approaches*, Cullompton, Devon: Willan.

TASK FORCE REPORT ON FEDERALLY SENTENCED PRISONERS (TFFSW) (1990), *Creating Choices—The Report of the Task Force on Federally Sentenced Women*, Ottawa: Solicitor General of Canada.

THOMAS, C. (2005), *Judicial Diversity in the United Kingdom and Other Jurisdictions*, London: Commission for Judicial Appointments.

THOMAS, D. (2002), 'Case Comment', *Criminal Law Review* (April): 331–3.

TITTLE, C. (1969), 'Inmate Organization: Sex Differentiation and the Influence of Criminal Sub Cultures', *American Sociological Review*, 34: 492–505.

VELIMESIS, M. (1975), 'The Female Offender', *Crime and Delinquency Literature*, 7(1): 94–112.

WADDINGTON, P. J. (1999), 'Police (Canteen) Sub-Culture: An Appreciation', *British Journal of Criminology*, 39(2): 287–309.

WALBY, S., and ALLEN, J. (2004), *Domestic Violence, Sexual Assault and Stalking: Findings from the British Crime Survey*, Home Office Research Study 276, London: Home Office.

WALKER, G. (2003), *Crime, Gender and Social Order in early Modern England*, Cambridge: Cambridge University Press.

WALKER, N. (1987), *Crime and Criminology. A Critical Introduction*, Oxford: Oxford University Press.

WALKLATE, S. (1989), *Victimology*, London: Unwin Hyman.

——(2004) *Gender, Crime and Criminal Justice*, Cullompton, Devon: Willan.

WALKOWITZ, J. (1980), *Prostitution and Victorian Society*, Cambridge: Cambridge University Press.

WARD, D., and KASSEBAUM, G. (1965), *Women's Prison*, London: Weidenfeld.

WEBB, D. (1984), 'More on Gender and Justice: Girl Offenders on Supervision', *Sociology*, 18.

WESTMARLAND, L. (2001), *Gender and Policing*, Cullompton, Devon: Willan.

WIENER, M. (1998), 'The Victorian Criminalization of Men', in P. Spierenburg (ed.), *Men and Violence: Gender, Honor and Rituals in Modern Europe and America*, Columbus, Ohio: Ohio State University Press.

WILLIS, P. (1977). *Learning to Labour*, Farnborough: Saxon House.

WOODBRIDGE, J., and FROSZTEGA, J. (1998), *Recent Changes in the Female Prison Population*, London: Home Office.

WORRALL, A. (1990). *Offending Women*, London: Routledge.

——(2002), 'Rendering them punishable', in P. Carlen (ed.), *Women and Punishment: The Struggle for Justice*, Cullompton, Devon: Willan.

——(2004), 'Twisted Sisters, Ladettes, and the New Penology: the Social Construction of "Violent Girls"', in C. Alder and A. Worrall (eds), *Girls' Violence*, New York: State University of New York Press.

YOUNG, A. (1990), *Femininity in Dissent*, London: Routledge.

——(1994), 'Feminism and the Body of Criminology', in D. Farrington and S. Walklate (eds), *Offenders and Victims: Theory and Policy*, London: British Society of Criminology and ISTD. British Criminology Conference Selected Papers, vol. 1.

YOUNG, J. (1999), *The Exclusive Society*, London: Sage.

YOUNG, M. (1991), *An Inside Job*, Oxford: Oxford University Press.

ZAPLIN, R. (ed) (1998), *Female Offenders: Critical Perspectives and Effective Interventions*, Gaithersburg, Md. Aspen.

ZEDNER, L. (1991), *Women, Crime and Custody in Victorian England*, Oxford: Oxford University Press.

14

ETHNICITIES, RACISM, CRIME, AND CRIMINAL JUSTICE

Coretta Phillips and Ben Bowling

This chapter aims to move beyond the narrow confines of the 'race and crime' debate—which for three decades has been concerned with explaining the over-representation of black people in prison—to consider other relevant issues. We examine violent racism, violence *within* minority communities, prison racism, and the experiences of minority practitioners, all of which form part of the picture of relations between minority ethnic groups and the criminal justice system. While broadening the agenda, we must still consider why black Britons, who comprise just over 2 per cent of the resident population, make up around 11 per cent of the prison population (Home Office 2006), so we examine how different ethnic groups fare at different stages of the criminal process and the links between crime and criminal justice practice set in the historical, social, and political context.

The social, political, and cultural landscape of Britain has changed significantly in the last decade. The fallout from the terrorist attacks of 11 September 2001, wars in Afghanistan and Iraq, suicide bombings in London in July 2005, and the expansion of criminal justice legislation have all had an impact. These events can be seen alongside wider global influences such as the rise of ethnic nationalism, the disintegration of the Soviet Union and Yugoslavia, and devastating natural disasters and famine displacing people to Western European countries including Britain. The hardened political response to asylum and immigration has shaped the experiences of people demonized as 'welfare scroungers', terrorists, or criminals in public discourse. The 2001 census provides new opportunities to explore the ethnic, cultural, and religious diversity of a country which remains a predominantly white society (92 per cent of the total population), but has minority ethnic communities which comprise up to a third of local populations in some cities and large towns (Lupton and Power 2004). Such diversity is a crucial backdrop to the study of ethnicities, racism, crime, and criminal justice.

SETTING THE CONTEXT: HISTORICAL, CONCEPTUAL, AND CONTEMPORARY

Taking a historical perspective helps to understand contemporary patterns by examining how racial ideologies have shaped thinking about ethnicity, crime, and criminal justice. The pseudo-scientific idea of 'race' and racial hierarchies originated in the ideas of European Enlightenment philosophers and physical scientists such as Hume, Kant, de Gobineau, Linne, and Blumenbach (Bowling and Phillips 2002). For these men, the Age of Reason and civilization were synonymous with the 'white people' of northern Europe, while those of supposedly 'other' racial origins were regarded as of naturally inferior moral, intellectual, and evolutionary potential (Kleg 1993). Stereotypes of people of African origin were different from those applied to people from Asia, but both were assumed to be fixed in a hierarchical position below the 'white race' (Eze 1997). Cesare Lombroso, the most influential of the new 'scientific criminologists', made a direct link between 'race' and crime in *Criminal Man* (1876), in which he concluded that 'many of the characteristics found in savages, and in the coloured races, are also to be found in habitual delinquents', including low cranial capacity, receding foreheads, darker skin, curly hair, and large or handle-shaped ears.

The themes of racist thinking—what Gilroy (2000) refers to as 'raciology'— legitimized practices of slavery and indentured labour, becoming embedded in imperialism and colonial policies covering Africa, Asia, and the West Indies. The inferior traits assumed to be innate to 'non-white' racial groups were also applied to racially 'othered' white ethnic groups, such as those of Irish and Jewish origin (see Pearson 1983; Swift 2002). A Liverpool newspaper referred to Irish Catholic immigrants in 1855 as 'the filthiest beings in the habitable globe . . . three-fourths of the crime perpetrated in this large town is by Irish papists. They are the very dregs of society.' Assumptions about the underworld criminality of Jewish peoples in England have also surfaced from time to time; Charles Dickens's depiction of Fagin in *Oliver Twist* epitomized common views of Jewish petty thievery in the early nineteenth century (see also Rubinstein 1996).

Following the Second World War and the extermination of a significant proportion of European Jewry, there was a sustained attempt within the academy to unpack the racial ideologies of the Nazi state. The 1951 UNESCO Statement by Experts on Race Problems—drawing on the expertise of natural and social scientists—concluded that there was no scientific basis for defining some racial groups as naturally inferior to others (Montagu 1943). Race came to be seen as a myth, a social construction, with its roots in historical processes of colonialism, rather than as an objective classification. The persistence of race in the public (and sociological) imagination, however, has meant that it has not yet been eclipsed by the less loaded term, ethnicity, which is preferred by some sociologists (Mason 2000). Ethnicity avoids an exclusive biological focus, referring to self-defined collectivities of people who share a common origin and culture, which unlike race, is variable according to local sociocultural systems (Barth 1969).

Despite this academic assault on the validity of the concept of 'race', the categories used in the UK census and for the purposes of 'ethnic monitoring' under section 95 of the 1991 Criminal Justice Act are a curious admixture of 'race' (White/Black/Mixed), nationality (Indian/Pakistani/Bangladeshi/Chinese), and geography (Black Caribbean/Black African). At the time of the 2001 census those of minority ethnic origin collectively made up 8.9 per cent of the population in England and Wales, with the Asian groups comprising 4.5 per cent, the black groups 2.4 per cent; and the Chinese and mixed-race groups about 1 per cent each. Although these administrative categories obscure the internal heterogeneity of these groups and are problematic for various other reasons (Bowling and Phillips 2002: 33–5), they offer the only opportunity to assess how experiences of crime and criminal justice vary among different ethnic groups.

Since the 1970s academic and political attention has centred on migrants from Britain's colonial territories who came to Britain in the post-war period, acting as a replacement labour force in urban areas that had suffered significant war casualties or population losses following upward white mobility (Solomos and Back 1996). Political and public discourses echoed earlier concerns about racial degeneration and the perceived problem of 'bad stock' assimilating into English culture. On occasion, as in Notting Hill and Nottingham in 1958, this hostility escalated into widespread racist violence (Bowling 1999). The local political backdrop was of widespread opposition to further post-colonial migration to the UK and in a notorious speech in Birmingham in 1968, Enoch Powell, MP, predicted that 'rivers of blood' would flow because of this 'alien element' who represented a direct threat to Britain's strong, white, national identity.

Daniel's (1968) survey found people from minority ethnic groups in Britain were consistently in jobs below the level to which they were qualified and were being overtly excluded from adequate public and private sector housing through what was known as the 'colour bar'. The legacy of early discrimination has contemporary resonance as social inequalities among Britain's minority ethnic groups have been sustained over time, although with increasing differentiation. Collectively, minority ethnic communities remain geographically concentrated in urban neighbourhoods where unemployment and social deprivation is greatest. Housing conditions are poorest for those of Pakistani and Bangladeshi origin, followed by Black Caribbeans and Black Africans, although there are some signs of suburbanization among those of Indian origin (Lakey 1997).

Secondary school attainment levels based on GCSE examination results present a complex picture with a high-attaining cluster of ethnic groups (pupils of Chinese, Indian, and Irish origin), a mid-range cluster (white British, mixed race, Bangladeshi, Irish Travellers, Pakistani, and Black African) and the lowest-attaining cluster of pupils of Black Caribbean and Gypsy/Roma origin (DfES 2005). Studies of labour market outcomes indicate higher levels of unemployment, lower occupational attainment, and lower earnings for minority ethnic individuals, but this is least marked for those of Indian and Chinese origin. In all these areas of social policy, there is cumulative evidence of a complex interplay of socio-economic, demographic, institutional, structural, and cultural factors—alongside direct and indirect racial discrimination—which contribute to these less favourable outcomes for minority ethnic groups (Phillips 2005a).

Structural inequalities and racial discrimination have coalesced and erupted into racialized riots between young minority ethnic men and the police at various times in recent history (see Bowling and Phillips 2002: 8–12). In late 2005, in a multi-ethnic suburb of Birmingham, there were violent clashes between black and Asian men, following allegations of a sexual assault against a Jamaican teenager. Before that, in spring and summer 2001, street violence erupted between young Pakistani, Bangladeshi, and white men, and the police, in the northern towns of Bradford, Burnley, and Oldham. In the aftermath, the official reports into the disturbances acknowledged the extreme levels of socio-economic deprivation experienced among Pakistani/Bangladeshi and white communities who nonetheless inhabited segregated residential, educational, occupational, and leisure spaces (see, for example, Cantle 2001). The disturbances thus reignited political concerns about the need for an inclusive sense of British identity to avoid social disorder (Phillips 2005a). The patterns of socio-economic disadvantage evident in the northern towns are clearly important too for interpreting patterns of victimization, offending, and the administration of criminal justice, and it is to these that we now turn.

REDRAWING THE PARAMETERS OF THE 'RACE AND CRIME' DEBATE: VICTIMIZATION AND OFFENDING

RACIST VICTIMIZATION

The experience of minority ethnic groups as victims of crime has rarely been at the heart of the 'race and crime' debate. For reasons that we discuss below, the Stephen Lawrence Inquiry was the moment when *racist* victimization—where an individual is selected as a target because of his or her race, ethnicity, or religion—gained full public recognition (Bowling 1999, Cathcart 1999). Racist violence was nothing new, of course; the reports of local groups have been highlighting the problem of racist and religiously motivated violence since the 1970s. In 1978, for example, the Bethnal Green and Stepney Trades Council (1978) report into violence and harassment against the Bangladeshi community led to official acknowledgement of a wider problem of racist violence in society (Bowling 1999). Similarly, Islamophobia—in verbal and violent forms—has been brought to the fore through the work of the European Monitoring Centre on Racism and Xenophobia (Allen and Nielsen 2002). Links between racist victimization and broader political events such as the Palestine–Israel conflict or the Iraq war have also been found by Iganski, Kielinger, and Paterson (2005) in their analysis of anti-Semitic incidents in London.

Extent and nature

Police-recorded racist incidents have increased dramatically from 4,383 incidents in 1988 to 52,694 incidents in 2003/4 (Home Office 2005a). Data from the British Crime Survey (BCS) show a drop in racist victimization since 1995, which given indications of both increased reporting to and recording by the police, may well represent a downward trend (Docking and Tuffin 2005). Whilst the perpetrators of racist violence are not exclusively white, elements of a defensive form of whiteness can assume significance in offending behaviour. Salisbury and Upson (2004) found 4 per cent of 'mixed-race' respondents interviewed in the 2002/3 BCS, 3 per cent of Asians, and 2 per cent of black and Chinese/other origin respondents had been the victim of racially motivated crime in the previous year, compared with less than 1 per cent of white respondents.

As might be expected, the volume of recorded racist incidents is likely to be higher in areas with relatively large minority ethnic populations, simply because there are more potential targets. However, Maynard and Read's (1997) study of police records found that *per capita rates* of racist victimization were highest in three provincial forces. This is consistent with accounts of rural racism and the victimization of asylum seekers/refugees dispersed outside Britain's centres of minority ethnic concentration (see Chakraborti and Garland 2004). Brimicombe *et al.*'s (2001) analysis of victimization allegations in Newham supported the hypothesis that attacks cluster where minority ethnic individuals form a small but growing proportion of the population (see also Hesse *et al.* 1992; Sampson and Phillips 1992, 1996; Bowling 1999, cf. Ray *et al.* 2004).

Although victimization surveys go some way further than official statistics in documenting the extent of racist violence they do not capture the process and nature of victimization, with its complex and repeated interactions and its cumulative impact on the victim (Bowling 1993, 1999). Sampson and Phillips (1992) showed that racist victimization tends to be of an ongoing nature, with both 'minor' abuse and incidents of physical violence interwoven in a pattern of harassment and intimidation— a fact often unacknowledged by statutory agencies who respond to single, discrete incidents (Bowling 1999; Phillips and Sampson 1998).

Responses to racist victimization

In response to their victimization people have been known to restrict their movements to safe spaces or to use situational measures to protect themselves, such as fireproof letterboxes, while collective self-defence campaigns aimed at physically defending neighbourhoods in the face of official inaction date back to the events in Notting Hill and Nottingham in 1958. Monitoring projects in Newham, Southall, and elsewhere across the country, formed in the late 1970s, continue to provide advice and support for victims of racist violence. The recent disorders in Bradford, Burnley, and Oldham in 2001 had their roots in the defensive counter-attacks by young Pakistani and

Bangladeshi men responding to organized racist violence by extreme right-wing groups, amidst perceptions of police under-protection (Webster 2003).

The statutory response to racist violence has focused on policing, multi-agency approaches, and new legislation. Research and community accounts have revealed low levels of satisfaction with the police, as victims have reported that the racist element of their victimization has been denied and presented as youthful misbehaviour, drunken pranks, or as neighbour disputes (Graef 1989; Sampson and Phillips 1992; Chahal and Julienne 1999). The police have blamed the victims for the violence directed against them, implying that traditional dress or speaking in a foreign language makes someone both more threatening and more vulnerable to attack (Bowling 1999). There has also been a consistent pattern of the police failing to record and investigate reported incidents, and ultimately of the criminal justice system failing to bring offenders to justice. The police have sometimes even viewed the victim as a suspect instead (ibid.).

The Macpherson Inquiry into the investigation of Stephen Lawrence's murder: an exemplar

The racist murder of Stephen Lawrence in south-east London in 1993 and the subsequent public inquiry into the failed Metropolitan Police murder investigation brought the issue of racist violence to the top of the political agenda at the end of the 1990s. It was perhaps the symbolic ingredients of blameless victim (Stephen Lawrence was aspiring, law-abiding, and religiously observant) and violent racist perpetrators (with criminal pasts) that crystallized the issue for the public and the establishment (Cathcart 1999; Rock 2004). The Inquiry concluded that the initial investigation into the murder was 'marred by a combination of professional incompetence, institutional racism and a failure of leadership by senior officers' (Macpherson 1999: 46.1). Institutional racism—defined as the 'collective failure of an organization to provide an appropriate and professional service to people because of their colour, culture, or ethnic origin'—could be 'seen or detected in processes, attitudes and behaviour which amount to discrimination through unwitting prejudice, ignorance, thoughtlessness and racist stereotyping which disadvantage minority ethnic people' (Macpherson 1999: 34). The report documented the denial of the racist motive for the murder among at least five police officers, and the racist stereotyping of Stephen's friend, Duwayne Brooks, at the scene, where he was wrongly assumed to be one of the protagonists in a fight between youths rather than a victim of an unprovoked attack (Hall *et al.* 1998). The Lawrence Inquiry criticized the use of inappropriate and offensive language, and the insensitive and patronizing handling of the Lawrence family throughout the investigation.

When the report was published, some police union representatives and right-wing commentators challenged the findings that the police service was institutionally racist (Dennis *et al.* 2000). Some criminologists argued that police incompetence in investigating murder was more salient than the issue of institutional racism (Innes 1999; Waddington 1999). Foster *et al.*'s (2005) assessment of the impact of the Lawrence Inquiry on policing shows that many police officers, particularly in London, still feel angry and resentful about the accusation of institutional racism which they perceive to be have been unfairly applied, and have wrongly assumed it refers to widespread individual racism. As numerous other commentators have noted, this largely reflects the conceptual imprecision of the Macpherson definition which conflated racisms at the level of the individual and of the institution (Miles and Brown 2003; Solomos 1999).

Nonetheless, the racist murder of Stephen Lawrence had an 'explosive impact on the workings of the criminal justice system' (Rock 2004: 481). The government response was to establish a ministerial priority for the police service 'to increase trust and confidence in policing amongst minority ethnic communities', as well as a range of other measures focusing on defining, reporting, recording, investigating, and prosecuting racist incidents, training for racism awareness and cultural diversity, police discipline, and enhancing the preventive role of education (Home Office 1999a). Oakley's (2005) analysis of EU member states' policing of racist crimes suggests that the reform programme has paid dividends. The report applauds the UK for having the most comprehensive and systematic approach enshrined in policy. Despite these accolades, Foster *et al.* (2005) suggest that any improvements need to be seen alongside continuing problems of sexist and homophobic exclusion and public expectations of discriminatory policing among minority ethnic groups (see also Criminal Justice System Race Unit 2005).

Another plank of New Labour's reforms was the introduction of enhanced penalties for racially aggravated offences in the Crime and Disorder Act 1998, ministers having been persuaded that such crimes attack the core identity of the victim and threaten the wider target community (Lawrence 2002). These laws, which are used widely in the USA, are controversial because some commentators claim that they censor free speech and thought and that they unfairly punish prejudice and hatred which are not, in themselves, criminal (see Jacoby 2002; Iganski 2002). Burney and Rose's (2002) study of the law's implementation found wide variation in the recording of racist incidents and their translation into racially aggravated offences, with only a tiny number being sentenced by the courts. Burney (2002) and Ray and Smith (2002) have also questioned the value of using the criminal law to punish offenders whose expression of racism may be slight or where localized cultures of racism and violence tacitly support such behaviour.

Explaining racist offending

Victims' accounts and case studies indicate that racist offenders are typically white males aged 16–25 years, but younger children and older adults are also sometimes involved. Incidents frequently involve groups of offenders, and sometimes include whole families (Percy 1998). Sibbitt's (1997) study in two London boroughs found that offenders' racist views were shared by the communities to which they belonged, and the offenders felt that this legitimated their actions. Ray *et al.*'s (2001) research in Manchester found that racist offenders rarely had knowledge of fascist political ideologies and most had engaged in other forms of non-racist crime. Offenders targeted minority ethnic individuals with whom they were acquainted, perceiving them to be receiving preferential treatment or access to scarce social and economic resources, such as housing, employment, education, and leisure facilities. This 'scapegoating' is a key explanation for racist offending (Bowling and Phillips 2002: 114–19). Ray *et al.* (2001) linked the display of violent racism to a sense of shame, grievance, and powerlessness experienced by offenders when comparing themselves to South Asians who formed the main victim group. South Asians were viewed by the offenders as self-interested and economically successful but not through revered manual labour, at the same time as being envied for their strong familial and communal cohesion, reinforced through cultural ties. The narratives of the offenders displayed a rage about the 'invisibility' and impoverishment of white culture and identity in Britain, a theme which has emerged in other sociological accounts (Nayak 2003). Elements of this narrative of whiteness frequently lament the end of Empire and of Britain's superiority as a world power, epitomized in both the presence of, and perceived success of, some minority ethnic groups in Britain (Parekh 2000; Gilroy 2004).

There have been over 150 racist murders in Britain in the last 35 years (Bowling 1999; Athwal and Kundnani 2006). However, most crime committed against minority ethnic communities, perhaps 85 per cent, is not racially motivated, and it is this 'ordinary' victimization to which we now turn.

VICTIMIZATION AND FEAR OF CRIME

Using data from the BCS, Salisbury and Upson (2004) estimate that in 2002–3, victimization risks for white, black, and Chinese/other people were similar (27 per cent, 26 per cent and 27 per cent), whilst those of Asian and 'mixed' origin experienced higher crime risks (30 per cent and 46 per cent). The overall greater risk of victimization for minority ethnic groups is also reflected in their having greater anxiety about crime (Clancy *et al.* 2001). The BCS data show that minority ethnic respondents were more likely to be victims of burglary and vehicle theft than white respondents, while those of mixed race experienced substantially higher levels of household and personal crimes.

The 2000 BCS found factors such as age, low income, unemployment, inner-city residence, and a lack of academic qualifications were more important than *ethnic origin* in explaining minority ethnic groups' higher levels of victimization (Clancy *et al.* 2001). Nevertheless, some of these factors, such as inner-city residence and unemployment, may themselves be partly explained by discrimination in housing and employment. Moreover, it is as yet unclear why risks are significantly higher for 'mixed' respondents, as this could not be explained on the basis of their age, type of area, levels of economic activity, or housing tenure (Salisbury and Upson 2004).

So far the discussion has centred on minority ethnic individuals as victims of crime. This must be viewed alongside an analysis of patterns of offending because victims and offenders tend to overlap and also because it is necessary to explore the inter- and intra-ethnic patterns of crime within minority ethnic and white communities.

THE SOCIAL CONSTRUCTION OF ETHNICITY AND CRIMINALITY

Pearson (1983) shows how crime has often been portrayed as something alien to the 'British way of life'. Media-fuelled 'crime panics' have often used imported words such as the Irish 'Hooligan', Spanish 'garotting', or American 'mugging' to describe supposedly foreign types of criminality (Pearson 1983; Hall *et al.* 1978; Bowling and Phillips 2002: 77). It was only in the last quarter of the twentieth century that crime in England began to be associated with black people and even today some white groups—such as Kosovans, Romanians, Russians, and other eastern European 'asylum-seekers' —are the focus of discussions of ethnicity and criminality. Historically, there has also been a racial undertone in discussions of 'English criminality', with home-grown crime and disorder seen as the result of the 'disease' of 'racial degeneration' (Pearson 1983: ix–xi, 69–73).

The 'race and crime' debate really heated up with the arrival of visible minority ethnic groups migrating from the former colonies. Although people from Africa, the Caribbean, and the Indian subcontinent were widely seen as inclined towards deviance when in the colonies, until the mid-1970s, the official view was that crime was not a problem among the people from Africa, the Caribbean, and the Indian subcontinent who were settling in Britain. As the 1972 House of Commons Select Committee put it: '[t]he conclusions remain beyond doubt: coloured immigrants are no more involved in crime than others; nor are they generally more concerned in violence, prostitution and drugs. The West Indian crime rate is much the same as that of the indigenous population. The Asian crime rate is very much lower' (House of Commons 1972: 71). Official views changed markedly soon afterwards, with some minority ethnic communities increasingly being seen as a crime and disorder problem (House of Commons 1976). From around the mid-1970s sensationalist media reports appeared, with headlines such as 'black crime shock', based on the publication of selective police statistics on robbery in inner city areas (Hall *et al.* 1978). Public discussion of the urban disorders and media images of 'ethnic criminality' served to lend credence to views about the pathological nature of minority ethnic communities, their family structure, values, and culture (Gilroy 1987a).

As a result, old and new images of black communities as prone to violence, drugs, and disorderly behaviour have become entrenched in the public consciousness (Gilroy 1982, 1987b). Asian communities have, in some accounts, been portrayed as conformist, passive, inward looking and self-regulating (Wardak 2000; Webster 1997). More recently, with media panics about 'Asian gangs' (Alexander 2000), Pakistani and Bangladeshi communities have been portrayed as increasingly violent and disorderly, culturally separatist and resisting integration within British society, and as the source of home-grown Islamic terrorism. The media representation of the bombings in London on 7 July 2005 and the fact that the perpetrators were Muslim and British citizens of

Pakistani and Jamaican origin have also served to cement the image of minority ethnic groups as a security threat. Numerous critics have also pointed out that ethnicity and culture always comes to the fore when black and Asian people commit crime (Gilroy 2003; Heaven and Hudson 2005: 376), a point which is reinforced by the absurdity of describing football violence, child sex abuse, serial killing, or corporate manslaughter as 'white on white' crimes (ibid.).

In May 2003, Chris Fox, then President of the Association of Chief Police Officers (ACPO), sparked controversy by commenting that criminals were using the cover of asylum to travel around the world. In fact, ACPO's own research indicated that the majority of asylum-seekers are law-abiding and are more likely to be victims than offenders. In October 2003, Beverley Hughes, then Home Office minister, reported to Parliament, 'there is no evidence to suggest that asylum seekers are disproportionately likely to commit crime'. Nonetheless, there have been numerous newspaper reports of 'crime waves' committed by refugees and asylum-seekers, many of which have been written in sensationalist fashion. This is not to say that asylum-seekers never commit crime. It would be surprising if people who have fled conflict situations and were vulnerable to poverty, homelessness, and victimization, were themselves never involved in crime. The key issue is that the media, sometimes on the basis of a selective use of police statistics, can create a distorted or exaggerated image of crime within particular groups in society.

CRIMINOLOGICAL RESEARCH ON ETHNICITY AND CRIME

SELF-REPORT SURVEYS

Self-report surveys rely on the honesty of interviewees to disclose dishonest and violent behaviour (see Maguire, Chapter 10 this volume). Nonetheless, large numbers of people do admit to their crimes, many providing great detail, and the method is generally agreed to be valid and reliable (Budd and Sharp 2005). Based on a sample of 2,500 young people, Graham and Bowling (1995) found white and black respondents had very similar rates of offending (44 per cent and 43 per cent), while those of Indian, Pakistani, and Bangladeshi origin (30 per cent, 28 per cent, and 13 per cent) had very much lower rates (see also Flood-Page *et al.* 2000). The Offending, Crime and Justice Survey of 12,000 people found that white people and those of 'mixed' ethnic origin were the most likely to say that they had committed a crime (around 40 per cent), compared with those of Asian, black, or 'other' ethnic origin (21 per cent, 28 per cent, and 23 per cent) (Sharp and Budd 2005: 8). Localized surveys in secondary schools in deprived areas found the highest rates of offending among the 'mixed' group (61 per cent) with white (55 per cent) and black (50 per cent) respondents having similar rates and those of Asian origin significantly lower (33 per cent) (Armstrong *et al.* 2005: 19).

Since the early 1990s, at least nine Home Office self-report surveys have compared drug use among different ethnic groups, producing remarkably similar findings.[1] Sharp and Budd (2005) found that amongst males, respondents of 'mixed' ethnicity were most likely to have used drugs–mostly cannabis—in the last year (27 per cent) compared with 16 per cent of both their black and white counterparts, 13 per cent of 'other' ethnic groups, and 5 per cent of Asians. Class A drug use in the last year reported was similar for males of white, mixed, and 'other' ethnic origins (6 per cent) and much lower for Asian and black males (1 per cent and 2 per cent respectively). Among females, drug use (both cannabis and Class A) was higher among white respondents and those of 'mixed' ethnic origin and lower among those of Asian and black origin.

SUSPECTS DESCRIBED BY VICTIMS AND WITNESSES

Victims of crime can also tell us about the ethnic origin of the people whom they suspect of committing crimes against them through their descriptions either to the police or in victimization surveys. About four out of 10 of the victims surveyed in the British Crime Survey were able to offer a description of the person they knew or believed to have committed a crime against them, typically in 'contact offences' such as assault, robbery, and theft (Clancy *et al.* 2001). Victims' descriptions should be treated with caution because the crimes in which they can describe the offender may not be representative of those where they cannot, and also because eye-witness identification is not entirely reliable (Coleman and Moynihan 1996).

Clancy *et al.* (2001) found that, where the victim could judge the offender's ethnic origin, 85 per cent described the offenders involved as white, while 15 per cent said that the offender was from a visible minority ethnic group. Individual minority ethnic groups make up a very small proportion of suspected offenders for most offences. This ranges from a small over-representation for burglary to a large over-representation for 'mugging'. Of the sample of 203 victims of 'mugging' identified in the 2000 BCS, 63 (three out of 10) described their assailant as black (ibid.). Mugging, a term without legal standing but comprising robbery, contact, and snatch thefts, accounts for 1.7 per cent of recorded crime (Dodd *et al.* 2004) and continues to be the focus of media panics as it has since the early 1970s (Hall *et al.* 1978).

The police have collected ethnically coded descriptions of offenders for selected offences—typically street robbery—since the mid-1970s (Hall *et al.* 1978; Bowling and Phillips 2002: 78–9). Several recent Home Office studies have examined victims' descriptions in police reports of particular crimes in selected locations. Harrington and Mayhew's (2001: 41) study of mobile phone theft found that in the London borough of Westminster two-thirds of suspects were black and three out of 10 were white, whereas in Stockport three-quarters of suspects were white and 10 per cent were black.

---

[1] Leitner *et al.* (1993), Mott and Mirrlees Black (1995), Graham and Bowling (1995), Ramsay and Percy (1996), Ramsay and Spiller (1997), Flood Page *et al.* (2000), Ramsay *et al.* (2001), Aust and Smith (2003), and Sharp and Budd (2005).

In Birmingham, only 10 per cent of suspects were white, compared with more than half who were black and one-third Asian. Smith's (2003: 26) study found that the majority of robbery suspects were black in six out of nine police areas, the exceptions being Stockport, Preston, and Blackpool where 99 per cent of the suspected offenders were white.

HOMICIDE AND GUN CRIME

Around 800 people were victims of murder, manslaughter, or infanticide in England and Wales in 2003–4. Among them is a marked over-representation of minority ethnic groups, particularly black people, who were five times as likely to be murdered as their white counterparts (Home Office 2005a). Those of 'other' ethnic origin were seven times more likely to be murdered than their white counterparts and people of Asian origin were nearly twice as likely (see Figure 14.1).

The detection rate for homicide is relatively high in comparison with other offences but it is more common for those involving black victims to remain unsolved (27 per cent) in comparison with Asian (18 per cent) or white victims (13 per cent) (Home Office 2005a). This may be because of the method of killing (e.g. those involving strangers and guns are less likely to be solved), or because witnesses are less likely to come forward being fearful of intimidation or reprisals. It may be, as it is widely perceived within minority ethnic communities, because the police are less interested in these cases, make mistakes, or mishandle investigations (Clancy *et al.* 2001). Among those in which a suspect was identified, the majority of homicides were intra-ethnic; that is, 92 per cent of white victims were killed by someone of the same ethnic group and this was true of 56 per cent of black victims and 66 per cent of those of Asian origin (Home Office 2005a). This pattern has remained more or less consistent since homicide data were first published in 1999.

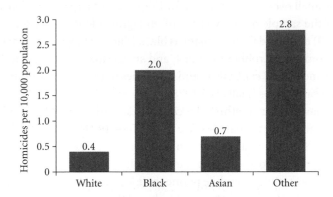

Fig. 14.1 Homicides per 10,000 Population, by ethnic group, combined data for 2001/01 to 2002/03

Notes: 1. Number of homicide victims: White 1,780; Black 254; Asian 160; Other 149.

2. Excludes Offences where ethnicity was unrecorded. A Further 172 offences committed by Dr Harold Shipman have also been excluded as these were committed before 2000, although they were discovered and recorded during the period. *Source*: Hearnden and Hough (2004).

Recent years have seen increased public anxiety about gun crime within black communities in the UK. While guns hardly featured in the crime scene until the late 1980s, murders involving guns became increasingly prevalent during the 1990s. Two of the most notorious instances of gun crime in recent years were double murders, both of which occured in 2003: teenage girls Charlene Ellis and Letisha Shakespeare were caught in gang crossfire in January and then, in October, 7-year-old Toni-Ann Byfield and her father Bertram Byfield were killed in an execution-style shooting. The public outcry around these murders intensified the development of anti-gun campaigns within black communities. Despite this public concern and media attention, there still remains only a very limited amount of research (Bullock and Tilley 2002) and only a handful of journalistic accounts of gun crime within black communities (McLagan 2005; Thompson 2004).

It is important to keep these crimes in perspective. Gun homicide remains relatively rare: over the past decade an average of 25 black people have been victims of gun murder each year compared with around 40 white people and seven Asians (Home Office 2005a: 22). Black murder victims are much more likely to have been shot (31 per cent) than white (6 per cent) or Asian (12 per cent) victims, accounting for one-third of gun murder victims in England and Wales. Bullock and Tilley's (2002) study of shooting in Manchester found that of the 32 offenders identified in 46 shooting incidents they examined, 22 were black, eight were white, and two were Asian. There was a clear overlap between victims and offenders. Of the 32 offenders, eight had previously been shot and three were subsequently shot dead.

Crime statistics paint a complex picture of patterns of crime within minority ethnic and white communities. On one hand, black people and those of 'other' ethnic groups are over-represented in stop and search, arrest, conviction, and prison statistics (the reasons for which are discussed later in the chapter). People of Asian origin are over-represented in some statistics and under-represented in others. Black people also appear substantially over-represented in victims' and witness descriptions of some forms of crime but not others and again, the picture for people of Asian origin is more mixed. On the other hand, self-report studies—based on admitted offending—are consistent with official data in indicating that offending rates are very much lower among the Asian population than among their white counterparts, but they contrast sharply with their indication that offending is no more common among the black population than among the white population. There are three possible explanations for this discrepancy.

• Self-report studies may accurately reflect the extent of crime within minority ethnic communities while arrest and other official statistics create a distorted picture as a result of racial discrimination in policing and the criminal justice process.

• People from minority ethnic groups may be less willing to admit their offending to crime surveys. No research evidence exists to support this view in the UK (Sharp and Budd 2005), although studies in the USA and the Netherlands have found that some ethnic groups are more likely to conceal their offending than others (Hindelang 1981; Junger 1989, 1990; cf. Bowling 1990).

- The two methods measure different things. Self-report surveys may be best suited to measuring the extent of criminal behaviour in the general population but less useful for shedding light on the small number of the most serious offenders who are often missed by household surveys.

This debate could be considered simply 'empiricist haggling' over crime statistics and we have sympathy with those who eschew the whole enterprise of classifying crimes according to the skin colour of their perpetrators (Gilroy 1982: 146). However, this debate will continue with or without the benefit of research evidence. Moreover, the question of patterns of crime within minority ethnic communities contributes to the framing of discussions about the fairness of policing and the criminal justice process and it is to these issues that we now turn our attention. We start with the police, usually the first and most frequent point of contact between citizen and state.

THE POLICE AND POLICING MINORITY COMMUNITIES

'Mistrust, resentment and suspicion' between the police and minority ethnic communities can be traced back to the anti-immigrant attitudes and insensitive policing of the early years of post-colonial migration to the UK (Whitfield 2004). Hunte's (1966: 12) West Indian Standing Conference report, for example, referred to police officers going 'nigger hunting . . . to bring in a coloured person at all costs'. Allegations of oppressive policing against African, Caribbean, and Asian communities—such as mass stop and search operations, the inappropriate use of paramilitary tactics, excessive surveillance, unjustified armed raids, police violence and deaths in custody, and a failure to respond effectively to racist violence—recur throughout the 1970s and 1980s (Institute of Race Relations 1987; Bowling and Phillips 2002: 128–9). The collective experience of minority ethnic communities—including marginalized 'white' minorities such as the Irish community—in the UK is of being 'over-policed and under protected' (Reiner 2000; Macpherson 1999).

STOP AND SEARCH

Among the various aspects of the relationship between the police and minority ethnic communities, it is the practice of 'stop and search' that has been the most contentious.[2] Under the 1824 Vagrancy Act, the so-called 'sus' law, a person could be arrested and prosecuted by the police and convicted at court for 'loitering with intent' to commit a

---

[2] Black deaths in custody has also been a very contentious issue, especially when a very disproportionate number occurred during the 1980s and 1990s (Institute of Race Relations 1991; Bowling and Phillips 2002: 131–5).

crime. This highly discretionary power was used extensively and often arbitrarily against black communities. In April 1981, the Metropolitan Police used these powers to conduct a mass stop and search operation called Operation Swamp which triggered the Brixton riots amid allegations of insensitive and discriminatory policing (Scarman 1981). After the abolition of 'sus' a new provision, section 1 of the Police and Criminal Evidence Act 1984 (PACE), permitted an officer to stop and search someone where he or she has 'reasonable suspicion' of wrongdoing (see also Sanders and Young, Chapter 28, this volume). However, allegations that minority ethnic groups were being targeted persisted and when the first 'ethnically coded' statistics on the use of PACE, section 1, were published, a clear picture of disproportionality was revealed, a pattern that persists to this day.

In the year ending April 2004, the police carried out almost 750,000 searches. Of the people stopped, 15 per cent were black, 7 per cent Asian, and 1 per cent of 'other' ethnic origin (Home Office 2005a). Relative to the population as a whole, black people were 6.5 times more likely to be stopped and searched than white people and Asians twice as likely (ibid.). While the number of searches carried out by individual police forces has varied, the level of disproportionality has increased steadily since the ethnic monitoring data were first made available in the mid-1990s (FitzGerald and Sibbitt 1997). It should also be borne in mind that these figures conceal very significant differences *within* these crude 'ethnic' categories (Waddington *et al.* 2004). In particular, the experiences of white minorities such as the Irish, Travellers, and migrants from eastern Europe—which differ markedly from those of the white majority community—are subsumed in the catch-all 'white' category (James 2005).

There are large differences among police forces in both the extent of the use of stop and search powers and the reasons for which people are searched (Home Office 2005a). Typically, about half are for drugs, with searches for stolen property and offensive weapons accounting for the majority of the remainder. Only a small proportion of searches result in an arrest; in the most recent statistics, 13 per cent of stops involving black and white people and 11 per cent involving Asian people. BCS data are consistent with police data and indicate that people from black and Asian communities were more likely to be stopped repeatedly both in vehicles and on foot (Clancy *et al.* 2001: 59–61), and are more frequently subject to intrusive searching (Skogan 1990; Newburn and Hayman 2001). Formal action is also more common in stops involving black people compared with other ethnic groups (Norris *et al.* 1992; Bucke and Brown 1997). Generally, people from minority ethnic groups are much less likely to think that the police acted politely and to believe that they were stopped fairly (Clancy *et al.* 2001: 68–70).

The police may also use section 60 of the Criminal Justice and Public Order Act 1994, which permits a search *without suspicion* in places and at times where serious violence is anticipated or to search for weapons. The use of this power tripled between 1998/99 and 2001/02, reaching rates per 1,000 population of 0.2 for white people, 5.5 for black people, and 3.6 for Asian people; thus black people were 28 times more likely to be searched and Asian people 18 times more likely to be searched than their white counterparts. In 2003/4, the use of this power fell for all groups but particularly for minority ethnic groups. Nonetheless, black people were still 13 times more likely and Asian people six times more likely than white people to be searched under these powers. An arrest was made in only 4 per cent of searches under section 60 (Home Office 2005a).

'Suspicionless searches' for 'articles of a kind which could be used in connection with terrorism' are also authorized under section 44 of the Terrorism Act 2000. Police data suggest that these powers were used disproportionately against black and Asian people prior to the bombings in London on 7 July 2005 (Home Office 2005a: 9–10). Since then, there has been a sharp increase in the use of these powers and they have been used very extensively against minority ethnic communities. Although there is no statistical evidence that Muslims are being targeted there is a widespread perception of this within the community. In March 2005, Home Office minister Hazel Blears commented that it was a 'reality' that anti-terrorist stops and searches would be 'disproportionately experienced by the Muslim community'.

EXPLAINING DISPROPORTIONALITY

Why are some communities more frequently stopped and searched by the police? One view is that police officers deliberately target minority groups because of widespread racial prejudice, stereotyping, and overt discrimination. Numerous well-known black people including John Sentamu (now Archbishop of York), senior civil servants, police officers, members of Parliament, musicians, and lawyers have been stopped without justification or on a flimsy pretext (Bowling and Phillips 2002: 128–130). Qualitative research on police culture in the 1980s found that derogatory language—such as 'Paki', 'nigger', 'coon', and 'spade'—was 'accepted and expected' and reflected deep-seated racist beliefs about ethnicity and criminality (Smith and Gray 1985; Holdaway 1983). Police officers used 'colour as a criterion for stops' and were unapologetic about targeting black people (Smith and Gray 1985). Recent research suggests that overt targeting continues though police officers are more hesitant in admitting to it (Quinton *et al.* 2000: 24; Cashmore 2002; FitzGerarald 1999). *Explicit* racist language is less common (Foster *et al.* 2005). Under greater scrutiny after the Lawrence Inquiry, officers felt less able to carry out unjustified stop and search 'fishing trips' without proper grounds for searching (ibid.: 30). However, racist attitudes and behaviour may simply have gone 'underground' (ibid.). For example, in October 2003 a BBC documentary *The Secret Policeman* covertly filmed extreme racist attitudes among a group of recruits, several of whom said quite explicitly that they were targeting people from minority ethnic communities for stop and search.

A second, and diametrically opposed, explanation put forward for disproportionality in stop and search figures is that they reflect ethnic differences in patterns of offending.

Smith (1994: 1092), for example, argues that 'police officers tend to make a crude equation between crime and black people, to assume that suspects are black and to justify stopping people in these terms'. Some commentators have dismissed this as inaccurate and serving to reinforce racial stereotyping (CARF 1999). Nonetheless, Smith (1994: 1092) argues that it may be a 'rational explanation' for police stop and search behaviour since it is in line with victims' descriptions of offenders and because the same proportion of people of all ethnic groups were arrested as a result of carrying out stop and search operations (ibid.).

A third explanation for the over-representation of minority communities in stop and search figures—that it arises *indirectly* from social and demographic factors—has been explored using a range of complex statistical analyses (Clancy *et al.* 2001). Minority ethnic communities have a young age structure and so at least some of the disparity arises from the fact that young people are more likely to be stopped and searched. Similarly, living in London (which has a high rate of stop and search activity), being unemployed, or working in a manual occupation, and being out after dark three or more times in a week have all been associated with higher rates of experiencing both stop and search and ethnicity (Clancy *et al.* 2001).

A related explanation is that people from minority ethnic communities, because of their patterns of employment and leisure activities, are more frequently 'available' at the times and in the places where stopping and searching occurs (MVA and Miller 2000; Waddington *et al.* 2004). Arguing that particular ethnic groups 'place themselves at risk of being stopped by the police through their differential use of public space', these studies focus not on the resident population as their baseline but the population 'available' to be stopped. They have found that white people tend to be stopped or searched at a higher rate than their presence in the available population, Asian people tend to be under-represented, and a mixed picture emerges for black people—who are in some places under- and in other places over-represented. This challenges the claim that police officers explicitly target minority ethnic groups for stop and search actions, particularly vehicle stops, where officers' visibility may be impaired by road and weather conditions, suggesting instead that bias is an unintended consequence of routine practices (Waddington *et al.* 2004). The authors conclude that disproportionality arises from the fact that policing bears down more heavily upon people who more frequently use public space and these happen to be black and Asian people. Clearly factors such as unemployment, homelessness, and employment in occupations involving evening and night work—each of which is more common in black and Asian communities—place individuals from these communities at greater risk of being stopped and searched. Therefore a more sophisticated analysis of structural or institutional racism is required to explain how racial disproportionality in the use of police powers comes about.

A useful distinction can be made between 'low-' and 'high-discretion' stops (FitzGerald 1999). Low-discretion stops refers to those conducted by officers where they have received relevant information about a particular offence—a suspect's description, for example—from a member of the public such as a crime victim. High-discretion searches are those where police officers are acting proactively without specific intelligence. It is the searches where officers have wide discretion to use their own intuition, stereotypes, and prejudices, which are most likely to be discriminatory (FitzGerald 1993). It is perhaps for this reason that disproportionality tends to be widest in drugs searches (Quinton *et al.* 2000: 16–17) and those that require no element of reasonable suspicion (Bowling and Philips 2002: 236).

Whatever the explanation, it is widely agreed that the disproportionate use of stop and search powers against minority communities is a problem: it seems inherently unfair and has a range of negative consequences in terms of public support for the police (Clancy *et al.* 2001) and willingness to join the criminal justice professions, and contributes to the criminalisation of minority ethnic communities (Macpherson 1999; Metropolitan Police Authority 2005). To solve these problems, the Lawrence Inquiry recommended improvements in recording and monitoring and increased public awareness of the right to receive a record of being stopped (Macpherson 1999 recommendations 61–3). A Home Office Stop and Search Action Team, including a 'challenge panel' of community representatives has been created to monitor the use of stop and search powers. Police Authorities have also undertaken their own scrutiny of stop and search recommending increased accountability, the reduction of disproportionality and more creative ways to inform the public about their rights on being stopped and searched (Metropolitan Police Authority 2004). The Home Office (2005b) has produced a new code of practice which came into effect on 1 January 2006 and a *Stop and Search Manual* (Home Office 2005c) and the Association of Chief Police Officers have produced new draft guidance in 2005. All of these initiatives emphasize the requirement that the power should be used fairly, responsibly, and without unlawful discrimination.

The acknowledgement that stop and search powers can be used unfairly is a step forward. The resulting increased accountability and scrutiny of the use of the power in the national and local sphere and in relation to the actions of individual constables has the potential to reduce its arbitrary and discriminatory nature. However, this process may serve to legitimate an intrusive and coercive power that makes only a limited contribution to public safety and which is still used far more extensively against minority ethnic communities. It is of concern that despite all the 'post-Lawrence' policy activity, stop and search powers continue to be used disproportionately against minority ethnic communities.

ARREST

The ethnic disproportionality evident in prison populations can be seen at the entry point to the criminal justice system. The figures for 2003/4 show an annual arrest rate of 26 per 1,000 for white people in England and Wales. The figures were 29 for Asians, 35 for those of 'other' ethnic origins, but over three times higher at 89 per 1,000 for black people (Home Office 2005a). As Figure 14.2 shows, the over-representation of black people in arrest statistics was evident in all offence categories, but was most

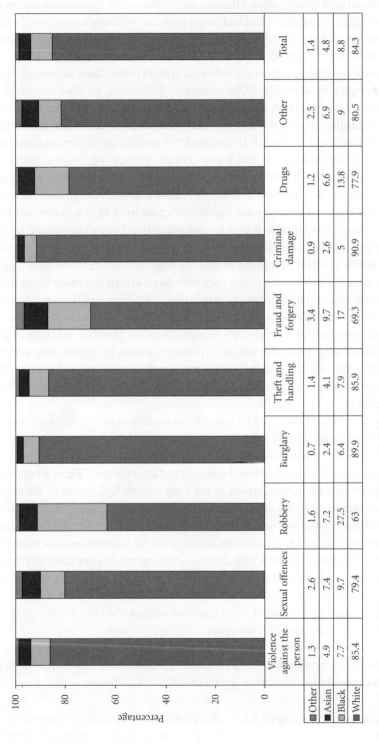

	Violence against the person	Sexual offences	Robbery	Burglary	Theft and handling	Fraud and forgery	Criminal damage	Drugs	Other	Total
Other	1.3	2.6	1.6	0.7	1.4	3.4	0.9	1.2	2.5	1.4
Asian	4.9	7.4	7.2	2.4	4.1	9.7	2.6	6.6	6.9	4.8
Black	7.7	9.7	27.5	6.4	7.9	17	5	13.8	9	8.8
White	85.4	79.4	63	89.9	85.9	69.3	90.9	77.9	80.5	84.3

Fig. 14.2 Arrest population by ethnic group and notifiable offences, 2003/4

Source: Home Office (2005a).

striking for fraud and forgery, drug offences, and robbery (27.5 per cent). Asians were over-represented in sexual and fraud and forgery arrests. With the exception of robbery and homicide, which have already been discussed, there has been no empirical research that has explored 'ethnic specialization' in particular types of offending.

Likely to be of continuing concern in the coming years is the ethnic disproportionality evident in samples held on the DNA database. Following an amendment to the Criminal Justice Act 2003, DNA samples can be retained for those arrested for a record-able offence regardless of whether they are then later released. According to one report, 37 per cent of black men in the UK have their DNA profile on the database compared with 13 per cent of Asian men and 9 per cent of white men.[3] Given higher case termination rates for black and Asian offenders (see below), this measure of 'genetic surveillance' may be one that impacts minority ethnic groups more than their white counterparts. Proposed new powers legislation contained in the Terrorism Bill to extend pre-charge detention will also be disproportionately experienced by those perceived to be potential Islamic terrorists.

Once in police custody, deciding to opt for legal advice, exercise their right of silence, and deny the offence for which they have been arrested is more likely in cases involving minorities and black suspects in particular (Phillips and Brown 1998; Bucke and Brown 1997). Such decisions function to the cumulative disadvantage of minor-ity ethnic suspects. To illustrate with an example, the least punitive outcome of police action following arrest—a caution or reprimand—can be given only where an offender admits the offence, and this partly explains the lower rates of cautioning for minority ethnic groups, particularly for black people (Home Office 2005a; Phillips and Brown 1998).

Whilst these decision points can be regarded as racially neutral—after all, it is up to individual suspects whether they decide to cooperate with police officers during their interview—historical tensions and a present-day mistrust of the police may often oper-ate to deny minority ethnic offenders the benefits of cooperation. Thus, an apparently non-discriminatory practice enshrined in the long-established rituals of the criminal justice system may work to the advantage of only some ethnic groups. This amounts to indirect racial discrimination but for the defence that such practices can be justified as necessary for the efficient and judicious running of the criminal justice system. For Smith (1997: 753), 'the question which decision-making criteria are justifiable or legit-imate raises deep and difficult problems in the philosophy of law'. These questions could now be revisited within the framework of the Race Relations (Amendment) Act 2000 which brought the criminal justice system within the laws prohibiting racial discrimination (Bowling and Phillips 2002).

In addition to indirect racial discrimination in police detention, Newburn et al.'s (2004) analysis of strip searches over a 17-month period in one London police station suggests direct racial discrimination. Being of African Caribbean origin doubled the

---

[3] 'DNA of 37% of black men held by police', James Randerson, science correspondent, *The Guardian*, 5 January 2006.

probability of being strip searched while in custody, even once the reason for the arrest, the outcome of the detention, and the age and sex of the offender had been taken into account. The probability of being strip-searched was halved for those described by the police as of 'Arab or Oriental' ethnic origin, with little discernible difference for those of Asian or Mediterranean origins, compared with that for white European or Irish suspects.

DISCRIMINATION IN PROSECUTORIAL DECISION-MAKING AND SENTENCING

The Crown Prosecution Service (CPS) may divert suspects from formal action when it examines case files to decide whether they should proceed to court. There is no evidence to indicate that quality of case review varies by ethnic origin of the suspect (HMCPSI 2002; Gus John Partnership 2003), but this is not true of decisions made at case review.

Case termination: a break on criminalization?

Phillips and Brown's (1998) study of 1,175 suspects found higher rates of termination in cases involving black suspects (20 per cent) and Asian suspects (27 per cent) compared with white suspects (12 per cent), with minority ethnic origin predicting an increased chance of case termination by the CPS, after controlling for type and seriousness of the offence, and whether the suspect had previous convictions. Mhlanga's (1999) analysis of a larger national sample of suspects aged under 22 years revealed the same pattern. Both studies raise questions about policing practices, suggesting that a presumption of guilt is being selectively applied by police officers in the case of some black and Asian suspects. Specifically, HM Inspector of Crown Prosecution Services (2002) reported higher levels of case discontinuance among minority ethnic suspects and speculated that the police may be making a less critical assessment of the reliability of complainants and witnesses in cases involving minority ethnic defendants. It seems likely that the CPS 'break' on criminalizing minority ethnic suspects occurs precisely because discretion and subjectivity are at a minimum as prosecutors are guided by the stringent Code (Crown Prosecution Service 2004).

Bail

Minority ethnic groups are more likely than average to fall into the socio-economic and demographic categories for whom a remand in custody is likely. Housing inequalities and a perceived lack of community ties, among black minority ethnic groups in particular, may be regarded as contributing to a risk of absconding leading to higher rates of remands and the added risk of a custodial sentence if convicted. Hudson (1993: 164) points to the irony of court decisions informed by socio-economic inequality when the 'characteristics of the penalized population are so often the very characteristics we are building in to various formalized decision-making criteria, adherence to which we take as evidence that we are dispensing impartial criminal justice'.

Committal to the Crown Court

Higher rates of committal to the Crown Court for minority ethnic, particularly black, defendants has long been documented, and this partially reflects their choice to elect for jury trial (Home Office 2005a). It has usually been assumed that this is because of a mistrust of magistrates' impartiality and a preference to be tried by peers. This decision, however, makes black defendants more vulnerable to a more severe sentence if found guilty, by virtue of being tried in the Crown Court rather than the magistrates' court where sentences are less severe. At the same time it can be argued that, since acquittal rates are higher in the Crown Court than in the magistrates' courts, black defendants' risk of conviction is minimized by this course of action which at least partially offsets their increased vulnerability to being given a prison sentence if convicted.

Acquittals

A mixed picture emerges in relation to acquittal rates—early studies found little difference in the acquittal rates of white and minority ethnic defendants (Walker 1989; Home Office 1989)—while national data for 1999 revealed higher that average acquittal rates for both black and Asian defendants. Rather than indicating the absence of bias, it again challenges previous actions taken by the police and the CPS in cases involving minority ethnic defendants (cf. Smith 1997). As the *Denman Report* (2001: 107) into racial discrimination in the CPS concluded, the CPS could be construed as 'discriminating against minority ethnic defendants by failing to correct the bias in police charging decisions and allowing a disproportionate number of weak cases against minority ethnic defendants to go to trial'.

Pre-sentence reports

The writing of pre-sentence reports (PSRs) by probation officers for magistrates to consider before passing sentence presents another opportunity for racial bias to creep in (see Bowling and Phillips 2002: 176–9 for a review of early studies). A recent thematic inspection of the probation service identified 16 per cent of pre-sentence reports written on black offenders and 11 per cent on Asian defendants as reinforcing stereotypical attitudes about race and ethnicity, although the impact on final sentencing was not measured (HMIP 2000). The inspection also found numerous instances in which the contextual information provided on black and (sometimes Asian) offenders was less comprehensive than was the case for PSRs prepared for white offenders (Morgan 2005). The implications of this are noted by Hudson and Bramhall (2005: 736) who have observed, under the new regime of offender risk assessment which privileges 'finely judged difference rather than equality of sentencing', it is more than possible that demographic, familial, cultural, and socio-economic differences between ethnic groups will come to be used by probation officers to delineate risky and difficult offenders.

In their analysis of report-writing in a North-West probation area, Hudson and Bramhall draw attention to the ways in which the presence of employment and family networks was problematized for Asian offenders who were perceived to be over-controlled and pressurized by family commitments. In contrast, it was unemployment and family separation which were regarded as explanatory factors in white offending. Probation officers were found to have highlighted assumed behavioural problems among Asian offenders more often than among white offenders. The language of reports on Asian offenders was more 'distancing', suggesting Asian offenders were less remorseful, perhaps because the pre-sentence report interview had not resulted in a negotiated account of offending between Asian offenders and probation officer in a way that occurred more routinely with white offenders. For Hudson and Bramhall, this bias against Asian offenders must be viewed within the context of societal demonization and 'othering', particularly in the wake of the events of 11 September and the riots in the northern England towns in 2001. Significantly, they argue that contrary to views about the objectivity of risk-assessment techniques, they are constructed in a way that allows discretion and unwitting discrimination to occur.

SENTENCING

The most sophisticated and robust study attempting to isolate the 'independent' effect of ethnic origin on sentencing was Roger Hood's (1992) pioneering research, conducted in five Crown Courts in the West Midlands in 1989. Hood's approach, while significantly improving on previous methods however, was unable to take account of the extent to which legal factors such as seriousness of the offence and previous convictions were themselves the result of discrimination earlier in the process. Hood estimated a 5 per cent greater probability of black people being sentenced to custody compared with their white counterparts. Where defendants pleaded not guilty, and once all other legally relevant factors had been controlled for, Asian defendants, on average, were sentenced to nine months longer and black defendants three months longer than white defendants. The differences in sentencing occurred most often in the middle range of offence seriousness where judicial discretion was high, and the unequal treatment of black defendants was more common at Dudley Crown Court than at the more urban Birmingham Crown Court (ibid.). Mhlanga (1997) reported similar findings, with young black defendants having an increased risk of custody being imposed.

Hood's findings represent a clear example of direct discrimination against black and Asian defendants which has clearly contributed to their disproportionality in the prison population. However, this study was conducted more than fifteen years ago. Calverley *et al.*'s (2004) more recent study of black and Asian offenders subject to probation supervision found lower levels of 'criminogenic need' among these offenders than among white offenders, leading to speculation that this was the result of discriminatory sentencing.

YOUTH JUSTICE

Most empirical studies of the criminal justice processing of young people have produced findings indicative of discrimination (Landau and Nathan 1983; Phillips and Brown 1998), but their relevance has been somewhat overshadowed by legislative changes; namely the Crime and Disorder Act 1998 which established multi-agency Youth Offending Teams (YOTs) to coordinate youth justice services to individual offenders (see Morgan and Newburn, Chapter 30, this volume). Feilzer and Hood's (2004) analysis of over 31,000 YOT records found that young black people were substantially over-represented and young Asian people under-represented in YOT caseloads, although this did vary by area. The outcomes which could not be explained by the different offence profiles of white and minority ethnic youths included: higher discontinuance and acquittal rates among black youths; higher levels of secure detention, committal to the Crown Court, and more severe PSR sentence recommendations for black and mixed-parentage males; lower custodial sentencing for black and mixed-parentage males and black females; higher custodial sentencing for Asian males; and higher tariff community penalties for Asian and mixed-parentage males. The complexity of these findings makes broad interpretation difficult, but overall, Feilzer and Hood (2004) conclude that these aggregate differences between ethnic groups, once legally and socially relevant differences had been acknowledged, were consistent with racially discriminatory treatment. In contrast to earlier findings on adult offenders, it is significant that sentencing outcomes appeared harsher for Asian young offenders than for those of black (or mixed) origin, but findings are consistent with studies which have shown that black offenders are disadvantaged at the pre-sentence stages of the criminal justice process.

PUBLIC PERCEPTIONS OF FAIRNESS AND EQUALITY

After the Lawrence Inquiry, increasing minority ethnic confidence in the agencies of the criminal justice system has been a key government objective. Yet with the exception of the police and prison services, the British Crime Survey has shown that minority ethnic respondents hold *more favourable* attitudes than white respondents towards the CPS, magistrates, judges, and the youth courts (Mirrlees-Black 2001; Allen, Lovbakke, and El Komy 2005). More negative assessments are made in relation to the systems' respecting the rights of the accused and treating them fairly, and this is particularly the case for young men of all ethnic groups and Black Caribbeans (see Criminal Justice System Race Unit 2005). These are, of course, the demographic groups most likely to come into contact with the police and other criminal justice agencies. This has significant implications since it remains the case that, if policing and criminal justice practices are seen as inequitable and illegitimate, this can breed defiance for authority which, in turn, can have the effect of undermining willingness to conform to the law.

Shute, Hood, and Seemungal (2004) explored the perceptions of (mostly convicted) minority ethnic defendants and witnesses in all adult courts in Manchester, Birmingham, and South London. A relatively small proportion, 10 per cent of black defendants and 12 per cent of Asian defendants in the magistrates' courts perceived some racial bias in their treatment; the figures were 20 per cent and 12 per cent respectively among Crown Court defendants. Complainants believed that similarly placed white defendants would not have received such harsh sentences. Almost two-thirds of solicitors and barristers reported that minority ethnic defendants were always treated equitably by the courts, although this figure was lower at 43 per cent among black lawyers. Fewer interviewees had personally witnessed incidents which they regarded as racist, but Shute *et al.* (2004) point to some examples where derogatory language was used by court staff often in relation to 'black criminality', or where black and Asian families were deemed inferior, and where witnesses perceived harsher treatment by judges.

PRISON AND PROBATION

PRISON POPULATIONS

Since the mid-1980s prison populations have consistently comprised a disproportionate number of black male and female prisoners, of both British and foreign nationality (see Morgan and Liebling, Chapter 32, this volume). Among British nationals, the white male prison population increased by 36 per cent between 1985 and 2002, while the black and Chinese/Other populations grew by 172 per cent and the Asian increase was 105 per cent, with even more dramatic increases for females. The exception is the number of Asian women in prison which has remained consistently low, at only 38 in 2002, of whom 16 were foreign nationals. A future area of research should aim to shed light on the factors that protect Asian women from criminalization.

On 31 December 2005 there were 18,961 people from minority ethnic groups held in custody in Prison Service establishments, amounting to 25 per cent of the male prison population and 30 per cent of the female prison population. These figures must be qualified by the fact that one-third of the male and over half of the female minority ethnic population in custody were foreign nationals (Home Office 2006; see also Morgan and Liebling, Chapter 32, this volume). Prison statistics in 2000 showed that rates of incarceration for the Indian, Bangladeshi, and Chinese communities were low (126, 183 and 135 per 100,000) compared with white people, who were imprisoned at a rate of 188 per 100,000, and the strikingly high rates for Black Caribbeans of 1,704 and Black Africans at 1,274 per 100,000. The incarceration rate for Pakistanis was double that for the other South Asian groups, but still remained significantly lower than that for the black groups. The disparate group of those from other Asian origins experienced a similarly high incarceration rate. We return at the end of the chapter to consider the reasons for the very different levels of incarceration among minority ethnic groups.

RACISM AND 'RACE RELATIONS' IN PRISON

The historical context for understanding 'race relations' in prison is one in which there was staunch support for the National Front among many prison officers in the 1970s, alongside incidents of brutality and harassment by prison officers (Gordon 1983), following which 'race relations' policies were introduced in the early 1980s. In their study of five prisons in the mid-1980s, Genders and Player (1989) found evidence of direct racial discrimination where black prisoners were stereotyped as arrogant, lazy, noisy, hostile to authority, with values incompatible with British society, and as having 'a chip on their shoulder' (see Chigwada-Bailey 1997 for similar findings in relation to women prisoners). These stereotypes explained patterns of work allocations, with black prisoners most often doing the least favoured jobs, and more often experiencing adjudication for disciplinary infractions (Coid *et al.* 2002).

Edgar and Martin's (2004) study of four local prisons, conducted over 15 years after Genders and Player's research, concluded that processes of 'informal partiality' may operate in prison whereby black and Asian prisoners feel they are negatively stereo-typed and more disadvantaged by prison officers' use of discretion in awarding priv-ileges or meting out discipline, and this occurs in the context of a lack of oversight or monitoring of prisoner officers' actions. Prison officers appear to live in a 'parallel world' to that occupied by prisoners, as they perceive race relations far more positively, with racism being seen as a problem among prisoners but not among staff (see the thematic inspection by HM's Inspectorate of Prisons 2005). Burnett and Farrell (1994) found that racist victimization by prisoners was a common occurrence, although Edgar, O'Donnell, and Martin's (2003) more recent study of violence and power relationships in prisons concluded that racial hatred does not typically result in phys-ical violence. Instead, on occasion, disputes occur where a lack of respect is assumed from particular cultural practices or ways of responding to conflict.

Serious claims of brutality and discrimination against minority ethnic prisoners and officers led to a formal investigation of the Prison Service by the Commission for Racial Equality (2003), which revealed 17 instances of unlawful racial discrimination at Brixton and Parc prisons and Feltham young offenders institution. These included failing to protect prisoners and staff from racist abuse, violence, and intimidation, not meeting the religious and cultural needs of Muslim prisoners, and disadvantaging some black prisoners in access to jobs and earned privileges, or in disproportionately taking disciplinary actions against them. The Prison Service was criticized for its management of race equality and its ineffective systems, procedures, and practices, which failed to provide equivalent protection for minority ethnic prisoners and staff (Commission for Racial Equality 2003). The failure of protection was brought graphically to light in 2000 by the murder of Zahid Mubarek, a young Londoner of Asian origin, beaten to death by his white racist cellmate, Robert Stewart (Gupta 2005). In October 2003 following resistance by the Home Office, the House of Lords ruled that an independent public investigation into Zahid's death had to be convened. The report's primary recommendation was that enforced cell-sharing should be eliminated and that if the resources currently available to the Prison Service are insufficient to produce a significant decrease in enforced cell-sharing, central government should allocate further funds to the Prison Service to enable more prisoners to be accommodated in cells on their own (the final report is available online at www.zahidmubarekinquiry.org.uk).

It is possible that prisoners' ethnic and religious identities provide a mechanism for resisting institutional control (see Bosworth 1999; Morgan and Liebling, Chapter 32, this volume). Wilson's (2003) young black male interviewees, for example, described drawing support from other black prisoners in the face of perceived discrimination by prison 'Govs' (see also Genders and Player 1989). In contrast, Sparks *et al.* (1996) claimed that the young black prisoners in their study chose to minimize the centrality of ethnicity to prison life, instead situating themselves within the prisoner collective. It is unclear how religious identities contribute to prisoner allegiances and coping with imprisonment, but Spalek and Wilson's (2002) work has noted the academic and policy neglect of religious discrimination against Muslim prisoners. Overall only 8 per cent of prisoners are Muslim, but among Asian prisoners the figure is 71 per cent (Councell 2004).

PROBATION

Until relatively recently, research on the probation experiences of minority ethnic groups has been relatively sparse compared with studies of other areas of criminal justice. Negative stereotyping of minority ethnic probation clients was noted in early studies of probation practice, leading to assumptions that there was less possibility of change and rehabilitation among black offenders (Green 1989; Denney 1992).

In the most recent thematic inspection on racial equality, concerns centred on the quality of supervision of black offenders, particularly in terms of reduced levels of contact during the later stages of probation orders (HMIP 2000, 2004). However, Calverley *et al.*'s (2004) interviews with 483 black and Asian probation clients reported that 86 per cent felt they had been treated fairly by their supervisor, most of whom were white. There were quite mixed views on whether having a minority ethnic supervisor would have positive benefits (one-third thought it would), and most who were subject to attendance on a structured groupwork programme felt mixed ethnic groups rather than separate provision were the best option.

A key issue has been the extent to which probation officers have considered the role of racism in contributing to the offending behaviour of minority ethnic offenders (Holdaway and Allaker 1990). Calverley *et al.*'s (2004) study found similar levels of socio-economic disadvantage among white and minority ethnic offenders, but one-fifth said they had experienced racism at school, and many claimed that racial discrimination in the labour market had reduced their opportunities to engage in legitimate activities. Black empowerment programmes have been implemented in a small number of probation areas, typically incorporating sessions on black and Asian history, the dynamics of racism, exclusion and offending, with some mentoring, training, or community support for participants to counteract negative self-beliefs. There is some indication that such programmes may have higher completion rates and contribute to reduced reoffending among participants, although evaluative evidence is scarce (Williams 2005). The gendered experiences and needs of minority ethnic female offenders, however, remains rather neglected in both the policy and academic arena (Gelsthorpe 2005).

MINORITY ETHNIC EMPLOYMENT IN THE CRIMINAL JUSTICE SYSTEM

Ensuring that the criminal justice organizations have a workforce that reflects the diversity of the communities they serve is substantively important in its own right and in its potential contribution to social justice more generally. It is considered to be a key element in increasing minority ethnic groups' confidence and trust in the criminal justice system. It is assumed that officers from minority ethnic communities will act in a more even-handed and sensitive way than white officers because of the greater understanding of, and respect for, minority ethnic citizens that they have (Bowling and Phillips 2002). Specific skills, such as being multilingual, offer further attributes necessary for policing multi-ethnic communities. Against this, in relation to policing, is the view that minority ethnic police officers are 'co-opted' into the police culture, which is all-encompassing, to the extent that the gulf between police officer and citizen is maintained regardless of the ethnicity of the police officer (Cashmore 1991, 2002; see also Walker, Spohn, and DeLone 2004).

In 1999 in the wake of the Lawrence Inquiry the Home Secretary published local or national targets for the increased recruitment, retention, career progression, and senior-level representation of minority ethnic operational and non-operational staff in the Home Office, police, prisons, and probation services (Home Office 1999b). Statistics on the representation of minority ethnic groups in criminal justice agencies in 2003/4 presented in Table 14.1 show their marked under-representation in the police and prison services, and in the judiciary. Recruitment efforts may continue to be hampered by negative perceptions of the police and prison service where minority ethnic employees have, in the past, experienced hostile working environments, alienation, and marginalization, punctuated by instances of racially abusive language and sometimes victimization or harassment (Holdaway 1996; Alfred 1992; McDermott 1990; cf. Sharp 2002). Abbas's (2005) review of access to the senior judiciary points to the significance of fewer minority ethnic students studying law at the elite universities from which the Bar recruits, as well as to the disadvantaging of minority ethnic candidates by secret soundings carried out to informally assess candidates.

Whilst progress reports suggest that the Home Secretary's interim recruitment targets have largely been met or even exceeded, retention and promotion rates still varied across the Home Office and its service areas, and levels of senior representation remained low in most (Home Office 2003). Moreover, even those criminal justice services such as the CPS with proportionate minority ethnic representation have uncovered unequal treatment by managers and a denial of support for career advancement, including 'acting up' opportunities (Denman Report 2001). This has resulted in increasing numbers of applications to employment tribunals and mounting compensation costs for discriminatory treatment. The Morris Inquiry (2004) into the management of race and diversity in the Metropolitan Police Service documented

Table 14.1 Proporation of minority ethnic officers in the criminal justice professions in 2003/4

Agency	%
Police	3.3
Crown Prosecution Service	11.3
Magistrates' court	6.8
Crown Court	6.2
Magistracy: Lay	6.3
Stipendiary	6.9
Solicitors: On the Roll	8.8
In private practice	7.5
Judiciary	3.5
Barristers in independent practice	8.9
Prison officers	4.1
Probation officers	10.8
Parole Board	6.8

Source: *Statistics on Race and the Criminal Justice System 2004*, London: Home Office, 2005.

'management by retreat' as managers expressed fear and anxiety when managing the performance and conduct of staff who were ethnically or culturally different (see also CRE 2005). Poor performance by minority ethnic officers was less likely to be tackled via structured supervision, development, or training, so there was no opportunity for improvement before formal action was taken. This must have contributed to the disproportionate numbers of minority ethnic officers being subjected to internal investigations and suspensions. The collapse of high-profile disciplinary cases against minority ethnic senior police officers adds further weight to claims of discriminatory treatment (see also Stone and Tuffin 2000).

In all of the criminal justice professions, minority ethnic-run support organizations have been set up to provide support networks and training, and in many cases they have a campaigning and lobbying function. Phillips' (2005b) interviews with chairpersons of seven minority ethnic-led professional associations (such as the Association of Black Probation Officers) revealed perceptions of subtle direct discrimination among members. Being given impossible work tasks, inadequate supervision and training, more severe judgements on work performance leading to disciplinary charges, were all cited in addition to those noted in the Denman and Morris inquiries. Such experiences may be further compounded by sexism and gendered harassment for minority ethnic female officers (Holder, Nee, and Ellis 2000).

CONCLUSION: CHALLENGES FOR THEORY, RESEARCH, AND PRACTICE

The over-representation of black people in Britain's prisons is a critical issue; as the prison population grows (Morgan and Liebling, Chapter 32, this volume) the imprisonment of people from minority ethnic communities grows faster still. The entrenchment of racial disparity in prison populations calls for a critical examination of the statistical and research evidence on differences in patterns of offending among different ethnic groups. The findings of self-report surveys show that black and white people have, in general, an equal likelihood of being involved in crime, with people of Asian origin being much less likely (Sharp and Budd 2005). However, police arrest data, victimization surveys, and witness descriptions all point to the conclusion that black people are, in comparison with their numbers in the population, more likely to commit some specific criminal offences, such as robbery. A stark example is gun murders, in which about one in three of both victims and suspects are black people (Home Office 2005a). A sense of proportion is also important; the forms of crime in which black people figure prominently are rare and exist alongside other serious crime—such as burglary and city centre violence—in which people from minority ethnic communities are only slightly over-represented, if at all.

At the same time, it appears that racial discrimination operates in various forms at each stage of the criminal justice process. Police stereotyping plays a role in the targeting of black people for stop and search action,on the basis of unjustified assumptions rather than reasonable suspicion (Bowling and Phillips 2002: 138–48; FitzGerald and Sibbitt 1997: 66; Quinton *et al.* 2000: 24). Direct racism is compounded by policing practices—such as extensive stop and search activity at the times and in the places when young people from minority ethnic groups are 'available'—with the effect that minorities are more frequently brought into contact with the criminal justice system. In addition to direct discrimination (e.g. Hood 1992), some groups experience cumulative disadvantage following the application of supposedly neutral criteria when police, magistrates, and judges make decisions about whether to caution or charge with an offence (Phillips and Brown 1998), grant bail or remand in custody (Bowling and Phillips 2002: 154–5, 169–71), and when sentencing (Hood 1992). For example, although there are strong legal arguments for the 'sentencing discount' for a guilty plea, this has led consistently to longer prison sentences for black defendants. As Smith (1997: 175) observes, '[t]he use of a criterion that has an adverse effect on a whole ethnic group will be seen as an attack on that group, unless the reasons for adopting it are extremely compelling'.

In his contribution to the early editions of *The Oxford Handbook of Criminology*, David Smith (1994, 1997) insisted that it was unhelpful to conceptualize disparity in criminal justice outcomes for people of African, Caribbean, and South Asian origin as part of a 'generalized racism'. Asian communities, for example, suffer racial discrimination in housing and employment, and yet they are not over-represented in

Britain's prisons: women of Pakistani or Bangladeshi origin are almost completely absent from any visible involvement in crime, despite being among the most disadvantaged groups in our society. Where we take issue with Smith is in the notion of 'generalized racism'. Racism has, since its origins in the Enlightenment, constructed very different images of particular ethnic groups and these have inspired markedly different social responses. In our view, conceiving of racism as a complex and socially situated phenomenon *can* explain the criminal justice experiences of different ethnic groups. Thus, patterns of selective enforcement and harsher criminal justice outcomes for black people are consistent with unjustified heightened suspicion of black people based on stereotypes. This contrasts sharply with the stereotype of Asians as passive, conformist, and self-regulating which—until recent anxiety about terrorism—reflects a very different criminal justice response. For this reason, we reject notions of a uniform, static, and monolithic form of racism in favour of one rooted in historical and spatial specificity (Goldberg 1993).

The problem remains, however, that minority ethnic communities in Britain, especially those of African and Caribbean origin, have become criminalized. The explanation most commonly put forward for ethnic differences in crime focuses on social and economic inequality in general and poverty in particular. The social geography of robbery (Hallsworth 2005) and homicide (Dorling 2005) shows the links between these crimes and social exclusion. From this perspective it is poverty rather than ethnicity that is the key explanatory variable. There are many variations on this line of theorizing, some emphasizing relative rather than absolute deprivation, others emphasizing unemployment, truancy, exclusion, and school failure, or family disharmony. Ultimately, individuals' lives may still be largely shaped by the structures of 'race' and class, even if other aspects of their identities come to the fore. Susan Smith (1989) and Paul Gilroy (1987a) argue that 'race', class, and ethnicity are not *ahistorical* essences, but socially constructed categories upon which iniquitous social structures are based. Racism interacts with class disadvantage to produce patterns of social inequality experienced differently by minority ethnic groups; that is to say, racism has relative autonomy from socio-economic and political relations (CCCS 1982). Minority ethnic groups' experiences of crime and criminal justice do not result *solely* from their socio-economic position, as shown by research on criminal justice decision-making—in relation to stop and search activity, police cautioning, case termination by the Crown Prosecution Service, bail, pre-sentence reports, acquittals, committals to the Crown Court, custodial sentencing, and prison life—as well as employment experiences among minority ethnic staff, which are consistent with patterns of direct and indirect, institutionalized discrimination. The example of racist victimization is a reminder of the 'fault line' between communities who otherwise share the same social and economic conditions.

In attempting to explain variations in the experience of crime and justice among different ethnic groups some theorists have explored cultural differences. At its simplest, some have argued that cultures of crime or of resistance are 'imported' to an otherwise peaceful United Kingdom (cf. Gilroy 1987b; Pearson 1983). This view can easily be criticized because it over-simplifies the cultural complexity of life in Britain and neglects the context of socio-economic inequality. Nonetheless, some support for the idea that patterns of crime have to be seen in a global context comes from the police evidence that many of the gun murders during the 1990s were committed by Jamaican nationals and the fact that many of the black women imprisoned in the UK are drug couriers from Jamaica and Nigeria (Heaven and Hudson 2005). On the other hand, Gilroy argues that the Birmingham shootings in 2003 were 'an entirely home-grown phenomenon', reflecting ruthless consumerism and an obsession with 'celebrity culture'. Individualistic and consumerist lifestyles—themselves a manifestation of British rather than black cultures—encourage offending where legitimate opportunities for achieving desires are thwarted (Young 1999; FitzGerald *et al.* 2003; Gilroy 2003; Hallsworth 2005). A related line of thinking turns the question on its head by considering why people *obey* the law. Tyler (1990), for example, argues that conformity stems from the strength of the bonds between individual and society that are underpinned by 'procedural justice' and a belief in the legitimacy of the state. From this perspective, crime within minority communities is, in part, a consequence of the experience of unfairness.

We have argued elsewhere that the commission of crime can best be explained through the process of *criminalization* (Bowling and Phillips 2002). Crime clusters in conditions of social and economic exclusion and these material conditions mean that offending among minority ethnic groups is more likely to occur in public places, and is more visible and subject to surveillance and police attention. Compounded by racial discrimination within the criminal justice process, a disproportionate number of people within black and other minority ethnic communities acquire stop and search histories, intelligence files, entries on the police national computer and the DNA database, criminal convictions, and prison records. The brutalizing experiences of racism, exclusion, and criminalization lead some young people living in the most dangerous places to carry weapons 'for security' and to engage in violence arising from self-defence and retributive 'street justice'.

Such issues have yet to be explored properly within criminological research. Framed within a 'minority perspective' (Phillips and Bowling 2003), researchers would involve practitioners, activists, and ordinary members of ethnic minority communities in research design, facilitating access, framing research questions, analysing, interpreting and disseminating findings, and developing good practice on the ground. Detailed research on specific types of crime in their geographical, social, and economic contexts is required, as is research to understand the factors protecting South Asian communities—especially women—from becoming involved in crime and the criminal justice process. Future research on policing should examine the use of discretion in stops and searches, and the quality of suspect descriptions provided by victims and other sources of intelligence that inform police decisions. We also need to know more about the quality of legal advice provided during the court process and how defendants come to their decisions on plea and opting for Crown Court trial.

The Lawrence Inquiry was hailed as a watershed in the pursuit of justice for minority ethnic groups in Britain, but despite the volumes of research, policy development, legislation, innovation, and training that followed in its wake, things have got worse rather than better for many members of minority ethnic communities. 'Tough' crime policies have resulted in funnelling increasing numbers of people through the criminal process and into prison, impacting particularly severely on minority ethnic communities. And yet these policies do not seem to have achieved the goal of making all communities safe and peaceful places to live. The challenge for criminologists is to envision ways to create a safer society without sacrificing freedom, fairness, and justice.

■ SELECTED FURTHER READING

This chapter develops the ideas explored in the authors' *Racism, Crime and Justice* (Longman, 2002). On ethnicity and victimisation, look at Bowling's *Violent Racism* (Clarendon Press, 1999) and *Hate Crime* by Nathan Hall (Willan, 2005). *Policing, Race and Racism* by Michael Rowe (Willan, 2005) provides an overview, and a historical perspective is provided by James Whitfield in *Unhappy Dialogue: The Metropolitan Police and London's West Indian Community* (Willan, 2004). For the other key areas of criminal justice see Roger Hood's *Race and Sentencing* (Oxford, 1992); Edgar *et al.*, *Prison Violence: Conflict, Power and Victimization* (Willan, 2003); *Race and Probation* by Lewis *et al.* (Willan, 2005). For a critical perspective see Stuart Hall and colleagues' *Policing the Crisis* (Macmillan, 1978).

■ REFERENCES

ABBAS, T. (2005), *Diversity in the Senior Judiciary: A Literature Review of Research on Ethnic Inequalities*, London: The Commission for Judicial Appointments

ALEXANDER, C. (2000), *The Asian Gang: Ethnicity, Identity, Masculinity*, Oxford: Berg.

ALFRED, R. (1992), *Black Workers in the Prison Service*, London: Prison Reform Trust.

ALLEN, C., and NIELSEN, J. S. (2002), *Summary Report on Islamaphobia in the EU after 11 September 2001*, Vienna: European Monitoring Centre on Racism and Xenophobia

ALLEN, J., LOVBAKKE, J., and EL KOMY, M. (2005), *Confidence and Perceptions of the Criminal Justice System*, Online Report 31/05, London: Home Office.

ARMSTRONG, D., HINE, J., HACKING, S., ARMAOS, R., JONES, R., KLESSINGER, N., and FRANCE, A. (2005), *Children, Risk and Crime: The On Track Youth Lifestyles Surveys*, Home Office Research Study 278, London: Home Office.

ATHWAL, H., and KUNDNANI, A. (2006), *Sixty eight racist murders since Stephen Lawrence*, London: Institute of Race Relations.

AUST, R., and SMITH, N. (2003), *Ethnicity and Drug Use: Key Findings from the 2001/2002 British Crime Survey*, Research Findings 209, London: Home Office.

BARTH, F. (1969), *Ethnic Groups and Boundaries: The Social Organisation of Cultural Difference*, London: George Allen and Unwin.

BETHNAL GREEN AND STEPNEY TRADES COUNCIL (1978), *Blood on the Streets*, London: Bethnal Green and Stepney Trades Council.

BHATTACHARYYA, G., GABRIEL, J., and SMALL, S. (2002), *Race and Power: Global Racism in the Twenty-First Century*, London: Routledge.

BOSWORTH, M. (1999), *Engendering Resistance: Agency and Power in Women's Prisons*, Aldershot: Dartmouth.

BOWLING, B. (1990), 'Conceptual and Methodological Problems in Measuring "Race" Differences in Delinquency: A Reply to Marianne Junger', *British Journal of Criminology*, 30: 483–92.

——(1993), 'Racial Harassment and the Process of Victimization: Conceptual and Methodological

Implications for the Local Crime Survey', *British Journal of Criminology*, 33(1) Spring.

—— (1999), *Violent Racism: Victimisation, Policing and Social Context*, revised edn, Oxford: Oxford University Press

—— and PHILLIPS, C. (2002), *Racism, Crime and Justice*, London: Longman.

—— and —— (2003), 'Policing Ethnic Minority Communities', in T. Newburn, *The Handbook of Policing*, 528–55 Cullompton, Devon: Willan.

——, GRAHAM, J., and ROSS, A. (1994), 'Self-Reported Offending among Young People in England and Wales', in J. Junger-Tas *et al.*, *Delinquent Behaviour Among Young People in the Western World*, Amsterdam: Kugler.

BRIMICOMBE, A., RALPHS, M., SAMPSON, A., and TSUE, H. (2001), 'An Analysis of the Role of Neighbourhood Ethnic Composition in the Geographical Distribution of Racially Motivated Incidents', *British Journal of Criminology*, 41(2), Spring.

BUCKE, T., and BROWN, D. (1997), *In Police Custody: Police Powers and Suspects' Rights Under the Revised PACE Codes of Practice*, Home Office Research Study 174, London: Home Office.

BUDD, T., SHARP, C., BULMER, M., and SOLOMOS, J. (eds) (1999), *Racism*, Oxford: Oxford University Press.

BULLOCK, K., and TILLEY, N. (2002), *Shootings, Gangs and Violent Incidents in Manchester: Developing a Crime Reduction Strategy*, Crime Reduction Research Series Paper 13, London: Home Office.

BURNETT, R., and FARRELL, G. (1994), *Reported and Unreported Racial Incidents in Prisons*, Occasional Paper No. 14, Oxford: University of Oxford Centre for Criminological Research.

BURNEY, E. (2002), 'The Uses and Limits of Prosecuting Racially Aggravated Offences', in P. Iganski (ed.), *The Hate Debate—Should Hate be Punished as a Crime?*, London: Profile Books.

—— and ROSE, G. (2002), *Racist Offences—How is the Law Working? The Implementation of the Legislation on Racially Aggravated Offences in the Crime and Disorder Act 1998*, Home Office Research Study 244, London: Home Office.

CALVERLEY, A., COLE, B., KAUR, G., LEWIS, S., RAYNOR, P., ASADEGHI, S., SMITH, D. A., VANSTONE, M., and WARDAK, A. (2004), *Black and Asian Offenders on Probation*, Home Office Research Study 277, London: Home Office.

CANTLE, T. (2001), *Community Cohesion: A Report of the Independent Review Team*, London: Home Office.

CARF (Campaign Against Racism and Fascism) (1999), 'The Politics of Numbers: Police Racism and Crime Figures, *CARF*, 50, June/July: www.carf.demon.co.uk/feat29.html

CASHMORE, E. (1991), 'Black Cops Inc.', in E. Cashmore and E. McLaughlin (eds), *Out of Order?: Policing Black People*, London: Routledge.

—— (2001), 'The Experiences of Ethnic Minority Police Officers in Britain: Under-Recruitment and Racial Profiling in a Performance Culture', *Ethic and Racial Studies*, 24(4): 642–59.

—— (2002), 'Behind the Window Dressing: Ethnic Minority Police Perspectives on Cultural Diversity', *Journal of Ethnic and Migration Studies*, 28(2): 327–41.

CATHCART, B. (1999), *The Case of Stephen Lawrence*, London: Viking.

CCCS (1982), *The Empire Strikes Back: Race and Racism in 70s Britain*, London: Hutchinson in association with the Centre for Contemporary Cultural Studies.

CHAHAL, K., and JULIENNE, L. (1999), *'We Can't All Be White!': Racist Victimisation in the UK*, York: York Publishing Services.

CHAKRABORTI, N. and GARLAND, J. (eds) (2004), *Rural Racism*, Cullompton, Devon: Willan.

CHIGWADA-BAILEY, R. (1997), *Black Women's Experiences of Criminal Justice: Discourse on Disadvantage*, Winchester: Waterside Press.

CLANCY, A., HOUGH, M., AUST, R., and KERSHAW, C. (2001), *Crime, Policing and Justice: The Experience of Ethnic Minorities: Findings from the 2000 British Crime Survey*, Home Office Research Study 223, London: Home Office.

COID, J., PETRUCKEVITCH, A., BEBBINGTON, P., BRUGHA, T., BHUGRA, D., JENKINS, R., FARRELL, M., LEWIS, G., and SINGLETON, N. (2002), 'Ethnic Differences in Prisoners 1: Criminality and Psychiatric Morbidity', *British Journal of Psychiatry*, 181. 473–80.

COLEMAN, C., and MOYNIHAN, J. (1996), *Understanding Crime Data: Haunted by the Dark Figure*, Milton Keynes: Open University Press.

COMMISSION FOR RACIAL EQUALITY (CRE) (2003), *A Formal Investigation by the Commission for Racial Equality into HM Prison Service of England and Wales—Part 2: Racial Equality in Prisons*, London: Commission for Racial Equality.

—— (2005), *The Police Service in England and Wales: Final Report of a Formal Investigation by the*

Commission for Racial Equality, London: Commission for Racial Equality.

COUNCELL, R. (2004), *Offender Management Caseload Statistics 2003, England and Wales*, Home Office Statistical Bulletin 15/04, London: Home Office.

CRIMINAL JUSTICE SYSTEM RACE UNIT (2005), *BME Communities' Expectations of Fair Treatment by the Criminal Justice System*, London: Criminal Justice System Race Unit.

CROWN PROSECUTION SERVICE (2004), *The Code for Crown Prosecutors*, London: CPS.

DANIEL, W. W. (1968), *Racial Discrimination in England*, Harmondsworth: Penguin.

DENMAN, S. (2001), *The Denman Report—Race Discrimination in the Crown Prosecution Service*, London: Crown Prosecution Service.

DENNEY, D. (1992), *Racism and Anti-Racism in Probation*, London: Routledge.

DENNIS, N., ERDOS, G., and AL-SHAHI, A. (2000), *Racist Murder and Pressure Group Politics: The Macpherson Report and the Police*, London: Institute for the Study of Civil Society.

DEPARTMENT FOR EDUCATION AND SKILLS (2005), *Ethnicity and Education: The Evidence on Minority Ethnic Pupils. Research Topic Paper Rtpo1–05*, London: Department for Education and Skills.

DOCKING, M., and TUFFIN, R. (2005), *Racist Incidents: Progress since the Lawrence Inquiry*, Online Report 42/05, London: Home Office.

DODD, T., NICHOLAS, S., POVEY, D., and WALKER, A. (2004), *Crime in England and Wales 2003/2004*, Statistical Bulletin 10/04, London: Home Office.

DORLING, D. (2005), 'Prime Suspect: Murder in Britain', in *Criminal Obsessions: Why harm matters more than Crime*, London: Crime & Society Foundation.

EDGAR, K., and MARTIN, C. (2004), *Perceptions of Race and Conflict: Perspectives of Minority Ethnic Prisoners and of Prison Officers*, RDS Online Report 11/04, London: Home Office.

——O' DONNELL, I., and MARTIN, C. (2003), *Prison Violence: The Dynamics of Conflict, Fear and Power*, Cullompton, Devon: Willan.

EZE, E. (1997), *Race and The Enlightenment: a reader*, Oxford: Blackwell.

FEILZER, M., and HOOD, R. (2004), *Differences or Discrimination?*, London: Youth Justice Board.

FENTON, S. (2003), *Ethnicity*, Cambridge: Polity.

FITZGERALD, M. (1993), *Ethnic Minorities in the Criminal Justice System*, Home Office Research and Statistics Department, Research Study No. 20, London: HMSO.

——(1999), *Searches in London under Section 1 of the Police and Criminal Evidence Act*, London: Metropolitan Police.

——and SIBBITT, R. (1997), *Ethnic Monitoring in Police Forces: A Beginning*, Home Office Research Study 173, London: Home Office.

——, STOCKDALE, J. E., and HALE, C. (2003), *Young People & Street Crime: Research into Young People's Involvement in Street Crime*, London: Youth Justice Board.

FLOOD-PAGE, C., CAMPBELL, S., HARRINGTON, V., and MILLER, J. (2000), *Youth Crime: Findings from the 1998/99 Youth Lifestyle Survey*, Home Office Research Study No. 209, London: Home Office.

FOSTER, J., NEWBURN, T., and SOUHAMI, A. (2005), *Assessing the Impact of the Stephen Lawrence Inquiry*, Home Office Research Study 294, London: Home Office.

GELSTHORPE, L. (2005), 'The Experiences of Female Minority Ethnic Offenders: The Other "Other" ', in S. Lewis, P. Raynor, D. Smith, and A. Wardak (eds), *Race and Probation*, Cullompton, Devon: Willan.

GENDERS, E., and PLAYER, E. (1989), *Race Relations in Prison*, Oxford: Clarendon Press.

GILROY, P. (1982), 'Police and Thieves', in Centre for Contemporary Cultural Studies, *The Empire Strikes Back*, London: Hutchinson.

——(1987a), *There Ain't No Black in the Union Jack: The Cultural Politics of Race and Nation*, London: Hutchinson.

——(1987b), 'The Myth of Black Criminality', in P. Scraton (ed.), *Law, Order and the Authoritarian State: Readings in Critical Criminology*, Milton Keynes: Open University Press.

——(2000), *Between Camps: Race, Identity and Nationalism at the End of the Colour Line*, London: Allen.

——(2003), 'A New Crime, but the Same Old Culprits', *The Guardian*, 8 January.

——(2004), *After Empire: Melancholia or Convivial Culture?*, London: Routledge.

GOLDBERG, D. T. (1993), *Racist Culture: Philosophy and the Politics of Meaning*, Oxford: Blackwell.

GORDON, P. (1983), *White Law: Racism in the Police, Courts and Prisons*, London: Pluto.

GRAEF, R. (1989), *Talking Blues: The Police in their own words*, London: Collins Harvill.

GRAHAM, J., and BOWLING, B. (1995), *Young People and Crime*, Home Office Research Study No. 145, London: Home Office.

GREEN, R. (1989), 'Probation and the Black Offender', *New Community*, 16(1): 81–91.

GUPTA, T (2005), *Gladiator Games*, London: Oberon.

GUS JOHN PARTNERSHIP (2003), *Race for Justice: A Review of CPS Decision Making for Possible Racial Bias at Each Stage of the Prosecution Process*, London: Gus John Partnership.

HALL, S., LEWIS, G., and MCLAUGHLIN, E. (1998), *The Report on Racial Stereotyping* (prepared for Deighton Guedalla, solicitors for Duwayne Brooks, June 1998), Milton Keynes: Open University.

——, CRITCHER, C., JEFFERSON, T., CLARKE, J., and ROBERTS, B. (1978), *Policing the Crisis: Mugging, the State and Law and Order*, London: Macmillan.

HALLSWORTH, S. (2005), *Street Crime*, Cullompton, Devon: Willan.

HARRINGTON, V., and MAYHEW, P. (2001), *Mobile Phone Theft*, Home Office Research Study 235, London: Home Office.

HEARNDEN, I., and HOUGH, M. (2004), *Race and the Criminal Justice System: An Overview to the Complete Statistics 2002/3*, London: Home Office.

HEAVEN, O., and HUDSON, B. (2005), 'Race, Ethnicity and Crime', in C. Hale, K. Hayward, A. Wahidin, and E. Wincup, *Criminology*, Oxford: Oxford University Press.

HER MAJESTY'S CROWN PROSECUTION SERVICE INSPECTORATE (HMCPSI) (2002), *Report on the Thematic Review of Casework Having a Minority Ethnic Dimension*, London: HMCPSI.

HER MAJESTY'S INSPECTORATE OF PRISONS (HMIP) (2005), *Parallel Worlds: A Thematic Review of Race Relations in Prisons*, London: Her Majesty's Inspectorate of Prisons.

HER MAJESTY'S INSPECTORATE OF PROBATION (HMIP) (2000), *Towards Race Equality. Thematic Inspection*, London: Home Office.

——(2004), *Towards Race Equality: Follow-Up Inspection Report*, London: Her Majesty's Inspectorate of Probation.

HESSE, B., RAI, D. K., BENNETT, C., and MCGILCHRIST, P. (1992), *Beneath the Surface: Racial Harassment*, Aldershot: Avebury.

HINDELANG, M., HIRSCHI, T., and WEIS, J. (1981), *Measuring Delinquency*, Beverly Hills, Cal.: Sage.

HOLDAWAY, S. (1983), *Inside the British Police*, Oxford: Blackwell.

——(1996), *The Racialisation of British Policing*, London: Macmillan.

——and ALLAKER, J. (1990), *Race Issues in the Probation Service: a Review of Policy*, Wakefield: Association of Chief Officers of Probation.

HOLDER, K. A., NEE, C., and ELLIS, T. (2000), 'Triple Jeopardy? Black and Asian Women Police Officers' Experiences of Discrimination', *International Journal of Police Science and Management*, 3(1): 68–87.

HOME OFFICE (1989), *The Ethnic Group of those Proceeded Against or Sentenced by the Courts in the Metropolitan District in 1984 and 1985*, Home Office Statistical Bulletin 6/89, London: Home Office Statistical Department.

——(1999a), *Action Plan. Response to the Stephen Lawrence Inquiry*, London: HMSO.

——(1999b), *Race Equality—the Home Secretary's Employment Targets: Staff Targets for the Home Office, the Prison, the Police, the Fire and the Probation Services, a Home Office Publication under Section 95 of the Criminal Justice Act 1991*, London: Home Office.

——(2003), *Race Equality: The Home Secretary's Employment Targets. Milestone Report: Staff Targets for the Home Office, the Prison, the Police and the Probation Services*, London: Home Office.

——(2005a), *Statistics on Race and the Criminal Justice System 2004: A Home Office publication under Section 95 of the Criminal Justice Act 1991*, London: Home Office.

——(2005b), *Code A. Police and Criminal Evidence Act Code of Practice for the Exercise of Statutory Powers of Stop and Search. Effective from 1 January 2006*, London: Home Office.

——(2005c), *Stop and Search Manual*, London: Home Office.

——(2006), *Offender Management Caseload Statistics quarterly brief—October to December 2005, England and Wales*, London: Home Office.

HOOD, R. (1992), *Race and Sentencing*, Oxford: Clarendon Press.

HOUSE OF COMMONS (1972), *Select Committee on Race Relations and Immigration Session 1971–2,*

Police/Immigration Relations, London: House of Commons.

—— (1976), *Select Committee on Race Relations and Immigration Session 1975–6, The West Indian Community*, London: House of Commons.

HUDSON, B. (1993), *Penal Policy and Social Justice*, Basingstoke: Macmillan.

—— and BRAMHALL, G. (2005), 'Assessing the Other: Constructions of "Asianness" in Risk Assessments by Probation Officers', *British Journal of Criminology*, 45(5): 721–40.

HUNTE, J. (1966), *Nigger Hunting in England?*, London: West Indian Standing Conference.

IGANSKI, P. (ed.) (2002), *The Hate Debate: Should Hate be Punished as a Crime?*, London: Profile Books in association with the Institute for Jewish Policy Research.

——, KIELINGER, V., and PATERSON, S. (2005), *Hate Crimes against London's Jews: An Analysis of Incidents Recorded by the Metropolitan Police Service 2001–04*, London: Institute for Jewish Policy Research.

INNES, M. (1999), 'Beyond the Macpherson Report: Managing Murder Inquiries in Context', *Sociological Research Online*, 4(1).

INSTITUTE OF RACE RELATIONS (1987), *Policing Against Black People*, London: IRR.

—— (1991), *Deadly Silence: Black Deaths in Custody*, London: Institute of Race Relations.

JACOBY, J. (2002), 'Punish Crime, Not Thought Crime', in P. Iganski (ed.), *The Hate Debate—Should Hate be Punished as a Crime?*, London: Profile Books.

JAMES, Z. (2005), 'Policing Space: Managing New Travellers in England', *British Journal of Criminology*, Advance Access, doi:10.1093/bjc/ azi077.

JUNGER, M. (1989), 'Discrepancies between Police and Self-Report Data for Dutch Racial Minorities', *British Journal of Criminology*, 29(3): 273–84.

—— (1990), 'Studying Ethnic Minorities in Relation to Crime and Police Discrimination: Answer to Bowling', *British Journal of Criminology*, 30(4): 493–502.

KLEG, M. (1993), *Hate Prejudice and Racism*, Albany, NY: State University of New York Press.

LAKEY, J. (1997), 'Neighbourhoods and Housing', in T. Modood, R. Berthoud, J. Lakey, J. Nazroo, P. Smith, S. Virdee, and S. Beishon (eds), *Ethnic Minorities in Britain: Diversity and Disadvantage*, London: Policy Studies Institute.

LANDAU, S. F., and NATHAN, G. (1983), 'Selecting Delinquents for Cautioning in the London Metropolitan Area', *British Journal of Criminology*, 23(2): 128–49.

LAWRENCE, F. (2002), 'Racial Violence on a "Small Island": Bias Crime in a Multicultural Society', in P. Iganski (ed.), *The Hate Debate—Should Hate be Punished as a Crime?*, London: Profile Books.

LEITNER, M., SHAPLAND, J., and WILES, P. (1993), *Drug Usage and Drugs Prevention: The Views and Habits of the General Public*, London: HMSO.

LOMBROSO, C. (1876), *L'Uomo Delinquente*, Turin: Fratelli Bocca.

LUPTON, R., and POWER, A. (2004), *Minority Ethnic Groups in Britain*, London: Centre for the Analysis of Social Exclusion.

MAC AN GHAILL, M. (1999), *Contemporary Racisms and Ethnicities: Social and Cultural Transformations*, Buckingham: Open University Press.

MCDERMOTT, K. (1990), 'We Have No Problem: The Experience of Racism in Prison', *New Community*, 16(2): 213–28.

MCLAGAN, G. (2005), Guns and Gangs: Inside Black Gun Crime, London: Allison and Busby.

MACPHERSON, W. (1999), *The Stephen Lawrence Inquiry*, Report of an Inquiry by Sir William Macpherson of Cluny, advised by Tom Cook, The Right Reverend Dr John Sentamu and Dr Richard Stone, Cm 4262–1, London: The Stationery Office.

MASON, D. (2000), *Race and Ethnicity in Modern Britain*, Oxford: Oxford University Press.

MAYHEW, P., AYE MAUNG, N., and MIRRLEES-BLACK, C. (1993), *The 1992 British Crime Survey*, Home Office Research Study No. 132, London: HMSO.

MAYNARD, W., and READ, T. (1997), *Policing Racially Motivated Incidents*, Police Research Group Crime Detection and Prevention Series, No. 59, London: Home Office.

METROPOLITAN POLICE AUTHORITY (2004), *Report of the MPA Scrutiny on MPS Stop and Search Practice*, London: Metropolitan Police Authority.

MHLANGA, B. (1997), *The Colour of English Justice: a Multivariate Analysis*, Aldershot: Avebury.

—— (1999), *Race and Crown Prosecution Service Decisions*, London: The Stationery Office.

MILES, R., and BROWN, M. (2003), *Racism*, 2nd edn, London: Routledge.

MILLER, J., BLAND, N., and QUINTON, P. (2000), *The Impact of Stops and Searches on Crime and the*

Community, Police Research Series Paper 127, London: Home Office.

MIRRLEES-BLACK, C. (2001), *Confidence in the Criminal Justice System: Findings from the 2000 British Crime Survey*, Research Findings No. 137, London: Home Office.

MONTAGU, A. (1943), *Man's Most Dangerous Myth: The Fallacy of Race*, Walnut Creek/London: AltaMira Press.

MORGAN, R. (2005), 'Race, Probation and Inspections', in S. Lewis, P. Raynor, D. Smith, and A. Wardak (eds), *Race and Probation*, Cullompton, Devon: Willan.

MORRIS, W. (2004), *The Report of the Morris Inquiry. The Case for Change: People in the Metropolitan Police Service*, London: Metropolitan Police Authority.

MOTT, J., and MIRRLEES-BLACK, C. (1995), *Self-Reported Drug Misuse in England and Wales: Findings from the 1992 British Crime Survey*, Research and Planning Unit Paper No. 89, London: Home Office.

MVA and MILLER, J. (2000), *Profiling Populations Available for Stops and Searches*, Police Research Series Paper No. 131, London: Home Office.

NAYAK, A. (2003), *Race, Place and Globalization: Youth Cultures in a Changing World*, Oxford: Berg.

NEWBURN, T., and HAYMAN, S. (2001), *Policing, Surveillance and Social Control: CCTV and Police Monitoring of Suspects*, Cullompton, Devon: Willan.

——, SHINER, M., and HAYMAN, S. (2004), 'Race, Crime and Injustice? Strip Search and the Treatment of Suspects in Custody', *British Journal of Criminology*, 44(5): 677–94.

NORRIS, C., FIELDING, N., KEMP, C., and FIELDING, J. (1992), 'Black and Blue: an Analysis of the Influence of Race on Being Stopped by the Police', *British Journal of Sociology*, 43(2): 207–23.

OAKLEY, R. (2005), *Policing Racist Crime and Violence: A Comparative Analysis*, Vienna: European Monitoring Centre on Racism and Xenophobia.

PAREKH, B. (2000), *The Future of Multi-Ethnic Britain*, London: Profile Books.

PEARSON, G. (1983), *Hooligan: A History of Respectable Fears*, London: Macmillan.

PERCY, A. (1998), *Ethnicity and Victimisation: Findings from the 1996 British Crime Survey*, Home Office Statistical Bulletin 6/98, 3 April, London: Home Office.

PHILLIPS, C. (2005a), 'Ethnic Inequalities under New Labour: Progress or Entrenchment?', in J. Hills and K. Stewart (eds), *A More Equal Society? New Labour, Poverty, Inequality and Exclusion*, Bristol: Policy Press.

——(2005b), 'Facing Inwards and Outwards? Institutional Racism, Race Equality and the Role of Black and Asian Professional Associations', *Criminal Justice*, 5(4): 357–77.

——and BOWLING, B. (2003), 'Racism, Ethnicity and Criminology: Developing Minority Perspectives', *British Journal of Criminology*, 43(2): 269–90.

——and BROWN, D. (1998), *Entry into the Criminal Justice System: A Survey of Police Arrests and Their Outcomes*, Home Office Research Study No. 185, London: Home Office.

——and SAMPSON, A. (1998), 'Preventing Repeated Victimisation: An Action Research Project', *British Journal of Criminology*, 38(1): 124–44.

POVEY, D., UPSON, A., and JANSSON, K. (2005). *Crime in England and Wales: Quarterly Update*, June 2005, Home Office Statistical Bulletin 18/05, London: Home Office.

QUINTON, P., BLAND, N., and MILLER, J. (2000), *Police Stops, Decision-Making and Practice*, Police Research Series Paper No. 130, London: Home Office.

RAMSAY, M., and PERCY, A. (1996), *Drug Misuse Declared: Results of the 1994 British Crime Survey*, Research Findings No. 33, London: Home Office Research and Statistics Directorate.

——and SPILLER, A. (1997), *Drug Misuse Declared in 1996: Latest Results from the British Crime Survey*, Home Office Research and Statistics Directorate, Home Office Research Study No. 172, London: Home Office.

——, BAKER, P., GOULDEN, C., SHARP, C., and SONDHI, A. (2001), *Drug Misuse Declared in 2000: Results from the British Crime Survey*, Home Office Research Study No. 224, London: Home Office.

RAY, L., and SMITH, D. (2002), 'Hate Crime, Violence and Cultures of Racism', in P. Iganski (ed.), *The Hate Debate — Should Hate be Punished as a Crime?*, London: Profile Books.

——SMITH, D., and WASTELL, L. (2001), 'Understanding Racist Violence', *Criminal Justice Matters*, 43.

——, ——, and —— (2004), 'Shame, Rage and Racist Violence', *British Journal of Criminology*, 44(3): 350–68.

REINER, R. (2000), *The Politics of the Police*, Oxford: Oxford University Press.

ROCK, P. (2004), *Constructing Victims' Rights: The Home Office, New Labour, and Victims*, Oxford: Oxford University Press.

ROWE, M. (2004), *Policing, Race and Racism*. Cullompton, Devon: Willan.

RUBINSTEIN, W. D. (1996), *A History of the Jews in the English-Speaking World: Great Britain*, Basingstoke: Macmillan.

SALISBURY, H., and UPSON, A. (2004), *Ethnicity, Victimisation and Worry About Crime: Findings from the 2001/2002 and 2002/2003 British Crime Surveys*, Findings 237, London: Home Office.

SAMPSON, A., and PHILLIPS, C. (1992), *Multiple Victimisation: Racial Attacks on an East London Estate*, Police Research Group Crime Prevention Unit Series Paper 36, London: Home Office.

—— and —— (1996), *Reducing Repeat Victimisation on an East London Estate*, Police Research Group Crime Prevention Unit Crime Prevention and Detection Paper 67, London: Home Office.

SCARMAN, L. (1981), *The Scarman Report*, London: HMSO.

SHARP, C., and BUDD, T. (2005), *Minority Ethnic Groups and Crime: The Findings from the Offending, Crime and Justice Survey 2003*, Home Office Online Report 33/05.

SHARP, D. (2002), 'Policing after Macpherson: The Experiences of Muslim Police Officers', in B. Spalek (ed.), Islam, Crime and Criminal Justice, Cullompton, Devon: Willan.

SHUTE, S., HOOD, R., and SEEMUNGAL, F. (2005), *A Fair Hearing: Ethnic Minorities in the Criminal Courts*, Cullompton, Devon: Willan.

SIBBITT, R. (1997), *The Perpetrators of Racial Harassment and Racial Violence*, Home Office Research Study No. 176, London: Home Office.

SKOGAN, W. G. (1990), *The Police and the Public in England and Wales: A British Crime Survey Report*, Home Office Research Study No. 117, London: HMSO.

SMITH, D. J. (1994), 'Race, Crime and Criminal Justice', in M. Maguire, R. Morgan, and R. Reiner (eds), *The Oxford Handbook of Criminology*, Oxford: Clarendon Press.

—— (1997), 'Ethnic Origins, Crime and Criminal Justice', in M. Maguire, R. Morgan, and R. Reiner (eds), *The Oxford Handbook of Criminology*, 2nd edn, Oxford: Oxford University Press.

—— and GRAY, J. (1985), *Police and People in London*, London: Policy Studies Institute.

SMITH, J. (2003), T*he Nature of Personal Robbery*, Home Office Research Study 254, London: Home Office.

SMITH, S. J. (1989), *The Politics of "Race" and Residence: Citizenship, Segregation and White Supremacy in Britain*, Cambridge: Polity.

SOLOMOS, J. (1999), 'Social Research and the Stephen Lawrence Inquiry', *Sociological Research Online*, 4(1).

—— and BACK, L. (1996), *Racism and Society*, London: Macmillan.

SPALEK, B., and WILSON, D. (2002), 'Racism and Religious Discrimination in Prison: The Marginalisation of Imams in Their Work with Prisoners', in B. Spalek (ed.), *Islam, Crime and Criminal Justice*, Cullompton, Devon: Willan.

SPARKS, R., BOTTOMS, A. E., and HAY, W. (1996), *Prisons and the Problem of Order*, Oxford: Oxford University Press.

STEVENS, P., and WILLIS, C. F. (1979), *Race, Crime and Arrests*, Home Office Research Study No. 58, London: HMSO.

STONE, V., and TUFFIN, R. (2000), *Attitudes of People from Minority Ethnic Communities towards a Career in the Police Service*, Police Research Series Paper 136, London: Home Office.

SWIFT, R. (ed.) (2002), *Irish Migrants in Britain, 1815–1914: A Documentary History*, Cork: Cork University Press.

THOMPSON, T. (2004), *Gangs: A Journey into the Heart of the British Underworld*, London: Hodder & Stoughton.

TYLER, T. (1990), *Why People Obey the Law*, London: Yale University Press.

VON HIRSCH, A., and ROBERTS, J. (1997), 'Racial Disparity in Sentencing: Reflections on the Hood Study', *Howard Journal*, 36(3): 227–36.

WADDINGTON, P. A. J. (1999), 'Discretion, "Respectability" and Institutional Police Racism', *Sociological Research Online*, 4(1).

——, STENSON, K., and DON, D. (2004), 'In Proportion: Race and Police Stop and Search', *British Journal of Criminology*, 44: 889–914.

WALKER, M. A. (1989), 'The Court Disposal and Remands of White, Afro-Caribbean, and Asian Men (London, 1983)', *British Journal of Criminology*, 29(4): 353–67.

WALKER, S., SPOHN, C., and DELONE, M. (2004), *The Color of Justice: Race, Ethnicity, and Crime in America*, 2nd edn, Belmont, Cal: Wadsworth.

WARDAK, A. (2000), *Social Control and Deviance: A South Asian Community in Scotland*, Aldershot: Ashgate.

WEBSTER, C. (1997), 'The Construction of British "Asian Criminality" ', *International Journal of the Sociology of Law*, 25: 65–86.

——(2003), 'Race, Space and Fear: Imagined Geographies of Racism, Crime, Violence and Disorder in Northern England.' *Capital & Class*, 80, 95–122.

WHITFIELD, J. (2004), *Unhappy Dialogue: The Metropolitan Police and black Londoners in post-war Britain*, Cullompton, Devon: Willan.

WILLIAMS, P. (2005), 'Designing and Delivering Programmes for Minority Ethnic Offenders', in S. Lewis, P. Raynor, D. Smith, and A. Wardak (eds), *Race and Probation*, Cullompton, Devon: Willan.

WILSON, D. (2003), ' "Keeping Quiet" or "Going Nuts": Some Emerging Strategies Used by Young Black People in Custody at a Time of Childhood Being Re-Constructed', *Howard Journal of Criminal Justice*, 42(5): 411–25

YOUNG, J. (1999), *The Exclusive Society: Social Exclusion in Crime and Difference in Later Modernity*, London: Sage.

15

VICTIMS, VICTIMIZATION, AND CRIMINAL JUSTICE

*Carolyn Hoyle and Lucia Zedner** *

INTRODUCTION

Our knowledge about victims is in a state of continuing development. Conventional conceptions of victimization have been challenged by new studies of previously invisible victims: of corporate and white-collar crime, of trafficking, genocide, armed conflict, torture, terrorism, and crimes of the state (Ruggiero 1992; Morgan and Evans 1999; Goodey 2005). Studies of secondary victimization and the collateral effects of crime and punishment draw attention to the families of primary victims (Young 2000), of prisoners (Travis and Waul 2004), and of those sentenced to capital punishment or executed in jurisdictions that retain the death penalty (Vandiver 2003; Sharp 2005). These studies both expand and render problematic the concept of victim so that the term victim has become a contested one, challenged by those who prefer 'survivor' (Rock 1998b; Lamb 1999) or favour reference to 'harms' (Hillyard *et al.* 2005). Our expanding knowledge is guided by both academic research and the political impact of legislation, policy-making, and lobbying by interest groups. The promotion of victims' interests on the national and international stage has driven radical policy development in respect of victims' service and procedural rights. Perhaps the most dramatic shift has been the emergence of restorative justice, commonly advanced in the name of victims. Restorative justice is, however, only the most prominent of many procedural changes made in recent years that purport to enhance justice for victims.

* The authors are grateful to the following colleagues for their comments on previous drafts of this chapter: Andrew Ashworth, David Miers, Rod Morgan, Julian Roberts, and Paul Rock, and to Emily Coates for her research assistance.

THE NATURE AND DISTRIBUTION OF VICTIMIZATION

SOURCES OF DATA

Survey data

The development of victim surveys was a key factor in generating criminological interest in victims. In America in the 1960s mass victimization surveys sought to quantify the unreported 'dark figure' of crime. Pilot studies (Reiss 1967) led, in 1972, to annual National Crime Surveys (NCSs) (now National Crime Victimization Surveys, NCVSs) carried out by the Bureau of Justice Statistics. The British Crime Survey (BCS) (Hough and Mayhew 1983) was modelled on the NCS and collected data on crime; factors predisposing people to victimization; impact of crime; fear of crime; victims' experiences of the police; and self-reported offending. From 2001 the BCS moved to an annual cycle, increased its sample size, and now interviews 50,000 people aged 16 or over. The BCS provides data at the level of individual police force areas and is published jointly with police recorded crime statistics to allow for direct comparison.[1] National crime surveys are also carried out in Scotland (McVie *et al.* 2004) and in Northern Ireland (French and Campbell 2005).

International data sources

Similar large-scale surveys are conducted in over 70 different countries. An important source of comparable data is the International Crime Victimization Survey programme (ICVS) carried out, originally in Europe, since 1989. From 1991, United Nations involvement increased the geographical coverage to 33 countries, rising to 48 in 2004 (Alvazzi del Frate and Van Kesteren 2004). In 2004–5, the fifth round of the ICVS in the 15 old member states of the European Union was carried out as the European Crime Survey. These surveys seek a better picture of victimization than police records supply and identify the social, economic, and demographic characteristics of victims (although for discussion of methodological limitations see Maguire, Chapter 10, this volume).

The many publications of the World Health Organization (WHO),[2] such as the 2002 *World Report on Violence and Health* (Krug *et al.* 2002), also provide valuable information, as do other WHO reports on domestic violence, and sexual violence and the prevention of violence, published since 2002. Non-governmental organizations (NGOs) also gather important information on criminal victimization. What follows is not an exhaustive list but rather an indication of the many types of data available.

Amnesty International (AI) campaigns for internationally recognized human rights and reports annually on human rights abuses and other forms of violence worldwide,

---

[1] Crime against retailers is the subject of periodic Commercial Victimisation Surveys (Shury *et al.* 2005).

[2] The WHO was established in 1948, as a specialized agency of the UN, to serve as the directing and coordinating authority for international health matters and public health.

including rape and sexual violence against women and children, violence against minorities, torture, 'disappearances', 'death squads', trafficking, terrorism; as well as on the justice system, including the death penalty, arbitrary detention, unlawful killings, unfair trials, and deaths in custody.

Other organizations, such as The Medical Foundation for the Care of Victims of Torture and the Aegis Trust, also document evidence of torture, genocide, and other offences. Human Rights Watch, the largest independent, non-governmental human rights organization is another source of valuable data, conducting fact-finding investigations into human rights abuses worldwide. In addition to these international bodies, countries with recent histories of severe human rights abuses have established regional organizations which gather data on victimization by interviewing witnesses and victims about killings, disappearances, torture, and other abuses within armed conflicts (for example, the Humanitarian Law Center based in Belgrade). Since 1998 the United Kingdom Foreign and Commonwealth Office has published an annual report on human rights, drawing on evidence from AI and other organizations. It is an important source of information on victims of torture, terrorism, and the death penalty, as well as on specific abuses against women and children.

Academic research

Von Hentig, *The Criminal and his Victim* (1948), is widely regarded as the seminal text in developing victim studies. Highly critical of the traditional offender-oriented nature of criminology, von Hentig proposed a dynamic, interactionist approach to victim precipitation and 'victim-proneness'. Others took up these notions. Mendelsohn (1956) developed victim typologies to denote degrees of culpability; Wolfgang (1958) applied the concept of victim precipitation to homicide data; and, most controversially, Amir (1971) studied victim–offender interaction as a precipitating factor, re-ascribing blame to the victim in rape cases. Whilst Amir's study attracted criticism on methodological and ideological grounds (Morris 1987: 173–4; Walklate 1989: 4–5), others have defended the idea of victim-precipitation, arguing that in a rigorously pursued, value-free social science there is no reason why it should entail victim blaming (Fattah 1991).

In an attempt to overcome the limitations of studies based on recorded data, Sparks, Genn, and Dodd's study (1977) of London sought to ascertain the extent and nature of unreported crime, victims' perceptions of crime, and attitudes towards the criminal justice system. It set the agenda for many subsequent surveys and smaller-scale, qualitative studies. By narrowing their geographical focus, local victim surveys document the uneven distribution of risk, by race, sex, age, class, and locale (see Maguire, Chapter 10, this volume). For example, rural victim surveys challenged the presumption that crime is primarily an urban problem (Koffman 1996: 89–114). Local surveys set crime in its broader social context by including questions about racial and sexual harassment, drug abuse, and other forms of anti-social behaviour (Crawford *et al.* 1990: 4), as well as victim perceptions of police priorities, service delivery, and accountability. Their success in revealing differential patterns of victimization has prompted changes also to the BCS (Percy and Mayhew 1997).

Securing sufficient numbers of victim groups, such as the elderly, the young, the disabled, or those subject to domestic or sexual violence, requires dedicated surveys directed at, among others residential homes, schools, refuges, or total institutions. For example, recent research in prisons has focused on victimization of male (Edgar and O'Donnell 1998) and female prisoners (Loucks 2005). There are, of course, limitations to these data: evidence of sexual victimization by both prison staff and prisoners draws almost entirely on US data and tends to ignore violence against the most vulnerable, such as sex offenders and homosexuals (O'Donnell 2004).

Studies of personal crimes against women seek to overcome their under-representation by mass victimization surveys (Hoyle and Sanders 2000; Loseke *et al.* 2005). Recent work examines domestic violence victims within ethnic minority and marginal communities (Parmar *et al.* 2005). This challenges the primacy of gender as an explanatory model of domestic violence, by exploring how structural inequalities such as racism, class privilege, and heterosexism, intersect with gender oppression (Sokoloff 2005). Academic research has also taken up the largely hidden phenomena of violence in same-sex relationships (Ristock 2002); violence against children in the home (Cavanagh *et al.* 2005), and domestic violence against men (Grady 2002) although the methodological difficulties associated with this research remain a matter of concern (Saunders 2002; Dobash and Dobash 2004).

Several local or specialized surveys suggest levels of sexual crime against women that are far higher than those revealed by national victim surveys and police records (Walby and Allen 2004). The chief difficulty with these studies is that differences in approach, wording, and categorization of responses have generated widely differing estimates of victimization. The sensitivity of survey questions and the approach and demeanour of the interviewer may also dramatically alter response rates. These limitations led many academics, particularly those committed to empirical study of the experiences of vulnerable groups, to abandon the survey for in-depth qualitative work.

The tendency of surveys to concentrate on the 'ideal victim', the weak, respectable, and innocent person harmed by the big, bad stranger (Christie 1986), prompted researchers to explore victimization amongst the less obviously 'worthy' or those in a relationship with their offenders. Examples include research on male rape (Allen 2002), date rape (Fisher *et al.* 2005), and rape within marriage (Painter and Farrington 1998). Miers (2000) shows that only 'innocent' victims are considered worthy of compensation, Hamill (2002) looks at the less than ideal status of victims of paramilitary punishments, whilst Borer (2003) challenges the discrete and binary approach to the concepts of victims and offenders through an analysis of the South African Truth and Reconciliation Commission. These studies make explicit the more general truth that there is considerable overlap between populations of victims and offenders.

'Radical' and 'critical' victimologists have analysed the wider political, economic, and social context of victimization (Mawby and Walklate 1994). A newly emerging area of 'radical-critical' academic research, as yet on the margins of criminological enquiry, concerns victims of crimes of the state, armed conflict, and crimes against humanity. A high proportion of the data about these victims derives from research in the adjacent disciplines of political science, international relations, anthropology, and history. Despite intense media coverage of atrocities such as the massacre of around 8,000 Bosniak (Bosnian Muslim) men and boys in Srebrenica in 1995 by the Bosnian Serb forces and the genocide of over half a million Tutsi in Rwanda around the same time, criminology is only now beginning to recognize the scale and effects of state crime and other political violence.

Less than a decade ago Cohen (2001) and Jamieson (1998) demonstrated the reluctance of criminologists to carry out research on crimes against humanity, despite the fact that conflicts involve colossal violence and victimization, and Hagan *et al.* (2005), in their critique of Sudanese state denial about the conflict in Darfur, consider how slow modern American criminology is to advance the study of genocide. A special issue of the *British Journal of Criminology* acknowledges that 'the space devoted to state crime in the literature of our discipline remains pitifully small' (Green and Ward 2005: 432). With some notable exceptions—Cohen, Ward, Green, Jamieson, Roche, McEvoy, and Bauman—criminologists have, as yet, paid little attention to state-sponsored aggression. Despite the scale and importance of the subject matter, criminologists are perhaps uneasy about entering into this new area, unsure whether their methodological expertise is up to the task. Following the approach of Bauman, Woolford examines some of the prevailing arguments for establishing a criminology of genocide and, showing the limitations of mainstream criminological frameworks for this endeavour, argues that criminologists must develop a critical and reflexive approach to this understudied area of criminal behaviour (Woolford 2006; Bauman 1989).

THE NATURE AND SCOPE OF VICTIMIZATION

National data

In respect of ordinary crimes, successive reports of the BCS have found that while the chance of being a victim of a minor offence is high, the risk of suffering a more serious offence is small. The 2004/05 BCS estimated that there were 2,412,000 violent incidents against adults in England and Wales, although 46 per cent of these did not result in any lasting injury to the victim. Violent crime rates have fallen by 43 per cent since reaching a peak in 1995, an estimated 1.8 million fewer incidents. Victimization falls unequally on particular individuals and groups. Risk of victimization generally is closely related to geographical area, and risk of personal victimization correlated with age, sex, and patterns of routine activity, such as going out in the evenings and consuming alcohol. People who had visited a pub or wine bar more than three times a week in the past month had a higher risk of victimization for all violent offences and were particularly likely to experience stranger violence: 3.2 per cent compared with 0.6 per cent of those who had not (Nicholas *et al.* 2005: 59). Much crime is endogenous—victims, witnesses and offenders are recruited from substantially the same groupings and are more likely to be (quite literally) in contact with one another. Age is a key determinant: young men between the ages of 16 and 24 are most at risk, with 14.6 per cent experiencing criminal violence in the past year (Nicholas *et al.* 2005: 71). Domestic violence is the only category for which the risks for women (0.7 per cent) are higher than for men (0.2 per cent). Risks of violence by strangers and acquaintances are substantially greater for men than for women; 2.3 per cent of men were victims of stranger violence in 2004/05 interviews, compared with 0.6 per cent of women (Nicholas *et al.* 2005).

Women are most likely to be raped by men they know: 54 per cent of rapes are committed by intimates, and 29 per cent by other known individuals, with 50 per cent of cases involving repeat offences by the same person (Walby and Allen 2004). Although 17 per cent more sexual offences were recorded by the police in 2004/05, this can be largely accounted for by the change in recording of indecent exposure. Within the 2004/05 total of 60,946 sexual offences, the police recorded 24,120 indecent assaults on women and 3,515 on men. There were 14,002 recorded rapes, 92 per cent of which were of women (Nicholas *et al.* 2005: 80).

The risk of being a victim of either burglary or vehicle-related theft has halved since 1995 and is much reduced for other property crimes. Household acquisitive crime has fallen by more than half (53 per cent) between 1995 and 2004/05 and domestic burglaries by 20 per cent between 2003/04 and 2004/05 (Nicholas *et al.* 2005: 49). Risks are much higher in inner-city areas, particularly those with high levels of physical disorder, and higher in rented accommodation than owner-occupied homes. Households with lower levels of disposable income, with single-adult, young, or unemployed heads of households, are also at greater risk.

For many types of crime, in particular personal crimes such as street robberies, both Afro-Caribbeans and Asians are more at risk than whites, possibly because they are over-represented in social and age groups particularly prone to crime. Ethnic minorities are disproportionately likely to be council tenants or to live in younger households in socially disadvantaged areas. The risk of being the victim of a racially motivated offence is highest among those of mixed ethnicity. Assaults, threats, and vandalism are those offences most often thought to be committed for racial reasons (Salisbury and Upson 2004: 1–3).

International data

Turning to the international data, the 2000 ICVS revealed that from 1990 to 1995 crime stabilized or fell in many respondent countries and from 1995 to 1999 the dominant pattern was of falling crime (Van Kesteren *et al.* 2000).[3] There was a consistent fall in property crime; changes in violent crime were more variable. In 2000 contact crime accounted for about a quarter of all crimes, with assaults and threats making up about two-thirds of these (or 15 per cent of all crime). Robbery formed a very small proportion of contact crime in all countries. Car vandalism made up nearly a quarter and theft of, and from, cars together comprised a third of all crimes. Assaults and threats comprised 15 per cent of crimes. Only just over 1 per cent of women (1.3 per cent) reported offensive sexual behaviour and only 0.6 per cent reported sexual assaults

---

[3] At the time of going to press data from the fifth IVCS (2005) were not yet available. See: http://www. unicri.it/wwd/analysis/icvs/index.php.

(including rape, attempted rape, and indecent assault), though for reasons discussed above these are undoubtedly under-representations.

The US National Crime Victimisation Survey (2004) shows that US residents, aged 12 or older, experienced an estimated 24 million violent and property victimizations. For crimes of violence aggregate rates for the period 2003–4 declined by 9 per cent from 2001–2 and, taken together, these years' estimates indicate that crime rates remain stabilized at the lowest levels experienced since 1973 (Catalano 2005). Nonetheless, it remains the case that in the USA, 700,000 women report being raped or sexually assaulted each year (Krug *et al.* 2002: 151). Evidence from other continents, particularly from Africa, suggests that high rates of sexual violence are not unique to America. For example, the South African police statistics for the years 2003/4 recorded 52,759 reported rapes (Amnesty International 2005).

Beyond surveys, supranational institutions and NGOs provide international data about various forms of violence. The World Heath Organization *World Report on Violence and Health* (Krug *et al.* 2002) estimated that in 2000 at least 1.6 million people worldwide died as a result of self-inflicted, interpersonal, or collective violence. Most deaths occurred in low- to middle-income countries, with less than 10 per cent in high-income countries. Children are at high risk of both physical and sexual abuse and homicide. There is a strong relationship between domestic violence and child abuse. Domestic violence is common and in some countries it is endemic: in Turkey it is estimated that between a third and a half of women are victims of physical violence in the home (Amnesty International 2005: 5), often accompanied by psychological and/or sexual abuse. Partner violence accounts for a significant proportion of female murder victims (between 40 and 70 per cent in Australia, Canada, Israel, South Africa, and America: Krug *et al.* 2002: 93). An important form of domestic violence is assaults, acid attacks, and murder as a consequence of dowry disputes. UN data show that dowry murder occurs predominantly in South Asia. In many societies, rape victims and women suspected of engaging in premarital sex or adultery are murdered by their male relatives in 'honour killings' (in Pakistan more than 1,000 women every year) (Coomaraswamy 2000; Warrick 2005).

An emerging area of criminological concern is victimization within armed conflicts and state-sponsored aggression. Some 70 per cent of casualties in recent conflicts were non-combatants, most women and children. Women are frequent victims of abduction, rape, sexual abuse, forced pregnancy, and slavery (Rehn and Johnson Sirleaf 2002). For example, in Rwanda, approximately half a million women were raped during the 1994 genocide; in Bosnia, 20,000–50,000 women were raped during five months of conflict in 1992. At any one time, according to data collated by the UK Foreign and Commonwealth office, there are over 300,000 children fighting in armed conflicts around the world. Over two million have been killed in conflict situations over the last decade and many more have been made orphans, maimed, abducted, and abused. Furthermore, trafficking thrives in conflict zones, with girls in particular being at a high risk of sexual violence. In South Asia, it is estimated by UNICEF that at least 500,000 children are involved in the sex industry, many of whom are victims of trafficking

(UK Foreign and Commonwealth Office 2005: 232–4). Trafficking of women from Eastern Europe, South America, Asia, and Africa remains widespread (Krug *et al.* 2002: 153–5).

IMPACT OF VICTIMIZATION

Victim surveys tell little about the impact of victimization. This is better captured by qualitative research focusing on particular types of crime or of victim, for example burglary victims (Mawby 2001); domestic violence (Hoyle and Sanders 2000); sexual assault and stalking victims (Kelly 1988); victims of violence (Shapland *et al.* 1985; Stanko and Hobdell 1993); rape victims (Scheppele and Bart 1983; Allen 2002); child victims (Hartless *et al.* 1995); ethnic minority victims (Salisbury and Upson 2004); and the elderly (Brogden and Nijhar 2000; Donaldson 2003). Together these studies highlight the acute stress and adverse physical, practical, or financial effects suffered by victims of more serious crimes. During the 1990s the grief and trauma suffered by relatives of murder victims and families of death row and executed prisoners was documented in the psychological literature (for example, the *Journal of Traumatic Stress*). Recent work has focused on the impact of large-scale political violence. As well as witnessing brutal attacks on and murder of family members, survivors often experience forced expulsion, rape, torture, and loss of their home and livelihood (Weine 1999). While reactions to victimization are highly crime-specific, most studies suggest that psychological distress is the dominant reaction. At its most severe, this has been formally recognized by psychologists as 'post-traumatic stress disorder'—a clinical condition the symptoms of which include anxiety, depression, loss of control, guilt, sleep disturbance, and obsessive dwelling on the crime (Falsetti and Resnick 1995). Industrial and environmental crimes may also have a massive effect, aptly captured by their common designation as disasters—witness Piper Alpha, Zeebrugge, Bhopal, and Three Mile Island (Ericson 1994).

Personal crimes such as physical and sexual assault and child abuse commonly entail long-term effects. For example, victims of sexual assault may suffer emotional disturbance, sleeping or eating disorders, feelings of insecurity or low self-esteem, or troubled relationships for months or years after the event. Even after counselling, psychological symptoms such as depression and somatic disorders persist (Kelly 1988). Child abuse victims may suffer impaired self-esteem, poor physical health, short- and long-term psychological damage, learning problems, withdrawal, and regressive behaviour. Some children suffer psychiatric illnesses that include post-traumatic stress disorder, major depression, and sleep disorders (Wolfe 1999). Child sexual abuse may induce profound feelings of fear, revulsion, shame, and guilt (Finkelhor and Araji 1986; Trowell *et al.* 1999).

Studies of abuse by intimate partners reveal immediate and lasting mental and physical health effects. In addition to physical injury, victims of domestic violence suffer depression, eating and sleeping disorders, self-harming behaviours, low self-esteem, and chronic physical disorders, and some even attempt suicide (Follette *et al.* 1996; Krug *et al.* 2002). Children who routinely witness abuse frequently exhibit similar behavioural and psychological disturbances to those who are abused (Krug *et al.* 2002: 103). The impact on victims and their children of this violence and the controlling behaviours that are part of most violent relationships (Hoyle and Sanders 2000) produces high attrition rates in the criminal process (Hoyle 2000; Ellison 2003). The failure of criminal justice to provide an effective response for some victims has led academics to consider alternative responses, including specialized domestic violence court processes (Eley 2005) and restorative justice (Strang and Braithwaite 2002).

In the context of armed conflict and state-sponsored aggression, victimization can affect morbidity and mortality, with high murder rates often in quite short periods of time. Approximately 191 million people lost their lives to collective violence in the twentieth century, more than half of whom were civilians. In just 100 days in 1994 approximately 800,000 people were killed in Rwanda. Not only are many survivors of conflicts seriously injured or permanently incapacitated as a result of attack, but there is an increase in deaths due to the concurrent rise in infectious and non-communicable diseases brought about by the collapse of public services, including health care and immunization programmes, during periods of conflict. Disruption to trade and business leads to shortages of food and other vital supplies (famine related to conflicts is estimated to have killed 40 million people in the twentieth century). Such conflicts also lead to further crimes. The increase in psychological and behavioural problems it causes (depression, suicide, and post-traumatic stress disorder) leads to more interpersonal violence amongst survivors. There is often a dramatic rise in HIV transmission, with military forces, and, sometimes, peacekeeping forces, demanding sexual services from local people and using rape as a weapon of war. Survivors of conflicts can suffer from depression and anxiety, psychosomatic ailments, suicidal behaviour, intra-familial conflict, and anti-social behaviour (Krug *et al.* 2002: ch. 8). These symptoms are often very severe amongst refugees who have experienced considerable upheaval and displacement (during 2004 over 25 million people were internally displaced by civil wars; see www.unhcr.ch).

Whilst the emotional impact of serious violent crimes is readily apparent, research suggests that property crimes can also take their toll on victims. Not only do they cause financial and practical harms, they also can create feelings of shock, insecurity, or violation (Maguire 1982). The BCS 2002/03 found that 83 per cent of burglary victims were emotionally affected, with 37 per cent reporting they had been strongly affected (Nicholas and Wood 2003). Elderly victims were particularly badly affected, with many experiencing deterioration in health following the crime (Donaldson 2003). The impact of white-collar, corporate, or business crime upon its victims, including corporations, can also be significant (Levi 2001; Slapper and Tombs 1999). High-profile fraud cases, such as Barings Bank, BCCI, Lloyds, the Maxwell pension fund, MCI Worldcom, and Enron drew attention to the financial and emotional impact upon their victims (Levi and Pithouse 1992). In turn, the impact of crime against corporations (businesses, local authorities, government agencies, and charitable or religious foundations) is by no means only financial (Young 2002: 136–42). The remote consequences of corporate crime may extend to employees, tenants, and consumers (Young 2000: 230).

In respect of both personal and property crime, the impact may extend beyond the incident itself. Considerable expenses may be incurred in replacing uninsured property, in medical care, counselling, or funeral costs. Some victims are driven to move house as a consequence of a traumatic burglary, or to escape continuing attacks, harassment, or stalking. Some lose earnings, or even their jobs, after missing time from work for court attendance or due to crime-related illness or depression (Shapland *et al.* 1985: 104–5).

The impact of victimization varies according to sociodemographic variables such as isolation, resources, vulnerability, and previous experience (Skogan 1986: 140–3). General feelings of vulnerability among women (in part because, at least in America, women may associate crime with the risk of rape, Ferraro 1995), ethnic minorities, and the poor also increase the impact of crime, although expectations of masculinity can inhibit men from expressing their reactions (Goodey 1997; Allen 2002). Multiple or series victimization compounds the impact suffered with each repeated occurrence. Research suggests that a very small percentage of victims experience a disproportionate amount of crime (Farrell and Pease 2001). A minority of victims are so repeatedly victimized that it becomes virtually impossible to distinguish the impact of discrete crimes from the generally impoverished quality of their lives (Hope *et al.* 2001: Commission for Racial Equality 1988: 7). Racial harassment is an important example here. Bowling suggests that violent racism is best seen as a 'process' that the mere counting of individual incidents cannot capture (Bowling 1998: ch. 5).

The wider impact of crime on secondary or indirect victims is increasingly recognized. The most telling example is immediate grief and long-term trauma experienced by the families of murder victims (Rock 1998a; Hoffmann 2003; Victim Support 2006). Spungen (1997) describes families' feelings of isolation and stigmatization within their communities, and of being overlooked by the criminal justice system. For those who witness homicide or other non-fatal assaults, the shock or guilt for failing to intervene may be profound (Victim Support 1991). Serious crimes place considerable stress on family relations, and may even lead to their break-up. The consequent dislocation also impinges on those other members of the household who are its 'indirect victims'— most commonly children (Morgan and Zedner 1992; Burman and Allen-Meares 1994). At its worst, the impact is such that they should properly be recognized as victims in their own right.

VICTIMS' MOVEMENTS AND VICTIMS' JUSTICE

In the United States, a strongly rights-based victim movement emerged in the 1960s and 1970s. Largely conservative in outlook, often seeking more punitive responses to offenders, it was in some states associated with demands for the retention or reintroduction of the death penalty (Hodgkinson 2004). Dissatisfied with the existing responses to victims, the movement demanded a reorientation of the criminal justice system in favour of victims. Latterly it has become more variegated, with groups like 'Parents of Murdered Children' eschewing political involvement, while other groups like 'Families and Friends of Murder Victims' engage in high-profile political lobbying.

In Britain, the central organ of the victim movement, Victim Support, has a very different history. Beginning life as a local initiative in Bristol in 1974, Victim Support grew dramatically in the following decades (Rock 1990). Its 370 local schemes now cover the entire country, with over 1,000 paid staff and 18,000 volunteers helping over one and a half million victims and over 235,000 witnesses in the criminal courts a year (Rock 2004a: 121). Traditionally, Victim Support has maintained a relatively low-key political profile. More recently it has adopted a proactive role promoting service rights for victims, though not rights of allocation, arguing that victims should 'be free of the burden of decisions relating to the offender' (www.victimsupport.org.uk). Lobbying by Victim Support contributed to the introduction of the Domestic Violence, Crime and Victims Act 2004, the provisions of which give statutory protections to victims' interests (see below).

The main thrust of Victim Support's endeavour remains in the provision of emotional support, practical services, and information to individual victims at a local level (Maguire and Kynch 2000: 13). The BCS suggests victims find contact with Victim Support very helpful or fairly helpful in 64 per cent of cases, especially where contact was made soon after the offence and by telephone, not letter. Of all BCS-recorded incidents, only 3 per cent resulted in some contact with Victim Support, and in 91 per cent of cases this contact was initiated by Victim Support (Ringham and Salisbury 2004: 11). Despite efforts to harmonize provision, there remains considerable diversity of local policy and practice, particularly as between inner-city and rural areas. The availability of volunteers also determines service provision; particularly since inner-city areas with the highest crime rates tend to furnish the fewest recruits. Although there has been a massive increase in government funding to Victim Support from £5,000 in 1979–80 to over £30 million in 2005 (although funding is now static) demand for services still outstrips resources. For example, the Victim Supportline launched in 1998 took over 15,500 calls during 2005, but more than double that number went unanswered for lack of volunteers (just over half of all calls were related to violent crime, while one-fifth came from people affected by domestic violence: www.victimsupport.org). Formally, Victim Support is committed to providing services to all victims and witnesses of crime (there has been, since 2003, a Witness Service in every criminal court in England and Wales): in practice it is obliged to balance this ideal with the targeting of limited resources to those most in need. Victim Support's focus has moved from concentrating on 'conventional' victims of burglary, robbery, and theft, to victims of sexual and violent crime and the families of murder victims (increasingly in cooperation with SAMM, see below) (Victim Support 2006).

Other established organizations include the National Society for the Prevention of Cruelty to Children (NSPCC) which, since 1884, has carried out campaigns, research, education, and community-based protection of abused children. The more recently founded (1986) Childline (which merged with the NSPCC in 2006) provides a free 24-hour helpline for children in distress or danger.

Refuges are an important source of support for victims of domestic violence. They grew out of the women's movement of the late 1960s and 1970s. The first refuge for battered women was established in 1972. Most local and regionally based services are coordinated through the Women's Aid Federation (founded in 1974). In 2001/02 refuges were provided for over 40,000 people, and nationally, over 140,000 women and their children were given outreach support. Another source is Refuge, an independent charity set up in 1979. It provides a home to 1,200 women and children, as well as helplines, outreach services, and advice centres, offering support, advice, and referrals to about 80,000 abused women and their children a year. In 2003/4 the National Domestic Violence Helpline answered approximately 74,000 calls. Funding of refuges is piecemeal and precarious with the result that provision is variable, heavily reliant on voluntary support, and often in poor-quality accommodation (Dobash and Dobash 1998).

Rape Crisis centres developed out of the same wave of re-emergent feminism in the 1970s, on a similar model to that of refuges. First opened in London and Birmingham, rape crisis centres spread nationwide offering emotional support and legal and medical advice to women who have been sexually assaulted or raped. With few funded posts, reliant mainly on the work of volunteers, rape crisis centres offered a 24-hour telephone helpline and provided face-to-face counselling. Committed also to educating and informing the public about rape, Rape Crisis has preferred the term survivor to victim. The Rape Crisis Federation was founded in 1996 as an umbrella organization for local rape crisis groups, a referral service to provide advice, information, and training to local groups, and campaigning on local issues of sexual violence. In 2003, however, the Home Office withdrew funding, forcing it to close, leaving many areas without support for rape victims (www.rapecrisis.org.uk). Support for victims of sexual offending is now channelled through the Victims' Fund introduced by the Domestic Violence, Crime and Victims Act 2004. Administered by the Home Office, the Victims' Fund provides £4 million, recovered from the proceeds of crime surcharge on all criminal convictions, and on fixed penalty notices, which could boost the total value of the Fund to up to £30 million. Priorities include developing and extending the network of Sexual Assault Referral Centres (SARCs) and grants of up to £50,000 to voluntary and community organizations (Home Office 2004).

New lobby groups promoting particular victims' interests continue to proliferate. The Zito Trust, which campaigns for victims of mentally disordered offenders; the tiny pressure group Justice for Victims, campaigning on behalf of the families of homicide victims; and Support After Murder and Manslaughter (SAMM), which primarily provides support after homicide, were launched in the mid-1990s. While some groups work with government for the advancement of victims' interests, others, notably Justice for Victims, are more confrontational and exigent in their promotion of victims' interests, and less mindful of the need to balance these against the rights of offenders. The victim movement is ideologically diverse. Relations between the groups range from close cooperation to outright hostility (Rock 1998a: 206–77). Despite, or perhaps because of, this heterogeneity, the combined impact of their endeavours has been considerable.

Although the victims movement in general has been careful to avoid political involvement in penal policy (indeed, Victim Support has eschewed the very title 'victims' movement'), certain victims organizations have been vociferous in their demand for greater severity in sentencing (Rock 1998a: 218). Vocal, determined, or resourceful victims can and have had a profound impact on politics and policy-making. Lobbying by some victim interest groups has contributed to a trend towards increasingly punitive policies. The victim has been invoked as a potent rhetorical device or symbolic tool to lever up punitiveness in what Ashworth calls 'victims in the service of severity' and Garland describes as 'the projected, politicized, image of "the victim" . . . as an all-purpose justification for measures of penal repression' (Ashworth 2000: 186; Garland 2001: 143; MacCormick and Garland 1998). Similarly, the naming of criminal laws and penal measures after individual victims (for example, 'Megan's Law' in America, and the (largely unsuccessful) campaign for 'Sarah's Law' in Britain) uses the plight of the victim to legitimate more extensive controls and new punitive measures (Wood 2005).

A more general political commitment to ' "rebalance" justice in favour of victims' and to promote 'victim's justice' is a central plank of government policy (Home Office 2002). One outcome is the Victims Advisory Panel (placed on a statutory footing by the Domestic Violence, Crime and Victims Act 2004). Chaired by the Minister of State with responsibility for victims' issues, the Panel brings together Ministers and officials, as well as representatives of victims' organizations, and 10 lay members, who have themselves been victims of crime, to discuss the impact of crime and to consider new government policies. It reports on the provision and implementation of victim and witness services and support (Victims Advisory Panel 2003/2004).

VICTIMS IN THE CRIMINAL JUSTICE PROCESS

The victim is fast becoming accepted as a key player in the criminal justice process. Acknowledgement of the victim's status as a party to the dispute (Christie 1977) and as an actor without whose cooperation in reporting crime, furnishing evidence, and acting as a witness in court, most crime would remain unknown and unpunished, has been a powerful driver of reform. Another is recognition that the process inflicts further or secondary psychological harms. Research has shown that insensitive questioning by police, poor information, delay, or unexplained decisions by the Crown Prosecution Service (CPS) to drop a case may compromise victims' willingness to cooperate and entail further suffering. This may lead them to withdraw from the criminal process and limit its ability to pursue cases effectively (Cretney and Davis 1997).

That victims' interests are not presently met is evidenced by, for example, by an international survey which suggests that about half of victims feel that the police 'did not do enough' about their crime (Van Kesteren et al. 2000: 7). Examination of Council of

Europe guidelines on the treatment of victims during criminal proceedings revealed that the majority of the 22 jurisdictions did not yet meet the criteria laid down (Brienen and Hoegen 2000). Such evidence has provided further support to efforts to grant victims' rights in the criminal process.

PUTTING RIGHTS INTO PRACTICE

To the extent it is possible to speak of rights for victims, they can be categorized under two headings. 'Service rights' refer to services to victims which do not affect procedure, such as information provided about case progress. 'Procedural rights', such as victims' rights of allocution, give victims a voice in the criminal process and may be detrimental to the defendant (Ashworth 2000; Cape 2004). Although we adopt this distinction as analytically useful, it breaks down in respect of those service rights that have procedural implications; for example, the screening of vulnerable victims in court may have an adverse impact on the defendant's right to a fair trial.

Service rights

In Britain, the Home Office has made progressive attempts to improve the ways in which victims are kept informed by police and prosecutors. Two *Victim's Charters* published in the 1990s (Home Office 1990 and 1996) set out standards of service to ensure that victims received better information about case progress, that their views were obtained and considered, and that they received proper facilities and assistance in court. The One Stop Shop (OSS) was introduced under the *Victim's Charter* 1996, partly in response to evidence that victims were dissatisfied with the quality of information about case progress. Under the OSS pilot the police were made responsible for providing victims with information throughout the case. In practice the scheme failed to live up to expectations. Information often came too late or the police were not able to explain decisions made by others (Hoyle *et al.* 1999: 41–2). Also, many serious crimes (including domestic violence) were excluded from the scheme, as were decisions relating to remands and bail conditions, leaving victims dissatisfied with information provision (Ringham and Salisbury 2004).

The Charters have been replaced by a Code of Practice introduced under the Domestic Violence, Crime and Victims Act 2004 (section 32). In force since April 2006, the Code sets out minimum standards of service that victims and witnesses can expect from criminal justice agencies. For example, most victims (the Code does not extend to corporate victims) have the right to information about the decisions relating to case progress. These include bail and remand decisions (whose omission under the OSS scheme had been a source of dissatisfaction to victims: Hoyle *et al.* 1998) which must be reported within specified timescales, shortened in the case of vulnerable or intimidated witnesses.[4]

---

[4] Vulnerable victims are defined as persons under the age of 17 and those with mental or physical disabilities. The definition of intimidated victims is very broad ranging, deriving from sociodemographic and offence-related factors that provide evidence of likely intimidation or potential further victimization.

For the small percentage of victims who are called as witnesses, there are further service rights: to render the trial less intimidating, prosecutors are supposed to introduce themselves and later explain the outcome. Yet witnesses remain at the mercy of questioning by defence counsel *and* prosecution alike. Attempts have been made to ameliorate the position of victims both through the provision of support and by statutory reform.

The Witness Service, run by Victim Support, covers all courts in England and Wales and provides advice, information, and support to help witnesses through the stress of a court appearance. It ensures better facilities, such as separate waiting areas, offers pre-trial visits to court, and helps witnesses make sense of the court process. Whilst improving the experiences of witnesses, especially immediately prior to the trial, arguably the Service is as much about improving witness attendance rates, thereby increasing the rate of timely guilty pleas and increasing successful prosecutions (indeed, much innovation done in the name of victims and witnesses has the ulterior purpose of increasing the efficiency of the system by encouraging victims to report crime and witnesses to testify more effectively and thereby increasing convictions). The Witness Service can do little to lessen the ordeal of cross-examination in the witness box and witness service volunteers may not be able adequately to explain court decisions (Riding 1999).

To resolve these problems, the Victims' Code of Practice introduced 165 Witness Care Units across England and Wales (Home Office 2005c). The units bring CPS and police together to provide 'better information, reassurance and support' to victims and witnesses and encourage their cooperation at trial. Witness Care Officers act as a single point of contact, providing information about case progress, and coordinating other support agencies. Pilot studies carried out in 2003 found that the Units improved witness attendance at court by nearly 20 per cent, reduced the number of trials adjourned due to witness difficulties by 27 per cent, and led to a 17 per cent drop in cracked trials. In addition, a 10-point Prosecutors' Pledge introduced in 2005 now provides for information, emotional and practical support, and court visits prior to trial (www.cps.gov.uk).

Recognition of the secondary victimization experienced by vulnerable witnesses such as rape victims, who can be subjected to intensive and degrading questioning, has led to many procedural innovations and changes in the rules of evidence (Temkin 2002; Hamlyn *et al.* 2004; Burton *et al.* 2006). Where children are witnesses, judges have long removed wigs and robes or come down from the bench; barristers have de-robed; quietly spoken victims or witnesses are provided with microphones; and provision has been made for the use of screens, of live video links, and pre-recorded videotaped interviews, all intended to reduce the stress to victims (Morgan and Zedner 1992: 128–44; Keenan *et al.* 1999; Choo 2006: 307–34). The government paper, *Speaking up for Justice* (Home Office 1998) made 78 recommendations to improve the treatment of vulnerable and intimidated witnesses in the criminal justice system. Some of these required administrative action, such as training, guidance, early police/CPS strategy meetings, and separate waiting areas. Others required legislation. The Youth Justice and Criminal

Evidence Act 1999, Pt II provides for vulnerable or intimidated witnesses to be screened in court, or to give evidence by live link or in camera; for the removal of gowns and wigs; for the clearing of the public gallery; for the use of communication aids; for the admissibility of video-recorded evidence-in-chief and cross-examination; and for the examination of witnesses through an intermediary (Ashworth 2000: 190–1; Birch 2000). It provides also for the protection of certain witnesses from cross-examination by the accused in person, and restricts the cross-examination of rape complainants about their sexual history. The Criminal Justice Act 2003 went further, allowing any witness to give evidence via a live video link.

National surveys of witnesses show that 78 per cent were fairly or very satisfied with their experience of the criminal justice system (Angle *et al.* 2003). Eighty-one per cent of witnesses had contact with the Witness Service and 95 per cent of these found it supportive. Fifty-seven per cent of witnesses had the opportunity to see the courtroom prior to trial and 83 per cent were kept in separate waiting rooms. Despite efforts to prevent intimidation, 26 per cent of witnesses still felt intimidated by individuals, and 21 per cent felt intimidated by the process or environment.

However, studies of vulnerable witnesses are not so encouraging. Whilst some research has shown that those who took advantage of 'special measures' introduced in the 1999 Act were less likely to feel anxious or distressed than those not using them, and that a third would not have been willing and able to give evidence without them (Hamlyn *et al.* 2004), a recent evaluation of provisions for vulnerable and intimidated witnesses suggests that the administrative and legislative measures in place are not fully implemented and leave significant unmet needs (Burton *et al.* 2006). These later findings are consistent with Hamlyn *et al.* in terms of increased satisfaction rates amongst witnesses, and show a greater use of special measures in court. Although Burton *et al.* suggest deficiencies in the implementation of measures, Cooper and Roberts (2005) found video-recorded evidence-in-chief, TV link and screens were commonly requested and made available. Early identification of vulnerable and intimidated witnesses by the police and CPS is vital if these measures are to be used appropriately. Burton *et al.* (2006) found that these organizations continue to experience difficulties identifying those in need. Although these various measures have improved the experience of giving evidence for some victims, they do not appear to have improved the conviction rate for rape victims, which has declined over the past few decades, with current figures showing that fewer than 6 per cent of rape cases reported to the police result in a conviction (Home Office 2006).

Procedural rights

Whilst few argue against service rights, procedural rights are contentious because they can threaten defendants' due process rights and undermine fairness (Hudson 2004). Arguments against allowing victims a greater say include: the intrusion of private views into public decision-making; limitations on prosecutorial discretion; the danger that the victim's subjective view undermines the court's objectivity; disparity in sentencing of similar cases depending on the resilience or punitiveness of the victim

(Ashworth 1993); and, lastly, that to increase their involvement may further burden victims while raising their expectations unrealistically (Justice 1998; Reeves and Mulley 2000: 138). Nevertheless, partly as a result of lobbying by some wings of the victims movement (Victim Support resolved from the first that it would not comment on sentences and sentencing), there has been a significant expansion of victims' rights to influence decisions in respect of cautioning and charging decisions, plea negotiations, sentencing, parole, and release. For example, witnesses are routinely consulted in respect of trial dates and bail decisions. Since 1990, the Probation Service has been under an obligation to contact the victims of life-sentenced prisoners, and since 1995 victims of other categories of prisoner, to ascertain if they have concerns about the conditions attached to the offender's release, which the Parole Board is required to take into account in determining licence conditions (Crawford and Enterkin 2001). The Code of Practice imposes more extensive obligations on the Probation Service to inform victims as to parole and release and take account of their wishes in respect of release conditions.

In Britain Victim Statements were introduced under the Victim's Charter 1996, inviting victims to state the physical, financial, psychological, social, or emotional effects the offence had on them or their family (Hoyle *et al*. 1999). The term 'victim statement' rather than 'victim impact statement' was deliberately chosen to distance the initiative from American statements of opinion (Morgan and Sanders 1999: 1). It is claimed that victim statements give victims a voice, enable their views to be heard and taken into account, and increase victim satisfaction, and thereby their cooperation (Sanders *et al*. 2001).

Advocates of victim input have argued that it promotes more informed, accurate, and democratic sentencing decisions; recognizes the victim's status as the person harmed by the offence; helps victims to recover; increases their satisfaction and cooperation with the criminal justice system; and can promote rehabilitation by confronting the offender with the impact of his or her crime (Tobolowsky 1999). Criminal justice practitioners generally welcomed victim statements, but were divided as to whether they should influence sentencing decisions, not least because information so provided was potentially irrelevant, exaggerated, or unverifiable (Hoyle *et al*. 1999: 3). It is unclear whether the fact that victim statements, appear seldom to influence sentencing decisions is a product of resistance by criminal justice professionals to victims' influence (Erez 1999; Erez and Rogers 1999), or because they are 'misconceived in principle and unsatisfactory in practice' (Sanders *et al*. 2001). Most opponents have argued that victim statements impair the objectivity of the process; shift the focus away from legitimate sentencing factors and towards inappropriate considerations of victim retaliation and vengeance; risk disparate and disproportionate sentencing; erode the prosecutor's function and control over the prosecution; or further traumatize victims by creating unmet expectations or by obliging them to participate in the sentencing process against their wishes (Ashworth 1993; Tobolowsky 1999).

The British government introduced a 'Victim Personal Statement Scheme' in 2001 (Home Office 2001) despite considerable weaknesses documented by researchers (Hoyle *et al*. 1999). Just four years later, the Victims' Code of Practice no longer requires the police to solicit victim personal statements,[5] except in respect of relatives of victims of murder and manslaughter who, it is proposed, should be able to make a personal statement in court (in person or via a public advocate) before sentence on how they have been affected by the crime (Home Office 2005a). Victim personal statements were introduced in Australia in the early 1990s (Cook *et al.* 1999) and have more recently been introduced in some European countries, for example the Netherlands and Poland (Wemmers 2005).

In the USA, the federal government and the majority of the states have constitutional or legislative provisions (or both) that require notification, to the victim, of important events and actions in the criminal process and allow, to varying degrees, crime victims to be present and to attend hearings at critical stages of the criminal process. Victims' right to be heard at sentencing has been widely adopted. The federal system and most states admit victim impact evidence though the prescribed content varies considerably. Some states explicitly authorize input only in regard to the direct physical, psychological, and financial impact of the crime whilst others admit opinions as to sentence (Blume 2003; Logan 2005). This latter right of allocution is clearly controversial (Bandes 1996; Arrigo and Williams 2003).

An area of particular controversy is the role of victim impact evidence in capital sentencing hearings. A recent decision of the US Supreme Court overruled previous judgments to pave the way for the admission of victim impact statements in death penalty cases (*Payne* v. *Tennessee*).[6] It remains unclear whether victims' opinions as to sentence are admissible, partly because the courts seem unable to distinguish between opinion testimony and victim impact evidence (Hoffmann 2003).

In Britain the emphasis has been on introducing procedural rights that do not involve victims in sentencing decisions. The Domestic Violence, Crime and Victims Act 2004 increased the protection, support, and rights of victims and witnesses, and created the role of Commissioner for Victims and Witnesses. The role of the Commissioner is to 'promote the interests of victims and witnesses' and 'take such steps as he considers appropriate with a view to encouraging good practice in the treatment of victims and witnesses' and to 'keep under review the operation of the Code of Practice' (section 49).

The extent to which these various reforms create rights for victims remains open to debate. The interests secured by the Victims' Charters of the 1990s were arguably better thought of as 'legitimate expectations' and 'standards' (Justice 1998). Similarly, the Human Rights Act 1998 lacks any clear statement of victims' rights (Ashworth 2000: 188; de Than 2003), although it has established that Articles of the European Convention on Human Rights (ECHR) relating to the protection of life, liberty, and security of a person may be invoked in relation to victims. In the prevailing rights culture, the balancing of victims' rights against the right of the defendant to a fair trial under Article 6 is a source of continuing academic debate and court jurisprudence (Ashworth 2000). Even though the Code of Practice sets out the 'obligations of service

---

[5] Personal communication from Lisa Vernon, Home Office, October 2005.

[6] 501 U.S. 808, 827 (1991).

providers' and institutes the office of Commissioner, failure to comply does not, of itself, result in liability to legal proceedings (Home Office 2005c). Although victims have the right to appeal to the Parliamentary Ombudsman should they feel that service providers have failed to abide by its provisions, the continuing limits of enforceability makes it questionable whether the Code generates substantive rights for victims.

Compensation

In Britain, victims retain their theoretical but rarely exercised right to damages against the offender in a civil action, but have no right in criminal proceedings to compensation. They have either to rely upon the court to make a compensation order or to make claims against the state Criminal Injuries Compensation Scheme. This said, state compensation in Britain receives more applicants and pays out more money than similar schemes in other European member states (Home Office 2005b).

Unlike in jurisdictions such as France or Germany where victims have the right to pursue civil claims for compensation within the criminal process, in Britain compensation is payable by the offender as an ancillary order to the main penalty in cases where 'injury, loss, or damage' had resulted (under the Criminal Justice Act 1972). The Criminal Justice Act 1982 made it possible to order compensation as the sole penalty and required that the payment of compensation take priority over the fine. These developments reflected the growing importance attached to reparation over retribution. The Criminal Justice Act 1988 further required courts to consider making a compensation order in every case of death, injury, loss, or damage and give reasons for not doing so. It also extended the range of injuries eligible for compensation.

Compensation orders may now be made in respect of personal injury; losses through theft of, or damage to, property; losses through fraud; loss of earnings while off work; medical expenses; travelling expenses; and pain and suffering. The court must take account of the offender's circumstances and ability to pay. In most cases, compensation orders are paid in full within 12 months, not least because the courts have wide powers to enforce payment, including imprisonment. In 2004 12,300 offenders were ordered to pay compensation. Over the period 1999 to 2004, the total number of offenders ordered to pay compensation at magistrates' courts decreased by 12 per cent from 43,800 to 38,400 for indictable offences and increased by 45 per cent from 54,800 to 79,300 for summary offences. At Crown Courts the total number of offenders ordered to pay compensation for indictable offences has remained stable for the past three years (Nicholas *et al.* 2005). The Criminal Justice Act 2003 makes it possible to order compensation pre-trial under conditional cautions.

Compensation is also made through the state-funded Criminal Injuries Compensation Scheme (CICS) set up in 1964 to make discretionary payments to victims, or the dependants of those who have died, of unlawful violence. Payments are made to reflect 'society's sense of responsibility for and sympathy with the blameless victims of crimes of violence' but explicitly not in recognition of any liability (CICA 2006). The scheme thus combines material compensation with a symbolic gesture of sympathy (Miers 1997: 12; Duff 1998: 107).

In an attempt to curb the spiralling cost of payments and improve administrative efficiency, a tariff scheme was introduced under the Criminal Injuries Compensation Act 1995 (Miers 2001b). The minimum award is set at £1,000 (effectively denying compensation to victims of minor assaults and robberies). The tariff groups injuries of comparable severity into 25 bands, each receiving a standard fixed payment (from £1,000 to £250,000). For those who are incapacitated as a result of their injury for 28 weeks or more, a separate payment for loss of earnings (or potential earnings) and for the cost of any necessary special care is available up to a maximum of £500,000. This leaves those unable to work for periods of less than 28 weeks without compensation (though they may receive relevant state benefits). Compensation is payable for loss of dependency in cases of fatal injury, together with a fixed award of £11,000 to the dependant (or £5,500 each if there is more than one). Critics argue that this is a derisory figure that demeans the value of the life that has been lost. But it is in fact marginally higher than the equally conventional sum payable in a civil action against the offender, against which the same criticism could be levelled.

The underlying issue concerns the scheme's purpose. It has been criticized for unduly limiting maximum awards, excluding consideration of the complexities of individual cases, failing to take full account of loss of earnings, and removing parity between state compensation payments and civil awards. When the tariff scheme was introduced in 1996, the Home Office was clear that it 'no longer tries to compensate victims in the same way as civil law damages, but simply provides a lump sum in recognition of the injury suffered' (Home Office 1999: 46). This clarity is, however, compromised by the continuing use of the word 'compensation' and of the provision of 'additional compensation'. These features inevitably create an expectation for victims that the scheme *will* deliver an award close to the outcome of a successful civil action, and equally inevitably invite criticism that victims of more serious and disabling injuries are under-compensated. Radical proposals to restructure the scheme (Home Office 2005b) create an opportunity to give its payments a name that does not use the word 'compensation' but which would both be more accurate as to their purpose and divorce them from unhelpful comparisons with civil actions (Miers 2006b).

Compensation is available only to victims of violence, though why they should be singled out for help denied other victims has long been a matter of debate (Ashworth 1986; Duff 1987; Miers 1997). The Domestic Violence, Crime and Victims Act 2004 (section 57) provides for the Criminal Injuries Compensation Authority to recover from offenders the money it has paid to their victims. The undoubted advantage of the CICS remains that victims are not dependent on the remote possibility that the offender will be identified, prosecuted, convicted, ordered to pay compensation, and have the means to pay.

A controversial aspect of the scheme is the regard given to the victim's character and history. The police play a significant role as gate-keepers: in deterring 'undeserving' victims from applying; failing to inform those they consider inappropriate claimants about the CICS; or giving information to the Authority which calls into question the legitimacy of claims (Newburn and Merry 1990; Miers 2000). Where an applicant behaved provocatively or has convictions for serious offences, however unconnected with the offence in question, compensation will generally be withheld. Those who fulfil the stereotypical picture of a deserving recipient or ideal victim may thus receive awards more readily than those who do not (Christie 1986; Miers 2000).

Recourse to the CICS by victims increased dramatically for most of its life, but numbers have declined in recent years. Whereas there were nearly 80,000 claims in 2001/02, the Criminal Injuries Compensation Authority (CICA) currently handles about 66,000 cases and pays out to victims approximately £170 million a year (Home Office 2005b). Concern about previous limitations of the scheme (Home Office 1999) led to the introduction of revisions in 2001, including an increase in the level of awards and some amendments to victims' eligibility. As claims continued to rise, so did expenditure on compensation payments. The government's response is the consultation document published in 2005 outlining plans to simplify the scheme. Whilst aiming to increase the amount of support provided to those most seriously injured by crime, it proposes to remove financial compensation to victims with less serious injuries and offer, in its place, practical support. This could include help with improving home security, immediate financial assistance with dental care and other costs, and access to counselling and other services for victims. The document also places an emphasis on more financial compensation from offenders and greater enforcement of compensation orders (Home Office 2005b).

Practical support for victims of crime will be managed by Victim Care Units to be established around the country. The government plans to work with Victim Support and other voluntary organizations to develop a range of help for victims including: paying for security upgrades in burglary cases; providing short-term financial help where the victim faces immediate hardship as a result of the crime; providing personal attack alarms to victims of violent crime; working with the local community and local authorities to improve security, e.g. CCTV and street lighting; liaising with housing, benefits, education, and social services to ensure that the victim's needs are fully understood and met; and help with claiming insurance or compensation, or dealing with other administration needed as a result of the crime (Home Office 2005b).

THE RISE OF RESTORATIVE JUSTICE

The proliferation of research about victims has raised larger questions about the purpose of criminal justice and the place of the victim within it. Victim surveys have consistently revealed that victims are no more punitive than the general public, and many are willing to engage in direct mediation, or to receive compensation from their offender (Mattinson and Mirrlees-Black 2000: 41). A recent poll shows that most victims want a criminal justice system that deters criminals and do not believe that custodial sentences do this. A majority favour community service and restorative meetings between victims and offenders over more punitive measures (http://www. icmresearch.co.uk/ reviews/2006; Travis 2006). There is clearly an appetite for restorative justice.

Restorative justice is an umbrella term for a variety of theories and practices which share the aim of repairing a wide range of harms, including material and psychological damage and damage to relationships and the general social order, caused by criminal behaviour (Hoyle and Young 2002b). Most restorative justice advocates agree that its core values include: respect; accountability; consensual participation and decision-making; and the inclusion and empowerment of all relevant parties (Young and Hoyle 2003a). The United Nations defines restorative justice as a process 'in which the victim, the offender and/or any other individuals or community members affected by a crime participate actively together in the resolution of matters arising from the crime' (Centre for International Crime Prevention (United Nations) 1999). In contrast to mediation, therefore, bi- or tri-partite resolution is replaced with a meeting of all those involved, however tangentially, facilitated by a youth justice coordinator, social worker, police officer, and occasionally a volunteer. The group discusses the offence, the circumstances underlying it, its effects on the victim and others, and how damaged relationships can be restored and the victim compensated.

BRIEF HISTORY OF RESTORATIVE JUSTICE

Restorative justice was primarily developed not from academic theory but by practitioners frustrated with conventional criminal justice practice (Johnstone 2003a). Practical attempts were made to draw on local indigenous practices with the aim of involving victims, reforming offenders, and repairing damaged communities (Marshall 1999). Nonetheless, some of those responsible for establishing and in particular promoting restorative practices have drawn on the work of academics who sought reorientation of the criminal justice system toward the victim. For example, the oft-cited article, 'Conflicts as Property', has been particularly influential (Christie 1977). Christie argued that crime not only is a wrong against society but often represents also a private wrong done by the offender to a specific victim and that to benefit from conflicts we must stop handing them over to professionals to resolve. This shift, it is claimed, would reduce reliance on punitive disposals and institute in their place positive attempts to rectify the harm caused by crime (Zehr 1990). Such writings have been used to justify practical attempts to put the victim at centre stage, a stakeholder, along with the offender and the wider community. They hark back to a mythical 'golden age' when victims were in control of the decision to prosecute and the presentation of their case (although the heyday of the victim was not quite as unsullied as some of its admirers imagine: Rock 2004b).

An important precursor to restorative justice was experiments with victim-offender mediation and reconciliation carried out in North America and Britain in the 1970s. The first victim-offender reconciliation programme was founded in Kitchener,

Ontario, in 1974 (Peachey 1989). Later, various community programmes brought victims and offenders together, usually after a court had passed sentence, to facilitate individual reparation and reconciliation. By the mid-1990s there were over 300 such programmes in North America and a number of similar schemes in England and Wales (Dignan and Marsh 2001). The 1980s saw the first attempts to include the wider community in such programmes. For example, sentencing circles, group mediation involving the affected parties and the wider community, were inspired by indigenous Canadian peacemaking processes (Lilles 1996). From these local, indigenous practices emerged family group conferences, meetings that involve the family of the offender, the victim, and a trained facilitator.

New Zealand was the first country to put family group restorative conferences into a statutory framework. The New Zealand Children, Young Persons and their Families Act introduced the new youth justice system in 1989, the same year that Braithwaite's seminal book, *Crime, Shame and Reintegration* was published. Conferencing in New Zealand, together with Braithwaite's theory of reintegrative shaming, led to the transfer of the New Zealand model to Wagga Wagga, New South Wales, albeit with conferences facilitated by the police (Daly 2001). In 1991 the renowned 'effective cautioning' scheme began in Wagga Wagga to caution juvenile offenders according to restorative principles (Moore and O'Connell 1994). This was later introduced to the UK, via the Thames Valley Police restorative cautioning scheme, and has since been influential in informing some restorative practices in the youth justice system, in particular the final warning scheme, introduced under the Crime and Disorder Act 1998 (Hoyle 2006) (although there are tensions between attempts to introduce restorative measures and the increasing use of prison for juveniles, see Morgan and Newburn, Chapter 30, this volume).

Unlike legislators in New Zealand and in most Australian states and territories, the UK Labour government strongly endorsed police-led restorative cautioning, as practised in Thames Valley (Young and Goold 1999). It introduced various new youth justice measures which involved the police and other key agencies in restorative justice (Crawford and Newburn 2003). The Crime and Disorder Act 1998 replaced police cautions for young offenders with reprimands and warnings, which are supposed to be delivered according to restorative principles under the auspices of youth offending teams (section 39), and it introduced reparation orders (section 67), which require young offenders to make reparation to the victim or community at large. In making the order, the court is reminded to take into account the victim's views, and reparation should not be ordered without their explicit consent (Fionda 2005). Following the advice of the report of the Home Office sentencing review (Halliday 2001: 21), and the Auld review of the criminal courts (Auld 2001), the government introduced the conditional caution under the Criminal Justice Act 2003 (Part 3, sections 22–7). This disposal for adult offenders includes reparative or restorative conditions stipulated by the police and approved by the Crown Prosecution Service. Indeed, this Act (section 142), reflecting the restorative principles endorsed in the White Paper, *Justice for All* (Home Office 2002), makes clear that one of the statutory purposes of sentencing in general is the making of reparation by offenders to persons affected by their offences.

Whilst academic and political attention has focused on restorative processes with young offenders (Hoyle *et al.* 2002; Fionda 2005), there has been less consideration of its potential in respect of adults and in difficult cases, such as sexual, racial, or domestic violence, or homicide. This has started to change with restorative experiments being carried out in prisons (Van Ness 2006), between victims and people convicted of serious offences (Shapland *et al.* 2006); with victims of sexual and racial crimes (Hudson 1998; Daly 2006); with victims of domestic violence (Strang and Braithwaite 2002); with families of homicide victims (Umbreit *et al.* 2003), including those cases where the offender is awaiting execution (Umbreit and Vos 2000); with disputes and bullying in schools (Morrison 2006); with complaints against the police (Young *et al.* 2005); and with victims of state-sponsored violence, human rights abuses, and even genocide (Drumbl 2002; Roche 2002; Froestad and Shearing 2006; Llewellyn 2006). These diverse initiatives share a commitment to bring victims, and others harmed by criminal or offensive behaviour, into contact with offenders and other interested members of the community, and to provide opportunities for material and symbolic reparation. This being so, they have the potential, at least, to restore victims and to reintegrate offenders (Hoyle and Young 2003).

RESTORATIVE JUSTICE: A VICTIM-CENTRIC APPROACH?

Restorative justice, more than any other initiative since the establishment of the modern criminal justice system, has the power to reinstate the victim centre stage with the offender, and the majority of victims claim that this is where they want to be (Travis 2006). Research suggests that many victims want a less formal process where their views count, more information about both the progress and the outcome of their case, to participate in its resolution, and to receive material reparation and emotional restoration, including an apology (Strang 2002).

Despite concerns expressed by both critics and advocates about the role of victims in restorative justice, a consistent picture of high aggregate victim satisfaction with police-led processes emerges from the research: for example, over 90 per cent of victims in the scheme in Wagga Wagga, New South Wales, were satisfied, and 96 per cent in a similar scheme in the USA (McCold and Wachtel 2002). At their best, restorative encounters appear to alleviate victims' feelings of anger or fear towards their offender, or crime more generally, and bring about genuine remorse on the part of the offender, encouraging a greater sense of victim empathy. Victims can, and often do, receive explanations, apologies, and occasionally compensation. In the Thames Valley Police restorative cautioning initiative the therapeutic benefits to victims of attending restorative sessions were clear. The overwhelming majority of victims who participated felt satisfied with the process, and fear of, or anger with, the offender had generally disappeared. Ninety-two per cent said that the meeting had been a good idea, with only one victim feeling marginally worse for having attended (Hoyle *et al.* 2002).

Levels of victim participation in restorative justice schemes are typically low. Research on youth offender panels, part of referral orders, established under the Youth

Justice and Criminal Evidence Act 1999, found that victims attended panel meetings in fewer than 7 per cent of cases, partly due to failures of communication (Newburn *et al.* 2002). A restorative cautioning scheme in Mountpottinger, Northern Ireland, also brought offenders together with victims in only 7 per cent of cases (O'Mahony *et al.* 2002). The Thames Valley Police restorative cautioning scheme was a little more successful, managing to get 14 per cent of victims to conferences (Hoyle *et al.* 2002). However one recent initiative achieved victim participation in 91 per cent of conferences (Shapland *et al.* 2006). Likewise, in New Zealand victims attended about half of all family group conferences (Morris and Maxwell 2000: 211), and in Canberra they attended in about 80 per cent of cases (Strang 2002: 121).

Since victims express an interest in meeting with offenders and generally benefit from those encounters, it is possible that the low victim participation rates in many schemes result from failures of communication. Data from the Thames Valley suggest that whilst some victims choose not to participate through fears of retaliation or because of practical constraints upon their time, others were not provided with sufficient information about the planned session to make an informed choice about whether to attend (Hoyle 2002). Hence, they were effectively excluded from the process.

Where victims want to communicate with the offender, but not to take part in a restorative session, alternative means of communication should be found. In the Thames Valley such processes were not carried out at all or were carried out inadequately. Often the facilitator failed accurately to reflect the victim's experiences and wishes in presenting a victim statement, and misleading information was passed on to the conference participants. Frequent failures to provide feedback information about the restorative sessions to those victims resulted in their feeling irate and excluded (Hoyle 2002).

To judge the success of restorative justice schemes by reference only to victim participation rates might encourage undesirable pressure upon victims to take part. But on current evidence it is far from clear that restorative justice is centrally, or even principally, about victims. One review of restorative justice programmes in 12 European countries found that only one country (Denmark) claimed to be victim oriented; a further five are offender oriented; in two countries the orientation varies with the particular programme; and in the remaining four the orientation is mixed (Miers 2001a: 79).

The question then arises: how much is restorative justice promoted in the interests of victims and how much in the interest of offenders or crime reduction? Certainly research on the latter is inconclusive. Data from New Zealand and Australia suggest that restorative justice may have some crime-reductive effect, at least in some types of case. Maxwell and Morris (2001), in New Zealand, found evidence consistent with a reduction in reoffending even when other important factors such as adverse early experiences and subsequent life events were taken into account. When compared to court, restorative conferences in Canberra were found to result in a substantial reduction in reoffending rates by violent offenders, a small increase in offending by drink drivers, and no difference in repeat offending by juvenile property offenders or shoplifters

(Sherman *et al.* 2000). However, research on the Thames Valley restorative cautioning scheme found insufficient evidence to prove it was more effective than traditional cautioning in reducing re-sanctioning rates. Furthermore, there were no significant differences in the frequency or seriousness of subsequent offending between offenders who met their victims and those who went through a restorative caution without the victim present (Wilcox *et al.* 2004).

Research suggests other benefits such as improvements in offenders' relationships with their families; reductions in truanting and exclusions from schools; and reductions in offending and/or changes in offending behaviour which, whilst not amounting to desistance, clearly indicate a move away from recidivism and towards cessation of particularly unacceptable behaviour (Hoyle and Young 2002b). But these are primarily benefits for offenders and the wider community. Ashworth has therefore warned of the dangers of 'victim prostitution' in restorative justice (Ashworth 2000: 186), whereby victims are used as a means to diversion and crime reduction, not as ends in themselves (Young and Goold 1999).

The most difficult questions, not yet answered to the satisfaction of either critics or advocates, concern the place of restorative justice in the criminal justice system and, in particular, its relationship to the state, including who should facilitate meetings and whether outcomes should be guided by principles of proportionality (Young and Hoyle 2003b; Hoyle 2006). Restorative principles have historically been incorporated somewhat awkwardly into the existing punitive framework (Zedner 1994; Brown 2001). Opinions differ as to the extent to which restorative justice should be bound by principles of due process. On the issue of proportionality, for example, there are those who regard it as paramount (Ashworth 2002) and those who do not (Braithwaite 2002), with others arguing for reparative processes and outcomes within upper and lower limits of proportionality (Cavadino and Dignan 1997; Ashworth 2002; Braithwaite 2002). Questions of proportionality and access to legal advice are not only relevant to offenders, they also concern victims, the wider community, and the public interest in cases where victims feel coerced into agreeing to disproportionately low reparation, where deliberative accountability has failed (Roche 2003).

The problems entailed in reorienting the criminal justice system towards the victim by means of restorative justice have not passed unobserved (Ashworth 1986; von Hirsch *et al.* 2003). Objections include: that it has no penal character; that to secure reinstatement to the victim is no more than the enforcement of a civil liability; and that by focusing on harm, it fails to take sufficient account of the offender's culpability. Looking at the sentencing practice of the Courts of Appeal in cases which have involved restorative processes, Edwards (2006) demonstrates potential incompatibilities between restorative values, in particular between allowing victims rights of allocution regarding sentence, and sentencing principles of proportionality, consistency, and objectivity. In practice the low participation of victims in many restorative initiatives leaves open the question of how far restorative justice practice, as opposed to theory, is victim centred.

CONCLUSION

Victims of conventional crimes now attract an unprecedented level of interest, both as a subject of criminological enquiry and as a focus of criminal justice policy. It remains the case that some victims of violence, such as those caught up in civil war, genocide, or other conflicts are only at the fringes of criminological concern, especially in the West. Far from being simply a compartmentalized topic, victim research has had an impact upon every aspect of criminological thinking and has profoundly altered our picture of crime by uncovering a vast array of hidden offences, many against the most vulnerable members of society. Academic scholarship has shifted, over the last few years, with less attention given to the impact of crime on victims, psychological or otherwise, and more focus on contentious questions about the role of victims in the criminal process. Political pressure, too, has raised the victim's profile, ensuring recognition of victim needs and stressing the importance of victim services. It has greatly expanded the role of compensation, provision of services, and information, and has allowed victims' interests to inform key decisions in the criminal justice process. At a time when the impulse to punish dominates, the current commitment to restorative justice, especially for young offenders, is an important countertrend. How far restorative justice serves the interests of victims, however, remains a matter of live debate.

■ SELECTED FURTHER READING

Goodey, *Victims and Victimology: Research, Policy and Practice* (Pearson Education, 2005) and Dignan, *Understanding Victims and Restorative Justice* (Open University Press, 2005) are both good overviews of the subject. On the problems entailed in researching victims see Walklate, 'Researching Victims', in King and Wincup (eds), *Doing Research on Crime and Justice* (Oxford University Press, 2000). For contemporary academic, policy, and political debates on the nature, extent, and impact of criminal victimization and policy responses to it see Walklate, *Handbook on Victims and Victimology* (Willan, 2007, forthcoming). On the development of the victims' movement, see Rock, *Constructing Victims' Rights: The Home Office, New Labour, and Victims* (Oxford University Press, 2004). Good collections of essays include Crawford and Goodey, *Integrating a Victim Perspective within Criminal Justice* (Ashgate Dartmouth, 2000) and Hoyle and Young, *New Visions of Crime Victims* (Hart Publishing, 2002). The role of the victim in the criminal justice system is an area of lively debate (Cape, *Reconcilable Rights? Analysing the Tension between Victims and Defendants*, Legal Action Group, 2004). Classic texts, including Christie's 'Conflicts as Property', can be found in Johnstone, *A Restorative Justice Reader: Texts, Sources, Context* (Willan, 2003). On restorative justice see Braithwaite, *Crime, Shame and Reintegration* (Cambridge University Press, 1989) and Braithwaite, 'Restorative Justice: Assessing Optimistic and Pessimistic Accounts', *Crime and Justice* (1999), and Strang, *Repair or Revenge: Victims and Restorative Justice* (Clarendon Press, 2002). For an overview of its international development see Miers, 'The International Development of Restorative Justice: A Comparative Review', in Johnstone and van Ness (eds), *Restorative Justice Handbook* (Willan, 2006). Of the many edited collections on restorative justice, its potential, and its limits, see von Hirsch *et al.*, *Restorative Justice and Criminal Justice: Competing or Reconcilable Paradigms?* (Hart Publishing, 2003) and Johnstone and Van Ness, *Handbook of Restorative Justice* (Willan, 2006).

■ REFERENCES

ALLEN, S. (2002), 'Male Victims of Rape: Responses to a Perceived Threat to Masculinity', in C. Hoyle and R. Young (eds), *New Visions of Crime Victims*, 23–48, Oxford: Hart.

ALVAZZI DEL FRATE, F., and VAN KESTEREN, J. N. (2004), *Criminal Victimisation in Urban Europe. Key Findings of the 2000 International Crime Victims Survey*, Turin: UNICRI.

AMIR, M. (1971), *Patterns of Forcible Rape*, Chicago: University of Chicago Press.

Amnesty International (2005), *Amnesty International Report 2005: the state of the world's human rights*, London: Amnesty International Publications.

ANGLE, H., MALAM, S., and CAREY, C. (2003), *Key Findings from the Witness Satisfaction Survey 2002*, London: HMSO.

ARRIGO, B. A., and WILLIAMS, C. R. (2003), 'Victim Vices, Victim Voices, and Impact Statements: On the Place of Emotion and the Role of Restorative Justice in Capital Sentencing', *Crime and Delinquency*, 49(4): 603–26.

ASHWORTH, A. (1986), 'Punishment and Compensation: Victims, Offenders and the State', *Oxford Journal of Legal Studies*, 6: 86–122.

——(1993), 'Victim Impact Statements and Sentencing', *Criminal Law Review*, 498–509.

——(2000), 'Victims' Rights, Defendants' Rights and Criminal Procedure', in A. Crawford and J. Goodey (eds), *Integrating a Victim Perspective within Criminal Justice*, Aldershot: Ashgate Dartmouth.

——(2002), 'Responsibilities, Rights and Restorative Justice', *British Journal of Criminology*, 42(3): 578–95.

AULD, R. (2001), *Review of the Criminal Courts of England and Wales, Summary*, www.criminal-courts-review.org.uk/summary.htm.

BANDES, S. (1996), 'Empathy, Narrative, and Victim Impact Statements', *University of Chicago Law Review*, 63(2): 361–412.

BIRCH, D. J. (2000), 'A Better Deal for Vulnerable Witnesses', *Criminal Law Review*, 223–49.

BLUME, J. H. (2003), 'Ten Years of Payne: Victim Impact Evidence in Capital Cases', *Cornell Law Review*, 88(2): 257–81.

BORER, T. A. (2003), 'A Taxonomy of Victims and Perpetrators: Human Rights and Reconciliation in South Africa', *Human Rights Quarterly*, 25(4): 1088–1116.

BOWLING, B. (1998), *Violent Racism: Victimization, Policing, and Social Context*, Oxford: Clarendon Press.

BRAITHWAITE, J. (1989), *Crime, Shame and Reintegration*, Cambridge: Cambridge University Press.

——(1999), 'Restorative Justice: Assessing Optimistic and Pessimistic Accounts', *Crime and Justice*, 25: 1–127.

——(2002), 'In Search of Restorative Jurisprudence', in L. Walgrave (ed.), *Restorative Justice and the Law*, 150–67, Cullompton, Devon: Willan.

BRIENEN, M. E. I., and HOEGEN, E. H. (2000), *Victims of Crime in 22 European Criminal Justice Systems: The Implementation of Recommendation (85)11 of the Council of Europe on the Position of the Victim in the Framework of Criminal Law and Procedure*, Nijmegen: Wolf Legal Productions.

BROGDEN, M., and NIJHAR, P. (2000), *Crime, Abuse and the Elderly*, Cullompton, Devon: Willan.

BROWN, S. P. (2001), 'Punishment and the Restoration of Rights', *Punishment and Society*, 3(4): 485–500.

BURMAN, S., and ALLEN-MEARES, P. (1994), 'Neglected Victims of Murder: Children's Witness to Parental Homicide', *Social Work Monographs*, 39: 28–34.

BURTON, M., EVANS, R., and SANDERS, A. (2006), 'Implementing Special Measures for Vulnerable and Intimidated Witnesses: The Problem of Identification', *Criminal Law Review*, 229–40.

CAPE, E. (ed.) (2004), *Reconcilable Rights? analysing the tension between victims and defendants*, London: Legal Action Group.

CATALANO, S. (2005), *Criminal Victimisation, 2004. Bureau of Justice Statistics National Crime Victimisation Survey*, Washington, DC: US Department of Justice.

CAVADINO, M., and DIGNAN, J. (1997), 'Reparation, Retribution and Rights', *International Review of Victimology*, 4(4): 233–54.

CAVANAGH, K., DOBASH, R., and DOBASH, R. P. (2005), 'Men Who Murder Children Inside and Outside the Family', *British Journal of Social Work*, 35(5): 667–88.

Centre for International Crime Prevention (United Nations) (1999), *Draft Declaration on Basic Principles on the Use of Restorative Justice Programmes in Criminal Matters*, New York: UN, United States. Office of Justice Programs. Office for Victims of Crime.

CHOO, A. (2006), *Evidence*, Oxford: Oxford University Press.

CHRISTIE, N. (1977), 'Conflicts as Property', *British Journal of Criminology*, 17(1): 1–15.

——(1986), 'The Ideal Victim', in E. Fattah (ed.), *From Crime Policy to Victim Policy*, 1–17, London: Macmillan.

CICA (2006), *Criminal Injuries Compensation Authority: ninth annual report and accounts for the year ended 31 March 2005*, London: The Stationery Office.

COHEN, S. (2001), *States of Denial: Knowing about Atrocities and Suffering*, Cambridge: Polity Press.

Commission for Racial Equality (1988), *Learning in Terror: A Survey of Racial Harassment in Schools and Colleges*, London: Commission for Racial Equality.

COOK, B., DAVID, F., and GRANT, A. (1999), *Victims' Needs, Victims' Rights: Policies and Programs for Victims of Crime in Australia, Research and Public Policy Series No.19*, Canberra: Australian Institute of Criminology.

COOMARASWAMY, R. (2000), *Integration of the Human Rights of Women and the Gender Perspective. Violence against Women, (Report of the Special Rapporteur on Violence against Women)*, New York: United Nations, Economic and Social Council, Commission on Human Rights.

COOPER, D., and ROBERTS, P. (2005), *Special Measures for Vulnerable and Intimidated Witnesses*, Nottingham: University of Nottingham School of Law.

CRAWFORD, A., and GOODEY, J. (eds) (2000), *Integrating a Victim Perspective within Criminal Justice*, Aldershot: Ashgate Dartmouth.

——and ENTERKIN, J. (2001), 'Victim Contact Work in the Probation Service: Paradigm Shift or Pandora's Box?', *British Journal of Criminology*, 41(4): 707–25.

——and NEWBURN, T. (2003), *Youth Offending and Restorative Justice: implementing reform in youth justice*, Cullompton, Devon: Willan.

——, JONES, T., WOODHOUSE, T., and YOUNG, J. (1990), *Second Islington Crime Survey*, Middlesex: Middlesex Polytechnic.

CRETNEY, A., and DAVIS, G. (1997), 'Prosecuting Domestic Assault: Victims Failing Courts, or Courts Failing Victims?', *Howard Journal of Criminal Justice*, 36(2): 146–57.

DALY, K. (2001), 'Conferencing in Australia and New Zealand: Variations, Research Findings and Prospects', in A. Morris and G. M. Maxwell (eds), *Restorative Justice for Juveniles: Conferencing Mediation and Circles*, Oxford: Hart.

——(2006), 'Feminist engagement with restorative justice', *Theoretical Criminology*, 10(1).

DE THAN, C. (2003), 'Positive Obligations under the European Convention on Human Rights: Towards the Human Rights of Victims and Vulnerable Witnesses?', *Journal of Criminal Law*, 67(2): 165–82.

DIGNAN, J. (2005), *Understanding Victims and Restorative Justice*, Maidenhead: Open University Press.

——and MARSH, P. (2001), 'Restorative Justice and Family Group Conferences in England', in A. Morris and G. Maxwell (eds), *Restorative Justice for Juveniles: Conferencing, Mediation and Circles*, 85–101, Oxford: Hart.

DOBASH, R. E., and DOBASH, R. P. (1998), *Rethinking Violence Against Women*, Thousand Oaks, Cal., London: Sage.

DOBASH, R. P. and DOBASH, R. E. (2004), 'Women's Violence to Men in Intimate Relationships', *British Journal of Criminology*, 44(3): 324–49.

DONALDSON, R. (2003), *Experiences of Burgled Older People, Home Office Findings 198*, London: Home Office.

DRUMBL, M. A. (2002), 'Restorative Justice and Collective Responsibility: Lessons For and From the Rwandan Genocide', *Contemporary Justice Review*, 5(1): 5–22.

DUFF, P. (1987), 'Criminal Injuries Compensation and "Violent" Crime', *Criminal Law Review*, 219–30.

——(1998), 'The Measure of Criminal Injuries Compensation: Political Pragmatism or Dog's

Dinner?', *Oxford Journal of Legal Studies*, 18(1): 105–42.

EDGAR, K., and O'DONNELL, I. (1998), 'Assault in Prison: The "Victim's" Contribution', *British Journal of Criminology*, 38(4): 635–50.

EDWARDS, I. (2006), 'Restorative Justice, Sentencing and the Court of Appeal', *Criminal Law Review*, 110–23.

ELEY, S. (2005), 'Changing Practices: The Specialised Domestic Violence Court Process', *Howard Journal of Criminal Justice*, 44(2): 113–24.

ELLISON, L. (2003), 'Responding to Victim Withdrawal in Domestic Violence Prosecutions', *Criminal Law Review*, 760–72.

EREZ, E. (1999), 'Who's Afraid of The Big Bad Victim? Victim Impact Statements as Victim Empowerment and Enhancement of Justice', *Criminal Law Review*, 545–56.

——and ROGERS, L. (1999), 'Victim Impact Statements and Sentencing Outcomes and Processes: The Perspectives of Legal Professionals', *British Journal of Criminology*, 39(2): 216–39.

ERICSON, K. (1994), *A New Species of Trouble: The Human Experience of Modern Disasters*, New York: W.W. Norton and Co.

FALSETTI, S. A., and RESNICK, S. H. (1995), 'Helping the Victims of Violent Crime', in S. E. Hobfoll (ed.), *Traumatic Stress: From theory to practice*, 263–85, New York: Plenum Press.

FARRELL, G., and PEASE, K. (2001), *Repeat Victimization*, Monsey, NY: Criminal Justice Press.

FATTAH, E. A. (1991), *Understanding Criminal Victimization : an introduction to theoretical victimology*, Scarborough, Ont.: Prentice-Hall Canada.

FERRARO, K. F. (1995), *Fear of Crime : Interpreting Victimization Risk*, Albany, NY: State University of New York Press.

FINKELHOR, D., and ARAJI, S. (1986), *A Sourcebook on Child Sexual Abuse*, Newbury Park: Sage Publications.

FIONDA, J. (2005), *Devils and Angels: Youth Policy and Crime*, Oxford: Hart.

FISHER, B. S., CULLEN, F. T., and DAIGLE, L. E. (2005), 'The Discovery of Acquaintance Rape', *Journal of Interpersonal Violence*, 20: 493–500.

FOLLETTE, V., POLUSNY, M., BECHTLE, A., and NAUGLE, A. (1996), 'Cumulative Trauma: The Impact of Child Sexual Abuse, adult sexual assault, and spouse abuse', *Journal of Traumatic Stress*, 925–35.

FRENCH, B., and CAMPBELL, P. (2005), *Crime Victimisation in Northern Ireland: Findings from the 2003/2004 Northern Ireland Crime Survey*, Northern Ireland Office.

FROESTAD, J., and SHEARING, C. (2006), 'Conflict Resolution in South Africa: a case study', in G. Johnstone and D. Van Ness (eds), *Handbook of Restorative Justice*, Cullompton, Devon: Willan.

GARLAND, D. (2001), *The Culture of Control: Crime and Social Order in Contemporary Society*, Oxford: Oxford University Press.

GOODEY, J. (1997), 'Boys Don't Cry: Masculinities, Fear of Crime and Fearlessness', *British Journal of Criminology*, 37(3): 401–18.

——(2005), *Victims and Victimology: Research, Policy and Practice*, Harlow: Pearson Education.

GRADY, A. (2002), 'Female-on-Male Domestic Abuse: Uncommon or Ignored?', in C. Hoyle and R. Young (eds), *New Visions of Crime Victims*, 71–96, Oxford: Hart.

GREEN, P., and WARD, T. (2005), 'Introduction', *British Journal of Criminology*, 45(4): 431–33.

HAGAN, J., RYMOND-RICHMOND, W., and PARKER, P. (2005), 'The Criminology of Genocide: The Death and Rape of Darfur', *Criminology*, 43: 525–62.

HALLIDAY, J. (2001), *Making Punishments Work: Report of the Review of the Sentencing Framework for England and Wales*, London: Home Office.

HAMILL, H. (2002), 'Victims of Paramilitary Punishment Attacks in Belfast', in C. Hoyle and R. Young (eds), *New Visions of Crime Victims*, 49–70, Oxford: Hart.

HAMLYN, B., PHELPS, A., and SATTAR, G. (2004), *Key Findings from the Surveys of Vulnerable and Intimidated Witnesses 2000/01 and 2003*, London: HMSO.

HARTLESS, J., DITTON, J., NAIR, G., and PHILLIPS, S. (1995), 'More Sinned Against than Sinning: A Study of Young Teenagers' Experience of Crime', *British Journal of Criminology*, 35(1): 114–33.

HILLYARD, P., PANTAZIS, C., TOOMBS, S., GORDON, D., and DORLING, D. (2005), *Criminal Obsessions: Why Harm Matters More than Crime*, London: Crime and Society Foundation.

HODGKINSON, P. (2004), 'Victims: Meeting the Needs of the Families of the Homicide Victim and the Condemned', in P. Hodgkinson and W. Schabas (eds), *Capital Punishment: Strategies for Abolition*, 332–58, Cambridge: Cambridge University Press.

HOFFMANN, J. L. (2003), 'Revenge or Mercy? Some Thoughts about Survivor Opinion Evidence in Death Penalty Cases', *Cornell Law Review*, 88(2): 530–42.

HOME OFFICE (1990), *Victim's Charter: A Statement of the Rights of Victims*, London: HMSO.

—— (1996), *Victim's Charter*, London: HMSO.

—— (1998), *Speaking up for Justice: Report of the Interdepartmental Working Group on the Treatment of Vulnerable and Intimidated Witnesses in the Criminal Justice System*, London: Home Office.

—— (1999), *Compensation for Victims of Violent Crime: Possible Changes to the Criminal Injuries Compensation Scheme*, London: Home Office.

—— (2001), *Victim Personal Statement Scheme: Circular 35/2001*, London: HMSO.

—— (2002), *Justice for All*, London, HMSO.

—— (2004), *Cutting Crime, Delivering Justice A Strategic Plan for Criminal Justice 2004–08*, London: Home Office.

—— (2005a), *Hearing the Relatives of Murder and Manslaughter Victims: Consultation Document*, London, Home Office, Criminal Justice System: 28.

—— (2005b), *Rebuilding Lives: supporting victims of crime*, London: Home Office, Criminal Justice System.

—— (2005c), *Victims' Code of Practice*, London: HMSO.

—— (2006), *Convicting Rapists and Protecting Victims—Justice for Victims of Rape, A Consultation Paper*, London: Home Office, Office for Criminal Justice Reform.

HOPE, T., BRYAN, J., TRICKETT, A., and OSBORN, D. R. (2001), 'The Phenomena of Multiple Victimization: The Relationship between Personal and Property Crime Risk', *British Journal of Criminology*, 41(4): 595–617.

HOUGH, M., and MAYHEW, P. (1983), *The British Crime Survey: First Report, HORS No. 76*, London: Home Office, HMSO.

HOYLE, C. (2000), *Negotiating Domestic Violence: police, criminal justice, and victims*, Oxford: Oxford University Press.

—— (2002), 'Securing Restorative Justice for the "Non-Participating" Victim', in C. Hoyle and R. Young (eds), *New Visions of Crime Victims*, 97–132, Oxford: Hart.

—— (2006), 'Policing and Restorative Justice', in G. Johnstone and D. Van Ness (eds), *Handbook of Restorative Justice*, Cullompton, Devon: Willan.

—— and SANDERS, A. (2000), 'Police Response to Domestic Violence: From Victim Choice to Victim Empowerment?', *British Journal of Criminology*, 40(1): 14–36.

—— and YOUNG, R. (2002a), *New Visions of Crime Victims*, Oxford: Hart.

—— and —— (2002b), 'Restorative Justice: assessing the prospects and pitfalls', in M. McConville and G. Wilson (eds), *The Handbook of the Criminal Justice Process*, 525–48, Oxford: Oxford University Press.

—— and —— (2003), 'Restorative Justice, Victims and the Police', in T. Newburn (ed.), *Handbook of Policing*, 680–706, Cullompton, Devon: Willan.

——, MORGAN, R., and SANDERS, A. (1999), *The Victim's Charter: an evaluation of pilot projects*, London: Home Office.

——, YOUNG, R., and HILL, R. (2002), *Proceed with Caution: an evaluation of the Thames Valley Police initiative in restorative cautioning*, York: York Publishing Services.

——, CAPE, E., MORGAN, R., and SANDERS, A. (eds), (1998), *Evaluation of the "One-Stop Shop" and Victim Statement Pilot Projects*, London: Home Office.

HUDSON, B. (1998), 'Restorative Justice: The Challenge of Sexual and Racial Violence', *Journal of Law and Society*, 25(2): 237.

—— (2004), 'Balancing the Rights of Victims and Offenders', in E. Cape (ed.), *Reconcilable Rights? Analysing the Tension between Victims and Defendants*, 125–36, London: Legal Action Group.

JAMIESON, R. (1998), 'Towards a Criminology of War in Europe', in V. Ruggiero, N. South, and I. Taylor (eds), *The New European Criminology*, 480–506, London: Routledge.

JOHNSTONE, G. (2003a), 'Introduction', in G. Johnstone (ed.), *A Restorative Justice Reader: Texts, Sources, Context*, 1–18, Cullompton, Devon: Willan.

—— (2003b), *A Restorative Justice Reader: Texts, Sources, Context*, Cullompton, Devon: Willan.

—— and VAN NESS, D. (eds) (2006), *Handbook of Restorative Justice*, Cullompton, Devon: Willan.

JUSTICE (1998), *Victims in Criminal Justice: Report of the Justice Committee on the Role of Victims in Criminal Justice*, London: Justice.

KEENAN, C., DAVIS, G., HOYANO, L., and MAITLAND, L. (1999), 'Interviewing Allegedly Abused Children with a View to a Criminal Prosecution', *Criminal Law Review*, 863–73.

KELLY, L. (1988), *Surviving Sexual Violence*, Cambridge: Polity Press.

KOFFMAN, L. (1996), *Crime surveys and victims of crime*, Cardiff: University of Wales Press.

KRUG, E. G., DAHLBERG, L. L., MERCY, J. A., ZWI, A. B., and LOZANO, R. (2002), *The World Report on Violence and Health*, Geneva: World Heath Organisation.

LAMB, S. (ed.) (1999), *New Versions of Victims*, New York: New York University Press.

LEVI, M. (2001), 'White-Collar Crime Victimisation', in N. Shover and J. P. Wright (eds), *Crimes of Privilege: Readings in White-Collar Crime*, Oxford: Oxford University Press.

——and PITHOUSE, A. (1992), 'The Victims of Fraud', in D. Downes (ed.), *Unravelling Criminal Justice*, London: Macmillan.

LILLES, H. (1996), 'Circle Sentencing: Part of the Restorative Justice Continuum', in A. Morris and G. Maxwell (eds), *Restorative Justice for Juveniles: Conferencing, Mediation and Circles*, Oxford: Hart.

LLEWELLYN, J. (2006), 'Truth Commissions and Restorative Justice', in G. Johnstone and D. Van Ness (eds), *Handbook of Restorative Justice*, Cullompton, Devon: Willan.

LOGAN, W. A. (2005), 'Victims, Survivors and the Decisions to Seek and Impose Death', in J. R. Acker and D. R. Karp (eds), *Wounds That Do Not Bind: Victim-Based Perspectives on the Death Penalty*, Durham, NC: Carolina Academic Press.

LOSEKE, D. R., GELLES, R. J., and CAVANAUGH, M. M. (eds), (2005), *Current Controversies on Family Violence*, Thousand Oaks, Cal.: Sage.

LOUCKS, N. (2005), 'Bullying Behaviour amongst Women in Prison', in J. Ireland (ed.), *Bullying Among Prisoners: Innovations in research and theory*, Cullompton, Devon: Willan.

MCCOLD, P., and WACHTEL, T. (2002), 'Restorative Justice Theory Validation', in E. Weitekamp and H.-J. Kerner (eds), *Restorative Justice: Theoretical Foundations*, 267–84, Cullompton, Devon: Willan.

MACCORMICK, N., and D. GARLAND (1998), 'Sovereign States and Vengeful Victims: The Problem of the Right to Punish', in A. Ashworth and M. Wasik (eds), *The Fundamentals of Sentencing Theory*, 11–29, Oxford: Oxford University Press.

MCVIE, S., CAMPBELL, S., and LEBOV, K. (2004), *Scottish Crime Survey 2003*, Edinburgh: Scottish Executive Social Research.

MAGUIRE, M. (1982), *Burglary in a Dwelling*, London: Heinemann.

——and KYNCH, J. (2000), *Public Perceptions and Victims' Experiences of Victim Support: Findings from the 1998 British Crime Survey. Home Office Occasional Paper*, London: Home Office.

MARSHALL, T. F. (1999), *Restorative justice: an overview*, London: Home Office.

MATTINSON, J., and MIRRLEES-BLACK, C. (2000), *Attitudes to Crime and Criminal Justice: Findings from the 1998 British Crime Survey*, London: Home Office.

MAWBY, R. (2001), *Burglary*, Cullompton, Devon: Willan.

——and WALKLATE, S. (1994), *Critical Victimology: International Perspectives*, London: Sage.

MAXWELL, G. M., and MORRIS, A. (2001), 'Family Group Conferences and Reoffending', in A. Morris and M. G. (eds), *Restorative Justice for Juveniles: Conferencing, Mediation and Circles*, 243–63, Oxford: Hart.

MENDELSOHN, B. (1956), 'Une nouvelle branche de la science bio-psycho-sociale: victimiologie', *Revue Internationale de Criminologie et de Police Technique*, 11(2): 95–109.

MIERS, D. (1997), *State Compensation for Criminal Injuries*, Oxford: Oxford University Press.

——(2000), 'Taking the Law into their own Hands: victims as offenders', in A. Crawford and J. Goodey (eds), *Integrating a Victim Perspective within Criminal Justice*, 77–95, Aldershot: Ashgate Dartmouth.

——(2001a), *An International Review of Restorative Justice*, London: Home Office.

——(2001b), 'Criminal Injuries Compensation: The New Regime', *Journal of Personal Injuries*, 4: 371–95.

——(2006a), 'The International Development of Restorative Justice', in G. Johnstone and D. Van Ness (eds), *Restorative Justice Handbook*, Cullompton, Devon: Willan.

——(2006b), 'Rebuilding Lives: Operational and Policy Issues in the Compensation of Victims of Violent and Terrorist Crimes', *Criminal Law Review*, August: 695–721.

MOORE, D. B., and O'CONNELL, T. (1994), 'Family Conferencing in Wagga Wagga: A Communitarian Model of Justice', in C. Adler and J. Wundersitz (eds), *Family Conferencing and Juvenile Justice: The Way Forward or Misplaced Optimism?*, 45–86, Canberra: Australian Institute of Criminology.

MORGAN, J., and ZEDNER, L. (1992), *Child Victims: Crime, Impact, and Criminal Justice*, Oxford: Oxford University Press.

MORGAN, R., and EVANS, M. E. (1999), *Protecting Prisoners: The Standards of the European Committee for the Prevention of Torture in Context*, Oxford: Oxford University Press.

——and SANDERS, A. (1999), *The Uses of Victim Statements*, London: Home Office.

MORRIS, A. (1987), *Women, Crime and Criminal Justice*, Oxford: Blackwell.

——and MAXWELL, G. (2000), 'The Practice of Family Group Conferences in New Zealand', in A. Crawford and J. Goodey (eds), *Integrating a Victim Perspective within Criminal Justice*, 207–25, Aldershot: Ashgate Dartmouth.

MORRISON, B. (2006), 'Schools and Restorative Justice', in G. Johnstone and D. Van Ness (eds), *Handbook of Restorative Justice*, Cullompton, Devon: Willan.

NEWBURN, T., and MERRY, S. (1990), *Keeping in Touch: Police-Victim Communication in Areas*, HORS No. 116, London: HMSO.

——, CRAWFORD, A., EARLE, R., GOLDIE, S., HALE, C., MASTERS, G., NETTEN, A., SAUNDERS, R., SHARPE, K., and UGLOW, S. (2002), *The Introduction of Referral Orders into the Youth Justice System: Final Report*, London: Home Office.

NICHOLAS, S., and WOOD, N. (2003), *Property Crime. Crime in England and Wales 2002/2003*, Home Office Statistical Bulletin, London: Home Office.

——, POVEY, D., WALKER, A., and KERSHAW, C. (2005), *Crime in England and Wales 2004/2005*, London: Home Office.

O'DONNELL, I. (2004), 'Prison Rape in Context', *British Journal of Criminology*, 44(2): 241–55.

O'MAHONY, D., CHAPMAN, T., DOAK, J., GREAT BRITAIN. Northern Ireland Office and Northern Ireland Statistics & Research Agency (2002), *Restorative Cautioning: A Study of Police Based Restorative Cautioning Pilots in Northern Ireland*, Belfast: Northern Ireland Office.

PAINTER, K., and FARRINGTON, D. F. (1998), 'Marital Violence in Great Britain and its Relationship to Marital and Non-marital Rape', *International Review of Victimology*, 5(3–4): 257–76.

PARMAR, A., SAMPSON, A., DIAMOND, A., and GREAT BRITAIN. Home Office. Research Development and Statistics Directorate (2005), *Tackling Domestic Violence: Providing Advocacy and Support to Survivors from Black and other Minority Ethnic Communities*, London: Home Office.

PEACHEY, D. E. (1989), 'The Kitchener Experiment', in M. Wright and B. Galaway (eds), *Mediation and Criminal Justice*, 14–26, London: Sage.

PERCY, A., and MAYHEW, P. (1997), 'Estimating Sexual Victimization in a National Crime Survey: A New Approach', *Studies in Crime and Crime Prevention*, 6: 125–50.

REEVES, H., and MULLEY, K. (2000), 'The New Status of Victims in the UK: Opportunities and Threats', in A. Crawford and J. Goodey (eds), *Integrating a Victim Perspective within Criminal Justice*, 125–45, Aldershot: Ashgate Dartmouth.

REHN, E., and JOHNSON SIRLEAF, E. (2002), *Women, War and Peace: The Independent Experts' Assessment on the Impact of Conflict on Women and Women's Role in Peace-building*, United Nations Development Fund for Women (UNIFEM).

REISS, A. J. (1967), *Studies in Crime and Law Enforcement in Major Metropolitan Areas*, Washington, DC: US Department of Justice.

RIDING, A. (1999), 'The Crown Court Witness Service: Little Help in the Witness Box', *Howard Journal of Criminal Justice*, 38(4): 411–20.

RINGHAM, L., and SALISBURY, H. (2004), *Support for victims of crime: findings from the 2002/2003 British Crime Survey*, London: Home Office.

RISTOCK, J. (2002), *No More Secrets: Violence in Lesbian Relationships*, New York: Routledge.

ROCHE, D. (2002), 'Restorative Justice and the Regulatory State in South African Townships', *British Journal of Criminology*, 42(3): 514–33.

——(2003), *Accountability in Restorative Justice*, Oxford: Oxford University Press.

ROCK, P. (1990), *Helping Victims of Crime: The Home Office and The Rise of Victim Support in England and Wales*, Oxford: Clarendon Press.

——(1998a), *After Homicide: Practical and Political Responses to Bereavement*, Oxford: Oxford University Press.

——(1998b), 'Murderers, Victims and "Survivors": The Social Construction of Deviance', *British Journal of Criminology*, 38(2): 185–200.

——(2004a), *Constructing Victims' Rights: the Home Office, New Labour, and Victims*, Oxford: Oxford University Press.

——(2004b), 'Victims, Prosecutors and the State in nineteenth century England and Wales', *Criminal Justice*, 4(4): 331–54.

RUGGIERO, V. (1992), 'Realist Criminology: A Critique', in R. Mathews and J. Young (eds), *Issues in Realist Criminology*, 123–40, London: Sage.

SALISBURY, H., and UPSON, A. (2004), *Ethnicity, Victimisation and Worry about Crime: findings from the 2001/02 and 2002/03 British Crime Surveys. Research Findings No. 237*, London: Home Office.

SANDERS, A., HOYLE, C., MORGAN, R., and CAPE, E. (2001), 'Victim Impact Statements: Don't Work, Can't Work', *Criminal Law Review*, 447–58.

SAUNDERS, D. (2002), 'Are Physical Assaults by Wives and Girlfriends a Major Social Problem? A Review of the Literature', *Violence Against Women*, 8(12): 1424–48.

SCHEPPELE, K., and BART, P. (1983), 'Through Women's Eyes: Defining Danger in the Wake of Sexual Assault', *Journal of Social Issues*, 39(2): 63–81.

SHAPLAND, J., WILLMORE, J., and DUFF, P. (1985), *Victims and the Criminal Justice System*, Aldershot: Gower.

——, ATKINSON, A., ATKINSON, H., CHAPMAN, B, COLLEDGE, E., DIGNAN, J., HOWES, M., JOHNSTONE, J., ROBINSON, G., and SORSBY, A. (2006), *Restorative Justice in Practice—Findings from the Second Phase of the Evaluation of Three Schemes. Home Office Findings No. 274*, London: Home Office.

SHARP, S. F. (2005), *Hidden Victims: The Effects of The Death Penalty on Families of The Accused*, New Brunswick, NJ: Rutgers University Press.

SHERMAN, L., STRANG, H., and WOODS, D. (2000), *Recidivism Patterns in the Canberra Reintegrative Shaming Experiments (RISE)*, Canberra: Centre for Restorative Justice, Research School of Social Sciences, Australian National University.

SHURY, J., SPEED, M., VIVIAN, D., KUECHEL, A., and NICHOLAS, S. (2005), *Crime against Retail and Manufacturing Premises: Findings from the 2002 Commercial Victimisation Survey, Online report 37/05*, London: Home Office.

SKOGAN, W. G. (1986), 'The Impact of Victimization on Fear', *Crime and Delinquency*, 33: 135–54.

SLAPPER, G., and TOMBS, S. (1999), *Corporate Crime*, Harlow: Longman.

SOKOLOFF, N. J. (2005), *Domestic Violence at the Margins: Readings in Race, Class, Gender, and Culture*, Piscataway, NJ: Rutgers University Press.

SPARKS, R., GENN, H., and DODD, D. J. (1977), *Surveying Victims*, London: Wiley.

SPUNGEN, D. (1997), *Homicide: The Hidden Victims: A Guide for Professionals*, Thousand Oaks, Cal., London: Sage.

STANKO, E. A., and HOBDELL, K. (1993), 'Assault on Men: Masculinity and Male Victimization', *British Journal of Criminology*, 33(3): 400–15.

STRANG, H. (2002), *Repair or Revenge: Victims and Restorative Justice*, Oxford: Clarendon Press.

—— and BRAITHWAITE, J. (eds), (2002), *Restorative Justice and Family Violence*, Cambridge: Cambridge University Press.

TEMKIN, J. (2002), *Rape and the Legal Process*, 2nd edn, Oxford: Oxford University Press.

TOBOLOWSKY, P. M. (1999), 'Victim Participation in the Criminal Justice Process: Fifteen Years After the President's Task Force on Victims of Crime', *New England Journal on Criminal and Civil Confinement*, 25(1): 21–106.

TRAVIS, A. (2006), 'Victims of Crime Reject Notion of Retribution', *The Guardian*, 16 January.

TRAVIS, J., and WAUL, M. (eds), (2004), *Prisoners Once Removed: The Impact of Incarceration and Reentry on Children, Families, and Communities*, Washington, DC: Urban Institute Press.

TROWELL, J., UGARTE, B., KELVIN, I., BERELOWITZ, M., SADOWSKI, H., and LE COUTEUR, A. (1999), 'Behavioural Psychopathology of Child Sexual Abuse in Schoolgirls Referred to a Tertiary Centre: A North London Study', *European Child and Adolescent Psychiatry*, 8(2): 107–16.

UK FOREIGN AND COMMONWEALTH OFFICE (2005), *Human Rights, Annual Report 2005*, London: HMSO.

UMBREIT, M. S., and VOS, B. (2000), 'Homicide Survivors Meet the Offender Prior To Execution: Restorative Justice Through Dialogue', *Homicide Studies*, 4(1): 63–87.

——, BRADSHAW, W., and COATES, R. (2003), 'Victims in Dialogue with the Offender: Key Principles, Practices, Outcomes, and Implications', in E. G. M. Weitekamp and H.-J. Kerner (eds), *Restorative Justice in Context: International practice and directions*, 123–44, Cullompton, Devon: Willan.

VAN KESTEREN, J. N., MAYHEW, P., and NIEUWBEERTA, P. (2000), *Criminal Victimisation in Seventeen Industrialised Countries*, The Hague: Ministry of Justice WODC.

VAN NESS, D. (2006), 'Prisons and Restorative Justice', in G. Johnstone and D. Van Ness (eds),

Restorative Justice in Policing, Cullompton, Devon: Willan.

VANDIVER, M. (2003), 'The Impact of the Death Penalty on the Families of Homicide Victims and of Condemned Prisoners', in J. R. Acker, R. M. Bohm, and C. S. Lanier (eds), *America's Experiment with Capital Punishment: Reflections on the Past, Present, and Future of the Ultimate Penal Sanction*, 2nd edn, 613–45, Durham, NC: Carolina Academic Press.

VICTIM SUPPORT (1991), *Supporting Families of Murder Victims*, London: Victim Support.

—— (2006), *In the Aftermath: the support needs of people bereaved by homicide*, London: Victim Support.

VICTIMS ADVISORY PANEL (2003/2004), *Listening to Victims—the first year of the Victims' Advisory Panel*, London: HMSO.

VON HENTIG, H. (1948), *The Criminal and his Victim*, New Haven, Conn.: Yale University Press.

VON HIRSCH, A., ROBERTS, J. V., BOTTOMS, A., ROACH, K., and SCHIFF, M. (eds), (2003), *Restorative Justice and Criminal Justice: competing or reconcilable paradigms?*, Oxford: Hart.

WALBY, S., and ALLEN, J. (2004), *Domestic Violence, Sexual Assault and Stalking: Findings from the British Crime Survey*, Home Office Research Study No. 276, London: Home Office Research, Development and Statistics Directorate.

WALKLATE, S. (1989), *Victimology: the victim and the criminal justice system*, London: Unwin Hyman.

—— (2000), 'Researching Victims', in R. D. King and E. Wincup (eds), *Doing Research on Crime and Justice*, 183–201, Oxford: Oxford University Press.

—— (2007, forthcoming), *Handbook on Victims and Victimology*, Cullompton, Devon: Willan.

WARRICK, C. (2005), 'The Vanishing Victim: Criminal Law and Gender in Jordan', *Law and Society Review*, 39(2): 315–48.

WEINE, S. M. (1999), *When History is a Nightmare: Lives and Memories of Ethnic Cleansing in Bosnia-Herzegovina*, Piscataway, NJ: Rutgers University Press.

WEMMERS, J. A. (2005), 'Victim Policy Transfer: Learning From Each Other', *European Journal on Criminal Policy and Research*, 11(1): 121–33.

WILCOX, A., YOUNG, R., and HOYLE, C. (2004), *An Evaluation of the Impact of Restorative Cautioning:*

Findings from a Reconviction Study, Home Office Research Findings 255, London: Home Office.

WOLFE, D. A. (1999), *Child Abuse: Implications for Child Development and Psychopathology*, 2nd edn, Thousand Oaks, Cal.: Sage.

WOLFGANG, M. (1958), *Patterns in Criminal Homicide*, Philadelphia, Pa.: University of Pennsylvania Press.

WOOD, J. K. (2005), 'In Whose Name? Crime Victim Policy and the Punishing Power of Protection', *National Women Studies Association Journal*, 17(3): 1–17.

WOOLFORD, A. (2006), 'Making Genocide Unthinkable: Three Guidelines for a Critical Criminology of Genocide', *Critical Criminology*, 14: 87–106.

YOUNG, R. (2000), 'Integrating a Multi-Victim Perspective into Criminal Justice through Restorative Justice Conferences', in A. Crawford and J. Goodey (eds), *Integrating a Victim Perspective within Criminal Justice*, 227–51, Aldershot: Ashgate Dartmouth.

—— (2002), 'Testing the Limits of Restorative Justice: The Case of Corporate Victims', in C. Hoyle and R. Young (eds), *New Visions of Crime Victims*, 133–72, Oxford: Hart.

—— and GOOLD, B. (1999), 'Restorative Police Cautioning in Aylesbury—From Degrading to Reintegrative Shaming Ceremonies?', *Criminal Law Review*, 126–38.

—— and HOYLE, C. (2003a), 'New, Improved Police-Led Restorative Justice?', in A. Von Hirsch, J. V. Roberts, A. Bottoms, K. Roach, and M. Schiff (eds), *Restorative Justice and Criminal Justice: Competing or Reconcilable Paradigms*, 273–91, Oxford: Hart.

—— and —— (2003b), 'Restorative Justice and Punishment', in S. McConville (ed.), *The Use of Punishment*, 199–234, Cullompton, Devon: Willan.

——, ——, COOPER, K., and HILL, R. (2005), 'Informal Resolution of Complaints Against the Police: A quasi-experimental test of restorative justice', *Criminal Justice*, 5(3): 279–317.

ZEDNER, L. (1994), 'Reparation and Retribution: Are they Reconcilable?', *Modern Law Review*, 57(2): 228–50.

ZEHR, H. (1990), *Changing Lenses: A New Focus for Crime and Justice*, Scottdale, Pa.: Herald Press.

16

MENTALLY DISORDERED OFFENDERS, MENTAL HEALTH, AND CRIME

Jill Peay

Mentally disordered offenders are, as Webb and Harris (1999: 2) observe, categorically awkward; being neither exclusively ill nor uncomplicatedly bad, such offenders 'totter between two not always compatible discourses of state intervention'. Are they offenders who have mental disorders, or people with mental disorders who have offended? Or both? When should we be treating illness and when punishing infractions? And where? Should such offenders be in penal institutions, in hospital, or in the community? This is a challenge faced alike by health and criminal justice personnel, and by criminologists. Can they agree about into whose remit mentally disordered offenders should fall? And if they could agree, is there any prospect of supportive and coherent legal reform given that the eminently sensible recommendations of the Butler Committee (Butler 1975) have remained in limbo for over thirty years?

While it is clear that mentally disordered offenders do not represent some single, easily identifiable group, not much else is straightforward about this field. This chapter charts a path through already muddied waters. It is perhaps unsurprising that, as a synopsis, it embodies much of the incoherence and many of the mixed philosophies evident in the responses of the law and of practitioners, policy-makers, and the caring professions to 'mentally disordered offenders'. However, one theme recurs. If mentally disordered offenders are not a distinct group, to treat them as such for reasons of beneficence exposes them, in an era when the shift to risk-based sentencing dominates policy, to being dealt with more harshly. An alternative approach, the plurality model (Peay 1993) might provide some guide to a less discriminatory approach, since it takes as its starting point the notion that 'mentally disordered offenders' ought to be treated alike with 'ordered' offenders. Proportionality in sentencing, access to therapeutic regimes and crime reduction interventions, and questions of reparation ought to apply equally. This would not be to suggest that a standard criminal justice model should simply embrace offenders with mental health problems, but rather that that model requires reform to be informed by issues pertinent to the capacity of the offender both to be held criminally responsible and to be a proper subject of treatment. And whilst our mental condition defences remain inadequate for properly distinguishing those who should be held responsible for their offending and those who should not (Mackay 1995), then we cannot begin to deal fairly even with the first issue.

The chapter is divided into seven sections; the primary focus is on England and Wales, although literature from other countries is used to flesh out ideas and principles. The first section reviews developments in policy and sets the context of conflicting themes. Questions of individual justice and the effectiveness of interventions, questions which rightly apply for all offenders, are writ large for those with mental disorder where the neutrality of an 'intervention' becomes imbued with the apparent beneficence of 'treatment'. The second section examines the concept of mentally disordered offenders: do such offenders constitute an isolated category meriting special provision, or do the issues this 'group' raises have wider implications for the study of criminology? The third addresses briefly the problem of definition: what is meant by a 'mentally disordered offender'? Fourthly, are mentally disordered offenders a minority group? What is their incidence, their impact on the criminal justice system, and what are the mechanisms for diverting offenders outwith the penal system? The fifth section examines the fundamental justification for separate provision, namely treatment. This section takes a critical look at evidence of the relationship between mental disorder and crime, and then focuses on a key problematic group—offenders suffering from psychopathic disorder—who straddle the ordered–disordered offending continuum. There is also a brief examination of the new pilot services for 'dangerous people with severe personality disorder' ('DSPD'). The sixth section tackles some hidden agendas—bifurcation, detention for protective purposes, due process in discharge and release mechanisms— and the final section formulates some conclusions.

POLICY DEVELOPMENT IN ENGLAND AND WALES: A CONTEXT OF CONFLICTING THEMES

Current policy in mental health and crime in England and Wales, as in many other Western countries, is not dominated by humanitarian concerns; rather, it is permeated by perceptions and attributions of risk (for a contrary view see Seddon 2006). Debates about the shift to a 'risk penality' are now commonplace in the criminological literature (see, for example, Loader and Sparks, Chapter 3, this volume; Brown and Pratt 2000). Offenders with mental disorders are peculiarly 'at risk' of being perceived as posing an unquantifiable danger, and thus, peculiarly apt for the ubiquitous focus on risk management. As risk is transposed into danger, dangerous individuals are singled out for special attention, and the responsibility for preventing and managing risk is transferred to those professionals dealing with or caring for them (Douglas 1992). While earlier editions of this *Handbook* stressed the importance of Home Office Circular 66/90 (encouraging the placement of mentally disordered offenders, wherever possible, into the care of health and personal social services), in the current risk-dominated climate, therapeutic considerations no longer hold sway. The impact of Circular 66/90 has been leavened by a series of risk-infused policy developments.

What evidence is there of this shift in policy? The prevailing policy had adopted a broadly treatment-based approach. Punishment and protection were not overriding criteria; diversion and treatment were paramount. This approach treated offenders who were mentally disordered primarily in terms of their mental disorder. While not wholly unproblematic, it did relegate questions of risk and reoffending to a lower order. In keeping with this, the report of the Government's Expert Committee on the necessary scope of mental health legislation (Richardson 1999) would, with its emphasis on patient autonomy, non-discrimination, and issues of capacity, have taken mental health law generally in the direction of medical law (Fennell 2001).

However, the Government's contrary emphasis on risk management, the reduction of reoffending and early intervention, rejected this approach. Its White Paper (Department of Health/Home Office 2000) took issues relating to the safety of the public as being of key importance, and built on proposals for new DSPD orders; in essence, a form of indefinite detention for some people with personality disorder (Home Office 1999). This attempt to push mental health law in the direction of 'penal law' has not yet been fully accomplished, since, at the time of writing, the government has still not brought forward final legislative proposals on mental health. However, it is notable that many of the Government's objectives have already been achieved with the introduction of indeterminate sentencing under the Criminal Justice Act 2003 (Ashworth 2005) and by the Multi-Agency Public Protection Arrangements (MAPPA) introduced in April 2001 (see generally Home Office/National Probation Service 2004).

The MAPPA are designed to ensure the identification of serious sexual and violent offenders in the community, the sharing of information among those agencies involved in the assessment of the risk, and the management of that risk as offenders move from conditions of security into the community. For the purposes of this chapter the scheme embodies many of the conflicting themes that will follow, for MAPPA embrace both registered sex offenders (that is, all those who satisfy the notification requirements of Part 2 of the Sexual Offences Act 2003, but including those whose offences may not be of the most serious character), violent and other sex offenders, either sentenced or disposed of as mentally disordered offenders, and some other offenders whom it is thought may cause serious harm to the public. In 2003–4, 39,492 offenders fell within this remit, of whom 2,152 had the highest risk classification and were referred to the Multi-Agency Public Protection Panels (MAPPPs) for face-to-face inter-agency consideration (National Probation Service 2004). These MAPPPs enjoy psychiatric representation and, since the passage of the Criminal Justice Act 2003, the various agencies involved have a duty placed on them to cooperate with the responsible authority in each of the 42 MAPPA areas. Yet psychiatrists' primary responsibility is to the health of their patients; and psychiatrists, like other health professionals, have a duty of confidentiality towards those patients, a duty that does not sit easily with the concepts of information sharing embraced by the MAPPPs. The tensions are evident, and not only in respect of information sharing (Royal College of Psychiatrists 2004), but also in respect of the very relevance of psychiatric knowledge to the broad ambit of general offending:

> the contribution of psychiatry to risk assessment and management is confined to those with a mental disorder, and that the ability of psychiatrists accurately to assess risk is limited. There is otherwise a danger of perceived risk being seen as a reason for psychiatric involvement. Any such tendency would result in the unjustified 'pathologising' of ex-prisoners, which would be both unethical and impractical in its service implications. (ibid.: 12).

The shift towards indeterminacy, of controlling offenders in the community, and of the role of risk in underpinning these developments, had been presaged by a number of warning signs evident in discussions about mentally disordered offenders. Questions of risk had always been present in the arrangements for discretionary life sentences for offenders of an 'unstable' character[1] who were in a 'mental state which makes them dangerous to the life or limb of members of the public'.[2] But risk also emerged in the Report on *Mentally Disturbed Offenders in the Prison System* (Home Office/DHSS 1987) where it was noted, in the context of transferring prisoners to hospital for treatment, that 'the response to the needs of individual mentally disturbed offenders has to take account of the legitimate expectation of the public that government agencies will take appropriate measures for its protection' (ibid.: para. 3.6). Similarly, the Criminal Justice Act 1991 had a limited but important exception to its central principle of proportionality, in its arrangements for violent and sexual offences, where 'longer than normal sentences' could be given if it was 'necessary to protect the public from serious harm' (section 2(2)(b)). These provisions had a disproportionate impact on mentally disordered offenders (Solomka 1996), as did the provisions for automatic life sentences under section 2 of the Crime (Sentences) Act 1997, since they could trump the court's discretion to impose a therapeutic disposal on offenders found to be disordered at the point of sentence.[3] The same Act also introduced the hospital and limitation direction, a hybrid order which permits the courts to sentence those suffering from psychopathic disorder to a period of imprisonment, but to direct that they be admitted to a psychiatric hospital with the option of return to prison if treatment was either impossible or unexpectedly effective. In conflict with over forty years of legal and psychiatric opinion (Eastman and Peay 1998) these developments illustrated a growing desire to maintain penal control over mentally disordered offenders.

This is, of course, only one manifestation of a wider trend towards greater repression (see Ashworth, Chapter 29, and Loader and Sparks, Chapter 3, this volume). But for mentally disordered offenders this trend may have been magnified by concerns about reoffending by former psychiatric patients, a concern fuelled by the introduction in

[1] *R v. Hodgson* (1967) 52 Cr. App. R. 113.
[2] *R v. Wilkinson* (1983) 5 Cr. App. R. (S.) 105, at 109.
[3] *Newman* [2000] 2 Cr. App. R. (S.) 227.

1994 of *mandatory* inquiries into homicides committed by those who had had contact with the specialist mental health services (Department of Health 1994; Peay 1996). The spate of negative publicity the inquiries brought to psychiatric patients, services, and personnel (see Rumgay and Munroe 2001) did much to kindle an underlying public misconception of a relationship between mental disorder and violence.

It was particularly galling to those involved in treating the mentally disordered that such concerns persisted despite repeated demonstrations that 'Re-offending rates are in fact no higher than for any other class of offender' (Murray 1989: iii); that the trend was in the direction of mentally ill people committing fewer homicides than mentally ordered people (Taylor and Gunn 1999); and the fact that when psychiatric patients killed, they were much more likely to kill themselves than others (Appleby *et al.* 2001). Finally, there is good evidence that those restricted patients discharged from hospital pose a much lower risk of serious reoffending than comparable offenders released from prison (Ly and Foster 2005). Perhaps in acknowledgement of the reality as opposed to the mythology surrounding mental disorder and crime, and in recognition that much of what was going to be learned had already been learned, in 2001 it was announced that inquiries after homicide were no longer to be mandatory.

It is thus not surprising that the policy context embodies both positive and negative messages. On the one hand, calls for diverting mentally disordered offenders from the damaging effects of the criminal justice system remain persistent. Moreover, the increasing popularity of early intervention in the lives of offenders is consistent with a philosophy that 'treatment works'; people can be changed, diverted, distracted, or protected from inappropriate or damaging experiences. Yet on the negative side, there appears to be a persistent distrust of therapeutic disposals for some mentally disordered offenders.

Much of the confusion arises because of the tensions inherent across the continuum both of ordered–disordered behaviour and that of law-abiding–law-breaking behaviour. Notions of care and treatment are seen as appropriate for the seriously disordered, provided this does not arise in conjunction with offending of a worrying nature. Similarly, notions of protection and custodial punishment have been traditionally reserved for serious offenders, again assuming an absence of obvious disorder. Yet these tensions are confounded where it is argued that disorder and offending exist side by side in one individual, or, more confusingly still, interact. Dilemmas are posed by the handling of those mentally disordered offenders isolated as meriting 'special' provision, whichever limb of the bifurcated policy (special care or special control) is adopted. Moreover, 'special' provision all too easily manifests itself in special discrimination (Campbell and Heginbotham 1991). Indeed, the discrimination and stigma faced by those with mental health problems is amplified when disorder and offending co-occur.

Another conflict arises between welfarism and legalism. Gostin (1986: v) distinguishes the two approaches thus: legalism occurs 'where the law is used to wrap the patient in a network of substantive and procedural protections against unjustified loss of liberty and compulsory treatment'; whereas welfarism occurs where 'legal safeguards are replaced with professional discretion which is seen as allowing speedy access to treatment and care, unencumbered by a panoply of bureaucracy and procedures'.

These two philosophies sit uneasily together in the Mental Health Act 1983. Moreover, this Act, the key statutory provision dealing with mentally disordered offenders, with its emphasis on treating people on the basis of who they are, has also sat uncomfortably alongside a criminal justice approach which has traditionally emphasized what people have done as the basis for a proportionate intervention. It is therefore notable that the Criminal Justice Act 2003 has the reform and rehabilitation of offenders as one of its five purposes of sentencing (section 142(1)). Arguably, therefore, there has been something of a fusion between mental health and criminal justice objectives, with both sets of professionals now being expected to engage in the potentially competing tasks of reformation and risk management, with the latter taking precedence where the former is in peril.

Finally, there is the impact of the Human Rights Act 1998. The European Convention on Human Rights (ECHR) has had a powerful influence on the relationship between the executive and the continuing detention of those with psychiatric disorders; an influence which has generally permeated discretionary decision-making. Yet, the ECHR is not a document that naturally lends itself to the protection of those with mental disorders. Indeed, it permits discrimination against those of 'unsound mind'. Nonetheless, the first declaration of incompatibility under the Human Rights Act occurred in a case concerning an offender-patient detained in a psychiatric hospital.[4] Perhaps this is mere coincidence. But perhaps it reflects the presence of conflicting tensions permeating the practices of all who work in this field, whether they are based in the police station or at the Court of Appeal (Eastman and Peay 1999).

MENTAL DISORDER AND OFFENDERS: A CASE FOR SPECIAL PROVISION?

Should mentally disordered offenders be treated as a separate topic, in the same way that gender, race, youth, and victims are isolated from the mainstream? Arguably not, since mental disorder is not a fixed characteristic of an offender. Yet what these topics do have in common is their 'inconvenience' for a criminology imbued with male, adult, mentally healthy, formerly non-victimized values. It is the premise of this chapter that the lessons to be learned from how we deal conceptually, practically, and in principle with those deemed 'mentally disordered offenders' have as much to say about topics regarded as central to, or ranging across, the scope of criminology as they have to say about 'marginal' groups. Thus, mentally disordered offenders should not be seen as a Cinderella area.

Indeed, to argue for the existence of a discrete group of mentally disordered offenders would presuppose a category of mentally ordered offenders. This falsely comforting

---

[4] *R v. Mental Health Review Tribunal, on the application of H* [2001] 3 W.L.R. 512.

tendency parallels that noted by Gilman (1988), that setting the sick apart sustains the fantasy that we are whole. Yet, the criminal law broadly adopts such an approach, presuming rationality in the absence of proof of its complete loss (see Smith and Hogan 1988: 200). But such a clear-cut division is problematic. Even the reasonable man on the Clapham omnibus can experience a seeming moment of madness if he alights at the Common. In turn, scientific advances in our understanding of the structure, functioning, and chemistry of the brain have generated a more medical approach to some forms of offending (Hare 1996; Hodgins and Muller-Isberner 2000) and to calls for the law to recognize new neurological syndromes which may underlie offending behaviour (Lewis and Carpenter 1999). In the area of so-called normal offending, defences are frequently advanced or mitigation constructed which draw on elements of 'diminished responsibility', 'unthinking' behaviour, or uncontrolled responses to extreme social stress. Concepts of limited rationality will be familiar to criminologists. Yet few of these offenders would wish for the special treatment that may follow a finding of 'defect of reason' integral to a finding of 'not guilty by reason of insanity'. Why not? Is it a recognition of the punishing aspects of such treatment? Or a desire not to be stigmatized along with those deemed mad (see, for example, Gardner and Macklem 2001, on the attractiveness of normal 'provocation' over 'abnormal' diminished responsibility)? As Porter (2004) observed, it might be preferable to be criminalized and maintain one's free will than to be psychiatrized and lose it.

Or is it that we recognize that some level of disordered thinking ought to alleviate punishment, if not excuse it altogether? Thus, 'complete absolution' is a legal nicety. Mentally disordered offenders find themselves confined in hospitals, prisons, therapeutic regimes within prisons, and, most notably, within the remand population. Mentally disordered offenders exist in one shape or form across the entire criminal justice system, and 'disorder' may be found to a greater or lesser extent—partly dependent on the incentives for its construction—throughout offending populations.

Accordingly, one dominant theme in this chapter concerns a plea that the component parts of the concept be disaggregated: mentally disordered offenders are first and foremost people; whether they may have offended or whether they may be disordered will be matters for individual resolution. Prioritization of one aspect (the mentally disordered element) of an individual's make-up readily leads to neglect of other, perhaps more pertinent, aspects. Mentally disordered people may have other needs deriving from other 'defining' features such as gender (see Care Services Improvement Partnership 2006), race, or age; particular offender groups such as sex offenders or substance misusers may need prioritization; similarly, people with personality (or psychopathic) disorders, or sensory disabilities, or brain damage, or learning disabilities may also require special provision. This range of offenders will manifest themselves amongst the homeless, amongst victims, and as witnesses to crime. Indeed, as James *et al.* (2002: 88–9) have noted from their study of court diversion, the majority of 'mentally disordered offenders' may be more aptly described as the 'offending mentally disordered' since they are known psychiatric patients who are, in essence, accessing care through the criminal justice system and who have more similarities with those being

25 per cent reported a decrease in their staffing levels and a third were operating with only one member of staff. These statistics support the reported sense that mentally disordered offenders were a low priority for agencies in almost a quarter of those schemes responding to the survey. No longer can these initiatives be described as 'burgeoning' (Cavadino 1999). Indeed, as NACRO asserts (2005: 14) the situation 'is far from ideal'.

In addition to the various diversion schemes, there are also formal powers under the 1983 Act to divert offenders into the hospital system. Sections 35 and 36 permit remand to hospital for reports and treatment respectively; section 38 initiated interim hospital orders, to avoid the difficulty that could arise out of the 'once and for all' disposal to hospital under a section 37 hospital order. The interim order permits the court to 'hedge its bets'. Although a punitive order should not follow where an offender responds to treatment and is returned to court for sentence, a punitive approach may be adopted where it becomes apparent that no 'cure' is possible. However, none of these orders has been frequently used (Department of Health 2004), in stark contrast with the numbers of psychiatric reports carried out in prison.

Should the mentally disordered be exempt from prosecution altogether? Some commentators believe that those with mental handicap should be prosecuted and held responsible where responsibility exists (Carson 1989). Others argue that defendants who have failed to seek psychiatric help when so advised, or who fail to take prescribed medication, should not then be able to rely upon their psychiatric condition to reduce their culpability (Mitchell 1999). The Code for Crown Prosecutors requires the CPS to consider a defendant's mental condition but notes, 'Crown Prosecutors must balance the desirability of diverting a defendant who is suffering from significant mental or physical ill health with the need to safeguard the general public'; disorder per se is not regarded as a sufficient basis for not proceeding (CPS 2004: para. 5.10g), although it is one of the factors that may make a prosecution less likely to be needed in the public interest, provided the offence is neither serious nor likely to be repeated. Home Office Circular 66/90 also distinguishes those forms of mental disorder made worse by the institution of proceedings and those which come about by reason of instituting proceedings. Lastly, Robertson (1988) suggests that the presence of disorder may make prosecution more likely where a guilty plea is anticipated. Hence, in the decision to prosecute, the presence of mental disorder may act as a mitigating factor and pre-empt action, or it may act as an incentive to proceedings being taken. The public interest in ensuring that the offence will not be repeated needs to be weighed against the welfare of the person in question.

Problems of due process also dog the diversion arena. Does the earlier involvement of psychiatrists inevitably favour welfarism over legalism? How is a balance to be achieved between the rights of the defendant and those of the victim (Laing 1999)? And, as Fennell notes (1991: 336–7), assuming an offender is prepared to be diverted, 'hospital authorities and local authorities have considerable discretion as to whether to accept responsibility for that person. If he is a persistent petty offender, or is potentially disruptive, he is unlikely to be afforded priority status in the queue for scarce resources.' Indeed, the James *et al.* (2002) study would suggest that those admitted to hospital via the courts are less needy than those admitted direct from the community, and it is only the trigger of criminal justice involvement that enables them to cross the threshold for admission. With the drop at district level in in-patient beds for the adult mentally ill, from around 150,000 in the 1950s to approximately 63,000 in the early 1990s, and a reluctance by some to see offender-patients integrated with 'non-offenders', diversion and community care may have real limits to their ability to absorb all those whom the courts might wish so to allocate. Shaw *et al.* (2001) also note that of those diverted to inpatient psychiatric services, one in three had lost contact at a one-year follow-up, while of those referred to psychiatric community teams or outpatient clinics, less than a third attended for their first appointment. Maintaining supervision and contact with those in the community is inherently problematic, but this looks like a case of needles returning to the haystack.

PRISON POPULATIONS

In discussing remands to hospital while awaiting trial, Hoggett (1996: 108) provocatively asks whether it is worse to languish in hospital without trial, or in prison without treatment. This question has real force, given the extent of mental disorder within the prison population. Examination of this (i) details the range of disorders recognized by psychiatrists amongst an offending population; (ii) underlines the 'irrelevance' to many of these offenders of their mental disorder (since it has not resulted in their being subject to special provisions); and (iii) re-emphasizes the central point that offenders with mental disorder are not some minority group of only marginal concern.

Studies of the prevalence of mental disorder in prison populations have consistently found substantial levels of disorder. Amongst the sentenced male population, Gunn *et al.* (1991) found that 37 per cent had a diagnosable mental disorder. Brooke *et al.* (1996), looking at the remand population, found an incidence of 63 per cent, with 5 per cent suffering from psychosis. The 1997 national survey of psychiatric morbidity, looking at 3,000 prisoners across England and Wales (Singleton *et al.* 1998), found 7 per cent of sentenced men and 10 per cent of men on remand probably to have functional psychotic disorders. Of the five disorders surveyed in the research (personality disorder, psychosis, neurosis, alcohol misuse, and drug dependence), fewer than one in ten prisoners showed no evidence of any of these disorders.

Are these figures shocking in absolute terms? Yes. First, because the problem is in no sense new. Over twenty years earlier, Gunn *et al.* (1978) reported an incidence of 31 per cent with psychiatric disorders in the south-east prison population, of whom 2 per cent were psychotic. This high level of disorder (in its broad sense) but 'low' level of psychosis (the latter then comparable with that in the community) is a common finding. Whether the increase over the last twenty years reflects more disorder or differential diagnostic practices is less clear; that it remains there at all to be diagnosed at these levels is the principal concern.

Secondly, the figures are shocking because of the incidence of suicide and self-harm in prison. Suicide in prison remains a persistent problem (Liebling 1999) despite laudable attempts to address the issue through suicide prevention policies and, more recently, such initiatives as first night centres and measures to improve multi-disciplinary work. Taking their most rigorous measure—suicide attempts in the week prior to interview— Singleton *et al.* (1998) note that 2 per cent of the male remand population reported attempting suicide (this is distinguished from para-suicide). One-third of 'successful' prison suicides have a history of mental disturbance (Dooley 1990).

Thirdly, the prison population is projected to grow to 92,400 by March 2009 (Cross and Olowe 2003). The figure of 75,030 on 13 January 2006 would, by extrapolation, mean a minimum of 5,252 prisoners with functional psychosis, prisoners certainly in need of treatment and probably in need of transfer to hospital. For even if services for people with personality, sexual, and substance misuse disorders were developed in prisons, and even with the new mental health 'in-reach' services to be provided by the NHS (Department of Health *et al.* 2001; Grounds 2000) transfer to hospital for the seriously mentally ill is the only current viable and humane option. Only in hospital can drugs be administered on a compulsory basis, victimization by other prisoners be avoided, and unpredictable violence or incidents of self-harm be better controlled. Yet hospital bed occupancy remains over 90 per cent and the available secure bed total falls manifestly short of the latent demand in the prison population. There simply are not enough secure beds.

However, considering the number and variety of hurdles that mentally disordered offenders have to jump in order not to be diverted from the prison population, the presence of over 5,000 seriously mentally ill people in prison suggests a number of additional hypotheses. First, these filters may fail either effectively to identify or, if identified, to divert these offenders into the hospital system. For example, Birmingham *et al.* (1996: 1523), in observing that fewer than a quarter of diagnosable mentally disordered remand prisoners were identified as such on initial screening at reception by the prison medical service, note: 'In a busy remand prison abnormal behaviour is often tolerated or perceived as a discipline problem and dealt with punitively, while the "quietly mad" are ignored.'

Secondly, the mismatch between the narrow criteria for Mental Health Act disposal at the point of sentence and the subsequent broad clinical diagnosis of disorder will substantially account for the finding of fewer than one in ten with no diagnosable disorder. Most offenders simply do not meet the 1983 Act criteria for hospital disposal or transfer. Moreover, the tautological relationship between personality disorder/drug/ alcohol and sexual problems, and offending behaviour will also skew the figures. Many of these offenders could benefit from transfer to a therapeutic community like Grendon. However, even with the new Grendon-type prison at Marchington, provision will fall short of demand.

Lastly, disagreements among doctors about treatability and the lack of suitable facilities for those suffering from personality disorder and sexual deviation will result in resort to prison by default. Treatment in hospital for some types of offender is simply not a probable outcome; difficult or violent behaviour will often discount a therapeutic disposal. While the courts may perceive a need for a psychiatric referral, this ultimately is not matched by those providing the services. Where the courts cannot force doctors to accept patients for treatment, prison sweeps up.

Thus, although the sentencing of mentally disordered offenders is predicated on notions of diversion and treatment, there has always been the possibility of recourse to a penal disposal where there are elements of culpability (or predicted dangerousness) that require punishment (or control). Indeed, even where doctors are willing and able to treat an offender, the courts may still insist upon a penal sentence.[6]

TRANSFER TO HOSPITAL

The development of mental disorder *after* imprisonment, together with a persistent failure to identify all those needing treatment at an earlier stage, makes necessary some transfer mechanism. Transfer from prison to hospital has a history plagued with problems. Again the basic premise is difficult to contest, namely that detention in prison is inappropriate for those whose mental disorder is sufficiently serious to justify transfer to hospital; yet transfer was historically consistently under-used (Grounds 1991). Bed-blocking in the special hospitals, attributable to problems with moving patients either to less secure hospitals, or back to prison, reduced bed availability for those coming from prison.

Notably, recent statistics covering a seven-year period (Ly and Foster 2005) show a significant and arguably welcome increase in the numbers of prisoners transferred to hospital. The increase has been most marked for sentenced prisoners, possibly attributable to the new DSPD beds, but even for unsentenced prisoners, the number transferred in the most recent year was the highest in the period reviewed. Indeed, transfers from prison in 2004 accounted for 63 per cent of all admissions of restricted patients. So, do the increased numbers suggest greater flexibility in the use of transfer provisions per se (Mackay and Machin 2000), or a growing reluctance by the courts to use therapeutic disposals in the first instance? The question is hard to answer. Nevertheless, figures relating to overall court and prison disposals (Department of Health 2004) show a decrease in admissions (from 2,100 in 1994/5 to 1,601 in 2003/4) and a decrease in the use of hospital orders (with or without restrictions) from 978 in 1994/5 to 554 in 2003/4.

Two aspects of transfer are noteworthy. First, transfer may be motivated by a desire to protect the public rather than by a wish to ensure that the patient receives the care needed (Grounds 1991). The use of transfer for prisoners reaching the end of their sentence would support this assertion, as does the drive for new orders and services in respect of 'DSPD' (see below). Secondly, transferred patients are in a potentially disadvantageous position. Although they would be detained on a notional hospital order (and hence dischargeable) once their prison sentence expired, in an era when indeterminacy in sentencing for the most serious offences is dominant, quite when this position will be reached is unclear; in the interim, patients on life sentences prior to the

---

[6] *R* v. *Birch* (1989) 90 Cr. App. R. 78.

expiry of their tariff period are reviewable by the Parole Board.[7] Moreover, the use of hospital and limitation directions (a sentence of imprisonment with a direction that the offender be admitted to hospital; Eastman and Peay 1998) is likely to be extended from those suffering from psychopathic disorder to those suffering from all mental disorders (Department of Health/Home Office 2000). Even though these orders have barely been used, they may yet prove attractive to a judiciary favouring concepts of 'punishment and public protection'; they can also impact on the mechanics and safeguards embodied in the current transfer arrangements.

As Fennell (1991: 333) concludes, 'it is likely that, despite current policies of diversion, significant numbers of mentally disordered offenders will remain in prisons, and therefore there is an urgent need to consider how a humane and therapeutic psychiatric service might be provided within the prison system'. And here is the nub of the problem; mentally disordered offenders cannot be neatly packaged and swept into the caring system, for, on a broad definition of the term, they make up some 90 per cent of the prison population. Thus, some means of offering effective 'treatment' (if not compulsory treatment) within prison has to be considered.

Hence the resurgence of a treatment movement within criminology. Although its genesis may lie equally in disillusionment with just deserts and humane containment for what is evidently a 'damaged' population, the presence and extent of mentally disordered offenders in the prison population constitutes a compelling force. While the view was ominously expressed in 1991 by the Home Office that 'offenders are not given sentences of imprisonment by the courts for the purposes of ensuring their rehabilitation' (para. 1.28), attempts to reduce subsequent offending by specific groups have grown in scale and importance over the last few years, especially through the cognitive behavioural programmes developed under the 'What Works' agenda (see Raynor, Chapter 31, this volume). Indeed, in the light of the Halliday Report (Halliday *et al.* 2001; Ashworth 2005, and Ashworth, Chapter 29, this volume), with its emphasis on the contribution that sentencing can make to crime reduction through working with offenders under sentence—both during and after a period of imprisonment—'rehabilitation' is back in vogue, even if it appears in a new and more instrumental guise.

MENTAL DISORDER, OFFENDING BEHAVIOUR, AND TREATMENT

Treatment is the fundamental justification for separate provision for mentally disordered people who have committed offences. But it is not readily clear what is meant by treatment, or what treatment is attempting to alter—the 'underlying disorder', the offending

[7] *Benjamin and Wilson* v. *UK* (2003) 36 EHRR 1 held the former 'technical lifer status' to be in breach of Article 5(4).

behaviour, or the link, if any, between the two? Or are our efforts really devoted largely to alleviating the distress and emotional problems offenders suffer, those either pre-existing or post-dating the offending? If it is the likelihood of criminal behaviour per se, the justification for treatment will not be confined to a 'mentally disordered' subgroup of offenders. Accordingly, an examination of the relationship between disorder and offending is critical. This leads into the final section of this chapter, on protection. Here, the argument is turned on its head: where mental disorder provides a basis, not for a therapeutic disposal but for a lengthier custodial disposal than would be proportionate to the seriousness of the offence. Should there then be a compensatory right to treatment for that disorder (Hale 2004)?

WHAT IS THE RELATIONSHIP BETWEEN MENTAL DISORDER AND OFFENDING BEHAVIOUR?

As Prins (1990) has amply demonstrated, the relationship between mental disorder and criminality is an uncertain one, concluding (ibid.: 256), 'Most psychiatric disorders are only very occasionally associated with criminality'. Prins also illustrates well the difficulties of establishing cause and effect in this troubled area: 'we are trying to make connections between very different phenomena, and these phenomena are the subject of much debate concerning both substance and definition' (ibid.: 247).

Another emphasis in the literature concerns the relationship between mental disorder and *violence* (Monahan *et al.* 2001; Wessely and Taylor 1991). The overwhelming correlates of violence are male gender, youth, lower socio-economic class, and the use/abuse of alcohol or drugs, and not the diagnosis of major mental disorder. However, the belief that mental disorder predisposes people to behave violently is widely held and enduring, resulting in discriminatory practices and attitudes towards those with mental disorder (see Crisp 2004). As Rubin (1972: 398) notes,

> certain mental disorders [are] characterized by some kind of confused, bizarre, agitated, threatening, frightened, panicked, paranoid or impulsive behaviour. That and the view that impulse (i.e. ideation) and action are interchangeable support the belief that all mental disorder must of necessity lead to inappropriate, anti-social or dangerous actions.

The relationship has been highly problematic to research. However, available now are the results from the MacArthur study of mental disorder and violence (Monahan *et al.* 2001), a study based on 1,000 male and female acute admission civil patients from three sites in the United States. Patients were contacted up to five times in the community after discharge, and official data collected in relation to their histories and progress. In addition to this, there were extensive self-report data and interviews conducted with 'patient collaterals'—that is people nominated by the patient as being most familiar with their behaviour in the community. This methodologically rigorous study comes to a number of important, albeit cautious, conclusions. With respect to criminological factors the authors observe, first, that men are no more likely to be violent than women over the course of a one-year follow-up, although the nature of their violence differs (this is consistent with other studies of mental disorder, but not with the criminological literature generally); secondly, that prior violence and criminality are strongly associated with post-discharge violence; thirdly, physical abuse as a child, but not sexual abuse, was associated with post-discharge violence; and neighbourhood disadvantage—in short, poverty—was significantly associated with violence. This finding helps us to understand why using individual-level predictors of violence—for example, race—can be so misleading. For although African-American racial status was associated with violence (odds ratio = 2.7), this was halved when neighbourhood disadvantage was taken into account, and in absolute terms the effect of 'poverty' was more significant (ibid.: 58–9). Thus, the authors conclude, 'violence by persons with mental disorders may be, in part, a function of the high-crime neighbourhoods in which they typically reside' (ibid.: 60), further noting that this has implications for the placement of half-way houses and other accommodation for people with mental illness.

With respect to clinical factors, the presence of a *co-occurring diagnosis of substance abuse or dependence* was critical. More surprising was that a diagnosis of schizophrenia was associated with lower rates of violence than either a diagnosis of depression, or, more significantly, *personality disorder*. Curiously, although psychopathy was a strong predictor of violence, the predictive power of the screening version of the Hare Psychopathy Checklist (Hart *et al*. 1995) derived from its 'antisocial behaviour' factor and not its 'emotional detachment' factor (the features more typically associated with those suffering from psychopathic disorder, see below). Notably, neither delusions, nor hallucinations, nor (controversially) command hallucinations were associated with higher rates of violence (making prescient Monahan and Steadman's (1983) question as to why those with paranoid delusions should be any more or less likely to attack their tormentors than those who are in fact being tormented). Failure to support the previous findings that lack of control and associated violent behaviour may be a prerogative of the *currently actively psychotic* (Swanson *et al*. 1990; Link *et al*. 1992) conflicts with some dearly held psychiatric notions. However, the authors point to the mediating factor of non-delusional suspiciousness, which may account for a tendency to interpret others' behaviour as hostile. Notably, even the relationship between violent thoughts and violence is not strong (although gaining an accurate measure of violent thoughts is inherently problematic), neither is that between anger and violence (although it was statistically significant).

While this litany of factors would seem to stack up against those with mental disorders, it is important to stress two matters. First, the complexity of the causes of violence amongst those with mental disorder (and, in all probability, amongst those without mental disorder) means that there will be no single solution to violence. Accordingly, any single treatment approach is likely to be of limited efficacy, and predictions of future violence will remain extremely hazardous. Secondly, mental disorders account for only a tiny proportion of violence.

In contrast, merely weighing the contribution of Bluglass and Bowden's *Principles and Practice of Forensic Psychiatry* (1990) might lead one to conclude that there is no form of *criminal* behaviour without a psychiatric element, with chapters on everything from Amok to Sexual Asphyxia. Tragically, the observation in earlier editions of this *Handbook* that it was regrettable that nothing was included on Zealotry remains all too apt. Two UK journals—*Criminal Behaviour and Mental Health* and *The Journal of Forensic Psychiatry*—have also focused on the relationship between mental ill-health and criminal behaviour. Although I could not do justice to this body of knowledge, some general observations follow which are pertinent to this path of medicalized explanations.

First, offence categories amongst 'disordered offenders' largely mirror those of 'normal' populations. Secondly, many of the offending population have themselves been offended against. Undoubtedly, the level of disorder and disadvantage amongst the prison population testifies to the inadequacies of the average confined population, but is it, in essence, an index of social failure, not criminogenic predispositions? Disentangling correlation and causation is highly problematic. How, for example, can it be determined what the relevance of the victimization was to the individual, if observations are based on psychiatric contact with those who have offended? Why should physical but not sexual abuse be related to subsequent violence (see Monahan *et al.* 2001, above)? Offenders may be only too willing to have their behaviour treated as something 'uncontrollable' if there is an anticipated benefit of so doing. The scene is set: offenders are prepared to incorporate psychiatric explanations of their behaviour; victimization in one form or another is a common, if not universal, experience; psychiatrists are peculiarly reliant on what their clients tell them; offending is widespread. All of the ingredients are present to permit a re-structuring of experiences as explanations or excuses.

Or is the victim/offending relationship merely coincidental? The danger is twofold. Once criminologists start down this path it is hard to see where it ends. Are not all offences equally open to medicalization? Even seemingly comprehensible property offences may, especially where trivial items are involved, require some less readily accessible explanation than mere acquisitiveness. Secondly, a medicalized explanation precedes a medicalized solution. But if treatment is adopted and then fails, what follows?

TREATMENT IN PRISON

In 1990 the Home Office observed, 'For most offenders, imprisonment has to be justified in terms of public protection, denunciation and retribution. Otherwise it can be an expensive way of making bad people worse' (para. 2.7). Since then, evidence-based treatment programmes, both in prison and in the community, have gained considerable momentum, under the general heading of the 'What Works' initiative (Home Office 2001). The latter has had a significant impact on the philosophy of imprisonment, even if the success of accredited programmes remains patchy.[8] However, it is worth noting here that the focus has largely been on treating offending,

[8] See e.g. Cann *et al.* (2003), reporting very mixed results for prison-based cognitive skills programmes.

rather than on mental disorder per se. Cognitive behavioural programmes for sex offenders, offence-focused problem-solving (the McGuire 'Think First' programme), substance-abuse treatment programmes, controlling and managing anger (CALM), and cognitive self-change programmes for violent offenders capture the flavour of these initiatives (see also Raynor, Chapter 31, and Hollin, Chapter 2, this volume; Grubin 2001).

However, the extent to which treatment endeavours can be both sustained and effective remains questionable. Achieving effectiveness will be jeopardized by two enduring factors: prison overcrowding and the use of short sentences, both of which can disrupt programme completion. Moreover, if sentencers come to believe that imprisonment will secure access to beneficial treatment programmes for persistent offenders, 'ordered' offenders may find themselves at as great a risk as disordered offenders of therapeutic sentencing, further accelerating the problem of overwhelming demand.

Emphasis is also shifting on to the importance of resettlement and providing through-care from prisons into the community, an initiative given further momentum by the establishment of the National Offender Management Service in 2004. But, this 'through-care' approach has had a worryingly narrow focus on crime reduction. Grant (1999) for example, observes multi-agency working in the community has had as its objective pragmatic restraint rather than treatment per se. He argues that it is no easy task to support the health needs of less serious offenders while managing the risk they pose and the fear they engender because of their perceived potential for harm (for further discussion of the expanding role of MAPPPs see Maguire *et al.* 2001; Kemshall and Maguire 2001). Such an approach will also involve criminal justice personnel in clinical decision-making (see Fennell and Yeates 2002) and create an enhanced emphasis on supervision in the community; one which is already placing the relevant agencies under strain.[9]

The shift from broadly based rehabilitation to offence-specific crime reduction initiatives has also had an impact on Grendon (psychiatric) Prison (Peay 2002: 776–7). Genders and Player (1995) admirably detail the way in which therapeutic endeavours and security considerations are difficult to reconcile. Yet Grendon's record of success in *controlling* problematic prisoners is notable. Similarly, Taylor (2003) has found statistically significant reductions in violent incidents amongst 55 prisoners held in the DSPD pilot assessment unit at HMP Whitemoor. Perhaps, as Genders and Player (1995) pointed out, knowledge by all concerned that the rest of the prison system provides a very different form of containment may have a positive effect on prisoner behaviour.

Lastly, prison remains an inappropriate location for patients with psychotic disorders. The inability to impose medication, together with the damning acceptance that there may be 'circumstances in which the standard of care falls below that which would be expected in a psychiatric hospital without the prison authority being negligent',[10] make this unarguable. Official reports continue to record the inadequacy of the care

---

[9] See 'Thousands freed from jail early will reoffend', *Observer*, 29 January 2006.
[10] *Knight* v. *The Home Office* [1990] 3 All E.R. 237.

provided in prisons with, for example, HM Inspectorate of Prisons noting after a visit to Holloway Prison that, of 25 in-patients in the health care centre 15 'were so ill that they should have been in an NHS facility as their health needs were far beyond the capacity of the staff on the ward' (2001: para. 2.109). And, most notably, the UK has now been found in violation of Article 2 of the ECHR—the right to life—following the killing of one mentally disordered man by another; both had been on remand and held in the same cell in Chelmsford Prison.[11]

This minefield may be crudely summarized:

1. 'Treatment' may mean many different things—ranging from the administration of anti-psychotic medication to the acquisition of social survival skills. There may be a mismatch between health and criminal justice personnel in respect of the objectives of treatment.

2. If the relationship between the disorder and the offending behaviour is not primarily causal, there is less justification for excusing from punishment, and offenders should remain entitled to protection of their rights as offenders while not being denied access to treatment.

3. Even if there is some causal element, punishment for the partially responsible (and hence, partially guilty) can be combined with treatment, where requested.

4. Successful treatment for a disorder may have no bearing on future criminality; mentally disordered offenders should be accorded proportionality in the length of confinement; release should not be determined on the basis of predictions of future offending.

5. As Campbell and Heginbotham (1991: 135) argue, where an offender is treatable and there is some causal connection between the disorder and his or her offending behaviour, there may be less (or no) justification for continued detention after treatment.

6. In the existing context, the balance between jurisprudential logic, which may sanction punishment for the 'culpable' mentally disordered offender, and decades of a humanitarian response endorsing a commonsense preference for treatment rather than punishment, ought to be reversed in favour of the former only where treatment can be demonstrated to be wholly inappropriate.

PSYCHOPATHIC DISORDER

Psychopathic disorder (a legal concept), personality disorder (a clinical concept), psychopathy (a trait measurable by the Hare Psychopathy Checklist: Hare 1991), and DSPD (dangerous severe personality disorder—a political/policy concept) are all terms used when exploring the association between disorders of personality and criminality. It is inevitable that there will be some association between personality and criminality since the concepts are, in varying formats, definitionally linked. Thus, the legal

---

[11] *Paul and Audrey Edwards* v. *The UK* (2002) Application No. 46477/99.

definition of psychopathic disorder under the 1983 Act includes the element that the disorder has resulted in 'abnormally aggressive or seriously irresponsible conduct'.

In addition to its interpersonal and affective elements, Hare's characterization of psychopathy includes the behavioural predisposition that 'psychopaths' are 'impulsive and sensation seeking, and they readily violate social norms' (Hare 1991: 3). Where the psychiatric profession employs clinical concepts of personality disorder, it is inevitable that therapeutic and conceptual difficulties will result (Grounds 1987). Moreover, forensic psychiatrists have been and remain deeply divided about whether psychopathic disorder should even be in the Mental Health Act (Cope 1993); compulsory admissions under this classification occur rarely, and even admission on restriction orders are infrequent (Ly and Foster 2005). Confusion thus seems endemic. Some argue that the label 'psychopathic disorder' adds nothing to an understanding of the condition, and indeed doubt the very existence of an underlying medical condition. Others regard it as a moral label not a clinical diagnosis, while some recognize a disorder but doubt whether any psychiatric intervention could be successful. Yet others argue that an attempt should be made to continue to treat selected psychopathic offenders since the 'sheer range of psychopathology makes it more appropriate . . . to think of the psychopathic disorders rather than a single entity' (Coid 1989: 755).

What is psychopathy? Roth's definition (1990: 449) is noteworthy:

> It comprises forms of egotism, immaturity, aggressiveness, low frustration tolerance and inability to learn from experience that places the individual at high risk of clashing with any community that depends upon cooperation and individual responsibility of its members for its continued existence. It has a characteristic sex distribution, age of onset, family history of similar symptoms and disorders and family constellations and influences that show a large measure of consistency in their course and outcome.

As noted above, people suffering from 'psychopathic disorder' rarely find themselves subject to civil commitment. So, are the traits associated with psychopathic disorder primarily troubling for the individual, or, more contentiously, advantageous?

From a criminological perspective, it is worth reiterating the findings of Monahan *et al.* (2001), above. 'Psychopathy' appears to have two dimensions: one relating to interpersonal and affective features (selfishness/callousness, etc.); and one to socially deviant behaviours (irresponsibility, antisocial behaviour, etc.). However, the relationship between psychopathy and violence appears, according to the Monahan *et al.* analysis (2001: 70), to be derived from the second dimension—the antisocial behaviour factor—and to tap personality traits associated with a consistent record of impulsive, irresponsible, antisocial acts. The underlying emotional pathology appears less important. If so, this would have obvious implications for the likely success of any treatment regime.

Psychiatrists find themselves in a dilemma. The era of psychiatric optimism which preceded the 1959 Act has been replaced, particularly in respect of the treatment of aberrant behaviour, by an era of psychiatric pessimism. Psychiatrists are wary of being asked to 'treat' psychopathic offenders. Some of the resultant slack has been taken up by psychologists, but even their enthusiasm may wane if the treatment is really containment and control. Paradoxically, psychiatrists have found themselves criticized both for a failure to offer treatment to those they regard as untreatable, and for releasing those they deem successfully treated. In this context, their opposition to the introduction of a formal 'community treatment order', which would entail further responsibilities in respect of controlling offender-patients in the community, is hardly surprising.

DANGEROUS PEOPLE WITH SEVERE PERSONALITY DISORDER

All of the difficulties outlined above are typified in the Government's DSPD initiative. This development (Home Office 1999; Department of Health/Home Office 2000) is the latest in a long line of legislative attempts to address the difficulties posed either by those with 'psychopathic disorder', or, in this case, by an ill-defined subset of them. While this group has been portrayed as having

> high rates of depression, anxiety, illiteracy, poor relationships and loss of family ties, homelessness and unemployment. They have high rates of suicide and high rates of death by violent means. They have high rates of substance misuse. Their behaviour is often violent. Their behaviour is of immense distress to themselves and they are frequently in the position where they are asking for help and yet finding it very difficult to access suitable help [Home Office 1999: 34],

it is hard to resist the sense that the initiative stems not from concerns about treatment, justice, or due process, but explicitly from anxiety about reoffending by those 'prematurely' released from the hospital or prison system.

The DSPD proposals have become, since the last edition of this *Handbook*, a prime focus for service development and legislative provision (see McAlinden 2001; Fennell 2001 and www.dspdprogramme.gov.uk/home_flash/index.php). This subset of the personality disordered/psychopathically disordered is thought to number some 2,400 men; at present, the initiative is focused on providing specialist facilities supported by new legislative powers in association with reform of the 1983 Act. Yet, cognitive behavioural programmes for 'psychopaths' are already part of the 'What Works' agenda in prisons. Moreover, of the four DSPD pilot schemes, two are sited in prisons. To what extent this reveals an emphasis on containment rather than treatment, or the tacit recognition that treatment may not be successful, is unclear. However, it is notable that the new national personality disorder programme (www.personalitydisorder.org.uk) seems to embrace the DSPD pilots in a low-key fashion; is it perhaps seeking to downplay DSPD and thereby distance the concept 'personality disorder' from 'dangerousness and violence'?

Generally, the DSPD initiative does not bode well. It shocked our North American counterparts, who have observed that even there such proposals had not been countenanced. And although a research programme has been initiated, there is a very strong sense that legislation will proceed in advance of any firm research findings. This is not to be an evidence-based programme. And how, anyway, could it be? If there is no agreed definition, no clear diagnosis, no agreed treatment, no means of assessing when the predicted risk may have been reduced, and no obvious link between the alleged underlying condition and the behaviour, how could outcome measures be agreed upon and then evaluated? Finally, the pilot programme recruits volunteers (and how could it be any other way, given the 'treatments' involved?); yet, if legislation were to be enacted to support the programme, offenders could be sent on a compulsory basis. Thus, any 'results' emerging from these pilots are likely to be fundamentally inapplicable to the target groups. Yet, the programme and all its associated publicity have the potential to further demonize this group; the possibility of discrimination against them thereafter is self-evident (see Crisp 2004: Part 6).

PROTECTIVE SENTENCING: PROCEDURAL SAFEGUARDS VERSUS TREATMENT

Reform in the area of the trial of offenders with mental disorder has been devoted primarily to increasing the court's sentencing options and not to addressing issues of prior culpability (Peay 2002: 765–72). This has a number of consequences for those who remain to be sentenced on a 'conventional' basis. Indeed, as Eastman and Peay (1999: 12) observe:

> Mentally disordered offenders may thus be doubly disadvantaged; hardly any gain benefit from their disorder by securing an acquittal on grounds of insufficient responsibility, whilst few of those who are sentenced are treated solely as mentally disordered when they are sentenced. Of those few sent to hospital, many then attract mental disorder attributions about their future offending in subsequent consideration of their discharge, sometimes thereby unjustifiably extending their period in (therapeutic) detention.

Thus, the bulk of offenders remain to be sentenced with their mental disorder having historically little, if any, mitigating effect. However, in an interesting development, the Sentencing Guidelines Council has identified 'mental illness or disability' as one of the four factors that may 'significantly lower culpability' when the seriousness of an offence is assessed (Sentencing Guidelines Council 2004: para. 1.25). Statutory reform however has, to date, done little to address the issue, and the presence of mental disorder can still lead to disproportionately long sentences where paternalistic assumptions about the 'mental disorder' element, and protective-predictive ones about the offending element, leave prisoner-patients with more than their 'just' deserts.

It is first worth reiterating that, like all offenders, those with mental disorder are overwhelmingly not dangerous. However, some are. Arguments favouring limited special measures have their attractions, if only to deal with that small but worrying group about whom fears of future offending abound; but their *quid pro quo* is that the preventive rationale should be tempered by procedural safeguards. Similarly, the arguments for bifurcation are inherently appealing, where diversion into humanitarian care protects offenders from damaging penal sentences. Yet the implications of these two propositions under our existing arrangements are that the route into confinement will affect both the route out, and whether and what type of treatment will be given.

Concepts of dangerousness and its alleged association with mental disorder pepper the academic literature and the rhetoric of sentencing (see generally Brown and Pratt 2000). Academics and policy-makers have been fiercely divided both on predictive grounds—will it work?—and on questions of rights—should it be allowed to work? The argument embodies the distinction between statistical and legal-clinical decision-making; crudely put, the difference between risk factors associated with groups of people who have common characteristics (much of the risk-prediction literature is of this nature), and the determination of whether any one individual within that group will be amongst those where risk is realized. These kinds of difficult decisions are faced regularly by courts, Mental Health Review Tribunals (MHRTs), discretionary lifer panels, the parole board, and clinicians (see, for example, Peay 1989; Padfield and Liebling 2000; Hood and Shute 2000). The findings of research concerning such decision-making bodies are consistent: despite actuarial evidence that would support the release of patients and prisoners, attributions of risk are central, overvalued, and very difficult to refute.

Should offenders be entitled to a proportional measure of punishment? Walker (1996: 7) argues that there may be no such 'right' where offenders have forfeited the presumption of being harmless because they have *previously* attempted or caused harm to others. In these circumstances precautionary sentencing may be justifiable. But how is such precautionary sentencing to be limited? And are mentally disordered offenders at greater risk of imposition of such a sentence? Dworkin (1977) described the restraint and treatment of the 'dangerously insane' as an insult to their rights to dignity and liberty—an infringement that could be justified not where crime reduction might result, but only where the danger posed was 'vivid'. Bottoms and Brownsword (1983: 21) unpacked the concept of vivid danger into its elements of seriousness, temporality (that is frequency and immediacy), and certainty. Certainty was pivotal to precautionary sentencing, but even a high probability of future offending should become relevant only if the behaviour anticipated involved causing or attempting 'very serious violence'. Thus, the right to a proportional measure of punishment would yield a '*prima facie* right to release for the prisoner at the end of his normal term', and this would apply— in the absence of 'vivid danger'—equally to the alleged 'dangerous offender'. But at this point theory and practice diverge.

The passage of the Criminal Justice Act 2003 (see Ashworth, Chapter 29, this volume), has made much of what has previously been written on the subject of sentencing redundant. The new emphasis on crime reduction, risk management, reparation, and deterrence, alongside rehabilitation and deserved punishment, is likely to place mentally disordered offenders in triple, if not quadruple, jeopardy. Treatment for their underlying disorders, attempts to reduce independently their potential for crime through 'measures to change the way offenders think and behave' (Halliday *et al.* 2001: 1), and a deterrence philosophy which may impact even less successfully on offenders with mental disorders, are all likely to contribute to a greater than proportionate use of incapacitation with 'mentally disordered offenders'.

Under the Criminal Justice Act 2003 psychiatric probation orders have been reinvented as community sentences with a mental health treatment requirement. All of the problems that bedevilled the original order remain (the need for both a willing practitioner and a consenting patient); whether permitting the order to extend beyond its former one-year constraint will make it more popular, remains to be established. At the other end of the spectrum, the introduction of indefinite sentences under section 225 (life sentence or imprisonment for public protection for serious offences), where the court is of the opinion that there is 'significant risk to members of the public of serious harm', is likely to draw more mentally disordered offenders into the net of indeterminacy. Conceding further this principle of preventive sentencing is likely to add to already existing difficulties; protective imperatives can infect the way in which decisions are made about the release even of non-offenders amongst the detained psychiatric population; fears of future offending can lead to inappropriate denial of release (Peay 1989: 184); they can also lead to inappropriate transfer (Grounds 1991); and to offender-patients being detained in hospital for periods commensurate with their offence rather than on the basis of assessed recovery from their disorders (Dell and Robertson 1988). Protective confinement is self-justifying and highly infectious.

One more positive development from the perspective of those mentally disordered offenders who commit serious offences is evident. The anomaly that the automatic life sentence for a second serious offence under the Crime (Sentences) Act 1997 could not be trumped by a disposal under the Mental Health Act 1983 (except for offenders suffering from psychopathic disorder, by way of the hospital and limitation direction) has now been remedied with the abolition of the automatic life sentence. And there is nothing to suggest that section 225 *prevents* the courts from making a hospital order with restrictions, where an offender satisfies the necessary conditions under the Mental Health Act 1983 (Law Commission 2005: Overview, paras 3.17–18). So, whilst the automatic life sentence would have trumped welfarist concerns, the obligatory discretionary life sentence and the indefinite sentence for public protection do not.

Spelling out the involvement of predictions of dangerousness is a first step in ensuring that such predictions are made with due regard to the rights of an offender not to be unjustifiably detained. A second necessary step is to ensure procedural fairness: the position of discretionary lifers has been somewhat improved by placing them on the same footing as restricted patients applying to MHRTs; equally though, all the problems which bedevil tribunals are likely to be replicated. Even given a reversed burden of proof, mentally disordered offenders seeking their release on the ground of non-dangerousness will have an uphill struggle when doing so from conditions of security.[12]

---

[12] The case of *H* (see note 4 above).

CONCLUSIONS

If the basic premise of this chapter is accepted—namely, that mentally disordered offenders are not, and should not be, treated as an isolated category—the conclusions that follow are of broader significance.

First, effort should be devoted to developing a pluralistic model of the criminal justice system. This has been discussed elsewhere (Peay 1993). Piecemeal tinkering may provide solutions for the problems posed by specific offenders; it is insufficient as a basis for addressing problems across the ordered–disordered offending continuum. Equally, the temptation to solve problems by addressing only the back end of the process (namely, sentencing and disposal issues) distracts attention from the urgent need for the prior issues of culpability to be resolved on a fairer basis than is currently achieved.

Secondly, if the mentally disordered cannot effectively be identified and marginalized, diversion and transfer can never be the solution. Resource allocation needs to be across the board, not only in respect of a limited number of beds for potentially difficult offender-patients.

Thirdly, and stemming from this, it is unrealistic to confine treatment to hospital settings. Treatment in prison, and in community settings, needs full consideration. The problem, of course, is the use of overt compulsion. What is clear is the need to think more carefully about the circumstances in which treatment will be offered, to whom, and what the consequences will be where it is deemed unwelcome, unsuccessful, or inappropriate. A pluralistic model would require the same limitations on intervention for all offenders, assuming they have the capacity to consent to treatment or undergo punishment. While adoption of a proportionality-based approach would constitute a sound foundation for greater fairness between offenders, the risk-based/treatment approach looks set to dominate the field; in this context more thought needs to be given to the problematic aspects of multi-agency working where confidential 'health' information will seep into criminal justice agencies.

Fourthly, the justifications are many for singling out subsections of 'disordered offenders' for special treatment. But special treatment can readily become special control; to be seduced by the notion that risk can be managed through the containment of identifiable individuals is to allow discriminatory treatment for that group, while failing to tackle the roots of the problem.

Lastly, the failure to agree on a definition of what constitutes a mentally disordered offender, or to apply it consistently even if criteria could be agreed, is likely to result in there being a mismatch of expectations amongst the various personnel and agencies dealing with such offenders. As Watson and Grounds (1993) have observed, greater liaison combined with overcoming the boundaries between different parts of the criminal justice and health agencies will be insufficient while the discrepancy in expectations remains.

■ SELECTED FURTHER READING

Herschel Prins' *Offenders, Deviants or Patients?* (3rd edition, Taylor & Francis, 2005) is both a good recent overview of the literature and a provocative read; similarly, Toby Seddon's *Punishment and Madness: Governing Prisoners with Mental Health Problems* (Cavendish, 2006) provides a contrasting picture to the themes pursued in this chapter. Littlechild and Fearns's edited collection, *Mental disorder and criminal justice. Policy, provision and practice* (Russell House, 2005) also contains a wealth of material and useful references to recent work on aspects of policy and practice in the field. The three Internet sites mentioned in the text, two relating to personality disorder—www.dspdprogramme.gov.uk/home_flash/index.php and www.personalitydisorder.org.uk—and one to the Joint Scrutiny Committee on the Draft Mental Health Bill 2004—www.publications.parliament.uk/pa/jt200405/ jtselect/jtment/ 79/7906.htm#a20—are all worth visiting. The Department of Health's plans for amending the Mental Health Act 1983 remain uncertain. However, if you would like to chart their labyrinthine progress, see—www.dh.gov.uk/PolicyAndGuidance/HealthAndSocialCareTopics/Mental Health/fs/en.

■ REFERENCES

APPLEBY, L., SHAW, J., SHERRATT, J., and AMOS, T. (2001), *Safety First: Five-Year Report of the National Confidential Inquiry into Suicide and Homicide by People with Mental Illness*, London: Department of Health.

ASHWORTH, A. (2005), *Sentencing and Criminal Justice*, 4th edn, Cambridge: Cambridge University Press.

AUDINI, B., and LELLIOTT, P. (2002), 'Age, Gender and Ethnicity of those Detained under Part II of the Mental Health Act 1983', *British Journal of Psychiatry*, 180: 222–6.

BARTLETT, P., and SANDLAND, R. (2000), *Mental Health Law: Policy and Practice*, London: Blackstone Press.

BIRMINGHAM, L., MASON, D., and GRUBIN, D. (1996), 'Prevalence of Mental Disorder in Remand Prisoners: Consecutive Case Study', *British Medical Journal*, 313: 1521–4.

BLUGLASS, R., and BOWDEN, P. (eds) (1990), *Principles and Practice of Forensic Psychiatry*, Edinburgh: Churchill Livingstone.

BOAST, N., and CHESTERMAN, P. (1995), 'Black People and Secure Psychiatric Facilities: Patterns of Processing and the Role of Stereotypes', *British Journal of Criminology*, 35: 218–35.

BOTTOMS, A., and BROWNSWORD, R. (1983), 'Dangerousness and Rights', in J. W. Hinton (ed.), *Dangerousness: Problems of Assessment and Prediction*, London: Allen and Unwin.

BROOKE, D., TAYLOR, C., GUNN, J., and MADEN, A. (1996), 'Point Prevalence of Mental Disorder in Unconvicted Male Prisoners in England and Wales', *British Medical Journal*, 313: 1524–7.

BROWN, M., and PRATT, J. (eds) (2000), *Dangerous Offenders: Punishment and Social Order*, London: Routledge.

BUCHANAN, A. (ed.) (2002), *Community Care of the Mentally Disordered Offender*, Oxford: Oxford University Press.

BURNEY, E., and PEARSON, G. (1995), 'Mentally Disordered Offenders: Finding a Focus for Diversion', *The Howard Journal*, 34: 291–313.

BUTLER, LORD (1975), *Report of the Committee on Mentally Abnormal Offenders*, Cmnd 6244, London: HMSO.

CAMPBELL, T., and HEGINBOTHAM, C. (1991), *Mental Illness: Prejudice, Discrimination and the Law*, Aldershot: Dartmouth.

CANN, J., FALSHAW, L., NUGENT, F., and FRIENDSHIP, C. (2003), *Understanding What Works: Accredited Cognitive Skills Programmes for Adult Men and Young Offenders*, Home Office Research Findings, No. 226, London: Home Office.

CARE SERVICES IMPROVEMENT PARTNERSHIP (2006), *Women at Risk: The Mental Health of Women in Contact with the Judicial System*, London: London Development Centre. Care Services Improvement Partnership. Available online at: www.london developmentcentre.org

CARSON, D. (1989), 'Prosecuting People with Mental Handicaps', *Criminal Law Review*: 87–94.

CAVADINO, P. (1999), 'Diverting Mentally Disordered Offenders from Custody', in D. Webb and R. Harris (eds), *Managing People Nobody Owns*, London: Routledge.

COID, J. (1989), 'Psychopathic Disorders', *Current Opinion in Psychiatry*, 2: 750–6.

COPE, R. (1993), 'A Survey of Forensic Psychiatrists' Views on Psychopathic Disorder', *Journal of Forensic Psychiatry*, 4: 215–35.

CRISP, A. (ed.) (2004), *Every Family in the Land. Understanding Prejudice and Discrimination against People with Mental Illness*, London: Royal Society of Medicine.

CROSS, I., and OLOWE, T. (2003), *Prison Population Brief: England and Wales: November 2003*, London: Home Office, Research Development Statistics.

CROW, I. (2001), *The Treatment and Rehabilitation of Offenders*, London: Sage.

CROWN PROSECUTION SERVICE (2004), *Code for Crown Prosecutors*, London: CPS.

DELL, S., and ROBERTSON, G. (1988), *Sentenced to Hospital: Offenders in Broadmoor*, Maudsley Monographs 32, London: Institute of Psychiatry.

DEPARTMENT OF HEALTH (1994), *Guidance on the Discharge of Mentally Disordered People and their Continuing Care in the Community*, NHS Executive HSG(94)27 and LASSL (94)4: 10 May 1994.

——(2004), *In-patients formally detained in hospitals under the Mental Health Act 1983 and other legislation, England: 1993–4 to 2003–4*, Bulletin 2004/22, London: Department of Health.

——,HM PRISON SERVICE, and NATIONAL ASSEMBLY FOR WALES (2001), *Changing the Outlook: A Strategy for Developing and Modernising Mental Health Services in Prisons*. London: Department of Health.

——, and HOME OFFICE (2000), *Reforming the Mental Health Act: Part II High Risk Patients*, Cm 5016-II, London: The Stationery Office.

DOOLEY, E. (1990), 'Prison Suicide in England and Wales, 1972–87', *British Journal of Psychiatry*, 156: 40–5.

DOUGLAS, M. (1992), *Risk and Blame: Essays in Cultural Theory*, London: Routledge.

DWORKIN, R. (1977), *Taking Rights Seriously*, London: Duckworth.

EASTMAN, N., and PEAY, J. (1998), 'Sentencing Psychopaths: Is the "Hospital and Limitation Direction" an Ill-Considered Hybrid?', *Criminal Law Review*: 93–108.

——and —— (eds) (1999), *Law Without Enforcement: Integrating Mental Health and Justice*, Oxford: Hart.

FENNELL, P. (1991), 'Diversion of Mentally Disordered Offenders from Custody', *Criminal Law Review*: 333–48.

——(2001), 'Reforming the Mental Health Act 1983: "Joined Up Compulsion"', *Journal of Mental Health Law*: 5–20.

——and YEATES, V. (2002), 'To serve which master? Criminal justice policy, community care and the mentally disordered offender', in A. Buchanan (ed.), *Community Care of the Mentally Disordered Offender*, Oxford: Oxford University Press.

GARDNER, J., and MACKLEM, T. (2001), 'Compassion without Respect? Nine Fallacies in *R v Smith*', *Criminal Law Review*: 623–35.

GENDERS, E., and PLAYER, E. (1995), *Grendon: A Study of a Therapeutic Prison*, Oxford: Clarendon Press.

GILMAN, S. (1988), *Disease and Representation. From Madness to AIDS*, Ithaca, NY: Cornell University Press.

GOSTIN, L. (1986), *Mental Health Services — Law and Practice*, London: Shaw and Sons.

GRANT, D. (1999), 'Multi-agency risk management of mentally disordered sex offenders: a probation case study', in D. Webb and R. Harris (eds), *Managing People Nobody Owns*, London: Routledge.

GROUNDS, A. (1987), 'Detention of "Psychopathic Disorder Patients" in Special Hospitals: Critical Issues', *British Journal of Psychiatry*, 151: 474–8.

——(1991), 'The Transfer of Sentenced Prisoners to Hospital 1960–1983', *British Journal of Criminology*, 31(1): 54–71.

——(2000), 'The Future of Prison Health Care', *Journal of Forensic Psychiatry*, 11: 260–7.

GRUBIN, D. (2001), 'Editorial. Treatment for mentally disordered offenders', *Criminal Behaviour and Mental Health*, 11: S109–S112.

GUDJONSSON, G., HAYES, G., and ROWLANDS, P. (2001), 'Fitness to be interviewed and psychological vulnerability: the views of doctors, lawyers and police officers', *Journal of Forensic Psychiatry*, 11: 74–92.

GUNN, J., DELL, S., and WAY, C. (1978), *Psychiatric Aspects of Imprisonment*, London: Academic Press.

——, MADEN, A., and SWINTON, M. (1991), 'Treatment Needs of Prisoners with Psychiatric Disorders', *British Medical Journal*, 303: 338–41.

HALE, LADY JUSTICE (2004), *What can the Human Rights Act do for my mental health?*, Paul Sieghart Memorial Lecture. Available from the British Institute of Human Rights website—www.bihr.org/archived-news.html

HALLIDAY, J., FRENCH, C., and GOODWIN, C. (2001), *Making Punishments Work: Report of a Review of the Sentencing Framework for England and Wales*, London: Home Office.

HARE, R. (1991) *The Hare Psychopathy Checklist—Revised*, Toronto: Multi-Health Systems.

—— (1996), 'Psychopathy: a clinical construct whose time has come', *Criminal Justice and Behaviour*, 23: 25–54.

HART, S., COX, D., and HARE, R. (1995), *The Hare Psychopathy Checklist: Screening Version*, Toronto: Multi-Health Systems.

HEALTHCARE COMMISSION, MENTAL HEALTH ACT COMMISSION, NATIONAL INSTITUTE FOR MENTAL HEALTH, CARE SERVICES IMPROVEMENT PARTNERSHIP (2005), *Count me in: Results of a national census of inpatients in mental health facilities in England and Wales*, London: Commission for Healthcare Audit and Inspection.

HM INSPECTORATE OF PRISONS (2001), *Report of an unannounced follow-up inspection of HM Prison Holloway 11–15 December 2000* (available on Home Office website).

HODGINS, S., and MULLER-ISBERNER, R. (eds) (2000), *Violence Crime and Mentally Disordered Offenders: Concepts and Methods for Effective Treatment and Prevention*, Chichester: Wiley.

HOGGETT, B. (1996), *Mental Health Law*, 4th edn, London: Sweet & Maxwell.

HOME OFFICE (1990), *Crime, Justice and Protecting the Public*, Cm 965, London: HMSO.

—— (1991), *Custody, Care and Justice*, London: HMSO.

—— (1999), *Managing Dangerous People with Severe Personality Disorder. Proposals for Policy Development*, London: Home Office.

—— (2001), *What Works: Second Report of the Joint Prison/Probation Service Accreditation Panel*, London: Home Office.

—— (2004), *The Police and Criminal Evidence Act 1984 Code of Practice C*, rev. edn, London: The Stationery Office.

—— and DEPARTMENT OF HEALTH (1996), *Mentally Disordered Offenders—Sentencing and Discharge Arrangements*, a discussion paper on a proposed new power for the courts, London: Home Office.

—— and DEPARTMENT OF HEALTH AND SOCIAL SECURITY (1987), *Report of the Inter-departmental Working Group of Home Office and DHSS Officials on Mentally Disturbed Offenders in the Prison System in England and Wales*, London: Home Office/DHSS.

—— and NATIONAL PROBATION SERVICE (2004), *The MAPPA Guidance*. Probation Circular reference No. 54/2004, 14 October.

HOOD, R., and SHUTE, S. (2000), *Parole decision-making: weighing the risk to the public*, Home Office Research Findings 144, London: Home Office, Research Development and Statistics Directorate.

JAMES, D., FARNHAM, F., MOOREY, H., LLOYD, H., BLIZARD, R., and BARNES, T. (2002), *Outcome of psychiatric admission through the courts*, London: Home Office, RDS Occasional Paper No. 79.

JOINT COMMITTEE ON THE DRAFT MENTAL HEALTH BILL (2005), *First Report*, House of Lords and House of Commons, 9 March. Also available from the Parliament website.

KEMSHALL, H., and MAGUIRE, M. (2001), 'Public Protection, Partnership and Risk Penality: The Multi-Agency Management of Sex and Violent Offenders', *Punishment and Society*, 3(2): 237–64.

LAING, J. (1999), 'Diversion of Mentally Disordered Offenders: Victim and Offender Perspectives', *Criminal Law Review*: 805–19.

LAW COMMISSION (2005), *A New Homicide Act for England and Wales?*, Consultation Paper No. 177, 20 December.

LEWIS, O., and CARPENTER, S. (1999), 'Episodic Dyscontrol and the English Criminal Law', *Journal of Mental Health Law*: 13–22.

LIEBLING, A. (1999), 'Prison suicide and prisoner coping', in M. Tonry and J. Petersilia (eds), *Prisons, Crime and Justice: A Review of Research*, Chicago: University of Chicago Press.

LINK, B., ANDREWS, H., and CULLEN, F. (1992), 'The Violent and Illegal Behaviour of Mental Patients Compared to Community Controls', *American Sociological Review*, 57: 275–92.

LITTLECHILD, B. (ed.), (2001), *Appropriate Adults and Appropriate Adult Schemes: Service User,*

Provider and Police Perspectives, Birmingham: Venture Press.

LITTLECHILD, B., and FEARNS, D. (eds) (2005), *Mental disorder and criminal justice. Policy, provision and practice*, Lyme Regis: Russell House Publishing.

LY, L., and FOSTER, S. (2005), *Statistics of mentally disordered offenders 2004 England and Wales*, Statistical Bulletin 22/05, London: Home Office, Research Development and Statistics Directorate.

MCALINDEN, A. (2001), 'Indeterminate Sentences for the Severely Personality Disordered', *Criminal Law Review*: 108–23.

MACKAY, R. D. (1995), *Mental Condition Defences in the Criminal Law*, Oxford: Clarendon Press.

—— and MACHIN, D. (2000), 'The Operation of Section 48 of the Mental Health Act 1983: An Empirical Study of the Transfer of Remand Prisoners to Hospital', *British Journal of Criminology*, 40: 727–45.

MAGUIRE, M., KEMSHALL, H., NOAKS, L., SHARPE, K., and WINCUP, E. (2001), *Risk Management of Sexual and Violent Offenders: The Work of Public Protection Panels*, Police Research Series Paper 139, London: Home Office.

MELTZER, H., GILL, B., PETTICREW, M., and HINDS, K. (1995), *OPCS Surveys of Psychiatric Morbidity in Great Britain, Report 1: The prevalence of psychiatric morbidity among adults living in private households*, London: The Stationery Office.

MITCHELL, E. M. (1999), 'Madness and meta-responsibility: the culpable causation of mental disorder and the insanity defence', *Journal of Forensic Psychiatry*, 10: 597–622.

MONAHAN, J., and STEADMAN, H. (1983), 'Crime and Mental Disorder An Epidemiological Approach', in M. Tonry and N. Morris (eds), *Crime and Justice: An Annual Review of Research*, vol. 4, 145–89, Chicago: University of Chicago Press.

——, STEADMAN, H., SILVER, E., APPELBAUM, P., ROBBINS, P., MULVEY, E., ROTH, L., GRISSO, T., and BANKS, S. (2001), *Rethinking risk assessment: The MacArthur study of mental disorder and violence*, New York: Oxford University Press.

MURRAY, D. J. (1989), *Review of Research on Re-offending of Mentally Disordered Offenders*, Research and Planning Unit Paper 55, London: Home Office.

NACRO (1993), *Mentally Disordered Offenders and Community Care*, Mental Health Advisory Committee Policy Paper No. 1, London: NACRO Publications.

—— (2005), *Findings of the 2004 Survey of Court Diversion/Criminal Justice Mental Health Liaison Schemes for mentally disordered offenders in England and Wales*, London: NACRO Publications.

NATIONAL PROBATION SERVICE (2004), *Public Protection from Dangerous Offenders Better than Ever*, News release, NPS.

PADFIELD, N., and LIEBLING, A. (2000), *An exploration of decision-making at discretionary lifer panels*, Home Office Research Study No. 213, London: Home Office, Research and Statistics Directorate.

PALMER, C., and HART, M. (1996), *A PACE in the Right Direction?*, Sheffield: Institute for the Study of the Legal Profession, Faculty of Law, University of Sheffield.

PEAY, J. (1989), *Tribunals on Trial: A Study of Decision-Making Under the Mental Health Act 1983*, Oxford: Clarendon Press.

—— (1993), 'A Criminological Perspective', in W. Watson and A. Grounds (eds), *Mentally Disordered Offenders in an Era of Community Care*, Cambridge: Cambridge University Press.

—— (ed.) (1996), *Inquiries after Homicide*, London: Duckworth.

—— (ed.) (1998), *Criminal Justice and the Mentally Disordered*, Dartmouth: International Library Series.

—— (2002), 'Mentally disordered offenders, mental health and crime', in M. Maguire R. Morgan, and R. Reiner (eds), *The Oxford Handbook of Criminology*, 3rd edn, Oxford: Oxford University Press.

—— (2003), *Decisions and Dilemmas: Working with Mental Health Law*, Oxford: Hart.

PENROSE, L. (1939), 'Mental Disease and Crime: outline of a comparative study of European statistics', *British Journal of Medical Psychology*, 18: 39–41.

PORTER, R. (2004), 'Is mental illness inevitably stigmatizing?', in A. Crisp (ed.), *Every Family in the Land. Understanding prejudice and discrimination against people with mental illness*, London: Royal Society of Medicine.

PRINS, H. (1990), 'Mental Abnormality and Criminality — an Uncertain Relationship', *Medicine, Science and Law*, 30(3): 247–58.

—— (2005), *Offenders, Deviants or Patients?*, 3rd edn, London: Taylor & Francis.

RICHARDSON, G. (1999), *Review of the Mental Health Act 1983*, Report of the Expert Committee, London: Department of Health.

ROBERTSON, G. (1988), 'Arrest patterns among mentally disordered offenders', *British Journal of Psychiatry*, 153: 313–16.

——, PEARSON, R., and GIBB, R. (1995), *The Mentally Disordered and the Police*, Research Findings No. 21, London: Home Office, Research and Statistics Department.

ROTH, M. (1990), 'Psychopathic (Sociopathic), Personality', in R. Bluglass and P. Bowden (eds), *Principles and Practice of Forensic Psychiatry*, Edinburgh: Churchill Livingstone.

ROYAL COLLEGE OF PSYCHIATRISTS (2004), *Psychiatrists and Multi-Agency Public Protection Panels: Guidelines on representation, participation, confidentiality and information exchange*, London: RCP.

RUBIN, D. (1972), 'Predictions of Dangerousness in Mentally Ill Criminals', *Archives of General Psychiatry*, 27: 397–407.

RUMGAY, J., and MUNROE, E. (2001), 'The Lion's Den: Professional Defences in the Treatment of Dangerous Patients', *Journal of Forensic Psychiatry*: 357–78.

SEDDON, T. (2006), *Punishment and Madness: Governing Prisoners with Mental Health Problems*, London: Cavendish.

SENTENCING GUIDELINES COUNCIL (2004), *Overarching Principles: Seriousness*, Final Guideline, London: SGC.

SHAW, J., TOMENSON, B., CREED, F., and PERRY, A. (2001), 'Loss of contact with psychiatric services in people diverted from the criminal justice system', *Journal of Forensic Psychiatry*, 12: 203–10.

SINGLETON, N., MELTZER, H., and GATWARD, R. (1998), *Psychiatric morbidity among prisoners in England and Wales*, Office for National Statistics, London: The Stationery Office.

SMITH, J. C., and HOGAN, B. (1988), *Criminal Law*, 6th edn, London: Butterworths.

SOLOMKA, B. (1996), 'The Role of Psychiatric Evidence in Passing "Longer than Normal" Sentences', *Journal of Forensic Psychiatry*, 7: 239–55.

STREET, R. (1998), *The Restricted Hospital Order: From Court to the Community*, Home Office Research Study No. 186, London: Home Office.

SWANSON, J., HOLZER, C., GANJU, V., and JONO, R. (1990), 'Violence and Psychiatric Disorder in the Community: Evidence from the Epidemiological Catchment Area Surveys', *Hospital and Community Psychiatry*, 41: 761–70.

TAYLOR, R. (2003) 'An assessment of violent incident rates in the Dangerous Severe Personality Disorder Unit at HMP Whitemoor', Home Office Research Findings, No. 210, London: Home Office.

TAYLOR, P., and GUNN, J. (1999), 'Homicides by people with mental illness: myth and reality', *British Journal of Psychiatry*, 174: 9–14.

VAUGHAN, P., KELLY, M., and PULLEN, N. (2001), 'The working practices of the police in relation to mentally disordered offenders and diversion services', *Medicine, Science and the Law*, 41: 13–20.

WALKER, N. (ed.) (1996), *Dangerous People*, London: Blackstone Press.

WATSON, W., and GROUNDS, A. (eds) (1993), *Mentally Disordered Offenders in an Era of Community Care*, Cambridge: Cambridge University Press.

WEBB, D., and HARRIS, R. (eds) (1999), *Managing People Nobody Owns*, London: Routledge.

WESSELY, S., and TAYLOR. P. (1991), 'Madness and Crime: Criminology versus Psychiatry', *Criminal Behaviour and Mental Health*, 1: 193–228.

17

PLACE, SPACE, CRIME, AND DISORDER

*Anthony E. Bottoms**

> For a woman to make an argument in favour of urban life may come as a surprise. Many women and much feminist writing have been hostile to the city, and recent feminist contributions to the discussion of urban problems have tended to restrict themselves narrowly to issues of safety, welfare and protection. This is a mistake, since it re-creates the traditional paternalism of most town planning. Women's experience of urban life is even more ambiguous than that of men, and safety is a crucial issue. Yet it is necessary also to emphasise the other side of city life and to insist on women's right to the carnival, intensity and even the risks of the city. Surely it is possible to be both pro-cities and pro-women, to hold in balance an awareness of both the pleasures and the dangers that the city offers women, and to judge that in the end, urban life, however fraught with difficulty, has emancipated women more than rural life or suburban domesticity.
>
> (Wilson 1992: 10)

In this quotation, Elizabeth Wilson provides a gendered perspective on a long-standing controversy, and affirms both the risks and the attractions and vitality of city life. It is a basic and long-established criminological truth that crime rates are higher in urban than in rural areas (Cressey 1964: ch. 3); but, since our life choices are made on many grounds, of which risk of victimization is just one, most of us prefer to live in cities rather than in the countryside.[1]

Cities can be understood in many ways. Town planners are obliged by their profession to take a holistic and somewhat abstract view of issues such as overall land use and transportation, or the juxtaposition of different kinds of urban activities (residential

---

* In the previous two editions of this *Handbook*, the corresponding chapter to this has been written jointly by Paul Wiles and myself. On this occasion, Paul Wiles's duties as Chief Scientific Adviser at the Home Office have made his continuing involvement impracticable, but many of the insights he contributed to earlier editions remain in the present text, to its considerable benefit.

[1] For this reason, rural crime has been largely ignored by criminology. For an attempt to begin to redress the balance, see the volume edited by Dingwall and Moody (1999). Note especially the comments by one of the editors (Susan Moody): 'The main problem continues to be the lack of engagement on the part of criminologists themselves with the rural...Rurality has something of significance to offer criminology. Sadly, however, criminology has offered little in return' (ibid.: 24).

areas, industry, shopping areas, parks, etc.). Demographers develop complex analyses of population patterns within cities, shifts over time, and so on. Ordinary citizens experience cities in a more direct way, drawn to different parts of the city for different activities (work, home, entertaining children, a 'night on the town'), often with very different emotional connotations. Ordinary citizens also do not shrink from describing different cities as having their own 'character' or 'feel'—'some are elegant, some unsightly, some intimidating and some mundane' (Hayward 2004: 1). Criminologists, somehow, need to draw upon all of these perspectives—and more besides—in understanding crime and responses to crime in the city: the town planner's view, the demographer's view, and the ordinary person's everyday experience of the city are all important in helping us to get to grips with issues relating to cities and crime.

The field of study commonly called 'urban sociology' has experienced a lengthy identity crisis in the last half-century. Some have argued that , since most people in advanced societies now live in cities, and the metropolitan elite dominate government, business, and the all-pervasive media, there is no longer a role for a distinctive 'urban sociology'—all sociology, even the sociology of rural areas, is suffused with urban preoccupations. Others, however, have pointed especially to what is sometimes called the 'embodiment' of human beings. By this is meant the fact that, despite the manner in which modern communications can now overcome traditional barriers of distance, human beings still exist only within human bodies, and human bodies can be located in only one place at a time. Moreover, it is a matter of common observation that human beings feel safe and comfortable in some locations, but not in others. Hence, it is argued, in studying modern social life (and certainly crime and disorder, to which the concept of safety is central), we cannot ignore the importance of the spatial, as well as the social, dimension of life in cities (Dickens 1990). The combination and interaction of the spatial and the social—the so-called *socio-spatial perspective*—is therefore now increasingly accepted as the conceptual bedrock of urban sociology (see Gottdiener and Hutchison 2006). It is also the central focus of what has often been called 'environmental criminology', but which I shall here call 'socio-spatial criminology'.[2] As Paul Wiles and I suggested in the previous edition of this *Handbook*, this field of research can usefully be defined as 'the study of crime, criminality, and victimization as they relate, first, to particular *places*, and, secondly, to the way that individuals and organizations shape their activities *spatially*, and in doing so are in turn influenced by *place-based* or *spatial* factors' Bottoms and Wiles 2002: 620).[3]

---

[2] In all previous editions of this *Handbook*, the term 'environmental criminology' has been used, but there are two reasons for altering this. First, 'environmental criminology' is increasingly being used to refer to the study of criminality in relation to 'green' issues, and it is sensible to avoid unnecessary confusion between these two separate research fields. Secondly, the term 'socio-spatial' captures the *interaction* between the social and the spatial—the central core of the subject—in a way that 'environmental criminology' arguably does not.

[3] As this definition implies, 'place' is not the same as 'space'. The former concept refers to a geographical location, with fairly definite boundaries, within which people may meet, engage in various activities, etc. 'Space' is a much broader concept, but socio-spatial criminologists are interested in it because some social activities have become quite markedly *spatially differentiated* (see for example the 'zoning' approach of much urban planning), and the spatial juxtaposition of individuals' and communities' routine social activities is, as we shall see, crucial to the explanation of some criminal phenomena.

Traditionally, the two central concerns of socio-spatial criminology have been *explaining the spatial distribution of offences* and *explaining the spatial distribution of offenders*, and these remain core topics in the field. To them must now be added, however, the *study of the spatial distribution of incivilities* (or 'anti-social behaviour'). But although some of the goals of scholars in this field have long remained unchanged, the object of study has not. Scholars studying Jane Austen's novels are studying the same texts in 2006 as in 1906, although of course they are doing so in a very different social context. But for urban sociologists and socio-spatial criminologists, it is not only the social context of study, but also the object of study ('the city') that has changed hugely in the last century. Increasingly, therefore, researchers recognize the need to consider the changed nature of the city in criminological study, and that perspective will emerge from time to time in this chapter.

The chapter is organized in the following way. Initially, there is a historical introduction and some brief methodological comments. This is followed by core sections on the spatial distribution of, respectively, offences, disorder, and offenders. Finally, the macro-social dimension will be considered, with an especial emphasis on the changing nature of contemporary cities.

PLACE, SPACE, AND CRIME: A BRIEF HISTORY

Although socio-spatial analyses of crime can be traced back to the first half of the nineteenth century, for present purposes the obvious starting point for a historical overview is the important criminological work carried out between the two World Wars from within the Chicago School of Sociology (on which see generally Bulmer 1984; Abbott 1997).

The main Chicagoan criminological contribution came from Clifford Shaw and Henry McKay, whose magnum opus on juvenile delinquency in urban areas is still read, sixty years on (Shaw and McKay 1942). Their main contribution to criminology was empirical, and their research embraced two very different styles, always seen by the authors themselves as complementary. In the first place, they meticulously mapped the residences of juvenile delinquents, initially in Chicago itself at different points in time, and then also in other American cities. Secondly, they also tried, in the tradition of the Chicago School more generally, to stay close to the life of the people and the communities they were writing about, particularly by producing life histories of offenders and low life in the city (see for example Shaw 1930).

We can concentrate here on Shaw and McKay's mapping of delinquent residences. In developing this research, they drew upon the more general work in urban sociology of the Chicago School, notably that of Robert E. Park and Ernest W. Burgess, the dominant concept of which was 'human ecology'. Human ecology was seen as the study of the spatial and temporal relations of human beings as affected by the selective, distributive, and accommodative forces of the environment; the concept was derived, by analogy, from the botanical subdiscipline of plant ecology. Shaw and McKay drew only to a limited extent upon the most explicitly quasi-biological elements of Park's urban sociology, but they made quite central use of Burgess's zonal theory of city development. According to this theory, the typical city could be conceptualized as consisting of five main concentric zones. The innermost zone was described as the non-residential central business district, which was then circled by a 'zone in transition', where factories and poorer residences were intermingled, and finally by three residential zones of increasing affluence and social status as one moved towards the outer suburbs. New immigrants, it was postulated, would move into the cheapest residential areas of the city (in the 'zone in transition') and then, as they became economically established, migrate outwards. This would be a continuous process, so that the 'zone in transition' would (as its name implies) have a high residential mobility rate and a rather heterogeneous population. In the case of a rapidly expanding city, particular districts which had once been peripheral and affluent might become, in time, part of the zone in transition within a larger metropolis.

Applying this zonal model to their empirical data, Shaw and McKay made three central discoveries (see Finestone 1976:25):

1. The rates of juvenile delinquency residence conformed to a regular spatial pattern. They were highest in the 'zone in transition', and then declined with distance from the centre of the city; and this was so not only in Chicago but in other cities as well.

2. The same spatial pattern was shown by many other indices of social problems in the city.

3. The spatial pattern of rates of delinquency showed considerable long-term stability, even though the nationality make-up of the population in the inner-city areas changed greatly from decade to decade (with successive waves of migration to American cities in the early twentieth century).

In seeking to explain these striking findings, Shaw and McKay focused especially upon the observed *cultural heterogeneity* and the *constant population movements* in the 'zone in transition'. Economic mobility lay at the heart of the process they described, but they did not posit a direct relationship between economic factors and rates of delinquency. Instead, the zone of transition, characterized as it was by economic deprivation, physical deterioration, population mobility, and population herterogeneity, was seen as containing both *social-structural weakness* (institutional incapacity to provide successful routes to valued societal goals; institutional discontinuities in socialization) and *cultural fragmentation* (Kornhauser 1978: 61–82). It was these factors, in Shaw and McKay's view, which especially influenced juvenile delinquency through a process that they called 'social disorganization' (although some later commentators have felt it might have been better described as 'weaknesses in social organization'). In their formulation, 'social disorganization exists in the first instance when the structure and culture of a community are incapable of implementing and expressing the values of its own residents' (Kornhauser 1978: 63), including the near-universal value of a non-delinquent future for one's children. The view was that, given the social fluidity and moral diversity[4] in the zone of transition, incoming immigrant communities could not provide for their young people common and clear non-delinquent values and control.[5]

It is a measure of the standing and achievement of Shaw and McKay that, in the quarter-century immediately after the end of the Second World War, there were relatively few major new developments in socio-spatial criminology, despite the publication of some significant individual research monographs (e.g. Lander 1954; Morris 1957). However, the 1970s were to see the subject given new impetus, mainly by two fresh developments.

The first of these can be described as the *rediscovery of the offence*. Shaw and McKay's work had been all about *area offender rates* (i.e. the rate of offenders per head of population in each area) but these are not necessarily the same as area offence rates (i.e. the rate of offences committed in each area), since we cannot necessarily assume that offenders commit offences close to their homes (see further below). Various different criminological developments combined to refocus attention on *crimes* rather than *offenders* in the 1970s (see generally Brantingham and Brantingham 1981a: Introduction). These included, in particular, the first-ever large-scale victim surveys (initiated in the USA in the late 1960s), and the early work of the Home Office Research Unit on 'crime as opportunity' (Mayhew *et al.* 1976), leading in due course to the more sophisticated development of 'situational crime prevention' approaches (see Clarke 1995; Smith and Cornish 2003), on which see further below.

The second major development of the 1970s came in the field of explaining offender rates. In his pioneering 1957 book, Terence Morris (1957) had shown that, given the existence in post-war Britain of a sizeable social housing sector (then called 'council housing'), and, as a part of this, some 'peripheral problem estates', the areal rates of offender residence in Croydon did not conform to the Chicago zonal hypothesis. This finding was confirmed and strengthened by work in Sheffield (Baldwin and Bottoms 1976) which indicated that, while there was something of a clustering of high-offender-rate areas around the central business district, for the city as a whole the data did not display any tidy zonal pattern. In seeking to explain these findings, the Sheffield researchers were drawn increasingly towards the exploration of the *direct and indirect consequences of the operation of housing markets* (see for example Bottoms and Wiles 1986). This emphasis on housing markets has been taken up by other researchers, and has been found to be of particular significance when assessing change in offender and offence rates in residential areas (see for example Wikström 1991; Foster and Hope 1993; Hancock 2001).

---

[4] The moral diversity arose not only from the presence in the zone in transition of several different immigrant groups, but also from the fact that 'many illegitimate enterprises and deviant moral worlds' (Finestone 1976: 28) found their natural home in this zone of the city.

[5] At various points in their writings, Shaw and McKay also speak of another and rather different theoretical approach to the explanation of criminality, namely that of *criminal subcultures*, linked to the cultural transmission of delinquent values. The precise relationship between these two varied theoretical strands of Shaw and McKay's work was not always made fully clear in their writings (see Kornhauser 1978: ch. 3).

The *rediscovery of the offence* and the *discovery of the significance of housing markets* between them did much to revivify socio-spatial criminology from the mid-1970s onwards. In more recent years, that revitalization has continued apace, with three fresh developments. The most obvious of these is the advent of computerized 'geographical information systems' (GIS), which has led to an explosion of interest in so-called 'crime mapping', and the development—particularly in the United States—of a new profession of 'crime analysts', mostly working in police departments. The study of the spatial dimensions of crime, offender, and victim data—which, within the professional memory of not-yet-retired criminologists, could literally only be accomplished by sticking pins in maps—has been completely transformed by the advent of GIS, although inevitably some of the applications of this technology have been, in practice, somewhat mundane.[6]

The second and third recent developments in the field are more theoretical, although involving different kinds of theory. One strand can be read as a continuing attempt to grapple with the issues raised by Shaw and McKay in their 'social disorganization' formulation; this strand of work has made us familiar with a new theoretical vocabulary of concepts such as 'collective efficacy' and 'control signals'. The other strand of work arises above all from the realization that the city of the early twenty-first century is in many ways very different from the city of the early twentieth century—a difference expressed in conceptual formulations such as 'the shift from modern to late modern society', or 'the change from a producer to a consumer society'. Both these approaches will be considered more fully later in this chapter.

These various recent developments in the field have led—perhaps inevitably—to some academic disputation, and it is not too difficult to identify at least three separate 'academic tribes' working in the field of socio-spatial criminology (see 'Selected further reading' at the end of this chapter). The text that follows tries to be fair to the various different traditions of work in the area (whilst not disguising the author's own preoccupations), within an overview that primarily concentrates on substantive issues. How far it succeeds in this aim is for others to judge.

PRELIMINARY METHODOLOGICAL ISSUES

Before we turn to substantive research findings, two key methodological issues must be briefly addressed: they are the distinction between the offence, the offender, and the victim, and the validity of official statistics.

The distinction between the offence rate and the offender rate has already been highlighted above. It is an absolutely central issue in socio-spatial criminology, as will

---

[6] An increasing number of introductory guides to the world of 'crime mapping' have been published in recent years: for good recent treatments see Chainey and Ratcliffe (2005) and Boba (2005).

quickly become apparent if one compares maps of offence locations in any given city (see for example Figure 17.1, discussed later) with a map of offender residences in the same year. Interestingly, however, research has shown that if one excludes non-residential areas such as the city centre, shopping malls, and industrial districts, there is often a strong (but not perfect) correlation between offender and offence rates in residential areas (Mawby 1979).

One should further note that, in any given geographical area, both the offence rate and the offender rate are in principle measurable both by official (police-recorded) data and by survey data (namely, victim surveys in respect of offence rates, and self-report surveys in respect of offender rates). In practice, however, self-report studies carried out on an areal basis are rare. One should also be aware that there is an important distinction in principle between an *area offence rate* and an *area victimization rate*. The former measures all offences committed in an area, whether against businesses, individual residents, or individuals who are visiting the area; the latter measures all offences committed against a defined population (e.g. respondents to a household victim survey living in a particular residential district), wherever those offences were committed. Because of this conceptual difference, particular care must be taken when comparing *total police-recorded offence rates* for a given area (which will be geographically limited to that area, but will include offences against businesses, and against individual visitors to the area) and *victimization rates generated from a household victim survey* in the same neighbourhood (which will exclude both crimes against businesses, and crimes against individual victims visiting the area, but will include crimes committed against residents of the area when they have ventured outside the district, e.g. to the city centre or their place of work).

These considerations take us straight to the second methodological issue, that of the validity of official criminal statistics in relation to area-based data. This is an important topic because, very often, the only easily available data for studying crime in a given local area are police-recorded statistics.[7] Over the years, there have been some lively debates surrounding this issue, with particular scepticism being expressed about the validity of official statistics during the heyday of labelling theory in the 1970s (for a useful historical overview of the debate, see Mawby 1989). Commenting on this debate in a short space is difficult, but to begin with the uncontroversial, there is now no doubt that, on a large-area basis—for example as between police forces—the message conveyed by official criminal statistics can be misleading, particularly because of different police investigative and recording practices in different areas (see for example Farrington and Dowds 1985; Burrows *et al.* 2000; HM Inspectorate of Constabulary 2000; see also Maguire, Chapter 10, this volume). On a smaller-area, within-city basis, where police recording practices are more often similar, there are good empirical grounds for believing that differential police-recorded offence and offender rates as

---

[7] Specially conducted local victimization surveys are by no means unknown, but have been conducted in only a small minority of areas. Large-scale national victimization surveys, such as the British Crime Survey, are—for reasons of sample size and error estimates—at best able to provide victimization estimates for large areas rather than small areas.

between different areas will frequently give basically true indications of neighbourhood differences in crime or criminality levels. However, one must always be very careful in interpreting even such data, and that is true especially (i) for offences that are recorded as a result of proactive policing, such as drug possession or soliciting for prostitution, and (ii) when one or more of the areas is severely socially disadvantaged, since the probability of the public reporting crimes to the police is significantly lower in such areas (Baumer 2002; Goudriaan *et al.* 2006).

EXPLAINING THE LOCATION OF OFFENCES

DESCRIPTIVE DATA

In turning to our substantive review of the issues, it is convenient to begin with the location of offences, not least because this is the topic that analysts using the new GIS technology have tended to prioritize.

Wikström's (1991) study of police-recorded offences in Stockholm provides one of the best illustrations of the way in which such offences are locationally distributed in a major city. Previous research work (see Baldwin and Bottoms 1976, using Sheffield data) had shown that offences tend, in traditional cities, to be clustered heavily around the city centre; and the offence data in Wikström's study (see Figure 17.1(a), (b), and (c)) show this to be especially the case for violence in public, vandalism in public, and theft of and from cars. (Wikström does not present data concerning shoplifting or thefts from the person, but other research studies have shown that these offences also are particularly located in city centres.) However, there is nothing necessarily immutable about such patterns. For example, in cities that develop large shopping or entertainment complexes on peripheral sites, some corresponding modification of this traditional geographical pattern may well occur; and in Sheffield the development of such a complex (the Meadowhall shopping mall) helped to reduce the proportion of all crime occurring in the city centre from 24 per cent in 1966 to 10 per cent in 1995 (Wiles and Costello 2000: 46). This is just one example of the changing nature of contemporary cities, highlighted in the introduction to this chapter.[8]

Turning to offences in residential areas, the distributions of family violence and residential burglaries in Wikström's study are shown in Figure 17.1(d) and (e). The highest rates of family violence were found in certain outer-city wards, and additional

---

[8] The Sheffield example is a small-scale manifestation of a development that Gottdiener and Hutchison (2006: 14) call the 'multicentered metro environment'—a process that has progressed further in the USA than in most other countries. According to Gottdiener and Hutchison (2006: 5), in contrast to the traditional city with its city centre or 'downtown', this 'new form of space can be typified by two features: it extends over a large [metropolitan] region, and it contains many separate centers, each with its own abilities to draw workers, shoppers and residents'.

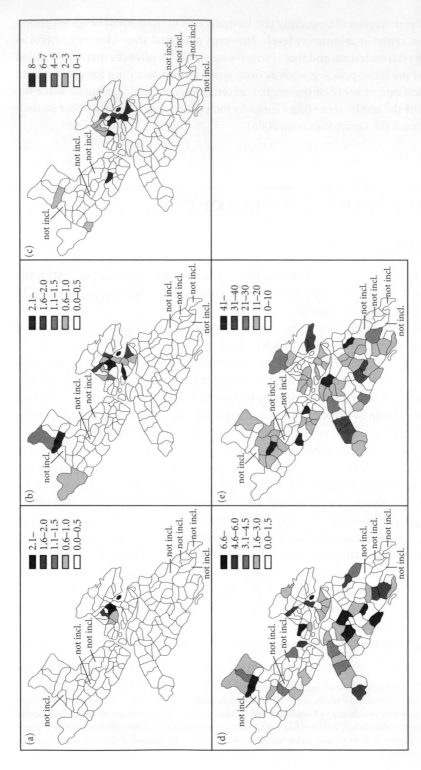

Fig. 17.1 Areal offence rates for selected types of crime, Stockholm, 1982: (a) violence in public per hectare; (b) vandalism in public per hectare; (c) thefts of and from cars per hectare; (d) family violence per 1,000 households; (e) residential burglaries per 1,000 residences

Source: Wikström (1991: 203–6).

analysis showed that this offence was heavily concentrated in the poorer public housing areas. A further inspection of the Stockholm maps indicates, however, that the distribution of offences of residential burglary was substantially different from that of family violence; indeed, Wikström (1991: 226–7) showed that recorded residential burglaries tended to occur disproportionately in areas of high socio-economic status, and especially in districts where there were nearby high offender-rate areas. This finding, while not unique in the literature,[9] conflicts with the results of many other research studies, which suggest that rates of residential burglary are greatest in, or in areas close to, socially disadvantaged housing areas (for a summary, see Mawby 2001: ch. 5). I will return to this contrast later.

Wikström's study demonstrates, at any rate as regards crimes measured by police data, first that there are marked geographical skews in the patterning of offence locations, and secondly that areal patterns can vary significantly by type of offence. This general message of locational variation has been heavily reinforced in other research. For example, Sherman *et al.* (1989), using police call data for Minneapolis for 1985–6, found (i) that just 3.3 per cent of specific locations in the city generated 50 per cent of crime-related calls, and (ii) that there was considerable variation in the victimization rate (as measured by call data) of specific micro-locations even within high crime rate areas—that is, even high-crime areas have their relatively safe specific locations, as well as their 'hotspots' where the public are likely to be especially vulnerable. Areas with different land-use patterns also often have different crime levels; city centres have already been mentioned, but other non-residential areas, such as industrial estates, can have burglary rates much higher than those of residential neighbourhoods, yet with significant variations which appear to be related especially to their proximity to high-offender-rate residential areas (see Johnston *et al.* 1994). Finally, even in high-offence-rate residential neighbourhoods, the chance of being victimized is not random, with some households not being victimized at all in a year, but others being repeatedly victimized. For example, in the worst tenth of areas studied in the 1988 British Crime Survey, only 28 per cent of respondents reported having been the victim of a property offence in the previous year, but the average number of incidents reported by property crime victims was 4.6, with some having been victimized only once, but others very frequently (Farrell 1995: 526). Spatial variations in offence-rate distributions are, in short, a pervasive feature of the crime-pattern landscape.

VEHICLE CRIME

To supplement the basic descriptive data in the previous subsection, let us take a closer look at one kind of crime—offences against vehicles. This will develop our description, and also begin to open up some theoretical issues.

---

[9] See, e.g., Baldwin and Bottoms (1976: 63), Winchester and Jackson (1982: 18–19). It should be pointed out that these studies, like Wikström's, are based on data recorded by the police, and it is likely that they proportionately overstate the number of high-value burglaries, since value is known to be related to the decision to report.

Wikström's (1991) offence maps of Stockholm clearly suggest a very high incidence of vehicle crime in the city centre area. However, closer consideration quickly reveals an underlying difficulty—namely, what is the best way to measure offence rates? Offender rates are straightforward to measure, because the appropriate denominator for such a rate is obviously the area population (or some subgroup of it such as a specified age/gender group). When measuring offence rates, however, using population denominators would often be highly misleading—and, as it happens, vehicle theft is an excellent example of this (for example, measuring city centre vehicle theft offences as a rate per 1,000 of the resident city centre population would clearly be inappropriate). Wikström's pragmatic solution to this difficulty, for vehicle crime, was to use a simple 'rate per hectare' measure.[10] However, this too has some difficulties.

Table 17.1 presents data from the British Crime Survey (BCS) for 2004–5 on the location and timing of vehicle-related thefts[11] in England and Wales. Column 3 of the table shows that as many as two-thirds of such thefts occur when the vehicle is located at or very near the victim's home. This gives a very different impression from the Stockholm data, but in fact the two data-sources are not necessarily incompatible (although of course they relate to different countries and different years) because vehicle thefts occurring near victims' homes will occur throughout a city or metropolitan area, and therefore will very likely not show up at all strongly when one analyses offences on an aggregate 'per hectare' basis.

There are additional subtleties in the data in Table 17.1. The vehicle-related thefts occurring near victims' homes are temporally very skewed, nearly 90 per cent of them occurring in the evenings or at night; conversely, most workplace-related vehicle crimes occur by day, while such offences in other locations are evenly split by day or night (column 4 of the table). Vehicle-related thefts from near victims' homes also very rarely occur in fully private areas (i.e. garages linked to the home); this seems to reflect the obvious fact that it is much easier to steal from cars parked on the driveway or in the street outside the home.

But there are further complications yet. If I park my car for the night on the driveway outside my home, it will probably be there for eight hours or more; if I park in a city centre car park when I go shopping, the car will be there for a much shorter period. Table 17.1 takes no account of these differing exposures to risk, but an analysis of earlier BCS data by Ronald Clarke and Pat Mayhew (1998) has attempted this. These authors calculated a rate of 'vehicle-related theft per 100,000 cars per 24 hours' for different locations; and on this basis, public car parks had the highest rate (454), followed by

---

[10] Wikström's (1991: 193–200) book contains a good short discussion of the technical problems of calculating valid area crime rates. For vehicle thefts, the best solution would be, as he recognizes, a denominator consisting of some kind of vehicle count, but this was unavailable in his Stockholm study. As the text near Figure 17.1 shows, the Stockholm study used different denominators for different offence types.

[11] This table includes both the taking of vehicles (i.e. theft of vehicles, plus taking without the consent of the owner) *and* theft from vehicles (for example, theft of car radios or property left inside vehicles). These might seem to be very different offences, but their general locational patterning is in fact usually (though not always) similar.

Table 17.1 British Crime Survey 2004–2005: Location and Timing of Vehicle-Related Thefts (%)

	Morning/Afternoon (6 a.m.–6 p.m.)	Evening/Night (6 p.m.–6 a.m.)	Total	% in category occurring in evening/night
Home area				
Private	2	2	2	
Semi-private*	11	28	24	
Street	15	49	41	
(Subtotal)	(28)	(79)	(67)	89.3%
Workplace				
Car park	9	1	3	
Street	6	1	2	
(Subtotal)	(15)	(2)	(5)	28.3%
Other				
Car park	33	11	16	
Street	20	8	11	
Other	4	1	2	
(Subtotal)	(57)	(20)	(29)	50.9%
Total	100	100	100	
Unweighted base	678	2,007	2,685	

* 'Semi-private' includes outside areas on the premises (house driveways, etc), and garages or car parks around but not connected to the home.
Source: Nicholas *et al*. (2005: 66).

street parking not outside the home or workplace (327), and—some way behind—by street parking outside the home and workplace (117 and 118 respectively). 'Semi-private' home locations (see Table 17.1) were well down the list on 40, with home garages on a rate of 2.

So, different measurement methods for offence rates yield different results, but it can be argued that each provides some valuable information. From the police viewpoint, it is useful to know that on a simple 'per hectare' basis, vehicle thefts are disproportionately concentrated in city centre areas. For the ordinary car owner wanting to avoid a vehicle-related theft, it is equally useful to know that the highest risk rate per hour of parking is to be found in public car parks. But since, if one parks outside one's home in the evening, it is almost always with the intention of leaving the vehicle there for several hours, it is also very important to recognize that *nearly two-thirds* of British vehicle-related thefts occur in such locations, overwhelmingly in the 6 p.m. to 6 a.m. period (Table 17.1).

The above examples do not exhaust the criminological interest of the locational study of vehicle thefts. Further examples from this crime type will be included as we begin to consider theoretical explanations for variations in offence locations, beginning with the concept of 'opportunity'.

OPPORTUNITY THEORY AND ROUTINE ACTIVITIES THEORY

Felson and Clarke (1998: 5) have usefully suggested that there are four main components of the concept of opportunity in property crimes, namely 'value, inertia, visibility and access', which can be easily remembered by the mnemonic 'VIVA'. These components, however, really group into two main aspects of opportunity. The first of these is *target attractiveness*, a concept which includes both value (monetary and/or cultural) and what Felson and Clarke call 'inertia', or portability (heavy goods such as washing machines are rarely stolen). 'Target attractiveness' thus relates to the intrinsic attractiveness of the object, from the point of view of the offender, leaving aside issues of access and guardianship (on which see further below). In explaining the location of offences, property value is the most important aspect of target attractiveness, since target values are often locationally skewed, both as regards the general affluence of different areas (see Wikström's data on residential burglary, above), and as regards the value of a particular target, by comparison with neighbouring potential targets. For example, in a 1993 analysis of vehicle crime using British Crime Survey data, it was found that, within a given residential area, the cars of the more obviously affluent residents were the more likely to be targeted.[12]

The second main dimension of opportunity can be described as *accessibility*, a concept that includes visibility, ease of physical access, and the absence of adequate guardianship. This dimension of opportunity is also well illustrated by a vehicle crime example, this time the vehicle theft rates from different multi-storey car parks in Croydon (see table in Bottoms 1994: 603). Three short-stay multi-storey car parks that were used primarily by shoppers (and which therefore had a constant stream of passers-by providing natural surveillance and guardianship) were found to have substantially lower crime rates per car park space than two long-stay car parks, primarily used by commuters from Croydon to London, which lacked such surveillance; it was the difference in the levels of natural guardianship that was apparently crucial. Many other similar examples of the importance of accessibility and natural surveillance can also be found in the literature.

Two interim observations should be made at this point about the concept of opportunity. First, if opportunities can be unintentionally *created* (for example, by building car parks with low natural guardianship), they can, at least in principle, also be intentionally *blocked*. This simple observation has given rise to what is now a sophisticated

---

[12] Specifically, in thefts of and from vehicles from immediately around the house, 'consumerist' households were more likely to be victimized, even when area and type of residence was controlled for (see Mayhew *et al.* 1993: 140–41). ('Consumerist' households were those owning three or more of five specified electronic consumer products.)

body of criminological literature organized around the concept of 'situational crime prevention'—that is, altering the physical and social environment ('situations') in an attempt to reduce the likelihood of crimes being committed (see Crawford, Chapter 26, this volume; also Clarke 1995, 1997; Smith and Cornish 2003). The concept of opportunity has an important, though not an exclusive, role to play within situational crime prevention; and when opportunity-blocking measures are successfully applied, this can itself lead both to overall crime reduction, and (importantly for the purposes of this chapter) to a change in the locational distribution of offences. For example, a few years ago analyses showed that in many house burglaries the offender(s) entered through the rear of the property; and this led to the installation, in suitable contexts, of gates and fences across alleyways or footpaths running behind houses (a process known as 'alley-gating'), with successful crime-preventive results (Chainey and Ratcliffe 2005: 28–31; Bowers *et al.* 2004).

Secondly, it will be apparent from the preceding discussion that opportunity theory uses, implicitly, a rational choice theory of offending, in which offenders are assumed to assess potential benefits (e.g. lucrative targets) and possible costs (e.g. an enhanced probability of getting caught if one attempts a vehicle theft in a car park with high natural surveillance, or a burglary through a front rather than a back window). This rational choice dimension of the opportunity approach (and of situational crime prevention theory more generally) has been explicitly embraced and developed especially by Derek Cornish and Ronald Clarke (1986, 2003).

Opportunity theory is often considered alongside 'routine activities theory', originally developed by Cohen and Felson (1979) and subsequently elaborated particularly by Marcus Felson (see for example Felson 2002). The central hypothesis of routine activities theory was originally stated as:

> the probability that a violation will occur at any specific time and place might be taken as a function of the convergence of likely offenders and suitable targets in the absence of capable guardians [Cohen and Felson 1979: 590].

However, of the three elements identified in the above quotation, in its early days routine activities theory in practice concentrated very heavily on the second and third (suitable targets and capable guardians).[13] That being so, the link with opportunity theory is self-evident—although (as will become clear shortly) by initially ignoring the offender dimension, advocates of routine activities theory closed off a promising approach. But, despite the similarities between routine activities and opportunity theory (see, more fully, Clarke and Felson 1993), there are nevertheless two features of the routine activities approach which usefully developed and extended the straightforward concept of 'opportunity'. These are as follows:

First, there is a strong interest within routine activities theory in *the day-to-day activities of potential victims of crime, and of those potentially able to offer 'natural surveillance'*. There is

---

[13] See Cohen and Felson (1979: 589): 'Unlike many criminological enquiries, we do not examine why individuals or groups are inclined criminally, but rather we take criminal inclination as given and examine the manner in which the spatio-temporal organisation of social activities helps people to translate their criminal inclinations into action.'

therefore seen to be an interdependence between the varied social organisation of daily life patterns (for example, in different decades, and/or in different places, and/or among different social groups in the same area) and the spatial-temporal patterns of illegal activities.

Secondly, routine activities theory has an explicitly spatial dimension, which, while implicitly present in simple opportunity theory, has not always been much developed by writers of that school. Routine activities theory, precisely because of its interest in the everyday lives of potential victims of crime, and of potential 'natural guardians', specific-ally emphasises 'the fundamental human ecological character of illegal acts as *events* which occur at specific locations in *space* and *time*, involving specific persons and/or objects' [Cohen and Felson 1979: 589, emphasis in original].

In sum, routine activities theory in effect embeds the simple concept of opportunity within the routine parameters of the day-to-day lives of ordinary people, and in doing so also emphasizes the spatial-temporal features of opportunity. Routine activities theory is also better able than opportunity theory to explain the location of offences against the person, rather than offences against property. For example, the common observation that offences of violence in public occur very disproportionately at weekends, and in or near places of public entertainment such as bars and clubs, is obviously more naturally explained by the concept of 'routine activities' than in the language of 'opportunity'.

Taking all the evidence of this subsection together, there is not much doubt that opportunities and routine activities powerfully influence crime locations. However, the research literature also suggests that matters are more complex than this. To begin to see why that is so, let us consider two pieces of evidence, one general and one specific. The general point is that, on their own, opportunities and the routine activities of victims and guardians seem unable to account for the overall distribution of victimization in residential areas in most cities. As already explained above, some affluent neighbour-hoods, with plenty of attractive targets, do have high victimization rates, but others do not (and this is not necessarily because they have effective guardianship). Moreover, often the highest victimization rates are found in the poorest neighbourhoods, with relatively low levels of target attractiveness. The more specific piece of evidence (one of many that could have been selected) is taken from an ethnographic study of convicted burglars in a Texas city (Cromwell *et al.* 1991). In this study it was found, congruently with opportunity theory, that offenders weighed potential gains, levels of guardianship (e.g. signs of occupancy) and risks of detection at possible sites of residential burglary. Hence, it appeared that *active weighing of the opportunity factor at the potential crime site* was indeed a significant factor in the ultimate decision whether or not to commit a particular crime. On the other hand, Cromwell and his colleagues also found that there was individual variation in the degree of planning as between different offenders (or groups of offenders); complex interactive effects (including emotional interactions) within groups of burglars; differences related to whether illicit drugs were used by the offenders; and interactions with fences that could affect the decision processes. What all this suggests is first, that we need to take a closer look at offenders and their routine activities; and secondly, that the rational-choice model of decision-making, implicitly or explicitly used by most opportunity and routine activities theorists, might need some modification. To consider these potential complexities, we will first look at the literature on offenders' perceptions and use of space, and then discuss more explicitly some apparently non-instrumentally-rational dimensions of offending.

OFFENDERS' PERCEPTIONS AND USE OF SPACE

It is a commonplace of criminological textbooks that much crime is committed close to offenders' homes. There are a number of 'crime and distance' studies, which explore detected offenders' distance from home when committing offences (for a brief review see Wiles and Costello 2000); however, it can reasonably be argued that this topic is rather less interesting than the related question of the relationship of the place of the offence to the offender's habitual use of space.

Let us first note that there are some purely *opportunist* property crimes, where a person responds 'there and then' to a set of attractive environmental cues; for example, a teenage boy calls at a friend's house, finds the back door open and £20 unguarded on the table. There are also some *affectively spontaneous* crimes, where a person commits, say, an assault in the course of a sudden heated argument with an acquaintance. These offences, by definition, must occur in the place where the offender happens to be, as a result of his/her daily life choices.

However, Patricia and Paul Brantingham (1981b) long ago proposed that offenders' daily life patterns might influence the location of offending behaviour even when the offender is engaging, to some degree, in a search pattern for a suitable target, having already decided in principle to commit an offence.[14] They argued that all of us carry in our heads 'cognitive maps' of the cities where we live. Some parts of the city we will know extremely well (e.g. the areas immediately around our home, near our workplaces and leisure sites, and in the city centre where we go for shopping and entertainment purposes); and we will also tend to know well the roads linking these various areas. On the other hand, there will be some areas of the city which we hardly know at all, such as residential areas (away from main roads) in which we have no social acquaintances and nothing else to attract us. The Brantinghams postulated that most offenders, preferring (like most people) to operate in contexts with which they are familiar, will not commit offences in poorly known areas. Hence, in their model, offences, even 'search pattern' offences, were thought to be most likely to occur where *criminal opportunities* (see earlier subsection) intersect with *cognitively known areas*—a hypothesis schematically illustrated in Figure 17.2. They also suggested that, where an individual is motivated to commit an offence, 'the actual commission of the offense is the end result of a multi-staged decision process which seeks out and identifies, within the general environment,

---

[14] For later refinements of this model see Brantingham and Brantingham (1993, 1999). The model is now usually referred to as 'crime pattern theory', and it has been argued that it incorporates rational-choice and routine-activities perspectives together with certain key principles from environmental psychology (Rossmo 2000).

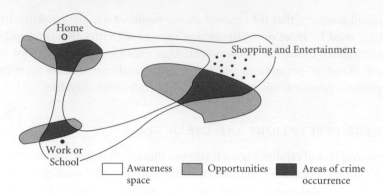

Fig. 17.2 The Brantinghams' hypothetical model of intersection of criminal opportunities with offenders' cognitive awareness space

Source: Newman, Charles L.; Brantingham, Paul J.; Brantingham, Patricia, *Patterns in Crime*, 1st edition © 1984. Reprinted by permission of Pearson Education, Inc., Upper Saddle River, NJ.

a target or victim positioned in time and space'. There will however be differences in this process depending on the motivation of the offender. In particular, it was suggested by the Brantinghams that in offences of 'high affect motivation', this decision process 'will probably involve a minimal number of stages', in which case one might reasonably expect that the distance travelled to commit the offence will usually be shorter than for more instrumentally calculated offences.

The degree of empirical testing of the Brantinghams' important model has not been as extensive or specific as one might wish; nevertheless, what evidence we have tends clearly to support it. To illustrate this, we may look briefly at two small-scale American studies, and then at some recent British research.

Rengert and Wasilchick (2000: ch. 3) carried out an interview study of imprisoned adult burglars from Delaware County, Pennsylvania, and showed that burglary sites were clustered disproportionately in areas closest to the offenders' normal routes to work and recreation. By contrast, a very different directional pattern was observed for the few burglaries in the sample committed not as a result of the offender's own search pattern, but because a secondary source (e.g. a fence) told the offender about an appropriate opportunity for crime. An earlier study in Oklahoma City had found some similar results (Carter and Hill 1979), though because Oklahoma City is a racially divided city, neither black nor white offenders ventured much into residential areas predominantly lived in by the other ethnic group. Based on their findings, Carter and Hill (1979: 49) proposed an interesting distinction between 'strategic' and 'tactical' choices in search-pattern property crimes. 'Tactics' refer to 'short-term operational considerations for a specific crime', and are likely to be influenced by (instrumentally rational) opportunity factors. However, these 'tactical' decisions, Carter and Hill suggest, will be taken only within a limited geographical framework already set by 'strategic' considerations. These 'strategic' considerations relate especially to the issue of familiarity, and are thus more likely to be based on affective factors (e.g. 'areas towards which he has a favorable feeling': Carter and Hill 1979: 49).

A recent study in Sheffield (Wiles and Costello 2000) found that offenders on average travelled only 1.93 miles from their homes to commit a crime—a finding similar to many other studies.[15] Interviews with Sheffield persistent offenders suggested that most of their travel was not in order to offend. More importantly, and congruently with the Brantinghams' model, most offending was not an outcome of criminally instrumental travel: less than a third of burglaries, for example, had involved travelling specifically in order to commit the offence (Wiles and Costello 2000: 36). The locations of offences were more usually the outcome of the offender's routine activities, which involved some travelling. Furthermore, these Sheffield offenders demonstrated the link between routine activities and crime in an additional way, since about 80 per cent of out-of-city travelling that involved offending was to places with strong traditional cultural links to Sheffield.

The studies considered above are of 'volume offenders', that is, those committing mainly property crimes. Not dissimilar results, however, have also been found for serious violent and sexual offenders, though where there is a serial pattern of such offences the publicity surrounding earlier offences can lead the offender to alter his initial locational preferences. For example, Figure 17.3 shows, in the order of their commission, the location of the murders and attempted murders committed by Peter Sutcliffe (the so-called 'Yorkshire Ripper') in the period 1975–81. As will be seen, the first three offences all occurred at points roughly equidistant from Sutcliffe's home, but in different directions (No. 1, NW; No. 2, S; No. 3, NE), and the next six crimes were clustered fairly close to the first three. After that, there was some diversification of location (Manchester, Huddersfield), and the final offence and arrest occurred in another city (Sheffield); presumably, by spreading his activities in this way Sutcliffe was, in the later stages of his offence sequence, trying to avoid the intense police hunt for him in areas closer to the sites of earlier victimizations. However that may be, the confirmation that a 'routine activities/cognitive spatial awareness' explanation seems often to apply to serious personal crimes has led to an important applied literature that reverses the logic of the Brantinghams' model, and uses the data on serial offences that are not cleared up in an attempt to predict the location of the offender's likely home or other familiar areas,[16] thus narrowing the scope of search for the detective team. This is known as 'geographic profiling' (see for example Canter 2003; Rossmo 2000).

In the light of the Brantinghams' model, it also becomes possible to explain why burglary patterns in different cities have produced conflicting results (see earlier subsection). The apparently conflicting findings may simply reflect the differing social geographies of the cities in which research has been carried out; that is, whether high-offender-rate areas are near affluent residential neighbourhoods, or the extent to

---

[15] Of course, average distance from home can vary by, for example, the age of the offender and the type of offence. However, the research literature on such factors does not always yield consistent results—see more fully Wiles and Costello (2000).

[16] In the majority of such offence sequences, including that of Peter Sutcliffe, the offender is found to live within 'an area that can be defined by a circle whose diameter [joins] the two furthest crimes: the "circle hypothesis"' (Canter 2003: 129). In a minority of cases, the offender seeks out targets away from a base—sometimes colloquially called a 'commuter'.

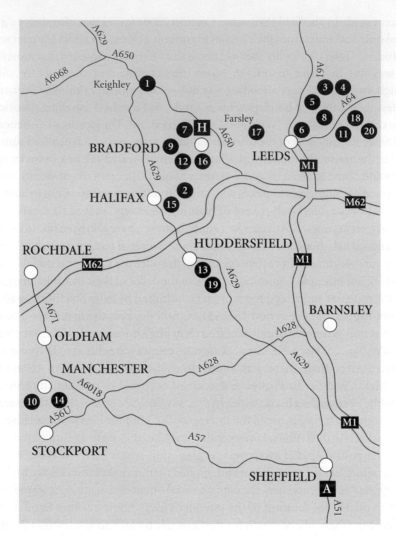

Fig. 17.3 Sequential locations of murders and attempted murders by Peter Sutcliffe 1975–1981

Notes: H = Sutcliffe's home; A = location of arrest.
Source: Copyright © David Carter 2003, Virgin Books Ltd.

which low-offender-rate areas act as 'social attractors' to offenders in their (non-criminal) routine activities.[17] Further support for this suggestion derives from British Crime Survey property-crime victimization data, when analysed by ACORN groups, which shows that whilst most better-off areas have low victimization rates, this is not true of those which are more likely to be located near to high-offender-rate areas

[17] For example, one low-offender/high-offence area in Sheffield (Wiles and Costello 2000: 53) is a fashionable small inner-suburban shopping and entertainment area surrounded by residential properties; it is likely that the high residential offence rate arises from offenders' familiarity with the area when visiting it for leisure purposes.

(Nicholas *et al.* 2005: 69).[18] The extent to which different cities have such better-off areas near to poorer areas with high offender rates will produce differing city maps of offence-rate distributions; in other words, the crime maps for a city will reflect the way in which the history of the city has relatively located different social groups, and facilities such as shopping and entertainment centres. Cities with the same degree of social differentiation can, therefore, have very different socio-spatial distributions of offences.

However, the proximity of offenders to offences and therefore to victims is not just geographical but also often social (a point that emphasizes the importance of considering the social as well as the spatial dimension in socio-spatial criminology). It has been known for some time, for example, in relation to crimes of violence, that individuals who choose to go out frequently at night, especially to certain areas or places of entertainment, have higher risks of personal victimization arising out of these social activities (see, e.g., Gottfredson 1984); and American data suggest that even robbery by acquaintances is far from unknown (Felson *et al.* 2000). Evidence is also now beginning to emerge that known offenders have high rates of property-crime victimization. An unpublished study in Sheffield has shown that, for police-recorded burglary, households which contained a (current) known offender had a higher rate of victimization than other households, even when the area offence rate is controlled for; and also that repeat victimization was higher in offender-households. A follow-up interview study suggested that one reason for these high victimization rates was that offender-victims were much more likely than the average burglary victim to be offended against by an acquaintance (Bottoms and Costello 2001). In short, the worlds of offending and victimization are not necessarily separate, and this is part of the explanation as to why high-offender-rate areas also have high offence rates.

BEYOND INSTRUMENTAL RATIONALITY

I have already several times referred to emotional or affective dimensions of offending—for example, in the within offending-group emotional interactions discussed by Cromwell *et al.* (1991), and in the Brantinghams' suggestion that offenders' search patterns will be truncated in crimes of 'high affect motivation'. Such comments suggest a need to move beyond straightforward instrumental rationality in studying the locational patterns of offences, but it has to be said that the literature on this topic remains underdeveloped.

Two main points can however be made, the first concerning offences committed for financial gain, and the second concerning 'crimes for excitement'. In an important ethnographic study of non-incarcerated persistent burglars, Wright and Decker (1994) reported that offenders usually decided to commit a residential burglary 'in response to

---

[18] ACORN ('A Classification Of Residential Neighbourhoods') classifies areas according to demographic, employment, and housing characteristics, based on small-area census data. There are five main ACORN area groups, amalgamated from 56 basic area types. Among the five main groups, BCS household victimization data for 2004–5 showed that, in general, victimization tended to be lowest in the richest areas ('Wealthy achievers'), rising as one went down the social scale to the poorest areas ('Hard Pressed'). The exception was the 'Urban Prosperity' area group (consisting of 'prosperous professionals', 'educated urbanities', and 'aspiring singles') who tend to live in inner-city areas. Their victimization rate was actually the *highest* for any of the five main ACORN groups for burglary, vehicle-related theft, and theft from the person.

a perceived need', typically an urgent need for money—for drugs, paying the rent, or for some other reason.[19] Because such needs were 'almost invariably regarded by the offenders as pressing', they were 'not disposed to consider unfamiliar, complicated or long-term solutions' (ibid.: 60) to the perceived problem. Having decided to commit a burglary in response to the need, offenders then had to choose an area, and a specific target. The choice of areas was, surprisingly often, restricted by the fact that some offenders did not (at the time of the pressing need) have access to a car. Additionally, however—and congruently with the Brantinghams' model—searches were constrained by a psychological need to search only in locations 'with which [offenders] were already intimately familiar', since committing any offence is 'alive with hazards', and familiarity with the area reduces the perceived hazards. Thus, the emotional dimensions of the urgency of the perceived need, and the desire to stay within areas where the offenders felt comfortable, significantly reduced the complexity of the 'search pattern' process, exactly as the Brantinghams had predicted. Such factors clearly help to explain data that are apparently anomalous from the perspective of simple rational choice theory, such as high victimization rates in the poorest communities.[20]

Secondly, and taking the non-instrumental dimension a stage further, Jack Katz (1988) has argued that at least part of the reason why many people—especially young people—offend lies in the excitement, or 'buzz', of the offending itself. Indeed, a current longitudinal study in Sheffield (see Bottoms *et al.* 2004) is examining desistance and persistence among a sample of (mostly) highly recidivistic offenders in their early twenties; at first interview, members of this sample were asked to rate various perceived 'obstacles to going straight or staying straight', and no fewer than 60 per cent of them rated 'the need for excitement' as such an obstacle. This 'excitement' dimension of offending is strongly stressed by those who describe themselves as 'cultural criminologists'; such scholars also usually link such issues, in contemporary societies, to the development of a consumer culture, with its emphasis on display. Thus, for example, Keith Hayward's (2004: 157) recent text on urban crime offers a number of tentative suggestions as to how 'various features associated with consumer culture are creating and cultivating— especially among young people—new forms of concomitant subjectivity based around desire, simultaneity, individualism and impulsivity that, in many instances, are finding expression in certain forms of transgressive behaviour'.

---

[19] Interestingly, Wright and Decker suggest that their work reveals more about the non-instrumental nature of burglars' actions than earlier studies because they interviewed active burglars who were not incarcerated. They argue that those in prison are more likely to rationalize the accounts of their previous actions.

[20] Rational choice theorists can and do respond to such observations by referring to the concept of 'bounded rationality'—for the truth is that none of us instrumentally calculates every decision in our lives; rather, we deploy rationality only within the limits (or bounds) of a set of habitual or working assumptions, and of the practical constraints that we face in seeking to put our plans into action (e.g. whether or not we have access to a car). Following such logics, many social scientists take the view that rational choice theory, using bounded rationality, can provide the basis of a unified and comprehensive theory of social behaviour. An alternative view, which is followed here, is that 'rational choice theory does provide empirically adequate explanations of certain social phenomena ... [b]ut such explanations are adequate only under precise conditions, and many of the unresolved problems of rational choice theory as a research program result from extending its explanations beyond their proper, restricted scope' (Bohman 1992: 207). On this view, both emotionality and norms require analytic separation from instrumental rationality.

The research literature does not yet contain many clear examples of the 'crime for excitement' phenomenon that can be specifically linked to particular locations, but one good case study can be found—again—in the sphere of vehicle crime. This example concerns the phenomenon of youth from West Belfast taking cars, prior to the mid-1990s Irish Republican Army (IRA) ceasefire. The 1989 International Victimization Study (a cross-national crime survey carried out in 14 jurisdictions) found that, over-all, in 1988 Northern Ireland had the lowest vitimization prevalence rates of all the participating countries; however, its prevalence of vehicle-taking (as distinct from theft from vehicles) was actually above the mean for the countries concerned (van Dijk *et al.* 1990: 48).[21] But the distribution of vehicle-taking across Northern Ireland was, at that time, very highly skewed: in 1987 no fewer than 42 per cent of all cars illegally taken in the whole of Northern Ireland were recovered in the small area of West Belfast (McCullough *et al.* 1990: 2), hence the rate of offending relating to that neighbourhood was very high. At the time, West Belfast was largely a 'no-go' area for the official police (the Royal Ulster Constabulary) unless they used armoured vehicles; this was because of the strong support for the republican movement (including its armed wing) within the local community. In these unusual circumstances, formal social control in the area was therefore largely exercised by the Republican movement itself, including punishment beatings and shootings administered by the IRA (Moran 2006).

A small study of vehicle crime in West Belfast (McCullough *et al.* 1990), including interviews with offenders, commented on 'the excitement in the area as a stolen car is raced about' (1990: 8). The offenders had very unfavourable social prospects (they typically had no educational qualifications, and no work experience except on Youth Training programmes), in the light of which, it was reported, 'the thrills and possibilities of car theft can become an exciting option' for them (op. cit.: 9). In a complex set of social processes, their 'joyriding' tended to isolate them from the rest of the West Belfast community (because of the distress that it caused, notably through racing cars in the streets); yet that community was at that time itself a somewhat embattled social group because of the political context. The punishment beatings or shootings that offenders received could also sometimes 'provoke an angry reaction from the joyriders'; indeed, 'it has even been known for a severe punishment shooting to be followed by a heightened spate of car thefts in West Belfast—a collective act of defiance' (op. cit.: 8).[22] It is clear that much of this evidence sits uneasily with the standard 'theory toolbox' of mainstream 'location of offence' researchers, based as it is on the rational-choice and routine-activities approaches. It is however important that our criminological imagination is broad enough to encompass such behaviour, as well as that more obviously

---

[21] A 'prevalence rate' in a crime victimization survey is the proportion of survey respondents reporting one or more victimizations for the offence(s) in question. For this measurement, therefore, single victims and multiple victims count equally. Prevalence rates are usually considered to be statistically more reliable than incidence rates.

[22] This is an example of a situation which itself seems to 'actively bring on behaviour' through a kind of provocation; that is, where 'the motivation to commit crime may itself be situationally dependent' (Wortley 2001: 63). Such observations have led to an important recent debate within situational crime prevention theory (Wortley 1998, 2001; Cornish and Clarke 2003).

motivated by instrumentally rational considerations. This is an important challenge for the socio-spatial criminology of the future.

REPEAT VICTIMIZATION

A final topic relating to the location of offences is repeat victimization. A few studies of this topic have reported analyses, using police-recorded data, over a five- or six-year period. Such analyses show that some revictimizations of the same target (e.g. a particular house in studies of residential burglary) can occur years after the first offence, but still at a level that is well above chance (Kleemans 2001; Costello and Bottoms 2004). It is very unlikely that such revictimizations are due to the same offender returning, and the most plausible explanation is that there are some targets that, over time, are repeatedly attractive to different offenders, acting—unknown to one another—on the same set of cues. Such an explanation is, of course, fully congruent with opportunity theory.

Of greater interest for present purposes are repeat victimizations where the *very fact of the first offence seems to have heightened the probability of the second*; such revictimizations usually occur within weeks of the initial offence. This is the type of repeat victimization that has attracted the greatest interest in the criminological literature (see generally Farrell and Pease 2001), and there is research evidence (reviewed in Everson and Pease 2001) that many such crimes are due to the same offender returning. From the point of view of socio-spatial criminology, such offences (which are by no means rare) shape the overall locational pattern of offences because of offenders' motivation to return to the same crime-site—a motivation that is not yet fully understood, although in general terms it is clearly compatible with the kind of evidence uncovered in, for example, Wright and Decker's study of burglary (see above). Further research using BCS data has shown that the higher the *area prevalence rate* (see note 21 above) for a given offence in a given area, the higher the rate of repeat victimization among those who are victimized (Trickett *et al.* 1992; Farrell 1995)—though again, the reasons for this are not yet fully understood. Establishing the full dimensions of this complex picture of repeat victimization (involving area characteristics, target characteristics, and offender motivation) remains an important challenge for socio-spatial criminology.

SOCIO-SPATIAL DIMENSIONS OF INCIVILITIES AND DISORDER

Around the turn of the millennium, an interesting conversation took place in Surrey between its then Chief Constable and researchers from the University of Surrey. The Chief Constable pointed out that the police seemed to be dealing with a new problem. Overall recorded crime rates, and BCS victimization data, suggested that most crime had been falling since the mid-1990s, but public anxiety about crime remained high, with, for example, surveys showing that most people believed crime rates were continuing to increase. Why, the Chief Constable asked, was this happening, and what should the police response be?

A key conceptual move made by the researchers in response to this puzzle was to argue that, as Martin Innes (2004: 336) later put it, the criminological literature lacked 'a coherent explanation of the public understanding of crime and disorder, and how such understandings are imbricated in the wider symbolic construction of social space'. To fill this gap, the researchers' 'central proposition' was that '*some crime and disorder incidents matter more than others to people in terms of shaping their risk perceptions*' (Innes 2004: 336, emphasis added). Thus, for example, three spouse murders in a medium-sized town in a year would be unusual, but would not necessarily create widespread fear, or a sense of threat, in the community at large, because they would be seen as 'private matters'. By contrast, the abduction and murder of a local schoolgirl on her way to school would almost certainly generate much more fear, and a sense of threat, in the area, because of the *signal* it would transmit about potential risks in the community. In the light of this signal, ordinary people might freshly consider as 'risky' certain places, people, or situations that they could easily encounter in their everyday lives; hence signals are 'social semiotic processes by which different crimes and disorders might have a disproportionate effect' in terms of fear and perceived threat (Innes and Fielding 2002: Abstract).

These core ideas were subsequently developed by Martin Innes in his work for the National Reassurance Policing Programme (NRPP). As part of that programme, Innes and colleagues conducted detailed qualitative interviews in 16 residential areas across England, asking representative respondents in each area what they would identify as the key *potential threats to neighbourhood safety* in their area. Some early results from six areas are shown in Figure 17.4 (later results are similar). For each area (here designated 'A' to 'F'), respondents' perceived threats to neighbourhood safety are listed in descending order of importance; thus, for example, in Area F 'drugs' were perceived as the principal threat to neighbourhood safety, followed by 'youths hanging around' and 'public drinking'.

Three points are especially striking about the information in this figure. First, there is some significant variation by area in the details of the responses. Secondly, however, there are some common themes that clearly emerge as the first three perceived 'signals' of lack of neighbourhood safety in the six areas: they are 'youths hanging around', drugs, litter/graffiti, damage, and public drinking. Thirdly, it is extremely interesting that burglary does not appear in the 'top three' in any of the six areas, and only features at all in three areas.

What explains the second and third points above? The answer seems to lie in the fact that the most commonly identified 'top signals' are all *disorderly events occurring in public space*. Thus, perhaps, these kinds of incidents send a powerful signal to residents (in a way that residential burglaries do not) that 'my area is out of control'. As one respondent put it to Innes (2004: 348):

> Yes, it is daft, it is almost daft, but graffiti is the thing that sort of bothers me more, because it is in my face every day. I mean obviously rape and murder are more horrendous crimes, but it is graffiti that I see.

Crime or Disorder 'Signal'*	Areas					
	A	B	C	D	E	F
1	Drugs	Youths hanging around	Youths hanging around	Youths hanging around	Youths hanging around	Drugs
2	Youths hanging around	Litter	Graffiti, litter and public urination	Vandalism and damage	Drugs	Youths hanging around
3	Assault	Damage	Damage	Public violence and drinking	Damage and graffiti	Public drinking
4	Burglary	Public drinking	Public violence and mugging	Racing vehicles and skateboarding	Abandoned /racing vehicles	Antisocial neighbours
5	Mugging	Public violence and speeding	Drugs	Murder	Burglary	Damage
6	Public drinking	Verbal abuse	Burglary		Verbal abuse	Gangs

Fig. 17.4 National Reassurance Policing Project: top 'crime and disorder signals' across trial areas

* Crime or disorder signals are listed in descending order of perceived importance in each area.
Source: Innes, M., Hayden, S., Lowe, T., Roberts, C., and Twyman, L. (2004), *Signal Crimes and Reassurance Policing (Volume 1)*, Guildford: University of Surrey.

In short, the Surrey data show that even quite minor incivilities in an area can, on occasion—and especially if persistent ('in my face every day')—be perceived as major threats to local safety.

National data on incivilities in residential areas can be derived from the British Crime Survey, and two findings from the Survey are of especial importance in the present context. First, since 1992 the BCS has continually tracked responses to questions asking people whether, in their view, certain matters constitute a 'very big' or 'fairly big' problem in their residential area: the chosen indicators are 'rubbish or litter', 'vandalism and graffiti', 'teenagers hanging around', 'drug use or dealing', and 'noisy neighbours'. For all of these indicators, perceived problem levels were static, or slightly increasing, in the 11 years 1992–2002 inclusive (Wood 2004: 12), by contrast to the decreases in both recorded crime and the victimization counts of the BCS; though since 2002 the 'disorder' indicators also show a small decrease (Nicholas *et al.* 2005: 23).

If these respondents' perceptions accurately reflect real disorder levels,[23] then—given the Surrey University results on the importance of disorders as perceived indicators of local threat—these data certainly help to answer the Chief Constable of Surrey's question about why public anxieties have remained high.

[23] This raises difficult methodological issues which cannot be fully discussed here.

Secondly, the BCS provides specific data on the perceptions of disorders in different kinds of neighbourhoods; these consistently show that respondents in economically deprived areas report a far higher incidence of both 'physical' and 'social' disorders than do those in better-off areas (Wood 2004).[24]

These various data pose two central explanatory questions for the socio-spatial criminologist. These are, first, *why* do disorders in the public spaces of neighbourhoods appear to be of such significance as threats to the perceived safety of residents—more so, for example, than residential burglary? And, secondly, what explains the preponderance of disorders in economically deprived areas?

On the first point, the best answer (see generally Innes 2004; Bottoms 2006) seems to focus upon relating incivilities to people's *general sense of order* in a locality, bearing in mind Goffman's (1972: 241) observation that the non-performance of conventional courtesies in public places can act as an 'alarming signal' to individuals that something is wrong. There is clear social-scientific evidence that human beings value a *degree of predictability and order in everyday routines*,[25] and where this is disturbed by, for example, social disorders such as youths shouting insults, or physical disorders such as encountering a pool of urine in the lift, this can lead to genuine emotional upset and concern. Jack Barbalet (1998: 141) has also cogently argued that the basic needs of human beings include not only physical and individual needs, but also 'the need for society, the need for collective and co-operative activity'. If all this is correct, it is not surprising that apparent threats to predictable and peaceable social order in communal spaces can generate what at first sight seem to be surprisingly strong empirical results, such as those shown in Figure 17.4. To use the language of Anthony Giddens (see note 25 above), it would seem that incivilities have the capacity to generate genuine 'ontological insecurities', that is, insecurities that can strike at the very roots of people's welfare and self-understanding as sentient beings. Or, to put the point slightly differently (as Girling *et al.* (2000: 170) did after a study of a small town in 'Middle England'), ordinary people's 'everyday talk about crime and order (its intensity, the vocabularies used, the imagery mobilized, the associations that are made), *both depends upon, and helps to constitute, their sense of place*' (emphasis added).

This leads us to the second question, namely, why are incivilities focused in the poorest areas? One possible answer to this question is that high offender rates are also concentrated in poor areas (see a later section of this chapter), and that high disorder in an area is simply a by-product of high local offender rates. However, this answer is less than fully convincing, given that (i) in England and Wales from the mid-1990s disorder

---

[24] The distinction between 'physical' disorders (litter, graffiti, the residue of vandalism, drugs needles on the street, etc.) and 'social' disorders (noisy neighbours, young people hanging around and being rude, prostitution, etc.), is well established in the US literature—see, e.g., Skogan (1990).

[25] See, e.g., for example Giddens (1984: 64): 'Ordinary day-to-day social life . . . involves an ontological security founded on an autonomy of bodily control within predictable routines and encounters. The routinized character of the paths along which individuals move in . . . daily life . . . is "made to happen" by the modes of reflexive monitoring of action which individuals sustain in circumstances of co-presence. The "swamping" of habitual modes of activity by anxiety that cannot be adequately contained by the basic security system is specifically a feature of critical situations.' On 'the problem of social order' see further Elster (1989) and Wrong (1995).

apparently did not decrease, whilst offending did (see above); and (ii) there is other evidence of disorder and offending not always being co-incident in local areas (Taub *et al.*1984). A possible alternative answer (see Bottoms 2006) focuses instead on recent social change—specifically, the social conditions of 'late modernity'. In the United Kingdom, traditional industries have declined, and long-term unemployment (especially for unskilled males) is much higher than it was before 1980, so those in the poorest areas often face the future with pessimism. Yet all this is occurring within a society where GDP continues to grow, the division between rich and poor has significantly widened, and a consumerist ethos places emphasis on desirable display and hedonism (Hayward 2004, Boutellier 2004). Not surprisingly, in these circumstances there is less social solidarity in the poorest areas, with (sometimes at least) a particular lack of understanding between old and young. And, as Bryan Turner has recently emphasized, 'the erosion of common values and shared sentiments undermines trust' (Turner 2006). Given all this, it is perhaps not surprising that much of the behaviour described as 'disorder' in the poorest residential areas is 'non-instrumental behaviour' by the young, 'undertaken to cause symbolic affront' (Turner 2006). This analysis has here been only briefly sketched; but if its general thrust is correct, then contemporary incivilities are very closely linked to the changing nature of contemporary economies and contemporary cities, discussed early in this chapter. The non-instrumental, expressive character of much disorderly behaviour also reinforces the case for socio-spatial criminologists to pay more attention than hitherto to this kind of behaviour (see earlier discussion).

There is one further matter relating to incivilities that requires discussion, and that is the famous thesis—known colloquially as the 'broken windows hypothesis'—which postulates that if disorders in an area are left unchecked, they will escalate, and this will lead inexorably to the arrival of much more serious crime (and criminal actors) in the neighbourhood. The best-known exponents of this thesis were Wilson and Kelling (1982) (see also Kelling and Coles 1996), and the thesis seemed to be supported by later research by Skogan (1990). More recent research, however, requires a more sceptical evaluation of the thesis, and here two contributions have been of special importance. First, Sampson and Raudenbush (1999) directly tested the assumption of the broken windows hypothesis that 'disorder [is] a fundamental cause of crime' against their own alternative hypothesis. Their postulated view was first, that 'disorder is a manifestation of crime-relevant mechanisms and that *collective efficacy* should reduce disorder *and* violence by disempowering the forces that produce both'; and secondly, that 'structural constraints such as resource disadvantage account for both crime and disorder' (ibid.: 614, emphasis added). Since Sampson and Raudenbush's empirical tests favoured their own hypothesis, it is quite important to understand exactly what they meant by 'collective efficacy'. We can reasonably speak, these authors argue, of an individual having or failing to have 'efficacy' (that is, being able to achieve what he or she wants to achieve); in a similar manner, they say, we can speak of differential 'collective efficacy' between areas, on the assumption that (among other things) all communities share the goal of wanting a safe neighbourhood. 'Collective efficacy' is then more precisely defined as comprising two linked elements: first, the willingness of local residents (as judged by survey responses) to intervene for the common good in defined situations (such as children spray-painting graffiti on a building); and secondly, the existence or otherwise of 'conditions of cohesion and mutual trust among neighbors' (since 'one is unlikely to take action in a neighborhood context where the rules are unclear and people mistrust each other'). Thus, the concept of collective efficacy incorporates both a static 'relations of trust' dimension and a more action-oriented 'willingness to intervene' dimension.

Although the empirical data in this study favoured Sampson and Raudenbush's hypothesis over Wilson and Kelling's, it is important to note that in their conclusions the authors emphasized that the results do not 'imply the theoretical irrelevance of disorder' (1999: 637). On the contrary, their results negate only the direct 'broken windows lead to serious crime' hypothesis. Since, however, the authors also consider that disorders 'comprise highly visible cues to which neighborhood observers respond', it follows that disorder might indeed 'turn out to be important for understanding migration patterns, investment by business and overall neighborhood viability', in which case it could 'indirectly have an effect on crime' (ibid.).

The second major evaluation of the 'broken windows' thesis was by Ralph Taylor (2001), based on research in Baltimore. It is more explicitly longitudinal than Sampson and Raudenbush's work, and uses data for 66 areas of the city in 1981, and in 30 of the same areas in 1994.

In one sense, Taylor's research results could be said to be more positive for the broken windows hypothesis than Sampson and Raudenbush's. He did find partial support for the thesis: 'incivilities do affect some later changes in crime rates, in neighborhood fabric and in reactions to crime' (2001: 231). But there were two crucial qualifications to be made. First, 'the pattern of results has not proved robust across indicators or outcomes'. Secondly, the inconsistency of the longitudinal results for incivilities contrasts with 'other, more consistent' findings in the analysis, in particular the strength of the initial economic status and the initial racial composition of the area in predicting later outcomes. Disorder, in short, is a less strong predictor of serious crime than neighbourhood structural context.

Taylor's more general conclusion, arising from his results, is forcefully made (2001: 20), and is consistent with Sampson and Raudenbush's results as well as his own. His important message is that theorizing on incivilities

> needs to reconnect more firmly with works in the areas of urban sociology, urban political economy, collective community crime prevention and organizational participation. Changes in neighborhood fabric, neighborhood crime rates and residents' safety concerns are each tangled topics with a range of causes. To gain a clearer picture of these processes, it is necessary to break away from [incivilities] per se, and broaden the lines of inquiry.

There is no doubt that the strong version of the 'broken windows' thesis has been severely damaged by the rigorous empirical analyses of Sampson and Raudenbush and Taylor. However, neither of these alternative analyses rejects the potential significance of disorders in affecting some social outcomes, such as residents' confidence in the neighbourhood, or moving decisions (and these outcomes were also previously emphasized by Skogan (1990)). That is an important conclusion because, as Innes (2004: 340) has reminded us, criminal justice agencies such as the police have traditionally tended to dismiss disorders as 'comparatively trivial' (by comparison with 'real crimes' such as burglary). The 'broken windows' thesis was faulty in claiming almost inevitable escalatory crime outcomes from the existence of disorder; but at least it can be said to have engaged 'with the problem of why, when asked about their experiences and anxieties concerning crime, members of the public consistently attach considerable significance to . . . physical and social disorder' (Innes 2004: 340). It would seem, therefore, that we need better theoretical guidance for policy than 'broken windows' has offered us, but without reverting to a trivialization of disorders in policy terms. We also need to make sure that disorders are considered not in isolation, but in their total social context, 'reconnecting' criminology with urban sociology, urban political economy, and so on.

A possible policy lead in these circumstances is provided by Innes's (2004) concept of 'control signals'. For Innes, just as a 'signal crime or disorder' acts as a warning signal to people about potential risks or threats in the community (see above), so a 'control signal' is said to be 'an act of social control that communicates an attempt to regulate disorderly and deviant behaviour'. A useful empirical example of 'control signals' in action derives from some Chicago research published twenty years ago by Taub *et al.* (1984). They found evidence of two city neighbourhoods (Lincoln Park and Hyde Park/Kenwood) which had high crime rates, but also (i) positive 'satisfaction with safety' scores in residents' surveys, and (ii) rapidly appreciating residential property values. Clearly, these results are unexpected: one would normally expect high crime rates to coincide with depressed property values and low feelings of safety. In both neighbourhoods, however, the authors reported that 'there [were] highly visible signs of extra community resources being used to deal with the crime problem' (ibid.: 172), and to generate confidence in the area. By no means all of this activity was initiated by the police; for example in Hyde Park/Kenwood, those managing the regeneration (including the University of Chicago, which is located in the area) themselves invested heavily in the urban infrastructure, and also helped to obtain substantial federal urban renewal funds for the neighbourhood; additionally, they directly addressed residents' 'safety in public space' issues by introducing a private security force, 24-hour 'safety buses', and emergency telephones on street corners. It is not hard to see how all this could send a strongly positive 'control signal' to residents; the message would be, 'powerful people in this neighbourhood are taking seriously the need to halt the decline of the urban infrastructure, and the need to make the area feel safe to residents'.

Is there any evidence that a 'control signals' approach of this kind actually works, empirically speaking? The best evidence is very recent, and comes from the Home Office's evaluation of the National Reassurance Policing Programme (Tuffin *et al.* 2006)—to which, it will be recalled, Martin Innes's own research has been closely linked. The NRPP was conducted in 16 sites, using Innes's conceptualization to guide police managers in consulting the public about 'threats to safety' (of the kind shown in Figure 17.4); in response to such perceived threats, police managers then tried to develop appropriate action strategies, closely targeted to the perceived threats. For six of the sites, Home Office researchers were able to identify viable control areas, and then to measure before/after changes in the experimental sites, by comparison with the designated control site. The results were encouraging, auguring well for the 'signal crimes' perspective, although further replication is needed before one treats the conclusions as definitive.

Seeking to build on this positive result, in an earlier essay (Bottoms 2006), I have also suggested the possibility—based on wider research evidence—that, in any given area the successful deployment by the powerful of effective 'control signals' will enhance the likelihood that ordinary citizens will exercise improved 'collective efficacy'. This suggestion also seems consistent with Sampson and Raudenbush's theorization, since 'relations of trust' are, for these authors, a component of collective efficacy, and it seems reasonable, on all the evidence, that effective control signals could generate enhanced trust within a community. These suggestions are tentative, but seem well worthy of further exploration.[26]

EXPLAINING THE LOCATION OF OFFENDER RESIDENCE

As seen in an earlier section, traditionally the study of the location of offender residence was dominated by the conceptualizations of the Chicago School; and their explanations were themselves strongly influenced by the facts of stability over time in the zonal distribution of area offender rates, the nature of land use in different zones of the city, and the social instability in the 'zone of transition'.

Post Second World War evidence, however, dealt a heavy blow to some of these underpinning assumptions. For example, as previously indicated, because of the location of some social housing, offender rates in post-war British cities have borne little resemblance to the Chicagoan concentric ring pattern; and evidence from Sheffield showed that high-offender-rate areas did not necessarily have high residential mobility rates (Baldwin and Bottoms 1976: ch. 7; Bottoms *et al.* 1989).[27] Hence, socio-spatial

---

[26] A topic much in the news in relation to incivilities (or 'antisocial behaviour') is the antisocial behaviour order (ASBO). This topic cannot be discussed fully here, but, in brief, while some might regard ASBOs as effective 'control signals', others argue (in effect) that their use to date falls foul of the trap identified by Ralph Taylor (2001); on this latter view, ASBOs take a high-profile 'enforcement' approach to individual cases, but such actions can too easily be taken in isolation from analysis of the more general social conditions and problems in the area. It is difficult to resolve this debate in the absence of convincing empirical evidence on the effect of ASBOs (cf. reassurance policing, which has been much more rigorously researched). See more fully the essays in von Hirsch and Simester (2006), including Bottoms (2006).

[27] Even in Chicago, careful analysis by Bursik (1986) showed that the old areal regularities had broken down, and that while the areas of the city that underwent the most rapid social change generally experienced considerable increases in delinquency, nevertheless there were some atypical areas where this relationship did not hold.

criminologists do not now utilize Burgess's zonal theory of city development, nor do they assume an axiomatic linkage of high area offender rates with high residential mobility. Interestingly, however, the Chicagoan 'social disorganization' tradition has a direct theoretical successor in the 'collective efficacy' research approach.[28]

As a prelude to any discussion of areal offender rates, it is initially useful to consider how, in principle, area of residence and offender rates might be statistically related. This might occur, first, because more or less crime-prone individuals or groups are distributed (by the dynamics of the local housing market) to certain areas. However, in this kind of correlation, the social life of the area does not itself affect the criminality levels of the residents. But secondly, in principle *the social life of the area might itself influence criminal motivation.* This possible influence might be transient—for example, acquaintance patterns among local residents might lead to some being influenced by others to commit offences. Alternatively, however, the social life of an area might have longer-term effects on a person's daily routines, social activities, thought processes, etc, such that his or her overall propensity to commit crime in certain situations is intrinsically affected. This kind of longer-term effect is obviously most likely to be manifested among young residents of an area, but the possibility of its occurring among older residents should not be ruled out.

DO NEIGHBOURHOOD EFFECTS ON OFFENDER RATES EXIST?

Some criminologists (e.g. Wilson and Herrnstein 1985) have expressed scepticism about the existence of neighbourhood effects on criminal careers. The argument of the sceptics is that research has uncovered a number of key 'risk factors' in the causation of offending which are individual in nature, such as low intelligence and ineffective parenting. They further argue that research on criminal careers shows that persistent offenders typically begin to offend early in life, well before communal factors—such as delinquent peers or neighbourhood processes—could play much of a role (Wilson and Herrnstein 1985: 311).

Using data from the Pittsburgh Youth Study (a major longitudinal research project on male criminal careers), Wikström and Loeber (2000) set out to assess this sceptical case. They divided their sample into those with high individual risk scores for criminality, those with high protective scores (the obverse of individual risk factors), and an intermediate

---

[28] Although there are clear continuities between the concepts of social disorganization and collective efficacy, there is also one important difference. In testing social disorganization theory in the late 1980s, Sampson and Groves (1989: 779) assumed that 'local friendship networks' were an important dimension of local community social organization, and hence that their absence indicated 'social disorganization'. The concept of 'collective efficacy' makes no such assumption, reflecting the dual realisation (i) that some middle-class areas have few friendship networks but can nevertheless—when necessary—organize well to produce 'collective efficacy', (ii) that 'what many impoverished and dangerous neighborhoods have in common is a relatively high degree of social integration (high levels of local neighboring while being relatively isolated from contacts in the broader mainstream society) and low levels of informal social control (feelings that they have little control over their immediate environment, including the environment's negative influence on their children' (Wilson 1996: 63).

group, which was numerically the largest. They also divided the sample into four groups by 'neighbourhood context': these comprised those living in advantaged, middle range, and disadvantaged areas, the latter being further subdivided into areas of public housing and non-public housing. Table 17.2(a) shows the principal results for serious juvenile offending. In the sample as a whole, the proportion of boys who became serious juvenile offenders rose rapidly as one moved from those with a high protective score to those with a high risk score (in advantaged and middle-range areas, from less than 10 per cent to over 70 per cent). Among individuals with high individual risk scores, there was no neighbourhood effect (all types of residential area had offending rates between 70 per cent and 80 per cent among high-risk boys). But for those outside the high risk group, living in a disadvantaged area with public housing tenure significantly increased the probability of offending; for these youths, therefore, there seemed to be a clear neighbourhood effect.[29] Further analysis showed, however, that in one respect Wilson and Herrnstein's scepticism was apparently correct: for a first serious offence at the age of 12 or less, no neighbourhood effect was discernible in any of the risk groups.

The results shown in Table 17.2(a) are, nevertheless, in an important sense incomplete, and they almost certainly understate the neighbourhood effects on juvenile offending in Pittsburgh. To understand this point, Table 17.2(b) should be examined. This shows, in detail, the percentage of research subjects in different types of neighbourhood who were assessed as 'high risk' on each of the six variables that comprised the 'risk-protective score'. As may be seen, the overall risk index (bottom row of table) produced markedly higher scores in the disadvantaged neighbourhoods, especially public housing areas; and these overall differences were predominantly the result of strong area differences in the individual variables of 'low school motivation', 'poor parental supervision', and 'lack of guilt'. It is obviously in principle possible that each of these allegedly 'individual' factors might have been significantly influenced by the community context in which the youths had been raised (e.g. parenting styles might have been learned, perhaps years ago, by parents from their relatives or neighbours; 'lack of guilt' might be influenced by the dominant norms of the local community, and so forth). Since, however, Table 17.2(a) controls for these 'individual' risk factors, it follows that it might in fact be 'overcontrolling'—that is, in effect Table 17.2(a) could be said to be unwarrantably discounting the possibility of such indirect neighbourhood effects. This possibility is explicitly recognized by Wikström and Loeber (2000: 1134).[30]

We may, therefore, reasonably conclude that neighbourhood effects on offending can and do sometimes exist. In a direct sense, they are weaker than the so-called 'individual risk factors', as Table 17.2(a) shows; but these 'individual' risk factors almost certainly

[29] It is also important to note that, in the disadvantaged public housing areas, there was little difference (and no statistically significant difference) in the offender rate by the number of risk or protective factors present. Thus, in these areas, the neighbourhood context appeared to 'swamp' the effects of individual risk factors that were—in other areas—highly significant.

[30] For interesting parallel work in psychology see Bronfenbrenner (1979); the relevance of Bronfenbrenner's work for criminologists is well discussed by Martens (1993).

Table 17.2 Key results from the Pittsburgh Youth Study

(a) Per cent having committed serious offence by risk/protective score and neighbourhood context

| | Neighbourhood context | | | | | |
| | | | Disadvantaged | | | |
	Advantaged	Middle-range	Non-public	Public	Gamma	N
High Protective Score	11.1	5.1	16.7	37.5	0.23	155
Balanced Risk and Protective Score	27.3	40.1	38.5	60.7	0.23	651
High Risk Score	77.8	71.3	78.3	70.0	n.s.	222
Gamma	0.70	0.74	0.69	n.s.		
N	142	556	188	142		

(b) Per cent subjects with high risk scores by neighbourhood context

| | Neighbourhood context | | | | | |
| | | | Disadvantaged | | | |
	Advantaged	Middle-range	Non-public	Public	Gamma	N
High Hyperactivity-Impulsivity-Attention Problems	13.8	20.9	28.7	20.1	0.15	1436
Lack of Guilt	19.2	30.0	35.5	46.0	0.26	1254
Poor Parental Supervision	15.8	22.8	29.1	39.7	0.28	1414
Low School Motivation	21.9	31.2	44.9	47.6	0.30	1432
Many Peer Delinquents	17.9	22.9	27.7	29.4	0.15	1323
Positive Perception of Anti-Social Behaviour	29.2	25.8	19.8	25.9	n.s.	1431
Risk Index	13.3	19.9	28.8	34.9	0.30	1148

Source: Wikström, P-O.H., and Loeber, R., 'Do Disadvantaged Neighbourhoods cause Well-adjusted Children to be Adolescent Delinquents? A Study of Male Serious Juvenile Offending, Individual Risk and Protective Factors and Neighbourhood Context', in *Criminology*, 38: 1109–42 © 2000. Reprinted by permission of Blackwell Publishing.

themselves often incorporate significant 'hidden' neighbourhood effects. We may finally note one further interesting feature of the Pittsburgh study, namely that the neighbourhood effect was particularly evident in 'public housing' areas. In the US context, 'public housing' means both severe and concentrated economic disadvantage, and a specific housing tenure; and that thought directs us to a fuller examination of both of these matters in the context of offender rates.

AREAS OF CONCENTRATED DISADVANTAGE

Is there evidence that areas of concentrated disadvantage have high offender rates? And, if they do, is there a causal link between the disadvantage and the offending?

On the first question, two recent British studies provide rather striking evidence. Roger Houchin (2005) conducted a study of the home addresses (prior to incarceration) of the Scottish male prison population on the night of June 30 2003. He found that a quarter of the prison population had lived in just 53 (4 per cent) of the 1,232 local government wards in Scotland; and, further, that taking all wards together, there was a close and positive relationship between each ward's number of prisoners and its score on the official Index of Multiple Deprivation. Craglia and Costello (2006) conducted a parallel study in South Yorkshire, though with two main differences: first, the geographical units they utilized were not wards but the much smaller 'census output areas'; and secondly, they studied the annual offender rate for each small area, thus including not only those sent to prison but also the much larger number of those dealt with non-custodially. Their findings were, nevertheless, strikingly similar to Houchin's. Box 17.1 shows the results, from this study, of a regression using the area offender rate as the dependent variable; the predominance of factors associated with either poverty or unpopular housing stock is very evident.[31]

So, economically and socially disadvantaged areas have high offender rates, but does the disadvantage cause the offending? In overall terms, the answer to this question is clearly in the negative, since known offenders (such as ex-prisoners) may and do gravitate to economically deprived areas in search of cheap accommodation, and criminal

---

Box 17.1 REGRESSION ON SMALL-AREA OFFENDER RATES IN SOUTH YORKSHIRE: INCLUDED VARIABLES

X1 = Per cent unemployed in economically active age-groups (excluding students, disabled, home carers, etc.).

X2 = Per cent of households renting from other (i.e. hostels, boarding houses, and other communal establishments)

X3 = Per cent of households with lone parents with dependent children

X4 = Per cent of residential spaces vacant ('voids')

X5 = Index of Multiple Deprivation 2004—Health Domain score

X6 = Index of multiple deprivation 2004—Crime Domain score

R^2 = 0.82

Source: Craglia and Costello (2005), 'A model of offenders in England' in F. Toppen and M. Painho.

---

[31] Note also that the final variable in the equation (X6) is an offence location variable, thus confirming that, in residential neighbourhoods, there is overall a positive correlation between offender rates and offence rates, at least on police data.

justice agencies such as the Probation Service often tend to locate their specialist hostel accommodation in such areas. Clearly, in such situations, the disadvantaged area acts as an attractor of existing offenders (some of whom may then reoffend), not as a causal creator of fresh offences. On the other hand, we have observed in the Pittsburgh example (above) what seems—in one city at least—to be a causal relationship between disadvantage and serious juvenile offending. Can we make any progress in disentangling what is clearly a very complex set of social circumstances in disadvantaged areas?

There have been a number of recent reviews of this issue, all of which agree that the empirical evidence is not wholly consistent across studies, probably because of the complexity of interacting factors, and variation in different cities. I shall select here some highlights from three different reviews, each of which makes a useful point.

First, Weatherburn and Lind (2001), after a careful review, suggest that effects of economic stress on criminality do exist, but these are mediated principally through parenting, since there is empirical evidence that both economic and social stress exert 'a very disruptive effect on the parenting process' (ibid.: 44).[32] Moreover, the housing market's concentration of deprived and stressed families in disadvantaged areas 'can be expected to produce adverse effects on parenting above and beyond those which would be expected if they were distributed across neighbourhoods independently of each other' (ibid.: 45). Nevertheless, according to these authors the effects of defective parenting on criminality are not all direct, but are probably mediated at least in part by association with delinquent peers, arising from the weaker parental supervision over childrens' leisure time in disadvantaged areas (ibid.: 66).

Secondly, Sampson *et al.* (2002: 465) concur with the view that 'social and institutional processes [such as parenting] mediate the association of neighborhood structural factors with crime'. The mediating process that they particularly emphasize is the 'construct of collective efficacy' (ibid.: 459), as previously developed by Sampson and others (see above). Despite such mediating factors, however, these authors note that, at least in the US context, 'factors such as concentrated disadvantage . . . remain direct predictors of many outcomes' (ibid.: 465). Like Weatherburn and Lind on parenting, they also point out that collective efficacy, while apparently very important in relation to local offending rates, is 'not produced in a vacuum', and is more easily generated 'in environments with a sufficient endowment of socioeconomic resources and residential stability' (ibid.: 465). To which one might add (see earlier discussion) that clear 'control signals', in Innes's sense, also appear—at least tentatively—to promote the exercise of collective efficacy by local residents.

A third review of this topic is by Oberwittler (2005). He suggests that the evidence for a 'concentrated disadvantage effect' on offending is greater from US research than from European studies, a conclusion that arguably might be related to the greater

---

[32] Weatherburn and Lind (2001: ch. 1) identify a number of problems with what they call the 'ESIOM' paradigm ('economic stress-induced offender motivation'); these include for example the 'non-utilitarian crime anomaly', i.e. that rates of violent crime are strongly statistically associated with economic disadvantage, but the motivation for violence is rarely economic. The authors believe that all the identified anomalies can be overcome when the effects of economic stress are seen as mediated through parenting.

economic inequality, and weaker welfare safety nets, in the USA. Presenting data from his own empirical study in Cologne and Freiburg (see also Oberwittler 2004), Oberwittler reports an overall neighbourhood contextual effect on serious youth crime after controlling for individual disadvantage, though there were a number of differential effects for specific sub-groups. Some of these effects were quite complex and interesting. For example, many native-born German youths spent much of their leisure time with friends from outside their immediate residential area, and in disadvantaged neighbourhoods it was above all the 'youths of low educational status and with a preference for unsupervised routine activities that have local friends'. Moreover, in this study, only if a youth's friends came from the (home) disadvantaged neighbourhood was there a neighbourhood contextual effect on offending. Oberwittler points out the very important implications of this kind of finding—scholars must, when studying potential neighbourhood effects on offending, cease to take 'the neighbourhood as a fixed environmental context', and start instead to trace in detail the actual 'daily itineraries' and social interactions of different groups of neighbourhood residents. This will include, in the case of adolescents, measuring potential 'school effects' as opposed to 'neighbourhood effects' (at least where, as is increasingly the case, school admissions policies are not simply based on geographical catchment areas). These last points are of great potential significance for the future of socio-spatial criminology. Traditionally, the 'environmental criminologists' of the past have tended to study only *neighbourhood* effects, but 'environments' are not simply neighbourhoods, as the 'socio-spatial' terminology (see note 3 above) emphasizes. The Brantinghams (see earlier section of this chapter) have very usefully drawn attention to offenders' routine activities (including non-criminal activities) in relation to the specific locations of offences— but, it is clear, we need to expand this approach to consider how the active use of space varies as between people from different kinds of neighbourhoods; and, within neighbourhoods, also people of different ages, males and females, young people from different schools, and so on. Research in this field has begun, but is still in its infancy (see, for example, Wikström and Sampson (2003) on 'ecometrics').

THE ROLE OF THE HOUSING MARKET

As indicated in an earlier section of this chapter, in the 1970s and early 1980s research studies in Sheffield strongly suggested that the operations of housing markets might be relevant to the spatial distribution of offender rates, over and above other relevant variables such as the social class distribution of households in the area (Baldwin and Bottoms 1976; Bottoms and Wiles 1986). Subsequently, Wikström (1991) produced similar results, based on a path model analysis for offender rates in different areas of Stockholm.

To illustrate housing market effects on offending levels more concretely, I will focus attention here on one particular case study—namely, research conducted by Janet Foster and Tim Hope (1993: ch. 8) on a public sector housing estate in Hull. This estate was studied as part of research into the so-called 'Priority Estates Project' (PEP) improvement initiative in selected difficult housing areas across England.

The PEP improvement programme on the Hull estate had two linked features. First, there were some management changes, focused especially on greater tenant consultation in the running of the estate. Secondly, a number of environmental improvements were also initiated in part of the estate, notably various 'defensible space' changes to some low-rise housing, including 'the addition of front gardens, fencing, and blocking off walkways' (Foster and Hope 1993: 36).[33] The researchers adopted a quasi-experimental evaluative design to assess these various changes, including comparing the estate with a 'control' estate; and they utilized both quantitative and qualitative research methods. In brief, they found a number of significant reductions in crime levels in the low-rise part of the estate, as a result of the PEP improvements, with both design and management changes apparently playing their part. Simultaneously, however, there was an unplanned-for change in the composition of the tenant population in three tower blocks on the same estate. In the past, these blocks had incorporated a substantial proportion (over 40 per cent) of elderly tenants; but during the study period, tenant vacancies in the tower blocks increased significantly—partly through natural causes (illness, deaths) and partly because of a planned transfer of some older tenants to low-rise housing. The resulting tower block vacancies were allocated to new tenants in accordance with the standard lettings rules of the local authority; but, as it happened, these allocations brought to the area new tenants who were disproportionately young, poor, unemployed, and single, including some who had recently been released from prison or a young offenders' institution. This influx of new tenants had the effect of increasing the number of criminal acts in that part of the estate simply because of the arrival of more criminally prone residents; but it also had more complex consequences, described by the researchers as follows:

> At the outset of the study, adolescent 'gang' members on the estate tended to be distinct from the adult criminal networks... but as the young people moved into the tower blocks on the estate, they began to form links between the estate adults and adolescents. Members of the adolescent gang started to use the youths' flats in the tower blocks... to 'hang out', while the youths began to establish or solidify contacts with older persons involved in offending. The consequence was a widening and deepening of the networks of adolescents, youths and adults engaged in criminal activities on the estate [Foster and Hope 1993: 76].

Thus, the operation of the housing market in the Hull estate had the unintended effect of producing what the authors describe as a 'deepening criminal network', linking previously separate groups in the area. It is an analytically telling (if substantively depressing) example of the way in which housing market processes can influence area criminality in broader ways than simply altering the composition of the resident population. Not dissimilarly, in Sheffield, a detailed case study was carried out in two adjacent housing areas, which were in demographic and social class terms very similar,

---

[33] 'Defensible space' is an architecturally based crime prevention approach originally developed by Oscar Newman (1973). Architectural crime prevention approaches are not always successful: see, e.g., Department of the Environment (1997).

but which had markedly different offending rates. In these areas, the operation of the housing market seemed to hold the key to the maintenance of this offending differential (Bottoms *et al.* 1989).[34] Hence, it is clear that in studying offender rates in a given local area, attention should always be paid to the possibility of both direct and indirect effects of housing market processes.

TOWARDS EXPLANATION

How can we develop the various strands noted above into an overall explanation of how community context might influence offender rates? This is an important question because, as Wikström and Sampson (2003: 119) have correctly noted, up to now 'research on environmental influences has largely failed to specify in any detail the causal mechanisms that link social context with crime and pathways into crime.'

Given the current state of research and theorization, no definitive explanatory framework can be offered. However, the tentative suggestions of Wikström and Sampson (2003) are summarized in Figure 17.5, and they provide the best available framework at the present time.

As will be seen, the two parts of Figure 17.5 each has a postulated outcome in a particular kind of *behaviour setting*—either behaviour settings promoting the development of self-control and morality (Figure 17.5(a)) or criminogenic behaviour settings (Figure 17.5(b)). The authors do not assume that behaviour settings are the only relevant variables in the generation of criminal acts—rather, they explicitly postulate that the behaviour setting will interact with the individual's developed morality, and his or her self-control, both of which could have been partly shaped by environmental influences. But individuals, with different propensities (morality and self-control), find themselves in (or actively seek out) different behaviour settings—and behaviour settings themselves vary on a continuum from the criminogenic to those which promote morality and self-control (Figure 17.5). Out of these interactions (propensity × behaviour setting) arise acts of crime or acts of conformity (Wikström and Sampson 2003: 122).

So, according to this theory, what helps to shape whether behaviour settings are criminogenic or otherwise? The two key postulated variables are *collective efficacy* and *community capital*. 'Collective efficacy' has been discussed in an earlier section of this chapter; clearly, if community residents are willing to intervene to, for example, 'nip in the bud' some emerging vandalism, this will constitute a setting less favourable to delinquency. 'Community capital' is defined by the authors as 'the aggregate of individual and institutional resources in a community' (ibid.: 128), and appears to equate to an amalgam of what others have referred to as the separate subspheres of economic,

---

[34] Both the Sheffield and Hull examples concern public-sector housing, from which some have inferred that housing market processes are relevant to the production of offender rates only in a public-sector context. This is wholly erroneous, as careful reflection on 'tipping' processes in private sector contexts will quickly reveal—see Taub *et al.* (1984) for an excellent discussion of the dynamics of 'tipping'.

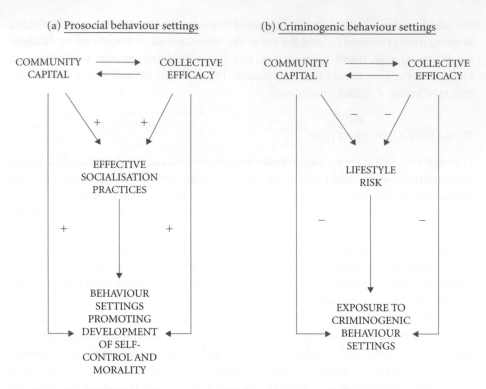

Fig. 17.5 Community contextual influences on two kinds of behaviour settings

Source: Wikström, P-O.H. and Sampson, R.J., 'Social Mechanisms of Community Influences on Crime and Pathways in Criminality', in B.B. Lahey, T.E. Moffitt, and A. Caspi, *Causes of Conduct Disorder and Juvenile Delinquency* © 2003. Reprinted by permission of Guilford Publications Inc.

human, and social capital;[35] the suggestion is that greater resources in the neighbourhood will promote fewer criminogenic behaviour settings.

As will be seen from Figure 17.5(a) and 17.5(b), Wikström and Sampson's argument is that collective efficacy and community capital have a *direct* effect on the generation of more pro-social or antisocial behaviour settings, but also some *mediated* effects. Specifically, it is suggested that pro-social behaviour settings are generated by collective efficacy and community capital mediated by *effective socialization practices* (cf. also Weatherburn and Lind 2001); while antisocial behaviour settings are generated by (negative) collective efficacy and community capital mediated by *lifestyle risk* among less well-supervised youths.

---

[35] 'Economic capital' (financial resources) and 'human capital' (human resources, especially those derived from formal education and industrial/professional experience) are straightforward concepts. 'Social capital' refers to the potentially positive effects of social interactions (including functioning social institutions such as voluntary organizations) within a given society or subsociety. People living in a particular community may benefit from social capital even if they do not contribute to it: 'if the crime rate in my neighborhood is lowered by neighbors keeping an eye on one another's homes, I benefit even if I personally spend most of my time on the road and never even nod to another resident on the street' (Putnam 2000: 20). See further Halpern (2005).

This important contribution to the 'area offender rate' research literature will need careful testing in the future. One brief comment, however, perhaps can and should be made here. As previously indicated, the 'collective efficacy' approach has some important continuities with the Chicagoan 'social disorganization' approach, one of the assumptions of which is that communities share the goal of crime prevention. That assumption is usually valid, but sometimes matters are more complex; for example, in some areas organized criminal gangs can exert an influence on neighbourhoods in a way which clearly demonstrates a degree of 'collective efficacy', but the results are not necessarily unambiguously desirable. A vivid recent British demonstration of this point arose in one of the two high-crime areas of Salford studied by Walklate and Evans (1999). In 'Oldtown' (an inner-city area with quite strong family and kinship ties, and a reputation for 'toughness') there was an organized criminal group known as the 'Salford Firm'. This group, while both practising and condoning criminal activity outside the local area, took it upon themselves to police local criminal incidents (such as burglaries) by giving the culprits (mostly local youth) a 'smacking' in a process of self-proclaimed 'street justice' (ibid.: 93). Moreover, 'grassing' by local residents to the police was discouraged by, for example, writing informants' names on a wall in a central location in the area. The researchers report that ordinary people felt intimidated by the presence of the gang and its activities, but also felt that it had at times afforded the community a degree of protection from criminal victimization, protection that was not always provided by the police (for example, the gang had apparently kept hard drugs out of the area). Residents were, as a result, often ambivalent about the area; they recognized that a particular kind of social order was in operation, and 'appreciated the personal advantage it afforded them', but they 'nevertheless worried about their children growing up in such an environment' (ibid.: 95). The complexities of this kind of situation are not adequately encompassed by unidimensional concepts of 'collective efficacy' and 'community capital', because of the element of normative tension clearly present in the Oldtown community, but not fully allowed for in most current theorization.

INTEGRATING SOCIO-SPATIAL CRIMINOLOGY

One of the most important criminological developments of the last twenty years, for which particular credit should be assigned to Per-Olof Wikström, is the attempt to produce a better integration between developmental criminology and socio-spatial criminology (Farrington *et al.* 1993; Wikström and Sampson 2006). Promising first steps have been made in that task, but—as all informed observers would agree—there remains also much to accomplish.

In the meantime, this chapter has, it is hoped also demonstrated that there remain significant and necessary steps to be taken to achieve better empirical and theoretical integration within socio-spatial criminology itself. The two traditional core topics in the field (explaining the locational distribution of offences and offenders) are, for the most part, tackled by different scholars, and sometimes with different theoretical approaches (for example, rational choice theory is more prominent among offence-focused scholars). The newer topic of areal disorder is of interest to both offence-based and offender-based scholars, but its relationship to each is not yet fully established—not least because the dust on the 'broken windows controversy' is perhaps only just settling. It should be clear, however, that the socio-spatial dimensions of offences, offending, and disorder need to be considered in relation to one another, and the linkages between the different subtopics need to be more securely established. This presents a large—but exciting—future research agenda for socio-spatial criminology.

MACRO-LEVEL ISSUES

Socio-spatial criminology necessarily focuses on variations in offences, offending, and disorder across relatively small areas; and, within these areas, on micro-locations such as exactly where cars are parked when an offence is committed (see Table 17.1). In dealing with such matters, it is sometimes easy to forget the macro-social dimension, but to do this is of course a serious mistake, since—especially in our contemporary, globalized world—macro-social issues can powerfully influence everyday life in local communities. For example, earlier in this chapter—in the course of discussing local crime rates, offender rates, and disorders—we have touched on macro-level phenomena such as the decline of traditional manufacturing industries (in the discussion of disorders) and the advent of an international consumer economy and consumer culture (Hayward 2004).

In an important text, Bursik and Grasmick (1993) noted that, in Shaw and McKay's early research in Chicago, the almost exclusive focus was upon the world of the residents themselves. Too often, later socio-spatial criminologists have followed this example. Bursik and Grasmick decisively corrected this tendency by drawing attention, first, to the links between residents and corporate and public bodies in local neighbourhoods, and secondly, to the links between the local neighbourhood and institutions and agencies external to the area itself (such as city governments; or decision-makers in large corporations, who might choose to invest, or cease to invest, locally). These are both potentially very important influences on local life, as Taub *et al.* (1984) also showed in their case study of the Hyde Park/Kenwood area of Chicago (see earlier discussion).

Bursik and Grasmick's work, however, is restricted to residential areas, and it focuses on specific corporate and/or external actors, and not on more general macro-social issues such as global economic change. A study which makes good these omissions is the important recent British research on crime and social control in the night-time economy by Dick Hobbs and his colleagues (2003). These authors note that, in cities in the north of England which suffered grievously from the economic transformations of the 1980s, one way of promoting economic regeneration has been to attempt to revitalize sites left redundant by the collapse of the traditional industrial base. This usually involves:

> a number of high-profile 're-imaging' and 'place-marketing' initiatives designed to secure investment from external and 'mobile' capital, to attract an influx of skilled and professional residents, and to boost the local tourism, leisure, and retail sectors. Such 'beauty contests' . . . often centre around 'flagship' projects such as waterfront developments, heritage and theme parks, concert halls, shopping centres, prestigious office and leisure complexes, and the hosting of major cultural or sporting events [Hobbs *et al.* 2003: 34].

In such circumstances, civic government usually takes it upon itself to attempt to promote the city, which in turn involves a significant reorientation of local government activities towards the needs of business (in—at least in intention—the longer-term interests of the city's residents). One aspect of such regeneration in many cities has been the growth of the 'night-time economy' of pubs, clubs, and the like. Indeed, 'the existence of a thriving night-time economy is now taken as a prerequisite for any city hoping to make a claim upon progressive profitability' (ibid.: 35), and major national and international leisure companies are keen to invest in such activities. These economic imperatives, however, quite frequently conflict with the requirements of crime prevention—since deliberately encouraging an alcohol-fuelled night-time economy, typically focused upon a small geographical area, and seeking to attract (in particular) young adult clients, is hardly an ideal recipe for an assault-free environment. Entrepreneurial local governments can then face a dilemma if there are high-profile, violent incidents, which might seem to threaten the city's carefully fostered image of regeneration; and this can lead to conflicts between local government and the police. So, for example:

> On 12 March 1998 the front cover of the *Manchester Evening News* carried details of a strongly worded letter sent by the Leader of the [City Council], Richard Leese, to the then Chief Constable of GMP [Greater Manchester Police] . . . The grim tone of the letter stood in stark contrast to the Council's usual '24-hour city' marketing rhetoric. Leese described a state of 'rampant lawlessness' in which problems of both street violence and the intimidation of licensees had reached 'critical' proportions. It was 'a crisis', Leese claimed, that GMP appeared 'either unable or unwilling to address' [Hobbs *et al.* 2003: 103–4].

As Hobbs and his colleagues emphasize, while pressures of this sort are very evident in a number of post-industrial cities, the ways in which they are resolved vary from place to place (see also Girling *et al.* 2000: 8–9). This is an important point, because scholars who are particularly interested in 'globalization', 'late modernity', and the like can display an unfortunate '*insensitivity to place*', and a 'tendency to *presume* that certain [issues] have global prevalence under late modern conditions, rather than to investigate how these mutations are received, resisted or altered in specific institutional and political settings, with all the *unevenness* that such enquiry is likely to reveal' (ibid.: 163 emphasis in original). Macro-social criminology which ignores socio-spatial criminology will, in short, be as impoverished as socio-spatial criminology which ignores the macro-social dimension. We need both.

■ SELECTED FURTHER READING

As indicated in the text of this chapter, there are at least three identifiably separate groups of scholars working in the field of socio-spatial criminology, and there is no good overall text that covers all three traditions. Students most interested in the routine activities/rational choice/crime pattern theory approach might begin further reading with Felson, *Crime and Everyday Life*, 3rd edn (Sage, 2002) and those parts of Chainey and Ratcliffe, *GIS and Crime Mapping* (John Wiley, 2005) that interest them; at a more advanced level they might then move on to the essays in Smith and Cornish, *Theory for Practice in Situational Crime Prevention* (Criminal Justice Press, 2003). Students who wish to acquaint themselves with the social disorganization tradition and its modern developments should begin by mastering Kornhauser's excellent chapter on early social disorganization theory in his *Social Sources of Delinquency* (University of Chicago Press, 1978: ch. 3); and then move on to strong recent essays such as those by Wikström and Sampson, *Social Sources of Delinquency* (University of Chicago Press, 2003) and Sampson and Raudenbush, 'Systematic Social Observation of Public Spaces: A New Look at Disorder and Crime', *American Journal of Sociology*, 105: 603–51 (1999). Finally, those interested in the more ethnographic and 'cultural criminology' approach to the subject are recommended to read Keith Hayward's textbook, *City Limits: Crime, Consumer Culture and the Urban Experience* (Glasshouse, 2004); and, in more empirical vein, the excellent study of the night-time economy by Dick Hobbs and his colleagues, *Bouncers: Violence and Governance in the Night-Time Economy* (Oxford University Press, 2003).

■ REFERENCES

ABBOTT, A. (1997), 'Of time and space: the contemporary relevance of the Chicago School', *Social Forces*, 75: 1149–82.

BALDWIN, J., and BOTTOMS, A. E. (1976), *The Urban Criminal*, London: Tavistock.

BARBALET, J. M. (1998), *Emotion, Social Theory and Social Structure: A Macrosociological Approach*, Cambridge: Cambridge University Press.

BAUMER, E. P. (2002), 'Neighborhood disadvantage and police notification by victims of violence', *Criminology*, 40: 579–617.

BOBA, R. (2005), *Crime Analysis and Crime Mapping*, London: Sage.

BOHMAN, J. (1992), 'The limits of rational choice explanation', in J. S. Coleman and T. J. Fararo (eds), *Rational Choice Theory: Advocacy and Critique*, Newbury Park, Cal.: Sage.

BOTTOMS, A., E. (1994), 'Environmental criminology', in M. Maguire, R. Morgan, and R. Reiner (eds), *The Oxford Handbook of Criminology*, 1st edn, Oxford: Oxford University Press.

—— (2006), 'Incivilities, offence and social order in residential communities', in A. von Hirsch and A. Simester (eds), *Incivilities: Regulating Offensive Behaviour*, Oxford: Hart.

—— and COSTELLO, A. (2001), 'Offenders as Victims of Property Crimes in a Deindustrialised City'. Plenary presentation at the First Annual Conference of the European Society of Criminology, Lausanne, Switzerland.

—— and WILES, P. (1986), 'Housing tenure and residential community crime careers in Britain', in A. J. Reiss and M. Tonry (eds), *Communities and Crime*, Chicago: University of Chicago Press.

—— and —— (2002), 'Environmental Criminology', in M. Maguire, R. Morgan, and R. Reiner (eds), *The Oxford Handbook of Criminology*, 3rd edn, Oxford: Oxford University Press.

—— MAWBY, R. I., and XANTHOS, P. (1989), 'A tale of two estates', in D. Downes (ed.), *Crime and the City*, London: Macmillan.

——Shapland, J., Costello, A., Holmes, D. J., and Muir, G. (2004), 'Towards desistance: theoretical underpinnings from an empirical study, *Howard Journal of Criminal Justice*, 43: 368–89.

Boutellier, H. (2004), *The Safety Utopia*, Dordrecht: Kluwer.

Bowers, K. J., Johnson, S. D., and Hirschfield, A. (2004), 'Closing off opportunities for crime: an evaluation of alley-gating', *European Journal of Criminal Policy and Research*, 10: 283–308.

Brantingham, P. J., and Brantingham, P. L. (1981a), *Environmental Criminology*, Beverly Hills, Cal.: Sage Publications.

——and —— (1981b), 'Notes on the geometry of crime', in P. J. Brantingham and P. L. Brantingham (eds), *Environmental Criminology*, Beverly Hills, Cal.: Sage Publications.

——and —— (1984), *Patterns in Crime*, New York: Macmillan.

——and —— (1993), 'Environment, routine and situation: toward a pattern theory of crime', in R. V. Clarke and M. Felson (eds), *Routine Activity and Rational Choice*, New Brunswick, NJ: Transaction.

——and —— (1999), 'A theoretical model of crime hot spot generation', *Studies on Crime and Crime Prevention*, 7: 31–60.

Bronfenbrenner, U. (1979), *The Ecology of Human Development*, Cambridge, Mass.: Harvard University Press.

Bulmer, M. (1984), *The Chicago School of Sociology*, Chicago: University of Chicago Press.

Burrows, J., Tarling, R., Mackie, A., Lewis, R., and Taylor, G. (2000), *Review of Police Forces' Crime Recording Practices*, Home Office Research Study 204, London: Home Office.

Bursik, R. J. (1986), 'Ecological stability and the dynamics of delinquency', in A. J. Reiss and M. Tonry (eds), *Communities and Crime*, Chicago: University of Chicago Press.

——and Grasmick, H. G. (1993), *Neighborhoods and Crime*, New York: Lexington.

Canter, D. (2003), *Mapping Murder: The Secrets of Geographical Profiling*, London: Virgin.

Carter, R. L. and Hill, K. Q. (1979), *The Criminal's Image of the City*, New York: Pergamon Press.

Chainey, S., and Ratcliffe, J. (2005), *GIS and Crime Mapping*, Chichester: John Wiley.

Clarke, R. V. (1995), 'Situational crime prevention', in M. Tonry and D. Farrington (eds), *Building a Safer Society*, Chicago: University of Chicago Press.

——(1997), *Situational Crime Prevention: Successful Case Studies*, 2nd edn, Guilderland, NY: Harrow and Heston.

——and Felson, M. (1993), *Routine Activity and Rational Choice*, New Brunswick, NJ: Transaction.

——and Mayhew, P. (1998), 'Preventing crime in parking lots: what we know and need to know', in M. Felson and R. Peiser (eds), *Crime Prevention through Real Estate Management and Development*, Washington, DC: Urban Land Institute.

Cohen, L. E., and Felson, M. (1979), 'Social change and crime rate trends: a routine activities approach', *American Sociological Review*, 44: 588–608.

Cornish, D. B., and Clarke, R. V. (eds) (1986), *The Reasoning Criminal: Rational Choice Perspectives on Offending*, New York: Springer.

——and —— (2003), 'Opportunities, precipitations and criminal decisions: a reply to Wortley's critique of situational crime prevention', in M. J. Smith, and D. B. Cornish (eds) *Theory for Practice in Situational Crime Prevention*, Monsey, NY: Criminal Justice Press.

Costello, A., and Bottoms, A. E. (2004), 'Repeat Residential Burglary Victimization in Sheffield'. Paper presented at the Third Annual Conference of the European Society of Criminology, Amsterdam.

Craglia, M., and Costello, A. (2005), 'A model of offenders in England', in F. Toppen and M. Painho (eds), AGILE 2005 (Association Geographic Information Laboratories Europe), Eighth Conference on Geographic Information Science— Conference Proceedings. Lisbon: Universidade Nova de Lisboa.

Cressey, D. (1964), Delinquency, Crime and Differential Association, The Hague: Martinus Nijhoff.

Cromwell, P. F., Olson, J. N., and Avary, D'A.W. (1991), *Breaking and Entering: An Ethnographic Analysis of Burglary*, Newbury Park, Cal.: Sage.

Department of the Environment (1997), *The Design Improvement Controlled Experiment: an evaluation of the impact, costs and benefits of estate remodelling*, London: Department of the Environment.

Dickens, P. (1990), *Urban Sociology: Society, Locality and Human Nature*, London: Harvester Wheatsheaf.

Dingwall, G., and Moody, S. (eds) (1999), *Crime and Conflict in the Countryside*, Cardiff: University of Wales Press.

ELSTER, J. (1989), *The Cement of Society: A Study of Social Order*, Cambridge: Cambridge University Press.

EVERSON, S., and PEASE, K. (2001), 'Crime against the same person and place: detection opportunity and offender targeting', in G. Farrell and K. Pease (eds), *Repeat Victimization*, Monsey, NY: Criminal Justice Press.

FARRELL, G. (1995), 'Preventing repeat victimization', in M. Tonry and D. Farrington (eds), *Building a Safer Society*, Chicago: University of Chicago Press.

—— and PEASE, K. (eds) (2001), *Repeat Victimization*, Monsey, NY: Criminal Justice Press.

FARRINGTON, D. P., and DOWDS, E. A (1985), 'Disentangling criminal behaviour and police reaction', in D. P. Farrington and J. Gunn (eds), *Reactions to Crime*, Chichester: Wiley.

——, SAMPSON, R. J., and WIKSTRÖM, P.-O. H. (eds) (1993), *Integrating Individual and Ecological Aspects of Crime*, Stockholm: National Council for Crime Prevention.

FELSON, M. (2002), *Crime and Everyday Life*, 3rd edn, London: Sage.

—— and CLARKE, R. V. (1998), *Opportunity Makes the Thief: Practical Theory for Crime Prevention*, Police Research Series 98, London: Home Office.

——, BAUMER, E. P., and MESSNER, S. F. (2000), 'Acquaintance robbery', *Journal of Research in Crime and Delinquency*, 37: 284–305.

FINESTONE, H. (1976), 'The delinquent and society: the Shaw and McKay tradition', in J. F. Short, Jr. (ed.), *Delinquency, Crime and Society*, Chicago: University of Chicago Press.

FOSTER, J., and HOPE, T. (1993), *Housing, Community and Crime: The Impact of the Priority Estates Project*, Home Office Research Study 131, London: HMSO.

GIDDENS, A. (1984), *The Constitution of Society*, Cambridge: Polity Press.

GIRLING, E., LOADER, I., and SPARKS, R. (2000), *Crime and Social Change in Middle England: Questions of Order in an English Town*, London: Routledge.

GOFFMAN, E. (1972), *Relations in Public: Microstudies of the Public Order*, New York: Harper Colophon.

GOTTDIENER, M., and HUTCHISON, R. (2006), *The New Urban Sociology*, 3rd edn, Boulder, Col.: Westview Press.

GOTTFREDSON, M. (1984), *Victims of Crime: The Dimensions of Risk*, Home Office Research Study 81, London: HMSO.

GOUDRIAAN, H., WITTEBROOD, K., and NIEUWBEERTA, P. (2006), 'Neighbourhood characteristics and reporting crime', *British Journal of Criminology*, 46: 719–42.

HALPERN, D. (2005), *Social Capital*, Cambridge: Polity Press.

HANCOCK, L. (2001), *Community, Crime and Disorder*, Basingstoke: Palgrave.

HAYWARD, K. J. (2004), *City Limits: Crime, Consumer Culture and the Urban Experience*, London: Glass/house.

HM Inspectorate of Constabulary (2000), *On the Record*, London: Home Office.

HOBBS, D., HADFIELD, P., LISTER, S., and WINLOW, S. (2003), *Bouncers: Violence and Governance in the Night-Time Economy*, Oxford: Oxford University Press.

HOUCHIN, R. (2005), *Social Exclusion and Imprisonment in Scotland*, Glasgow: Glasgow Caledonian University.

INNES, M. (2004), 'Signal crimes and signal disorders: notes on deviance as communicative action', *British Journal of Sociology*, 55: 335–55.

—— and FIELDING, N. (2002), 'From community to communicative policing: "signal crimes" and the problem of public reassurance', *Sociological Research Online*, 7(2). see www.socresonline.org.uk/7/2/innes.html.

JOHNSTON, V., LEITNER, M., SHAPLAND, J., and WILES, P. (1994), *Crime on Industrial Estates*, Home Office Crime Prevention Unit Paper 54. London: Home Office.

KATZ, J. (1988), *Seductions of Crime*, New York: Basic Books.

KELLING, G., and COLES, C. M. (1996), *Fixing Broken Windows*, New York: Free Press.

KLEEMANS, E. R. (2001), 'Repeat burglary victimization: results of empirical research in the Netherlands', in G. Farrell and K Pease (eds), *Repeat Victimization*, Monsey, NY: Criminal Justice Press.

KORNHAUSER, R. R. (1978), *Social Sources of Delinquency*, Chicago: University of Chicago Press.

LANDER, B. (1954), *Towards an Understanding of Juvenile Delinquency*, New York: Columbia University Press.

McCULLOUGH, D., SCHMIDT, T., and LOCKHART, W. (1990), *Car Theft in Northern Ireland*, Belfast: Extern.

MARTENS, P. L. (1993), 'An ecological model of social-isation in explaining offending', in D. P. Farrington, R. J. Sampson, and P.-O. H. Wikström (eds), *Integrating Individual and Ecological Aspects of Crime*, Stockholm: National Council for Crime Prevention.

MAWBY, R. I. (1979), *Policing the City*, Farnborough, Hants: Saxon House.

—— (1989), 'Policing and the criminal area', in D. J. Evans and D. T. Herbert (eds), *The Geography of Crime*, London: Routledge.

—— (2001), *Burglary*, Cullompton, Devon: Willan.

MAYHEW, P., AYE MAUNG, N., and MIRRLEES-BLACK, C. (1993), *The 1992 British Crime Survey*, Home Office Research Study 132, London: HMSO.

——, CLARKE, R. V., STURMAN, A., and HOUGH, J. M. (1976), *Crime as Opportunity*, Home Office Research Study 34, London: HMSO.

MORAN, J. (2006), 'Informal Justice: The Local Governance of Anti-Social Behaviour in Republican Communities in West Belfast', Unpublished PhD thesis, University of Cambridge.

MORRIS, T. P. (1957), *The Criminal Area: a Study in Social Ecology*, London: Routledge & Kegan Paul.

NEWMAN, O. (1973), *Defensible Space: People and Design in the Violent City*, London: Architectural Press.

NICHOLAS, S., POVEY, D., WALKER, A., and KERSHAW, C. (2005), *Crime in England and Wales 2004/2005*, Home Office Statistical Bulletin 11/05, London: Home Office.

OBERWITTLER, D. (2004), 'A multilevel analysis of neighbourhoood contextual effects on serious juvenile offending: the role of subcultural values and social disorganisation', *European Journal of Criminology*, 1: 201–35.

—— (2005), 'Social Exclusion and Youth Crime in Europe——The Spatial Dimension'. Plenary presentation at the Fifth Annual Conference of the European Society of Criminology, Krakow, Poland.

PUTNAM, R. D. (2000), *Bowling Alone: The Collapse and Revival of American Community*, New York: Simon and Schuster.

RENGERT, G., and WASILCHICK, J. (2000), *Suburban Burglary: A Tale of Two Suburbs* 2nd edn, Springfield, Ill.: Charles C. Thomas.

ROSSMO, D. K. (2000), *Geographical Profiling*, Boca Raton, Fla: CRC Press.

SAMPSON, R. J., and GROVES, W. B. (1989), 'Community structure and crime: testing social disorganisation theory', *American Journal of Sociology*, 94: 774–802.

——and RAUDENBUSH, S. W. (1999), 'Systematic social observation of public spaces: a new look at disorder and crime', *American Journal of Sociology*, 105: 603–51.

—— MORENOFF, J. D., and GANNON-ROWLEY, T. (2002), 'Assessing "neighborhood effects": social processes and new directions in research', *Annual Review of Sociology*, 28: 443–78.

SHAW, C. R. (1930), *The Jack Roller*, Chicago: University of Chicago Press.

——and MCKAY, H. D. (1942), *Juvenile Delinquency and Urban Areas*, Chicago: University of Chicago Press.

SHERMAN, L. W., GARTIN, P. R., and BUERGER, M. E. (1989), 'Hot spots of predatory crime: routine activities and the criminology of place', *Criminology*, 27: 27–55.

SKOGAN, W. G. (1990), *Disorder and Decline: Crime and the Spiral of Decay in American Neighborhoods*, New York: Free Press.

SMITH, M. J., and CORNISH, D. B. (eds) (2003), *Theory for Practice in Situational Crime Prevention*, Monsey, NY: Criminal Justice Press.

TAUB, R., TAYLOR, D. G., and DUNHAM, J. D. (1984), *Paths of Neighborhood Change*, Chicago: University of Chicago Press.

TAYLOR, R. B. (2001), *Breaking Away from Broken Windows: Baltimore Neighborhoods and the Nationwide Fight against Crime, Grime, Fear and Decline*, Boulder, Col.: Westview.

TRICKETT, A., OSBORN, D. R., SEYMOUR, J., and PEASE, K. (1992), 'What is different about high crime areas?', *British Journal of Criminology*, 32: 81–9.

TUFFIN, R., MORRIS, J., and POOLE, A. (2006), *An Evaluation of the Impact of the National Reassurance Policing Programme*, Home Office Research Study 296, London: Home Office.

TURNER, B. S. (2006), 'Social capital, trust and offensive behaviour', in A. von Hirsch and A. Simester (eds), *Incivilities: Regulating Offensive Behaviour*, Oxford: Hart.

VAN DIJK, J. J. M., MAYHEW, P., and KILLIAS, M. (1990), *Experiences of Crime Across the World: Key Findings from the 1989 International Crime Survey*, Deventer: Kluwer Law.

VON HIRSCH, A., and SIMESTER, A. (eds) (2006), *Incivilities: Regulating Offensive Behaviour*, Oxford: Hart.

WALKLATE, S., and EVANS, K. (1999), *Zero Tolerance or Community Tolerance?*, Aldershot: Ashgate.

WEATHERBURN, D., and LIND, B. (2001), *Delinquent-Prone Communities*, Cambridge: Cambridge University Press.

WIKSTRÖM, P.-O. H. (1991), *Urban Crime, Criminals and Victims: The Swedish Experience in an Anglo-American Comparative Perspective*, New York: Springer-Verlag.

——and LOEBER, R. (2000), 'Do disadvantaged neighborhoods cause well-adjusted children to become adolescent delinquents?: a study of male serious juvenile offending, individual risk and protective factors, and neighborhood context', *Criminology*, 38: 1109–42.

——and SAMPSON, R. J. (2003), 'Social mechanisms of community influences on crime and pathways in criminality', in B. B. Lahey, T. E. Moffitt, and A. Caspi (eds), *Causes of Conduct Disorder and Juvenile Delinquency*, New York: Guilford Press.

——and—— (eds) (2006), *The Explanation of Crime: Context, Mechanisms and Development*, Cambridge: Cambridge University Press.

WILES, P., and COSTELLO, A. (2000), *The 'Road to Nowhere': the Evidence for Travelling Criminals*, Home Office Research Study 207, London: Home Office.

WILSON, E. (1992), *The Sphinx in the City: Urban Life, The Control of Disorder, and Women*, Berkeley, Cal.: University of California Press.

WILSON, J. Q., and HERRNSTEIN, R. J. (1985), *Crime and Human Nature*, New York: Simon and Schuster.

——and KELLING, G. (1982), 'Broken windows', *Atlantic Monthly*, March: 29–38.

WILSON, W. (1996), *When Work Disappears: The World of the New Urban Poor*, New York: Knopf.

WINCHESTER, S., and JACKSON, H. (1982), *Residential Burglary*, Home Office Research Study 74, London: Home Office.

WOOD, M. (2004), *Perceptions and Experience of Antisocial Behaviour: Findings from the 2003/2004 British Crime Survey*, Home Office Online Report 49/04. London: Home Office.

WORTLEY, R. (1998), 'A two-stage model of situational crime prevention', *Studies on Crime and Crime Prevention*, 7: 173–88.

——(2001), 'A classification of techniques for controlling situational precipitations of crime', *Security Journal*, 14: 63–82.

WRIGHT, R. T., and DECKER, S. H. (1994), *Burglars on the Job: Street Life and Residential Break-ins*, Boston, Mass.: Northeastern University Press.

WRONG, D. H. (1995), *The Problem of Order: What Unites and Divides Society*, Cambridge, Mass.: Harvard University Press.

18

YOUTH CRIME AND YOUTH CULTURE

Tim Newburn

YOUTH AND CRIME IN HISTORICAL CONTEXT

For at least the last century the key representation of young people has been to see them as a 'problem'—either as a source of difficulties, or as being 'at risk'. Indeed, Pearson (1983) has charted generalized complaints about 'juvenile delinquency' since at least pre-industrial seventeenth-century 'Merrie' England. More distinctively 'modern' forms of complaint about juveniles began to appear during the urban and industrial revolutions of the early nineteenth century. Although youth cultures in Britain are generally thought of as a post-Second World War phenomenon, they have been observable for far longer. However, just as we must guard against the assumption that the problems of youth are a peculiarly post-war phenomenon so, having discovered parallels for our modern concerns as far back as the seventeenth century, we must not fall into the trap of thinking that it was ever thus. Both continuity and change are visible, and it is important to pay due regard to each. In this chapter I begin by exploring the emergence of the idea of 'adolescence' as a distinct period in individual development, before moving on to consider youth culture in post-war Britain. The chapter concludes by looking at patterns of youth crime.

In England and Wales no child may be guilty of a criminal offence below the age of 10. Moreover, between the ages of 10 and 18 young offenders are dealt with in the youth justice system largely separately from adult offenders. Such a separation is relatively new (see Morgan and Newburn, Chapter 30, this volume) and reflects, in part, increasing concerns about the particular vulnerability of young people. By contrast, as the French historian Philippe Aries has argued, in the Middle Ages childhood was a considerably foreshortened period: 'Children were mixed with adults as soon as they were considered capable of doing without their mothers or nannies, not long after a tardy weaning (in other words at about the age of seven)' (Aries 1973: 395). Society was divided by status which, generally speaking, was not age related (Stone 1979). However, from the seventeenth century onward, childhood was progressively extended and increasingly separated from adulthood. In Aries' view, it is only since that time that we have become preoccupied with the physical, moral, and sexual development of young people. As childhood as a separate category evolved, so there developed with it the idea that children were a responsibility—that they required protection—and, moreover, that children were creatures with the potential for good and evil, discipline being required to ensure that the former predominated over the latter (Anderson 1980).

Furthermore, as these two phases in the life cycle were progressively separated and the transition between them was extended through restrictions on work and the formalization of education, so the opportunity for the development of a further, intermediary phase increased. This is the phase that has come to be referred to as 'adolescence'. The meaning of this term changed considerably during the course of the twentieth century (Coleman and Hendry 1990). Much of this was a consequence of the emergence and development of formal education in schools, the progressive privatization of the family, and the separation of work from domestic life (Shorter 1976; Stone 1979).

The distinctively modern adolescent started to appear in the nineteenth century. The Factory Acts limited working hours, compulsory education began to develop from the 1870s—albeit slowly—and urban working-class young people were developing what can perhaps be regarded as the first modern youth subcultures (Davis 1990), such as the 'scuttlers' and 'peaky blinders' (Humphries 1981; Pearson 1983). Institutions were developed for delinquents and for those *at risk* of delinquency—the 'perishing classes'—and it was out of these that the modern juvenile justice system grew. By the turn of the century, young people in the new cities and manufacturing towns were experiencing considerable economic independence and leisure time was expanding. It was at this time that heightened concerns about delinquency and hooliganism emerged (Rook 1899; Booth 1902).

It is the work of the American psychologist G. Stanley Hall that is most closely associated with the 'discovery' of 'adolescence' (as understood as a physiological stage triggered by the onset of puberty). In his 'storm and stress' model, adolescence was conceived as a time of 'hormonal turmoil' (Griffin 1993: 16), in which young people required freedom in order to fulfil their potential, and control to instil discipline. Early theories of 'delinquency', such as Cyril Burt's, owed much to Hall's work and shared elements of its biological determinism. Although theories of delinquency broadened in their approach during the course of the last century, the ways in which adolescence is conceived remain heavily influenced by the 'storm and stress' model. Nonetheless, even Burt's predominantly psychological theory of delinquency recognized the secondary influence of the social and cultural environment. Juvenile crime was generally perceived as resulting from deficient self-control and control by others, particularly parents. Poor social conditions and inadequate opportunities for constructive use of leisure were also seen as problematic, and the response to the problem of 'delinquency' was primarily via youth movements which sought to improve the leisure activities of working-class, or more particularly, 'rough' working-class, youth. Most of these movements were voluntary, often attached to churches.

Most official indicators of the level of juvenile crime suggested that it rose fairly steadily during the 1930s, and rose sharply, though with some ups and downs, during the Second World War. War-time conditions—the black-out, high wages for youth labour, family disruption, the closure of schools and youth clubs—were blamed for much delinquency (Bailey 1987). Indeed, family disruption or dysfunction is one of the few 'factors' that appears with regularity in much of the theorizing about delinquency, including psychoanalytic approaches (Schoenfeld 1971), social control theories (Hirschi 1969), and social learning theories (Bandura 1977). With the end of the War and the advent of the welfare state, there was some expectation that crime would return to its pre-war levels. This proved not to be the case, though for the first decade or so the rate of increase in crime was not sharp. This was a time of broad political consensus, generally referred to as Butskellism. After a period in which consumption was held back by rationing and wage restraint, it eventually also became a time of optimism and increasing affluence (see Downes and Morgan, Chapter 9, this volume).

YOUTH IN POST-WAR BRITAIN

A vast army of scientists and professionals played a central role in supporting the state in its task of post-war social reconstruction. Part of this project involved the creation and maintenance of a new social order. The causes of disorder were believed to lie in the consequences of the war and in the continuing inequalities of the post-war era, the solutions in successful economic management and the reduction of inequality. Of great concern were the effects of the war on the family, and this became increasingly central to the understanding of delinquency in the 1950s; such work involved the ' "discovery" (and persistent rediscovery)' of the 'problem family' (Clarke 1980: 73), together with the continuing influence of the work of Cyril Burt, that of John Bowlby, the ecological work of John Barron Mays, and the beginnings of community studies which identified the family as the 'central transmitting agency of social values and behaviour'.

The number of known juvenile offenders began to rise substantially from about 1955, as did public concern about youth in general. Young people were beginning to enjoy a degree of autonomy that was significantly greater than that of previous generations, and at the heart of this was their generally increasing affluence (Abrams 1959; Pinto-Duschinsky 1970). This led to the growth of increasingly spectacular youth styles based around the conspicuous consumption of 'leisure and pleasure' (Frith 1983), linked with the emergence of what became known as 'mass culture' and the development of its most spectacular offshoot, youth culture.

In some respects, however, 'youth' in post-war Britain appeared to transcend class. Although the subcultural styles that developed were, seemingly, distinctly class based, there was wide concern over youth as a whole, and the development of phrases such as the 'generation gap' gave expression to the prevalent feeling that it was the differences between age groups as opposed to classes that were the more problematic. This received some support in sociological quarters from those who believed that traditional class divisions were being broken down by increasing affluence (Goldthorpe *et al.* 1969). Crucially, 'youth' were perceived to be one of the most striking indications of social change. For the moral entrepreneurs of the period, 'youth' was a problem. Most importantly, youth was 'a cornerstone in the construction of understandings, interpretations and quasi-explanations *about* the period' (Clarke *et al.* 1976: 9).

The first of the major post-war subcultures was the 'Teds'. The appearance of rock 'n' roll in Britain lit the touchpaper of respectable moral outrage (Gillett 1983), and the quiff, 'Duck's Arse', long jackets with velvet collars, bootlace ties, drainpipe trousers, and suede shoes defined the style. Moral concern was focused in the main on the sporadic violence at rock 'n' roll fims, on the occasional confrontations between rival groups of 'Teds', and on the so-called 'race riots' of the late 1950s. However, concerns about the general behaviour of young people in post-war British society focused on both sexual and criminal behaviour, and images of juvenile delinquency, and more generalized forms of rebellion or resistance, were closely intertwined. It was not just violence associated with the 'Teds', therefore, but the blatant sexuality of what Melly (1972: 36) called 'screw and smash' music ('a contemporary incitement to arbitrary fucking and mindless vandalism'), which terrified older generations. Though post-war thinking—influenced by Fabianism and positivism—looked for solutions in increasing prosperity, it seemed clear that 'consensus, affluence and consumerism had produced, not the pacification of worry and anxiety—their dissolution in the flux of money, goods and fashion—but their reverse: a profound, disquieting sense of moral unease' (Hall *et al.* 1978: 233). The more liberal atmosphere of the 1960s, illustrated in the reform of the laws on obscenity, abortion, theatre censorship, capital punishment, homosexuality, divorce, and licensing, was counterbalanced, at least in part, by moral campaigns to check the 'permissive revolution' (Newburn 1991).

A succession of white working-class subcultures followed in the wake of the Teds, and with what appeared to be increasing speed. These included 'Mods'—of various sorts—whose style was 'sharp but neat and visually understated' (Hebdige 1976: 88) and broad enough to encompass sharp suits, parkas, and the seemingly ubiquitous Vespa (Cohen 1972). In opposition, sometimes literally, always stylistically, were the Rockers. Similar to the Teds, in that they originated from lower down the social scale than the Mods (Barker and Little 1964), they were unfashionable, unglamorous, and associated with leather, motor bikes, and an aggressive, often violent, masculinity (Willis 1978). Perhaps the most starkly aggressive of all subcultural styles were the skinheads, who appeared in the late 1960s. The skinheads espoused traditional, even reactionary, values and, through their association with football violence and attacks on ethnic minorities and gays, quickly obtained folk devil status. Their racism, defence of territory, opposition to hippy values, their social origins (unskilled working class) and particular construction of style or 'bricolage' (Clarke 1976b)— Doc Marten boots, cropped hair, braces—were seen by subcultural theorists as representing 'an attempt to recreate through the "mob" the traditional working class community' (Clarke 1976a: 99).

Subcultural theory grew out of a more generally functionalist sociology of delinquency, the origins of which lay in the Chicago School in the 1920s–1940s (see Rock, Chapter 1, this volume). It was not until the late 1960s that a distinctly British school of subcultural theory emerged. Its distinctiveness lay in taking traditional subcultural theory and locating it within cultural and historical time and place. This was in part a response to the perceived shortcomings of anomie theory, but also because North American theory was felt inapplicable to the British context in a number of ways (Downes and Rock 1982). Nevertheless, as Stan Cohen (1980: iv) noted, despite any differences, the two waves shared a great deal: 'Both work with the same "problematic" ... growing up in a class society; both identify the same vulnerable group: the urban male working-class late adolescent; both see delinquency as a collective solution to a structurally imposed problem'. Early British work, such as John Barron Mays's *Growing Up in the City* and Terry Morris's *The Criminal Area*, formed the basis of a distinctly British form of sociological criminology which really took off from the late 1960s after the publication of Downes's work. In Downes's view, delinquency is not at heart rebellious, but conformist. The conformity is to working-class values. Consequently, he effectively rejected the idea—so far as the area he was studying was concerned—of delinquent subcultures and, rather, saw delinquency as a 'solution' to some of the structural problems faced by young men. In this, in part, he was aligning himself with American sociologists such as Matza and Sykes. For Downes, many of the young people he studied dissociated themselves from school and work and emphasized leisure goals:

> In the absence of work-orientation and job-satisfaction, and lacking the compensations accruing from alternative areas of non-work, such as home-centredness, political activity and community service, the 'corner boy' attaches unusual importance to leisure. There is no reason to suppose that the delinquent 'corner boy' does not share the more general, technically classless 'teenage culture', a culture whose active pursuit depends on freedom from the restraints of adult responsibility, but which reflects the 'subterranean values' of the conventional adult world. There is some reason to suppose, however, that the working-class 'corner boy' both lays greater stress on its leisure goals, and has far less legitimate access to them, than male adolescents differently placed in the social structure. This discrepancy is thought to be enough to provide immediate impetus to a great deal of group delinquency, limited in ferocity but diversified in content [Downes 1966: 250].

As British subcultural theory developed, so its focus moved gradually away from delinquency and increasingly towards leisure and style (the main exceptions being Patrick 1973; Parker 1974; and Gill 1977). Parker's is a study of criminal subculture in which theft from cars provided a profitable adolescent interlude before the onset of a more respectable adult life or a more serious and long-term criminal career. Both his and Patrick's studies—in which the focus was on the machismo of the 'hard man'— brought insights from labelling theory to bear on the study of subcultures. Parker's 'boys' used theft as a means of dealing with some of the problems they faced, dissociating themselves in part from the values of the dominant social order and, like the delinquents in Downes's pathbreaking (1966) study, responding within the physical and material conditions which constrained their range of choice and freedom.

Subcultures emerged not just as a response to the problems of material conditions — their class circumstances, schooling, and so on. They were also taken to represent a symbolic critique of the dominant culture in which 'style' was read as a form of resistance. Subcultures, at least from the viewpoint of the more radical commentators of the 1970s, were essentially oppositional rather than subordinate. It was this opposition which gave rise to the kinds of societal reaction that Stan Cohen, utilizing interactionism, labelling theory, and the idea of deviancy amplification, described as 'moral panics', wherein 'a condition, episode, person or group of persons emerges to become defined as a threat to societal values and interests' (1980: 9).

The most recurrent forms of moral panic in Britain since the war have been those surrounding youthful forms of deviance—from subcultural styles, through football hooliganism, to drug use (Thornton 1995). For their members, subcultures allowed the possibility of providing solutions to material and sociocultural problems, albeit through solutions that were symbolic. In a seminal essay on working-class youth culture, Phil Cohen (1972: 23) argued that the latent function of subculture was to:

> express and resolve, albeit 'magically', the contradictions which appear in the parent culture. The succession of subcultures which this parent culture generated can thus all be considered as so many variations on a central theme—the contradiction, at an ideological level, between traditional working-class puritanism and the new hedonism of consumption; at an economic level between a part of the socially mobile elite or a part of the new lumpen proletariat.

The solution, however, is largely expressed through style rather than crime. The style of each subculture involves the creation of identities and images built upon objects appropriated from other cultures and eras. Jefferson (2004: 29–30) argues that Cohen also understood such subcultural style in Freudian terms as a 'compromise solution between the needs of adolescents to be autonomous of and different from their parents as well as to be able to hang onto the security of existing parental identifications'. It was at this point that the vocabulary of cultural studies met various strands of the sociology of deviance. Discerning 'the hidden messages inscribed in code on the glossy surfaces of style, to trace them out as maps of meaning' (Hebdige 1979: 18), became the key task.

Though the bulk of youthful styles in the 1960s were of working-class origin, the last years of the decade also saw the development of a middle-class counter-culture which, associated with both permissiveness and drug use, was guaranteed a hostile reaction from 'respectable' society. Brake argues that hippy culture in Britain was made up largely of students and ex-students and 'provided a moratorium for its members of approximately five years in which to consider one's identity and relationship to the world' (1985: 95). Drugs and sex were the focuses of moral concern, and the late 1960s saw significant increases in prosecutions for possession of marijuana and a concerted campaign of prosecutions against the underground press (Palmer 1971; Newburn 1991).

The dominant focus of British subcultural theory in the 1970s was on white, working-class, male culture (Dorn and South 1982). There were, at least in the earliest years of such writing, few attempts to understand either female delinquency or the styles associated with female subcultures, though the work of Angela McRobbie was both an early and a consistent exception to this (McRobbie and Garber 1976; McRobbie 1980, 1991). According to McRobbie and Garber (1976), because of their position within public and private worlds, girls tend to be pushed to the periphery of social activities, and much 'girl culture' becomes a culture of the bedroom rather than the street (see also Frith 1983). It is this, McRobbie (1980: 40) argues, that most subcultural theorists ignore:

> in documenting the temporary flights of the Teds, Mods or Rockers, they fail to show that it is monstrously more difficult for women to escape (even temporarily) and that these symbolic flights have often been at the expense of women (especially mothers) and girls. The lads'... peer-group consciousness and pleasure frequently seem to hinge on a collective disregard for women and sexual exploitation of girls.

Subcultural theory had little to offer by way of explanation of the involvement of young women in criminal activity. In the 1980s, however, as the youth cultural scene went quiet, so the sociological students of style moved their focus away from youth and towards sexuality and ethnicity (McRobbie 1994a; see also Heidensohn and Gelsthorpe, Chapter 13, this volume). Although contemporary sociological work on youth cultures pays significantly more attention to young women than its 1970s precursor, it continues to be dominated by a preoccupation with the activities and style of white youth, though there is much less concern with ideas of subculture (see for example the essays in Epstein 1998, and Bennett and Kahn-Harris 2004a).

By comparison with the 1960s, the early 1970s were a relatively quiet time on the youth subcultural front, though they did see the blossoming of Afro-Caribbean cultural resistance, in part associated with, and reinforced by, the mugging panic of the mid-1970s (Hall *et al.* 1978). Up to this point there appears to have been no explicit association between black youth and crime. Such an association became firmly established, and the 'view of the blacks as innately criminal, or at least more criminal than the white neighbours whose deprivation they share, which became "common sense" during the early 1970s, is crucial to the development of new definitions of the black problem and new types of racial language and reasoning' (Gilroy 1987: 109). In subcultural terms, Hebdige (1987) argues that as the mood of some black British youth became more angry and bitter, so the central messages of reggae and of Rastafarianism became increasingly relevant (see Cashmore 1983).

In the late 1970s reggae also attracted punks 'who wished to give tangible form to their alienation' (Hebdige 1979: 63). First visible around 1976, punk was visually and verbally violent, but less frequently physically so than was publicly portrayed (Savage 1991; 1996). Moreover, with its links with Malcolm McLaren and Vivienne Westwood's King's Road shop, 'Sex', it incorporated a degree of commercialism which some commentators viewed as distinguishing it from previous, more 'authentic' subcultural styles (though for criticisms of this view, see McRobbie 1994b; Thornton 1995). Punk attempted to undermine 'every relevant discourse' (Hebdige 1979: 108). It used bin liners, safety pins, PVC, graffiti, ripped clothing, and bondage gear as a counterpoint to conventional dress style; and its music, dancing, band names, song titles, and language (Laing 1985) provided further shock tactics to reinforce the sought-after outcast status. 'Things were never the same after punk' (McRobbie 1994b: 159), and if hippies were a direct product of the permissive 1960s and early 1970s, and punk was, in part, a reaction to hippy romanticism, youth culture in the 1980s and after was profoundly shaped by the conservatism, economic depression, and the highly individualized consumerism of the times.

Subcultural studies began to change from this period. In part this was a result of a mounting critique of the Centre for Contemporary Cultural Studies (CCCS) approach, which was perceived as overly preoccupied with males, with style, and with a rather monochrome and mechanistic portrayal of working-class 'resistance'. The shift in subcultural studies was also a product of the changing nature of the social world and what was perceived as the consequent fragmentation of 'youth cultures' and the construction of new identities that were a part of the emergent late modern social world. Through the late 1970s and into the 1980s, social and economic conditions for many young people became dramatically tougher (Williamson 2004). The key defining features were unemployment and racism, and it was against this background that African-Caribbean cultural resistance burgeoned and that 'punk' appeared. From the late 1970s onward, youth unemployment became a permanent feature of the social landscape: by the mid-1980s less than three-tenths of 16- to 17-year-olds had full-time jobs (Roberts 1995). In parallel with the precipitous decline in youth employment, especially full-time youth employment, and the withdrawal of entitlement to benefits for most 16- to 17-year-olds, there was also a significant expansion in the late 1980s of youth training schemes, though these have declined once more, and a massive rise in the numbers 'staying on' in education. The major consequence of these structural changes was to extend and complicate the transition from dependent childhood to independent adulthood (Furlong and Cartmel 1997). The developing gap between 'work-rich' and 'work-poor' families meant that at least a proportion of young people faced increased difficulty in negotiating the extended transition into adult life (Wallace 1987; Jones 1995). A further small group about whom relatively little is known are those not in education (often having been excluded), training, or work. Many disappear from the system altogether, some temporarily, others permanently; and it is around these young people that many concerns about future criminal activity coalesce (Hagell and Newburn 1994; Newburn and Shiner 2005; Williamson 2004).

The extended and altered nature of education, and the extended and increasingly problematic character of the transition from adolescence to adulthood has had a number of consequences (MacDonald *et al.* 2005). Arguably, it has problematized the notion of 'youth'. As Frith (2004: 177) observes in his overview of subcultural studies in the past thirty years, this is possibly the most significant shift in youth studies before and after subculture. At the height of subcultural studies, 'youth was an age category;

now, it seems, it isn't, or isn't necessarily'. In addition, it has almost certainly had an impact not just on subcultural style but on youth offending and the rising age of peak offending from 14 forty years ago to 18 today (see below). This shift reflects the changing nature of youth transitions.

The increasingly reflexive and commodified nature of late modernity fragmented youth cultural styles and led to the emergence of a new approach that has been characterized, perhaps predictably, as 'post-subcultural theory' (Bennett and Kahn-Harris 2004b). This approach largely rejects a structurally based account of subculture and argues, by contrast, for the importance of understanding the creative 'pick'n'mix' nature of much contemporary identity formation. At its most extreme this view was captured by Polhemus (1997: 150) who argued that we 'now inhabit a Supermarket of Style where, like tins of soup lined up on endless shelves, we can choose between more than fifty different styletribes. Jumbling geography as well as history, British punk circa 1976 sits on the shelf next to 1950s American Beatnik or late Jamaican reggae'. A slightly more restrained version of post-subcultural theory can be found, however, in the work of writers such as Muggleton (2000) and Redhead (1990). In this view it is argued that as the world of work has retreated as a realistic prospect for many, so lifestyles dominated by consumption have come closer to the foreground. This was reflected in youth culture in the 1980s which 'became more of an advertising medium than ever before; it was notable not for opposition, but for its role in selling everything from Levi 501 jeans to spot cream' (Redhead 1990: 105). As a consequence, much was made of the supposed 'end of youth culture'. Bottoms and Wiles (1995), following Giddens, suggest that one of the consequences of the increasing dominance of consumption is a gradual relocation of sources of trust in late modern society from groups or collectivities— kin, local community, religious group—to individualized relations. Given the importance of collective norms in limiting individual deviant actions, the criminogenic consequences of the relocation of trust are easy to see. Furthermore, they argue, this decline in traditional collectivities has had a negative impact on age-integrated leisure patterns, and this, linked to globalization of aspects of youth culture and consumption, is likely to reinforce both age-specific activities and the boundaries between 'youth' and other social groups. In such circumstances, 'respectable fears' about young people become exacerbated. The most recent and most consistent of respectable fears about youth arguably concern drugs and drug use (South, Chapter 24, this volume).

The late 1980s and 1990s saw the emergence of dance-based, drug-associated youth cultural styles, to which the acid house subculture and subsequent rave 'movement' or 'scene' were central. With its origins in Chicago House music and Euro-Pop (the Balearic Beat), acid house enjoyed a brief moment of approbation in the media before its drug connections led to inevitable backlash. Acid house parties and, more particularly, the use of the drug Ecstasy were the focal point of moral campaigns. Such partying—or 'hedonism in hard times' (Redhead 1993: 4)—was somewhat in contrast with the drabber youth culture of the late 1970s and early 1980s. Where 'punk had rejected such obvious pleasure a decade before . . . youth hedonism was now back, with a vengeance. A fortnight's holiday in the sun became packed into a single weekend—then the next weekend and the next' (McKay 1996: 105). Rave culture inspired considerable moral indignation—at least in the press—and was also subject to increasing legislative attention. Initially, the Entertainments (Increased Penalties) Act 1990—which had been introduced as a Private Member's Bill—restricted the holding of 'raves' or large-scale parties. This was followed by the Criminal Justice and Public Order Act 1994, which contained provisions for dealing with raves, together with other forms of 'collective trespass', particularly those associated with 'new age travellers'.

As should be clear by now the bulk of British sociological attention during the 1960s to 1980s, and beyond, was devoted to the study of white youth, though various 'Birmingham School'[1] authors, notably Stuart Hall, Dick Hebdige, and Paul Gilroy, applied elements of the subcultural style approach both to black youth culture and to questions of racism and crime. From 'rude boys' and ska to reggae and Rastafarianism, Hebdige sought to explain elements of black youth culture as expressions of resistance, and as products of an increasingly problematic relationship with elements of British society—not least the police. Of particular interest and concern was the 'mugging crisis' of the early 1970s and the politicization of the problem of 'black crime' of which it was emblematic (Hall *et al.* 1978). It was from this point, Gilroy (1987: 109) argues, that a common-sense view emerged which saw 'blacks as innately criminal, or at least more criminal than the white neighbours whose deprivation they share'. Black youth cultural styles had a profound effect on numerous white, working-class youth cultures and undoubtedly the increasingly explicit cross-over that was evident in the 1970s and 1980s contributed significantly to the moral panics of the time (Gilroy and Lawrence 1988). More recently, sociological attention has turned to Asian youth and the emergence of new folk devils: the 'Asian gang' and radical Muslim youth (Alexander 2000). Indeed, the growing focus on diversity and difference has led to an increasing focus on religion as a source of identity, and one almost indistinguishable from 'race' in some accounts. As a consequence, as Alexander (2000:15) puts it, 'Muslims have then, ironically, become the new "black", with all the associations of cultural alienation, deprivation and danger that come with this position'. Signs of youthful Asian disaffection were already visible by the mid-1980s with disturbances having taken place in London and Bradford early in the decade. Subsequent disturbances, again in Bradford in 1995 (Bradford Commission 1996) and in Bradford, Burnley, and Oldham in 2001 (Cantle 2001) have focused considerable attention on young Muslims (Webster 1997), concerns which have had an altogether more dramatic focus since the suicide bombings in London in July 2005.

Despite the declining frequency in recent times with which new subcultural styles have emerged and been played out as a form of 'symbolic guerrilla warfare' (Thompson 1998: 48) moral panics around youth, and especially youthful deviance and criminality, continue to be a regular feature of the political and cultural landscape. For a time,

---

[1] Named after the Centre for Contemporary Cultural Studies at the University of Birmingham. At its height the CCCS was directed by Stuart Hall (its first director was Richard Hoggart) and among its members it included John Clarke, Chas Critcher, Phil Cohen, Paul Gilroy, Dick Hebdige, Dorothy Hobson, Tony Jefferson, Angela McRobbie, Brian Roberts, Paul Willis, and Janice Winship.

however, the study of youth culture and sociological enquiry into the ways in which deviance and transgression acquire meaning became somewhat unfashionable. Criminology became increasingly preoccupied with, and focused upon, governmental and administrative concerns. There are signs of a re-emergence of interest in the ethnographic study of deviance, however, most notably under the banner of 'cultural criminology' (see Ferrell and Sanders 1995; Ferrell 2006). Ironically, given that much such cultural criminology is designed as a counterpoint to so-called administrative criminology, it is to primarily survey-based empirical studies of the relationship between youth and crime, most produced by government, that we turn next.

YOUNG PEOPLE, CRIME, AND VICTIMIZATION

A significant proportion of crime is committed by young people. Indeed, Hirschi and Gottfredson (1983: 552) argue that the age-crime distribution 'represents one of the brute facts of criminology'. This, in tandem with adult fears about youthful deviance, leads to young offenders occupying the 'dubiously privileged position', in changing guises, as society's number one folk devil (Muncie *et al.* 1995). Though official statistics can only ever provide a crude estimate of juvenile offending, they nevertheless suggest that at least one-fifth of all those cautioned or convicted in any one year are aged between 10 and 17 and well over one-third (37 per cent) are aged under 21 (Nicholas *et al.* 2005). Self-report studies confirm the by now largely accepted fact that offending in the teenage years is relatively common. Research conducted by the Home Office in the mid-1990s found that over half of males and almost one-third of females aged between 14 and 25 admitted to committing one or more criminal offences at some point in their lives (Home Office 1995). A more recent self-report study found that 10- to 17-year-olds were responsible for 35 per cent of the incidents measured even though they comprised 14 per cent of the sample (Budd *et al.* 2005b). The same study found that approximately one-third of young males and just under one-fifth of young females aged between 10 and 25 reported having committed at least one offence in the past year (see Figure 18.1).

Estimates of the peak age of offending vary but generally place it somewhere between 15 (MORI 2004) and 18 (Home Office 2005). The estimated peak age of offending is higher for males than it is for females. Home Office self-report survey data identify the 16–17- year age group as that with the highest prevalence of offending for males, with that for females being slightly younger at approximately 14–15 (see Figure 18.2). Official statistics also suggest that the peak age of known male offending has increased; it was 14 years in 1971, 15 in 1980, and increased to 18 by 1990, where it has since remained. The location of the peak age of offending in the mid- to late adolescent years has traditionally been taken as indicating that a significant proportion of young people will simply 'grow out of crime' (Rutherford 1992).

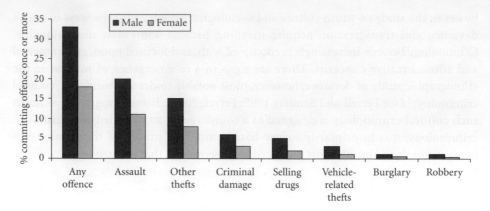

Fig. 18.1   10–25-year-olds committing offences in the last 12 months by sex (%)
Source: Budd *et al.* 2005b.

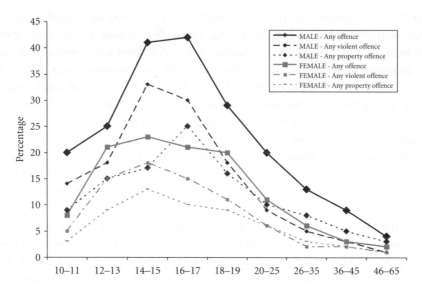

Fig. 18.2   Last-year prevalence of offending by age (%)
Source: Budd *et al.* 2005b.

The first Youth Lifestyles Survey (YLS) provided new evidence about the prevalence of offending for different age groups (Graham and Bowling 1995). The data showed the peak age of offending for males to be 14 for 'expressive property offences', 16 for violent offences, 17 for serious offences, and 20 for drug offences. Among females, the peak age of offending was 15 for property, expressive, and serious offences, 16 for violent offences, and 17 for drug offences. Looking, however, at the proportions of males at different ages who admitted to having committed various offences within a one-year period, Graham and Bowling found that expressive and violent offences were most prevalent among 14–17-year-olds, property offences (excluding fraud and theft from work) among 18–21-year-olds, and theft of motor vehicles among 22–25-year-olds. When fraud and theft from work were included within the property crime category, 22–25-year-olds had the highest rate of offending. They concluded that, among males, while the rate of participation in offending does not change significantly between the ages of 14 and 25, it does change markedly in character. Most particularly, they suggested that young men did not appear to be desisting from property offences in their early twenties. They cast some doubt, therefore, on the idea that young people tend to 'grow out of crime'.

This thesis was explored again in the second YLS, which had an extended age range (12–30) and a larger sample size. Though this again found that rates of property offending differed from rates of criminal damage and violence, remaining fairly stable between the ages of 18 and 25, it found that the proportion declined thereafter, possibly suggesting a somewhat delayed pattern of 'desistance' (Flood-Page *et al.* 2000). Finally, there is a considerable body of data that points to the disproportionate involvement of working-class males in offending when compared with other social groups. Work in the mid-1990s on persistent young offenders found under one-tenth to come from households whose head was in non-manual employment (Hagell and Newburn 1994). Although self-report studies tend to show less of a gap in levels of offending by social class (Graham and Bowling 1995), the 1998/9 YLS found that young males in social classes IV and V were more likely to be persistent offenders (12 and 17 per cent respectively) than those from social classes I–III (10 per cent) (Flood-Page *et al.* 2000).

THE NATURE OF MALE AND FEMALE OFFENDING

The predominance of property crime among those offences committed by young people is confirmed by official statistics and by self-report studies. Juveniles, irrespective of age or sex, are most likely to be cautioned or convicted for theft and handling stolen goods. Until relatively recently burglary was the second most common source of cautions and convictions for male juvenile offenders, but the rise in recorded violent offending has seen such offences displace burglary in second place (see Table 18.1).

Self-report data confirm the general picture available from *Criminal Statistics* (Home Office 2005) and help us provide a little more detail about patterns of male and female offending. Both male and female juvenile offenders are significantly more likely to commit a violent offence than a property offence, albeit that males have considerably higher prevalence rates than females. The Home Office Crime and Justice Survey (CJS) (Budd *et al.* 2005a) found the peak age of violent offending to be 14 to 15 for both males and males, with one-third of males and 18 per ent of females having committed such an offence in the previous year. The peak age of property offending remains 14 to 15 for females, and peaks at around 13 per cent, whereas it is both slightly older (16–17 years old) and higher (25 per cent) for males. According to such surveys over the age of 16, most of these offences decline in frequency, though fraud and buying stolen goods tend to become more common among females (Flood-Page *et al.* 2000).

Table 18.1 Offenders found guilty or cautioned, by offence type, sex and age (%)

	Male 10–11	Female 10–11	Male 12–14	Female 12–14	Male 15–17	Female 15–17
Theft and handling	52	78	45	70	34	60
Violence against the person	19	11	19	17	18	18
Burglary	13	4	13	3	10	3
Criminal damage	10	4	8	3	5	4
Robbery	2	1	3	1	4	2
Fraud and forgery	0	1	1	1	2	3
Sexual offences	1	0	2	0	1	0
Drug offences	1	0	6	2	18	6
Other (excl. motoring)	2	1	4	2	8	5
Motoring	0	0	0	0	1	0

Source: Home Office 2005: Table 3.10.

The frequency of offending varies markedly and there is now a considerable criminological literature looking at persistent and serious offending by juveniles. Early research by Wolfgang and colleagues (1972) identified what they described as 'chronic offenders'. This small group—representing just over 6 per cent of the cohort being studied—accounted for more than half of all the arrests experienced by the whole group. There has been considerable policy interest in such offenders for a decade or more and a large body of longitudinal and cross-sectional research has examined the backgrounds and offending histories of such 'frequent', 'high rate', or 'life course persistent' offenders (West and Farrington 1977; Farrington and West 1993; Huizinga *et al.* 1995; Smith, Chapter 20, this volume). Similarly, the 2004 CJS uses self-report data to distinguish between *prolific* and *frequent* offending. *Prolific* offending was defined as having committed six or more offences in the previous year, whereas *serious* offending was defined as having committed any of the following offences in the previous year: theft of a vehicle; burglary; robbery; theft from the person; assault resulting in injury; and selling Class A drugs. Figure 18.3 breaks down the 2004 CJS juvenile cohort into those that have and those that have not offended in the previous year, and then subdivides the offenders into *prolific*, *serious*, and *prolific and serious* offenders.

The survey found that using such definitions, approximately one-quarter of juveniles that had offended in the previous year would be defined as being *serious and prolific* and 60 per cent would be defined as either *serious* or *prolific*. On this basis the researchers estimate that there are approximately 420,000 *serious* or *prolific* juvenile offenders in England and Wales, rather reinforcing the difficulties highlighted by previous research in identifying what is often thought to be a *small* group responsible for a disproportionate amount of crime (see Hagell and Newburn 1994).

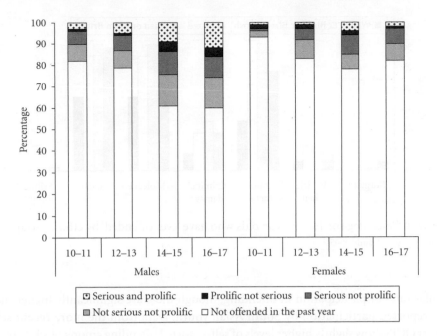

Fig. 18.3 Offending profile of juveniles, *Crime and Justice Survey*, 2004
Source: Budd *et al.* 2005a.

ETHNIC MINORITY YOUTH AND CRIME

It was not until the 1970s that there was any explicit association made between black youth and crime (see Phillips and Bowling, Chapter 14, this volume). The increased concern that arose was partly a result of the 'mugging panic' early in the decade, and other signs of poor or deteriorating relationships between the police and black youth. This was reinforced by the release of statistics by the Metropolitan Police suggesting that crime rates were particularly high among African-Caribbean youth in the capital. Other sources of data showed black youth to be over-represented at all other stages of the criminal justice process, and subsequent research has confirmed such over-representation. Thus, African-Caribbean youth are more likely to be prosecuted than are white youth, who are more likely to be cautioned (Landau and Nathan 1983); they are more likely to be charged with offences which must be heard in the Crown Court (Audit Commission 1996); and they are more likely to be remanded in, and sentenced to, custody (Phillips and Bowling, ibid.).

Given the now strong popular association between black youth and crime, it is perhaps surprising how little rigorous, empirical research has been conducted in the area. There are a number of useful exceptions to this; one is the first YLS which included a booster sample of 808 young people from ethnic minorities (Graham and Bowling 1995); another is the recent Offending Crime and Justice Survey (OCJS) conducted by the Home Office (Sharp and Budd 2005). The data from the YLS were striking. They suggested that, in general, white and African-Caribbean youth have

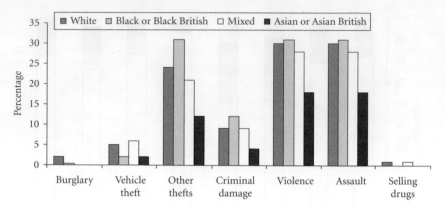

Fig. 18.4 Percentage of 10–15-year-olds who have 'ever offended' by ethnic group
Source: Sharp and Budd 2005.

similar rates of participation in offending, though these are significantly higher than self-reported participation by South Asian youth. Data from the more recent self-report OCJS show slightly higher levels of self-reported offending among black or black British respondents compared with white respondents (see Figure 18.4).

Both groups report higher levels of lifetime offending than either Asian or Asian British respondents or those of mixed ethnic origin (see Figure 18.3). However, a slightly higher proportion of white respondents (23 per cent) reported having ever committed a 'serious' offence compared with mixed (20 per cent), black or black British (20 per cent), or Asian or Asian British respondents (15 per cent). The OCJS also included a series of questions about antisocial and other 'problem' behaviours. The results show slightly higher overall levels of antisocial behaviour among white young people aged 10 to 15, but these differences were not significant. The more sizeable differences appeared to be in relation to treatment within the criminal justice system which, in some instances at least, was 'consistent with discriminatory treatment' (Feilzer and Hood 2005; see also Morgan and Newburn, Chapter 30, this volume).

YOUNG PEOPLE, DRUGS, ALCOHOL, AND CRIME

Close associations between youth subcultures and illicit drug use have been noted since at least the hippy counter-culture of the 1960s (Young 1971). However, far from being perceived as problematic, 'during the 1960s and 1970s it was fashionable in social science and liberal circles to question whether the prevailing concern about drug use might not be an example of ... "moral panic" ' (Dorn and South 1987: 2). This all changed in the late 1970s, and the years 1979–81 were the watershed during which 'the heroin habit' really began to take off and when, for the first time, its use became associated with the young unemployed (Pearson 1987). The number of known addicts trebled between 1979 and 1983, and research in the late 1980s confirmed the impression of a significant spread of heroin use (Parker *et al.* 1988). Public concern about increasing heroin use was followed by fears of a possible 'crack' epidemic, though, in the main, the worst of these fears have not been realized. Research in the 1990s suggests that 'the picture now is one of continuing widespread availability of a great variety of drugs, use being shaped by familiar factors such as local supply, contexts of use, preferred styles of consumption and purpose or intent' (South 1994: 399; see also South, Chapter 24, this volume).

Data on the incidence and prevalence of illicit drug use among young people are now available as a result of a number of important surveys (inter alia Plant *et al.* 1985; Balding 1994; Measham *et al.* 1994; Mott and Mirrlees-Black 1993; Miller and Plant 1996; Ramsay and Percy 1996; Ramsay *et al.* 2001; Goulden and Sondhi 2001). Prevalence for 15- to 20-year-olds varies between approximately 10 and 35 per cent in the national samples and 5 and 50 per cent in local samples. The surveys show cannabis to be the most popular illicit drug, though use of LSD, amphetamines, and Ecstasy has increased since the late 1980s, as has polydrug use (Parker *et al.* 1995). Figure 18.5 shows the last-year prevalence of drug use by males and females aged 10 to 25.

Drug use and age are clearly linked. Use of illicit drugs is rare in early teenage years, increases sharply in the mid-teens, and is generally shown to peak in the late teens or early twenties (ISDD 1994). It has been the annual surveys conducted by Howard Parker and colleagues since the early 1990s that have probably been most influential in framing contemporary understandings of youthful drug use (Measham *et al.* 1994; Parker and Measham 1994; Parker *et al.* 1995; Parker *et al.* 1988, 2001). Conducted in schools in the North-West of England, the surveys provide data on use of illicit drugs among samples of children aged approximately 14 in the first survey through to the age of 18. The surveys indicate relatively high prevalence rates of 'lifetime use' reported by over a third (36 per cent) of 14-year-olds to almost two-thirds (64 per cent) of 18-year-olds (Parker *et al.* 1998).

Both national and local surveys indicate that, at least until recently, drug use by young people appears to have been on the increase. Mott and Mirrlees-Black (1993), for

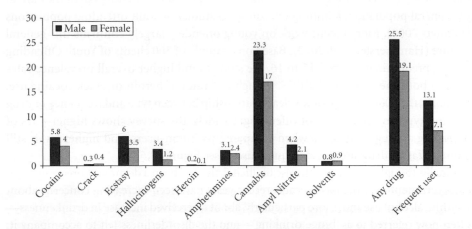

Fig. 18.5 Drug use among 10–25-year-olds in the last 12 months by age and sex
Source: Budd *et al.* 2005b: Table A7.1.

instance, note that the percentage of 16- to 19-year-olds reporting cannabis use more than doubled between 1983 and 1991. The late 1980s and early 1990s witnessed an increase in the use of dance drugs. Though this increase started from a relatively low baseline, by the mid-1990s dance drugs had become an important part of the youth drug scene (Measham *et al*. 1993). Moreover, according to Parker *et al*. (1995), unlike the situation a decade previously, there were no longer any significant differences in the prevalence of illicit drug use by young men and women, though the authors recognize that in terms of the quantities, the frequency, and the repertoire of drug use, gendered differences may still remain. Parker *et al*. (1995) conclude that the ways in which young people perceive and relate to illicit drugs is changing quite dramatically, and that adolescents now live in a world in which the availability of drugs is unexceptional, even 'a *normal* part of the leisure-pleasure landscape' (1995: 25; though for a critical review see Shiner and Newburn 1997, 1999). The most recent national surveys of youthful illicit drug use (Ramsay *et al*. 2001) suggest that there has been some stabilizing of prevalence rates, though there appears to have been a significant increase in cocaine use since the mid-1990s.

Against the background of rising levels of illicit drug use in the 1990s it is perhaps not surprising that faith in primary prevention diminished and that attention increasingly turned to forms of secondary prevention, particularly the reduction or minimization of harm associated with drug use (Lloyd and Griffiths 1998). Recent years have seen growing attention, both at an official level and academically, paid to levels and types of drug use among 'vulnerable groups' (Lloyd 1998). A growing body of research has high-lighted the particularly 'vulnerable' position of young offenders (Collison 1994; Newburn 1998, 1999; Becker and Roe 2005; Wincup *et al*. 2003). The second YLS found that three-quarters (74 per cent) of 'persistent offenders' reported lifetime use of drugs, and almost three-fifths (57 per cent) reported having used drugs in the past year (Goulden and Sondhi 2001). In addition to reporting raised general prevalence rates, the survey also suggested that the rates of use of drugs such as crack and heroin are significantly higher among young serious and/or persistent offenders than they are in the general population, a finding reinforced by studies of adult offending populations (Bennett 2000). More recent work on young offenders largely confirms this general picture (Hammersley *et al*. 2003). Based on a sample of 300 clients of Youth Offending Teams, predominantly aged 15 to 16, the study found higher overall prevalence rates than in both the YLS and the BCS, though low rates of heroin or crack cocaine use. Similarly, the 2004 OCJS shows a clear relationship between type and frequency of drug use and type and frequency of offending. Crudely, the survey shows higher rates of offending among drug-users when compared with non-users, and higher levels still among Class A drug-users and frequent users (see Figure 18.6).

Finally, though the issue of the use of illicit drugs has been a dominant preoccupation of government over the past decade, recent years have seen increasing concerns about youthful alcohol use and, more particularly, about a perceived increase in drunkenness—often now referred to as 'binge drinking'—and the disorderliness felt to accompany it. Young people's experiences with alcohol vary sharply with age (Newburn and Shiner 2001), typically with levels and frequency of use being relatively low during the early

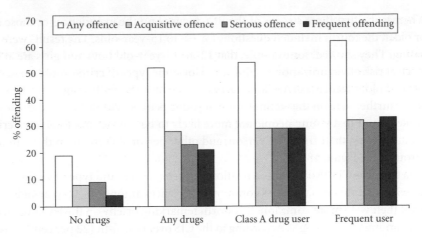

Fig. 18.6 Proportion of 10–25-year-olds committing different types of offences, by drug status

Source: Budd *et al.* 2005b: Table A7.3.

teenage years and increasing markedly during the mid- to late teens (Turtle *et al.* 1997; Harrington 2000). Experiences of intoxication follow a similar pattern. Patterns of youthful alcohol consumption appeared to be relatively stable during the 1970s and 1980s (Goddard 1991; Lister-Sharp 1994). During the 1990s, however, there was evidence of an increase in the frequency of underage alcohol consumption together with an increase in the amounts being consumed (Goddard 1996). Within this there was also some evidence of higher rates of intoxication and binge drinking (Roberts *et al.* 1997). As with illicit drugs the precise nature of the relationship between alcohol and crime is difficult to determine. Evidence from the YLS appears to show a general association between 'binge drinking' and offending, especially violent offending (Richardson *et al.* 2003), and also with persistent offending (Flood-Page *et al.* 2000). Not only is drinking associated with offending, it is also linked to victimization. People injured in cases of assault are more likely to have been drinking at the time that those injured in other ways (Hayden 1995) and those assaulted are likely themselves to be occasionally 'heavy' or 'binge' drinkers (Shepherd and Brickley 1996; Yates 1987).

YOUNG PEOPLE, VICTIMIZATION, AND THE POLICE

When the words 'youth' and 'crime' are linked, the picture in most minds is generally of the young person as an offender. Given the frequency and prevalence of offending by young people this is perhaps not surprising. Young people, however, are frequently victims of crime. Outside those studies which have focused specifically on child abuse and domestic violence, most criminological studies of victimization have paid scant attention to young people's experiences as victims of crime (though for some exceptions see Morgan and Zedner 1992; Anderson *et al.* 1994; Aye Maung 1995; Hartless *et al.* 1995; Loader 1996; see also Hoyle and Zedner, Chapter 15, this volume).

Whereas the first three sweeps of the BCS focused on the experiences of those aged 16 or older, the fourth included questions for 12- to 15-year-olds. The results were illuminating. They showed, for example, that 12- to 15-year-old boys and girls are at least as much at risk of victimization as adults, and for some types of crime, more at risk than adults and older teenagers (Aye Maung 1995). The more recently conducted CJS 2003 provides further data on the victimization of young people (Wood 2005). The study, for example, found that young people are more likely to be the victim of personal crimes (assault, robbery, theft from the person, and other personal theft) than those in older age groups (see Figure 18.7).

Data from the CJS also indicate a relationship between age and type of victimization. Thus, whereas robberies were less common experiences among 10–11-year-olds, other types of theft were more common. It is worth remarking briefly on the levels of victimization among young people. According to the CJS over one-fifth (22 per cent) of 10- to 15-year-olds report having experienced some form of violence in the past year and over a third (35 per cent) report some form of personal crime. Unusually, in addition to investigating criminal victimization the CJS also sought information on 'bullying'. Asking 10- to 17-year-olds if they had been 'bullied in a way that frightened or upset them', the CJS reported that 19 per cent answered in the affirmative. Those most at risk were 10- to 11-year-olds, of whom 27 per cent said they had been bullied. In over half the cases, bullying involved face-to-face abuse or 'verbal offensiveness' and in a third of cases it involved physical assault. Not only were young people more likely to be victimized than older age groups, they were also more likely to experience repeat victimization. Thus, 60 per cent of 10- to 15-year-olds that had experienced violence in the previous year did so more than once compared with 51 per cent of 16- to 25-year-olds and 44 per cent of 26- to 65-year-olds (Wood 2005). Although the CJS does not break

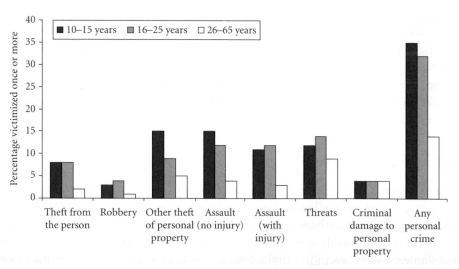

Fig. 18.7 Percentage of age groups victimized once or more in the last 12 months
Source: Wood 2005.

down such experience by ethnic origin, data from the British Crime Survey (BCS), conducted by the Home Office, suggest that African-Caribbeans generally face higher risks than young people from other ethnic groups. The BCS found that only about one in ten incidents were brought to the attention of the police, though the proportion rose to one in five of the more serious incidents experienced. In contrast, one in three members of the sample said that they had had some form of contact with the police in the previous six to eight months. About one-fifth had been stopped and 8 per cent said they had been searched, a higher rate than is the case for older age groups (Aye Maung 1995). Juveniles were also less likely to be told why they were being stopped than were their elders. This, combined with the not infrequent experience for many of being 'moved on', contributed to the apparently paradoxical position in which young people feel both over-controlled and under-protected by the police (Anderson *et al.* 1994; Aye Maung 1995; Hartless *et al.* 1995; Loader 1996).

Despite the often-made assumption that young people are more likely to hold negative views of the police than older people, the 1992 BCS found that 88 per cent of 12- to 15-year-olds agreed with the statement, 'We need a police force in this country to keep law and order', and 63 per cent thought that the police did a very (10 per cent) or fairly (53 per cent) good job in their area. Less than one-tenth said they felt the police did a very poor job. The second YLS (Flood-Page *et al.* 2000) found that over half (53 per cent) of young people aged 12 to 18 felt that the police did a 'fairly good job', and a further 12 per cent felt they did a 'very good' job. Paralleling the attitudes within the black adult population, the least favourable views of the police were held by young African-Caribbeans and, indeed, the views expressed by young people generally were found to correspond closely with the views expressed by the adults in the same households. The study was not able to explore such links in detail, but nevertheless concluded that 'how the police treat both young people *and* adults may well influence the attitudes the other group holds' (Aye Maung 1995: 57).

CONCLUSION

The study of youth culture and deviance was initially dominated by a highly sociological approach that focused on the nature of growing up in post-war America and Britain and the adaptive behaviours that resulted. Early concerns with explaining delinquent behaviour gradually gave way, especially in Britain, to a preoccupation with style and the role of subculture as a 'magical solution' to the generally class-based problems faced by the young and disadvantaged. Slowly but surely such work has been superseded by a less sociologically concerned criminology focusing more on the nature and patterning of criminal careers and the risk and protective factors associated with the onset, persistence of, and desistance from, such offending. Recent years, however, have seen something of a re-emergence of interest in youth culture and subculture, with those working under the banner of 'cultural criminology' (Hayward and Young, Chapter 4, this volume) rediscovering and revitalizing many of the elements of sociological criminology that were in danger of being submerged by governmental concerns about the control of juvenile behaviour. These latter concerns have undoubtedly resulted in the gradual accumulation of a vast wealth of important data—with more emerging all the time. Whilst this information is hugely valuable, one cannot help but feel that it is the work that draws together all of these data with the insights that derive from (sub) cultural and interactionist sociology that holds the greatest promise.

■ SELECTED FURTHER READING

Anyone concerned to understand the history of adult concerns about the young should start with Geoffrey Pearson's *Hooligan: A History of Respectable Fears* (Macmillan, 1983). On subcultures, there are good collections of readings in the Centre for Contemporary Cultural Studies' *Resistance through Rituals* (Hall and Jefferson, Hutchinson, 1976) and Sarah Thornton's *The Subcultures Reader* (Routledge, 1997). Dick Hebdige's *Subculture: The Meaning of Style* (Methuen, 1979) remains the classic cultural studies text on 'style'. David Downes's *The Delinquent Solution* (Routledge & Kegan Paul, 1966) and Howard Parker's *View From the Boys* (David and Charles, 1974) set the standard in Britain for the sociological study of male delinquency. Anyone interested in finding out what cultural criminology can provide, rather than listening to claims on its behalf, should turn to Jeff Ferrell's remarkable *Empire of Scrounge* (State University of New York Press, 2006). The changing nature of being young in the second half of the twentieth century was accompanied by a noisy soundtrack, and should be understood in that context. Writing on popular music is even more a matter of taste than is criminological literature. However, to my mind, it is pretty hard to beat Nik Cohn's *Awopbopaloobop Alopbambboom* (Paladin, 1970), Charlie Gillett's *The Sound of the City* (Souvenir Press, 1983), Jon Savage's *England's Dreaming: Sex Pistols and Punk Rock* (Faber & Faber, 1991), Mark Neal and Murray Foreman's *That's the Joint: the Hip Hop Studies Reader* (Routledge, 2004) and (once again) Nik Cohn's *Triksta* (Harvill Secker, 2005). Anyone interested in exploring patterns of youthful offending, drug use, and victimization should consult the reports from the two Youth Lifestyles Surveys, the recent Crime and Justice, and Offending, Crime and Justice Surveys, as well as the annual MORI surveys commissioned by the Youth Justice Board (all of which are available on the Home Office and YJB websites).

■ REFERENCES

ABRAMS, M. (1959), *The Teenage Consumer*, London: Routledge & Kegan Paul.

ALEXANDER, C. E. (2000), *The Asian Gang: Ethncity, Identity, Masculinity*, London: Berg.

ANDERSON, M. (1980), *Approaches to the History of the Western Family, 1500–1914*, London: Macmillan.

ANDERSON, S., KINSEY, R., LOADER, I., and SMITH, C. (1994), *Cautionary Tales*, Aldershot: Avebury.

ARIES, P. (1973), *Centuries of Childhood*, Harmondsworth: Penguin.

AUDIT COMMISSION (1996), *Misspent Youth: Young people and crime*, London: Audit Commission.

AYE MAUNG, N. (1995), *Young people, victimisation and the police: British Crime Survey findings on the experiences and attitudes of 12–15 year olds*, Home Office Research Study No. 140, London: HMSO.

BAILEY, V. (1987), *Delinquency and Citizenship: Reclaiming the young offender 1914–1948*, Oxford: Clarendon Press.

BALDING, J. (1994), *Young people and illegal drugs*, Exeter: Health Education Unit, University of Exeter.

BANDURA, A. (1977), *Social Learning Theory*, Englewood Cliffs, NJ: Prentice Hall.

BARKER, P., and LITTLE, A. (1964), 'The Margate offenders — a survey', *New Society*, 4(96): 6–10.

BECKER, J., and ROE, S. (2005), *Drug use among vulnerable groups of young people: Findings from the 2003 Crime and Justice Survey*, London: Home Office.

BENNETT, A., and KAHN-HARRIS, K. (2004a), *After Subculture: Critical studies in contemporary youth culture*, Basingstoke: Macmillan.

—— and —— (2004b), 'Introduction', in A. Bennett and K. Kahn-Harris, K. (eds), *After Subculture: Critical studies in contemporary youth culture*, Basingstoke: Macmillan.

BENNETT, T. (2000), *Drugs and Crime: The results of the second developmental stage of the NEW-ADAM programme*, Home Office Research Study No. 205, London: Home Office.

BOOTH, C. (1902), *Life and Labour of the People of London*, London: Macmillan.

BOTTOMS, A. E., and WILES, P. (1995), 'Crime and insecurity in the city', in C. Fijnaut, J. Goethals, T. Peters, and L. Walgrave (eds), *Changes in Society: Crime and Criminal Justice in Europe*, 2 vols, The Hague: Kluwer.

BRADFORD COMMISSION (1996), *The Bradford Commission Report*, London: The Stationery Office.

BRAKE, M. (1985), *Comparative Youth Culture*, London: Routledge.

BUDD, T., SHARP, C. and MAYHEW, P. (2005a), Offending in England and Wales: First results from the 2003 Crime and Justice Survey, London: Home Office.

——, ——, WEIR, G., WILSON, D., and OWEN, N. (2005b), *Young People and Crime: Findings from the 2004 Offending, Crime and Justice Survey*, Home Office Statistical Bulletin 20/05, London: Home Office.

CANTLE, T. (2001), *Community Cohesion: A report of the independent review team*, London: Home Office.

CASHMORE, E. (1983), *Rastaman: The Rastafarian Movement in England*, London: Unwin.

CLARKE, J. (1976a), 'The skinheads and the magical recovery of community', in S. Hall and T. Jefferson (eds), *Resistance Through Rituals*, London: Hutchison.

——(1976b), 'Style', in S. Hall and T. Jefferson (eds), *Resistance Through Rituals*, London: Hutchison.

——(1980), 'Social democratic delinquents and Fabian families', in National Deviancy Conference (ed.), *Permissiveness and Control: The fate of sixties legislation*, London: Macmillan.

——and JEFFERSON, T. (1976), 'Working class youth cultures', in G. Mungham and G. Pearson (eds), *Working Class Youth Culture*, London: Routledge & Kegan Paul.

——, HALL, S., JEFFERSON, T., and ROBERTS, B. (1976), 'Subcultures, cultures and class: A theoretical overview', in S. Hall and T. Jefferson (eds), *Resistance Through Rituals: Youth subcultures in post-war Britain*, London: Hutchison.

COHEN, P. (1972), 'Subcultural conflict and working class community', in S. Hall *et al.* (eds), *Culture, Media, Language*, London: Hutchison.

COHEN, S. (1980), *Folk Devils and Moral Panics*, London: Martin Robertson.

COLEMAN, J., and HENDRY, L. (1990) *The Nature of Adolescence*, London: Routledge.

COLLISON, M. (1994), 'Drug offenders and criminal justice: careers, compulsion, commitment and penalty', *Crime, Law and Social Change*, 21: 49–71.

DAVIS, J. (1990), *Youth and the Condition of Britain*, London: Athlone Press.

DORN, N., and SOUTH, N. (1982), 'Of males and markets: A critical review of youth culture theory', *Research Paper 1*, Centre for Occupational and Community Research, London: Middlesex Polytechnic.

——and —— (eds) (1987), *A Land Fit for Heroin? Drug policies, prevention and practice*, Basingstoke: Macmillan.

DOWNES, D. (1966), *The Delinquent Solution*, London: Routledge & Kegan Paul.

——and ROCK, P. (1982), *Understanding Deviance*, Oxford: Oxford University Press.

EPSTEIN, J. S. (ed.) (1998), *Youth Culture: Identity in a Postmodern World*, Oxford: Blackwell.

FARRINGTON, D., and WEST, D. J. (1993), 'Criminal, penal and life histories of chronic offenders: Risk and protective factors and early identification', *Criminal Behaviour and Mental Health*, 3: 492–523.

FEILZER, M., and HOOD, R. (2005), *Differences or Discrimination: Minority Ethnic Young People in the Youth Justice System*, London: Youth Justice Board.

FERRELL, J. (2006), *Empire of Scrounge: Inside the underground of dumpster diving, trash picking and street scavenging*, New York: State University of New York Press.

——and SANDERS, C. S. (1995), *Cultural Criminology*, Boston, Mass.: Northeastern University Press.

FLOOD-PAGE, C., CAMPBELL, S., HARRINGTON, V., and MILLER, J. (2000), *Youth Crime: Findings from the 1998/99 Youth Lifestyles Survey*, Home Office Research Study No. 209, London: Home Office.

FRITH, S. (1983), *Sound Effects: Youth, leisure and the politics of rock and roll*, London: Constable.

——(2004), 'Afterword', in A. Bennett and K. Kahn-Harris (eds), *After Subculture: Critical studies in contemporary youth culture*, Basingstoke: Macmillan.

FURLONG, A., and CARTMEL, F. (1997), *Young People and Social Change*, Buckingham: Open University Press.

GILL, O. (1977), *Luke Street: Housing policy, conflict and the creation of the delinquent area*, London: Macmillan.

GILLETT, C. (1983), *The Sound of the City*, London: Souvenir Press.

GILROY, P. (1987), *There Ain't No Black in the Union Jack*, London: Hutchinson.

——and LAWRENCE, P. (1988), 'Two tone Britain: white and black youth and the politics of anti-racism', in P. Cohen and H. S. Bains (eds), *Multi-Racist Britain*, London: Macmillan.

GODDARD, E. (1991), *Drinking in England and Wales in the late 1980s*, London: HMSO.

——(1996), *Teenage Drinking in 1994*, London: HMSO.

GOLDTHORPE, J., LOCKWOOD, D., BECHOFER, F., and PLATT, J. (1969), *The Affluent Worker in the Class Structure*, Cambridge: Cambridge University Press.

GOULDEN, C., and SONDHI, A. (2001), *At the margins: drug use by vulnerable young people in the 1998/99 Youth Lifestyles Survey*, Home Office Research Study No. 228, London: Home Office.

GRAHAM, J., and BOWLING, B. (1995), *Young People and Crime*, London: Home Office.

GRIFFIN, C. (1993), *Representations of Youth: A study of youth and adolescence in Britain and America*, Cambridge: Polity Press.

HAGELL, A., and NEWBURN, T. (1994), *Persistent Young Offenders*, London: Policy Studies Institute.

HALL, S. (1969), 'The hippies: An American moment', in J. Nagel (ed.), *Student Power*, London: Merlin Press.

——(1980), *Drifting into a Law and Order Society*, London: Cobden Trust.

——and JEFFERSON, T. (eds) (1976), *Resistance through Rituals*, London: Hutchison.

——, CRITCHER, C., JEFFERSON, T., CLARKE, J., and ROBERTS, B. (1978), *Policing the Crisis. Mugging, the State and Law and Order*, London: Macmillan.

HAMMERSLEY, R., MARSLAND, L., and REID, M. (2003), *Substance use by young offenders: the impact of the normalization of drug use in the early years of the 21st century*, London: Home Office.

HARRINGTON, V. (2000), *Underage Drinking: Findings from the 1998/99 Youth Lifestyles Survey*, Research Findings No. 125, London: Home Office.

HARTLESS, J., DITTON, J., NAIR, G., and PHILLIPS, S. (1995), 'More sinned against than sinning: A study of young teenagers' experiences of crime', *British Journal of Criminology*, 35(1): 114–33.

HAYDEN, D. (1995), *Young People and Alcohol-related Incidents*, Executive Summary No. 45, London: Centre for Research on Drugs and Health Behaviour.

HEBDIGE, D. (1976), 'The Meaning of Mod', in S. Hall and T. Jefferson (eds), *Resistance Through Rituals*, London: Hutchison.

——(1979), *Subculture: The meaning of style*, London: Methuen.

——(1987), *Cut 'n mix: Culture, Identity and Caribbean Music*, London: Methuen.

HIRSCHI, T. (1969), *Causes of Delinquency*, Berkeley, Cal.: University of California Press.

——and GOTTFREDSOHN, M. (1983), 'Age and the Explanation of Crime,' *American Journal of Sociology*, 89: 552–84.

HOME OFFICE (1995), *Criminal Careers of those Born between 1953 and 1973*, Home Office Statistical Bulletin 14/95, London: Home Office Research and Statistics Department.

——(2005), *Criminal Statistics 2004*, Home Office Statistical Bulletin 19/05, London: Home Office.

HUIZINGA, D., LOEBER, R., and THORNBERRY, T. (1995), *Recent Findings from the Program on the*

Causes and Correlates of Delinquency, Report to the Office of Juvenile Justice and Delinquency Prevention, Washington DC.

HUMPHRIES, S. (1981), *Hooligans or Rebels? An oral history of working class childhood and youth, 1889–1939*, Oxford: Basil Blackwell.

ISDD (1994), *Drug misuse in Britain 1994*, London: ISDD.

JEFFERSON, T. (2004), 'From cultural studies to psychosocial criminology: an intellectual journey', in J. Ferrell, K., Hayward, W. Morrison, and M. Presdee (eds), *Cultural Criminology Unleashed*, London: Glasshouse Press.

JONES, G. (1995), *Family Support for Young People*, London: Family Policy Studies Centre.

LAING, D. (1985), *One Chord Wonders: Power and meaning in punk rock*, Milton Keynes: Open University Press.

LANDAU, S., and NATHAN, G. (1983), 'Selecting delinquents for cautioning in the London metropolitan area', *British Journal of Criminology*, 23(2): 128–49.

LISTER-SHARP, D. (1994), 'Underage drinking in the UK since 1970: public policy, the law and adolescent drinking behaviour', *Alcohol and Alcoholism*, 29(5): 555–63.

LLOYD, C. (1998), 'Risk factors and problem drug use: identifying vulnerable groups', *Drugs: Education, Prevention and Policy*, 5(3): 217–32.

—— and GRIFFITHS, P. (1998), 'Problems for the future: Drug use among vulnerable groups of young people', *Drugs: Education, Prevention and Policy*, 5(3): 213–16.

LOADER, I. (1996), *Youth, Policing and Democracy*, Basingstoke: Macmillan.

MACDONALD, R., SHILDRICK, T., WEBSTER, C., and SIMPSON, D. (2005), 'Growing up in poor neighbourhoods: The significance of class and place in the extended transitions of "socially excluded" young adults', *Sociology*, 39: 873–91.

McKAY, G. (1996), *Senseless Acts of Beauty: Cultures of resistance since the sixties*, London: Verso.

McROBBIE, A. (1980), 'Settling accounts with subcultures: A feminist critique', *Screen Education*, 39.

—— (1991), *Feminism and Youth Culture: From 'Jackie' to 'Just Seventeen'*, London: Macmillan.

—— (1994a), 'A cultural sociology of youth', in A. McRobbie (ed.), *Postmodernism and Popular Culture*, London: Routledge.

—— (1994b), 'Shut up and dance: youth culture and the changing modes of femininity', in A. McRobbie

(ed.), *Postmodernism and Popular Culture*, London: Routledge.

—— and GARBER, J. (1976), 'Girls and subcultures: An exploration', in S. Hall and T. Jefferson (eds), *Resistance Through Rituals*, London: Hutchison.

MEASHAM, F., NEWCOMBE, R., and PARKER, H. (1993), 'The Post-Heroin Generation', *Druglink*, May/June: 16–17.

——, ——, and —— (1994), 'The normalization of recreational drug use amongst young people in North-West England', *British Journal of Sociology*, 45(2): 287–312.

MELLY, G. (1972), *Revolt into Style*, Harmondsworth: Penguin.

MILLER, P., and PLANT, M. (1996), 'Drinking, smoking and illicit drug use among 15 and 16 year olds in the United Kingdom', *British Medical Journal*, 17 August, 313: 394–7.

MORGAN, J., and ZEDNER, L. (1992), *Child Victims: Crime, impact and criminal justice*, Oxford: Oxford University Press.

MORI (2004), *MORI Youth Survey 2004*, London: Youth Justice Board.

MOTT, J., and MIRRLEES-BLACK, C. (1993), *Self-reported Drug Misuse in England and Wales: Main finding from the 1992 British Crime Survey*, London: Home Office.

MUGGLETON, D. (2000) *Inside Subculture: The Postmodern Meaning of Style*, Oxford: Berg.

MUNCIE, J., COVENTRY, G., and WALTERS, R. (1995), 'The politics of youth crime prevention: developments in Australia and England and Wales', in L. Noaks, M. Levi, and M. MAGUIRE (eds), *Issues in Contemporary Criminology*, Cardiff: University of Wales Press.

NEWBURN, T. (1991), *Permission and Regulation: Law and morals in post-war Britain*, London: Routledge.

—— (1998), 'Young offenders, drugs and prevention', *Drugs, Education, Prevention and Policy*, 5(3): 233–43.

—— (1999), 'Drug Prevention and Youth Justice: Issues of Philosophy, Politics and Practice', *British Journal of Criminology*, 39(4): 609–24.

—— and SHINER, M. (2001), *Teenage Kicks? Young people and alcohol: A review of the literature*, York: Joseph Rowntree Foundation.

—— and —— (2005), *Dealing with Disaffection: Young People, Mentoring and Social Inclusion*, Cullompton, Devon: Willan.

NICHOLAS, S., POVEY, D., WALKER, A., and KERSHAW, C. (2005), Crime in England and Wales, Home Office Statistical Bulletin 11/05, London: Home Office.

PALMER, T. (1971), The Trials of OZ, London: Blond and Briggs.

PARKER, H. (1974), View From The Boys, London: David and Charles.

——, ALDRIDGE, J., and MEASHAM, J. (1998), Illegal Leisure: The normalization of adolescent recreational drug use, London: Routledge.

——and MEASHAM, F. (1994), 'Pick 'n mix: changing patterns of illicit drug use among 1990s adolescents', Drugs, Education, Prevention and Policy, 1(1): 5–13.

——, —— and ALDRIDGE, J. (1995), Drug Futures: Changing patterns of drug use amongst English youth, London: ISDD.

——, NEWCOMBE, R., and BAKX, K. (1988), Living With Heroin: The impact of drugs 'epidemic' on an English community, Milton Keynes: Open University Press.

PATRICK, J. (1973), A Glasgow Gang Observed, London: Methuen.

PEARSON, G. (1983), Hooligan: A history of respectable fears, Basingstoke: Macmillan.

——(1987), 'Social deprivation, unemployment and patterns of heroin use', in N. Dorn and N. South (eds), A Land Fit for Heroin? Drug policies, prevention and practice, Basingstoke: Macmillan.

PINTO-DUSCHINSKY, M. (1970), 'Bread and circuses? The Conservatives in power 1951–64', in V. Bogdanor and R. Skidelsky (eds), The Age of Affluence, London: Macmillan.

PLANT, M., PECK, D., and SAMUEL, E. (1985), Alcohol, Drugs and School Leavers, London: Tavistock.

POLHEMUS, T. (1997), 'In the Supermarket of Style', in S. Redhead, D. Wynne, and J. O'Connor (eds), The Clubcultures Reader, Oxford: Blackwell.

RAMSAY, M., and PERCY, A. (1996), Drug Misuse Declared: Results of the 1994 British Crime Survey, Home Office Research Study 151, London: Home Office.

——, BAKER, P., GOULDEN, C., SHARP, C., and SONDHI, A. (2001), Drug Misuse Declared in 2000: Results from the British Crime Survey, Home Office Research Study 224, London: Home Office.

REDHEAD, S. (1990), The End of the Century Party: Youth and pop towards 2000, Manchester: Manchester University Press.

——(1993), 'The end of the end-of-the-century party', in S. Redhead (ed.), Rave Off, Avebury: Aldershot.

RICHARDSON, A., BUDD, T., ENGINEER, R., PHILLIPS, A., THOMPSON, J., and NICHOLLS, J. (2003), Drinking, Crime and Disorder, London: Home Office.

ROBERTS, C., BLAKEY, V., and TUDOR-SMITH, C. (1997), The Impact of Alcopops on the Drinking Patterns of Young People in Wales, Findings from the 1996 Welsh Youth Health Survey, Briefing Report No. 12, Cardiff: Health Promotion Wales.

ROBERTS, K. (1995), Youth and Employment in Modern Britain, Oxford: Oxford University Press.

ROOK, C. (1899), The Hooligan Nights, London: Grant Richards.

RUTHERFORD, A. (1992), Growing Out of Crime: The New Era, Winchester: Waterside Press.

SAVAGE, J. (1991), England's Dreaming: Sex Pistols and Punk Rock, London: Faber & Faber.

——(1996), Time Travel, From the Sex Pistols to Nirvana: Pop, media and sexuality 1977–1996, London: Chatto and Windus.

SCHOENFELD, C. G. (1971), 'A psychoanalytic theory of juvenile delinquency', Crime and Delinquency, 17: 479–80.

SHARP, C., and BUDD, T. (2005), Minority Ethnic Groups and Crime: Findings from the Offending, Crime and Justice Survey 2003, London: Home Office.

SHEPHERD, J., and BRICKLEY, M. (1996), 'The relationship between alcohol intoxication, stressors and injury in urban violence', British Journal of Criminology, 36(4): 546–66.

SHINER, M., and NEWBURN, T. (1997), 'Definitely, May be Not? The normalization of recreational drug use amongst young people', Sociology, 31(3): 511–29.

——and —— (1999), 'Taking Tea With Noel: The place and meaning of drug use in everyday life', in N. South (ed.), Drugs: Cultures, controls and everyday life, London: Sage.

SHORTER, E. (1976), The Making of the Modern Family, London: Collins.

SOUTH, N. (1994), 'Drugs and crime', in M. Maguire, R. Morgan, and R. Reiner (eds), The Oxford Handbook of Criminology, 1st edn, Oxford: Oxford University Press.

STONE, L. (1979), The Family, Sex and Marriage in England 1500–1800, Harmondsworth: Penguin.

THOMPSON, K. (1998), Moral Panics, London: Routledge.

THORNTON, S. (1995), Club Cultures: Music, media and subcultural capital, Oxford: Polity Press.

TURTLE, J., JONES, A., and HICKMAN, M. (1997), *Young People and Health: The Health Behaviour of School-Age Children*, London: HEA/BMRB.

WALLACE, C. (1987), *For Richer, For Poorer: Growing up in and out of work*, London: Tavistock.

WEBSTER, C. (1997), 'The construction of British "Asian" criminality', *International Journal of the Sociology of Law*, 25: 65–86.

WEST, D. J., and FARRINGTON, D. (1977), *The Delinquent Way of Life*, London: Heinemann Educational.

WILLIAMSON, H. (2004), *The Milltown Boys Revisited*, London: Berg.

WILLIS, P. (1978), *Profane Culture*, London: Routledge & Kegan Paul.

WINCUP, E., BUCKLAND, G., and BAYLISS, R. (2003), *Youth homelessness and substance use: report to the drugs and alcohol research unit*, London: Home Office.

WOLFGANG, M., FIGLIO, R. M., and SELLIN, T. (1972), *Delinquency in a Birth Cohort*, Chicago: University of Chicago Press.

WOOD, M. (2005) *The victimisation of young people: findings from the Crime and Justice Survey 2003*, Home Office Findings 246, London: Home Office.

YATES, D. W. (1987), 'The detection of problem drinkers in the accident and emergency department', *British Journal of Addiction*, 82: 163–87.

YOUNG, J. (1971), *The Drugtakers*, London: Paladin.

19

CHILDHOOD RISK FACTORS AND RISK-FOCUSED PREVENTION

David P. Farrington

INTRODUCTION

The main aim of this chapter is to review key information about childhood risk factors and risk-focused prevention. It focuses on individual and family risk factors for offending and antisocial behaviour, and on the results of prevention initiatives targeting these risk factors. The emphasis is on offending by males; most research on offending has concentrated on males, because they commit most of the serious predatory and violent offences (for reviews of risk factors for females, see Moffitt *et al.* 2001). This review focuses on research carried out in the United Kingdom (especially), the United States, and similar Western industrialized democracies.

Within a single chapter, it is obviously impossible to review everything that is known about childhood risk factors and risk-focused interventions. I will be very selective in focusing on some of the more important and replicable findings obtained in some of the more methodologically adequate studies: especially, prospective longitudinal studies of large community samples and randomized experiments conducted to evaluate the impact of prevention techniques. (For more extensive reviews, see Farrington and Welsh 2007).

Tonry and Farrington (1995) distinguished four major prevention strategies. *Developmental prevention* (reviewed in this chapter) refers to interventions designed to prevent the development of criminal potential in individuals, especially those targeting risk and protective factors discovered in studies of human development (Tremblay and Craig 1995). *Community prevention* refers to interventions designed to change the social conditions and institutions (e.g. families, peers, social norms, clubs, organizations) that influence offending in residential communities (Hope 1995). *Situational prevention* refers to interventions designed to prevent the occurrence of crimes by reducing opportunities and increasing the risk and difficulty of offending (Clarke 1995).

Criminal justice prevention refers to traditional deterrent, incapacitative, and rehabilitative strategies operated by law-enforcement and criminal justice agencies. The term 'risk-focused prevention' is now used more generally than 'developmental prevention', but the two terms essentially have the same meaning.

This chapter is structured as follows. This section introduces the key concepts of developmental criminology, risk factors, and risk-focused prevention. This is followed by more detailed discussions of individual and family risk factors for offending, including reviews of explanations and possible intervening processes and a description of a wide-ranging integrative developmental theory. The next section reviews risk-focused prevention programmes that have been proved to be effective in high-quality evaluation research, and the concluding section outlines recommendations for research and policy.

DEVELOPMENTAL CRIMINOLOGY

Developmental criminology is concerned with three main issues: the development of offending and antisocial behaviour, risk factors at different ages, and the effects of life events on the course of development (Loeber and LeBlanc 1990; LeBlanc and Loeber 1998; Farrington 2007a). Developmental topics are reviewed only briefly here, as the focus is on risk factors and on risk-focused prevention (see also Smith, Chapter 20, this volume).

In studying development, efforts are made to investigate the prevalence of offending at different ages, the frequency of offending by offenders, the ages of onset and desistance, and specialization and escalation of offending over time (for reviews of criminal career research, see Piquero *et al.* 2003, 2007). There are many studies of the persistence of offending and characteristics of persistent offenders (e.g. Farrington and West 1993). There is an emphasis on investigating within-individual change over time, for example when people graduate from hyperactivity at age 2 to cruelty to animals at 6, shoplifting at 10, burglary at 15, robbery at 20, and eventually spouse assault, child abuse and neglect, alcohol abuse, and employment and mental health problems later on in life. Attempts are made to study developmental pathways and sequences over time, for example where one type of behaviour facilitates or acts as a kind of stepping stone to another (Loeber *et al.* 1993). It is desirable to identify non-criminal behaviours that lead to criminal behaviours, and early indicators of later frequent and serious offending that might suggest opportunities for early prevention.

It seems that offending is often part of a larger syndrome of antisocial behaviour that arises in childhood and tends to persist into adulthood (West and Farrington 1977). There is significant continuity over time, since the antisocial child tends to become the antisocial teenager and then the antisocial adult, just as the antisocial adult then tends to produce another antisocial child. Typically, researchers find relative stability (the relative ordering of people on measures of antisocial behaviour is significantly stable) but changing behavioural manifestations over time, as individual capacities, opportunities, and social contexts change (Farrington 1990a). For example, only children at school can truant or be excluded from school, only older people can beat up their spouses,

70-year-olds have difficulty committing burglaries, and so on. There is a great deal of interest in different types of behavioural trajectories, for example the distinction between adolescence-limited and life-course persistent antisocial behaviour (Moffitt 1993; Nagin *et al.* 1995). Many of the results on offending that are reviewed in this chapter may be primarily driven by the more persistent offenders, who tend to be more extreme in many ways.

In developmental criminology, risk factors at different ages are studied, including biological, individual, family, peer, school, neighbourhood, and situational factors. In general, similar results are obtained when studying risk factors for either self-reported or officially recorded offending (Farrington 1992b). As mentioned, it is only possible to review individual and family factors within the scope of this chapter (for more wide-ranging reviews, see Rutter *et al.* 1998; Farrington 2007b).

Many risk factors for offending are well established and highly replicable. For example, a systematic comparison of two longitudinal surveys in London and Pittsburgh (Farrington and Loeber 1999) showed numerous replicable predictors of delinquency over time and place, including impulsivity, attention problems, low school attainment, poor parental supervision, parental conflict, an antisocial parent, a young mother, large family size, low family income, and coming from a broken family. Vazsonyi *et al.* (2001) found that the patterns of association between measures of self-control (e.g. impulsivity, risk-taking, getting angry) and measures of antisocial behaviour (e.g. theft, assault, vandalism, drug use) were highly similar across four countries (Hungary, the Netherlands, Switzerland, and the United States). Less well established are the causal mechanisms linking risk factors and offending. For example, does large family size predict offending because of the consequent poor supervision of each child, over-crowded households, poverty, or merely because more antisocial people tend to have more children than others?

There is a great deal of interest in the early prediction of later offending, and in risk factors that might form the basis of risk (and needs) assessment devices (e.g. Augimeri *et al.* 2001). Typically, prospective prediction (e.g. the percentage of high-risk children who become persistent offenders) is poor but retrospective prediction (e.g. the percentage of persistent offenders who were high-risk children) is good. The fact that many children at risk have successful lives inspires the search for protective factors and individual resilience features that might inform prevention techniques. There is a great deal of interest in cumulative, interactive, and sequential effects of risk factors. For example, the probability of becoming a persistent offender increases with the number of risk factors (Farrington 2002), almost independently of which particular risk factors are included. There are also attempts to study individual development in different neighbourhood and community contexts (Wikström and Loeber 2000).

In researching development, risk factors, and life events, it is essential to carry out prospective longitudinal surveys. I will refer especially to knowledge gained in the Cambridge Study in Delinquent Development, which is a prospective longitudinal survey of over 400 London males from age 8 to age 48 (Farrington and West 1990; Farrington 1995, 2003b; Farrington *et al.* 2006). In general, results obtained in British longitudinal surveys of offending (e.g. Wadsworth 1979: Kolvin *et al.* 1990) are highly concordant with those obtained in comparable surveys in North America (e.g. Capaldi and Patterson 1996; Loeber *et al.* 2003), the Scandinavian countries (e.g. Pulkkinen 1988; Klinteberg *et al.* 1993), and New Zealand (e.g. Fergusson *et al.* 1994; Henry *et al.* 1996), and indeed with results obtained in British cross-sectional surveys (e.g. Graham and Bowling 1995; Flood-Page *et al.* 2000). For more information about the longitudinal surveys mentioned in this chapter, see Farrington and Welsh (2007).

RISK FACTORS

Risk factors are prior factors that increase the risk of occurrence of the onset, frequency, persistence, or duration of offending (Kazdin *et al.* 1997). Longitudinal data are required to establish the ordering of risk factors and criminal career features. The focus in this chapter is on risk factors measured in childhood that predict the onset or prevalence of offending; few studies have examined risk factors for persistence or duration. For simplicity, risk factors are reviewed one by one in this chapter. However, many risk factors tend to be interrelated, and it is of course necessary to investigate which factors are independent predictors of offending. This is discussed later in the section on 'Explaining Development and Risk Factors'.

It is difficult to decide if any given risk factor is an indicator (symptom) or a possible cause of offending. For example, are heavy drinking, truancy, unemployment, and divorce symptoms of an antisocial personality, or do they cause people to become more antisocial? Similarly, to the extent that delinquency is a group activity (Reiss and Farrington 1991), delinquents will usually have delinquent friends, and this does not necessarily show that delinquent friends cause delinquency. It is important not to include a measure of the dependent variable (e.g. delinquent friends) as an independent variable in causal analyses, because this will lead to false (tautological) conclusions and an over-estimation of explanatory or predictive power (Amdur 1989).

It is possible to argue that some factors may be both indicative and causal. For example, long-term variations *between* individuals in an underlying antisocial tendency may be reflected in variations in alcohol consumption, just as short-term variations *within* individuals in alcohol consumption may cause more antisocial behaviour during the heavier drinking periods. In other words, heavy drinking may be viewed as a situational trigger rather than a long-term cause. The interpretation of other factors may be easier. For example, being exposed as a child to poor parental child-rearing techniques might cause (or even be a consequence of) the child's antisocial behaviour but would not be an indicator of it.

One methodological problem is that most knowledge about risk factors is mainly based on variation between individuals, whereas prevention requires variation (change) within individuals. Kraemer *et al.* (1997) argued that only risk factors that can change within individuals can have causal effects. It is not always clear that findings within individuals would be the same as findings between individuals. To take a specific example, unemployment is a risk factor for offending between individuals, since unemployed people are more likely than employed people to be offenders (West and Farrington 1977). However, unemployment is also a risk factor for offending within individuals, since people are more likely to offend during their periods of unemployment than during their periods of employment (Farrington *et al*. 1986). The within-individual finding has a much clearer implication for prevention, namely that a reduction in unemployment should lead to a reduction in offending. This is because it is much easier to demonstrate that a risk factor is a cause in within-individual research. Since the same individuals are followed up over time, many extraneous influences on offending are controlled (Farrington 1988).

In the Pittsburgh Youth Study, in which 1,500 Pittsburgh males were followed up from age 7 to age 25, risk factors for delinquency were compared both between individuals and within individuals (Farrington *et al*. 2002). Peer delinquency was the strongest correlate of delinquency in between-individual correlations but did not predict delinquency within individuals. In contrast, poor parental supervision, low parental reinforcement, and low involvement of the boy in family activities predicted delinquency both between and within individuals. It was concluded that these three family variables were the most likely to be causes, whereas having delinquent peers was most likely to be an indicator of the boy's offending.

RISK-FOCUSED PREVENTION

The basic idea of risk-focused prevention is very simple: identify the key risk factors for offending and implement prevention methods designed to counteract them. There is often a related attempt to identify key protective factors against offending and to implement prevention methods designed to enhance them. Typically, longitudinal surveys provide knowledge about risk and protective factors, and experimental and quasi-experimental studies are used to evaluate the impact of prevention and intervention programmes. Thus, risk-focused prevention links explanation and prevention, links fundamental and applied research, and links scholars, policy-makers, and practitioners (Farrington 2000). The book *Serious and Violent Juvenile Offenders: Risk Factors and Successful Interventions* (Loeber and Farrington 1998) contains a detailed exposition of this approach as applied to serious and violent juvenile offenders.

Risk-focused prevention was imported into criminology from medicine and public health by pioneers such as Hawkins and Catalano (1992). This approach has been used successfully for many years to tackle illnesses such as cancer and heart disease. For example, the identified risk factors for heart disease include smoking, a fatty diet, and lack of exercise. These can be tackled by encouraging people to stop smoking, to have a more healthy low-fat diet, and to take more exercise. Interventions can be targeted on the whole community or on persons at high risk. Typically, the effectiveness of risk-focused prevention in the medical field is evaluated using the 'gold standard' of randomized controlled trials, and there has been increasing emphasis in medicine on cost–benefit analyses of interventions. Not surprisingly, therefore, there has been a similar emphasis in criminology on high-quality evaluations and on cost–benefit analyses (Welsh *et al.* 2001; Sherman *et al.* 2006).

Risk factors tend to be similar for many different outcomes, including violent and non-violent offending, mental health problems, alcohol and drug problems, school failure, and unemployment. Therefore, a prevention programme that succeeds in reducing a risk factor for offending will in all probability have wide-ranging benefits in reducing other types of social problems as well. Because of the interest in linking risk factors with prevention programmes, risk factors that cannot be changed feasibly in such programmes (e.g. gender and race) are excluded from consideration in this chapter, except to the extent that they act as moderators (e.g. if the effect of a risk factor is different for males and females).

A major problem of risk-focused prevention is to establish which risk factors are causes and which are merely markers or correlated with causes (Farrington 2000). It is also desirable to establish mediators (intervening causal processes) between risk factors and outcomes (Baron and Kenny 1986). Ideally, interventions should be targeted on risk factors that are causes; interventions targeted on risk factors that are markers will not necessarily lead to any decrease in offending. The difficulty of establishing causes, and the co-occurrence of risk factors, encourages the blunderbuss approach: interventions that target multiple risk factors. However, there is also evidence that integrated or multi-modal intervention packages are more effective than interventions that target only a single risk factor (Wasserman and Miller 1998).

In principle, a great deal can be learned about causes from the results of intervention experiments, to the extent that the experiments establish the impact of targeting each risk factor separately (Robins 1992). For example, Najaka *et al.* (2001) attempted to draw conclusions about causality by analysing relationships between risk factors and antisocial behaviour in school-based experiments. Ideally, intervention experiments need to be designed to test causal hypotheses, as well as to test a particular intervention technology. However, there is a clear tension between maximizing the effectiveness of an intervention (which encourages a multiple component approach) and assessing the effectiveness of each component and hence drawing conclusions about causes (which requires disentangling of the different components).

Risk-focused prevention includes protective factors. Ideally, risk and protective factors should be identified and then risk factors should be reduced while protective factors are enhanced. However, both the definition and existence of protective factors are controversial. On one definition, a protective factor is merely the opposite end of the scale to a risk factor. Just as a risk factor predicts an increased probability of offending, a protective factor predicts a decreased probability. However, to the extent that explanatory variables are linearly related to offending, researchers may then object that risk and protective factors are merely different names for the same underlying construct.

Another possible definition of a protective factor is a variable that interacts with a risk factor to minimize the risk factor's effects. Such interactive variables are often termed 'moderators' (Baron and Kenny 1986). If poor parental supervision predicted a high risk of offending only for males from low-income families, and not for males from high-income families, then high income might be regarded as a protective factor counteracting the effects of the risk factor of poor parental supervision. Problems associated with the definition of protective factors may be alleviated by focusing on resilience or psychosocial skills and competencies. More research is needed to identify protective factors, linked to the use of interventions targeted on protective factors.

INDIVIDUAL RISK FACTORS

Among the most important individual factors that predict offending are low intelligence and attainment, low empathy, and impulsiveness, as the meta-analysis by Lipsey and Derzon (1998) showed. These factors are reviewed in this section, which concludes by discussing social cognitive skills and cognitive theories (see also Hollin, Chapter 2, this volume).

LOW INTELLIGENCE AND ATTAINMENT

Low intelligence is an important predictor of offending, and it can be measured very early in life. For example, in a prospective longitudinal survey of about 120 Stockholm males, Stattin and Klackenberg-Larsson (1993) reported that low intelligence measured at age 3 significantly predicted officially recorded offending up to age 30. Frequent offenders (with four or more offences) had an average IQ of 88 at age 3, whereas non-offenders had an average IQ of 101. All of these results held up after controlling for social class. In the Perry pre-school project in Michigan, Schweinhart et al. (1993) found that low intelligence at age 4 significantly predicted the number of arrests up to age 27. Also, in the Providence (Rhode Island) site of the National Collaborative Perinatal project, Lipsitt et al. (1990) showed that low IQ at age 4 predicted later juvenile delinquency.

In the Cambridge Study, one-third of the boys scoring 90 or less on a non-verbal intelligence test (Raven's Progressive Matrices) at age 8–10 were convicted as juveniles, twice as many as among the remainder (Farrington 1992b). Low non-verbal intelligence was highly correlated with low verbal intelligence (vocabulary, word comprehension, verbal reasoning) and with low school attainment at age 11, and all of these measures predicted juvenile convictions to much the same extent. In addition to their poor school performance, delinquents tended to be frequent truants, to leave school at the earliest possible age (15), and to take no school examinations.

Low intelligence and attainment predicted both juvenile and adult convictions (Farrington 1992a). Low intelligence at age 8–10 was also an important independent predictor of spouse assault at age 32 (Farrington 1994). Also, low intelligence and attainment predicted aggression and bullying at age 14 (Farrington 1989, 1993b), and low school attainment predicted chronic offenders (Farrington and West 1993). Low non-verbal intelligence was especially characteristic of the juvenile recidivists (who had an average IQ of 89) and those first convicted at the earliest ages (10–13). Furthermore, low intelligence and attainment predicted self-reported delinquency almost as well as it did convictions (Farrington 1992b), suggesting that the link between low intelligence and delinquency was not caused by the less intelligent boys having a greater probability of being caught.

Low non-verbal intelligence was about as strong a predictor of juvenile convictions as other important childhood risk factors (low family income, large family size, poor parental child-rearing behaviour, poor parental supervision, and poor concentration or restlessness) but it was a weaker predictor than having a convicted parent or a daring (risk-taking) personality. Measures of intelligence and attainment predicted measures of offending independently of other risk factors such as family income and family size (Farrington 1990b).

The key explanatory factor underlying the link between intelligence and delinquency may be the ability to manipulate abstract concepts. People who are poor at this tend to do badly in intelligence tests such as the Matrices and in school attainment, and they also tend to commit offences, probably because of their poor ability to foresee the consequences of their offending and to appreciate the feelings of victims (i.e. their low empathy). Certain family backgrounds are less conducive than others to the development of abstract reasoning. For example, lower-class, economically deprived parents tend to talk in terms of the concrete rather than the abstract and tend to live for the present, with little thought for the future, as Cohen (1955: 96) pointed out many years ago. In some ways, it is difficult to distinguish a lack of concern for future consequences from the concept of impulsiveness (discussed later).

Low intelligence may be one element of a pattern of cognitive and neuropsychological deficits. For example, the 'executive functions' of the brain, located in the frontal lobes, include sustaining attention and concentration, abstract reasoning and concept formation, anticipation and planning, self-monitoring of behaviour, and inhibition of inappropriate or impulsive behaviours (Morgan and Lilienfeld 2000). In the Montreal longitudinal-experimental study, Seguin *et al.* (1995) found that a measure of executive functioning based on cognitive-neuropsychological tests at age 14 was the strongest neuropsychological discriminator of violent and non-violent boys. This relationship held independently of a measure of family adversity (based on parental age at first birth, parental education level, coming from a broken family, and low socio-economic status). In the Pittsburgh Youth Study, the life-course-persistent offenders had marked neurocognitive impairments (Raine *et al.* 2005).

Alternatively, it might be argued that IQ tests are designed to measure ability to succeed in school (which may be a different construct from 'intelligence'). Hence, low IQ predicts school failure, and there are many criminological theories suggesting that school failure leads to delinquency (for example, through the intervening construct of status deprivation: see Cohen 1955). Lynam *et al.* (1993) completed one of the most important attempts to test these and other possible explanations, using data collected in the Pittsburgh Youth Study. Their conclusions vary according to the ethnicity of the boys. For African American boys, they found that low verbal intelligence led to school failure and subsequently to self-reported delinquency, but for Caucasian boys the relationship between low verbal intelligence and self-reported delinquency held after controlling for school failure and all other variables. It may be that poor executive functioning and school failure are both plausible explanations of the link between low intelligence and offending.

EMPATHY

There is a widespread belief that low empathy is an important personality trait that is related to offending, on the assumption that people who can appreciate or experience a victim's feelings (or both) are less likely to victimize someone. This belief also underlies cognitive-behavioural skills training programmes that aim to increase empathy (see later). However, its empirical basis is not very impressive. There are inconsistent results, measures of empathy are not well validated or widely accepted, and there are no prospective longitudinal surveys relating early empathy to later offending.

A distinction has often been made between cognitive empathy (understanding or appreciating other people's feelings) and emotional empathy (actually experiencing other people's feelings). Jolliffe and Farrington (2004) carried out a systematic review of 35 studies comparing questionnaire measures of empathy with official record measures of delinquent or criminal behaviour. They found that low cognitive empathy was strongly related to offending, but low affective empathy was only weakly related. Most importantly, the relationship between low empathy and offending was greatly reduced after controlling for intelligence or socio-economic status, suggesting that they might be more important risk factors or that low empathy might mediate the relationship between these risk factors and offending.

The best studies of the 1990s that have related empathy to offending in relatively large samples are as follows. In Australia, Mak (1991) found that delinquent females had lower emotional empathy than non-delinquent females, but that there were no significant differences for males. In Finland, Kaukiainen *et al.* (1999) reported that empathy (cognitive and emotional combined) was negatively correlated with aggression (both measured by peer ratings). In Spain, Luengo *et al.* (1994) carried out the first project that related cognitive and emotional empathy separately to (self-reported) offending, and found that both were negatively correlated.

Jolliffe and Farrington (2006) developed a new measure of empathy called the Basic Empathy Scale. An example of a cognitive item is, 'It is hard for me to understand when my friends are sad', and an example of an emotional item is, 'I usually feel calm when other people are scared'. In a study of 720 British adolescents aged about 15, they found that low affective empathy was related to self-reported offending and violence for both males and females, and to an official record for offending for females (Jolliffe and Farrington 2007). Low cognitive empathy was related to self-reported serious theft (including burglary and car theft) for males. Low affective and cognitive empathy was related to fighting and vandalism for males and to theft from a person for females. Therefore, low empathy may be an important risk factor for delinquency.

IMPULSIVENESS

Impulsiveness is the most crucial personality dimension that predicts offending. Unfortunately, there are a bewildering number of constructs referring to a poor ability to control behaviour. These include impulsiveness, hyperactivity, restlessness, clumsiness, not considering consequences before acting, a poor ability to plan ahead, short time horizons, low self-control, sensation-seeking, risk-taking, and a poor ability to delay gratification. Virtually all these constructs, measured in different ways, are consistently related to measures of offending (see, e.g., Blackburn 1993: 191–6; Pratt *et al.* 2002).

Many studies show that hyperactivity predicts later offending. In the Copenhagen Perinatal project, Brennan *et al.* (1993) discovered that hyperactivity (restlessness and poor concentration) at age 11–13 significantly predicted arrests for violence up to age 22, especially among boys experiencing delivery complications. More than half of those with both hyperactivity and high delivery complications were arrested for violence, compared to less than 10 per cent of the remainder. In the Mater University Study of Pregnancy in Brisbane, Australia, Bor *et al.* (2004) found that problems of attention and restlessness at age 5 more than doubled the risk of delinquency at age 14.

In the Orebro longitudinal study in Sweden, Klinteberg *et al.* (1993) reported that hyperactivity at age 13 predicted police-recorded violence up to age 26. The highest rate of violence was among males with both motor restlessness and concentration difficulties (15 per cent), compared to 3 per cent of the remainder. In another Swedish longitudinal study, Eklund and Klinteberg (2003) concluded that attention problems were the most important components of hyperactivity that predicted later violent offending.

In the Cambridge Study, boys nominated by teachers as lacking in concentration or restless, those nominated by parents, peers, or teachers as the most daring or risk-taking, and those who were the most impulsive on psychomotor tests at age 8–10, all tended to become offenders later in life. Later self-report measures of impulsiveness were also related to offending. Daring, poor concentration, and restlessness all predicted both official convictions and self-reported delinquency, and daring was consistently one of the best independent predictors (Farrington 1992b). A combined measure of HIA ('hyperactivity-impulsivity-attention deficit') significantly predicted juvenile convictions independently of conduct problems at age 8–10 (Farrington *et al.* 1990). Lynam (1996) argued that children with both HIA and conduct problems were at greatest risk of later chronic offending.

The most extensive research on different measures of impulsiveness was carried out in the Pittsburgh Youth Study by White *et al.* (1994). The measures that were most strongly related to self-reported delinquency at ages 10 and 13 were teacher-rated impulsiveness (e.g. 'acts without thinking'), self-reported impulsiveness, self-reported under-control (e.g. 'unable to delay gratification'), motor restlessness (from videotaped observations), and psychomotor impulsiveness (on the Trail Making Test). Generally, the verbal behaviour rating tests produced stronger relationships with offending than the psychomotor performance tests, suggesting that cognitive impulsiveness (based on thinking processes) was more relevant to delinquency than behavioural impulsiveness (based on test performance). Future time perception and delay of gratification tests were only weakly related to self-reported delinquency.

SOCIAL COGNITIVE SKILLS AND COGNITIVE THEORIES

Many researchers have argued that offenders use poor techniques of thinking and problem-solving in interpersonal situations (Blackburn 1993: 204–9). Offenders are often said to be self-centred and callous, with low empathy. They are relatively poor at role-taking and perspective-taking, and may misinterpret other people's intentions. Their lack of awareness or sensitivity to other people's thoughts and feelings impairs their ability to form relationships and to appreciate the effects of their behaviour on other people. They show poor social skills in interpersonal interactions, fidgeting and avoiding eye contact rather than listening and paying attention.

It is further argued that offenders tend to believe that what happens to them depends on fate, chance, or luck, rather than on their own actions. Such thinking makes them feel that they are controlled by other people and by circumstances beyond their control. Hence, they think that there is no point in trying to succeed, so that they lack persistence in aiming to achieve goals. Arguably, offenders often externalize the blame for their acts to other people rather than taking responsibility themselves, and expect people to believe far-fetched stories. Furthermore, they fail to stop and think before acting and fail to learn from experience. These social cognitive deficits are linked to offenders' concrete as opposed to abstract thinking and their poor ability to manipulate abstract concepts (Ross and Ross 1995). While this constellation of features fits in with many previously cited characteristics of offenders, it has to be said that the evidence in favour of some of them (e.g. the poor social skills of delinquents) is not convincing.

Perhaps the best developed theory to explain the development of social cognitive skills in relation to aggressive behaviour is the social information processing model of Dodge (1991). According to this, children respond to an environmental stimulus by (a) encoding relevant cues, (b) interpreting those cues, (c) retrieving possible behavioural responses from long-term memory, (d) considering the possible consequences of alternative responses, and (e) selecting and performing an act. According to Dodge, aggressive children are more likely to interpret cues as hostile, to retrieve aggressive alternative responses, and to evaluate the consequences of aggression as beneficial.

Huesmann and Eron (1984) put forward a cognitive script model, in which aggressive behaviour depends on stored behavioural repertoires (cognitive scripts) that have been learned during early development. In response to environmental cues, possible cognitive scripts are retrieved and evaluated. The choice of aggressive scripts, which prescribe aggressive behaviour, depends on the past history of rewards and punishments, and on the extent to which children are influenced by immediate gratification as opposed to long-term consequences. According to Huesmann and Eron, the persisting trait of aggressiveness includes a collection of well-learned aggressive scripts that are resistant to change. Other theories focusing on the thinking processes of offenders are not reviewed here (e.g. the rational choice theory of Clarke and Cornish 1985), but the whole topic of cognition and crime is discussed in more detail by Hollin, Chapter 2, this volume.

FAMILY RISK FACTORS

In this section, family factors are grouped into five categories: (a) criminal and antisocial parents; (b) large family size; (c) child-rearing methods (poor supervision, poor discipline, coldness and rejection, low parental involvement with the child); (d) abuse (physical or sexual) or neglect; and (e) disrupted families. Excluded are socio-economic factors such as low family income, low social class of the family, living in a poor neighbourhood, and the residential mobility of the family.

CRIME RUNS IN FAMILIES

Criminal and antisocial parents tend to have delinquent and antisocial children, as shown in the classic longitudinal surveys by McCord (1977) in Boston and Robins (1979) in St Louis. The most extensive research on the concentration of offending in families was carried out in the Cambridge Study. Having a convicted father, mother, brother, or sister predicted a boy's own convictions, and all four relatives were independently important as predictors (Farrington *et al.* 1996). For example, 63 per cent of boys with convicted fathers were themselves convicted, compared with 30 per cent of the remainder. Same-sex relationships were stronger than opposite-sex relationships, and older siblings were stronger predictors than younger siblings. Only 6 per cent of the families accounted for half of all the convictions of all family members.

Similar results were obtained in the Pittsburgh Youth Study. Arrests of fathers, mothers, brothers, sisters, uncles, aunts, grandfathers, and grandmothers all predicted the boy's own delinquency (Farrington *et al.* 2001). The most important relative was the father, whose arrest predicted it independently of all other arrested relatives. Only 8 per cent of families accounted for 43 per cent of arrested family members.

In the Cambridge Study, having a convicted parent, or a delinquent older sibling, by the tenth birthday was consistently among the best age 8–10 predictors of the boy's later offending and antisocial behaviour. Apart from behavioural measures such as troublesomeness, they were the strongest predictors of juvenile convictions (Farrington 1992b). Having a convicted parent, or a delinquent older sibling, was also the best predictor, after poor parental supervision, of juvenile self-reported delinquency.

There are several possible explanations (which are not mutually exclusive) for why offending tends to be concentrated in certain families and transmitted from one generation to the next. First, there may be intergenerational continuities in exposure to multiple risk factors. For example, each successive generation may be entrapped in poverty, disrupted families, single and/or teenage parenting, and living in the most deprived neighbourhoods.

Secondly, the effect of a criminal parent on a child's offending may be mediated by environmental mechanisms. In the Cambridge Study, it was suggested that poor parental supervision was one link in the causal chain between criminal fathers and delinquent sons (West and Farrington 1977: 117).

Thirdly, the effect of a criminal parent on a child's offending may be mediated by genetic mechanisms (Raine 1993). In a convincing design comparing the concordance of identical twins reared together and identical twins reared apart, Grove *et al.* (1990) found that heritability was 41 per cent for childhood conduct disorder and 28 per cent for adult antisocial personality disorder, showing that the intergenerational transmission of offending was partly attributable to genetic factors. Fourthly, criminal parents may tend to have delinquent children because of official (police and court) bias against criminal families, who also tend to be known to official agencies because of other social problems. At all levels of self-reported delinquency in the Cambridge Study, boys with convicted fathers were more likely to be convicted themselves than were boys with unconvicted fathers (West and Farrington 1977: 118). However, this was not the only explanation for the link between criminal fathers and delinquent sons, because boys with criminal fathers had higher self-reported delinquency scores and higher teacher and peer ratings of bad behaviour.

LARGE FAMILY SIZE

Large family size (a large number of children in the family) is a relatively strong and highly replicable predictor of delinquency (Ellis 1988). It was similarly important in the Cambridge and Pittsburgh studies, even though families were on average smaller in Pittsburgh in the 1990s than in London in the 1960s (Farrington and Loeber 1999). In the Cambridge Study, if a boy had four or more siblings by his tenth birthday, this doubled his risk of being convicted as a juvenile (West and Farrington 1973: 31), and large family size predicted self-reported delinquency as well as convictions (Farrington 1992b). It was the most important independent predictor of convictions up to age 32 in a logistic regression analysis; 58 per cent of boys from large families were convicted up to this age (Farrington 1993a).

In the National Survey of Health and Development, Wadsworth (1979) found that the percentage of boys who were officially delinquent increased from 9 per cent for families containing one child to 24 per cent for families containing four or more children. The Newsons in their Nottingham study also concluded that large family size was one of the most important predictors of offending (Newson *et al.* 1993). A similar link between family size and antisocial behaviour was reported by Kolvin *et al.* (1988)

in their follow-up of Newcastle children from birth to age 33, by Rutter *et al.* (1970) in the Isle of Wight survey, and by Ouston (1984) in the Inner London survey.

There are many possible reasons why a large number of siblings might increase the risk of a child's delinquency. Generally, as the number of children in a family increases, the amount of parental attention that can be given to each child decreases. Also, as the number of children increases, the household tends to become more overcrowded, possibly leading to increases in frustration, irritation, and conflict. In the Cambridge Study, large family size did not predict delinquency for boys living in the least crowded conditions (West and Farrington 1973: 33). This suggests that household overcrowding might be an important intervening factor between large family size and delinquency.

Brownfield and Sorenson (1994) reviewed several possible explanations for the link between large families and delinquency, including those focusing on features of the parents (e.g. criminal parents, teenage parents), those focusing on parenting (e.g. poor supervision, disrupted families), and those focusing on economic deprivation or family stress. Another interesting theory suggested that the key factor was birth order: large families include more later-born children, who tend to be more delinquent. Based on an analysis of self-reported delinquency in a Seattle survey, they concluded that the most plausible intervening causal mechanism was exposure to delinquent siblings. In the Cambridge Study, co-offending by brothers was surprisingly common; about 20 per cent of boys who had brothers close to them in age were convicted for a crime committed with their brother (Reiss and Farrington 1991).

CHILD-REARING METHODS

Many different types of child-rearing methods predict a child's delinquency. The most important dimensions of child-rearing are supervision or monitoring of children, discipline or parental reinforcement, warmth or coldness of emotional relationships, and parental involvement with children. Parental supervision refers to the degree of monitoring by parents of the child's activities, and their degree of watchfulness or vigilance. Of all these child-rearing methods, poor parental supervision is usually the strongest and most replicable predictor of offending (Smith and Stern 1997; Farrington and Loeber 1999). Many studies show that parents who do not know where their children are when they are out, and parents who let their children roam the streets unsupervised from an early age, tend to have delinquent children. For example, in the classic Cambridge-Somerville study in Boston, poor parental supervision in childhood was the best predictor of both violent and property crimes up to age 45 (McCord 1979).

Parental discipline refers to how parents react to a child's behaviour. It is clear that harsh or punitive discipline (involving physical punishment) predicts a child's delinquency, as the review by Haapasalo and Pokela (1999) showed. In their follow-up study of nearly 700 Nottingham children, John and Elizabeth Newson (1989) found that physical punishment at ages 7 and 11 predicted later convictions; 40 per cent of offenders had been smacked or beaten at age 11, compared with 14 per cent of non-offenders. Erratic or inconsistent discipline also predicts delinquency (West and

Farrington 1973: 51). This can involve either erratic discipline by one parent, sometimes turning a blind eye to bad behaviour and sometimes punishing it severely, or inconsistency between two parents, with one parent being tolerant or indulgent and the other being harshly punitive. It is not clear whether unusually lax discipline predicts delinquency. Just as inappropriate methods of responding to bad behaviour predict delinquency, low parental reinforcement (not praising) of good behaviour is also a predictor (Farrington and Loeber 1999).

Cold, rejecting parents tend to have delinquent children, as McCord (1979) found twenty years ago in the Cambridge-Somerville study. More recently, she concluded that parental warmth could act as a protective factor against the effects of physical punishment (McCord 1997). Whereas 51 per cent of boys with cold physically punishing mothers were convicted in her study, only 21 per cent of boys with warm physically punishing mothers were convicted, similar to the 23 per cent of boys with warm non-punitive mothers who were convicted. The father's warmth was also a protective factor against the father's physical punishment.

Low parental involvement in the child's activities predicts delinquency, as the Newsons found in their Nottingham survey (Lewis *et al.* 1982). In the Cambridge Study, having a father who never joined in the boy's leisure activities doubled his risk of conviction (West and Farrington 1973: 57), and this was the most important predictor of persistence in offending after age 21 as opposed to desistance (Farrington and Hawkins 1991).

Most explanations of the link between child-rearing methods and delinquency focus on attachment or social learning theories. Attachment theory was inspired by the work of Bowlby (1951), and suggests that children who are not emotionally attached to warm, loving, and law-abiding parents tend to become delinquent (Carlson and Sroufe 1995). The sociological equivalent of attachment theory is social bonding theory, which proposes that delinquency depends on the strength or weakness of a child's bond to society (Catalano and Hawkins 1996).

Social learning theories (Patterson 1982, 1995) suggest that children's behaviour depends on parental rewards and punishments and on the models of behaviour that parents represent. Children will tend to become delinquent if parents do not respond consistently and contingently to their antisocial behaviour and if parents themselves behave in an antisocial manner. These theories have inspired the use of parent training methods to prevent delinquency (see later).

CHILD ABUSE AND NEGLECT

Children who are physically abused or neglected tend to become offenders later in life (Malinosky-Rummell and Hansen 1993). The most famous demonstration of this was completed by Widom (1989) in Indianapolis. She used court records to identify over 900 children who had been abused or neglected before age 11, and compared them with a control group matched on age, race, gender, elementary school class, and place of residence. A 20-year follow-up showed that the children who were abused or neglected were more likely to be arrested as juveniles and as adults than were the controls, and they were more likely to be arrested for juvenile violence (Maxfield and Widom 1996). Child sexual abuse, and child physical abuse and neglect, also predict adult arrests for sex crimes (Widom and Ames 1994).

Similar results have been obtained in other studies. In the Cambridge-Somerville study in Boston, McCord (1983) found that about half of the abused or neglected boys were convicted for serious crimes, became alcoholics or mentally ill, or died before age 35. In the Rochester Youth Development Study, which is a prospective longitudinal survey of about 1,000 children originally aged 12–14, Smith and Thornberry (1995) showed that recorded child maltreatment under age 12 (physical, sexual, or emotional abuse or neglect) predicted later self-reported and officially noted delinquency. Furthermore, these results held up after controlling for gender, race, socio-economic status, and family structure.

Numerous theories have been put forward to explain the link between child abuse and later offending. Brezina (1998) described three of the main ones. Social learning theory suggests that children learn to adopt the abusive behaviour patterns of their parents through imitation, modelling, and reinforcement. Attachment or social bonding theory proposes that child maltreatment results in low attachment to parents and hence to low self-control. Strain theory posits that negative treatment by others generates negative emotions such as anger and frustration, which in turn lead to a desire for revenge and increased aggression. Based on analyses of the Youth in Transition study, Brezina found limited support for all three theories.

DISRUPTED FAMILIES

Most studies of broken homes have focused on the loss of the father rather than the mother, because the loss of a father is much more common. In general, it is found that children who are separated from a biological parent are more likely to offend than children from intact families. For example, in their birth cohort study of over 800 children born in Newcastle-upon-Tyne, Kolvin et al. (1988) discovered that boys who experienced divorce or separation in their first five years of life had a doubled risk of conviction up to age 32.

McCord (1982) in Boston carried out an interesting study of the relationship between homes broken by loss of the biological father and later serious offending by boys. She found that the prevalence of offending was high for boys from broken homes without affectionate mothers (62 per cent) and for those from unbroken homes characterized by parental conflict (52 per cent), irrespective of whether they had affectionate mothers. The prevalence of offending was low for those from unbroken homes without conflict (26 per cent) and—importantly—equally low for boys from broken homes with affectionate mothers (22 per cent). These results suggest that it might not be the broken home which is criminogenic but the parental conflict which often causes it. They also suggest that a loving mother might in some sense be able to compensate for the loss of a father.

In the Cambridge Study, both permanent and temporary (more than one month) separations before age 10 predicted convictions and self-reported delinquency, provided that they were not caused by death or hospitalization (Farrington 1992b). However, homes broken at an early age (under age 5) were not unusually criminogenic (West and Farrington 1973). Separation before age 10 predicted both juvenile and adult convictions (Farrington 1992a), and was an important independent predictor of adult social dysfunction and spouse assault at age 32 (Farrington 1993a, 1994).

The importance of the cause of the broken home is also shown in the National Survey of Health and Development, which is a survey of over 5,000 children born in one week in England, Scotland, or Wales (Wadsworth, 1979). Boys from homes broken by divorce or separation had an increased likelihood of being convicted or officially cautioned up to age 21 (27 per cent) in comparison with those from homes broken by death of the mother (19 per cent) or of the father (14 per cent), or from unbroken homes (14 per cent). Homes broken while the boy was under age 5 especially predicted delinquency, while homes broken while the boy was between ages 11 and 15 were not particularly criminogenic. Remarriage (which happened more often after divorce or separation than after death) was also associated with an increased risk of delinquency, suggesting a negative effect of step-parents. The meta-analysis by Wells and Rankin (1991) also shows that broken homes are more strongly related to delinquency when they are caused by parental separation or divorce rather than by death.

In the Dunedin study in New Zealand, boys from single-parent families were disproportionally likely to be convicted; 28 per cent of violent offenders were from single-parent families, compared with 17 per cent of non-violent offenders and 9 per cent of unconvicted boys (Henry et al. 1996). Based on analyses of four surveys (including the Cambridge Study), Morash and Rucker (1989) concluded that the combination of teenage child-bearing and a single-parent, female-headed household was especially conducive to the development of offending in children. Later analyses of the Cambridge Study showed that teenage child-bearing combined with a large number of children particularly predicted offending by the children (Nagin et al. 1997).

Much research suggests that frequent changes of parent figures predict offending by children. In a longitudinal survey of a birth cohort of over 500 Copenhagen males, Mednick et al. (1990) found that divorce followed by changes in parent figures predicted the highest rate of offending by children (65 per cent), compared with divorce followed by stability (42 per cent) and no divorce (28 per cent). In the Dunedin study in New Zealand, Henry et al. (1993) reported that both parental conflict and many changes of the child's primary caretaker predicted the child's antisocial behaviour up to age 11. However, in the Christchurch study in New Zealand, Fergusson et al. (1992) showed that parental transitions in the absence of parental conflict did not predict an increased risk of child offending. Also, in the Oregon Youth Study, Capaldi and Patterson (1991) concluded that antisocial mothers caused parental transitions which in turn caused child antisocial behaviour.

Explanations of the relationship between disrupted families and delinquency fall into three major classes. Trauma theories suggest that the loss of a parent has a damaging effect on a child, most commonly because of the effect on attachment to the parent.

Life-course theories focus on separation as a sequence of stressful experiences, and on the effects of multiple stressors such as parental conflict, parental loss, reduced economic circumstances, changes in parent figures, and poor child-rearing methods. Selection theories argue that disrupted families produce delinquent children because of pre-existing differences from other families in risk factors such as parental conflict, criminal or antisocial parents, low family income, or poor child-rearing methods.

Hypotheses derived from the three theories were tested in the Cambridge Study (Juby and Farrington 2001). While boys from broken homes (permanently disrupted families) were more delinquent than boys from intact homes, they were not more delinquent than boys from intact, high-conflict families. Interestingly, this result was replicated in Switzerland (Haas *et al.* 2004). Overall, the most important factor was the post-disruption trajectory. Boys who remained with their mother after the separation had the same delinquency rate as boys from intact, low-conflict families. Boys who remained with their father, with relatives or with others (e.g. foster parents) had high delinquency rates. It was concluded that the results favoured life-course theories rather than trauma or selection theories.

EXPLAINING DEVELOPMENT AND RISK FACTORS

KEY INDEPENDENT PREDICTORS

In explaining the development of offending, a major problem is that most risk factors tend to coincide and tend to be interrelated. For example, adolescents living in physically deteriorated and socially disorganized neighbourhoods disproportionally tend also to come from families with poor parental supervision and erratic parental discipline and tend also to have high impulsivity and low intelligence. The concentration and co-occurrence of these kinds of adversities makes it difficult to establish their independent, interactive, and sequential influences on offending and antisocial behaviour. Hence, any theory of the development of offending is inevitably speculative in the present state of knowledge.

A first step is to establish which factors predict offending independently of other factors. In the Cambridge Study, it was generally true that each of six categories of variables (impulsivity, intelligence or attainment, poor parenting, criminal family, socio-economic deprivation, child antisocial behaviour) predicted offending independently of each other category (Farrington 1990b). For example, the independent predictors of convictions between ages 10 and 20 included high daring, low school attainment, poor parental child-rearing, a convicted parent, poor housing, and troublesomeness (Farrington and Hawkins 1991). Hence, it might be concluded that impulsivity, low intelligence, poor parenting, a criminal family, and socio-economic deprivation, despite their interrelations, all contribute independently to the development of delinquency. Any theory needs to give priority to explaining these results.

THE INTEGRATED COGNITIVE ANTISOCIAL POTENTIAL (ICAP) THEORY

The modern trend is to try to achieve increased explanatory power by integrating propositions derived from several earlier theories (Catalano and Hawkins 1996). My own theory of male offending and antisocial behaviour (Farrington 2005b) is also integrative, and it distinguishes explicitly between the development of underlying antisocial tendencies and the occurrence of antisocial acts.

Figure 19.1 shows the key elements of this theory, which was primarily designed to explain offending by lower-class males. I have called it the 'Integrated Cognitive Antisocial Potential' (ICAP) theory. It integrates ideas from many other theories,

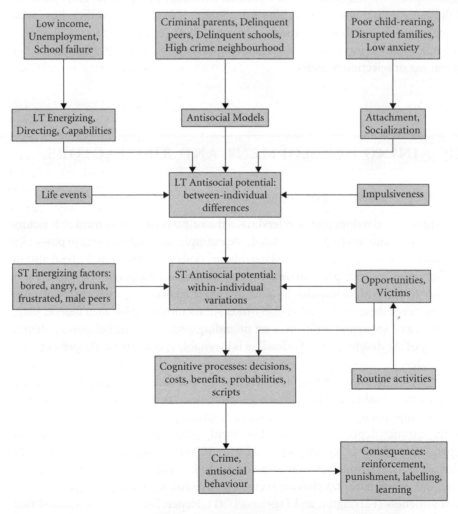

Fig. 19.1 The Integrated Cognitive Antisocial Potential (ICAP) Theory

Note: LT = Long-Term; ST = Short-Term.

including strain, control, learning, labelling, and rational choice approaches (see Agnew 2002); its key construct is antisocial potential (AP); and it assumes that the translation from antisocial potential to antisocial behaviour depends on cognitive (thinking and decision-making) processes that take account of opportunities and victims. Figure 19.1 is deliberately simplified in order to show the key elements of the ICAP theory on one sheet of paper; for example, it does not show how the processes operate differently for onset compared with desistance or at different ages.

The key construct underlying offending is antisocial potential (AP), which refers to the potential to commit antisocial acts. 'Offending' refers to the most common crimes of theft, burglary, robbery, violence, vandalism, minor fraud, and drug use, and to behaviour that in principle might lead to a conviction in Western industrialized societies such as the United States and the United Kingdom. Long-term, persisting, between-individual, differences in AP are distinguished from short-term, within-individual, variations in AP. Long-term AP depends on impulsiveness, on strain, modelling, and socialization processes, and on life events, while short-term variations in AP depend on motivating and situational factors.

Regarding long-term AP, people can be ordered on a continuum from low to high. The distribution of AP in the population at any age is highly skewed; relatively few people have relatively high levels of AP. People with high AP are more likely to commit many different types of antisocial acts including different types of offences. Hence, offending and antisocial behaviour are versatile, not specialized. The relative ordering of people on AP (long-term, between-individual variation) tends to be consistent over time, but absolute levels of AP vary with age, peaking in the teenage years, because of changes within individuals in the factors that influence long-term AP (e.g. from childhood to adolescence, the increasing importance of peers and decreasing importance of parents).

Figure 19.1 shows how risk factors are hypothesized to influence long-term AP. Following strain theory, the main energizing factors that potentially lead to high long-term AP are desires for material goods, status among intimates, excitement, and sexual satisfaction. However, these motivations only lead to high AP if antisocial methods of satisfying them are habitually chosen. Antisocial methods tend to be chosen by people who find it difficult to satisfy their needs legitimately, such as people with low income, unemployed people, and those who fail at school. However, the methods chosen also depend on physical capabilities and behavioural skills; for example, a 5-year-old would have difficulty in stealing a car. For simplicity, energizing and directing processes and capabilities are shown in one box in Figure 19.1. Ideally, I should develop an electronic map of my theory that allows people to click on different boxes to see more underlying detail, as with electronic street maps.

Long-term AP also depends on attachment and socialization processes. AP will be low if parents consistently and contingently reward good behaviour and punish bad behaviour. (Withdrawal of love may be a more effective method of socialization than hitting children.) Children with low anxiety will be less well socialized, because they care less about parental punishment. AP will be high if children are not attached to (prosocial) parents, for example if parents are cold and rejecting. Disrupted families (broken homes) may impair both attachment and socialization processes.

Long-term AP will also be high if people are exposed to and influenced by antisocial models, such as criminal parents, delinquent siblings, and delinquent peers, for example in high-crime schools and neighbourhoods. Long-term AP will also be high for impulsive people, because they tend to act without thinking about the consequences. Also, life events affect AP; it decreases (at least for males) after people get married or move out of high-crime areas, and it increases after separation from a partner.

According to the ICAP theory, the commission of offences and other types of antisocial acts depends on the interaction between the individual (with his immediate level of AP) and the social environment (especially criminal opportunities and victims). Short-term AP varies within individuals according to short-term energizing factors such as being bored, angry, drunk, or frustrated, or being encouraged by male peers. Criminal opportunities and the availability of victims depend on routine activities. Encountering a tempting opportunity or victim may cause a short-term increase in AP, just as a short-term increase in AP may motivate a person to seek out criminal opportunities and victims.

Whether a person with a certain level of AP commits a crime in a given situation depends on cognitive processes, including considering the subjective benefits, costs and probabilities of the different outcomes, and stored behavioural repertoires or scripts. The subjective benefits and costs include immediate situational factors such as the material goods that can be stolen and the likelihood and consequences of being caught by the police. They also include social factors such as likely disapproval by parents or female partners, and encouragement or reinforcement from peers. In general, people tend to make decisions that seem rational to them, but those with low levels of AP will not commit offences even when (on the basis of subjective expected utilities) it appears rational to do so. Equally, high short-term levels of AP (e.g. caused by anger or drunkenness) may induce people to commit offences when it is not rational for them to do so.

The consequences of offending may, as a result of a learning process, lead to changes in long-term AP and in future cognitive decision-making processes. This is especially likely if the consequences are reinforcing (e.g. gaining material goods or peer approval) or punishing (e.g. receiving legal sanctions or parental disapproval). Also, if the consequences involve labelling or stigmatizing the offender, this may make it more difficult for him to achieve his aims legally, and hence may lead to an increase in AP. (It is difficult to show these feedback effects in Figure 19.1 without making it very complex.)

Farrington (2003a, 2005b) has described how this theory explains and predicts key results from developmental and life-course criminology. For reviews of other developmental and life-course theories, see Farrington (2005a).

RISK-FOCUSED PREVENTION

Within the limited space available, it is not feasible to present an exhaustive or systematic review of the effectiveness of risk-focused interventions to reduce crime. In particular, I will not focus on interventions that do not work. Instead, a selection of some of the most effective programmes will be described, with special reference to programmes that have carried out a cost–benefit analysis. As far as possible, programme elements will be linked to risk factors, but there is often only a tenuous link between risk factors and prevention programmes. As mentioned, many programmes have multiple components, making it difficult to isolate their 'active ingredients'.

The most important risk-focused prevention programmes that have been targeted on individual and family risk factors use skills training, general parent education, parent training, pre-school intellectual enrichment programmes, and some combination of these (multi-component programmes). The most convincing evidence of the effectiveness of these programmes has been obtained in randomized experiments (for reviews of such experiments, see Farrington and Welsh 2005, 2006). Programmes that have proved to be effective in high-quality evaluation research are reviewed here (see also Lipsey and Wilson 1998; Farrington and Welsh 2003).

SKILLS TRAINING

The most important prevention techniques that target the risk factors of impulsiveness and low empathy are cognitive-behavioural skills training programmes (see also Hollin, Chapter 2, this volume). For example, Ross and Ross (1995) devised a programme that aimed to teach people to stop and think before acting, to consider the consequences of their behaviour, to conceptualize alternative ways of solving interpersonal problems, and to consider the impact of their behaviour on other people, especially victims. It included social skills training, lateral thinking (to teach creative problem, solving), critical thinking (to teach logical reasoning), values education (to teach values and concern for others), assertiveness training (to teach non-aggressive, socially appropriate ways to obtain desired outcomes), negotiation skills training, interpersonal cognitive problem-solving (to teach thinking skills for solving interpersonal problems), social perspective training (to teach how to recognize and understand other people's feelings), and role-playing and modelling (demonstration and practice of effective and acceptable interpersonal behaviour).

Ross and Ross (1988) implemented this 'Reasoning and Rehabilitation' programme in Ottawa, and found (in a randomized experiment) that it led to a large decrease in reoffending for a small sample of adult offenders in a short 9-month follow-up period. Their training was carried out by probation officers, but they believed that it could be carried out by parents or teachers. This programme has been implemented widely in several countries, and forms the basis of many accredited cognitive-behavioural programmes used in the UK prison and probation services, including the Pathfinder projects (McGuire 2001).

A similar programme, entitled 'Straight thinking on Probation', was implemented in Mid-Glamorgan by Raynor and Vanstone (2001; see also Raynor, Chapter 31, this volume). Offenders who received skills training were compared with similar offenders who received custodial sentences. After one year, offenders who completed the programme ('experimentals') had a lower reconviction rate than control offenders ('controls') (35 per cent as opposed to 49 per cent), although both had the same predicted reconviction rate of 42 per cent. The benefits of the programme had worn off at the two-year follow-up point, when reconviction rates of experimentals (63 per cent) and controls (65 per cent) were similar to reach other and to predicted rates. However, the reconvicted experimentals committed less serious crimes than the reconvicted controls.

Tong and Farrington (2006) completed a systematic review of the effectiveness of 'Reasoning and Rehabilitation' in reducing offending. They located 26 comparisons of experimental and control groups in four countries. Their meta-analysis showed that, overall, there was a significant 14 per cent decrease in offending for programme participants compared with controls.

Lösel and Beelmann (2006) completed a systematic review of the effectiveness of skills training with children. They located 89 comparisons of experimental and control groups. Their meta-analysis showed that, overall, there was a significant 10 per cent decrease in delinquency in follow-up studies for children who received skills training compared with controls. The greatest effect was for cognitive-behavioural skills training, where there was an average 25 per cent decrease in delinquency in seven follow-up studies.

PARENT EDUCATION

Many types of parent education programmes have been implemented to tackle family risk factors such as poor child-rearing and poor parental supervision. In the most famous intensive home-visiting programme, Olds *et al.* (1986) in Elmira (New York) randomly allocated 400 mothers either to receive home visits from nurses during pregnancy, or to receive visits both during pregnancy and during the first two years of life, or to a control group who received no visits. Each visit lasted about one and a quarter hours, and the mothers were visited on average every two weeks. The home visitors gave advice about prenatal and postnatal care of the child, about infant development, and about the importance of proper nutrition and the avoidance of smoking and drinking during pregnancy.

The results of this experiment showed that the postnatal home visits caused a decrease in recorded child physical abuse and neglect during the first two years of life, especially by poor unmarried teenage mothers; 4 per cent of visited versus 19 per cent of non-visited mothers of this type were guilty of child abuse or neglect. This last result is important because (as mentioned above) children who are physically abused or neglected tend to become violent offenders later in life. In a 15-year follow-up, the main focus was on lower-class unmarried mothers. Among these mothers, those who received prenatal and postnatal home visits had fewer arrests than those who received prenatal visits or no visits (Olds *et al.* 1997). Also, children of these mothers who received prenatal and/or postnatal home visits had less than half as many arrests as children of mothers who received no visits (Olds *et al.* 1998).

Several economic analyses show that the monetary benefits of this programme outweighed its costs for the lower-class unmarried mothers. The most important are by Greenwood *et al.* (2001) and Aos *et al.* (2004). However, both measured only a limited range of benefits. Greenwood and his colleagues measured only benefits to the government or taxpayer (welfare, education, employment, and criminal justice), not benefits to crime victims consequent upon reduced crimes. Aos and his colleagues measured benefits to crime victims (tangible, not intangible) and benefits to the government or taxpayer from savings in criminal justice, welfare, education, and unemployment costs. Nevertheless, both studies reported a benefit : cost ratio greater than 1 for this programme: 4 according to Greenwood *et al.* and 2.9 according to Aos *et al.*

To test the generalizability of the results of the Elmira study, two urban replications are currently under way: one in Memphis, Tennessee (Olds *et al.* 2004a), and the other in Denver, Colorado (Olds *et al.* 2004b). Early follow-up results from both replications (four and two years after programme completion, respectively) show improvements on a wide range of outcomes for both nurse-visited mothers and their children compared to their control counterparts.

PARENT TRAINING

Parent training is also an effective method of preventing offending. Many different types of parent training have been used, but the behavioural parent management training developed by Patterson (1982) in Oregon is one of the best known approaches. His careful observations of parent-child interaction showed that parents of antisocial children were deficient in their methods of child-rearing. These parents failed to tell their children how they were expected to behave, failed to monitor their behaviour to ensure that it was desirable, and failed to enforce rules promptly and unambiguously with appropriate rewards and penalties. The parents of antisocial children used more punishment (such as scolding, shouting, or threatening), but failed to make it contingent on the child's behaviour.

Patterson attempted to train these parents in effective child-rearing methods, namely noticing what a child is doing, monitoring behaviour over long periods, clearly stating house rules, making rewards and punishments contingent on behaviour, and negotiating disagreements so that conflicts and crises did not escalate. His treatment was shown to be effective in reducing child stealing and antisocial behaviour over short periods in small-scale studies (Dishion *et al.* 1992; Patterson *et al.* 1982, 1992).

Other important parent training programmes that have been used in the United Kingdom include Triple-P (Sanders *et al.* 2000) and The Incredible Years (Webster-Stratton 2000). The Webster-Stratton programme was shown to reduce childhood antisocial behaviour in an experiment conducted by Scott *et al.* (2001) in London and Chichester. About 140 mainly poor, disadvantaged children aged 3–8 referred for aggressive and antisocial behaviour were allocated to experimental (parent training) or control (waiting list) groups. The parent training programme, based on videotapes, was given for two hours a week over 13–16 weeks, covering praise and rewards, setting limits, and handling misbehaviour. Follow-up parent interviews and observations showed that the antisocial behaviour of the experimental children decreased significantly compared to that of the controls. Furthermore, after the intervention, experimental parents gave their children far more praise to encourage desirable behaviour, and used more effective commands to obtain compliance.

The Montreal longitudinal-experimental study used a multi-modal intervention based on child skills training and parent management training. Tremblay *et al.* (1995) identified disruptive (aggressive/hyperactive) boys at age 6, and randomly allocated over 300 of these to experimental or control conditions. Between ages 7 and 9, the experimental group received training designed to foster social skills and self-control. Coaching, peer-modelling, role-playing, and reinforcement contingencies were used in small group sessions on such topics as 'how to help', 'what to do when you are angry', and 'how to react to teasing'. Also, their parents were trained using the parent management training techniques developed by Patterson (1982). Parents were taught to provide positive reinforcement for desirable behaviour, to use non-punitive and consistent disciplinary practices, and to develop family crisis management techniques.

This prevention programme was quite successful. By age 12, the experimental boys committed less burglary and theft, were less likely to get drunk, and were less likely to be involved in fights than the controls (according to self-reports). Also, the experimental boys had higher school achievements. At every age from 10 to 15, the experimental boys had lower self-reported delinquency scores than the control boys. Interestingly, the differences in antisocial behaviour between experimental and control boys increased as the follow-up progressed. The experimental boys were also less likely to be gang members and to take drugs, but they were not significantly different from the controls in having sexual intercourse by age 15 (Tremblay *et al.* 1995, 1996). Later analyses have shown differences between experimental and control boys in trajectories of delinquency (Vitaro *et al.* 2001) and aggression, vandalism, and theft (Lacourse *et al.* 2002).

PRE-SCHOOL PROGRAMMES

Several pre-school programmes have been designed to enhance cognitive abilities, intelligence, and attainment. The most famous pre-school intellectual enrichment programme is the Perry project carried out in Ypsilanti (Michigan) by Schweinhart and Weikart (1980). This was essentially a 'Head Start' programme targeted at disadvantaged African American children, who were allocated to experimental and control groups. The experimental children attended a daily pre-school programme, backed up by weekly home visits, usually lasting two years (covering ages 3–4). The aim of the 'plan—do—review' programme was to provide intellectual stimulation, to increase thinking and reasoning abilities, and to increase later school achievement.

This programme had long-term benefits. Berrueta-Clement *et al.* (1984) showed that, at age 19, the experimental group was more likely to be employed, more likely to have graduated from high school, more likely to have received college or vocational training, and less likely to have been arrested. By age 27, the experimental group had accumulated only half as many arrests on average as the controls (Schweinhart *et al.* 1993). Also, they had significantly higher earnings and were more likely to be home owners. More of the experimental women were married, and fewer of their children were born out of wedlock.

The most recent follow-up of this programme at age 40 found that it continued to make an important difference in the lives of the participants (Schweinhart *et al.* 2005). Compared to the control group, those who received the programme had significantly fewer life-time arrests for violent crimes (32 per cent vs 48 per cent), property crimes (36 per cent vs 58 per cent), and drug crimes (14 per cent vs 34 per cent), and they were significantly less likely to be arrested five or more times (36 per cent vs 55 per cent). Improvements were also recorded in many other important life-course outcomes. For example, significantly higher levels of schooling (77 per cent vs 60 per cent graduating from high school), better records of employment (76 per cent vs 62 per cent), and higher annual incomes were reported by the programme group compared to the controls.

Several economic analyses show that the monetary benefits of this programme outweighed its costs. The Perry project's own calculation (Barnett 1993) included crime and non-crime benefits, intangible costs to victims, and projected benefits beyond age 27. This generated an often quoted benefit : cost ratio of 7.2. Most of the benefits (65 per cent) were derived from savings to crime victims. A cost–benefit analysis at age 40 found that the programme produced just over US$17 in benefits per dollar of cost, with 76 per cent of this accruing to the general public because of savings in crime, education, and welfare costs and increased tax revenue, and 24 per cent resulting from benefits to programme participants.

Desirable results were also obtained in evaluations of other pre-school programmes (e.g. Reynolds *et al.* 2001; Campbell *et al.* 2002). Also, a large-scale study by Garces *et al.* (2002) found that children who attended Head Start programmes (at ages 3 to 5) were significantly less likely to report being arrested or referred to court for a crime by ages 18 to 30 compared to their siblings who did not attend these programmes.

MULTIPLE-COMPONENT PROGRAMMES

One of the most important school-based prevention experiments was carried out in Seattle by Hawkins *et al.* (1991). This was a multiple-component programme combining parent training, teacher training, and child skills training. About 500 first-grade children (aged 6) in 21 classes in eight schools were randomly assigned to be in experimental or control classes. The children in the experimental classes received special treatment at home and school which was designed to increase their attachment to their parents and their bonding to the school. Also, they were trained in interpersonal cognitive problem-solving. Their parents were trained to notice and reinforce socially desirable behaviour in a programme called 'Catch them being good'. Their teachers were trained in classroom management, for example to provide clear instructions and expectations to children, to reward children for participation in desired behaviour, and to teach children prosocial (socially desirable) methods of solving problems.

This programme had long-term benefits. O'Donnell *et al.* (1995) focused on children in low-income families and reported that, in the sixth grade (age 12), experimental boys were less likely to have initiated delinquency, while experimental girls were less likely to have initiated drug use. In the latest follow-up, Hawkins *et al.* (1999) found that, at age 18, the full intervention group (receiving the intervention from grades 1 to 6) admitted less violence, less alcohol abuse, and fewer sexual partners than the late intervention group (grades 5–6 only) or the controls. The benefit : cost ratio of this programme according to Aos *et al.* (2001) was 4.3.

In general, multiple-component programmes, including individual, family, school, and community interventions, are more effective than programmes with only one of these components (Wasserman and Miller 1998). Multi-Systemic Therapy (MST) is an increasingly popular multiple-component intervention designed for serious juvenile offenders (Henggeler *et al.* 1998). The particular type of treatment is chosen according to the needs of the young person, and it may include individual, family, peer, school, and community interventions (including parent training and skills training).

Henggeler *et al.* (1993) completed the first experimental test of MST. This evaluation, with 84 juvenile offenders, showed that (compared with out-of-home placement) MST was followed by fewer arrests (at immediate outcome and at two years post-treatment), lower self-reported delinquency, less peer-oriented aggression, and improvements in the functioning of the family unit as a whole, as measured by the outcome of family cohesion.

There have been five later large-scale experiments on MST. Four of the five trials, all carried out by Henggeler (the originator of this treatment) and his colleagues, found that the intervention was effective in reducing later offending (Borduin *et al.* 1995; Henggeler *et al.* 1997, 1999, 2002). Borduin and his colleagues (1995) reported that MST caused a 63 per cent reduction in the prevalence of arrests, while the reduction was 56 per cent in the Henggeler *et al.* (2002) study. For two of the programmes (Borduin *et al.* 1995; Henggeler *et al.* 1999), improvements were also found in the functioning of the family unit as a whole, as measured by the outcome of family cohesion.

However, the one large-scale independent evaluation of MST, by Leschied and Cunningham (2002) in Canada, did not find that it was effective in reducing later convictions (compared with the usual community services, which typically involved probation supervision); the MST group were 10 per cent more likely to be convicted within 12 months. Also, two meta-analyses of the effectiveness of MST came to diametrically opposite conclusions. Curtis *et al.* (2004) found that it was effective, while

Littell (2005) concluded that it was not. Nevertheless, MST is a promising intervention technique, and it is being used in the United Kingdom (Jefford and Squire 2004).

One of the best ways of achieving risk-focused prevention is through multiple-component community-based programmes including several of the successful interventions listed above, and 'Communities That Care' (CTC) has many attractions (Farrington 1996). Perhaps more than any other programme, it is evidence based and systematic: the choice of interventions depends on empirical evidence about what are the important risk and protective factors in a particular community and on empirical evidence about 'What works'. It has been implemented in at least 35 sites in England, Scotland, and Wales, and also in the Netherlands and Australia (Communities that Care 1997; Utting 1999). Unfortunately, it is difficult to draw any conclusions from the evaluation of three UK CTC projects by Crow et al. (2004) because of implementation problems. While the effectiveness of the overall CTC strategy has not yet been demonstrated, the effectiveness of its individual components is clear (Harachi et al. 2003).

CONCLUSIONS

RESEARCH IMPLICATIONS

A great deal has been learned in the last twenty years, particularly from prospective longitudinal surveys, about childhood risk factors for offending and other types of anti-social behaviour. Offenders differ significantly from non-offenders in many respects, including impulsiveness, intelligence, family background, and socio-economic deprivation. These differences are often present before, during, and after criminal careers. More research is needed to elucidate the causal chains that link these factors with antisocial behaviour, the ways in which these factors have independent, interactive, or sequential effects, and developmental sequences leading to persistent offending. Since most is known about risk factors for prevalence and onset, more research is needed on risk factors for frequency, duration, escalation, and desistance.

Existing British longitudinal surveys of offending were often conducted many years ago when social conditions were very different, and results are often based on Caucasian males living in cities. New prospective longitudinal surveys are needed to take account of the increasing ethnic diversity of the population, to advance knowledge about risk factors for girls and in non-urban areas, and especially to advance knowledge about protective factors that prevent offending. The new Peterborough longitudinal survey directed by P.-O. H. Wikström is particularly welcome. However, new surveys are also required that begin in childhood, preferably under age 5. In addition, it would be highly desirable to collect information about delinquency in an existing survey such as the Avon Longitudinal Study of Parents and Children (e.g. O'Connor et al. 2002).

Particular efforts should be made to investigate the effects of life events on the course of development of offending.

Only recently have longitudinal researchers begun to pay sufficient attention to neighbourhood and community factors, and there is still a great need for them to investigate immediate situational influences on offending (Farrington *et al.* 1993; Wikström *et al.* 1995). Existing research tells us more about the development of criminal potential than about how that potential becomes the actuality of offending in any given situation. Research on immediate situational influences on offending should be included in new longitudinal studies, to link up the developmental and situational approaches.

High-quality experimental and quasi-experimental evaluations of the effectiveness of crime reduction programmes are needed in the United Kingdom. Most knowledge about the effectiveness of prevention programmes, such as cognitive-behavioural skills training, parent training, and pre-school intellectual enrichment programmes, is based on American research. Ideally, prevention programmes should aim not only to tackle risk factors but also to strengthen protective factors, and both risk and protective factors should be measured and targeted. An important development in recent years has been the increasing use of cost–benefit analysis in evaluating prevention programmes. Cost–benefit analyses of the effectiveness of prevention programmes should be given some priority, and a standard how-to-do-it manual should be developed.

It is hard to evaluate large-scale crime reduction strategies, and to answer questions about whether it is better (in terms of crimes saved per pound spent, for example) to invest in risk-focused early prevention, in physical or situational prevention, in more police officers, or in more prison cells. Nevertheless, this question is of vital importance to government policy-makers and to the general population. Therefore, research is needed to investigate the cost-effectiveness of risk-focused prevention in comparison with other general crime reduction strategies.

POLICY IMPLICATIONS

Consideration should be given to implementing a multiple-component risk-focused prevention programme such as CTC more widely throughout Great Britain. This programme could be implemented by existing Crime and Disorder Partnerships. However, they would need resources and technical assistance to conduct youth surveys and household surveys to identify key risk and protective factors for both people and places. They would also need resources and technical assistance to measure risk and protective factors, to choose effective intervention methods, and to carry out high-quality evaluations of the effectiveness of programmes in reducing crime and disorder.

The focus should be on primary prevention—offering the programme to all families living in specified areas—not on secondary prevention—targeting the programme on individuals identified as at risk. Ideally, the programme should be presented positively, as fostering safe and healthy communities by strengthening protective factors, rather than as a crime prevention programme targeting risk factors.

Nationally and locally, there is no agency whose main mandate is the primary prevention of crime. A national prevention agency could provide technical assistance, skills, and knowledge to local agencies in implementing prevention programmes, could provide funding for such programmes, and could ensure continuity, coordination, and monitoring of local programmes. It could provide training in prevention science for people in local agencies, and could maintain high standards for evaluation research. It could also act as a centre for the discussion of how policy initiatives of different government agencies influence crime and associated social problems. It could set a national and local agenda for research and practice in the prevention of crime, drug, and alcohol abuse, mental health problems, and associated social problems. National crime prevention agencies have been established in other countries, such as Sweden (Andersson 2005) and Canada (Sansfacon and Waller 2001).

A national agency could also maintain a computerized register of evaluation research and, like the National Institute of Health and Clinical Excellence, advise the government about effective and cost-effective crime prevention programmes. Medical advice is often based on systematic reviews of the effectiveness of health care interventions organized by the Cochrane Collaboration and funded by the National Health Service. Systematic reviews of the evaluation literature on the effectiveness of criminological interventions, possibly organized by the Campbell Collaboration (Farrington and Petrosino 2001), should be commissioned and funded by government agencies.

Crime prevention also needs to be organized locally. In each area, a local agency should be established to take the lead in organizing risk-focused crime prevention. In Sweden, 80 per cent of municipalities had local crime prevention councils in 2005 (Andersson 2005). The local prevention agency could take the lead in measuring risk factors and social problems in local areas, using archival records and local household and school surveys. It could then assess available resources and develop a plan of prevention strategies. With specialist technical assistance, prevention programmes could be chosen from a menu of strategies that have been proved to be effective in reducing crime in well-designed evaluation research. This would be a good example of evidence-based practice.

Recent promising developments in the UK, such as 'Sure Start' and 'Every Child Matters' (Chief Secretary to the Treasury 2003) have clearly been influenced by recent research on childhood risk factors and risk-focused intervention strategies. The time is ripe to expand these experimental programmes into a large-scale, evidence-based, integrated national strategy for the reduction of crime and associated social problems, including rigorous evaluation requirements.

■ **SELECTED FURTHER READING**

Farrington and Welsh (2007) have completed a book-length review of risk factors and effective interventions, entitled *Saving Children from a Life of Crime* (Oxford University Press). Several of the most important prospective longitudinal surveys are described in detail in *Taking Stock of Delinquency* edited by Thornberry and Krohn (Kluwer/Plenum, 2003). Criminal career research is reviewed in *Key Issues in Criminal Career Research* by Piquero *et al.* (Cambridge University Press, 2007). Developmental criminology and its theories are explained in *Integrated Developmental and Life-course Theories of Offending* edited by Farrington (Transaction, 2005). Wide-ranging reviews of what works to prevent crime can be found in *Evidence-Based Crime Prevention* edited by Sherman *et al.* (Routledge, 2006). More recent systematic reviews of the effectiveness of interventions are presented in *Preventing Crime* edited by Welsh and Farrington (Springer, 2006). Much information about risk factors and effective interventions can be found in *Serious and Violent Juvenile Offenders* (Sage, 1998) and *Child Delinquents* (Sage, 2001), both edited by Loeber and Farrington. Early prevention techniques in the childhood years are reviewed in *Early Prevention of Adult Antisocial Behaviour* edited by Farrington and Coid (Cambridge University Press, 2003) and *Support from the Start* edited by Sutton *et al.* (DFES, 2004). Cost–benefit analyses are reviewed in *Costs and Benefits of Preventing Crime* edited by Welsh *et al.* (Westview, 2001) and in *Changing Lives* by Greenwood (University of Chicago Press, 2006).

■ REFERENCES

AGNEW, R. (2002), 'Crime causation; Sociological theories' in J. Dressler (Editor-in-chief), *Encyclopedia of Crime and Justice*, 1: 324–34, New York: Macmillan.

AMDUR, R. L. (1989), 'Testing causal models of delinquency: A methodological critique', *Criminal Justice and Behaviour*, 16: 35–62.

ANDERSSON, J. (2005), 'The Swedish National Council for Crime Prevention: A short presentation', *Journal of Scandinavian Studies in Criminology and Crime Prevention*, 6: 74–88.

AOS, S., LIEB, R., MAYFIELD, J., MILLER, M., and PENNUCCI, A. (2004), '*Benefits and Costs of Prevention and Early Intervention Programmes for Youth*', Olympia, Wash.: Washington State Institute for Public Policy.

——, PHIPPS, P., BARNOSKI, R., and LIEB, R. (2001), *The Comparative Costs and Benefits of Programs to Reduce Crime* (version 4.0), Olympia, Wash.: Washington State Institute for Public Policy.

AUGIMERI, L. K., KOEGL, C. J., WEBSTER, C. D., and LEVENE, K. S. (2001), *Early Assessment Risk List for Boys (EARL-20B), Version 2*, Toronto: Earlscourt Child and Family Centre.

BARNETT, W. S. (1993), 'Cost-benefit analysis', in L. J. Schweinhart, H. V. Barnes, and D. P. Weikart, *Significant Benefits: The High/Scope Perry Preschool Study Through Age 27*: 142–73, Ypsilanti, Mich.: High/Scope Press.

BARON, R. M., and KENNY, D. A. (1986), 'The moderator-mediator variable distinction in social psychological research: Conceptual, strategic and statistical considerations', *Journal of Personality and Social Psychology*, 51: 1173–82.

BERRUETA-CLEMENT, J. R., SCHWEINHART, L. J., BARNETT, W. S., EPSTEIN, A. S., and WEIKART, D. P. (1984), *Changed Lives: The Effects of the Perry Preschool Programme on Youths Through Age 19*, Ypsilanti, Mich.: High/Scope Press.

BLACKBURN, R. (1993), *The Psychology of Criminal Conduct*, Chichester: Wiley.

BOR, W., McGEE, T. R., and FAGAN, A. A. (2004), 'Early risk factors for adolescent antisocial behaviour: An Australian longitudinal study', *Australian and New Zealand Journal of Psychiatry*, 38: 365–72.

BORDUIN, C. M., MANN, B. J., CONE, L. T., HENGGELER, S. W., FUCCI, B. R., BLASKE, D. M., and WILLIAMS, R. A. (1995), 'Multisystemic treatment of serious juvenile offenders: Long-term prevention of criminality and violence', *Journal of Consulting and Clinical Psychology*, 63: 569–87.

BOWLBY, J. (1951), *Maternal Care and Mental Health*, Geneva: World Health Organization.

BRENNAN, P. A., MEDNICK, B. R., and MEDNICK, S. A. (1993), 'Parental psychopathology, congenital factors, and violence', in S. Hodgins (ed.), *Mental*

Disorder and Crime, 244–61, Newbury Park, Cal.: Sage.

BREZINA, T. (1998), 'Adolescent maltreatment and delinquency: The question of intervening processes', *Journal of Research in Crime and Delinquency*, 35: 71–99.

BROWNFIELD, D., and SORENSON, A. M. (1994), 'Sibship size and sibling delinquency', *Deviant Behaviour*, 15: 45–61.

CAMPBELL, F. A., RAMEY, C. T., PUNGELLO, E., SPARLING, J. and MILLER-JOHNSON, S. (2002), 'Early childhood education: Young adult outcomes from the Abercedarian Project', *Applied Developmental Science*, 6: 42–57.

CAPALDI, D. M., and PATTERSON, G. R. (1991), 'Relation of parental transitions to boys' adjustment problems', *Developmental Psychology*, 27: 489–504.

——and —— (1996), 'Can violent offenders be distinguished from frequent offenders? Prediction from childhood to adolescence', *Journal of Research in Crime and Delinquency*, 33: 206–31.

CARLSON, E. A. and SROUFE, L. A. (1995), 'Contribution of attachment theory to developmental psychopathology', in D. Cicchetti and D. J. Cohen (eds), *Developmental Psychopathology, vol. 1: Theory and Methods*, 581–617, New York: Wiley.

CATALANO, R. F. and HAWKINS, J. D. (1996), 'The social development model: A theory of antisocial behaviour', in J. D. Hawkins (ed.), *Delinquency and Crime: Current Theories*, 149–97, Cambridge: Cambridge University Press.

CHIEF SECRETARY TO THE TREASURY (2003), *Every Child Matters*, Cm. 4860, London: The Stationery Office.

CLARKE, R. V. (1995), 'Situational crime prevention' in M. Tonry and D. P. Farrington (eds), *Building a Safer Society: Strategic Approaches to Crime Prevention*, 91–150, Chicago: University of Chicago Press.

——and CORNISH, D. B. (1985), 'Modelling offenders' decisions: A framework for research and policy', in M. Tonry and N. Morris (eds), *Crime and Justice*, vol. 6: 147–85, Chicago: University of Chicago Press.

COHEN, A. K. (1955), *Delinquent Boys: The Culture of the Gang*, Glencoe, Ill.: Free Press.

COMMUNITIES THAT CARE (1997), *Communities that Care (UK): A New Kind of Prevention Programme*, London: Communities that Care.

CROW, I., FRANCE, A., HACKING, S. and HART, M. (2004), *Does Communities That Care Work? An Evaluation of a Community-Based Risk Prevention Programme in Three Neighbourhoods*, York: Joseph Rowntree Foundation.

CURTIS, N. M., RONAN, K. R., and BORDUIN. C. M. (2004), 'Multisystemic treatment: A meta-analysis of outcome studies', *Journal of Family Psychology*, 18: 411–19.

DISHION, T. J., PATTERSON, G. R., and KAVANAGH, K. A. (1992), 'An experimental test of the coercion model: Linking theory, measurement and intervention', in J. McCord and R. E. Tremblay (eds), *Preventing Antisocial Behaviour: Interventions from Birth through Adolescence*, 253–82, New York: Guilford.

DODGE, K. A. (1991), 'The structure and function of reactive and proactive aggression', in D. J. Pepler and K. H. Rubin (eds), *The Development and Treatment of Childhood Aggression*, 201–18, Hillsdale, NJ: Lawrence Erlbaum.

EKLUND, J., and KLINTEBERG, B. A. (2003), 'Childhood behaviour as related to subsequent drinking offences and violent offending: A prospective study of 11 to 14-year-old youths into their fourth decade', *Criminal Behaviour and Mental Health*, 13: 294–309.

ELLIS, L. (1988), 'The victimful-victimless crime distinction, and seven universal demographic correlates of victimful criminal behaviour', *Personality and Individual Differences*, 3: 525–48.

FARRINGTON, D. P. (1988), 'Studying changes within individuals: The causes of offending', in M. Rutter (ed) S*tudies of Psychosocial Risk: The Power of Longitudinal Data*, 158–83, Cambridge: Cambridge University Press.

——(1989), 'Early predictors of adolescent aggression and adult violence', *Violence and Victims*, 4: 79–100.

——(1990a), 'Age, period, cohort, and offending', in D. M. Gottfredson and R. V. Clarke (eds), *Policy and Theory in Criminal Justice: Contributions in Honour of Leslie T. Wilkins*, 51–75, Aldershot: Avebury.

——(1990b), 'Implications of criminal career research for the prevention of offending', *Journal of Adolescence*, 13: 93–113.

——(1992a), 'Explaining the beginning, progress and ending of antisocial behaviour from birth to adulthood', in J. McCord (ed.), *Facts, Frameworks and Forecasts: Advances in Criminological Theory*, 3: 253–86, New Brunswick, NJ: Transaction.

——(1992b), 'Juvenile delinquency', in J. C. Coleman (ed.), *The School Years*, 2nd edn, 123–63, London: Routledge.

FARRINGTON, D. P. (1993a), 'Childhood origins of teenage antisocial behaviour and adult social dysfunction', *Journal of the Royal Society of Medicine*, 86: 13–17.

—— (1993b), 'Understanding and preventing bullying', in M. Tonry and N. Morris (eds), *Crime and Justice*, 17: 381–458, Chicago: University of Chicago Press.

—— (1994), 'Childhood, adolescent and adult features of violent males', in L. R. Huesmann (ed.), *Aggressive Behaviour: Current Perspectives*, 215–40, New York: Plenum.

—— (1995), 'The development of offending and antisocial behaviour from childhood: Key findings from the Cambridge Study in Delinquent Development. *Journal of Child Psychology and Psychiatry*, 36: 929–64.

—— (1996), *Understanding and Preventing Youth Crime*, York: Joseph Rowntree Foundation.

—— (2000), 'Explaining and preventing crime: The globalization of knowledge', *Criminology*, 38: 1–24.

—— (2002), 'Multiple risk factors for multiple problem violent boys', in R. R. Corrado, R. Roesch, S. D. Hart and J. K. Gierowski (eds), *Multi-problem Violent Youth: A Foundation for Comparative Research on Needs, Interventions and Outcomes*, 23–34, Amsterdam: IOS Press.

—— (2003a). 'Developmental and life-course criminology: Key theoretical and empirical issues', *Criminology*, 41: 221–55.

—— (2003b), 'Key results from the first 40 years of the Cambridge Study in Delinquent Development', in T. P. Thornberry and M. D. Krohn (eds), *Taking Stock of Delinquency: An Overview of Findings from Contemporary Longitudinal Studies*, 137–83, New York: Kluwer/Plenum.

—— (2005a), (ed.) *Integrated Development and Life-Course Theories of Offending*, (Advances in Criminological Theory, vol. 14), New Brunswick, NJ: Transaction.

—— (2005b), 'The Integrated Cognitive Antisocial Potential (ICAP) theory', in D. P. Farrington (ed.), *Integrated Developmental and Life-Course Theories of Offending*, 73–92, New Brunswick, NJ: Transaction.

—— (2007a), 'Developmental and life-course criminology', in H.-J. Schneider (ed.), *International Handbook of Criminology*, Berlin: De Gruyter, in the press.

—— (2007b), 'Origins of violent behaviour over the life span', in D. J. Flannery, A. T. Vaszonyi and I. Waldman (eds), *The Cambridge Handbook of Violent Behaviour*, Cambridge: Cambridge University Press, in the press.

—— and COID, J. W. (eds) (2003), *Early Prevention of Adult Antisocial Behaviour*, Cambridge: Cambridge University Press.

—— and HAWKINS, J. D. (1991), 'Predicting participation, early onset, and later persistence in officially recorded offending', *Criminal Behaviour and Mental Health*, 1: 1–33.

—— and LOEBER, R. (1999), 'Transatlantic replicability of risk factors in the development of delinquency', in P. Cohen, C. Slomkowski, and L. N. Robins (eds), *Historical and Geographical Influences on Psychopathology*, 299–329, Mahwah, NJ: Lawrence Erlbaum.

—— and PETROSINO, A. (2001), 'The Campbell Collaboration Crime and Justice Group', *Annals of the American Academy of Political and Social Science*, 578: 35–49.

—— and WELSH, B. C. (2003), 'Family-based prevention of offending: A meta-analysis', *Australian and New Zealand Journal of Criminology*, 36: 127–51.

—— and —— (2005), 'Randomized experiments in criminology: What have we learned in the last two decades?', *Journal of Experimental Criminology*, 1: 9–38.

—— and —— (2006), 'A half-century of randomized experiments on crime and justice', in M. Tonry (ed.), *Crime and Justice*, vol. 34, 55–132, Chicago: University of Chicago Press.

—— and —— (2007), *Saving Children from a Life of Crime: Early Risk Factors and Effective Interventions*, Oxford: Oxford University Press.

—— and WEST, D. J. (1990), 'The Cambridge Study in Delinquent Development: A long-term follow-up of 411 London males', in H.-J. Kerner and G. Kaiser (eds), *Criminality: Personality, Behaviour and Life History*, 115–38, Berlin: Springer-Verlag.

—— and —— (1993), 'Criminal, penal and life histories of chronic offenders; Risk and protective factors and early identification', *Criminal Behaviour and Mental Health*, 3: 492–523.

—— BARNES, G., and LAMBERT, S. (1996), 'The concentration of offending in families', *Legal and Criminological Psychology*, 1: 47–63.

——, COID, J. W., HARNETT, L., JOLLIFFE, D., SOTERIOU, N., TURNER, R., and WEST, D. J. (2006),

Criminal Careers and Life Success: New Findings from the Cambridge Study in Delinquent Development, London: Home Office (Research Findings No. 281).

——, GALLAGHER, B., MORLEY, L., St. LEDGER, R. J., and WEST, D. J. (1986), 'Unemployment, school leaving, and crime', *British Journal of Criminology*, 26: 335–56.

——, JOLLIFFE, D., LOEBER, R., STOUTHAMER-LOEBER, M., and KALB, L. M. (2001), 'The concentration of offenders in families, and family criminality in the prediction of boys' delinquency', *Journal of Adolescence*, 24: 579–96.

——, LOEBER, R., and VAN KAMMEN, W. B. (1990), 'Long-term criminal outcomes of hyperactivity-impulsivity-attention deficit and conduct problems in childhood', in L. N. Robins and M. Rutter (eds), *Straight and Devious Pathways from Childhood to Adulthood*, 62–81, Cambridge: Cambridge University Press.

——, ——, YIN, Y. and ANDERSON, S. (2002), 'Are within-individual causes of delinquency the same as between-individual causes?', *Criminal Behaviour and Mental Health*, 12: 53–68.

——, SAMPSON, R. J. and WIKSTRÖM, P.-O. H., (eds) (1993), *Integrating Individual and Ecological Aspects of Crime*, Stockholm: National Council for Crime Prevention.

FERGUSSON, D. M., HORWOOD, L. J. and LYNSKEY, M. T. (1992), 'Family change, parental discord and early offending', *Journal of Child Psychology and Psychiatry*, 33: 1059–75.

——, —— and —— (1994), 'The childhoods of multiple problem adolescents: A 15 year longitudinal study', *Journal of Child Psychology and Psychiatry*, 35: 1123–40.

FLOOD-PAGE, C., CAMPBELL, S., HARRINGTON, V. and MILLER, J. (2000), *Youth Crime: Findings from the 1998/99 Youth Lifestyles Survey*, London: Home Office (Research Study No. 209).

GARCES, E., THOMAS, D., and CURRIE, J. (2002), 'Longer-term effects of Head Start', *American Economic Review*, 92: 999–1012.

GOTTFREDSON, D. C. (2001), '*Schools and Delinquency*', Cambridge: Cambridge University Press.

GRAHAM, J. and BOWLING, B. (1995), '*Young People and Crime*', London: H.M.S.O. (Home Office Research Study No. 145).

GREENWOOD, P. W. (2006), *Changing Lives: Delinquency Prevention as Crime-Control Policy*, Chicago: University of Chicago Press.

——, KAROLY, L. A., EVERINGHAM, S. S., HOUBÉ, J., KILBURN, M. R., RYDELL, C. P., SANDERS, M., and CHIESA, J. (2001), 'Estimating the costs and benefits of early childhood interventions: Nurse home visits and the Perry Preschool', in B. C. Welsh, D. P. Farrington, and L. W. Sherman (eds), *Costs and Benefits of Preventing Crime*, 123–48, Boulder, Col.: Westview Press.

GROVE, W. M., ECKERT, E. D., HESTON, L., BOUCHARD, T. J., SEGAL, N., and LYKKEN, D. T. (1990), 'Heritability of substance abuse and antisocial behaviour: A study of monozygotic twins reared apart', *Biological Psychiatry*, 27: 1293–1304.

HAAPASALO, J. and POKELA, E. (1999), 'Child-rearing and child abuse antecedents of criminality', *Aggression and Violent Behaviour*, 1: 107–27.

HAAS, H., FARRINGTON, D. P., KILLIAS, M., and SATTAR, G. (2004), 'The impact of different family configurations on delinquency', *British Journal of Criminology*, 44: 520–32.

HARACHI, T. W., HAWKINS, J. D., CATALANO, R. F., LAFAZIA, A. M., SMITH, B. H., and ARTHUR, M. W. (2003), 'Evidence-based community decision making for prevention: Two case studies of Communities That Care', *Japanese Journal of Sociological Criminology*, 28: 26–37.

HAWKINS, J. D., and CATALANO, R. F. (1992), *Communities that Care*, San Francisco: Jossey-Bass.

——, ——, KOSTERMAN, R., ABBOTT, R., and HILL, K. G. (1999), 'Preventing adolescent health risk behaviours by strengthening protection during childhood', *Archives of Pediatrics and Adolescent Medicine*, 153: 226–34.

——, VON CLEVE, E., and CATALANO, R. F. (1991), 'Reducing early childhood aggression: Results of a primary prevention programme', *Journal of the American Academy of Child and Adolescent Psychiatry*, 30: 208–17.

HENGGELER, S. W., CLINGEMPEEL, W. G., BRONDINO, M. J., and PICKREL, S. G. (2002), 'Four-year follow-up of multisystemic therapy with substance-abusing and substance-dependent juvenile offenders', *Journal of the American Academy of Child and Adolescent Psychiatry*, 41: 868–74.

——, MELTON, G. B., BRONDINO, M. J., SCHERER, D. G., and HANLEY, J. H. (1997), 'Multisystemic therapy with violent and chronic juvenile offenders and their families: The role of treatment fidelity in successful dissemination', *Journal of Consulting and Clinical Psychology*, 65: 821–33.

HENGGELER, S. W., MELTON, G. B., SMITH, L. A., SCHOENWALD, S. K., and HANLEY, J. H. (1993), 'Family Preservation using Multisystemic Treatment: Long-Term Follow-Up to a clinical Trial with Serious Juvenile Offenders', *Journal of Child and Family Studies*, 2: 283–93.

—— ROWLAND, M. D., RANDALL, J., WARD, D. M., PICKREL, S. G., CUNNINGHAM, P. B., MILLER, S. L., EDWARDS, J., ZEALBERG, J. J., HAND, L. D., and SANTOS, A. B. (1999), 'Home-based multisystemic therapy as an alternative to the hospitalization of youths in psychiatric crisis: Clinical outcomes', *Journal of the American Academy of Child and Adolescent Psychiatry*, 38: 1331–9.

——, SCHOENWALD, S. K., BORDUIN, C. M., ROWLAND, M. D. and CUNNINGHAM., P. B. (1998), *Multisystemic Treatment of Antisocial Behaviour in Children and Adolescents*, New York: Guilford.

HENRY, B., CASPI, A., MOFFITT, T. E., and SILVA, P. A. (1996), 'Temperamental and familial predictors of violent and non-violent criminal convictions: Age 3 to age 18', *Developmental Psychology*, 32: 614–23.

——, MOFFITT, T. E., ROBINS, L. N., EARLS, F. E. and SILVA, P. A. (1993), 'Early family predictors of child and adolescent antisocial behavior: Who are the mothers of delinquents?', *Criminal Behaviour and Mental Health*, 3: 97–118.

HOPE, T. (1995), 'Community crime prevention', in M. Tonry and D. P. Farrington (eds), *Building a Safer Society: Strategic Approaches to Crime Prevention*, 21–89, Chicago: University of Chicago Press.

HUESMANN, L. R., and ERON, L. D. (1984), 'Individual differences and the trait of aggression', *European Journal of Personality*, 3: 95–106.

JEFFORD, T., and SQUIRE, B. (2004), 'Multi-Systemic Therapy: Model practice', *Young Minds*, 71: 20–1.

JOLLIFFE, D., and FARRINGTON, D. P. (2004), 'Empathy and offending: A systematic review and meta-analysis', *Aggression and Violent Behaviour*, 9: 441–76.

—— and FARRINGTON, D. P. (2006), 'Development and validation of the Basic Empathy Scale', *Journal of Adolescence*, 29, 589–611.

—— and —— (2007), 'Examining the relationship between low empathy and self-reported offending', *Legal and Criminological Psychology*, in the press.

JUBY, H., and FARRINGTON, D. P. (2001), 'Disentangling the link between disrupted families and delinquency', *British Journal of Criminology*, 41: 22–40.

KAUKIAINEN, A., BJORKVIST, K., LAGERSPETZ, K., OSTERMAN, K., SALMIVALLI, C., ROTHBERG, S., and AHLBOM, A. (1999), 'The relationships between social intelligence, empathy, and three types of aggression', *Aggressive Behaviour*, 25: 81–9.

KAZDIN, A. E., KRAEMER, H. C., KESSLER, R. C., KUPFER, D. J., and OFFORD, D. R. (1997), 'Contributions of risk-factor research to developmental psychopathology', *Clinical Psychology Review*, 17: 375–406.

KLINTEBERG, B. A., ANDERSSON, T., MAGNUSSON, D., and STATTIN, H. (1993), 'Hyperactive behaviour in childhood as related to subsequent alcohol problems and violent offending: A longitudinal study of male subjects', *Personality and Individual Differences*, 15: 381–8.

KOLVIN, I., MILLER, F. J. W., FLEETING, M., and KOLVIN, P. A. (1988), 'Social and parenting factors affecting criminal-offence rates: Findings from the Newcastle Thousand Family Study (1947–1980)', *British Journal of Psychiatry*, 152: 80–90.

——, ——, SCOTT, D. M., GATZANIS, S. R. M., and FLEETING, M. (1990), *Continuities of Deprivation? The Newcastle 1000 Family Study*, Aldershot: Avebury.

KRAEMER, H. C., KAZDIN, A. E., OFFORD, D. R., KESSLER, R. C., JENSEN P. S., and KUPFER, D. J. (1997), 'Coming to terms with the terms of risk', *Archives of General Psychiatry*, 54: 337–43.

LACOURSE, E., COTE, S., NAGIN, D. S., VITARO, F., BRENDGEN, M., and TREMBLAY, R. E. (2002), 'A longitudinal-experimental approach to testing theories of antisocial behaviour development', *Development and Psychopathology*, 14: 909–24.

LEBLANC, M., and LOEBER, R. (1998), 'Developmental criminology updated', in M. Tonry (ed.), *Crime and Justice*, 23: 115–98, Chicago: University of Chicago press.

LESCHIED, A. and CUNNINGHAM, A. (2002), '*Seeking Effective Interventions for Serious Young Offenders: Interim Results of a Four-Year Randomized Study of Multisystemic Therapy in Ontario, Canada*', London, Canada: London Family Court Clinic.

LEWIS, C., NEWSON, E., and NEWSON, J. (1982), 'Father participation through childhood and its relationship with career aspirations and delinquency', in N. Beail and J. McGuire (eds), *Fathers: Psychological Perspectives*, 174–93, London: Junction.

LIPSEY, M. W., and DERZON, J. H. (1998), 'Predictors of violent or serious delinquency in adolescence and early adulthood: A synthesis of longitudinal research', in R. Loeber and D. P. Farrington (eds), *Serious and Violent Juvenile Offenders: Risk Factors and Successful Interventions*, 86–105, Thousand Oaks, Cal.: Sage.

——and Wilson, D. B. (1998), 'Effective intervention for serious juvenile offenders: A synthesis of research', in R. Loeber and D. P. Farrington (eds), *Serious and Violent Juvenile Offenders: Risk Factors and Successful Interventions*, 313–45, Thousand Oaks, Cal.: Sage.

Lipsitt, P. D., Buka, S. L., and Lipsitt, L. P. (1990), 'Early intelligence scores and subsequent delinquency: A prospective study', *American Journal of Family Therapy*, 18: 197–208.

Littell, J. H. (2005), 'Lessons from a systematic review of effects of multisystemic therapy', *Children and Youth Services Review*, 27: 445–63.

Loeber, R., and Farrington, D. P. (eds) (1998), *Serious and Violent Juvenile Offenders: Risk Factors and Successful Interventions*, Thousand Oaks, Cal.: Sage.

——and ——(eds) (2001), *Child Delinquents: Development, Intervention and Service Needs*, Thousand Oaks, Cal.: Sage.

——, and LeBlanc, M. (1990), 'Toward a developmental criminology', in M. Tonry and N. Morris (eds), *Crime and Justice*, 12: 375–473, Chicago: University of Chicago Press.

——, Farrington, D. P., Stouthamer-Loeber, M., Moffitt, T. E., Caspi, A., White, H. R., Wei, E., and Beyers, J. M. (2003), 'The development of male offending: Key findings from 14 years of the Pittsburgh Youth Study', in T. P. Thornberry and M. D. Krohn (eds), *Taking Stock of Delinquency: An Overview of Findings from Contemporary Longitudinal Studies*, 93–136, New York: Kluwer/Plenum.

——, Wung, P., Keenan, K., Giroux, B., Stouthamer-Loeber, M., van Kammen, W. B., and Maughan, B. (1993), 'Developmental pathways in disruptive child behaviour', *Development and Psychopathology*, 5: 101–31.

Lösel, F., and Beelmann, A. (2006), 'Child social skills training', in B. C. Welsh and D. P. Farrington (eds), *Preventing Crime: What Works for Children, Offenders, Victims, and Places*, 33–54, Dordrecht, Netherlands: Springer.

Luengo, M. A., Otero, J. M., Carrillo-de-la-Pena, M. T., and Miron, L. (1994), 'Dimensions of antisocial behaviour in juvenile delinquency: A study of

personality variables', *Psychology, Crime and Law*, 1: 27–37.

Lynam, D. (1996), 'Early identification of chronic offenders: Who is the fledgling psychopath?', *Psychological Bulletin*, 120: 209–34.

——, Moffitt, T. E., and Stouthamer-Loeber, M. (1993), 'Explaining the relation between IQ and delinquency: Class, race, test motivation, school failure or self-control?', *Journal of Abnormal Psychology*, 102: 187–96.

McCord, J. (1977), 'A comparative study of two generations of native Americans', in R. F. Meier (ed.), *Theory in Criminology*, 83–92, Beverly Hills, Cal.: Sage.

——(1979), 'Some child-rearing antecedents of criminal behaviour in adult men', *Journal of Personality and Social Psychology*, 37: 1477–86.

——(1982), 'A longitudinal view of the relationship between paternal absence and crime', in J. Gunn and D. P. Farrington (eds), *Abnormal Offenders, Delinquency, and the Criminal Justice System*, 113–28, Chichester: Wiley.

——(1983), 'A forty year perspective on effects of child abuse and neglect', *Child Abuse and Neglect*, 7: 265–70.

——(1997), 'On discipline', *Psychological Inquiry*, 8: 215–17.

McGuire, J. (2001), 'What works in correctional intervention? Evidence and practical implications', in G. A. Bernfeld, D. P. Farrington, and A. W. Leschied (eds), *Offender Rehabilitation in Practice: Implementing and Evaluating Effective Programmes*, 25–43, Chichester: Wiley.

Mak, A. S. (1991), 'Psychosocial control characteristics of delinquents and non-delinquents', *Criminal Justice and Behaviour*, 18: 287–303.

Malinosky-Rummell, R., and Hansen, D. J. (1993), 'Long-term consequences of childhood physical abuse', *Psychological Bulletin*, 114: 68–79.

Maxfield, M. G., and Widom, C. S. (1996), 'The cycle of violence revisited 6 years later', *Archives of Pediatrics and Adolescent Medicine*, 150: 390–95.

Mednick, B. R., Baker, R. L., and Carothers, L. E. (1990), 'Patterns of family instability and crime: The association of timing of the family's disruption with subsequent adolescent and young adult criminality', *Journal of Youth and Adolescence*, 19: 201–20.

Moffitt, T. E. (1993), 'Adolescence-limited and life-course-persistent antisocial behaviour: A developmental taxonomy', *Psychological Review*, 100: 674–701.

——, CASPI, A., RUTTER, M., and SILVA, P. A. (2001), *Sex Differences in Antisocial Behaviour*, Cambridge: Cambridge University Press.

MORASH, M., and RUCKER, L. (1989), 'An exploratory study of the connection of mother's age at child-bearing to her children's delinquency in four data sets', *Crime and Delinquency*, 35: 45–93.

MORGAN, A. B., and LILIENFELD, S. O. (2000), 'A meta-analytic review of the relation between antisocial behaviour and neuropsychological measures of executive function', *Clinical Psychology Review*, 20: 113–36.

NAGIN, D. S., FARRINGTON, D. P., and MOFFITT, T. E. (1995), 'Life-course trajectories of different types of offenders', *Criminology*, 33, 111–39.

NAGIN, D. S., POGARSKY, G., and FARRINGTON, D. P. (1997), 'Adolescent mothers and the criminal behaviour of their children', *Law and Society Review*, 31: 137–62.

NAJAKA, S. S., GOTTFREDSON, D. C., and WILSON, D. B. (2001), 'A meta-analytic inquiry into the relationship between selected risk factors and problem behaviour', *Prevention Science*, 2: 257–71.

NEWSON, J., and NEWSON, E. (1989), *The Extent of Parental Physical Punishment in the UK*, London: Approach.

——, —— and ADAMS, M. (1993), 'The social origins of delinquency', *Criminal Behaviour and Mental Health*, 3, 19–29.

O'CONNOR, T. G., HERON, J., GOLDING, J., BEVERIDGE, M., and GLOVER, V. (2002), 'Maternal antenatal anxiety and children's behavioural/emotional problems at 4 years', *British Journal of Psychiatry*, 180: 502–8.

O'DONNELL, J., HAWKINS, J. D., CATALANO, R. F., ABBOTT, R. D., and DAY, L. E. (1995), 'Preventing school failure, drug use, and delinquency among low-income children: Long-term intervention in elementary schools', *American Journal of Orthopsychiatry*, 65: 87–100.

OLDS, D. L., ECKENRODE, J., HENDERSON, C. R., KITZMAN, H., POWERS, J., COLE, R., SIDORA, K., MORRIS, P., PETTITT, L. M., and LUCKEY, D. (1997), 'Long-term effects of home visitation on maternal life course and child abuse and neglect: Fifteen-year follow-up of a randomized trial', *Journal of the American Medical Association*, 278: 637–43.

——, HENDERSON, C. R., CHAMBERLIN, R., and TATELBAUM, R. (1986), 'Preventing child abuse and neglect: A randomized trial of nurse home visitation', *Pediatrics*, 78: 65–78.

——, ——, COLE, R., ECKENRODE, J., KITZMAN, H., LUCKEY, D., PETTITT, L., SIDORA, K., MORRIS, P., and POWERS, J. (1998), 'Long-term effects of nurse home visitation on children's criminal and antisocial behaviour: 15-year follow-up of a randomized controlled trial', *Journal of the American Medical Association*, 280: 1238–44.

——, KITZMAN, H., COLE, R., ROBINSON, J., SIDORA, K., LUCKEY, D. W., HENDERSON, C. R., HANKS, C., BONDY, J., and HOLMBERG, J. (2004a), 'Effects of nurse home-visiting on maternal life course and child development: Age 6 follow-up results of a randomized trial', *Pediatrics*, 114: 1550–9.

——, ROBINSON, J., PETTITT, L. M., LUCKEY, D. W., HOLMBERG, J., NG, R. K., ISACKS, K., SHEFF, K. L., and HENDERSON, C. R. (2004b), 'Effects of home visits by paraprofessionals and by nurses: Age 4 follow-up results of a randomized trial', *Pediatrics*, 114: 1560–8.

OUSTON, J. (1984), 'Delinquency, family background, and educational attainment', *British Journal of Criminology*, 24: 2–26.

PATTERSON, G. R. (1982), *Coercive Family Process*, Eugene, Oreg.: Castalia.

—— (1995), 'Coercion as a basis for early age of onset for arrest', in J. McCord (ed.), *Coercion and Punishment in Long-Term Perspectives*, 81–105, Cambridge: Cambridge University Press.

——, CHAMBERLAIN, P., and REID, J. B. (1982), 'A comparative evaluation of a parent training programme', *Behavior Therapy*, 13: 638–50.

——, REID, J. B., and DISHION, T. J. (1992), *Antisocial Boys*, Eugene, Oreg.: Castalia.

PIQUERO, A. R., FARRINGTON, D. P., and BLUMSTEIN, A. (2003), 'The criminal career paradigm', in M. Tonry (ed.), *Crime and Justice*, 30: 359–506, Chicago: University of Chicago Press.

——, ——, and —— (2007), *Key Issues in Criminal Career Research: New Analyses of the Cambridge Study in Delinquent Development*, Cambridge: Cambridge University Press.

PRATT, T. C., CULLEN, F. T., BLEVINS, K. R., DAIGLE, L., and UNNEVER, J. D. (2002), 'The relationship of attention deficit hyperactivity disorder to crime and delinquency: A meta-analysis', *International Journal of Police Science and Management*, 4: 344–60.

PULKKINEN, L. (1988), 'Delinquent development: Theoretical and empirical considerations', in M. Rutter (ed.), *Studies of Psychosocial Risk: The*

Power of Longitudinal Data,184–99, Cambridge: Cambridge University Press.

RAINE, A. (1993), *The Psychopathology of Crime: Criminal Behaviour as a Clinical Disorder* , San Diego, Cal.: Academic Press.

——, MOFFITT, T. E., CASPI, A., LOEBER, R., STOUTHAMER-LOEBER, M., and LYNAM, D. (2005), 'Neurocognitive impairments in boys on the life-course persistent antisocial path', *Journal of Abnormal Psychology*, 114: 38–49.

RAYNOR, P., and VANSTONE, M. (2001), ' "Straight thinking on Probation": Evidence-based practice and the culture of curiosity', in G. A. Bernfeld, D. P. Farrington, and A. W. Leschied (eds), *Offender Rehabilitation in Practice: Implementing and Evaluating Effective Programmes*, 189–203 Chichester: Wiley.

REISS, A. J., and FARRINGTON, D. P. (1991), 'Advancing knowledge about co-offending: Results from a prospective longitudinal survey of London males', *Journal of Criminal Law and Criminology*, 82: 360–95.

REYNOLDS, A. J., TEMPLE, J. A., ROBERTSON, D. L., and MANN, E. A. (2001), 'Long-term effects of an early childhood intervention on educational achievement and juvenile arrest: A 15-year follow-up of low-income children in public schools', *Journal of the American Medical Association*, 285: 2339–46.

ROBINS, L. N. (1979), 'Sturdy childhood predictors of adult outcomes: Replications from longitudinal studies', in J. E. Barrett, R. M. Rose, and G. L. Klerman (eds), *Stress and Mental Disorder*, 219–35, New York: Raven Press.

—— (1992), 'The role of prevention experiments in discovering causes of children's antisocial behaviour', in J. McCord and R. E. Tremblay (eds), *Preventing Antisocial Behaviour: Interventions from Birth through Adolescence*, 3–18, New York: Guilford.

ROSS, R. R., and ROSS, B. D. (1988), 'Delinquency prevention through cognitive training', *New Education*, 10: 70–5.

—— and —— (eds) (1995), *Thinking Straight: The Reasoning and Rehabilitation Programme for Delinquency Prevention and Offender Rehabilitation*, Ottawa: Air Training and Publications.

RUTTER, M., GILLER, H., and HAGELL, A. (1998), *Antisocial Behaviour by Young People*, Cambridge: Cambridge University Press.

——, TIZARD, J., and WHITMORE, K. (1970), *Education, Health and Behaviour*, London: University of London Press.

SANDERS, M. R., MARKIE-DADDS, C., TULLY, L. A., and BOR, W. (2000), 'The Triple-P Positive Parenting Programme: A comparison of enhanced, standard and self-directed behavioural family intervention for parents of children with early onset conduct problems', *Journal of Consulting and Clinical Psychology*, 68: 624–40.

SANSFAÇON, D., and WALLER. I. (2001), 'Recent evolution of governmental crime prevention strategies and implications for evaluation and economic analysis', in B. C. Welsh, D. P. Farrington, and L. W. Sherman (eds), *Costs and Benefits of Preventing Crime*, 225–47, Boulder, Col.: Westview Press.

SCHWEINHART, L. J., and WEIKART, D. P. (1980), *Young Children Grow Up: The Effects of the Perry Preschool Programme on Youths Through Age 15*, Ypsilanti, Mich.: High/Scope Press.

——, BARNES, H. V., and WEIKART, D. P. (1993), *Significant Benefits: The High/Scope Perry Preschool Study Through Age 27*, Ypsilanti, Mich.: High/Scope Press.

——, MONTIE, J., ZONGPING, X., BARNETT, W. S., BELFIELD, C. R., and NORES, M. (2005), *Lifetime Effects: The High/Scope Perry Preschool Study Through Age 40*, Ypsilanti, Mich.: High/Scope Press.

SCOTT, S., SPENDER, Q., DOOLAN, M., JACOBS, B., and ASPLAND, H. (2001), 'Multicentre controlled trial of parenting groups for child antisocial behaviour in clinical practice', *British Medical Journal*, 323: 194–6.

SEGUIN, J., PIHL, R. O., HARDEN, P. W., TREMBLAY, R. E., and BOULERICE, B. (1995), 'Cognitive and neuropsychological characteristics of physically aggressive boys', *Journal of Abnormal Psychology*, 104: 614–24.

SHERMAN, L. W., FARRINGTON, D. P., WELSH, B. C., and MACKENZIE D. L. (eds) (2006), *Evidence-Based Crime Prevention* (rev. edn), London: Routledge.

SMITH, C. A., and STERN, S. B. (1997), 'Delinquency and antisocial behaviour: A review of family processes and intervention research', *Social Service Review*, 71: 382–420.

——, and THORNBERRY, T. P. (1995), 'The relationship between childhood maltreatment and adolescent involvement in delinquency', *Criminology*, 33: 451–81.

STATTIN, H., and KLACKENBERG-LARSSON, I. (1993), 'Early language and intelligence development and their relationship to future criminal behaviour', *Journal of Abnormal Psychology*, 102: 369–78.

SUTTON, C., UTTING, D., and FARRINGTON, D. P. (eds) (2004), *Support from the Start: Working with*

Young Children and their Families to Reduce the Risks of Crime and Antisocial Behaviour, London: Department for Education and Skills (Research Report 524).

THORNBERRY, T. P., and KROHN, M. D. (eds) (2003), *Taking Stock of Delinquency: An Overview of Findings from Contemporary Longitudinal Studies*, New York: Kluwer/Plenum.

TONG, L. S. J., and FARRINGTON, D. P. (2006), 'How effective is the Reasoning and Rehabilitation programme in reducing offending? A meta-analysis of evaluations in four countries', *Psychology, Crime and Law*, 12: 3–24.

TONRY, M., and FARRINGTON, D. P. (1995), 'Strategic approaches to crime prevention', in M. Tonry and D. P. Farrington (eds), *Building a Safer Society: Strategic Approaches to Crime Prevention*, 1–20, Chicago: University of Chicago Press.

TREMBLAY, R. E., and CRAIG, W. M. (1995), 'Developmental crime prevention', in M. Tonry and D. P. Farrington (eds), *Building a Safer Society: Strategic Approaches to Crime Prevention*, 151–236, Chicago: University of Chicago Press.

——, MÂSSE, L. C., PAGANI, L., and VITARO, F. (1996), 'From childhood physical aggression to adolescent maladjustment: The Montreal prevention experiment', in R. D. Peters and R. J. McMahon (eds), *Preventing Childhood Disorders, Substance Use, and Delinquency*, 268–98, Thousand Oaks, Cal.: Sage.

——, PAGANI-KURTZ, L., MASSE, L. C., VITARO, F., and PIHL, R. O. (1995), 'A bimodal preventive intervention for disruptive kindergarten boys: Its impact through mid-adolescence', *Journal of Consulting and Clinical Psychology*, 63: 560–8.

UTTING, D. (ed.) (1999), *A Guide to Promising Approaches*, London: Communities that Care.

VAZSONYI, A. T., PICKERING, L. E., JUNGER, M., and HESSING, D. (2001), 'An empirical test of a general theory of crime: A four-nation comparative study of self-control and the prediction of deviance', *Journal of Research in Crime and Delinquency*, 38: 91–131.

VITARO, F., BRENDGEN, M., and TREMBLAY, R. E. (2001), 'Preventive intervention: Assessing its effects on the trajectories of delinquency and testing for mediational processes', *Applied Developmental Science*, 5: 201–13.

WADSWORTH, M. E. J. (1979), *Roots of Delinquency: Infancy, Adolescence and Crime*, London: Martin Robertson.

WASSERMAN, G. A., and MILLER, L. S. (1998), 'The prevention of serious and violent juvenile offending', in R. Loeber and D. P. Farrington (eds), *Serious and Violent Juvenile Offenders: Risk Factors and Successful Interventions*, 197–247, Thousand Oaks, Cal.: Sage.

WEBSTER-STRATTON, C. (2000), *The Incredible Years Training Series*, Washington, DC: Office of Juvenile Justice and Delinquency Prevention.

WELLS, L. E., and RANKIN, J. H. (1991), 'Families and delinquency: A meta-analysis of the impact of broken homes', *Social Problems*, 38: 71–93.

WELSH, B. C., and FARRINGTON, D. P. (eds) (2006), *Preventing Crime: What Works for Children, Offenders, Victims and Places*, Dordrecht: Springer.

——, ——, and SHERMAN, L. W. (eds) (2001), *Costs and Benefits of Preventing Crime*, Boulder, Col.: Westview Press.

WEST, D. J., and FARRINGTON, D. P. (1973), *Who Becomes Delinquent?*, London: Heinemann.

—— and —— (1977), *The Delinquent Way of Life*, London: Heinemann.

WHITE, J. L., MOFFITT, T. E., CASPI, A., BARTUSCH, D. J., NEEDLES, D. J., and STOUTHAMER-LOEBER, M. (1994), 'Measuring impulsivity and examining its relationship to delinquency', *Journal of Abnormal Psychology*, 103: 192–205.

WIDOM, C. S. (1989), 'The cycle of violence', *Science*, 244: 160–6.

—— and AMES, M. A. (1994), 'Criminal consequences of childhood sexual victimization', *Child Abuse and Neglect*, 18: 303–18.

WIKSTRÖM, P.-O. H., and LOEBER, R. (2000), 'Do disadvantaged neighbourhoods cause well-adjusted children to become adolescent delinquents? A study of male juvenile serious offending, individual risk and protective factors, and neighbourhood context', *Criminology*, 38: 1109–42.

——, CLARKE, R. V., and McCORD, J. (eds) (1995), *Integrating Crime Prevention Strategies: Propensity and Opportunity*, Stockholm: National Council for Crime Prevention.

20

CRIME AND THE LIFE COURSE

David J. Smith

Crime is mostly committed by young people—by adolescents and adults in their twenties. Criminal offending, therefore, is closely linked to the life course. It is one of a number of psychosocial disorders that are characteristic of youth, in the sense that they rise in prevalence or frequency, or reach a peak, in adolescence or early adulthood. Other examples are problem drinking, use of illegal drugs, depression (especially in females), suicide (especially in males), and eating disorders (Rutter and Smith 1995; Smith and Rutter 1995).

Statements about the relationship between age and crime are usually based on a simple count of offences, without taking account of their monetary or symbolic value. It is possible to argue that crimes of the powerful, usually committed by older men, are far more important than their showing in conventional crime statistics. Nevertheless, there is a large body of 'ordinary' crime, some of it serious, some relatively trivial, which undeniably has a major impact on victims, and which indirectly structures people's lives: this is mostly committed by young men.

Any theory of criminal offending should explain how it fits with the course of individual development from infancy to old age, because the relationship between age and offending is so striking. Gottfredson and Hirschi (1990) argued that it is enough to state that there exists an invariant relationship between age and offending. Their argument is unconvincing for several reasons. First of all, the relationship is not invariant: for example, the peak age of offending varies considerably according to the type of offence (Farrington 1986: 199). More important, to state that age 'causes' crime is empty. Gottfredson and Hirschi quoted the analogy of Boyle's Law, which expresses the relationship between the temperature, volume, and pressure of a gas, yet this analogy self-destructs, because Boyle's Law describes a regularity, but does not provide a deeper explanation of the underlying physical processes. Such an explanation was provided later by molecular physics, which interprets heat, temperature, and pressure in terms of the movement of particles in a container. An equally important point is that age is not a personal characteristic, but an index of the likely stage that someone has reached in a partly predictable sequence of development, and an indicator of social standing. As Rutter (1989) has argued, the explanation for 'age effects' must therefore lie in the detailed process of development, and in associated social meanings and social roles. For example, there is a fundamental difference between behavioural change arising from maturation (e.g. puberty) and from experience.

The evolution of offending over the life course is a story of both continuity and change. On the one hand, there is considerable stability in the differences between individuals at succeeding stages of the life cycle: the most disruptive child is likely to become the most serious and persistent adult offender. On the other hand, the likelihood of offending, and the forms that antisocial behaviour takes, change radically with advancing years, and these striking changes are reflected in the age/crime curve. The predictability and persistence of offending in the same individuals over the years need to be explained. Because criminal behaviour appears to be dysfunctional for most people, explaining why they persist in it poses a challenge. Possible explanations span constitutional factors, personality, cognitive processes, social interactions, victimization-offending loops, labelling and stigmatization, and constraints imposed by social structure. Equally, the dramatic change in offending over the life course needs to be explained, and it is remarkable that most classic criminological theories have not even tried to explain it. Possible realms of explanation are changing social responses to misbehaviour in people of different ages, changing social bonds and peer influence, changing social roles, activities, and associated opportunities for offending, and changing cultural definitions.

Stability and change over the life course are two of the organizing concepts of this chapter, but before analysing continuity or change in offending, it is necessary to consider whether criminal behaviour is so diverse that generalizations are not possible. After a section reviewing methodological problems in collecting information about offending over the life course, the first main section therefore considers the extent of specialization in offending, and the strength of the evidence that different criminal behaviours are closely linked. The following section analyses the *extent* of stability in offending over the life course, and the extent of change. The next two sections are concerned with *explaining* stability and change . The first of these examines how features of the social environment as well as the make-up of the individual can keep the course of life to a well-defined path. The second focuses on explaining why people sooner or later stop offending. The conclusion argues that a number of central problems in criminology, such as the explanation for the contrast in offending between males and females, and the influence of the penal system on offending, can only be tackled by further research adopting a life course perspective.

PROBLEMS OF METHOD

The two main sources of information used on offending over the life course are official statistics (usually convictions, occasionally arrests or police contacts) and self-reports (information that people give about their own offending in personal interviews or self-completion questionnaires). Official records have a special importance because an offence officially recorded against someone's name has a legal, social, and symbolic significance that sets it apart from an offence that was not known to the authorities. Their severe limitation is that they cover only a small fraction of criminal incidents, because only a minority of offences are reported to the police and recorded by them, and only a minority of recorded offences lead to an arrest or charge. Statistics for England and Wales in 1997 show that cases where action was successfully taken against an offender (cautions and convictions) accounted for only 2.97 per cent of offences (estimated from victims' reports in the British Crime Survey) (Barclay and Tavares 1999). Also, official statistics are distorted, because these rates of attrition vary widely between types of offence. From the early 1960s onwards, a huge number of studies have been carried out using self-report methods, and these provide a much more complete account of offending. The criticism that people will generally not admit to having committed offences in a confidential survey has long been disproved: self-report studies reveal far more offences, including serious ones, than are shown in official records (Huizinga 1991; Elliott 1994). A considerable number of studies have tested the validity of self-reports against the criterion of official records, a 'bootstrapping' method of validation, since self-reports aim to improve on official records. These studies generally show a significant correlation between self-reports and official records (e.g. Farrington 1973) but the correlation cannot be high, since self-reported offending is so much more common than official offending, and the complex, partly probabilistic processes of the criminal justice system mediate between the two. A particularly thorough study of this kind was carried out by Dunford and Elliott (1984) using five annual sweeps of data from the US National Youth Survey (the subjects were aged 11–17 at the first sweep, and 16–22 at the fifth). First, youths were divided into four groups reflecting the level and seriousness of their self-reported delinquency in a given year. Then they were further classified into four groups reflecting the delinquency types they belonged to over the sequence of years: for example, serious career offenders were defined as those who had committed at least three of the more serious[1] offences in two or more consecutive years. The same youths were then classified into comparable groups using official arrest data. The results showed that the proportion who had been arrested in the first three years of the study varied regularly across the four groups, from 1.9 per cent among self-reported non-offenders to 24.3 per cent among self-reported serious career offenders. All the officially defined career offenders (serious and non-serious) were also identified as career offenders from self-reports. However, only 14 per cent of the self-reported career offenders had a record of arrest, and among these only 2 per cent were identified as career offenders from their arrest records. This both supports the validity of the self-report measures, and shows that they reveal far more offending and offenders than the arrest records.

As Bowling (1990) has pointed out, a limitation of this form of validation is that the self-reports of those without an official record remain untested, and this is a major

---

[1] UCR (Uniform Crime Report) Part 1 offences were the ones regarded as more serious for this purpose.

weakness because a high proportion of self-reported offenders have no official record. The point was earlier addressed by Farrington (1973), who showed that among youths with no official record, self-reported offending was a good *predictor* of whether they would acquire an official record in future. This finding also demonstrates that the correlation between self-reports and official records does *not* arise merely because those without a record are more likely to conceal their offending in answers to survey questions.

The studies mentioned above compared official records and self-reports for the same individuals, but did not try to match particular acts (e.g. the burglary at 12 Beechgrove Crescent on 3 June). Where this has been done, studies have found that offences known to the police are self-reported in 80 to 90 per cent of cases (Huizinga 1991: 60). However, the important finding from this back-check method is that there may be systematic differences between ethnic groups. Huizinga and Elliott (1986) in a US study found that white males reported 84 per cent of their officially recorded offences, whereas African American males reported 61 per cent of theirs. Junger (1989) in a Dutch study also found a difference between ethnic groups in level of disclosure, and found a much lower level of disclosure than the American studies. In his review, Huizinga (1991) quotes several other US studies that found a higher level of under-reporting among African American males than other groups, and also several that found more under-reporting among males than females.

In broad terms, these findings suggest that the self-report method is the best available for collecting information about criminal offending in the life course. Like other research instruments, it has important defects and limitations, but these are offset in the best studies by combining official records and self-reports, and by collecting information from various informants (parents, teachers, peers) as well as the individual included in the study. The findings on differential disclosure among males and females, and among different ethnic groups, show that self-reports introduce some systematic bias. However, the systematic biases in official records are probably at least as serious.

A different challenge for researchers is obtaining samples that adequately represent serious and persistent offenders, who account for a high proportion of offences, but a small proportion of the population. The problem is that serious and persistent offenders are likely to lead unconventional, unstable lives, and are therefore unlikely, for a variety of reasons, to be included in conventional data collection exercises. For example, they may be absent from school when a questionnaire is administered, they may escape selection in a random sample because they often move house or have no fixed abode, they may be in prison when the interviewer calls, and they may often refuse to be interviewed. Some classic studies of offending in the life course have used a sample of institutionalized youths in order to ensure that heavy-end offenders are properly studied: the best example is the Gluecks' study in Boston (Glueck and Glueck 1950: Sampson and Laub 1993). Most have simply over-sampled neighbourhoods with high levels of social and economic stress: for example, the Cambridge Study in Delinquent Development (Farrington and West 1990), or the Pittsburgh Youth Study (Loeber *et al.* 1998).

A study by Cernkovich *et al.* (1985) compared two groups: a sample designed to be representative of all young people aged 12 to 19 in a US metropolitan area; and a sample of the populations of three male juvenile institutions within the same state, together with the entire population of the only female juvenile institution in the state. The same self-reported delinquency questions, based on the US National Youth Survey, were applied to both samples. The group defined as 'high frequency major offenders' accounted for 13.6 per cent of neighbourhood youths, but 80 per cent of the institutional sample. When comparisons were confined to this group of chronic offenders, they were found to be far more delinquent among the institutional than among the neighbourhood sample. For example, 41 per cent of the institutional chronic offenders reported breaking and entering more than once a month, compared with none of the neighbourhood chronic offenders at that frequency. The study is far from conclusive, because the sampling method used for the neighbourhood survey may well have been inadequate.[2] Nevertheless it points to a fundamental problem which has not been fully addressed even by the most elaborate recent studies. The problem is even more challenging for the small number of studies that cover mature adults than for the much larger number that concentrate on adolescents.

The method favoured by most contemporary researchers is the prospective longitudinal study. In the best examples, information is obtained regularly (say, once a year) about a cohort of young people from a number of informants (the cohort members, their parents, teachers, and friends) and records (school records, police, and criminal records). The advantage of this approach is that information is obtained soon after the event, so that sequences in time can be used to establish the priority of cause versus effect. Also, to the extent that many individual characteristics and circumstances remain stable, those few that have changed can be identified as the likely cause of a change in behaviour; or in other words, as longitudinal researchers often put it, individuals act as their own controls. However, these advantages are not as decisive as they seem at first. Supposing that the interval between sweeps of data collection is 12 months, an enormous sequence of interactions will have taken place over that period, for example, between a 16-year-old girl and her friends. It will be wholly impossible to establish which came first: the girl's delinquency, or her friends' delinquency. This is because a so-called prospective longitudinal study is actually a series of retrospective surveys, and the period of retrospection is enormously long in relation to the complexity of social interactions in people's lives. It turns out, therefore, that even in longitudinal studies, evidence supporting or contradicting causal explanations is usually indirect, and seldom wholly conclusive.

[2] Sampling methods are not fully reported, but it seems that a quota sampling method was used at the final stage. This would have allowed interviewers to carry out interviews with those who were easiest to find. No response rates are quoted, and there is no information about the number of recalls made by interviewers, which suggests that a quota sampling method was used.

THE EXTENT OF SPECIALIZATION IN OFFENDING

Criminal offending covers a wide diversity of actions: some serious, others trivial; some direct, overt, symbolically transgressive, others covert, deceptive, avoiding open conflict; some violently aggressive, others (the majority) non-violent; some involving special knowledge or complex techniques (safe-blowing, embezzlement, computer fraud), others simple (hand-bag snatching, wife-battering); some involving unusual or abnormal impulses (paedophilia), others (the majority) springing from universal frustrations and needs. A decision to generalize about such a wide variety of behaviours reflects the theoretical position that despite surface differences, there are fundamental similarities beneath. In fact, nearly all research in the developmental tradition takes the generalization further, by treating antisocial behaviour in children as essentially similar to offending in adults. This approach is underpinned by the assumption that the law and a common moral fabric provide a unifying framework. Diverse forms of criminal, antisocial, even unconventional behaviour have in common that they are all infractions of the law, a moral code, or social conventions and expectations. This could mean that these varied forms of behaviour have some common origins. For example, Gottfredson and Hirschi (1990) and Hirschi and Gottfredson (1994) have argued that 'the generality of deviance' encompasses not only criminal offending, but also road accidents, which are similarly related to age, and that the common origin is a lack of self-control. Alternatively, it is possible to argue that a wide range of deviant behaviour springs from aggression, even though aggression is often not manifest in the act: a burglar who breaks into an empty house must be prepared to confront the owner if necessary, and there is often an edge of aggression in the behaviour of a child who refuses to eat his supper.

Although the idea of the generality of deviance is certainly a theoretical position, there is also a considerable weight of evidence to show that offenders are predominantly versatile rather than specialized. Yet there is some degree of specialization, and a key question is whether this tends to increase as the criminal career lengthens.

An important early contribution was Wolfgang and colleagues' pioneering study of a cohort of Philadelphia boys (Wolfgang *et al.* 1972: the findings on specialization are summarized in Farrington *et al.* 1988). They classified offences into five broad types, then constructed 'transition matrices' showing for example the probability that a boy who had committed an injury offence at the first arrest would commit another injury offence at the next arrest. The general pattern clearly showed more versatility than specialization: for example, the probability that the next arrest would be for a minor ('non-index') offence was over .5 regardless of the current offence. There was, however, some specialization superimposed on this versatility: for example, the probability that the next arrest would be for theft was .271 where the current arrest was for theft, but only .128 where the current arrest was for causing injury. A number of further studies in the 1980s produced essentially similar conclusions. The study by Farrington *et al.* (1988) used a different statistic (the 'forward specialization coefficient') to trace the linkages between one offence and the next known offence committed by the same person. Using a database of nearly 70,000 juvenile offenders in Utah and in Maricopa County, Arizona, the study found a small degree of specialization overall, but there were notable variations according to the offence: for example, specialization was relatively high for burglary and motor vehicle theft, and relatively low for trespassing, weapons, and vandalism.

The two major studies mentioned above were of juveniles. A study of a large Danish cohort of 28,884 men aged 27 to 30 demonstrated a modest degree of specialization in violent offending (Brennan *et al.* 1989). The main conclusion (that there is far more versatility than specialization) was confirmed for adults in a study by Stander *et al.* (1989). This time the database was a 10 per cent sample survey of adult males (aged 21 and above) under sentence in 21 prisons in the south-east of England in 1972 (N = 811). Offences were classified into just six categories (violence, sex, burglary, theft, fraud, other). The transition matrices for this adult sample showed a greater degree of specialization than for the juvenile samples discussed above, but there was still much more versatility than specialization. The analysis also showed that specialization could best be described by identifying a sequence of at least three convictions, and not just considering the links between one conviction and the next. Forward specialization coefficients (calculated as described in Farrington *et al.* 1988) were considerably higher for fraud and for sexual offences than for other offence types. These findings confirmed the picture of predominant versatility, but with partial exceptions for certain offences.

In an early review of specialization in juvenile offending, Klein (1984) referred to several studies that had made use of self-report data, but these had not analysed the question in the detailed way described above. Most detailed studies of offending patterns have used official data on convictions or arrests. Self-report data could be used in principle, although they carry the limitation that the exact date of the offence is usually not known. In practice, they have generally been used in rather a different way, to investigate how far some 'general deviance factor' will go to explain different forms of deviance or offending. For example, McGee and Newcomb (1992) analysed self-reports of a wide range of behaviours among a cohort of young people studied at four developmental stages: early adolescence (aged around 13), late adolescence (aged around 17), young adulthood (aged around 21), and adulthood (aged around 25). Factor analysis was used to identify 'latent constructs' or in other words general tendencies underlying the specific forms of deviant behaviour. For example, four such general tendencies were identified at the young adulthood and adulthood stages: drug use, social conformity, sexual involvement, and criminal behaviour. It was found that the fit of the model could be improved by adding a 'general deviance' factor representing the overlap between the four general tendencies. This general deviance factor explained 63 per cent of the variance in the four more specific factors in early adulthood, and 43 per cent in adulthood. These findings show that there is a general tendency towards antisocial behaviour which underlies a wide range of criminal as well as unconventional or rebellious behaviours. They also suggest that the importance of this general factor declines with age, which is equivalent to the idea that criminal specialization increases as the criminal career lengthens. A considerable number of other studies (e.g. Donovan and Jessor 1985) have used factor analysis on self-report data to confirm the existence of a 'general deviance' factor, which usually accounts for about half of the variance in specific forms of deviance or offending. Among the most interesting are those that extend this approach to high-risk juvenile offenders (Dembo *et al.* 1992) and to different time periods and cultural groups (Le Blanc and Girard 1997).

More recent work by Soothill *et al.* (2002a, 2002b) is a new approach to the problem of classifying offending behaviour. The study made use of the Offenders Index, a court-based reporting system of convictions for standard-list offences in England and Wales ('standard-list offences' do not include less serious ones that are not centrally recorded). The data used were for two cohorts of all offenders born in four specified weeks in 1953 and 1958, although findings quoted here will be from the 1953 cohort (N = 11,402). For most of the analysis, a very detailed offence classification was used (71 separate offences for the 1953 males and 29 for the 1953 females). The task that Soothill and colleagues set themselves was to describe the structure of offending activity in a way that would show how different offence types were related, but allow for changes in the pattern of offending at different points in the criminal career. They approached this problem by finding typologies of criminal activity within *five-year periods* of the offender's criminal history up to the age of 40. A form of latent class analysis was used to identify clusters of offences within these five-year strips. The structure of these clusters was held constant across the whole period up to the age of 40, but an individual was allowed to move from one cluster to another at different stages of the life cycle. Clusters can be described by showing how offence types are distributed between them, although a description of this kind can be enormously complex. With some inevitable simplification, this can be boiled down to an outline description. For example, the authors provided the following description of cluster D in the analysis of males from the 1953 cohort:

> Involved in wounding, assault, and criminal damage. Also those most likely to be in possession of an offensive weapon. 16–25 year olds.
>
> *So to sum up:* **General violence**

Figure 20.1 shows how male offenders were assigned to clusters, by age group, for the 1953 cohort. Figure 20.2 shows the same for females. These figures immediately demonstrate major differences between the age profiles of offenders included in the clusters. In the case of the males, for example, cluster B (non-violent property, especially burglary) is heavily dominated by very young offenders, whereas cluster C (fraud and general theft) has a much older profile, with a peak between the ages of 26 and 30. Another interesting contrast is that cluster D (general violence) is heavily concentrated in two age groups, 16–20 and 21–25, whereas cluster I (shoplifting) is much more evenly distributed across the full age range. These striking differences show that among convicted offenders the clusters of offences they commit vary widely between the ages of 16 and 40. Hence any theory that sees offending as flowing from a single factor such

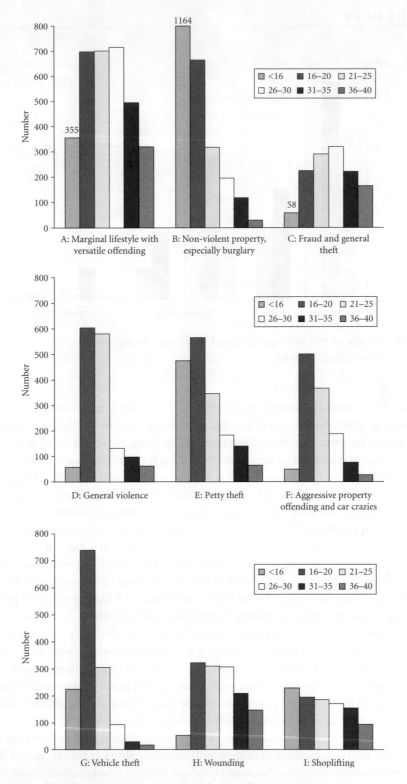

Fig. 20.1 Profile of 1953 males assigned to clusters, by age group

Source: Soothill *et al.* 2002b: Table 5.1.

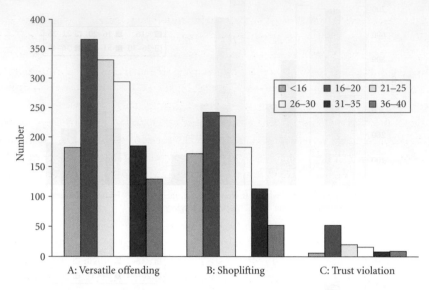

Fig. 20.2 Profile of 1953 females assigned to clusters, by age group
Source: Soothill *et al.* 2002b: Table 5.3.

as lack of self-control (Gottfredson and Hirschi 1990; Hirschi and Gottfredson 1994) is incomplete, at best. In the case of females, there are only three clusters, and differences between the age profiles of these clusters are not striking. Hence the analysis reveals far less evidence of patterned or specialized offending for females than it does for males. Among females, the shoplifting cluster is heavily concentrated in the 16–20 age group, and numbers in this cluster fall off quite rapidly in later age groups. There is also a shoplifting cluster for males, but this has a much flatter age distribution.

Having assigned offenders to clusters, Soothill *et al.* considered how they moved from one cluster to another at different ages. They found that a majority of offenders had convictions in only one age strip. Of the male offenders, 63.5 per cent had convictions in only one age strip, and a total of 83.0 per cent had convictions in only one or two. It was rare for male offenders to have convictions in all five age strips (.9 per cent) or in five out of the six (2.5 per cent) (Soothill *et al.* 2002b: Table 6.1). 'Age-strip recidivism' defined in this way was much rarer still among females. Because most criminal careers were confined to one or two age strips, most offenders could by definition appear in only one or two offence clusters. In fact, 68.0 per cent of the males in the 1953 cohort appeared in only one cluster, while a further 20.4 per cent appeared in just two, 8.3 per cent in three, and 3.3 per cent in four or more (Soothill *et al.* 2002b: Table 6.2). In one sense this illustrates a high degree of specialization in criminal careers, because it shows that most offenders only ever belong to one offence cluster. However, this is potentially misleading, since offenders with relatively short criminal careers do not have the opportunity to move between clusters. A more detailed analysis (Soothill *et al.* 2002b: Table 6.3) showed that offenders with longer criminal careers had commonly moved between offence clusters. This can be illustrated by reference to the statistics for the 1953 cohort of males. One-fifth of the men had convictions in two age strips, and of these, 79.8 per cent were assigned to two different clusters in these two age groups. A further 8.6 per cent had convictions in three age strips, and of these more than half (53.2 per cent) were assigned to three different clusters, 41.4 per cent to two different clusters, and only 5.4 per cent to the same cluster throughout.

Offenders with careers extending across several age strips were more likely to switch than to stay within the same offence cluster: the proportion assigned to the same cluster from one age strip to the next seldom rose above 40 per cent, and for many cells it was 10 per cent or lower. There was no overall trend towards increasing specialization as people grew older—instead this depended on the cluster of offences where people started.

On the whole, the evidence suggests that it is fruitful to think of the great diversity of antisocial and criminal behaviour as closely related at a deeper level. This approach is supported by the many studies showing a single factor underlying more specific forms of deviance, and by the widely corroborated finding that arrests and convictions show more versatile than specialized patterns of offending. Specific offences do tend to cluster into patterns within criminal careers, but because those with long careers typically switch between clusters, it is unlikely that clusters of offences correspond to well-defined criminal types.

THE EXTENT OF STABILITY AND CHANGE OVER THE LIFE COURSE

Until recently, longitudinal studies of criminal offending have focused on the relatively short span from childhood to early adulthood. That was partly because these studies were typically carried out by psychologists with an interest in the way that individual characteristics develop through childhood, and partly because it becomes much harder to track cohort members once they have passed through education and left their parents' home. This focus on the earlier stages of the life cycle has been accompanied by an emphasis on individual differences in the propensity to criminal and antisocial behaviour and on finding individual characteristics and experiences that are associated with the development of antisocial tendencies. Researchers in this tradition usually advocate early intervention with children and families at risk to prevent the development of criminal propensities (see Farrington, Chapter 19, this volume).

Research carried out within this framework, with the emphasis on childhood and adolescent development, has usually found a considerable degree of stability over time in the differences between individuals, although as pointed out by Robins (1978) the pattern is different depending on whether we look forwards or backwards over people's early lives. Looking forwards, most antisocial children do *not* become antisocial or criminal adults. Looking backwards, most criminal young adults *were* antisocial children. This asymmetry exists because antisocial and criminal behaviour peaks in mid- to late adolescence then falls throughout the life course.

It now seems that individual differences in offending looked moderately stable only because researchers concentrated on the early part of the life course. A few recent research projects have followed people through a much longer span: in the case of Laub and Sampson (2003) between the ages of 7 and 70. A far less stable and predictable pattern is shown over the full life course.

To the extent that there is stability, it is stability in the differences between individuals, but this is superimposed on a pattern of massive change in the behaviour of the same individuals at different ages. Gottfredson and Hirschi (1990) proposed that differences in offending behaviour between individuals at any particular stage of the life cycle correspond to differences in an underlying propensity to antisocial behaviour, and that the pattern of change in offending from one stage of the life cycle to another is the same in everyone regardless of their underlying propensity to offend. On this theory, the base level of offending varies between individuals, but the pattern of ups and downs at different ages is the same. As we shall see, this idea has been rigorously tested by two recent research projects (Ezell and Cohen 2005; Laub and Sampson 2003) which have found, instead, that the pattern of ups and downs in offending varies between different groups.

STABILITY OF INDIVIDUAL DIFFERENCES

A good illustration of the predictability of antisocial behaviour up to the teenage years is provided by an article entitled 'How early can we tell?' by White *et al.* (1990), based on analysis of a longitudinal study of a birth cohort of over 1,000 children in Dunedin, New Zealand. These children were divided into three groups on the basis of reports by parents, teachers, and the children themselves at the ages of 9, 11, and 13. The 50 children designated AD were pervasively antisocial at two of the three age points at least, and as rated by at least two of the three informants; the 37 children designated OD had other diagnoses at age 11 (e.g. attention deficit disorder with no conduct disorder symptoms); the remaining 837 children designated ND were those with no disorder. Five characteristics of the children collected at the ages of 3 and 5 were used to predict which group they would fall into. This analysis correctly classified 70 per cent of the AD cases and 81 per cent of the ND cases at ages 9–13. The three strongest predictors were parent-reported behaviour problems at age 5 and 'difficult to manage' and 'externalizing behaviour problems' at age 3. The other two predictors were a test of motor coordination, and a cognitive test (involving drawing), both at age 5. As the authors stated, 'the results . . . suggest that behavioural problems are the best preschool predictors of antisocial behaviour at age 11, and that behavioural problems as early as age 5, especially when rated by parents, can be predictive of future conduct problems' (White *et al.* 1990: 519).

The analysis was extended to predict delinquency at the age of 15. At that age, variety of self-reported delinquency and police contacts were more than twice as high among the AD as among the ND group. Delinquents at age 15 were defined as those with a high self-report score and at least one police contact, and there were 38 adolescents in this group. Using the five preschool predictors as before, the analysis correctly predicted 65 per cent of the delinquents and 67 per cent of the non-delinquents. This still showed considerable stability in individual differences from the preschool years, but also indicated that predictability declined in the adolescent years, which suggests that new causes of delinquency start to be influential at that time.

In interpreting these findings it has to be borne in mind that the ND group is much larger than the AD group, which means that even though the predictors are powerful, there are many false positives. For example, 19 per cent of the ND cases at age 11 were wrongly predicted from the pre-school assessments, meaning that 159 children were incorrectly predicted to be pervasively antisocial—three times as many as the 50 children who actually turned out to be pervasively antisocial at age 11. This would be a severe limitation on use of the findings for targeted intervention (whether ethical or unethical). Nevertheless these findings do demonstrate substantial continuity of individual differences in antisocial and delinquent behaviour from a very early age up to adolescence. This confirms findings from a considerable number of other studies (e.g. Robins 1966, 1978; Loeber and Dishion 1983; Robins and Regier 1991; Farrington 1995), some of which show that prediction from an early age continues to be powerful into adulthood.

The stability of aggressiveness, and its pervasive influence, have been particularly well studied. Reviewing 16 studies, Olweus (1979) found that the correlation between early aggressive behaviour and later criminality averaged .68. Huesman *et al.* (1984) in a longitudinal study over a 22-year period found that early aggressiveness predicted traffic violations, as well as spouse abuse, other criminal behaviour, and self-reported physical aggression. It seems that violent offenders in adulthood had very often shown aggression in early childhood, although of course many aggressive children do not become violent offenders later. Farrington (1978) found that seven out of ten males arrested for a violent offence by the age of 21 had been rated as highly aggressive between the ages of 12 and 14. In spite of the high level of continuity overall, West and Farrington (1977) showed that a minority of adult criminals were free of conduct disturbance during childhood, and that late onset was associated with low social status and criminality of the parents. Again Magnusson *et al.* (1983) found that nine out of ten males who had committed violent offences by the age of 26 had been rated as highly aggressive between the ages of 10 and 13. However, Magnusson (1987) later found from the same longitudinal study in Stockholm that the apparent link between aggressiveness in childhood and later criminality arose because there was a group of boys having a combination of characteristics including both aggressiveness and hyperactivity. Boys who were hyperactive and aggressive were likely to become persistent offenders, whereas those who were aggressive but not hyperactive had no more than an average chance of offending later.

AGE AND CRIME

The simplest way to illustrate the age/crime curve is to show the age distribution of officially recorded offenders in a given year. For any time in the second half of the twentieth century this shows a very sharp peak in offending around the age of 14 to 18 both in England (based on cautions and convictions) and in the USA (based on arrests). The rise up to this peak, starting from the age of criminal responsibility, is very steep, whereas the fall is steep up to the age of about 24, then flattens into a very long and slow decline from the age of 35 continuing indefinitely into old age (Farrington 1986: 192–3). As pointed out by Hirschi and Gottfredson (1983) and Gottfredson and Hirschi (1990), this pattern is strikingly similar for different countries and historical epochs and among different population groups, such as males and females (even though the base rate of offending is many times higher in males). Longitudinal analyses of a single age cohort show a broadly similar pattern. Thus Farrington (1990) showed that for his sample of 411 London males, mostly born in 1953, the peak age for convictions was 17; there was a sharp decline in convictions between the ages of 18 and 23, then a level, lower rate up to the age of 30, when a further slow decline began. Findings for a national cohort of individuals born in 1953 were similar.

As set out earlier, a more recent study by Soothill *et al.* (2002a, 2002b) divided histories of recorded convictions into 'strips'. Figure 20.3 shows for a 1953 birth cohort the rate of conviction per 1,000 population within each five-year strip. To facilitate the comparison between males and females, the results have been indexed on the last strip (age 36–40) which is always set to 100. The findings show that when local year-on-year variations are averaged out, there was a sharp rise to a peak between the ages of 16 and 20,

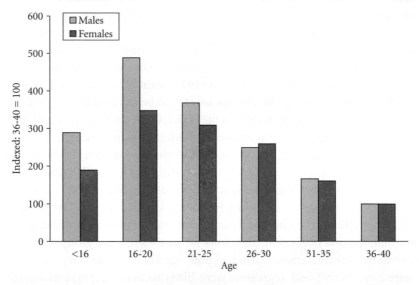

Fig. 20.3 Rate of conviction of 1953 birth cohort by age band: England and Wales

Note: Convictions expressed per 1,000 population, then indexed.

Source: Soothill *et al.* (2002b), calculated from Table 3.1 and 3.2.

followed by a steady decline in a straight line thereafter. This pattern applied to males and females, but the peak was less pronounced for females than for males.

Figure 20.4, which is confined to males, shows similar graphs for ten broad offence categories. These illustrate sharp differences in the age/crime curve according to the offence. It is striking that the rate of conviction for burglary before the age of 16 was so high that there was little further rise in the 16–20 age strip, and a very sharp fall thereafter. Both motoring and drug convictions, by contrast, peaked between the ages of

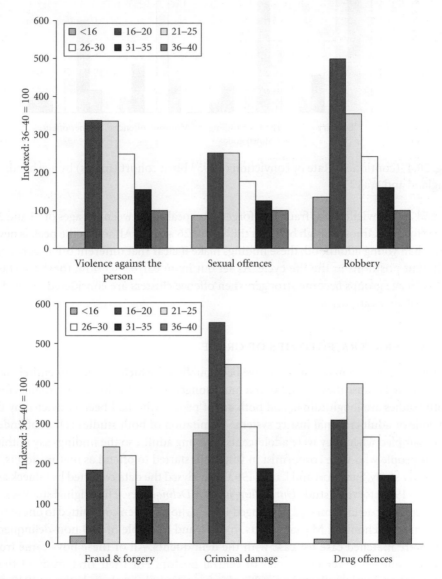

Fig. 20.4 Rate of conviction of 1953 birth cohort (males) by age band: England and Wales

Note: Convictions expressed per 1,000 population, then indexed.
Source: Soothill *et al.* (2002b), calculated from Table 3.1.

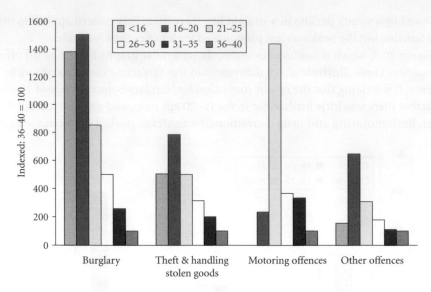

Fig. 20.4 (continued) Rate of conviction of 1953 birth cohort (males) by age band: England and Wales

21 and 25. Convictions for fraud and forgery also peaked between the ages of 21 and 25, but remained almost as high between the ages of 26 and 30. Although the peak is never later than young adulthood, these findings make it clear that different offences occupy different positions in the life cycle. As set out in an earlier section, these contrasts between age groups become stronger when offence clusters are considered, instead of broad offence categories.

LONG-TERM TRAJECTORIES OF CRIME

In recent years two major studies have been published which provide an entirely new perspective because they extend over a much longer part of the life course than before. Both studies are longitudinal, and both are of people who had been convicted by the juvenile or adult criminal justice system. A limitation of both studies is that offenders were sampled when they were adolescents or young adults, so the findings say nothing about people who were conformist in youth but started to offend as mature adults. In an earlier study, Sampson and Laub (1993) reanalysed the data collected by Glueck and Glueck (1950) for their study *Unravelling Juvenile Delinquency*. The original study was of 500 'persistent delinquents', all males aged 10–17, who had been committed to one of two correctional schools in Massachusetts in 1939, and a sample of 500 non-delinquents who were matched case for case with the delinquents. All of these boys came from underprivileged lower-class areas of central Boston. For their first study of these groups, the Gluecks collected a wealth of information about them between 1939 and 1948. Between 1949 and 1963 they followed up the same individuals at the age of 25, then again at the age of 32. Sampson and Laub (1993) in their reanalysis made use of all the information about these men available up to the age of 32, including data that had been retrospectively collected about their childhood. For their later study, Laub and Sampson (2003) tracked down the official criminal records of the original delinquent group (but not the matched non-delinquent group) up to the age of 70 and conducted interviews with a sample of 52 surviving men from the same group.

A basic finding from this analysis was that 'the classic age/crime pattern . . . is replicated even within a population that was selected for its serious, persistent delinquent activity' (Laub and Sampson 2003: 86). Among these serious juvenile delinquents, there was a rapid drop in offending between the ages of 16 and 20, then a long, steady fall all the way up to the age of 60. This overall pattern was dominated by property crimes, which are much the most common. The peak age for alcohol and drug-related crimes came much later, in the mid-thirties. The average length of the official criminal career of these men was 25.6 years, so even though the peak age of offending came early, they typically continued offending for many years after that: on average, their officially recorded offending stopped at the age of 37.5, which means that for many the process of desisting from crime continued into their forties and fifties. The earlier analysis by Sampson and Laub (1993) had shown that a range of variables capturing individual characteristics and behaviour in childhood and adolescence were useful predictors of offending in young adulthood. In the later analysis, Laub and Sampson (2003) combined the 13 sturdiest predictors of offending into a single childhood risk indicator; this included measures of personality, temperament, cognitive abilities, childhood behaviours, and early and frequent involvement in crime and delinquency. This summary measure continued to predict offending even up to the late fifties. The high-risk group (the top 20 per cent on the summary measure) accounted for twice as many recorded offences at ages 50–59 as the rest (Laub and Sampson 2003: 93). This shows that there is a substantial degree of stability and predictability of behaviour across most of the life course. On the other hand, the pattern of change over the life course was remarkably similar for the high-risk and low-risk groups. In youth and early adulthood, the probability of official offending was substantially greater among the high-risk than low-risk group; the probability began to decline among the two groups at almost the same age and according to the same pattern, although the decline was somewhat steeper for the high-risk group, so that the gap between them was greatest in youth and smallest at a later age. Even by adopting various other strategies to define in advance (based on the data from childhood and adolescence) a group of high-rate chronic offenders, Laub and Sampson were unable to find any group that continued to offend steadily throughout the life course: instead, all of these groups showed the familiar age/crime curve. From this, Laub and Sampson concluded that 'desistance is a general process' which affects even the highest-risk groups within a sample of serious and persistent juvenile offenders. Although there was an important degree of predictability in the individual differences in offending over the life course, this should not be over-stated. For example, among the 11 men with the highest scores on the summary measure of childhood and family risk, and whose adolescent offending rates were high, six were nonetheless among the bottom 25 per cent in terms of offending between the ages of 25 and 60.

ARE THERE DISTINCT OFFENDING TRAJECTORIES?

The second major study to have been published in recent years (Ezell and Cohen 2005) covered a smaller part of the life course than Laub and Sampson (2003), but still took the analysis well beyond the teenage and early adult years. The study covered three samples of men who on conviction for a criminal offence had been committed to the California Youth Authority either as juveniles (aged 11–17) or as young adults (aged 18–21). The samples were of those released in 1981–2, 1986–7, and 1991–2. Information about their previous criminal records and other background data were collected from their files, and post-release arrest data were collected up to June 2000. The average ages at the end of the follow-up period were 37, 33, and 27 for the three groups respectively (although the maximum age to which individuals were observed was 43), while life history information started at the age of 7. Like the Gluecks' cohort of juvenile delinquents, Ezell and Cohen's sample consisted of official offenders only, but it included a higher proportion of 'high-end' serious and frequent offenders. Among other indicators, over 80 per cent of the sample had been arrested for at least one serious violent offence; furthermore, nearly 10 per cent had been arrested for homicide.

The analysis by Laub and Sampson (2003) described above was prospective, meaning that high-risk and low-risk groups were defined on the basis of childhood characteristics and early behaviour, then the later pattern of offending by age was compared between these groups. By contrast, Ezell and Cohen looked retrospectively at the evolution of offending (as indexed by arrests) between the ages of 7 and 40 to find whether it was possible to identify distinct groups that had followed different trajectories. To do this, they used statistical methods earlier developed by Nagin and Land (1993) and Land, McCall, and Nagin (1996). The aim of these methods is to identify latent classes of individuals grouped according to the similarity in their trajectories of arrests. Corresponding to each class there is an equation that specifies how offending varies according to age for members of that class. In itself, the model says nothing about why offending varies with age, or why it varies between the different latent classes. The method can be regarded as simply a systematic procedure for finding patterns. For each of the three samples, the best solution was one that identified six latent classes, and individuals in these classes had strikingly different offending trajectories, even though most of them on commitment to the California Youth Authority had been serious and frequent offenders. Looking, for example, at the sample of those released in 1981–2, there was a class whose offending peaked at the age of 17 then rapidly declined to a very low level by the age of 21; and in contrast a class whose offending steadily rose to a high peak at the age of 30 and only then started to decline, remaining high even at the age of 38.

It may be argued that a blind statistical procedure of this kind is bound to find patterns in any data because it is programmed to do so, but this would not be a valid criticism. A number of tests were used to demonstrate that the differences between the trajectories of the six classes were statistically significant, and moreover the results were robust: they did not change substantially when changes were made to the detailed specification of the model. Perhaps more important, the differences between the trajectories are substantively important: as mentioned above, one class had stopped offending by the age of 21, whereas another was still offending at a high rate at the age of 38. These results amount to a refutation of Gottfredson and Hirschi's theory of age and crime. According to that theory, individuals vary in their propensity to antisocial and criminal behaviour, but the rate of offending and antisocial behaviour varies by age in the same way for everyone. In other words, if age is on the horizontal axis of a graph, and the rate of offending is on the vertical axis, according to Gottfredson and Hirschi there are a number of age/crime curves with just the same shape but located higher or lower on the vertical axis. Ezell and Cohen's analysis shows, instead, that there are several groups of offenders whose age/crime curves have entirely different shapes. Corresponding to those curves are equations that specify how offending changes according to age in a different way for each of these latent classes. Laub and Sampson (2003) carried out a similar analysis of the offending trajectories of the delinquent group from the Gluecks' study which they had tracked up to the age of 70. They also produced six clearly distinguished latent classes. The groupings and shape of the trajectories were found to be substantially different depending on whether total crime was considered, or one or other of three broad types (property crime, violent crime, and alcohol- and drug-related crime).

Although the patterns that these procedures find are statistically robust, it does not follow that the people belonging to the different classes are different 'types'—that they are inherently different in some way. To put the point more precisely, there must presumably be some explanation for the different trajectories, but two broad kinds of explanation are possible. The first is that there are stable characteristics that explain why someone follows one trajectory or another. These could be personal characteristics, such as impulsivity or intelligence, or things to do with location in the social structure that are hard to change, such as social class. The second broad kind of explanation is that something happened at a particular point in someone's life to nudge them into one trajectory or another: for example, they got married or got a steady job. If the explanation for having followed one trajectory rather than another is time-varying factors, like marriage or employment, we will not be tempted to say that the members of the different classes are different 'types' but rather that some people got lucky or made a good decision whereas others didn't.

In fact, Ezell and Cohen (2005) found that membership of their six latent classes was not predicted by any of the individual characteristics of offenders on which they had information. Similarly, Laub and Sampson (2003: 110) found that 'group membership is not easily, if at all, predictable from individual, childhood, and adolescent risk factors'. Instead, they pursued a separate analysis of dynamic factors driving change in people's lives, as further discussed in a later section. In summary, the evidence from these recent studies strongly suggests that offending trajectories over the life cycle, and not just overall levels of offending, can vary widely between individuals, but that people following a particular trajectory of offending do not belong to a type with definable, stable characteristics. These findings contrast rather strongly with Terrie Moffitt's theory of offender types.

MOFFITT'S THEORY OF OFFENDER TYPES

Moffitt (1993, 1997) has proposed that there are two distinct categories of antisocial behaviour and offending: life-course persistent, and adolescence-limited. According to this taxonomy, life-course-persistent antisocial behaviour starts very early, and continues throughout life, but the forms in which it is expressed, the ways it is perceived and described, and the social reactions to it, change at different stages of the life cycle. By contrast, adolescence-limited antisocial behaviour increases rapidly in early adolescence, then declines rapidly after the peak age at around 18. The two groups of offenders are hard to distinguish in adolescence from their rates or patterns of offending, but they are entirely different in terms of their behaviour in childhood and in maturity. The substantial stability of offending over the life course is entirely due to life-course-persistent offenders, whereas the substantial change in rates of offending is entirely due to adolescence-limited offenders. When the two groups are superimposed, as in most statistics, the result is the observed age/crime curve. The second element of the theory is that the causes of offending are different among the two groups. Life-course-persistent offending is pathology. It is caused by constitutional factors, specifically a deficit in the brain's executive functions, in combination with neglectful or inadequate parenting in the preschool years. Adolescence-limited offending is normal. It is a way in which teenagers demonstrate their autonomy and maturity, so once they have manifestly reached adult status it stops (Caspi and Moffitt 1995).

In formulating the theory, Moffitt was relying on a considerable body of evidence to show that early onset of antisocial behaviour predicts more serious offending persisting into adulthood (e.g. Blumstein *et al.* 1985; Tolan and Thomas 1995; Fergusson *et al.* 1996). However, the idea is *not* that early offending locks young people into a cycle of reoffending. Instead, the theory is that early onset is an *indication* that certain children have a range of *other* characteristics that will cause them to behave antisocially throughout their lives. Hence, the theory is not disturbed by Nagin and Farrington's (1992b) finding that age of onset has no independent effect on later convictions, after allowing for the effects of other variables. (However, it is worth noting that Fergusson *et al.* (1996), using a different data set and statistical approach, came to the opposite conclusion.)

Moffitt (2003) reviewed the state of the evidence ten years after the publication of the original paper. In doing so, she split up the theory into a number of more specific hypotheses. The first was that 'life-course-persistent antisocial development emerges from early neurodevelopmental and family-adversity risk factors', and here there is an increasing emphasis on the interaction between inherited neurophysiological deficits and harmful features of the early social environment. She quoted studies from eight countries in support of the link between neurological abnormalities and cognitive deficits and antisocial behaviour persisting beyond childhood. She also pointed to a few studies that had provided indications that a constitutional vulnerability such as hyperactivity can interact with an aspect of the early environment such as poor parenting to produce an escalating pattern of antisocial behaviour that has an early onset (Patterson *et al.* 2000). The second hypothesis identified was that genetic factors contribute more to life-course-persistent than to adolescence-limited antisocial development. She quoted three groups of recent behavioural genetic studies in support of this claim. The first group compared the heritability of different dimensions of antisocial behaviour. Three studies had found that a measure of aggression, thought to be associated with the life-course-persistent prototype, was more heritable than a measure of delinquency, thought to be associated with the adolescence-limited prototype. A second group of behavioural genetic studies had found that antisocial behaviour emerging in childhood was more heritable than delinquency emerging in adolescence, which was more subject to environmental influences. A third group of four studies of very young twins had found high levels of heritability (50–80 per cent) of aggressive behaviour in infants up to the age of 3, which compares with a considerably lower level of heritability of adolescent and adult antisocial behaviour, according to a recent meta-analysis of relevant studies (Rhee and Waldman 2002).

An important hypothesis among those proposed by Moffitt (2003) is that most female antisocial behaviour belongs to the adolescence-limited type, because the neurophysiological deficits giving rise to life-course-persistent antisocial behaviour are much more common in males than in females. Analysis of the Dunedin, New Zealand study has shown that the difference between males and females is much greater for antisocial behaviour persisting into adulthood than for adolescence-limited antisocial behaviour, and this has been confirmed by a range of other studies (Moffitt 2003: 66–7). Moffitt also quoted further, more recent evidence that early starters were more likely than late starters to persist in a range of antisocial behaviours into middle adulthood, a finding that was the original spark for the theory.

Moffitt's idea has the virtues of boldness and simplicity, and it is stimulating a growing body of research. Some of this suggests that reality may be fuzzier than Moffitt's theory proposes. Nagin *et al.* (1995), using West and Farrington's London data, defined four offending trajectories rather than two. They found that the adolescence-limited offenders were intermediate in their personal characteristics between those who had never been convicted and the groups of high-level and low-level chronic offenders. Although they had ceased being convicted, they continued (from their self-reports) to commit certain kinds of offence, such as thefts from employers, to use drugs, to drink heavily, and to get involved in fights. Again, analysis of the Christchurch, New Zealand cohort by Fergusson *et al.* (1996) showed that the adolescence-limited group had scores on a range of risk factors that were intermediate between the non-offenders and the life-course-persistent offenders.

The theory was challenged in a more fundamental way by the recent studies of Laub and Sampson (2003) and Ezell and Cohen (2005). There are, in fact, two challenges. One concerns the trajectories themselves, the other the way of explaining why people follow one trajectory rather than another. Perhaps because they continued much further into the life cycle than most of the studies on which Moffitt relies, these two studies identified six trajectories rather than two. One of the trajectories identified in each study is adolescence-limited offending, but the other five are varied and contrasting, and cannot possibly be summarized as life-course persistent. The central point is that all of the trajectories show a strong decline in offending after a certain age, although the timing varies widely. There is no pure life-course-persistent group, and instead offenders on all trajectories desist, so change over the life course is not confined to the adolescence-limited group. The strongest challenge, however, comes from Laub and Sampson (2003) and concerns the explanations for the different trajectories. These authors argued that distinct offending trajectories do not correspond to distinct types of person. Although their analysis of the Gluecks' data confirmed a vast number of other studies in showing that childhood risk factors are moderately good predictors of the later *level* of offending, they also found that these childhood factors do not predict offending *trajectory*. This is directly contrary to the predictions of Moffitt's theory. On the views both of Moffitt and of Laub and Sampson, some of the influences on offending are characteristics of the individual and social setting that are stable over time, such as an explosive temperament, whereas others are dynamic factors that operate only at certain times, such as getting a job or trying to move from being a teenager to being an adult. Moffitt argued that only time-varying factors apply to one group (adolescence-limited offenders) whereas only time-constant factors apply to the other (life-course-persistent offenders). Laub and Sampson argued, instead, that a blend of time-varying and time-constant factors influences all groups. Laub and Sampson (2001) summed this up as the contrast between two accounts: one describes antisocial behaviour as arising from a process of law-like development in which the potential of a given type of person is realized in actual behaviour, a process analogous to the execution of a programme; the other describes offending as rising and falling in response to variable influences from the social environment.

EXPLAINING STABILITY

Although a few offenders, perhaps those who misuse powerful positions in legitimate organizations, successful fraudsters, or leading lights in criminal networks, may achieve wealth, status, and power—the chief explanation of offending according to Merton (1938)—most persistent offenders who end up in prison seem to lead miserable lives: as recently illustrated by the narratives that committed offenders told Shadd Maruna (2001), they typically persist in spite of low incomes, insecurity, fragile relationships, physical injury, and mind-numbing and brutalizing spells of imprisonment. It is easy to explain why people persist in successful behaviour that brings outcomes they desire. Explaining why people persist in behaviour that seems inflexible and maladaptive poses more of a challenge. Surprisingly, however, several theoretical traditions in criminology and psychology suggest that criminal behaviour is 'an amplifying process that leads to further and more serious deviance' (Gove 1985: 118, quoted in Maruna 2001: 20). It can be argued that there are too many explanations for stability of offending behaviour, and too few explanations for desistance, given that the level of stability is modest, and all groups of offenders tend to give up.

THE IDEA THAT OFFENDING CAUSES MORE OFFENDING

As Matsueda and Heimer (1997) have pointed out, the theoretical traditions in criminology that can most readily be used to explain life-course continuity in offending are symbolic interactionism and labelling theory. On Lemert's classic account, everyone performs deviant acts from time to time, but usually they escape formal censure. When other people notice and disapprove, the matter is often resolved by negotiation and accommodation on both sides. When a deviant act does lead to formal censure, the offender may choose to stop or conceal the deviant behaviour in future. However, a person stigmatized as deviant may respond by embracing the new role, and may reorganize the self around this new identity. From this point, the person will find new associates, and learn new offending skills and techniques of self-justification. Now each new criminal act will take the person further down a road that leads to more offending, and will make it more and more difficult to return. On this account, offending, in conjunction with the response to offending by other people and institutions, leads to more offending, and this interactive process embeds the individual in a criminal way of life. As well as symbolic interactionism and labelling theory, such an account makes use of learning theory (Sutherland and Cressey 1955) and of Sykes and Matza's (1957) 'techniques of neutralization. Becoming criminal is partly a matter of learning from associates how to commit the crime and how to stop feeling guilty about it. Alternatively, in the tradition of social control theory (Hirschi 1969) it can be argued that involvement in crime weakens social bonds which then have less influence in restraining people from further offending.

If any of these theories are true, then offending should tend to increase after a first conviction. Farrington (1977) found that boys first convicted between the ages of 14 and 18 increased their self-reported delinquency compared with a matched group of unconvicted boys. The same result was obtained in studying the effect of first convictions between the ages of 18 and 21 (Farrington et al. 1978). This supports the view that offending causes more offending, but later researchers have been dissatisfied with this form of analysis, because of the possibility that the experimental group (those who were convicted) may not be similar to the control group (those who were not convicted) in all relevant respects. Nagin and Paternoster (1991) argued that stability in offending could arise from 'persistent heterogeneity'—fixed differences between individuals explained by either known or unknown variables. Alternatively, stability could arise from 'state dependence'—offending now causes further offending in the future, so the future state of the system is dependent on its present state. The 1990s saw a new generation of studies that deployed more powerful statistical methods to take account of unobserved as well as observed characteristics of offenders when estimating the effect of past on future offending (Nagin and Paternoster 1991; Nagin and Farrington 1992a, 1992b; Sampson and Laub 1993; Land *et al.* 1996; Paternoster *et al.* 1997; Paternoster and Brame 1997; Bushway *et al.* 1999). In these analyses, persistent heterogeneity is estimated from the correlations between unexplained variations in delinquency at one time and another. The logic underlying this procedure is that if there are unknown differences between individuals that cause offending at both times, then unexplained variations during the two periods should be correlated, as they flow from the same unknown stable characteristics. In broad terms, three findings have emerged from these studies: controlling for people's known characteristics, past offending strongly predicts future offending; there is considerable unobserved heterogeneity, in other words there are individual characteristics not captured by the studies which have an influence on people's offending; the effect of past on future offending is considerably reduced by controlling for these unobserved variables, but it remains significant and substantial in most of the studies. Ezell and Cohen (2005) carried out a particularly thorough analysis, using the California Youth Authority data set discussed earlier, and confirmed these conclusions. After they tested various different statistical approaches, the findings remained robust.

CONSTITUTIONAL FACTORS

By the mid-1990s it was already clear that there is an important heritable component in criminal behaviour, although the evidence base was rather slender—in their review, Carey and Goldman (1997) listed seven twin studies and six adoption studies. Over the past ten years, a new generation of studies in behavioural genetics has confirmed those findings and begun to ask new questions and provide new answers about the interplay between genetic factors and the social environment. Three broad types of interaction can be distinguished: passive, evocative, and active (Scarr 1992). First, parents' genes make the children's genes, but also help to construct the children's environment, which brings about a passive correlation between the children's genes and their environment. Secondly, people evoke responses from others that are correlated with their own characteristics: for example, a person who behaves aggressively (influenced by a genetic predisposition) evokes aggressive behaviour in others, so that his aggressive nature is correlated with an aggressive microsocial environment. Thirdly, people actively select environments that are correlated with their interests, tastes, and preferences, so that the genotype finds a suitable ecological niche. Because of these processes, studies that do not take account of genetic factors may easily over-state the influence of the social environment. For example, abusive parents tend to have aggressive children, but this may be only partly because of the effect of the parents' behaviour on child development. It may also be because children inherit an aggressive temperament from their abusive parents, and because children with an inherited tendency to aggression tend to evoke abusive behaviour in their parents. Finally, another important kind of gene-environment interaction has been highlighted by recent research: there are genes that make people resistant to specific kinds of environmental influence. In a landmark paper, Caspi *et al.* (2002) reported that a feature of the gene that controls the activity of the neurotransmitter MAOA moderates the effects of child abuse. Maltreated children with this genetic feature were less likely to develop antisocial behaviour.

Moffitt (2005) has recently reviewed the evidence from the new behavioural genetics on the interplay between genes and environment in the development of antisocial behaviour. She cited about 200 papers, and readers interested in that growing body of evidence should consult her review. As she reported, meta-analyses of more than 100 studies (Miles and Carey 1997; Rhee and Waldman 2002) have concluded that genes influence 40 to 50 per cent of population variation in antisocial behaviour. It is these genetic studies, rather than the purely sociological ones, that unequivocally prove the importance of environmental influences, because they take account of confounds with genetic factors and parcel them out. At the same time it is clear that the substantial genetic influence on antisocial behaviour is a major cause of stability in offending over the life course.

FAMILY AND PARENTING

A very large number of studies have produced evidence on the relation between family functioning and crime or antisocial behaviour in children, and many of these have used longitudinal methods to provide relatively strong evidence that family factors have a causal influence. In a review of the evidence then available, Loeber and Stouthamer-Loeber (1986) concluded that the influence of neglect (lack of supervision and involvement) was strongest, followed by conflict (including inappropriate or inconsistent discipline and rejection). Deviant behaviour and values in the parents themselves was the third strongest influence, and family disruption (including absence of the father and illness of a parent) was a significant influence, but less strong than the others. Many subsequent studies, such as the Edinburgh Study (Smith 2004b) have essentially confirmed these findings. However, a serious weakness is that these studies did not control for the possible confounding effects of genetic factors. One possible confound is that parents' genes influence parenting but also (when passed to offspring) influence antisocial behaviour in their children. Another is that children who have inherited a tendency to aggressive or antisocial behaviour evoke punitive or hostile parenting. Moffitt (2005: 540) concluded in her recent review that the association between child aggression and parenting styles within the normal range (that is, not including serious abuse) is in large part a spurious artefact of the child's genotype, which causes both. Nevertheless, she also considered that analyses of several twin samples had recently established that bad parenting has some effect on children's aggression after genetic factors have been controlled. This does not apply to all aspects of bad parenting, however. For example, use of corporal punishment (short of abuse or injury) is strongly associated with child aggression, but this association disappears after controlling for genetic factors. As mentioned earlier, interactions between genetic influences and parenting may be crucial: there is evidence that child abuse is far more damaging to some children than to others, depending on their genotype (Caspi *et al.* 2002).

These findings suggest that family functioning is often the start of a process that leads to continuity of antisocial behaviour. Sampson and Laub (1993) in their reanalysis of the Gluecks' longitudinal data were able to show that family factors had an important influence on whether the boy was delinquent in adolescence. They also found that the family process variables were related to adult criminality, but that this relationship was entirely mediated by adolescent delinquency. On the basis of these findings, they suggested that much of the linkage between the childhood family experiences and adult criminality may be due to interactional and cumulative continuity through the responses of other people and institutions, and not to stable dispositions formed in childhood as a result of family experiences.

Gerald Patterson and colleagues at the Oregon Social Learning Center (Patterson *et al.* 1992) have argued that ineffective parents reward coercive behaviour and do not consistently reward cooperative behaviour, so that their children learn to get what they want by behaving coercively. The child's coercive behaviour then evokes coercive and unpredictable behaviour in the parent, and so the cycle continues. This account of parenting, based on social learning theory, is backed up by findings from longitudinal multi-method studies of 200 families. The logic of the theory is that individual coercive acts are functional for the child (and later for the adolescent and adult) in the short term, but dysfunctional in the longer term, because a person without self-discipline will never be successful in the wider world. This kind of theory constitutes an important attempt to explain why criminal and antisocial behaviour, viewed as maladaptive, should persist over the life course.

Analysis of the London and Pittsburgh cohorts (Farrington *et al.* 1996; Farrington *et al.* 2001) has shown close links in terms of convictions or arrests between parents and children, between siblings, and between other relatives, to the extent that 6 per cent of families in the London cohort accounted for half of the convictions. This says nothing about causal mechanisms, but it does show that in one way or another continuity in offending is brought about through the family.

THE OFFENDING/VICTIMIZATION LOOP

A feature of crime patterns that has been emphasized too little is the tendency for victims and offenders to share some characteristics. For example, both victimization and offending rates are elevated among African Caribbeans in Britain (Smith 2005a), and among African Americans in the USA (Sampson and Lauritsen 1997) and this is explained by an elevated rate of black-on-black crime. Fattah (1991) summarized evidence from studies in Canada, the USA, Australia, and Britain showing that victim and offender populations tended to be similar in several respects: young, male, unmarried, and unemployed. Hoyle and Zedner (Chapter 15, this volume) summarize the long history of the idea that much crime arises out of an interaction between victim and offender, and Fattah (1991) reviewed the scattered evidence that offending and victimization are linked. Farrall and Maltby (2003) uncovered high levels of victimization among a sample of convicted offenders on probation. A current study of a cohort of 4,300 young people in Edinburgh has found a correlation of .421 between victimization and offending over the same time period (Smith 2004a). Smith and Ecob (submitted) identified three broad types of explanation: that crime arises from interactions within a social circle; that victimization and offending have common causes either within the individual or in the social environment; and that victimization causes offending (for example, victims retaliate) and offending causes victimization (for example, offenders make themselves vulnerable). Their analysis showed strong links between trajectories of victimization and offending between the ages of 12 and 17. High delinquency at an earlier time was related to rising victimization later, and vice versa. These relationships held after controlling for interactions within the social circle and common origins of victimization and delinquency. This constitutes strong evidence for a true causal relationship between victimization and offending, running in both directions. This is likely to reinforce the stability of individual offending patterns, because interactions between victims and offenders set up repeating feedback loops which continually refresh the motives and opportunities for crime.

IMPULSIVITY OR LACK OF SELF-CONTROL

It is well established that impulsivity, viewed as inability to plan ahead and to defer gratification (Mischel 1983), predicts antisocial behaviour and delinquency (Pulkkinen 1986; Krueger *et al.* 1994). There is evidence that impulsivity is specifically related to aggression and delinquency, and not to 'internalizing' disorders such as anxiety and depression (Krueger *et al.* 1996). In fact, impulsivity is probably the best example of a personality characteristic that can help to explain continuity in antisocial behaviour and delinquency over the life course. It can be argued that, for those who find it difficult to delay gratification, impulsive behaviour is self-reinforcing because by definition it involves achieving immediate gratification. Hence, a pattern of impulsive behaviour, once established, should tend to persist. Building in part on these findings, Gottfredson and Hirschi (1990) put forward a general theory of crime as a lack of self-control, but such a theory goes well beyond the psychological evidence, which shows that many other factors help to predict delinquency after lack of impulse control has been taken into account.

SOCIAL INFORMATION PROCESSING

There is evidence that antisocial persons have different conceptions of themselves and the world from other people, and different beliefs about what kind of behaviour is acceptable and effective in achieving results (for a summary of the evidence on social information processing and self-concepts, see Dodge and Schwartz 1997). In particular, aggressive persons tend to believe that aggression will produce tangible rewards, that it is a legitimate way of solving problems, that it is a normal and acceptable means of guarding and improving one's reputation, and that victims don't suffer (Caspi and Moffitt 1995: 486). These psychological findings describe something similar to the 'techniques of neutralization' described by Sykes and Matza (1957) and the 'moral disengagement' described by Bandura (1991). These self-concepts and beliefs about the world tend to be self-sustaining, because of certain very general, conservative features of the system for processing social information, that tend to reinforce already existing personal theories of reality. Dodge (1980; Crick and Dodge 1994; Dodge and Schwartz 1997) has developed a more detailed theory of the steps through which social information is processed. In particular, he proposed that aggressive people tend to attribute hostile intent to neutral social signals, to put the worst inter-pretation on other people's behaviour, and to focus on aggressive cues while ignoring non-aggressive ones.

The evidence shows that individual differences in social information processing predict differences in antisocial behaviour. At the same time, biased processing is a powerful mechanism through which these differences can be maintained and accentu-ated. Individuals who wrongly attribute hostility to others will behave aggressively towards them, bringing about this time an actual aggressive response. This in turn will tend to confirm the personal theory of reality that supports the biased processing, and increase the likelihood of wrong attribution of hostility the next time round. Dodge *et al.* (1995) showed from a longitudinal study that similar patterns of social information processing are partly responsible for the linkage between early child abuse and later conduct problems.

ALCOHOL AND DRUGS

Use of alcohol and drugs is very closely related to offending careers, and this link starts from an early age. The Edinburgh Study has recently shown that criminal offending is substantially higher among users of drugs (mainly cannabis) and alcohol between the ages of 12 and 15; crime victimization is substantially higher among drug and alcohol users, too (McVie and Bradshaw 2005). Research among people arrested in four English towns showed that 69 per cent of them tested positive for at least one drug (excluding alcohol), and 36 per cent for two or more; 29 per cent of those arrested tested positive for opiates, and 20 per cent for cocaine (including crack). Average weekly expenditure on drugs among the arrested who were users was £129 (in 1999), and £308 among users of both heroin and crack cocaine. Those arrested reported that they met much of this cost through income from crime. The arrested people who tested positive on drugs reported far more offences than those who did not (Bennett 2000). The link between alcohol and violent crime has been documented by a large body of research (Fagan 1990). Although the causal sequences have not been fully clarified, the causal arrows probably point both ways from substance use towards offending and from offending towards substance use. The recent qualitative study by Maruna (2001) vividly illustrated how persistent offending in Liverpool was closely intertwined with drug addiction and how drug use and offending were part of the same social scene. It is clear enough that drugs and alcohol are important factors that keep people offending and make it hard for them to stop.

SOCIAL STRUCTURE

As detailed elsewhere (Bottoms, Chapter 17, this volume) there are substantial differences in both offending and victimization between neighbourhoods, and these differences have some relationship to social class composition, levels of deprivation, types of housing, features of the physical environment, and the functioning of communities. Differences in offending between individuals within neighbourhoods are much greater than differences between neighbourhoods, however, so that statistical models that include both neighbourhood and individual characteristics find that neighbourhood characteristics significantly predict offending, but the effects of individual characteristics are much larger (Sampson *et al.* 1997). Nevertheless, existing studies may underestimate the importance of social context because nearly all of them are cross-sectional. Longitudinal studies may eventually show that the cumulative effects on the developmental process of growing up in a particular kind of neighbourhood are larger than shown by earlier cross-sectional studies. A complicating factor is that individual and neighbourhood influences interact. Analysis of the Pittsburgh Study has suggested that neighbourhood influences are greatest for the *least* vulnerable individuals (Wikström 1998).

In their reanalysis of the Gluecks' (1950) longitudinal study in Boston, Sampson and Laub (1993) showed that social structure factors, such as unemployment or low income, had little direct effect on the development of offending in young people. Instead, they had an important indirect effect, through influencing family functioning. Parents with insecure employment, low incomes, or poor housing have little time and energy to supervise and control their children, to do things with them, or to discuss their projects and problems. The view that social and economic deprivation has a crucial effect through its influence on family functioning and parenting is supported by a large number of other studies (e.g. Dodge *et al.* 1994; Larzelere and Patterson 1990; Bank *et al.* 1993; Brody *et al.* 1994; Conger *et al.* 1992, 1993; Kolvin *et al.* 1988). Maruna (2001) has documented how the collapse of the local economy in Liverpool in the 1970s created a generation of people with little hope and a local culture of exceptionally high drug use and property crime.

EXPLAINING DESISTANCE

If there are too many explanations for continuity in offending behaviour, there are too few explanations for change. The problem is underlined by the recent studies (Laub and Sampson 2003; Ezell and Cohen 2005) which have shown that all observed types of offending trajectory involve substantial change, and all show a major decline in offending sooner or later. In seeking to explain this decline, most writers (e.g. Laub and Sampson 2001) have started with a discussion about how to define desistance. The recent work on trajectories may be a better starting point. Although both Laub and Sampson (2003) and Ezell and Cohen (2005) contested Moffitt's (1993) 'dual taxonomy' of antisocial behaviour, their analyses at least confirmed that there is a group whose criminal offending is confined to adolescence. In place of Moffitt's life-course-persistent group, they proposed a range of offending trajectories, all eventually desisting, but some much sooner than others. The first section below briefly discusses desistance among adolescence-limited offenders. The remaining sections tackle the problem of explaining change among more persistent and serious offenders.

ADOLESCENCE-LIMITED OFFENDERS

Why does offending rise to a peak in the mid-teens then rapidly fall among a large group of young people who for the most part do not share the disadvantages and problems of more persistent offenders? One theoretical tradition explains this by changes over the life course in the strength of social bonds (Sampson and Laub 1990, 1993). From the perspective of social control theory, reciprocal relationships lock people into conventional society, and restrain them from committing deviant acts. Children have very strong bonds with the adults who are responsible for them, are utterly dependent on them, and are more or less effectively controlled by them. Conventional adults have bonds to a spouse, children, employer, friends. Adolescence is the period when young people loosen the bonds with family and school, and before the time when they have formed a new set of adult relationships, and acquired new commitments. People are therefore less constrained during the period of adolescence than at any other time of their lives, and hence more likely to be involved in crime and deviance. As set out later, there is solid evidence to support the theory that social bonds help to explain desistance. A much broader argument for social control theory draws attention to historic change in the nature of adolescence (Rutter and Smith 1995). At the beginning of the twentieth century, young people normally left school at about 12, to work often in mixed-age groups. Although sexual maturity, financial independence, and forming an independent household followed after several years, from an early age young people spent much of their time with adults and were locked into reciprocal relationships with them. In the second half of the twentieth century, as full-time education lengthened, so the time when young people started work was postponed for longer and longer. This created a lengthy period during which young people possessed an ambiguous status, a period which for the first time in history came to be perceived as a separate stage of life. During this adolescent phase, teenagers spent most of their time with other teenagers, and had weak ties to adults or adult institutions. It can be argued, therefore, that the rise in crime in the period 1950–80 coincided with a weakening of conventional social bonds among young people and an expansion of their relationships with peers.

Caspi and Moffitt (1995) and Moffitt (1997) have argued instead that adolescence-limited offending arises out of the autonomy wars associated with youth transitions. Teenagers need to show they are mature, and freely choosing to engage in behaviour that is forbidden to youth is one way of showing it. In doing so, they mimic life-course-persistent offenders who have started to engage in these behaviours sooner. For the 'normal', adolescence-limited offenders, there is no more need for these gestures of independence once they have actually reached maturity, so they stop. Although Caspi and Moffitt proposed this theory as an alternative to social control theory, there is no conflict between the two ideas, and they can instead be regarded as complementary.

A third explanation for the fall in offending from the peak in adolescence has been proposed by Mark Warr (1993, 1998, 2002). Much youth offending is carried out in groups. Typically it involves young people imitating and emulating each other (Reiss 1988), competing, fighting, and committing offences on one another (Smith 2004a). From analysis of the (US) National Youth Survey for respondents aged 11–21, Warr (1993) found that exposure to delinquent peers, time spent with peers, and loyalty to peers increased dramatically in adolescence, then fell in line with desistance from offending. Warr argued that the decline in offending in the late teens was largely explained by the decline in peer associations rather than strengthened conventional social bonds across age groups, because the effect of social bonds was greatly weakened after controlling for peer associations. Graham and Bowling (1995) also concluded from their analysis of a British youth survey that disengagement from deviant peers was a precondition for desistance from crime.

A final possible explanation for declining offending after adolescence—although this is an explanation of a negative kind—is that most adolescent offenders are not captured by the criminal justice system or therefore stigmatized as official offenders. Evidence from the Edinburgh Study (McAra and McVie, 2005) shows that the actual level and seriousness of offending, as reflected in self-reports, cannot explain why some young people and not others are captured by the Scottish youth justice system. After controlling for offending, young people belonging to certain categories (male, working class, living in a deprived neighbourhood, out on the streets) had a higher than average chance of being picked up by the police and referred to the children's hearings. In a further analysis McAra and McVie (submitted) demonstrated that offending declined more slowly from its adolescent peak among young people captured by the system than among a matched group of young people who had not been captured although they earlier had shown the same offending patterns. In line with labelling theory, these findings suggest that young offenders who are not stigmatized may easily come to regard themselves as normal and integrate into adult society.

PERSISTENT OFFENDERS

Among those who continue to offend after the teenage years, there are widely varying trajectories of offending, as shown by the two recently published long-term follow-up studies (Laub and Sampson 2003; Ezell and Cohen 2005). These studies are agreed in finding that the particular trajectory—or in other words, how soon offenders desist—cannot be predicted from their individual characteristics and family background. This finding is particularly powerful in the case of Laub and Sampson's continuation of the Gluecks' study, because this database includes rich and detailed information from multiple sources about individual offenders and their families. If the finding is definitive, it follows that explanations for desistance have to be sought in personal transformations and changes in the social environment. Gottfredson and Hirschi's (1990) idea that desistance reflects an ageing process that affects everyone in the same way is not sustainable once it is accepted that there are widely different age/crime trajectories. An alternative theory might be that biological and psychological maturation is pre-programmed (and influences offending) but the programme varies between individuals, so some come to maturity sooner than others. This does not seem likely, given that a wide range of psychological characteristics in youth do not predict later offending trajectories. Hence we are thrown back on dynamic theories that explain desistance in terms of things that change in people's lives.

Desistance is not an event but a process that does not have a definitive end, so that any definition of when it has been achieved is liable to be arbitrary. Even if people are no longer officially recorded offenders, their lives may not be transformed in a positive way. Shover concluded from his interviews with persistent thieves that 'Most ex-convicts live menial or derelict lives and many die early of alcoholism or drug use, or by suicide' (Shover 1996: 146, cited in Laub and Sampson 2001). One possibility is that their antisocial and self-destructive behaviour takes a different form at different times in their lives, so that desistance from crime is really a switch to other forms of disruptive conduct and another equally miserable style of life. That is, in fact, a central tenet of Moffitt's (1993) theory. However, it has not yet been backed by much evidence, especially not evidence relating to the later part of the life course.

Rutter (1988) discussed whether the explanations for desistance are just the converse of the explanations for offending. Laub and Sampson (2001) argued that so far most predictors of desistance that have been identified are, in fact, just the opposite of known predictors of offending, yet it is clear that the *process* of going straight cannot be conceptualized as the process of becoming deviant running in reverse. The reformed thief does not become a choirboy again; instead, he becomes a garage mechanic who remembers very well that he used to be a thief. Both in social and in psychological terms, the process of making good, in Maruna's (2001) phrase, cannot be a return to a former existence: it can only be a new life that takes in and transforms earlier identities and relationships.

Social engagement

There is good evidence from both quantitative and qualitative research that engagement in conventional social roles is a critical factor leading towards desistance from crime. In their reanalysis and continuation of the Gluecks' (1950) study, Sampson and Laub (1993) and Laub and Sampson (2003) have set this conclusion within the frame of social control theory. On an expansive interpretation of this theory, social bonds not only constrain the individual from doing anything that might threaten them, but also confer a secure identity and locus to the person who lies at the nexus of a network of relationships. Also, reciprocal relationships, which constitute social bonds, are the source of freedom and power, even though they also exercise restraints. It is through our relationships with other people that we exercise the power of choice and fulfil our desires.

In their continuation of the Gluecks' study, Laub and Sampson (2003) showed that marriage, military service, and getting a job were all associated with desisting from crime. Men who got married were more likely to desist from crime than those who did not. In addition, men who got married were more likely to desist at times when they were married than at other times. These conclusions remained the same whether all crime, violent crime, or property crime was considered. They also remained constant after controlling for a summary of all of the childhood risk factors associated with offending. In support of one of these conclusions, Quinton *et al.* (1993) found that offenders who formed a supportive cohabiting relationship in early adulthood were more likely to desist from crime than those who did not. Qualitative research by Maruna (2001), Farrall and Calverley (2005), and Laub and Sampson (2003) shows, further, that these ties both restrain and confer a sense of purpose and identity.

Although the link between social engagement and desistance is well established, there is room for discussion about the linking mechanisms and the larger framework in which they should be located. On Hirschi's (1969) social control theory, social bonds have an emotional component (attachment), a rational component (commitment), a moral component (strength of belief in widely shared conventional values), and a routine activities component (involvement). This provides a rich variety of linking mechanisms. The general pattern of debate is that other writers have emphasized one or other of these mechanisms and sought to develop it into a more general theory. On a rational choice account, for example, shifts in the perceived costs and benefits of crime account for desistance (Clarke and Cornish 1985), but these shifts may be associated with getting a steady job or making a good marriage, because these milestones increase investment in a conventional way of life and the benefits from it. Whether it is helpful to analyse the matter in cost–benefit terms is questionable, however, since the decision will always critically depend on how far ahead the offender is prepared to look. Alternatively, on a routine activities account, people with strong conventional bonds become engrossed in everyday activities and situations that simply exclude the possibility of offending. A fruitful line for future research would be to establish whether all or only some of these linking mechanisms are important. Warr (2002) has argued, instead, that desistance is related to conventional social bonds only because peer relationships become less frequent and intense as marriage and work relationships grow stronger.

Remaking the self

If the process of becoming criminal involves the 'reorganization of the self' around the deviant label (Lemert 1967) the process of desisting from crime must involve remaking the self again. As pointed out earlier, this process cannot be regression to a former self, because the earlier person, without experience of crime and punishment, would not be able to understand or cope with the long-lasting consequences of a past criminal career. Qualitative studies of offenders and former offenders have repeatedly confirmed that giving up crime does involve deep changes in the way that individuals see themselves and their relations to others (Maruna 2001; Laub and Sampson 2003; Farrall and Calverley 2006). The process of remaking the self can stretch over years, but it can be marked by a sudden shift when everything is seen in a new light (sometimes called an 'epiphany'). At some point in this process, offenders can reach the point of repudiating and morally condemning their former conduct, and feeling deep shame when they contemplate their former self. The qualitative research confirms that work and intimate relationships are critical, but also shows how they have an effect through helping to reconstitute the self. Maruna (2001) particularly emphasized that former offenders need to do something constructive to help others in order to start feeling better about themselves, and take the first steps towards a different way of life. On this account, it is being able to envisage the possibility of a different life that is the key to starting the process of change. A changing perception of the risks of criminal conduct for self, partner, and children may be an important aspect of the reorientation associated with the desistance process.

To emphasize the importance of remaking the self is not to minimize habits, routine activities, and social or institutional structures. There is scope for the self to be reorganized around a 'straight' identity to the extent that the person is enmeshed in a pattern of life that leaves little room for offending. Although the lives of most former offenders are bound to be hard, the chance to get jobs and housing is probably a minimum condition for the process of personal change to take place.

CONCLUSION

The importance of the life course perspective in tackling the central issues in criminology can best be demonstrated by three examples of problems that remain to be solved. First, the large difference in rates of offending between males and females cannot be explained from what is currently known. Various longitudinal studies have now started to tackle the problem (Moffitt *et al.* 2001; Smith and McAra 2004). The Edinburgh Study findings at age 12 and 13 suggested that the explanatory models that focus on teenage experiences apply to males and females in much the same way, but a substantial difference in offending remains after controlling for these variables. This fits with the findings of Moffitt *et al.* (2001) from their literature review and analysis of the Dunedin Study. They concluded that the gender gap in offending arose because males are 'more likely to experience neuro-cognitive deficits, undercontrolled temperamental features, weak constraint (poor impulse control) and hyperactivity' and that these risks accounted for most of the sex difference in offending (Moffitt *et al.* 2001: 7). There was little difference between males and females in the impact of adolescent developmental processes on offending, as also shown by the early Edinburgh Study findings. Thus, in the terms of Moffitt's taxonomy, there was a substantial difference between the sexes in life-course-persistent offending, but little difference in adolescence-limited offending. Substantial further developmental research is needed to refine and check these findings.

Secondly, there is limited understanding of the interactions between individual life histories and the communities and institutions in which they are located. Current analyses appear to show only small effects of neighbourhood characteristics as opposed to individual characteristics on crime rates. That seems to be in tension with what is known about rapid secular change in crime rates, and large differences between countries, which can only arise from social institutions and social structure. Also, analyses of the Pittsburgh Study (Wikström 1998) suggest that neighbourhood influences may be quite different according to the problems ('risk factors') experienced by the individual adolescent.

Thirdly, it has proved extremely difficult to assess the effects of the criminal justice system on rates of crime (Smith 2005b). The most popular methods have involved building statistical models, on the pattern of those used by economists, in order to show how changes in the activity of the criminal justice system (arrests, convictions, sentences of imprisonment) are mathematically related to changes in the level of crime, after allowing for the effects of other variables. This approach has often failed to produce clear results. In order to make progress with the problem it will be important to compare the natural histories of offenders who are and are not captured by the official system (McAra and McVie 2005) and describe the actual mechanisms that may link crime and punishment: for example, deterrence depends on potential offenders becoming aware of the risks they are taking. Longitudinal research is needed to show how direct and indirect knowledge of the activities of the criminal justice system influences offenders' decision making over the life course.

■ SELECTED FURTHER READING

For a general review of the topics covered in this chapter, see M. L. Benson, *Crime and the Life Course* (Los Angeles: Roxburg, 2002).

The best source for contemporary theoretical approaches to crime and the life course is T. P. Thornberry (ed.) (1997), *Advances in Criminological Theory Vol 7: Developmental Theories of Crime and Delinquency*, 11–54. (New Brunswick, N.J. and London: Transaction). This is a series of essays, each one covering one of the major theoretical traditions.

For a treatment of patterns of convictions over the life course (up to age 40) see K. Soothill, B. Francis, and R. Fligelsone (2002), *Patterns of Offending Behaviour: A New Approach* (London: Home Office, Research Findings No 171).

For a comprehensive review of the evidence on the effect of family factors on delinquency, see R. Loeber and M. Stouthamer-Loeber (1986), 'Family Factors as Correlates and predictors of juvenile conduct problems and delinquency', in M. Tonry and N. Morris (eds), *Crime and Justice: An Annual Review of Research*, 7: 29–149 (Chicago: University of Chicago Press). More recent research, which does not always confirm these earlier conclusions, has not yet been conveniently summarized in a similar review.

For a succinct review of the evidence on genetic influences on antisocial behaviour, see G. Carey and D. Goldman (1997), 'The Genetics of Antisocial Behaviour', in D. M. Stoff (ed.), *Handbook of Antisocial Behaviour*, 243–54, (New York: Wiley). A more recent review is provided by S. H. Rhee and I. D. Waldman (2002), 'Genetic and Environmental Influences on Antisocial Behavior: A meta-analysis' (*Psychological Bulletin*, 128: 490–529). A much more detailed treatment is provided by T. E. Moffitt (2005), 'The New Look of Behavioral Genetics in Developmental Psychopathology: Gene-Environment Interplay in Antisocial Behaviors' (*Psychological Bulletin*, 131(4): 533–54). For a review of the influence of factors rooted in the central nervous system (whether or not inherited) see T. E. Moffitt (1990), 'The Neuropsychology of Juvenile Delinquency: A Critical Review', in M. Tonry and N. Morris (eds), eds., *Crime and Justice: An Annual Review of Research*, 12: 99–169 (Chicago: University of Chicago Press).

For a conspectus of the voluminous output from the Cambridge Study, see D. P. Farrington (2002), 'Key Findings from the First Forty Years of the Cambridge Study of Delinquent Development', in T. P. Thornberry and M. D. Krohn (eds), *Taking Stock of Delinquency: An Overview of Findings from Contemporary Longitudinal Studies* (New York: Kluwer/Plenum).

Some of the most important findings from longitudinal research on crime in recent years are from the reanalysis of the earlier study in Boston by Sheldon and Eleanor Glueck. This work is brought together in an accessible way, and related to a developed theoretical framework, in R. J. Sampson and J. H. Laub (1993), *Crime in the Making: Pathways and Turning Points through Life* (Cambridge, Mass.: Harvard University Press). Findings from very long-term follow-ups of members of the same cohort, focusing particularly on desistance from crime, are presented in J. H. Laub and R. J. Sampson (2003), *Shared Beginnings, Divergent Lives: Delinquent Boys to Age 70* (Cambridge, Mass.: Harvard University Press). A thorough review of the research literature on desistance and a new analysis is provided by M. E. Ezell and L. E. Cohen (2005), *Desisting from Crime: Continuity and Change in Long-Term Crime Patterns of Serious Chronic Offenders* (Oxford: Oxford University Press). For a new approach to desistance based on qualitative research, see S. Maruna (2001), *Making Good: How Ex-Convicts Reform and Rebuild their Lives* (Washington DC: American Psychological Association).

The original statement of Moffitt's developmental taxonomy is to be found in T. E. Moffitt (1993), ' "Life-course-persistent" and "Adolescence-limited" Antisocial Behaviour: A Developmental Taxonomy' (*Psychological Review*, 100: 674–701), although several longer treatments are also referred to in this chapter. Moffitt reviewed the theory in the light of subsequent research in (2003), 'Life-Course Persistent and Adolescence-Limited Antisocial Behavior: A 10-Year Research Review and a Research Agenda', in B. B. Lahey, T. E. Moffitt, and A. Caspi (eds), *Causes of Conduct Disorder and Juvenile Delinquency*, 49–75 (New York and London: The Guilford Press).

Readers who are interested in analytical and empirical work on gender issues and offending should consult T. E. Moffitt, A. Caspi, M. Rutter, and P. A. Silva (2001), *Sex Differences in Antisocial Behaviour* (Cambridge: Cambridge University Press). A review of research on the influence of peers on offending can be found in M. Warr (2002), *Companions in Crime: The Social Aspects of Criminal Conduct* (Cambridge: Cambridge University Press).

■ REFERENCES

BANDURA, A. (1986), *Social Foundations of Thought and Action: A Social Cognitive Theory*, Englewood Cliffs, N.J.: Prentice-Hall.

—— (1991), 'Social Cognitive Theory of Moral Thought and Action', in W. M. Kurtines and J. L. Gewirtz (eds), *Handbook of Moral Behaviour and Development, Vol I: Theory*, 45–103, Hillsdale, N.J.: Lawrence Erlbaum.

—— (1997), *Self-Efficacy: The Exercise of Control*, New York: W. H. Freeman and Co.

BANK, L. FORGATCH, M. S., PATTERSON, G. R., and FETROW, R. A. (1993), 'Parenting Practices of Single Mothers: Mediators of Negative Contextual Factors', *Journal of Marriage and the Family*, 55: 371–84.

BARCLAY, G. C., and TAVARES, C. (1999), *Digest 4*, London: Home Office Research and Statistics Directorate.

BENNETT, T. (2000), *Drugs and Crime: The Results of the Second Developmental Stage of the NEW-ADAM Programme* (Home Office Research Study 205), London: Home Office.

BLUMSTEIN, A., FARRINGTON, D. P., and MOITRA, S. (1985), 'Delinquency Careers: Innocents, Desisters, and Persisters', in M. Tonry and N. Morris (eds), *Crime and Justice: An Annual Review of Research*, 6: 187–219, Chicago: University of Chicago Press.

——, COHEN, J., ROTH, J., and VISHER, C. A. (eds) (1986), *Criminal Careers and "Career Criminals", Vol 1. Report of the Panel on Research on Criminal Careers*, Washington DC: National Research Council.

BOWLING, B. (1990), 'Conceptual and Methodological Problems in Measuring "Race" Differences in Delinquency: A Reply to Marianne Junger', *British Journal of Criminology*, 30: 483–92.

BRENNAN, P., MEDNICK, S., and JOHN, R. (1989), 'Specialization in Violence: Evidence of a Criminal Subgroup', *Criminology*, 27(3): 437–53.

BRODY, G. H., STONEMAN, Z., FLOR, D., McCRARY, C., HASTINGS, L., and CONYERS, O. (1994), 'Financial Resources, Parent Psychological Functioning, Parent Co-Caregiving, and Early Adolescent Competence in Rural Two-Parent African-American Families', *Child Development*, 65: 590–605.

BRONFENBRENNER, U. (1979), *The Ecology of Human Development: Experiments by Nature and Design*, Cambridge, Mass.: Harvard University Press.

BUSHWAY, S., BRAME, R., and PATERNOSTER, R. (1999), 'Assessing Stability and Change in Criminal Offending: A Comparison of Random Effects, Semiparametric, and Fixed Effects Modeling Strategies', *Journal of Quantitative Criminology*, 15; 23–61.

CAREY, G., and GOLDMAN, D. (1997), 'The Genetics of Antisocial Behaviour', in D. M. Stoff (ed.), *Handbook of Antisocial Behaviour*, 243–54, New York: Wiley.

CASPI, A., and MOFFITT, T. (1995), 'The Continuity of Maladaptive Behaviour: From Description to Understanding in the Study of Antisocial Behaviour', in D. Cicchetti and D. Cohen (eds), *Developmental Psychopathology*, 2: 472–511, New York: Wiley.

——, LYNAM, D., MOFFITT, T. E., and SILVA, P. A. (1993), 'Unravelling Girls' Delinquency: Biological, Dispositional, and Contextual Contributions to Adolescent Misbehaviour', *Developmental Psychology*, 29: 19–30.

——, McCLAY, J., MOFFITT, T. E., MILL, J., MARTIN, J., CRAIG, I. W., TAYLOR, A., and POULTON, R. (2002), 'Role of Genotype in the Cycle of Violence in Maltreated Children', *Science*, 297: 851–4.

CERNKOVICH, S. A., GIORDANO, P. C., and PUGH, M. D. (1985), 'Chronic Offenders: The Missing Cases in Self-Report Delinquency Research', *The Journal of Criminal Law and Criminology*, 76(3): 705–32.

CLARKE, R. V., and CORNISH, D. B. (1985), 'Modeling Offenders' Decisions: A Framework for Research and Policy', in M. Tonry and N. Morris (eds), *Crime and Justice: An Annual Review of Research*, 6: 147–86.

CONGER, R. D., CONGER, K. J., ELDER, G. H., LORENZ, F. O., SIMONS, R. L., and WHITBECK, L. B. (1992), 'A Family Process Model of Economic Hardship and Adjustment of Early Adolescent Boys', *Child Development*, 63: 526–41.

——, ——, ——, ——, ——, and —— (1993), 'Family Economic Stress and Adjustment of Early Adolescent Girls', *Developmental Psychology*, 29(2): 206–19.

CRICK, N. R., and DODGE, K. A. (1994), 'A Review and Reformulation of Social Information-Processing Mechanisms in Children's Social Adjustment', *Psychological Bulletin*, 115(1): 74–101.

DEMBO, R., WILLIAMS, L., WOTHKE, W., SCHMEIDLER, J., GETREU, A., BERRY, E., and WISH, E. (1992), 'The Generality of Deviance: Replication of a Structural Model Among High-Risk Offenders', *Journal of Research in Crime and Delinquency*, 29(2): 200–16.

DILALLA, L. F., and GOTTESMAN, I. I. (1989), 'Heterogeneity of Causes for Delinquency and Criminality: Lifespan Perspectives', *Development and Psychopathology*, 1: 339–49.

DISHION, T. J., PATTERSON, G. R., and KAVANAGH, K. A. (1992), 'An Experimental Test of the Coercion Model: Linking Theory, Measurement, and Intervention', in J. McCord and R. Tremblay (eds), *Preventing Antisocial Behaviour*, 253–82, New York and London: Guilford Press.

DODGE, K. A. (1980), 'Social Cognition and Children's Aggressive Behaviour', *Child Development*, 51: 162–70.

—— and SCHWARTZ, D. (1997), 'Social Information Processing Mechanisms in Aggressive Behaviour', in D. M. Stoff (ed.), *Handbook of Antisocial Behaviour*, 171–80, New York: Wiley.

——, PETTIT, G. S., and BATES, J. E. (1994), 'Socialization Mediators of the Relation between Socioeconomic Status and Child Conduct Problems', *Child Development*, 65: 649–65.

——, ——, ——, and VALENTE, E. (1995), 'Social Information-Processing Patterns Partially Mediate the Effect of Early Physical Abuse on Later Conduct Problems', *Journal of Abnormal Psychology*, 104(4): 632–43.

DONOVAN, J. E., and JESSOR, R. (1985), 'Structure of Problem Behaviour in Adolescence and Young Adulthood', *Journal of Consulting and Clinical Psychology*, 53(6): 890–904.

DUNFORD, F. W., and ELLIOTT, D. S. (1984), 'Identifying Career Offenders Using Self-Reported Data', *Journal of Research in Crime and Delinquency*, 21: 57–86.

EASTERLIN, R. A. (1968), *Population, Labor Force and Long Swings in Economic Growth: The American Experience*, New York: National Bureau of Economic Research.

EAVES, L. J., SILBERG, J., MEYER, J., MAES, H., SIMONOFF, E., PICKLES, A., RUTTER, M., TRUETT, T. R., and HEWITT, J. K. (1997), 'Genetics and Developmental Psychopathology: 2. The Main Effects of Gene and Environment on Behavioural Problems in the Virginia Twin Study of Adolescent Development', *Journal of Child Psychology and Psychiatry*, 38: 965–80.

ELLIOTT, D. S. (1994), 'Serious Violent Offenders : Onset, Developmental Course, and Termination —

The American Society of Criminology 1993 Presidential Address', *Criminology*, 32(1): 1–21.

——, AGETON, S. S., HUIZINGA, D., KNOWLES, B. A., and CANTER, R. J. (1983), *The Prevalence and Incidence of Delinquent Behavior: 1976–1980*, National Youth Survey Report, no. 26, Boulder, Col.: Behavioral Research Institute.

ESBENSEN, F.-A., and HUIZINGA, D. (1993), 'Gangs, Drugs, and Delinquency in a Survey of Urban Youth', *Criminology*, 31(4): 565–87.

EZELL, M. E., and COHEN, L. E. (2005), *Desisting from Crime: Continuity and Change in Long-Term Crime Patterns of Serious Chronic Offenders*, Oxford: Oxford University Press.

FAGAN, J. (1990), 'Intoxication and Aggression', in M. Tonry and J. Q. Wilson (eds), *Drugs and Crime: Crime and Justice 13*: 241–320, Chicago: University of Chicago Press.

FARRALL, S., and CALVERLEY, A. (2006), *Understanding Desistance from Crime: Theoretical Directions in Resettlement and Rehabilitation*, Maidenhead: Open University Press.

—— and MALTBY, S. (2003), 'The Victimization of Probationers', *Howard Journal of Criminal Justice*, 42: 32–54.

FARRINGTON, D. P. (1973), 'Self-Reports of Deviant Behavior: Predictive and Stable?', *The Journal of Criminal Law and Criminology*, 64: 99–110.

—— (1977), 'The Effects of Public Labelling', *British Journal of Criminology*, 17: 122–35.

—— (1978), 'The Family Backgrounds of Aggressive Youths', in L. A. Hersov, M. Berger, and D. Shaffer (eds), *Aggression and Antisocial Behaviour in Childhood and Adolescence*, 73–93, Oxford: Pergamon.

—— (1979), 'Longitudinal Research on Crime and Delinquency', in N. Morris and M. Tonry (eds), *Crime and Justice: An Annual Review of Research*, 1: 289–348, Chicago: University of Chicago Press.

—— (1983), 'Offending from 10 to 25 Years of Age', in K. T. Van Dusen and S. A. Mednick (eds), *Prospective Studies of Crime and Delinquency*, Boston: Kluwer-Nijhoff.

—— (1986), 'Age and Crime', in M. Tonry and N. Morris (eds), *Crime and Justice: An Annual Review of Research*, 7: 189–250, Chicago: University of Chicago Press.

—— (1990), 'Age, Period, Cohort and Offending', in D. M. Gottfredson and R. V. Clarke (eds), *Policy and Theory in Criminal Justice*, 51–75, Aldershot: Avebury.

——(1995), 'The Twelfth Jack Tizard Memorial Lecture: The Development of Offending and Antisocial Behaviour from Childhood: Key Findings from the Cambridge Study in Delinquent Development', *Journal of Child Psychology and Psychiatry*, 36: 929–64.

——and WEST, D. J. (1990), 'The Cambridge Study in Delinquent Development: A Long-Term Follow-Up of 411 London Males', in H.-J. Kerner and G. Kaiser (eds), *Criminality: Personality, Behaviour, Life History*, 115–38, Berlin: Springer-Verlag.

——, BARNES, G. C., and LAMBERT, S. (1996), 'The Concentration of Offending in Families', *Legal and Criminological Psychology*, 1: 47–63.

——, JOLLIFFE, D., LOEBER, R., STOUTHAMER-LOEBER, M., and KALB, L. M. (2001), 'The Concentration of Offenders in Families, and Family Criminality in the Prediction of Boys' Delinquency', *Journal of Adolescence*, 24: 579–96.

——, OSBORN, S. G., and WEST, D. J. (1978), 'The Persistence of Labelling Effects', *British Journal of Criminology*, 18: 277–84.

——, SNYDER, H. N., and FINNEGAN, T. A. (1988), 'Specialization in Juvenile Court Careers', *Criminology*, 26(3): 461–87.

FATTAH, E. (1991), *Understanding Criminal Victimization: An Introduction to Theoretical Victimology*, Englewood Cliffs, N.J.: Prentice-Hall.

FERGUSSON, D. M., HORWOOD, L. J., and LYNSKEY, M. T. (1993), 'The Effects of Conduct Disorder and Attention Deficit in Middle Childhood on Offending and Scholastic Ability at Age 13', *Journal of Child Psychology and Psychiatry*, 34(6): 899–916.

——, LYNSKEY, M. T., and HORWOOD, L. J. (1996), 'Factors Associated with Continuity and Changes in Disruptive Behaviour Patterns', *Journal of Abnormal Child Psychology*, 24: 533–53.

GLUECK, S., and GLUECK, E. (1950), *Unravelling Juvenile Delinquency*, New York: The Commonwealth Fund.

GOTTFREDSON, M., and HIRSCHI, T. (1986), 'The True Value of Lambda Would Appear to be Zero: An Essay on Career Criminals, Criminal Careers, Selective Incapacitation, Cohort Studies, and Related Topics', *Criminology*, 24: 213–33.

——and —— (1990), *A General Theory of Crime*, Stanford, Cal.: Stanford University Press.

GOVE, W. (1985), 'The Effect of Age and Gender on Deviant Behavior: A Biopsychosocial Perspective', in A. S. Rossi (ed.), *Gender and the Life Course*, 115–144. New York: Aldine.

GRAHAM, J., and BOWLING, B. (1995), *Young People and Crime*, Home Office Research Study No. 145, London: Home Office.

HARRINGTON, V., and MAYHEW, P. (2001), *Mobile Phone Theft*, Home Office Research Study 235, London: Home Office Research, Development and Statistics Directorate.

HINSHAW, S. P. (1992), 'Externalizing Behaviour Problems and Academic Underachievement in Childhood and Adolescence: Causal Relationships and Underlying Mechanisms', *Psychological Bulletin*, 111(1): 127–55.

HIRSCHI, T. (1969), *Causes of Delinquency*, Berkeley, Cal.: University of California Press.

——and GOTTFREDSON, M. (1983), 'Age and the Explanation of Crime', *American Journal of Sociology*, 89: 552–84.

——and —— (1994), 'The Generality of Deviance', in T. Hirschi and M. R. Gottfredson (eds), *The Generality of Deviance*, 1–22, New Brunswick, N. J. and London: Transaction Publishers.

HORNEY, J. D., OSGOOD, W., and HARSHALL, I. H. (1995), 'Criminal Careers in the Short-Term: Intra-individual Variability in Crime and Its Relations to Local Life Circumstances', *American Sociological Review*, 60: 655–73.

HUESMANN, L. R., ERON, L. D., LEFKOVITZ, M. M., and WALDER, L. D. (1984), 'Stability of Aggression over Time and Generations', *Developmental Psychology*, 20: 1120–34.

HUIZINGA, D. (1991), 'Assessing Violent Behavior with Self-Reports', in J. S. Milner (ed.), *Neuropsychology of Aggression*, 47–66, Boston: Kluwer.

——and ELLIOTT, D. S. (1986), 'Reasserting the Reliability and Validity of Self-Report Delinquency Measures', *Journal of Quantitative Criminology*, 2(4): 293–327.

JUNGER, M. (1989), 'Discrepancies between police and self-report data for Dutch racial minorities', *British Journal of Criminology*, 29: 273–84.

KANDEL, D. B. (1978), 'Homophily, Selection, and Socialization in Adolescent Friendships', *American Journal of Sociology*, 84(2): 427–36.

KEENAN, K., LOEBER, R., ZHANG, Q., STOUTHAMER-LOEBER, M., and VAN KAMMEN, W. B. (1995), 'The Influence of Deviant Peers on the Development of Boys' Disruptive and Delinquent Behaviour: A Temporal Analysis', *Development and Psychopathology*, 7: 715–26.

KLEIN, M. W. (1984), 'Offence Specialization and Versatility Among Juveniles', *British Journal of Criminology*, 24(2): 185–94.

KOLVIN, I., MILLER, F. J. W., FLEETING, M., and KOLVIN, P. A. (1988), 'Social and Parenting Factors Affecting Criminal-Offence Rates: Findings from the Newcastle Thousand Family Study (1947–1980)', *British Journal of Psychiatry*, 152: 80–90.

KRUEGER, R. F., CASPI, A., MOFFITT, T., and WHITE, J. (1996), 'Delay of Gratification, Psychopathology, and Personality: Is Low Self-Control Specific to Externalizing Problems?', *Journal of Personality*, 64: 107–29.

——, SCHMUTTE, P. S., CASPI, A., MOFFITT, T., CAMPBELL, K., and SILVA, P. A. (1994), 'Personality Traits are Linked to Crime Among Men and Women: Evidence from a Birth Cohort', *Journal of Abnormal Psychology*, 103(2): 328–38.

KUHN, T. F. (1962), *The Structure of Scientific Revolutions*, Chicago: University of Chicago Press.

LAND, K. C., MCCALL, P. L., and NAGIN, D. S. (1996), 'A Comparison of Poisson, Negative Binomial, and Semiparametric Mixed Poisson Regression Models', *Sociological Methods and Research*, 24: 387–442.

LARZELERE, R., AND PATTERSON, G. R. (1990), 'Parental Management: mediator of the Effect of Socioeconomic Status on Early Delinquency', *Criminology*, 28(2): 301–24.

LAUB, J. H., and SAMPSON, R. J. (2001), 'Understanding Desistance from Crime', in M. Tonry (ed.), *Crime and Justice: A Review of Research*, 28: 1–70.

—— and —— (2003), *Shared Beginnings, Divergent Lives: Delinquent Boys to Age 70*, Cambridge, Mass.: Harvard University Press.

LEBLANC, M., and GIRARD, S. (1997), 'The Generality of Deviance: Replication Over Two Decades With a Canadian Sample of Adjudicated Boys', *Canadian Journal of Criminology*: 171–83.

LEMERT, E. (1967), *Human Deviance, Social Problems and Social Control*, Englewood Cliffs, N.J.: Prentice-Hall.

LERNER, R., CASTELLINO, D. R., PATTERSON, A. T., VILLARRUEL, F. A., and MCKINNEY, M. H. (1995), 'Developmental Contextual Perspective on Parenting', in M. H. Bornstein, *Handbook of Parenting*, 2: 285–309, Mahwah, N.J.: Lawrence Erlbaum.

LEVY, F., HAY, D. A., MCSTEPHEN, M., WOOD, C., and WALDMAN, I. (1997), 'Attention-Deficit Hyperactivity Disorder: A Category or a Continuum? Genetic Analysis of a Large-Scale Twin Study', *Journal of the American Academy of Child and Adolescent Psychiatry*, 36(6): 737–44.

LOEBER, R., and DISHION, T. J. (1983), 'Early Predictors of Male Adolescent Delinquency: A Review', *Psychological Bulletin*, 94: 68–99.

—— and STOUTHAMER-LOEBER, M. (1986), 'Family Factors as Correlates and predictors of juvenile conduct problems and delinquency', in M. Tonry and N. Morris (eds), *Crime and Justice: An Annual Review of Research*, 7: 29–149, Chicago: University of Chicago Press.

——, FARRINGTON, D. P., STOUTHAMER-LOEBER, M., MOFFITT, T., and CASPI, A. (1998), 'The Development of Male Offending: Key Findings from the First Decade of the Pittsburgh Youth Study', *Studies on Crime and Crime Prevention*, 7(2): 141–71.

MCARA, L., and MCVIE, S. (2005), 'The Usual Suspects? Street Life, Young Offenders and the Police', *Criminal Justice*, 5(1): 5–36.

—— and —— (submitted), 'Youth Justice: The Impact of System Contact on Patterns of Desistance', *European Journal of Criminology*.

MCGEE, L., and NEWCOMB, M. D. (1992), 'General Deviance Syndrome: Expanded Hierarchical Evaluations at Four Ages From Early Adolescence to Adulthood', *Journal of Consulting and Clinical Psychology*, 60(5): 766–76.

MCVIE, S., and BRADSHAW, P. (2005), *Adolescent Smoking, Drinking and Drug Use* (Edinburgh Study of Youth Transitions and Crime, report no. 7), Edinburgh: Centre for Law and Society. Available at www.law.ed.ac.uk/cls/esytc/7Smoking_Drinking_Drug_Use.pdf.

MAGNUSSON, D. (1987), 'Adult Delinquency in the Light of Conduct and Physiology at an Early Age: A Longitudinal Study', in D. Magnusson and A. Öhman (eds), *Psychopathology*, 221–34, Orlando, Fla.: Academic Press.

——, STATTIN, H., and DUNER, A. (1983), 'Aggression and Criminality in a Longitudinal Perspective', in K. T. Van Dusen and S. A. Mednick (eds), *Antecedents of Aggression and Antisocial Behaviour*, 277–301. Boston, Mass.: Kluwer-Nijhoff.

MARUNA, S. (2001), *Making Good: How Ex-Convicts Reform and Rebuild their Lives*, Washington DC: American Psychological Association.

MATSUEDA, R. L., and HEIMER, K. (1997), 'A Symbolic Interactionist Theory of Role-Transitions, Role-Commitments, and Delinquency', in T. P. Thornberry (ed.), *Advances in Criminological Theory, vol. 7: Developmental Theories of Crime and*

Delinquency, 163–213. New Brunswick, N.J. and London: Transaction.

MENARD, S., and ELLIOTT, D. S. (1994), 'Delinquent Bonding, Moral Beliefs, and Illegal Behaviour: A Three-Wave Panel Model', *Justice Quarterly*, 11(2): 173–87.

MERTON, R. K. (1938), 'Social Structure and Anomie', *American Sociological Review*, 3: 672–82.

MILES, D. R., and CAREY, G. (1997), 'The Genetic and Environmental Architecture of Human Aggression', *Journal of Personality and Social Psychology*, 72: 207–17.

MISCHEL, W. (1983), 'Delay of Gratification as Process and as Person Variable in Development', in D. Magnusson and V. L. Allen (eds), *Human Development: An Interactional Perspective*, 149–65, New York: Academic Press.

MOFFITT, T. (1990), 'Juvenile Delinquency and Attention Deficit Disorder: Boys' Developmental Trajectories from Age 3 to Age 15', *Child Development*, 61: 893–910.

—— (1993), ' "Life-course-persistent" and "Adolescence-limited" Antisocial Behaviour: A Developmental Taxonomy', *Psychological Review* 100: 674–701.

—— (1997), 'Adolescence-Limited and Life-Course Persistent Offending: A Complementary Pair of Developmental Theories', in T. P. Thornberry (ed.), *Advances in Criminological Theory, Vol 7: Developmental Theories of Crime and Delinquency*, 11–54, New Brunswick, N.J. and London: Transaction.

—— (2003), 'Life-Course Persistent and Adolescence-Limited Antisocial Behavior: A 10-Year Research Review and a Research Agenda' in B. B. Lahey, T. E. Moffitt, and A. Caspi (eds), *Causes of Conduct Disorder and Juvenile Delinquency*, 49–75, New York and London: The Guilford Press.

—— (2005), 'The New-Look Behavioral Genetics in Developmental Psychopathology: Gene-Environment Interplay in Antisocial Behaviors', *Psychological Bulletin*, 131(4): 533–54.

——, CASPI, A., RUTTER, M., and SILVA, P. A. (2001), *Sex Differences in Antisocial Behaviour: Conduct Disorder, Delinquency, and Violence in the Dunedin Longitudinal Study*, Cambridge: Cambridge University Press.

NAGIN, D. S., and FARRINGTON, D. P. (1992a), 'The Stability of Criminal Potential from Childhood to Adulthood', *Criminology*, 30(2): 235–60.

—— and —— (1992b), 'The Onset and Persistence of Offending', *Criminology*, 30(4): 501–23.

—— and LAND, K. C. (1993), 'Age, Criminal Careers, and Population Heterogeneity: Specification and Estimation of a Nonparametric, Mixed Poisson Model', *Criminology*, 31(3): 327–62.

—— and PATERNOSTER, R. (1991), 'On the Relationship of Past to Future Participation in Delinquency', *Criminology*, 29(2): 163–89.

——, FARRINGTON, D. P., and MOFFAT, T. (1995), 'Life-Course Trajectories of Different Types of Offenders', *Criminology*, 33(1): 111–39.

OLWEUS, D. (1979), 'Stability of Aggressive Reaction Patterns in Males: A Review', *Psychological Bulletin*, 86: 852–75.

PATERNOSTER, R., and BRAME, R. (1997), 'Multiple Routes to Delinquency? A Test of Developmental and General Theories of Crime', *Criminology*, 35: 49–84.

——, DEAN, C. W., PICKQUERO, A., MAZEROLLE, P., and BRAME, R. (1997), 'Generality, Continuity, and Change in Offending', *Journal of Quantitative Criminology*, 13: 231–66.

PATTERSON, G. R. (1993), 'Orderly Change in a Stable World: The Antisocial Trait as a Chimera', *Journal of Consulting and Clinical Psychology*, 61(6): 911–19.

——, DEBARYSHE, B. D., and RAMSEY, E. (1989), 'A Developmental Perspective on Antisocial Behaviour', *American Psychologist*, 44(2): 329–35.

——, DEGARNO, D. S., and KNUTSON, N. (2000), 'Hyperactive and Antisocial Behaviors: Comorbid or Two Points in the Same Process?', *Development and Psychopathology*, 12: 91–106.

——, REID, J. B., and DISHION, T. J. D. (1992), *Antisocial Boys*, Eugene, Oreg.: Castalia Publishing Company.

PLOMIN, R., DE FRIES, J. C., McCLEARN, G. E., and RUTTER, M. (1997), *Behavioural Genetics*, 3rd edn, New York: Freeman.

PULKKINEN, L. (1986), 'The Role of Impulse Control in the Development of Antisocial and Prosocial Behaviour', in D. Olweus, J. Block, and M. Radke-Yarrow (eds), *Development of Antisocial and Prosocial Behaviour*, 149–63, Orlando, Fla.: Academic Press.

QUINTON, D., PICKLES, A., MAUGHAN, B., and RUTTER, M. (1993), 'Partners, Peers, and Pathways: Assortative Pairing and Continuities in Conduct Disorder', *Development and Psychopathology*, 5: 763–83.

Reiss, A. J. (1988), 'Co-offending and Criminal Careers', in M. Tonry and N. Morris (eds), *Crime and Justice: An A Review of Research*, 10: 117–70, Chicago: University of Chicago Press.

Rhee, S. H., and Waldman, I. D. (2002), 'Genetic and Environmental Influences on Antisocial Behavior: A meta-analysis', *Psychological Bulletin*, 128: 490–529.

Robins, L. N. (1966), *Deviant Children Grown Up : A Sociological and Psychiatric Study of Sociopathic Personality*, Baltimore, Md.: Williams and Wileus.

——(1978), 'Sturdy Childhood Predictors of Adult Antisocial Behaviour: Replications from Longitudinal Studies', *Psychological Medicine*, 8: 611–22.

——and Regier, D. A. (eds) (1991), *Psychiatric Disorders in America: The Epidemiological Catchment Area Study*, New York: Free Press.

Rowe, D. C., Woulbroun, E. J., and Gulley, B. L. (1994), 'Peers and Friends as Nonshared Environmental Influences', in E. M. Hetherington, D. Reiss, and R. Plomin, *Separate Social Worlds of Siblings: The Impact of Nonshared Environment on Development*, 159–73, Hillsdale, N.J.: Lawrence Erlbaum.

Rutter, M. (1988), 'Longitudinal Data in the Study of Causal Processes: Some Uses and Some Pitfalls', in M. Rutter (ed.), *Studies in Psychosocial Risk: The Power of Longitudinal Data*, Cambridge: Cambridge University Press.

——(1989), 'Age as an Ambiguous Variable in Developmental Research: Some Epidemiological Considerations from Developmental Psychopathology', *International Journal of Behavioural Development*, 12: 1–24.

——(1995), 'Causal Concepts and Their Testing', in M. Rutter and D. J. Smith (eds), *Psychosocial Disorders in Young People: Time Trends and Their Causes*, 7–34, Chichester: Wiley.

——and Smith, D. J. (eds) (1995), *Psychosocial Disorders in Young People: Time Trends and Their Causes*, Chichester: Wiley.

——, Giller, H., and Hagell, A. (1998), *Antisocial Behaviour by Young People*, Cambridge: Cambridge University Press.

Sampson, R. J., and Laub, J. H. (1990), 'Crime and Deviance over the Life Course: The Salience of Adult Social Bonds', *American Sociological Review*, 55: 609–27.

——and ——(1993), *Crime in the Making: Pathways and Turning Points through Life*, Cambridge, Mass.: Harvard University Press.

——and ——(1997), 'A Life-Course Theory of Cumulative Disadvantage and the Stability of Delinquency', in T. Thornberry (ed.), *Developmental Theories in Crime and Delinquency: Advances in Theoretical Criminology*, vol. 7, New Brunswick, N.J.: Transaction.

——and Lauritsen, J. L. (1997), 'Racial and Ethnic Disparities in Crime and Criminal Justice in the United States', in M. Tonry (ed.), *Ethnicity, Crime, and Immigration: Crime and Justice*, 21: 311–74, Chicago: University of Chicago Press.

——, Raudenbush, S. W., and Earls, F. (1997), 'Neighbourhoods and Violent Crime: A Multilevel Study of Collective Efficacy', *Science*, 277: 918–24.

Scarr, S. (1992), 'Developmental Theories for the 1990s: Development and Individual Differences', *Child Development*, 63: 1–19.

Sherman, D. K., Iacono, W. G., and McGue, M. (1997), 'Attention-Deficit Hyperactivity Disorder Dimensions: A Twin Study of Inattention and Impulsivity-Hyperactivity', *Journal of the American Academy of Child and Adolescent Psychiatry*, 36(6): 745–53.

Silberg, J., Rutter, M., Meyer, J., Maes, H., Hewitt, J., Simonoff, E., Pickles, A., Loeber, R., and Eaves, L. (1996), 'Genetic and Environmental Influences on the Covariation between Hyperactivity and Conduct Disturbance in Juvenile Twins', *Journal of Child Psychology and Psychiatry*, 37: 803–16.

Simons, R. L., Wu, C., Conger, R., and Lorenz, F. (1994), 'Two Routes to Delinquency: Differences Between Early and Late Starters in the Impact of Parenting and Deviant Peers', *Criminology*, 32: 247–76.

Smith, D. J. (2004a), *The Links between Victimization and Offending* (Report no. 5, The Edinburgh Study of Youth Transitions and Crime). Edinburgh: Centre for Law and Society. Available at www.law.ed.ac.uk/cls/esytc/5Victimization.pdf.

——(2004b), *Parenting and Delinquency at Ages 12–15* (Report no. 3, The Edinburgh Study of Youth Transitions and Crime). Edinburgh: Centre for Law and Society. Available at www.law.ed.ac.uk/cls/esytc/3Parenting.pdf.

——(2005a), 'Ethnic Differences in Intergenerational Crime Patterns', in M. Tonry (ed.), *Crime and Justice: A Review of Research*, 32: 59–127.

——(2005b), 'The Effectiveness of the Juvenile Justice System', *Criminal Justice*, 5(2): 181–95.

——and Bradshaw, P. (2005), *Gang Membership and Teenage Offending* (Report no. 8, Edinburgh Study of Youth Transitions and Crime). Edinburgh: Centre for Law and Society. Available at www.law.ed. ac.uk/cls/esytc/8Gang_ Membership. pdf.

——and Ecob, R. (submitted), 'The Links between Victimization and Offending', *British Journal of Sociology*.

——and McAra, L. (2004), *Gender and Youth Offending* (Report no. 2, The Edinburgh Study of Youth Transitions and Crime). Edinburgh: Centre for Law and Society. Available at www.law.ed.ac.uk/ cls.esytc/2Gender.pdf.

——and Rutter, M. (1995), 'Time Trends in Psychosocial Disorders of Youth', in M. Rutter and D. J. Smith (eds), *Psychosocial Disorders in Young People: Time Trends and Their Causes*, 763–81, Chichester: Wiley.

Soothill, K., Francis, B., and Fligelsone, R. (2002a), *Patterns of Offending Behaviour: A New Approach*, Home Office Research Findings, No. 171, London: Home Office.

——and ——(2002b), *Patterns of Offending Behaviour: A New Approach*, London: Home Office. Available online at www.homeoffice. gov.uk/rds/pdfs2/patternsrevisedr171.pdf.

Soussignan, R., Tremblay, R. E., Schall, B., Laurent, D., Larivée, S., Gagnon, C., Leblanc, M., and Charlebois, P. (1992), 'Behavioural and Cognitive Characteristics of Conduct Disordered-Hyperactive Boys from Age 6 to 11: A Multiple Informant Perspective', *Journal of Child Psychology and Psychiatry*, 33(8): 1333–46.

Stander, J., Farrington, D. P., Hill, G., and Altham, P. M. E. (1989), 'Markov Chain Analysis and Specialization in Criminal Careers', *British Journal of Criminology*, 29(4): 317–35.

Sykes, G. M., and Matza, D. (1957), 'Techniques of Neutralization: A Theory of Delinquency', *American Sociological Review*, 22: 664–70.

Taylor, E., Chadwick, O., Heptinstall, E., and Danckaerts, M. (1996), 'Hyperactivity and Conduct Problems as Risk Factors for Adolescent Development', *Journal of the American Academy of Child and Adolescent Psychiatry*, 35(9): 1213–26.

Thornberry, T., and Krohn, M. D. (1997), 'Peers, Drug Use, and Delinquency', in D. M. Stoff (ed.), *Handbook of Antisocial Behaviour*, 218–33, New York: Wiley.

——, ——, Lizotte, A. J., and Chard-Wierschem, D. (1993), 'The Role of Juvenile Gangs in Facilitating Delinquent Behaviour', *Journal of Research in Crime and Delinquency*, 30, 1: 55–87.

——, Lizotte, A. J., Krohn, M. D., Farnworth, M., and Jang, S. J. (1994), 'Delinquent Peers, Beliefs, and Delinquent Behaviour: A Longitudinal Test of Interactional Theory', *Criminology*, 32(1): 47–83.

Tolan, P. H., and Thomas, P. (1995), 'The Implications of Age of Onset for Delinquency Risk II: Longitudinal Data', *Journal of Abnormal Child Psychology*, 23(2): 157–81.

Tremblay, R. E., Mâsse, L. C., Vitaro, F., and Dobkin, P. L. (1995), 'The Impact of Friends' Deviant Behaviour on Early Onset of Delinquency: Longitudinal Data from 6 to 13 Years of Age', *Development and Psychopathology*, 7: 649–67.

Warr, M. (1993), 'Age, Peers, and Delinquency', *Criminology*, 31: 17–40.

——(1998), 'Life-Course Transitions and Desistance from Crime', *Criminology*, 36: 183–216.

——(2002), *Companions in Crime: The Social Aspects of Criminal Conduct*, Cambridge: Cambridge University Press.

West, D. J., and Farrington, D. P. (1977), *Who Becomes Delinquent?*, London: Heinemann.

White, J. L., Moffitt, T. E., Earls, F., Robins, L., and Silva, P. A. (1990), 'How Early Can We Tell?: Predictors of Childhood Conduct Disorder and Adolescent Delinquency', *Criminology*, 28(4): 507–33.

Wikström, P.-O. H. (1998), 'Communities and crime', in M. Tonry (ed.), *The Oxford Handbook of Criminal Justice*, 269–301, New York: Oxford University Press.

Wilson, J. Q., and Herrnstein. R. (1985), *Crime and Human Nature*, New York: Simon and Schuster.

Wolfgang, M. E., Figlio, R. M., and Sellin, T. (1972), *Delinquency in a Birth Cohort*, Chicago: University of Chicago Press.

PART IV

FORMS OF CRIME

21

VIOLENT CRIME

Michael Levi, Mike Maguire, and Fiona Brookman

INTRODUCTION

Violent crime is a deeply emotive topic and graphic illustrations of it abound on television and cinema screens and in newspapers, colouring the political and criminal justice responses not just to violence but to crime in general. Yet despite its prominence in both fiction and the news, the attention it has received from criminologists has been surprisingly patchy, focused mainly on a few specific forms of offending (in recent years, notably domestic and sexual violence, and street robberies and assaults) or particular kinds of offender (especially those who commit frequent or extreme acts of violence). It appears to be a self-evident category of behaviour, but there are disputes around whether to define as 'violence', for example, deaths and injuries caused through dangerous driving or through corporate negligence (such as breaches of health and safety regulations in factories or on the railways, or breaches of public health legislation in the food industry). The numbers involved are considerable:

- in 2005, 3,201 people were killed and 28,954 seriously injured on British roads (Department for Transport 2006) with some 500 prosecutions for causing death or bodily harm, 10,300 for dangerous driving, 40,900 for careless driving, and 107,100 actions taken for the high-risk offences of driving after consuming alcohol or drugs (Fiti and Murray 2006);

- In 2004/2005 in the UK, employees at work suffered 220 deaths and 20,213 major injuries, and members of the public 361 deaths and 14,321 injuries connected with the workplace (Health and Safety Commission 2006). We have excluded here deaths and injuries from longer-term industrial diseases caused by, for example, asbestos and coal dust inhalation.

- In addition, 70,311 cases of food poisoning were recorded by the Health Protection Agency in 2004, five times the figure in 1982 (HPA 2006).[1]

---

[1] There are no reliable mortality data available because food poisoning is not an official cause of death (personal communication, HPA Centre for Infections, June 2006). Of course, some food poisoning cases (and

The 'corporate injury' cases might be defined as 'violent crime' on the grounds that, although employers hardly ever *intend* harm either to staff or to the public, harms commonly result from paying 'piece-work' which encourages workers to take risks with their own welfare, or from economies such as poor rail track maintenance, or from employing poor English speakers and untrained staff in roles where loss of life represents a real but infrequent risk. In that sense, they are not mere accidents but the result of a *process* of profit-maximization by corporations (or governments) which define as acceptable the levels of risk to themselves or others (see Brookman 2005 for a discussion of the extent of such deaths, and Tombs 2006 for a discussion of their ideological context as part of a wider critique of the limits of criminology).[2]

Indisputably 'violent', but contested as to whether they constitute 'crime', are other kinds of conduct claimed by some as legitimate. For example, there have been numerous arguments over the years about whether certain violent acts count as 'terrorism' or as 'freedom fighting', or whether government-sponsored violence (including prolific use of the death penalty—Hood 2003) constitutes law enforcement or crimes by the state. In some countries, too, it is not fully accepted that child- or wife-beating constitute 'crime'. Therefore to arrive at a broad understanding of violent crime, we are obliged to do some careful 'unpicking' and to be clear about what components of violence we are addressing.

This chapter first explores some of the ways in which our perceptions of violence, and our attitudes towards its perpetrators, are moulded by a variety of social and cultural influences. We then look at evidence about how much violent crime of various kinds there may be, and at issues surrounding the risk of victimization and its distribution. This is followed by an examination of the different ways in which scholars from different disciplines—biology, socio-biology, psychology, psychiatry, and sociology—have tried to account for the existence, level, and forms of violent crimes. To provide a more concrete example of the issues involved, a closer look is taken at recent work on homicide. Finally, recent trends and developments in attempts to control or reduce violence are briefly reviewed. The principal focus will be on England and Wales, but we will include some comparative dimension.

---

industrial deaths and injuries) are attributable to ignorance or mistakes by citizens, rather than negligence by businesses.

[2] Homicide charges have rarely been brought against large corporations or their directors, and most of the corporate homicide prosecutions that have succeeded have been those in which the smallness of the firms has made it easier to prove that the person responsible was the 'directing mind' of the company (Wells 2001). Due to business opposition and priority given to street crime issues, there has been a persistent lack of political motivation for reform of the law to facilitate prosecutions of corporate killing as recommended by the Law Commission in 1998, despite media and victim criticism for failure to prosecute successfully after rail crashes. In 2006, after years of prevarication (and lobbying by business about unfair risks to directors), the government introduced the Corporate Manslaughter and Corporate Homicide Bill.

ATTITUDES TO VIOLENCE AND CONSTRUCTIONS OF BLAME

The results of surveys in Western countries tend to show quite a high degree of consensus in the public's ratings of the relative seriousness of property and violent offences, the latter consistently emerging as more serious (Levi and Jones 1985; Pease 1988; O'Connell and Whelan 1996). However, despite the well-tested methodology of such surveys, there can be major variations—much better captured by qualitative research than by surveys—in how seriously different forms of violence are viewed in specific contexts, particularly where justifiability and excusability are involved. For example, accounts in court or in the media of the character and behaviour of both parties may influence whether a sexual assault is viewed as a 'real rape' (Adler 1987; Lees 2002) or a homicide as a murder (as in a highly publicized English case in which a householder shot a young burglar in the back at night). Again, although the law defines 'provocation' in homicide as requiring a *sudden and temporary* loss of self-control by the killer, feminists and other campaigners have gradually won sympathy for the argument that the experience of long-term abuse by some women who kill ought to be construed as provocation. As a result, the courts have slowly shifted towards a looser construction of loss of self-control, and changes to the law on provocation are in prospect (Law Commission 2004). By contrast, provocation tends to be widely ignored in relation to violence in public places, which tends to be misleadingly stereotyped as a conflict between a guilty offender and an innocent victim, especially where there is an age or status difference: in fact, it is often an escalating interactive process (Luckenbill 1977; Athens 1980; Toch and Adams 1994).

More generally, it could be argued that we over-inculpate street violence and under-inculpate corporate and motoring 'violence' and, despite the tougher attitude to corporate negligence reflected in the long fought-over Corporate Manslaughter and Corporate Homicide Bill 2006, this pattern is unlikely to change greatly. Various attempts have been made over the years to explain this, as well as other aspects of our conceptions of, and attitudes towards, violent crime. Some radical accounts have put forward the claim that political and corporate interest groups consciously use the power of the media to promote certain images of violence and influence reactions to it. For example, Hall *et al.* (1978) argued that such factors lie behind periodic over-reactions that take place in relation to street violence: in particular, 'governments in trouble' try to distract attention from financial or political crises by stirring up unfounded fears about young (particularly black) males attacking people in the street (see also Bowling 1993; Brownstein 1996; Curran *et al.* 2005). Conversely, large companies are said to be adept at ensuring that relatively little serious media attention is paid to workplace deaths (Tombs 2006). However, even if such deliberate intentions exist, many criminologists would not only question the extent to which the media can actually be manipulated, but argue that public attitudes to crime are influenced by many factors other than media representations alone.

In this context, it is worth referring briefly to Stan Cohen's (2002, originally 1971) concept of 'moral panics'—anxieties about particular social problems amplified by the media under the encouragement of 'moral entrepreneurs'. This has proved a useful conceptual tool for criminology, and is still relevant to many recent 'scares' about violent crime. The tabloid media remain obsessed by allegedly new or growing 'threats' such as, in recent years, knife crime, gun crime, violence in and around schools, 'road rage', 'binge drinking', young people in 'hoodies', and of course 'paedophiles'. Media reports of the new phenomenon of 'happy slapping', in which an unsuspecting victim is attacked while accomplices record the assault (commonly with a camera phone) were particularly prevalent in the UK throughout 2005. Such panics can be triggered by individual incidents and become 'self-fulfilling prophecies': for example, in 2001 in the USA, one father killing another in a quarrel over their children's ice hockey game triggered off a spate of stories about parental competitiveness and 'rink rage'. Pearson (1983) wrote of 15-year cycles of moral panic about youth since the Victorian era, but fuelled by the growth of the media and their constant need for audience-grabbing copy, the cycles appear to have become much shorter in recent years. The political imperative to do something (including over-hasty new legislation) about these newsworthy crimes tends to be greater than in the case of common offences which are neither 'new' nor technologically soluble enough to merit urgent attention. To the extent that the media drive political and policing responses—though the media usually claim that they merely *reflect* 'public opinion'—such coverage is consequential in practical terms (see Reiner's 'media-made crime', Chapter 11 in this volume). While it should not be forgotten that in some cases there is evidence of real increases in serious criminal behaviour (some incidents of so-called 'happy slapping' have resulted in serious and even lethal violence),[3] the cumulative effect on the public is the continual stoking of fears of exaggerated threats (see Hough 1995 for a good empirical review of anxiety about crime; for recent British Crime Survey (BCS) data on worry about crime, including violence, see Patterson and Thorpe 2006: 36–8).

In short, how the police, courts, media, and different groups of the population respond to violence—and, indeed, what they construe as violent behaviour meriting a strong response and what they construe as excusable—is shaped by a wide variety of individual, social, and cultural influences, which may change significantly over time. The type of media coverage afforded to violent crime is clearly an important factor, and this can be influenced by government, police, and corporate efforts to get the media to reflect particular perceptions and attitudes. However, public attitudes are affected by many other factors, including people's own (and their friends' and neighbours') personal experiences of crime. It also appears, as already intimated, that determined campaigning can change public thinking considerably. Notably, feminists have had a major influence on both public and professional attitudes to domestic violence and sexual assault (reflected in allegations being treated more seriously by the police, and in

---

[3] For example, in October 2004 a gang of six youths from Lambeth in central London undertook and filmed several separate attacks on random victims, one of whom died (see BBC News Online, 23 January 2006).

increased sentence lengths for rape), while other pressure groups have helped to transform attitudes to child sexual abuse (see Hoyle and Zedner, Maguire, Chapters 15 and 10, respectively, this volume).

Before leaving the subject of attitudes to violence, it is important to consider those which may develop in times of war or serious civil unrest—or, indeed, when terrorism is seen as a major threat. In such circumstances, perceptions depend heavily on where one stands in the conflict. Killings of people 'on the other side' are likely to be regarded as relatively unimportant, as they will have been to some extent dehumanized through various forms of propaganda. Desensitization to the killing of 'combatants' (or 'terrorists') can quickly extend into attitudes towards the deaths of civilians. Few Britons, for example, expressed serious qualms about the deaths of large numbers of German civilians in the (militarily unnecessary) bombing of Dresden in the Second World War; similar comments could be made about the Americans and Hiroshima. In present circumstances, many in the West (and certainly Americans) might rank the thousands of deaths caused by planes hijacked by al-Qaeda in 2001 as more serious than the same number of innocent civilians killed in a more dispersed fashion by American bombing in Iraq or Afghanistan; many in the Middle East (and many Muslims in the West) might take the reverse view. Again, whether specific violent incidents are even regarded as 'criminal' may vary with the standpoint of the observer.

At times, particularly in the case of civil wars, the basic humanity of whole populations can be eradicated by deep-seated racial, ethnic, or religious prejudices, which can blind them to even the most blatant atrocities. Labels such as 'war criminal' and 'genocide' are not widely applied by people (let alone by criminal justice systems) against their own leaders, at least until they are out of power. Equally, those who commit 'crimes of obedience' (Kelman and Hamilton 1989) define themselves, and are commonly defined in their culture (or at least their narrower reference group), as 'loyal' rather than as being violent conspirators in acts of genocide. Such a state of denial was commonplace in the murder of some 800,000 Tutsis in Rwanda during the 1990s (Gourevitch 2000)—more than the total UK homicides in the past two centuries—the millions killed in the Nazi Holocaust, and the killing of mostly innocent civilians in countless insurgency conflicts. How did so many Rwandans and Germans (and citizens in other death camp locations and Jew-exporting countries: see Bovenkerk 2000) manage 'not to notice' that this genocide was going on, or manage not to view the dead or 'disappeared' as full humans, and thus avoid being, in their own eyes, blameworthy? In accounting for genocide, a socio-biologist might argue that 'not noticing' represents a personal survival-enhancing factor, while psychoanalysts and sociologists from the 'Frankfurt school' might stress the impact of authoritarian child-rearing with its emphasis on social conformity, plus the learned hatred of and contempt for particular ethnic, religious, or national categories of (non)person. These remain areas of intense dispute between genocide studies scholars (see, for example, Goldhagen 1997; Gourevitch 2000; Browning 2001; and Burleigh 2001), although as Cohen (2000) powerfully reminds us, the whole topic of crimes against humanity has remained strangely neglected by criminologists.

EXTENT OF VIOLENT CRIME AND RISKS OF VICTIMIZATION

Risk has become a central theme in social explanation and in discourse analysis. Indeed, some sociologists go as far as to regard it as a central organizing principle of late modern societies (Giddens 1990; Beck 1992; Bauman 1998; Loader and Sparks, Chapter 3, this volume). Where crime is concerned, the concepts of risk assessment and risk management pervade policing and penal practice (Ericson and Haggerty 1997; O'Malley 1998; Kemshall and Maguire 2001) and are key factors in decisions about, for example, police resource allocation and crime reduction interventions. Risk of becoming the victim of crime is also an important consideration for many people in organizing their daily lives (Stanko 1990).

However, most individuals' assessments of their risks of victimization bear little resemblance to traditional calculations of mathematical probability. They are affected by factors such as the voluntariness, personal controllability, and familiarity of the criminal activity in question. Perceptions about the frequency of occurrence of specific crimes are also closely tied up with perceptions of their seriousness. Numerous studies have shown or suggested that the easier it is to recall or imagine an event—a process made easier by dramatic media reporting, as well as popular crime fiction—the more likely we are to judge that it happens frequently or that it might happen to us (Kahneman *et al.* 1982; Freudenberg 1988; Slovic 1992; see also Kemshall and Maguire 2003). Thus, because dramatic crimes are more memorable, we are more frightened of them than we 'need' to be. For example, Lichtenstein *et al.* (1978) found that, in estimating the risks of various forms of death, people tend to grossly overestimate risk in relation to the most vivid or imaginable events, especially homicide. Chadee *et al.* (2006: 21) likewise found that, in 1999, 585,000 Trinidadians thought it likely that they would be murdered: 120 actually were murdered that year.

As a counterweight to such distorted images, calculations of risk can be based on either recorded crime figures or the results of public surveys of victimization, such as the British Crime Survey (BCS)—though both of these, of course, are themselves products of particular perceptions and definitions of violence, and should not be held up as the 'true picture' (Maguire, Chapter 10, this volume). The above two sets of data are now published together annually in *Crime in England and Wales* (Walker *et al.* 2006) and to some extent compared against one another. While both have important limitations, particularly in relation to violence between partners and acquaintances, they at least give us a broad picture of the numbers of people who are willing to report having been physically assaulted each year, and the levels of injuries they sustained. These figures can then be translated into 'risks' of being seriously assaulted, in comparison to, for example, being burgled, injured in a car accident, or whatever. However, as will become clear later, global figures of this kind can be seriously misleading.

RECORDED VIOLENT CRIME AND BCS ESTIMATES

The recorded crime statistics on violence cover a disparate collection of offences that have reached the statute books over the years, ranging from murder to harassment, and including some historical anomalies such as bigamy, concealment of birth, and 'endangering life at sea'.[4] They currently divide violent crime into three main categories: *violence against the person*, *sexual offences*, and *robbery* (see Thorpe and Robb 2006: Table 2.04). The first group is subdivided into 'more serious' offences (principally, homicide, threats/conspiracy to murder, and 'more serious wounding')[5] and 'other offences'. The latter have included since 1998 offences of common assault, harassment, and assault on a constable, many of which result in little or no injury (this change in the counting rules artificially raised the recorded totals of 'violent crime' by over 250,000 in the first year). The BCS, now based on interviews with over 47,000 people annually, allows estimates of how many incidents are not brought to official notice. However, BCS estimates are not all directly comparable with police figures, because the BCS does not measure, for example, sexual offences or offences against children under 16. Only a so-called 'comparable subset' can be directly compared.

More details on both recorded violence and BCS findings—as well as warnings about their limitations as measures of both the extent of, and trends in crime—can be found in Maguire (Chapter 10, this volume), but it is worth setting out here the main figures for 2005/6. As shown in Table 21.1, over the 12 months of the financial year, the police in England and Wales officially recorded about 1.2 million 'violent crimes'. Over one million (84 per cent) of these consisted of the less serious kinds of violence against the person: indeed, 183,000 were cases of common assault with no injury. Robberies (98,000), sexual offences (62,000), and serious non-sexual assaults (40,000) were all much smaller in number. In the same year, however, the BCS produced estimates of over two million non-sexual assaults (wounding and common assault category combined) and over 300,000 robberies. The comparable subsets indicate that only around a fifth of the BCS robberies and common assaults, and less than half of BCS wounding incidents, were recorded by the police (Table 21.2).

Translated into crude 'risk' figures, the BCS results suggest at first sight that about one in 25 adults are likely to fall victim to violent offences (and 1 in 60 to violence by a *stranger*) each year. However, as we shall see, such figures have little relevance at the individual level, as some people will fall victim several times, and the distribution of risk among different social groups is highly skewed. We shall return to this issue after taking a broad-brush look at data on violence (and comparative risk of victimization) from other countries.

[4] A Home Office review identified over 70 different uses of the term 'assault' in law. The draft Offences Against the Person Bill 1998—never put before Parliament to date—contained a set of relatively simple and straightforward new offences to replace the various existing offences of grievous and actual bodily harm and assault: intentional serious injury; reckless serious injury; intentional or reckless injury; and assault. This scales penalties according to a combination of motivation and outcome.

[5] These consist mainly of acts defined under the Offences Against the Person Act 1861 as 'wounding with intent' or 'inflicting grievous bodily harm' (GBH).

Table 21.1 Violent offences recorded by the police, England and Wales, 2005/6

Offence group	Number
Violence against the person	1,059,913
(More serious offences)	(40,330)
(Other offences)	(1,019,583)
Robbery	98,204
(Business property)	(8,762)
(Personal property)	(89,442)
Sexual offences	62,081
(Rape 16 and over)	(9,253)
(Rape under 16)	(5,196)
(Sexual assault 13 and over)	(18,598)
(Sexual assault under 13)	(5,039)
(Other)	(23,995)
Total	1,220,198

Source: Adapted from Walker *et al.* (2006), *Crime in England and Wales 2005/06*, London: Home Office.

Table 21.2 Recorded violent crimes and BCS violence, comparable subset, 2005/6

	Offence totals (to nearest 1,000)		
	BCS estimate	Police recorded	Ratio Police–BCS
Comparable offences			
Common assault	919,000	175,000	1:5.3
Wounding	1,119,000	477,000	1:2.3
Robbery	311,000	66,000	1:4.7
Totals	2,349,000	718,000	1:3.3

Source: Adapted from Walker *et al.* (2006) *Crime in England and Wales 2005/06*, London: Home Office.

COMPARATIVE DATA

As Nelken (Chapter 22, this volume) indicates, comparing crime figures between countries is by no means a straightforward task, owing to major cultural and legal differences in definitions and understandings. The most commonly compared violence figures are those on homicide, where these problems may be less serious (though they are certainly still present). Table 21.3 shows official homicide rates per million population between 2000 and 2002 in selected countries and cities across the world.

Table 21.3 Homicide rates per million population, selected countries and cities, 2000–2002

EU Country/City	Rate	EU Country/City	Rate
Scotland	22.7	Hungary	21.8
Edinburgh	15.6	Budapest	21.1
Dundee	29.9	Latvia	50.7
Glasgow	62.9	Riga	136.6
England & Wales	17.5	Lithuania	104.5
London	26.7	Vilnius	88.8
Northern Ireland	28.5	Malta	11.8
Belfast	62.4	Poland	21.4
Austria	9.0	Warsaw	32.3
Vienna	14.6	Slovakia	24.8
Belgium	71.1	Bratislava	39.4
Brussels	30.3	Slovenia	12.2
Germany	10.9	Ljubljana	10.7
Berlin	21.7	EU Average	25.8
Ireland (Eire)	18.9		
Dublin	21.2	**Other Country/City**	**Rate**
Italy	13.3	Australia	17.8
Rome	13.6	Canberra	5.4
France	17.5	Sydney	15.3
Paris	18.1	Canada	17.9
Denmark	9.8	Ottawa	7.5
Copenhagen	16.0	Japan	10.8
Sweden	6.6	Tokyo	11.2
Stockholm	n/a	New Zealand	16.4
Spain	11.3	Wellington	6.3
Madrid	18.1	Norway	9.6
Netherlands	14.7	Oslo	18.7
Amsterdam	31.3	Russia	223.6
Greece	11.3	Moscow	117.9
Athens	12.8	South Africa	739.3
Portugal	11.3	Pretoria	373.5
Lisbon	15.0	Switzerland	11.0
Finland	27.7	Berne	5.4
Helsinki	19.2	Geneva	16.9
Cyprus	13.9	USA	55.4
Lefkosia	3.6	New York	80.8
Czech Republic	25.2	San Francisco	82.6
Prague	43.3	Washington DC	427.8
Estonia	103.3		
Tallinn	94.3		

Source: Adapted from Table 18, *Scottish Executive Statistical Bulletin*, Criminal Justice Series 2005/12, December 2005. Edinburgh: Scottish Executive.

There are some major variations amongst the countries listed, from a staggering rate of nearly 740 per million population in South Africa to less than seven per million population in Sweden. Washington D.C. (427) emerges as the city with the highest rate. Amongst the EU cities listed, London ranks twelfth (of 28) and comes out as 'safer' than Amsterdam, Brussels, and Berlin. Perhaps most striking are the very high homicide rates of several Eastern European and former Soviet bloc countries and cities: in particular, Latvia, Estonia, and Lithuania and their respective capital cities of Riga, Tallin, and Vilnius, have among the highest rates in Europe. There is also significant variation amongst cities in the UK, with Belfast and Glasgow exhibiting high rates of 62 per million population compared to London's average of 26.7.

THE DISTRIBUTION OF RISK: GENDER, AGE, SOCIAL CLASS, AND RACE

As already hinted, within England and Wales (as elsewhere) there are wide variations in the risk of victimization between different social groups. In this section, we look at the distribution of risk of becoming a victim of violence in terms of the four basic social categories of gender, age, social class, and race; we then look briefly at other risk factors such as location, occupation, and 'lifestyle' (a broader discussion of risk of crime victimization can be found in Hoyle and Zedner, Chapter 15, this volume). It is important to note that some of these factors—notably, gender, age, and social class—are also strong predictors of *offending*. This will be discussed in the section on 'explanations of crime'.

Gender

According to the BCS, as in other sources of data on the subject, there are more male than female victims of violence. The overall risk of being a victim of violent crime in the 2005/06 BCS was 3.4 per cent, but this rose to 4.3 per cent for males in comparison with 2.5 per cent for females.

Domestic violence was the only category of violence for which the risks to women (0.6 per cent) were higher than for men (0.2 per cent). However, the general BCS survey is not a good instrument for picking up domestic violence, so these figures are clearly under-representations (see Maguire, Chapter 10, this volume). On the basis of computerized self-completion questionnaires, where the responses are not seen by the interviewer, the 2004/05 BCS found that partner violence (excluding sexual violence) had been experienced in the previous year by 4.7 per cent of women and 3.6 per cent of men (Finney 2006: 4, 16)—an unexpectedly high proportion in the latter case. Indeed, in terms of prevalence (i.e. the proportions of males and females reporting having been assaulted), evidence from several studies suggests that the gender differences in domestic violence are not as great as one might think.[6] On the other hand, most indicate that

---

[6] Greater differences tend to emerge from local surveys in inner city areas, especially where interviewers have been specially trained to ask questions in this area (see, for example, Jones *et al.* 1986; Mooney 1993; for further discussion, see Maguire, Chapter 10, this volume).

women suffer both *more serious* and *more frequent* domestic assault than men. For example, in an earlier self-completion BCS exercise (Walby and Allen 2004: 33), women were found to be four times more likely than men to have sustained severe physical injuries such as broken bones or teeth (8 per cent compared to 2 per cent) or severe bruising (21 per cent compared to 5 per cent). A major exception to such findings emerged in the USA in a report by Straus and Gelles (1990), based on two large national surveys exclusively on violence in the home. This caused considerable controversy when it appeared to show not only as many male as female victims, but that men were more likely than women to be victims of *severe* violence by their partner. As one might expect, the research came under methodological attack, but more importantly, Straus and Gelles' discussion of the findings was criticized for its failure to take account of the essentially 'gendered' nature of domestic violence: in particular the key difference between women's violence, which is often provoked by genuine male threats, and men's violence, which is based more often on power-control fantasies than on women's threats or 'unreasonable' taunting (Dobash *et al.* 1992, 2004; Archer 1994; Dobash and Dobash 2004). As Young (1988) pointed out in a similar debate with the designers of the BCS, the same action (a punch, or kick, or slap) can have a very different 'meaning' and impact depending on the vulnerability of the victim and the social context in which it is delivered. Nevertheless, the Straus and Gelles research has helped to focus attention on the fact that both female-on-male and same-sex domestic violence are significant social problems.

Age

Young people are more at risk than older people of becoming victims of any form of violence except spouse abuse. Among males, 13 per cent of 16–24-year-olds interviewed by the BCS said they had been assaulted at least once in 2005/06, compared with 5 per cent of those aged 25–44. The equivalent figures for females were 7 per cent and 3 per cent (Jansson *et al.* 2006: 81). Such patterns are often explained in terms of differences in 'lifestyle' (see later), it being noted for example that young people tend to go out drinking at night more often (Tuck 1989; Mattinson 2001). The BCS does not include those aged less than 16, though some specialist surveys of young people have been conducted. The Offending, Crime and Justice Survey (OCJS) found that slightly higher proportions of those aged 10–15 than those aged 16–25 had suffered assault with injury in the previous 12 months (13 per cent compared to 11 per cent) and that the former were also more likely to suffer repeat victimization: 62 per cent compared with 54 per cent had been assaulted more than once (Budd *et al.* 2005: 112). These high levels in the younger group may also be explained by 'lifestyle' factors, although probably different ones to those affecting the victimization of 16–25-year-olds.

Social class

The BCS indicates further significant differences in victimization rates by social class. A range of factors can be drawn upon as indicators of social class including income, type of housing, and employment status. The BCS provides measures of each of these along with the ACORN classification (which groups postcodes according to demographic, employment, and housing characteristics). These data indicate that housing status and the area one lives in are more important risk predictors of violent victimization than income level per se. Private renters were found in the 2005/06 BCS to be almost three times more likely than owner-occupiers to be victims of violence. This was particularly evident when the violence involved strangers. Similarly, those living in areas characterized as suffering high levels of physical disorder were twice as likely to fall victim to violence as those in 'wealthy achiever' areas (as defined by the ACORN classification). The unemployed were also almost twice as likely to fall victim to violence as those in employment (Jansson *et al.* 2006: 81–2).

Other research in the both the UK and the USA has indicated strong social class differences in violence between spouses (Gelles 1998), marital rape (Painter 1991) and child abuse (Straus *et al.* 1980), as well as in violence outside the family (Weis 1989). Moreover, most violence has been found to be both intra-class and intra-race, partly reflecting lifestyles in which males engage in honour contests or domestic oppression. It is also likely that violence—and particularly multiple victimization—affecting the most socially excluded members of society is seriously 'under-counted', relative to other groups, by either national surveys or police crime statistics. This has again been a key finding in specialized local crime surveys in inner city areas, as well as in qualitative research (Jones *et al.* 1986; Genn 1988; Evans and Fraser 2003; Croall forthcoming; see also Maguire, Chapter 10, this volume).

Finally, homicide offers potentially the most accurate *recorded* crime data set for ascertaining the social class of victims. The indications from the Homicide Index in England and Wales are that it largely involves people from lower-class backgrounds as both victims and offenders (Brookman 2005). Both Australian (National Committee 1990; Polk 1994a) and American (Green and Wakefield 1979) studies also indicate that homicide victims come disproportionately from the lower social classes and since most homicides—a fortiori the 'family killings'—are 'cleared up' and are intra-class, it seems evident that it is the poor who are most likely to be injured and killed, whether by violence as conventionally defined or by injury at work.

Race and ethnicity

The 2004/05 BCS indicated that ethnicity was not independently associated with risk of victimization for violent crime. Previous analysis of the 2002/03 BCS had shown that people from black and minority ethnic groups (BME) were at greater risk of household and personal crime than white people. However, this was largely explained by the younger age profile of the BME population and the fact that younger people experience higher rates of victimization (Home Office 2006: 8). The exception was individuals of 'mixed race' whose elevated risk could not be explained on the basis of their age, place of residence, or levels of economic activity (see also Salisbury and Upson 2004). Nevertheless, it should be noted that racist motives greatly magnify the impact of many offences of violence on BME groups—including apparently 'minor' offences such as common assault and harassment. The police have recently become much more assiduous in recording 'racially motivated' incidents, which numbered almost 58,000 in 2004/05 (Home Office 2006: 18; for further discussion of all the above issues, see Phillips and Bowling, Chapter 14, this volume).

That said, there is clear evidence that people from BME groups are more likely to fall victim to homicide than white people. These differences are less striking in England and Wales than in the USA, but 11 per cent of the victims of homicide between 2002 and 2005 were black and 6 per cent were Asian, both figures significantly above the proportions of black and Asian people in the population (Home Office 2006: 18; Brookman 2005). Black victims (32 per cent) were also much more likely than white victims (5 per cent) or Asian victims (10 per cent) to have been shot.

SPATIAL, SITUATIONAL, AND 'LIFESTYLE' RISK FACTORS

In addition to the basic social characteristics of individuals, the distribution of risk of victimization is affected by a number of environmental, situational, and so-called 'lifestyle' factors. Analysis of such factors has been encouraged and made much easier by the growth of crime surveys, as well as improvements in police incident data (Maguire, Chapter 10, this volume). There is space here for only a few brief examples: examples will be given of findings in relation to area and location, occupation, and frequency of going out drinking at night.

Area and location

A great deal of attention has been paid in recent years to the distribution of risks of crime and victimization across different *areas and locations*—to the extent that a whole subdiscipline, what Bottoms (Chapter 17, this volume) calls 'socio-spatial criminology'—has grown up around it. Some of this has examined broad areal patterns, revealing, for example, that the incidence of violent crime, like all 'conventional' types of crime, is strongly correlated with population density (i.e. it occurs disproportionately in metropolitan areas) and, in the main, in city centres rather than in peripheral areas, although this can vary with housing patterns (McLintock and Avison 1968; Baldwin and Bottoms 1976; Wikström 1991). More recently, much more detailed analysis has been conducted at local level, where it is operationally useful to police and partnerships engaged in targeted operations or 'situational' crime reduction activity such as the provision of better lighting in 'violence hotspots' (see Crawford, Maguire, Chapters 26 and 10, respectively, this volume). However, as the literature on areas and locations is well covered elsewhere in the volume (especially by Bottoms), we shall say no more about it here.

Occupation

In empirical research (though far less so in theoretical analyses of masculinities to which the topic is clearly relevant: Archer 1994; Collier 1998), increasing attention is being paid to the differential risks of violence among occupational groups while at work. This has not generally addressed the sorts of 'corporate violence' risks discussed earlier (as we noted, the exclusion of workplace accident and avoidable industrial illness data from victimization surveys is understandable, but reflects the conventional construction of violent crime). Rather, it has focused mainly on attacks on staff by members of the public. Campaigns by social security officials against the removal of security screens from job centres, by teachers to make it easier to exclude 'violent pupils', and by hospitals to exclude violent patients, demonstrate the emotive heat of this issue and the potential it has for disruption of public services.

It is not always conceptually clear whether the best way of looking at these risks is in relation to the numbers of people doing a particular job, or the numbers of people with whom they have to deal. Ideally, one might want to look at assaults as a ratio of encounters with the public, thus allowing for time spent away from risky places and people. Waddington *et al.* (2005) thoughtfully examined violence against the police, Accident and Emergency Unit medical staff, social workers, and mental health professionals, but did not have sufficient data to make such calculations.

A special analysis of responses to the 2002/03 British Crime Survey produced an estimate that there were 849,000 incidents of violence at work in England and Wales in that year, roughly half of these being threats. Put differently, just under 1 per cent of working adults were the victims of actual assaults and a further 1 per cent had been threatened in the workplace (Upson 2004: 5). Table 21.4 illustrates the relative dangerousness of various types of occupation, combining data from the 2001/02 BCS and the 2002/03 BCS. Here, it is clear that those working for 'protective services' (principally the police) have a much higher risk than any other group, with 'health and social welfare associate professionals' (mainly nurses, paramedics, and youth officers) the next highest. The findings are not broken down by specific professions. However, previous analysis of BCS data from the late 1990s (Budd 1999) showed that the police had by far the highest annual risk of assault (25 per cent), followed by social workers and probation officers (9 per cent), publicans and bar staff (8 per cent), and nurses (5 per cent). This does not of course tell us what the relative severity patterns were in the various groups. Also, as in other areas of violence, such physical risk data understate the impact of implicit and explicit threats, and the proportion of such threats or insults that lead to violent incidents is unknown.

Where fatal incidents are concerned, 15 police officers were killed in the line of duty in Great Britain between 1995 and 2005 (see www.policememorial.org.uk for details). This is a much lower figure than in many other countries, including the USA, but an increase on previous decades. A corresponding growth in lethal violence *by* police officers—though rarely found to be criminal violence—is reflected in the fact that, over the same period, there were 27 fatal shootings by the police in England and Wales. There were also at least 13 cases of unlawful killing verdicts and manslaughter prosecutions in relation to the wider category of prison, police custody, or police pursuits, in the ten years after 1995 (www.inquest.org.uk/)

Table 21.4 Risks of assault and threats among occupational groups: data from British Crime Survey, 2001/02 and 2002/03

High risk of assaults	High risk of threats
Protective services (12.6 per cent)	Protective services (3.0 per cent)
Health and social welfare associate professionals (3.3 per cent)	Health and social welfare associate professionals (2.3 per cent)
Transport and mobile machine drivers and operatives (1.9 per cent)	Managers and proprietors in agriculture and services (2.2 per cent)
Managers and proprietors in agriculture and services (1.8 per cent)	Health professionals (2.3 per cent)
Health professionals (1.4 per cent)	Skilled agricultural trades (1.6 per cent)
Caring personal services (1.3 per cent)	Management and personnel (2.6 per cent)
Leisure/personal service providers (1.1 per cent)	Leisure/personal service providers (1.5 per cent)
Teaching and research professionals (1.0 per cent)	Sales (1.3 per cent)
Elementary administration and services (0.9 per cent)	Teaching and research professionals (1.2 per cent)
Corporate managers (0.8)	Elementary administration and services/culture, media and sports/and business and public service (1.0 per cent)

Source: Upson (2004: 30).

Frequency of going out drinking

According to the 2005/06 BCS, respondents who had visited pubs or wine bars in the evening more than three times a week in the month prior to interview were almost three times more likely to fall victim to violence than those who had not visited a pub/wine bar (Jansson *et al.* 2006: 81). Earlier BCS data also indicate that around a quarter of all incidents of stranger violence occur in pubs or clubs on weekend evenings (Mattinson 2001: 3). This is the main 'lifestyle' factor identified by crime surveys as a major determinant of risk. Of course, it is closely tied up with other factors, especially age and location, as young people are more likely than older people to go out drinking in city centres late at night, but it also emerges as independently significant in statistical analyses.

CHANGES IN VIOLENT CRIME RATES

Finally, is British society 'more violent' now than it was in the past, and are more people at greater risk of becoming victims, as the media constantly suggest? If one takes a very long-term view, even leaving aside periods of war and social upheaval, the answer is probably 'no'. The homicide rate in England and Wales today is thought to be roughly half what it was in the mid-seventeenth century, though the *pattern* of homicide is very different, being much more intra-familial now than then. Gatrell (1980) has argued that the Victorian era did witness a significant fall in the level of violent crime (at least outside the home). Similar claims have been made about other Western countries. For example, Gurr's review (1990) points to large American and English fluctuations within a general decline attributable to the 'civilizing process'. Eisner (2001) uses data from several European countries to suggest that a range of disciplinary arrangements in schooling, religious reform, and manufacturing promoted modern individualism and reduced individual-level violence.

Over the medium term, however, the evidence points mainly in the other direction—though the picture has become very unclear in the past few years. According to the official crime statistics in England and Wales (supported since 1982 by the BCS), there was a strong and sustained increase in violent offences, as in most other types of crime, between the mid-1950s and the mid-1990s. Since then the picture has become more complicated. BCS figures suggest that the incidence of violent crime has been declining substantially, with a reduction of 43 per cent between 1995 and 2005/6 (a trend mirrored in the USA, where victimization surveys indicate that it has returned to 1973 levels: see Catalano 2005). By contrast, police-recorded offences have indicated some rises, particularly during the early 2000s. The latter are to a large extent a consequence of changes to the counting rules in 1998 and the introduction of the National Crime Recording Standard in 2002. Nevertheless, as discussed in more depth by Maguire (Chapter 10, this volume), these do not explain the discrepancy entirely. It may also be significant that rises have occurred not just in minor offences such as common assault, but also in the more serious offence categories, where reporting and recording rates are usually less volatile.

It also seems likely, from a range of sources of evidence, that *particular forms* of violent crime—some of which are suffered disproportionately by particular social groups—have increased over this period (see Hough *et al.* 2005). In particular, the rapid expansion of the 'late night economy', based around large increases in alcohol sales to young people, has almost certainly brought with it an increase in alcohol-related violence and disorder (see Hobbs *et al.* 2000; Maguire and Nettleton 2003; Maguire and Brookman 2005; Hough *et al.* 2005; Measham and Brain 2005).[7] Finally, there is some evidence that offences involving firearms have been increasing. For example, recorded offences involving firearms in England and Wales increased from around 7,000 in 2000/01 to over 11,000 in 2005/06 (Jansson *et al.* 2006: 72)—though a high proportion of the increase involved air weapons rather than more lethal weapons. At present, then, careful analysis is needed to tease out trends in different kinds of violent behaviour from a variety of data sources—an excellent illustration of the need for caution in drawing conclusions from any one set of official crime statistics (see Maguire, Chapter 10, this volume).

---

[7] Measham and Brain (2005: 276) provide evidence, from their interviews with 350 respondents at various drinking locations in Manchester, that excessive or 'binge-drinking' is not merely a media-manufactured concern. They state that 'whilst the media may amplify and distort our understanding through their coverage of binge drinking, there is evidence that a significant change is underway in terms of what young people drink, how and why, in that they are psychoactive consumers pursuing a bounded but determined drunkenness within a developing culture of intoxication'.

PREDICTING AND EXPLAINING
VIOLENT BEHAVIOUR

Just as with victimization, rates and seriousness of violent offending vary among different social groups and individuals, and much research has been conducted over the years in order to determine what kinds of people are most likely to commit violent offences. We outline below some of the 'risk factors' that have been identified in the course of such research. However, it is important to bear in mind that, while identifying such factors may be of some use for predicting future violent behaviour (and hence for probabilistically targeted strategies to try and prevent it), it does not help us make sense of violent behaviour and therefore is no substitute for *explanation*. Patterns of offending, like patterns of victimization, should be regarded as evidence with which to develop or test theories about *why* particular people, or categories of people, are more likely than others to use violence—and, moreover, why they do so only on some occasions or in particular situations. As we shall see later, it is the basic kinds of explanation put forward that distinguish different disciplinary and theoretical approaches to the study of violence. Thus while socio-biologists may seek to explain it largely in terms of genetic effects, psychiatrists and psychologists tend to focus on the feelings, thoughts, or attitudes (and the origins of these) that propel some people towards violence, often against particular types of victim. Again, criminologists with a sociological background tend to look at the influence of social structure, culture, or social ordering on patterns of offending. Of course, such distinctions are by no means so clear-cut in practice, and writers in apparently different disciplines can account for violence in ways that look quite similar, though their terminologies and references may differ markedly. For example, sociologists who adopt a sociocultural or ethnographic approach, like many social psychologists, tend to focus on ways in which social interactions at the micro-level can generate violent responses in particular kinds of situation (though, ultimately, their views of the underlying reasons for the nature of these interactions may differ, one from another). The second part of this section will provide examples of different kinds of explanation of violent behaviour that have been developed in each of the above disciplinary traditions.

PREDICTORS OF VIOLENT BEHAVIOUR

In some very broad respects, violent offenders resemble victims of violence. This is particularly true of offenders involved in street violence who, like their victims, tend to be young, male, and from the lower social classes: higher than average proportions, too, have criminal records (Aye Maung 1995; Flood-Page *et al.* 2000). However, this is only the beginning of the story. First of all, perpetrators of domestic violence (and particularly domestic homicide) are overwhelmingly male while the majority of their victims are female. Equally important for attempts at explanation, by no means all of those in particular 'risk categories' actually commit any violence. This is obviously true of huge categories such as 'young lower-class males', but it is also true of even the most refined categories one can devise, such as those who score high on psychopathy scales or sex-offending prediction instruments. Again, while those who have committed violent offences in the past are more likely than most other people to commit them in the future, only a minority actually do so. Where the most serious kinds of violent offending are concerned, the proportions are very small: for example, of a sample of rapists convicted in 1951, only 6 per cent had been reconvicted of sex crimes by 1973 (Soothill *et al.* 1976) and of 264 people convicted of rape in 1972, 4.5 per cent had been reconvicted of rape by 1985 (Home Office 1989; for general overviews of the prospects and limits of prediction, see Monahan 1981; Morris and Miller 1985; Monahan and Steadman 1994). Such figures, together with the fact that the *majority* of 'violent offenders' are not convicted of more than one violent offence, suggest that concepts such as 'careers of violence' are not very useful except for relatively small numbers of serious offenders, including some 'serial' abusers of their own families (repeat violence being most common in domestic situations)[8] and some extra-familial rapists and paedophiles. These findings of low recidivism for violence have, or ought to have, important implications for those who believe in 'incapacitating the violent offender'.

Some researchers have set out to identify predictors of future violent offending among very young children, focusing less on group attributes such as low income or educational level than on aspects of individual temperament or of parenting practice. For example, from studies of cohorts of children followed up over a long period, Farrington (1989, 1991) found that children who are high on hyperactivity-impulsivity-attention deficit, who are restless and lacking in concentration, who lack empathy, and who find it difficult to defer gratification, have a relatively high risk of becoming violent offenders when older. This may look like a caricature of the 'feckless poor', but it does achieve a prediction of who *within a class* is most likely to display persistent and/or serious aggression (see further, Farrington, Chapter 19, this volume).

Alcohol and drugs

Researchers have increasingly drawn attention, not only to social and individual factors, but also to high correlations between violent offending and substance misuse, especially alcohol (Ramsay 1996). For example, victims in the 2005/06 BCS believed the offender or offenders to have been under the influence of alcohol in 44 per cent of all violent incidents: this figure increased to 54 per cent for incidents involving strangers. American research likewise indicates a strong relationship between alcohol use and violent offending, both against partners (Frieze and Browne 1989) and generally. Adolescents who drink heavily or use drugs are more likely than those who do not to commit violent acts (Herrnstein 1995).

---

[8] Even within the family violence context, it is far from clear what proportion of men who have hit their wives do so again, let alone escalate the level of violence. Fagan's (1989) review of the cessation of family violence notes that three-quarters of spouse abusers stop following legal sanctions (though for how long they stop is uncertain, since the follow-up periods are not long).

While such findings are important, it is reiterated that they do not *explain* violence in causal terms and one should be careful not to jump to conclusions in this respect. Most people know others who behave much more aggressively when they have been drinking heavily. However, it is very rare for such people to be violent *every* time that they consume alcohol, so it cannot be said, for example, that the drink is a sufficient or even a necessary explanation of their violence. Heavy drinking among violent adolescents may reflect the risk-taking mental set of those who begin their criminal careers early, rather than there being a direct causal link between the drinking and the violence. Equally, the concentrations of violent incidents late at night in city centres (Tuck 1989; Deehan 1999; Maguire and Nettleton 2003) *could* be a product of problems such as overcrowded bars and disputes over scarce transport, rather than a direct effect of alcohol per se (as argued by the Social Issues Research Centre 2002). Notwithstanding this, the opportunities for certain types of interaction offered by heavy alcohol use, combined with an aggressive male 'drinking culture' (Tomsen 1997), strongly implicate alcohol in the process of becoming violent and hence offer a useful starting point from which to build theoretical explanations of at least some forms of violence[9] (for a comprehensive discussion of the possible causal relationships between substance misuse (including alcohol) and crime, see Bennett and Holloway 2006).

Illicit drugs are less prominent than alcohol as a risk factor in survey results, though offenders were perceived as being under the influence of drugs in nearly a quarter of all violent incidents reported to the 2005/06 BCS, and a slightly higher proportion of 'muggings' (Jansson *et al.* 2006). Moreover, Bennett and Holloway (forthcoming) found, as part of their NEW-ADAM research, that almost 60 per cent of individuals who had been arrested for assault (between 2000 and 2002) had used an illicit drug in the last 12 months, including 35 per cent who said they had used at least one Class A drug. Of those who provided urine specimens, 47 per cent tested positive for any illicit drug, 44 per cent tested positive for alcohol, and 17 per cent tested positive for Class A drugs. In the USA, too, strong positive correlations have been found between the seriousness and frequency of violent delinquency and the level and frequency of drug-taking (Fagan 1990).

As with alcohol, except in so far as there may be 'commercial' violence resulting from a desire to dominate drugs distribution or extort money from sellers, there is little evidence that the *pharmacological* effects of cannabis, hallucinogens, or opiates makes people violent, at least when taken alone (Bennett and Holloway 2006). There is a more plausible link between violence and amphetamines and solvents (and with steroids often associated with body-building) but, again, demonstrating the causal link is problematic, and confounded by the intervening personality variables. The effects of crack cocaine in increasing the risks of mental illness (one side-effect of which may be violence) are difficult to separate out from the need to get funds to obtain a 'fix', which

[9] Of course, there are many types of violence for which it offers *no* explanation: for example, most political, corporate and state sponsored violence. It should also be noted that most Muslims neither drink nor take illegal drugs, yet violence is by no means unknown in Muslim countries.

can lead to robbery as well as to non-violent crimes for gain. A thoughtful overview by Fagan concludes (1990: 299) that:

> intoxication affects cognitive processes that shape and interpret perceptions of both one's own physiology (i.e. expectancy) and the associated behavioral response. The cognitive processes themselves are influenced by cultural and situational factors that determine the norms, beliefs, and sanctions regarding behaviors following intoxication . . . Propensity toward aggression reflects explanations regarding the use of personal power to resolve perceived conflicts.

EXPLAINING VIOLENCE

Setting out to 'explain violence' immediately raises some basic questions. Given the enormous heterogeneity of forms of violence discussed earlier in this chapter, is it plausible that any one theory or theoretical paradigm can account for all these manifestations, or even serve as a common thread in all of them? Should we therefore be seeking only for explanations of particular 'types' of violence (such as 'domestic' violence, or 'gang violence')? And should we restrict ourselves to 'criminal' violence, or include violence that is widely regarded as 'legitimate' (such as violence in wartime, violent sports, or executions of criminals)? Equally important, what sort of explanation are we looking for? An explanation of why this person committed that act in a particular place and time?[10] Or why particular 'kinds of individual' tend to acquire criminal histories of violent offending? Alternatively, are we searching for an explanation of different *rates* of violence in different locations, geographical areas, or countries, and/or over time? Or of different rates of offending or victimization, by occupation, age, ethnicity, and gender? Or of patterns in relationships between offenders and victims, in these or other terms? Different sorts of answers are required for different aims and levels of explanation, which partly explains why attention has been paid to such a variety of factors as autonomic nervous systems, hormones, food metabolization, electroencephalogram readings, social and economic status (absolute, or by level of social inequality), gender, ethnicity, media coverage, and level of 'victim-precipitation'.

The conceptual issue of 'what acts count as violence' does not cause too many difficulties for criminologists in practice, because they often ignore it. Much of the criminological literature on explaining violent crime takes as its field of enquiry the 'conventional' kinds of assault which dominate the 'offences against the person' officially recorded by the police (see Maguire, Chapter 10, this volume). A significant proportion of the psychological literature (and that by psychologically oriented criminologists) has a narrower focus on individuals who frequently assault others, or on the

---

[10] Much of the ubiquitous literature on serial killers and rapists takes this form. It seldom explores, however, whether and/or why there are variations over time and between cultures in the frequency of the phenomenon, or even the psychopathology of suspects, except inasmuch as it helps to narrow down the range of plausible suspects. For a good review in this genre, see Holmes and Holmes (1996). For a deeply sceptical view of the social construction of serial homicide, see Jenkins (1994). Especially since the television series *Cracker*, there has been a vogue for books on profiling and about profilers (e.g. Canter 1995; Britton 1998, 2001).

more extreme kinds of violence, such as homicide and rape. Both approaches are perfectly defensible. Some people have a frankly psychotic or psychopathic view of the world and their relationship with it, and it seems appropriate in these extreme cases to take as the object of explanation 'why and in what respects are these people so different?' (see, for example, Hare 2001). Other violent offenders are closer to normal behaviour for their gender and age, and the appropriate focus is on social learning, situational interaction, cognitive processing, and opportunity factors. However, such approaches are limited in terms of explaining violence in a wider sense, leaving out areas such as corporate or state violence, and often not taking sufficient account of the gendered nature of much violence.

Another persistent difficulty with many approaches to explaining violence (and, for that matter, victimization risks) is that they seldom generate anything close to a causal account which makes sense of *non*-violence as well as of violence. The accounts that come closest to helping us understand why this person committed that crime on that particular occasion are retrospective reviews: but the motivating factors they reveal are much more common than violent behaviour, even if one takes into account opportunity variables.

Those who write about violence understandably reflect their background disciplines, and although most will acknowledge that heredity, personality, family conflicts, cultural (including gendered) and situational factors all influence violent behaviour, it is the *relative* salience of these variables that produces a clear divide. Although severely constrained by space limits, we shall attempt to give a least a flavour of this multiplicity of perspectives, by commenting very briefly in turn on a range of biological, psychoanalytic, (social) psychological, and sociological (including feminist) explanations of violence. We shall restrict our focus here mainly to explanations of *individual* violence, saying relatively little about the subject of *collective* violence. It is, however, important to recognize that the two can be closely linked: particularly violent individuals can influence the behaviour of a crowd (Waddington 1992). Moreover, the presence of 'significant others' can be a factor in individuals becoming violent in certain situations—for example, through not wishing to 'lose face' in front of a peer group. We shall also leave aside terrorism, some aspects of which are discussed elsewhere in this volume by Levi (Chapter 23).

In order to provide a more concrete illustration of how some of the theoretical perspectives outlined can be used by researchers to help understand patterns of violence, this section will be followed by a discussion of recent work on a specific form of violent crime, homicide.

BIOLOGY, SOCIO-BIOLOGY, AND EVOLUTIONARY THEORY

We begin with a few very brief comments on biological theories of violence. These tend to focus either on disorders of the brain (which may be permanent or temporary) caused by physical damage or environmental factors which affect its physiology, or on the influence of genetic and/or evolutionary factors on individual behaviour.

Research in the first of the above areas has identified a huge range of both endogenous and exogenous factors said to affect the physiology of the brain, leading under certain circumstances to loss of self-control (Moir and Jessell 1995). Such factors have included releases of testosterone (Archer 1990), the metabolization of glucose (Raine *et al*. 1994), the menstrual cycle (Fishbein 1992), and even eating chocolate (Lester 1991) and the weather (Cheatwood 1995). One of the main problems that such theories come up against—in common with many other theories, it should be said—is that they find difficulty in accounting both for the non-violence of many people who have been exposed to the factors in question, and for the infrequency of violence among those who *sometimes* behave violently. Work which, for example, associates the post-pubertal adolescent 'testosterone rush' with the rise in aggression among boys (e.g. Olweus 1987) does at least provide some plausible account for age variation in aggression levels, but less so differences within the age group. Of course, it is fairly easy to make fun of the *general* value of the impact, for example, of chocolate on suicide and homicide—should we ban chocolate as well as guns?—but for some individuals, particular physiological triggers may apply under rare combinations of conditions that one may only discover after the violent incident. Understanding such cases can be extremely valuable to clinical work with patients already identified as having serious violent propensities, although it is arguably less valuable as a basis for general theories of violence.

Wilson and Herrnstein (1985; see also Herrnstein 1995) are among the most prominent academics who argue that *genetic* factors are important to the understanding of violent behaviour. They have found some empirical support, particularly in studies following up the criminal records of monozygotic (identical) versus dizygotic twins (Brennan *et al*. 1995; Mednick *et al*. 1987; Rowe 1990). Genetic theories may help to explain why some people behave violently for a long time in a variety of settings: although the manifestations of aggression vary, a child who is top of the distribution for aggression at the age of 8 is likely to be near the top twenty years later (see Farrington, Chapter 19, this volume). However, they have difficulty in accounting for changes in violent crime rates in the same society over time or, again, for the infrequency of violence among those who sometimes behave violently.

There are socio-biological approaches—mainly those which adopt evolutionary explanations—which are more dynamic and therefore can accommodate changing violence rates to some degree. For example, Burgess and Draper (1989) examine family violence in evolutionary terms, arguing that under certain conditions, child maltreatment has a benefit in helping the fittest survive; hostility towards stepchildren may also be explicable in terms of our being prepared to act in a more hostile way towards people who share none of our genes.[11] (See Felson 2006, for a recent approach to explaining *all*

---

[11] Natural selection arguments take into account epidemiological data but, like most functionalist explanations, tend towards the tautological. Selection operates at the level of the individual person or even the individual gene, rather than in terms of 'reproducing the population': the latter is simply an aggregated consequence of individual selections. One problem posed for natural selection theory is the high prevalence of unrecorded incest. Another problem is how to account for variations in violence such as the alleged increase in attacks upon 'disabled' people in Germany during the 1990s.

crimes including violence in terms of adaptation to environments.) Brownmiller (1975) is one of the few feminists to argue that rape is the result of *biological drives* (rather than being 'learned masculinity', which is functional for male hegemony) and a historical adaptation deriving from lack of lawful access to reproductive mates. However, it might be argued in response that many rapists also enjoy access to consenting (or at least uncomplaining) females; moreover, the generalized aggressiveness they often display to people and to property suggests that 'the selfish gene' is not restricted to the desire to reproduce genetically. Finally, analyses of homicide by Daly and Wilson (1988, 1994; see also Wilson and Daly 1992) emphasize the different evolutionary selection pressures on men and women which favour male risk-taking and female risk-avoidance. However, they also concede that situational circumstances have a major effect on whether the evolutionary drives are translated into actual violent behaviour. Thus for example, Daly and Wilson (1988: 128) write:

> A seemingly minor affront is not merely a 'stimulus' to action, isolated in time and space. It must be understood within a larger social context of reputation, face, relative social status, and enduring relationships. Men are known by their fellows as 'the sort who can be pushed around' or 'the sort who won't take any shit', as guys whose girlfriends you can chat up with impunity or guys you don't want to mess with. In most social milieus, a man's reputation depends in part upon the maintenance of a credible threat of violence.

As this passage shows, socio-biologists such as Daly and Wilson have superficially quite a lot in common with ethnographers and others who adopt a sociocultural approach to the study of violence (discussed below). However, the difference lies in their breadth of perspective and analysis of the *origins* of attitudes. We may conclude that although *some* biologists may be trapped in a static framework which obviously cannot account for the enormous variations in the extent of violence across societies and over time, the more sophisticated do take such variability into account. Even so, their analysis of the reasons behind such changes tends to produce what are essentially functionalist and teleological explanations of violent behaviour.

PSYCHIATRIC AND CLINICAL APPROACHES TO VIOLENCE

There is a self-evident quality in the proposition that people who commit especially vile acts have 'something wrong with them': the very abnormality of the acts make it unsurprising that people should look for something abnormal about those who performed them. However, while some killers and rapists are obviously highly disturbed, many appear quite normal most of the time (Jefferson 1997). Dobash *et al.* (2001) found that of all men then serving sentences for homicide in Great Britain, just over a third came from broken homes, a quarter had a father who was violent to their mother, over half had alcohol problems, half had abused drugs, and a quarter had mental health problems. One of the interesting things that may be inferred from these findings—which are reminiscent of analyses of the general prison population, not just serious violent offenders—is the surprisingly large percentage that do *not* appear to be mentally disturbed or to come from a severely dysfunctional family or personal background.

For this reason, while they may be of considerable value in guiding the treatment of individual patients (for example, in high-security mental hospitals), psychiatric analyses of violent offenders tend to have relatively narrow explanatory power. To the non-clinician, indeed, some accounts of 'the mind of the murderer' (for example, Guttmacher 1973) amount to little more than a list of mental states and some *ex post facto* interpretation of how their family interactions may have generated their 'compulsion to kill', without any obvious reason as to why the crimes occurred at that time and place, nor consideration of why similarly disturbed individuals never kill or cause serious harm to others. Gresswell and Hollin (1994) have provided a more helpful typology of multiple murderers, breaking motivation into four areas:

1. Visionary killers, who suffer from delusional beliefs about particular victims.
2. Missionary killers, who have decided to rid society of certain types of people (such as prostitutes).
3. Hedonistic or lust killers, who seek to remove the memory of humiliation by projecting rage on to their victims.
4. Power and control killers, who use killing as a form of domination.

However, for some, even this kind of motivational typology fails to illuminate the development of violent behaviour over time within the individual's life cycle. A more dynamic kind of explanation is provided by Brown (1991; see also Raine 1993; Malmquist 1995), who argues that serial killers develop a taste for killing which relieves anxieties and is positively reinforced by the dissolution of anxiety, rather like other forms of addiction. This is compatible with the emotional 'high' that offenders sometimes get from sexual or violent acts which is emphasized by Katz (1988) and which, others have noted, can change the pattern and intensity of their violence (Canter 1995; Britton 1998, 2001).

With a somewhat different orientation to psychiatrists, clinical psychologists tend to focus on the determinants of behaviour rather than offenders' emotions. However, their explanations remain strongly concentrated on individual pathology and pay little attention to structural or cultural influences. For example, while acknowledging our very limited understanding of why some people turn out that way, Hare (2001: 27) asserts that:

> the aggression and violence of the psychopath are instrumental, predatory and cold-blooded, and owe more to the nature of the individual than to the social and environmental forces that help to drive most other types of violence.

Hare has developed a rigorous set of criteria into a psychopathy checklist in which high scores are given to people who display lack of empathy, guilt, or remorse and who use others only as tools for their own interests. People thus diagnosed have a significantly higher reconviction rate than people who score low: a situation made worse rather than better by the sort of therapeutic community awareness regime sometimes recommended to increase empathy. Hare (1998) agrees that many people who receive high scores do not commit violent crimes or (by implication) any crimes: indeed, as classical psychiatric accounts also make clear, many would make successful captains of industry or politicians. So these are enhanced risk predictive factors rather than being either necessary or sufficient conditions for violent or any other crime (see also Peay, Chapter 16, this volume).

In conclusion, the episodic and non-recidivistic nature of most violent crime remains a difficulty for the general explanatory powers of both psychiatric and clinical psychological accounts, focusing as they do (understandably) on the most serious cases. Such accounts are also open to criticism from sociologists (and feminists) on the grounds that their focus on factors internal to the individual underestimates the importance of cultural and structural influences on behaviour.[12] As Jones (2000: 43) concludes:

> [I]t is not clear that any association between mental disorder and violent crime means that the offending occurred as a result of the disorder. The mental disorder may have been related to wider social problems which themselves precipitated the offending. Moreover, even where an association is apparent, it does not provide an explanation for the vast majority of violent crimes.

SOCIAL PSYCHOLOGICAL EXPLANATIONS

Social psychological approaches to the explanation of violence have in common with micro-level sociological or sociocultural approaches (see below) a focus on interpersonal dynamics that 'produce' violent behaviour in particular situations, although they tend to locate its ultimate origins in the offender's cognitive processes and earlier influences which shaped them. Cognitive theories, which have dominated the field for some years, are discussed in some detail by Hollin, Chapter 2 in this volume, so only brief comments will be made here.

In essence, cognitive explanations of offending behaviour, including violence, entail the argument that individuals who have failed to mature normally and develop empathy and 'moral reasoning' remain in a self-centred world in which they acquire 'cognitive distortions' which cause them to misunderstand and misinterpret both their own and other people's behaviour (see Andrews and Bonta 1998). They are also likely to lack social and interpersonal skills which assist people to resolve potential conflicts.

---

[12] Such a criticism is implicit in the work of Freedman and Hemenway (2000), who studied the precursors to lethal violence amongst a death row sample. They found injury or deficit present across four distinct 'ecological' levels—*the individual* (e.g. brain injury); *the family* (e.g. experiencing or witnessing physical or sexual abuse at home); *the community* (e.g. isolation from the community); and *social institutions* (e.g. failure by such institutions to recognize abuse or neglect and react accordingly). What was striking amongst the men they studied was the constellation of predisposing factors that had been experienced by these killers.

Some learn to interpret social 'cues' as signs of hostility which require a (to them, entirely legitimate) violent response.

Another related concept is that of 'scripts' (Huessman and Eron 1989) which are learned by an individual about what events are likely to occur, how s/he should react to the events, and what will result. These 'scripts' have been learned during the child's early development (influenced by parents' own cognitive processes, so people who view the world as hostile tend to reinforce this construct in the child's scripts) and are retrieved from memory on the appropriate environmental cues. However, psychologists stress that this is not a mechanical process, and is influenced by many other factors in any interaction, including the responses of others and previous relationships between those involved. For example, in research on marital violence (Frude 1994) stresses the importance of:

1. relationship dissatisfaction, which leads to more negative evaluation of the partner's behaviour and to anger;

2. the couple's power relationship, which can be exacerbated when the male has fewer resources than the female (Straus and Gelles 1990); and

3. the couple's conflict style. Violence is particularly common in relationships which have high 'ambient conflict', involving frequent rows and the absence of inhibitions in attacking the self-esteem of their partner.

As discussed by both Hollin and Raynor in this volume (Chapters 2 and 31, respectively), cognitive theories (together with some ideas from behavioural psychology, particularly concerning the reinforcement of behaviour) have been extremely influential in the development of 'offending behaviour programmes', which are currently attended by large numbers of offenders in prisons and probation areas across England and Wales. These include programmes aimed specifically at high-risk violent and sexual offenders, in which participants are taught to recognize and overcome their own cognitive distortions and practise more appropriate ways of handling situations through exercises and role-plays.

An interesting aspect of such theories, with important implications for programmes, is their tendency to focus on *impulsive* behaviour, and on violence characterized by anger and a loss of self-control. In the latter regard, the work of Novaco (1994) has been particularly influential, linking cognitive misinterpretations of social cues with the triggering of angry thoughts and hence violent responses. This has informed the development of 'anger management' programmes for violent offenders, in which participants are taught mechanisms to avoid or control angry reactions. However, this can draw attention away from a rather different kind of violence in which anger may be largely absent: broadly speaking, what Megargee (1983) called 'instrumental' (as opposed to 'expressive') violence. Such violence may be committed in order to obtain an economic benefit—for example, to keep other drug dealers off one's territory or away from one's crime proceeds (Stelfox 1998) or to obtain money or valuables through robbery. A reputation for violence can also be economically functional in, say, protection rackets or other activities involving 'gangsters' or organized criminal groups (Reuter 1983; Gambetta 1994): indeed, where reputation is strong enough, there may be no need actually to hurt anyone, at least until violent competitors come along.

Admittedly, such a bifurcation of motives is far too crude. On the one hand, many robbers also obtain a 'high' from the apparently instrumental violence or threats they employ (Katz 1988), and gangsters may consider that 'it is just business' when mutilating and/or murdering their victims, but actually they may be psychopathic or psychotic revellers in violence also. Vice versa, apparently 'expressive' violence can also be used (instrumentally) as a means of controlling people. For example, it can generate domestic and sexual services from partners who are afraid to leave the aggressor; a reputation as an unpredictable 'nutter' or 'psychopath' can also be advantageous in dealings among local criminals, as amply demonstrated by the Kray twins in the 1960s (it also used to be handy for getting work as a 'bouncer' or club doorman (Hobbs *et al.* 2000), though this has changed since the introduction of vetting). Nevertheless, there is some truth in the distinction, and it may be that different kinds of explanation are required to take account of differences in motives. In practical terms, this issue raises questions about the suitability of 'anger management' programmes for people who already use violence in a very controlled manner when, for example, committing robberies or rape: should we be teaching them to do so more effectively?

SOCIOLOGICAL AND SOCIOCULTURAL APPROACHES

In contrast to the micro-level focus of social psychological accounts, most early sociological accounts of violence—as of crime in general—focused on aggregate data sets and broad-scale cultural trends, and sought explanations in fundamental structural problems in society such as 'social disorganization', social inequality, and blocked opportunities for advancement. Thus, in Mertonian anomie theory and its later development, 'rebellion' was one mode of adaptation, and violent gangs arose where there was no organized crime to offer a ladder of economic mobility. These theories are extensively discussed by Rock elsewhere in this volume (Chapter 1), so no more will be said about them here. Where violence is concerned, this tradition has continued particularly in comparative research, such as cross-national and cross-regional studies of homicide rates which attempt to explain the differences as the effects of, for example, differences in levels of inequality or rurality, or of race or religion (see, for example, Archer and Gartner 1984; Braithwaite and Braithwaite 1980; Gartner 1990; Rahav 1990; Smith and Zahn 1999). However, from the early 1960s onwards, much greater attention has been paid by sociologists, as well as social anthropologists and ethnographers, to how social interactions at the micro-level may produce violence (see, for example, Luckenbill 1977; Athens 1980; Felson 2002; Felson 1983 also offers a social interactionist approach to understanding sexual coercion). At the same time, interest began to grow in the influence of 'culture' on individual behaviour. An important milestone in this respect was the 'subculture of violence' theory of Wolfgang and Ferracuti (1967). In line with other subcultural theories of the time, the authors argued that violent behaviour is learned from other members of peer groups who espouse certain sets of values that differ from those of the dominant culture of conventional society. Their main focus was on subcultures made up of young black people in inner cities, which appeared to produce higher rates of homicide and serious violence than those found elsewhere in the USA. Such subcultures, they argued, promoted value systems in which violence comes to be regarded as *normal and expected* in certain social situations. Indeed, violence is valued to such an extent that those who avoid it are 'punished' by becoming ostracized or treated with no respect. Thus, they wrote:

> The significance of a jostle, a slightly derogatory remark, or the appearance of a weapon in the hands of an adversary are stimuli differently perceived and interpreted by Negroes and whites, males and females. Social expectations of response in particular types of social interaction result in differential 'definitions of the situation' [Wolfgang and Ferracuti 1967: 153].

The theory has been heavily criticized subsequently on both empirical and theoretical grounds: for example, it has variously been argued that the supposed 'subculture' is by no means as homogeneous as implied by the authors, that poverty and social inequality are better predictors of violence than race, and that it fails to explain satisfactorily why such a culture grew up in the first place. Nevertheless, it had a considerable influence on later work. For example, Curtis (1975) developed the theory by arguing that black people were expected to have a lower 'boiling point' precisely because of the racism and economic discrimination in the wider society: an argument made also by Blau and Blau (1982) and Currie (1985). It also helped inform a rich variety of what might broadly be called 'sociocultural' studies of violent behaviour. These include studies of subcultures other than those defined around race, such as the alienated working class youth cultures in the UK explored by Cohen (1972) and later by Segal (1990), studies of North American gang cultures (e.g. Vigil 1988; Huff 1990; Jankowski 1992; for a compendium of key articles, see Maguire 1996) and 'cross-cultural' studies, such as that by Sanday (1981) on the 'socio-cultural context of rape'. Particularly powerful studies of individual violent (sub)cultures have included Bourgois's (1996) ethnography of crack dealers, and Strong's (1995) study of parts of Colombian society in which young men on motorcycles are willing to assassinate anyone for a few dollars, simply to prove themselves in a country where 'reputation' is crucial both for dignity and for sexual display. A common element of many of the above cultures is the high value they place on 'masculine' (or 'macho') behaviour—a point to which increasing importance has been attached since the development of theoretical work on 'masculinities' in the 1990s by writers such as Connell and Messerschmidt (see below).

FEMINIST THEORY AND 'MASCULINITIES'

Finally, it is important to point out that feminist writers have had a major influence on theoretical approaches to violent crime and, unlike even ten years ago, it is now rare to find serious discussions of the topic without some attention to the implications of the fact that most violence is committed by *men*.[13] Again, this issue is discussed elsewhere in the volume (by Heidensohn and Gelsthorpe, Chapter 13, and to some extent by Rock, Chapter 1), so only brief comments will be made here (though the topic will be raised again specifically in our discussion of homicide).

Early feminist theories of male violence against women stressed the social construction of masculinity, violence, and sexuality in patriarchal society, whose object is to reproduce and maintain men's relative status and authority over women (Hanmer *et al.* 1989; Scully 1990; Dobash and Dobash 1979, 1992; Newburn and Stanko 1994). Wife-beating, for example, was seen as closely tied up with men's attempts to maintain control or 'patriarchal rights' over their partners (Dobash and Dobash 1979). However, such accounts were not only somewhat sweeping and one-dimensional in their portrayal of men, but also unsatisfactory in illuminating variations in violence against women over time or in different societies. They also tended to pay little attention to the other key dimensions of social class and race. Nevertheless, they helped to focus theorists' attention on critical questions that had previously been neglected in explanations of crime, such as what it was about men that caused so many of them to commit crime, and conversely (a variation on the central question raised by control theory) why so many women did *not* commit crime.

New and fruitful thinking on the first of these issues was set in motion by the introduction of the dynamic and fluid concept of 'masculinities'. The core of the argument here is that gender is socially constructed, the dominant gender structure (male hegemony) being constantly reproduced, negotiated, and 'played out' by men 'doing gender' in a variety of ways in a variety of situations: different masculinities are thus created and learned (see Connell 1995). Importantly, too, theories around masculinities are able to take more account than previous feminist theories of both race and class, focusing particularly on the relationship between the powerlessness of young lower-class—and, in some studies, black—males and the particular ways in which such groups 'do gender', including committing criminal and violent acts (such as 'doing violence to women': Websdale and Chesney-Lind 1998). Important publications in this area include those by Messerschmidt (1993, 1997), Newburn and Stanko (1994), Jefferson (1994), Miller (2002), Chesney-Lind (2006) and Mullins (2006). A more detailed overview can be found in Heidensohn and Gelsthorpe (Chapter 13, this volume). The value of the concept to the understanding of phenomena such as violent crime is that it maintains attention to major structural forces, but at the same time takes full account of the role of human agency in determining what happens in specific situations, thus helping to explain variation and change.

---

[13] This is not to deny the importance of work such as that by Campbell (1991, 1993) on violence by women, including by female gangs.

MAKING SENSE OF HOMICIDE

Having given a very brief and broad flavour of the various approaches that have been adopted over the years in attempts to 'explain' violent crime, we now illustrate in a more concrete fashion the kinds of issues that face anyone embarking upon such a path, by taking a more detailed look at one specific category of violence—homicide. This offence has been surprisingly little discussed over the years by academic criminologists (particularly British criminologists) in comparison with several other forms of violence, although it has recently seen an increase in scholarly attention. In the course of the discussion, the relevance will be shown of a number of the theoretical perspectives discussed above. Our general conclusion will be that no one theory can adequately 'explain homicide': rather, a better understanding can be reached through a combination of perspectives.

As indicated earlier, compared to other forms of violent crime, homicide is relatively rare (in most of the last ten years, there have been between 700 and 900 homicides recorded in England and Wales, well under 0.1 per cent of all violent crimes recorded by the police). The relative rarity of this offence does not, however, make it any easier to explain. Homicides are more diverse in character than some other forms of violent crime, including robbery. For example, making sense of why a mother kills her newborn child, why 'partners' kill one another, why a man sexually assaults and kills an unknown woman, or why a drinker kills another during a brawl in a pub, may all require different forms of explanation. These, of course, are the more conventional forms of homicide that comprise the bulk of the official homicide statistics. Understanding what causes serial or spree killers or terrorists to kill, or corporations to engage in deadly risk-taking behaviour, raises further challenges still.

A useful starting point to try to make sense of homicide is gender—not least because both the extent and patterns of homicide vary considerably depending upon the sex of those involved. For example, over 90 per cent of all homicides are committed by males, around 70 per cent of the victims of homicide are male and over half of all homicides occur amongst males (see Brookman 2005). Males are more likely to kill strangers and acquaintances than intimates, whereas the reverse is the case for women (Jensen 2001). In addition, there are many more examples of serial and spree killings perpetrated by males than females and the major players in corporate homicide are male (Messerschmidt 1997). However, gender is not the only major social dimension in which the incidence of homicide is skewed in relation to the general population. As with other forms of violence, both offenders and victims are disproportionately young and from lower social classes (Polk 1994a; Dobash *et al.* 2004; Brookman 2005). Any adequate account of homicide has to take account of these structural issues as well as important situational factors.

Two major forms of male-on-male homicide have been identified by scholars—to some extent influenced by the work of Connell and Messerschmidt, discussed above—which revolve around masculine displays of honour, power, and control (see Polk

1994b, 1995; Brookman 2003). On the one hand there are '*confrontational* homicides' that occur fairly spontaneously amongst men who are not known to one another, often in response to fairly trivial disagreements. These often occur in and around pubs and clubs, and alcohol often permeates the encounters. Several researchers have observed that what might seem trivial to the outside observer is in fact integral to many of the assailants' (and often victims') need to feel in control and their sense of being men. In contrast, '*revenge* homicides' are planned attacks. The offender seeks out the victim in order to 'punish' him for some perceived wrongdoing (against himself or a third party). Once again, the issue of power and control is critical. These men have to 'right the wrong' in the best way they know how—by violent means. Not only are formal avenues of redress less available to marginalized men (as compared to men well integrated into roles of economic success) but such a route would often be considered inappropriate among their peers. This may not be simply a matter of 'subcultural values' (as discussed earlier in relation to Wolgang and Ferracuti's work), but may also have financial implications. For example, Topalli *et al.* (2002) studied retaliatory violence in the context of street drug-dealers in St Louis, Missouri and found that the volatile social setting that these males inhabit makes them key targets for robbery and violence. This 'occupational hazard', that is devoid of legal protection, has ensured that the men project a 'menacing and capable' reputation. Clearly image, status, and reputation are powerful protectors of their livelihood and lives.

As noted earlier, it is not completely clear why men from disadvantaged backgrounds are more likely to resort to violence as a way of controlling other men (or, for that matter, women)—though some of the theoretical work referred to above provides valuable insights into the relationships between powerlessness (in the conventional sense), fragile masculine status, and cultures in which violence is accepted or even expected as a response to challenges. It is even less clear why only *some* of these men engage in violence (lethal or otherwise): we must always be mindful of the fact that only a very small proportion of marginalized lower-class men ever commit serious violence, let alone homicide.

For many years, most theories purporting to explain *female* violence and homicide tended to pathologize and medicalize women: see, for example, Walker's (1984) *The Battered Woman Syndrome* or d'Orban (1979) on filicide. More recent accounts have provided evidence that female violence can often have a more purposive nature (see, for example, Jurik and Gregware 1992, on female homicide). However, they also indicate that women's violence is less about gaining or asserting control than that of men. Female perpetrators of violence (including homicide) often state that it was linked to some form of perceived 'failure' (as a mother or wife for example). They also tend to view their own displays of aggression as a loss of self-control, rather than as a means of gaining control of a situation or person (see, for example, Campbell 1993).

Whilst gender, class, and age are clearly critical in explaining variations in homicide, there are also many situational and environmental factors to consider. Using data on individual cases from the Homicide Index, Brookman (2005) explores the part played by, for example, alcohol and drugs, the availability of lethal weapons, and the attitudes of 'audiences', in order to develop a broad typology of homicide events and an explanatory framework based on a variety of structural, dispositional, and situational factors which play a different role in different kinds of homicide (in this, she to some extent follows the approach adopted by Wolfgang (1958), in his pioneering work *Patterns in Criminal Homicide*). An important distinction she makes is between, on the one hand, homicide that is essentially an extreme outcome of violent behaviour similar to that which often results 'only' in serious injury (e.g. the person did not initially set out to kill, but lost control, or the fact that the victim died rather than survived was due to ill-luck in a blow hitting a vital organ or medical assistance being delayed); and, on the other hand, homicide where the intention is to make absolutely sure that the victim dies. The former, she argues, can often be explained through theories which apply to violence in general, but the latter may require a different form of interpretation—and by implication, different preventive strategies (on the latter point, see Brookman and Maguire 2005). Overall, like other recent writers in this field (notably Polk 1994a, 1994b, 1995), she accords particular importance to explanations based on gender and 'masculinities'. Nevertheless, a central message from her work is that no one perspective is adequate on its own, and that any satisfactory theoretical account of homicide will have to take into account a combination of structural, cultural, situational, and interactional factors (see Weiner *et al.* 1990, for a similar argument in relation to violence in general).

RESPONSES TO VIOLENCE: RECENT TRENDS

As with any other type of crime, social and legal responses to crimes of violence vary widely over time and place, as penological thinking, priorities, and fashions change and as levels of public, media, and political concern rise or fall. There is no space here to cover the range of current responses to violence in any depth, and the *Handbook* already contains comprehensive reviews of developments in sentencing (Ashworth, Chapter 29), offending behaviour programmes (Raynor; Hollin, Chapters 31 and 2, respectively), multi-agency crime prevention measures (Crawford, Chapter 26) and both the 'risk management' and psychiatric treatment of 'dangerous' offenders (Peay, Chapter 16), which are all highly relevant to the issue. However, it is worth very briefly outlining some recent trends.

Over the past decade or so, violent crime (never long out of the headlines in any era) has been exceptionally high on the political agenda in England and Wales, and has been at the forefront of debates about penal policy. The 'headline' debates, and many of the legislative, policy, and practice changes which they have influenced, have been largely concerned with sentencing—in particular, 'tougher' and 'preventive' sentencing. However, other (and perhaps ultimately more effective) approaches have been developing in a quieter fashion.

SENTENCING AND POST-RELEASE CONTROL

The basic trend in the sentencing of violent offenders has been towards more and longer custodial sentences. Among those convicted of offences of violence against the person, the proportion sent to immediate custody rose from 22 per cent in 1994 to 31 per cent in 2004; a similar rise was apparent for sexual offences, from 44 to 59 per cent. The total number sent to custody for any kind of violent offence also increased from under 14,000 in 1994 to over 20,000 in 2004. Moreover, over the same period, the average length of custodial sentence passed by the Crown courts for violence against the person increased from 22 to 26 months, and for sexual offences from 38 to 43 months. Indeed, among all the main offence groups, sexual offences and robbery (along with drugs offences) attract by far the longest average sentences in the higher courts: by comparison, the average Crown court sentence in 2004 for theft and handling offences was 12 months and for fraud and forgery it was 15 months (Home Office 2005a: Ch. 2).

Averaging sentences in this way, however, conceals major differences in the sentencing of people at the top and bottom of the range. A trend towards 'bifurcation' (Bottoms 1977) has been evident for many years, whereby, in essence, long sentences get longer and short sentences get shorter. This has manifested itself in some very tough sentences, both for the more serious types of violence and for people considered 'dangerous' (Peay, Chapter 16, this volume). It has also had a significant impact on the size and structure of the prison population. By 2004, for example, 45 per cent of the entire sentenced prison population, and over four-fifths of the *long-term* prison population were there for violence, including sexual violence (Home Office 2005c: Ch. 8; for further discussion, see Morgan and Liebling, Chapter 32, this volume). Such figures are particularly striking when one remembers that violent and sexual offences make up only about 19 per cent of officially recorded crime (Maguire, Chapter 10, this volume).

Long prison sentences for violence are often justified in terms of retribution and deterrence, but they have increasingly been aimed as much—if not more—at 'public protection' or (the more graphic American term) *'incapacitation'*. Indeed, this objective has been written into important statutes directed at both violent and sexual offending: notably the Criminal Justice Act 1991, which, despite enshrining 'just deserts' principles to limit sentence lengths for most types of offence, allowed much longer sentences for sexual and violent offenders on the grounds of public protection; and the Crime (Sentences) Act 1997, which introduced the presumption of a life sentence on second conviction for a serious violent or sexual crime. This utilitarian approach to sentencing (which, perhaps tellingly, has hardly impacted upon responses to either corporate or motoring 'violence') has caused considerable argument and unease—at least among academics, who are usually more troubled than politicians about justifications for punishment. The so-called 'dangerousness debate' has continued on and off since the 1970s, mainly about the extent to which future serious offending by particular individuals can be predicted, and what level of risk and what accuracy of prediction would justify keeping people in custody indefinitely to prevent future crimes (see, for example, Bottoms 1977; Monahan 1981; Floud and Young 1981; Morris and

Miller 1985; Haapanen 1990; Monahan and Steadman 1994; Kemshall 2001; Peay; Ashworth, Chapters 16 and 29, respectively, this volume). As Morris and Miller (1985: 21) observe:

> the societal decision, the moral decision, is . . . how to balance the risk of harm to society and the certain intrusion on the liberty of each member of the preventively detained group. At some level of predicted harms from the group, the intrusions on each individual's liberty may be justified.

Of course, we seldom have the opportunity of discovering what those incapacitated would have done had they been released, thereby making it difficult to test the validity of our expectancy rates.

In addition to sentences passed in court, statutory controls over sexual and violent offenders on completion of custodial sentences have also been tightened considerably. Since 1983, when the Home Secretary virtually applied a blanket veto on the early release of violent and sexual offenders serving over five years (see Maguire 1992), parole for such offenders has been greatly restricted. Moreover, once they are released, they are increasingly subject to risk assessment and 'risk management' (including police surveillance) by multi-agency 'public protection panels' (Maguire et al. 2001; Kemshall and Maguire 2001, 2002). Sex offenders are also subject to extended licence periods, as well as being placed on the sex offender register and obliged to notify the police of their whereabouts for a minimum of five years; they can also be placed under a civil Sex Offender Order, breach of which is a criminal offence carrying imprisonment for up to five years. Those assessed as high risk are subject to multi-agency public protection arrangements (MAPPA), which can involve police surveillance, regular home visits, and other control measures (Home Office 2005b).

ALTERNATIVE APPROACHES

Not all recent developments have been based on the pessimistic view that violence reduction can only be achieved by 'incapacitating' known offenders—primarily by locking them away for lengthy periods. In particular, there has been a revival of belief in the effectiveness of 'correctional' methods, in the shape of structured programmes for offenders in prison or on probation. There has also been increasing experimentation with various forms of situational crime prevention, including efforts to 'design out' or 'manage' violence through altering 'risky' environments.

Offending behaviour programmes

As discussed in depth by both Raynor and Hollin in this volume (Chapters 31 and 2, respectively), the 'what works' initiative in England and Wales has produced a rapid increase in the use of 'offending behaviour programmes', most of them based on cognitive-behavioural approaches. These are tightly structured 'courses' in which tutors (in prisons and in probation offices) work through a sequence of modules intended essentially to teach offenders to avoid 'distorted thinking' and to improve their skills in handling social situations. Some of those designed specifically for violent offenders set out to teach them 'anger management' and self-control, although it is recognized that this approach is not appropriate for all: as discussed earlier, violent behaviour can also be highly instrumental and controlled (Megargee 1983; Polk 1994a; Brookman 2005). The best programmes are now accredited by the Correctional Services Accreditation Panel (CSAP 2005), which also monitors the quality of their delivery: 'what works' research suggests that quality in both design and delivery is essential to effectiveness. Substantial claims have been made, based mainly on evidence from the United States, for the success of such programmes in reducing reconviction rates (see Raynor, Chapter 31, this volume), although there is little evidence about their impact specifically on violent behaviour.

Accredited programmes for sex offenders have a longer history than those for violent offenders. There is also more evidence of their effectiveness, although reconviction rates for sex offences are generally very low anyway, and it is difficult to identify significant changes brought about by 'treatment' (Hedderman and Sugg 1996; Beech *et al.* 1998; Friendship *et al.* 2001). In the case of domestic violence, too, there is some evidence that specially tailored programmes can make a difference, at least in the short term, to behaviour as well as to attitudes (Dobash *et al.* 2000).

Crime reduction initiatives

Finally, violent offending is now the target of numerous crime reduction initiatives, particularly where efforts are made to identify and target specific 'hotspots' of violent behaviour and to 'manage' these through various forms of inter-agency cooperation. Most Crime and Disorder Reduction Partnerships now have subgroups dedicated to violence reduction through multi-agency working, and their efforts are subject to increasingly demanding target-setting and monitoring by the Home Office (see Crawford, Chapter 26, this volume).

Among the most prominent such initiatives have been efforts to manage the disorder and violence associated with the 'night time economy' (Hobbs *et al.* 2000). These include, for example, training and registration of door staff and bar staff, better design of pubs and clubs, staggering of closing times, and provision of late night transport (Deehan 1999; Maguire and Nettleton 2003; Finney 2004). Such initiatives are not primarily about tough policing and threats of punishment, but involve strategic interventions instigated through partnerships between, for example, local councils, town planners, managers of licensed premises, police licensing officers, and taxi or bus companies. Where domestic violence is concerned, too, risk-based preventive strategies are being developed as alternatives (or complements) to enforcement strategies such as automatic arrest and prosecution. For example, MARACs (Multi-Agency Risk Assessment Conferences) are now a central element of the Home Office's national domestic violence plan, which encourages multi-agency interventions to provide holistic support to very high-risk victims and to end chronic abuse (see Robinson 2006).

CONCLUSIONS

Much of the criminological progress during the last twenty years has been in refining our understanding of the risks of crime for different groups in different locations, and how this relates to their lifestyles. By contrast with this focus on the victim (and to some extent the location), the causes of violence have received comparatively little recent criminological attention. This is not simply because victims are easier to get to, both physically and mentally, than are offenders and because the discovery of the victim has been a major area of criminal policy interest. It partly reflects also the greater theoretical simplicity of generating interesting facts about patterns of victimization than of explaining fundamentally why certain people use violence against others in particular circumstances. We have stressed, perhaps ad nauseam, the enormous variation within that all too often simplified term, 'violent crime', but one implication of this is that we may need different explanatory accounts for those who commit what everyone agrees are highly abnormal and unacceptable acts compared with those who behave in ways that are less condemned or even are approved by people in their reference groups or subcultures. We may also need to look differently at 'one-off' violence that occurs in the street and the varied forms of violence (especially family violence, but also institutional violence) which occurs behind closed doors between 'repeat players'.

The concept of 'masculinities' is one analytical thread that has run through much of the aetiological discussion. As has now been widely demonstrated, men's resources for accomplishing masculinity vary with their class and to some extent race positions. Thus, one of the only arenas in which young men from poor backgrounds or marginalized ethnic minority groups can display masculinity is the world of violent gangs,[14] whereas more affluent boys can find other areas to express themselves—including, later on in life, corporate aggression (Levi 1994). As Polk (1994a) argues, when overlaid with social class, the concept helps to account not just for 'typical' homicides but also for homicides for predatory gain and, as Kersten (1996) adds, for many sexual crimes too. However, while this perspective has greatly advanced our understanding of violence, it should not exclude attention to motives not directly connected with the expression of masculinity (cf. Jones 2000). For example, Bourgois' (1996) ethnography of crack use and dealing in an American *barrio* shows that the huge importance attached to the search for 'respect' may well have its psychodynamic roots in miserable (and/or misogynistic) family relationships and lack of 'men's work', but can also often bring financial benefits and enhanced status and control within the family and/or peer group. This has echoes of the problem with Megargee's (1983) distinction between 'expressive' and 'instrumental' violence: in many cases, violent acts can fulfil both functions at once.

---

[14] 'Masculinity' also offers an outlet for some young and poor women who want to show their rejection of their received roles (Messerschmidt 1997).

Another key theme that has emerged is that almost all forms of explanation come up against the basic problem of accounting for the non-violence of most males—including young and socially marginalized males—most of the time. Some predatory individuals go out in search of people to attack, but however dangerous they are, these are the minority of assailants, rapists, and even killers. The fact that a substantial proportion of killers do *not* come from broken homes, have *not* had violent parents, were *not* unemployed at the time of the offence, or do not possess any of the other identified risk factors (Dobash *et al.* 2001) indicates the complex dynamics that go into the making of serious violence. Clearly, sociological and sociocultural explanations grossly *overpredict* violence, while personality-based explanations alone cannot account for the variations in violence over time and place. We now have a better understanding of the interplay between early family experiences, temperament, valuation by society, and situational factors in creating sets of violent behaviour that together constitute violent crime rates. But no existing clear theoretical model can make sense of all the data or account for all violent crime, nor should we expect to discover one that will.

Finally, societies and sectors of society undoubtedly vary over time in the extent to which violent or aggressive behaviour of particular types is tolerated or approved of. This has consequences for the extent to which we can regard violence as 'normal' and—given the regulating effects of both social and subcultural approval or disapproval—for the corresponding levels of offending. For example, in the UK, sexual offences against children are now reacted to with a much greater level of opprobrium than they were only twenty years ago, while the police are no longer permitted to tolerate spousal violence or rape as they once did. At the other extreme, serious violence—including gun crime—seems to have become regarded as more 'normal' than it used to be among some groups (particularly those engaged in drug dealing). Nevertheless, there are limits to the elasticity of such attitudes. Outside of a wartime or quasi-wartime context of ethnic or national oppression, serial killers or rapists are not likely to be considered as 'normal' personalities, even by their 'peers' (whoever they may be). Equally—at least in many European democracies—subcultures which are regarded as having 'gone too far' in their approval of serious violence are likely eventually to be targeted by determined state interventions, These, in turn, may have a variety of impacts (positive or negative) on the attitudes and behaviours in question. In other words, 'subcultures' should not be seen as static entities, totally disconnected from mainstream society. Most individuals develop different attitudes to violence as they grow older, while each new generation will react to wider changes in society by developing new ways of expressing their 'masculinity' or of gaining advantages over others, which may involve greater or less violence, or different forms of violence.

■ SELECTED FURTHER READING

Recent British books providing general overviews of theories of violence include Jones's *Understanding Violent Crime* (Open University Press, 2000) and Brookman's *Understanding*

Homicide (Sage, 2005). Also useful is Stanko's summary of an ESRC-funded research pro-gramme on violence, 'Theorizing About Violence: Observations From the Economic and Social Research Council's Violence Research Program' (*Violence Against Women*, Vol. 12, 2006). There are numerous North American texts which discuss explanations of violence in the USA, among the more interesting and readable being Barak's *Violence and Nonviolence: Pathways to Understanding* (Sage, 2003) and Gilligan's *Violence: Reflections on our Deadliest Epidemic* (Jessica Kingsley, 2000). Among older books, *Pathways to Criminal Violence* (Weiner and Wolfgang, Sage, 1989) is still a useful resource, while both Katz's *The Seductions of Crime: the Moral and Sensual Attractions of Doing Evil* (Basic Books, 1988) and Athens's *Violent Criminal Acts and Actors: Revisited* (University of Illinois Press, 1997) are rich texts providing good summaries of conventional approaches as well as putting forward original theories of their own.

Key books that focus on 'masculinities' include Messerschmidt's *Masculinities and Crime: Critique and Reconceptualization* (Rowman & Littlefield, 1993), Archer's *Male Violence* (Routledge, 1994) and Polk's *When Men Kill: Scenarios of Masculine Violence* (Cambridge, 1994). Three edited books are also recommended: Newburn and Stanko's *Just Boys Doing Business* (Routledge, 1994); Bowker's *Masculinities and Crime* (Sage, 1998); and *Understanding Masculinities*, edited by Mac An Ghaill (Open University Press, 1996). A good example of empirical research exploring masculinities is Messerschmidt's *Nine Lives* (Westview Press, 2000), which discusses in detail the life histories of nine adolescent boys and unravels why some commit acts of violence or sexual offences, whilst others do not. Where female violence is concerned, Miller's *One of the Guys: Girls, Gangs, and Gender* (Oxford University Press, 2000) and Campbell's classic study, *The Girls in the Gang* (Blackwell, 1991) are among the most important studies of gang violence, while violence by women in domestic situations is discussed in Browne's *When Battered Women Kill* (Free Press, 1991), Jensen's *Why Women Kill: Homicide and Gender Equality* (Lynne Reiner, 2001) and a thought-provoking journal article by Dobash and Dobash, 'Women's Violence Against an Intimate Male Partner: Working on a Puzzle' (*British Journal of Criminology*, 2004).

There is a huge literature on domestic or family violence more generally. Dobash and Dobash's *Violence against Wives* (Free Press, 1979) was a pioneering study in the area and is still well worth reading, although much of the same authors' later work, including *Women, Violence, and Social Change* (Routledge, 1992) has developed their ideas further. Gelles *et al*.'s *Current Controversies on Family Violence* (Sage, 2004) gives a good flavour of current debates, while Hanmer *et al*.'s reader *Home Truths about Domestic Violence: Feminist Influences on Policy and Practice* (Routledge, 2000) provides a good range of examples of feminist approaches.

In regard to other specific forms of violence, there is a rich North American literature on gang violence (useful overviews can be found in Huff's *Gangs in America* (Sage, 1990) and Jankowski's *Islands in the Street: Gangs and American Urban Society* (University of California Press, 1992), while perhaps the classic British study remains Patrick's *A Glasgow Gang Observed* (Eyre Methuen, 1973). There has been a considerable amount of recent attention in the UK to alcohol-related violence, and particularly recommended is Hobbs *et al*.'s *Bouncers: Violence and Governance in the Night time Economy* (Oxford University Press, 2005). On corporate 'violence' Wells's *Corporations and Criminal Responsibility* (Oxford University Press, 2001) is a key text. Finally—but very importantly—on large-scale political violence and abuses of human rights, Cohen's *States of Denial* (Polity Press, 2000) is essential reading.

The British Crime Survey and other Home Office commissioned surveys have produced a great deal of quantitative data about the extent and distribution of specific forms of violent crime, and numerous studies can be found on the Home Office website. Examples include *Violence at Work: Findings from the 2002/03 British Crime Survey* (Upson, 2004); *Violence in the Night-time Economy: Key Findings from Research* (Finney, 2004); *Young People and Crime: Findings from the 2004 Offending, Crime and Justice Survey* (Budd et al., 2005) and *Domestic Violence, Sexual Assault and Stalking: Findings from the 2004/05 British Crime Survey* (Finney, 2006).

Recent British publications on responses to violent crime include a broad overview by Maguire and Brookman, 'Violent and Sexual Crime', in *Handbook of Crime Prevention* (ed. Tilley: Willan, 2005) and (specifically on homicide) Brookman and Maguire's 'Reducing Homicide in the UK: A Review of the Possibilities' *(Crime, Law and Social Change*, 2005). Where specific kinds of intervention are concerned, Strang and Braithwaite's edited volume, *Restorative Justice and Family Violence* (Cambridge University Press, 2000), Dobash et al.'s edited volume, *Changing Violent Men* (Sage, 2000) and *Managing Sex Offenders in the Community: Contexts, Challenges and Responses*, edited by Matravers (Willan, 2003) are all valuable contributions. Police and criminal justice responses to domestic violence in England and Wales are well covered in Hoyle's *Negotiating Domestic Violence: Police, Criminal Justice and Victims* (Oxford University Press, 1998) and in the USA in Buzawa and Buzawa's *Domestic Violence: The Criminal Justice Response* (University of Massachusetts, 2003).

■ REFERENCES

ADLER, Z. (1987), *Rape on Trial*, London: Routledge.

ANDREWS, D. A., and BONTA, J. (1998), *The Psychology of Criminal Conduct*, Cincinnati: Anderson.

ARCHER, D., and GARTNER , R. (1984), *Violence and Crime in Cross-National Perspective*, New Haven: Yale University Press.

ARCHER, J. (1990), 'The influence of testosterone on human aggression', *British Journal of Psychology*, 82: 1–28.

—— (1994), 'Violence between men', in J. Archer (ed.), *Male Violence*, London: Routledge.

ATHENS, L. (1980), *Violent Criminal Acts and Actors*, London: Routledge.

AYE MAUNG, N. (1995), *Young People, Victimisation and the Police*, Research Study No. 140, London: Home Office.

BALDWIN, J., and BOTTOMS, A. E. (1976), *The Urban Criminal*, London: Tavistock.

BAUMAN, Z. (1998), *Globalization*, Oxford: Polity Press.

BECK, U. (1992), *Risk Society: Towards a New Modernity*, London: Sage.

BEECH, A., FISHER, D., BECKETT, R., and SCOTT-FORDHAM, A. (1998), *An evaluation of the prison sex offender treatment programme*, Home Office Research Findings No. 79, London: Home Office. Available at www.homeoffice.gov.uk/rds/pdfs/r79.pdf.

BENNETT, T., and HOLLOWAY, K. (2006), *Understanding drugs, alcohol and crime*, London: McGraw Hill/Open University Press.

—— and —— (forthcoming), *Drug-Crime Connections*, Cambridge: Cambridge University Press.

BLAU, J., and BLAU, P. (1982), 'The cost of inequality: metropolitan structure and violent crime', *American Sociological Review*, 47: 114–29.

BOTTOMS, A. E. (1977), 'Reflections on the Renaissance of Dangerousness', *Howard Journal*, 16(2): 70–96.

BOURGOIS, P. (1996), *In Search of Respect: Selling Crack in El Barrio*, Cambridge: Cambride University Press.

BOVENKERK, F. (2000), 'The other side of the Anne Frank story: The Dutch role in the persecution of the Jews in World War Two', *Crime, Law and Social Change*, 34(3): 237–58.

BOWLING, B. (1993), 'Racial harassment and the process of victimisation: conceptual and methodological implications for the local crime survey', *British Journal of Criminology*, 33: 231–50.

BRAITHWAITE, J., and BRAITHWAITE, V. (1980), 'The effects of income inequality and social democracy on homicide', *British Journal of Criminology*, 20: 45–53.

BRENNAN, P., MEDNICK, S., and VOLAVKA, J. (1995), 'Biomedical factors in Crime', in J. Wilson and J. Petersilia (eds), *Crime*, San Francisco: ICS Press.

BRITTON, P., (1998), *The Jigsaw Man*, London: Corgi.

—— (2001), *Picking up the Pieces*, London: Corgi.

BROOKMAN, F. (2003), 'Confrontational and Grudge Revenge Homicides in England and Wales', *The Australian and New Zealand Journal of Criminology*, 36(1): 34–59.

—— (2005), *Understanding Homicide*, London: Sage.

—— and MAGUIRE, M. (2005), 'Reducing Homicide: A Review of the Possibilities', *Crime, Law and Social Change*, 42: 325–403.

BROWN, J. (1991), 'The psychopathology of serial sexual homicide: a review of the possibilities', *American Journal of Forensic Psychiatry*, 12: 13–21.

BROWNING, C. (2001), *Ordinary Men*, London: Penguin.

BROWNMILLER, S. (1975), *Against Our Will*, Harmondsworth: Penguin.

BROWNSTEIN, H. (1996), *The Rise and Fall of a Violent Crime Wave: Crack Cocaine and the Social Construction of a Crime Problem*, New York: Harrow and Heston.

BUDD, T. (1999), *Violence at Work: findings from the British Crime Survey*, London: Home Office.

——, SHARP, C., WEIR, G., WILSON, D., and OWEN, N. (2005), *Young People and Crime: Findings from the 2004 Offending, Crime and Justice Survey*, HOSB 20/05, London: Home Office.

BURGESS, R., and DRAPER, P. (1989), 'The explanation of family violence: the role of biological, behavioral, and cultural selection', in L. Ohlin and M. Tonry (eds), *Family Violence*, Chicago: University of Chicago Press.

BURLEIGH, M. (2001), *The Third Reich: a New History*, London: Pan.

CAMPBELL, A. (1991), *The Girls in the Gang*, 2nd edn, Oxford: Basil Blackwell.

—— (1993), *Out of Control: Men, Women and Aggression*, London: Harper Collins.

—— and MUNCER, S. (1994), 'Men and the meaning of violence', in J. Archer (ed.), Male Violence, London: Routledge.

CANTER, D. (1995), *Chasing the Shadows*, London: Harper Collins.

CATALANO, S. (2005), *Criminal Victimization 2004*, Washington DC. Bureau of Justice Statistics.

CHADEE, D., AUSTEN, L., and DITTON, J. (2006), 'The relationship between likelihood and fear of criminal victimization', *British Journal of Criminology*, Advance Access published 30 May 2006.

CHEATWOOD, D. (1995), 'The effects of the weather on homicide', *Journal of Quantitative Criminology*, 11: 51–70.

CHESNEY-LIND, M. (2006), 'Patriarchy, Crime, and Justice: Feminist Criminology in an Era of Backlash', *Feminist Criminology*, 1(1): 6–26.

COHEN, S. (2000), *States of Denial*, Cambridge: Polity Press.

—— (2002), (originally 1972), *Folk Devils and Moral Panics*, 3rd edn, London: Routledge.

COLLIER, R. (1998), *Masculinities, crime and criminology*, London: Sage.

CONNELL, R. (1995), *Masculinities*, Oxford: Blackwell.

CRAVEN, D. (1996), *Female Victims of Violent Crime: Select Findings*, Washington DC: US Department of Justice.

CROALL, H. (forthcoming), 'Social Exclusion and Victimisation', in P. Davies., P. Francis., and C. Greer (eds), *Victims, Crime and Society*, London: Sage.

CSAP (2005), *The Correctional Services Accreditation Panel Annual Report*, London: Home Office.

CURRAN, C., DALE, M., EDMUNDS, M., HOUGH, M., MILLIE, A., and WAGSTAFFE, M. (2005), 'Street Crime in London: Deterrence, Disruption and Displacement', London: Government Office for London.

CURRIE, E. (1985), *Confronting Crime: an American Challenge*, New York: Pantheon Books.

CURTIS, L. (1975), *Violence, Race and Culture*, Lexington, Mass.: Lexington Books.

DALY, M., and WILSON, M. (1988), *Homicide*, New York: de Gruyter.

—— and —— (1994), 'Evolutionary psychology of male violence', in J. Archer (ed.), *Male Violence*, London: Routledge.

DEEHAN, A. (1999), *Alcohol and Crime: Taking Stock*, Crime Reduction Research Series Paper 3, London: Home Office.

DEPARTMENT FOR TRANSPORT (2006), *Road Casualties in Great Britain. Main Results: 2005*, Transport Statistics Bulletin, London: Department for Transport.

DOBASH, R. E., and DOBASH, R. D. (1979), *Violence against Wives*, New York: Free Press.

—— and —— (1992), *Women, Violence, and Social Change*, London: Routledge.

——, ——, DALY, M., and WILSON, M. (1992), 'The myth of sexual symmetry in marital violence', *Social Problems*, 39(1): 71–91.

——, ——, CAVANAGH, K., and LEWIS, R. (2000), *Changing Violent Men*, Thousand Oaks, Cal.: Sage.

——, ——, ——, —— (2001), *Homicide in Britain*, Research Bulletin No.1, University of Manchester.

——, ——, ——, —— (2004), 'Not an Ordinary Killer—Just an Ordinary Guy: When Men Murder an Intimate Woman Partner', *Violence Against Women* (Special Issue), 10: 577–605.

DOBASH, R. P., and DOBASH, R. E. (2004), 'Women's Violence Against an Intimate Male Partner: Working on a Puzzle', *British Journal of Criminology*, 44: 324–49.

d'ORBAN, P. T. (1979), 'Women who kill their children', *British Journal of Psychiatry*, 134: 560–71.

EISNER, S. (2001), 'Modernization, self-control and lethal violence', *British Journal of Criminology*, 41: 618–38.

ERICSON, R. V., and HAGGERTY, K. D. (1997), *Policing and the Risk Society*, Oxford: Oxford University Press.

EVANS, K., and FRASER, P. (2003), 'Communities and Victimisation', in P. Davies, P. Francis, and V. Jupp (eds), *Victimisation: Theory, Research and Policy*, Basingstoke: Palgrave Macmillan.

FAGAN, J. (1989), 'Cesssation of Family Violence: Deterrence and Dissuasion', in L. Ohlin and M. Tonry (eds), *Family Violence*, Chicago: University of Chicago Press.

—— (1990), 'Intoxication and aggression', in M. Tonry and J. Wilson (eds), *Drugs and Crime*, Chicago: University of Chicago Press.

FARRINGTON, D. (1989), 'Early predictors of adolescent aggression and adult violence', *Violence and Victims*, 4: 307–31.

—— (1991), 'Childhood aggression and adult violence: early precursors and later life outcomes', in D. Pepler and K. Rubin (eds), *The Development and Treatment of Childhood Aggression*, Hillsdale, N J: Erlbaum.

FELSON, M. (2002), *Crime and Everyday Life*, 3rd edn, London: Sage.

—— (2006), *Crime and Nature*, London: Sage.

FELSON, R. (1993), 'Sexual coercion: a social interactionist approach', in R. Felson and J. Tedeschi (eds), *Aggression and Violence: Social Interactionist Perspectives*, Washington DC: American Psychological Association.

FINNEY, A. (2004), *Violence in the Night-time Economy: Key Findings from Research*, Findings 214, London: Home Office.

—— (2006), *Domestic Violence, Sexual Assault and Stalking: Findings from the 2004/05 British Crime Survey*, Home Office online report 12/06.

FISHBEIN, D. (1992), 'The psychobiology of female aggression', *Criminal Justice and Behaviour*, 19: 99–126.

FITI, R., and MURRAY, L. (2006), *Motoring Offences and Breath Test Statistics England and Wales 2004*, Home Office Statistical Bulletin, London: Home Office.

FLOOD-PAGE, C., CAMPBELL, S., HARRINGTON, V., and MILLER, J. (2000), *Youth Crime: Findings from the 1998/99 Youth Lifestyles Survey*, Home Office Research Study 209, London: Home Office.

FLOUD, J., and YOUNG, W. (1981), *Dangerousness and Criminal Justice*, London: Heinemann.

FREEDMAN, D., and HEMENWAY, D. (2000), 'Precursors of Lethal Violence: A Death Row Sample', *Social Science and Medicine*, 50: 1757–70.

FREUDENBERG, W. R. (1988), 'Perceived risk, real risk: social science and the art of probabilistic risk assessment' *Science*, 242, October: 44–9.

FRIENDSHIP, C., BLUD, L., ERIKSON, M., TRAVERS, R., and THORNTON, D. (2001), 'Cognitive-behavioural treatment for imprisoned offenders: an evaluation of H.M. Prison Services cognitive skills programmoo', Roport to the Joint Prison/Probation Accreditation Panel (mimeo).

FRIEZE, I., and BROWNE, A. (1989), 'Violence in marriage', in L. Ohlin and M. Tonry (eds), *Family Violence*, Chicago: University of Chicago Press.

FRUDE, N. (1994), 'Marital violence: an interactional perspective', in J. Archer (ed), *Male Violence*, London: Routledge.

GAMBETTA, D. (1994), *The Sicilian Mafia*, Cambridge, Mass.: Harvard University Press.

GARTNER, R. (1990), 'The victims of homicide', *American Sociological Review*, 55(1): 92–107.

GATRELL, V. (1980), 'The decline of theft and violence in Victorian and Edwardian England', in V. Gatrell, B. Lenmna, and G. Parker (eds), *Crime and the Law: the Social History of Crime in*

Western Europe since 1500, London: Europa Publications Ltd..

GELLES, R. (1998), 'Family violence', in M. Tonry (ed.), *The Handbook of Crime and Punishment*, New York: Oxford University Press.

GENN, H. (1988), 'Multiple victimisation', in M. Maguire and J. Pointing (eds), *Victims of Crime: a New Deal?*, Milton Keynes: Open University Press.

GIDDENS, A. (1990), *The Consequences of Modernity*, Cambridge: Polity Press.

GOLDHAGEN, D. (1997), *Hitler's Willing Executioners*, London: Abacus.

GOUREVITCH, P. (2000), *We Wish to Inform You That Tomorrow We Will be Killed with Our Families*, London: Picador.

GREEN, E., and WAKEFIELD, R. (1979), 'Patterns of Middle and Upper Class homicide', *Journal of Criminal Law and Criminology*, 70(2): 172–81.

GRESSWELL, D., and HOLLIN, C. (1994), 'Multiple murder: a review', *British Journal of Criminology*, 34: 1–29.

GURR, T. (1990), 'Historical trends in violent crime: a critical review of the evidence', in N. Weiner, M. Zahn, and R. Sagi (eds), *Violence: Patterns, Causes, Public Policy*, San Diego: Harcourt Brace Jovanovich.

GUTTMACHER, M. (1973), *The Mind of the Murderer,*. New York: Arno.

HALL, S., CRITCHER, C., JEFFERSON, T., CLARKE, J., ROBERTS, B. (1978), *Policing the Crisis*, London: Macmillan.

HAAPANEN, R. (1990), *Selective Incapacitation and the Serious Offender*, New York: Springer-Verlag.

HANMER, J., RADFORD, J., and STANKO, E. (1989), *Women, Policing, and Male Violence: an International Perspective*, London: Routledge.

HARE, R. (1998), *Without Conscience: the disturbing world of the psychopaths amongst us*, New York: Guilford Press.

—— (2001), 'Psychopathy and risk for recidivism and violence', in N. Gray, J. Laing, and L. Noaks (eds), *Criminal Justice, Mental Health and the Politics of Risk*, 27–48, London: Cavendish.

Health Protection Agency (2006), *Food Poisoning Notifications—Annual Totals England and Wales, 1982–2004*. Available at: www.hpa.org.uk/infections/topics_az/noids/food_poisoning.htm.

HEALTH AND SAFETY COMMISSION (2006), *Statistics, 2004/05*, London: Health and Safety Commission.

HEDDERMAN, C., and SUGG, D. (1997), *Does Treating Sex Offenders Reduce Reoffending?*, Research Findings, No. 45, London: Home Office.

HERRNSTEIN, R. (1995), 'Criminogenic traits', in J. Wilson and J. Petersilia (eds), *Crime*, San Francisco: ICS Press.

HOBBS, D., LISTER, S., HADFIELD, P., WINLOW, S. and HALL, S. (2000), 'Receiving shadows: governance and liminality in the night-time economy' *British Journal of Sociology*, 51(4): 682–700.

HOLMES, R., and HOLMES, S. (1996), *Profiling Violent Crimes: an Investigative Tool*, Thousand Oaks, Cal.: Sage.

HOME OFFICE (1989), *Statistics on Offences of Rape 1977–87*, Statistical Bulletin 4/89, London: Home Office.

—— (2000), *First Report from the Joint Prison/ Probation Accreditation Panel*, London: Home Office.

—— (2005a), *Sentencing Statistics 2004 England and Wales*, Statistical Bulletin 15/05, London: Home Office.

—— (2005b), *Strengthening Multi-Agency Public Protection Arrangements (MAPPAs)*, Development and Practice Report 45, London: Home Office.

—— (2005c), *Offender Management Caseload Statistics 2004*, Statistical Bulletin 17/05, London: Home Office.

—— (2006), *Statistics on Race and the Criminal Justice System 2005*, London: Home Office. Available at: www.homeoffice.gov.uk/rds/pdfs06/s95race05.pdf.

HOOD, R. (2003), *The Death Penalty: A Worldwide Perspective*, Oxford: Oxford University Press.

HOUGH, M. (1995), *Anxiety about Crime: Findings from the 1994 British Crime Survey*, Research Study 147, London: Home Office.

—— MIRRLEES-BLACK, C., and DALE, M. (2005), *Trends in Violent Crimes Since 1999/2000*, London: Institute for Criminal Policy Research. Available at www.kcl.ac.uk/depsta/law/research/icpr/publications/ViolenceReport. pdf.

HUESSMAN, L., and ERON, L. (1989), 'Individual differences and the trait of aggression', *European Journal of Personality*, 3: 95–106.

HUFF, C. R. (ed) (1990), *Gangs in America*, Newbury Park, Cal.: Sage.

JANKOWSKI, M. S. (1992), *Islands in the Street: Gangs and American Urban Society*, San Francisco: University of California Press.

JANSSON, K., COLEMAN, K., and KAIZA, P. (2006), 'Violent Crime', in A. Walker, C. Kershaw, and S. Nicholas (eds), *Crime in England and Wales 2005/2006*, London: Home Office.

JEFFERSON, T. (1994), 'Theorising Masculine Subjectivity', in T. Newburn and E. A. Stanko (eds), *Just Boys Doing Business? Men, Masculinities and Crime*, London: Routledge.

——(1997), 'Masculinities and Crime', in M. Maguire, R. Morgan, and R. Reiner (eds), *The Oxford Handbook of Criminology*, 2nd edn, Oxford: Clarendon Press.

JENKINS, P. (1994), *Using Murder: the Social Construction of Serial Homicide*, New York: de Gruyter.

JENSEN, V. (2001), *Why Women Kill: Homicide and Gender Equality*, London: Lynne Reiner.

JOHNSON, A. (1980), 'On the prevalence of rape in the United States', *Signs*, 6: 136–46.

JONES, S. (2000), *Understanding Violent Crime*, Milton Keynes: Open University Press.

JONES, T., MACLEAN, B., and YOUNG, J. (1986), *The Islington Crime Survey: Crime, Victimization and Policing in Inner City London*, Aldershot: Gower.

JURIK, N. C., and GREGWARE, P. (1992), 'A Method for Murder: The Study of Homicides by Women', *Perspectives on Social Problems*, 4: 179–201.

KAHNEMANN, D., SLOVIC, P., and TVERSKY, A. (1982), *Judgment under Uncertainty: Heuristics and Biases*, Cambridge: Cambridge University Press.

KATZ, J. (1988), *The Seductions of Crime: the moral and sensual attractions of doing evil*, New York: Basic Books.

KELMAN, H. C., and HAMILTON, V. L. (1989), *Crimes of obedience: Toward a social psychology of authority and responsibility*, New Haven, Conn.: Yale University Press.

KEMSHALL, H. (2001), *Risk Assessment and Management of Known Sexual and Violent Offenders: A Review of Current Issues*, Police Research Series Paper 140, London: Home Office.

——and MAGUIRE, M. (2001), 'Public Protection, Partnership and Risk Penality: The Multi-Agency Risk Management of Sexual and Violent Offenders', *Punishment and Society: The International Journal of Penology*, 5(2): 237–64.

——and —— (2002), 'Community Justice, Risk Management and the Role of Multi-Agency Public Protection Panels', *Journal of Community Justice*, 1: 11–27.

——and —— (2003), 'Sex offenders, risk penality and the problem of disclosure to the community', in

A. Matravers (ed.), *Managing Sex Offenders in the Community: Contexts, Challenges and Responses*, Cullompton, Devon: Willan.

KERSTEN, J. (1996), 'Culture, Masculinities and violence against women', *British Journal of Criminology*, 36: 381–95.

KILLIAS, M., and AEBI, M. (2000), 'Crime trends in Europe from 1990 to 1996: how Europe illustrates the limits of the American experience', *European Journal on Criminal Policy and Research*, 8: 43–63.

Law Commission (2004), *Partial Defences to Murder*. Final Report, Law Commission Report No. 290, London: Law Commission. Available at: www.lawcom.gov.uk/docs/lc290(1).pdf.

LEES, S. (2002), *Carnal Knowledge*, London: The Women's Press.

LESTER, D. (1991), 'National consumption of chocolate and rates of personal violence (suicide and homicide)', *Journal of Orthomolecular Medicine*, 6: 81–2.

LEVI, M. (1994), 'Masculinities and white-collar crime', in T. Newburn and B. Stanko (eds), *Just Boys Doing Business*, London: Routledge.

——and JONES, S. (1985), 'Public and Police Perceptions of Crime Seriousness in England and Wales', *British Journal of Criminology*, 25(3): 234–50.

LICHTENSTEIN, S., SLOVIC, P., FISCHHOFF, B., LAYMAN, M., and COMBS, B. (1978), 'Judged frequency of lethal events', *Journal of Experimental Psychology (Human Learning and Memory)*, 4: 551–78.

LUCKENBILL, D. F. (1977), 'Criminal Homicide as a Situated Transaction', *Social Forces*, 25: 176—86.

McLINTOCK, F., and AVISON, N. (1968), *Crime in England and Wales*, London: Heinemann.

MAGUIRE, M. (1992), 'Parole', in E. Stockdale and S. Casale (eds), *Criminal Justice Under Stress*, London: Blackstone Press.

——(ed.) (1996), *Street Crime*, International Library of Criminology, Aldershot: Dartmouth.

——and BROOKMAN, F. (2005), 'Violent and Sexual Crime', in N. Tilley (ed.), *Handbook of Crime Prevention: Theory, Policy and Practice*, Cullompton, Devon: Willan.

——and NETTLETON, H. (2003), *Reducing alcohol-related violence and disorder: an evaluation of the 'TASC' project*, Home Office Research Study 265, London: Home Office.

——, KEMSHALL, H., NOAKS, L., and WINCUP, E. (2001), *Risk Management of Sexual and Violent Offenders: The work of Public Protection Panels*,

Police Research Series paper 139, London: Home Office.

MALMQUIST, C. (1995), *Homicide: a Psychiatric Perspective*, Washington DC: American Psychiatric Press, Inc.

MATTINSON, J. (2001*), Stranger and Acquaintance Violence: Practice Messages from the British Crime Survey*, Briefing Note 7/01, London: Home Office.

MEASHAM, F., and BRAIN, K. (2005), ' "Binge" drinking, British alcohol policy and the new culture of intoxication', *Crime, Media and Culture*, 1(3): 262–83.

MEDNICK., S. A., MOFFITT, T. E., and STACK, S. (eds) (1987), *The causes of crime: new biological approaches*, Cambridge: Cambridge University Press.

MEGARGEE, E. (1983), 'Undercontrolled and over-controlled personality types in extreme anti-social aggression', *Psychological Monographs*, 80(3, whole No. 611).

MESSERSCHMIDT, J. (1993), *Masculinities and Crime: Critique and Reconceptualization*, Lanham, Md.: Rowman and Littlefield.

—— (1997), *Crime as Structured Action*, Thousand Oaks, Cal.: Sage.

MILLER, J. (2002), 'The Strengths and Limits of "Doing Gender" for Understanding Street Crime', *Theoretical Criminology*, 6(4): 433–460.

MOIR, A., and JESSEL, D. (1995), *A Mind to Crime: the Controversial Links between the Mind and Criminal Behaviour*, London: Michael Joseph.

MONAHAN, J. (1981), *Predicting Violent behavior: An Assessment of Clinical Techniques*, Beverly Hills, Cal.: Sage.

—— and STEADMAN, H. (1994), *Violence and Mental Disorder: Developments in Risk Assessment*, Chicago: Chicago University Press.

MOONEY, J. (1993), *The Hidden Figure: Domestic Violence in North London*, London: Islington Council.

MORRIS, N., and MILLER, M. (1985), 'Predictions of dangerousness', in M. Tonry and N. Morris (eds), *Crime and justice: An annual review of research*, 1–50, Chicago: University of Chicago Press.

MULLINS, C. (2006), *Holding your Square: Masculinities, Streetlife and Violence*, Cullompton, Devon: Willan.

NATIONAL COMMITTEE (1990), *Violence: Directions for Australia*, Canberra: Australian Institute of Criminology.

NEWBURN, T., and STANKO, B. (eds) (1994), *Just Boys Doing Business*, London: Routledge.

NOVACO, R. W. (1994), 'Anger as a risk factor for violence among the mentally disordered' in J. Monahan

and H. J. Steadman (eds), *Violence and mental disorder: Developments in risk assessment*, Chicago: University of Chicago Press.

O'CONNELL, M., and WHELAN, A. (1996), 'Taking wrongs seriously: Public perceptions of crime seriousness', *British Journal of Criminology*, 36(2): 299–318.

OLWEUS, D. (1987), 'Testosterone and Adrenaline: Aggression and Antisocial Behaviour in Normal Adolescent Males', in S. Mednick, T. Moffitt, and S. Stack (eds), *The Causes of Crime: New Biological Approaches*, New York: Cambridge University Press.

——, MATTERSON, A., SHALLING, D., and LOW. H. (1988), 'Circulating testosterone levels and aggression in adolescent males: A causal analysis', *Psychosomatic Medicine*, 50: 261–72.

O'MALLEY, P. (ed.) (1998), *Crime and the Risk Society*, Aldershot: Ashgate.

PAINTER, K. (1991), *Wife Rape, Marriage and the Law*, Manchester: Manchester University Press.

PATTERSON, A., and THORPE, K. (2006), 'Public Perceptions', in A. Walker, C. Kershaw, and S. Nicholas, *Crime in England and Wales 2005/06*, London, Home Office.

PEARSON, G. (1983), *Hooligan*, London: Macmillan.

PEASE, K. (1988), *Crime seriousness: findings from the British Crime Survey*, London: Home Office Research and Planning Unit.

POLK, K. (1994a), *When Men Kill: Scenarios of Masculine Violence*, Cambridge: Cambridge University Press.

—— (1994b), 'Masculinity, Honour and Confrontational Homicide', in T. Newburn and E. A. Stanko (eds), *Just Boys doing the Business?*, London: Routledge.

—— (1995), 'Lethal Violence as a Form of Masculine Conflict Resolution', *The Australian and New Zealand Journal of Criminology*, 28(1): 93–115.

RAHAV, G. (1990), 'Cross National Variations in Homicide', *Aggressive Behavior*, 16: 69–76.

RAINE, A. (1993), *The Psychopathology of Crime: Criminal Behaviour as a Clinical Disorder*, London: Academic Press.

——, BUCHSBAUM, M., STANLEY, J., and LOTTENBERG, S. (1994), 'Selective reductions in prefrontal glucose metabolism in murderers', *Biological Psychiatry*, 36: 365–73.

RAMSAY, M. (1996), 'The relationship between alcohol and crime', *Home Office Research Bulletin*, 38: 37–44.

REUTER, P. (1983), *Disorganized Crime*, Cambridge, Mass.: MIT Press.

ROBINSON, A. L. (2006), 'Reducing Repeat Victimisation among High-Risk Victims of Domestic Violence: The Benefits of a Coordinated Community Response in Cardiff, Wales', *Violence Against Women: An International and Interdisciplinary Journal*, 12(8): 761–88.

ROWE, D. C. (1990), 'Inherited dispositions towards learning delinquency and criminal behaviour: new evidence', in L. Ellis and H. Hoffman (eds), *Crime in biological, social and moral context*, New York: Praeger.

SALISBURY, H., and UPSON, A. (2004), *Ethnicity, Victimisation and Worry about Crime: Findings from the 2001/02 and 2002/03 British Crime Surveys*, Home Office Research Study 237, London: Home Office.

SANDAY, P. (1981), 'The socio-cultural context of rape: a cross-cultural study', *Journal of Social Issues*, 37(4): 5–27.

SCULLY, D. (1990), *Understanding Sexual Violence*, London: Harper Collins.

SEGAL, L. (1990), *Slow Motion: Changing Masculinities, Changing Men*, London: Virago.

SLOVIC, P. (1992), 'Perceptions of risk: reflections on the psychometric paradigm', in S. Krimsky and D. Golding (eds), *Social Theories of Risk*, Westport, Conn.: Praeger.

SMITH, M., and ZAHN M. (eds) (1999), *Homicide: A Sourcebook of Social Research*, Thousand Oaks, Cal.: Sage.

Social Issues Research Centre (2002), *Counting the Cost: The Measurement and Recording of Alcohol-Related Violence and Disorder*, London: The Portman Group.

SOOTHILL, K., JACK, A., and GIBBENS, T. (1976), 'Rape: A 22-Year Cohort Study' *Medicine, Science, and the Law*, 16(1): 62–9.

STANKO, E. (1990), *Everyday Violence*, London: Unwin Hyman.

STELFOX, P. (1998), 'Policing Lower Levels of Organised Crime in England and Wales', *Howard Journal of Criminal Justice*, 37: 393–406.

STRAUS, M., and GELLES, R. (1990), 'How violent are American families? Estimates from the National Family Violence Survey and other studies', in M. Straus and R. Gelles (eds), *Physical Violence in American Families*, New Brunswick, N.J.: Transaction.

——, ——, and Steinmetz, S. (1980), *Behind Closed Doors*, New York: Anchor Press.

STRONG, S. (1995), *Whitewash: Pablo Escobar and the Cocaine Wars*, London: Pan.

THORPE, K., and ROBB, P. (2006), 'Extent and Trends', in A. Walker, C. Kershaw, and S. Nicholas, *Crime in England and Wales 2005/06*, London, Home Office.

TOCH, H., and ADAMS, K. (1994), *The Disturbed Violent Offender*, Washington DC: American Psychological Association.

TOMBS, S. (2006), 'Workplace harm and the illusion of law', in S. Tombs *et al.* (eds), *Criminal Obsessions: why harms matter more than law*, London: Crime and Society Foundation.

TOMSEN, S. (1997), 'A Top Night: Social Protest, Masculinity and the Culture of Drinking Violence', *British Journal of Criminology*, 37(1): 90–102.

TOPALLI, V., WRIGHT, R., and FORNANGO, R. (2002), 'Drug Dealers, Robbery and Retaliation', *British Journal of Criminology*, 42: 337–51.

TUCK, M. (1989), *Drinking and Disorder: a study of non-Metropolitan violence*, London: HMSO.

UPSON, A. (2004), *Violence at Work: Findings from the 2002/03 British Crime Survey*, Home Office online report 04/04.

VIGIL, J. D. (1988), *Barrio Gangs: Street Life and Identity in Southern California*, Austin: University of Texas Press.

WADDINGTON, D. (1992), *Contemporary Issues in Public Disorder*, London: Routledge.

WADDINGTON, P., BADGER, D., and BULL, R. (2005), *The Violent Workplace*, Cullompton, Devon: Willan.

WALBY, S., and ALLEN, J. (2004), *Domestic Violence, Sexual Assault and Stalking: Findings from the British Crime Survey*, London: Home Office.

WALKER, A., KERSHAW, C., and NICHOLAS, S. (2006), *Crime in England and Wales 2005/06*, London, Home Office.

WALKER, L. E. (1984), *The Battered Woman Syndrome*, New York: Springer.

WEBSDALE, N., and CHESNEY-LIND, M. (1998), 'Doing Violence to Women', in L. H. Bowker (ed.), *Masculinities and Violence*, London: Sage.

WEIS, J. (1989), 'Family violence research methodology and design', in L. Ohlin and M. Tonry (eds), *Family Violence*, Chicago: University of Chicago Press.

WEINER, N., ZAHN, M., and SAGI, R. (1990), *Violence: Patterns, Causes, Public Policy*, San Diego: Harcourt Brace Jovanovich.

WELLS, C. (1993), *Corporations and Criminal Responsibility*, Oxford: Oxford University Press.

——(2001), *Corporations and Criminal Responsibility*, 2nd edn, Oxford: Oxford University Press.

WIKSTRÖM, P.-O. H. (1991), *Urban Crime, Criminals and Victims: The Swedish Experience in an Anglo-American Comparative Perspective*, New York: Springer.

WILSON, J., and HERRNSTEIN, R. (1985), *Crime and Human Nature*, New York: Simon & Schuster.

WILSON, M., and DALY, M. (1992), 'Who kills whom in spouse killings: on the exceptional sex ratio of spousal homicides in the United States', *Criminology*, 30(2): 189–214.

WOLFGANG, M. (1958), *Patterns in Criminal Homicide*, Philadelphia: University of Philadelphia Press.

——and FERRACUTI, F. (1967), *The Subculture of Violence*, London: Tavistock.

YOUNG, J. (1988), 'Risk of crime and fear of crime: a realist critique of survey-based assumptions', in M. Maguire and J. Pointing (eds), *Victims of Crime: a New Deal?*, Milton Keynes: Open University Press.

22

WHITE-COLLAR AND CORPORATE CRIME

David Nelken

INTRODUCTION

The media increasingly report cases of business or professional people caught out in serious offences, sometimes for behaviour that they did not expect to be treated as criminal, and for which it is often difficult to secure a conviction. Such Jekyll and Hyde contradiction between respectability and crime raises questions that are unlike those posed by other types of criminal behaviour. Why do they do it when they have so much to lose? How representative are they or their practices of other businessmen, or of business life in general? Is there one law for the rich and another for the poor?

One of the biggest difficulties in approaching this subject is to find a way of putting dramatic and newsworthy cases of business misbehaviour into some sort of context and proportion. Study of the distribution and frequency of white-collar crimes is made problematic by the fact (not in itself unimportant) that, especially in the common law countries where the concept was first formulated, most white-collar crimes are not included in the official statistics which serve as the basis for debates about 'the crime problem'. The usual difficulties of interpreting the statistics of crime are greatly magnified here (Levi 1985). The information recorded by specialized enforcement agencies (often not even made public) serves mainly as a source for describing methods of control rather than the misbehaviour being controlled. Neither can it be assumed that there is any uniformity in the meaning of data obtained in this way. A few agencies are reactive, and depend on complaints; others are proactive, but the level of enforcement is restricted by limited resources (in Britain factories are inspected for safety offences on average once every four years). Much regulation is geared to using prosecution as a last resort—thus the number of prosecuted offenders says little about the theoretical level of crime; conversely, the number of visits or warnings cannot be used as an index of the incidence of deliberate law-breaking. There is a danger of double-counting where the same behaviour is dealt with by different agencies, or where one firm has more subunits than another. This also creates problems about defining recidivism—which were ignored by Sutherland in his pioneering study (Sutherland 1949). There are problems of classifying the date and location of some of these offences (a factor which often helps secure their immunity). Shifts in legislative mandates, and in the number, expertise, politics, and motivation of enforcers, make a treacherous basis for studies of changes in offending patterns over time. Lastly, supplementing official statistics with victim reports is difficult because the victims are often unaware of their victimization; and even where this is not the case, as in organizations subject to fraud, there is often unwillingness to admit to vulnerability.

These difficulties mean that discussions of the subject in textbooks are often forced to rely unduly on newspaper reports or on the activities of crusading journalists (see, e.g. Coleman 1985; but see now Punch 1996). Obtaining information in this way complicates the task of assessing the accuracy, frequency, or representativeness of the cases reported. Are 'scandals' by definition unrepresentative of normal life, or should we rather see them, as Punch does, as occasions which expose typical practices and mechanisms of deviance—especially the way 'illicit solutions are found to managerial dilemmas' (Punch 1996)? What is clear is that newspapers, or those who feed them their stories, initiate crime control campaigns for reasons which may have little to do with the long-term trend in the misbehaviour at issue. It is therefore often hard to tell, here as elsewhere, whether business or financial crimes are increasing or are just more newsworthy, or to decide if apparent change is the result of an increase in a given kind of misbehaviour or more the consequence of a trend towards the use of formal and legal, rather than informal, means to deal with it.

Despite these problems there have been some useful studies drawing on agency records to survey the rate of corporate offending (Clinard and Yeager 1980), or even on court records to establish the type of offenders normally apprehended for what the authors call 'middle-class crimes' (Weisburd *et al.* 1991). What we know about white-collar crime also comes from interviews with enforcers as well as observation of their work (e.g. Carson 1970; Hawkins 1984; Hutter 1988, 1997; and cf. Nelken 1991); interviews with businessmen (e.g. Lane 1953; Braithwaite 1984); biographies of and retrospective accounts by offenders (e.g. Geis 1968); participant observation in offending organizations (e.g. Nelken 1983: ch. 2); experimental techniques such as those used by consumer organizations (Green 1990: ch. 2), as well as other sources (and for useful methodological hints on researching these type of offences, see Levi 1985).

Although most of the literature on white-collar crime is American, major contributions have been made by other English-language scholars, such as Braithwaite, Carson, and Levi. The equivalent term for 'white-collar crime' is also widely found in other languages, and even used in foreign court proceedings. There are also interesting contributions, sometimes in foreign languages, which could serve as a useful starting point for comparative research (e.g. Tiedemann 1974; Cosson 1978; Magnusson 1985; Clarke 1990b; Delmas-Marty 1990; Zigler 1990; Van Duyne 1993; Passas and Nelken 1993; Savelsberg 1994). But the common use of the term can be misleading. Despite the similarities of modern industrialized economies, there are important differences in general and legal culture that affect the meaning of and response to white-collar crime (and its contrasting category of ordinary crime). These contrasts have not yet been sufficiently explored (see Nelken 1994a; Levi and Nelken 1996; Nelken 2000). In civil law countries such as Italy there are few of the special enforcement agencies used to deal with occupational offences found, for example, in America, Britain, and Australia. Instead, normal police forces, often spearheaded by specialized financial police, conduct investigations of economic crime, and businessmen or politicians with white collars regularly see the inside of prisons (though few seem to stay there for long). American outrage over business misbehaviour may be connected to what Wright-Mills (1943/1963) saw as the small-town values of American social reformers, as well as to a peculiar, American love–hate relationship with big businesses (are they the ultimate proof of capitalist success, or a threat to the market and to the individual?). In countries with a strong Catholic heritage the respectability attached to capitalist profit-making may be less secure than in Protestant countries (Ruggiero 1996).

Much of the literature on white-collar crime continues to be concerned to demonstrate the seriousness and diffuseness of such offending, and to show that its costs and damages dwarf those of conventional, or ordinary, crime (for a recent summary of attempts to measure the impact of white-collar crime, see Slapper and Tombs 1999: 37–41, 54–84). More than any other type of crime, white-collar offences are also attacked for undermining the basis of trust that holds society together (for example, by discrediting those in authority or positions of privilege who are supposed to be models of respectability). Colossal fines and settlements are imposed in cases of some financial crimes, for example, Michael Milken, the junk bond king, paid over $650 million in court-ordered restitution even before sentence. The collapse of the savings and loan institutions (similar to what in Britain are described as building societies) in the United States in the late 1980s may end up costing a trillion dollars. This is many times the cost of the Marshall Plan or the Korean War; but the real impact is blunted because the costs are to be covered by a US government fifty-year loan (Pontell and Calavita 1993; Calavita et al. 1997; Zimring and Hawkins 1993). Contrary to what is supposed by some definitions (e.g. Edelhertz 1970), there is also no reason to exclude violence and death from the province of white-collar crime. There are a number of case studies which document this, even without going into more controversial but important calculations of the overall number of fatal accidents or diseases occurring at work which could have been prevented and prosecuted (Box 1983: 28ff.; Hills 1988; Slapper 1991). Carson's study of the loss of life in the exploration for oil in the North Sea (confirmed by later events such as the blowing up of the Piper Alpha oil rig in 1988 with the loss of 168 lives), for instance, showed that many lives could have been saved with rudimentary attention to safety considerations (Carson 1982). The devastating consequences of the nuclear disaster at Chernobyl, the chemical explosion at Bhopal, the suffering caused by the sale of the drug thalidomide, or the contraceptive known as the Dalkon shield, are other well-known examples.

Despite all this evidence, white-collar crimes are still subjected to very different interpretations. It might seem odd that sociologists, familiar with Durkheim's argument that society considers dangerous those behaviours it responds to as criminal, rather than the other way round, should keep trying to prove that white-collar crime is really criminal simply because it causes great harm. The answer must be that they hope in this way to influence the social definition of such conduct. Debates over the causes and control of white-collar crime do connect to different political evaluations of the misdeeds of business or capitalism. Political conservatives tend to favour structural explanations of business malpractice rather than personal guilt—thus changing places with liberals in comparison with their positions on ordinary crime (Zimring and Hawkins 1993). But even authors with very different political views argue that corporate crime requires 'a shift from a humanist to a structuralist problematic'—though they continue nonetheless to apply the criminal label to the behaviour which results from such a structural problematic (Slapper and Tombs 1999: 17).

SEVEN TYPES OF AMBIGUITY

Why is there still so much disagreement over white-collar crime? As with the equivocal designs produced by Gestalt psychologists, do we find it difficult to see 'the criminal' and 'the respectable person' in one and the same figure? Following Aubert (1952) I shall argue that ambiguity about the nature of white-collar crime, and the best way of responding to it, forms an essential key to the topic and can be used to provide insights into this type of crime as well as the 'ordinary' crime to which it is contrasted. As the subject has become more established scholars have either tended to abandon Aubert's insight, or to concentrate on only one or two of the sources of ambiguity that will be considered here. They also tend to divide into those, on the one hand, who point to the ambiguous features of white-collar crime so as to explain and justify special treatment for this misbehaviour, and those, on the other hand, who claim that ambiguity is a socially constructed smoke-screen that ought to be dispelled. In this chapter I do not purport to settle the question of how far the features that supposedly make white-collar crime more ambiguous than ordinary crime are (merely) socially constructed. I shall, however, try to do something to clarify the uncertainties produced by the literature itself by offering a critical review both of those arguments which assert that ambiguity is intrinsic to the misbehaviour itself and of those which attempt to prove that white-collar crime is 'essentially' the same as ordinary crime but is transformed by the social reaction to it.

To provide a common thread to the following overview of what has been written about the definition of, causes of, and responses to, white-collar crime, I shall seek to illustrate seven different sources of ambiguity that surround this topic. (I use the term 'ambiguity' loosely to embrace the various forms of equivocalness, uncertainty, and ambivalence referred to in and produced by discussions of the characteristics of white-collar crime.) The first ambiguities that I shall consider arise in trying to define what is meant by 'white-collar crime'. The ambiguous way the concept is used in the criminological literature means that it is not clear what range of crimes is being referred to. From the outset, Sutherland's concept has also been criticized for seeking to apply the crime label to behaviours whose definition as crime is legally or sociologically controversial. The second set of ambiguities belongs more to discussions of the causes of white-collar crime. While many scholars try to apply the usual criminological frameworks of explanation to this kind of offending, others have used the topic precisely so as to place these schemes in doubt. Ambiguity also surrounds discussions of the commission of these offences. Thus some writers stress the point that this type of offending behaviour takes place in a more respectable context than most other crimes, and that it is the product of more ambiguous intentions than is the case for ordinary crime. The third set of ambiguities derives from the regulation and handling of white-collar crime. White-collar crimes are often controlled in a different, and more ambivalent, way than ordinary crime, and it is controversial how far this reflects, reinforces, or even creates its ambiguity. The uncertain status of these crimes may also be seen to reflect a process of transition and social change in which the public is not yet ready for more outright criminalization of these behaviours. It is also argued that control of these offences is hampered by problems of competing values and social costs that do not arise in repressing ordinary crime.

I shall be taking these various ambiguities one by one, partly for purposes of exposition and partly because there are important differences amongst the sources and types of ambiguity. Taken as a whole, however, many of these ambiguities are mutually reinforcing and thus help to shape the perceived character of white-collar crime as a social phenomenon. If, for example, different and predominantly administrative methods of enforcement are used in dealing with white-collar as opposed to ordinary crimes, this will shape public opinion concerning their relative seriousness. But at the same time, such (alleged) differences in public attitudes also serve as justifications offered by legislators and regulators for their different treatment of white-collar crimes. On the other hand, any given source of ambiguity may have implications under a number of different headings. For example, the fact that white-collar crimes generally take place in private settings represents a special feature of their causation that may facilitate their commission. This also serves as an impediment to normal policing methods, which helps to explain the use of other forces and forms of enforcement. Lastly, the importance of respecting 'privacy' as a value also figures as an argument in policy debates over the appropriateness or otherwise of strengthening controls. For this edition I have abbreviated some of my discussions of these questions in order to make room for a final section in which I examine the applicability of this framework to the recent spate of financial scandals in the USA (whereas for an excellent overview of the physical harm carried out by corporations readers should consult Gobert and Punch's *Rethinking Corporate Crime* (2003)).

WHITE-COLLAR CRIME AS A
CONTESTED CONCEPT

If Sutherland merited a Nobel prize, as Mannheim thought, for pioneering this field of study, he certainly did not deserve it for the clarity or serviceableness of his definition. What, if anything, is there in common between the marketing of unsafe pharmaceuticals, the practice of insider trading, 'long-firm' fraud, computer crime, bank embezzlement, and fiddling at work? Though Sutherland claimed to be interested in reforming criminological theory, rather than changing society, the appeal of this topic, particularly through the 1970s and 1980s, was unquestionably linked to its progressive connotations and its implicit accusations of bias in the making and enforcing of criminal law (Yeager 1991). The apparent success of the label in finding public acceptance, while lacking a clear or agreed referent, may testify less to its coherence than to its capacity to name a supposed threat. Not all examples of white-collar crime are ambiguous (e.g. embezzlement), just as not all ambiguous deviance is white-collar crime. But considerable disagreement over the range of misbehaviour referred to, as well as doubts about the coherence of those behaviours it does include, makes the category as a whole rather ambiguous. And, peculiarly enough, those white-collar offences whose criminal character seems most unambiguous—such as bank embezzlement or (on some definitions) credit card fraud—are the ones least likely to illustrate the theoretical or policy-relevant features of white-collar crime in which Sutherland and his successors have been most interested.

We will not deal here with the intrinsic difficulties built into Sutherland's definition of white-collar crime as a crime committed by 'a person of high status in the course of his occupation' (1949: 9), a matter that was discussed in the first edition of this *Handbook*. Nor will we illustrate the point that the problem of definition cannot just be put aside in order to get on with more interesting matters, because the solution found for this problem ultimately determines the findings of any investigation (see earlier editions of this work). If at one extreme there can be problems in distinguishing ordinary business behaviour from business crime, at the other, there continues to be uncertainty about where to draw the line between white-collar crime and organized crime. As predicted in the first edition of this *Handbook* (Nelken 1994b), the overlap between these types of enterprise crime has become an important new focus of research (though one already anticipated in the theory of illegal enterprises put forward by Smith and others in the 1980s). Ruggiero, for example, claims that Sutherland created an unsatisfactory distinction between these two types of criminal behaviour (leaving only gangsters in the category of organized crime) that has wrongly been taken over by later criminologists. He argues that white-collar/organized crime should be seen as a normal rather than pathological aspect of business life, and its causes should be sought in wealth and power rather than greed as such. Organized crime, he insists, once we get away from ethnic stereotypes, involves the same flexible consumer-oriented behaviour that characterizes all successful business behaviour. Offering a wealth of examples of business-type crimes, Ruggiero argues that both white-collar and organized criminals use similar techniques, share the same illegal know-how, and share the same values—even if perpetrators come from different backgrounds. Their crimes are performed in or by organized structures, thrive on collusion, and normally enjoy the connivance of administrators and legislators (Ruggeiro 1996).

In part we may be witnessing real changes in the phenomena pointed to by these different criminological labels. In the first place, business crime may be taking on some of the characteristics of organized crime. As Reichman observes, 'insider trading as practiced in the 1980s is a form of crime that combines elements of the traditional categories of occupational and organizational crime' (Reichman 1992: 56). Likewise, traditional organized crime groups, such as the Mafia or the Camorra in Italy, or the Chinese or Taiwanese Triads, have become increasingly capitalistic in orientation and ethos (see, e.g., Arlachi 1985 on the Mafia and the Protestant ethic, or Gambetta's (1994) thesis of the Mafia as an industry of private protection). In Post-communist countries which are without a recent history of capitalist markets, it may indeed be artificial to draw a line between business and organized crime. More broadly, globalization may be leading to similar forms of structural integration of legitimate and illegitimate business activities, making regular collaboration between business and organized criminals both more possible and more necessary (Nelken 1997a). An important topic for research is global tax avoidance and evasion, and the role of professionals such as lawyers and accountants on both sides of the fence as facilitators and enforcers (see e.g. Levi *et al.* 2005).

On the other hand, this thesis should not be pushed too far. Claims concerning a symbiotic relationship between ordinary business, white-collar crime, and organized crime presuppose important differences rather than total overlap. Organized crime groups are able to gain legitimacy, respectability, protection, access, expertise, suppliers, customers, investment opportunities, or various other advantages from such relationships, and these benefits would be attenuated if the differences were to disappear. Both white-collar crime and organized crime cover such a continuum of activities that there will clearly be some that fall outside any attempt to categorize them together (think, on the one hand, of a small food shop breaking hygiene regulations, and, on the other, of a classical protection racket based on territorial domination). What is certainly true is that the distinction between these types of crime will vary according to the type of crime and the structure of the industry under consideration.

By common agreement, Sutherland's definition is not considered a helpful starting point for doing research into white-collar crime. Apart from its internal contradictions (for example, are we dealing with crimes committed for or against organizations?), changes in class structure, forms of business activity, organizational forms, and cultural valuations all threaten to undermine its empirical coherence. But what other definitions can be found which do not simply rely on selecting the most appropriate-seeming crimes from the official criminal statistics? One common inductive strategy is to start from the data produced by the non-police administrative agencies generally entrusted with dealing with business offences (especially in common law countries). This was the source of data used in the comprehensive Clinard and Yeager study which focused on various federal regulatory bodies (Clinard and Yeager 1980). Non-police agencies in Britain included the Post Office, British Transport Police, Customs, water authorities, local government, Ministry of Agriculture, etc. (See Royal Commission 1980.) But though these agencies may have some enforcement practices in common it would be quite wrong to describe all the types of offenders they prosecute (many from poor backgrounds) as white-collar criminals.

Another strategy is to seek to develop typologies of different kinds of crime which fit under the general heading of 'white-collar crime'. Many writers work with subcategories such as crimes against the environment, crimes in the workplace, and economic crimes. The difficulty here is that the categories thus created are still likely to end up as containers for somewhat disparate behaviours. Green (1990) distinguishes organizational occupational crime, state authority occupational crime, professional occupational crime, etc. But these headings cannot pretend to be either theoretically defined, or even coherent classifications of types of crime. The offences considered as state crime range from bribe-taking to genocide; whilst the chapter on individual occupational crime—which is admitted to be a 'catch-all' category—includes behaviours as different as employee theft and securities crimes. The drawbacks to inductivism are evident in the artificial distinctions that lead Green to discuss the crimes committed by bribe-givers in a different chapter from those of bribe-takers. Nonetheless, the range of crimes brought under the rubric of the white-collar crime concept continues to grow: Friedrichs (2003) devotes chapters to state corporate crime, enterprise crime, contrepreneurial crime, avocational crime, finance crime, and 'techno crime'.

There are also various attempts to rethink Sutherland's concept in a more deductive fashion. Some of these are deliberately modest, such as Clarke's extended definition of business crime in terms of its distinguishing features (Clarke 1990a: ch. 3). In the rest of the book Clarke seeks to illustrate the applicability of his definition to a series of different areas of misbehaviour (and justifies a refusal to develop typologies partly on the somewhat odd grounds that opting for any one typological scheme would exclude another which might be more appropriate for other purposes). Despite the richness of his descriptions his approach can be criticized for already building in as part of his definition of business crime those controversial features of the social response that are less geared to prosecution than in the case of ordinary crime. It is also unclear why the book is entitled *Business Crime* when the thrust of the argument is intended to undermine this label.

Of greater value are the more ambitious efforts aimed at finding a key theoretical variable which could produce a coherent focus for further research. Recent examples (which go beyond the somewhat unimaginative 'crimes of the powerful', 'crimes of the upperworld', or 'elite crimes') include Shapiro's focus on the increasing need to trust agents and the consequent exposure to various forms of abuse of such trust in which agents subordinate the interests of their principals to their own gain (Shapiro 1989). Coleman and others stress the importance of the growth of organizational actors in what has been called the 'asymmetric society' (Gross 1980; Coleman 1992). These approaches may include more or less than the offences that Sutherland covered: Shapiro's proposal, for example, seems to be derived from her previous empirical research interests in securities frauds and would not be applicable, say, to pollution crimes; its focus on agents also lets principals off the hook. But such approaches promise to be theoretically more productive than Sutherland's concept.

IS WHITE-COLLAR CRIME REALLY CRIME?

If there are basic uncertainties about what is being referred to when talking of white-collar crime, there are also long-standing doubts whether or not all the misbehaviours discussed under this rubric can be considered to count as crime. Most of the continuing controversy, as well as the stimulus, generated by this topic is due to the fact that it appears to straddle the crucial boundary between criminal and non-criminal behaviour. Since this is a well-aired problem, and the debates can be found in all the readers on this subject (e.g. Geis 1968), I will confine myself to drawing out their relevance to the issue of ambiguity. Many scholars have argued that the misbehaviours discussed by Sutherland or his followers do not always satisfy the legal criteria for crime; some even go so far as to insist on the necessity for a penal conviction at court (e.g. Tappan 1947). It is, admittedly, ironic that Sutherland himself was unable to publish the names of the companies whose administrative violations he described in his book, because of his publisher's fears that he would then be exposed to claims of libel for describing them as criminal (this was remedied only in the uncut version published much later: Sutherland 1983). Restricting attention to those crimes found in the ordinary criminal statistics, however, too easily robs the term of all its sense. The results of following such a definition make it possible to argue that white-collar crime is an otiose category and that white-collar criminals, like most ordinary criminals, are young, feckless, and unsuccessful (see Hirschi and Gottfredson 1987, 1989; and the criticism by Steffensmeier 1989). Others have made virtually the opposite attack, complaining that many white-collar crimes are merely technically criminal and are not socially considered on a par with ordinary crimes; hence they do not satisfy the requirements of a sociological definition of crime (see, e.g. Burgess 1950, criticizing Hartung 1950). While this is a more acute criticism, it tends to assume the unchanging circularity of social definitions and underestimates the potential for change (a process in which criminology can play a part).

The fact that such opposite criticisms can be raised is confirmation of the ambiguity of this concept—which is also reflected in the use of descriptions such as 'regulatory crimes' or 'mala prohibita'. Sutherland, and many later scholars, chose to include in their definition of white-collar crime not only misbehaviours with criminal penalties, but also those that carried only civil or administrative sanctions. This was done precisely so as not to invoke the question whether the choice of these different and generally lighter sanctions was justified (or only a sign of the political and economic power of the offenders involved). But it is only a small (if significant) step from this to argue for the inclusion in the category of white-collar crime of other types of harmful business behaviour that have succeeded (through much the same political and economic pressures) in avoiding being subject to any sanctions at all.

Must we use law to draw the line? One of the contributions made by the topic of white-collar crime to criminology lies in this very difficulty of assimilating all that Sutherland was getting at without breaking the boundaries of the discipline. Should the definition of crime adopted for sociological purposes be the same as that of the law? What are the dangers of tying criminology to a starting point defined by another—politically conditioned—discipline? If we allow the political process to define what counts as crime, is this a politically conservative choice? Or is it just good tactics—a way to avoid alienating the 'liberals' (as Box 1983 argues)? Leading writers insist that we must refer to the law because otherwise it would be impossible to decide who is to define what should count as business deviance (Coleman 1987). But this was exactly the decision that the labelling perspective tried to force criminologists to face. The topic of white-collar crime thus illustrates the possibility of divergence between legal, social, and political definitions of criminality—but in so doing it reminds us of the artificiality of all definitions of crime.

EXPLAINING THE CAUSES OF WHITE-COLLAR CRIME

Can white-collar crime be explained using the normal frameworks of criminological explanation? In previous editions I argued that the motives usually attributed to white-collar criminals (greed and power) were too often left unexplored and that more effort needed to be made to 'appreciate' the perspective of those engaged in white-collar crime, however politically distasteful this might be for some scholars (Nelken 1994b, 1997b). Some progress is being made. The insider stories which emerge from former participants, especially in the world of high finance, describe a subculture where the excitement for young men of living life in the fast lane is as important as the money benefits themselves (Portnoy 1997). Punch tries to get behind the 'surface solidity of the business organisation' so as to examine 'the fluctuating and even turbulent reality of managerial "backstage" ' behaviour. In this 'world of power struggles, ideological debate, intense political rivalry, manipulation of information, and short term problem solving . . . managers emerge as something of amoral chameleons, buffeted by moral ambiguity and organizational uncertainty; they survive this "messy not to say dirty" environment by engaging in Machiavellian micro-politics' (Punch 1996). He finds that business studies students can get as indignant as the next person about the social and human costs of business misbehaviour. But once they are asked to role-play as managers having to make hard choices in risky situations, the same students regularly opt for 'macho', high-risk strategies. In the 'real world' of the organization the pressure 'to deliver the goods' or protect market share or just one's own career are potent motivations. And there are numerous ways of seeking to justify such behaviour as not really reprehensible.

More generally, however, the problem of what exactly needs to be explained continues to confuse the search for causes. Is white-collar crime conventional or unconventional behaviour for those who commit it? If it is conventional, why is so much effort put into keeping criminal activities secret even from other members of the same organization (Hirschi and Gottfredson 1987)? Where the explanatory approach adopted is to look for the individual motivations of what is taken to be clearly criminal behaviour, white-collar crime becomes just another test of standard theories of crime causation. Its novelty, if any, is tied to the emergence of new opportunities, for new groups, to commit old offences—for example, through the use of computers to carry out frauds. Where, instead, the issue becomes the criminogenic properties of business, of capitalism, or organizational behaviour in general, then the normative fabric of everyday business life seems placed in doubt and the actual evidence of white-collar crime seems to fall short of what would be possible.

These difficulties have not discouraged a series of attempts to explain the causes of white-collar crime, and there are even a number of good reviews of such work (see, e.g. Braithwaite 1985, who concludes, however, that 'only banal generalisations are possible', or Coleman 1987, who furnishes a (banal?) synthesis of existing work in terms of opportunity and motivation theory). I shall comment on explanations concerned with the whole area of white-collar crime. But, as already noted, the search for causes may be limited to typologies of crime, such as crimes by professional people, or even to specific offences. And obviously, where the topic is theoretically reformulated this will affect what needs to be explained. For Shapiro, for example, the study of white-collar crime belongs to the wider study of the maintenance and abuse of trust (see also Nelken 1994a; Friedrichs 2003). Attention should focus on the rising need to rely on agents and the consequent increased exposure to the risks of their malpractices. Trust is required in so far as it is difficult to tell when agents are putting their self-interests above those of their principals, especially as they tend to be the 'repeat players', and to act at a distance; but efforts to limit their discretion are self-defeating. To understand causation there therefore needs to be 'the marriage of a systematic understanding of the distribution of structural opportunities for trust abuse with an understanding of the conditions under which individual or organisational fiduciaries seize or ignore these illicit opportunities' (Shapiro 1989: 353).

The concept of white-collar crime was certainly not invented in order to provide comfort for standard approaches to causation in criminology. Sutherland hoped to use these misbehaviours as ammunition against the reigning tendency to explain crime in terms of individual or social pathology. By ridiculing the idea that businesses or businessmen could be said to misbehave because of their difficult childhoods, he intended to reform criminological theory and show that only his theory of 'differential association' could account for all forms of criminal behaviour. There is ample evidence of the diffusion of definitions favourable to white-collar forms of law-breaking in business circles, whether these are based on loyalty to the firm, the alleged requirements of business life, or dislike of government regulation. But Sutherland's theory is nevertheless now regarded as flawed and superficial, and the search for a universal theory of crime has lost its attractions. Ironically, those who are most committed to the subject of white-collar crime are now under attack by criminologists who argue that there is no need for this special category of criminal behaviour precisely because it gets in the way of general explanations of the crime phenomenon (Hirschi and Gottfredson 1987; Gottfredson and Hirschi 1990: ch. 9).

Proponents both of 'strain' and of 'control' theories have tried to make sense of white-collar crime. Whatever his original focus may have been, most strain theories of corporate crime find their inspiration in Merton's concept of anomie. White-collar crimes can be seen, for example, as an 'innovative' response on the part of businesses (or particular roles such as middle management) to the strain of conforming to cultural prescriptions to maintain profits even in difficult circumstances (Passas 1990; Vaughan 1996; Slapper and Tombs 1999). The strain may be located in the business environment as such, in particular industries, or in particular firms. A classical study of the conditions under which the major car manufacturers in the USA constrain their car dealers to operate showed the pressure put on dealers to cut corners if they wanted to survive economically (Leonard and Weber 1970); other situations may 'facilitate' rather than directly 'coerce' criminal solutions (Needleman and Needleman 1979). More could be made of these ideas (Nelken 1994c; Slapper and Tombs 1999).

Control theories, on the other hand, are premised on the initial question: why don't we all commit crimes when the temptations are so strong? The reply given is that most of us, the generally law-abiding, have too much invested in relationships and in legitimate society. The best way to rob a bank may indeed be to own one—or work in one—but, we assume, most of those in this position do not take advantage of it. This approach is a weak candidate for explaining white-collar crime because it finds it difficult to account for how middle-class criminals (and even most of those who find themselves in a position to embezzle) ever achieved their social positions in the first place. It also needs to show why they would be willing to risk their investment (Wheeler 1992). One neglected argument that is suggested here is based on the idea of 'over-investment'. The findings of Weisburd and his colleagues in their sample of middle-class criminals were that 'many of our offenders have the material goods associated with successful people but may barely be holding their financial selves together' (Weisburd *et al.* 1991: 65). This could be interpreted as meaning that such offenders are, if anything, so strongly tied to social expectations and obligations that they are even willing to offend to maintain their position (and so anomie and control theories meet up)! In any case, whatever its general bearing, more specific ingredients of control theory, such as the importance of 'neutralization' of social controls through the use of justifications (learned within or outside the company), are regularly adopted in explaining white-collar crime. Typical theoretical syntheses in textbooks dealing with white-collar crime in fact draw both on the 'strain' elements of capitalist competition and striving for business or individual success, and on the large possible variety of such 'techniques of neutralization' (see, e.g. Box 1983; Coleman 1987; Green 1990).

The labelling approach has, strangely, been comparatively neglected in the study of white-collar crime. One reason for this could be that criminologists here line up with those doing the labelling (see Katz 1980; Yeager 1991: ch. 1). There is of course the apparent paradox that it is the 'insiders' rather than the 'outsiders' who are being labelled—but the paradox normally disappears once the details of who is really affected become clearer. In any case, few would now want to deny the importance of legislative or other battles over the labelling of business misbehaviour. The perspective would seem peculiarly relevant given the relative recency of many laws regulating business, the sharp swings between political projects of regulation and deregulation, and the divergent views of different groups as to the appropriateness of criminalization. Some attention has been given to the success of techniques of 'non-labelling' or 'de-labelling' used by lawyers and accountants in diluting or avoiding the imposition of the criminal label, for example in shaping the (mis)behaviour involved in some tax-avoidance schemes (McBarnet 1991; McBarnet and Whelan 1999). In my study of the social construction of landlord crime (Nelken 1983) I examined the process of criminal labelling and de-labelling in this area of business misbehaviour. I showed that those actually apprehended for landlord crime were small, immigrant landlords involved in disputes with their tenants (for similar findings for other white-collar crimes, see Hutter 1988; Croall 1989). With some effort it was possible to portray their self-help methods as criminal, but the malpractices characteristic of large business landlords stayed immune to criminalization because of their similarity to ordinary business behaviour—a 'limit' of the legal process which was, paradoxically, concealed by actually exaggerating the capacity of law to control such behaviour (Nelken 1983). White-collar crimes and the reaction to them seem, perhaps more than other crimes, to be subject to interrelated cycles of expansion and reform. The apparent growth of political corruption in the 1980s, followed by widespread crackdown in the 1990s, is a good example (Nelken and Levi 1996).

The attempt to explain white-collar crime within the 'normal science' approaches used in criminology shows itself not only in theories of causation, but also in the effort to follow the 'careers' of such criminals (Weisburd and Waring 2001). Many writers adopt a positivist search for the peculiar characteristics that distinguish offenders from non-offenders. Sutherland (1949, 1983) was keen to show the widespread nature of white-collar offences but also to identify the major culprits. He examined infringements of rules governing fair labour practices by General Motors and others, violations of rules against the restraint of trade, especially common in the major companies in the film industry, infringements of patents, and misrepresentation in advertising involving household names such as Bayer aspirin, Quaker Oats, Carnation milk, Phillips milk of magnesia, Hoover vacuum cleaners, and Encyclopedia Britannica. He particularly stressed the duration of some offences and the 'recidivism' of some of the companies concerned.

Clinard and Yeager (1980), in the most wide-ranging documentary study of corporate crime to date, examined all the federal administrative, civil, and criminal actions initiated in 1975 and 1976 by 25 federal agencies against 582 of America's largest corporations. The violations they examined were divided into non-compliance with agency regulations; environmental pollution; financial crimes, such as illegal payments or tax offences; labour discrimination, including unsafe working practices; manufacturing offences, such as the distribution of unsafe products; and unfair trading practices, including price-fixing arrangements. Going beyond Sutherland, they tried to control comparisons for the time available to commit offences and the different size of the companies they investigated. They found that three-fifths of their sample had charges brought against them in those years. While 13 per cent of the companies accounted for just over half the violations, large, medium, and small companies were all well represented amongst the violators. Where Sutherland had found the film, mercantile, and railroad industries particularly engaged in violations, Clinard and Yeager found their black sheep in the oil, pharmaceutical, and motor vehicle industries, which all had more than their proportional share of violations. The oil industry, for example, was involved in three-fifths of all serious violations, with 22 of 28 oil-refining firms guilty of at least one violation in the period under consideration; car manufacturers were responsible in all for one-sixth of all the violations discovered and for a third of the manufacturing violations overall; pharmaceutical manufacturers accounted for one-tenth of all violations, and all 17 companies were found to have committed at least one violation.

Some of Clinard and Yeager's findings were artefacts which resulted from using data which depended on the vagaries of regulatory regimes: the higher offending rates of diversified firms, for example, may simply mean that they were more exposed to different regulatory agencies (though the firms concerned may also have faced problems in maintaining oversight of their different operations). Their investigation produced some statistical support for the proposition that violations increased as financial performance became poorer; this was particularly marked for environmental and labour offences. On the other hand, firms with higher than average growth rates were more likely to have engaged in manufacturing violations. The authors admitted that the causal variables on which they concentrated—size, growth rate, diversification, and market power and resources—had only limited predictive power. Even the more confident of their claims concerning crime rates and economic performance have been questioned in the later literature (Braithwaite 1985). Their study was unable to allow for the complicating factor of why and when agencies choose to uncover violations, and has been criticized for taking agency records as the measure of corporate crime and for failing to see such behaviour as endemic to capitalism (Young 1981). A valuable study by Haines (1997) examines the way companies react after they have been involved in safety violations on the hypothesis that the same causes which explain violation would also account for what was done or not done afterwards to put things right. Her findings were that managers in larger companies were less likely to take a 'blinkered' view of what should be done to avoid recurrence and could afford to take a broader and longer-term approach to the problem of reconciling profit and safety.

A central debate amongst scholars of white-collar crime in fact concerns the extent to which corporate and business crime should be seen as an inevitable consequence of capitalism. Box (1983), in a Marxist-influenced application of Merton, argues that corporations are criminogenic because, if legal means are blocked, they will resort to illegal means so as to maintain or increase profitability. As and when necessary, they will use techniques aimed at competitors (e.g. industrial espionage or price fixing), at consumers (e.g. fraud or misleading advertising), or at the public at large (e.g. environmental pollution). Those recruited to work in corporations learn to justify such behaviour on the grounds that 'business is business' (cf. Pearce 1976; Punch 1996). This is particularly true for those who rise to the top and who then have a disproportionate influence over the ethos of their firms (although they generally take care not to be directly involved or informed of the illegal activities made necessary by their drive for profit). For those who subscribe to this theory businessmen comply with the law in so far as they see it enforced strictly (thereby denying competitive advantage to those who would break it). Where there are few effective controls, as in the Third World, capitalism shows its true face, selling unsafe products, paying low wages, and exploiting the complaisance of poor and corrupt governments and regulators (see Slapper and Tombs 1999: ch. 7).

On the other hand, it is well to bear in mind some reservations about the idea that capitalism as such is criminogenic. If Merton's anomie theory is to be pressed this far it is at least necessary to go on to discuss the alternative, non-criminal modes of responding to 'strain', and (what Merton did not do) offer an explanation of when and why each mode is chosen. The argument appears to predict too much crime and makes it difficult to explain the relative stability of economic trade within and between nations, given the large number of economic transactions, the many opportunities for committing business crimes, the large gains to be made, and the relative unlikelihood of punishment. This theory also has difficulty in accounting for improvements in safety and increases in the quality of goods under capitalism. If it is somewhat oversimplified to argue that only a small proportion of businessmen are 'bad apples', it is not much more convincing to assume that all businesses act as 'amoral calculators' and would choose to offend but for the availability of serious sanctions (Pearce and Tombs 1990, 1991). The desires to continue in business, and to maintain self-respect and the good will of fellow businessmen, go a long way to explaining reluctance to seize opportunities for a once-only windfall. Trading competitors (as well as organized consumer groups, unions, and others) can serve as a control on illicit behaviour for their own reasons. Law-abidingness can often be definitely in the competitive interests of companies. Braithwaite (1985) illustrates how American pharmaceutical companies able to obtain Federal Drug Administration authorization for their products are in this way guaranteed lucrative markets in countries that cannot afford their own expensive drug-testing facilities. It could be said that the clear evidence of exploitation and the sale of dangerous goods in Third World countries reflects an anomalous situation which is at least partly the result of the excessive freedom of manoeuvre of powerful multinational companies which are not exposed to sufficient competition. On the other hand, we should not underestimate the role of state regulation in all this. Current pressures of globalization that may be leading to a 'de-coupling' of politics and economics, both at home and abroad, could have dire consequences.

Marxist theory has no need to assume that all business crime will be tolerated. Many forms of business misbehaviour made into crimes may reflect changing forms of capitalism or inter-class conflict. At any given period, some corporate crimes, such as anti-trust offences, will not be in the interest of capitalism as a whole, so it is important to distinguish what is in the interests of capitalism from what suits particular capitalists. Even if the latter may succeed in blocking legislation or effective enforcement, at least in the short term, this does not prove that it is capitalism as such which requires the continuation of specific forms of misbehaviour. Moreover, capitalism is a set of practices and not just an important set of social actors. Practices may remain free from effective control even if the group concerned is not particularly economically powerful. Thus the relative immunity from control of abuses of the Rent Acts committed by private business landlords in Britain has been attributed less to their importance within the social structure and more to objective difficulties in controlling their behaviour without affecting normal commercial transactions (Nelken 1983). When professional criminals succeed in getting away with serious forms of business-related crime such as 'long-firm' fraud, it is implausible to say that this is in the interest of any capitalist group (Levi 1985). The same can be said of many of the large frauds carried out by previously respected insiders against companies.

We should not underestimate the fruitfulness of hypotheses based on the capacity of capitalism to generate business crime. But care needs to be taken in connecting macro and micro levels of explanation. All organizations, and not only the corporate form of trading, can be criminogenic in so far as they tend to reward achievement even at the expense of the outer environment (Kramer 1992). This would help to explain why public organizations such as the army, the police, or government bureaucracies also generate crime and corruption (these behaviours are increasingly being included in textbooks on white-collar crime). Likewise, the far from positive record of the former communist regimes in matters of worker safety, environmental pollution, or corruption cannot be blamed on the pressures of competition. Even in capitalist societies it is often the absence of market pressures that explains some types of business misbehaviour, such as the ease with which government subsidy programmes are diverted to improper uses (Passas and Nelken 1993; Nelken 2002).

WHITE-COLLAR CRIME IN ITS EVERYDAY SETTINGS

We have seen so far that there are, on the one hand, doubts about how far the same explanations will work for white-collar crime as for ordinary crime, and, on the other hand, risks of over-explanation in accounts which relate it too closely to ordinary business behaviour. For some commentators, however, the central issue concerns the extent to which white-collar crimes come about in similar ways to other criminal behaviour. Clarke's book on business crime, for example, argues strongly that these misbehaviours are typically 'less criminal' in their inception and motivation than much ordinary crime (Clarke 1990a). Whereas many textbook presentations of white-collar crime simply list a variety of dangerous behaviours in a way that emphasizes their harmful consequences and implies that these are incurred deliberately, or at least recklessly, Clarke attempts to recover their sense by putting them back into their everyday business context.

For Clarke there is a series of factors that distinguish the commission of business crimes. Their location in the midst of ordinary business and occupational activity both facilitates their achievement and helps to prevent their detection by colleagues and superiors as well as outside authorities. As compared to ordinary crimes such as burglary, the perpetrator has every justification to be present at the scene of the crime. Indeed, Clarke claims that unlike ordinary crimes, where a crucial clue is presence at the scene, with white-collar crimes the problem is to discover whether there has been an offence rather than to identify the culprit. Police or regulatory agencies are reluctant to enter private settings without invitation, and are often not called upon even where an offence has been committed. White-collar crimes are frequently what we could call 'complainantless crimes', and those who suffer the consequences of them cannot be relied upon to act as a reliable source of criminal intelligence. Clients of professionals are often unable to assess their performance—this is why they need to turn to them in the first place. Workers may simply be unaware of the risks to which they have been exposed; consumers will often not appreciate what they have lost; competitors will be unaware of collusive practices. The behaviour that constitutes white-collar crime is often indistinguishable on its surface from normal legal behaviour. For example, for fraud to be accomplished, it must obviously succeed in mimicking the appearance of legitimate transactions, and it is not unusual for those guilty of this crime to remain undetected for years or even a lifetime. Unlike all except 'victimless crimes' the involvement of the victim is apparently voluntary (though sometimes the result of the lure of easy money).

A further claim concerning the supposed distinctiveness of white-collar crime is virtually true by definition. The criminal aspects of the business or occupational activities under consideration are often secondary or collateral features, both in priority and in the succession of events, of an undertaking pursued for other, legitimate purposes. Criminal consequences, such as damage to the health of workers or to the environment, often come about either as a result of omissions, or because of financial pressures or unanticipated opportunities for gain; they are not inherent to the economic activity as such. Such criminality is difficult to recognize (in time) because of the narrow and constantly changing line between acceptable and unacceptable business behaviour. Even such essential features of outright crooked schemes as the deliberate withholding of payment to creditors may exist as practices in the legitimate world of business—for example, as a desperate manoeuvre by small businesses trying to survive on tight margins, or as a more cynical use of market strength by large enterprises exploiting the dependence on their patronage of small contractors. This makes it difficult for all concerned—creditors, regulators, and others—to tell whether, or at what point, the intention permanently to avoid payment was formed.

Ambiguity surrounds not only the goals of the activity in the midst of which white-collar crime is encountered, but also, it is argued, the degree of intentionality involved. There are certainly notorious cases of cold-blooded calculation, such as the way Ford went ahead with its dangerous design for the Ford Pinto rear engine because it estimated that the potential payment of damages would be less than the cost of recalling the cars (Dowie 1988), or the manner in which the P&O shipping company disregarded repeated requests for the installation of bow warning-lights to improve safety on their 'on-off' ferries (see Punch 1996; Slapper and Tombs 1999). But, it is claimed, these are the exceptions (and even these cases did not end in criminal convictions). More commonly it is difficult to distinguish malevolence from incompetence; and, as Clarke insists, in business and professional life, we are often more concerned about the harmful effects of the latter. Professionals are specifically valued for their competence rather than for their honesty as such (which is perhaps taken for granted); in large organizations and bureaucracies there is considerable scope for laziness or disinterest that may have tragic consequences. These points, it is said, are less true of ordinary crime.

On the other hand, many scholars insist that these aspects of the setting and commission of white-collar crimes mainly point to problems of detection and do not negate the essential similarities between these and ordinary crimes. Businesses involved in offending behaviour often do their best to organize so as to minimize the costs of their infractions (concealing compromising knowledge from directors, 'appointing vice presidents responsible for going to jail', etc.). Conversely, as explained in previous editions of this *Handbook*, there are also occasions where enforcement against ordinary crime has to overcome similar difficulties of categorization. Like so much concerning the social definition of white-collar crime, the question of intention therefore easily lends itself to social construction. Much ambiguity, or, conversely, the provision of a cover of ostensible legality, is a contingent product of social processing. Thus accountants and barristers may use their professional skills to help businesses construct tax-avoidance schemes which must then appear as anything but deliberate attempts to evade tax (McBarnet 1991; McBarnet and Whelan 1999). Even if a case reaches trial, defence lawyers work hard to redefine the misconduct as not having been deliberate (Mann 1985). White-collar criminals may even find that they have allies in the redefinition of their behaviour in those trying their misbehaviour. In the course of research into deviance by professionals I made a study of the (confidential) proceedings of English family practitioner tribunals, which deal with cases where dentists (and other professionals) are alleged not to have complied with their National Health Service contracts. Here everything is done to avoid the impression that potentially criminal behaviour is at issue even though, in cases where misconduct is proved, fixed withholdings from payment serve the function of fines. In one case, for example, a dentist admitted to 'fraud' in deliberately claiming for more work than he had done, only to find the tribunal members pleading with him to retract his admission (and claim inadvertence) so that they could retain jurisdiction.

While it is debatable how far the ambiguous aspects alleged to characterize the commission of white-collar crime are intrinsic features restricted to this type of misbehaviour, there are certainly some important cases where criminals deliberately exploit the appearance of legitimate business. In fact the overlap between white-collar crime and more clear-cut kinds of crime, such as organized crime, has so far been relatively neglected in comparison to the attention given to the boundary between white-collar crime and ordinary business behaviour. Professional or organized criminals may create ambiguity by fostering the impression of genuine business enterprises, if necessary by trading normally for an initial period. At other times they may penetrate legitimate companies, especially when these have fallen on hard times, and use them to launch purely criminal activities such as 'long-firm' frauds (Levi 1981). Organized criminal businesses may seek to monopolize the market for legitimate goods and services, such as public construction projects or waste-processing, beating their competitors with their lower marginal costs and using violence or corruption against competitors or those with the power to award lucrative contracts, as with Camorra enterprises in the Campania area of Italy and the activities of many of the cosche of the New Mafia (Arlachi 1985).

The division of labour between legitimate and illegitimate business can represent an attempt to disguise the criminal presuppositions of legal enterprises. Legitimate businesses may call upon the service of criminals for particular operations such as loan repayment, money laundering, or tax evasion (Block 1991: chs 5 and 6). They may also take indirect advantage of the operation of international criminals. For example, major electrical companies apparently find it financially profitable to buy and resell (at the expense of other wholesalers) examples of their own products illegally smuggled on to the market (Van Duyne 1993). Legal enterprise may rely on organized criminals to supply a disciplined workforce, as in the New York construction industry (New York State Organized Crime Task Force 1988), or to get rid of industrial waste products in illegal ways so as to reduce their external costs of production (Szasz 1986). Conversely, organized criminals may call upon legitimate businesses, such as printers or supermarkets, in developing major frauds like those against the EEC agricultural subsidy programmes (Passas and Nelken 1993); such symbiosis is also essential for the purpose of recycling money earned in illegal activities. The steady growth in international and transnational trading—and the changing face of national and economic borders in Europe—is also leading to an increase in different types of criminals seeking to profit from the opportunities these changes offer them (Passas and Nelken 1993; Van Duyne 1993; Nelken 2002). Current research on white-collar crime is increasingly concerned with exploring the relationship between legal, semi-legal, and illegal economic activities—and such enquiry is likely to be intensified as regional groupings increasingly use harmonized crime control as a badge of identity. This requires giving attention to the comparative dimension, because the relationships between businessmen, professionals, and organized criminals vary in different countries and because many of these crimes have an international dimension which exploits differences between national legal systems (Ruggiero 1996; Nelken 1997a). Appreciation of the political and economic structures conducive to such operations requires the criminologist to be open to concepts pioneered in disciplines other than sociology, including ideas about clientilism in political science, legal and illegal monopolies in economics, and risk analysis in accounting and management science.

THE AMBIVALENT RESPONSE TO WHITE-COLLAR CRIME

The above discussion will have already illustrated various ways in which the control of white-collar crime can also play a part in its causation. Government and business may share similar imperatives that coincide to favour offending. Carson's description of the importance of 'speed' in the calculations of both the Treasury and the oil companies in the exploitation of North Sea oil, and the consequent sacrifice of ordinary safety standards, is an extreme example of such objective coincidence of interests (Carson 1981). The Bank of England may be caught between its duties as regulator of the banking system and its desire not to compromise the credibility of one of the major clearing banks (*The Economist* 1992). But, even where government and offenders are clearly opposed, weak regulatory regimes or moves towards deregulation can still provide an incentive to offending. One common strategy that leads to increased crime is the combination of removing legal or informal constraints on a business sector with the simultaneous use of (new) criminal penalties to be available as a last resort. Complex and changing regulatory regimes, especially those involving government payment schemes, may in themselves provide the opportunity for crime (Calavita, *et al.* 1997; Nelken 2002; Passas and Nelken 1993; Vaughan 1983).

The methods adopted in responding to white-collar crime play a particularly important part in shaping this type of behaviour, inasmuch as the difficulty of relying on complainants means that the accent must be put on prevention and proactive enforcement. In this way our information about these types of misbehaviour often tells us more about the theories and priorities of the controllers than anything else (for example, the belief that small firms are more likely than large ones to bend the rules will inevitably find confirmation in the statistics of violations discovered). New forms of enforcement contribute to the construction of ' "postmodern" policing' (Spalek 2001). When dealing with the type of offence which is seen to overlap with organized crime (such as international fraud or money-laundering) the (often misleading) accounts of who is responsible for such activity which are put forward by enforcers have a large role in creating the type of policing then put in place (see Nelken 1997a).

But the main issue that needs to be discussed under this heading is the charge that the different enforcement methods used to respond to white-collar as compared to ordinary crimes reinforce their ambiguous status and indirectly contribute to their causation. Is the difference in handling the cause or consequence of the distinctiveness of white-collar crime? Many scholars stress the fact that white-collar crimes are difficult to detect and control. It is difficult to prove intention when dealing with decisions taken within an organization (and legal thinking has not yet caught up with the importance of organizations); trials are long and expensive; juries have problems in understanding the evidence in complex fraud cases; professional advisers acting for businessmen can delay or defeat prosecution. Extra powers for obtaining evidence given to the Department of Trade and Industry inspectors or the Serious Fraud Office go only some of the way to dealing with these difficulties. A premium is therefore placed on achieving compliance without the need for prosecution (although this is used as a threat, the need actually to resort to it is seen as failure). It is considered still better to rely on self-regulation by an industry or by the business itself. But reliance on self-policing can easily lead to conflicts of interest. For example, banks find themselves both as potential participators in money-laundering and as required to detect and deter it (Levi 1991a, 1991b).

Some scholars (such as Clarke 1990a, but here his views are more widely shared) argue that the way white-collar crimes are handled reflects the special circumstances of these offences. It makes sense to use compliance in the regulation of occupations because the offender can easily be found at his or her place of occupation and it is feasible to put repeated pressure on him. Violations of safety or pollution standards are difficult and costly to conceal. Even the apparently self-defeating practice of giving advance warning of inspection visits does not therefore lead to concealment of offending. The difficulty in other business offences, Clarke argues, is to identify the commission of an offence rather than find the offender. But even here offenders in organizations do tend to leave a 'paper trail' of their actions.

Different interpretations of the nature of white-collar crime lead to corresponding views concerning the best way to handle them. Clarke argues that an approach based on criminal prosecution is inappropriate for all but a few cases of business crime because complainants are mainly interested in recompense and go to the police only if all else fails; the criminal process polarizes the parties, involves delay, carries risks of failure, and, above all, does nothing to secure future improvement in the relevant working practices. Existing enforcement practices make more sense; suggestions for improvement should be based mainly on trying to internalize better methods of control within businesses themselves rather than to increase prosecution (Stone 1975 is a classic discussion of this theme). But the opposite point of view is also well supported. Green summarizes an extensive American literature that offers various proposals for improving the effectiveness of prosecution against white-collar crimes (Green 1990: ch. 8; see also Groves and Newman 1986). The assumption behind much of this work is that business behaviour is in fact particularly well suited to the application of deterrent criminal sanctions. Offences ('it is alleged') are strictly instrumental and offenders have much to lose from prosecution; prison, if only it were to be used regularly, would be more potent than for ordinary criminals. The main problem in current practice is that of producing a level of fines sufficient actually to deter business. Solutions such as stock dilution, equity fining, or ceding shares to the state may all work, but in cases where there has been physical injury they may give the wrong message that everything can ultimately be paid for. Informal and formally initiated negative publicity is unlikely to put a firm out of business, but it can and does have collateral effects and may help to produce beneficial procedural changes within firms (Fisse and Braithwaite 1985).

For many observers the difficulties of controlling white-collar crime, and the need to rely on compliance techniques, should rather be attributed to a lack of political will to provide the resources necessary for a full-blown prosecution approach. In Britain proportionally few policemen are assigned to the Fraud Squad; the prestige of such assignments is low and term of service short (Levi 1987). For the United States, Calavita and Pontell argue that the savings and loans crash was partly due to the lack of trained thrift examiners and the overloaded FBI agents directed to clear up the scandal (Calavita and Pontell 1992; Calavita *et al.* 1997). Even the famous and feared American Securities and Exchange Commission (SEC), according to Shapiro, is forced to choose between detection or enforcement and uses the criminal sanction only in around 11 per cent of its cases (Shapiro 1984).

The actual combination of objective difficulties and political priorities in decisions over prosecution is often concealed by ideologically loaded communication. Much white-collar crime is subject to regulation under the heading of strict liability by which, in theory, even unintentional offending can be held criminally culpable. Criminal law textbooks and philosophic writers discuss whether or not this is justified by the difficulty of proving intention in complex, modern, industrial processes. However, investigations of the 'logic in use' of the inspectorates responsible (at least in common law countries) for some of the most important areas of social regulation, such as those concerning worker safety or environmental pollution, tell a different story. In practice, apart from cases in which accidents have taken place, breaches of rules will normally be subject to sanctions only if *mens rea*—and even recidivism—has been shown by a refusal to correct matters pointed out by the inspector in warning visits and letters (Carson 1970; Hawkins 1984; Hawkins and Thomas 1984; Hutter 1988, 1997). The inspectors involved in such enforcement activity refuse to see themselves as 'industrial policemen', seeing their role rather as one geared to advising and cajoling the majority of fundamentally law-abiding businessmen.

One consequence (perhaps even an intended one, see Carson 1974, 1980) of this difference between theory and practice is that the imposition of strict liability reduces the stigma associated with these offences so as to reinforce the impression that they represent behaviour that is merely 'mala prohibita' rather than 'mala in se'. Enforcement techniques that concentrate on consequences rather than intentions, by collapsing the distinction between incompetence and deliberateness, thus often end up diluting rather than extending criminal stigma. Recent efforts to convict corporations for crime, especially in the area of safety, have had some success. But despite a series of disasters, moves towards more effective regulation have been slow (Wells 1993; Slapper 1999). How far criminal law can help is a moot point: in Italy, employers found guilty of serious safety offences at work are regularly subject to sanctions in the ordinary courts. But Italy has one of the highest rates in Europe of what they refer to as 'white death' (a point missed by Gobert and Punch (2003) when they praise the relevant Italian legislation).

Difficulties of enforcement may often be exaggerated to conceal other decisions (or non-decisions) about responding to crimes committed by economically influential groups. In an important study, Carson argued convincingly that the causes of accidents on North Sea oil-rigs were little different from those which lead to accidents in factories or construction (Carson 1981). The claim that the high level of injuries was due to the difficulty of regulating activities operating 'at the frontiers of technology' at hitherto untried depths of oil exploration at sea was not supported by his careful examination of the relevant case records. The crucial issue was the fact that the responsibility for ensuring compliance with the normal standards of safety had not been assigned to the factory inspectors of the Health and Safety Inspectorate (here being seen in more heroic light than in Carson's earlier work) but to the Department of Energy. But since this was also the body responsible for encouraging oil exploration to proceed as fast as possible in the interests of the British balance of payments, there was an inevitable conflict of interests in which those of the weakest groups were sacrificed.

Since Sutherland, the subject of white-collar crime has also been the focus of attempts to prove that the rich and powerful are treated more favourably by the criminal justice system. Some caveats should be entered here. The main basis for the relative immunity of businessmen in the criminal process (at least in Anglo-American jurisdictions) derives from political choices regarding which behaviour to make criminal in the first place, and only to a lesser extent from the way their offences are categorized. Those effectively criminalized for business-related offences tend to be small businessmen, quite often from immigrant backgrounds (Nelken 1983; Croall 1989). It is thus a mistake to confuse the macro (legislative) and micro (enforcement) logics which keep criminality and respectability apart. Many of those working in the criminal justice system would actually be interested in (and have an interest in) successful prosecutions of 'the powerful'. Thus apparently ineffective legislative outcomes are often best studied as a product of 'coherence without conspiracy' (Nelken 1983). This does not mean, of course, that there cannot also be more explicit cases of prejudice, and there have rightly been many attacks on alleged bias and injustice in the handling of white-collar crimes, from enforcement to trial and beyond. As with most accusations of bias, however, the difficulty is in ensuring that like is being compared with like.

A well-known debate over the alleged leniency involved in using 'compliance' methods for dealing with white-collar regulatory offences is that between Pearce and Tombs, on the one hand, and Hawkins on the other (Pearce and Tombs 1990, 1991; Hawkins 1990, 1991). Pearce and Tombs began by criticizing Hawkins's and other descriptions of the compliance approach, for giving the appearance of being persuaded by the 'logic in use' of those whose enforcement strategy they described. In this way, it was alleged, they (indirectly) confirmed an unfair status quo instead of supporting the adoption of stricter methods that could reduce the level of harm caused by such offences. Hawkins fiercely challenged this as a misreading of the role of interpretive sociology (which was not directed towards policy evaluation), but then went on to endorse the compliance strategy in general terms without necessarily agreeing with all its tactics or the level of severity of the sanctions applied. For their part, Pearce and Tombs recommended that prosecution should begin at an earlier stage; they favoured the imposition of (low) fines rather than simply warning notices and wanted there to be more use of other sanctions such as the withdrawal of licences. In his reply, Hawkins pointed out that very few of the violations noted in routine proactive enforcement do eventually turn out to be the cause of serious harm and that it is not possible to predict which will do so. In his view, unless Pearce and Tombs really want to cut back sharply on enforcement discretion, their proposals are unlikely to produce much change in current practice. And to insist on legal action each time a violation is revealed, as was tried for a time by the American OSHA mines authority, tends to be counterproductive in terms of alienating the good will of those being regulated. It also risks producing a political backlash leading to deregulation, as happened in the case of this agency.

As this summary suggests, this and similar debates fail to make progress mainly because the policy arguments of Hawkins and others like him assume as givens exactly those political realities which their critics would like to see changed (see now Slapper and Tombs 1999). A useful study which points to this moral is Cook's comparison of the harsh response to those suspected of social security fraud with that met by those engaged in tax frauds of very similar kinds (Cook 1989). The very different treatment received by each group relates less to the practical possibilities of enforcement (more or less the same), or to fears of counterproductive effects from tougher penalties, but rather follows from a set of associated beliefs about the relative worth and importance of maintaining the good will of each set of offenders.

Some of the most fruitful proposals for strengthening the control of white-collar crime, which acknowledge the force of both sides of this debate, are those developed by Braithwaite on the basis of his research into the successes and failures of regulation in very different industries and businesses, such as drug-manufacturing, coalmining, and nursing homes. He suggests that businesses (beyond a certain size) should be obliged by government to write a set of rules tailored to the unique contingencies of their firm. These rules should be submitted for comment and amendment to interest groups, including citizen groups. Firms should have their own internal compliance unit with statutory responsibility on the director to report cases of violation, and the function of government inspectors would be to audit and (if necessary) sanction the performance of this unit (see Braithwaite 1995; Hutter 1997; Haines 1997).

It might be thought that the study of bias in the prosecution and trial of white-collar crimes should be more straightforward than an evalution of the justifiability of its special style of enforcement; but even here there is no consensus. Analysis of the penalties meeted out for serious frauds in Britain, as compared to other types of crime, certainly suggests that these are the crimes which are the most rewarding (Levi 1991c). Shapiro, in her study of securities offenders in the USA, detected a tendency for higher-status offenders to be less likely to receive criminal penalties instead of being dealt with by administrative and civil measures (Shapiro 1984, 1989). But in their more comprehensive American study, Weisburd *et al.* (even after double-checking) found that higher-status offenders were more likely to get prison sentences (Weisburd *et al.* 1991: 7). In their earlier study Wheeler *et al.*, using a sample of pre-1980 American social enquiry reports and case files, showed that penalties for white-collar crimes depended on the normal criteria for other crimes: prior record, seriousness of crime, degree of involvement of offender, the nature of harm to the victim, etc. There was, however, some limited evidence of judges identifying with the offender more than in cases of ordinary crimes, especially if the latter involve personal violence (Wheeler *et al.* 1988). The authors left it open whether the judges were merely reproducing (unconsciously or deliberately) the biases of the wider population.

Instead of demanding that white-collar criminals be treated like ordinary criminals, we could argue the reverse (though this is rarely done). Why not apply the methods used for dealing with businessmen and professionals to ordinary criminals? Much of what purports to be regulation or self-regulation of white-collar crime is bogus or ineffectual, and deserves to be attacked as such. But there is also much to be learned from the variety of forms of regulation and self-regulation designed to reduce violations without criminalizing the offender. Even if it would probably be impossible to model the handling of ordinary crime too closely on that used for businessmen, the differences are not always as great as made out. All non-police agencies—even when not dealing with powerful offenders—put the emphasis on recovering money rather than securing convictions (Royal Commission on Criminal Procedure 1980). The problem of apprehending and maintaining pressure on ordinary criminals (who are not linked to their place of work as white-collar criminals are) is not as great as it seems: the police do know just where to lay their hands on juvenile delinquents—and quite a few other criminal suspects. And white-collar criminals have even more resources than ordinary criminals for covering their tracks when it becomes necessary.

In a sense compliance does already get used with ordinary criminals; Pearce and Tombs (1991) mention police control of prostitution and gambling as an example of compliance methods. But they use this to show the danger of collusion and corruption in the use of such methods. The role of social work and diversion (before trial) and probation or other techniques of rehabilitation (after conviction) is a better example. The choice between cooperation or compulsion is repeatedly offered to ordinary criminals from the stage of pleading guilty to obtaining parole. A crucial difference, however, is that it is usually necessary for an offender accused of ordinary crime to suffer the stigma of a conviction before consideration is given to compliance, whereas the opposite is true for business offenders handled in this way. We may be tempted to believe that, beyond a certain point, enforcement against ordinary crime is geared precisely to maximizing stigma even at the expense of effectiveness.

Pearce and Tombs do seem correct in tracing the difference in approach to the (untested) assumption that businessmen are basically disposed to respond well to a compliance approach whereas ordinary criminals are presumed to require punishment. But they prefer the equally untested assumption that businessmen should be dealt with as 'amoral calculators'. The evidence from interviews, however, is that managers say that they do not, for the most part, think in deterrence terms because only unethical managers are seen to respond to deterrence. Interviewees do concede that this process can get out of control and that it is difficult to be ethical when not running at a profit (Simpson 1992; Yeager 1995). But they insist that 'reputable' managers 'cut corners' only to try to save the company; they may bend the rules but do not violate them and they do not act for personal gain. It is reasonable to conclude that practical considerations regarding effective enforcement provide insufficient justification for the extent of the present contrast between methods used for ordinary and business crimes. A considerable merit of Braithwaite's long-standing search for an effective as well as just approach to the control of all types of crime—what he calls 're-integrative shaming' (Braithwaite 1989, 1995)—is that it builds in a series of attempts at compliance as a prelude to prosecution.

WHITE-COLLAR CRIME AS AN INDEX OF SOCIAL CHANGE

Whatever the reasons or justifications for the methods used to control white-collar crime, the ambivalence of the social response to this sort of behaviour is also related to wider social factors which have both objective and subjective dimensions. For Aubert (as well as for writers such as E. A. Ross, who anticipated Sutherland's ideas on this topic) the ambiguity of white-collar crimes reflected the objective fact that they were the index of important transitions in social structure. A good example of this phenomenon is the practice of 'insider trading' on the stock exchange and in other financial institutions, which has only relatively recently come to be penalized in Britain. Even now practitioners can have difficulty in drawing the line between legal and illegal conduct (a problem exploited by defence lawyers) and can justify as good business the competitive testing of the limits of legality (Reichman 1992). As Clarke brilliantly puts it: 'It would have perplexed leading members of these institutions up to the end of the 1950s to be told that they were doing anything reprehensible in acting on such information. It was precisely because of the access to such information that one was part of the City, and one was part of the City in the clear expectation of making a considerable amount of money' (Clarke 1990a: 162). The crime of insider trading therefore nicely symbolizes the change from a time when there were only 'insiders' (see also Stanley 1992). The attacks on political corruption in the 1990s are a further example of white-collar crime as an index of changing social structure.

Ambiguity and ambivalence are inevitable results of situations in which previously legal behaviour has only recently been redefined, and this is exacerbated when the boundaries are changed in ways that are to some extent outside the control of the community being regulated. We could also extend Aubert's analysis by saying that social and legal definitions of crime may be out of joint either because public attitudes have not yet caught up with the legal recognition of important economic and social changes, or because the law has not yet recognized the seriousness of behaviour which causes public concern (in both cases these processes will be fanned, resisted, or mediated by interest and pressure groups). As a further complication we should note that economic and legal definitions will not always coincide (insider trading is still seen as economically useful by some economists). Conversely, at any given time there will be some practices which are quite legal but of dubious economic value, a current example being corporate raiding so as to bid up the price of a business and sell on at a profit. It is therefore not always easy to tell when the time has arrived at which certain business practices have lost all economic justification.

In their stimulating work on the savings and loans frauds, Calavita and Pontell discuss the economic justifications of the type of practices which were the subject of prosecutions during and after the period of Reaganite relaxation of economic controls in the 1980s (Calavita and Pontell 1992; Calavita *et al.* 1997). This period saw the breaking down of barriers between banks and other financial institutions, and a great increase in the scale and internationalization of financial transactions. Drawing on the idea of the French economist Allais, they argue that much of what is produced in what he calls the 'casino economy' is of illusory economic benefit. If, for example, it takes only $12 billion of commercial trade to generate $400 billion of foreign exchange transactions, the opportunities for manipulating money are far in excess of the goods to which they correspond. The system is kept going only by trust in the backing of these transactions, but an excess of confidence can equally bring about disaster if it allows the production of 'junk bonds' or helps sustain unsound financial institutions. They point to various characteristic abuses of this period, such as corporate takeovers, currency trading and futures trading, 'land flips', 'daisy chains' and other forms of property speculation, and the switching of loans to confuse auditors regarding actual assets. Emblematic for them was the accumulation of enormous uncollectable loans relying on federal deposit insurance that were at the heart of the massive 'savings and loans' losses.

An interesting question is how far the practices that Calavita and others describe (which they associate with finance capital as opposed to industrial capital) can be controlled severely without putting at risk jobs and economically sound activities. Much of what they criticize, shorn of obvious abuses, may point to changes in what makes economic sense in a world where the costs of production increasingly favour countries other than the USA and Western Europe. It should also be noted that the savings and loans fiasco was as much the result of too generous government guarantees to bank investors, as it was of speculation and financial mismanagement. They themselves may be relying on an outdated model of industrial capitalism as the only proper conception of a functioning economy. This said, much white-collar and financial crime grows out of the opportunities to exploit objective changes in organizational forms of business trading (particularly marked in a period of increasing global competition) in ways which the law, especially national laws, are slow to deal with or incapable of catching in time. (See, for example, Pearce and Snider 1995; Tombs 1995.) Other crimes are connected to the cycles of boom and bust that seem inherent in global capitalist expansion.

A more subjective source of ambivalence in the social response to white-collar crime is the assumption that there is less public concern about these behaviours—and therefore less support for severe sanctions, than is the case with more familiar street crimes—especially those involving violence (though this may be the result of existing methods of control). A series of studies has therefore sought to demonstrate that the public in fact ranks examples of these crimes quite severely as compared to ordinary crimes (see, e.g. Cullen *et al.* 1983; Green 1990: 47–57). Harsh attitudes towards such conduct, going well beyond the penalties actually imposed, can be documented in cases of culpable disasters caused by white-collar offenders (Calavita *et al.* 1991). On the other hand, some other attempts to measure public attitudes to white-collar crime do reveal greater leniency in public attitudes (see, e.g. Goff and Nason-Clarke 1989). Much depends on the way questions about different crimes are phrased and the extent to which an effort is made to refer to the possible side-effects of the use of certain sanctions. But even if it were to be shown that there was greater public ambivalence towards white-collar crimes than towards ordinary crimes, writers such as Box would only regard this as a further challenge 'to sensitize people to not seeing processes in which they are victimised as disasters or accidents' (Box 1983: 233).

THE COLLATERAL COSTS OF CONTROL

Many of the ambiguities discussed so far point to value conflicts and awkward policy dilemmas that are often cited as explaining, and even justifying, caution in seeking to curb white-collar crime. If risk-taking is really the motor of the capitalist economy then someone has to pay the price of the inevitable failures. The pursuit of greater health and safety (or even of greater bank transparency) has costs in terms of national and international competitiveness and jobs; it is not always easy to juggle competing pressures, and the interests of business and/or employment can be used to try to justify the acceptance of no more than a 'reasonable' level of safety or pollution. In many areas of business crime enforcers are obliged to choose between going for punishment (and stigmatization), or else achieving compliance or maximizing the amount of revenue recovered. Other dilemmas are more particular. If we are worried about money-laundering, does this mean that we want to see banks become a crucial part of the justice system? What about the rights to privacy and confidentiality (Levi 1991a, 1991b)?

But we should not be too quick to assume that such post hoc philosophical dilemmas or justifications are the actual movers of political action. To explain the social weight given to these conflicting values we also need to provide a sociology of public policy choices. Starting from a Marxist perspective, Snider, for example, examines the dialectic between the state, business interests, pressure groups, public opinion (etc.) in an attempt to explain the contrasting fate of different types of regulation (Snider 1991; but see also the more hopeful analysis by Braithwaite 1995). She argues that the resistance to effective implementation of legislation concerning health and safety at work is explicable in terms of the fact that these laws are not in the interest of business itself (except where they can be used by large businesses to beat off the competition of smaller firms). Industry tends—with the collusion of the state—to balance the safety of workers against the increased costs of production. The victims of these crimes are diffuse, though not as diffuse as the victims of crimes against the environment. Anti-trust legislation has more success because the state is interested in bringing down its costs as a major purchaser from the private sector, and at least parts of the business world are in favour of such laws. On the other hand, the monopolies and cartels that already control many major markets provide firm resistance, and, of less importance, unions may be ambivalent because of the threat to jobs which could follow the break-up of large conglomerations. Insider trading and stock market fraud, Snider claims, should encounter least resistance (as the success of the American Securities and Exchange Commission supposedly illustrates) because here the interests of the state and business coincide. Business needs to be able to raise money on the stock market, and government does not want to have to bail out defrauded investors. We will be reminded of the political dimension of these policy dilemmas if we accept that the control of ordinary crime may also have a number of negative side-effects—on the offender, his family, and the community—which tend to be ignored when the crucial criterion of policy choice is reduced to the need to continue business as usual.

The potential of criminology to contribute to shaping public policy concerning the best way to regulate white-collar crime is likely to increase in importance, but it is unlikely to be univocal in its recommendations. There will always be a need for denouncing the 'crimes of the powerful' and their many illegal (as well as semi-legal and legal) ways of causing harm. But practical experience as well as theoretical considerations would suggest that there are severe difficulties in using the criminal law to control the groups most powerful within a given society. It is extremely difficult to get laws passed which represent a real threat to current economic interests. And there is always the danger that, in given political circumstances, tougher measures may have counter-productive effects for victims or consumers in general. Yet we should not assume that treating white-collar crime as crime, or trying to fit it into the usual paradigm of criminological explanation, necessarily goes hand in hand with the belief that we must use criminal sanctions to reduce the behaviour.

THE ENRON STAGE OF CAPITALISM?

In this final section I shall address the crisis in corporate governance that was brought to light by the crimes committed by leading US companies such as Enron, Worldcom, and Tyco, many of which ended in bankruptcies at the cost of billions of dollars to shareholders, workers, and customers. Can these cases be analysed using the framework set out in this chapter? Or do they mean that corporations are now seen to be essentially criminal? Much 'anti-global' social activism is motivated by radical suspicion towards multinational companies in particular. A forceful argument that would seem to support this view is found in the recent runaway best-seller (and accompanying documentary film) by Joel Bakan, a Canadian law professor. Bakan (2004) claims that the legal implication of limited liability is that corporations must only serve the interests of their shareholders. This leads them to seek to 'externalize' the costs of their operations. Social responsibility, despite protestations to the contrary, can never be allowed to get in the way of profit. Interestingly, Bakan makes little use of criminological work (there is no obeisance to Sutherland, despite a listing of the crimes of General Electric, nor reference to the thesis so similar to his own, put forward by Box). And whereas Sutherland chose to use crimes by corporations to demonstrate the error of explaining crime by pathology, Bakan says that corporations should be compared to psychopaths because of their single-minded focus only on what is in their interest, irrespective of the damage to others. On the other hand, it is not so easy to define the self-interest of corporations once we factor in considerations of commercial reputation and social acceptance. The extreme cases we shall be considering usually ended with the implosion of the corporation. We need to ask when and why self-interest and public interest conflict (a corporation published Bakan's book!) and what can be done about this. The same urge for survival at the expense of others could not be attributed to the state as well as to other organizations and agencies. Hence, suitably reinforced, as Bakan helpfully shows, they could be used to counter-balance the power of corporations.

If most corporations still manage to avoid being seen as essentially criminal this is in large part because they are able to exploit and benefit from types of ambiguity that are not possible for street criminals. For purposes of illustration I shall concentrate mainly on Enron about which more than 60 books have already been published, and which has been the subject of a number of films and documentaries. Its bankruptcy in 2001 at one trillion dollars was the largest to date (one billion went to lawyers and others as fees just to wind it up). Aside from the losses to shareholders, Enron's collapse also led to thousands of lost jobs as well as pensions, including those of its workers who were 'locked in'. Enron has become a metaphor for all that went wrong with American capitalism. Hardly a day has passed over the last three years without Google reporting further newspaper commentary, much of this affirming that this case was just the tip of the iceberg, and discussing how far we were dealing with 'bad apples' or with a 'dying orchard'. By 2002 in fact over 24 large public companies had admitted inflating revenue by improper accounting practices, with directors living lavish lifestyles at their shareholders' expense.

As far as the definition of white-collar and corporate crime is concerned, the Enron case shows that it can be problematic to distinguish in practice crime committed by a corporation (for its shareholders), crime using the corporation as an instrument (for example against competitors or consumers), and crime committed against the corporation itself. More important is the difficulty of drawing the line between business and criminal behaviour. For many years, Enron was a story of successful innovation, having grown from its origins as a gas pipeline company to a trader in 1,800 products or types of contracts and 13 currencies, selling almost everything and insuring against everything—including the risk of bankruptcy! (As reported in one film for television, 'they eat risk for breakfast, they crap out monster earnings by lunch'.) After deregulation in the 1980s Enron hedged price swings using customized, and often highly complex, physical contracts and financially settled derivatives contracts, which by the end were in conflict with reporting rules or business logic or both. From 1990 it expanded abroad. The mixed verdict on Enron's businesses contrasts with the apparently similar Parmalat bankruptcy in Italy, where huge losses were incurred through expanding into unprofitable sidelines such as travel agencies and football clubs, thanks to the protection of banks, politicians, ineffectual regulators, and a poorly functioning stock exchange (Sapelli 2004). At its peak Enron was the seventh biggest company in the USA, and figured in the list of *Fortune* magazine's best companies for seven years in a row. As late as 1999, Andrew Fastow, its chief accounting officer, received an excellence award for his ability in capital management, but plea-bargained a prison sentence of ten years (and forfeited more than 23 million dollars) only a few years later. Despite their substantial personal enrichment, those who left the company before the bankruptcy were rarely charged with any offences.

On the other hand, in order to be able to convict the managing directors (as I write, the trial is reaching its climax) the prosecution must of course be able to show that their behaviour was NOT normal business behaviour. Kenneth Lay faces six counts of fraud and conspiracy, and Richard Skilling is charged with 28 counts of fraud, conspiracy, insider trading, and lying to auditors; Skilling faces a maximum of 275 years in prison. Their fate turns on whether it can be shown that they approved of and covered up schemes designed to inflate apparent earnings. In a recent radio interview Bethany McLean, the *Fortune* journalist who first voiced suspicions of Enron in 2001, tried to reconcile this contradiction saying, 'unfortunately, American business is all about meeting quarterly earnings targets, and that's the obsession that brought Enron down. But I don't think other companies take it to the extreme that Enron did. At Enron, most of its business was manufacturing earnings. Maybe that's 10 per cent of the business of most other companies.'

As with other white-collar crime, some relevant misbehaviour was legally criminal but not widely stigmatized socially, other misconduct was socially disapproved of, but not technically criminal, and the line between these was a changing one. The techniques used at Enron to increase the apparent value of the stock (and mortgage the future) ranged from duplicitous methods of moving debt off the books via special-purpose entities, hedging, and the use of derivates, to controversial 'mark to market' accounting methods. The executive at Arthur Andersen, Enron's auditors, who gave the order to shred incriminating documents, withdrew his plea bargain after a higher court decided that this behaviour did not count as crime. Some of Enron's losses were due to bad business judgement (e.g. over its investment in Broadband), foolish investments, and the pursuit of pharaonic international projects, while some of its gains were achieved thanks only to the manipulation of energy shortages in California and elsewhere. Its credit rating, and the value of its expanding business in insurance, telecommunications, and finance, was easy to talk up, but as easy to see collapse once confidence waned.

What of the causes? As in analyses of ordinary crime we can point to motivation, opportunity, and lack of guardians. 'Greed' was certainly a key factor, with managers' stock options linked to the stock exchange price, three million dollar bonuses, the chance of getting your children into the best private schools, and living in the better Houston condominiums. But it would be wrong to see this as just a pathological feature of certain individuals, given that greed is supposed to be what drives the entire capitalist system. And these same individuals were also public benefactors on a large scale, coaching youngsters' baseball teams, even teaching religion. One account of Enron, written by an ex-employee, tries to draw a line between greed which is acceptable, greed at the expense of others, which is not good, and, 'worst of all', what he calls 'a culture of boundless greed'. The fiercely competitive organizational culture (as shown in hiring and firing), with its heavy macho overtones, led to de-responsibilization with respect to harm caused in pursuit of the organization's goals. Given that this culture started at the top, Durkheim's original idea of anomie, as a sense of there being no limits, seems as pertinent as Merton's idea of anomie as 'strain'. Opportunity was provided by the difficulty for outsiders (and even many insiders) to understand what was going on amidst the complexities of the trades and the general climate of expectations of ever-rising stock prices. A crucial role was played by the lack of effective guardians (Coffee 2002). Deregulation gave Enron its chance, and 'Kenny boy', as Lay was known to the Bush administration, was able to place his nominee on the federal energy regulatory commission and helped shaped policy for the industry. Handsome campaign contributions were paid to both Republican and Democrat politicians. Non-executive directors, auditors ('billing their brains out') who earned more via their consulting arms than through traditional accounting, investment bankers, and industry analysts (often the recipients of targeted largesse) all played a part in keeping Enron's share price artificially high, ignoring any potential conflicts of interest. An activist Supreme Court, with a conservative majority, had earlier weakened protection of investors in case of bankruptcy, and made it more difficult to deal with borderline, so-called 'SCUM' methods of selling stock involving (un)Suitability, Churning, Unauthorised trading, and Misrepresentation. The SEC, for its part, had not reviewed Enron since 1997.

But these financial scandals have brought into being the toughest reaction since the 1929 crash. From 2002 to 2005 there were more than 700 corporate crime convictions. As compared to the 1980s, there are more lengthy prison sentences, which are clearly aimed at deterrence, and intended to show that financial malpractice on this scale constitutes highly serious crime (though arguably some penalties have been inconsistently harsh). There have also been various attempts at court-organized social engineering of company compliance. The SEC now targets a higher proportion of large companies, the Sarbanes–Oxley Act set a much higher standard of governance (which has even been used by some foreign governments to constrain the behaviour of US companies abroad), and accountancy and auditor responsibilities have been reconfigured. There were almost a third more financial restatements in the period from 2003 to 2004 and the number of boards on which a majority of directors are independent rose from 61 per cent in 2001 to 89 per cent in 2005. But it is difficult to know how far public opinion has been affected. After all, the desire to get rich quick was the essential fuel for the stock market bubble, and it is striking that the value of stock in Martha Stewart's company went *down* when she recently came out of prison. Immediately following a scandal it is normal to ignore fears of collateral costs in enforcing laws against corporate criminals. In any case there are already pressures to undo some of these regulations (and it should also be borne in mind that there has been no similar crackdown on the safety risks caused by corporations; on the contrary, business interests in the USA have recently made enormous gains in de-legitimizing personal injury tort plaintiffs, and getting their claims 'capped' by numerous state legislatures. The backlash against financial crime, it is said, is having negative effects on the small businesses market, with costs for compliance with the standards set by the Sarbanes–Oxley Act estimated at six billion dollars per year, out of a total regulatory burden of 27 billion dollars. For some economists the problem at Enron is claimed to have been essentially bad business judgement, which then led to attempts to cover up. The market, it is claimed, had it not been manipulated, could and would have brought Enron down to its right price, just as the stock exchange in the end is self-correcting; the main deterrent to business misbehaviour will always be the desire to avoid bad publicity. More subtly, it has been argued that there is a danger that rules devised at one turn of the business cycle could have counterproductive effects when enforced at another (Coffee 2002).

At the other end of the political spectrum, however, any attempt by capitalism to reform itself is seen as yet more of the problem rather than any part of the solution. The harm caused by Enron should be sought less in its eventual failure than in its period of success! Enron is described as 'a high flying symbol for an entire industry that has gone mad through the black magic of deregulation'. Enron's ability to convert almost all risks into saleable commodities illustrates the way corporations are spearheading the commodification of everything, including DNA. But the 'disembedding' of the economy from politics that characterizes neo-liberalism is especially important because of the heady opportunities offered by globalization (Passas 2000). When we focus on its role outside the United States, Enron emerges as an important player in the 'second enclosure movement', a new stage of capitalism (Prashad 2002), in which natural resources, such as water, oil, and gas are being bought up *legally* in a new form of predatory imperialism (US government agencies offered considerable assistance to Enron in its foreign adventures). The view that 'flows' of capital are now out of the control of single nation state is shared by many observers on the Right and the Left. This does not necessarily mean that single companies can do as they wish; it may not be coincidence that Enron collapsed shortly after taking on a battle over energy with the state of California. But observers of the Right and the Left also tend to agree on another point. For both, the criminalization of a few failed company directors is unlikely to affect such transnational processes.

■ SELECTED FURTHER READING

An essential starting point for studying what was originally meant by the label of white-collar crime remains Edwin H. Sutherland, *White-collar Crime: The Uncut Version* (New Haven: Yale University Press, 1983). Useful overviews of the field include Steven Box, *Power, Crime and Mystification* (London: Tavistock, 1983); Michael Clarke, *Business Crime: Its Nature and Control* (Oxford: Polity Press, 1990); Hazel Croall, *White-collar Crime* (Milton Keynes: Open University Press, 1994); David Nelken (ed.), *White-collar Crime* (Aldershot: Dartmouth, 1994); David O. Friedrichs, *Trusted Criminals: White-collar Criminals in Contemporary Society* (Belmont: Wadsworth, 2nd edn, 2003); and Gary Slapper and Steve Tombs, *Corporate Crime* (Harlow: Longman, 1999). The organization of the Slapper and Tombs volume—the most comprehensive recent UK text—roughly follows the expository order of this chapter. But the authors take a resolutely Marxist approach which links white-collar crime to the imperatives of capitalist social structure; and at the same time also wish to remove any ambiguity from the (capitalist) legal response to such behaviour. James Gobert and Maurice Punch in *Rethinking Corporate Crime* (London) Butterworths 2003, drawing on pioneering research by David Bergman, Celia Wells, and others, offer a thorough and balanced analysis of the ways corporations may be held legally accountable for the safety risks they create. More detailed (mainly USA) case studies can be sampled in Kip Schlegel and David Weisburd (eds), *White-Collar Crime Reconsidered* (Boston: Northeastern University Press, 1992) and Michael Tonry and Albert Reiss Jnr (eds), *Beyond the Law: Crime in Complex Organizations* (Chicago: University of Chicago Press, 1993) and Maurice Punch, *Dirty Business: Exploring Corporate Misconduct* (London: Sage, 1996). On the response to the sort of white-collar crime which gets dealt with by the ordinary courts in Britain the best work is that by Mike Levi, *Regulating Fraud* (London: Tavistock, 1987). An original and controversial approach to the increasingly important problem of the overlap between white-collar and organized crime is Vincenzo Ruggiero, *Organised Crime and Corporate Crime in Europe* (Aldershot: Dartmouth, 1996).

■ REFERENCES

ARLACHI, P. (1985), *Mafia Business*, Oxford: Oxford University Press.

AUBERT, V. (1952), 'White-collar Crime and Social Structure', *American Journal of Sociology*, 58: 263–71.

BAKAN, J. (2004), *The Corporation: The Pathological Pursuit of Profit and Power*, New York: Free Press.

BLOCK, A. (1991), *Perspectives on Organising Crime*, Boston/London: Kluwer.

BOX, S. (1983), *Power, Crime and Mystification*, London: Tavistock.

BRAITHWAITE, J. (1984), *Corporate Crime in the Pharmaceutical Industry*, London: Routledge & Kegan Paul.

——(1985), 'White-collar crime', *Annual Review of Sociology*, 11: 1–25.

——(1989), *Crime, Shame and Integration*, Cambridge: Cambridge University Press.

——(1995), 'Corporate Crime and Republican Criminological Praxis', in F. Pearce and L. Snider (eds), *Corporate Crime*, 48–72, Toronto: University of Toronto Press.

BURGESS, E. (1950), 'Comment to Hartung', *American Journal of Sociology*, 56: 25–34.

CALAVITA, K. *et al.* (1991), 'Dam Disasters and Durkheim', *International Journal of the Sociology of Law*, 19: 407–27.

——and PONTELL, H. (1992), 'The Savings and Loans Crisis', in M. Erdmann and R. Lundman (eds), *Corporate and Governmental Deviance*, Oxford: Oxford University Press.

——, ——and TILLMAN, R. (1997), *Big Money Crime*, Berkeley, Cal.: University of California Press.

CARSON, W. G. (1970), 'White-collar Crime and the Enforcement of Factory Legislation', *British Journal of Criminology*, 10: 383–98.

—— (1974), 'Symbolic and instrumental dimensions of early factory legislation', in R. Hood (ed.), *Crime, Criminology and Public Policy*, 107–38, London: Heinemann.

—— (1980), 'The Institutionalisation of Ambiguity: The Early British Factory Acts', in G. Geis and E. Stotland (eds), *White-collar Crime: Theory and Research*, 142–73, London and New York: Sage.

—— (1981), *The Other Price of Britain's Oil*, Oxford: Martin Robertson.

CLARKE, M. (1990a), *Business Crime: Its Nature and Control*, Oxford: Polity Press.

—— (1990b), 'The Control of Insurance Fraud: A Comparative View', *British Journal of Criminology*, 30: 1–23.

CLINARD, M., and YEAGER, P. (1980), *Corporate Crime*, New York: Free Press.

COFFEE JNR, J. C. (2002), 'Understanding Enron: It's About the Gatekeepers, Stupid', *Columbia Law & Economics Working Paper* No. 207 (30 July).

COLEMAN, J. W. (1985), *The Criminal Elite: The Sociology of White-Collar Crime*, New York: St Martin's Press.

—— (1987), 'Toward an Integrated Theory of White-collar Crime', *American Journal of Sociology*, 93(2): 406–39.

—— (1992), 'The Asymmetric Society', in M. Erdmann and R. Lundman (eds), *Corporate and Governmental Deviance*, 95, Oxford: Oxford University Press.

COOK, D. (1989), *Rich Law, Poor Law*, Milton Keynes: Open University Press.

COSSON, J. (1978), *Les Industriels de la Fraude Fiscale*, Paris: Editions du Seuil.

CROALL, H. (1989), 'Who is the white-collar criminal?', *British Journal of Criminology*, 29: 157–74.

CULLEN, F. *et al.* (1983), 'Public Support for Punishing White-Collar Criminals', *Journal of Criminal Justice*, 11: 481–93.

DELMAS-MARTY, M. (1990), *Droit Pénal des Affaires*, Paris: Presses Universitaires de France.

DOWIE, M. (1988), 'Pinto Madness', in Stuart L. Hills (ed.), *Corporate Violence: Injury and Death for Profit*, Totowa, N. J.: Rowman and Littlefield.

Economist, The (1992), 'The Blue Arrow Affair', 7 March: 23.

EDELHERTZ, H. (1970), *The Nature, Impact and Prosecution of White-Collar Crime*, Washington DC: US Government Printing Press.

FISSE, B., and BRAITHWAITE, J. (1985), *The Impact of Publicity on Corporate Offenders*, Albany, N.Y.: State University of New York Press.

FRIEDRICHS, D. (2003), *Trusted Criminals: White-collar Criminals in Contemporary Society*, 2nd edn, Belmont: Wadsworth.

GAMBETTA, D. (1994), *The Sicilian Mafia: An Industry of Private Protection*, Oxford: Oxford University Press.

GEIS, G. (1968), 'The Heavy Electrical Equipment Anti-Trust Cases of 1961', in G. Geis (ed.), *White-Collar Crime*, New York: Atherton Press.

GOBERT, J., and PUNCH, P., *Rethinking Corporate Crime*, London: Butterworths.

GOFF, C., and NASON-CLARKE, N. (1989), 'The Seriousness of Crime in Fredericton, New Brunswick: Perceptions toward White-collar Crime', *Canadian Journal of Criminology*, 31: 19–34.

GOTTFREDSON, M., and HIRSCHI, T. (1990), *A General Theory of Crime*, Stanford, Cal.: Stanford University Press.

GREEN, G. S. (1990), *Occupational Crime*, Chicago: Nelson Hall.

GROSS, E. (1980), 'Organisational Structure and Organisational Crime', in G. Geis and E. Stotland (eds), *White-Collar Crime: Theory and Research*, New York: Sage.

GROVES, W. B., and NEWMAN, G. (eds) (1986), *Punishment and Privilege*, Albany, N.Y.: Harrow and Heston.

HAINES, F. (1997), *Corporate Regulation: Beyond Punish or Persuade*, Oxford: Clarendon Press.

HARTUNG, F. (1950), 'White-collar Offences in the Wholesale Meat Industry in Detroit', *American Journal of Sociology*, 56: 25–34.

HAWKINS, K. (1984), *Environment and Enforcement: Regulation and the Social Definition of Pollution*, Oxford: Clarendon Press.

—— (1990), 'Compliance Strategy, Prosecution Policy and Aunt Sally: A Comment on Pearce and Tombs', *British Journal of Criminology*, 30: 444–66.

—— (1991), 'Enforcing Regulation: More of the same from Pearce and Tombs', *British Journal of Criminology*, 31: 427–30.

—— and THOMAS, J. M. (eds) (1984), *Enforcing Regulation*, Boston/London: Kluwer.

HILLS, S. L. (ed.) (1988), *Corporate Violence: Injury and Death for Profit*, Totowa, N J: Rowman and Littlefield.

HIRSCHI, T., and GOTTFREDSON, M. (1987), 'Causes of White-Collar Crime', *Criminology*, 25: 949–74.

—— and —— (1989), 'The Significance of White-Collar Crime for a General Theory of Crime', *Criminology*, 27: 359–72.

HUTTER, B. (1988), *The Reasonable Arm of the Law?*, Oxford: Clarendon Press.

—— (1997), *Compliance: Regulation and the Environment*, Oxford: Clarendon Press.

KATZ, J. (1980), 'The Social Movement Against White-collar Crime', *Criminology Review Yearbook*: 161–84.

KRAMER, R. C. (1992), 'The Space Shuttle Challenger Explosion: A Case Study of State–Corporate Crime', in K. Schlegel and D. Weisburd, *White-Collar Crime Reconsidered*, 214–43, Boston, Mass.: Northeastern University Press.

LANE, R. (1953), 'Why Businessmen Violate the Law', *Journal of Criminal Law, Criminology and Police Science*, 44: 151–65.

LEONARD, W. N., and WEBER, M. G. (1970), 'Automakers and Dealers: A Study of Criminogenic Market Forces', *Law and Society Review*, 4: 407–24.

LEVI, M. (1981), *The Phantom Capitalists*, London: Gower Press.

—— (1985), 'A Criminological and Sociological Approach to Theories of and Research into Economic Crime', in D. Magnuson (ed.), *Economic Crime—Programs for Future Research*, Report No. 18: 32–72, Stockholm: National Council for Crime Prevention, Sweden.

—— (1987), *Regulating Fraud*, London: Tavistock.

—— (1991a), 'Pecunia Non Olet: Cleansing the Money Launderers from the Temple', *Crime, Law and Social Change*, 16: 217–302.

—— (1991b), 'Regulating Money Laundering', *British Journal of Criminology*, 31: 109–25.

—— (1991c), 'Fraudulent Justice? Sentencing the Business Criminal', in P. Carlen and D. Cook (eds), *Paying for Crime*, 86–108, Milton Keynes: Open University Press.

—— and NELKEN, D. (eds) (1996), 'The Corruption of Politics and the Politics of Corruption', special issue of the *Journal of Law and Society*, 23: 1.

—— and NELEN, H., and LANKHORST, F. (2005), 'Lawyers as crime facilitators in Europe: An introduction and overview,' *Crime, Law and Social Change*, 42 (2–3): 117–121(5).

McBARNET, D. (1991), 'Whiter than White-collar Crime: Tax, Fraud Insurance and the Management of Stigma', *British Journal of Sociology*, 42: 323–44.

—— and WHELAN, C. (1999), *The One Eyed Javelin-Thrower*, London: Wiley.

MAGNUSSON, D. (ed.) (1985), *Economic Crime—Programs for Future Research*, Report No 18, Stockholm: National Council for Crime Prevention, Sweden.

MANN, M. (1985), *Defending White-collar Crime*, New Haven, Conn.: Yale University Press.

NEEDLEMAN, M. L., and NEEDLEMAN, C. (1979), 'Organizational Crime: Two models of Crimogenisis', *Sociological Quarterly*, 20: 517–28.

NELKEN, D. (1983), *The Limits of the Legal Process: A Study of Landlords, Law and Crime*, London: Academic Press.

—— (1991), 'Why Punish?', *Modern Law Review*, 53: 829–34.

—— (1994a), 'Whom can you Trust? The Future of Comparative Criminology', in D. Nelken (ed.), *The Futures of Criminology*, 220–44, London: Sage.

—— (1994b), 'White-Collar Crime', in M. Maguire, R. Morgan, and R. Reiner (eds), *Oxford Handbook of Criminology*, 1st edn, 355–93, Oxford: Oxford University Press.

—— (ed.) (1994c), *White-collar Crime*, Aldershot: Dartmouth.

—— (1997a), 'The Globalisation of Criminal Justice', in M. Freeman (ed.), *Law and Opinion at the End of the Century*, 251–79, Oxford: Oxford University Press.

—— (1997b), 'White-Collar Crime', in M. Maguire, R. Morgan, and R. Reiner (eds), *Oxford Handbook of Criminology*, 2nd edn, 891–924, Oxford: Oxford University Press.

—— (2000), 'Telling Difference', in D. Nelken (ed.), *Contrasting Criminal Justice*, 233–64, Aldershot: Dartmouth.

—— (2002), 'Corruption in the European Union', in M. Bull and J. Newell (eds), *Corruption and Scandal in Contemporary Politics*, London: Macmillan.

—— and LEVI, M. (1996), 'Introduction' to 'The Corruption of Politics and the Politics of Corruption', special issue of the *Journal of Law and Society*, 23(1): 1–17.

NEW YORK STATE ORGANIZED CRIME TASK FORCE (1988), *Corruption and Racketeering in the New York City Construction Industry*, New York, Cornell University Press.

PASSAS, N. (1990), 'Anomie and Corporate Deviance', *Contemporary Crises*, 14: 157–78.

—— (2000), 'Global Anomie, Dysnomie and Economic crime', *Social Justice*, 27: 16–44.

—— and NELKEN, D. (1993), 'The thin line between legitimate and criminal enterprises: subsidy frauds in the European Community', *Crime, Law and Social Change*, 19: 223–43.

PEARCE, F. (1976), *Crimes of the Powerful: Marxism, Crime and Deviance*, London: Pluto.

—— and SNIDER, L. (1995), 'Regulating Capitalism', in F. Pearce and L. Snider (eds), *Corporate Crime*, 19–48, Toronto: University of Toronto Press.

—— and TOMBS, S. (1990), 'Ideology, Hegemony and Empiricism: Compliance Theories of Regulation', *British Journal of Criminology*, 30: 423–43.

—— and —— (1991), 'Policing Corporate "Skid Rows" ', *British Journal of Criminology*, 31: 415–26.

PONTELL, H. N., and CALAVITA, K. (1993), 'The Savings and Loan Industry', in M. Tonry and A. Reiss Jnr (eds), *Beyond the Law: Crime in Complex Organizations*, 203–47, Chicago: University of Chicago Press.

PORTNOY, F. (1997), *F.I.A.S.C.O: Blood in the Water on Wall Street*, London: Profile Books.

PUNCH, M. (1996), *Dirty Business: Exploring Corporate Misconduct*, London: Sage.

PRASHAD, V. (2002), *Fat Cats and Running Dogs: the Enron Stage of Capitalism*, London: Zed Books.

REICHMAN, N. (1992), 'Moving Backstage: Uncovering the Role of Compliance Practices in Shaping Regulatory Practices', in K. Schlegel and D. Weisburd, *White-Collar Crime Reconsidered*, 244–68, Boston, Mass.: Northeastern University Press.

ROSOFF, S. M., PONTELL, H. N., and TILLMAN, R. (1998), *Profit Without Honour: White Collar Crime and the Looting of America*, Upper Saddle River, N. J.: Prentice Hall.

ROYAL COMMISSION ON CRIMINAL PROCEDURE (1980), *Prosecutions by Private Individuals and Non-Police Agencies*, Research Study No. 10, London: HMSO.

RUGGIERO, V. (1996), *Organised Crime and Corporate Crime in Europe*, Aldershot: Dartmouth.

SAPELLI, G. (2004), *Giochi Proibiti: Enron e Parmalat; capitalismi a confronto*, Milan: Mondadori.

SAVELSBERG, J. (1994), *Constructing White-Collar Crime: Rationalities, Communication, Power*, Philadelphia, Pa: University of Pennsylvania Press.

SHAPIRO, S. (1984), *Wayward Capitalists*, New Haven, Conn.: Yale University Press.

—— (1989), 'Collaring the Crime, not the Criminal: Reconsidering "White-Collar Crime" ', *American Sociological Review*, 55: 346–65.

SIMPSON, S. S. (1992), 'Corporate Crime Deterrence and Corporate Control Policies, Views from the Inside', in K. Schlegel and D. Weisburd, *White-Collar Crime Reconsidered*, 289–308, Boston, Mass.: Northeastern University Press.

SLAPPER, G. (1991), *Blood in the Bank*, Aldershot: Dartmouth.

—— and TOMBS, S. (1999), *Corporate Crime*, Harlow: Longman.

SMITH, D. J. Jnr (1980), 'Paragons, Pariahs and Pirates: A Spectrum-Based Theory of Enterprise', *Crime and Delinquency*, 26: 358–86.

SNIDER, L. (1991), 'The Regulatory Dance: Understanding Reform Processes in Corporate Crime', *International Journal of the Sociology of Law*, 19: 209–36.

SPALEK, P. (2001), 'Policing the UK Financial System: The Creation of the New Financial Services Authority and its Approach to Regulation', *International Journal of the Sociology of Law*, 29(1): 75–88.

STANLEY, C. (1992), 'Serious Money: Legitimation of Deviancy in the Financial Markets', *International Journal of the Sociology of Law*, 20: 43–60.

STEFFENSMEIER, D. (1989), 'On the Causes of White-collar Crime: An Assessment of Hirschi and Gottfredson's Claims', *Criminology*, 27: 345–58.

STONE, C. (1975), *Where the Law Ends: The Social Control of Corporate Behaviour*, New York: Harper and Row.

SUTHERLAND, E. H. (1949), *White-collar Crime*, New York: Holt, Rinehart and Winston.

—— (1983), *White-collar Crime: the Uncut Version*, New Haven, Conn.: Yale University Press.

SZASZ, D. (1986), 'Corporations, Organised Crime and the Disposal of Hazardous Waste: An Examination of the Making of a Criminogenic Regulatory Structure', *Criminology* 24: 1–27.

TAPPAN, P. (1947), 'Who is the Criminal?', *American Sociological Review*, 12: 96–102.

TIEDEMANN, K. (1974), 'Kriminologische und Kriminalistiche Aspekte der Subventionseschtei-chung', in H. Schafer (ed.), *Grundlagen der Kriminalistik*, 13(1), Wirtschaftskriminalitat, Weissen-Kragen Kriminalitat, Hamburg: Steinton.

Tombs, S. (1995), 'Corporate Crime and New Organizational Forms', in F. Pearce and L. Snider (eds), *Corporate Crime*, 132–47, Toronto: University of Toronto Press.

Van Duyne, P. (1993), 'Organised Crime and Business Crime Enterprises in the Netherlands', *Crime, Law and Social Change*, 19: 103–43.

Vaughan, D. E. (1983), *Controlling Unlawful Organizational Behaviour*, Chicago: University of Chicago Press.

——(1996), *The Challenger Launch Decision*, Chicago: University of Chicago Press.

Weisburd, D., and Waring, E. J. (2001), *White Collar Crime and Criminal Careers*, Cambridge: Cambridge University Press.

Wheeler, S., Waring, E., and Bode, N. (1991), *Crimes of the Middle Classes: White-collar Offenders in the Federal Courts*, New Haven, Conn.: Yale University Press.

Wells, C. (1993), *Corporations and Criminal Responsibility*, Oxford: Clarendon Press.

Wheeler S. (1992), 'The Problem of White-Collar Crime Motivation', in K. Schlegel and D. Weisburd, *White-Collar Crime Reconsidered*, 108–24, Boston, Mass.: Northeastern University Press.

——, Mann, K., and Sarat, A. (1988), *Sitting in Judgement: The Sentencing of White-Collar Crimes*, New Haven, Conn.: Yale University Press.

Wright-Mills, C. (1943/1963), 'The Professional Ideology of Social Pathologists', in C. Wright-Mills, *Power, Politics and People*, 525–52, New York: Oxford University Press.

Yeager, P. C. (1991), *The Limits of Law: The Public Regulation of Private Pollution*, Cambridge: Cambridge University Press.

——(1995), 'Management, Morality and Law, Organizational Forms and Ethical Deliberations', in F. Pearce and L. Snider (eds), *Corporate Crime*, 147–68, Toronto: University of Toronto Press.

Young, T. R. (1981), 'Corporate Crime: A Critique of the Clinard Report', *Contemporary Crises*, 5: 323–36.

Zigler, J. (1990), *La Suisse Lave Plus Blanc*, Amsterdam: Uitgeverij Balanss.

Zimring, F., and Hawkins, G. (1993), 'Crime, Justice and the Savings and Loans Crisis', in M. Tonry and A. Reiss Jnr (eds), *Beyond the Law: Crime in Complex Organizations*, 247–92, Chicago: University of Chicago Press.

23

ORGANIZED CRIME AND TERRORISM

*Michael Levi**

INTRODUCTION

In this chapter, we will briefly critique legal and operational definitions of organized crime and terrorism, and suggest more meaningful ways of thinking about them; discuss how criminals organize themselves and how criminal markets work; and finish with a brief appreciation of the importance of understanding the interrelationship between crime control mechanisms—criminal justice and prevention, including private sector controls—and the ways in which criminals get together to commit serious crimes for profit or social transformation.

During the last two decades, in many countries, governments and citizens have expressed increasing concern about the growing threat from crime. Although both crimes and their governance remain primarily local, electronic and print media accounts have brought to the fore the *transnational* components of drugs, illegal labour/people trafficking, frauds, and terrorism, and action against these phenomena has been sought in international political marketplaces, both regional and global. One indicator of this interest has been the fact that in the past two decades, no fewer than four United Nations Conventions have been devoted to serious crime issues.[1] At a European level, there has been a proliferation of measures attending to the threat of money-laundering and organized crime, starting with the 1990 Council of Europe Convention and the first EC Money Laundering Directive of 1991, and accelerating in the late 1990s and early part of this century, to (in 2005) the EC Third Directive and the

* I am grateful to Nicholas Dorn at Cardiff University for comments on drafts of this chapter.

[1] The UN Conventions are the Vienna Drugs Convention 1988; the Convention for the Suppression of the Financing of Terrorism 2000; the Transnational Organized Crime Convention 2000; and the Convention against Corruption 2003, all of which are now in force.

Council of Europe Convention No. 198,[2] which also cover the financing of terrorism. Reflecting the raised profile of transnational 'law and order' issues within the EU, from a lower base rate than other Directorates General, the Justice, Liberty and Security portfolio has become one of the most active areas of the European Commission's work, in terms of numbers of legislative proposals. These legislative framework changes have been accompanied by the unprecedented growth of (often informal, 'soft law') international bodies whose task is to monitor compliance with a multitude of rules—a quite new phenomenon of transnational governance, whose limits remain unclear (Levi and Gilmore 2002). As regards the USA, internationalization of law enforcement and intelligence has proceeded apace from an already substantial anti-drugs and anti-insurgency presence in the 1970s. The Serious Organised Crime Agency, established in the UK in 2006 specifically as a harm-reduction rather than law enforcement body (to emphasize its broader strategic intervention role),[3] is second only to the USA in the number of its intelligence/liaison staff working overseas.

However, this is not an essay reviewing those fascinating and socially important developments in international law-making, policing, and criminal justice.[4] Nor is it a critique of what van Duyne (1996, 2004, 2005, 2007) has caustically termed the 'threat assessment industry' or of particular theories of organized crime or terrorism *control* (see contributors to Biersteker and Eckert 2007; Naylor 2003, 2006). Rather it represents an attempt to look at the nature of the criminal phenomena that are said to have motivated changes in law creation and crime control—and that, to the extent that the controls have had an impact, have also been moulded by them.[5] It will be seen that in the case of both organized crime and terrorism, there is a spectrum of academic opinion, ranging from those who see them as widespread and very well *organized* (a term of art that should lead us to ask, how organized particular sorts of crime have to be?) to those who see them as intermittent, weakly and variably *networked*.

'Organized crime' has been a significant part of the popular discourse of American politicians and films since the 1920s. From the 1970s, the European components of this

---

[2] These are the EC Third Directive on the prevention of the use of the financial system for the purposes of money-laundering or terrorist financing, and the Council of Europe Convention No. 198 on laundering, search, seizure, and confiscation of the proceeds from crime and on the financing of terrorism. (See Fijnaut and Paoli 2004 and Gilmore 2004, for some rich description of these policy trends.) Note the way that financing of terrorism has been tacked on to what previously would have been money-laundering measures devoted only to reducing organized crime, with disputed effects—see Cuellar (2003); Levi (2007a); Napoleoni (2004); Passas and Jones (forthcoming).

[3] See Harfield (2006) for a good early discussion of SOCA. The complexities of harm assessment are too great to be discussed here, nor is there space in this chapter for more than a cursory review of the control of organized crime or terrorism.

[4] This arena has been one of severe legislative overload as a multitude of bodies have sought to transform substantive legislation and national/mutual legal assistance powers to assist in combating transnational crimes. For more than descriptive accounts of developments in the regulation of organized crime and terrorism, see, e.g., Andreas and Nadelmann (2006), Beare (2003), Dorn and Levi (forthcoming), Levi and Wall (2004), several contributors to Reichel (2005) and to Sheptycki and Wardak (2005), and Woodiwiss (2005).

[5] See, e.g., Black *et al.* (2001); Levi and Maguire (2004); Levi and Reuter (2006) for discussions of this difficult issue of the relationship between controls and criminal behaviour. There is a more substantial literature on drugs than on other areas of 'organized crime' control impact.

international 'connection' have been popularized by films such as *The Godfather* and *The French Connection*, although less 'Hollywoody' national versions (e.g. British films such as *The Krays* and *The Long Good Friday*) portrayed a more banal and parochial reality more similar to the racecourse gangs depicted in *Brighton Rock* (1947) than their American counterparts.[6] Italy excepted, the place of organized crime in the western European cultural lexicon has been less prominent, although it has had a higher profile in some ex-communist countries (and of course several countries, East and West, have had prolonged experience of domestic terrorism). It is intriguing to analyse why Europeans have become so interested in it since the mid-1990s and whether this policy and (to a more limited extent) resources explosion has been merited by 'the evidence' of the harm and patterns of criminal conduct. What do we mean by the term 'organized' and what is so different and harmful about 'organized' crimes for economic and/or political gain, compared with other crimes? These are issues that we will seek to address in this chapter, constrained as we are by space in dealing with multi-layered problematics.

Since the '9/11' attacks on America and the subsequent less dramatic[7] bombings in Africa, Asia, and Europe, the threat posed by 'organized crime' appears to have receded somewhat in official circles, to be replaced by that of 'terrorism', some of which is funded by crime, leading to emotive phrases such as 'narco-terrorism' (though the latter phenomenon preceded the twenty-first century). The shift of intelligence agencies towards dealing with 'transnational organized crime' after the collapse of Communisn and the IRA political threat was reversed post '9/11' (in the USA) and post-'7/7' (in the UK). However it would be wrong to infer that the threats from organized criminality (and, for that matter, terrorism) were or are illusions: (a) people really do get murdered and property blown up, and (b) millions of people really do use illegal drugs that have been transported sometimes through long distances and through multiple jurisdictions, before being covertly sold to people who (mostly) want to use them, some of whom commit crimes to be able to afford to buy them. Others buy counterfeit products such as cigarettes or sex with women transported by[8] and sometimes controlled by criminals. We thus start this chapter from the 'realist' premises: (i) that there are a lot of profitable crimes about, (ii) that some (*perhaps* an increasing number of) people are

---

[6] This may have reflected differences in the nature of criminal organization (influenced by Prohibitionist policies) in the USA and the UK.

[7] The dramaturgy of '9/11' does not reflect the aggregate totals killed compared with other nations, but the political and terrorist recruiting impacts of 'spectaculars'. Each nation or other (e.g. religious) reference group typically sees the death of its own members as more salient than those of others. (For some interesting discussions of violence and cultural identity, see Gray 2003; Sen 2006).

[8] In the cultural struggle over harm prioritization, the terminology can become blurred. If the women know at the point of transportation that they are going to become sex workers, the proper term is 'smuggling'; if they do not, it is 'trafficking' or even (when sold by their relatives, 'slavery'). In practice, adults are often told lies about the nature of their future employment. Some feminist groups consider that women cannot validly consent to become sex workers and therefore that all such transportation is trafficking. Much migrant sex work involves exploitation, but it is unlikely that any transporting network would survive long if those who paid to emigrate typically failed to reach their destinations alive or to send funds back to repay and help their families. Home Office analysis (unpublished) ranks people-trafficking as the most harmful of 'organized crimes'.

motivated to pursue their cultural/political/religious grievances through the use of violence, and (iii) that these crimes need 'organizing' (throughout, we prefer the connotations of the verb 'organizing crime' to that of the noun 'organized crime') *in some form* if they are to be performed effectively. Furthermore, some components of these crimes—from financing through obtaining the tools of crime to laundering proceeds—*usually* involve moving money, people, and chemicals/ weaponry across national borders. Not that any of this is so surprising, since most licit economic activities have similar requirements, down to those that enable us to buy at the corner shop the high-energy bar required to get readers through this chapter.

One of the main aims of this chapter is to try to shift us away from the over-simplified focus on organizational *structures* of offending that is part of the emotional baggage of hierarchy associated with terms like 'Organized Crime' or, to a lesser extent, 'Al-Qā'idah'.[9] Both (a) power relations between offenders and (b) the number of people available and motivated to commit serious crimes for financial or political gain are important. However the organizational forms by which crimes are 'delivered' are issues that require empirical investigation, and to do that we have to deconstruct stereotypes while recognizing that there was some underlying criminal behaviour or threat, as Stan Cohen (2002) attempted in his classic study of 'Mods and Rockers' in the 1960s, *Folk Devils and Moral Panics*. There is no 'criminal organization gene' whose DNA it is our task to unravel. Crimes and their organization develop, most fruitfully by mutual cooperation but often in practice by a mixture of this and distrust/domination. Individuals vary in their access to resources, personalities, and technical and organizational aptitudes, as well as in the networks of which they are already a part: these affect their ability to exploit and flourish in the environments in which they find themselves.[10]

The concern with the form of crime delivery is one justification for connecting these dimensions of the chapter title: what, after all, do crimes for profit and political power/resistance have in common (apart from both being included in the European

---

[9] Unlike many common terms used for organized crime in the Roman alphabet, Arabic transliterations give rise to a bewildering set of Anglo-American spellings, as staff in the financial services industry—who have to check bank accounts against the inconsistently transliterated list of individuals whose accounts are frozen—know to their cost. The difficulty here is not just translation, however, but also conceptual. As the stimulating Rand analysis of learning by terrorist organizations (Jackson *et al.* 2005a: 3 footnote 5) observes:

> Al Qaeda was deliberately *not* selected to be a case study group. The goal of the study was to examine organizational learning across different types of terrorist organizations to find commonalities and differences among their experiences. The rapid change occurring in al Qaeda during the study period and the volume of information available made it such a complex subject that we would not have been able to satisfactorily examine a sufficient number of other terrorist groups.

Of course, this begs the difficult question of when one can properly consider a network or a set of collaborative activities to constitute 'an organization'.

[10] Varese (2006) argues that features of the local economy — the presence of significant sectors of the economy unprotected by the state and a local rather than export orientation — generate a demand for criminal protection, and lead to successful transplantation. Contrary to established theories of social capital and trust, a high level of interpersonal trust among local law-abiding residents is not sufficient to stop the Mafia from establishing itself elsewhere. Whether this is true outside Italy or other places where images of Mafia remain credible remains to be tested.

Union's definition of organized crime)? Some terrorism (but not much of that which currently preoccupies developed nations) may have as its sole or partial objective material gain—even the socialist *redistribution* of existing wealth may be thus construed—but this is straining the relationship somewhat. Indeed, the editors and I had some debate as to whether terrorism should be more appropriately located exclusively within the 'violent crime' chapter of the Handbook. However we decided that its *form*, and its relationship with the tools of late modernity (transnational air travel and communications, the Internet and the spread of information about weapons construction, globalization of financial services and commerce including the arms trade and covert networking), have a sufficient linkage with organizational questions traditionally raised in relation to 'organized crime' to make discussion here appropriate. Both embody the 'glocal'—the link between the global and the local—and are delivered locally. In the case of terrorism (like extortion), the targets do not want what is delivered, and this is a major distinction from many forms of organized crime that involve the supply of desired but illegal products, whether they be

- wholly illegal (like criminalized drugs);
- counterfeit (on a spectrum from poor-quality pharmaceuticals—such as antibiotics or 'stamina pills' that do not work as advertised—to high-quality digital DVDs and copied generic pharmaceuticals that do work well), or
- tax-evaded but otherwise legal (smuggled genuine alcohol, fuel oil, or tobacco).

Some communities or subgroups want or applaud acts of terrorism *ex post facto*, and there is widespread tolerance of the purchase of stolen goods, excise-evaded goods, and counterfeit goods so long as they do not do actual harm other than reduce some corporate profits and correspondingly reduce the state's tax incomes. However, whereas if asked beforehand, people (suicide bombers excepted) who are blown up would see themselves as victims, most people who purchase illegal goods and services do not. Comparison can clarify the points of difference not always apparent in political rhetorics about the 'War on Terror' and the 'War on Organized Crime'. (Readers might consider how we would know when we were winning or losing such wars.)

The levels and organization of crimes in any given society are affected by controls, irrespective of how competently/vigorously those controls are implemented: this simple insight is the general contribution of interactionist perspectives in criminology, and is an implicit message of routine activities and situational crime prevention models. 'Controls' here include not just legal norms and their enforcement but the broader sets of activities that shape crime opportunities, Taking some issues 'organized' for political as well as economic reasons, these opportunities might include political campaign finances, the geopolitics of oil, or anti-Communism/'fundamentalism' (though if even one mosque or madrassah was transforming every worshipper into a terrorist, the rate of violence would be far greater). Taking issues of primarily economic concern that lack strong political alignment, they might include technological factors such as the introduction in Europe of Chip and Pin technology to neutralize the skimming of data from the magnetic stripes on our credit and debit cards; or measures to frustrate 'key logging' as a way of capturing our passwords for online banking. What is more difficult to address is the ways in which criminal justice practices (as well as history, motivations, and skills) shape the *organization* of offending, but we have insufficient space for this issue and, except for the impact of corruption within criminal justice systems, the research evidence to date is poor.

As with legitimate products—many products supplied by 'organized criminals' are grown and/or manufactured in far-distant parts of the world—it is difficult to retain the nation state as a meaningful bounded unit of analysis for understanding the organized crime issue as a whole, even though most individuals involved in drug-dealing, extortion, credit card fraud, armed robberies, sex work, etc. may not do any international business as part of their daily routines. On the control side, since police and intelligence agencies have their *national* interests as their rationale for intervention, this requires them to subordinate short-term to strategic cooperation. These cross-border dimensions[11] are what makes both organized crime and white-collar crime different from other crimes for gain. Yet there is much variation within this nexus, calling into question the coherence of what is talked about. It is hard to avoid discussing 'organized crime' as if it were a coherent common noun describing a well-understood set of arrangements to commit crime: this term indeed is part of the problem for critics. Precisely what is one criticizing or defending? Is it the notion of a hierarchical organization dominating global activity (by analogy with Microsoft or Google), or a set of giant firms competing but acting more or less in tandem (like the oil industry)? Or, as we will go on to see in most parts of western Europe (Dorn *et al.* 2005; Fijnaut and Paoli 2004), are the arrangements to supply illegal goods and services and to commit crimes for gain more like a network—within which there are many forms of organiz*ing*—in which case why should we call 'it' 'organized crime' or, for that matter, 'disorganized crime'? Or, as we shall suggest, does it make more sense to include all of these?

This review will *not* argue either that organized crime/terrorism are insignificant in their social implications or that the amount of money-laundering is small (see van Duyne and Levi 2005; Levi and Reuter 2006).[12] However, it is as well to take into account the huge propaganda element (from all sides) in modern media treatment of these issues and, above all, that our images of organized crime and terrorism often rely on policing images, which themselves depend on the way in which intelligence and enforcement are organized, as well as on pervasive social mythologies about what sort of persons and what sorts of behaviour constitute a 'threat to society'.[13] Where the

---

[11] Including multinational pressures for manpower movement and trade liberalization across national borders (Naylor 2002; Berdal and Serrano 2002; Andreas and Nadelmann, 2006)

[12] Money-laundering in legal terms means any act of concealment of proceeds of crime, including thieves placing funds in their own bank accounts in their own names. However, given the lifestyles of most offenders, they typically save very little so to calculate laundering we would need to know something about the distribution of profits from crime (subtracting operational costs including corruption), how much offenders save, and in what media they do so. From a country's point of view, one might need to know how much of other countries' proceeds of crime they handle and how much of their gross domestic criminal product gets exported.

[13] Sometimes, those policing agencies may underestimate the connections between criminals by failing to develop intelligence leads on networks. Furthermore, given the $40 billion or so collapse (despite bankrolling a

mistake lies is in moving from the (defensible) proposition that harmful impacts are considerable, to the (indefensible) proposition that these impacts arise from a common delivery mechanism called 'organized crime'.

ANALYTICAL ISSUES IN DEFINING THE NATURE OF 'ORGANIZED CRIME'

The term 'organized crime' denotes not just a set of criminal *actors* but also a set of criminal *activities* (Cohen 1977). Nowadays, these for-profit activities would be taken to include drugs-trafficking; trafficking in people; extortion; kidnapping for profit; illegal toxic waste dumping (environmental crime); sophisticated credit card fraud; fraud against the European Union; smuggling to evade excise tax on alcohol and tobacco; intellectual property theft (video and audio piracy and product-counterfeiting); VAT evasion (including Missing Trader Intra-Community frauds); corruption to achieve these offences, etc.[14] (Council of Europe 2005; Europol 2006; OCTF 2006; SOCA 2006). Problematically, the term is usually used to describe those activities *only when carried out by underworld-type figures*, though all four of the reports (and much of the terrorism literature) broaden out this conventional imagery to include activities and people that facilitate and underpin serious crime. Thus the collective noun 'organized crime' is constituted by both 'full-time' and 'part-time' criminals, many of whom may have multiple partners. The UK Serious Organised Crime Agency website (www.soca.gov.uk/orgCrime/index.html) answers the question 'What is organized crime?' by saying

Organised crime covers a very wide range of activity and individuals involved in a number of crime sectors.

The most damaging sectors to the UK are judged to be trafficking of Class A drugs, organised immigration crime and fraud.

In addition, there are a wide range of other threats, including high tech crime, counterfeiting, the use of firearms by serious criminals, serious robbery, organised vehicle crime, cultural property crime and others.

large percentage of American congressmen) at the end of 2001 of the once seventh largest American corporation, Enron, accompanied by revelations of serious financial mis-statements and shredding of documents by auditors Arthur Andersen, which plunged the unfortunate company pension-holders into penury while some directors offloaded their shares at a huge profit, it is tempting to ask which organized crime groups are doing more *economic* harm than Enron did.

[14] Politicians find it difficult to resist adding to the list of competencies of agencies charged with organized crime control. Following feminist, human rights, and media campaigns, trafficking of women rose to a high priority in the USA and the UN and, to a perhaps lesser extent, the EU, despite real concerns about whether some of this was just economic migration, despite low wage rates in host countries and the fact that many become sex workers and therefore part of the quasi-consensual crime market.

In the context of analysing business conspiracies to fix contracts in the Dutch building industry, van Duyne (2005) raises the issue of why we do not label corporate cartels as organized crime in the same way that we do the Colombian Cali cocaine cartel. It seems easier to generate negative labels for people who (we believe) do only bad things; when people are engaged in some socially positive activities, they get less condemnation or even get support. Thus it is with individual terrorists and 'terrorist organizations' that are involved in community service and are not corrupt (like Hamas);[15] and drugs-traffickers may be popular if they are generous in their neighbourhoods and spend liberally in local car dealerships, liquor stores, and restaurants. However, these 'Robin Hood' cultural observations do not constitute an analytical justification for not viewing business cartels differently, nor a coherent rationale for accepting a lower level of enforcement for 'white-collar' crime generally.

How do we know how 'organized crime' is constituted? Cressey (1969), using the surveillance tapes and interviews with Joseph 'the Canary that Sang' Valachi, set out the official version of Italian-American Mafia as a line management, vertically integrated, and horizontally coordinated organization (though it was left unstated how widely crime groups' 'licence to operate' charges extended to burglaries, robberies, credit card frauds, etc.). (There are parallels with the ways that unreliable informant testimonies plus government/enforcement agency preconceptions helped to construct a convenient but quite inaccurate model of 'Al-Qā'idah' as a hierarchical organisation with Usama bin Lāden at its head—see Burke 2004, 2006 and Naylor 2006 for detailed, if controversial deconstructions of such oversimplified accounts.) Few academics have been convinced by the Valachi Boss—Underboss—Soldier model as a portrait of organized crime in America: although Jacobs *et al.* (1994) and Jacobs and Gouldin (1999) put up a spirited defence that LCN (La Cosa Nostra) organized crime families do exist in cities like New York (as confirmed by wiretap evidence as well as informants), there is little confirmed evidence of such gang *domination* of criminal activity, even in the north-east USA. Analysts[16] have noted that 'organized crime' falsely implies a discontinuity between the 'organized criminal' and other criminals, and between organized criminals and the state, whereas studies of criminal markets and drugs/vice pricing data suggest otherwise—at least for developed countries.

In relation to illicit markets and crimes within them, the situation may vary from country to country. Work done in Italy and the United States discredits the alien-importation conventional history and emphasizes the coalition between business people, politicians, and crime groups in organizing and tolerating crime against the public interest.[17] Indeed Woodiwiss (2005) inverts the normal model and attributes most 'organized crime' to business people. However, this radical view that business and

---

[15] At the time of writing, despite being elected as the government of the Palestinian Authority, Hamas remained officially labelled as a terrorist organization. The use of quotation marks in parts of the text should not be viewed as the author's personal judgement but merely a reflection of the deeply contested nature of such judgements.

[16] For example, Reuter (1983); Reuter and Rubinstein (1978) and Smith (1980).

[17] Pearce 1976; Block and Chambliss 1981; Paoli 2002, 2003; Stille 1996; Woodiwiss 2001.

criminals are symbiotic in turn ignores the often unwanted parasitical and predatory crimes committed *against* business by crime groups, in which business people get locked into a system of paying both to obtain contracts and to avoid active harm from regulators and enforcement personnel. The latter discontents led to complaints by business people that helped to trigger the *mani pulite* ('Clean Hands') judicial investigations in Italy that convulsed the Italian polity and led to the prosecution of the then current and previous Italian prime ministers. (The symbiotic model also has difficulty in accounting for high-profile corporate and individual prosecutions such as Enron and Parmalat—see the discussion of white-collar crime by Nelken, Chapter 22, this volume.) A useful perspective is to think about the control of crimes (including Grand Corruption by kleptocratic politicians) as a particular context in which interlocking patron-client relationships lead to compromises and trade-offs.

In a sense, the wrong question has often been asked about 'organized crime' (as it has about delinquent gangs), which is to ask if 'it' is organized in a particular way, whereas the more sensible question is to ask what factors over time shape the ways in which crimes of certain types are organized and who gets involved in them? (See Mack and Kerner 1975 for some early European analysis of 'full-time criminals'; Hobbs 1997, 2001 for a view of 'the Firm' as being first rooted in and then uprooted from its English class and local environment that could not be more different from the Cressey model; and Dorn *et al.* 1992, for indications both of heterogeneity and change.) Later British work stresses the linkages between serious crimes for gain (especially drugs, extortion, and sex work) and the night-time economy, which flourishes in the relatively unsurveilled, age-segregated geographic sectors of our towns and cities.[18] While criminal organizations do exist in Italy, Mafia is more a method of patron/client relationships and extortion than it is a specific body 'in charge' of all serious criminality.[19]

Nevertheless, such critiques do not seem to have dented media or policy-makers' enthusiasms either for the term or for action against 'it', and this enthusiasm has led to *legal* definitions that generate the boundaries of punishment both within nation states and, increasingly, outside them. To the pragmatist seeking a rationale for necessary action, a visualizable enemy is valuable: 'organized crime', like terrorism, has become defined as a transnational threat requiring transnational action(and indeed, even if such crimes are often 'disorganized' it is difficult to see how they could be tackled without cross-border action).[20] Legal definitions of organized crime, like other social labels such as 'antisocial behaviour', are based around the measures that legislators want to

---

[18] As Levi, Maguire and Brookman note, Chapter 21, this volume, high alcohol consumption in this setting has also fuelled street violence, though in a smaller proportion of drunkenness cases than one might expect from media accounts.

[19] See Arlacchi (1986, 1998); Gambetta (1994); Paoli (2002, 2003).

[20] A dramatic example was the arrest in August 2006 of a British senior executive of a Costa Rica-run online betting firm for 'wire fraud', allegedly because the firm accepted telephone and other bets from American citizens. One of the complaints of the extraordinary campaign mounted in the summer of 2006 by British business people against the extradition of the 'NatWest Three' to the USA on Enron-related charges was that fast-track extradition arrangements passed in part to deal with terrorism were being used mainly for (organized?) white-collar crime cases (Levi 2006).

take against evils, both activities and 'sorts of people', especially combinations of people. In domestic and international legal definitions, which bind countries to action, there is often a tension between: (a) those who want the legislation to cover a wide set of circumstances to avoid the risk that any major criminal might 'get away with it', and (b) those who want the law to be quite tightly drawn to avoid the overreach of powers which might otherwise criminalize groups who are only a modest threat. Typically, organized criminals have few supporters willing to stand up for them in the public sphere, so definitions tend to be loose. This may be witnessed in the European Union definitions (in the Joint Action of 1998) and in the UN Transnational Organised Crime Convention 2000, as well as in US Racketeer Influenced Corrupt Organizations (RICO) legislation 1970 (Levi and Smith 2002; Morselli and Kazemian 2004). There is no space here to discuss these legal definitions.[21] The key thing to note is that provided that criminals work over a 'prolonged' period of time—however long (or short) that is— 'organized crime' as defined by the EU and UN can mean anything from major Italian syndicates in sharp suits or Sicilian peasant garb to three very menacing-looking burglars with a window-cleaning business who differentiate their roles by having one act as look-out, another as burglar, and a third as money-launderer! By UN criteria, for example, a group that engages in 'skimming' credit card details with a small and inexpensive piece of software and re-encoding them on to plastic cards to be used in another country qualifies as a transnational organized crime group. Almost all drugs and fraud money-laundering beyond simple self-laundering by placing funds in a local bank account also qualifies. The scale of transnational crime correspondingly is very large.

In the case of terrorism, definition is even more controversial, which is one reason why the UN has been unable to come to an agreed one in the way that (however unsatisfactorily from an analytical viewpoint) they did with transnational organized crime. The UN ended up resignedly regarding terrorism as the equivalent of a war crime in peacetime. Pondering these issues, the excellent analysis by journalist Burke (2004: 22) states:

> There are multiple ways of defining terrorism, and all are subjective. Most define terrorism as 'the use or threat of serious violence' to advance some kind of 'cause'. Some state clearly the kinds of group ('sub-national', 'non-state') or cause (political, ideological, religious) to which they refer. Others merely rely on the instinct of most people when confronted with an act that involves innocent civilians being killed or maimed by men armed with explosives, firearms or other weapons. None is satisfactory, and grave problems with the use of the term persist. Terrorism is after all, a tactic. The term 'war on terrorism' is thus effectively nonsensical . . . [m]y preference is, on the whole, for the less loaded term 'militancy'.

The nature and extent of 'organized crime' and 'terrorism' threats remains deeply contested terrain. Students should also pay close attention to the use of the term 'transnational': it is helpful to think of the tasks that need to be performed to commit

---

[21] For a discussion of the UN Convention, see www.unafei.or.jp/english/pdf/PDF_rms/no59/ch23.pdf and the UNODC website.

serious crimes over a long period, most of these tasks being as easily accomplished at a local level as transnationally. These are:

1. Obtain finance for crime.

2. Find people willing and technically/socially competent to commit crimes (though this may not always be necessary).

3. Obtain equipment and transportation necessary to commit the crimes.

4. Convert, where necessary, products of crime into money or other usable assets.

5. Find people and places willing to store proceeds (and perhaps transmit and conceal their origin).

6. Neutralize law enforcement by technical skill, by corruption, and/or by legal arbitrage, using legal obstacles to enforcement operations and prosecutions which vary between states.

These procedural elements can be broken down further into much more concrete steps, when analysing the dynamics of particular crimes and/or criminal careers.[22] Some similarities exist with the process of terrorism, depending on whether it is suicide bombing or the more conventional paramilitary terrorism emanating from the Irish/Basque ETA conflicts, *except that the funds may come from entirely lawful activities*. In the case of suicide bombers, the process ends with the third stage above; with non-suicides, there is normally a link with crime because (a) many logistical support services—including people—may need to be paid for over a long period of time, perhaps decades; and (b) though less so in the case of state-sponsored terrorism, the purchase of logistics for armed struggle will usually require robbery, black market purchases, and/or fraudulent documentation on identities and end-user certificates for weapons.

States with a role in the production or supply of illegal commodities (drugs or people) or in the storing and laundering of proceeds of crime can sometimes be said to be 'captured' by organized crime, while other 'collapsed states' (such as Afghanistan at times, following intervention by many international actors) are too weak and/or corrupted to deal with crime entrepreneurs and/or political rebels in their midst.[23] This makes 'State-Organized Crime' (Chambliss 1989) sometimes a more appropriate term than mere 'organized crime', for the latter tends to focus us exclusively towards the threat posed by some (usually alien) group of low-lifes.[24] In practice, provided they are deemed to assist in restraining communism[25] or terrorism, anti-crime measures may be subordinated to wider foreign and economic policy interests: covert military operations overseas, especially in support of military regimes or guerrillas, have led to toleration of or even active support for some illegal drugs producers or distributors, for

[22] See Cornish (1994), Tremblay *et al.* (1994, 2001), and Morselli (2005).

[23] Arquilla and Ronfeldt 2001; Friman and Andreas 1999; Mitsilegas 2003; Tilly 1985; Williams 2001; Wright 2006; Zartman 1995.

[24] See Sterling (1991, 1994) and Robinson (2002) for examples of the global conspiracy theory end of this spectrum.

[25] See, for a particularly critical account, Woodiwiss (2001, 2005).

example in Afghanistan (Naylor 2006; Thoumi 2007). Indeed, some observers may be tempted to dismiss the existence of organized crime altogether (Hawkins 1969; van Duyne 1996, 2007),[26] because 'its' manifestations are not obvious in the West, and/or because of suspicions that claims of 'threats to society' are being crafted to suit the bureaucratic and personal interests of police centralizers, international justice harmonizers, and intelligence agencies.

Specialized information sources may be tainted and the perspectives drawn from them partial. Some law enforcement officials may have *idées fixes* about 'organized crime', may lack adequate analytical skills or resources to carry out network analysis,[27]—or they may simply pragmatically find 'it' a convenient myth to get more resources from politicians. Data matching and more sophisticated data-mining techniques may reveal connections in, for example, insurance, social security, or tax fraud claims that were not otherwise apparent but this does not mean that all crimes or other types of fraud are 'organized'. There is no obviously 'correct' view on these issues: if the organization of clandestine behaviour was so obvious, it would not be secret! But ethnographic and interview studies, especially of drug markets (Hobbs 2000, 2001; Pearson and Hobbs 2001; Rawlinson 2000; Wright 2006; for a review, Dorn *et al.* 2005); reviews of completed but not always prosecuted case files (Fijnaut *et al.* 1998; van Duyne and Miranda 1999; van Duyne and Levi 2005); and economic pricing analysis (Reuter 1983; Reuter and Kleiman 1986; Fiorentini and Peltzman 1995) can give us some clues as to which accounts are more plausible.

THE NATURE OF ORGANIZED CRIME AND 'ITS' MARKETS

There is no *a priori* reason why the organization of crime should be constant over time or between societies at any given moment, or should embody a trend towards syndicated crime. This is the point stressed by McIntosh (1975) in her classic account of modes of organization, shifting from *picaresque* banditry, through routinized *craft* crime (like pickpocketing of handkerchiefs in Victorian times), to *project* crime (like major robberies and thefts such as Brink's Mat in 1984, the Northern Bank in 2005, and the break-in by earth-remover to attempt to steal valuable jewellery from the De Beers exhibition at the London Dome and to transport it away by speedboat—see Shatford and Doyle 2005) and *business* organization (such as the continuous supply of illegal goods and services). The organization of crime depends on the stage of historical development and also on the counter-measures to crime. The key point is that people

---

[26] For the avoidance of doubt, neither author denies that there is crime and drug use in abundance: the denial is of the hierarchically 'organized' nature of crime delivery.

[27] For glimpses of what is required, see Klerks (2003) or Coles (2001), the latter critiqued by Chattoe and Hamill (2005).

contemplating particular forms of crime find themselves in different situations, depending on the city, or country, and their own embeddedness in concrete networks, in a criminal and/or 'respectable' elite: this was implicit in the model of responses to *anomie* developed by Cloward and Ohlin (1960). (See, for a particularly useful effort at analytical integration, Morselli 2005). There is insufficient space to deal with all of these questions here, but they demonstrate how varied is the range of issues associated with organized crime (and terrorism), and also the range of academic areas encompassed by its study, including banking and market economics, political science, international relations, strategic studies, international law, media studies, social psychology, and sociology.

The Italian (or more precisely, Italian-American) model has embedded itself in popular culture, mediated through Hollywood. Yet all ethnographic accounts focus on a more complex set of patron/client relationships in which ethnic networks can sometimes supply a trust level that is important for smoothly functioning crime as it is for commerce. This research, including interesting studies of networks of Colombians (Zaitch 2002), Japanese (Hill 2003), and Turks (Bovenkerk and Yesilgöz 1998; Fijnaut *et al.* 1998), as well as Hobbs's (1997, 2001, 2004) work in the UK, collectively demonstrates the subtle linkages between the organization of crime and the organization of ordinary social relations and work.

In brief, the accident of geography (where particular drugs can be easily produced, people want/need to emigrate, and direct supply routes), combined with the skill and contact set (including local corrupt contacts) and (variable) trust values that offenders bring to the table, has led a variety of ethnic groups to become involved in 'organized crime'. Even a decade ago in the USA, despite their growing involvement in securities fraud, there was hardly an Italian name in the FBI 'most wanted' list of targets (Reuter 1995), and unsurprisingly, a variety of ethnicities (including whites) have become involved in supplying criminal goods and services in the USA (Chin 1996; Finckenauer and Waring 1999; Finckenauer and Albanese 2005). Such groups make less use than previously of Italian-American Mafia dispute-resolution services (including their former near-monopoly of corrupt law enforcement and political contacts). Nor is there much vertical integration of organized crime groups, either in the USA or Europe, even in drugs markets[28]: street-level criminals are normally independent of major crime syndicates, even where the latter do exist.

As Block and Chambliss (1981) suggest, without denying ethnic involvement in criminality, rather than being viewed as an alien group of outsiders coming in and perverting society, organized crime in America is best viewed as a set of shifting coalitions between groups of gangsters, business people, politicians, and union leaders, normally local or regional in scope. Many of these participants have legitimate jobs and sources of income. Similar observations would apply in some other countries such as Mexico (Geopolitical Drug Dispatch 2001, Gomez-Cespedes 1999), where—though this has

---

[28] (Dorn *et al.* 1992, 1998, 2005; Gruter and van de Mheen 2005; Pearson and Hobbs 2001; Ruggiero and South 1995; Paoli 2001; Zaitch 2002; Zaitch *et al.* 2003).

changed somewhat in the past five years—a small elite historically dominated the economy and political system and shared favours out among themselves. Ironically, the privatization of the economy in former communist countries in the name of freedom enabled oligarchs—whether connected or not to organized crime groups—to buy former state assets for far below their true value and to buy up cheaply the shares given to the workers and public. Privatization also provides easy avenues for money-laundering where the authorities and banks cannot afford to be too inquisitive about the source of the funds. (Though sensible criminals may not wish to leave their funds too long in countries with no depositor or investor protection schemes, or where a liquidator of a bank that goes bust might demand to know the beneficial ownership and origin of the funds before paying compensation.) The era of ultra-violent entrepreneurship may have ended and consolidation occurred in Russia (Galeotti 2004; Volkov 2002), but there remains a substantial amount of economic crime emanating from Russian criminals, some of them—like Nigerians—from diasporas outside the country.

Among advanced industrial nations, the closest similarities to this 'political coalition' organizational model have been reported for Australia, where extensive narcotics, cargo theft, and labour-racketeering rings with ties to state-level politicians and police were discovered during the 1970s and 1980s; and for Japan, where Yakuza and other racketeers specialize in vice and extortion (Hill 2003). Both of these illustrations, however, also suggest that the coalition—in which campaign funds also play an important role—is not entirely by consent: business people would rather not pay the blackmail if they felt they had any realistic alternative. In Britain, by contrast, though there were allegations in 2006 about large (illegal) donations in exchange for the promise of a seat in the unelected House of Lords, this appears to have been more for social status in legitimate society than for direct political control on behalf of criminal purposes;[29] and Serious Fraud Office investigations into alleged transnational corruption/cartels involving BAE, Halliburton, and National Health Service suppliers have not involved organized crime groups connected with illegal drugs, extortion, etc. The disconnect is partly because of a more conservative social and political system in the UK than in some other countries, but principally because the supply and consumption of alcohol, gambling, and (in some respects) prostitution remain legal and partly regulated (as was the case, for a while, for opiates). This reduces the profitability of supplying these goods and services criminally, although large profits can still be made by traffickers in women, who make them work in near-slavery conditions in massage parlours, saunas, and the like, in suburbia as well as in traditional red-light districts;[30] and worldwide (including intra-EU), differences in tax levels on alcohol make wide-spread evasion profitable. A host of groups are important in the supply of illegal drugs to and via Britain.[31] But

---

[29] Though in societies—the majority—where networking and 'being seen in the right places' is vital to economic prestige, the line between status and political power is an elastic one.

[30] There is enormous dispute about the proportion of women who are trafficked as contrasted with smuggled as economic migrants. For European research on trafficking in women, see Aronowitz 2001; Kelly 2005; Kelly and Regan 2001; Laczko 2005; Monzini 2005; Vocks and Nijboer 2000.

[31] (Dorn *et al.* 1992, 1998; Stelfox 2003; Pearson and Hobbs 2001; SOCA 2006).

except for drug importers and wholesalers, cargo thieves who work at airports, and local vice, protection, and pornography syndicates, the historic evidence suggests that British and German 'organized criminals' tend to be relatively short-term groups drawn together for specific projects, such as fraud and armed robbery, from a pool of long-term professional criminals on a within-force or regional basis.[32]

Instead of making routine comparisons with the USA, it may be better to look at organized crime in Europe from its own set of economic and social landscapes in which organized crime *trade* takes place. As van Duyne (1996) observes, Europe has a large diversity of economies, extensive economic regulations, many loosely controlled borders to cross, and relatively small jurisdictions. This means that the largest illegal profits for European crime-entrepreneurs are to be gained in the drug market and in the area of organized business crime, with asymmetries in excise and value-added tax and the modest controls over fraud against the EU offering many opportunities. If the normal (licit) business nucleus in southern Italy, Turkey, or Pakistan is the extended family (Ianni and Reuss-Ianni 1972; Fijnaut *et al.* 1998), in northern Europe such socio-economic family units are much rarer and social bonds more restricted, for example to people bound by loyalties of place (Hobbs 1997, 1998, 2001; Pearson and Hobbs 2001), though the very fracturing of the social fabric that has led to so much concern about social exclusion also paradoxically may inhibit *criminal* solidarity. The exceptions are the crime-enterprises of minorities in Europe whose businesses are family matters, which should not be equated with impersonal 'syndicates' (Ianni 1974; Bovenkerk 2007).

In order to make profits, those who offer illegal goods and services must advertise, if only to selected 'affinity groups' derived from other sources and activities. This generally means that in the long run, the police will come to know about the criminality too. To ensure freedom from the law, unless they can rely on police tolerance without a financial motivation, the criminals must therefore subvert the policing agencies and/or the courts, and this is a major reason for concern about the impact of organized crime. (Though in reality, it is a side effect of the prohibition of goods and services in popular demand, without which organized criminals would be operating in this area only as extorters from business.) In the Italian case, it seems clear that the state itself has at times in some sense collaborated with organized crime groups, though there is an unfortunate tendency to mix this up with the cosy or sometimes parasitic corrupt deals between business people and both national and northern politicians investigated mainly by the Milan magistrates (with very modest final criminal justice outcomes). But arguably, whatever the patron-client relationships that permeate Italian society—noted for instance in the favour network that generated corrupt refereeing and led to sanctions against several top Italian Soccer clubs (most notably Juventus) in 2006—the Mafia (or Christian Democrat/Mafia) supremacy probably required the tolerance of US foreign policy to survive.[33]

---

[32] See McIntosh (1975) and Mack and Kerner (1975) for some early discussions along these lines, and Porter (1996) and Fijnaut and Paoli (2004) for later examples.

[33] See Nelken 1996; Stille 1996; Thoumi 2003; Woodiwiss 2001, 2005.

Alternatively, those crime entrepreneurs who are not confident about their abilities to subvert or sidestep the law might rationally choose to operate on a fairly small scale, in keeping with the illegality of the products, while the supply of criminal labour generates the total volume of product demanded by the marketplace. The result is a far more differentiated set of people and groups involved in supplying illegal goods and services than the organized crime imagery would lead us to expect (Paoli 2002; contributors to Fijnaut and Paoli 2004). This applies even to the so-called Cali and Medellin drug 'cartels', where collaborative authority structures made it most unlikely that long-term price-fixing could ever be accomplished (Thoumi 2003; Naylor 2004). Finally, the consensus[34] suggests that the success of organized crime in Italy and Russia (and, one might further argue, in many parts of Latin America) depends also on the more general lack of trust in society and between citizens and government. This imposes some limits on expansionism by serious crime groups, since when they come up against societies in which trust between citizens and governments/policing institutions operates well, Mafia-type organizations find an infertile soil in which to grow and—as far as we can tell—are unsuccessful in the long term, despite having substantial funds at their disposal. The importance of generating trust between citizens and government (sometimes where none has ever existed) is one reason why, if they want to succeed, attempts to combat organized crime in low-trust countries require more than a merely institutional focus on governance, i.e. more than whether these countries have something called an Independent Commission against Corruption and a panoply of intrusive surveillance and anti-laundering/asset forfeiture laws.

SKILLS AND PREREQUISITES FOR CRIME

Naylor (2003) has developed a typology of profit-driven crimes in which he argues that the kinds of skills needed and the organizational forms that crime takes depend on what the criminals need to do: predatory crimes involve winners and losers, whereas in market offences, criminals supply a mostly willing market with legal-source tax-evaded goods or illegal-source prohibited goods, and in commercial offences, mostly legitimate corporations commit offences (e.g. cheat customers and investors as part of profit-seeking). In predatory acts such as robbery, violence or its threat is a key element, and professional robbers—whether of commercial premises (Gill 2001; Shover 1996) or of passengers in the street—become highly skilled in its dramaturgy. In market offences, violence occurs mostly in disputes over territory or over proceeds of crime stored in cash. In most Western societies, such violence is an artefact of the criminalization of popular goods and services; though elsewhere, extortion or 'protection' ('roof' in eastern Europe) can take place where there is a weak state incapable of protecting all its people from such threats *and* where criminals (who can include police or even senior politicians and officials) have the motivation and aptitude to make

---

[34] Good contributions to the trust and organized crime issue include Gambetta (1994); von Lampe and Johansen (2004); Nelken (1997); and Varese (2001, 2006).

convincing threats. In all of these cases, violence is instrumental, but it can simultaneously also express a need/wish to be shown 'respect' (Levi, Maguire and Brookman,
Chapter 21, this volume).

Despite the general social movement against corruption,[35] in profit-driven crime,
corrupt payments are not central, because predatory crimes do not require them, while
market offences give value to more or less voluntary purchasers (except for those
addicted persons who really want to give up). However, corruption may occur either as
a one-off or as a regular payment to neutralize law enforcement and, in some societies,
it may move from individual to group to systemic corruption (Sherman 1974; Punch
2000) from where, once established, 'good governance' campaigns will not generate
ready change without an internal seismic shift in patron-client relationships as has happened—at least temporarily—in Indonesia and the Philippines.

Once the offences have occurred, an integral part of the crime process involves fencing
(resale) of goods—where goods or traceable money have been obtained—and laundering those proceeds that have not been spent and need to be stored. Sutton (1998) has
shown how stolen goods tend to be recycled through pubs and informal neighbourhood networks: one might add that this reduces local hostility to people otherwise
depicted as dangers to 'society'. This focus on the embeddedness of crime with the local
economy[36] may understate somewhat the use of supermarkets and local shops to sell
(unaccounted-for) produce from large hauls. In the 1970s, I interviewed someone who
had stolen without knowing its content a truckload of yoghurt, which he would have
had great difficulty disposing of without it becoming spoiled had he got that far: selling
alcohol and tobacco smuggled in from the Continent is relatively easy, not just because
there is a bigger market but also because there are fewer storage problems and easy
rationalizations for both sellers and purchasers that 'the amount of duty the government makes people pay is diabolical'.

In his study of the global market for looted antiquities, Mackenzie (2005a, 2005b)
notes the importance of 'techniques of neutralization' that are given some protection in
law and by the inactivism of law enforcement and victims: unless a provenance (history
of ownership and/or documented circumstances of excavation) adds to the value of an
object, it usually is not mentioned. In terms of looted antiquities, Mackenzie identifies
three types of buyers: those who have no qualms about buying looted antiquities, those
who will buy 'chance finds' but not other looted antiquities (as in heads ripped off
statues), and the 'angels' who never buy looted antiquities — none of whom was found
in his study. Auction houses' and dealers' warranties of title are used in the place of due
diligence investigations into the origins of antiquities. Dealers' self-justifications
include: source countries' laws preventing export of antiquities are 'draconian' and
'unfair'; dealers and collectors are 'saving' objects for posterity and for education of all
humankind; source countries are merely the geographical accidental owners, since
territorial boundaries have shifted; and, finally, we are not the type of people who do

---

[35] Transparency International 2006; Pieth 1998/99; Anechiarico and Jacobs 1998; World Bank 2006.
[36] See also Hobbs 2001; von Lampe 2006 and Ruggiero 2000.

criminal acts and therefore we will continue to do as we have always done before. However, in my view, shifts in enforcement practices (e.g. in Greece during 2006) may have an effect on the market, whether on key nodal intermediaries or on private and public institutions for whom respectability is important.

As for money-laundering, this has been the subject of much mystification. Laundering in legal terms is simply the concealment of proceeds of crime (see Alldridge 2003) but more analytically ought to be viewed as the cleansing of funds so that they can be used in a way indistinguishable from legitimate money. What most people appear to mean by money-laundering is the hiding of funds in accounts somewhere outside of the *current* surveillance capabilities of enforcement agencies and/or professional intermediaries such as accountants, bankers, and lawyers who may have a legal duty to sensitize themselves to laundering typologies and to report suspicions or 'unusual' transactions to the authorities, on pain of lengthy imprisonment and large fines. If and when those official surveillance capabilities increase—as they did steadily during the 1990s, accelerating after the millennium and especially after the plane-bomb attacks on New York and Washington on 11 September 2001—funds that were just hidden become vulnerable to enforcement intervention and perhaps confiscation (ARA 2006; Kennedy forthcoming; Levi and Reuter 2006). Those 'organized criminals'—the great majority by volume, it appears (Shover 1996)—who make themselves popular with local car dealers, restaurateurs/publicans, and lovers by spending their money as they go along have no such problems of working out how to hide and store their money (though they may be hit subsequently by proceeds of crime confiscation and civil forfeiture orders that they may never repay). Van Duyne and Levi (2005) show that few convicted major criminals in the Netherlands and the UK have carried out very sophisticated laundering techniques: this should become less true as the financial investigation resources and skills of the authorities increase.

DRUG-TRAFFICKING NETWORKS

Much of the rising concern about organized criminality around the world has been because of its association with illegal drugs (see South, Chapter 24, this volume). There has been a gradual improvement in our understanding of drugs networks, where the greatest profits are thought to be in the 'middle market' in the supply chain. However, it is not certain what is sometimes meant by network and the literature review of upper-level drug-trafficking by Dorn *et al.* (2005) is helpful in this respect (see Box 23.1).

Dorn *et al.* (2005) opt for the first meaning—networking within the market—because the research best supports it. By contrast, an implication of the second meaning, that upper-level drug-trafficking lacks larger and/or 'harder-edged' organizations, is not well supported by the literature or interviews. Similarly, although some traffickers are very much in a state of flux, many others are not, and may function for decades (see the typology in Box 23.2 drawn from Dorn *et al.*). Hence, here, 'networking' is a

Box 23.1 NETWORKING IN THE MARKET: A CONCEPTUAL CRITIQUE

Terminology found in the literature is sometimes ambiguous. This is especially so in relation to 'network'/'networking'. The overwhelming consensus within the criminological literature is that networks are very important. On inspection, however, it appears that there are at least three common uses of this term.

(1) As a way of describing the structure and/or everyday workings of *the market as a whole*, in the sense that the market can be regarded as a complex social network (singular noun), within which different participants have to network (verb) (to carefully seek out and interact with traffickers who may be like or unlike themselves, etc.: see, for example, Coles 2001; Pearson and Hobbs 2001). In other words, through networking, traffickers construct the market.

(2) As a way of describing drug markets as made up of *independent small groups or individuals*, sometimes called 'disorganized crime', sometimes simply 'networks' (plural). Doubt is cast upon the existence of larger and/or 'harder' criminal organizations operating in the UK or other European contexts, partly because it is posited that law enforcement agencies break up larger groups. In other words, in drug trafficking, 'small is beautiful'.

(3) As a way of referring to the durability or otherwise of criminals' organizational and other arrangements, when these are seen as *ever-changing*. In other words, impermanence is the name of the game. (This approach often co-exists with number (2) above, although they are analytically separable.)

Source: Dorn *et al.* (2005).

term equally applicable to all traffickers, not a type in itself. One probable consequence of increased mixing between hitherto different traffickers is the breakdown of linguistic, national, and cultural barriers between traffickers. Shared experience facilitates new bonds, trust, and, on release from prison, closer cooperation between 'different' groups, and the easier formation of multicultural/multinational teams. As a result, the old barriers are breaking down fast. Whilst in the past it may have made sense for law enforcement agency (LEA) reports to categorize some varieties of criminality along ethnic, national, or related lines, to do so today is open increasingly to question: networking has spilt over traditional channels. This does not mean that there are no risks in dealing with other cultural groups and with strangers, and for all the casual discourse about globalization of organized crime (and terrorism), insufficient is known about the barriers to successful integration of criminals across national and international borders (Dorn *et al.* 2005). According to these authors, the table in Box 23.2 summarizes what on the basis of the literature may be said about each main type, its positioning in drug and other crime markets, degrees of permanence, typical business practices, and specific vulnerabilities. Some of these aspects bring us back to terrorism.

Box 23.2 A TYPOLOGY OF UPPER-LEVEL DRUG-TRAFFICKING ORGANIZATIONS, THEIR PRIORITIES, MARKET POSITIONING, DEGREES OF PERMANENCE, AND BUSINESS PRACTICES

Traffickers' priorities	Positioning in crime markets	Structures and degrees of permanence	Business practices
Politico-military			
Support for political objectives	Specific level or niche in a drug market is typical: production, export, transit and/or distribution (depending on political base)	Strongly defended hierarchy in own areas, cells outwith. Permanence: high	Aggressive: tendency to use violence against competitors and state; also political bargaining and/or coup attempts
Business criminals			
Personal enrichment	Vertical integration is common: from source zone, through transit zones, and sometimes on to distribution (but only rarely on to retail). Groups based in source zones may have discrete European representatives.	Core group is durable over several years, other criminals are drawn in, or external resources contracted, as and when needed for specific projects. Permanence: Medium	Very careful: principals 'cut out'; strong counter-surveillance; penetration of LEAs. Europe-based groups opportunistically involved in other criminal markets. Violence is a last resort—draws too much attention
Adventurers			
Risk is part of life	Opportunistic positioning—may arrange importation one time, at other times providing linkages or acting as a courier. Any part of the market.	Individuals and friends. Permanence of arrangements: low—mutating by the month	Risk-taking: individuals work for self or others (depending on events), are quite exposed in both cases

Source: Dorn *et al.* 2005: 36.

TERRORISM AND THE ALLEGED ORGANIZED CRIME-TERRORISM NEXUS

Different terrorist groups began with different cultural and economic resources, and also are tuned into the international 'community' in different ways. A decade ago, this section would not have focused at all on the global 'Jihad'—often used loosely in contemporary discourse—for a European or American audience. It has been culturally convenient to believe that terrorism (like organized crime) involves foreign 'invaders', but though this might seem to be supported by '9/11' and by the Madrid 2004 bombings, it is not supported by the Oklahoma City or London 2005 bombings (and subsequent alleged British attempts) or indeed by nationalist movements such as the IRA or the Basque ETA. Likewise, although some terrorists and organized criminals have obtained documentation by 'identity theft', many others—including some involved in '9/11'—have used their genuine names and have toured or worked legally in the countries they have attacked.

Particularly after the London bombings of 2005 and the alleged 'liquid explosives' plot of August 2006, it is now appreciated that much terrorism affecting the UK is home grown, yet influenced by (a) global events such as attacks on Muslim countries or communities and (b) by relationships/training at home and abroad (such as in Bosnia or Pakistan, where many of those 'converted' to terrorism spent some time). The global availability of video pictures of atrocities and particular constructions of blame for them has shaped anger and 'availability' for terror attacks and logistical support in many countries. In Northern Ireland, by contrast, the focus has been on the 'progression' of former paramilitary terrorists into mere organized criminals, the criminal behaviour being similar (though the bombings have stopped), the motivations shifting from ideology to personal financial accumulation. (Though—disputed by Sinn Fein and Loyalist politicians—the Independent Monitoring Commission (2006 and in earlier reports) remains concerned about the influence of paramilitaries' intimidation and illicit wealth upon security and the political process in Northern Ireland.) Thus, there is a widespread belief that Irish republican elements were behind the robbery (assisted by kidnapping bank staff) of £26.5 million in banknotes from the Northern Bank in December 2004, but there was far less concern that the funds would go into violence against the British state than there would have been a few years earlier.[37] The arrest in 2001 in Colombia of three people alleged to be senior figures connected to the PIRA, for allegedly assisting the FARC Marxist guerrillas, gave rise to much speculation about global alliances (drugs for terrorist expertise), almost sabotaging the Anglo-Irish Peace Agreement; despite their acquittal on the more serious terrorism charges being overturned by the Colombian Court of Appeal in 2004, they returned to the Irish Republic and have not been extradited.

---

[37] There was even less concern when the Northern Bank recalled and changed its banknotes, making most of the stolen ones valueless. Republicans in the South were raided in connection with the robbery, and large quantities of different notes seized.

As so often is the case, the linkages remain open to serious question. There is much debate in the literature as to the strength of the organized crime-terrorism nexus (or continuum), some arguing that differences in motives mean there is little relationship, while others focus on similarities in methods (see Picarelli 2006 for a useful review). As with the general organized crime literature, there is a tendency to over-generalize the relationship and to try to upgrade the harmfulness of undesired activities by stating that it (e.g. product counterfeiting, fraud, or Internet gambling) could finance terrorism (as indeed it sometimes does). One major difference between organized criminals and some terrorists is the role played by suicide bombers in what is often viewed as the 'new Islamic terrorism': yet to the extent that the motives can properly be distinguished, nationalism and resistance to what is seen as Western cultural imperialism/invasion can be more significant than religious extremism. (Though recent attackers in Britain have been devout Muslims, revulsion at decadent Western values is common among British and non-British terrorists.) Page (2006) shows that of 41 Lebanese suicide bombers, only eight were Islamic fundamentalists; 27 were from leftist political groups; three were Christians; all were born in Lebanon. (See, for a good general review of what terrorists want, Richardson 2006.)

MONEY TALKS?

Much is made of the economic, 'money flow' links involved in terrorism: Napoleoni (2004) and Robinson (2002, 2003) write in terms of trillions of dollars. The truth is that almost any licit or illicit income-generating activity could finance terrorism. Here we ought to distinguish financing of (i) the infrastructure of global persuasion towards particular intolerant interpretations of Islam (e.g. Sunni Salafism, more often called Wahhabism); (ii) the infrastructure of terror—training camps, transporting people for general indoctrination and specific training (though this need not be overseas) as with white-collar and organized crimes, terrorist plots have been hatched during sporting activities or on 'adventure holidays' in the UK —and (iii) the usually modest operational expenditure on attacks. Whereas the first category involves major expenditure and the second significant costs, the third is more difficult. It is tempting to focus upon Western explosions: immediate operational costs totalled less than a thousand pounds in the case of the London bombings of 2005, a few thousand euros for the Madrid bombings of 2004, and US$400,000–500,000 for the '9/11' 'spectacular' (Levi 2007a). However, depending on one's definition of terrorism, weaponry used in the Middle East for rocket attacks does require more substantial expenditure, some of it being state-sponsored, as do gifts of around US$12,000 by Hizbollah to owners of every house in Lebanon totally destroyed by Israel in 2006. The National Commission (2004) indicates that prior to '9/11', the largest single al-Qāʿidah expense was support for the Taliban, estimated at about US$20 million per year. Bin Lāden (though not alone) also used money to train operatives in camps in Afghanistan, create terrorist networks and alliances, and support the jihadists and their families. These funds came primarily from Saudi business people and Bin Lāden's fabled but actually rather modest wealth, rather than from crime. Initial ideological persuasion and training may have come from such sources, but the London bombers needed no money from crime. There have been arrests for involvement in payment card fraud in the UK of Algerians, Sri Lankan Tamils, and other nationals involved in international networks supportive of terrorism (often nationalist rather than for the Muslim Caliphate), but it remains crucial to understand that financing a large movement and financing an individual suicide-bombing attack involve very different orders of magnitude of cost. Even the loosely applied term 'Islamic terrorism' covers a range of political affiliations, in addition to the conflicts between Sunni and Shi'a believers, that are most publicized in civil strife in contemporary Iraq. The tendency to conflate or ignore these conflicts in some official interpretations of linkages is criticized by Naylor (2006), who demonstrates in detail the complexities of ever-shifting relationships between Eastern and Western politicians, warlords, smugglers, and illicit markets, as well as the unintended consequences of American bankrolling of anti-Russian activists in Asia. He also stresses the contribution made by the USA, in particular, to funding the *mujahideen* and to supplying them with arms to fight the Russians, which later became unintended financing of terrorism against the West.[38]

The Provisional IRA (PIRA) and loyalist paramilitaries have traditionally obtained significant funds from crime ranging from extortion and owning/operating fruit machines to, at least from the 1990s, cross-border fuel-oil smuggling; but PIRA and Sinn Fein also obtained much funding from the Irish diaspora, at least until '9/11' shifted cultural awareness and legal controls over Noraid in the USA. (The same process led to action against Muslim aid to jihadists and, more controversially, to the prohibition in the USA and Europe of Islamic charities such as the Holy Land Foundation which was alleged to have given aid to banned organizations and to the families of suicide bombers.) Logically, the prohibition of legitimate political and charitable donations should reduce the scale of support for terrorists and for their families after the attacks and indoctrination, but drive potential terrorists to greater involvement in illegal-source activities: hence the interest in payment card fraud, which has fewer technical or social barriers to entry than other forms of blue/white-collar crime.

The terminology used to describe terrorism committed by those claiming to act in the name of Islam has shifted from the initial concept of Bin Lāden as orchestrating terrorism from the top of the 'Al-Qāʿidah' pyramid to seeing it as a combination of 'Al-Qāʿidah core', other (often conflicting) long-standing networks, and self-starting individuals and networks who are 'Al-Qāʿidah-inspired' but operate independently and without funding from Bin Lāden. Thus, Gunaratna (2007) argues that (as of 2006) what he describes as 'the al Qaeda movement' consists of three parts:

- the al-Qaeda group, founded by bin Laden and Abdullah Azzam in the late 1980s and severely weakened in the aftermath of the US invasion of Afghanistan;

- the al-Qaeda network, which is composed of the al-Qaeda group and thirty to forty associated groups located primarily in Africa, Asia, and the Middle East; and

- ideologically affiliated cells worldwide acting in the name of or inspired by al-Qaeda in pursuit of global jihad.

---

[38] For a critical review of Naylor's earlier work on terrorism, see Finckenauer (2006).

Although the global jihadi movement embodies the ambitions of al-Qaeda, he asserts, it is broader than the al-Qaeda movement and has surpassed al-Qaeda as the most significant threat to international security. Whereas Gunaratna (2007) and many other commentators see this as an evolution occurring as a response to improved international controls over terrorism, Naylor (2006) sees the entire 'Al-Qā'idah' issue as self-serving mythology created by Western intelligence agencies and politicians. Somewhere in between, Jackson *et al.* (2005a, 2005b) show how variable have been these changes in their review of evidence on the learning processes of terrorist organizations, while Caulkins *et al.* (forthcoming) indicate some sobering lessons from the War on Drugs to the War on Terror. This interpretative tension is endlessly reprised in media commentaries, for example in the course of the arrests in August 2006 of many people suspected of involvement in plots to blow up a dozen aircraft, with connections to Pakistan and alleged connections to 'Al-Qā'idah', but declared by all to be primarily plots by British Muslims in Britain. Many Muslims, especially young ones, are reportedly disposed to disbelieve these official accounts, citing as 'evidence' that many of the alleged plotters seemed quite normal in their daily behaviour (failing to comprehend that they themselves may be victims of the stereotyping of terrorists as being 'not like us', since the acknowledged '7/7' London bombers were also viewed as normal by their neighbours and families). What seems plain is that although there are transnational elements to terrorism (as it affects Europe), and both cultural inspiration and the learning of techniques may come from abroad (e.g. roadside bombings in Iraq, spreading elsewhere), terrorist attacks are no longer *dependent* on transnational migration by bombers themselves

THE EVOLUTION OF CRIME AND TERRORISM ORGANIZATION: SOME TENTATIVE CONCLUSIONS

The explanation of how and why crime groups develop in the way that they do is important, but the argument here has been that a focus on definitions of 'organized crime' and on which groups might or might not qualify as such[39] is unilluminating: it imposes a false (fantasy) grid of coherence on what is really a very diverse set of people and activities. As Wright (2006), Stelfox (2003), and Dorn *et al.* (1992) note, most of the images of criminal organization generated by the police—so often imported into policy-making, the media, and hence popular discourse—tend to reflect their own institutional organization, e.g. drugs squads. One may add that resource allocation also plays a part in shaping criminal opportunities and hence organization. Although the development of multi-crime-type 'serious/major crime units' looks as if it takes into account the complexity of criminal activities of crime networks, in practice such squads

---

[39] See Gregory (2003) for a critical and thoughtful discussion of the earlier UK classification system.

are dependent on where they can get human and technical intelligence from, and this may be more likely to come from the anti-drugs than from the anti-fraud arena. If the same criminal personnel are active in both types of crime, this may not matter (except in crime statistics) but if they are not, then this advantages some groups—particularly specialist fraudsters—against others.

The organization of crimes results from the interaction of crime opportunities, offender and prospective offender motivations, skills and networks, and control efforts (whether through the criminal law, administrative law or disruption). It is thus a *dynamic* process that evolves as offenders adapt (or fail to adapt) to their changing environment, including facilities offered by the legal commercial environment, such as air travel, container lorries and ships, car repair firms (Tremblay *et al.* 2001), payment card issuers and merchants (Levi 1998), telemarketing of 'investment opportunities' (Shover *et al.* 2003), and relationships with financial institutions and professionals (INCSR 2006; contributors to the Special Issue introduced by Levi *et al.* 2005; Levi and Reuter 2006). In some cases, for example 'missing trader' or 'carousel' VAT frauds, the opportunities result from structural weaknesses in EU regulations on how VAT is administered in intra-EU trades, resulting in billions of pounds of losses annually in the UK, only some of them known to be attributable to 'organized crime' figures in the conventional sense,[40] though they do meet the EU criteria for organized crime and feature as a major issue in the UK's Organized Crime Threat Assessment (SOCA 2006). HM Revenue and Customs in 2006 won permission from the EU to change the way it applies VAT to trades of mobile phones and computer chips, the favourites among fraudsters because they are of high value but are small in bulk. From early 2007, VAT is chargeable when the phones arrive at a retailer and will not be refundable when the goods cross an EU border: however the fraudsters may simply change the scam to products that are not covered by this change in regulations. There are many cases where crime networks adapt to police preventative tactics even in the course of one series of frauds; and the losses of drugs or excise-evaded shipments constitute mainly opportunity costs, from which higher members of crime groups either develop counter-intelligence strategies or just accept risks and losses of (often poor Third World female) 'mules'.

In this respect, in the shuffling of the pack of cards that constitutes the policy process, the prevention/enforcement tactic of 'disruption' may turn out to the joker. One of the

---

[40] Information from author interviews with Revenue and Customs officials. Missing trader fraud is a complex VAT scam, involving cross-border sales, typically of high-value products such as mobile phones or computer chips. The fraud is perpetrated by an importer who supposedly collects VAT on behalf of the government when the goods are sold in the UK. Instead, the importer becomes a 'missing trader' who pockets the tax and disappears. The goods can then be exported, at which point the government is expected to pay a VAT refund. When the fraud is repeated many times, it is known as 'carousel fraud'. Goods are imported repeatedly and re-exported in a series of contrived transactions, with VAT stolen by the importer and a refund claimed by the exporter every time the goods are moved to another state. Sometimes, the goods are non-existent and are simply created on paper. Trade figures have shown a rapid escalation in fraudulent cross-border trade, suggesting that the Exchequer's losses from the fraud were two to three billion pounds in 2005–6. In August 2006, official data showed that exports linked to missing trader fraud rose by almost 50 per cent in the second quarter to a record £9.7bn. About £1 in every £10 of Britain's exports in 2006 have been linked to the fraud.

many unanswered questions about the policy shift to disruption is whether it may reinforce (reward) tendencies for 'organizing' criminals to build greater redundancy, subcontracting, and disposability into their activities, with stronger 'cut-outs' (Dorn *et al.* 1998) between core and non-core human assets, aiming at greater protection for the former (whom disruption regimes may find it unnecessary and not cost-effective to prosecute) whilst accepting 'shrinkage' in the latter (costs of doing business). If so, one might ask about the costs and benefits of such policies: is a durable 'network' (as seen from the police/intelligence point of view) better or worse than a passing 'organization', and if so, why? Similar thoughts are beginning to surface in relation to anti-terrorist policies, where a shift from political dialogue to the elimination of exposed elements, etc. might be expected to elicit not only a series of mistakes but also the creation of defences-in-depth. (Doing nothing is not an option.) The question of the impacts of enforcement on the forms of organization of illegal activities is not a new one but it is a troublesome one and, unfortunately, it is typically posed after the event. (Never have we read a timely policy-orientated discussion of how a proposed innovation in control arrangements might re-shape crime, although there have been such discussions in relation to international security, even if the warnings sometimes have not been heeded.)

Aggregate changes in routine activities, fashion, decriminalization, and prevention technology—as well as in criminal networks—may produce changes or apparent changes in modes of 'organized criminality'. Yet though all the ethnographic, policing, and survey data point to the dramatic rise in the size of illegal drug markets, the periodization of criminal organization is not easy.

If the world of crime were to parallel Elias's analysis of the civilizing process, one might expect a drift away from *macho* criminality to the softer arts of the fraudster, where less police interest and lower sentences can be found. However though there has been a significant rise in frauds available to traditional criminals, such as insurance and payment card fraud, there appear to be cultural and skill barriers to entry into many areas of fraud which have inhibited this transformation for most predatory and market criminals. Several armed robbers turned to long-firm (bankruptcy) frauds as early as the late 1960s, and later to credit card fraud, social security fraud, and even to carousel, VAT, and other frauds against the European Union—either alongside or subsequent to drug-dealing—but this move into the moderately upmarket areas of fraud has hardly dented those other types of crime, so arguably it is expansion rather than displacement. In focusing on these shifts by criminals with 'previous', we may risk neglecting systematic frauds and other crimes by people who are not previously known to the authorities. Some Russian crime syndicates (including wealthy business people in the USA) have shown the capacity to engage in vast international frauds, but so too have long-term Caribbean and Swiss residents operating businesses globally for decades without being defined as part of the 'organized crime problem' (Block and Weaver 2004; van Duyne and Block 1994; Williams 2001).

An interview-based study of bankruptcy fraudsters found substantial variations in the organization of that form of crime during the 1960s and 1970s, but since the sixteenth century, fraudsters in particular have found cross-border crime attractive because it creates problems of legal jurisdiction, investigative cost, and practical interest by police, prosecutors, and even creditors themselves (Levi 1981, 2007b). European Union harmonization and expansion does not itself make any difference to this, except (1) in providing new pretexts or 'storylines' for fraudsters to use to get credit or investment, and (2) inasmuch as it changes the structures of control, e.g. changing customs regulations makes missing trader intra-Community frauds or VAT evasion easier or harder, or the UK's ratification of the European Convention on Mutual Assistance makes cooperation and conviction easier.

Hobbs (1997) and Coles (2001) stress the importance to serious crime group activity in the UK of fluidity and brokerage roles—of temporary social arrangements—in putting people and skills together. Indeed, it is these connectors or 'nodes' rather than the most central or highest-ranking figures who may be the most crucial lubricants of serious crime (Jackson *et al.* 1996). The rapid career development of some major criminals demonstrates that the rewards (and risks) of playing such a key entrepreneurial role can be very high (Barnes *et al.* 2000). Thus, while acknowledging the importance of missing data about the waxing and waning of relationships over time and place (Sparrow 1991; McAndrew, 1999), Coles (2001: 586) argues:

> It is possible to contemplate the situation where unsophisticated groups fail to use brokers and have no links to other groups; more sophisticated groups, particularly large and stable groups might employ a number of relatively static individuals as brokers; and, the most sophisticated, aggressively entrepreneurial groups would utilise a range of capable brokers operating themselves in chains of brokers. The identification of any varying usage of brokers in this way might provide an indication of the sophistication or degree of 'organization' of a criminal network.

The role of fences, criminal professionals (accountants, lawyers), money-launderers, and transportation firms may be important in facilitating networks, though they themselves may have to be 'brokered'. Such an enforcement intelligence methodology may bring increased risks for those upperworld members whose connections with the underworld may not previously have been noticed: but if neither the person nor the activity is part of the police and intelligence surveillance set, they may still remain safe from intervention (see Gill 2000).

Gradually (and see Sutton 1998, for a valuable analysis of this in relation to stolen property markets), criminologists have begun to see 'the causes of crime' as including an analysis of how crime is organized socially and technically. This fuses the neglected traditions of gang/subculture theory with situational opportunity theory, especially in its improved recent formulations (Clarke 1997; Clarke and Homel 1997; Clarke and Guerette 2003) in showing how the forms of crime are shaped by the motivational and cultural environments in which they occur, which facilitate and/or inhibit the development of highly organized crime, whether or not accompanied by offender versatility. To understand how this is possible, we need to examine crime as a business process, requiring funding, technical skills, distribution mechanisms, and money-handling facilities. The larger the criminal business, the more likely it is that all these elements will be required, with the special business problem that what they are doing is illegal and, if caught and convicted, they—and their bankers or lawyers—could all go to jail for very long times as 'organized criminals' or 'organizers of terrorism'[41]. On the other hand, if they manage all of these business functions well, then jail is less than likely—even though their business may be buffeted by disruption from post-policing agencies such as SOCA. (See, for example, the Organised Crime Prevention Orders proposed by the Home Office (Home Office 2006) and other private and public sector preventative measures discussed by Levi and Maguire (2004) and by van De Bunt and van der Schoot (2003).)

This chapter acknowledges that there are international groupings engaged in the commission of very serious social harms, though not all of them are labelled 'organized criminals' or 'terrorists'. Despite the apocalyptic visions not only of the political Right but of sociologists such as Castells (1998), however, it seems unlikely that Albanian, Chinese, Colombian, and/or Russian crime 'cartels' will dominate the West with their economic power (though other states may be captured by corrupt kleptocracies). More likely is an increasing number of financial attacks on economic targets—by infiltration and corruption of staff domestically and in outsourced locations overseas, as well as via e-attacks—and a continuing devolved and networked supply of illegal goods and services, with some larger operators in countries where the evidential rules or the inefficiency/corruption of officials make proof of involvement too difficult. Though judgements of incidence and prevalence of threats may differ, there is general agreement that (at least in the context of well-established and non-corrupt states with effective policing and regulatory agencies) networked crime is more efficient than hierarchical 'planned centralism' for long-term criminal survival (Levi and Naylor 2000; Williams 2001): this may also apply to terrorism (Arquilla and Ronfeldt 2001; Jackson *et al.* 2005a, 2005b). For past decades, many criminologists felt safe enough making observations to the effect that, for criminals intending to stay in business for a long time, unless they are extraordinarily gifted and/or live in an extraordinarily corrupt haven, 'small is beautiful' (Dorn *et al.* 1992; Levi 1981, 2007b).

However, all these 'either/or' judgements (is there a high level of organization or not?) may be undermined by modern communications, one of the effects of which is to dissolve notions of place, belonging, cooperating, and organizing. If young men in the north or Midlands of England watch television or videos and decide to take a hand in international relations by bombing central London, then perhaps old categories are breaking down and one should expect some diversity in economic crime too. This is aided by the relatively risk-free zone of experimentation in economic crime attempts, whether by e-crime or more conventional forms, so long as experiments do not involve hacking into defence establishments or other critical national infrastructure, which arouse the concern of the authorities transnationally.

As the legal economy demonstrates, the existence of global markets does not imply that multinational conglomerates are the only or even best-suited organizations to

---

[41] Roach *et al.* (2005) and Clarke and Newman (2005) seek to apply this sort of model to terrorism, though it remains to be seen how fruitful this will be in practice.

supply criminal consumer needs. When the illegality of the activities imposes severe constraints on financing, recruitment, advertising, sales, and the collection and consolidation of funds, criminal growth may be inhibited. What is important (for crime control as well as academic understanding) is to appreciate the subtlety, complexity, and depth of field of the organization of crimes. In doing so, we should bear in mind that many different forms of organization can coexist in parallel, and that to be an 'organized criminal' does not mean that one has to be a member of an 'organized crime syndicate'. There is no Blofeld figure or SMERSH collective organizing 'crime' or 'terrorism' worldwide: rather there are layers of different forms of enterprise criminal, some undertaking wholly illegal activities and others mixing the legal and illegal depending on contacts, trust, and assessment of risks from enforcement in particular national markets. Which of these we choose to call 'organized criminals' is a matter of judgement (and libel laws),[42] and we need to be clearer about which segments of the criminal market we are referring to before we can be sure we are discussing the same thing when we use the tern 'organized crime'. In fact, it might be better not to rely on the term, or alternatively to rely on the fact that it does not have a stable meaning. As for terrorism, unlike most forms of organized criminality, there are often diasporas, indeed world-wide communities—either sharing religious or other ideological affinity or, more broadly, sharing a disgust at state policies—who may regard violence as heroic or at least as rational, given closures of other avenues: a key issue is what potential terrorists and their supporters regard as 'legitimate targets'. There is an active process of social redefinition/disinformation by media-savvy people on both sides of every 'war'. Suicide bombers need no infrastructure to protect their identities after the fact, and the availability of recipes for explosives on the Internet as well as underground literature means that there is less need of skilled engineers than used to be the case in 'liberation wars' in

---

[42] A fascinating insight into some of the problems of media commentary in the UK, contrasted with the USA, is provided by the case of *Loutchansky* v. *Times Newspapers Ltd and others* (QBD, 27 April 2001) [2001] All E.R. (D.) 207 (Apr.); *Loutchansky* v. *Times Newspapers (Nos 2–5)* [2001] EWCA Civ 1805, CA. In that case, the judge found that *The Times* had libelled an Uzbekhi businessman in 1999 over reported links with Russian organized crime, despite media reports of the involvement of the Bank of New York in laundering the proceeds of criminal activity in Russia; media reports of suspicions about and investigations into serious crimes allegedly committed by Dr Loutchansky, which have resulted in his exclusion from various jurisdictions (including the UK); a statement by the then director of the CIA about the claimant's company, Nordex, being associated with Russian criminal activity; convictions of Dr Loutchansky by a Latvian court in 1983 for offences of dishonesty; various reports in the media and the contents of reports by intelligence services. (Information provided to and by the author Jeffrey Robinson, 2002, was rejected as a well-researched and reasonable foundation for the articles.) In *Loutchansky* v. *Times Newspapers Ltd and others* (*No. 2*), 5 December 2001, the Court of Appeal partially rejected the judge's conclusions, but in this and other cases (e.g. involving the former Conservative Party Treasurer, Lord Ashcroft, and his corporate dealings in Belize), the perils of even suggesting that a prominent public figure is suspected of organized crime activities are plain. Recently, limiting the libel-friendly image discussed above, the House of Lords held in *Jameel and others* v. *Wall Street Journal Europe* [2006] UKHL 44 that 'where the topic of a media investigation was of public importance, relevant allegations that could not subsequently be proved true should not attract libel damages if they had been published responsibly. The media was entitled to publish defamatory allegations as part of its duty of neutral reporting of news, or if, after investigation, they were believed to have substance and to raise matters of public interest'. It remains to be seen what the impact of this will be in practice, but it brings the UK closer to the USA and perhaps was influenced by the risk that the UK would become the global forum of choice for the suppression of critical media reportage.

Northern Ireland or Spain, or in many developing countries. The relative success of Hizbollah in the 2006 Lebanese conflict illustrates the ways that well-organized but dispersed networks can outwit conventional techniques.

The proposition that criminal organization/networking has changed over the years—with a shift from solid hierarchy or collegiality to the chameleon-like flexible networks —may reflect dominant academic and law enforcement opinion (though the latter, like governments, appears publicly glued to the language of 'organized crime'). However this proposition is by no means proven. To test it, we would need the following: (i) a distinct and replicable method for exploring and demonstrating criminals' management of their affairs, in relation to organization/networking; (ii) sufficient confidence in that method to be able to say that it could track changes over time in forms of organization/networking; (iii) to be clearer than perhaps we are at present whether the proposition would refer to 'all' forms of serious crime (corporate, public corruption, terrorism, state crime) or only to particular aspects (drugs- and people-trafficking, major VAT/excise tax frauds); and (iv) to delineate to which periods of time and corresponding crime control/policing/private-sector regulatory policies we are referring. For example, we might wish to contrast 1990s developments (including regulation and policing, national and EU Third Pillar and international cooperation), with the current period, post-'9/11', with its mix of (a) US-driven policies connecting 'failed states', anti-terrorism, the terrorism-OC linkage, and business clean-up agendas, and (b) continuing tendencies to European integration (Frontex border guards, Europol Joint Investigation Teams, European Court of Justice (2005), etc.).

As things stand, in spite of the abundant scholarship reviewed here, we have barely set out the methods for such testing, let alone applied them to specific periods, policies, and crime sectors: hence no generalization is safe. The field is open for research students as well as established scholars to make a real contribution here, both in fine-tuning methodology and in terms of careful focused efforts to fill the knowledge gaps. It could be useful to focus our professional communication capabilities—websites, journal special issues, etc.—on first attaining some degree of common language on this recurrent question, moving on to collate sectoral and then possibly general answers. The fruits should be of interest in a practical policy sense as well as moving forward the discipline of explaining patterns of serious criminality.

All areas of criminological explanation are difficult, but accounting for changes in how and why people get together to commit a large range of serious crimes for profit and (by violence and the threat of violence) for political/religious change is indeed challenging. This chapter has involved us in thinking, first, about concepts and the utility of many terms in common use; second, the epistemology of how we would recognize 'organized crime' if we saw it; third, what similarities plausibly exist between the forms of organization of terrorism and of organized crime; and finally, what we would need to get a better appreciation of the influences (including criminal justice and prevention influences) on the patterning of serious crime. The fact that many of these questions are not conceptually or empirically settled may distress readers looking for the sort of confident clarity conveyed in some textbooks and media accounts: but as eyewitness testimony research shows, there is no correlation between confidence and accuracy, and if understanding is to increase, it is better to start with an awareness of what we do not reliably know.

■ SELECTED FURTHER READING

There are several sorts of approach to the study of organized crime and its control, spanning political science, international criminal law and international relations, social network analysis, socio-legal studies, etc.

Clear analysis of the organization of crime is to be found in Naylor, R. Tom (2003), 'Towards a general theory of profit-driven crimes', *British Journal of Criminology*, 43: 81–101. A useful textbook (though conceptually underdeveloped) is Wright, A. (2006), *Organized Crime* (Cullompton, Devon: Willan), and good collections of essays may be found in Edwards, A., and Gill, P. (eds) (2003), *Transnational Organized Crime: Perspectives on Global Security* (London: Routledge); Reichel, P. (ed.) (2005), *Handbook of Transnational Crime & Justice* (Thousand Oaks, Cal.: Sage) and the annual European collections edited by Van Duyne and colleagues, published by Wolf Legal Publishers, www.wolfpublishers.nl/.

In addition to national governmental websites, useful websites and bibliographic sources include www.american.edu/traccc/resources/publications.html (especially for material on corruption and on eastern Europe), the Canadian Nathanson Center (www.yorku.ca/nathanson/default.htm); www.organized-crime.de/; www.assessingorganisedcrime.net/; and the United Nations (www.unodc.org/unodc/index.html).

A short historical overview that has never been bettered is McIntosh, M. (1975), *The Organization of Crime* (London: Macmillan). Also useful is von Lampe, K. (2006), 'The Interdisciplinary Dimensions of the Study of Organized Crime', *Trends in Organized Crime*, 9(3): 77–95. Key works on the Italian Mafia and Mafia-type associations are Gambetta, D. (1994), *The Sicilian Mafia* (Cambridge, Mass.: Harvard University Press); and Arlacchi, P. (1986), *Mafia Business: the Mafia Ethic and the Spirit of Capitalism* (London: Verso) (though this was given a certain piquancy by criticism of Dr Arlacchi's governance style prior to his resignation as Executive Director of the UN Drugs and Crime Programme at the end of 2001). These Italian issues are nicely if densely integrated into general organized crime literature in Paoli, L. (2002), 'The paradoxes of organized crime', *Crime, Law and Social Change*, 37: 51–97.

The threat assessment issues are more clearly divided between those who consider that there is a serious threat from organized crime (whether in a hierarchical or a networked form) and those who are sceptical and see it as a loose market mechanism. Good sophisticated exemplars of the former may be found in Williams, P. (2001), 'Transnational criminal networks', in J. Arquilla and D. Ronfeldt (eds), *Networks and Netwars: the Future of Terror, Crime and Militancy* (Santa Monica, Cal.: RAND) (and in other publications in the journals *Transnational Organized Crime* and *Global Crime*). Good illustrations of the sceptical position may be found in Beare, M. (ed.) (2003), *Critical Reflections on Transnational Organized Crime, Money Laundering and Corruption* (Toronto: Toronto University Press); van Duyne, P. (1996), 'The Phantom and Threat of Organized Crime', *Crime, Law and Social Change*, 24: 341–77; and Naylor, R. (2004), *Wages of Crime: Black Markets, Illegal Finance, and the Underworld Economy* (Ithaca, N.Y.: Cornell University Press) (and in other publications in *Crime, Law and*

Social Change). A classic American sceptical empirical review is Reuter, P. (1983), *Disorganized crime: Illegal markets and the Mafia* (Cambridge, Mass.: MIT Press). There has been a shift from historical 'organized crime situation reports' to more forward-looking 'organized threat assessments', and official annual Threat Assessments by the Council of Europe, Europol, and the UK Serious Organised Crime Agency are available from their websites and are cited in the References. There are also reports elsewhere, for example the US State Department's International Narcotics Control Strategy Report.

For those interested in the financial aspects of organized crime and terrorism, good reviews may be found in Blum, J., Levi, M., Naylor, R. T., and Williams, P. (1998), *Financial Havens, Banking Secrecy and Money-Laundering* (New York, N.Y.: United Nations Office for Drug Control and Crime Prevention); van Duyne, P., and Levi, M. (2005), *Drugs and Money* (London: Routledge); Levi, M., and Reuter, P. (2006), 'Money Laundering: A Review of Current Controls and their Consequences', in M. Tonry (ed.), *Crime and Justice: an Annual Review of Research*, vol. 34 (Chicago: Chicago University Press), and in Naylor's *Wages of Crime* (above). For particular focuses on terrorism, see contributions to T. Biersteker and S. Eckert (eds) (2007), *Countering the Financing of Terrorism* (London: Routledge) and Naylor, R. (2006), *Satanic Purses: Money, Myth, and Misinformation in the War on Terror* (Montreal: McGill-Queen's University Press), though these perspectives are heavily disputed.

For British material on the organization of crime and networks, useful articles are: Coles, N. (2001), 'It's not *what* you know—it's *who* you know that counts: analysing serious crime groups as social networks', *British Journal of Criminology*, 41: 580– 94; Hobbs, D. (1998), 'Going Down the Glocal: the local context of organised crime', *The Howard Journal*, 37(4): 407–22; and Hobbs, D. (2001), 'The Firm: organizational logic and criminal culture on a shifting terrain', *British Journal of Criminology*, 41: 549–60.

For good drugs-focused work on organization of crime, see Dorn, N., Oette, L., and White, S. (1998), 'Drugs Importation and the Bifurcation of Risk: Capitalization, Cut Outs and Organized Crime', *British Journal of Criminology*, 38: 537–60; Dorn, N., Levi, M., and King, L. (2005), *Literature review on upper level drug trafficking*, Home Office RDS OLR 22/05, www.homeoffice.gov.uk/rds/pdfs05/rdsolr2205.pdf; and Pearson, G., and Hobbs, D. (2001), *Middle Market Drug Distribution*, Home Office Research Study 227 (London: Home Office). See also the Royal Society of Arts' review of drug supply in the UK, www.rsadrugscommission.org.uk/pdf/supply_of_drugs_0605.pdf, and the drugs reports of the Beckley Foundation, www.beckleyfoundation.org/policy/reports.html. For an illuminating journalistic account, see Barnes, T., Elias, R., and Walsh, P. (2000), *Cocky: The Rise and Fall of Curtis Warren, Britain's Biggest Drug Baron* (London: Milo).

Those interested in the development of criminal techniques might find useful: Gill, M. (2001), 'The Craft of Robbers of Cash-in-transit Vans: Crime Facilitators and the Entrepreneurial Approach', *International Journal of the Sociology of Law*, 29: 277–91; Levi, M. (1998), 'Organising plastic fraud: enterprise criminals and the side-stepping of fraud prevention', *The Howard Journal*, 37(4): 423–38; and Tremblay, P., Talon, B., and Hurley, D. (2001), 'Body Switching and related adaptations in the resale of stolen vehicles', *British Journal of Criminology*, 41: 561–79.

Dutch criminology has generated some excellent criminological work, and a good overview in English is Fijnaut, C., Bovenkerk, F., Bruinsma, G., and van der Bunt, H. (1998), *Organised Crime in the Netherlands* (The Hague: Kluwer). For a more specialized study, see Zaich, D. Zaitch, D. (2002), *Trafficking Cocaine. Colombian Drug Entrepreneurs in the Netherlands* (The Hague: Kluwer Law International).

The policing of organized crime has been examined mostly in the context of drugs, but useful reviews include contributions to Beare (above), Harfield, C. (2006), 'SOCA: A paradigm shift in British policing', *British Journal of Criminology*, 46(4): 743–61; Levi, M. (2003), 'Organised and Financial Crime', in T. Newburn (ed.), *Handbook of Policing* (Cullompton, Devon: Willan), and Sheptycki, J. (2000), *Issues in Transnational Policing* (London: Routledge). For the policing of terrorism, see T. Newburn and M. Matassa (2003), 'Policing and Terrorism', in T. Newburn (ed.), *Handbook of Policing* (Cullompton, Devon: Willan).

For discussions of organized crime prevention, see, reviewing the Dutch experience, Bunt, H. van de, and Schoot, C. van der (2003), *Prevention of Organised Crime: a Situational Approach* (Cullompton, Devon: Willan), and Schoot, C. van der (2005), *Organised Crime Prevention in the Netherlands*, https://ep.eur.nl/bitstream/1765/7385/1/manuscript_proefschrift_cathelijne_4_december_2005_bladwijze.pdf; and, more generally, Levi, M. and Maguire, M. (2004), 'Reducing and preventing organised crime: An evidence-based critique', *Crime, Law and Social Change*, 41(5): 397–469. See also Hicks, D. C. (1998), 'Thinking about Organized Crime Prevention', *Journal of Contemporary Criminal Justice*, 14(4): 325–51.

Finally, on terrorism, Richardson, L. (2006), *What Terrorists Want* (London: John Murray) is a well written and intelligent overview by an Irish-born academic working in the USA. Burke, J. (2004), *Al-Qaeda* (London: Penguin) and Atwan, A. (2006), *The Secret History of Al-Qa'ida* (London: Saqi) provide good, readable analysis based on journalistic ethnography and interviews. For stimulating, in many ways diametrically opposed accounts, see Napoleoni, L. (2004), *T£rror Inc.* (London: Penguin) and Naylor (above), *Satanic Purses* (2006). In a more conventional mode, see a review by Wilkinson, P. www.st-andrews.ac.uk/intrel/research/cstpv/pdffiles/ Foreign%20Affairs%20Commission.pdf, and the attempt to apply situational crime prevention to terrorism by Clarke, R., and Newman, G. (2005), *Outsmarting Our Enemies*, New York: Praeger. There are a plethora of terrorism websites, mostly American, but British ones include: www.chathamhouse.org.uk and www.rusi.org/.

■ REFERENCES

ALLDRIDGE, P. (2003), *Money Laundering Law—a Liberal Critique*, Oxford: Hart Publishing.

ANDREAS, P. (2000), *Border Games: Policing the US-Mexico Divide*, New York: Cornell University Press.

——and NADELMANN, E. (2006), *Policing the Globe: Criminalization and Crime Control in International Relations*, New York: Oxford University Press.

ANECHIARICO, F., and JACOBS, J. (1998), *The Pursuit of Absolute Integrity*, Chicago: University of Chicago Press.

ARA (2006), *Annual Report 2005/06*, London: Assets Recovery Agency. Available at www.assetsrecovory.gov.uk/NR/rdonlyres/8D8413B8-B0FE-4A9F-AA02-2E2A9771A809/0/ARAAnnual Report06_new.pdf.

ARLACCHI, P. (1986), *Mafia Business: the Mafia Ethic and the Spirit of Capitalism*, London: Verso.

——(1998), 'Some observations on illegal markets', in V. Ruggiero, N. South, and I. Taylor (eds), *The New European Criminology*, London: Routledge.

ARONOWITZ, A. (2001), 'Smuggling and Trafficking in Human Beings: The Phenomenon, the Markets that Drive it and the Organisations that Promote it', *European Journal on Criminal Policy and Research*, 9(2): 163–95.

ARQUILLA, J., and RONFELDT, D. (2001), 'The advent of netwar (revisited)', in J. Arquilla and D. Ronfeldt (eds), *Networks and Netwars: the Future of Terror, Crime and Militancy*, Santa Monica, Cal.: Rand Corporation.

BARNES, T., ELIAS, R., and WALSH, P. (2000), *Cocky: the Rise and Fall of Curtis Warren Britain's Biggest Drug Baron*, London: Milo.

BEARE, M. (ed.) (2003), *Critical Reflections on Transnational Organized Crime, Money Laundering and Corruption*, Toronto: Toronto University Press.

BERDAL, M., and SERRANO, M. (eds) (2002), *Transnational Organized Crime: New Challenges to International Security*, Boulder, Cal.: Lynne Rienner.

BIERSTEKER, T., and ECKERT, S. (2007), *Countering the Financing of Global Terrorism*, London: Routledge.

BLACK, C., VAN DER BEKEN, T., and de RUYVER, B. (2000), *Measuring Organised Crime in Belgium*, Antwerp: Maklu.

BLOCK, A., and CHAMBLISS, W. (1981), *Organizing Crime*, New York, Elsevier.

BLUM, J., LEVI, M., and NAYLOR, R. T. (1998), *Financial Havens, Banking Secrecy and Money-Laundering*, New York, N.Y.: United Nations Office for Drug Control and Crime Prevention.

BOVENKERK, F. (2007), 'Half-baked Legalization Won't Work', in F. Bovenkerk and M. Levi (eds), *The Organized Crime Community*, Dordrecht: Springer.

——and YESILGÖZ, Y. (1998), *De Maffia van Turkije*, Amsterdam: Meulenhoff.

BUNT, H. VAN DE, and SCHOOT, C. VAN DER (2003), *Prevention of Organised Crime: a Situational Approach*, Cullompton, Devon: Willan.

BURKE, J. (2004), *Al-Qaeda*, London: Penguin.

——(2006), *On The Road to Kandahar*, London: Penguin.

CASTELLS, M., (1998), *End Of Millennium*, Oxford: Blackwell.

CAULKINS, J., KLEIMAN, M., and REUTER, P. (forthcoming), 'Lessons of the "War" on Drugs for the "War" on Terrorism', in A. Howitt and R. Pangi (eds), *Preparing for Domestic Terrorism*, Cambridge, Mass.: MIT Press.

CHAMBLISS, W. (1989), 'State-Organized Crime—the American Society of Criminology, 1998 Presidential Address', *Criminology*, 27: 183–208.

CHATTOE, E., and HAMILL, H. (2005), 'It's Not *Who* You Know' — It's What You Know About People You *Don't* Know That Counts: Extending the Analysis of Crime Groups as Social Networks', *British Journal of Criminology*, 45: 860–76.

CHIN, KO-LIN (1996), *Chinatown Gangs: Extortion, Enterprise, and Ethnicity*, New York, N.Y.: Oxford University Press.

CLARKE, R. (1997), 'Introduction', in R. Clarke (ed.), *Situational Crime Prevention: Successful Case Studies*, New York: Harrow and Heston.

——and GUERETTE, R. (2003), 'Product life cycles and crime: automated teller machines and robbery', *Security Journal*,16(1): 7–18.

——and HOMEL, R. (1997), 'A revised classification of situational crime prevention techniques', in S. Lab (ed.), *Crime Prevention at a Cross-roads*, Cincinnati, Ohio: Anderson.

——and NEWMAN, G. (2002), *Outsmarting Our Enemies*, New York: Praeger.

CLOWARD, R., and OHLIN, L. (1970), *Delinquency and Opportunity*, Glencoe, Ill.: Free Press.

COHEN, A. K. (1977), 'The concept of criminal organisation', *British Journal of Criminology*, 17: 97–111.

COHEN, S. (2002), *Folk Devils and Moral Panics: Creation of Mods and Rockers*, London: Routledge.

COLES, N. (2001), 'It's not *what* you know—it's *who* you know that counts: analysing serious crime groups as social networks', *British Journal of Criminology*, 41: 580—594.

COUNCIL OF EUROPE (2005), *Organised Crime Situation Report 2005*, Strasbourg, Council of Europe. Available at www.coe.int/t/e/legal_affairs/legal_co%2Doperation/combating_economic_crime/8_organised_crime/documents/Report2005E.pdf.

CORNISH, D. (1994), 'The procedural analysis of offending and its relevance for situational prevention', in R. Clarke (ed.), *Crime Prevention Studies*, Monsey: Criminal Justice Press.

CRESSEY, D. (1969), *Theft of the nation; the structure and operations of organised crime in America*, New York: Harper & Row.

CUELLAR, M. (2003), 'The Tenuous Relationship Between the Fight Against Money Laundering and the Disruption of Criminal Finance', *Journal of Criminal Law and Criminology*, Winter/Spring, 93(2–3): 311–466.

DOIG, A. (2006), *Fraud*, Cullompton, Devon: Willan.

DORN, N. (2003), 'Proteiform criminalities: the formation of organised crime as organisers' responses to developments in four fields of control', in A. Edwards, and P. GILL, (eds), *Transnational Organised Crime*, London: Routledge.

——and LEVI, M. (forthcoming), 'European private security, corporate investigation and military services: collective security, market regulation and structuring the public sphere', *Policing and Society*.

——, ——, and KING, L. (2005), *Literature review on upper level drug trafficking*, Home Office RDS OLR 22/05.

——MURJI, K., and SOUTH, N. (1992), *Traffickers*, London: Routledge.

——OETTE, L., and WHITE, S. (1998), 'Drugs Importation and the Bifurcation of Risk: Capitalization, Cut Outs and Organized Crime', *British Journal of Criminology*, 38: 537–60.

EUROPEAN COURT OF JUSTICE (2005), Judgment Of The Court (Grand Chamber), Action for annulment—Articles 29 EU, 31(e) EU, 34 EU and 47 EU—Framework Decision 2003/80/JHA, 13 September, Luxemburg: European Court of Justice. Available at http://curia.europa.eu.

EUROPOL (2006), *Organised Crime Threat Assessment 2006*, The Hague: Europol.

FIJNAUT, C., and PAOLI, L. (eds) (2004), *Organised Crime in Europe*, Dordrecht: Springer.

——, BOVENKERK, F., BRUINSMA, G., and VAN DER BUNT, H. (1998), *Organised Crime in the Netherlands*, The Hague : Kluwer.

FINCKENAUER, J. (2006), 'Review of Wages of Crime', *Crime, Law and Social Change*, 45(3): 27–30.

——and ALBANESE, J. (2005), 'Organized crime in North America', in P. Reichel (ed.) *Handbook of Transnational Crime & Justice*, Thousand Oaks, Cal.: Sage.

——and WARING, E. (1999), *Russian Mafia in America*, Boston, Mass.: Northeastern University Press.

FIORENTINI, G., and PELTZMAN, S. (eds) (1995), *The Economics of Organised Crime*, Cambridge: Cambridge University Press.

FRIMAN, R., and ANDREAS, P. (eds) (1999), *The Illicit Global Economy and State Power*, Lanham, Md.: Rowman and Littlefield.

GALEOTTI, M. (2004), 'The Russian "Mafiya": Consolidation and Globalisation', *Global Crime*, 6(1): 54–69.

GAMBETTA, D. (1994), *The Sicilian Mafia*, Cambridge, Mass.: Harvard University Press.

GEOPOLITICAL DRUG DISPATCH (2001), Special issue of *Crime, Law and Social Change*.

GILL, M. (2001), 'The Craft of Robbers of Cash-in-transit Vans: Crime Facilitators and the Entrepreneurial Approach', *International Journal of the Sociology of Law*, 29: 277–91.

GILL, P. (2000), *Rounding Up the Usual Suspects?*, Aldershot: Ashgate.

GILMORE, W. (2004), *Dirty Money: The Evolution of Money Laundering Counter-Measures*, 3rd edn, Strasbourg: Council of Europe Publishing.

GOMEZ-CESPEDES, A. (1999), 'Organised crime in Mexico', in F. Brookman, L. Noaks, *et al.* (eds),

Qualitative Research in Criminology, Brookfield, Vt.: Ashgate.

GRAY, P. (2003), *Al-Qaeda and What it Means to be Modern*, London: Faber and Faber.

GREGORY, F. (2003), 'Classify, Report and Measure: the UK Organised Crime Notification Scheme', in A. Edwards and P. Gill (eds), *Transnational Organised Crime*, London: Routledge.

GRUTER. P., and VAN DE MHEEN, D. (2005), 'Dutch cocaine trade: the perspective of Rotterdam cocaine retail dealers', *Crime, Law and Social Change*, 44(1): 19–33.

GUNARATNA, R. (2007), 'The evolution of Al Qaeda', in T. Biersteker and S. Eckert (eds), *Countering the Financing of Terrorism*, London: Routledge.

HARFIELD, C. (2006), 'SOCA: A paradigm shift in British policing', *British Journal of Criminology*, 46(4): 743–61.

HAWKINS, G. (1969), 'God and the Mafia', *The Public Interest*, 14: 24–51.

HICKS, D. C. (1998), 'Thinking About Organized Crime Prevention', *Journal of Contemporary Criminal Justice*, 14(4): 325–51.

HILL, P. (2003), *The Japanese Mafia: Yakuza, Law and the State*, Oxford: Oxford University Press.

HOBBS, D. (1997), 'Professional crime: change, continuity, and the enduring myth of the Underworld', *Sociology*, 31(1): 57–72.

——(1998), 'Going Down the Glocal: the local context of organised crime', *The Howard Journal*, 37(4): 407–22.

——(2000), 'Researching Serious Crime', in R. D. King and E. Wincup (eds), *Doing Research on Crime and Justice*, Oxford: Oxford University Press.

——(2001), 'The Firm: organizational logic and criminal culture on a shifting terrain', *British Journal of Criminology*, 41: 549–60.

——(2004), 'Organised Crime in the UK: in C. Fijnaut and L. Padi (eds), *Organised Crime in Europe*, Dordrecht: Springer.

HOME OFFICE (2006), *Consultation on New Powers Against Organised and Financial Crime*, London: Home Office.

IANNI, F. A. (1974), 'Authority, power and respect: the interplay of control systems in an organised crime "family" ', in S. Rottenberg (ed.), *The economics of crime and punishment*' Washington DC: American Enterprise Institute for Public Policy Research.

IANNI, F. A., and REUSS-IANNI, E. (1972), *A Family Business; Kinship and social control in organised crime*, London, Routledge & Kegan Paul.

INCSR (2006), *International Narcotics Control Strategy Report Volume II: Money Laundering and Financial Crimes*, Washington DC: US Department of State. Available at www.state.gov/p/inl/rls/nrcrpt/2006/vol2/.

INDEPENDENT MONITORING COMMISSION (2006), *10th Report*, Belfast and Dublin. Available at www.independentmonitoringcommission.org/documents/uploads/ACFEF3.pdf.

JACKSON, B., BAKER, J., CRAGIN, K., PARACHINI, J., TRUJILLO, H., and CHALK, P. (2005a), *Aptitude for Destruction, vol.2: Case Studies of organizational learning in Five Terrorist Groups*, Washington DC: Rand Corporation.

——, ——, ——, ——, ——, —— (2005b), *Aptitude for Destruction, vol.1: Organizational learning in Terrorist Groups and Its Implications for Combating Terrorism*, Washington DC: Rand Corporation.

JACKSON, J., HERBRINCK, J., and JANSEN, R. (1996), 'Examining criminal organisations: possible methodologies', *Transnational Organized Crime*, 2(4): 83–105.

JACOBS, J., and GOULDIN, L. (1999), 'Cosa Nostra's Last Stand?', in Tonry, M. (ed.), *Crime & Justice: An Annual Review of Research*, 24: 129–90, Chicago: Chicago University Press.

—— WORTHINGTON, J., and PANARELLA, C. (1994), *Busting the Mob*, New York: New York University Press.

KELLY, L. (2005), ' "You Can Find Anything You Want": A Critical Reflection on Research on Trafficking in Persons within and into Europe', *International Migration*, 43(1–2): 235–65.

—— and REGAN, L. (2000), *Stopping Traffic: Exploring the Extent of, and Responses to, Trafficking in Women for Sexual Exploitation in the UK*, Police Research Series Paper 125, London: Home Office.

KENNEDY, A. (forthcoming), 'Civil recovery of criminal proceeds : A troubling loss of faith in the criminal law?', *The Company Lawyer*.

KLERKS, P. (2003), 'The network paradigm applied to criminal organizations: theoretical nitpicking or a relevant doctrine for investigators? Recent developments in the Netherlands', in A. Edwards and P. Gill (eds), *Transnational Organised Crime: Perspectives on global security*, London: Routledge.

LACZKO, F. (2005), 'Data and Research on Human Trafficking', *International Migration*, 43(1–2): 5–16.

VON LAMPE, K. (2006), 'The cigarette black market in Germany and in the United Kingdom', *Journal of Financial Crime*, 13(2): 235–54.

—— and JOHANSEN, P. (2004), 'Organised Crime and Trust: On the conceptualization and empirical relevance of trust in the context of criminal networks', *Global Crime*, 6(2): 159–84.

LASCOUMES, P., and GODEFROY, T. (with contributions by CARTIER-BRESSON, J., and LEVI, M.) (2002), *Emergence du Problème des "Places Off Shore" et Mobilisation Internationale*, Paris: CEVIPOP-CNRS.

LEVI, M. (1981), *The Phantom Capitalists*, London: Heinemann.

—— (2003), 'Organising and controlling payment card fraud: fraudsters and their operational environment', *Security Journal*, 16(2): 21–30.

—— (2002), 'Money Laundering and its Regulation', *The Annals of the American Academy of Social and Political Science*, July.

—— (2006), 'The Media Construction of Financial White-collar Crimes', *British Journal of Criminology*, 46: 1037–57.

LEVI, M. (2007a), 'Lessons for countering terrorist financing from the war on serious and organized crime, in T. Biersteker and S. Eckert (eds), *Countering the Financing of Terrorism*, London: Routledge.

—— (2007b), *The Phantom Capitalists*, 2nd edn, Aldershot: Ashgate.

—— and GILMORE, B. (2002), 'Terrorist finance, money laundering and the rise and rise of mutual evaluation: a new paradigm for crime control?', *European Journal of Law Reform*, 4(2): 337–64.

—— and MAGUIRE, M. (2004), 'Reducing and preventing organised crime: An evidence-based critique', *Crime, Law and Social Change*, 41(5): 397–469.

—— and NAYLOR, T. (2000), *Organised crime, the Organisation of Crime, and the Organisation of Business*, Essay for the Crime Foresight Panel, London: Department of Trade and Industry.

—— and REUTER, P. (2006), 'Money Laundering: A Review of Current Controls and their Consequences', in M. Tonry (ed.) *Crime and Justice: an Annual Review of Research*, vol. 34: 289–375, Chicago: Chicago University Press.

—— and SMITH, A. (2002), *A Comparative Analysis of Organised Crime Conspiracy Legislation and Practice and their Relevance to England and Wales*, Research Findings, London: Home Office.

—— and WALL, D. (2004), 'Technologies, security and privacy in the post 9/11 European Information

Society', *Journal of Law & Society*, 31(3): 194–220.

——, NELEN, H., and LANKHORST, F. (2005), 'Lawyers as crime facilitators in Europe: An introduction and overview', *Crime, Law and Social Change*, 42(2–3): 117–21.

MCANDREW, D. (1999), 'The structural analysis of criminal networks', in D. Canter and L. Alison (eds), *The Social Psychology of Crime: Groups, Teams and Networks*, Aldershot: Ashgate.

MCINTOSH, M. (1975), *The Organisation of Crime*, London: Macmillan.

MACK, J., and, KERNER, H. (1975), *The Crime Industry*, Lexington: Saxon House.

MACKENZIE, S. (2005a), *Going, Going, Gone: Regulating the Market in Illicit Antiquities*, Leicester: Institute of Art and Law.

—— (2005b), 'Dig a Bit Deeper: Law, Regulation and the Illicit Antiquities Market', *British Journal of Criminology*, 45(3): 249–68.

MITSILEGAS, V. (2003), *Money Laundering Counter-Measures in the European Union: A New Paradigm of Security Governance versus Fundamental Legal Principles*, Amsterdam: Kluwer Law International.

MONZINI, P. (2005), *Sex Traffic: Prostitution, Crime and Exploitation*, London: Zed.

MORSELLI, C. (2005), *Contacts, Opportunities and Criminal Enterprise*, Toronto: University of Toronto Press.

—— and KAZEMIAN, L. (2004), 'Scrutinizing RICO', *Critical Criminology*, 12(3): 351–69.

NAPOLEONI, L. (2004), *T£rror Inc.*, London: Penguin.

NAYLOR, R. (2003), 'Towards a general theory of profit-driven crimes', *British Journal of Criminology*, 43: 81–101.

—— (2004), *Wages of Crime: Black Markets, Illegal Finance, and the Underworld Economy*, Ithaca, N.Y.: Cornell University Press.

—— (2006), *Satanic Purses: Money, Myth, and Misinformation in the War on Terror*, Montreal: McGill-Queen's University Press.

NCIS (2001), *UK Threat Assessment, 2001*, London: NCIS.

NELKEN, D. (1996) 'The judges and political corruption in Italy', in M. Levi and D. Nelken, (eds), *The Corruption of Politics and the Politics of Corruption*, Special Issue, *Journal of Law and Society*, 23: 95–112.

—— (1997), 'The Globalization of crime and criminal justice: prospects and problems', in M. Freeman (ed.) *Law and Opinion at the end of the 20th Century*, 251–79, Oxford: Oxford University Press.

OCTF (2006), *Organised Crime Task Force Annual Report and Threat Assessment 2006*. Available at, www.octf.gov.uk/publications/PDF/OCTF%20Annual%20Report%20and%20Threat%20Assessment%202006.pdf.

PAGE, R. (2006), *Dying to Win: Why Suicide Terrorists Do It*, London: Gibson Square.

PAOLI, L. (2001), *Illegal Drug Markets in Russia*, Freibourg: Max Planck Institut.

—— (2002), 'The paradoxes of organized crime', *Crime, Law and Social Change*, 37: 51–97.

—— (2003), *Mafia Brotherhoods*, New York: Oxford University Press.

PASSAS, N., and JONES, K. (forthcoming), 'Commodities and terrorist finance: diamonds, Al Qaeda and Hizbullah', *European Journal of Criminal Policy and Research*.

PEARCE, F. (1976), *Crimes of the Powerful*, London: Pluto.

PEARSON, G., and HOBBS, D. (2001), *Middle Market Drug Distribution*, HORS 227, London: Home Office.

PICARELLI, J. (2006), 'The Turbulent Nexus of Transnational Organised Crime and Terrorism: A Theory of Malevolent International Relations', *Global Crime*, 7(1): 1–24.

PIETH, M. (1998/99), 'The Harmonisation of Law against Economic Crime', *The European Journal of Law Reform*, , 527ff.

PORTER, M. (1996), *Tackling Cross Border Crime*, Crime Prevention and Prevention Series Paper 79, London: Police Research Group.

PUNCH, M. (2000), 'Police Corruption and its Prevention', *European Journal on Criminal Policy and Research*, 8(3): 301–24.

RAWLINSON, P. (2000), in R. King and E. Wincup (eds), *The Oxford Handbook of Criminological Research Methods*, Oxford: Oxford University Press.

REICHEL, P. (ed.) (2005), *Handbook of Transnational Crime & Justice*, Thousand Oaks, Cal.: Sage.

REUTER, P. (1983), *Disorganized crime: Illegal markets and the Mafia*, Cambridge, Mass.: MIT Press.

—— (1995), 'The decline of the American Mafia', *The Public Interest*, 120: 89–99.

—— and KLEIMAN, M. (1986), 'Risks and Prices: An Economic Analysis of Drug Enforcement', in M. Tonry and N. Morris (eds), *Crime and Justice:*

A Review of Research, vol. 7, Chicago: Chicago University Press.

REUTER, P., and RUBINSTEIN, J. (1978), 'Fact, Fancy, and Organized Crime', *The Public Interest*, 53: 45–68.

RICHARDSON, L. (2006), *What Terrorists Want*, London: John Murray.

ROACH, J., EKBLOM, P., and FLYNN, R. (2005), 'The Conjunction of Terrorist Opportunity: A Framework for Diagnosing and Preventing Acts of Terrorism', *Security Journal*,18: 7–25.

ROBINSON, J. (2002), *The Merger: The International Conglomerate of Organized Crime*, London: Penguin.

—— (2003), *The Sink*, London: Constable.

RUGGIERO, V. (2000), *Crime and Markets: Essays in Anti-Criminology*, Oxford: Clarendon Press.

—— and SOUTH, N. (1995), *Eurodrugs*, London: Routledge.

SEN, A. (2006), *Identity and Violence*, London: Allen Lane.

SHATFORD, J., and DOYLE, W. (2005), *Dome Raiders: How Scotland Yard Foiled the Greatest Robbery of All Time*, London: Virgin.

SHEPTYCKI, J. (2000), *Issues in Transnational Policing*, London: Routledge.

—— and WARDAK, A. (eds) (2005), *Transnational and Comparative Criminology*, Glasshouse Press.

SHERMAN, L. (1974), *Police Corruption: A Sociological Perspective*, Garden City, N.J.: Doubleday.

SHOVER, N. (1996), *Great Pretenders: Pursuits and Careers of Persistent Thieves*, Boulder, Col.: Westview Press.

——, COFFEY, G., and HOBBS, D. (2003), 'Crime on the line: Telemarketing and the changing nature of professional crime', *British Journal of Criminology*, 43 (July): 489–505.

SMITH, D. (1980), 'Paragons, pariahs and pirates: a spectrum-based theory of enterprise', *Crime and Delinquency*, 26: 358–86.

SOCA (2006), *Organised Crime Threat Assessment 2006–7*, London: Serious Organised Crime Agency.

SPARROW, M. (1991), 'The application of network analysis to criminal intelligence: an assessment of the prospects', *Social Networks*, 13: 251–74.

STELFOX, P. (2003), 'Transnational Organised Crime: a police perspective', in A. Edwards and P. Gill, *Transnational Organized Crime: Perspectives on Global Security*, London: Routledge.

STERLING, C. (1991), *The Mafia*, London: Grafton.

—— (1994), *Crime without Frontiers*, London: Warner.

STILLE, A. (1996), *Excellent Cadavers*, London: Vintage.

SUTTON, M. (1998), *Handling stolen goods and theft: A market reduction approach*, Home Office Research Study 178, London: Home Office.

THOUMI, F. (2003), *Illegal Drugs, Economy and Society in the Andes*, Baltimore, Md.: Johns Hopkins University Press.

—— (2007), 'The Rise of Two Drug Tigers: the development of the illegal drugs industry and drug policy failure in Afghanistan and Colombia', in F. Bovenkerk and M. Levi (eds), *The Organized Crime Community*, Dordrecht: Springer.

TILLY, C. (1985), 'War making and State making as Organized Crime', in P. Evans, D. Reuschemeyer, and T. Skocpol (eds), *Bringing the State Back In*, Cambridge: Cambridge University Press.

TRANSPARENCY INTERNATIONAL (2006), *Global Corruption Report*, Berlin: Transparency International.

TREMBLAY, P., CLERMONT, Y., and CUSSON, M. (1994), 'Jockeys and joyriders: changing car theft opportunity structures', *British Journal of Criminology*, 34(3): 307–21.

——, TALON, B., and HURLEY, D. (2001), 'Body Switching and related adaptations in the resale of stolen vehicles', *British Journal of Criminology*, 41: 561–79.

VAN DUYNE, P. (1993), 'Organised Crime and Business-Crime Enterprises in the Netherlands', *Crime, Law and Social Change*, 19: 103–42.

—— (1996), 'The Phantom and Threat of Organised Crime', *Crime, Law and Social Change*, 24: 341–77.

—— (1998), 'Money-Laundering: Pavlov's Dog and Beyond', *The Howard Journal*, 37(4): 359–74.

—— (2004), 'The creation of a threat image: media, policy making and organised crime', in P. van Duyne, M. Jager, K. von Lampe, and J. Newell (eds), *Threats and phantoms of organised crime, corruption and terrorism*, 21–51, Nijmegen: Wolf Legal Publishers.

—— (2005), 'Criminal subcontracting in the Netherlands: the Dutch "koppelbaas" as crime-entrepreneur', in P. C. van Duyne and K. von Lampe (eds), *The organised crime economy* 163–88, Nijmegen: Wolf Legal Publishers.

—— and BLOCK, A. (1994), 'Organized Cross Atlantic Crime', *Crime, Law and Social Change*, 22 (2): 127–47.

—— and DE MIRANDA, H. (1999), 'The emperor's clothes of disclosure. Hot money and suspect disclosures', *Crime, Law and Social Change*, 3: 245–71.

——, GROENHUIJSEN, M. S., and SCHUDELARO, A. A. P. (2005), 'Balancing financial threats and legal interests in money-laundering policy', *Crime, Law and Social Change*, 43(2): 117–47.

——and LEVI, M. (2005), *Drugs and Money: Managing the Drug Trade and Crime-money in Europe*, London: Routledge.

——and VAN DIJCK, M. (2007), 'Assessing Organised Crime: The Sad State of an Impossible Art', in F. Bovenkerk and M. Levi (eds), *The Organized Crime Community*, Dordrecht: Springer.

VARESE, F. (2001), *The Russian Mafia*, Oxford: Oxford University Press.

——(2006), 'How Mafias Migrate: The Case of the 'Ndrangheta in Northern Italy', *Law & Society Review*, 40: 411–44.

VOCKS, J., and NIJBOER, J. (2000), 'The promised land: a study of trafficking in women from central and eastern Europe to the Netherlands', *European Journal on Criminal Policy and Research*, 8(3): 379–88.

VOLKOV, V. (2002), *Violent Entrepreneurs*, Ithaca, N.Y.: Cornell University Press.

WILLIAMS, P. (2000), 'Transnational criminal networks', in J. Arquilla and D. Ronfeldt (eds), *Networks and Netwars: the Future of Terror, Crime and Militancy*, 61–97, Santa Monica, Cal.: RAND.

WOODIWISS, M. (2001), *Organized Crime and American Power: a History*, Toronto: University of Toronto Press.

——(2005), *Gangster Capitalism: The United States and the Global Rise of Organized Crime*, London: Constable and Robinson.

WORLD BANK (2006), *The Many Faces of Corruption: Tracking Vulnerabilities at the Sector Level*, Washington DC: World Bank.

WRIGHT, A. (2006), *Organized Crime*, Cullompton, Devon: Willan.

WRIGHT, R., DECKER, S., REDFERN, A., and SMITH, D. (1992), 'A Snowball's Chance in Hell: Doing Fieldwork with Active Residential Burglars', *Journal of Research in Crime and Delinquency*, 29(2): 148–61.

ZAITCH, D. (2002), *Trafficking Cocaine. Colombian Drug Entrepreneurs in the Netherlands*, The Hague: Kluwer Law International.

——,BOVENKERK, F., and SIEGEL, D. (2003). 'Organized crime and ethnic reputation manipulation', *Crime, Law & Social Change*, 2003(1): 23–38.

ZARTMAN, W. (1995), *Collapsed States*, Boulder, Col.: Lynne Rienner.

24

DRUGS, ALCOHOL, AND CRIME

Nigel South

INTRODUCTION

This chapter is concerned with illegal drugs and the most popular legal drug, alcohol. The illegal status of some drugs but not others (e.g. medicines) reflects judgements and classifications in domestic laws and international agreements (Bennett and Holloway 2005: 2–5; McAllister 2000; Drugscope 2006). In Britain the classification of illegal drugs is a tiered system reflecting official perceptions of their relative harmfulness. Thus Class A includes heroin and other strong opiates, cocaine, LSD, and Ecstasy (MDMA); Class B includes amphetamines and barbiturates while Class C includes tranquillizers and some mild stimulants. In January 2004 cannabis was moved from Class B to Class C, retaining its status as a controlled drug with a reduction in maximum penalty for possession from five to two years and an increase for supply and dealing from five to 14 years. Generally, maximum penalties are highest for Class A, lowest for Class C.

In terms of general effects, alcohol and drugs such as tranquillizers and heroin have a depressant effect on the nervous system; caffeine, amphetamines, cocaine, and tobacco are stimulants; cannabis, LSD, and Ecstasy distort perception. However, in relation to all drug use, actual behaviour and subjective experience will be strongly shaped by other influences, such as culture, context, and expectations (Dalgarno and Shewan 2005), as well as strength (e.g. alcohol content) or relative purity versus adulteration.

This chapter reviews trends in drug and alcohol use; situates drug control in the British and global contexts; and discusses data and debates concerning drugs and alcohol, crime, and criminal justice.

A REVIEW OF TRENDS IN DRUG AND ALCOHOL USE: 1950S TO 2005

Although most public and political attention tends to focus on illegal drugs as a source of social problems, this should not overshadow the significance of problems associated with legal drugs. For example, mass marketing and wide availability of prescribed and 'over the counter' pharmaceutical drugs, as well as solvents, may lead to misuse or dependency. Undoubtedly, however, alcohol remains the drug most widely used and misused. Alcohol consumption today is far higher than in the post-war years of the mid-twentieth century. Increased consumption from the 1950s onward is probably related to increases in disposable income, changes in leisure patterns, the rise in social acceptability of female drinking, and the proliferation of outlets for sales and consumption. There are recurrent concerns about increased alcohol consumption, health problems posed (e.g rise in liver disease among young people) (Alcohol Concern 2006), and offending (e.g. 'It is estimated that alcohol related crime costs the UK £7.3 billion per annum in terms of policing, prevention services, processing offenders through the criminal justice system and human costs incurred by the victims of crime. Overall alcohol-related harm costs the UK around £20 billion per year with alcohol-related crime accounting for the single largest area of expenditure' (ibid.: 1; see also Richardson and Budd 2003).

Mortality associated with tobacco and alcohol is considerably higher than deaths resulting from causes related to illegal drug misuse and complications. Deaths from the latter (mostly accidents) are difficult to determine, with various ways in which data may be recorded, misrecorded, or missed entirely. Office of National Statistics figures indicate a rise in drug-related deaths for England and Wales from about 860 in 1993 to around 1,620 in 2001 (Drugscope, 2005). According to Alcohol Concern (2003: 2), 'Overall trends show that the rates of alcohol-related deaths, where alcohol has been identified as an underlying cause of death, have risen in England and Wales since World War II (1945). The number of deaths more than doubled from 2,506 in 1979 to 5,543 in 2000'.

However, such comparison should not be interpreted as clear support for the view that illegal drugs should be legalized because 'they cause less harm than legal drugs'. Instead, there is an argument for trying to minimize the harm associated with all forms of drug misuse (Taylor 1999: 85). The point is that legal drugs (even if restricted) are widely available, illegal drugs are not; the health-related consequences of widespread legal availability of presently illegal drugs are not known. Taylor (ibid.) remarks that 'a selective decriminalisation of certain drugs could be one dimension in a serious campaign of harm reduction, not least in disrupting the process of production of "outsider cultures"' formed by those suffering disadvantage and social exclusion related to forms of substance misuse. However, Taylor also notes Currie's (1993: 68) conclusion, based on the US inner-city experience, that 'Proponents of full-scale deregulation of hard drugs ... tend to gloss over the very real primary costs of hard drug use ... and to exaggerate the degree to which the multiple pathologies surrounding drug use in America are an intended consequence of a "prohibitionist" regulatory policy'.

The legality of some drugs does not mean that they do not contribute to 'legal harms'. Drink and driving offences (including manslaughter deaths) (Corbett 2003) and alcohol-related violence and social disturbance result in high costs to the community and to health and police services (Shepherd and Lisles 1998; Pirmohamed *et al.* 2000). Despite their legal status, both alcohol and tobacco are attractive commodities for criminals engaged in theft, hijacking or smuggling activity.

A SHORT HISTORY OF DRUG USE TRENDS—1900S–1940S

Historically, illegal drug use has always crossed class boundaries. During the early years of the twentieth century and into the 1920s, drug users included: medical-professionals who had abused their access to opiates and other drugs; 'therapeutic addicts' of different class backgrounds who had become dependent during the course of pain-killing treatment with opiate-type drugs; and working-class users of opiate-based patent medicines. In London, there were small numbers of recreational and addicted users on the bohemian fringes of high society, within circles of young, white, male criminals and female prostitutes using cocaine in the West End, as well as in the East End 'opium dens' (Parssinen 1983: 216–17; Kohn 1992). However, while there was some considerable concern over drugs in this period (Kohn op. cit.), evidence suggests that the extent of use was limited and, by the end of the 1920s, in decline.

In the interwar years illegal drug use attracted little attention in the UK. However, subsequently, the paramount concern of nations at war was to secure drugs for medical purposes, and the entry of the USA into the Second World War brought unusual developments. The USA became a repository, producer, and supplier of pain-killing opiate-type drugs for the allied war effort and on the international scene played a coordinating role in the strategy of purchasing opium for allied stocks and denying such supply to the Axis powers (McAllister 2000: 147–9).

THE 1950S

During the early 1950s in Britain, both drug availability and official activity were minimal: 'The number of addicts known to the Home Office, most in medically related professions, remained low at between 300 and 400 ... But prosecutions for the use of cannabis began to rise' (Berridge 1999: 281). By the late 1950s a drug subculture seemed to be emerging in the West End of London linked to bohemian and jazz cultures (Tyler 1995: 169–70, 315–16). The availability of cannabis and heroin in these circles moved the Ministry of Health to establish the 1958 Inter-Departmental Committee on Drug Addiction under Sir Russell Brain, reporting in 1961. In the USA, popular anxieties and legislative responses were rather more pronounced. Accounts of the new youth fashions of the 1950s and purported links between rock and roll, the mixing of black and white youth, communism, and drugs (Shapiro 1999) were seen as alarms about America's vulnerability not only to external threats but also to subversion from within (Blackman 2004: 11–19).

THE 1960S

Examining trends for the late 1950s, the 1961 Brain Committee reported that drug supply was 'almost negligible', and Britain had no drug problem of significance. However, the 1960 Home Office addict statistics had not been available for the Committee and rising numbers of addicts (from 454 in 1960 to 753 in 1964) (Mott 1991: 78–9) suggested that a new trend was emerging.

The period of the 1960s is now culturally represented as one of post-war release, artistic innovation, anti-establishment sentiments, and alternative cultures (Shapiro 1999). In this context alarm about drugs was partly related to the emergence of new, young, working-class users of heroin and amphetamines. Middle-class youth also used heroin, but were particularly associated with images of a counter-culture—the 'hippy' lifestyle and drugs such as cannabis and LSD (Young 1971)—but it should also be remembered that for most youth, the intoxicant most widely used was (and remains) alcohol

Official, medical, and other observers identified the irresponsible prescribing of opiate drugs by a small minority of either gullible or profit-motivated private practitioners as the cause of the rise in addicts centred on London's West End (Ruggiero and South 1995: 19–23; Mott 1991). The Brain Committee was re-convened in 1964 to report on changes and in 1965 made recommendations of considerable importance for the future of the British response to drug misuse (Pearson 1991: 176–8).

FROM THE 1970S TO THE 1990S

With regard to use of opiates much of the 1970s presented a picture of relative stability and localized concentration, predominantly in the London area. By the tail of the decade, however, there were signs of further change and the 1980s saw a quite dramatic rise in use compared to the modest increases of the 1960s. Contrary to initial official perceptions, an increase in the availability of heroin was not a consequence of over-prescribing feeding the illegal market but of far less parochial developments. It was now the geo-politics of the international drug trade that demanded analysis and intervention. Cheap, high purity heroin was now becoming readily available from the Golden Crescent region of South West Asia (Iran, Pakistan, and Afghanistan) and with a tighter prescribing policy adopted by the new Drug Dependency Units (DDUs; see below), the new sources of availability stimulated the market. Of crucial importance was that the new heroin imports could be *smoked*, the prepared drug being heated and the smoke inhaled ('Chasing the dragon'), snorted, or sniffed (Auld *et al.* 1986). These methods overcame the deep psychological barrier associated with injecting and seemed familiar and 'ordinary' (Mott 1991: 85–6). Studies in various areas of England,

Scotland, and Wales confirmed the rapid spread of heroin use, now cheaper in real terms than five years previously. At the same time, official and popular concern gathered around the 'threat' of 'crack' as a new form of cocaine. Initially a threat with little substance, a decade later the crack situation had changed. In the meantime, from 1988, Acid House music had heralded a dance-drug culture, chemically fuelled by LSD and Ecstasy (MDMA) and generating a new mix of hedonism and consumerism, clubbing, and night-time escapism (Measham *et al.* 2000; Hobbs *et al.* 2005; South 2004).

THE 1990S AND INTO THE TWENTY-FIRST CENTURY

By the early 1990s, Britain had developed what remains a 'poly drug' culture. Of course, mixing drugs, selection for different effects, and/or use of alternatives to the preferred 'drug of choice' in times of scarcity, were not new phenomena. What was new was the integration into young people's drug cultures of a pick 'n' mix approach to available legal and illegal drugs (Davis and Ditton 1990; Parker *et al.* 1998; South 1999b). The Ecstasy dance-culture proved distinctive, not least in involving relatively 'ordinary' people whose 'deviance' lay in being enthusiasts of dance and particular dance-drugs (Shapiro 1999; Sanders 2005). Meanwhile, cocaine, crack, and heroin also saw increasing availability and use, generating serious crime and health problems, particularly in inner-city areas.

PREVALENCE AND AVAILABILITY

There is a huge literature on 'why people take drugs' (Sumnall *et al.* 2006: 6–7) with the World Health Organization employing the following categories of use:

> Experimental use that might or might not continue; Functional use that serves some purpose, such as recreation, but does not cause problems for the user; Dysfunctional use that leads to impaired psychological or social functioning; Harmful use that causes damage to the user's physical or mental health; Dependent use that could involve tolerance and/or withdrawal symptoms if use is ceased, and continued use' [ibid.: 6].

A major preoccupation has been with drug users' careers and the question of 'when did drug (legal and illegal) use start'? Evidence suggests that teen (and early teen) years are significant; that for most young people, experimentation (and little more) with illegal drugs involves cannabis (Class C), amphetamine and other Class B drugs, and from the early 1990s onward, occasional to regular use of Ecstasy and LSD (Class A). In the career of most drug users, 'escalation' to 'harder' drugs and long-term continuation of use is confined to a minority. Sumnall *et al.* (2006: 4) usefully note that:

> While there are no current data on the drugs used by children under 10 years old, in 2004 10 per cent of 11–15 year olds reported taking drugs in the previous month (NCSR/NFER 2005). UK schoolchildren (15–16 year olds) consistently report higher levels of lifetime use of any illegal drug than other European citizens (36 per cent versus 16 per cent) (Hibell *et al.* 2004).

This review also refers to British Crime Survey (BCS) data indicating that young people, aged 16–24 'are more likely than older people to have used drugs in the last year and in the last month (Condon and Smith 2003)'.

A major change from the 1990s onward has been the increase in use of cocaine generally and by young people aged 16–24 in particular although use appears to have stabilized since 2000 (Chivite-Matthews *et al.* 2005). Falling price (Corkery 2000; ISDD 1999) related to increased supply and hence easier availability, fashion, and social acceptability (Boys *et al.* 2001) may all be part of the explanation for this development. From the early 1990s to 2000, most crack or cocaine users in Britain seemed to be poly-drug users, not using excessively and not developing heavy dependence (Druglink 1992: 6), but perhaps ill-informed about differences between cocaine and crack, and about risks, particularly taking cocaine and alcohol together (Boys *et al.* 2001).

Importantly, Raistrick *et al.* (1999: 47) observe that 'as drug use has become prevalent among adolescents, it has ceased to be a simple matter clearly to separate out the role of alcohol from the role of other substances. Drug misusers tend to have misused alcohol under age, younger than their peers and prior to use of most or all illegal drugs'. Parker *et al.* (1998) have suggested that a pattern of 'normalization' of drug use is under way within the lifestyles and attitudes of those they surveyed. 'Normalization' does not mean that all young people are now drug users, nonetheless acquaintance with 'recreational' drugs and/or users is no longer unusual. Others have been critical of this suggestion and its implications, arguing that prohibitions, peer-group resistance, parental attachment, and preference for alternative activities remain central and act as deterrents to drug use (Shiner and Newburn 1999). Both viewpoints have validity and this is reflected in arguments suggesting that we are seeing, if not a widespread normalization of use, at least a process of 'cultural normalisation' (Pearson 2001). The debate is significant (South 1999b, 2004), 'shaped by two conflicting discourses which understand drugs in terms of cultural separation or cultural integration' (Blackman 2004: 147) but the idea of 'normalization' is, as Blackman (op. cit.) observes, 'an untidy concept' with 'problems in relation to overgeneralization' and difficulties in drawing distinctions between 'different drugs and different drug users'.

In the late 1980s and at the start of the 1990s, heroin availability was still high. Signs and predictions that its use was in decline were short-lived, and since the mid-1990s heroin use has seen a significant resurgence. Injection is a major method of administration and in this respect, as well as many others, it is essential to note the health concerns associated with drug use and misuse which may include, for example, mental health problems or homelessness (Carrabine *et al.* 2004, 206–27; Green *et al.* 2005). Injecting is a dangerous practice per se, and in the 1980s its association with the spread of HIV/AIDS was a key policy and practice issue. However, Hepatitis C is now well established as a virus transmitted via shared injecting equipment and yet receives far less media and health service attention.

SOCIAL DIVISIONS AND SOCIAL EXCLUSION

Gender, drugs, and alcohol

Studies of women's use of drugs (legal or illegal) remain relatively rare compared to the volume of work focused on men and even then reproduce a narrow research agenda covering, for example, the role of men in introducing women to drug use and in assisting them in injecting, women drug users and their roles as mothers and partners, and their involvement in prostitution. Informal care and support for alcohol and drug misusers is generally provided by women, and as Henderson (1999: 38) notes: 'A concern with women's drug use as it affects others still appears to dominate the gender and drug use literature'. Nonetheless, excellent studies do now exist (Taylor 1993; May *et al.* 1999; Maher 1997; Rosenbaum 1981). It is no longer true that drug *use* is predominantly male to the extent that it has been in the past (Parker *et al.* 1998; Sharp *et al.* 2001) and the usually cited ratio of 3:1 male to female users is probably an underestimate of the numbers of women users. As Best and Abdulrahim (2005: 3) note, this ratio may reflect uptake of services but underestimate actual prevalence: 'The underlying debate around representation offers two broadly opposing possibilities: more men use drugs problematically than women, so the numbers seeking treatment and in treatment are broadly proportional, or drug-using women are "hidden" and are under-represented in treatment, because of barriers that apply only to them, possibly relating to stigma and the structuring of treatment provision.' Possible barriers to women seeking treatment have now been examined quite systematically and are now better understood, including factors such as:

> stigmatisation and child protection issues; poor social support networks; weakness in maternity services; negative attitudes of health professionals; and ineffective inter-agency working. Those women who do access drugs services often find that there are significant shortcomings in the provision they receive. From the literature review, we noted a lack of: childcare and transport facilities; women-only services; provision for black and ethnic minority women, and services within the Criminal Justice System [Becker and Duffy 2002: 11].

Drug *dealing* probably remains a mainly masculine territory, and there are familiar and predictable characteristics of criminal enterprise as well as sociocultural prejudices operating against women in the drugs economy that explain this. In addition, it has been argued that women drug users and dealers may be particularly harshly treated when they come to official and media attention (Boyd 2004). US research (Fagan 1994: 186; Maher 1997) indicates openings in cocaine and crack markets for women dealers, albeit with varying degrees of autonomy while Denton and O'Malley (1999) report on Australian research on women dealers within the drug economy. In terms of alcohol, women's consumption has increased although this does not mean that gender-specific differences have disappeared; rather they continue to reflect prevailing norms and stereotypes (Plant *et al.* 2005; on women and alcohol, McDonald 1994 and Hunt *et al.* 2000; also Ettorre and Riska 1995).

Ethnicity

Drug use within ethnic minorities remains a story largely hidden from the record (Akhtar and South 2000; Pearson and Patel 1998; Daly 2005; Whittington 1999). When the topic has received attention it has frequently been discussed in terms of 'the depiction of dangerous places defined by the linking of drugs, crime, race and violence' (Murji 1999: 49), a process that can sensationalize stories about drugs and minorities, 'racialize' certain forms of drug use and drug culture, and pathologize the places where 'the mugger' and the 'drug trafficker' are said to reside (ibid.: 50–61).

Survey data on this subject face problems regarding reliability and coverage and although methods are increasingly sophisticated it remains worth noting that, as Murji (ibid.: 52) observes, while 'Some surveys report that some ethnic or racial minority groups declare higher drug use ... [others] have found the opposite'. Illustratively, Patel (1999: 18) remarks that

> Surveys suggest that South Asians are less likely to use illicit drugs than their white counterparts, and very few South Asian drug users approach drug services. In contrast, qualitative research studies of perceptions, experiences and nature of drug use among Britain's South Asian communities suggest increasing levels of harmful drug use, particularly heroin, among South Asians (predominantly Pakistani and Bengali young men).

A 2005 Addaction survey report confirmed the latter trend, reporting that 'nearly four in five Bengalis seeking help for drugs are problem heroin users' and many started 'using heroin aged 13–15' (although this finding is based on only 463 Bengali clients in a larger survey) (Druglink 2005: 4). Parker *et al.* (1998: 57) note that surveys of race and religion in relation to young people and alcohol use show relatively insignificant differences between the self-reported drinking of white and Afro-Caribbean youth but higher abstinence among young Muslims.

According to Edmonds *et al.* (2005: 16) 'community drug misuse needs assessments suggest distinct patterns of drug use exist between ethnic groups (Bashford *et al.* 2003)' and such patterns can be summarized: 'Drug use by South Asians was more characterised by the use of heroin than crack, and also the use of a wide range of drugs including ecstasy and LSD'; Black African reported use 'was characterised by the use of both heroin and crack, while Black Caribbean use was more characterised by crack, amphetamine and ecstasy'; 'Middle Eastern respondents reported no use of ecstasy, crack or heroin'. Across all ethnic groups, cannabis tends to be the most widely reported in terms of use. Key findings from the 2001/2002 BCS (Research Development and Statistics Directorate 2003) included data on 'mixed background' respondents and reported that 26 per cent in this category had taken an illicit drug in the past year, this being a higher result than for other categories (white, 12 per cent; black, 12 per cent; Chinese/other, 8 per cent; or Asian, 5 per cent). Levels of drug use were higher for those from white or mixed backgrounds than for those from a black background.

Drugs, deprivation, and social exclusion

Overall there seems to be some correlation between drug use and high rates of deprivation. The 1998 ACMD report on *Drug Misuse and the Environment* acknowledged that 'research points strongly to a statistical association between deprivation and problematic drug use' (ibid.: 3), and Foster (2000) revisited the site of a study undertaken ten years previously and found deterioration on most measures of deprivation and a parallel increase in crime and drug use. In the case of Scotland, McCarron (2006: 29) reports that 'Between 1999 and 2001, in the 10 per cent most deprived areas there was a yearly average of 460 admissions to hospital for drug conditions per 100,000 population compared with 20 per 100,000 in the 10 per cent least deprived areas'. However, there may also be inverse relationships. Localities with high indices of deprivation may have low rates of use, while there are socially advantaged, middle-class areas with high rates of use. Data from the 2000 BCS illustrated this mixed picture well, showing 'consistently higher levels of drug use among 16–29s living in affluent urban areas. Similar patterns are found for cocaine and Class A drugs. Heroin on the other hand, is more common in less affluent areas' (Sharp *et al.* 2001: 3).

From the late 1990s the Labour administration has pursued a series of policy initiatives aimed at reducing drug use and dealing by addressing social exclusion, improving the living environment in run-down areas, and focusing on localities with concentrations of long-term and high youth unemployment with the aim of assisting the successful transition of young people (16–25) to adulthood (MacGregor 1998: 190; Social Exclusion Unit 2004).

THE CONTROL OF DRUGS: BRITAIN AND THE GLOBAL CONTEXT

During the nineteenth century, opiate preparations were commonly marketed and widely used throughout Europe and North America (Berridge 1999), for example as medicines and tonics, as an analgesic, as a sedative, as a remedy for cholera, and as children's 'quieteners'. Apart from such therapeutic use, reports between the 1830s and 1860s describe the recreational use of opiates in factory districts, seaports, and the Fenlands (Parssinen 1983: 212), and the literature of the period indicates experimentation and familiarity with opium in literary and bohemian circles (Berridge 1999). However, the question of *control* was emerging.

The Industrial Revolution and other socio-economic developments promoted interest in the subject of public health, particularly in relation to the fitness of the urban working class. The common use of opiate preparations gave rise to some concern (although use for pleasure and pain relief among the middle class apparently received less disapproval and attention at this point Berridge 1999). A different provocation of public discussion about opiates was their common use as a means of sedating children—a practice resulting in many cases of children dying of opium poisoning (Parssinen 1983: 207; Pearson 1991: 170). Additionally, from around the 1870s onward, sensational accounts of Chinese 'Opium Dens' in the Limehouse area of London's East

End provided sinister stereotypes of Oriental conspiracies and clandestine organizations (Kohn 1992: 18–20). There was, of course, considerable hypocrisy in the promotion of such images.

The original traffickers in the opium trade were the great colonial powers such as Britain and the Netherlands (McAllister 2000: 9–39) and Britain had invested heavily and engaged in two conflicts known as the Opium Wars (1839–42 and 1856–58) to secure the conditions of 'free trade' that enabled export of opium from India (then part of the British Empire) to China. China had sought to ban importation and when forced to accept this suffered a major trade deficit which it only managed to turn around by allowing domestic production of opium from 1880 (Chawla and Pietschmann 2005: 161). This investment in the opium trade makes the limited extent of domestic control over opiate use in Britain less surprising. Nonetheless, in the latter half of the century, moral opposition to Britain's opium trade was growing. Further, there was a shift in perception of opium use, from seeing it as an indulgence or habit to viewing it as a 'problem', classifiable in various ways by the new medical discourses (Berridge 1979, 1999). The 1868 Pharmacy Act removed morphine and opium derivatives from the shelves of general stores and gave pharmacists the monopoly of dispensing. Medical practitioners attempted, but failed, to bring the treatment and control of those dependent upon opium within the provisions of the 1888 Inebriates Act, already covering the voluntary detention of 'habitual drunkards'. 'Insanity' certified to be the result of addiction could lead to institutionalization and the 1890 Lunacy Act was sometimes applied, but only with the passing of the 1913 Mental Deficiency Act did legislation embrace 'any sedative, narcotic or stimulant drug' within the definition of an 'intoxicant' and thereby allow for the detention of 'moral imbeciles' in asylums or under the guardianship of another (Pearson 1991: 171).

As well as 'medical entrepreneurs', 'moral crusaders' were also active in seeking the introduction of new control measures. In 1874, the Society for the Suppression of the Opium Trade was formed, largely supported by Quaker campaigners, and subsequently securing Parliamentary support from the Radical wing of the Liberal party (Berridge 1999). The later Report of the Royal Commission on Opium published in 1895 was something of a 'whitewash' (ibid.: 186–7) but the important *economic* development was that, even as moral and political debates waxed and waned, by the early 1880s the 'signs of decline in the importance of opium as an Indian revenue item were already visible' and 'by 1885, China was probably producing just as much opium as she imported . . . . In the 1890s, exports of Indian opium began to decline absolutely as well as relatively' (ibid.: 178). By 1906, it was neither a great act of moral conviction nor one incurring great financial loss for a new Liberal government to commit Britain to phasing out opium exports from India to China.

By the early years of the twentieth century a polarity had emerged between the medical view of drug use as addictive or a 'disease' and a moral view of it as a vice to be controlled by law and punishment (Berridge 1979; Smart 1984). However, the concerns about vice that finally introduced the first real penal response to drug use in Britain arose not as a result of peacetime lobbying but in the context of wartime emergency.

During the early years of the First World War, press and public were aroused by accounts of prostitution and cocaine posing a threat to the discipline of allied troops (Kohn 1992: 23–66). Similarly, concern about the productivity of war workers in the factories prompted calls for restriction of alcohol availability. In 1916, Regulation 40B of the Defence of the Realm Act (DORA), made possession of cocaine or opium a criminal offence except for professionals such as doctors, or where supplied on prescription (Kohn 1992: 44). DORA regulations also introduced licensing laws restricting opening times of public houses and regulating alcohol sales. Of course, alcohol controls had the greatest long-term consequences but with regard to the cocaine 'threat', legal control was now exercised and unauthorized possession was criminalized. A significant step had been taken and the role of the Home Office was brought to centre stage in the control of drugs, both domestically (Tyler 1995: 312–13; Pearson 1991: 172; Berridge 1978: 293) and internationally (McAllister 2000).

Subsequently, various influences, such as the ambitions of the USA regarding prohibitionism and the agenda for drug control, as well as the final ratification of the 1912 Hague Convention on Opium via the post-war Versailles Treaty (Article 295) (Bruun *et al.* 1975: 12; McAllister 2000), all encouraged further government legislation in the form of the Dangerous Drugs Acts of 1920 and 1923. These confirmed possession of opiates and cocaine as illegal except where prescribed by a doctor. The Home Secretary gained powers to regulate the manufacture, distribution, and legitimate sale of these drugs, and policing practice and public perception reflected the new status of illegal drugs as a criminal matter (Parssinen 1983: 217; Pearson 1991: 172; Lee and South 2003).

Problems relating to alcohol misuse or dependence have also been a source of moral, medical, and penal concern since the nineteenth century. Fines, imprisonment, or treatment programmes have been employed (Johnstone 1996: 33–100; Cabinet Office Strategy Unit 2004). However, while control regarding opium and cocaine was now set on a path of increasing prohibition, control in relation to alcohol has largely been a story of increasing liberalization. DORA regulations were at first ignored and then lifted. The Licensing Act 1964 laid out the system for discretionary granting of licences to sell alcohol, originally by licensing magistrates but since the Licensing Act 2003 by licensing committees of local authorities. This Act brings together several licensing arrangements (for providing alcohol, entertainment, and late-night food and drink) under one arrangement and furthermore places a duty on all licensing authorities to carry out four principal functions: the prevention of crime and disorder; public safety; the prevention of public nuisance; and the protection of children from harm.

Liberalization of the alcohol laws began in the 1980s and since then successive governments have relaxed controls on availability. A variety of laws have defined and specified responses to drunken behaviour, from the 1839 Metropolitan Police Act and the 1872 Licensing Act to the 1964 Act and subsequent amendments. Certain Acts have been particularly concerned with public order and providing powers to police and others, while provisions of local by-laws can also be used to enforce prohibition of drinking in designated places. In November 2005 new arrangements allowed licensed premises to apply for permission to remain open later and in some cases for the sale of alcohol 24 hours a day. Critics predicted increases in 'binge drinking' and alcohol-related crime and a Home Office Minister conceded that the policy might lead to increase in arrests and fixed penalty notices. Early indicators suggest the degree of alarm was unfounded although evaluation data are not yet available.

THE 'BRITISH SYSTEM' OF DRUG CONTROL

Following DORA and then the 1920 Act, the Home Office made 'consistent attempts to impose a policy completely penal in direction' (Berridge 1984: 23). The response from the medical lobby was to result in a report to the Ministry of Health that laid the foundation for the 'British system' of response to drugs and indeed for a 'harm reduction' approach. Chaired by Sir Humphrey Rolleston, President of the Royal College of Physicians, the 1926 Report of the Departmental Committee on Morphine and Heroin Addiction (known as the 'Rolleston Report') aimed to define the circumstances in which prescription was appropriate and the precautions to be taken to avoid the possibility of abuse (Ministry of Health 1926: 2; Tyler 1995: 313–14; Pearson 1991: 173). Hence, the Committee recommended prescription of heroin and morphine to enable gradual withdrawal, or to 'maintain' a regulated supply to those judged unable to break their dependence or those whose lives would otherwise suffer serious disruption.

Given the influential view that this development represents a profoundly different path to that taken by the USA, it is important to make two points. First, the view that Rolleston held of addicts was resolutely that they were 'middle class, middle aged, often from the medical profession and invariably an abuser of morphine. About five hundred such individuals existed nation-wide and rather than representing a threat they were to be pitied' (Tyler 1995: 313); only as 'an afterthought' was passing consideration given to the existence of working-class use of opiate-based patent medicines (ibid.). Secondly, looking at when such criminality actually emerged in the USA can challenge the idea that it was the nature of the British response that avoided duplication of the US experience. As Parssinen (1983: 219) suggests:

> Although the Harrison Act [of 1914] probably strengthened the connections between narcotics addiction and the urban underworld, these connections were firmly in place long before 1914. The increasingly hard-line American enforcement and treatment policy during the 1920s was less cause than effect of the emerging criminal-addict.

In other words, in terms of numbers of drug users, and the drugs-crime relationship, the British and US experiences were divergent already, ahead of the passing and subsequent interpretation of legislation. In Britain the drugs issue was receding in significance even as the Rolleston Committee deliberated: medical and recreational addiction was in decline. Press and public fascination persisted and sensational stories still made news (Kohn 1992) but, generally, such subcultures of use as had existed were fragile. Scarcity, related expense, and law enforcement efforts deterred both users and suppliers of cocaine and opiates. As Parssinen (1983: 220) argues, 'in Britain as in America, drug policy was less a cause than it was the effect of the addict population. Put simply, narcotic drug maintenance was accepted in Britain in the 1920s because the addict population was small, elderly and dying off.'

Various commentators (Smart 1984; Pearson 1991; Kohn 1992) agree that apparently dominant medical discourses of this time were in fact influenced by, and framed within, strong moral and penal positions. Nonetheless, one reason for a general acceptance of the success of 'Rolleston' is that through the 1930s to the late 1950s, Britain did indeed experience no serious problems with illegal drugs. Policy was seen as a continuing success despite being, in the words of Downes's (1977: 89) famous assessment, 'little more than masterly inactivity in the face of ... an almost non-existent ... problem'. As Berridge and Edwards (1987: 254) observed, the contrast between the American and British experience had rather less to do with the triumph of the Rolleston philosophy than with the 'enormously different social conditions in the cities of the two countries—different patterns of poverty, urban decay, ethnic underprivilege and entrenched criminal organization'. Despite this, for various reasons the 'British system' was idealized by others, particularly a line of influential American commentators, thereby distorting debate in the USA and promoting 'an atmosphere of self-congratulation and complacency within the British medical elite' (Blackman 2004: 26).

Even so, between 1920 and 1964, Britain was a signatory to a long string of control measures, largely carried along by the momentum of international initiatives (McAllister 2000; Ruggiero and South 1995: 99–101). The 1960s, however, saw developments on the domestic scene. Nationally as well as internationally, drugs became a challenging social problem, associated with cultural and political change. In 1961, the UN Single Convention on Narcotic Drugs drew together provisions of nine previous treaties signed between 1912 (Hague Convention) and 1953, and extended control to cover the plants poppy, coca, and cannabis.

In Britain, the 1964 Drugs (Prevention of Misuse) Act was introduced to control possession, production, and supply of amphetamine (later adding control of LSD). In 1965, the Dangerous Drugs Act ratified the Single Convention and the reconvened Brain Committee published a new report. This was to lead to major legislation in the form of the Dangerous Drugs Act 1967. Prescribing was to continue but general medical practitioners were to be more tightly controlled by regulations and were to 'notify' to the Home Office new addicts not previously in treatment. The aim was to intervene to prevent seepage of prescribed opiates (and similar drugs) into the illicit market. Specialist Drug Dependency Units or 'clinics' were opened from 1968, initially in and around London, as the centres of expertise in treatment of addiction and with psychiatrists playing a leading role. Prescription of heroin and cocaine was now limited although general practitioners could still prescribe other drugs for treatment and there has been a long debate about the extent to which they are, can be, or should be involved in such specialist clinical work. Under new funding arrangements for general practitioners, drug treatment will be a 'National Enhanced Service' that will be provided by a few, rather than many, specializing practices in each area.

In practice, the new clinics sought to break client dependence on street drugs by prescribing methadone as a 'substitute' drug, thought less attractive than heroin and suitable for detoxification or 'maintenance'. Thus medical *management* of addiction was endorsed, placing doctors in a role with responsibility for regulating supply and controlling the spread of dependence (Pearson 1991: 178–81; MacGregor 1999).

Debates aired around the dichotomies of 'soft' and 'hard' drugs, and 'users' and 'dealers', during the 1960s, were reflected in the distinction made by the 1971 Misuse of Drugs Act between the offences of possession and supply. Drug users could be characterized as sad and weak types corrupted by drug dealers who were very bad types; the former needed counselling or treatment, the latter deserved harsh punishment. Hence, despite the liberalization of much legislation in these 'permissive' years, drugs received quite conservative treatment; even a call by the respectable Advisory Council on Drug Dependence (the Wootton Committee 1968) for relaxation of the law on cannabis, was dismissively rejected (Young 1971: 198–201).

The status of drug control as a 'war' can be traced to President Nixon's mobilization of American public and official sentiment in the 1970s when crime was ranked as pre-eminent among the problems facing US cities, with drugs close behind. In the 1980s President Reagan launched a renewed 'War on Drugs', and the coincidence of the conservative politics of the President and the new British Prime Minister, Mrs Thatcher, set the tone for the rhetoric—but not all of the practice—of drug control in that decade. Drugs in Britain in the 1980s became a political and politicized issue attracting a political consensus that largely persists.

The Conservative government's 'strategy document' *Tackling Drug Misuse* (1985) proposed five fronts for action, largely organized around enforcement but including prevention and treatment. In the mid-1990s, the Conservative government introduced a further set of 'drugs strategies' for England, Scotland, Wales, and Northern Ireland, with some regional variation in emphasis. The England strategy, *Tackling Drugs Together* (1995), adopted a community crime prevention emphasis and established multi-agency Drug Action Teams to promote local initiatives. These elements were continued in the most recent national strategy produced by the post-1997 Labour government, *Tackling Drugs to Build a Better Britain* (HM Government 1998; updated 2002). This set four aims:

(i) to help young people resist drug misuse in order to achieve their full potential in society;
(ii) to protect our communities from drug-related anti-social and criminal behaviour; (iii) to enable people with drug problems to overcome them and live healthy and crime-free lives;
(iv) to stifle the availability of illegal drugs on our streets.

Law enforcement and crime reduction are central features of this agenda, but so too are aspirations to address social exclusion and community-oriented drugs prevention, and to improve drug-related education and treatment. It is noteworthy that the strategy, and hence policy priorities and resources, focused on illegal drugs and not alcohol and it was not until 2004 that a 'Alcohol Harm Reduction Strategy for England' was published (Cabinet Office Strategy Unit 2004).

Following Labour's re-election in 2001, commitment to cross-departmental, 'joined-up' thinking has appeared patchy, with some return to traditional departmental divisions, a central role for the Home Office, and the creation of the National Treatment Agency. The Chief Executive of the NTA offered the rationale that a shared agenda would continue but be shaped by the national strategy: 'It is sound criminal justice policy to invest in drug treatment. At the same time, we have to look at the drugs strategy as a whole. It is just as important that putting more money into treatment will provide better health care for the user and address the public health agenda by continuing to support harm minimisation' (Hayes 2001). Some of this view is present in the Drugs Act 2005 (in force from 1 January 2006) but it is clear that the criminal justice emphasis remains paramount. The Act draws together several elements of past strategy and action, allowing testing of drug offenders when arrested, providing for intervention orders to be attached to Anti-Social Behaviour Orders (created under the Anti-Social Behaviour Act 2003) and requiring drug counselling, and allowing presumption of 'intent to supply' in cases of possession of a certain quantity of controlled drugs. It is also designed to support the aims of the Drugs Interventions Programme, established in 2003, to help adult drug-misusing offenders move from involvement in crime and into treatment. In Scotland, drugs strategy has been less dominated by a criminal justice approach (McCarron 2006: 32) though there have been innovations in this area including adaptations of the American Drug Court for the Scottish context (Glasgow and Fife) and creation of the Scottish Drug Enforcement Agency to coordinate both police and customs activities.

LAW ENFORCEMENT AND DRUGS PREVENTION: CRIMINAL JUSTICE AND MULTI-AGENCY INITIATIVES

Various police forces and strategy commentators have supported the idea of 'low level policing' aimed at disrupting street markets (Lee and South 2003: 433–6), diverting users from criminalization to counselling and treatment (Edmunds *et al.* 1999; Green *et al.* 2005), and more recently, the targeting of the 'middle market' (Pearson and Hobbs 2001; May and Hough 2004). Intelligence-led policing, use of informants, and collation of data have long been recognized as key features of effective drug law enforcement (Dorn *et al.* 1992; Lee and South 2003). This has been reflected in the creation of a series of bodies from the 1973 Central Drugs and Illegal Immigration Unit onward. The 2005 Serious Organised Crime and Police Act created the latest in the line, establishing, from 1 April 2006, the Serious Organised Crime Agency (SOCA), merging the National Crime Squad, the National Criminal Intelligence Service, the drug investigation and intelligence arms of HM Customs and Excise, and taking on responsibility for organized immigration crime. Transnational law-enforcement cooperation has grown extensively as well as in terms of sophistication since the 1980s. Drugs, money-laundering, and latterly terrorism have been key targets (Lee and South 2003: 429–31; Matassa and Newburn 2003).

Given the volume of drugs now produced for the international market, modest improvement in enforcement effectiveness may make little difference to availability. It is recognized that there seems to be no clear relationship between the size of seizures and either general availability or price and that even 'successful' enforcement—whether domestic or cross-border—will be ineffective in conditions where time and resource constraints mean that sections of a trafficking network are removed but quickly and easily replaced as the structure rebuilds itself. Views have been changing regarding the success that can be attributed to supply-side interventions against trafficking outside, and importation into, the UK, or targeting of retail-level dealing. In 2003, the Strategy Unit of the Cabinet Office produced a Drugs Report, primarily focusing on harms caused by crack and heroin but with wider implications for drugs policy and policing. The report was originally a confidential document and parts were released only after leaks to the media and submissions under the Freedom of Information Act (see RSA Drugs Commission website, News). According to the report, 'The drugs supply market is highly sophisticated, and attempts to intervene have not resulted in sustainable disruption to the market at any level. As a result: the supply of drugs has increased; prices are low enough not to deter initiation; but prices are high enough to cause heavy users to commit high levels of crime to fund their habits (Strategy Unit 2003: 105). Despite investment in anti-drugs measures of around £450 million per year (£18m on action in source countries; £49m on countering trafficking; £222m on 'import investigation'; £75m on UK border policing; £85m on anti-retail activity), the report notes that 'Over the past 10–15 years, despite interventions at every point in the supply chain, cocaine and heroin consumption has been rising, prices falling and drugs have continued to reach users—government interventions against the drug business are a cost of business, rather than a substantive threat to the industry's viability—however, by increasing risk, government interventions are likely to have slowed the decline in prices' (ibid.: 94). Future, more effective strategy should aim to reduce harms, targeting organized criminals who are the major importers and wholesalers, but also assisting with development projects to effect change in producer countries and support drug treatment at home. Hence, the Strategy Unit proposals place a version of 'harm reduction' at the heart of future drugs law enforcement, with impacts being evident in the establishment of SOCA and in the Metropolitan Police adoption of a 'new approach' to criminal networks in 2006 (Cowan 2006).

Enforcement statistics

A reappraisal of evidence of success has far-reaching implications. For example, politicians and the media like to see targets and impact measures, for example detection as reflected in annual seizure statistics. Of course this has always been recognized as a partial measure: years of high seizure have been greeted as either a sign of increased success of enforcement efforts, and/or a reflection of an increasing incoming volume of drugs requiring further enforcement resources. It is now widely acknowledged that seizure statistics tell us relatively little—a few seizures of very large amounts can inflate the figures unrepresentatively while low seizures do not mean low levels of importation or distribution. Evidently numerous consignments avoid detection and the Customs and police services of most countries are unlikely to feel able to claim much more than a 10 per cent interception rate. Drawing on global data for 2002, Chawla and

Pietschmann (2005) note that 'nearly 1.1 million seizure cases were reported in the world' and that this represented a 'considerable increase from the 300,000 cases reported in 1992'. Nonetheless, seen in the context of increasing production and trafficking in heroin, cocaine, and cannabis this ten-year increase in seizures is not impressive. Law enforcement statistics are subject to severe limitations.

Drug offences sentencing

As Bennett and Holloway (2005: 4) remark, 'In practice, most official data on the drugs-crime connection come from government statistics on drug offences. Much less is known about drug-related crime other than drug offences.' Home Office data on 'Offenders dealt with' show a consistent rise in the number of persons found guilty, cautioned, or 'dealt with by compounding' for drugs offences under the Misuse of Drugs Act. In 1998, the total number was 127,700 rising in 2003 to 133,970 but then seeing a fall in 2004 to 105,570 (Mwenda 2005: 2). Nearly 85 per cent of these offences in 2004 related to drug possession, 56 of which were specifically cannabis related although Class A offences had risen from 13,900 in 1995 to 36,500 in 2004. Interestingly and importantly, the 2004 statistics are the first to reflect the change of status of cannabis from Class B to Class C which came into effect on 29 January that year. The statistics treat cannabis as Class C for the whole year preventing year-by-year comparison but with the obvious effect that 'Class B offences fell by 92 per cent to 7,260 between 2003 and 2004, and class C offences rose from 1,660 to 59,050 in the same period' (ibid.: 2). It is worth noting that 'In 2004, 55 per cent of all drug offenders were cannabis possession offenders while four per cent were cannabis-dealing offenders' (ibid.: 4) The majority of drug offenders are male and the 2004 data confirm this trend, with just 12 per cent being female.

Unsurprisingly, the proportion of offenders known to the criminal justice system who have some form of alcohol or illicit drug problem is significantly high. According to the Office of National Statistics (Singleton *et al.* 1999), 58 per cent of remand and 63 per cent of sentenced prisoners reported hazardous levels of drinking in the year prior to entering prison while drug-testing of arrested people in eight sites across England and Wales found that 65 per cent tested positive for at least one illegal drug, 29 per cent for opiates and/or cocaine/crack (Bennett *et al.* 2001).

Penalties and sentencing trends have risen since the 1970s, reflecting ever-increasing political prioritization of drugs/crime as a social and electoral issue. In line with the original dichotomy in the 1971 Misuse of Drugs Act, possession offences are still treated rather differently to drug dealing. For example, according to Home Office figures for 2004 (Mwenda 2005: 5–6), only:

> Eleven per cent of drug offences were dealt with by custodial sentences, with the average sentence length being 32 months. Class A drug offences (such as cocaine) were likely to attract more and longer custodial sentences. ... The most common disposals used for known possession offences ... were cautions (44 per cent), followed by fines (22 per cent) and absolute or conditional discharges (11 per cent). Only five per cent were sentenced to immediate custody while nine per cent were given a community sentence.

By contrast, for those involved in drug dealing offences, the Class A to C system is reflected in harshness of sentencing and immediate custody follows in 61 per cent of cases, community sentences in 17 per cent, and cautions in only 9 per cent, although immediate custody sentences for dealing in cocaine, crack, or heroin occur in 82 per cent, 82 per cent, and 81 per cent of cases respectively (ibid.: 8).

Assessment of the threat from organized serious crime is now undertaken on a frequent and sophisticated basis and it is recognized that criminal entrepreneurs will not necessarily be engaged in drugs-related activity alone. A range of techniques and targets are required and one that has become central, albeit with only partial success, is asset confiscation. The 1986 Drug Trafficking Offences Act meant that sentences could include asset confiscation and this was followed by the 2002 Proceeds of Crime Act, which was accompanied by a government pledge to meet higher confiscation targets. The Act empowers the Assets Recovery Agency in several ways, including the freezing of assets at the start of an investigation to avoid their sudden disappearance from sight or jurisdiction and the granting of monitoring orders to the police and other investigators to trace transactions taking place on a given bank account. This has proved a less effective tool than hoped despite allowing the presumption that assets are the proceeds of trafficking or other crime unless the defendant can prove otherwise. Legal challenges employing human rights legislation have recently slowed progress with various cases.

Conclusions about the impact of sentencing are difficult to draw but imprisonment probably has little positive effect on drug or drug-related crime behaviour. Drugs are widely available in prisons and the sharing of injecting equipment makes risk of HIV/AIDS, or forms of hepatitis, a serious problem. Mandatory drug testing has encouraged use of drugs that are harder to detect, including a shift from cannabis to opiates. The Prison Reform Trust (2005: 20) reports that

> Drug use amongst prisoners in custody is reported to be high. A recent Home Office study found that four out of ten prisoners said they had used drugs at least once whilst in their current prison, a quarter had used in the past month and 16 per cent in the past week. Cannabis and opiates were the drugs most often used.

Treatment, rehabilitation, and diversion

The issue of *treatment* of drug and alcohol users raises several key criminological questions, such as: what kinds of treatment are most efficacious in (a) reducing reliance on the illegal market for drug supply, and (b) reducing related criminal activity engaged in to generate funds for purchasing drugs? Some studies indicate that maintenance prescribing has little clear impact on criminal activity, though there is some evidence that methadone treatment can help to reduce acquisitive crime rates in areas of heroin-based drug markets and that 'tailored' or 'flexible' therapeutic programmes can be effective. The most significant review of efficacy has been the National Treatment Outcomes Research Study (NTORS) and Gossop (2005: 5) notes that:

> Even without the numerous other tangible and intangible benefits in addition to the reductions in costs of crime to society, the financial costs of treating drug dependent patients provide a return that more than justified the cost of treatment [and that] Initial

calculations based upon savings associated with victim costs of crime and reduced demands upon the criminal justice system, estimated that for every extra £1 spent on drug misuse treatment, there was a minimum return of more than £3 in terms of savings to the economy.

Even so, NHS funding is under constant pressure and drug and alcohol misusers are not a widely popular group; hence it is not inconceivable that at some point in the future, treatment funding could be reduced and/or expensive treatment resources be rationed.

Drug Testing and Treatment Orders (DTTOs) were introduced as a new community sentence under the Crime and Disorder Act 1998 and while their use has increased there have been concerns about failure rates as well as variations by geography in terms of operational resources and practice. There is always some difficulty in determining whether success linked to such interventions can be attributed to the treatment per se or to personal history and situation (for example, users feeling that they are 'growing out of drugs' or are weary of the lifestyle). In practice, the argument for flexibility is precisely about being able to draw users into treatment at the point where they feel willing or need to change. It is also important to emphasize a further finding from NTORS, 'that crime and drug misuse do not inevitably go together. Half of the clients were not involved with acquisitive crime and more than two-thirds were not involved with drug selling crimes during the period before admission. Of those who were involved in crime, the majority were relatively infrequent offenders' (Gossop 2005: 3).

Treatment, abstinence, and tailored programmes seem to be able to improve social conditions and personal relationships but have had a poor record in improving labour market skills or housing, financial, and personal circumstances. Increasingly treatment, rehabilitation, and diversion schemes are incorporating opportunities for gaining vocational skills-training and qualifications (South *et al.* 2001) and McCarron (2006: 31) notes the particular progress made in Scotland with this approach where the 'high rate of unemployment, low level of qualifications and relatively low working age of drug users entering treatment' led to development of 'research and guidance integrating access to education, training and employment with care pathways'. In relation to serious alcohol misusers, Alcohol Concern (2000: 15) suggests that opportunities for treatment and prevention of reoffending are largely missed because of the absence of effective sentencing options. Many other problems here parallel those relevant to drugs, for example the need for specialist services within prisons and improved support arrangements on release from prison.

DRUGS, ALCOHOL, AND CRIME

Decriminalization versus prohibition

Possession, supply or preparation and manufacture of certain drugs are illegal. However some drugs are argued to be relatively harmless compared to the Class A 'dangerous drugs' such as crack and heroin. These points give rise to questions about whether the law is sensible, or whether legalization or other options are desirable

(Police Foundation 2000). Proponents argue that the costly, counterproductive, and unsuccessful efforts of law enforcement as a response to drug use suggest that legalization is a wiser alternative. It is suggested that availability would not mean unacceptable rises in use, and that taxation of legal supply would provide funds for educational, health, and counselling responses. Regulation would ensure purity levels and hence reduce health hazards caused by adulterants; and legal availability would remove the profit motive that drives the criminal market (Nadelman 1989; *The Economist* 2001; see also Husak and de Marneffe 2005, where Husak argues in favour and de Marneffe against; and the analysis in MacCoun and Reuter 2001). Opponents (Inciardi and McBride 1989; Wilson 1990) argue that legalization *would* increase use, thereby increasing serious costs to society. The decriminalization of cannabis use in the Netherlands has often been misunderstood, particularly by US prohibitionists. This is actually a case of a policy aimed at preserving 'market separation', keeping cannabis supply distinct from supply of drugs with an 'unacceptable risk', decriminalizing possession, and simply reflecting the flexibility that recent commentators have emphasized the 1961 UN Single Convention allows (Dorn 2004).

Drugs and crime

The European Monitoring Centre for Drugs and Drug Addiction (2003: 33) has suggested that the term 'drug-related crime' might include 'criminal offences in breach of drug legislation, crimes committed under the influence of illicit drugs, crimes committed by users to support their drug habit (mainly acquisitive crime and drug dealing) and systemic crimes committed as part of the functioning of illicit markets (fight for territories, bribing of officials, etc.)' (see, e.g, McElrath 2004). Debates about the drugs/crime relationship generally follow one or other of the following propositions: 'criminal lifestyles may facilitate involvement with drugs'; or 'dependence on drugs then leads to criminal activity to pay for further drug use' (South 1995; Bennett and Holloway 2005: 11–12). There is no dispute that there is an association between drugs and crime but this is not straightforward (Roberts 2003). It is straightforward that the very illegality of drugs will make their possession and supply an offence. Thereafter things are more complicated—does drug use lead to crime or does involvement in a criminal lifestyle lead to use of drugs? Heroin and crack users with a serious addiction may be committing a considerable amount of acquisitive crime to fund their habit (Bennett *et al.* 2001) but at the same time, as Seddon (2002) argues, 'a link between drugs and crime is in fact only found among a minority of drug users—the 3 per cent or so of illicit drug users who are termed "problem" users. Within this group, the association is primarily between use of heroin and/or crack cocaine and commission of certain economic/property offences (especially drug selling, shoplifting, burglary and other theft)'. For others, the route to drug use may be through involvement in an array of delinquent and criminal lifestyles (Auld *et al.* 1986; Pudney 2002), and drugs are just one commodity bought and sold in the pleasure markets of the late-modern illicit economy (Ruggiero and South 1997; Hobbs *et al.* 2005). Some work (Collison 1996; Parker 1996, South 2004) has noted a greater hedonistic attachment to a consumption-oriented lifestyle among young offenders using illegal drugs and/or alcohol, and that petty crime was routinely engaged in for support. Typically, drug-related crime is non-violent and acquisitive, involving theft, shoplifting, forgery, burglary, or prostitution. More serious drug-related crimes of violence and murder have been increasing in Britain, although still on a small scale by comparison with the USA.

'Involvement in criminal activity leads to drug use'

Some studies provide evidence that heroin or other serious drug misusers would already have been involved in delinquent or criminal activities before they started using these drugs. The argument on this side is that: (a) involvement in deviant/criminal-oriented subcultures or groups would be likely to lead a person to encounter the availability of drugs sold within that culture; (b) they would have a deviant lifestyle which would accommodate deviant drug use with relative ease; and (c) while money from criminal activity might then pay for the drugs, it was not drug addiction or use per se which led to the perpetration of crime.

'Involvement in drug use causes crime'

Of course, other studies argue that there *is* a *causal* link, and that drug use (particularly of heroin) causes crime. Some crimes seem to have a clear relationship with drug use, for example where drugs are stolen or where shoplifting or burglary generates funds that are used immediately to purchase drugs. There is a huge body of work supporting this proposition, albeit principally from the USA. The evidence is convincing but so too is the evidence from studies supporting the opposing proposition; furthermore and quite predictably, studies may uncover patterns in which 'participation in acquisitive crime (which mainly involves petty shoplifting) tends to precede the first use of drugs such as heroin and crack cocaine' but that 'participation in more serious crimes, such as street crime' may tend to occur after regular use has been established (Allen 2005: 356). The simple resolution of this debate is to agree with Nurco *et al.* (1985: 101), who twenty years ago sensibly suggested that 'the long and continuing controversy over whether narcotic addicts commit crimes primarily to support their habits or whether addiction is merely one more manifestation of a deviant and criminal life-style seems pointless in view of the fact that addicts cannot be regarded as a homogeneous group'.

Alcohol and crime

Concerns about the relationship between alcohol and crime are not new. According to Lombroso (1911/1968: 95–6):

> Alcohol ... is a cause of crime, first because many commit crime in order to obtain drinks, further, because men sometimes seek in drink the courage necessary to commit crime, or an excuse for their misdeeds; again, because it is by the aid of drink that young men are drawn into crime; and because the drink shop is the place for meeting of accomplices, where they not only plan their crimes but squander their gains ... it appears that alcoholism occurred oftenest in the case of those charged with assaults, sexual offences, and insurrections. Next came assassinations and homicide; and in the last rank those imprisoned for arson and theft, that is to say, crime against property.

Contemporary studies and debates concerning the extent to which alcohol consumption is responsible for certain forms of criminal behaviour are extensive but inconclusive (Raistrick *et al.* 1999; All Party Group on Alcohol Misuse 1995), and have some similarities and some dissimilarities with those concerning drugs and crime. Nonetheless, the National Alcohol Harm Reduction Strategy (Cabinet Office Strategy Unit 2004: 44) argues that 'Alcohol misuse is a major contributor to crime, disorder and anti-social behaviour, with alcohol-related crime costing society up to £7.3bn per annum. The most visible areas of concern for most people include: alcohol-related disorder and anti-social behaviour in towns and cities at night; and under-age drinking. Less visible but equally significant concerns are: crime, disorder and anti-social behaviour—often caused by repeat offenders; domestic violence; and drink-driving.'

It is alcohol rather more than illegal drugs that tends to be linked to aggression and violent crime, and hence, potentially, to crime with longer-term effects for victims and society (Alcohol Concern 2001; *Lancet* 1999). Estimates from the British Medical Association suggest that the offender or victim had been drinking in 65 per cent of murders, 75 per cent of stabbings, 70 per cent of beatings, and 50 per cent of fights or domestic assaults (ibid.). Raistrick *et al.* (1999: 54) similarly note that

> many perpetrators and victims of crimes of disorder or violence, including murder, as well as perpetrators of acquisitive crimes, such as burglary and theft, have alcohol in their blood at the time of the offence . . . . Furthermore, as with other drugs, heavier users of alcohol are more likely to have criminal records and to admit to criminal acts than are lighter users or abstainers.

However, the existence of a causal relationship between alcohol and violent crime remains difficult to substantiate (Alcohol Concern 2001). Perhaps the key conclusion is that 'alcohol may be neither a necessary nor sufficient *cause* of crime, but may nonetheless *affect* crime' (Raistrick *et al.* 1999: 55). Research findings suggest that a variety of co-factors may play a significant role in alcohol-related aggression. As with illegal drug consumption, *belief* about how alcohol is 'supposed' to affect behaviour, *coupled* with the influences of immediate social context and wider culture, are as important for the behavioural outcome as the amount of alcohol consumed. A Home Office review of research concludes that situational and cultural variables may play a role in the relationship between alcohol and aggression, and that no direct pharmacological link between alcohol and violent behaviour is supported. More probably, alcohol influences the social and cognitive processes that may lead to aggression (Deehan 1999). Hence, socialization and cultural expectations, stereotypes and labelling, circumstances and significant others, all play their part in shaping people's identities as 'aggressive' and as 'drinkers' (Borrill and Stevens 1993). Such definitions change across time and cultures, and are also strongly influenced by positive and negative images of alcohol use in entertainment media and alcohol advertising. The relationship between masculinity, alcohol, and violence is complex and deserves more attention (Tomsen 1997; Taylor 1999: 85–6). Hunt and Joe-Laidler (2001), for example, show how alcohol plays a significant role in gang life, contributing to cohesion, solidarity, and ways of maintaining group boundaries, but also being associated with internal violence including fights caused by rivalries or disputes over honour and respect. Alcohol may have a relationship with crime in other ways, for example:

> intoxication may shift some people over the threshold from contemplating crime to committing it; ... public disorder is commonly linked to open-air drinking by young people; ... alcohol use can serve as a financial motive for crime; alcohol problems can produce a home environment conducive to anti-social behaviours; ... drunk people may be amnesic regarding the negative consequences of their criminal actions, thus failing to learn from them; and alcohol intoxication can reduce inhibitions and judgement [Raistrick *et al*. 1999: 55].

Some of these factors may contribute to crimes in which there is a potential but unknown association with alcohol; in other words, there has been considerable research on alcohol and violence, sexual assault, and acquisitive crimes, but little on crimes such as 'fraud, tax evasion, smuggling, ... and other white-collar crimes' and the influence of alcohol (Raistrick *et al*. 1999: 56).

As Raistrick *et al*. (1999: 47) note, 'it is not known why some substance misusers become dependent on one substance, such as alcohol, and others on another, such as heroin, while most avoid dependence and grow out of substance misuse, or grow into a relatively stable and controlled pattern of alcohol or other drug use as adults'. Long-term, follow-up studies examining criminal careers and drinking careers suggest that 'criminality and alcohol abuse tend to run in parallel, as both have their peak incidence in young adults and tend to diminish with age' (d'Orban 1991: 298). Persistence of heavy drinking and petty crime into mid-life characterizes 'habitual drunkenness offenders' (ibid.), and some studies show a disproportionately higher level of alcohol problems among those arrested and prisoners than found in the general population (Raistrick *et al*. 1999). Cautions about inferring causality will still apply however: regardless of whether alcohol consumption precedes or succeeds offences (property or violent) and whatever the alcohol consumption levels involved (be it higher or lower than average) the drinking must still be considered in relation to specific criminal events.

CONCLUSIONS

In a new century of globalization, it is more urgent than ever that we should improve our knowledge and understanding of both the domestic and global contexts of the production and use of intoxicants in non-Western societies. The dominant discourse is Western-led and neglects comparative work that throws light upon portraits of drug use, cultures, and ways of managing matters in other contexts (Coomber and South 2004). On the one hand, such work can inform anti-trafficking strategies but, on the other, it will demonstrate that identifying the 'villains versus the victims' is not an easy task (Macdonald 2001). A comparative approach could also help to illuminate why 'international conventions and national laws can be inappropriate and ineffective in preventing traditional substance use' (Saxena 1995: 14) or tradition-based drug-crop cultivation. Lastly, knowing more about other societies can probably 'teach us much that is relevant to prevention in our own' (Gossop 1995: 16).

On the domestic front, policy-makers and expert committees have reconsidered drugs law and treatment with some acknowledgement of morality, religion, diversity, and so on but they commonly manoeuvre themselves around the legality/illegality distinction. Despite a central role for health concerns, twenty-first-century drug policy in the UK has so far shown no sign of a shift away from the legality/illegality anchor and the criminal justice preoccupations that accompany this. This distinction and state of affairs is rooted in legislation that is now over thirty years old (the 1971 Misuse of Drugs Act), the product of times quite different from today.

In terms of our knowledge base, there is (as usual) much more to be done. Despite improved evidence there is still much to learn about drug and alcohol use, links to crime, and about the reasons for successes and failures in prevention, treatment, and criminal justice interventions. Recognizing this, the UK Office of Science and Technology 'Foresight Programme on Brain Science, Addiction and Drugs' commissioned several studies to consider current and emerging knowledge that could help to predict the shape of 'Drugs Futures 2025'. The results hold promise but also grounds for caution. For example, as noted in work on 'ethical aspects of developments in neuro-science and drug addiction' (Foresight Project 2006),

> Advances in our knowledge of brain function, and the effects drugs have on this, raise ethical issues. These include the possible use of vaccinations against certain addictive drugs (with consideration of issues which would need to be taken into account before compulsory use could be considered), the ways in which genetic information about vulnerability to addiction could be used, and the possibility of drugs being developed for the enhancement of mental performance.

As the twenty-first century unfolds, the 'problems' that drugs (legal and illegal) will pose will not fade away. However it should by no means be assumed that the problems of the future and the ways in which society responds will always remain the same as in the past.

■ SELECTED FURTHER READING

Useful websites with links to further sites are provided by Drugscope: www.drugscope.co.uk; by Alcohol Concern: www.alcoholconcern.org.uk; and by the Royal Society of Arts Drugs Commission: www.rsadrugscommission.org/ . The Drugscope website provides access to *Drugsearch*, an online drugs encyclopaedia. P. Bean (2004), *Drugs and Crime* (Willan) focuses on law enforcement and criminal justice debates; T. Bennett and K. Holloway (2005), *Understanding Drugs, alcohol and crime* (Open University Press) and M. Simpson *et al.* (eds)

(2006), *Drugs in Britain* (Palgrave) provide good general overviews. N. South (ed.) (1995), *Drugs, Crime and Criminal Justice*, vols 1 and 2 (Dartmouth) reprint various classic and recent articles.

■ REFERENCES

ADVISORY COUNCIL ON MISUSE OF DRUGS (1998), *Drug Misuse and the Environment: A Summary*, Supplement to *Druglink*, 13.

AKHTAR, S., and SOUTH, N. (2000), 'Hidden from heroin's history: heroin use and dealing within an English Asian community', in M. Hough and M. Natarajan (eds), *International Drug Markets: From Research to Policy*, Crime Prevention Studies, vol. 11, New York: Criminal Justice Press.

ALCOHOL CONCERN (2001), www.alcoholconcern. org.uk/.

—— (2003), 'Alcohol and Mortality: Acquire: Alcohol Concern's Quarterly Information and Research Bulletin, Summer. London: Alcohol Concern. Available at www.alcoholconcern.org.uk/files/ 20030807_172030_mortality.pdf.

—— (2006), Health Impacts of Alcohol (Factsheet), London: Alcohol Concern, www.alcoholconcern. org.uk/.

ALL PARTY GROUP ON ALCOHOL MISUSE (1995), *Alcohol and Crime: Breaking the Link*, London: Alcohol Concern.

ALLEN, C. (2005), 'The links between heroin, crack cocaine and crime', *British Journal of Criminology*, 45(3): 355–72.

AULD, J., DORN, N., and SOUTH, N. (1986), 'Irregular Work, Irregular Pleasures: Heroin in the 1980s', in R. Matthews and J. Young (eds) *Confronting Crime*, London: Sage.

BACHUS, L., STRANG, J., and WATSON, P. (2000), 'Pathways to Abstinence: Two-Year Follow-up Data on 60 Abstinent Former Opiate Addicts', *European Addiction Research*, 6: 141–7.

BASHFORD, J., BUFFIN, J., and PATEL, K. (2003), *The Department of Health's Black and Minority Ethnic Drug Misuse Needs Assessment Project, Report 2: The Findings*, Preston: Centre for Ethnicity and Health.

BEAN, P. (2004), *Drugs and Crime*, Cullompton, Devon: Willan.

BECKER, J., and DUFFY, C. (2002), *Women Drug Users and Drugs Service Provision*, DPAS paper 17, London: Home Office.

BENNETT, T., and HOLLOWAY, K. (2005), *Understanding drugs, alcohol and crime*, Maidenhead: Open University Press.

——, ——, and WILLIAMS, T. (2001), 'Drug Use and Offending', *Findings*, 148, London: Home Office.

BERRIDGE, V. (1978), 'War Conditions and Narcotics Control: The Passing of the Defence of the Realm Act Regulation 40B', *Journal of Social Policy*, 7(3): 285–304.

—— (1979), 'Morality and Medical Science: Concepts of Narcotic Addiction in Britain, 1820–1926', *Annals of Science*, 36: 67–85.

—— (1984), 'Drugs and social policy: the establishment of drug control in Britain, 1900–1930', *British Journal of Addiction*, 79: 1.

—— (1999), *Opium and the People*, rev. edn, London: Free Association.

—— and EDWARDS, G. (1987), *Opium and the People*, 2nd edn, New Haven, Conn.: Yale University Press.

BEST, D., and ABDULRAHIM, D. (2005), *Women in Drug Treatment Services*, Research Briefing 6, London: National Treatment Agency.

BLACKMAN, S. (2004), *Chilling Out*, Maidenhead: Open University Press.

BORRILL, J., and STEVENS, D. (1993), 'Understanding human violence: the implications of social structure, gender, social perception and alcohol', *Criminal Behaviour and Mental Health*, 3: 129–41.

BOYD, S. (2004), *From Witches to Crack Moms: Women, Drug Law and Policy*, Durham, N.C.: Academic Press.

BOYS, A., DOBSON, J., MARSDEN, J., and STRANG, J. (2001), *Cocaine Trends: A Qualitative Study of Young People and Cocaine Use*, London: National Addiction Centre.

BRUUN, K., PAN, L., and REXED, I. (1975), *The Gentlemen's Club: International Control of Drugs and Alcohol*, Chicago, Ill.: University of Chicago Press.

CABINET OFFICE STRATEGY UNIT (2004), *Alcohol Harm Reduction Strategy for England*, London: Cabinet Office.

CARRABINE, E., IGANSKI, P., LEE, M., PLUMMER, K., and SOUTH, N. (2004), *Criminology: A Sociological Introduction*, London and New York: Routledge.

CHAWLA, S., and PIETSCHMANN, T. (2005), 'Drug trafficking as a transnational crime', in P. Reichel (ed.), *Handbook of Transnational Crime and Justice*, Thousand Oaks, Cal.: Sage.

CHIVITE-MATTHEWS, N., RICHARDSON, A., O'SHEA, J., BECKER, J., OWEN, J., ROE, S. and CONDON, J. (2005), *Drug misuse declared: Findings from the 2003–04 British Crime Survey*, London: Home Office Statistical Bulletin 04/05.

COLLISON, M. (1996), 'In search of the high life: drugs, crime, masculinity and consumption', *British Journal of Criminology*, 36(3): 428–44

CONDON, J., and SMITH, N. (2003), *Prevalence of Drug Use: Key Findings from the 2002/2003 British Crime Survey*, London: Home Office.

COOMBER, R., and SAITH, N. (eds) (2004), *Drug Use in Cultural Contexts 'Beyond the West': Tradition. Change and Post-Colonialism*, London: Free Association Books.

CORBETT, C. (2003), *Car Crime*, Cullompton, Devon: Willan.

CORKERY, J. (2000), *Drug Seizure and Offender Statistics, UK, 1998*, Statistical Bulletin 3/00, London: Home Office.

COWAN, R. (2006), 'Police raid Vietnamese cannabis factory', *Guardian Unlimited*, 16 March.

CURRIE, E. (1993), 'Towards a policy on drugs', *Dissent* (Winter): 65–71.

DALGARNO, P., and SHEWAN, D. (2005), 'Reducing the risks of drug use: the case for set and setting', *Addiction Research and Theory*, 13(3): 259–65.

DALY, M. (2005), 'Alien nation', *Druglink*, 20(4): 6–8.

DAVIS, J., and DITTON, J. (1990), 'The 1990s: Decade of the Stimulants?', *British Journal of Addiction*, 85: 811–13.

DEEHAN, A. (1999), *Alcohol and Crime: Taking Stock*, Policing and Crime Reduction Unit, London: Home Office.

DENTON, B., and O'MALLEY, P. (1999), 'Gender, trust, and business. Women drug dealers in the illicit economy', *British Journal of Criminology*, 39: 513–30.

D'ORBAN, P. (1991), 'The Crimes Connection: Alcohol', in I. Glass (ed.), *The International Handbook of Addiction Behaviour*, London: Routledge.

DORN, N. (2004), 'UK policing of drug traffickers and users: policy implementation in the contexts of national law, European traditions, international drug conventions and security after 2001', *Journal of Drug Issues*.

——, MURJI, K., and SOUTH, N. (1992), *Traffickers: Drug Markets and Law Enforcement*, London: Routledge.

DOWNES, D. (1977), 'The Drug Addict as a Folk Devil', in P. Rock (ed.), *Drugs and Politics*, New Brunswick, N.J.: Transaction.

DRUGLINK (1992), 'Low Dependence and Use Typical of British Cocaine/Crack Users', *Druglink*, 7(3): 6.

—— (2005), 'Bengalis face heroin problem', Druglink, 20(4): 4.

DRUGSCOPE (2005), 'How many people die from using drugs?', Drugscope FAQs, www.drugscope.org.uk.

——(2006), *Druglink Guide to Drugs (updated)*, London: Drugscope.

ECONOMIST, THE (2001), 'The case for legalisation', *The Economist*; available at www.economist.com/opinion/.

EDMONDS, K., SUMNALL, H., MCVEIGH, J., and BELLIS, M. (2005), *Drug Prevention Among Vulnerable Young People*, Liverpool: National Collaborating Centre for Drug Prevention.

EDMUNDS, M., HOUGH, M., TURNBULL, P., and MAY, T. (1999), *Doing Justice to Treatment: Referring Offenders to Drug Services*, DPAS paper 2, London: Home Office.

ETTORRE, E., and RISKA, E. (1995), *Gendered Moods: Psychotropics and Society*, London: Routledge.

EUROPEAN MONITORING CENTRE FOR DRUGS AND DRUG ADDICTION (2003), *The State of the Drugs Problem in the European Union and Norway*, Luxembourg: EMCDDA.

FAGAN, J. (1994), 'Women and drugs revisited: female participation in the cocaine economy', *Journal of Drug Issues*, 24(2): 179–225.

FORESIGHT PROJECT (2006), 'Ethical aspects of developments in neuroscience and drug addiction-Summary', *Drugs Futures 2025*, London: Office of Science and Technology.

FOSTER, J. (2000), 'Social Exclusion, Crime and Drugs', *Drugs: Education, Prevention and Policy*, 7(4): 317–30.

GOSSOP, M. (1995), 'Counting the Costs as well as the Benefits of Drug Control Laws', *Addiction*, 90: 16–17.

—— (2005), *Drug Misuse Treatment and Reductions in Crime*, Research Briefing 8, London: National Treatment Agency for Substance Misuse.

GREEN, G., SMITH, R., and SOUTH, N. (2005), 'Court based psychiatric assessment: a case for an integrated and diversionary public health role', *Journal of Forensic Psychiatry and Psychology*, 16(3): 577–91.

GRINSPOON, L. (1999), 'Medical Marijuana in a Time of Prohibition', *International Journal of Drug Policy*, 10(3): 145–56.

HAYES, P. (2001), 'Driving up treatment standards: interview', *Access*, 4 (Drugs Prevention Advisory Service newsletter).

HENDERSON, S. (1999), 'Drugs and Culture: the Question of Gender', in N. South (ed.), *Drugs: Cultures, Controls and Everyday Life*, London: Sage.

HM GOVERNMENT (1998), *Tackling Drugs to Build a Better Britain*, London: Stationery Office.

HIBELL, B., ANDERSSON, B., BJARNASSON, T. *et al.* (2004), *Alcohol and other Drug Use among Students in 35 European Countries*, The ESPAD Report, 2003, Stockholm: Swedish Council for Information on Alcohol and Other Drugs.

HOBBS, R., HADFIELD, P., LISTER, S., and WINLOW, S. (2005), *Bouncers: violence and governance in the night time economy*, Oxford: Oxford University Press.

HUNT, G., and JOE-LAIDLER, K. (2001), 'Alcohol and violence in the lives of gang members', *Alcohol Research and Health*, 25(1): 66–71.

——, ——and MACKENZIE, K. (2000), ' "Chillin', Being Dogged and Getting Buzzed": Alcohol in the lives of female gang members', *Drugs: Education, Prevention and Policy*, 7(4): 331–53.

HUSAK, D., and DEMARNEFFE, P. (2005), *The Legalization of Drugs*, Cambridge: Cambridge University Press.

INCIARDI, J., and MCBRIDE, D. (1989), 'Legalisation: A High Risk Alternative in the War on Drugs', *American Behavioural Scientist*, 32(3): 259–89.

INSTITUTE FOR THE STUDY OF DRUG DEPENDENCE (1999), 'Coke in the UK', *Druglink*, 14(6): 4.

JOHNSTONE, G. (1996), *Medical Concepts and Penal Policy*, London: Cavendish.

KOHN, M. (1992), *Dope Girls: The Birth of the British Drug Underground*, London: Lawrence and Wishart.

LANCET, THE (1999), 'Alcohol and Violence', *The Lancet*, 336: 1223–24, 17 November.

LEE, M., and SOUTH, N. (2003), 'Policing and drugs', in T. Newburn (ed.), *The Handbook of Policing*, Cullompton, Devon: Willan.

LOMBROSO, C. (1968), *Crime: Its Causes and Remedies*, Montclair, N. J.: Patterson Smith, originally published 1911.

MCALLISTER, W. (2000), *Drug Diplomacy in the Twentieth Century*, London: Routledge.

MCCARRON, M. (2006), 'Drugs: which policies work?', *RSA Journal*, February, 29–33.

MACCOUN, R., and REUTER, P. (2001), *Drug War Heresies: Learning from Other Vices, Times, and Places*, Cambridge: Cambridge University Press.

MACDONALD, D. (2001), 'Death, Destruction and Depression: Understanding Afghanistan', *Druglink*, 16(5): 23–6.

MCDONALD, M. (ed.) (1994), *Gender, Drink and Drugs*, Oxford: Berg.

MCELRATH, K. (2004), 'Drug Use and Drug Markets in the Context of Political Conflict: The Case of Northern Ireland: *Addiction Research and Theory*, 12(6): 577–90.

MACGREGOR, S. (1998), 'Reluctant Partners: Trends in Approaches to Urban Drug-taking in Contemporary Britain', *Journal of Drug Issues*, 28(1): 185–98.

——(1999), 'Medicine, Custom or Moral Fibre: Policy Responses to Drug Misuse', in N. South (ed.), *Drugs: Cultures, Controls and Everyday Life*, London: Sage.

MAHER, L. (1997), *Sexed Work: Gender, Race and Resistance in a Brooklyn Drug Market*, Oxford: Clarendon Press.

MATASSA, M., and NEWBURN, T. (2003), 'Policing and terrorism', in T. Newburn (ed.), *The Handbook of Policing*, Cullompton, Devon: Willan.

MAY, T., and HOUGH, M. (2004), 'Drug markets and distribution systems', *Addiction Research and Theory*, 12(6): 549–63.

——, EDMUNDS, M., and HOUGH, M. (1999), *Street Business: Links Between Sex and Drug Markets*, Crime Prevention Series Paper, London: Home Office Police Research Group.

MEASHAM, F., PARKER, H., and ALDRIDGE, J. (2000), *Dancing on Drugs: Risk, Health and Hedonism in the British Club Scene*, London: FABooks.

MINISTRY OF HEALTH (1926), *Report of the Departmental Committee on Morphine and Heroin Addiction*, London: HMSO.

MOTT, J. (1991), 'Crime and Heroin Use', in D. Whynes and P. Bean (eds), *Policing and Prescribing: The British System of Drug Control*, London: Macmillan.

MURJI, K. (1999), 'White Lines: Culture, "Race" and Drugs', in N. South (ed.), *Drugs: Cultures, Controls and Everyday Life*, London: Sage.

MWENDA, L. (2005), *Drug Offenders in England and Wales*, Statistical Bulletin, 23/05, London: Home Office.

NADELMAN, E. (1989), 'Drug Prohibition in the United States: Costs, Consequences and Alternatives', *Science*, 245: 939–47.

NCSR/NFER (National Centre for Social Research/National Foundation for Education Research) (2005), *Smoking, Drinking and Drug Use among Young People in England in 2004*, London: Department of Health.

NURCO, D., BALL, J., SHAFFER, J., and HANLON, T. (1985), 'The Criminality of Narcotic Addicts', *The Journal of Nervous and Mental Disease*, 173(2): 94–102.

PARKER, H. (1996), 'Alcohol, persistent young offenders and criminological cul-de-sacs', *British Journal of Criminology*, 36(2): 282–99.

—— and MEASHAM, F. (1994), 'Pick 'n Mix: changing patterns of illicit drug use amongst 1990s adolescents', *Drugs: Education, Prevention and Policy*, 1(1): 5–14.

——, ALDRIDGE, J., and MEASHAM, F. (1998), *Illegal Leisure: The Normalization of Adolescent Recreational Drug Use*, London: Routledge.

PARSSINEN, T. (1983), *Secret Passions, Secret Remedies: Narcotic Drugs in British Society, 1820–1930*, Manchester: Manchester University Press.

PATEL, K. (1999), 'Watching brief', *Druglink*, 14(5): 18–19.

PEARSON, G. (1987a), *The New Heroin Users*, Oxford: Basil Blackwell.

—— (1987b), 'Social Deprivation, Unemployment and Patterns of Heroin Use', in N. Dorn and N. South (eds), *A Land Fit for Heroin?: Drug Policies, Prevention and Practice*, London: Macmillan.

—— (1991), 'Drug Control Policies in Britain', in M. Tonry and J. Q. Wilson (eds), *Drugs and the Criminal Justice System, Crime and Justice*, 14: 167–227.

—— (2001), 'Normal drug use', *Substance Use and Misuse*, 36 (1 & 2): 167–200.

—— and HOBBS, D. (2001), *Middle Market Drug Distribution*, Research Study 27, London: Home Office.

—— and PATEL, K. (1998), 'Drugs, Deprivation and Ethnicity: Outreach among Asian Drug Users in a Northern English City', *Journal of Drug Issues*, 28(1): 199–224.

PIRMOHAMED, M., BROWN, C., OWENS, L., LUKE, C., GILMORE, I., BRECKENRIDGE, A., and PARK, B. (2000), 'The burden of alcohol misuse on an inner-city general hospital', *QJM: International Journal of Medicine*, 93(5): 291–5.

PLANT, M., MILLER, P. and PLANT, M. (2005), 'The relationship between alcohol consumption and problem behaviours: gender differences among British adults', *Journal of Substance Use*, 10(1): 22–30.

POLICE FOUNDATION (2000), *Drugs and the Law: Report of the Independent Inquiry*, London: Police Foundation.

PRISON REFORM TRUST (2005), *Prison Factfile, May 2005*, London: PRT; www.prisonreformtrust.org.uk.

PUDNEY, S. (2002), *The Road to Ruin? Sequences of Initiation into Drug Use and Offending by Young People in Britain*: Home Office Research Studies 252, London: Home Office.

RAISTRICK, D., HODGSON, R., and RITSON, B. (eds) (1999), *Tackling Alcohol Together: The Evidence Base for a UK Alcohol Policy*, London: Free Association Books.

RESEARCH DEVELOPMENT AND STATISTICS DIRECTORATE (2003), *Ethnicity and drug use: key findings from the 2001/2002 British Crime Survey*, London: Home Office.

RICHARDSON, A., and BUDD, T. (2003), *Alcohol, crime and disorder: a study of young adults*, Home Office Research Study 263, London: Home Office.

ROBERTS, M. (2003), *Drugs and Crime: From Warfare to Welfare*, London: NACRO.

ROSENBAUM, M. (1981), *Women on Heroin*, New Brunswick, N.J.: Rutgers University Press.

ROYAL COLLEGE OF PHYSICIANS AND BRITISH PAEDIATRIC ASSOCIATION (1995), *Alcohol and the Young*, London: Royal College of Physicians.

ROYAL SOCIETY OF ARTS (RSA) Drugs Commission (2006), 'News page' at www.rsadrugscommission.org/.

RUGGIERO, V., and SOUTH, N. (1995), *Eurodrugs: Drug Use, Markets and Trafficking in Europe*, London: UCL.

—— and —— (1997), 'The Late–Modern City as a Bazaar: Drug Markets, Illegal Enterprise and "the Barricades"', *British Journal of Sociology*, 48(1): 55–71.

SANDERS, B. (2005), 'In the club: ecstasy use and supply in a London nightclub', *Sociology*, 39(2): 241–58.

SAXENA, S. (1995), 'A Stroke of Distinctive Colour', *Addiction*, 90: 13–14.

SEDDON, T. (2002), 'Five Myths about Drugs and Crime', *Safer Society*, 14, Autumn.

SHAPIRO, H. (1999), 'Dances with Drugs', in N. South (ed.), *Drugs: Cultures, Controls and Everyday Life*, London: Sage.

SHARP, C., BAKER, P., GAILDEN, C., RAMSAY, M., and SANDHI, A. (2001), *Drug Misuse Declared in*

2000: Results from the British Crime Survey, Findings 149, London: Home Office.

SHEPHERD, J., and LISLES, C. (1998), 'Towards Multi-Agency Violence Prevention and Victim Support', *British Journal of Criminology*, 38(3): 351–70.

SHINER, M., and NEWBURN, T. (1999), 'Taking Tea with Noel: The Place and Meaning of Drug Use in Everyday Life', in N. South (ed.), *Drugs: Cultures, Controls and Everyday Life*, London: Sage.

SINGLETON, N., FARREL, M., and MELTZER, H. (1999), *Substance Misuse among Prisoners in England and Wales*, London: Office of National Statistics.

SMART, C. (1984), 'Social Policy and Drug Addiction: A Critical Study of Policy Development', *British Journal of Addiction*, 79: 31–9.

SOCIAL EXCLUSION UNIT (2004), *A New Direction for the Social Exclusion Unit 2004–5: Improving Service Delivery to the Most Disadvantaged*, London: Office of the Deputy Prime Minister.

SOUTH, N. (ed.) (1995), *Drugs, Crime and Criminal Justice, vol. 1*, Aldershot: Dartmouth.

——(ed.) (1999a), *Drugs: Cultures, Controls and Everyday Life*, London: Sage.

——(1999b), 'Debating Drugs and Everyday Life', in N. South (ed.), *Drugs: Cultures, Controls and Everyday Life*, London: Sage.

——(2004), 'Managing work, hedonism and the borderline between the legal and illegal markets', *Addiction Research and Theory*, 122(6): 525–38.

——, AKHTAR, S., NIGHTINGALE, R., and STEWART, M. (2001), 'Idle Hands: The Role of Employment in Addiction Treatment', *Drug and Alcohol Findings*, 1(6): 24–30.

STRATEGY UNIT (2003), *Drugs Report, Parts 1 and 2*, London: Cabinet Office.

SUMNALL, H., MCGRATH, Y., MCVEIGH, J., BURRELL, K., WILKINSON, L., and BELLIS, M. (2006), *Drug Use Prevention Among Young People*, London: National Institute for Health and Clinical Excellence.

TAYLOR, A. (1993), *Women Drug Users*, Oxford: Clarendon Press.

TAYLOR, I. (1999), *Crime in Context: A Critical Criminology of Market Societies*, Cambridge: Polity.

TOMSEN, S. (1997), 'A Top Night: Social Protest, Masculinity and the Culture of Drinking Violence', *British Journal of Criminology*, 37(1): 90–102.

TYLER, A. (1995), *Street Drugs*, London: Hodder & Stoughton.

WHITTINGTON, D. (1999), 'Nang Tien Nan: Princess Opium in Deptford', *Druglink*, 14(5): 13–14.

WILSON, J. (1990), 'Drugs and Crime', in M. Tonry and J. Q. Wilson (eds), *Drugs and Crime*, Chicago, Ill.: University of Chicago Press.

WOOTTON COMMITTEE (1968), *Cannabis: Report by the Advisory Committee on Drug Dependence*, London: HMSO.

YOUNG, J. (1971), *The Drugtakers: The Social Meaning of Drug Use*, London: Paladin.

PART V

REACTIONS TO CRIME

25

THE GOVERNANCE OF SECURITY: PLURALIZATION, PRIVATIZATION, AND POLARIZATION IN CRIME CONTROL

*Trevor Jones**

The way in which the security of citizens is organized and delivered in contemporary polities has undergone dramatic shifts over recent decades. These changes pose challenging theoretical questions about how we conceptualize security and its provision, as well as raising important normative issues about its contribution to the 'good society' and the most appropriate institutional arrangements for delivering this. This chapter provides an overview of recent debates about apparent transformations in the ways in which security is conceptualized and provided. It considers how security is being reconfigured, and what this implies for its current models of governance and how it might be better governed in the future. The chapter is divided into three main sections. The first discusses the two central concepts of the chapter, 'governance' and 'security'. The second section explores a number of key contemporary developments in the governance of security with a particular focus upon *diversification, the emergence of risk-based approaches, social polarization and exclusion*, and *expansion*. The third section considers debates about what is to be done. The fragmentation, transformation, polarization, and expansion of security pose a number of threats to equity, effectiveness, and accountability. However, these developments also provide opportunities to move towards a more democratic, just, and effective organization of security provision.

* I would like to thank Adam Edwards, Mike Maguire, and Tim Newburn for their helpful comments on an earlier draft of this chapter.

CLARIFYING KEY TERMS

GOVERNANCE

'Governance' has now become a central theme within writing about crime control, security, and order (Edwards 2006, Loader and Sparks, Chapter 3, this volume). Literally, the term denotes the activity (or activities) of 'governing'—self-conscious attempts to promote various collective outcomes. Such activities are an intrinsic part of social life, and governing arrangements of some form emerge wherever human beings associate with each other (Roberts 2005). Within criminological writing, the term was originally used in a straightforward way, for example to denote the constitutional and institutional arrangements for the formulation and direction of police policy (Lustgarten 1986). More recently, however, a different use of the term has emerged within writing about crime and crime control, arising from two distinct bodies of thought that challenge state-centred conceptions of the way that governing power is exercised.

First, work within the 'governmentality' tradition has highlighted the complex forms of rule by which authorities govern populations in contemporary societies. From this viewpoint, social life is regulated by the deployment of technologies of the self through which individuals work on themselves to shape their own conduct (Foucault 1991). In contemporary societies, governmental power aims to construct individuals who are capable of choice and action, but at the same time seeks to align their choices with the objectives of governing authorities. Thus, individuals and non-state organizations are configured as active participants in their own government, and increasingly governance involves the reshaping of institutions in ways that encourage individuals to regulate themselves (Braithwaite 2000). Governmentality theorists highlighted the ways in which various neo-liberal reform programmes have separated the 'steering' and 'rowing' elements of governing (Osborne and Gaebler 1993), and taking this a step further have suggested that there is a whole realm of government that is undertaken 'beyond the state'. As Rose and Miller (1992: 174) have stated: '[P]olitical power is exercised today through a profusion of shifting alliances between diverse authorities in projects to govern a multitude of facets of economic activity, social life and individual conduct'. The social is thus reconfigured as a realm of government and the governmental process is dispersed throughout the social field, permeating a network of agencies rather than remaining concentrated in the institutions of the state.

Similar themes are visible within a second body of work that has proposed new ways of thinking about the ways in which societies are governed. In the UK, this has been most widely associated with the work of Rod Rhodes and his critique of what he termed the 'Westminster model' of government. Rhodes (1997) deployed the term 'governance' to capture the complexity and fragmentation of contemporary government, and in particular to denote the emergence of governmental strategies originating from both inside and outside of the state. Governing power operates via what he termed 'self-organizing inter-organizational networks'. In Rhodes's terms, '[g]overnance signifies a *change* in the meaning of government, referring to a *new* process of governing; or a *changed* condition of ordered rule; or the method by which society is governed' (1997: 46, emphasis in original). Rhodes links these changes to familiar developments associated with neo-liberal reforms (of different kinds) such as privatization, contracting out, and the creation of semi-autonomous service delivery agencies. The governmental picture has been further complicated by the growing influence of supranational institutions such as the European Union. These developments have, it is argued, led to a fragmentation of the state, reducing the central state's control over the implementation of policy and further encouraging the development of inter-organizational networks. Relationships between the various parties within networks are characterized by 'power dependence' (Stoker 1998). Since policy actors have access to different types and levels of resources—financial, political, legal, or administrative—the policy process is characterized by negotiation and bargaining between a myriad of bodies, both state and non-state. Inevitably, some actors have greater resources than others, and in most cases the central state maintains a key position because of greater financial and legal resources when compared with other actors. Despite the growing complexity of the policy process, the state retains an important capacity to define various interests as legitimate, give shape to political organization, and incorporate some societal actors (and not others) into the policy-making process. The relationship between state organizations and other parts of policy networks is thus characterized by 'asymmetric interdependence'. The governmental authorities rule via attempting to steer networks in the required direction, via a process of negotiation and bargaining rather than central command.

Both the governmentality and the new governance literatures highlight the importance of non-state actors in governing processes, and suggest a more limited role for state institutions, in contrast with traditional constitutional analyses of the process of government (see, for example, Marshall 1984). Of course, the developments that they discuss are not novel. Only in the simplest of societies could a central governing power rule by direct command, and even at an early stage of development of sovereign nation states, central and local state institutions always needed to interact and bargain with other policy actors in order to develop and implement policy. There is a long tradition of pluralist analysis within both US and UK political science, the starting point of which was that a formal (state) institutional focus obscured the reality of how political power is exercised in modern polities. The emergence of pluralist accounts within political science was in part a reaction against the idea that constitutional factors (ministers, parties, separation of powers, etc.) were the key to understanding the way government worked. Instead, pluralists focused upon the interplay of a range of groups competing to organize and represent different interests shared by overlapping segments of society (Atkinson and Coleman 1992). In these models, the lobbying activities of interest groups were presented as a necessary condition for good governance, rather than a corrupting threat to democracy (Dahl 1961; Polsby 1963). Political scientists in this tradition suggested the primary role of state institutions in governing was in setting the 'rules of the game' for interest-group intermediation, and then attempting to aggregate and implement the policy preferences arising out of interest-group interactions.

Thus, the term 'governance' should be viewed as a different approach to *thinking about* the way that government operates, rather than denoting a fundamentally new and transformed mode of governing. However, the fragmentation of the policy process has clearly become more marked in recent years, in terms of both the numbers of actors involved in policy-making, and the complexity of the interrelationships between them. Two points in particular are worth bearing in mind for the later discussion. First, although these approaches to understanding the networked nature of contemporary governance have been extremely influential within political science, little of this work has paid attention to the policy domain of crime control and security provision (although see Ryan *et al.* 2001 for an exception). The deployment of the concepts of governance to this sphere has largely been undertaken by scholars working within the field of criminology and related subject areas (Johnston and Shearing 2003). The second point is that the clear implication of much new governance writing is that the role of the state in modern polities not only has been reconfigured but has been significantly limited. However, important though these trends clearly are, we should caution against overplaying the idea of state fragmentation and note that many writers emphasize the continued importance of national state institutions in the development of policy (Atkinson and Coleman 1992).

SECURITY

What is 'security', and why should we wish to pursue it? The term can denote a range of distinct meanings: it is used to describe an objective state of being protected from threats or danger, a subjective feeling of safety, or the means of pursuit of either of these (Zedner 2003). Johnston and Shearing (2003) note the range of meanings that are covered by the term, from states of physical safety, to those of emotional, psychological, and financial well-being. The focus here is upon the more immediate physical aspects of safety associated with the subjective and psychological concerns about possibilities of future threats to such safety. Following Johnston and Shearing, the promotion of security can be defined as 'intentional actions whose purpose is to provide guarantees of safety to subjects, both in the present and in the future' (2003: 15). A central feature of security provision is therefore future orientation, in that its main concern is to reduce the potential for current or future harms. This contrasts with the primarily retrospective vision of punishment which seeks to exact retribution for past wrongs. Two further features of the term security are worth mentioning here. First, in one common usage the term tends to have strong sectoral connotations and brings to mind commercial providers of security (for example, 'private security' or the 'security industry'). Secondly, within discussions of policing, the term is closely associated with 'high' policing of 'state security' (for example, see references to the 'security services' and 'national security') rather than the everyday 'low' policing functions of regulating crime and disorder in local communities (Bowling and Newburn 2006). There is not space here to discuss the international dimension of security governance (Dorn and Levi, forthcoming), although current debates about police restructuring in

England and Wales demonstrate how forms of security provision (for example, counter-terrorism versus neighbourhood policing) and levels of security (global, national, regional, and local) are increasingly entwined (O'Conner 2005). For further discussion of global developments in the governance of crime and security, see Loader and Sparks (Chapter 3, this volume), and Newburn and Reiner (Chapter 27, this volume).

A key question, and one that may appear odd given the current climate of security obsession, is how far do we want to go to achieve security? Surely it is self-evident that governments and citizens would wish to do the utmost to reduce the risk of future harms? However, security cannot be automatically assumed to be a universal and unqualified good (Zedner 2003). Unchecked attempts to quench the thirst for more security can have serious negative effects on civil liberties and on social life in general. The pursuit of security is not always compatible with, and must be balanced against, other valued social goods, such as liberty and privacy (Johnston 2000; Johnston and Shearing 2003). The promotion of security entails costs, and therefore requires explicit moral justification (Zedner 2003). Zedner draws upon the philosophy of punishment to develop a principled framework that can guide the pursuit of security, one that seeks to reconcile the important principle of minimalism (security arrangements often restrict the freedom of citizens in important ways) with the demands of social defence (in that citizens reasonably expect a degree of protection from harm as they go about their everyday lives). We shall return to these normative arguments in the last part of the chapter.

Thus, we cannot assume that the pursuit of security is unequivocally a good thing. However, whilst we must remain mindful of its actual and potential costs, security also clearly does have major social benefits. Loader and Walker (2006) highlight three beneficial public dimensions of security. First, the instrumental dimension reflects the fact that a degree of security is a necessary condition (or 'foundational presence') for the effective liberty of citizens and the attainment of other important social goods:

> the various infrastructural goods, which we may associate with the production of a more positive conception of freedom, such as widespread distribution of education, health provision, and social security, cannot be conceived of without the baseline of security—of negative freedom—and the stability of democratic politics and public administration which flows from this [Loader and Walker 2006: 184].

Secondly, security has an important social dimension, in so far as the security of any particular individual depends in some essential way upon the security of others. A person's sense of their own security cannot be viewed independently of others: the very notion of 'private security' is a contradiction in terms (Loader 1997). The reconfiguration of security as a private commodity—something that can be and should be purchased by individual consumers in the marketplace—raises a number of tensions, as we will see later. Thirdly, security has an important constitutive dimension, in that the promotion of security is fundamental to the establishment and sustenance of a sense of the social or the collective. The desire for protection from threats, and the ways in which collectivities realize such desires, plays a central role in establishing and maintaining trust, social identity, and a sense of community. In this sense, the pursuit of security 'helps to construct and sustain our "we feeling"—our very felt sense of "common publicness"' (Loader and Walker 2006: 191).

There are, then, important reasons why we should promote security and why it is viewed as a positive social good. However, the costs of security, and in particular the ways in which its pursuit can impinge negatively on other social goals, remind us of the need for a parsimonious and principled framework to shape and optimize our security arrangements. Many commentators suggest that recent shifts in security governance have exacerbated the danger of ineffective and inequitable provision of security to citizens, and had negative impacts upon other social goals such as liberty and justice.

KEY FEATURES OF CONTEMPORARY SECURITY GOVERNANCE

DIVERSIFICATION

The authorization and provision of security have become increasingly fragmented over recent years, and this can be seen on a number of distinct levels (Loader 2000). The focus here is on three levels in particular. There is growing diversification within the institutions of state government itself, beyond the state (primarily in terms of the commercialization of policing services), and below the level of the state (with the emergence of localized community-led forms of security authorization and provision). These trends are also clearly visible at the global level (above the nation state), and are discussed further by Loader and Sparks (Chapter 3, this volume).

Within state government

Although until the late twentieth century the provision of security and crime control remained primarily associated with the formal institutions of the state criminal justice system, this picture has become increasingly blurred in recent decades. Even within the realm of national state government itself, there has been a growth in the authorizers and providers of security services and a growing complexity in the arrangements for its effective promotion. There has been a significant pluralization of policing in terms of a proliferation of different providers within the field (Loader 2000; Crawford *et al.* 2005; Jones and Newburn 2006). There is now a range of forms of policing provision operating within the remit of national and local government. Some of these bodies are clearly new additions to the policing landscape. Others, however, have been around for many years but simply been rather invisible to academic scrutiny. During the 1980s and 1990s, a number of local authorities set up uniformed patrol services, and several established specialist bodies of constables (Jones 2003). The Police Reform Act 2002 enabled chief constables to designate police authority support staff as 'Police

Community Support Officers' (PCSOs) in order to support police officers in tackling low-level crime and antisocial behaviour. At the time of writing there are over 6,000 such officers in England and Wales, but the government plans to expand this number to 25,000 by 2008. Writers in the policing field have also come to recognize other long-established organizations operating largely within the public sector as important policing providers within the security networks. These bodies include special police forces (such as the British Transport Police (BTP)), and specialist investigatory and regulatory bodies attached to national and local government (such as the Health and Safety Executive, Post Office Investigation and Security Services, environmental health officers, trading standards officers, benefit fraud investigators, etc.) (Jones and Newburn 2006; Newburn and Reiner, Chapter 26, this volume). In addition to the growing number of providers, relationships within and between these different policing organizations have become more complex due to a long-term programme of marketization of public policing that dates back to the early 1980s. Key themes within this have been budgetary devolution, contracting out, and the provision of sponsorship and commercial funding (Crawford 2003). Overall then, the picture of who pays for and who provides public policing is becoming ever more complex and blurred.

Beyond state government

The growth of commercial security provision, and the increasing influence of corporate forms of private governance, has been a central element in debates about the diversification of security provision. Commercial provision of staffed security services, security equipment, and investigatory services in the UK has grown substantially in recent years. Although it is difficult to obtain reliable international comparative data in this area, there is strong evidence that similar trends have been experienced in many countries across the globe. Commercial provision has not just been restricted to the sphere of low policing, but a growing transnational security industry is engaged in the provision of military hardware and personnel, corrections and policing (Bowling and Newburn 2006; Dorn and Levi, forthcoming). Various factors lie behind such trends, including the growing demands for policing and security services outstripping the resources of public providers, a degree of direct privatization and hiving off of policing functions as part of central government reform programmes, the changing nature of urban space, and a range of broader structural changes in contemporary industrial societies that have contributed to growing concerns about risk and insecurity (Jones and Newburn 2006).

This substantial expansion of commercial security is not confined to the proliferation of providers. There has also been an expansion of the various auspices under which security is organized, with a growing number of authorizers of security functions (Bayley and Shearing 2001). This reflects a more fundamental shift in governance generally, with the expansion of domains of non-state governments that not only contract in security provision themselves (sometimes from state providers), but substantially determine the nature of the order to be protected, the kinds of rules necessary to do this, and the manner in which compliance is achieved (Shearing 2006).

Clifford Shearing has noted that much existing policing research—including work on the commercial security industry—overlooks the growing importance of private governments (McCauley 1986). These are defined as 'non-state entities that operate not simply as providers of governance on behalf of state agencies but as auspices of government in their own right' (Shearing 2006: 11). It is argued that, increasingly, social life takes place within non-state zones of governance, and this brings into question the meaning of citizenship and the notion of a public sphere. Some such developments are related to the deliberate policies of privatization and responsibilization adopted by state governments, but many have emerged completely independently of the state realm. The growing influence of private governance renders the notion of citizenship—tied to the idea of sovereign nation states—increasingly problematic. Indeed, it is argued that people should increasingly be thought of as 'denizens' of a range of distinct governmental domains, rather than citizens of a single, territorially defined, sovereign state (Shearing and Wood 2003). Much of the initial discussion about the rise of commercial policing related its expansion to the growth of 'mass private property' (Shearing and Stenning 1981) in many countries. This is defined as large, geographically connected holdings of commercially owned property to which access is open to large numbers of people, such as shopping centres, holiday complexes, retail parks, educational campuses, leisure parks, and private residential complexes (or 'gated communities') (Jones and Newburn 1998). Shearing and Stenning (1981, 1987) have linked the growth of mass private property to the emergence of corporate feudalism, whereby private governments exist alongside state government and where responsibility for guaranteeing and defining the peace progressively shifts from the state to corporate entities (Shearing 1992: 425). Thus, many citizens increasingly live, work, shop, and spend their leisure time in these commercially owned and governed spaces, rather than in the traditional public sphere.

It is clear that the spatial configuration of contemporary urban environments has important implications for the governance of security. Recent work has suggested a growing degree of spatial complexity, with a continuum of spatial types varying in terms of legal ownership and openness (Wakefield 2003; Kempa *et al.* 2004). In England and Wales, case law has confirmed the right of the owners of mass private property to arbitrarily exclude people from their land (Wakefield 2003). In 1995, the Court of Appeal upheld the right of the owners of an English shopping centre to permanently ban a group of youths from their property.[1] It is cases such as this that have led Crawford (2006) to conclude that the courts in England and Wales have provided private property owners with an almost unqualified right to exclude, which has major implications for the powers of private governments over citizens' lives. As von Hirsch and Shearing (2000) have argued, the use of exclusionary powers in this way can effectively exclude citizens from a major part of public life, given the increasing location of a range of employment, retail, and leisure facilities on such property. Such policies evade due process safeguards that limit the application of the criminal law, and also

---

[1] *CIN Properties Ltd* v. *Rawlins* (CA) [1995] 2 EGLR 130.

allow for disproportionate 'punishment' in relation to the initial offence. More recently, a residents' group in the north-east of England have brought a case before the European Court of Human Rights, regarding their rights within the privately owned Washington town centre in Tyne and Wear. The town centre houses a police station, health centre, and library as well as shops and other amenities. It was sold to a private property company during the 1970s, but residents only became aware of this when a pressure group began to collect signatures in the town centre for a petition about a controversial local development. Security agents prevented this because the owners of the property (a large insurance company) banned political activity on their land.

Thus, sovereignty itself—the authority to govern—is increasingly exercised by corporate private governments. Such developments call into question the involvement of the state not only in security provision, but in governing social life more generally. The work of Shearing and colleagues has therefore been vital in focusing attention upon the under-researched issue of non-state governing auspices and their implications for governance generally. An important objective of future research is to explore the extent and nature of the growth of these new communal spaces, and within this to identify what is novel and significant about current developments. There is certainly some evidence of significant growth in such spaces in many countries, particularly those with substantial amounts of available land and relatively less stringent state planning regulations (MacLeod 2003; Glasze *et al.* 2006). In other national contexts, not least the UK and other European countries, the limited data available suggest that these trends are less marked, but are certainly still significant, particularly in the retail sector (Minton 2002; Jones and Newburn 1999). Further research is also required to help us explore what is new about contemporary forms of non-state governance, since, as Shearing (2006) himself points out, private governments have always been with us. For example, as Roberts notes (2005: 16):

> [T]he size of these shifts should not be exaggerated; there has sometimes been a tendency to express their discovery in apocalyptic terms . . . These spaces are always there in centralized polities . . . this configuration is certainly not a unique feature of late capitalism, even if it takes on distinctive forms.

As is further developed in the next section, the expansion of some commercial types of private government has been accompanied by a substantial decline of many other forms of governance 'below the state' over the past century. What is novel is not private government per se, but the distinctive nature and form that it takes in late modern societies. The most significant development is perhaps the corporatization of private governance. Many of the new communal spaces that are discussed in the literature are established and governed by commercial profit-making organizations (as compared with the greater influence of non-market forms of private government for earlier generations, such as chapels/churches, trade unions, community clubs, and organizations, etc.). This is reflected in the changed nature of activities that occur under the gaze of private governments, with perhaps more leisure, travel, and shopping activities from the late twentieth century, as compared with cultural, working, and religious activities in previous eras. It may well be the case, given these other shifts, that there has been a change in the nature of the populations subject to private forms of security governance. Much contemporary private governance is concerned with promoting a safe and amenable environment for the consumption activities of the better off. Working-class and impoverished communities are therefore less likely to be members of privately governed organizations, and more likely to be subject to active exclusion from the spaces they cover. Finally, a key difference from former eras concerns the transnationalization of private government, which reflects the growing corporatization of social life more broadly. Many of these zones of governance operate not only within nation states, but across and outwith national boundaries (Shearing 2006).

Below state government

An important element of the proliferation of security providers and authorizers has occurred below national state institutions, in the form of order-definition and maintenance, rule-making, and enforcement exercised by non-commercial community and voluntary organizations. Part of this has involved the 'responsibilization' of non-state organizations to take control of their own security, and the language of partnership (Garland 1996). Whilst much of this activity has involved commercial organizations, an important objective of such approaches is to access the resources of community and voluntary organizations also. A number of authors have highlighted the growth of 'citizen-led' policing in a number of countries. For example, Bayley and Shearing have highlighted the expansion of neighbourhood watch schemes, crime prevention associations, protective escort services, and monitors around schools, shopping malls, and public parks (1996: 587). Activities that might once have been viewed as vigilantism are now actively encouraged by state organizations. Although there are no data to measure trends in the frequency of vigilante-type actions, it has been suggested that such phenomena are increasing (Johnston 1992, 1996). Against this, however, many formerly influential forms non-state governance below the level of the nation state have been in sharp decline, at least for the majority of working-class people in the UK.

To take a personal example, the extent to which the life of my grandfather was governed by non-state auspices below government was far greater than is the case for many members of the current generation. He was a 'denizen' of a number of distinct zones of governance covering most aspects of his life in the first half of the twentieth century. He spent his working day in the mass communal space of a South Wales steelworks, a huge industrial site that included its own private security force and internally organized ambulance and fire services. Within this working environment and many others like it, trade unions exerted significant governing influence over workers' day-to-day lives. Outside the workplace, religious and cultural life was dominated by non-state auspices. Daily life was organized around a host of chapel-related activities, and also by membership of other community organizations (not least the male voice choir, sporting clubs and, in his latter years, charitable bodies). For the majority of the British working-class population, these forms of non-state governance, many of which were connected directly or indirectly to the existence of secure lifetime employment, have literally collapsed during the latter part of the twentieth century (Mount 2005). The long-term decline of mass industrial employment, trade union membership, religious observance, and involvement in community and voluntary organizations is a well-documented feature of late modern societies (see, for example, Putnam 2000).

Whilst the declining influence of private governance is clearly true for much of the white working class, for some communities in the UK, non-state forms of private governance—many built around business and religious networks in particular communities—have become increasingly important. From the 1960s onwards, some immigrant communities responded to widespread disadvantage and discrimination in the housing and labour markets by developing high levels of home ownership and self-employment (Jones 1996; Modood *et al.* 1997). As a range of working-class institutions and forms of community organization have disintegrated amongst the white population in the former industrial areas of the UK, the influence of religious and community groups as forms of non-state governance has arguably expanded amongst more recently arrived groups to those areas (Edwards 2002). Recent debates about how to manage tensions between minority (often religious-based) sensitivities, and the broader liberal secular values (for example, regarding women's rights, freedom of expression, etc.) have highlighted the fact that, at least in some cases, non-state auspices are increasingly challenging the order that the state seeks to uphold.

RISK-BASED FORMS OF SECURITY GOVERNANCE

Contemporary security governance not only has been diversified in its authorization and provision, but there is evidence that it is changing in its fundamental nature. In particular, there has been a marked shift in the mentalities, technologies, and practices of security governance towards proactive and risk-oriented approaches (Loader and Sparks, Chapter 3, this volume). The commodification of security (and the expansion-ary dynamic of capitalism generally) has come to engender a forward-looking loss-reduction mentality that goes against the grain of traditional criminal justice approaches based on the retrospective punishment of past wrongs. This chimes with broader theories suggesting that contemporary social life is increasingly organized around attempts to predict and prevent (or at least ameliorate) future harms (Beck 1992). Feeley and Simon (1994) have suggested that contemporary penality is charac-terized by a 'New Penology' focused around risk-based discourses, objectives, and tech-niques. Rather than seeking to punish offenders for past wrongs, or even to rehabilitate them as law-abiding and productive citizens, contemporary criminal justice systems increasingly seek to place offenders (and, crucially, potential offenders) into particular risk categories, and then manage them in the most cost-effective way possible. Garland (2001) has linked shifts to risk-oriented thinking to a range of broader developments. Within academic criminology, there has been a growing influence of 'economic' the-ories of crime that present offenders as utility-maximizing individuals responding rationally to opportunities for crime. These 'criminologies of everyday life' include rational choice theory, and routine activities theory, and they underpin the idea of situational crime prevention. This approach seeks to manipulate the physical environment to minimize opportunities for crime and disorder, reduce the perceived rewards, or increase the potential risks of such behaviour (Clarke 1997).

These new risk-based mentalities and practices exist alongside more traditional punishment-oriented practices. For example, Kemshall and Maguire's (2001) analysis of the risk management of sex offenders in the community demonstrates the contested nature of such developments at the level of policy implementation. Although the language of risk looms large in policy documents and the discourse of managers, in practice this has been subject to a significant degree of resistance and reworking within and between particular criminal justice agencies. Similarly, Johnston (2000) shows how, within contemporary public policing, risk-based forms of thinking compete and coexist in complex ways with more traditional disciplinary approaches. Johnston and Shearing (2003) demonstrate how punitive enforcement-oriented means are used to address more preventive, future-oriented ends in the form of zero tolerance policing. Other key contemporary developments in public policing display this complex mingling of disciplinary and risk-oriented mentalities, technologies, and practices (Loader 1999). Developments in the corporate sector are central to all these trends. Shaped by the instrumental objective of loss reduction, Johnston and Shearing (2003) show how risk-oriented forms of thinking have a certain fit with market sensibilities, but do not sit comfortably with more traditional punitive approaches. This has resulted in a proliferation of different kinds of security provision, which are more hidden and consensual than traditional forms. For example, they place more emphasis on surveillance (often using new technologies such as CCTV), and deploy a range of other interventions to modify behaviour. On this view, security is increasingly embedded, both occupationally and functionally, throughout organizations. It is also designed in to the physical structure of premises, so that the architecture and layout of the built environment reduces the possibility of non-compliance (Newman 1972; Coleman 1985).

These developments are certainly important. However, it is also clear that neo-liberal reforms have simultaneously promoted contradictory trends. In some cases, the introduction of cost-cutting technology has removed the human element from areas of life that were at one time covered by a greater degree of natural surveillance. Rather than spread responsibility for security throughout organizations, such trends can actually result in a greater formalization of security provision. There has been a huge fall in occupations that traditionally offered a degree of 'secondary social control', in the form of authority figures—sometimes uniformed—who were present and visible in many public and quasi-public spaces (Jones and Newburn 2002). Such occupations include bus and tram conductors, receptionists, ticket collectors and guards, rail and bus station staff, roundsmen and women, and park-keepers. In part, this has been a consequence of the development and spread of new labour-saving technologies such as self-purchase ticket machines, automatic barriers, CCTV, and automated access control. Research on public and private policing in a London borough during the 1990s found that commercial security was undertaking activities that had previously been undertaken not by public police officers, but by caretakers, receptionists, teachers, school prefects, and park-keepers (Jones and Newburn 1998).

SOCIAL POLARIZATION AND EXCLUSION

One of the key features of the contemporary governance of security concerns its exclusionary and polarizing tendencies. This is one of the key paradoxes of security: that although security is often promoted as a universal good for the benefit of all, in practice its pursuit assumes and exacerbates social exclusion (Zedner 2003). It involves identification, targeting, and exclusion of those groups deemed to pose a threat. The growth of actuarial mentalities and practices, as outlined above, necessarily widens the gaze of those concerned with promoting security. We are now no longer simply concerned with investigating past wrongs and finding evidence about perpetrators but must consider the wider audience of all those who might *potentially* cause harms in the future. Due to a combination of economic forms of reasoning that present all individuals as potential offenders, and the marked tendency to overstate exposure to risk, the suspect population expands. At the same time, this mentality continues to focus upon traditional suspect populations: the poor, unemployed, homeless people, and ethnic minorities. They are regarded as prime candidates against whom security-oriented measures are deployed, partly because of the threat they are seen to pose to the established order and the safety of the better off, but also because traditional forms of punishment are seen as being inevitably less effective with them. Such groups often operate on the margins of capitalist society, have little purchasing power, and are less likely to be involved in regular legal employment. Thus, the cost–benefit rationality is likely to be less deeply embedded in their psyche. In addition, excluded and marginalized populations literally have much less to lose (Zedner 2003). A key theme within the new penology literature is the suggestion that policy-makers are increasingly operating on the pragmatic assumption that the best that can be done is to contain the 'dangerous classes' as efficiently and economically as possible. Thus, the penal system performs a kind of waste- anagement function for the better-off majority (Lynch 1998).

All the same, whilst risk-based approaches expand and exclude, they have not completely displaced traditional punitive forms of intervention. On the contrary, as will be discussed in more detail in the next section, a key characteristic of contemporary security governance is the simultaneous and linked expansion of punitive, state-based forms of intervention alongside corporate, proactive forms of security provision. Traditional punitive forms of intervention are increasingly applied to certain categories of the population, whilst the better off are more likely to experience the embedded and consensual forms of security governance. A key impact of some of the contemporary trends in urban space discussed above is social polarization. Whilst the rich are increasingly protected within commercially governed and safe spaces, the have-nots are left to fend for themselves in increasingly dangerous 'public' spaces, policed by an increasingly militarized public police force (Davis 1990). Increasingly effective crime prevention in middle-class districts and the spread of commercial forms of private governance both work to actively exclude the poor at the same time as further displacing crime and disorder to disadvantaged areas. In addition, even in those public spaces that remain, security governance is increasingly following the exclusionary and risk-based policies of private government. The spread of crime prevention by environmental design, exclusionary use of 'anti-social behaviour orders' (ASBOs) and other such interventions (such as youth curfews), is working to privatize public space (Crawford 2006). Although the spread of 'gated communities' in Britain is significantly less than has been the case in the USA, nevertheless there is some evidence of increasing residential segregation of this type (Webster 2002). Such developments have major implications for the development of social trust and civic life in general (Blakeley and Snyder 1997). They also have the effect of exacerbating security concerns in the long run, a paradox to which we turn in the following section.

EXPANSION

Contemporary forms of security governance bring with them a strong expansionist dynamic. Although security promises general reassurance, in practice its pursuit often further fuels public anxieties (Zedner 2003; Loader 1997). The devolution of security provision away from state institutions via privatization and other forms of responsibilization may have actually helped to further expand the state penal apparatus. Whereas in many other policy fields, the growth of privatization and contracting out has been accompanied by a decline in state provision, in the field of criminal justice these activities have been accompanied by a huge expansion of state expenditure and involvement (Braithwaite 2000). In many countries, public police forces now employ more staff than ever before. Public expenditure on the police, courts, and penal system continues to spiral; record numbers of people are incarcerated, and the penal sphere penetrates ever further into the family and civil society. Twenty years on, Stan Cohen's (1985) analysis of the dispersal of disciplinary control from the prison into wider society still has strong relevance. These apparently contradictory trends may be linked in a number of important ways. Privatization has been an addition to, not a replacement for, public policing and punishment. It has allowed an expansion of surveillance, and is partly responsible for an increase in the formal reporting of matters to the police for processing via the criminal justice system. There are more CCTV cameras, private security guards, wardens, and active citizens to direct police attention to incidents that at one time would have escaped official attention. Evaluations of some neighbourhood warden schemes have shown that their introduction was associated with an increase in recorded crime, because the existence of wardens actually meant that more previously unreported incidents were being dealt with by the police (NACRO 2003). In addition, moves towards pragmatic and managerial ways of managing security and crime control may have inadvertently added to the thirst for more punishment. The emergence of highly technical, apparently value-neutral, approaches to crime and punishment (and managerialist approaches such as reclassification of cannabis, and crime screening) may actually exacerbate punitive sentiments in the general public. The pragmatic concerns of cost effectiveness, system coordination, risk management, value for money, etc. are profoundly dissatisfying to fearful members of the public, and help to fuel demands for dramatic and expressive forms of punishment. As Garland (1990) has argued, managerial approaches to dealing with offenders that effectively demoralize (literally) the process of punishment may have the effect of pushing punitive feelings into the subconscious and serve to exacerbate them further.

In a more general sense, it may be that official responses to crime, public awareness campaigns about crime prevention, and a host of situational and target-hardening measures ultimately heighten subjective feelings of anxiety and insecurity. The increased visibility of security hardware and personnel sharpens the social perception of threat. This feeds into the desire for yet more security. Michael Tonry (2004) has argued that the emphasis of New Labour's anti-crime policies on disorder and anti-social behaviour may have actually served to make members of the public more sensitive to (and less tolerant of) minor infractions and incivilities. There are also other ways in which current approaches to security are inherently expansionist. Ian Loader (1997) argues that commercial security companies are active in constructing their own demand, by contributing through advertising to public insecurity. Similar claims can be made about senior public police officers who, whilst wanting to claim credit for reductions in crime, also may perceive some benefit from increased levels of crime and disorder in terms of support for resource claims. All these developments, along with a range of other structural and cultural changes, have contributed to 'insatiable demands' for more security (Morgan and Newburn 1997). Nils Christie (2000) has demonstrated how the commodification of crime control in capitalist societies and the growing commercial corrections market has a self-generating dynamic. Christie argues that penal policy in many countries is increasingly influenced by the prison-industrial complex, an international alliance of commercial penal and industrial interests that profits from expansionist penal policies. These developments are the 'natural outgrowth of our type of society, not an exception to it' (2000: 178). There is strong evidence, at least in the USA, that commercial corrections corporations have been active in promoting greater demand for prison places, via helping to fund campaigns for tougher sentencing laws (Jones and Newburn 2005).

The growing spatial polarization discussed in the previous section also contributes to heightened fear of crime and increases in crime itself. By displacing crime and disorder away from richer areas, it exacerbates economic disadvantage and social disorganization in disadvantaged neighbourhoods, and increases the likelihood of further expansion of offending and incivilities. These trends also increase social distance, and the tendency to perceive people from other social and economic groups as a threat. As Zedner (2003) points out, many contemporary attempts to govern security actually erode levels of trust and social solidarity: 'The question is whether trust is in practice further diminished by the late means that arise to compensate for its apparent demise . . . If we cannot trust the stranger, we can at least limit his opportunity to do us harm' (2003: 171). At a broader level still, a number of writers have observed a range of social developments that gathered pace in the latter part of the twentieth century that have contributed to a more generalized sense of 'ontological insecurity'. Such developments include: labour market restructuring and the virtual disappearance of secure lifetime employment; growing social and spatial mobility that has weakened the individual's ties with local places; the decline of participation in intermediate-level institutions such as trade unions, local shops, churches, community groups, and clubs; and growing economic inequality and social polarization that leads to a heightened sense of (and fear of) the 'other' (Garland 2001). Whereas people used to see themselves primarily as members of one or more groups, increasingly people are defining their life goals in terms of individual personal development. The increased privatism and individualization of social life have expanded opportunities for many people in a host of ways. But they have also eroded traditional bases of trust and stability, and individuals have increasingly become disembedded and insecure. These processes are likely to have contributed significantly to the growing demands for more security.

PROSPECTS FOR DEMOCRATIC SECURITY GOVERNANCE: NODAL GOVERNANCE OR RE-STATING SECURITY?

This section considers debates about the best way of attempting to govern security in democratic, just, and effective ways in the face of the major changes outlined above. Increasing levels of social diversity are currently being accompanied by growing fragmentation and inequity, in terms of both authorizers and providers of security. Furthermore, the increasing influence of risk-based thinking leads to a further proliferation of policing and security providers (Johnston and Shearing 2003). This may lead to a patchwork that amounts to the 'worst of all possible worlds' that combines ineffectiveness with inequity. The task is to establish a system of security governance that is neither quantitatively excessive nor qualitatively invasive, and meets the requirements of public accountability, justice, and effectiveness (Johnston 2000). Most would agree that this is a desirable goal, but differences emerge on how best to address it. Should we accept that the state has had its day in dominating the governance of security, and that the interests of citizens would be best served by embracing and further encouraging non-state forms of security provision? Alternatively, how far is it still realistic to see security as a public good, and in what ways is it possible and desirable for state-organized arrangements to assert more direction and control over its governance?

NODAL GOVERNANCE

As discussed above, private governments are now doing more than 'rule at a distance', and both steering and rowing functions are increasingly being undertaken by non-state actors (Shearing 2006). However, much of the extant literature on the governance of security continues to give conceptual priority to state institutions, and thus obscures the important role played by commercial and other non-state auspices of governance. In challenging this, a number of authors have suggested that empirically the concept of 'nodal governance' best captures the way in which governing is now undertaken in contemporary societies. They further suggest, normatively, that this conception should form the basis of future policy directions. Under conditions of nodal governance, collective outcomes are pursued within a network of nodes, some of which are state institutions, but many others of which are made up of commercial or community actors. This has clear parallels with the new governance literature outlined earlier. However, discussions about policing and security have remained rather unaffected by these approaches, even though growing governmental complexity is an established feature of approaches to understanding other policy spheres. For example, Shearing (2006) argues that much writing on policing exhibits what amounts to a 'state fetishism', and that we need to move away from this 'tenacious paradigm' in order to render new forms of security provision and governance both thinkable and doable. On his view, a collective 'myopia' on the part of many writers about policing and security about the key contribution of private governance has had important consequences in terms of equity. The failure to acknowledge private governance allows the relatively unfettered expansion of these forms of governance for privileged groups, who increasingly live their lives in the privately governed spaces of gated communities, shopping malls, holiday complexes, and leisure parks. Thus, we need to facilitate the participation of less advantaged groups within security markets, and to develop their own locally designed forms of private governance (Wood 2006).

This approach goes beyond merely arguing that the state can continue to set the overall framework for security governance but should devolve implementation to a range of non-state providers. It takes us further, beyond state governance and towards the acceptance and encouragement of forms of government in which social orders are defined, rules are made, and compliance achieved by non-state bodies. On this view, the central state is increasingly ill-equipped for the organization and delivery of effective security provision. State-organized provision has at best reflected the inefficiencies of large, centralized public bureaucracies. At its worst, state policing has actively contributed to oppression of disadvantaged groups. Therefore, security provision based on locally designed and organized interventions, with minimal central state input, is more suited to current political conditions and more likely to achieve just and effective outcomes (Wood 2006). This viewpoint suggests that contemporary trends in governance provide important opportunities for improving the governance of security for the less powerful. In particular, it rejects the position of those on the Left who simply attack neo-liberal policy programmes on principle and call for a return to the good old days of state provision. Furthermore, it goes much further than abstract theorizing. As outlined below, some of the leading writers in the 'nodal governance' school are actively involved in the design, establishment, and promotion of new arrangements for security governance in local communities in various parts of the world, most notably to date in South Africa and South America. Their approach is based on the implicit assumption that reversal of the dominant neo-liberal reform direction of recent decades is not politically feasible in the medium term. However, they share the concerns of many on the Left about the inequities and social polarization that seem to arise from these developments. In effect, current security governance arrangements favour those with the loudest voices and the deepest pockets. At the same time, the nodal governance theorists also accept much of the Hayekian critique of the problems of state provision (Hayek 1944). Rather than this centralized, bureaucratic, and inefficient approach, they emphasize the need to empower local communities to build their own security arrangements that draw upon local capacities and knowledge. They argue that policy-makers should promote frameworks that allow the poor and the weak to develop the power to compete and bargain effectively in a marketized world. What is required, therefore, is a radical devolution of governance, and the establishment and development of nodes governed by and for less advantaged communities.

These approaches have been applied in a number of practical developments. Much of the recent work on nodal governance has been conducted under the auspices of the Security 21 project at the Australian National University. This work has an avowed policy-focus, and has promoted imaginative new kinds of security provision based on the principles of nodal governance. A key example was developed in the community of Zwelethemba in South Africa. This involved the establishment of 'peace committees'— made up of members of the local community—to engage in conflict resolution (peace-making) and preventive intervention to avoid similar conflicts arising again (peace-building). The key aim is to draw upon local knowledge and capacity to develop imaginative, forward-looking solutions to community problems, rather than rely on the punitive and backward-looking mechanisms of traditional state policing. This has parallels to the way that security is managed in corporate settings, in that the main aim is to manage risks in order to better govern the future (rather than simply seek to punish past wrongs). When there is a conflict or problem in a local community, members of the local community can convene a Peace Gathering. These, chaired by a member of the Peace Committee, involve the range of relevant interested parties and seek to develop restorative solutions to these problems without recourse to formal criminal justice institutions (Shearing and Wood 2003; Johnston and Shearing 2003). Similar projects have been developed in Brazil and Argentina (Wood 2006; Wood and Cardia 2006).

The nodal governance approach has also been applied to policing reform within the United Kingdom. Clifford Shearing was a member of the Patten Commission on reform of the police in Northern Ireland, and actively promoted the practical development of a nodal conception of policing governance. His involvement was probably crucial in its recommendation for the establishment of District Policing Partnership Boards—a committee of the local authority that would have the power to buy in extra local policing resources from providers other than the public police (Shearing 2000). The Commission also recommended that at force level, a Policing Board (not a Police Board) should be established that would have substantially more powers than the existing police authority (Walker 2000). It was suggested that this body might be given responsibility for regulating all policing providers including commercial firms, and coordinating provision across policing networks. The UK Government's legislative response to the Patten Commission ultimately held back from some of these elements.

However, although perhaps its time had not yet come, the model laid down by Patten provides a highly interesting way of approaching the problem of governing local security networks.

RESTATING SECURITY GOVERNANCE: BRINGING THE STATE BACK IN

The work on nodal governance provides important challenges to the ways in which we conceptualize policing and security, but also a practical vision for a more just and effective governance of security in the future. However, concerns have been raised about the approach and its wider implications. There are a number of specific areas where it is difficult to imagine how effective and equitable outcomes might be advanced under the nodal governance model predicated upon an extremely limited (or absent) state. For example, where would responsibility lie for the monitoring and implementation of obligations under international law? What forms of intervention could deal with major environmental harms? How would serious and organized crimes that cross local community borders be effectively countered? How would the human rights of unpopular minorities be monitored and protected? With regard to this last point, Marks and Goldsmith (2006) suggest the nodal governance model is based on rather rosy assumptions about local community cohesiveness and the existence of a shared moral code that can act as the basis for locally organized security provision.

In response to these potential problems, it has been suggested that the central problem with contemporary security governance is the absence of effective state institutions that have the necessary resources and legitimacy to coordinate and control security provision (Loader and Walker 2006). Put another way, the central problem to be addressed is the growing *impotence* of state institutions, rather than their unjust or ineffective deployment. Marks and Goldsmith (2006) argue that, rather than further devolve sovereignty, the state should reassert itself as 'the anchor of collective security provision'. Even if we accept the broader arguments of the nodal governance approach—that many aspects of local security provision can be better organized and provided by devolving responsibility and resources to local communities—it does appear that state institutions (or something akin to them) must continue to play a central role. This appears to be accepted in practice in the particular nodal governance initiatives discussed above. First, there is at least a degree of (indirect) state funding via international aid. Although better local governance arrangements may in future facilitate growing local prosperity and an expanded local tax base, in the immediate future the kinds of disadvantaged communities where improvements in governance are most needed are likely to continue to be dependent upon resources raised through central taxation. There are two necessary conditions for this to work. First, local communities—although they have their own particular concerns and interests—must be seen as part of a wider political community that is bonded by some general uniting principles or values. Secondly, there must be institutional arrangements that allow for the collection of taxes and some redistribution of resources to poorer communities, and there must be at least a degree of support for (or at least acquiescence to) such arrangements on the part of the wider political community. It is difficult to see how such an arrangement could work in the absence of some form of wider collective political institutional framework, or a more general sense of a public interest (Loader and Walker 2004). The nodal governance model works within a framework that requires local processes and outcomes to conform to human rights principles. This is necessary, for example, to guard against the development of localized forms of justice and security provision that might discriminate unfairly against minority groups. Such a framework of universal standards must ultimately be enforced if necessary by a body that transcends local community boundaries. Finally, individual members of local communities within the current nodal governance models always have the option of recourse to the formal state institutions of policing and criminal justice if they are dissatisfied with the local community forms of intervention. Thus, even within the nodal governance model, state-organized arrangements remain vital, albeit in the background. It is difficult to see how improvements in security provision are possible in the absence of collective, state-type political institutions.

In a normative sense, we have already seen that there are strong arguments to suggest that we *should* retain and develop a generalized sense of security as a public good, and facilitate the development of collective political institutions to promote it (Loader and Walker 2006). Arguably, the nodal governance approach dismisses too readily the idea of the public interest in security and, in the extreme, it risks exacerbating the current polarization and expansion in security provision. As outlined above, Loader and Walker have convincingly argued, security should be conceived of as a social good, one that is essentially foundational for the development of other public goods and the effective operation of citizens' liberties. There have clearly been huge problems with the ways in which states have historically attempted to deliver this public good, particularly in countries such as Argentina and South Africa, where many communities have good reason to remain suspicious of state-centred arrangements. However, it remains the case that in most polities the state both is, and arguably should be, more than one node amongst many (Crawford 2006).

Clearly, current state-centred arrangements remain problematic in a range of ways. One possible way forward, and one that pays due respect to the changed conditions of contemporary security governance but that also seeks to reassert the notion of security as a public good, has been suggested by Ian Loader (2000). He suggests the establishment of significant new accountability institutions—Policing Commissions—to take responsibility for coordinating and monitoring the range of bodies involved in policing and security provision at the local, regional, and national levels. Such Commissions would be democratically driven and inclusive, with part of the membership being directly elected, but the other part appointed to ensure adequate representation from a range of social groups. The proposed Policing Commissions would have a formidable range of powers and functions, including the role of formulating and coordinating policy, licensing security providers, subsidizing extra provision in under-serviced areas, and the monitoring and evaluation of standards. They would have a statutory responsibility to ensure that all citizens receive a 'fair' share of policing services, which would require attention to both over-policing and under-protection of particular social groups. These proposals appear to offer an imaginative way forward in promoting the effective involvement of local community knowledge and capacities in security governance. At the same time, they offer the possibility of public, democratic forums that can provide more effective coordination of the complex networks that now make up security governance, whilst at the same time promoting more equitable provision that balances the demands of security against those of other valued social goods.

CONCLUSION

The governance of security has clearly changed in very significant ways. The fragmentation and complexity that characterizes contemporary governance more generally is now clearly visible within the realm of security. However, much research and writing in this field has yet to reflect this. The nodal governance approach has played a key role in addressing this deficit. It has provided a detailed analysis of the ways in which the security world has been transformed and drawn attention to the dangers inherent in these developments. At the same time, it has identified the possibilities these changes bring for positive reforms to security governance. This work has drawn helpfully upon the broader work of political scientists about the networked nature of contemporary governance. Nevertheless, it might be argued that the nodal governance approach also shares the limitations of some of the new governance literature. In particular, it overstates the limitations of state action and underplays the possibilities for collective political institutions to promote the effective and equitable provision of public goods. In particular, it too easily concedes to the neo-liberal critique of public provision and its narrow conception of security as something that can be delivered by market mechanisms. In communities characterized by polarization, economic disadvantage, social disorganization, low trust, and attendant problems of crime and disorder, what is required is more governmental action by state authorities, not less. A key challenge for the future is to develop effective public forms of political participation within which the governance of security in the narrow sense is more closely integrated with the promotion of security in its broader sense, in terms of the wider social and economic well-being of citizens.

■ SELECTED FURTHER READING

Readers who are interested in the broader sociological applications of the concept of governmentality are referred to the work of Nikolas Rose, in particular, *Powers of Freedom: Reframing Political Thought* (Cambridge University Press, 1999). David Garland's 1997 paper, 'Governmentality and the Problem of Crime' (*Theoretical Criminology*, 1(2)) provides an extremely helpful application of these ideas to criminological thinking. The starting point for the 'new governance' literature in political science is Rod Rhodes' 1997 book, *Understanding Governance: Policy Networks, Governance, Reflexivity and Accountability* (Open University Press). A more recent discussion of governance and its implications for the study of government in contemporary Britain, is provided in Bevir and Rhodes's *Interpreting British Governance* (Routledge, 2003). The key text for criminologists interested in applying the idea of networked governance to the realm of policing and security is Johnston and Shearing's *Governing Security* (Routledge, 2003) which provides an extensive treatment of many of the themes covered by this chapter. These themes are further discussed and developed by leading supporters and critics of the nodal governance approach in the excellent edited collection by Jennifer Wood and Benoî Dupont (2005), *Democracy, Society and the Governance of Security* (Cambridge University Press). To keep up to date with current thinking in these fields readers are advised to consult regularly the leading criminological journals, in particular *Criminology and Criminal Justice*, the *British Journal of Criminology*, *Punishment and Society*, *Theoretical Criminology*, and *Policing and Society*. In addition, it is clear that political scientists have important things to say about the subjects discussed in this chapter that are not always picked up upon by criminological audiences. Political science journals such as *Governance* and the *British Journal of Political Science* are extremely useful starting points for readers who are interested in applying some of the ideas and concepts of political studies to criminological subjects and vice versa.

■ REFERENCES

ATKINSON, M., and COLEMAN, W. (1992), 'Policy Networks, Policy Communities and the Problems of Governance', *Governance*, 5(2): 15–180.

BAYLEY, D., and SHEARING, C. (1996), 'The Future of Policing', *Law and Society Review*, 30(3): 585–606.

—— and —— (2001), *The New Structure of Policing*, Washington, DC: The National Institute of Justice.

BECK, U. (1992), *Risk Society: Towards a New Modernity*, London: Sage.

BLAKELEY, E., and SNYDER, M. (1997), *Fortress America: Gated Communities in the United States*, Washington, DC: Brookings Institution Press.

BOWLING, B., and NEWBURN, T. (2006), 'Policing and National Security'. Paper presented at London–Columbia, *Police, Community and the Rule of Law Workshop*, London, 16–17 March.

BRAITHWAITE, J. (2000), The New Regulatory State and the Transformation of Criminology, in D. Garland and R. Sparks (eds), *Criminology and Social Theory*, Oxford: Oxford University Press.

CHRISTIE, N. (2000), *Crime Control as Industry*, 3rd edn, London: Routledge.

CLARKE, R. (1997), *Situational Crime Prevention: Successful Case Studies*, 2nd edn, Albany, N.Y.: Harrow and Heston.

COHEN, S. (1985), *Visions of Social Control: Crime, Punishment and Classification*, Cambridge: Polity Press.

COLEMAN, A. (1985), *Utopia on Trial: Vision and Reality in Planned Housing*, London: Hilary Shipman.

CRAWFORD, A. (2003), 'The Pattern of Policing in the UK: Policing Beyond the Police', in T. Newburn (ed.), *The Handbook of Policing*, Cullompton, Devon: Willan.

—— (2006), 'Policing and Security as "Club Goods": The New Enclosures?', in J. Wood and B. Dupont (eds), *Democracy, Society and the Governance of Security*, Cambridge: Cambridge University Press.

——, LISTER, S., BLACKBURN, S., and BURNETT, J. (2005), *Plural Policing: The Mixed Economy of Visible Patrols in England and Wales*, Bristol: The Policy Press.

DAHL, R. (1961), *Who Governs? Democracy and Power in an American City*, New Haven, Conn.: Yale University Press.

DAVIS, M. (1990), *City of Quartz: Imagining the Future in Los Angeles*, London: Verso.

DORN, N., and LEVI, M. (forthcoming), 'European Private Security, Corporate Investigation and Military Services: Collective Security, Market Regulation and Structuring the Public Sphere', *Policing and Society*.

EDWARDS, A. (2002), Learning from Diversity: The Strategic Dilemmas of Community Based Crime Control', in G. Hughes and A. Edwards (eds), *Crime Control and Community: The New Politics of Public Safety*, Cullompton, Devon: Willan

—— (2006), 'Governance'. in E. McLaughlin and J. Muncie (eds), *The Sage Dictionary of Criminology*, 2nd edn, London: Sage.

FEELEY, M., and SIMON, J. (1994), 'Actuarial Justice: The Emerging New Criminal Law' in D. Nelken (ed.), *The Futures of Criminology*, London: Sage.

FOUCAULT, M. (1991), 'Governmentality' in G. Burchill, C. Gordon, and P. Miller (eds), *The Foucault Effect: Studies in Governmentality*, Hemel Hempstead: Harvester Wheatsheaf.

GARLAND, D. (1990), *Punishment and Modern Society*, Oxford: Oxford University Press.

—— (1996), 'The Limits of the Sovereign State', *British Journal of Criminology*, 36(4): 445–71.

—— (2001), *The Culture of Control: Crime and Social Order in Contemporary Society*, Oxford: Oxford University Press.

GLASZE, G., WEBSTER, C., and FRANTZ, K. (eds) (2006), *Private Cities: Global and Local Perspectives*, London: Routledge.

HAYEK, F. (1944), *The Road to Serfdom*, London: Routledge.

JOHNSTON, L. (1992), *The Rebirth of Private Policing*, London: Routledge.

—— (1996), 'What is Vigilantism?', *British Journal of Criminology*, 36(2): 220–36.

—— (2000), *Policing Britain: Risk, Security and Governance*, London: Longman.

—— and SHEARING, C. (2003), *Governing Security: Explorations in Policing and Justice*, London: Routledge.

JONES, T. (1996), *Britain's Ethnic Minorities: An Analysis of the Labour Force Survey*, 2nd edn, London: Policy Studies Institute.

—— (2003), 'The Governance and Accountability of Policing', in T. Newburn (ed.), *The Handbook of Policing*, Cullompton, Devon: Willan.

—— and NEWBURN, T. (1998), *Private Security and Public Policing*, Oxford: Clarendon Press.

—— and —— (1999), 'Urban Change and Policing: Mass Private Property Reconsidered', *European Journal on Criminal Policy and Research*, 7(2): 225–44.

—— and —— (2002), 'The Transformation of Policing? Understanding Current Trends in Policing Systems', *British Journal of Criminology*, 42(1): 129–46.

—— and —— (2005), 'Comparative criminal justice policy-making in the US and UK: the case of private prisons', *British Journal of Criminology*, 45(1): 58–80.

—— and —— (eds) (2006), *Plural Policing: A Comparative Perspective*, London: Routledge.

KEMPA, M., STENNING, P., and WOOD, J. (2004), 'Policing Communal Spaces: A Reconfiguration of the Mass Private Property Hypothesis', *British Journal of Criminology*, 44(4): 562–81.

KEMSHALL, H., and MAGUIRE, M. (2001), 'Public protection, partnership and risk penalty: The multiagency risk management of sexual and violent offenders', *Punishment and Society*, 3(2): 237–64.

LOADER, I. (1997), 'Private Security and the Demand for Protection in Contemporary Britain', *Policing and Society*, 7: 143–62.

—— (1999), 'Consumer Culture and the Commodification of Policing and Security', *Sociology*, 33(2): 373–92.

—— (2000), 'Plural Policing and Democratic Governance', *Social and Legal Studies*, 9(3): 323–45.

—— and WALKER, N. (2001), 'Policing as a Public Good: Reconstituting the Connections *between* Policing and State', *Theoretical Criminology*, 5(1): 9–35.

—— and —— (2004), 'State of Denial? Rethinking the Governance and Security', *Punishment and Society*, 6(2): 221–8.

—— and —— (2006), 'Necessary Virtues: The Legitimate Place of the State in the Production of Security', in J. Wood and B. Dupont (eds), *Democracy, Society and the Governance of Security*, Cambridge: Cambridge University Press

LUSTGARTEN, L. (1986), *The Governance of Police*, London: Sweet & Maxwell.

LYNCH, M. (1998), 'Waste Managers? The New Penology, Crime-Fighting and Parole Agent Identity', *Law and Society Review*, 32(4): 839–69.

MCAULEY, S. (1986), 'Private Government', in L. Lipson and S. Wheeler (eds), *Law and the Social Sciences*, New York: Russell Sage Foundation.

MACLEOD, G. (2003), *Privatizing the City? The Tentative Push Towards Edge Urban Developments and Gated Communities in the United Kingdom*, Report for the Office of the Deputy Prime Minister, Durham: University of Durham.

MARKS, M., and GOLDSMITH, A. (2006), 'The State, the People and Democratic Policing: The Case of South Africa', in J. Wood and B. Dupont (eds), *Democracy, Society and the Governance of Security*, Cambridge: Cambridge University Press.

MARSHALL, G. (1984), *Constitutional Conventions: The Rules and Forms of Political Accountability*, Oxford: Clarendon Press.

MINTON, A. (2002), *Building Balanced Communities: The US and UK Compared*, London: Royal Institute of Chartered Surveyors.

MODOOD, T. *et al.* (1997), *Ethnic Minorities in Britain: The Fourth National Survey*, London: Policy Studies Institute.

MORGAN, R., and NEWBURN, T. (1997), *The Future of Policing*, Oxford: Oxford University Press.

MOUNT, F. (2005), *Mind the Gap: The New Class Divide in Britain*, London: Short Books.

NACRO (2003), *Eyes and Ears: The Role of Neighbourhood Wardens*, Community Safety Practice Briefing, London: NACRO.

NEWMAN, O. (1972), *Defensible Space: Crime Prevention Through Urban Design*, New York: Macmillan.

O'CONNER, D. (2005), *Closing the Gap: A Review of the 'Fitness for Purpose' of the Current Structure of Policing in England and Wales*, London: Her Majesty's Inspectorate of Constabulary.

OSBORNE, D., and GAEBLER, T. (1993), *Reinventing Government: How the Entrepreneurial Spirit is Transforming the Public Sector*, New York: Penguin.

POLSBY, N. (1963), *Community Power and Political Theory*, New Haven, Conn.: Yale University Press.

PUTNAM, R. (2000), *Bowling Alone: The Collapse and Revival of American Community*, New York: Simon & Schuster.

RHODES, R. (1997), *Understanding Governance: Policy Networks, Governance, Reflexivity and Accountability*, Buckingham: Open University Press.

ROBERTS, S. (2005), 'After Government? On Representing Law Without the State', *The Modern Law Review*, 68(1): 1–24.

ROSE, N., and MILLER, P. (1992), Political Power Beyond the State: Problematics of Government', British Journal of Sociology, 43(2): 173–205.

RYAN, M., SAVAGE, P., and WALL, D. (eds) (2001), *Policy Networks in Criminal Justice*, Basingstoke: Palgrave.

SHEARING, C. (1992), 'The Relation Between Public and Private Policing', in M. Tonry and N. Morris (eds), *Modern Policing*, Chicago: University of Chicago Press.

—— (2000), ' "A New Beginning" for Policing', *Journal of Law and Society*, 27(3): 386–93.

—— (2006), 'Reflections on the Refusal to Acknowledge Private Governments', in J. Wood and B. Dupont (eds), *Democracy, Society and the Governance of Security*, Cambridge: Cambridge University Press.

—— and BERG, J. (2006), 'South Africa', in T. Jones and T. Newburn (eds), *Plural Policing: A Comparative Perspective*, London: Routledge.

—— and STENNING, P. (1981), 'Modern Private Security: Its Growth and Implications', in M. Tonry and N. Morris (eds), *Crime and Justice: An Annual Review of Research, Volume 3*. Chicago, Ill.: University of Chicago Press.

—— and —— (eds) (1987), *Private Policing*, Newbury Park, Cal.: Sage.

—— and WOOD, J. (2003), 'Nodal Governance, Democracy and the New "Denizen" ', *Journal of Law and Society*, 30(3): 400–19.

STOKER, G. (ed.) (1998), *The New Politics of British Local Governance*, Basingstoke: Macmillan.

TONRY, M. (2004), *Punishment and Politics: Evidence and Emulation in the Making of English Crime Control Policy*, Cullompton, Devon: Willan.

VON HIRSCH, A., and SHEARING, C. (2000), 'Exclusion from Public Space', in. A. Von Hirsch, D. Garland, and A. Wakefield (eds), *Ethical and Social Perspectives on Situational Crime Prevention*, Oxford: Hart.

WAKEFIELD, A. (2003), *Selling Security: The Private Policing of Public Space*, Cullompton, Devon: Willan.

WALKER, N. (2000), *Policing in a Changing Constitutional Order*, London: Sweet & Maxwell.

WEBSTER, C. (2002), 'Property Rights and the Public Realm: Gates, Green Belts, and Gemeinschaft', *Environment and Planning B: Planning and Design*, 29: 397–412.

WOOD, J. (2006), 'Research and Innovation in the Field of Security: A Nodal Governance View', in J. Wood and B. Dupont (eds), *Democracy, Society and the Governance of Security*, Cambridge: Cambridge University Press.

——, and CARDIA, N. (2006), 'Brazil', in T. Jones and T. Newburn (eds), *Plural Policing: A Comparative Perspective*, London: Routledge.

——, and DUPONT, B. (eds) (2006), *Democracy, Society and the Governance of Security*, Cambridge: Cambridge University Press.

ZEDNER, L. (2003), 'Too much security?' *International Journal of the Sociology of Law*, 31(3): 155–84.

26

CRIME PREVENTION AND COMMUNITY SAFETY

Adam Crawford

This chapter presents an overview of the contemporary rise of crime prevention and its institutionalization, specifically in England and Wales. Whilst similar developments are to be found in other advanced capitalist countries (Crawford 1998; Hughes *et al.* 2002), often reflecting the global 'transfer' of crime prevention ideas and practices, the manner in which these have been implemented in different jurisdictions (and within jurisdictions) has been significantly shaped by divergent local political and cultural traditions and socio-legal contexts. The reception of preventive strategies and technologies, in large part, has been conditioned by their alignment with political struggles and their resonance with cultural values. The chapter begins by locating the contemporary rise of a preventive mentality in a historical context. It then explores the conceptions of crime, order, and security that inform key developments in crime prevention and community safety. It considers the claims and implications of different approaches to prevention and critically analyses these, using illustrations from practical examples. It will be argued that this shift to prevention, together with the discourses, practices, and technologies that accompany it, is premised not upon a wholly coherent theoretical framework but a number of (sometimes competing) assumptions. In this light, the chapter considers the infrastructure that has been assembled to deliver crime prevention over the last quarter of a century and the policy initiatives and political debates that have surrounded its implementation.

Technological change has played a crucial role in crime prevention. Nevertheless, however commonsensical they may appear at first sight, all crime prevention technologies and strategies have embedded within them powerful claims about human agency and the possibilities for governing conduct. Crime prevention not merely is a value-free 'toolkit' derived from practice, but is deeply rooted in conceptual assumptions and provokes vexed ethical and social issues. Consequently, this chapter does not dwell upon a delineation of 'what works' in crime prevention. This is not to suggest that the evaluation of preventive outcomes does not matter. On the contrary, learning from implementation and outcomes is crucial in building an understanding of the possibilities and costs implicit in a preventive approach and how to improve them. The complexities inherent in evaluating a 'non-event' such as the prevention of crime are significant and warrant careful treatment in their own right (Pawson and Tilley 1997; Eck 2005).[1] Where relevant, reference will be made to the findings of evaluations. However, evaluation remains probably the weakest aspect of crime prevention studies. The meaning of 'success' is itself highly contested. Debates about 'what works' are often struggles over the status of different criteria and public values that are not easily reducible to a universally accepted component of efficiency.

THE FALL AND RISE OF PREVENTION

It is widely acknowledged that the last thirty years have seen an explosion in crime reduction initiatives focused upon prevention rather than cure; consequences rather than causes and offences rather than offenders. This contemporary emphasis prioritizes future governance (i.e. security) over reordering the past (i.e. justice) (Johnston and Shearing 2003). According to some, the 'ascent' of crime prevention represents a 'major shift in paradigm' in criminal justice and crime control (Tuck 1988), fundamentally altering the way in which we manage crime and structure social relations. Consequently, 'preventive partnerships' have become a defining face of contemporary crime control. As Garland notes:

> Over the past two decades . . . a whole new infrastructure has been assembled at the local level that addresses crime and disorder in a quite different manner . . . The new infrastructure is strongly oriented towards a set of objectives and priorities—prevention, security, harm-reduction, loss-reduction, fear-reduction—that are quite different from the traditional goals of prosecution, punishment and 'criminal justice'. [2001: 16–17].

Conceptions of preventive governance, however, are by no means new. Classical liberal thought in the eighteenth century promoted the governance of future life choices on the basis of rational calculations of the relative balance between pleasure and pain; reward and risk. The liberal subject at the heart of Bentham's writings was a prudent forward-planning rational actor—a *homo prudens*. Colquhoun, amongst others, advocated forms of crime prevention aimed at reducing opportunities and temptations that resonate with contemporary trends. It was inspired by this kind of thinking that Peel's conception of the 'new police' emerged. Their primary task was to be the 'prevention of crime', as made explicit in the Metropolitan Police's first instruction book published in 1829. Prior to this the term 'police' was seen as a broad aspect of political economy and good governance. From the sixteenth until the early nineteenth century in Europe 'policing' referred to a general schema of regulation that included diverse institutions

---

[1] There exist valuable of overviews findings from evaluation studies which readers should consult in this regard (Sherman *et al.* 1997; Goldblatt and Lewis 1998; see also Pease 2002).

engaged in the promotion of public tranquillity and ensuring efficient trade and commerce. Crime was marginal to this body of police regulation. It was only with the combination of the institutional birth of the modern professional police and liberalism's intellectual claim to define policing in terms of the question of crime and the rule of law, that a narrow conception of policing, and concomitantly prevention, over time, firmly became located within the state. Its paid agents ultimately were to be responsible for the nature and form of policing. The 'myth' of the monopolistic sovereign state, as expressed in the figure of Hobbes's Leviathan, found particular manifestation in the new police. The modern state was to be built on claiming and accumulating the legitimate monopoly of physical force.

The period from the late nineteenth century saw the slow growth of an elaborate and complex division of labour in relation to the tasks of crime control. The resultant criminal justice infrastructure was built around responding to, processing, and seeking to know and correct, its object—the apprehended offender. Proactive crime prevention had little place, except as an element of the lingering general or individual deterrence engendered by the limited prospects of apprehension and punishment for those who transgressed criminal laws. Despite the explicit emphasis on prevention within Peel's vision of policing, the subsequent organizational history of the British police saw the increasing marginalization of crime prevention as an object of police activity and as a focus of governmental attention. Within the police, crime prevention was reduced to a small number of dedicated officers and the residual 'scarecrow' function of visible uniformed patrols (Newburn and Reiner, Chapter 27, this volume).

The failure of Peel's vision of prevention-oriented policing, which Garland (2001: 30) terms the 'path not taken', may be explained by a convergence of factors:

• As the 'new police' sought public acceptance and legitimacy, against a background of social and political conflict, there was an ever-present danger that crime prevention would become synonymous with the more intrusive forms of surveillance associated with the spectre of French policing, with its centralized connotations of government spies, agents provocateurs, and secret police. By contrast, the English police were to be constituted in a different image: localized, unarmed, and accountable. The subsequent 'grudging acceptance' of the police was secured on the basis of locally 'negotiated compromise' often implying a downgrading of activities that might conjure up images of sinister surveillance.

• The spread of professional policing encountered a degree of scepticism about the effectiveness and cost of the Peelian model of preventive policing, notably in rural areas with large distances and dispersed populations.

• The growth of statistical data from the late nineteenth century onwards placed an emphasis on tangible outcomes in professional practice. As the prevention of crime could not easily be measured, resources dedicated to it were harder to justify.

• The evolution of a police organizational subculture with an 'action orientation' and 'macho' cultural values celebrated crime detection and thief-taking, whilst devaluing preventive work as 'unglamorous'.

• The Peelian legacy embodied a tension. Whilst its philosophy lay in notions of prevention, its legitimacy was 'legalistic', professional, and bureaucratic, as institutionalized through greater standardization of practice and centralization of command. This often pulled policing away from its preventive functions, notably local intelligence-gathering.

This overview reminds us that a contemporary understanding of crime prevention is intrinsically coupled with the history of modern policing and the ambitions of the modern state. As the police claimed ownership of crime prevention they subsequently shaped how it came to be understood. By the mid-1980s, Weatheritt observed: 'Whatever the expressed commitment of senior police officers and successive governments to the view that prevention is the primary objective of policing, the crime prevention job remains an activity performed on the sidelines while the main action takes place elsewhere' (1986: 49).

In explaining the revival of crime prevention in the late-twentieth century the following are noteworthy:

• Recorded crime rates increased dramatically from the 1960s onwards, placing growing strain upon the reactive criminal justice system.

• Victimization surveys prompted the growing realization that most crimes do not come to the attention of formal institutions, raising fundamental questions about the uncertain deterrent effects of state-administered punishments.

• The importance of institutions and processes of informal control in sustaining order and conformity were increasingly acknowledged. This coincided with social and cultural trends in the post-war period that appeared to be loosening and undermining traditional bonds of family, kinship, and community.

• With the economic crisis of the mid-1970s, governments began to look to fiscal savings and cost efficiencies. Established modes of crime control came to be seen as representing a significant financial burden upon the public purse, prompting consideration of alternatives.

Associated with the above was a realization of the limited effectiveness of traditional institutions of criminal justice and the thinking that informed them, notably a loss of faith in the 'rehabilitative ideal'. This new-found pessimism was most starkly evoked in Martinson's (1974) infamous phrase 'nothing works'. As faith in the traditional criminal justice establishment began to ebb and wane, practitioners and policy-makers looked elsewhere (Home Office 1977: 9–10). This shift also reflected a broader crisis of public confidence, raising questions about the wider legitimacy of the crime control enterprise and prompting a growing politicization of crime and criminal justice. Previously, crime control had been shielded from the gaze of political criticism by a broad consensus that it was best served by 'expert' judgement rather than public opinion. This insulation was increasingly breached as law and order became the subject of debate, notably with the growth of social movements that championed the previously ignored victims of crime. With declining clear-up rates, congested courts, and overcrowded prisons, the realization grew that welfarist promises ran ahead of government performance. Politics came to embrace views about the limited capacity of government to effect significant social change, particularly in the realm of behavioural modification. By the 1979 general election, issues of law and order had reached the top of the political agenda, where they have largely remained.

Hugely influential was the publication of James Q. Wilson's (1975) *Thinking About Crime*. In place of ideas about reforming offenders through welfare-based programmes was a revival of classicist notions of deterrence combined with an emphasis on informal mechanisms of control and a new pragmatic realism. Wilson contended that criminology should be tied more closely to public policy goals and that these should be achievable. To his mind, it had been preoccupied with questions of broad social and structural causation. Theories of crime relating to sociological causes, he argued, remain unproven or impracticable. Policy should focus on what can be changed or manipulated. The new logic was to seek interventions that could reduce the supply of criminal opportunities and increase the likelihood of apprehension. Motivational questions, whether social, structural, or psychological, were to be pushed into the background. In Ekblom's (2000) terms they are 'distal factors'. In the 'new criminologies of everyday life' (Garland 1996) at the vanguard of a preventive mentality, 'proximal' factors were to be accorded greater salience. This precipitated a criminological shift away from the offender as the object of knowledge towards the offence—its situational and spatial characteristics—as well as the place and role of the victim (see also Maguire; Hoyle and Zedner; and Bottoms, Chapters 10, 15 and 17, this volume).

CONCEPTUALIZING PREVENTION

The development of a preventive mentality saw a number of conceptual shifts and innovations that began to chart the terrain, focus, and technologies of governing through prevention. Brantingham and Faust's (1976) typology serves as a forceful reminder of the narrowness of the prevailing thinking about prevention. Drawing on an analogy with public health-care, they identified three typologies:

- *Primary prevention* entails work directed at general populations and places to address potentially criminogenic factors before the onset of the problem.

- *Secondary prevention* involves work with people or places identified as 'at risk' because of some predispositional factor.

- *Tertiary prevention* is directed towards preventing the recurrence of criminal events, by targeting known offenders, victims, or places that are already part of the crime pattern.

Rather like a health service that only focuses upon treating ill people rather than ensuring that people live healthily, the modern state had put all its crime-preventive eggs in the tertiary basket. The criminal justice enterprise with its collection of specialists, professionals, and experts, when looked at through this lens, appeared to be concentrating nearly all its resources in a narrow field. In the mid-1970s, very little explicit work could be said to be focused around secondary prevention and even less concerned with primary prevention. Reflecting this, van Dijk defined crime prevention as 'the total of all policies, measures and techniques, outside the boundaries of the criminal justice system, aiming at the reduction of the various kinds of damage caused by acts defined as criminal by the state' (1990: 205). This is somewhat misleading as it obscures the tertiary preventive role of criminal justice and the considerable contemporary criminal justice focus on 'at risk' groups and a more porous involvement of the wider community. Under the 1998 Crime and Disorder Act (section 37) 'preventing offending' became the overarching priority of Youth Offending Services throughout England and Wales (Morgan and Newburn, Chapter 30, this volume). Likewise, in an echo of Peel's initial injunctions, the Association of Chief Police Officers in *A Crime Prevention Strategy for the New Millennium* committed police services 'to seek to change the culture of the police service so that crime prevention and community safety enjoys a higher status and is accepted as a responsibility of all officers' (ACPO 1996).

Drawn broadly, crime prevention includes all pre-emptive interventions into the social and physical world with the intention, at least in part, of altering behaviour or the flow of events in a way that reduces the likelihood of crime or its harmful consequences. The purposive dimension highlights a broader transformation heralded by the ascendancy of preventive thinking. The inflated cultural, social, and political salience accorded to crime and insecurity since the 1970s has resulted in policies and strategies previously defined in terms of other outcomes increasingly redefined in terms of their possible crime-preventive effects. Through this lens, the quality of education, nutrition, health, environment, housing, and social provisions more generally, frequently come to be viewed in terms of their criminogenic consequences or crime potential, rather than merely as important public goods in their own right. Consequently, a preventive mentality has fostered a 'criminalization of social policy', hereby life is increasingly 'governed through crime and insecurity' or at least social policies are justified in terms of their crime reductive potential (Crawford 1997a: 228). The shift to prevention accords to crime an elevated place in the construction of social order such that fundamental public issues may become marginalized, except in so far as they are defined in terms of their crime-preventive qualities. The Perry/Pre-school project in the USA is an example of the manner in which a social good, namely education, can become redefined or at least accorded new salience on the basis of its possible preventive effects rather than its educational merits per se. The initiative targeted pre-school children identified as 'at risk' of entering into criminality because of the situation of their parents and provided them with highly structured pre-school educational and cognitive enrichment programmes. The positive longitudinal research findings highlighted reduced levels of arrest and drug use amongst the cohort by the time they were 27 as compared with a control group (Schweinhart *et al.* 1993).

The most enduring differentiation with regard to types of intervention focuses on the nature of the initial processes or mechanisms to be altered in the anticipation of producing a preventive effect. *Situational prevention* involves the management, design, or manipulation of the immediate physical environment to reduce the opportunities for specific crimes. *Social prevention* entails changing social processes. It is primarily concerned with measures aimed at tackling the causes of crime and the dispositions of individuals to offend. This distinction is more fluid than appears at first, as situational features might be targeted in the anticipation that they will affect social interactions. Conversely, social processes may be targeted with the intention of shaping or improving the environment.

SITUATIONAL CRIME PREVENTION

Situational crime prevention is often identified as the brainchild of Ronald Clarke and colleagues in the Home Office Research and Planning Unit during the early 1980s. Whilst their work was undoubtedly instrumental in conceptualizing and rationalizing disjointed developments, as well as fostering research and policy interest, situational prevention is probably better understood as an assortment of practices in search of a theory. It emerged through a plethora of locally based and small-scale initiatives, innovations, and technological advances often arising from attempts to solve very specific problems. Many of these had their origins in the commercial sector. Simultaneously, a new band of researchers became interested in conceptualizing the crime-preventive potential of practical initiatives. The pragmatic connection between emerging theory and practice made this interactive process a particularly vibrant one, driving innovation forward. Clarke captured this in claiming situational crime prevention to be a 'framework for some practical and commonsense thinking about how to deal with crime' (1995: 93).

A formative step in the systemization of the dispersed fragments and developing techniques was flagged by the publication of *Crime as Opportunity* (Mayhew *et al.* 1976). It drew together a number of studies that appeared to indicate the potential for altering people's decisions to commit certain acts by changing the opportunities immediately available to individuals. Situational, unlike social, factors are believed to be more subject to manipulation. It is easier to reduce opportunities and temptations than to change human dispositions. In place of a 'nothing works' pessimism is a renewed optimism that some things, however small, do impact upon the commission of crimes in specific locations, at particular times.

Researchers began to analyse, often through retrospective studies, the impact of situational modifications upon behaviour. The detoxification of domestic gas, for example, was shown to have impacted on the overall number of people committing suicide (Clarke and Mayhew 1988). Researchers concluded that once the most common means of committing suicide, through asphyxiation using the domestic gas supply, was no longer available, the overall incidence of suicide declined. Whilst this much debated example did not actually involve a crime, its portent was considerable. If an intervention could affect a decision as fundamental as the possible termination of one's own life, simply by changing the opportunities available, then how much more powerful could situational prevention be in contexts involving less serious decisions with more mundane repercussions? From this perspective, opportunity reduction can take three interrelated forms by:

- *increasing the perceived effort* involved in crime by making the targets of crime harder to get at or otherwise hindering the commission of crime;

- *increasing the perceived risks* of detection and apprehension;

- *reducing the anticipated rewards* of crime; in some cases this may involve removing the targets of crime altogether (Clarke 1995).

Pease (2002: 952) notes that the early emphasis on achieving these aims through 'bars, bolts and barriers' promoted misconceptions that primary prevention equates with target hardening and physical intervention. Partly in response to these perceptions, Cornish and Clarke (2003) added two further dimensions to include *reducing provocation* and *removing excuses* (Table 26. 1). Reducing the provocative elements in situations seeks to understand and limit the immediate triggers for criminal events. Removing excuses, by contrast, seeks to eliminate the possibility of someone responding that they did not know they were committing an offence or that they had no alternative but to do so. Examples include efforts to make compliance as easy as possible by reminding people of rules and their obligations through notification and alerting them to the consequences of their actions. This constitutes a form of 'regulated self-regulation' that dovetails with the wider use of behavioural contracts (in schools, housing, and youth justice) in governing future conduct (Crawford 2003). As Brantingham *et al.* note, 'many of the specific techniques in this category of situational crime prevention represent activities typical of municipal government' (2005: 280). Here, we have a concept of prevention that is both extensive in its reach and accords more closely with pre-nineteenth-century concepts of policing. Prevention of crime is restored to an integral aspect of everyday good governance.

It is incorrect to suggest, as some critics do, that situational prevention does not seek to change people. Rather it seeks to do so through such routine and mundane modifications to the physical world that they become almost imperceptible. Control is embedded in the design and arrangement of things in a way that it is taken for granted, but nonetheless demands small adjustments to behaviour. The sleeping policeman (or hump) in the road does not require the motorist to engage in a finely grained calibration of the costs and benefits that attain from travelling at different speeds. It triggers a slight alteration of behaviour, in this instance with regard to speed. Collectively, situational prevention represents the confluence of a number of different theoretical strands.

Table 26.1 Techniques of situational crime prevention

Increase the perceived effort	Increase the perceived risk	Reduce the anticipated reward	Reduce provocations	Remove excuses
Target harden: Steering locks; Anti-robbery screens; Tamper-proof packaging	*Extend guardianship:* Baggage screening; Merchandise tags; Automatic ticket gates at stations	*Conceal targets:* Off-street parking; Gender neutral phone directories	*Reduce stress and frustrations:* Efficient queuing; Polite service; Soothing music/lighting	*Set rule:* Harassment codes; Contractual agreements; Customs declaration; Hotel registration
Access control: Entry phones; Electronic card access; Car park barriers; Computer passwords	*Assist natural surveillance:* 'Defensible space' designs; Street lighting; Windows; 'Cocoon' neighbourhood watch	*Remove targets:* Removable car stereo; Pre-paid phone-cards; Women's refuges	*Avoid disputes:* Segregating rival football fans; Fixed taxi fares; Reduce overcrowding	*Post instructions:* Notices highlighting rules—i.e. 'No parking', 'Private property'
Screen exits: Ticket needed for exit; Electronic merchandise tag	*Reduce anonymity:* Taxi driver IDs; Caller ID; 'How's my driving' contacts; School uniforms	*Identify property:* Property marking; Vehicle licensing and parts marking; Product serial numbers; Cattle tagging	*Reduce temptation and arousal:* Controls on violent pornography; Enforce good behaviour on football pitches; Prohibit racial slurs	*Stimulate conscience:* Roadside speed displays; Drink driving campaigns
Deflect offenders: Cul-de-sacs, street closures; Segregate rival football fans; Separate facilities for women	*Employee surveillance/Place managers:* CCTV; Park wardens; Club doormen	*Disrupt markets:* Monitor pawn shops & car boot sales; Control on classified ads; Licensed street vendors	*Neutralize peer pressure:* 'Idiots drink and drive' & 'It's OK to say No' campaigns; Disperse trouble-makers at school	*Facilitate compliance:* Easy library checkout to discourage theft; Provide ample bins and public toilets
Controlling means/Facilitators: Restricting availability/sale of knives, guns, spray paint; 'Smart' guns	*Formal surveillance:* Speed cameras; Burglar alarms; Automatic number plate recognition	*Deny benefits:* Ink merchandise tags; Graffiti cleaning; Disabling stolen mobile phones	*Discourage imitation:* Rapid repair of damaged property and removal of abandoned vehicles; V-chips in TVs	*Control disinhibitors:* Drinking age laws; Breathalysers in pubs/car ignition; Parental controls on Internet

Source: Adapted from D. B. Cornish and R. V. Clarke: 'Opportunities, Precipitators and Criminal Decision', 16 *Crime Prevention Studies* (2003: 90).

ENVIRONMENTAL DESIGN

In the USA, Jacobs (1961) presented a powerful critique of post-war urban planning, emphasizing its destructive impact on the natural processes of ordering within neighbourhoods. Drawing on these insights, Newman sought to identify architectural designs that would discourage criminality and foster preventive social controls. He elaborated a theory of 'defensible space' as 'a model for residential environments which inhibits crime by creating the physical expression of a social fabric that defends itself' (1972: 3). He argued that architectural design can release the latent sense of territoriality and community among inhabitants, so that these become accepted parts of residents' assumption of responsibility for preserving a safe and well-maintained living environment. Newman identified four key constituents of good design to encourage social control networks: territoriality, surveillance, image, and environment. Crucially, territoriality demands physical spaces that demarcate areas of control, whilst surveillance requires the design of buildings so as to allow and enable easy observation of territorial areas. The mass housing projects of the post-war period, he contended, squeezed out important processes of social control. In their place 'indefensible spaces' proliferated, including: anonymous walkways, underpasses, lifts, stairwells, and long dark corridors, all with easy access to the public. They constitute 'confused' areas which belong to no one, are cared for by no one, and which are observed by no one. Smaller units which householders could supervise and be seen to be responsible for should engender a sense of ownership and community spirit, reviving important processes of control.

Newman's ideas had close affinity with a looser array of design practices which clustered under the heading of 'crime prevention through environmental design' (CPTED). Most prominent in the work of Jeffery (1971), CPTED sought to apply notions of environmental change and design to foster territoriality in situations beyond residential areas. These ideas attracted significant federal US funding to implement and evaluate. However, the results proved very disappointing. Subsequently, the interest in CPTED waned, in the USA at least. More generally, the works of both Newman and Jeffery were accused of architectural determinism in their failure to consider the role of social variables and behaviour both directly and in mediating the effects of architectural designs.

In the UK, these ideas were resurrected by Coleman (1985), who identified a number of 'design disadvantages', the presence of which correlates with high levels of antisocial behaviour. She claimed empirical support for her thesis from the study of numerous public sector housing estates. She sought to explain the social processes through which design affects crime. For her, situational and dispositional aspects of crime are identified, not as mutually independent but as 'two sides of the same coin'. Poor design encourages an environment in which crime is a 'learned response'. She argued that: 'Architectural situations that are highly vulnerable to crime can teach children to adopt criminal decisions, and this learned disposition can then cause them to see all situational weaknesses as rational opportunities for crime' (1989: 109–110). In sum,

Coleman offers a vision of crime prevention in which situational modifications *cause* social and cultural change.

However, Coleman's analysis largely ignored the impact of wider social and cultural factors that influence the make-up of the people housed in poorly designed mass housing estates, such as the social stigma attached to certain estates, local authority allocation policies, and the character of housing estate management (Bottoms and Wiles 1986). Nevertheless, her work, along with that of Newman and Jeffery, has had an enduring legacy (Ekblom 1995) and been widely applied in planning designs by central and local governments.[2] In this light, police forces regularly employ architectural liaison officers to promote crime-prevention thinking in planning designs. Furthermore, new houses are kite-marked as 'Secured by Design' if they conform to certain architectural standards.[3] Home Office research claims to have shown 30 per cent lower burglary rates in new Secured by Design homes as compared to similar housing that does not meet the same standards (Armitage 2000).

The introduction of planned housing around cul-de-sacs is probably the most notably example of 'defensible space'. Cul-de-sacs are designed to foster small group community cohesion, enhance surveillance, and limit access to those with legitimate purposes for visiting the dwellings. However, Hillier and Shu contend that the debate on urban layout and crime over the past two decades has been 'long on ideology . . . but short on evidence' (2000: 224). They claim their research findings 'challenge many aspects of the current defensible space orthodoxy' and show that the built-in security advantages that defensible space proponents argue belong to cul-de-sacs 'in fact belong to the street, with its greater potential for movement, its greater mutual visibility for higher numbers of neighbours, and greater protection from the rear' (ibid.). Problematically, defensible space theory does not inform us how places are actually used by people. Spaces may be defensible but not defended if the social apparatus and personnel for effective defence is lacking. If people living in a cul-de-sac leave during the day to commute to work elsewhere they leave behind no active surveillance, especially as any other natural surveillance that passers-by might have asserted will have been removed by the segregation of the residential area and lack of pedestrian flow. Cul-de-sac designs, like defensible space more generally, foster an impoverishment of the public realm by creating exclusive 'clubs' that reduce the number of people occupying public spaces, rendering them potentially more, rather than less, vulnerable (Hillier and Hanson 1984).

ROUTINE ACTIVITY THEORY

Routine activity theory is a macro-level attempt to identify the supply of criminal opportunities and to understand crime patterns (Cohen and Felson 1979). It focuses on criminal events, their distribution and clustering over time and space, rather than

[2] For example, Department of the Environment circular 5/94 on 'Planning Out Crime'.
[3] www.securedbydesign.com.

criminal inclinations. The latter are not denied but rather the theory takes the supply of offenders as given. Routine activity theory identifies three minimal elements for a crime to occur:

- A *'likely offender'*—anyone who for any reason might commit a crime.
- A *'suitable target'*—an object or person likely to be taken or attacked by the offender.
- The *absence of a 'capable guardian'*—someone who might intervene to stop or bear witness to an offence.

In this light, the rise in crime since the 1960s is explained by reference to the increasing proportion of empty homes in the day, in part due to the greater number of single-person households and expanded participation of women in the workplace, and the increased availability of valuable, lightweight, portable electronic goods. Social changes have produced more targets and fewer capable guardians. Conversely, it is proposed that the removal of any of the three constituent elements will disrupt criminal events. By implication, the supply of 'capable guardians' is crucial to prevention efforts. The most likely guardians against crime are not necessarily the police but rather neighbours, friends, and bystanders.

Routine activity theory has fostered meso-level crime pattern analysis, significantly facilitated by technological developments in geo-spatial mapping. This has allowed preventive energies to be targeted at high-crime 'hotspots'. However, as routine activity theory dwells solely on the supply of opportunities provided by specific time-place conjunctions, it is unable to disentangle the conundrum as to whether places vary in their capacity to cause crime or merely serve to attract crime that would have occurred regardless. Sherman *et al.* phrase the question as follows: 'Are the routine activities of some hot spots criminogenic *generators* of crime, or merely more attractive *receptors* of crime?' (1989: 46, emphasis in original). The answer is far from being resolved either theoretically or empirically but goes to the heart of situational prevention. Nonetheless, there has been considerable practical application of routine activity theory, in part due to its apparent simplicity and the pragmatic optimism it affords.

RATIONAL CHOICE THEORY

At a micro level, rational choice theory attempts to explain human decision-making. It revives neo-classical ideas about human motivations. At their base, people are pleasure maximizers. They seek out avenues and opportunities that increase their individual pleasure and avoid those that may cause pain. This assumes that offenders choose to commit specific offences for the benefits they bring. Prevention is aimed at altering decision-making processes so as to increase the risks or effort involved in the commission of a crime and decrease any rewards associated with it. This challenges the established criminological wisdom that devoted attention to dispositional theories of crime. Notably, situational approaches presuppose crime to be a normal aspect of modern life and criminals to be essentially 'like us': no different from other rational actors. 'The reality', Felson opines, 'is that ordinary people can do ordinary crime—young and old. Everybody could do at least some crime some of the time' (1998: 11). He suggests that dominant criminological understandings and policy discourses tend to conform to a 'not me' fallacy: the idea that people who commit crime are somehow different from ordinary people 'like me'. By seeking to differentiate between criminals and law, abiding citizens, the focus has been on differences rather than similarities.

Possibly the most valuable insight provided by situational perspectives is that 'context matters'. Situational theory demands not merely that interventions are targeted at appropriate places rooted in an understanding of their specific crime problems but also that these should be regularly reviewed and renewed or adapted. As situational interventions are intended to affect behaviour, they need to be continuously checked, for their ongoing effectiveness will depend upon how crime patterns adapt and change over time. This acknowledges that crime patterns—like the social, cultural, and technological worlds—are not static. From within a situational frame of reference, new criminal opportunities are being created all the time, notably through scientific innovations. Crime opportunities are highly specific, are concentrated in time and space, depend on everyday movements of activity, and are interconnected in such a manner that one crime may produce opportunities for another (Felson and Clarke 1998). As some opportunities may be closed or restricted consequent to situational endeavours others may be opened. Crucially, however, continual adaptation and evolution 'makes knowledge of what works in crime prevention a wasting asset' (Ekblom 2005: 230).

In essence, situational prevention privileges a particular kind of knowledge that is practical, empirical, and reflexive. This context specificity and temporal impermanence questions the generalizing claims about situational interventions made by many proponents of 'crime science' (Laycock 2003) and 'international crime prevention' (Farrington 2000). Situational prevention is essentially a 'bottom-up' approach that needs to be grounded in local knowledge and a reflexive engagement with the ongoing interactions between situations and people. This is very different from the scientific, evidence-based quest for 'what works'. Hence, situational prevention fits uneasily with efforts to generalize and provide evidence for rules distilled into universal 'toolkits'. Yet, as Shapland (2000) notes, many of its proponents view situational prevention from a top-down governmental perspective which belies its knowledge-based assumptions. The inferences of contextual specificity are frequently lost in the application and imple-mentation of situational prevention. Techniques developed in one context are often transferred to others with little regard to context. One reason for this disjunction between theory and practice may lie in the fact that situational prevention embodies a universal image of human decision-making—that of the 'amoral' rational choice actor—which is easily and eminently generalizable. It evokes a 'de-differentiating' logic that cannot be housed in different, specialist, professional state institutions and that 'implies the generalization of crime control to meet the generality of crime' (Garland 2000: 13).

Nevertheless, situational crime prevention has proved attractive at a number of levels. As well as its pragmatism and its appeal to commonsense, piecemeal change with tangible results, situational prevention (re-)emerged at a favourable political moment. Its language of economic reasoning, personal choice, responsibility, and rationality fitted very well with the growing neo-liberal consensus within government, first articulated by the Thatcher governments in the 1980s, but subsequently reinforced and extended by later governments. Its appeal to the responsibilities of people and organizations throughout civil society meshed well with the growing political will to downsize and roll back the state, in order to free up entrepreneurial initiative. The neo-liberal mantra demanded a retreat from the 'illusion' that governments can provide social goods (Garland 1996; Loader and Sparks, Chapter 3, this volume). In this context, situational prevention offered the promise of short-term and cost-effective, albeit small-scale, impacts in stark contrast to the 'nothing works' pessimism connected with the grand-scale, social engineering projects circulating within criminal justice. A situational mentality speaks the language of the market, of supply and demand, risk and reward, opportunities and costs, whilst appealing to regulation beyond the state through private and quasi-private auspices. It focuses as much on victims as on offenders. Furthermore, it contrasted with apparently discredited social welfare models of policy provision and resonated with a particular political ideology.

Whilst situational prevention was originally promoted by a Conservative government, Clarke (2000: 107–9) is correct to note that the ideas that inform such an approach is by no means 'conservative'. Far from it, is eschews a moral agenda at the heart of conservative political philosophy, in preference for an instrumental understanding of both behaviour and the role of government. Neo-conservative ideas are to be found more clearly associated with community-based crime prevention (explored later), which sees the role of government as implicated not merely in freeing autonomy but crucially, also, in shaping it by inculcating a moralized vision of civic virtue.

DISPLACEMENT—THE ACHILLES HEEL?

One of the central objections to situational prevention is that as it fails to address the 'root causes of crime' or individual dispositions it merely deflects crime. Displacement can take a number of different forms including: *spatial, temporal, tactical, target,* and *type of crime* (Hakim and Rengert 1981). To complicate matters further, these forms of displacement may occur simultaneously or in combination. Clearly, displacement constitutes a major challenge for situational approaches and presents considerable difficulties for evaluating their effectiveness. However, it would be wrong to assume that displacement is either inevitable or complete. To do so would be to see crime prevention as analogous to squeezing a balloon which subsequently changes shape and distribution but does not change in volume. However, this 'hydraulic' interpretation assumes complete displacement which is unlikely in relation to many forms of crime, notably burglary, where the demands of time and effort are considerable. Displacement makes certain assumptions about crime. It presumes that incentives to commit a crime are sufficiently strong to survive the initial thwarting of intention—that 'bad will out'. Cornish and Clarke (1987) suggest that displacement is contingent upon the belief that different crimes can serve a functional equivalence for offenders. Instead, they claim that the willingness of an individual to substitute one offence for another depends upon the extent to which the alternative corresponds with the offender's goals and abilities. They point to the different 'choice structuring properties' of crimes, defined as the type and amount of pay-off, perceived risk, and skills needed that are 'perceived by the offender as being especially salient to his or her goals, motives, experience, abilities, expertise, and preferences' (ibid.: 935). The legitimate assumption is that displacement will not be random but is likely to be structured, or clustered, by certain factors.

A significant difficulty arises where displaced crime shifts to a more serious offence or results in more harmful consequences. This 'malign' displacement might occur where offenders choose to use greater force or more harmful techniques in adapting to preventive interventions or where more vulnerable people are affected as a result of crime prevention. There was some evidence that the introduction of steering column locks in the UK—initially introduced on new cars only—whilst reducing theft of new cars made older cars almost twice as vulnerable. By implication, this shifted the risk of car theft on to those more likely to be less affluent, those who bought second-hand cars. In recognizing malign displacement, we also need to acknowledge the possibility of 'benign' displacement, where a less serious offence or non-criminal act is committed or an act of similar seriousness is committed upon a victim for whom, or in a place where, it has less serious consequences.

Proponents of situational approaches point to a possible reverse effect by which crime-reductive impacts may extend beyond the intended target in a 'diffusion of benefits' (Clarke and Weisburd 1994: 169). This 'halo' or 'free-rider' effect highlights the processes that spread the crime-reduction benefits beyond its primary targets. Poyner's (1992) evaluation of CCTV introduced in car parks at Surrey University found that neighbouring car parks outside the camera's field of vision also benefited from reductions in crime. Matthews' (1992) study of the introduction of street closures to stop kerb-crawling near Finsbury Park, north London, found that not only did prostitution decline but so did other offences indirectly associated with prostitution including burglary and car theft. This case study was also held to be an example of benign displacement. Where prostitutes were displaced they often moved off the streets and into areas where the nuisance element was reduced and the prostitutes were likely to be safer.

Despite criticisms, the phenomenon of displacement points to the power of policy interventions, not their weakness. Crime displacement might be seen as a potential tool of crime control policy rather than as an unwanted constraint upon crime-prevention programmes (Barr and Pease 1990: 279). The displacement of crime, produced by forms of deliberate prevention, might be used to redistribute the burden of victimization in a more equitable manner. However, the attraction of explicit policies of crime redistribution is unlikely to be politically acceptable. Few people would welcome redistributed crime into their neighbourhood. Nevertheless, this illuminates the political choices that constitute present patterns of crime.

CRITIQUES OF SITUATIONAL CRIME PREVENTION

Situational crime prevention has evoked considerable critique from within established criminology in part due to its radical reframing of policy concern, research enquiry, and practical effort. It does not seek to explain, nor is it interested in, questions of aetiology—criminology's traditional focus. Offenders are constructed as 'abiographical individuals', abstracted from their social or structural contexts and personal histories (O'Malley 1992). Clarke and Cornish (1985) acknowledge the reality of 'limited rationality' in decision-making, in that choice is constrained by limits of time, ability, and the availability of relevant information. Nonetheless, this largely fails to address non-opportunistic crimes or the proposition that not all actors are economically self-interested. Situational prevention has little to say about non-instrumental factors, expressive crime, and the role of emotions. The attractions of risk-laden criminal acts that may express moral or cultural preferences are not easily comprehended within a framework of rational choice. In some contexts, the risk may itself be the attraction. Hence, situational approaches have less to say about crimes, such as joyriding, drug-taking, hate crime, violence associated with binge-drinking and gang membership, that may evoke some expressive dimension.

A further critique focuses on the lack of an ethical dimension to situational crime prevention theory. It appears to have no explicit concerns for equity built into it and affords no boundaries to its use or implications. Many proponents of situational approaches prefer to strip crime and prevention of any association with moral or normative debates (Felson 1998). Nevertheless, the way that situational prevention is used in an unequal society may well increase inequalities. Its practical implementation raises fundamental social and ethical questions. One retort to this objection has come in the form of linking situational approaches to work with victims of crime (Pease 1998a). Buttressed by research that shows victimization is a good predictor of 'repeat victimization' (Farrell 1995), the introduction of situational methods as a prompt response to victimization (a kind of tertiary victim prevention programme) enables such interventions to constitute a form of social compensation: 'To acknowledge that the best predictor of the next victimization is the last victimization is to acknowledge that victim support and crime prevention are two sides of the same coin' (Forrester *et al.* 1990: 45). As crime compounds other social disadvantages, crime prevention linked to repeat victimization allows for a targeting of those most disadvantaged without labelling them as such. Rather than adding to inequalities, this allows for the non-contentious targeting of need.

Nevertheless, situational prevention has become associated, by some, with the rise of a 'fortress society' in which the logic of 'target-hardening' is taken to its extreme in the form of 'gated communities' where people live secured behind walls, gates, and other security paraphernalia. Whilst the extent of gating in the UK has often been over-exaggerated (and is clearly less than in the USA, South Africa, and parts of Latin America), a recent survey of planning authorities identified around 1,000 gated communities in England (Atkinson *et al.* 2004). Developers spearheading market development in city-centre living in the UK acknowledge that the privatization and gating of communal space has become an accepted design and selling feature (Webster 2001). Less dramatic are the potential long-term cultural implications and effects of a defensive mentality which often serves to undermine and obstruct social trust relations (Crawford 2000).

Situational approaches also raise ethical issues with regard to civil liberties and human rights. Many situational mechanisms are intrusive, entail the collection of personal data and invade traditional notions of privacy, notably CCTV and identity-based security systems. It is perhaps ironic that in the same country where concerns over civil liberties and fears of intrusive surveillance helped to define a particular vision of prevention and police work nearly two centuries ago, these arguments largely have been ignored in the proliferation of preventive technology. There is an exclusionary logic accompanying the instrumental thinking that informs situational approaches. Denying access to, and excluding potential troublemakers from, places where crime opportunities present themselves is likely to be more cost-effective than making goods so hard to get to for 'good consumers' that it would get in the way of business. This is certainly the lesson that large retail outlets and shopping centres have learned. Exclusion through diverse formal and informal banning orders and private policing strategies are prominent crime-prevention strategies. Frequently, this entails the use of 'profile-based exclusions' which often target young people (von Hirsch and Shearing 2000).

DEVELOPMENTAL CRIME PREVENTION

Social crime prevention is usefully subdivided into those that target individual motivations and those that seek to change communal interactions or collective processes of control. These are often referred to as *developmental* and *community* crime prevention respectively. As developmental crime prevention is well covered elsewhere (Farrington, Chapter 19, this volume), what follows is limited to a few critical observations. Much developmental prevention focuses on young people perceived to be 'at risk' of offending (secondary prevention) rather than universal social and educational policies (primary prevention). Secondary developmental prevention, by identifying 'risk factors' which cluster among groups of known delinquents, is premised upon a differentiating logic that focuses upon a targeted group as a sub-population from those who do not occupy the same risk groupings (Homel 2005). This marks it out as distinct from primary situational prevention with its de-differentiating logic and neo-classical influences. Developmental prevention is infused with a heavy dose of positivism. It draws causal inferences from assessments of risks. Hence, it is concerned with identifying, classifying, differentiating, and seeking to correct 'risk factors', in much the same way that early positivist criminologists sought to study the predispositional attributes of 'criminality'.

Developmental prevention seeks to highlight risk factors that may signal the future onset of criminality, protective factors that may reduce the likelihood of criminality, and desistence factors which may usher young people out of crime. It is heavily reliant therefore upon predictive tools in assessing the likelihood that a given person with certain risk factors will go on to commit specific crimes. However, calculation of future risks can never be an exact science. There will always be 'false positives', those targeted for intervention, but who would not have gone on to commit crime. There is a financial logic behind this differentiation in that targeting resources at those most 'at risk' rather than providing universal services is inherently more cost-effective. Another implication of differential treatment is the possibility of stigmatization by association.

There is a dynamic within developmental approaches to seek ever earlier forms of intervention and to identify ever more (potentially remote) risk factors. One problem is to establish which risk factors are causes and which are merely markers or correlated with causes; correlation is not the same as causation. Most knowledge about risk factors is based on variation between individuals, whereas prevention requires variation (change) within individuals. It is not always clear that findings within individuals are the same as findings between individuals (Farrington, Chapter 19, this volume). Ideas of 'nipping crime in the bud' have pushed criminological concern further and earlier into child—and even foetal—development, elaborating more complex chains of causation. The impact of this logic is to expand the range and reach of state interventions deeper into the social fabric. These may be in the interests of the individuals concerned and society more generally, in terms of reductions in crime, but raise ethical issues about the appropriate limits of government intervention, the balance between potential crime-preventive benefits and other social goods, and the impact on those targeted who might never have developed into criminality. This begs the question, where does social policy end and criminal policy begin? Targeting those 'at risk' for special services may be more politically acceptable than providing services to people who have offended, which raises objections that wrongdoers should not benefit from their misdeeds. Nevertheless, a weaker version of this objection may come into play. Why should those who may be teetering on the edge of criminality, whose behaviour may be problematic but not yet criminal, be given resources unavailable to their well-behaved peers?

More generally, developmental prevention is an example of 'risk-thinking' that has become more pervasive and is associated with the rise of 'actuarial justice' with an emphasis upon risk-assessment techniques and the elaboration of insurance-based technologies (Feeley and Simon 1994). However, the distinction between 'old' needs-based interventions and the 'new' language of risk-based programmes is not as marked as some critics suggest (Hannah-Moffat 2005). O'Malley notes that 'much developmental crime prevention of late has begun explicitly to identify as risk factors the kinds of "social conditions" identified under welfare programmes' (2001: 97–8).

COMMUNITY CRIME PREVENTION

A risk-based dynamic is also evident in some community-level prevention programmes (of a secondary preventive type). Targeting a community or neighbourhood with high aggregate risk factors avoids the aforementioned objections about giving special resources to those perceived to be undeserving because of their association with criminality. Because high levels of criminality often coexist alongside high levels of victimization, such programmes can be 'sold' as targeting the most vulnerable social groups, rather like crime prevention focused on 'repeat victimization'. This may deflect charges of favouritism, but does not necessarily eliminate the stigmatizing potential of such programmes. Communities may develop reputations which can be hard to shed, with consequent implications for their attractiveness as a place to live. *Communities That Care* (CTC) is a prominent example of a risk-based programme aimed at working with all young people in targeted areas.

The theoretical basis for CTC is what Catalano and Hawkins (1996) call a 'social development model', which purports that child development is influenced by the quality of the interaction between children and adults. They echo Hirschi's (1969) ideas about the role of social bonds in encouraging individuals to forgo their selfish motivations and conform to rules. It is believed that children who are given clear standards of behaviour and have positive social bonding with adults are less likely to get involved in crime. The development of pro-social factors is seen as a means of protecting children from the consequences of risk factors. Importantly, these protective factors do not rest just in individuals but in social interactions too.

However, much that passes as community crime prevention has little to do with communities as collective entities, but rather deploy a community focus in order to reach individuals or households. Community-based interventions frequently lack a clear sense of purpose beyond improving the locality and the well-being of residents or a theory of how change could be achieved. Various forms of community prevention might better be interpreted 'not only as applications of criminological theory, but also as complex pieces of sociopolitical action that also have a defining ideological and ethical character' (Hope 1995: 22). Implicitly, community crime prevention seeks to strengthen latent social control mechanisms and/or provide people with a stake in their own conformity through a diverse array of interventions (Crawford 1998: 124).

One factor that informs much of the community-based prevention is the assumption that the rise in crime since the 1960s is attributable, in part, to the breakdown in traditional social ties and the obligations that derive from them. From an American context, Putnam (2000) has sought to demonstrate declining 'civic engagement' and social capital as symptoms and causes of impoverished democracy and social breakdown. He defines social capital as the 'connections among individuals—social networks and the norms of reciprocity and trustworthiness that arise from them' (2000: 19). This definition emphasizes the norms and networks that enable people to act collectively. Unlike some other forms of economic or human capital, social capital lies between individuals and organizations in relationships. It is not reducible to individual possession. This relational quality means that social capital is believed to operate as a form of social glue that fosters integration, cohesion, and order. It provides a conceptual tool that policy-makers can deploy in promoting strong communities.[4]

However, in much of the policy debate, the linkages between social capital and economic and human capital are often left under-developed. Extra-community (top-down) resources and bottom-up capacity building are often entwined. The sources of social capital are frequently confused with the benefits or assets that are believed to derive from them. Some disadvantaged neighbourhoods have high levels of sociability but are unable to utilize or exploit this in ways that produce tangible benefits that address their deprivation. As Sampson and colleagues (1999) suggest, the concentration of multiple forms of disadvantage tend to depress shared expectations for collective action, particularly regarding children.

Woolcock (2001) distinguishes between three different forms of social capital:

- *Bonding social capital* consists of the strong social ties that exist among groups of people that share similar values, interests, and backgrounds.

- *Bridging social capital* relates to bonds between different social groups—between generations, cultural, ethnic, and religious groups. These are generally weaker, less intense, attachments.

- *Linking social capital* refers to the ties that connect people to local service providers and resources. This alludes to vertical relations that link people and communities to sources of power and resources that lie beyond the neighbourhood in the wider society, notably in formal institutions.

Linking social capital draws particular attention to the importance of the manner in which neighbourhoods connect with, and are situated within, a wider social environment. The ability of residents to engage with local authorities and access extra-communal resources is influenced by local political-economies and the manner in which areas are viewed and responded to by outsiders, notably official agencies and the media. Different combinations of social capital will generate divergent outcomes. Some may be more or less important to different communities at various times and for achieving different purposes. These diverse forms of social capital can operate in mutually reinforcing, but also in competing, ways. Linking social capital can foster intra-group bonding and inter-group bridging. However, by creating strong in-group loyalty and affective relations, bonding capital may also create strong out-group antagonism within and between local communities.

---

[4] Understandings of social capital have significantly influenced New Labour thinking and policy initiatives, especially within the Civil Renewal Unit in the Home Office and the Neighbourhood Renewal Unit in the Office of the Deputy Prime Minister.

BROKEN WINDOWS, FEAR, AND DISORDER

Possibly the most influential contribution to debates about communities, informal social control, and crime prevention is Wilson and Kelling's (1982) 'broken window' thesis. They argue that minor incivilities—such as vandalism, graffiti, rowdy behaviour, drunkenness, begging—if unchecked and uncontrolled will set in train a series of linked social responses, as a result of which 'decent' neighbourhoods can tip into fearful ghettos of crime. Untended property and unchecked behaviour, they argue, produce a breakdown of community controls, by a spiralling process, whereby: incivilities lead to fear which promotes avoidance, withdrawal, and flight by local residents which, in turn, leads to reduced informal social control which results in more serious crime, which leads to increased fear, and so on. As the neighbourhood declines, so disorder, fear, and crime spiral upwards. The 'broken window' is a powerful metaphor for the absence of order and control.

The proposed solution is to stop and reverse the 'cycle of decline' in its earliest stages by focusing upon 'order maintenance' through the policing of incivilities and other 'signs of crime' (Kelling and Coles 1996). What is deemed necessary is for the community to reassert its 'natural forces' of moral authority and control through early intervention in disorderly conduct. The logic is that if one tackles low-level disorders, it is possible to impact upon more serious types of crime. Implicit is the belief that the police have neglected their order-maintenance functions in preference for their crime-fighting tasks. These ideas have found particular favour with communitarians, such as Etzioni (1993), who articulate a need to revive the moral authority of communities and call for a greater emphasis on social responsibilities rather than individual rights. Strong communities, it is argued, can speak to us in moral voices. They allow the policing *by* communities rather than the policing *of* communities.

However, Wilson and Kelling offer little empirical support for their claims regarding a causal relationship between disorder, fear, and increased crime. Taylor's (2001) findings challenge the assumption that signs of incivility (particularly physical signs) influence crime and fear of crime in any simplistic manner. What is more, 'broken windows' and disorder do not necessarily have the same effects or meanings in different neighbourhoods. They may be interpreted in different ways. Taylor shows how 'fear of crime' differences are greater between individuals than between neighbourhoods. In most cases, fear arises because of differences between residents responding to roughly comparable ecological conditions. Levels of disorder tend to be highest in areas with high poverty, as well as heterogeneous and transient populations (Skogan 1990). Sampson and Raudenbusch (1999) argue that disorder and crime both stem from certain neighbourhood structural qualities, notably concentrated poverty. Disorder does not directly promote crime. Rather, they both stem from a lack of 'collective efficacy', defined as the presence or absence of social cohesion, mutual trust, and a willingness to intervene in support of informal social control, which is itself conditioned by the structural characteristics of neighbourhoods.

Nevertheless, the 'broken window' thesis has passed into established 'orthodoxy' within British government policy, regularly cited in documentation in support of new initiatives. Most prominently, it has focused attention upon interventions aimed at disorder and incivilities as preludes to more serious crime. This has informed the antisocial behaviour agenda and Respect Action Plan (Home Office 2003; 2006a), as well as specific new powers like ASBOs and dispersal orders.[5] It has also influenced the contemporary emphasis on fear reduction as the object of policy in its own right.[6] The 'broken windows' thesis directly informed the development of 'zero-tolerance policing' both in the USA and the UK, which proponents claimed led to significant reductions in serious crime in New York in the 1990s (Bratton 1997; Kelling and Bratton 1998). Whilst the empirical evidence for this remains the subject of debate (Harcourt 2001), it alerted attention to the policing of minor 'quality of life' issues.

LIMITATIONS OF COMMUNITY

In essence, the 'broken windows' thesis and the 'defensible space' theory, as well as the policies to which they give rise, are premised on a notion of 'community defence' in that they envisage the community to be under attack, notably from 'outsiders'. There is little sense in which offenders are understood as members of, and belonging to, communities—as neighbours, husbands, or sons (Currie 1988). Hence, they have little to say about crimes involving intimate insiders, such as domestic violence and corporate crime. There is an assumption that community members share moral values and conceptions of order, thus marginalizing intra-communal differences. The reality, in many urban areas, is not the homogeneous communities of nostalgia but a cosmopolitan mix of age groups, ethnicities, cultures, and social identities. Here, (dis)orderly behaviour itself may be differently interpreted and experienced.

Contrary to communitarian assumptions, 'more community' does not equate in any simple way with 'less crime'. Community and its shared normative values may well be criminogenic. Strong social ties, networks, and mutual trust all sustain organized crime, gang cultures, and hate crime. Deviant social networks can foster antisocial behaviour, transmitting values, skills, and knowledge that constitute 'criminal capital'. Inversely, a lack of strong social ties and bonds of community does not inevitably promote disorder. Affluent, low-crime areas that may display an appearance of civility do not always exhibit characteristics of intimacy, connectedness, and mutual support, as Baumgartner's (1988) research on the moral order of American suburbs testifies. Rather than rely on informal control, suburbanites are likely to call rapidly upon the intervention of formal mechanisms to which they have greater access than more deprived areas, and which respond more readily to them than to the latter. Middle-class suburbs may be lacking in community ties and yet orderly. By contrast, informal control mechanisms are not necessarily absent in all high-crime areas (Hope and Foster 1992). The structural attributes of communities—the manner in which they connect

[5] ASBOs were first introduced by the Crime and Disorder Act 1998 (s.1) and dispersal orders by the Anti-Social Behaviour Act 2003 (s.30).

[6] This was first signalled by the Grade Working Group Report (Home Office 1989) into *Fear of Crime* and reinforced more recently through the 'reassurance policing' agenda in 2004.

with, and are situated within, sources of power and resources in the wider environment—may be more important than community as a sense of belonging.

Assumptions about the nature of community and the relations between communities and offenders produce dilemmas for implementation. Strategies are more likely to be successful in low-crime, organized, and homogeneous communities that perceive themselves under threat from 'outsiders'. This has been the fate of Neighbourhood Watch. Research confirms that it is easiest to establish Neighbourhood Watch in affluent, suburban areas with low crime rates involving people who hold favourable attitudes towards the police rather than in inner-city, crime-prone, public sector housing estates with heterogeneous populations (Hope 2000). This reflects a more general observation that there is generally an inverse relationship between prevention activity and need (Rosenbaum 1988). Many community-based schemes, like Neighbourhood Watch, rather than simply relieving the police of burdens can generate new demands. Evidence shows that in order to establish and sustain Neighbourhood Watch police assistance and support are vital (Hussain 1988). Hence, community-based prevention can have the perverse effect of skewing public resources towards those places which may least need them and those people most capable of protecting themselves.

Paradoxically, the contemporary focus on communities has emerged at a historic time at which empirically communities are declining in relevance as a source of strong bonds. In much of the policy rhetoric around community crime prevention there is often a slippage between community as a sense of something lost and community as a focus for building modern democratic institutions. The ideals of community—reciprocity, intimacy, and trustworthiness—sit awkwardly with contemporary concerns for individuality, freedom, and mobility. Accordingly, community-based initiatives tend to hold unrealistic expectations of what communities can do to reduce crime. There is a danger that communities have become a site around which individuals and groups can be mobilized to take on greater responsibility for their own well-being and security. This shedding of responsibility from the state has implications for where the cost for providing security should lie as well as the blame for failure. With a burgeoning security market and the growing purchase by communities of additional security patrols (Crawford *et al.* 2005), the worry is that some communities are better able to carry this burden, whilst others might become blamed for their incapacity to prevent crime.

The focus on community-level governance begs a more fundamental question: to what extent are the 'community' and the 'social' complementary aspects of the same broad rationality of government or different and potentially competing levels of government? Community justice is not the same as social justice. Community-based solutions tend to be particularistic and parochial, with little concern for externalities and wider social ramifications. Well-defended communities may serve to displace crime on to less-well-defended residential areas. Hence, one community's safety may come at the expense of others'. Is it desirable that safety as a public good is transformed into a parochial or exclusive good?

In this vein, Pease has argued that community safety is something of a misnomer (2002: 948). Safety, he notes, incorporates harms that extend far beyond crime; including traffic, health, food, pollution, product design, planning, etc. A pan-hazard approach would see crime as only a small element of harm reduction. From this perspective, placing community safety in the context of crime and disorder legislation is rather like the tail wagging the dog. More appropriately, crime and disorder should be housed within an overarching community safety legislative framework. Pease is undoubtedly correct, in that seeing harm through a crime lens is unhelpful and skews the notion of safety by its implications with crime. It fuels an unhelpful focus upon crime-related risks—such as those presented by predatory strangers—at the expense of more immanent yet mundane risks such as those presented by traffic and pollution. As Adam (2005) dryly notes, the risk of being killed by a suicide bomber in Britain is minuscule compared to that presented by the motor car. The way people respond to risks is mediated by their cultural and political salience. A consequence of community safety debates is that risks have become simultaneously conflated and confused—the risk of burglary, disorder, incivility, and disrespect regularly intermingle with sexual abuse and mass murder. Yet, crime and disorder related risk have also become segregated from many other social harms.

Community safety is less a misnomer in so far as it offers space for a politics and ethics of collective security which is more than the sum of individual security initiatives. Against a background in which security has become commodified, it is potentially the notion of 'private security' that is the more problematic misnomer (Loader 1997). Not only is private security an oxymoron because one person's security initiatives or behaviours impact upon other people's safety, but also because an individual's security depends in some significant manner upon the security of others. People are intimately reliant upon others for their security, both how they feel and how at risk they are. Regardless, community safety has come to be the defining discourse within which much of contemporary policy in the UK has been couched.

POLICY DEVELOPMENTS IN THE UK

As an adaptation to the crisis within criminal justice, crime-prevention thinking heralded a fundamental shift in the object of enquiry, ways of conceiving, and methods of responding to the threat of crime. Table 26.2 provides an overview of key policy developments since 1980 that sought to advance this preventive logic. A major declaration of the shift to a preventive mentality within government came with the publication of Interdepartmental Circular 8/84. It constituted a decisive statement of the new philosophy, declaring that 'preventing crime is a task for the whole community'. The vehicle to deliver this new message was the Safer Cities Programme and its predecessor the Five Towns Initiative which together ran from the mid-1980s to

Table 26.2 Timeline of key policy developments in Britain since 1980

Year	Event	Key relevance
1980	Gladstone Report published	Outlines a problem-oriented methodology for implementing crime prevention
1983	Crime Prevention Unit established	Set up with the Home Office to encourage crime-prevention activity
1984	Interdepartmental Circular 8/84	Elaborates a multi-agency approach to crime prevention
1986	Five Towns Initiative	Initial government attempt to sponsor local multi-agency partnerships
1988	Safer Cities Programme	Key vehicle for institutionalizing local crime-prevention partnerships through short-term government funding for targeted urban areas. 20 projects funded—extended to 32 more under phase 2 launched in 1992
1988	Crime Concern established	Funded through the Home Office to foster private-sector involvement in crime prevention and disseminate good practice
1989	Grade Report on the Fear of Crime	Standing Conference on Crime Prevention acknowledges fear as a policy concern
1990	Interdepartmental Circular 44/90	Sets terms of reference for the Morgan Committee 'to consider and monitor progress', and accompanied by a good practice booklet, *Partnership in Crime Prevention*, reviewing developments since 8/84
1991	Morgan Report published	Advocates the use of the term 'community safety' in preference to 'crime prevention' and proposes local authorities be given a statutory duty to establish community safety partnerships and set local strategies
1992	Car Theft Index published	Home Secretary invites manufacturers to discuss its implications
1994	CCTV Challenge Competition	Partnership bids with matched funding for open-street CCTV schemes
1994	Circular 5/94 'Planning Our Crime'	Encourages crime prevention in planning decisions as a 'material consideration'
1997	General Election	Labour Government elected with a commitment to implement Morgan Report
1998	Crime and Disorder Act	Places a duty on local authorities and police to coordinate and promote Crime and Disorder Reduction Partnerships (CDRPs). Section 17 requires local authorities to consider the crime and disorder implications of all their activities. Introduces ASBOs, parenting orders, and youth offending teams

1998	Social Exclusion Unit set up	Establishes 18 cross-departmental policy action teams to address social exclusion, 'narrow the gap' between the worst estates and the rest, and join up government policies
1999	Crime Reduction Programme	£400 million allocated to 'evidence-based' experimentation over 3 years
2000	National Strategy for Neighbourhood Renewal launched	Highlights antisocial behaviour as a significant urban problem and gives rise to Neighbourhood Renewal Fund and New Deal for Communities, targeting 39 most deprived estates in England and Wales. Neighbourhood warden schemes launched
2002	Police Reform Act	Extends legal responsibility for formulating and implementing CDRPs to Police and Fire Authorities and Primary Care Trusts. Fire Authorities covered by s.17. Introduces community support officer as new police employee dedicated to patrol
2003	Anti-Social Behaviour Act and Action Plan	Extends the legal responsibility of CDRPs to 'anti-social behaviour' (ASB), expands the use of fixed penalty notices to ASB, and creates new powers for police to disperse groups. The ASB Action Plan launches a national campaign coordinated by a Home Office ASB Unit
2004	*Building Communities, Beating Crime* White Paper	Commits the government to undertake a review of CDRPs and publish a community safety strategy
2005	Clean Neighbourhoods and Environment Act	Extends 1998 Act to cover 'anti-social and other behaviour adversely affecting the local environment' for the purposes of the work of CDRPs
	National Community Safety Plan	Promises central government commitment to deliver joined-up community safety strategy and incorporates National Policing Plan within wider safety agenda
2006	Respect programme launched	Plans to go 'broader, deeper, and further' than previous initiatives to address antisocial behaviour and restore 'respect'. Coordinated centrally
	Government Response to its Review of CDRPs	Outlines plans to replace CDRP's triennial review cycle with 6-monthly strategic intelligence assessments to inform annual rolling 3-year community safety plans, to create a duty on partners to share depersonalized data, and expand s.17

the mid-1990s. By providing limited short-term funding and a coordinator these local projects sought to draw together emergent partnerships and ignite crime-prevention activities. The intention was to incorporate a wide range of organizations and interests including representatives of businesses, the voluntary sector, and the public sector to consider local crime problems and preventive measures. The symbolic ownership of, and dominant voice within, these partnerships lay with the police and the types of crime prevention promoted tended to be of a police-led situational kind.

The Morgan Committee, established in 1990 to review developments since Circular 8/84, fostered a significant shift in the emerging discourse. It advanced a series of significant recommendations (Morgan 1991). The two most important were conceptual and institutional. Conceptually, it suggested that the term 'community safety' be preferred to 'crime prevention'. The latter was seen to be too narrow and too closely associated with police-related responsibilities. Community safety, by contrast, was perceived to be open to wider interpretation which could encourage 'greater participation from all sections of the community in the fight against crime' (ibid.: 13). It was also seen as an umbrella term under which situational and social approaches could be combined rather than juxtaposed.

Institutionally, the Morgan Report recommended that local authorities should be given 'statutory responsibility', working with the police, for the development and promotion of community safety. It also highlighted the lack of central government coordination. Largely for ideological reasons, the Conservative government refused to implement the Report's central recommendations and subsequently ran out of significant crime prevention ideas beyond promoting active citizenship through the special constabulary and Neighbourhood Watch and sponsoring the expansion of CCTV across the country.[7] It is estimated that in the mid-1990s in England some 78 per cent of the Home Office's crime prevention budget was being spent on CCTV systems alone (Koch 1998). This growth has continued, with Britain leading the world in the installation of CCTV. According to the British Security Industry Association (BSIA), by 2004 there were over 4.25 million CCTV cameras installed in the UK.[8]

The dramatic expansion of CCTV was initially rooted in a political ideology that favoured a situational approach and technological solutions whilst visibly demonstrating that (local and national) government was 'doing something' about crime. However, it also reflects a deeper cultural attraction in that CCTV cameras not only evoke symbols of security by appearing to perform preventive tasks, but also facilitate the acting out of more traditional expressive and punitive sentiments provoked by the footage derived from CCTV cameras where criminal acts and disorder are captured on film. In this manner, CCTV straddles both a preventive logic and a punitive one (Norris and McCahill 2006). It enables both a governance of the present and future through surveillance and deterrence and a reordering of the past by witnessing and recording

[7] In 1994, the first of four CCTV Challenge Competitions was launched to support the expansion of city-centre CCTV.

[8] www.bsia.co.uk/industry.html.

events. Not only are CCTV cameras tangible reminders that someone is trying to secure personal safety but also they serve to prompt moral indignation at the acts they portray. As town centres, shopping malls, and other locations have increasingly vied to present themselves as safe havens to attract mobile populations to visit, use, or shop, the CCTV now constitutes an indispensable symbol of security.

Over the intervening years, community safety has become entangled with wider influences on public policy promoted in the name of a 'modernization agenda':

- Neo-liberal-inspired reforms to the public sector through the contracting out of service delivery to the private sector, the separation of purchaser/provider roles, the introduction of internal markets and competition, and the incorporation of private sector management methods into the public sector.

- A managerialist impulse to measure performance by results set against clear objectives.

- A rhetorical emphasis on 'evidence-based policy' and the promotion of 'what works' in the rational and cost-effective use of resources.

- A desire to provide joined-up solutions to complex social problems that transcend the competency of traditional departments, professional expertise, and disciplinary boundaries.

COMMUNITY SAFETY PARTNERSHIPS—THE INFRASTRUCTURE

As the Morgan Report noted, crime prevention and community safety are peripheral concerns of diverse agencies but 'a truly core activity of none of them' (1991: 15). In response, it articulated and advanced a partnership approach that advocates the co-production of community safety. Prevention demanded a novel holistic approach that transcends the competencies of specific professional groups and associations and cuts across disciplinary boundaries. In theory, if not in practice, this new politics:

- recognizes that the levers and causes of crime lie far from the traditional reach of the criminal justice system;

- acknowledges that there is no single agency solution to crime and disorder—it is multifaceted in both its causes and its effects;

- recognizes the need for social responses to crime which reflect the nature of the phenomenon itself and its multiple aetiology;

- allows for a holistic approach to crime, community safety, and associated issues which is 'problem-focused' rather than 'bureaucracy-premised';

- affords the potential coordination and pooling of knowledge, capacity, and resources.

In this new local governance of public safety, partnership has become a defining locus for the rearticulation of responsibilities within and among public sector organizations, voluntary agencies, private businesses, and individuals. Citizens are now cast as 'partners against crime' in a new corporate approach, involving a fundamental realignment of professional 'expertise'. The Crime and Disorder Act 1998 created the institutional framework for implementing a partnership approach. It diverged from the Morgan proposals in that it placed a joint duty on local councils and the police to work with a wide range of other agencies from the public, private, voluntary, and community sectors to develop and implement strategies to reduce crime and disorder.[9] Each of the 376 Crime and Disorder Reduction Partnerships (CDRPs; called in Wales Community Safety Partnerships, or CSPs) in England and Wales is required to conduct a triennial audit of crime and disorder within its area, to consult the local community on the findings, and to deliver a strategic response (Home Office 1998). The Act also provides a power to partners to disclose information for the purposes of the Act (section 115).

Section 17 of the 1998 Act also imposes a duty on local authorities, in exercising their various functions, to consider the crime and disorder implications and the need to do all that they reasonably can to prevent crime and disorder in their area. The purpose of the duty was to 'give the vital work of preventing crime a new focus across a very wide range of local services . . . putting crime and disorder considerations at the very heart of decision making, where they have always belonged' (Home Office 1997: para. 33). It was intended as an 'enabling device' to promote the embedding of a crime-prevention mentality in the everyday activities of the police and local authorities. Some commentators saw this as the most radical element of the 1998 Act. As anticipating crime could pervade 'every aspect of local authority responsibility, it is difficult to conceive of any decision which will remain untouched by section 17 considerations' (Moss and Pease 1999: 16).

Soon after the establishment of CDRPs the government launched its ambitious Crime Reduction Programme. Local partnerships were to be centrally involved in the implementation which allocated significant funding through which to advance the work of preventive partnerships. Initially, the programme was intended to run for ten years. The programme benefited from a specific 'window of opportunity' in which it appeared attractive to a range of politicians, administrators, researchers, and practitioners (Maguire 2004). The programme was unique in British history in its scale and scope, the extent of the funding, and its commitment to evaluation. Its aim was to use research-based knowledge and accumulate new knowledge about the effectiveness of a wide range of interventions for dissemination. To this end, some 10 per cent of the initial £250 million budget was to be allocated to evaluation.

In the event, however, the programme only ran from 1999 to 2002 and few projects were fully implemented. Many suffered from slow-moving bureaucratic procedures, cultural resistance from practitioners, unfeasible timescales, and a lack of capacity on the part of relevant organizations. In the event, less was learned about what works than

---

[9] The discussion that follows applies primarily to England and Wales. Obligations set out in the Crime and Disorder Act 1998 do not apply to Scotland, where a voluntaristic approach to partnerships has prevailed. Northern Ireland has followed a slightly different route.

about the reasons for implementation failure. Maguire (2004) suggests that the unravelling of the crime-reduction programme, in part, lay in the manner in which it got sucked into the wider reform agenda of achieving performance targets and delivering crime-reduction outcomes. The initial long-term aim of learning through experimentation and evaluation became sidetracked by the shorter-term objectives of meeting challenging crime-reduction targets set by government. At the outset of the programme, the government announced targets including a 30 per cent reduction in vehicle crime by 2004 and a 25 per cent reduction in burglary by 2005.

CRIME REDUCTION FUNDING

The crime reduction programme was replaced by the Safer Communities Initiative, under which funds were distributed to partnerships through Regional Government Offices. Between 1999 and 2004, grants of £927 million were dedicated to specific crime-reduction projects by the Home Office. During this period, the Home Office introduced 14 different types of crime-reduction grants, each with different conditions and requiring separate audit certificates. In its review of the work of CDRPs and their relations with the Home Office, the National Audit Office (NAO 2004: 1) concluded that 'complex funding systems have placed an administrative burden on partnerships' and 'the Home Office could have achieved bigger reductions in crime by minimizing the administrative work done by partnerships, so that more monies can be spent on successful crime prevention initiatives instead'. The Report also noted problems engendered by short-term funding, which often resulted in the early termination of successful initiatives once the funding dried up. In response to the NAO's criticisms, the Safer and Stronger Communities Fund, rolled out in England in 2005–6, sought to bring together some of the existing grants into a single fund.

One predicament generated by the shift to an inter-agency approach within government has been the proliferation of diverse partnerships around different cross-cutting issues often benefiting from differing funding sources. The broad field of crime prevention rapidly became congested with CDRPs, Drug and Alcohol Action Teams (DAATs), youth offending teams, Local Strategic Partnerships (LSPs), Local Criminal Justice Boards, and many others. This has created overlapping competencies, confused responsibilities, friction, coordination deficits, and the duplication of effort. There have been efforts to rationalize these 'tangled webs' including the merger of CDRPs and DAATs, but there remain considerable uncertainties over relations between different partnerships, such as CDRPs and LSPs. This fragmented local landscape has often been exacerbated by conflicting and competing central government programmes, notably where initiated by different government departments. Particular tensions over the direction of community safety have emerged from the Office of the Deputy Prime Minister (ODPM), responsible for urban regeneration and civil renewal, and the Home Office, responsible for policing and criminal justice. More generally, the logic of the 1998 Act, coupled with privatization, contracting out of local service delivery, and other government initiatives, has been to foster greater fragmentation and complexity. This is particularly evident, for example, in the burgeoning mixed economy of visible uniformed patrol personnel (see Crawford *et al.* 2005).

ASSESSING COMMUNITY SAFETY PARTNERSHIPS

Despite their initial promise, the 'honeymoon' period of CDRPs was short-lived (Phillips 2002). They have largely not lived up to early expectations. The main barriers to successful partnership include a reluctance of some agencies to participate (especially health, education, and social services); the dominance of a policing agenda; unwillingness to share information; conflicting interests, priorities, and cultural assumptions on the part of different agencies; local political differences; lack of inter-organizational trust; desire to protect budgets; lack of capacity and expertise; and over-reliance on informal contacts and networks which lapse if key individuals move on (Skinns 2005; Hughes 2006). The involvement of the private sector has often been patchy and the role of the voluntary sector is frequently marginalized. Despite section 115 of the 1998 Act, which gives partners the legal power to exchange information, in practice partnerships experienced considerable problems in reaching agreements or protocols about what data they could legitimately share and on what basis. Along with data protection legislation, the implications of section 115 have been differently interpreted. As a result, concerns over confidentiality have often stymied partnership working and problematized inter-organizational trust relations.

Central government responded to the perceived unwillingness of some key agencies to participate actively in CDRPs by expanding the list of organizations under a legal duty to participate. Since the original legislation, a similar statutory responsibility has been extended to police authorities and fire authorities as of April 2003 and Primary Care Trusts (representing the health service) a year later.[10] Demands for such legislative obligations emerged largely because these partners were not deemed to be contributing to partnerships around the country. Similarly, the implementation of section 17 has fallen considerably below expectations. One area where it might have had direct and immediate implications was in the realm of planning applications, where police architectural liaison officers and crime prevention design advisors might have been able to use it as a lever into planning decisions. A significant number of test cases revolved around applications for licensed premises associated with the expansion of the night-time economy. Despite the well-documented attendant crime and disorder implications of large numbers of alcohol outlets in city centres (Home Office 2001), the Planning Inspectorate has been largely unwilling to uphold decisions to reject applications on the grounds of section 17 where these have been made by local authorities (Moss 2006). As a branch of central government rather than the local council, the Planning Inspectorate has not felt itself bound by the legislation which applies to local authorities alone. This reflects more general tensions between responsibilities at central and local government levels.

---

[10]   Under the Police Reform Act 2002.

In practice, the focus of many partnerships has been compliance with national performance indicators, notwithstanding the requirement upon them to identify and pursue local priorities. Under central pressures, the community safety remit of CDRPs narrowed significantly in the late 1990s to a focus on crime reduction as measured against police-recorded crime figures (Audit Commission 2002: 12). Despite the rhetoric of localism, central government appears to have been unable and unwilling to adopt a more 'hands off' approach to local partnerships. In the politically sensitive arena of crime and disorder, government desires to be seen to be responding to immediate problems often encourage a 'hands on' approach to micro-management. A notable example was the Street Crime Initiative. In response to a rise in street robbery, a centrally directed initiative was set up, challenging ten police forces with short-term reduction targets. This ambiguous stance of central government reflected the dilemma of government pertaining to govern at 'arm's length' but ending up 'hands on' (Crawford 2001).

Such has been the political disappointment with community safety partnerships—despite the steady decline of aggregate crime rates since the mid-1990s—that in late 2004, the government announced a major review of their activities, governance, and accountability, acknowledging that: 'a significant number of partnerships struggle to maintain a full contribution from key agencies and even successful ones are not sufficiently visible, nor we think accountable, to the public as they should be' (Home Office 2004: 123). The review prompted two developments focused respectively around the role of central government and of local partnerships in delivering community safety. First, the government published a National Community Safety Plan (Home Office 2005), which signals the incorporation of the National Policing Plan within a wider community safety agenda. It also represents an attempt to achieve similar results at central government level to those demanded of local authorities via their section 17 obligations. In the plan, the government has committed itself to deliver a more co-ordinated national approach by requiring ministers to prioritize community safety policies and consider community safety dimensions of new and existing policies (ibid.: 15). However, the plan creates no new obligations. It falls considerably short of either the section 17 duties on local authorities or the proposals put forward in the Morgan Report for government to provide 'a community safety impact statement' for all new legislation and major policy initiatives.

Secondly, in early 2006, the government published a response to its review which made a number of proposals for the future development of CDRPs (Home Office 2006b):

- To replace the triennial audit and review cycle with six-monthly strategic intelligence assessments.
- To require CDRPs to produce annual rolling three-year community safety plans informed by intelligence assessments.
- To strengthen section 115 of the 1998 Act and place a duty on responsible authorities to share depersonalized data relevant for community safety purposes.

- To broaden the definition of section 17 to require agencies to take account of antisocial behaviour.

- To set national standards on a range of issues to establish a consistent approach to partnership working across all CDRPs, for which compliance is to be compulsory.

The review appears to offer 'more of the same' with regard to central steering of local partnerships, propped up by statutory duties. Impatience at the pace of change has provoked an acceleration of the review cycle with little regard for the extensive burdens that partnerships are under to respond to the frenetic pace of new initiatives and the burdens of meeting central targets.

There remain a number of broader dilemmas facing partnerships that the government's review did not adequately address. First, the managerialist emphasis on target-setting and performance measurement has fostered an *intra*-organizational focus on meeting narrow goals that pays little attention to the task of managing *inter*-organizational relations and networks (Crawford 2001). The myopic implications of performance measurement afford scant regard to the complex process of negotiating shared purposes, particularly where there is no hierarchy of control. In such a wider policy climate, it is difficult to encourage partners for whom crime is genuinely a peripheral concern to participate actively in community safety endeavours whilst they are being assessed for their performance in other fields.

Government impatience with community safety partnerships alludes to a political conundrum. On the one hand, since their establishment there has been a significant and sustained reduction in aggregate crime levels. According to the 2004/05 BCS, since peaking in 1995, the overall crime rate fell by 44 per cent, with vehicle crime and burglary declining by 57 per cent, and violent crime falling by 43 per cent (Nicholas *et al.* 2005; see also Maguire, Chapter 10, this volume). Whilst the beginning of this decline preceded the implementation of CDRPs, it nevertheless coincided with the implementation of diverse crime-prevention measures. Inevitably, there are difficulties in attributing cause for the decline in crime rates to the various preventive programmes promoted by government, particularly as the decline preceded the current government's prevention drive and has been mirrored in other jurisdictions where different strategies have developed. Nevertheless, the National Audit Office (2004) concluded its review declaring that the government's crime prevention funding through CDRPs and the police had contributed to this decline.

What appears hard to explain, at first glance, is that there has been very little political attribution of the reduction in crime to preventive efforts. Despite what appears to be a 'success story' on a grand scale, politicians have been unwilling to credit prevention. There may be a number of reasons for this. First, much of the (potentially effective) prevention activity actually lies beyond government control and may be more attributable to commercial security initiatives such as the design of products that are harder to steal (for example, cars and consumer tagged goods) and the preventive actions of individuals by introducing alarms and locks on their property. Secondly, it may reflect an acknowledgement that good news about crime is not particularly newsworthy, as well as a political preference to talk 'tough on crime and disorder', by focusing on an alleged growing tide of lawlessness, antisocial behaviour, and lack of respect. Thirdly, there has been a realization that crime risks are not directly related to public perceptions and that changing perceptions may be as important as changing actual risks (or more so).

FEAR OF CRIME

There is an awkward relationship between fear and crime prevention. Fear can provoke preventive activities. It can encourage people to take precautions; to lock doors, fit alarms, and avoid certain situations. However, crime-preventive initiatives do not necessarily reduce fear and initiatives that fail to reduce crime may successfully impact upon reported levels of fear. Furthermore, prevention activities can remind people of their own insecurities and anxieties. It is ironic that quests for security tend to increase subjective insecurity by 'alerting citizens to risk and scattering the world with visible reminders of the threat of crime' (Zedner 2003: 163). Crime risks and fear of crime do not march to the same drum. Subjective fear of crime may be high amongst those people with little objective risk of victimization.

Despite the reduction in crime rates, recent BCS findings show that nearly two-thirds of the public thought crime across the country had increased over the previous two years. Concerns over low-level incivilities and antisocial behaviour have continued to increase. The percentage of people perceiving young people as a problem increased from 20 per cent to 31 per cent between 1992 and 2004/5 (Nicholas *et al.* 2005). Paradoxically, with police officer numbers at an all-time high and more civilian staff than ever, public insecurity and fear of crime remain stubbornly unaffected. In talking up law and order concerns, the government's successive campaigns against antisocial behaviour appear to have fanned public fears rather than reduced them. With the launch of the 'reassurance policing' programme and the commitment to deliver dedicated 'neighbourhood policing teams' (Home Office 2004), fear reduction has moved centre stage, not only within policing but in community safety more generally. The then Home Secretary, David Blunkett, reflected this when launching the programme: 'If you don't feel it, you don't believe it—only when people begin to feel safer will we know that we are beginning to make a real difference'.[11] If 'feeling is believing', fear reduction may be as important as crime reduction for perceptions of security, if not more so.

FOLDING IN AND OPENING OUT

There have been a number of ambiguous shifts in policies broadly related to crime prevention. Whilst the 1990s saw a shift in terminology from a narrow, police-centred understanding of crime prevention to 'community safety' in order to broaden debate to include the adverse impact of fear of crime, disorder, and incivilities, the years from

[11]   www.reassurancepolicing.co.uk/Latest_Details.asp?id=28.

1999 onwards saw a subsequent shift to 'crime reduction' as the overriding narrative. Accompanying this narrowing of the preventive lens have been the more capacious concerns with securing public reassurance, tackling antisocial behaviour, and promoting civility and respect. This reflects a much deeper ambivalence about the appropriate tasks and capacities of contemporary government. At one instance, government policy has sought to devolve responsibilities on to others and to acknowledge the limited effectiveness of governmental interventions. Since Circular 8/84 this has been a common refrain within policy. Yet, at the next moment, governments have sought to reassert ambitious intentions to regulate behaviour in ways that often appear to lie far beyond the reach of the state. This tension is evident in the recent 'Respect' Action Plan launched in January 2006, which plans to go 'broader, deeper and further' than previous initiatives in addressing antisocial behaviour. By this, the government means 'addressing anti-social behaviour in every walk of life . . . tackling the causes of disrespectful behaviour . . . introducing new powers and taking action to make a difference in the short-term and embedding those changes into the mainstream to create cultural change so that everyone sees and expects a robust response to anti-social behaviour' (Home Office 2006a: 7). The moral agenda implicit in the 'broken windows' thesis is evident.

In a context in which the cultural salience of crime is prominent and crime-related anxieties dominate public debate, governments are caught in something of a *Catch 22* situation; simultaneously needing to be seen to be doing something about something over which government has little control. More often than not, 'doing something' means reasserting state authority, or at least attempting to do so by invoking 'more law' and, frequently, more criminal law. The number and range of new laws that have been created in recent years is testimony to the enduring recourse to sovereign command. The politics of crime prevention and community safety over the past decade reflect 'hyper-innovation' in a context of 'hyper-politicization'. We have seen the 'frenetic selection of new institutional modes, and their equally frenetic replacement by alternatives' (Moran 2003: 26). This frantic quest for diverse ways of regulating social life has been premised upon an incoherent conception of 'state craft' embedded in a clash between ambitious central state interventionism and limited capacities. The resultant developments have been both contradictory and volatile as the preventive face of government jostles with its punitive counterpart (O'Malley 1999).

INSURANCE, BUSINESS, AND PREVENTION

The story of the contemporary genesis and growth of crime prevention is often written as if it was something imposed by governments upon the citizenry through programmes of 'responsibilization'—emanating outwards from the centre—and evidenced by key policy initiatives. Yet, much of the credit should properly be attributed to small-scale, local, and pragmatic developments within civil society and the business sector. In reality, both criminology and government policy were relative latecomers to a preventive way of thinking. By contrast, insurers have acted as key 'agents of prevention', helping to spread actuarial logics and technologies of prediction as well as fostering networks with state agencies that have been instrumental in the ascendancy of crime prevention (Ericson *et al.* 2003). However, the logic of insurance can encourage and restrain preventive thinking. It absorbs responsibility by spreading the effect of risks across the community of risk-takers. The incentives to protect against future loss can be reduced as the economic cost is covered by the insurance—producing a 'moral hazard'. Insurance can also responsibilize in that the terms of the insurance contract may require the insured to engage in activities that reduce or eliminate risks rather than merely spreading their effects.

In the UK, the insurance industry was relatively slow to recognize and use its potential power to influence behaviour with regard to crime risks by providing incentives to take preventive measures (Litton 1982). A combination of the event of mass consumerism and the rise in crime risks prompted insurers to narrow their risk pools and foster a preventive mentality on the part of insurers. The willingness of insurance companies, citizens, and businesses to weigh the costs of crime against the costs of prevention only became apparent where there were significant incentives to do so. In the ensuing years, the insurance industry played a significant part in fostering preventive governance through networks with the police, government agencies, and diverse forms of insurance cover. In the field of domestic and vehicle insurance, significant incentives to reduce risks have been introduced for designers, manufacturers, and consumers. Insurance companies have been crucial in promoting the spread and use of certain situational measures, making these a requirement of certain policies.

Yet, it would be wrong to suggest that crime prevention inevitably preoccupies businesses. For many years, car manufacturers were unmoved by police and government concerns about the relative ease of stealing cars. It was only after the Home Office published a Car Theft Index (Houghton 1992) and the Home Secretary invited manufacturers to discuss its implications, that manufacturers actively took notice and subsequently incorporated anti-theft designs into cars. Many businesses prefer not to acknowledge—especially publicly—their crime-related risks. Much crime or fraud is tolerated simply because it costs less than the efforts required to prevent it. The cost of crime may be accepted as an overhead expense which is part of the business calculation. Prevention unless embedded in an unobtrusive manner can literally get in the way of business. Over-policing can be counterproductive to the smooth flow of commercial relations, whilst visible symbols of prevention can suggest a threatening environment. Some businesses are wary of presenting an image of a place where preventive security is necessary, as it may indicate to customers that their business is an unsafe place (Crawford *et al.* 2005: 53). For retail outlets, there is a fine balance between making goods prominent, highly accessible, and alluring at the same time as minimizing the risks of loss through theft. There is an enduring ambiguity between the liberality of businesses' inclusive invitation to the public and their commercial desire to keep out 'risky or undesirable' people. The tension between crime prevention and business goals alerts us to the fact that ultimately crime prevention must be weighed against other social, cultural, or economic goals.

A further dynamic in the relationship between crime, security, and business is that crime, and fear of crime, 'sells'. Insurance companies and businesses have often exploited the market that insecurities about crime and disorder generate. It is not surprising that the rise in crime prevention has coincided with the commercialization of security. There is a booming private security industry manufacturing, promoting, and selling diverse kinds of preventive technologies and security hardware. The security industry in the UK had an estimated annual turnover of £5.15 billion in 2004, employing approximately 600,000 people.[12] In many instances, the private sector is at the vanguard of developments in preventive innovation and the spread of preventive thinking. The security industry has a vested interest in both promoting technological solutions and stimulating public anxieties.

BLIND SPOTS

The preceding discussions have largely focused upon the principal areas of governmental activity, namely the prevention of crimes and disorder which occur in public places rather than corporate or white-collar crime. This is not to suggest that crime prevention has little to say about such crime. It does, notably in the fields of fraud, money-laundering, and cybercrime (Levi, Chapter 23, this volume). Nevertheless, crime prevention in relation to corporate crime raises different questions about appropriate responsibility and competence. For example, the New Zealand government identified 'white-collar crime' as one of seven priorities in its crime prevention strategy published in 1994 (Crime Prevention Unit 1994). However, when the New Zealand government tasked its local partnerships, the Safer Community Councils, with the responsibility for implementing the strategy, it became apparent that most local practitioners found it very difficult to generate much interest or activity around 'white-collar crime'. This was less a lack of will and more a lack of competency on their part (Crawford 1997b). Some elements of crime prevention may be better served by specialist and centralized authorities than dispersed to local communities.

Likewise, the implications of gender for crime prevention remain largely under-developed (Walklate 2002). Much of the preventive focus has been restricted to the prevention of violence against women, notably in public spaces (Stanko 1990). Crime, responsibility, and avoidance all have different implications in private spaces where crime occurs within relations that are familiar or familial. The event-orientation of situational crime sits less well with relational crimes, notably those perpetrated against children. Shaw and Andrew conclude a recent international review of crime prevention

[12] www.bsia.co.uk/industry.html.

noting: 'Crime prevention in general continues to pay little attention to the significance of gender in the behaviours of potential or actual offenders or victims' (2005: 302). In part, this reflects the limitations of a rational choice model, when confronted with the significant differences in behaviour patterns of women and men.

DESIGNING THE FUTURE

A central implication of a preventive mentality is to 'design out crime', by introducing preventive thinking into the very earliest stages of product development. Pease notes, traditionally 'our world innovates first and thinks of crime consequences later' (1998b: 58). Crime prevention demands that we should anticipate crime consequences and seek to incorporate 'counter-moves' at the point of innovation. This insight has particular implications for private businesses as well as the public sector and prompts questions about how best to increase incentives for crime prevention, particularly for dealing with innovation.

The Department of Trade and Industry's Foresight Directorate in a document entitled *Just Around the Corner* highlighted two extreme scenarios for the year 2020 (DTI 2000). The pessimistic scenario is one in which people live in walled estates with screening and security patrols, and where people avoid public spaces and public transport because they are seen as potentially hostile. The optimistic scenario is one in which advances in crime-prevention technology outpace advances in crime-promotion technology. It depicts a world in which identity theft is kept in check by all-pervasive surveillance technology, DNA fingerprinting, odour detectors, and probabilistic profile-matching, and where much crime has been rendered impossible by technological advances. Whilst the pessimistic scenario has already found expression in the growth of gated communities and degraded public spaces, the optimistic scenario is one in which the very nature of social relations has become transformed by crime prevention. Ironically, there appears to be little concern for the social inconveniences, erosion of civil liberties, cultural decimation, and technological overload that all the preventive paraphernalia constitute. The optimistic scenario is evidently a society in which trust in people has been all but annihilated and replaced by trust in systems, and where interpersonal obligations have little, if any, meaning unless they can be interpreted as benefiting to the self. In both scenarios, the increased technological sophistication of prevention measures leaves people as the most vulnerable link in the chain of crime opportunities.

The observation that the DTI's scenarios should provoke is whether a society that places the prevention of crime first and foremost may be less appealing given the burdens, restrictions, and cultural values implicit. Ultimately, some things are more important than crime prevention. Assessing the relative benefit of preventive technologies against other public goods and social values means reconnecting crime prevention with its ethical and moral implications. This is not a plea to put the technological genie back in the bottle but rather to shape the direction it takes.

CONCLUSIONS

If the rise of a preventive mentality constitutes a 'paradigm shift', we need to be wary that paradigms, as well as bringing new things to light also shade from view those aspects of the world that do not fit neatly within their outlook (Kuhn 1967). Ways of seeing invariably imply ways of not seeing. Just as ideas about crime prevention and broader conceptions of policing slipped from view after the late eighteenth century, so too the new orthodoxy is in danger of shielding certain issues from sight. Crime prevention often implies certain assumptions about human motivations and associations, crime causation and appropriate responses to them, as well as values and ethics for the 'good society'.

There is a need to be careful not to over-exaggerate the influence of preventive ideas. Whilst, as we have seen, considerable government funding and effort has been invested in situational approaches, this pales in the shade of the vast amounts of money that are consumed by the traditional criminal justice estate. Despite the refocusing of the youth justice system towards preventing crime, only a small amount of its budget is dedicated to what might be categorized as primary or secondary prevention. Furthermore, research suggests that the new cadre of community safety workers remains largely wedded to ideas of social prevention in preference to situational approaches (Hughes 2006). Proponents of situational crime prevention, rather than celebrating its institutional successes, frequently bemoan the lack of influence of situational ideas and the indifference with which they have been received by many criminologists and politicians (Clarke 2000). Situational ideas have received a greater reception in the UK than in many other parts of the world. They have had comparatively less impact in the USA, notably since 'defensible space' and CPTED concepts fell out of favour in the late 1970s. Australia and New Zealand, by contrast, have seen considerable acceptance of situational ideas (O'Malley and Sutton 1997). However, when the New Zealand government sought to develop a crime-prevention strategy in the late 1980s it deliberately looked to the French model with its greater emphasis on social prevention than the English approach that was so closely associated with situational prevention (Bradley and Walters 2002).

Contemporary crime prevention, rather than conforming to a fundamental rupture or 'epistemological break' (Garland 2000) in the way we think about and practise crime control, might be better thought of in terms of the adage: 'something old, something new, something borrowed, something blue'. 'Something old' alludes to the classical liberal ideas that inform much pre-nineteenth-century preventive thinking. 'Something new' represents a predictive, future-oriented mentality concerned with loss reduction, new technologies of control, and the novel infrastructure of local partnerships. By contrast, 'something borrowed' refers to both the repackaging of needs-based approaches in the language of risk-based interventions and the significant influence of policy transfer between jurisdictions from 'zero-tolerance policing' through 'communities that care' to privatized criminal justice. Finally, 'something blue' denotes the enduring role of the police within much crime prevention theory, policy, and practice.

■ SELECTED FURTHER READING

The literature on crime prevention and community safety, like the topic itself, has expanded considerably. Good overviews are available in Crawford, *Crime Prevention and Community Safety* (Longman, 1998) and Hughes, *Understanding Crime Prevention* (Open University Press, 1998). These texts situate crime prevention within a broader political and theoretical backdrop. Recent policy developments are well covered in Hughes, *Crime and Community* (Palgrave, 2006). Tilley's edited *Handbook of Crime Prevention and Community Safety* (Willan, 2005) is a useful collection of essays covering a wide range of subjects and includes contributions from many key proponents in contemporary debates. Felson, *Crime and Everyday Life* (3rd edn, Sage, 2002) presents the arguments for situational prevention with everyday illustrations of practical ways to reduce crime opportunities. Clarke's edited collection, *Situational Crime Prevention: Successful Case Studies* (Criminal Justice Press, 1997) and the various volumes of *Crime Prevention Studies* provide further practical insights. The Home Office Crime Reduction website is a useful resource (www.crimereduction.gov.uk/), with links to Home Office funded evaluation findings and updates on policy initiatives.

The volume edited by von Hirsch and colleagues, *Ethical and Social Perspectives on Situational Crime Prevention* (Hart, 2000) presents a wide-ranging and excellent analysis of situational crime prevention, particularly with regard to its normative implications. The collection of essays in *Crime Prevention and Community Safety: New Directions* (Sage, 2002) edited by Hughes and colleagues offers a particularly valuable insight into comparative developments, as does Duprez and Hebberecht's edited volume *The Prevention and Security Policies in Europe* (Brussels University Press, 2002).

■ REFERENCES

ADAM, J. (2005), '7/7: What kills you matters—not numbers', *Times Higher Education Supplement*, 29 July, 18–19.

ARMITAGE, R. (2000), *An Evaluation of Secured by Design Housing in West Yorkshire*, Home Office Briefing Note 7/00.

ASSOCIATION OF CHIEF POLICE OFFICERS (1996), *Towards 2000: A Crime Prevention Strategy for the New Millennium*, Lancaster: ACPO.

ATKINSON, R., BLANDY, S., FLINT, J., and D. LISTER (2004), *Gated Communities in England*, London: ODPM.

AUDIT COMMISSION (2002), *Community Safety Partnerships*, London: Audit Commission.

BARR, R., and PEASE, K. (1990), 'Crime Placement, Displacement and Deflection', *Crime and Justice*, 12: 277–318.

BAUMGARTNER, M. (1988), *The Moral Order of the Suburbs*, Oxford: Oxford University Press.

BOTTOMS, A. E., and WILES, P. (1986), 'Housing Tenure and Residential Community Crime Careers in Britain', *Crime and Justice*, 8: 101–62.

BRADLEY, T., and WALTERS, R. (2002), 'The Managerialization of Crime Prevention and Community Safety: The New Zealand Experience', in G. Hughes, E. McLaughlin and J. Muncie (eds), *Crime Prevention and Community Safety: New Directions*, London: Sage, 240–59.

BRANTINGHAM, P. J., and FAUST, L. (1976), 'A Conceptual Model of Crime Prevention', *Crime and Delinquency*, 22: 284–96.

BRANTINGHAM, P. L., BRANTINGHAM, P. J., and TAYLOR, W. (2005), 'Situational Crime Prevention as a Key Component in Embedded Crime Prevention',

Canadian Journal of Criminology and Criminal Justice, 47(2): 271–92.

BRATTON, W. (1997), 'Crime is down in New York City: Blame the Police', in N. Dennis (ed.), *Zero Tolerance: Policing a Free Society*, 29–42, London: IEA.

CATALANO, R., and HAWKINS, J. D. (1996), 'The Social Development Model: a theory of antisocial behaviour', in J. D. Hawkins (ed.), *Delinquency and Crime*, 149–97, Cambridge: Cambridge University Press.

CLARKE, R. V. (1980), 'Situational Crime Prevention: Theory and Practice', *British Journal of Criminology*, 20(2): 136–45.

—— (1995), 'Situational Crime Prevention', *Crime and Justice*, 19: 91–150.

—— (2000), 'Situational Prevention, Criminology and Social Values', in A. Von Hirsch, D. Garland, and A. Wakefield (eds), *Ethical and Social Perspectives on Situational Crime Prevention*, 97–112, Oxford: Hart.

—— and CORNISH, D. B. (1985), 'Modelling Offenders' Decisions', *Crime and Justice*, 6: 147–85.

—— and MAYHEW, P. (1988), 'The British Gas Suicide Story and Its Criminological Implications', *Crime and Justice*, 10: 79–116.

—— and WEISBURD, D. (1994), 'Diffusion of Crime Control Benefits', *Crime Prevention Studies*, 2: 165–83.

COHEN, L., and FELSON, M. (1979), 'Social Change and Crime Rate Trends: A Routine Activity Approach', *American Sociological Review*, 44: 588–608.

COLEMAN, A. (1985), *Utopia on Trial*, London: Hilary Shipman.

—— (1989), 'Disposition and Situation: Two Sides of the Same Crime', in D. J. Evans and D. T. Herbert (eds), *The Geography of Crime*, 108–34, London: Routledge.

CORNISH D. B., and CLARKE R. V. (1987), 'Understanding Crime Displacement', *Criminology*, 25(4): 933–47.

—— and —— (2003), 'Opportunities, precipitators and criminal decision', *Crime Prevention Studies*, 16: 41–96.

CRAWFORD, A. (1997a), *The Local Governance of Crime*, Oxford: Clarendon Press.

—— (1997b), *A Report on the New Zealand Safer Community Councils*, Wellington: Ministry of Justice.

—— (1998), *Crime Prevention and Community Safety: Politics, Policies and Practices*, Harlow: Longman.

—— (2000), 'Situational Crime Prevention, Urban Governance and Trust Relations', in A. Von Hirsch, D. Garland, and A. Wakefield (eds), *Ethical and Social Perspectives on Situational Crime Prevention*, 193–213, Oxford: Hart.

—— (2001), 'Joined-Up but Fragmented', in R. Matthews and J. Pitts (eds), *Crime, Disorder and Community Safety: A New Agenda?*, 54–80, London: Routledge.

—— (2003), 'Contractual Governance of Deviant Behaviour', *Journal of Law and Society*, 30(4): 479–505.

—— LISTER, S., BLACKBURN, S., and BURNETT, J. (2005), *Plural Policing*, Bristol: Policy Press.

CRIME PREVENTION UNIT (1994), *The New Zealand Crime Prevention Strategy*, Wellington: CPU.

CURRIE, E. (1988), 'Two Visions of Community Crime Prevention', in T. Hope and M. Shaw (eds), *Communities and Crime Reduction*, 280–6, London: HMSO.

DEPARTMENT OF TRADE AND INDUSTRY (2000), *Just Around the Corner*, London: DTI.

ECK, J. E. (2005), 'Evaluation for Lesson Learning', in N. Tilley (ed.), *Handbook of Crime Prevention and Community Safety*, 699–733, Cullompton, Devon: Willan.

EKBLOM, P. (1995), 'Less Crime By Design', *The Annals*, 539: 114–29.

—— (2000), 'The Conjunction of Criminal Opportunity', in S. Ballintyne, K. Pease, and V. McLaren (eds), *Secure Foundations*, 30–66, London: IPPR.

—— (2005), 'Designing Products Against Crime', in N. Tilley (ed.), *Handbook of Crime Prevention and Community Safety*, 203–44, Cullompton, Devon: Willan.

ERICSON, R., DOYLE, A., and BARRY, D. (2003), *Insurance as Governance*, Toronto: University of Toronto Press.

ETZIONI, A. (1993), *The Spirit of Community*, New York: Simon & Schuster.

FARRELL, G. (1995), 'Preventing Repeat Victimization', Crime and Justice, 19: 469–534.

FARRINGTON, D. (2000), 'Explaining and Preventing Crime: The Globalization of Knowledge', *Criminology*, 38(1): 1–24.

FEELEY, M., and SIMON, J. (1994), 'Actuarial Justice', in D. Nelken (ed.), *The Futures of Criminology*, 173–201, London: Sage.

FELSON, M. (1998), *Crime and Everyday Life*, 2nd edn, London: Sage.

—— and CLARKE, R. V. (1998), *Opportunity Makes the Thief: Practical Theory for Crime Prevention*, London: Home Office.

FORRESTER, D., FRENZ, S., O'CONNELL, M., and PEASE, K. (1990), *The Kirkholt Burglary Project: Phase II*, London: Home Office.

GARLAND, D. (1996), 'The Limits of the Sovereign State', *British Journal of Criminology*, 36(4): 445–71.

—— (2000), 'Ideas, Institutions and Situational Crime Prevention', in A. von Hirsch, D. Garland, and A. Wakefield (eds), *Ethical and Social Perspectives on Situational Crime Prevention*, 1–16, Oxford: Hart.

—— (2001), *The Culture of Control*, Oxford: Oxford University Press.

GOLDBLATT P., and LEWIS C. (eds) (1998), *Reducing Offending*, London: Home Office.

HAKIM, S., and RENGERT, G. F. (1981), *Crime Spillover*, Beverly Hills, Cal.: Sage.

HANNAH-MOFFAT, K. (2005), 'Criminogenic needs and the transformative risk subject: Hybridizations of risk/need in penality', *Punishment and Society*, 7(1): 29–51.

HARCOURT, B. (2001), *Illusion of Order*, London: Harvard University Press.

HILLIER, B., and HANSON, J. (1984), *The Social Logic of Space*, Cambridge: Cambridge University Press.

—— and SHU, S. (2000), Crime and Urban Layout: the need for evidence', in S. Ballintyne, K. Pease, and V. McLaren (eds), *Secure Foundations*, 224–48, London: IPPR.

HIRSCHI, T. (1969), *Causes of Delinquency*, Berkeley, Cal.: University of California Press.

HOMEL, R. (2005), 'Developmental Crime Prevention', in N. Tilley (ed.), *Handbook of Crime Prevention and Community Safety*, 71–106, Cullompton, Devon: Willan.

HOME OFFICE (1977), *Review of Criminal Justice Policy 1976*, London: Home Office.

—— (1989), *Report of the Working Group on the Fear of Crime*, London: Home Office.

—— (1997), *Getting to Grips with Crime: A New Framework for Local Action*, London: Home Office.

—— (1998), *Guidance on Statutory Crime and Disorder Partnerships*, London: Home Office.

—— (2001), *Fighting Violent Crime Together: An Action Plan*, London: Home Office.

—— (2003), *Respect and Responsibility—Taking a Stand Against Anti-Social Behaviour*, London: Home Office.

—— (2004), *Building Communities, Beating Crime*, London: Home Office.

—— (2005), *National Community Safety Plan 2006–2009*, London: Home Office.

—— (2006a), *Respect Action Plan*, London: Home Office.

—— (2006b) *Review of Partnership Provisions of the Crime and Disorder Act 1998, Report of Findings*, London: Home Office.

HOPE, T. (1995), 'Community Crime Prevention', *Crime and Justice*, 19: 21–89.

—— (2000), 'Inequality and the Clubbing of Private Security', in T. Hope and R. Sparks (eds), *Crime, Risk and Insecurity*, 83–106, London: Routledge.

—— (2005), 'The New Local Governance of Community Safety in England and Wales', *Canadian Journal of Criminology and Criminal Justice*, 369–87.

—— and FOSTER, J. (1992), 'Conflicting Forces: Changing the dynamics of crime and community', *British Journal of Criminology*, 32: 488–504.

HOUGH, M. (2004), 'Modernization, Scientific Rationalism and the Crime Reduction Programme', *Criminal Justice*, 4(3): 239–53.

HOUGHTON, G. (1992), *Car Theft in England and Wales: The Home Office Car Theft Index*, London Home Office.

HUGHES, G. (2006), *Crime and Community*, London: Palgrave.

——, McLAUGHLIN, E., and MUNCIE J. (eds) (2002), *Crime Prevention and Community Safety: New Directions*, London: Sage.

HUSSAIN, S. (1988), *Neighbourhood Watch in England and Wales: A Locational Analysis*, London: Home Office.

JACOBS, J. (1961), *The Death and Life of Great American Cities*, New York: Random House.

JEFFERY, C. R. (1971), *Crime Prevention Through Environmental Design*, Beverly Hills, Cal.: Sage.

JOHNSTON, L., and SHEARING, C. (2003), *Governing Security*, London, Routledge.

KELLING, G., and BRATTON, W. (1998), 'Declining Crime Rates: Insiders, views of the New York Crime Story', *Journal of Criminal Law and Criminology*, 88(4): 1217–31.

—— and COLES, C. M. (1996), *Fixing Broken Windows*, New York: Touchstone.

KOCH, B. (1998), *The Politics of Crime Prevention*, Aldershot: Ashgate.

KUHN, T. (1967), *The Structure of Scientific Revolutions*, Chicago: University of Chicago Press.

LAYCOCK, G. (2003), 'Launching Crime Science'. Available at: www.jdi.ucl.ac.uk/publications/crime_science_series/launching.php.

LITTON, R. A. (1982), 'Crime Prevention and Insurance', *Howard Journal*, 21: 6–22.

LOADER, I. (1997), 'Private Security and the Demand for Protection in Contemporary Britain', *Policing and Society*, 7(3): 143–62.

MAGUIRE, M. (2004), 'The Crime Reduction Programme in England and Wales', *Criminal Justice*, 4(3): 213–37.

MARTINSON, R. (1974), 'What Works?—Questions and Answers about Prison Reform', *The Public Interest*, 35(1): 22–54.

MATTHEWS, R. (1992), 'Developing More Effective Strategies for Curbing Prostitution', in R. V. Clarke (ed.), *Situational Crime Prevention: Successful Case Studies*, 89–98, Albany, N.Y.: Harrow and Heston.

MAYHEW, P., CLARKE, R. V., STURMAN, A., and HOUGH, M. (1976), *Crime as Opportunity*, London: HMSO.

MORAN, M. (2003), *The British Regulatory State*, Oxford: Oxford University Press.

MORGAN, J. (1991), *Safer Communities: The Local Delivery of Crime Prevention Through the Partnership Approach*, London: Home Office.

MOSS, K. (2006), 'Crime Prevention as Law', in K. Moss and M. Stephens (eds), *Crime Reduction and the Law*, 1–13, London: Routledge.

—— and PEASE, K. (1999), 'Crime and Disorder Act 1998: Section 17 a Wolf in Sheep's Clothing?', *Crime Prevention and Community Safety*, 1(4): 15–19.

NATIONAL AUDIT OFFICE (2004), *Reducing Crime: the Home Office working with Crime and Disorder Reduction Partnerships*, London: Stationery Office.

NEWMAN, O. (1972), *Defensible Space: People and Design in the Violent City*, London: Architectural Press.

NICHOLAS, S., POVEY, D., WALKER A., and KERSHAW, C. (2005), *Crime in England and Wales 2004/2005*, London: Home Office.

NORRIS, C., and MCCAHILL, M. (2006), 'CCTV: Beyond Penal Modernism', *British Journal of Criminology*, 46(1): 97–118.

O'MALLEY, P. (1992), 'Risk, Power and Crime Prevention', *Economy and Society*, 21(3): 252–75.

—— (1999), 'Volatile and Contradictory Punishment', *Theoretical Criminology*, 3(2): 175–96.

—— (2001), 'Risk Crime and Prudentialism Revisited', in K. Stenson and R. Sullivan (eds), *Crime, Risk and Justice: The politics of crime control in liberal democracies*, 89–103, Cullompton, Devon: Willan.

—— and SUTTON, A. (eds), (1997) *Crime Prevention in Australia: Issues in Policy and Research*, Sydney: Federation Press.

PAWSON, R., and TILLEY, N. (1997), *Realistic Evaluation*, London: Sage.

PEASE, K. (1998a), *Repeat Victimization: Taking Stock*, London: Home Office.

—— (1998b), 'Crime, Labour and the Wisdom of Solomon', *Policy Studies*, 19(3/4): 255–65.

—— (2002), 'Crime Reduction', in M. Maguire, R. Morgan, and R. Reiner (eds), *The Oxford Handbook of Criminology*, 3rd edn, 949–79, Oxford: Oxford University Press.

PHILLIPS, C. (2002), 'From Voluntary to Statutory Status', in G. Hughes, E. McLaughlin, and J. Muncie (eds), *Crime Prevention and Community Safety: New Directions*, 163–81, London: Sage.

POYNER, B. (1992), 'Situational Crime Prevention in Two Parking Facilities', in R. V. Clarke (ed.), *Situational Crime Prevention: Successful Case Studies* 174–84, Albany, N.Y.: Harrow and Heston.

PUTNAM, R. (2000), *Bowling Alone: The Collapse and Revival of American Community*, New York: Simon & Schuster.

ROSENBAUM, D. P. (1988), 'Community Crime Prevention: A Review and Synthesis of the Literature', *Justice Quarterly*, 5(3): 323–93.

SAMPSON, R., and RAUDENBUSH, S. (1999), 'Systematic Social Observations of Public Spaces: A New Look at Disorder in Urban Neighborhoods', *American Journal of Sociology*, 105(3): 603–51.

——, MORENOFF, J., and EARLS, F. (1999), 'Beyond Social Capital', *American Sociological Review*, 64(5): 633–60.

SCHWEINHART, L. J., BARNES, H. V., and WEIKART, D. P. (1993), *Significant Benefits: the High/Scope Perry Preschool Study Through Age 27*, Ypsilanti, Mich: High/Scope.

SHAPLAND, J. (2000), 'Situational Prevention: Social Values and Social Viewpoints', in A. von Hirsch, D. Garland, and A. Wakefield (eds), *Ethical and Social Perspectives on Situational Crime Prevention*, 113–23, Oxford: Hart.

SHAW, M., and ANDREWS, C. (2005), 'Engendering Crime Prevention', *Canadian Journal of Criminology and Criminal Justice*, 47(2): 293–316.

SHERMAN, L., GOTTFREDSON, D., MACKENZIE, D., ECK, J., REUTER, P., and BUSHWAY, S. (1997), *Preventing Crime: What Works, What Doesn't, What's Promising*, Washington DC: NIJ.

SHERMAN, L. W., GARTIN, P. R., and BUERGER, M. E. (1989), 'Hot Spots of Predatory Crime', *Criminology*, 27(1): 27–55.

SKINNS, L. (2005), 'Cops, Councils and Crime and Disorder: A critical review of three community safety partnerships', Unpublished PhD thesis, Cambridge University.

SKOGAN, W. (1990), *Disorder and Decline*, New York: Free Press.

STANKO, E. (1990), 'When Precaution is Normal: A Feminist Critique of Crime Prevention', in L. Gelsthorpe and A. Morris (eds), *Feminist Perspectives in Criminology*, 173–83, Milton Keynes: Open University Press.

TAYLOR, R. B. (2001), *Breaking Away from Broken Windows*, Boulder, Col.: Westview Press.

TUCK, M. (1988), 'Crime Prevention: A Shift in Concept', *Home Office Research and Planning Unit Research Bulletin, No. 24*, London: Home Office.

VAN DIJK, J. (1990), 'Crime Prevention Policy: Current State and Prospects', in G. Kaiser and H. -J. Albrecht (eds), *Crime and Criminal Policy in Europe*, 205–20, Frieburg: Max Planck Institute.

VAN HIRSCH, A., and SHEARING, C. (2000), 'Exclusion from Public Space', in A. von Hirsch, D. Garland, and A. Wakefield (eds), *Ethical and Social Perspectives on Situational Crime Prevention*, 77–96, Oxford: Hart.

WALKLATE, S. (2002), 'Gendering Crime Prevention', in G. Hughes, E. McLaughlin, and J. Muncie (eds), *Crime Prevention and Community Safety: New Directions*, 58–76., London: Sage

WEATHERITT, M. (1986), *Innovations in Policing*, London: Croom Helm.

WEBSTER, C. (2001), 'Gated Cities of Tomorrow', *Town Planning Review*, 72(2): 149–69.

WILSON, J. Q. (1975), *Thinking About Crime*, New York: Vintage.

—— and KELLING, G. (1982), 'Broken Windows', *The Atlantic Monthly*, March: 29–37.

WOOLCOCK, M. (2001), 'The Place of Social Capital in Understanding Social and Economic Outcomes', *Isuma: Canadian Journal of Policy Research*, 2(1): 11–17.

ZEDNER, L. (2003), 'Too Much Security?', *International Journal of the Sociology of Law*, 31: 155–84.

27

POLICING AND THE POLICE

Tim Newburn and Robert Reiner

INTRODUCTION: CRIMINOLOGY AND POLICING

In popular culture cops and robbers are a conceptual couple, but for most of its history criminology has focused only on the latter. It was tacitly assumed that the police were a straightforward, mechanistic response to crime.

In the eighteenth and early nineteenth centuries there had flourished a branch of political economy known as the 'science of police' (see Chapter 12 on political economy, in this volume). The term 'police' was used then in a much broader way to connote the whole craft of governing a social order (Neocleous 2000; Dubber 2005; Zedner 2006). The police in our contemporary sense were seen as merely a small part of this.

The positivist 'science of criminology' in the late nineteenth century excluded the functioning of policing and criminal justice from its intellectual province. During the early 1960s, however, the epistemological break in the criminological enterprise designated as 'labelling theory' paved the way for new critical criminologies (Taylor, *et al.* 1973: chs 5–9; Rock, Chapter 1, and Loader and Sparks, Chapter 3, in this volume), that saw the structure and functioning of criminal justice agencies as problematic (Becker 1964, 1967). This intellectual conjuncture, together with changes in the politics of law and order, brought the police on to the research agendas of criminologists (Reiner and Newburn 2006; McLaughlin 2006).

This chapter will review the development and findings of police research. The next section will explore the growth of research on the police over the last half-century. The third section of the chapter will address the fundamental conceptual questions: What is policing and who are the police? The fourth section will analyse police discretion, how the 'law in the books' gets translated into the 'law in action' of policing practice. Three dimensions of discretion will be examined: (1) The patterns of police discretion; (2) The sources of these patterns; (3) The governance of police discretion. The fifth section will look at the emergence in the last twenty years of new, innovative policing tactics, seeking to overcome the limitations of traditional approaches. The sixth section examines the pluralization of policing, the proliferation of forms of policing beyond the police. The next section charts the growing internationalization of policing in an era of globalization. The concluding section of the chapter considers possible future trends in policing.

THE DEVELOPMENT OF POLICE RESEARCH

Systematic research on the police developed at roughly the same time, the early 1960s, on both sides of the Atlantic.[1] In the USA the key motor driving early police research was concern with civil rights. It was recognized that police practice often departed from legal standards, and the Supreme Court sought to close the gap by tighter specification of due process legality (Sklansky 2005: 1728–56). Socio-legal researchers began to analyse how the police role, organization, and culture structured deviation from due process values.

In 1968 'law and order' displaced 'civil rights' as the key domestic political issue in the USA (Beckett 1997). Concern moved away from police malpractice to their effectiveness in controlling crime and disorder. The civil libertarian impulses that had given birth to police research were largely eclipsed by policy-oriented, managerial work.

In the 1980s the increasing influence of 'community policing' concepts resulted in a synthesis of these approaches. Instead of police efficiency and democratic accountability being seen as contradictory concerns, police leaders, policy-makers, and researchers argued that they were inextricably interdependent (Skolnick and Bayley 1986, 1988; Skogan 2006; Sklansky 2005: 1810–4). During the 1990s, however, there was a resurgence of interest in tougher policing styles, notably so-called 'zero tolerance', tighter managerial accountability and performance measurement, encapsulated in the iconic legend of the New York City crime drop (Karmen 2000; Dixon and Maher 2005).

The sources of British police research were also a combination of changes in the politics of law and order and theoretical developments in criminology (Reiner 2000; Reiner and Newburn 2006). The 1950s were the heyday of cross-party consensus on law and order (Downes and Morgan, Chapter 9, this volume). The pedestal on which the police then stood was illustrated by the popularity of the TV series *Dixon of Dock Green*, encapsulating the cosy stereotype of the British bobby (Sydney-Smith 2002; Leishman and Mason 2003; Reiner 2003; McLaughlin 2006: ch. 1). In 1959, following a series of scandals, a Royal Commission was established to look at the role, organization, and accountability of the police (Royal Commission 1962).

Research on the police in Britain developed in this context. Banton's pioneering empirical study (Banton 1964) found the police role was primarily 'peace-keeping', not law enforcement. This has been echoed in subsequent work around the world (Bayley 1994). Banton's key analytic theme, the dependence of formal on informal social

---

[1] There had been one influential sociological study of the police conducted earlier, by William Westley for his PhD in the late 1940s. This was only published as a book in 1970 (Westley 1970).

control, has often been re-discovered, as in much current discussion about partnership, the wider policing family, and the 'respect' agenda. Despite eschewing any concerns with scandal, Banton was acutely aware that there were severe threats to the benign and consensual mode of policing he described. He anticipated that the British police might lose their sacred aura, and needed to reconstruct their authority.[2]

These themes were developed by a number of young British researchers in the early 1970s (Holdaway 1979). Their observations found that the backstage life of the police—apparently the acme of a bureaucratic, rule-bound organization, disciplined to discipline others—was in fact a fluid world, seething with tensions, spontaneity, and deviance.

In the later 1970s 'law and order' became a central political issue, and was crucial to the 1979 Conservative General Election victory. The police themselves were becoming an overt pressure group on the political stage (Reiner 1978). This politicization of policing was reflected in the emergence of two new strands of research. In the academic and political worlds overtly critical or Marxist work on the police proliferated (e.g. Hall *et al.* 1978; Hain 1979, 1980; Brogden 1982; Scraton 1985; Grimshaw and Jefferson 1987). The other new strand of police research in the late 1970s was policy-oriented research commissioned by government bodies. Official policy-oriented research is not necessarily uncritical, but the fastest growth since the mid-1980s is in managerialist studies of immediate practical relevance, often conducted by the police themselves (Brown 1996; Reiner and Newburn 2006).

'POLICE' AND 'POLICING'

Until recently, most research rested on a taken-for-granted notion of the police (Cain 1979). The police were assumed to be a state agency with a broad mandate of crime control, order maintenance, and service work.

Understanding the nature of *policing* requires conceptual deconstruction of this assumed idea of *the police*. Modern societies are characterized by what can be termed 'police fetishism': the ideological assumption that the police are a functional prerequisite of social order, the thin blue line defending against chaos. In fact many societies have existed without a formal police force of any kind. The limitations of thinking in terms of *the* police are increasingly apparent, as contemporary societies are experiencing a pluralization of policing (cf. the section on pluralization below, and Jones, Chapter 25, this volume).

The idea of policing is an aspect of the more general concept of social control, itself a complex notion (Innes 2003). In some sociological theories social control is seen as

---

[2] In the optimistic scientistic mood of the mid-1960s Banton sees more sociology in police training as a possible tool for this. If only PC Dixon had read some Durkheim he might never have turned into Dirty Harry!

everything that contributes to the reproduction of social order, including the formation of culture and socialization into it. Cohen acerbically dismissed this all-embracing, amorphous usage as 'a Mickey Mouse concept'. He restricted the concept to 'the organised ways in which society responds to behaviour and people it regards as deviant, problematic, worrying, threatening, troublesome or undesirable' (Cohen 1985: 1–2).

Social control may be regarded positively or negatively by different social philosophies. In conservative functionalist sociology, it was seen as the necessary bulwark of the consensus underpinning social order. Adequate control mechanisms against deviance were a functional prerequisite of any viable society. The development of critical criminologies changed the evaluation of social control institutions. Social control came to be regarded as *producing* deviance through the effects of labelling. It was condemned as oppressive, preserving unjust power and privilege.

The concept of policing is closely related to that of social control. Policing is a set of activities *directed* at preserving the security of a particular social order; but it does not encompass all activities intended to produce order. It excludes post hoc punishment, as well as processes creating the conditions of social order (for example socialization, family, religion, or other internalized ethical controls).

The specificity of policing as a subset of control processes is the creation of systems of surveillance coupled with the threat of sanctions. Policing refers to 'organised forms of order-maintenance, peace-keeping, rule or law enforcement, crime investigation and prevention and other forms of investigation and information-brokering' (Jones and Newburn 1998: 18). Diverse policing strategies are proliferating today (see the section on pluralization below), even though it is only the state agency with the omnibus mandate that is popularly understood by the label *the* police.

Until modern times policing functions were primarily carried out as a by-product of other social relationships. Anthropological studies show that many pre-literate societies have existed without any formalized system of policing. A well-known study of 51 pre-industrial societies found police in the sense of a 'specialised armed force used partially or wholly for norm enforcement' in only 20 of these (Schwartz and Miller 1964: 161). Police appeared 'only in association with a substantial degree of division of labour' (ibid.:166), and were preceded by other elements of a specialized legal and governmental system like money, mediation, and damages.

Policing may originate in collective and communal processes of social control, but specialized police forces develop hand in hand with the emergence of social inequality, hierarchy, and more centralized, dominant state systems (Spitzer 1975). Anthropological studies show that the emergence of specialized police 'is linked to economic specialisation and differential access to resources that occur in the transition from a kinship-to a class-dominated society' (Robinson and Scaglion 1987: 109). During this transition communal policing forms are converted in incremental stages to state-dominated ones, which begin to function as agents of class control in addition to more general social control. The complex and contradictory function of contemporary police, as simultaneously embodying the quest for general and stratified order—'parking tickets' as well as 'class repression' (Marenin 1983)—is thus inscribed in their origins.

British police ideology postulates a fundamental distinction between British community-based policing and an alien, 'Continental', state-controlled system (Mawby 1991, 2003). Conventional histories of the British police attempt to trace a direct lineage between ancient tribal forms of collective self-policing and the contemporary Bobby (Reith 1956). Such claims have been characterized aptly as 'ideology as history' (Robinson 1979). It is true that many European systems of police did develop overtly as instruments of state control. Revisionist histories, however, have emphasized that modern police development in Britain and the USA is also shaped by class and state structures and strategies (Silver 1967; Storch 1975; Miller 1977; Emsley 1996; Reiner 2000: chs 1 and 2). The supposedly benign 'British' model was in any case for home consumption only. A more militaristic and coercive model was exported to colonial situations (Brogden 1987; Palmer 1988).

Although contemporary patterns of police vary in detail, they have converged increasingly around fundamentally similar organizational and cultural lines, without the qualitative distinctions of kind implied in traditional British police ideology (Bayley 1985; Brodeur 1995). This is facilitated by the emergence of a new international cadre of experts who facilitate the diffusion of fashions in police thinking around the globe (Newburn and Sparks 2004).

The police are called upon routinely to perform a bewildering miscellany of tasks, from traffic control to terrorism. The uniting feature of police work is not a particular social function, whether it be crime control, social service, order maintenance, or political repression. Rather, it is that all demands on the police involve 'something that ought not to be happening and about which someone had better do something **now**!' (Bittner 1974: 30, emphasis in original). In other words, policing tasks arise in emergency situations, usually with an element of social conflict.

The police normally resort to a variety of ways and means to keep the peace without initiating legal proceedings (Kemp, Norris, and Fielding 1992). Underlying all their tactics is the bottom-line power to wield legal sanctions, ultimately the use of legitimate force (Bittner 1970, 1974: 35). 'A benign bobby . . . still brings to the situation a uniform, a truncheon, and a battery of resource charges . . . which can be employed when appeasement fails and fists start flying' (Punch 1979: 116). Indeed, over the past thirty years or so public order and anti-terrorist policing have been characterized by a gradual process of militarization (Waddington 2003). Nonetheless, successful policing has usually been seen as the craft of handling trouble without resort to coercion, usually by skilful verbal tactics (Muir 1977; Bayley and Bittner 1984).

To sum up, 'policing' is an aspect of social control processes involving surveillance and sanctions intended to ensure the security of the social order. The order in question may be based on consensus, conflict, or an ambiguous amalgam of the two—as is usually the case in modern societies. The 'police' as a specialized, state-organized body with the primary responsibility for deploying legitimate force to safeguard security exist only in relatively complex societies. The police developed as 'domestic missionaries' in the endeavours of modern states to propagate and protect a dominant conception of peace and propriety (Storch 1976; Zedner 2006). They have not been mere tools of the state, however, performing tasks determined from above: a considerable element of police discretion is inevitable.

POLICE DISCRETION: ITS NATURE, OPERATION, AND CONTROL

Many jurisdictions have denied the legitimacy of police discretion, requiring the police to initiate criminal proceedings whenever there is evidence of an offence. However discretion is both routine and inevitable. Breaches of the law outstrip police capacity to process them, so choices about priorities are inescapable. Discretion is also logically necessary as legal rules require interpretation in unpredictable fact situations. Discretion could also be desirable to avoid oppressiveness, as British law recognized (Reiner and Leigh 1992).

The recognition that the police do not adhere mechanistically to the rule of law raised the prospect of discrimination and malpractice. Police discretion was hard to regulate, however, because the dispersed character of routine police work gave it 'low visibility' (Goldstein 1960). Thus 'the police department has the special property . . . that within it discretion increases as one moves down the hierarchy' (Wilson 1968: 7). There was a gulf between 'street' and 'management' cops, and it was the culture of the former that shaped practice (Ianni and Ianni 1983).

In the late 1970s a structuralist critique argued that such rule scepticism made the street cops 'the "fall-guys" of the legal system' (McBarnet 1978, 1979). Although a degree of discretion was inevitable, British law took an unnecessarily permissive stance to police powers by formulating elastic and vague rules. This paved the way for more detailed studies of the interaction between legal rules and police practice (Dixon 1997; Reiner 2000: ch. 6; Sanders and Young 2003).

THE OPERATION OF POLICE DISCRETION

The Scarman Report on the 1981 Brixton disorders (Scarman 1981) influentially argued that public tranquillity should have priority over law enforcement. Discretion was the better part of police valour. But police discretion is not an equal opportunity phenomenon. It disguises the disproportionate use of police powers against unpopular and powerless minorities, 'police property' (Lee 1981: 53–4). The police also tend to neglect the victimization of the powerless: they are over-policed *and* under-protected. Unsurprisingly, such groups have the most negative views of the police (Smith *et al.* 1983; Fitzgerald *et al.* 2002: chs 4–7).

The characteristic deployment of the police underpins this practical concentration on policing the underclass. Most police resources are devoted to uniformed patrol of public space, but privacy has a class dimension (Stinchcombe 1963). The lower the social class of a person, the more their social lives take place in public space, and the more 'available' they are to come to police attention (Fitzgerald 1999; Quinton *et al.* 2000; Waddington *et al.* 2004). Adversarial policing falls disproportionately on young men in the lowest socio-economic groups.

Racial discrimination

Numerous studies have shown that the police disproportionately exercise their powers against black people (Bowling and Phillips 2002, 2003, and Phillips and Bowling, Chapter 14, this volume; Shiner and Delsol 2006). A complex interaction between police discrimination, and social pressures which generate disproportionate offending by young black men, is the most plausible explanation (Reiner 1993; Bowling and Phillips 2002, 2003).

It is also widely documented that ethnic minorities are disproportionately victimized by crime of all kinds, and that they often perceive the police response as inadequate (Bowling 1999; Foster *et al.* 2005). These problems are related to the issue of racial discrimination within the police force in the treatment of ethnic minority officers (Holdaway 1996).

Gender and policing

A difference between debates about race and sex discrimination in policing is that whereas black people are disproportionately at the receiving end of police powers, the opposite is true of women. The very small proportion of female suspects at every stage of the process is probably the most consistent pattern in criminal justice. Feminist criminologists have rightly underlined the maleness of the overwhelming majority of processed offenders as perhaps the most important though usually overlooked feature of crime (see Heidensohn and Gelsthorpe, Chapter 13, this volume).

It does not follow, however, that the police do not deal with women suspects or potential suspects in discriminatory ways. Police officers have tended to regard women with a conventional imagery bifurcating them into either 'whores' or 'wives' (Heidensohn 1985: 58). The low rate of formal processing of women as suspects masks a complex web of discrimination. Some women escape suspicion because 'chivalry' places them outside the frame of likely offenders in the stereotypes of investigating officers. Yet others, such as teenage girls behaving in sexually precocious or deviant ways, or prostitutes, may be dealt with by the police at a lower threshold of entry into the system because they violate the officers' codes of acceptable behaviour, or may be seen paternalistically as in need of 'protection' from themselves.

There is much clearer evidence of discrimination against women in their treatment by the police as victims (Gregory and Lees 1999; Heidensohn 2003). Calls to domestic disturbances have always been a significant part of the police workload, but tended to be treated by officers without recourse to criminal proceedings even where evidence of assault is present. 'Domestics' are seen as messy, unproductive, and not 'real' police work in traditional cop culture. This issue has become highly charged in the last three decades around the world, and police forces have attempted to improve their response to domestic assaults, with debatable results (Sherman 1992; Hoyle 1998). There has also been much concern about insensitive or even hostile treatment of rape victims, an issue dramatically highlighted 25 years ago by Roger Graef's TV documentary on the Thames Valley Police which filmed the interrogation of a rape victim (BBC 1, 18 January 1982). Despite considerable improvements since then (Blair 1985), the treatment of rape victims by police remains problematic (Temkin 2002).

Women are also discriminated against as police officers. Until thirty years ago discrimination within police forces was institutionalized: separate women's divisions carried out radically different functions. The Sex Discrimination Act 1975 formally integrated women into the same units as male officers, but discrimination survived in a variety of ways (Jones 1987). Although the recruitment of women officers has increased over time, as has their presence in senior ranks (several women chief constables have been appointed in the last ten years), the continuation of discrimination has been documented by numerous studies (Heidensohn 1992, 2003; Brown and Heidensohn 2000).

Police discretion and the rule of law

In a liberal democracy the police are subject to a tension between the values of crime control and due process (Packer 1968; Sklansky 2005; Sanders and Young, Chapter 28, this volume). When subject to pressure to produce results in terms of effective law enforcement the police will frequently cut corners (Skolnick 1966).

THE EXPLANATION OF POLICE DISCRETION

Three broad approaches to explaining how police discretion operates can be distinguished: individualistic, cultural, and structural.

Individualistic explanations

It has frequently been alleged that police work attracts people with distinctive personalities, in particular authoritarianism. Most research does not support the view that police recruits are more authoritarian than comparable civilian samples (Waddington 1999a). Studies of the socialization of recruits suggest that training has a temporary liberalizing effect (Brown and Willis 1985; Fielding 1988), but exposure to practical policing results in a more authoritarian perspective. This is better understood as a cultural adaptation to the exigencies of police work than the unfolding of a set of basic personality traits, and anyway is not directly translated into policing practice (Waddington 1999b).

Cultural explanations

The impact of the informal culture of the rank and file is the most common explanation of police working practices found in the research literature. Tensions associated with the police task in liberal democracies are said to generate a distinctive subculture to handle them. In Skolnick's classic formulation, police in a liberal democracy are faced with a basic dilemma: they are under pressure to achieve results in the form of law enforcement, but the rule of law restricts the methods they can use (Skolnick 1966: ch. 3). They are also visible embodiments of social authority, exposing them to danger from deviants, and creating tensions in all their social relationships. These pressures of the police condition are coped with by the development of a set of informal rules, rites, and recipes. This subculture is transmitted by storytelling, a toolkit of examples for dealing with police work (Shearing and Ericson 1991).

Skolnick identified three main aspects of cop culture: suspiciousness, internal solidarity coupled with social isolation, and conservatism. Suspiciousness arises from the pressure to achieve results by catching offenders, and the concern with danger: people and places are constantly scrutinized for signs of crime or risk. Suspiciousness makes the police prone to operate with prejudiced stereotypes of potential 'villains' and 'troublemakers'. Internal solidarity and social isolation are mutually reinforcing. Solidarity is knitted from the intense experience of confronting shared dangers, and the need to be able to rely on colleagues in tight spots. Isolation is the product of organizational aspects of the work such as the shift system, and people's wariness in interacting with authority figures. Solidarity can become a device for shielding wrongdoing, whilst isolation may exacerbate prejudiced stereotypes. Moral and social conservatism is inherently related to the core police function of symbolizing and safeguarding authority. Charged with upholding law and maintaining order, police are likely to have an elective affinity with the values underpinning them. Sympathizing with deviants or dissidents is likely to generate cognitive dissonance in police officers. This is not to say that police officers cannot be liberal but it is unlikely to be the norm.

Political conservatism is less universal a feature of police culture, although it is certainly much more common than radicalism. Police officers have generally inclined to the political Right, despite having working-class origins (Reiner 2000: 191–4). The formation of modern police organizations involved a complex process of *de-radicalization*, culturally distancing officers from their labour roots (Robinson 1978).

Many studies have observed racism and machismo in police culture (Holdaway 1983; Graef 1989; Young 1991; Brown and Heidensohn 2000). Others have emphasized officers' strong commitment to what they see as 'real' policing—fighting crime and catching criminals. Police often have a sense of mission concerning their work, masked by a veneer of cynicism (Reiner 2000: 111–14).

The classic studies of police culture have been attacked for presenting a monolithic picture, overlooking differences between and within forces (Chan 1997; Foster 2003). However, many researchers since Skolnick have analysed such variations (Reiner 2000: ch. 3).

Cultural variations within forces

The rank hierarchy and division of labour within police organizations structure different subcultures. There are also variations due to age, gender, ethnic group, educational and social background, as well as individual personality.

The most obvious cultural gulf is between the street level and the management ranks, with conflicting interests and perspectives[3] (Punch 1983). Senior ranks are mainly concerned with administration, and with presenting a public face of acceptable conduct to external audiences. Senior officers will often be in an adversarial role vis-à-vis the rank and file, who tend to hold derogatory images of the managerial levels as parasitic pen-pushers rather than 'real' police.

Nonetheless it is important not to lose sight of the common interests uniting all ranks. They share a stake in the status, reputation, and resources of the organization. The cultural gulf between street and management cops may be analysed as something of a cynical, Faustian bargain. It allows management cops to present acceptable glosses of police practice to influential public audiences whilst being shielded from the more sordid aspects of street policing.

The organizational division of labour also produces systematic differences in the subcultures associated with specialisms. The most hallowed is the perennial rivalry between uniform and detective branches. Each has a characteristic ideology emphasizing the greater importance of its own role and an associated negative image of the other. Uniform branches will often see themselves as the bedrock of the organization, and argue that contrary to public impressions they apprehend the majority of offenders. The CID will be resented for taking over cases for court processing after the hard work of capture has already been accomplished, grabbing the glamour and the glory. For their part detectives pride themselves on being dedicated to 'real' policing, dealing with crime and criminals, in particular the more serious cases (Hobbs 1988: chs 4, 8; Maguire and Norris 1992). They will look down on the humdrum peace-keeping and service work of the patrol branches, and castigate those stuck there as plodding 'woodentops'. In turn, both operational patrol and CID officers will have negative images of administrative personnel or branches like training or community relations, who are perceived as removed altogether from 'real' police work. There are also differences in outlook and style amongst patrol officers, reflecting different career aspirations and trajectories, variations in educational and social background, as well as individual personality and choice[4] (Reiner 2000: 101–3).

Cultural variations between forces

The cultures of different forces vary over time and between places. They are shaped by law, external social contexts, management strategies, and government policy.

James Q. Wilson's comparative research on eight US forces (Wilson 1968) distinguished three departmental cultures, related to departmental policy choices, and varying social and political contexts. The watchman style emphasized order maintenance rather than law enforcement. Patrol officers had wide discretion in how they handled their beats, with little bureaucratization. The legalistic style enjoined

---

[3] This is accentuated when (as was the case in British county forces until the Second World War) there is lateral entry of senior ranks and they come from more privileged social and educational backgrounds (Reiner 1991: ch. 2; Wall 1998).

[4] Senior officers are not a monolithic group either (Reiner 1991: ch. 12).

universalistic law enforcement, minimizing officers' discretion. The service style encouraged the provision of helpful services to citizens. The favoured reaction to deviance was the formal caution, rather than the (often benign) neglect of the watchman approach, or the automatic prosecution of legalism. Each style was rooted in particular social and political preconditions. Cultural variations between forces have been demonstrated by several subsequent US studies, related to social context and political choices (e.g. Rossi *et al.* 1974).

British research has also identified cultural variations between forces. Cain demonstrated significant differences in the cultures of a rural and a city force (Cain 1973). Rural police were strongly integrated into their communities, city officers more alienated (Jones and Levi 1983; Shapland and Vagg 1988; Shapland and Hobbs 1989; Young 1993 found similar rural/urban variations). An ethnographic study comparing two inner-city London police stations showed that management strategy could achieve discernible cultural change even in unpropitious circumstances (Foster 1989).

It seems that although there are common tendencies generated by the basic features of police work in any contemporary industrial society, their cultural expression can differ. This is partly because of varying social and political contexts, partly because of management philosophies. Police culture is neither monolithic nor invariant, but responsive to social structure and official policy (Foster 2003).

Structural explanations

Structural explanations of policing supplement rather than supplant cultural accounts. The major analyses of police culture do not represent it as a freestanding phenomenon into which successive generations of police are socialized as passive cultural dopes. The culture is generated and sustained by the problems and tensions of the police role, structured by legal and social pressures.

The culturally supported values and beliefs of police officers are an important element in explaining their practices, but not the whole story. These values and beliefs are translated into action in concrete situations where other pressures have to be taken account of. For example, officers who are racially prejudiced may nonetheless be restrained from acting in overtly discriminatory ways by clear and effectively sanctioned rules barring this (Waddington 1999b).

Police work is shaped by the core mandate and organization of the police. The modern police are primarily organized for the regular uniform patrol of public space, coupled with post hoc investigation of reported or discovered crime or disorder. Police practice is structured by the legal and social institution of privacy, patterned by class, race, and gender. There is an isomorphism between the structure of social power and the mapping of the population as potential trouble and hence suspicious in police culture (Reiner 2000: 92–5). The racism, sexism, impatience with legal formality, and other characteristics of police culture that have alarmed liberal critics are not simply manifestations of pathological authoritarian personalities, excessive exposure to *The Sun*, or a self-sustaining canteen cowboy ethos. The basic determinant is the role the police are assigned in the social order: moral street-sweeping. Their control powers are primarily directed against the young, male, disproportionately black, economically marginal, street population who threaten the tranquillity of public space as defined by dominant groups. Police prejudices are more a product than a cause of the differential use of police powers, which embodies the socially structured nature of the police mandate.

THE CONTROL OF POLICE DISCRETION

The formal control of police discretion in Britain is limited by the common law doctrine of constabulary independence. As stated by Lord Denning, this holds that a 'constable . . . is not the servant of anyone, save of the law itself. No Minister of the Crown can tell him that he must, or must not, keep observation on this place or that; or that he must, or must not, prosecute this man or that one. Nor can any police authority tell him so. The responsibility for law enforcement lies on him.' (*R v. Metropolitan Police Commissioner, ex p. Blackburn* [1968] 2 Q.B. 136)[5] The doctrine gives British police officers a strong measure of legitimate discretion, by contrast with jurisdictions where there is an ideal of full enforcement. Two levels of decision-making can be distinguished: individual officers' discretion in routine police work; and general policy decisions. These are not hermetically sealed categories. The myriad discretionary decisions by officers in individual incidents may contradict formal policy. On the other hand, policy decisions have some effect on the structuring of individual discretion— even if it is only the need for street cops to find ways of covering up deviant practices.

Individual accountability

There are two principal channels for holding individual officers to account for alleged wrong-doing: the courts and the complaints process.

Legal accountability

Statute and common law provide powers to the police to accomplish their duties, but also set limits to their legitimate use (Dixon 1997). The main statutory powers of the police are codified in the Police and Criminal Evidence Act 1984 (PACE), although they have been expanded since.

PACE attempted for the first time to develop a comprehensive set of police powers and safeguards for suspects,[6] aiming to achieve a 'fundamental balance' between them (this was the axiom of the 1981 Royal Commission on Criminal Procedure (RCCP) Report which led to PACE). The safeguards are set out partly in the Act itself, partly in Codes of Practice accompanying it. PACE sought to overcome the perennial problem of the low visibility of police work by requiring that each exercise of a power had to be

[5] It should be noted that these oft-cited words of Lord Denning are strictly speaking obiter dicta, as emphasized by Lustgarten's corrosive analysis that 'seldom have so many errors of law and logic been compressed into one paragraph' (Lustgarten 1986: 64). Nonetheless, the doctrine of constabulary independence is now so firmly embedded that the judiciary are unlikely to abandon it easily.

[6] Prior to PACE there was limited protection for suspects afforded by the Judges' Rules, a set of non-statutory administrative directions laying down procedures for questioning and taking statements originally formulated in 1912.

recorded contemporaneously. For example, section 1 extended the power to stop and search, but this must be grounded in 'reasonable suspicion', with a record written as soon as possible, and made available to the suspect. All the safeguards are underpinned by section 67 of PACE, which makes failure to comply with them a disciplinary offence. Judges were given a broad discretion to exclude evidence gathered in ways that would render the proceedings as a whole unfair (section 78). In addition, PACE includes sections purporting to enhance police accountability more generally, for example through the complaints process and by community consultation.

During its protracted Parliamentary passage critics of PACE were particularly vexed about its reliance on internal police recording and discipline. But after the Act came into operation criticism came primarily from the police, who complained that the recording and other procedural requirements hampered effective investigation.

There has been extensive research evaluating the impact of PACE on police practice (for summaries see Dixon 1997; Brown 1997; Reiner 2000: ch. 6; Sanders and Young, Chapter 28, this volume). Some studies suggest that suspects systematically fail to receive their rights (McConville *et al.* 1991). They argue that the Act does not fundamentally erode the structural advantage the police have in the investigation process, especially after a suspect is in police custody. Others suggest that the new procedures have achieved substantial changes in the treatment of suspects. It also appears to be the case that the courts in general have been more vigorous in excluding evidence gathered in violation of PACE procedures than they were under the old Judges' Rules (Feldman 1990).

When the government was forced to establish the Royal Commission on Criminal Justice in 1991 in the wake of the successful appeals by the Birmingham Six and Guildford Four, it was hoped by civil libertarians that the protection of suspects would be boosted even further. In the event its recommendations on police powers and safeguards (Royal Commission 1993) amounted only to detailed footnotes to PACE, 'an almost endless list of recommendations for administrative, piecemeal changes, many of which have been ignored' (Rose 1996: 16).

Most of the new powers recommended by the 1993 Royal Commission Report, such as those to take samples for DNA analysis, were incorporated into the Criminal Justice and Public Order Act 1994. The Act also extended stop and search powers (section 60), and gave new powers to control trespassers and raves. Most fundamentally, it introduced the right for the prosecution to comment adversely on a suspect's exercise of the right to silence in police interviews, with a corresponding change in the caution given beforehand. This overturned the recommendations of both the Royal Commissions on Criminal Procedure (1981) and Criminal Justice (1993), which had seen the right to silence as a cornerstone safeguard for suspects. It resulted in a decline in the proportion of suspects exercising their right of silence in relation to some or all questions (Bucke *et al.* 2000).

The legislative trend since 1993 has been extensions of police powers without corresponding safeguards, with the Human Rights Act of 1998 constituting the only exception. New powers to intercept communications, conduct covert operations, stop and search and arrest, and new public order offences were created by the Police Act 1997, the Crime and Disorder Act 1998, the Regulation of Investigatory Powers Act 2000, the Terrorism Act 2000, and the Criminal Justice and Public Order Act 2001.

In 2002 the Home Office conducted a review of PACE, premised on the view that the regime of safeguards it had instituted created a regime of procedures adequately protecting suspects. The concern was to provide a 'useful tool supporting the police and providing them with the powers they need to combat crime'. It was deemed necessary to 'simplify police procedures; reduce administrative burdens on the police; save police resources; speed up the process of justice'. Accordingly the Review floated a number of proposals to dilute the safeguards of PACE. The Criminal Justice Act 2003 authorized detention for 36 hours for all (not just 'serious') arrestable offences, and added criminal damage to the possible grounds for stop and search. The Serious Organised Crime and Police Act 2005 created a power of arrest for *all* offences, not just the more serious ones hitherto deemed 'arrestable'. It enhanced powers of search and finger-printing. It also allowed for the creation of civilian custody officers, overturning the PACE requirement that they should normally be police sergeants. The clear trend is for enhanced powers and reduced safeguards, reflecting the law and order politics that have prevailed since the early 1990s.

In sum, the regime of safeguards established since PACE had a substantial impact on police practice, inhibiting gross violations of suspects' rights. However, the pressures on the police to achieve results have intensified in the new crime control climate, and they are increasingly armed with new powers unfettered by safeguards. This is likely to reduce the legal accountability of the police in future.

The complaints process

A statutory procedure for handling complaints against the police was first established by the Police Act 1964. It relied on police investigation and adjudication, and there was much criticism of the absence of any independent element. The Police Act 1976 established an independent Police Complaints Board (PCB) to adjudicate complaints. This failed to command public (or police) confidence. An element of independence in the investigation of complaints was achieved by PACE in 1984. This replaced the PCB by the Police Complaints Authority (PCA), with powers to supervise some police investigations. A major study evaluating the PCA suggested that it could operate effectively in its supervisory role, although resource constraints normally prevented more than token supervision (Maguire and Corbett 1991). However the same research—as well as other studies—showed that the system failed to command confidence (ibid.). In 1999 Police (Conduct) Regulations enhanced the position of complainants by lowering the standard of proof from 'beyond reasonable doubt' to 'on the balance of probabilities'.

The Police Reform Act 2002 established an independent body empowered to investigate complaints against the police, the Independent Police Complaints Commission. This achieved the long-standing central demand of civil libertarians, but it remains to be seen what effect it will have on the substantiation of complaints, and on public confidence in the system (Smith 2004). Experience in other countries suggests independent investigation of complaints is not a panacea for regulating police misconduct (Goldsmith and Lewis 2000). No matter who does the investigating, complaints against the police are hard to sustain, because of the low visibility of most encounters. This turns most cases into a head-on collision of testimony in which the complained-against police officer usually has the advantage.[7]

Policy accountability

The discretion of the rank-and-file police officer is structured by the management style and policies developed by the chief officer in a force. What avenues are there for the public accountability of these policy decisions?

The present formal structure of police governance in England and Wales is set out in the Police Act 1964 (following recommendations of the 1962 Report of the Royal Commission on the Police) and the Police and Magistrates' Court Act 1994, consolidated as the Police Act 1996. The 1964 Act enshrined the so-called 'tripartite' system of accountability for the (currently 41) provincial forces in England and Wales, comprising local police authorities, the Home Secretary, and chief constables.

The two London forces differed from this pattern. The Metropolitan Police had the Home Secretary as their police authority from 1829 until 1999, when the Greater London Authority Act created a police authority for the Met. The City of London force is accountable to the Common Council of the City of London (the Aldermen and Mayor), as well as the Home Secretary.

The 1964 Police Act divided accountability for provincial policing between chief constables, responsible for 'direction and control' of their forces; local police authorities, with the duty of 'maintenance of an adequate and efficient police force for the area' (section 4); and the Home Secretary, who was expected to use a variety of powers to further the efficiency of policing throughout the country. Under the 1964 Act police authorities consisted two-thirds of elected local councillors, and one-third of JPs (who are selected by the Lord Chancellor).

There has been vigorous debate about what the 1964 Act's provisions really meant (Lustgarten 1986; Reiner 1991: ch. 2; Walker 2000). Until the late 1970s it seemed to be accepted that the role of the police authority was as a sounding board for the professional expert, the chief constable. Police authorities might exercise some influence over broad policy matters such as how the budget should be spent, but even on this, and certainly on 'operational' issues, they were generally content to accept the chief's guidance. The Home Secretary's powers remained dormant.

This cosy consensus was shattered by the politicization of policing issues in the late 1970s. In 1981 radical Labour councils were elected in most large cities, and the

---

[7] Another significant avenue of legal redress for individuals subject to wrongful exercise of police powers is civil action (Dixon and Smith 1998). Extension of legal aid, coupled with the Police Act 1964 which exposed police authorities to vicarious liability for the wrongful actions of constables, made it possible and worthwhile for people to take civil actions against the police. Substantial damages have sometimes been awarded to successful litigants, but in the last decade restrictions on legal aid and on the size of damages have limited civil actions (Smith 2003).

metropolitan police authorities began to try and influence policing policy in controversial areas, notably public order tactics, especially during the 1984–5 miners' strike. Highly publicized conflicts occurred between chief constables and police authorities, notably in Greater Manchester and Merseyside. The clashes underlined the impotence of local police authorities. Home Secretaries invariably supported the chief constables against police authority attempts to influence 'operational' matters.

In the late 1980s the almost complete powerlessness of the local authority leg of the tripartite structure was highlighted by legal developments. In 1988 the Northumbria Police Authority sought a judicial review of a decision by the Home Secretary, which provided plastic bullets for riot-control training in local forces where the police authority refused to sanction their purchase. The Court of Appeal rejected the Authority's case, holding that both under the 1964 Police Act, and under the Royal Prerogative, the Home Secretary had a duty to preserve the Queen's Peace entitling him to override the police authority (*R* v. *Secretary of State for the Home Department, ex p. Northumbria Police Authority* [1988] 2 W.L.R. 590). Local police authorities enjoyed only such influence as the other two parties, the chief constable and the Home Secretary, deemed it wise to allow. Most chief constables, however, accepted policies emanating from the Home Office as binding, even though they were formally merely advisory (Reiner 1991: ch. 11).

The centralizing trend has become more apparent following recent reforms of police governance. The Police and Magistrates' Courts Act 1994, consolidated with the 1964 Police Act into the Police Act 1996, made substantial steps in a centralizing direction. The specified functions of police authorities were subtly altered from 'maintenance of an adequate and efficient' force to 'efficient and effective' (Police Act 1996, section 6). The precise scope of this responsibility remains as gnomic as in the 1964 version, but the symbolism is obvious. The prime purpose of the new-fangled police authorities is to be local watchdogs of the managerialist, value-for-money ethos that successive governments have injected into the whole public sector (Power 1999; McLaughlin and Murji 2001; McLaughlin *et al.* 2001).

The most controversial changes were to the structure of police authorities. The democratically elected councillor component of police authorities was reduced from two-thirds to just over a half (nine out of the normal total of 17 members: Police Act, 1996 Schedule 2, para. 1(1)(a)). Three members are magistrates (i.e. just over one-sixth instead of one-third: para. 1(1)(b)). The remaining five members are appointed under the complex and arcane procedures detailed in Schedule 3 to the 1996 Act. Overall the Act left police authorities with a slight preponderance of elected members, as a fig leaf to hide growing centralization.

The explicit intention was to make police authorities more 'businesslike'. They acquired new duties to issue an annual policing plan for their area (Police Act 1996, section 8) and local policing objectives (section 7). The chief constable has the same general function of 'direction and control' of the force as in the 1964 Act, but this must be exercised with regard to the local policing plan and objectives which the authority draws up in liaison with him (section 10). This is an empowerment of the authority compared to the 1964 Act, but it largely has to act as a conduit for the Home Secretary's priorities (sections 37–9). Overall the Police and Magistrates' Courts Act continued the long-term process of shifting the balance of power towards central government.

This conclusion is reinforced when the changes in governance are considered in the context of other elements of successive governments' police reforms. The Sheehy Inquiry into Police Responsibilities and Rewards (the Sheehy Report 1993) had recommended that all police officers should be appointed on short-term contracts and subject to performance-related pay (PRP), assessed by the Home Secretary via the new police authorities. This would have constituted a formidably centralized system of control over policing. Without abandoning the constabulary independence doctrine in any formal way, the Home Secretary could colour the use of discretion by constables by regulating the criteria determining pay and job security. The police would no longer be accountable in the gentlemanly 'explanatory and co-operative' style which (in Geoffrey Marshall's words) characterized the impact of the 1964 Police Act (Marshall 1978). Nor would they be subject to the 'subordinate and obedient' style of accountability to democratically elected local authorities that had been demanded by the Act's radical critics. Instead they would be subject to a new market-style 'calculative and contractual' discipline (Reiner and Spencer 1993), capable of penetrating the parts of policing which earlier models could not reach, the day-to-day operation of discretion. The toughest aspects of Sheehy were defeated by a storm of opposition from police representative associations, just as the centralizing impact of the Police and Magistrates' Courts Act had been modified in the House of Lords. The diluted versions of these measures that resulted left a lot open to detailed argument and development. As Newburn and Jones show, 'the nexus of control is a complicated one, and how it works in practice will, like the previous arrangements, be heavily dependent on how the relevant parties choose to use their powers' (Newburn and Jones 1996: 125).

The significance of the national policing plan and objectives that the 1994 Act mandated the Home Secretary to issue was underlined by the House of Lords judgment in the 1998 *International Trader's Ferry* case. This upheld the legality of a chief constable's decision to restrict the level of police protection for live animal exporters against protestors, despite the general public duty to keep the peace, and EC Treaty obligations to protect the free movement of goods. The decision was based partly on the old constabulary independence doctrine, but also on the need to achieve the Home Secretary's crime control objectives, which would be jeopardized by allocating more personnel to deal with the dispute.

The centralizing trend continued with the Police Reform Act 2002. This requires the Home Secretary to issue an annual National Policing Plan and objectives. A Home Office 'Police Standards Unit' was established to improve the performance of all basic command units across the country. This process will be further consolidated as a result of the creation of the National Policing Improvement Agency that will become operational in early 2007. It will almost certainly oversee a substantially restructured policing landscape. The government had planned a sweeping amalgamation programme (HMIC 2005; Loveday 2006). These plans have been frustrated, and the future scenario is highly uncertain ('New Blow to Clarke As Police Mergers Programme Scrapped', *The Guardian*, 13 July 2006), but they are likely to be resuscitated in some form. Although the government has pledged to reinvigorate local police governance in the 2004 White Paper *Building Communities: Beating Crime*, there must be grave doubt about whether the overall centralizing trajectory will be reversed (McLaughlin 2005).

There has certainly been a profound transformation in the formal organization of police governance in the years since 1994, with a clear trend to enhancing central control. Unlike previous major changes in police accountability there has been no Royal Commission (as many commentators advocated). The reforms emanated from internal Home Office enquiries with minimal outside consultation. The measures were predicated on a clear but contentious conceptualization of the police role as being primarily 'catching criminals' (para. 2.2 of the 1993 White Paper, *Police Reform*). In theory and practice the police mandate had traditionally encompassed a much broader spectrum of concerns, including crime prevention and management, order mainten-ance and peace-keeping, emergency and other services (Bayley 1994; Morgan and Newburn 1997). The narrow emphasis on crime control had hitherto been seen by most official enquiries, notably the Scarman Report of 1981, as a deformation of rank-and-file police culture, not actively promoted by policy and performance targets. The police capacity to control crime is inherently limited by the deep roots of policing problems in wider social, political-economic, and cultural processes (Bayley 1994; Morgan and Newburn 1997; Reiner 2000: ch. 4). However, the major trend since the 1990s has been to emphasize crime control as the key role of the police, encouraging the pursuit of innovative strategies of crime reduction.

'NEW TRICKS': INNOVATIVE POLICING STRATEGIES

The original mandate of Peel's Metropolitan Police placed greatest emphasis on the prevention of crime (Emsley 1996). This was to be achieved primarily through visible patrol. During the course of the nineteenth century a detective function was added and these two strategies—preventive patrol and criminal investigation—have continued to form the core of policing over the past century or more. Nevertheless, recent decades have witnessed some important developments in policing, many prompted by the pressures under which all criminal justice agencies were placed by governments increasingly concerned to secure 'value for money' and 'economy, efficiency and effectiveness' in public services (Rawlings 1991; Reiner and Spencer 1993). Additionally, they were also partly a reaction against the 'nothing works' penal pessimism of the 1970s and the apparently precipitous declines in public confidence in policing during roughly the same period. New developments in policing are almost always as much about police legitimation as they are about police effectiveness (Reiner 2000; Smith 2006).

From the 1970s research, primarily in the USA, had begun seriously to question the efficacy of patrol (for a summary of much contemporary British research see Clarke and Hough 1984). The Kansas City experimental study of preventive patrol found little impact on reported crime, levels of fear of crime, or confidence in the police (Kelling *et al.* 1974). One response to the Kansas City findings—which were a study of car patrol—was to reaffirm faith in some quarters in the perceived benefits of foot patrol and further large-scale research in Newark in the USA found some evidence of impact on fear of crime, and ratings of the police, though not on crime levels (Pate and Skogan 1985). Nevertheless, through its influence on Wilson and Kelling's subsequent (1982) 'Broken Windows' article, which argued strongly that police action against minor incivilities and nuisances was an important factor in preventing the development of more significant and less tractable problems, it has played a significant role in maintaining faith in routine visible patrol as a cornerstone of contemporary policing (for a thorough critique, see Harcourt 2001).

In recent years policing has seen the regular appearance of what are alleged to be new 'models' of police work, each claiming to reorient and refashion policing in ways that represent a more or less radical departure from traditional methods. Many have been nothing more than fancy labels and promotional devices rather than genuine developments in policing styles and tactics. However, from among the morass it is possible to identify a number of developments in policing that are worthy of more sustained analysis. Weisburd and Eck (2004) in a recent review of American policing draw attention to three—community policing, problem-oriented policing, and hotspots policing—to which a fourth, British, variant might be added—intelligence-led policing. What links all these innovations is the diagnosis that policing hitherto has been too reactive and should become more proactive (Tilley 2003).

In assessing these innovations, Weisburd and Eck (2004) distinguish policing strategies along two dimensions: the diversity of approaches involved and the level of focus. Traditional law-enforcement approaches, involving a fairly standardized set of tactics, score fairly low on the diversity dimension. Similarly, strategies that are applied relatively uniformly across circumstances, times, and places by policing agencies score relatively low on the level of focus dimension. They argue that traditional policing methods—what they call the standard model—have rarely been characterized by a diversity of approaches or by being particularly targeted or focused. By contrast, innovations in policing over the last decade or so have tended to move outward along one or both of the dimensions.

COMMUNITY POLICING

Of the various innovations it is undoubtedly community policing that has spread the furthest or, at least, is the most frequently and prominently talked about. Although the precise characteristics of community policing are often rather difficult to pin down (Klockars 1988), broadly speaking such approaches propose that there be greater citizen involvement in the identification of the problems that should form priorities for police attention as well as in the responses to those problems (Trojanowicz and Bucqueroux 1990). Community policing emerged from the growing acceptance that at best the police could often only offer a very partial solution to the difficulties they confronted (Morgan and Newburn 1997). In both the USA and the UK community policing emerged from the recognition that police-community relations had deteriorated significantly, particularly with some minority ethnic communities (Skogan and Hartnett 1997). Community policing initiatives proliferated in the 1980s, though the available evidence suggests many were of very limited if any impact. Research on community constables (Brown and Iles 1985), directed patrolling (Burrows and Lewis 1988), focused patrolling (Chatterton and Rogers 1989), neighbourhood policing (Irving *et al.* 1989) and Neighbourhood Watch (Husain 1988; Bennett 1990; McConville and Shepherd 1992) shows that all suffered from considerable problems in relation to planning and implementation. Consequently, evaluation results were generally poor. Nevertheless, in the UK in the aftermath of the urban riots of the early 1980s, and Lord Scarman's plea for greater police-community consultation, ideas associated with community policing became the accepted policing orthodoxy, at least amongst senior officers (Reiner 1991) and policy-makers. Indeed, continuing senior police scepticism about aggressive police patrol tactics was a very significant stumbling block when politicians began extolling the virtues of 'zero tolerance policing' in the mid-to late 1990s (Jones and Newburn 2007). So well established has community policing become in the USA that it has been described as the 'national mantra of the American police' (Greene 2000: 301).

In essence community policing seeks to reorient relationships between police and community, placing much greater emphasis on working for and with local communities, and downplaying the extent to which policing is a set of activities imposed upon communities. The major difficulties are contained in the term itself. It is sufficiently awkward to define to allow for almost any policing activity to be included under its rubric (Bayley 1994). Moreover, with its connotations of inclusiveness, consensus, communication, and consultation, an idea such as community policing, however difficult to pin down, is almost impossibly seductive (Brogden 1999). Nevertheless, there have been numerous attempts both to define, and to evaluate, community policing. Bayley (1994) for example suggests that its core elements include community consultation, the decentralization of police departments in order that local priorities can be responded to, and the adoption of a problem-solving approach in which the police endeavour to reorient away from reactive incident-focused activity toward a more analytical framework. It is clear that the intention behind community policing is that it should be geared to locally identified priorities and, moreover, that it should adopt tactics and styles that are appropriate to local needs. Consequently, it is a model of policing in which there is expected to be a wide array of approaches and which is therefore very distinct from the more uniform policing styles that dominated much of the twentieth century. Such variety is partly what makes it difficult to define and contributes to difficulties in evaluation.

The largest and arguably most successful community policing experiment to date has been the Chicago Alternative Policing Strategy (CAPS). This programme, carried out in five experimental districts, involved all elements of the police department in community policing—not just patrol officers—and aimed to reduce officer resistance to such approaches. It sought to stimulate citizen involvement through 'beat meetings', and to solve the twin problems of only attracting the 'usual suspects' to community meetings and police domination of the problem-solving elements of such meetings. Finally, it endeavoured to integrate policing with other city services in order that local problem-solving was not undermined by the ability to act across institutional boundaries. The results in Chicago, as in many other evaluated community policing initiatives, have been mixed. According to Skogan and Hartnett (1997) elements of the CAPS initiative, as with others, were found in the aggregate to have succeeded about half the time. The significance of CAPS undoubtedly lies in its scale. Whereas the majority of other community policing evaluations have been based on relatively small-scale experiments, the CAPS experiment has been both sizeable and ongoing. The tension in community policing lies in the danger that even the most well-meaning community-oriented programmes may easily revert to more classic police approaches which use them as a means either of securing legitimacy for police actions or of increasing police information and intelligence (Mastrofski 2006).

PROBLEM-ORIENTED POLICING

At the heart of many community policing initiatives is the idea of police as 'problem-solvers' (Eck and Spelman 1987). Often considered a variant of community policing, 'problem-oriented policing' is somewhat easier to describe. Emanating from the work of Herman Goldstein (1990), problem-oriented policing (POP) is an explicit attempt to make police work more analytical in the identification of the 'problems' to be addressed, and constructive in the solutions applied to the problems identified. The underlying assumption is that much policing treats incidents brought to its attention as if they were discrete—having no connection or pattern. By contrast, POP looks for connections and patterns, with the aim of finding lasting solutions to ongoing problems (Moore 1992). As a consequence a number of 'tools' have come to be associated with this approach, notably the problem analysis triangle (the PAT, consisting of the offender, the victim, and the location) and the SARA process in which four sequenced stages—scanning, analysis, response, and assessment—form the basis for problem-solving (Tilley 2003).

A focus on problem-solving has given rise to a number of linked policing strategies concentrating on such patterning as repeat or prolific offenders (Everson and Pease 2001), repeat victimization (Farrell and Pease 2001), and hotspots (Sherman 1990) among others. Indeed, there is a growing literature particularly around 'hotspots policing'. There have been a number of experimental studies in which focused and increased police patrols in areas where there are particular problems have had a measurable impact on levels of crime and disorder (Sherman and Weisburd 1995;

Braga *et al.* 1999). However, as with community policing, there has also been consider-able cultural resistance within the police to POP (Read and Tilley 2000; Scott 2000). There remains a very strong enforcement orientation in policing and an attachment to the excitement and glamour of the flashing blue lights of emergency response. The potentially more sedate world of data collection and analysis holds fewer attractions. It is also something that few police departments are well equipped to deal with. Although the police are increasingly concerned with information brokerage and knowledge production (Ericson and Haggerty 1997), they tend still to be short on those skills that would make for successful problem-solving (Bullock and Tilley 2003), meaning that much policing practice falls well short of the ideals espoused by Goldstein (Eck 2006).

INTELLIGENCE-LED POLICING

Arguably, it is precisely the identification of such limitations that lay behind the emergence of a further variation—so-called 'intelligence-led policing' (ILP). This approach departs somewhat from problem-oriented and community policing in its tendency to privilege crime fighting and enforcement over other policing functions. Moreover, its underlying assumption is that these functions can be performed more efficiently and effectively through greater stimulation and use of intelligence. The link with POP lies in its emphasis upon the search for patterns in offending and victimization. Although ILP is now firmly established as the intended template for the organization of policing in England and Wales through the vehicle of the National Intelligence Model (NIM) (Maguire 2000) a number of other recent developments have occurred simultan-eously to complicate the picture. Centrally, there have been the continuing problems associated with high levels of public anxiety about crime and the perception—public and political—that high-visibility policing is important in addressing such anxieties.

One of the most recent variants on the community policing and intelligence-led policing theme in Britain is the development of 'reassurance policing' (Dalgleish and Myhill 2004). A significant programme was established under this rubric between 2003 and 2005, arising in part from survey research which showed that despite year-on-year falls in crime since the mid-1990s a significant proportion of the public continued to believe that crime was still rising. In government circles this became known as the 'reassurance gap'. In parallel with this, there was also political concern that despite dropping crime levels there were continued demands in many communities for tough and more visible action against a range of activities—some criminal, some not. The government's 'antisocial behaviour agenda' (see Morgan and Newburn, Chapter 30, this volume) developed strongly from about 2000 onward and, in due course, fed into the emerging reassurance policing experiment.

The idea of 'signal crimes' was the intellectual glue that allowed concerns about the 'reassurance gap' to be linked with the antisocial behaviour agenda (Innes and Fielding 2002; Innes 2006). Although argued to be quite distinct from the notion of 'broken windows', the signal crimes idea nevertheless contains resonances of Wilson and Kelling's original thesis. At the heart of 'broken windows' is the observation that signs of disorder and lack of guardianship, if left untended, lead to escalating disorder and crime. At the core of the signal crimes idea is that there are particular crimes and disorders that act as warning signals to people about the nature of risk. One highlights the signal that disorder sends to potential offenders, the other the signal it sends to local citizens. In many respects reassurance policing is an amalgam of elements of community policing and POP. At the core of its approach is the assumption that a visible presence is important to local feelings of security. The community should be involved in both the identification of local problems and the action taken in response and, centrally, policing activity should be targeted at those problems that appear to matter most. An early evaluation claims considerable success both in terms of crime reduction and in feelings of safety (Tuffin *et al.* 2006) though as with all developments in the area of police 'innovations' the extent to which the programme is sustainable and replicable remains a key question.

PLURALIZATION

It is no longer possible to argue or imagine that policing and the police are largely synonymous. Liberal democracies in the twenty-first century are policed by what often appears to be a bewildering array of organizations (Crawford 2003; Walker 2003; Jones and Newburn 2006a). Such has been the pace and extent of change in this area that two leading commentators have argued that 'future generations will look back on our era as a time when one system of policing ended and another took its place' (Bayley and Shearing 1996: 585). The period since the mid-1960s they argue has seen the 'end of a monopoly' by the public police (though see Jones and Newburn 2002) and the emergence of what they call a 'multilateralized' system of security provision (Bayley and Shearing 2001). Through this term they seek to draw attention to the increasing complexity of policing, in terms not just of its provision, but also of its authorization or governance (Shearing 2006; and Jones, Chapter 25, this volume). One of the consequences of these changes to the landscape of policing is that a number of observers have increasingly come to talk of policing as having become 'pluralized' (Crawford *et al.* 2005; Jones and Newburn 2006a) and others have argued for the use of the term 'governance of security' in preference to the term 'policing' (Johnston and Shearing 2002).

In essence 'pluralization' may be taken to refer to three related sets of developments. First, the increasing size and pervasiveness of the commercial security sector that is visible in many countries (see the contributions in Jones and Newburn 2006c). Secondly, there has been the growing 'commodification' of public policing. Commodification itself may be broken down into three distinct processes (Loader 1999): 'managerialism' (becoming more 'business-like'); 'consumerism' (the re-presentation of public policing as a 'service' and of the public as 'consumers'); and, 'promotionalism' (the increasingly professional promotion of the 'product'). Relatedly, from the 1980s onwards we have seen successive waves of 'civilianization' and the beginning of discussions about possibilities of privatization. In addition, many countries have seen the emergence of forms of policing provision that can be distinguished both from commercial security and from traditional state constabularies. Key examples include the recent introduction of '(police) community support officers' and 'neighbourhood wardens' in the UK (Crawford 2003), the establishment of local municipal police organizations in France (Roche 2002), and the introduction of police auxiliaries (politie-surveillanten) and 'city guards' (stadswachten) in the Netherlands (van Steden and Huberts 2006). Finally, criminologists in some countries have come to pay increasing attention to the activities of a range of governmental regulatory and investigatory agencies undertaking important 'policing' tasks (e.g. Hutter 1988). However, undoubtedly the most visible manifestation of pluralization has been the growing visibility and variety of private, municipal, and civilian guards, officers, and wardens on the streets of every major city and many smaller communities.

PRIVATE SECURITY

In recent decades an increasingly complex division of labour has emerged in which private security personnel far outstrip police in numerical terms (Jones and Newburn 1998, 2006b)—and have access to increased powers in some cases—in which civilian employees and auxiliaries have become an accepted part of state policing, and in which the police and numerous other agencies—public, private, and voluntary—work in 'partnership' (Button 2007).

The proliferation of private security has involved the spread of new technologies, such as closed-circuit television (CCTV) (Lyon 2001), and the growing incursion of the private sector into forms of work, or areas of activity, more usually associated with public policing such as the enforcement of parking and traffic regulations, the transport and guarding of prisoners, and most importantly—certainly for the way we view policing—the patrolling of public streets. Though some of these are relatively recent developments, a degree of caution has to be exercised when discussing the degree to which this is a departure from previous arrangements (Zedner 2006). In fact, there is good evidence to suggest that by the late 1950s/early 1960s the numbers employed in the private security industry already exceeded the number of police officers (Jones and Newburn 1998). Despite this, it is arguably only in the last two decades that the police service's dominant position in the public mind as the 'thin blue line' protecting the public from crime and lawlessness has come under successful challenge.

The private security sector is generally broken down into three main elements: staffed services; security equipment; and investigation. Staffed services—guarding, asset protection, door supervision, debt collection, and the like—is undoubtedly the most visible part of the sector (Jones and Newburn 1998; Wakefield 2003). Investigative services—tracing missing persons, matrimonial work, industrial espionage, credit checking, and fraud investigation—is the least visible though areas such as forensic accounting may now well be one of the fastest-growing parts of the private sector (Williams 2005). However, the most significant growth area in recent times has been in the proliferation of security hardware and, in particular, the expansion of the use of CCTV (McCahill 2002; Coleman 2004). The first major city-centre CCTV systems were introduced as part of the 'Safer Cities' initiative in the mid-1980s and a small number of towns went ahead with such installations at around the same time using local authority rather than central government funding. By the mid-1990s fewer than 80 towns and cities had CCTV schemes (Fyfe and Bannister 1996). By May 1999 there were over 530 town and city-centre CCTV systems in operation and further government funding since then has further fuelled expansion, with the latest estimates suggesting that there are now in excess of four million cameras in operation in Britain (Norris *et al.* 2004).

It is extremely difficult to provide accurate estimates of the size of the private security sector (Jones and Newburn 2006b). Although a number of estimates have appeared since the late 1980s, the majority of these either have been little more than informed guesswork or, where they are based on evidence, are limited to the established and licensed parts of the industry. Recent research (Crawford *et al.* 2005) using industry data suggests the turnover in the sector had reached close to £2 billion by 2003 and subsequent work (Keynote Report 2004) estimates that the figure may be closer to £5 billion. The private security sector now employs somewhere in the region of 217,000 (Button 2002) to 333,000 people (Jones and Newburn 1998) depending on how the measurement is done.

EXPLAINING THE GROWTH OF PRIVATE SECURITY

Explaining the re-emergence of private security is also far from straightforward. Some have argued that it is the result of increasing financial constraints on the police who, as a consequence, are unable to meet the demands placed upon them (Spitzer and Scull 1977). In recent decades, however, public expenditure on the police has increased markedly and the number of police officers has grown steadily in recent years (Kirwan and Bibi 2006). Nevertheless, it is clear that a 'demand gap' exists (Morgan and Newburn 1997). Despite recent downward trends in crime, public perceptions of safety and security have not followed suit and demands for increased policing provision continue. Another factor is undoubtedly the growing privatization of urban space, notably the growth of 'mass private property' (Shearing and Stenning 1981; though see Jones and Newburn 1999) and the gradual emergence of gated residential communities. Though such changes are undoubtedly contributing to the continued expansion of the private policing sector they would not appear to have been as significant in the UK as in the USA and Canada (Blakely and Snyder 1997).

A third factor is the direct privatization of public functions by government. Although the private security sector was a very substantial presence much earlier, it was not until the 1980s that privatization emerged as a formal element of government policy and began to have an effect on the police. The initial battleground was police funding. From

1982/3 onwards the government began vigorously to pursue its 'Financial Management Initiative' (FMI), designed to encourage efficiency and cost savings by applying private-sector management methods to the public sector, and imposing market disciplines on them (Rawlings 1991). Although initially it looked as if the police might be safe from such scrutiny, the publication of Home Office Circular 114/1983 (and later the even tougher 106/1988), largely without consultation with police representative bodies, signalled that the financial climate had changed.

The pace of change really picked up in the 1990s, beginning with the 1993 White Paper on Police Reform (Home Office 1993) and the subsequent Police and Magistrates' Courts Act 1994 which introduced national league performance tables. This was quickly followed by the report of the Sheehy Inquiry into Police Responsibilities and Rewards which recommended the introduction of fixed-term contracts and performance-related pay for senior officers, the flattening of the police hierarchy through the removal of certain ranks, and the reduction of starting pay and the linking of pay rates to non-manual private-sector earnings (Sheehy 1993).

The most explicit consideration of privatization came with the establishment of the 1993 Core and Ancilliary Tasks Review to 'examine the services provided by the police, to make recommendations about the most cost-effective way of delivering core police services and to assess the scope for relinquishing ancillary tasks' (Posen 1995). The clear intention behind the review was to seek to identify non-essential tasks that could be provided by agencies other than the police. In the event the final report was a damp squib, merely recommending the contracting out of a small number of peripheral duties, such as escorting wide loads. By contrast, the 2004 HMIC Thematic Inspection on Modernization concluded, 'the likelihood is that the police will increasingly focus on the core, exclusive roles, contracting or commissioning other organisations to deliver the remainder' (HMIC 2004).

In fact, privatization—directly or by contracting out—has been a more minor factor in the changing face of policing in contemporary Britain than appeared likely in the early 1990s. Some functions have been transferred entirely to the private sector. The Criminal Justice Act 1991 (sections 80–6) transferred responsibility for security arrangements for prisoners in transit from the police and prison service to private contractors, and also (section 76) made provision for magistrates' courts to contract-in security officers to maintain order. Individual forces have contracted out such activities as the construction and management of custody centres, reception duties, and post-charge administration—including the taking of fingerprints, photographs, DNA samples, and PNC checks. Nevertheless, rather than direct privatization, it has been growing civilianization, including that of the custody officer role (section 120 of the Serious Organised Crime and Policing Act 2005), the encouragement of police partnership with other providers such as the Highways Agency in traffic policing, and most recently the introduction of a new tier of auxiliaries, that has had the greatest impact on the contemporary policing landscape.

CIVILIANIZATION AND THE 'NEW AUXILIARIES'

The police have long been encouraged to 'civilianize' posts that do not require the training and legal powers of a police officer. The significant drive to civilianize began during the 1980s (Jones *et al.* 1994) with the Home Office encouraging forces to recruit civilian staff into financial management, legal services, research, forensics, and human resources jobs within the police service (Mawby and Wright 2003). Some are now employed at senior levels (ACPO rank) and are part of force management teams and civilians make up over a third of the total police workforce. The last decade has seen the mushrooming of what has been the termed the 'new public auxiliaries' (Crawford and Lister 2004). It was the introduction of community support officers that was the most radical of the proposals however. Almost a decade earlier, a committee established by the Police Foundation and the Policy Studies Institute had recommended experimentation with alternative forms of police patrol (Cassels 1994; Morgan and Newburn 1997), only to be roundly criticized by ACPO and by New Labour in opposition for recommending 'policing on the cheap'. By 2002, however, the fiscal realities were such that it was difficult for any politician to avoid the conclusion that the level of policing seemingly demanded by local communities could not easily be met from the public purse. A form of public-private partnership was proposed and underpinned by the Broken Windows philosophy (Wilson and Kelling 1982). The White Paper proposed, and the Police Reform Act 2002 incorporated, proposals that agents and agencies such as neighbourhood and street wardens, security guards in shopping centres, park keepers, and 'other authority figures' (Home Office 2001: para. 2.31) could be accredited by, and work alongside, the police in a formal capacity. More controversially, the government proposed a power to enable chief constables to appoint support staff to provide a visible presence (i.e. to patrol) in the community. These 'community support officers' would be under the control of the chief constable and would have limited powers to detain suspects, to stop vehicles, and to issue fixed-penalty notices. Introduced only a few years ago there are now well over 6,000 PCSOs in England and Wales (Kirwan and Bibi 2006), with numbers anticipated to rise to 24,000 by 2008.

Directly and indirectly, through a number of measures, successive governments have stimulated further moves in the direction of a more complex and fragmented policing division of labour. The Police Reform Act 2002, via the creation of community support officers and the accreditation of extended police family members, is the most visible of the recent measures, though the neighbourhood policing programme launched in 2005 seeks to place the new auxiliaries at the heart of all neighbourhood policing teams. How plural policing arrangements are to be governed is an issue that remains not only unresolved but largely ignored (for an exception see Crawford 2003). Certainly, government has shown little interest to date in such matters. Of all the recent inquiries into policing, the most explicit recognition of the increasingly 'plural' nature of policing and security provision was contained in the proposals advanced by The Independent Commission on Policing in Northern Ireland (the Patten Inquiry) which was set up as part of the Good Friday Agreement (10 April 1998) (Patten 1999). The

Patten Commission recommended a radical overhaul of accountability structures, including the introduction of a Police Ombudsman and a new Policing Board (not Police Board) to replace the largely discredited Police Authority. Beneath the Policing Board it recommended the establishment of District Policing Partnership Boards (DPPB) as a committee of district councils with a majority elected membership. In particular, it was envisaged that these boards would have responsibility for promoting partnership of community and police in the collective delivery of community safety. Perhaps most radically in this regard the Inquiry recommended that district councils should have the power to contribute financially towards the improved policing of the district. This could enable DPPBs to purchase additional services from the police or other statutory agencies, or indeed from the private sector. Critics suggested that this would be exploited in such a way as to enable services involving, or even controlled by, paramilitaries to be purchased by DPPBs. Though by no means enacted in full in Northern Ireland (McEvoy *et al.* 2002; Mulcahy 2006), and unlikely to be enacted on the mainland in the near future given the police reform programme that is under way, the approach to policing and to police accountability was considered by some to have considerable potential (Neyroud 2001, outlined in Patten (1999)).

INTERNATIONALIZATION

The bulk of criminological literature focuses on policing as a set of domestic activities undertaken by agents of the state within particular national boundaries. This is hardly surprising given that the maintenance of internal order by the police is generally viewed as one of the defining characteristics of the modern nation state. However, if the rise of the police was paradigmatic of the modern then the changing socio-political conditions characteristic of globalization are slowly making such a conception appear increasingly anachronistic. That this is so can be seen in the gradual pluralizing of policing already described, and also in the increasing visibility of what is now generally referred to as 'transnational policing' (Sheptycki 2000a). By transnational policing, what is generally meant is those activities undertaken by policing bodies that draw their authority from polities that lie beyond individual nation states.

EUROPEAN DEVELOPMENTS

Early European initiatives in transnational policing activity date back to the late nineteenth century (Deflem 2002). The first permanent body was the International Criminal Police Commission established in Vienna in 1923, succeeded after the Second World War by the International Criminal Police Office or Interpol (Walker 2000). From small and informal beginnings Interpol has expanded significantly and has participating bureaux in nearly two hundred countries. Despite this Interpol is no longer the primary site of transnational policing activity. In particular European countries began making other arrangements because of Interpol's perceived shortcomings in relation to anti-terrorist policing, as well as concerns about the security of its communications network (House of Commons 1990). Very significant expansions in the area of European transnational police cooperation have taken place in the last two decades. A number of factors have been important in stimulating such activity, notably the growing international reach of US law-enforcement activities (Nadelmann 1993) and the growing visibility and power of the European Union (Anderson *et al.* 1995). The internationalization of policing was given particular impetus by America's 'War on Drugs' and its use of the military as well as its Drug Enforcement Agency and the FBI in its interdiction efforts (Nadelmann 1993), though non-state actors also appear to have played an important role (Sheptycki 2000b). As part of this effort a series of Mutual Legal Assistance Treaties were signed providing a legal basis for cross-border police activity, particularly covert activity (Manning 2000). According to Bigo (2000) the 1970s were the watershed in the process of Europeanization of crime and policing issues. A series of small 'security clubs' emerged in this period. These were mainly bilateral and trilateral agreements between European nations and were partly a reaction to increasing American influence over Interpol. The establishment of TREVI in 1976 was followed by the initial Schengen Agreement in 1985, comprising five member states, and a more extensive Implementation Agreement in 1990 which established the computerized Schengen Information System and police cooperation in activities such as 'hot pursuit' (Walker 2000).

Since the signing of the Maastricht Treaty in 1992 police cooperation has been established as a formal part of the 'Third Pillar' of Justice and Home Affairs within the European Union. Centrally, Europol was established as the Europe-wide police intelligence agency that would receive and supply information to the police forces of member states. Realizing such objectives was far from straightforward in practice and Europol did not become fully operational until 1999 (Walker 2003). There has been significant expansion of European policing activity since that point, not least as the repercussions of the attacks in the United States on 11 September 2001 were felt across the Atlantic. The European security agenda which is driving such developments is now focused primarily on transnational organized crime (see Chapter 23, this volume) and the threat of international terrorism. In particular, the scale of the terrorist threat seems to have overcome the majority of remaining national concerns about the growing power of Europol and related EU institutional arrangements. Moreover, the post-9/11 security agenda has vastly increased EU cooperation with the USA in relation to the exchange of intelligence and personal data and significantly enhanced US involvement in EU border policing and security planning (Den Boer and Monar 2002).

In the last five years Europol's mandate has been extended to allow it to investigate murder, kidnapping, hostage-taking, racism, corruption, unlawful drug-trafficking, people-smuggling, and motor vehicle crime (Lavranos 2003). European Union sharing of information and intelligence with the USA has occurred primarily through Europol, but also through the establishment of Eurojust—the EU inter-governmental institution responsible for judicial cooperation around crime (Dubois 2002). Moreover, criminal investigations involving two or more member states have been facilitated since June 2002 by an EU Council decision to enable the creation of 'joint investigation teams' comprising terrorist experts, members of Europol and Eurojust, and, potentially, also US officials. The European arrest warrant came into force in 15 member states in January 2004 enabling the transnational transfer of accused persons (Walker 2003). Although such developments fall some way short of the emergence of a European FBI, domestic reforms suggest that this is the direction in which European policing is heading.

SERIOUS AND ORGANIZED CRIME

The transnationalizing effects of the twin concerns of international terrorism and global organized crime can also be seen in domestic developments in British policing organization and activity (Edwards and Gill 2003; Hobbs 1998; Levi 2003; Matassa and Newburn 2003). The policing of serious and organized crime has led to the gradual centralization of core detective functions, initially through the emergence of Regional Crime Squads, and subsequently the National Crime Squad (NCS) and the National Criminal Intelligence Service (NCIS) (Maguire 2003). However, these two have now been disbanded and wrapped up into the newly created Serious and Organised Crime Agency (SOCA) as a result of the Serious Organised Crime and Policing Act 2005. The Agency, established initially with 4,200 staff, amalgamated the functions of NCIS and NCS, together with the investigative branches from the Immigration Service and the Revenue and Customs Service. SOCA has a number of other important characteristics that set it apart from the main constabularies in the UK. Although SOCA's first Director General was drawn from the police service, having previously headed up the NCS, its first chair, Sir Stephen Lander, was previously the Head of MI5, indicating the emergence of a hybrid agency working as a policing body but specializing in covert and intelligence-gathering activity. SOCA will have officers permanently stationed abroad working with and within intelligence agencies in other jurisdictions and similarly will house investigators from other agencies within the UK. SOCA is a non-departmental public body, not a police force, and its staff are civilians not police officers, although they have considerable designated powers. As a NDPB it is governed by a Board with a majority of non-executive members and, unlike the majority of police forces, is answerable directly to the Home Secretary rather than to a police authority.

TRANSNATIONAL PRIVATE SECURITY

It is not only public policing but also commercial security that can increasingly be found operating transnationally. Indeed, this trend is arguably clearer in relation to private policing. By the turn of the century Johnston (2000: 22) was able to note that 'While transnational public policing is a relatively new phenomenon, the commercial security market is already dominated by a small number of transnational companies'.

This includes traditional contract security operations but also less frequently studied areas such as risk management, business intelligence, and military services (Johnston 2006). Such companies, he suggests, are able to generate high revenues, high rates of growth, and huge profits. Group 4 Securicor is a good example. It currently employs over 400,000 people and operates in over 100 countries, describing itself as having an 'unrivalled geographic footprint'. Its activity is divided among three sectors: what it calls 'security services', which includes manned guarding and other activities relating to justice systems such as running custodial institutions, immigration detention, prisoner transfer, and electronic monitoring; security systems including alarms, entry systems, CCTV, and biometrics; and the guarding and transfer of cash and other valuables. Its turnover in 2004 was £3.8 billion, making it one of the world's largest security companies. The company produces weekly global 'security reports' that it publishes on its website detailing events and perceived risks of which clients, or potential clients, ought to be aware. These tend to include civil disturbances and disputes, concerns over violent crime, other civil emergencies related for example to extreme weather, and increasingly the problems related to the threat of international terrorism. Indeed, it is in this area that one of the more remarkable developments in transnational security has been taking place over the past decade and a half.

The end of the Cold War and more recently the growing impact of the 'War on Terror' have progressively blurred the boundary between internal and external threats. One of the more significant consequences of these developments has been the growth of the private military industry. It is generally held to consist of three main sectors (Singer 2003): 'military support firms' which provide logistical and intelligence services; 'military consulting firms' that provide strategic advice and training; and 'military provider firms' which offer tactical military assistance including the defence of key installations and individuals together with combat services. In terms of the scale of such activity, the UK Foreign Office confirmed that it alone had paid £30m during 2004 to private security companies, about two-thirds of it in Iraq (*Independent on Sunday*, 19 March 2005), having paid £20m in 2003. To the extent that it is possible to identify the emergence of a 'new structure' of 'multilateralized' policing (Bayley and Shearing 2001), it is clear that this encompasses 'high' as well as 'low' policing activities (Bowling and Newburn forthcoming).

Transnational policing is undoubtedly set to increase markedly. We are witnessing the gradual emergence of a new global political order in which the liberal democratic nation state occupies a different position from that which gave birth to the policing arrangements that dominated the bulk of the nineteenth and twentieth centuries. The rise of other sources of supranational and subnational authority poses an important challenge to the sovereignty of the nation state. Moreover, the nature of the 'late modern' world involves increasing transnational trade—both legal and illegal—providing a challenge to police organizations that have traditionally been geared toward the local and national stage. It also appears to bring with it new threats and risks, not the least of which are those associated with international terrorism. Terrorism itself is less and less defined and constrained by national borders. Moreover, for some at least, the traditional constraints on high-impact/high-casualty methods seem to have been removed. The most dystopian reading of these trends suggests that the traditional nation state is so ill-equipped to deal with these problems that it will itself necessarily undergo a fairly radical transformation in which risk and opportunity replace welfare and safety as the core concerns of the state (Bobbitt 2002). Whatever else occurs, these trends will undoubtedly provide the basis for the continued expansion of transnational policing networks and, almost certainly, the gradual transformation of what have largely been networks for the diffusion of intelligence into transnational operational police forces.

GOVERNING TRANSNATIONAL POLICING

As we described earlier, there has been a significant shift in debates around British police governance over the past thirty years or so. By contrast, as yet there has been relatively little debate about the governance and oversight of transnational policing bodies. However, as McLaughlin (1992) pointed out some years ago the potential for the emergence of a multi-tiered policing system independent of the political process—or at least a political process which is perceived by citizens to have any immediate bearing on their everyday concerns—gives rise to some very obvious concerns. This remains a complex field. Whilst it is clearly the case that both public and commercial transnational policing activities appear to be growing, the idea of policing as a core function of the state retains great power, and some of the limits, or at least barriers, to the development of truly transnational operational policing bodies are illustrated in the very significant political problems evident in attempts to create a European federal state. There is an emerging debate in academic criminology over how best to imagine—practically and normatively—what appropriate structures for the governance of transnational security might look like and, more particularly, within this what the role of the nation state should be (Johnston and Shearing 2002; Loader and Walker 2006; Johnston 2006).

CONCLUSION: FUTURES OF POLICING

British policing is facing momentous changes. This conclusion will attempt to analyse its predicament, and hazard a glance at the future. Although the concentration will be on the British police, the underlying pressures to which they are subject are found in other jurisdictions too.

The modern British police were established during the first half of the nineteenth century against widespread opposition across the social and political spectrum (Emsley 1996, 2003; Reiner 2000: ch. 1; Rawlings 2003). As a way of overcoming this, the architects of the British police tradition strove to construct a distinctive organizational style and image (Miller 1977; Emsley op. cit.; Reiner op. cit.: ch. 2). This emphasized the idea of the police as an essentially civilian body, minimally armed, relying primarily on the same legal powers to deal with crime as all citizens shared, strictly subject to the rule of law, insulated from governmental control, and drawn from a representative range of working-class backgrounds to facilitate popular identification. An official inquiry by the police staff associations succinctly summarized this conception: 'traditional British policing is relatively low in numbers, low on power, and high on accountability; . . . it is undertaken with public consent.' (Operational Policing Review 1990: 4).

This image of British policing did not develop because of some peculiar affinity of British culture for civic values. The pacific image of the British bobby was a myth deliberately constructed in order to defuse the virulent opposition which existed to the very idea of police in early nineteenth century Britain. That it succeeded owed at least as much to the long-term process of greater social integration and consensus over the century between the 1850s and the 1950s as to any actions of the police themselves.

By the mid-1950s, however, the police had negotiated a huge degree of public support. This is attested to by the evidence of surveys and much contemporary documentation, indicating a high degree of popular trust for the police, who stood as symbols of the nation. Behind this facade there is much evidence from oral histories and memoirs that in the 'Golden Age' of consent to policing, the treatment of the 'police property' groups at the base of the social hierarchy was rough, ready, and uninhibited by notions of legality or justice (Mark 1978: chs 2–4; Young 1991; Weinberger 1995). Nonetheless the high regard the population in general accorded the police in Britain was unparalleled in the experience of any other country.

In the last thirty years the process of growing acceptance of the police in Britain has been reversed, although the police still remain central symbols of security (Loader and Mulcahy 2003). A number of changes have plunged them into acute controversy and conflict: corruption and miscarriage of justice scandals; accusations of race and sex discrimination; increasing public disorder and the militarization of police tactics (Jefferson 1990; Waddington 2003); rising crime and an apparently declining police ability to deal with it (Morgan and Newburn 1997); decreasing public accountability as forces have grown larger, more centralized, and more reliant on technology (Reiner 2000: ch. 2). Police leaders recognized this problem and introduced reforms to deal with it, professionalizing management, improving training, streamlining working procedures, and becoming more open to the public through consultation of various kinds. None of this self-engineered change has been sufficient to satisfy recent governments.

The political space for government reform of the police comes from the decline in public support (Fitzgerald *et al.* 2002), although this remains resilient compared to other institutions (Loader and Mulcahy 2003). In recent times the police have been widely perceived as guilty of systematic malpractice as well as falling down on the job, despite generous treatment in terms of pay and conditions compared to other public services. The prospects for reversing this decline by the government's reform agenda are doubtful. Their strategy rests upon a fundamental misconception of policing, which whilst commonly shared, has for many years been called into question by research. The premise underlying current initiatives is that—if properly organized—policing *can* have a significant impact on crime levels, deterring crime in the first place by uniform patrol, and detecting criminals efficiently after the event if crimes do occur. This can be referred to as the rational deterrent model of policing.

By this standard it certainly seems at first sight that the police in Britain are far less efficient and effective than they used to be, despite large increases in resources. In the period since the Second World War recorded crime levels have increased inexorably, albeit with some decline in recent years. The proportion of crimes cleared up by the police has fallen dramatically over the same period. Whilst the clear-up rate is a notoriously inadequate measure of police performance, the decline in it has been politically damaging for the police, and exposed them to the government's current policing initiatives.

There is, however, a substantial body of research evidence, much of it emanating from the Home Office Research and Planning Unit, suggesting that policing resources and tactics have a tenuous relationship to levels of crime or the clear-up rate (Clarke and Hough 1980, 1984; Bayley 1994; Morgan and Newburn 1997; Reiner 2000: ch. 4). Innovative strategies may have some impact, as reviewed earlier, but are unlikely to have a major effect on the overall levels of crime. The police are primarily managers of crime and keepers of the peace, not a vehicle for reducing crime substantially. Crime is the product of deeper social forces, largely beyond the ambit of any policing tactics, and the clear-up rate is a function of crime levels and other aspects of workload rather than police efficiency.

Underlying the many specific causes of controversy over policing, such as malpractice, militarization, or apparently declining effectiveness, there is a deeper and more fundamental change in contemporary society, variously characterized as 'post' or 'late' or 'liquid' modernity, globalization, neo-liberalism, or risk society (see Loader and Sparks, Chapter 3, this volume). We saw earlier that the rise of a specific organization specializing in policing functions coincided with the development of modern nation states, and was an aspect of the process by which they sought to gain centralized control over a particular territory. This was particularly true of the British case where bureaucratic police organizations came into being comparatively late by European standards and coincided with the historical trajectory towards greater social integration after the initial impact of the Industrial Revolution. The British police have always been unique on a comparative scale for concentrating in the same organization a variety of policing functions—crime prevention, detection, peace-keeping, public order maintenance, and the preservation of state security, which in other countries are divided between separate bodies. In all societies the symbolic functions of the police are at least as important as their direct instrumental effectiveness in dealing with crime and disorder. This is particularly true in Britain, where the police came to stand—together with the monarchy whose peace they are sworn to protect—as symbols of consensual and legitimate order.

The position of the police as an organization symbolizing national unity and order is threatened by social changes transforming the modern world economically, socially, politically, and culturally. Consumerism becomes the driving force of action, and the social structure follows a dynamic of fragmentation, dis-organization, pluralism, and de-centring (Giddens 1990). Economic changes have transformed the economic and social framework, dispersing and globalizing the centralized 'Fordist' production systems of modern times, and increasing economic inequality. Whilst the majority participate, albeit very unevenly and insecurely, in unprecedented levels of consumption, a substantial and growing 'underclass' is permanently and hopelessly excluded (Taylor 1999; Young 1999). Certainly with the political dominance of free-market economic policies there is no prospect at all of their incorporation into the general social order. In other words, the 'police property' group grow far larger than ever before, and more fundamentally alienated. This economic fragmentation interacts with a long and complex process of cultural diversification, declining deference, erosion of moral absolutes, 'desubordination' (Miliband 1978), and growing anomie to create a more turbulent, disorderly social world.

In this context, the British conception of the police as a body with an omnibus mandate, symbolizing order and harmony, becomes increasingly anachronistic but also more vital to many as the sole remaining national symbol (Loader and Mulcahy 2003). The British police are likely to move more towards the international pattern of specialist national units for serious crime, terrorism, public order, large-scale fraud, and other national or international problems. Local police providing services to particular communities will remain, but with sharp differences between 'service'-style organizations in stable suburban areas, and 'watchman' bodies with the rump duties of the present police, keeping the lid on underclass crime in symbolic locations.

For those in society who can afford it, provision of security will be increasingly privatized, either in residential areas or in the 'mass private property' sector where more and more middle-class leisure and work takes place (Shearing and Stenning 1983; South 1988; Johnston 1992, 2000; Jones and Newburn 1998; Button 2007). Specialized human policing in any form, however, will become a smaller part of an array of impersonal control processes built into the environment, technological control, and surveillance devices, and the guarding and self-policing activities of ordinary citizens. *The* police will be replaced by a pluralized assortment of bodies with policing functions, and a more diffuse array of policing processes, as discussed above. The extent to which this represents a qualitative transformation to a fundamentally new mode of policing can be debated (Bayley and Shearing 1996; Jones and Newburn 2002; Johnston and Shearing 2002). But the profound changes in social structure, culture, crime, and order in an age of increasing global interdependence and insecurity are bound to have momentous implications for the policing that seeks to regulate them.

■ SELECTED FURTHER READING

The most comprehensive coverage of policing issues is in the *Handbook of Policing* edited by Tim Newburn (Cullompton: Willan, 2003), its accompanying reader, *Policing: Key Readings*, (Cullompton: Willan, 2005), and in the third edition of Robert Reiner's single authored text,

The Politics of the Police (Oxford: Oxford University Press, 2000). Other single authored volumes with a more specific focus include N. Fielding, *The Police and Social Conflict*, 2nd edn (London: Glasshouse, 2005); P. A. J. Waddington, *Policing Citizens*, (London: UCL Press, 1999), and L. Johnston, *Policing Britain: Risk, Security and Governance* (London: Longman, 2000). A comprehensive collection of classic and recent articles is R. Reiner (ed.), *Policing Vols. I and II* (Aldershot: Dartmouth, 1996).

■ REFERENCES

ANDERSON, M., DEN BOER, M., CULLEN, P., WILLMORE, W., RAAB, C., and WALKER, N. (1995), *Policing the European Union*, Oxford: Oxford University Press.

BANTON, M. (1964), *The Policeman in the Community*, London: Tavistock.

BAYLEY, D. (1985), *Patterns of Policing*, New Brunswick, N.J.: Rutgers University Press.

—— (1994), *Police For The Future*, New York: Oxford University Press.

—— and BITTNER, E. (1984), 'Learning the Skills of Policing', *Law and Contemporary Problems* 47(4)::35–60.

—— and SHEARING, C. (1996), 'The Future of Policing', *Law and Society Review*, 30(3):586–606.

—— and —— (2001), *The Worldwide Restructuring of the Police*, Washington DC: National Institute of Justice.

BECKER, H. (1964), *Outsiders*, New York: Free Press.

—— (1967), 'Whose Side Are We On?', *Social Problems*, 14(3): 239–47.

BECKETT, K. (1997), *Making Crime Pay*, New York: Oxford University Press.

BENNETT, T. (1990), *Evaluating Neighbourhood Watch*, Aldershot: Gower.

BIGO, D. (2000), 'Liaison Officers in Europe: New Officers in the European Security Field', in J. W. E. Sheptycki, *Issues in Transnational Policing*, London: Routledge.

BITTNER, E. (1974), 'Florence Nightingale in Pursuit of Willie Sutton: A Theory of the Police', in H. Jacob (ed.), *The Potential for Reform of Criminal Justice*, Beverly Hills Cal.: Sage.

—— (1970), *The Functions of the Police in Modern Society*, Chevy Chase, Md.: National Institute of Mental Health.

BLAIR, I. (1985), '*Investigating Rape: A New Approach for Police*, London: Croom Helm.

BLAKELY, E. J., and SNYDER, M. G. (1997), *Fortress America: Gated Communities in the United States*, Washington DC: Brookings Institution.

BOBBITT, P. (2002), *The Shield of Achilles*, London: Penguin.

BOWLING, B. (1999a), 'The Rise and Fall of New York Murder', *British Journal of Criminology*, 39(4): 531–54.

—— (1999b), *Violent Racism*, Oxford: Oxford University Press.

—— and NEWBURN, T. (forthcoming), 'Policing and national security', in B. Bowling and J. Fagan (eds), *Police, Community and the Rule of Law*, Oxford: Hart.

—— and PHILLIPS, C. (2002), *Racism, Crime and Justice*, London: Longman.

—— —— (2003), 'Policing Ethnic Minority Communities', in T. Newburn (ed.), *Handbook of Policing*, Cullompton, Devon: Willan.

BRAGA, A. A., WEISBURD, D., WARING, E. J., MAZEROLLE, L., SPELMAN, W., and GAJEWSKI, F. (1999), 'Problem-oriented policing in violent crime/places: A randomized controlled experiment', *Criminology*, 37(3): 541–80.

BRODEUR, J. -P. (ed.) (1995), *Comparisons in Policing*, Aldershot: Avebury.

—— (ed.) (1998), *How to Recognise Good Policing*, Thousand Oaks, Cal.: Sage.

BROGDEN, M. (1982), *The Police: Autonomy and Consent*, London: Academic Press.

—— (1987), 'The Emergence of the Police: The Colonial Dimension', *British Journal of Criminology*, 27(1): 4–14.

—— (1999), 'Community Policing As Cherry Pie', in R. Mawby (ed.), *Policing Across the World*, London: UCL Press.

BROWN, D. (1997), *PACE Ten Years On: A Review of the Research*, Home Office Research Study 155, London: HMSO.

—— and ILES, S. (1985), *Community Constables*, London: Home Office.

BROWN, J. (1996), 'Police Research: Some Critical Issues', in F. Leishman, B. Loveday, and S. Savage (eds), *Core Issues in Policing*, London: Longman.

—— and HEIDENSOHN, F. (2000), *Gender and Policing: Comparative Perspectives*, London: Macmillan.

BROWN, L., and WILLIS, A. (1985), 'Authoritarianism in British Police Recruits: Importation, Socialisation or Myth?',' *Journal of Occupational Psychology*, 58(1): 97–108.

BUCKE, T., STREET, R, and BROWN, D. (2000), *The Right of Silence: The Impact of the CJPO 1994*, Home Office Research Study 199, London: HMSO.

BULLOCK, K., and TILLEY, N. (eds) (2003), *Crime Reduction and Problem-Oriented Policing*, Cullompton, Devon: Willan.

BURROWS, J., and LEWIS, H. (1988), *Directed Patrolwork*, London: HMSO.

BUTTON, M. (2002), *Private Policing*, Cullompton, Devon: Willan.

—— (2007), *Security Officers and Policing*, Aldershot: Avebury.

CAIN, M. (1973), *Society and the Policeman's Role*, London: Routledge.

—— (1979), 'Trends in the Sociology of Police Work', *International Journal of Sociology of Law*, 7(2): 143–67.

CASSELS, J. (1994), *The Role and Responsibilities of the Police: Report of an Independent Inquiry*, London: Police Foundation/Policy Studies Institute.

CHAN, J. (1997), *Changing Police Culture*, Cambridge: Cambridge University Press.

CHATTERTON, M., and ROGERS, M. (1989), 'Focused Policing', in R. Morgan and D. Smith (eds), *Coming to Terms With Policing*, London: Routledge.

CLARKE, R., and HOUGH, M. (eds) (1980), *The Effectiveness of Policing*, Farnborough: Gower.

—— and —— (1984), *Crime and Police Effectiveness*, London: Home Office Research Unit.

COHEN, S. (1985), *Visions of Social Control*, Cambridge: Polity.

COLEMAN, R. (2004), *Reclaiming the Streets*, Cullompton, Devon: Willan.

CRAWFORD, A. (2003), 'The Pattern of Policing in the UK: Policing Beyond the Police', in T. Newburn, *Handbook of Policing*, Cullompton, Devon: Willan.

—— and LISTER, S. (2004), *The Extended Policing Family*, York: Joseph Rowntree Trust.

——, ——, BLACKBURN, S., and BURNETT, J. (2005), *Plural Policing: The Mixed Economy of Visible Patrols in England and Wales*, Bristol: Policy Press.

DALGLEISH, D., and MYHILL, A. (2004), *Reassuring the Public: A review of international policing interventions*, London: Home Office.

DEFLEM, M. (2002), *Policing World Society: Historical Foundations of International Police Co-operation*, Oxford: Clarendon Press.

DELSOL, R., and SHINER, M. (2006), 'Regulating Stop and Search: A Challenge for Police and Community Relations in England and Wales', *Critical Criminology*, 14: 241–63.

DEN BOER, M., and MONAR, J. (2002), '11 September and the Challenge of Global Terrorism to the EU as a Security Actor', *Journal of Common Market Studies*, 40(1): 11–28.

DIXON, B., and SMITH, G. (1998), 'Laying Down the Law: The Police, The Courts and Legal Accountability', *International Journal of the Sociology of Law*, 26: 419–35.

DIXON, D, (1997), *Law in Policing*, Oxford: Oxford University Press.

—— and MAHER, L. (2005), 'Policing, Crime and Public Health: Lessons for Australia From the "New York Miracle" ', *Criminal Justice*, 5: 115–44.

DUBBER, M. (2005), *The Police Power*, New York: Columbia University Press.

DUBOIS, D. (2002), 'The attacks of 11 September: EU-US cooperation against terrorism in the field of justice and home affairs', *European Foreign Affairs Review*, 7: 317–35.

ECK, J. (2006), 'Science, values and problem-oriented policing: why problem-oriented policing?', in D. Weisburd and A. A. Braga (eds), *Police Innovation: Contrasting Perspectives*, Cambridge: Cambridge University Press.

—— and SPELMAN, W. (1987), 'Who ya gonna call? The police as problem-busters', *Crime and Delinquency* January, 31–52.

EDWARDS, A., and GILL, P. (2003), *Transnational Organised Crime*, London: Routledge.

EMSLEY, C. (1996), *The English Police: A Political and Social History*, 2nd edn, Hemel Hempstead: Harvester Wheatsheaf.

—— (2003), 'The Birth and Development of the Police', in T. Newburn (ed.), *Handbook of Policing* Cullompton, Devon: Willan.

ERICSON, R., and HAGGERTY, K. (1997), *Policing Risk Society*, Oxford: Oxford University Press.

EVERSON, S., and PEASE, K. (2001), 'Crime against the same person and place: detection, opportunity and offender targeting', in G. Farrell and K Pease (eds), *Repeat Victimization: Crime Prevention Studies Series 12*, Monsey, N.Y.: Criminal Justice Press.

FARRELL, G., and PEASE, K. (eds) (2001), *Repeat Victimization: Crime Prevention Studies Series 12*, Monsey, N.Y.: Criminal Justice Press.

FELDMAN, D. (1990), 'Regulating Treatment of Suspects in Police Stations: Judicial Interpretation of Detention Provisions in the Police and Criminal Evidence Act 1984', *Criminal Law Review*, 452–571.

FIELDING, N. (1988), *Joining Forces*, London: Routledge.

—— (2005), *The Police and Social Conflict*, 2nd edn, London: Glasshouse.

FITZGERALD, M. (1999), *Searches in London Under Section 1 of the Police and Criminal Evidence Act*, London: Metropolitan Police.

—— HOUGH, M., JOSEPH, I., and QURESHI, T. (2002), *Policing for London*, Cullompton, Devon: Willan.

FOSTER, J. (1989), 'Two Stations: An Ethnographic Analysis of Policing in the Inner City', in D. Downes (ed.), *Crime and the City*, London: Macmillan.

—— (2003), 'Police Cultures', in T. Newburn (ed.), *Handbook of Policing*, Cullompton, Devon: Willan.

—— NEWBURN, T., and SOUHAMI, A. (2005), *Assessing the Impact of the Stephen Lawrence Enquiry*, London: Home Office.

FYFE, N. R., and BANNISTER, J. (1996), 'City watching: closed circuit television in public spaces', *Area*, 28(1): 37–46.

GIDDENS, A. (1990), *The Consequences of Modernity*, Cambridge: Polity Press.

GOLDSMITH, A., and LEWIS, C. (2000), *Civilian Oversight of Policing*, Oxford: Hart.

GOLDSTEIN, H. (1990), *Problem-Oriented Policing*, New York: McGraw Hill.

GOLDSTEIN, J. (1960), 'Police Discretion Not To Invoke the Criminal Process: Low Visibility Decisions in the Administration of Justice', *Yale Law Journal*, 69, March: 543–94.

GRAEF, R. (1989), *Talking Blues*, London: Collins.

GREENE, J. (2000), 'Community Policing in America', in J. Horney (ed.), *Criminal Justice 2000 Vol. 3: Policies, Processes and Decisions of the Criminal Justice System*, Washington, DC: National Institute of Justice.

GREGORY, J., and LEES, S. (1999), *Policing Sexual Assault*, London: Routledge.

GRIMSHAW, R., and JEFFERSON, T. (1987), *Interpreting Policework*, London: Unwin.

HAIN, P. (ed.) (1979), *Policing the Police*, London: Calder.

—— (ed.) (1980), *Policing the Police 2*, London: Calder.

HALL, S., CRITCHER, C., JEFFERSON, T., CLARKE, J., and ROBERTS, B. (1978), *Policing the Crisis*, London: Macmillan.

HARCOURT, B. (2001), *Illusion of Order: The False Promise of Broken Windows Policing*, Cambridge, Mass.: Harvard University Press.

HEIDENSOHN, F. (1985), *Women and Crime*, London: Macmillan.

—— (1992), *Women in Control? The Role of Women in Law Enforcement*, Oxford: Oxford University Press.

—— (2003), 'Gender and Policing', in T. Newburn (ed.), *Handbook of Policing*, Cullompton, Devon: Willan.

HER MAJESTY'S INSPECTORATE OF CONSTABULARY (2004), *Modernising the Police Service*, London: HMIC.

—— (2005), *Closing the Gap*, London: HMIC.

HOBBS, D. (1988), *Doing the Business: Entrepr-eneurship, The Working Class and detectives in the East End of London*, Oxford: Oxford University Press.

—— (1998), 'Going down the Glocal: the local context of organized crime', *Howard Journal of Criminal Justice*, 37(4): 407–22.

HOLDAWAY, S. (ed.) (1979), *The British Police*, London: Edward Arnold.

—— (1983), *Inside the British Police*, Oxford: Blackwell.

—— (1996), *The Racialisation of British Policing*, London: Macmillan.

HOME OFFICE (1993), *Police Reform White Paper*, London: Home Office.

—— (2001), *Secure Borders, Safe Haven: Integration with diversity in modern Britain*, London: Home Office.

HOUSE OF COMMONS (1990), *Practical Police Cooper-ation in the European Community*, Home Affairs Committee (7th Report), Session 1989–90, London: HMSO.

HOYLE, C. (1998), *Negotiating Domestic Violence: Police, Criminal Justice and Victims*, Oxford: Oxford University Press.

HUSAIN, S. (1988), *Neighbourhood Watch in England and Wales*, Crime Prevention Unit Paper No.12, London: Home Office.

HUTTER, B. (1988), *The Reasonable Arm of the Law? Law Enforcement Procedures of Environmental Health Officers*, Oxford: Oxford University Press.

IANNI, E. R., and IANNI, F. (1983), 'Street Cops and Management Cops: The Two Cultures of Policing', in M. Punch (ed.), *Control in the Police Organisation*, Cambridge, Mass.: MIT Press.

INNES, M. (2003), *Understanding Social Control*, Maidenhead: Open University Press.

—— (ed.) (2006), 'Reassurance and the "New" Community Policing', Special Issue, *Policing and Society* 16(2).

—— and FIELDING, N. (2002), 'From Community to Communication Policing: "Signal Crimes" and the Problem of Public Reassurance', *Sociological Research Online*, 7(2).

IRVING, B., BIRD, C., HIBBERD, M., and WILLMORE, J. (1989), *Neighbourhood Policing*, London: Police Foundation.

JEFFERSON, T. (1990), *The Case Against Paramilitary Policing*, Milton Keynes: Open University Press.

JOHNSTON, L. (1992), *The Rebirth of Private Policing*, London: Routledge.

—— (2000), *Policing Britain*, London: Longman.

—— (2006), 'Transnational security governance', in J. Wood and B. Dupont (eds), *Democracy, Society and the Governance of Security*, Cambridge: Cambridge University Press.

—— and SHEARING, C. (2002), *Governing Security*, London: Routledge.

JONES, S. (1987), *Policewomen and Equality*, London: Macmillan.

—— and LEVI, M. (1983), 'The Police and the Majority: The Neglect of the Obvious', *Police Journal*, 56(4): 351–64.

JONES, T., and NEWBURN, T. (1998), *Private Security and Public Policing*, Oxford: Oxford University Press.

—— and —— (1999), 'Urban Change and Policing: Mass Private Property Reconsidered', *European Journal of Criminal Policy and Research*, 7(2): 225–44.

—— and —— (2002), 'The Transformation of Policing? Understanding Current Trends in Policing Systems', *British Journal of Criminology*, 42(1): 129–46.

—— and —— (2006a), 'Understanding plural policing', in T. Jones and T. Newburn (eds), *Plural Policing: A Comparative Perspective*, London: Routledge.

—— and —— (2006b), 'The United Kingdom', in T. Jones and T. Newburn (eds), *Plural Policing: A Compara-tive Perspective*, London: Routledge.

—— and —— (2007), *Policy Transfer and Criminal Justice*, Buckingham: Open University.

—— —— and SMITH, D. (1994), *Demo-cracy and Policing*, London: Policy Studies Institute.

KARMEN, A. (2000), *New York Murder Mystery*, New York: New York University Press.

KELLING, G. *et al.* (1974), *The Kansas City Preventive Patrol Experiment*, Washington, DC: Police Foundation.

KEMP, C., NORRIS, C., and FIELDING, N. (1992), *Negotiating Nothing: Police Decision-Making in Disputes*, Aldershot: Avebury.

KEYNOTE REPORT (2004), *The Security Industry: Industry Report*, September 2004 (see also www.keynote.co.uk).

KIRWAN, S., and BIBI, N. (2006), *Police Service Strength, England and Wales, 30th September 2005*, London: Home Office.

KLOCKARS, C. (1988), 'The Rhetoric of Community Policing', in J. R. Greene and S. D. Mastrofski (eds), *Community Policing: Rhetoric or Reality?*, New York: Praeger.

LAVRANOS, N. (2003), 'Europol and the fight against terrorism', *European Foreign Affairs Review*, 8: 259–75.

LEE, J. A. (1981), 'Some Structural aspects of Police Deviance in Relations With Minority Groups', in C. Shearing (ed.), *Organisational Police Deviance*, Toronto: Butterworth.

LEISHMAN, F., and MASON, P. (2003), *Policing and the Media*, Cullompton, Devon: Willan.

LEVI, M. (2003), 'Organised and Financial Crime', in T. Newburn (ed.), *Handbook of Policing*, Cullompton, Devon: Willan.

LOADER, I. (1999), 'Consumer Culture and the Commodification of Policing and Security', *Sociology*, 33(2): 373–92.

—— and MULCAHY, A. (2003), *Policing and the Condition of England*, Oxford: Oxford University Press.

—— and WALKER, N. (2006), 'Necessary virtues: the legitimate place of the state in the governance of security', in J. Wood and B. Dupont (eds), *Democracy, Society and the Governance of Security*, Cambridge: Cambridge University Press.

LOVEDAY, B. (2006), *Size Isn't Everything: Restructuring Policing in England and Wales*, London: Policy Exchange.

LUSTGARTEN, L. (1986), *The Governance of the Police*, London: Sweet & Maxwell.

Lyon, D. (2001), *Surveillance Society*, Maidenhead: Open University Press.

McBarnet, D. (1978) 'The Police and the State', in G. Littlejohn, B. Smart, J. Wakeford, and N. Yuval-Davis (eds), *Power and the State*, London: Croom Helm.

—— (1979) 'Arrest: The Legal Context of Policing', in S. Holdaway (ed.), *The British Police*, London: Edward Arnold.

McCahill, M. (2002), *The Surveillance Web*, Cullompton, Devon: Willan.

McConville, M., and Shepherd, D. (1992), *Watching Police, Watching Communities*, London: Routledge.

——, Sanders, A. and Leng, R. (1991), *The Case for the Prosecution: Police Suspects and the Construction of Criminality*, London: Routledge.

McEvoy, K., Gormally, B., and Mika, H. (2002), 'Conflict, crime control and the "re"-constitution of state-community relations in Northern Ireland', in G. Hughes, E. McLaughlin, and J. Muncie (eds), *Crime Prevention and Community Safety: New Directions*, London: Sage.

McLaughlin, E. (1992), 'The Democratic Deficit: European Unity and the Accountability of the British Police', *British Journal of Criminology*, 32(4): 473–87.

—— (2005), 'Forcing the Issue: New Labour, New Localism and the Democratic Renewal of Police Accountability', *Howard Journal*, 44(5): 473–89.

—— (2006), *The New Policing*, London: Sage.

—— and Murji, K. (2001), 'Lost Connections and New Directions: Neo-liberalism, New Public Managerialism, and the "Modernisation" of the British Police', in K. Stenson and R. Sullivan (eds), *Crime, Risk and Justice*, Cullompton, Devon: Willan.

—— Muncie, J., and Hughes, G. (2001), 'The Permanent Revolution: New Labour, New Public management and the Modernization of Criminal Justice', *Criminal Justice*, 1: 301–18.

Maguire, M. (2000), 'Policing By Risks And Targets: Some Dimensions and Implications of Intelligence-led Crime Control', *Policing and Society*, 9: 315–36.

—— (2003), 'Criminal Investigation and Crime Control', in T. Newburn, *Handbook of Policing*, Cullompton, Devon: Willan.

—— and Corbett, C. (1991), *A Study of the Police Complaints System*, London: HMSO.

—— and Norris, C. (1992), *The Conduct and Supervision of Criminal Investigations*, London: HMSO.

Manning, P. K. (2000), 'Policing new social spaces', in Sheptycki, J. W. E. (ed.), *Issues in Transnational Policing*, London: Routledge.

Marenin, O. (1983), 'Parking Tickets and Class Repression: The Concept of Policing in Critical Theories of Criminal Justice', *Contemporary Crises*, 6(2): 241–66.

Mark, R. (1978), *In the Office of Constable*, London: Collins.

Marshall, G. (1978), 'Police Accountability Revisited', in D. Butler and A. H. Halsey (eds), *Policy and Politics*, London: Macmillan.

Mastrofski, S. (2006), 'Community policing: A sceptical view', in D. Weisburd and A. A. Braga (eds), *Police Innovation: Contrasting Perspectives*, Cambridge: Cambridge University Press.

Matassa, M., and Newburn, T. (2003), 'Policing and Terrorism', in T. Newburn (ed.), *Handbook of Policing*, Cullompton, Devon: Willan.

Mawby, R. I. (1991), *Comparative Policing Issues*, London: Unwin.

—— (2003), 'Models of Policing', in T. Newburn (ed.), *Handbook of Policing*, Cullompton, Devon: Willan.

—— and Wright, A. (2003), 'The Police Organisation', in T. Newburn (ed.), *Handbook of Policing*, Cullompton, Devon: Willan.

Miliband, R. (1978), 'A State of Desubordination', *British Journal of Sociology*, 29(4): 399–409.

Miller, W. (1977), *Cops and Bobbies*, Chicago: Chicago University Press.

Moore, M. (1992), 'Problem-Solving and Community Policing', in M. Tonry and N. Morris (eds), *Modern Policing*, Chicago: Chicago University Press.

Morgan, R., and Newburn, T. (1997), *The Future of Policing*, Oxford: Oxford University Press.

Muir, W. K. (1977), *The Police: Streetcorner Politicians*, Chicago: Chicago University Press.

Mulcahy, A. (2006), *Policing Northern Ireland: Conflict, legitimacy and reform*, Cullompton, Devon: Willan

Nadelmann, E. (1993), *Cops Across Borders: The internationalization of U.S. criminal law enforcement*, University Park, Pa.: Penn State Press.

Neocleous, M. (2000), *The Fabrication of Social Order*, London: Pluto.

Newburn, T. (ed.) (2003), *Handbook of Policing*, Cullompton, Devon: Willan.

—— (ed.) (2005), *Policing: Key Readings*, Cullompton, Devon: Willan.

NEWBURN, T., and JONES, T. (1996), 'Police Accountability', in W. Saulsbury, J. Mott, and T. Newburn (eds), *Themes in Contemporary Policing*, London: Police Foundation: Policy Studies Institute.

—— and SPARKS, R. (eds) (2004), *Criminal Justice and Political Cultures*, Cullompton, Devon: Willan.

NEYROUD, P. (2001), *Public Participation in Policing*, London: Institute for Public Policy Research.

—— and BECKLEY, A. (2001), *Policing, Ethics and Human Rights*, Cullompton, Devon: Willan.

NORRIS, C., MCCAHILL, M., and WOOD, D. (2004), 'The growth of CCTV: a global perspective on the international diffusion of video surveillance in publicly accessible space', *Surveillance and Society*, 2 (2/3): 111–35.

OPERATIONAL POLICING REVIEW (1990), Joint Consultative Committee of the Police Staff Associations, Surbiton, Surrey: The Police Federation.

PACKER, H. (1968), *The Limits of the Criminal Sanction*, Stanford, Cal.: Stanford University Press and Oxford University Press.

PALMER, S. H. (1988), *Police and Protest in England and Ireland 1780–1850*, Cambridge: Cambridge University Press.

PATE, A. M., and SKOGAN, W. G. (1985), *Coordinated community policing: The Newark experience. Technical report*, Washington, DC: Police Foundation.

PATTEN, C. (1999), *A New Beginning: Policing Northern Ireland*, The Report of the Independent Commission on Policing For Northern Ireland. Norwich: HMSO.

POSEN, I. (1995), *Review of Police Core and Ancillary Tasks*, London: HMSO.

POWER, M. (1999), *The Audit Society*, Oxford: Oxford University Press.

PUNCH, M. (1979), 'The Secret Social Service', in S. Holdaway (ed.), *The British Police*, London: Edward: Arnold.

—— (1983), 'Officers and Men' in M. Punch (ed.), *Control in the Police Organisation*, Cambridge, Mass.: MIT Press.

QUINTON, P., BLAND, N., and MILLER, J. (2000), Police Stops, Decision-Making and Practice, *Police Research Paper 130*, London: Home Office.

RAWLINGS, P. (1991), 'Creeping Privatisation? The Police, the Conservative Government and Policing in the Late 1980s', in R. Reiner and M. Cross (eds), *Beyond Law and Order*, London: Macmillan.

—— (2003), 'Policing before the Police', in T. Newburn (ed.), *Handbook of Policing*, Cullompton, Devon: Willan.

READ, T., and TILLEY, N. (2000), *Not Rocket Science: Problem-solving and Crime Reduction*, Crime Reduction Series Paper No. 6, London: Home Office.

REINER, R. (1978), *The Blue-Coated Worker*, Cambridge: Cambridge University Press.

—— (1991), *Chief Constables*, Oxford: Oxford University Press.

—— (1993), 'Race, Crime and Justice: Models of Interpretation', in L. Gelsthorpe and W. McWilliams (eds), *Minority Ethnic Groups and the Criminal Justice System*, Cambridge: Institute of Criminology.

—— (2000), *The Politics of the Police*, 3rd edn, Oxford: Oxford University Press.

—— (2003), 'Policing and the Media', in T. Newburn, ed., *Handbook of Policing*, Cullompton, Devon: Willan.

—— and LEIGH, L. (1992), 'Police Power', in G. Chambers, and C. McCrudden (eds), *Individual Rights in the UK Since 1945*, Oxford: Oxford University Press/Law Society.

—— and NEWBURN, T. (2006), 'Police Research', in R. King and E. Wincup (eds), *Doing Research on Crime and Justice*, 2nd edn, Oxford: Oxford University Press.

—— and SPENCER, S. (eds) (1993), *Accountable Policing: Effectiveness, Empowerment and Equity*, London: Institute for Public Policy Research.

REITH, C. (1956), *A New Study of Police History*, London: Oliver and Boyd.

ROBINSON, C. D. (1978), 'The Deradicalisation of the Policeman', *Crime and Delinquency*, 24(2): 129–51.

—— (1979), 'Ideology As History', *Police Studies*, 2(2): 35–49.

—— and SCAGLION, R. (1987), 'The Origin and Evolution of the Police Function in Society', *Law and Society Review*, 21(1): 109–53.

ROCHE, S. (2002), 'Towards a new governance of crime and insecurity in France', in A. Crawford (ed.), *Crime and Insecurity: The governance of safety in Europe*, Cullompton, Devon: Willan

ROSE, D. (1996), *In the Name of the Law: The Collapse of Criminal Justice*, London: Cape.

ROSSI, P., BERK, R., and EIDSON, B. (1974), *The Roots of Urban Discontent*, New York: Wiley.

ROYAL COMMISSION ON THE POLICE (1962), *Final Report*, Cmnd. 1728, London: HMSO.

ROYAL COMMISSION ON CRIMINAL JUSTICE (1993), *Report*, Cm. 2263, London: HMSO.

SANDERS, A., and YOUNG, R. (2003), 'Police Powers', in T. Newburn (ed.), *Handbook of Policing*, Cullompton, Devon: Willan.

SCARMAN, LORD (1981), *The Brixton Disorders*, Cmnd. 8427, London: HMSO.

SCHWARTZ, R. D., and MILLER, J. C. (1964), 'Legal Evolution and Societal Complexity', *American Journal of Sociology*, 70(1): 159–69.

SCOTT, M. (2000), *Problem-oriented Policing: Reflections on the First 20 Years*, Washington, DC: Department of Justice.

SCRATON, P. (1985), *The State of the Police*, London: Pluto.

SHAPLAND, J., and HOBBS, R. (1989), 'Policing on the Ground', in R. Morgan and D. Smith (eds), *Coming To Terms with Policing*, London: Routledge.

—— and VAGG, J. (1988), *Policing By the Public*, London: Routledge.

SHEARING, C. (1996), 'Reinventing Policing: Policing as Governance', in O. Marenin (ed.), *Policing Change, Changing Police*, New York: Garland.

—— and ERICSON, R. (1991), 'Culture As Figurative Action', *British Journal of Sociology*, 42: 481–506.

—— and STENNING, P. (1981), 'Modern Private Security: Its Growth and Implication', in M. Tonry and N. Morris (eds), *Crime and Justice 3*, Chicago: Chicago University Press.

—— and —— (1983), 'Private Security: Implications for Social Control', *Social Problems*, 30(5): 493–506.

SHEEHY, P. (1993), *Inquiry Into Police Responsibilities and Rewards*, London: Home Office (the Sheehy Report).

SHEPTYCKI, J. (ed.) (2000a), *Issues in Transnational Policing*, London: Routledge.

—— (2000b), 'Policing the virtual launderette: money laundering and global governance', in J. Sheptycki (ed.), *Issues in Transnational Policing*, London: Routledge.

SHERMAN, L. W. (1990), 'Police crackdowns: Initial and residual deterrence', in *Crime and justice: A review of research*, vol. 12, ed. by M. Tonry and N. Morris, Chicago: University of Chicago Press.

—— (1992), *Policing Domestic Violence: Exper-iments and Policy Dilemmas*, New York: Free Press.

—— and WEISBURD, D. (1995), 'General deterrent effects of police patrol in crime "hot spots": A randomized, controlled trial', *Justice Quarterly*, 12(4): 625–48.

SILVER, A. (1967), 'The Demand For Order in Civil Society', in D. Bordua (ed.), *The Police*, New York: Wiley.

SINGER, P. W. (2003), *Corporate Warriors, The Rise of the Privatized Military Industry*, Ithaca, N.Y.: Cornell University Press.

SKLANSKY, D. (2005), 'Police and Democracy', *Michigan Law Review*, 103(7): 1699–1830.

SKOGAN, W. (2006), 'The promise of community polic-ing', in D. Weisburd and A. A. Braga (eds), *Police Innovation: Contrasting Perspectives*, Cambridge: Cambridge University Press.

—— and HARTNETT, S. (1997), *Community Policing, Chicago Style*, New York: Oxford University Press.

SKOLNICK, J. (1966), *Justice Without Trial*, New York: Wiley.

—— and BAYLEY, D. (1986), *The New Blue Line*, New York: Free Press.

—— and —— (1988), *Community Policing: Issues and Practices Around the World*, Washington, DC: National Institute of Justice.

SMITH, D., (ed.) (2006), *Police and People Twenty Years On*, Aldershot: Ashgate.

——, GRAY, J., and SMALL, S. (1983), *Police and People in London*, London: Policy Studies Institute.

SMITH, G. (2003), 'Actions for Damages Against the Police and the Attitudes of Complainants', *Policing and Society*, 13(4): 413–22.

—— (2004), 'Rethinking Police Complaints', *British Journal of Criminology*, 44(1): 15–33.

SOUTH, N. (1988), *Policing For Profit*, London: Sage.

SPITZER, S. (1975), 'Punishment and Social Organisation: A Study of Durkheim's Theory of Evolution', *Law and Society Review*, 9(4): 613–37.

—— and SCULL, A. (1977), 'Social Control in Historical Perspective', in D. Greenberg (ed.), *Corrections and Punishment*, Beverly Hills Cal.: Sage.

STINCHCOMBE, A. (1963), 'Institutions of Privacy in the Determination of Police Administrative Practice', *American Journal of Sociology*, 69(2): 150–60.

STORCH, R. (1975), 'The Plague of Blue Locusts: Police reform and Popular resistance in northern England 1840–1857', *International Review of Social History*, 20(1): 61–90.

STORCH, R. (1976), 'The Policeman as Domestic Missionary', *Journal of Social History*, 9(4): 481–509.

SYDNEY-SMITH, S. (2002), *Beyond Dixon of Dock Green*, London: I.B. Taurus.

TAYLOR, I. (1999), *Crime in Context*, Cambridge: Polity.

——, WALTON, P. and YOUNG, J. (1973), *The New Criminology*, London: Routledge.

TEMKIN, J. (2002), *Rape and the Legal Process*, 2nd edn, Oxford: Oxford University Press.

TILLEY, N. (2003), 'Community Policing, Problem-Oriented Policing and Intelligence-Led Policing', in T. Newburn (ed.), *Handbook of Policing*, Cullompton, Devon: Willan.

TROJANOWICZ, R., and BUCQUEROUX, B. (1990), *Community Policing*, Cincinnati, Ohio: Anderson Publishing.

TUFFIN, R., MORRIS, J., and POOLE, A. (2006), *An Evaluation of the Impact of the National Reassurance Policing Programme*, London: Home Office.

VAN STEDEN, R., and HUBERTS, L. (2006), 'The Netherlands', in T. Jones and T. Newburn (eds), *Plural Policing: A Comparative Perspective*, London: Routledge.

WADDINGTON, P. A. J. (1999a), *Policing Citizens*, London: UCL Press.

—— (1999b), 'Police (Canteen) Sub-culture: An Appreciation', *British Journal of Criminology*, 39(2): 287–309.

—— (2003), 'Policing Public Order and Political Contention', in T. Newburn, (ed.), *Handbook of Policing*, Cullompton, Devon: Willan.

——, STENSON, K., and DON, D. (2004), 'In Proportion: Race and Police Stop and Search', *British Journal of Criminology*, 44(6): 889–914.

WAKEFIELD, A. (2003), *Selling Security*, Cullompton, Devon: Willan.

WALKER, N. (2000), *Policing in a Changing Constitutional Order*, London: Sweet & Maxwell.

—— (2003), 'The Pattern of Transnational Policing', in T. Newburn (ed.), *Handbook of Policing*, Cullompton, Devon: Willan.

WALL, D. (1998), The Chief Constables of England and Wales, Aldershot: Avebury.

WEINBERGER, B. (1995), *The Best Police in the World*, London: Scolar.

WEISBURD, D., and ECK, J. E. (2004), 'What can the police do to reduce crime, disorder and fear?', *The Annals*, 593, (May): 42–65.

WESTLEY, W. (1970), *Violence and the Police*, Cambridge, Mass.: MIT Press.

WILLIAMS, J. W. (2005), 'Reflections of the private versus public policing of economic crime', *British Journal of Criminology*, 45(3): 316–39.

WILSON, J. Q. (1968), *Varieties of Police Behaviour*, Cambridge, Mass.: Harvard University Press.

—— and KELLING, G. (1982), 'Broken Windows', *Atlantic Monthly*, 249(3): 29–42.

YOUNG, J. (1999), *The Exclusive Society*, London: Sage.

YOUNG, M. (1991), *An Inside Job*, Oxford: Oxford University Press.

—— (1993), *In the Sticks: An Anthropologist in a Shire Force*, Oxford: Oxford University Press.

ZEDNER, L. (2006), 'Policing Before the Police', *British Journal of Criminology*, 46(1): 78–96.

28

FROM SUSPECT TO TRIAL

Andrew Sanders and Richard Young

This chapter looks at the use of legal powers in the criminal justice system of England and Wales. The principles underlying different criminal justice systems vary according to history, culture, and ideology. The adversary principle underpins the English system, other common law systems such as those of Australia, Canada, and the United States, and 'hybrid' systems such as in Scotland. Thus, much of what follows draws upon what we know of, and applies to, these other systems, although the focus is domestic.

We examine various models of criminal justice, police decisions 'on the street' (primarily to stop/search and to arrest), aspects of police station detention (including police questioning, the right of silence, and access to legal advice), decisions to prosecute and caution, and the pre-trial process (bail, plea bargaining, and disclosure). Although we do not look at trials as such, the main processes in most cases are covered as the overwhelming majority of prosecutions are settled by guilty pleas or (more rarely) are dropped by the Crown Prosecution Service (CPS). Throughout the chapter we contrast the police with other enforcement agencies, and the 'law in the books' with the way law-enforcement bodies actually work.

Most police actions and court cases are in all probability unproblematic. Inevitably, though, this chapter highlights the problems—for it is little consolation to someone who is constantly stop-searched, or to an innocent person who is found guilty, that they are unusual and that the system generally works well. Unfortunately space constraints mean that we cannot discuss appeals and remedies for police malpractice although these are covered in Sanders and Young (2006 chs 11 and 12). However, we draw attention to some of the faults of these review systems in the conclusion, where we identify the main operating aims of the criminal justice system.

MODELS OF CRIMINAL JUSTICE

The adversary principle is often characterized as embodying the search for 'proof' rather than 'truth' (Damaska 1973). The search for 'truth' is usually said to be embodied in 'civil law' systems (such as the French), which are 'inquisitorial'. It would be nice if 'proof' and 'truth' were synonymous and sought with equal vigour, as a leading Chief Constable once advocated (Pollard 1996). But, using the 'due process' and 'crime control' models developed by Packer (1968), we will see that this is unrealistic.

'Due process' values prioritize civil liberties in order to secure the maximal acquittal of the innocent, risking acquittal of many guilty people. 'Crime control' values prioritize the conviction of the guilty, risking the conviction of some (fewer) innocents and infringement of the liberties of some citizens to achieve the system's goals. Due-process-based systems tightly control the actions and effects of crime-control agencies, while crime-control-based systems, with their concern for convictions, do not. No system can correspond exactly with either model (just as no system is entirely adversarial or entirely inquisitorial), but in most systems the values of one or the other model appear to predominate.

As soon as the police challenge any individual whom they have any reason to suspect, an adversarial relationship is formed. In Britain, this triggers due-process protections, such as the caution against self-incrimination and the usual requirement of 'reasonable' suspicion for the exercise of coercive powers. On arrest the suspect is generally taken to a police station and detained. This triggers further due-process protections, such as a right of access to lawyers, as civil liberties are further eroded by detention, interrogation, search of the suspect's home, fingerprinting, and so forth. At the prosecution stage, further evidence is required and further protections are provided: the CPS to vet the case and legal aid to prepare a defence. In order to convict there must be yet more evidence. So, due-process requirements become more stringent at each stage, in parallel with the increased coerciveness of suspicion, accusation, and trial. Suspects may be believed to be guilty by the police, and may indeed be guilty 'in truth'. But in the absence of sufficient evidence (i.e. sufficient proof) due process requires that they be exonerated. At the final stage proof need not be absolute, but only 'beyond reasonable doubt'. Legal guilt and actual guilt are therefore not synonymous. Even in a due process system there will occasionally be legally guilty persons who are not 'actually' guilty, and many actually guilty persons who are not legally guilty. This means that all systems will produce some cases like the infamous 'miscarriage' cases of the last twenty-five years: the Birmingham Six, Guildford Four, Bridgewater Four, West Midlands Police Serious Crime Squad cases, and so forth. Whether or not these are evidence of system failure depends on how often they occur, why they occur, and whether there are adequate systems of review and appeal.

One difference between the different models lies in their methods of discovery of the truth and their degrees of success. Doubts about, for instance, the way each side in the adversarial trial guards 'its' evidence lead critics to argue for more 'transparency' in the pursuit of truth (Pollard 1996), while doubts about the impartiality of inquisitorial systems reveal different ways in which the truth can be obscured (Hodgson 2001). Similarly, doubts about police efficiency and propriety on the part of advocates of due process lead them to argue for the process of legal proof; while advocates of crime control argue that court processes and legal protections obstruct truth discovery.

Despite the clarification provided by Packer's models, their value is limited. In particular, they do not attempt to prescribe what the goals of the criminal process should be. Ashworth and Redmayne (2005) make such an attempt by developing a framework of ethical principles derived from the European Convention on Human Rights (ECHR). This is valuable, particularly as the Human Rights Act 1998 makes the ECHR applicable to all areas of UK law, but it creates as many problems as it solves. For example, Ashworth and Redmayne's principles include rights for victims ('to respect' and 'to compensation') that are major lacunae in Packer's models, but little guidance is provided on how to reconcile these rights with those of suspects and defendants when conflicts occur (Cape 2004). Other rights are reformulations of key due-process principles. Many of them are vague, such as 'to be treated fairly and without discrimination' and 'reasonable grounds for arrest and detention'. Those that are precise, such as the 'right of innocent persons not to be convicted', are not absolute, but may be undercut by the kinds of considerations one finds in the crime-control model.

Another promising framework is that of social integration and exclusion. Faulkner (1996) characterizes the 'exclusion' approach as one whereby 'crime is to be prevented by efficiency of detection, certainty of conviction and severity of punishment. . . . "criminals" are to be seen as an "enemy" to be defeated and humiliated, in a "war" in which the police are seen as the "front line" '. He contrasts this with Locke's view, that 'the end of law is not to abolish or restrain but to preserve and enlarge freedom'. On this inclusionary approach, 'authority will not be respected if it is simply imposed: it has to be accountable and it has to be legitimate. . . . solutions to the problem of crime have to be sought by inclusion within the community itself' (ibid.: 6). This position is compatible with forms of 'restorative justice' that bring together all 'stakeholders' in an offence (including the victim) to discuss how the harm caused by the offender can be 'repaired' (there is no space in this chapter to discuss restorative justice, but see Hoyle and Zedner, and Morgan and Newburn, Chapters 15 and 30, respectively, this volume). The inclusion/exclusion model has now been fleshed out by several analysts (for example, J. Young 1999; Garland 2001) and the difficulties in reorienting the system towards inclusion have been recognized, both in general (Faulkner 2001) and in relation to specific issues such as victims (Sanders 2002). It offers more than the other models discussed, for the inclusion approach combines the comprehensiveness of the human rights model with a clear sense of purpose.

This sense of purpose is at the centre of our own 'freedom model'. It starts by recognizing that the criminal process involves conflicting values, aims, and interests, such as: convicting the guilty; protecting the innocent from wrongful conviction; protecting human rights by guarding against arbitrary or oppressive treatment; protecting victims; maintaining order; securing public confidence in, and cooperation with, policing and prosecution; and achieving these goals without disproportionate cost and consequent harm to other public services. Whilst politicians often pretend that these goals are all equally achievable, the reality is that choices have to be made over which are to have priority. Such choices inevitably express a particular philosophical standpoint—in recent years, Prime Minister Blair has been arguing that the potentially innocent receive excessive protection at the expense of the majority (see Downes and Morgan, Chapter 9, this volume).

Unusually for a politician, Blair was expressing a philosophical standpoint. We too adopt a clear standpoint. Unlike that of Blair, it makes freedom the overriding purpose of the criminal justice system. All the interests and goals of criminal justice in a liberal democracy can be seen as connected to this underlying goal. Prosecution is not a valuable activity in itself: by censuring wrongdoing it should reinforce law-abiding instincts and habits, and the punishment or treatment of offenders aims to reduce their propensity to commit crime. Either way, the freedom of past and potential future victims should be enhanced through having their fear of crime reduced. Similarly we expect prosecutors to respect the rights of suspects and defendants not because protection is a goal in itself but to promote their freedom. And prosecutions are brought as one method of upholding order not because an orderly society is desirable in itself but because a degree of order is needed to enable individuals and communities to pursue their own ends. Whilst the various interests described will still come into conflict, at least under this model we keep in focus the ultimate aim of the system and can opt for compromises that are likely to maximize overall freedom. 'Freedom' is, of course, a deeply contestable notion that means very different things within different political traditions. Our use of the term 'freedom' is deliberately loose and unspecific because we concentrate attention here on the need for change instead of getting bogged down regarding exactly what that change should be, although we are more prescriptive elsewhere (e.g. Young and Sanders 2004; Sanders and Young 2006).

POLICE DECISIONS 'ON THE STREET'

The due process origins of our system can be seen in the fact that, in the first decades after the establishment of the modern police in the nineteenth century, sufficient evidence to prosecute was needed before street powers could be exercised. Stop and search powers did not exist (as such) and arrested persons had to be taken directly before the magistrates, who decided whether to prosecute. In theory, then, police investigation had to take place *before* arrest, although in reality many people used to be held by the police without formal arrest (supposedly 'helping the police with their enquiries'). Arrests are now often made to *facilitate* investigation, bringing the formal rules into line with a crime-control reality. Moreover, a large range of stop-search powers has been provided to the police, and incremental additions to arrest and stop-search powers have been a common feature of the last twenty years (for details see Sanders and Young 2006: chs 2–3).

The current legal position is now somewhere between the crime-control and due-process polarities but heading firmly in the direction of crime control. Stop and search without judicial warrant is allowed for most 'normal' crimes (theft, drugs offences, criminal damage, possession of offensive weapons, etc.), and the Serious Organised Crime and Police Act 2005 abolished the concept of an 'arrestable' (i.e. serious) offence by giving the police the power to arrest for *any* offence (again, without judicial warrant). Most of these powers require 'reasonable suspicion'—a somewhat open-ended concept—of a specific offence. The Code of Practice on stop and search (Code A) issued by the Home Office to accompany the Police and Criminal Evidence Act 1984 (PACE) states that 'there must be an objective basis' for the suspicion which 'can never be supported on the basis of personal factors alone without reliable supporting intelligence or information or some specific behaviour by the person concerned' (paragraph 2.2). The Code has been tightened up in successive editions since 1984 in an attempt to deal with the problem of the police stereotyping some types of people (especially young ethnic minority males) as inherently criminogenic, but the problem remains that the police have a wide latitude in deciding when 'supporting information' (i.e. 'intelligence') is 'reliable' and in interpreting 'specific behaviour' as suspicious.

Other recent stop-search powers do not require reasonable suspicion—e.g. under section 44 of the Terrorism Act 2000, which applies wherever and whenever a senior officer decides that use of stop and search will be expedient for the prevention of acts of terrorism (subject to subsequent approval by the Home Secretary); and under several pieces of legislation, there are special provisions to stop and search for weapons in areas designated by an inspector. These powers were initially presented as exceptional in nature but they are now being used extensively by the police. In 2004/05 there were 41,300 special weapons searches and 35,800 section 44 searches (Ayres and Murray 2005: 11–12). Moreover, it emerged in *Gillan & Anr* v. *Commissioner of Police of the Metropolis & Anr* [2004] EWCA Civ 1067 that in practice rolling (successive) authorizations covering the whole of London have been made by the police and approved by the Home Secretary since section 44 came into force. The Court of Appeal saw nothing wrong with this.

DISCRETION

Discretion is at the root of criminal justice practice. Police officers necessarily exercise discretion in deciding whether to stop and search and arrest. Some people look less 'suspicious' than others, and multitudes of actual or likely offences have to be prioritized. Arrest is less frequent than informal action even for relatively serious violence (Clarkson *et al.* 1994; HMIC and HM CPSI 2004; Paradine and Wilkinson 2004). Similarly, when officers are able to be proactive (as compared to their usual reactive mode) they have to use discretion about the offences or offenders in which to invest scarce time. Discretion is also created as a consequence of the way offences are defined. Most offences require *mens rea* (a 'guilty mind') that, broadly, amounts to intent or advertent recklessness. Thus knocking someone to the ground would be a crime if done deliberately, but not if done accidentally or in self-defence. However, since *mens rea* is so difficult to assess, officers have ample scope to arrest or not according to their preference. Moreover, the definition of many offences, particularly in the realm of public order, are inherently vague. So, stop-and-search and arrest decisions are constrained only loosely by law: the powers themselves, even if requiring reasonable suspicion, are ill-defined and subjective, the offences for which the powers are exercised are similarly ill-defined, and the police set their own priorities.

There are four levels at which discretion is structured, none of which have much to do with the law. First, there are general policing goals. To say that a prime function of the police is to maintain order, control crime, and catch criminals may be trite, but it identifies a fundamental conflict between policing goals and the due-process model. In so far as that model is an obstacle course, it can only get in the way of policing goals. To expect the police to abide by due process standards voluntarily—without coercion through 'inhibitory' rules—is therefore unrealistic. The second level is force policy, which can vary considerably from locality to locality (Miller *et al.* 2000: 13). Then there is 'cop culture' (see Chan 1996; Foster 2003). Its elements of sexism and racism, and its stereotyping of people and groups of certain types (on 'rough' estates, with certain lifestyles, etc.) affect the way officers view society. Take the Code of Practice's reference to 'specific behaviour' such as 'obviously trying to hide something'. How one views such matters depends on prevailing culture and individual officers' own ways of mediating that culture. To marginalized youths spending much of their lives on the street, hooded clothing may be a fashion choice or simply a way of keeping warm. To police officers, 'hoodies' may be perceived as 'obviously trying to hide something'. The final level, then, is that of the individual. Police officers are not representative of the population. They tend to be disproportionately white, male, and conservative. The homogeneity of this group, coupled with police training and socialization processes, enables 'cop culture' to be easily reproduced (Reiner 2000: esp. ch. 3).

PATTERNS OF BIAS AND POLICE WORKING RULES

Research prior to the implementation of PACE in the mid-1980s found that the weak constraints imposed on discretion by law allowed huge bias in policing. Stops were often based on classic stereotypes leading to patterns of bias on lines of class, gender, and race (see Sanders and Young 2006: ch. 2 for details). The introduction of PACE in the mid-1990s was intended to make some difference. For although PACE gave more, not less, power to the police, it also incorporated more controls than before. These include requirements to tell suspects why they are being arrested or stop-searched and to make records of the incident. However, stop-and-search and arrest decisions are of intrinsically low visibility (Goldstein 1960). Thus written records can be constructed after the event (McConville *et al.*: 991: ch. 5). As one officer put it to McConville *et al.* (1991), he would stop a suspect 'instinctively and then think about how he would satisfy a disinterested third party' (field notes).

This suggests that the Code has altered the way officers *account* for their exercise of discretion, but not the way they *actually* exercise it. Accounts of incidents can correspond as much with legal expectations as with the reality of the incidents (Scott and Lyman 1968; Ericson 1981). Thus officers are aware that the precise way in which forms are completed may either help or hinder the public making a complaint about their actions (Bland *et al.* 2000: 73) and formulaic wording is routinely used to cloak stop-searches in apparent legality (NACRO 1997; Fitzgerald 1999). It is hardly realistic to expect an officer to record on his stop-search form that his reason for exercising a power was that he had come across a 'Rastafarian out at night', or 'because he's a fucking paki' (BBC 2003) yet we know that such reasoning does take place (see below). On the other hand, at least the requirement to record has the *potential* to focus officers' minds on the limits of their legal powers, and some officers do claim this has an influence on them (Bland *et al.* 2000: 71–72). However, when scrutiny of forms reveals the reasons for searches to be sometimes recorded in such vague terms as 'drugs search', 'info received', and 'acting furtively' (ibid.: 44) the extent to which there has been a genuine shift in police reasoning remains open to question. The recently imposed requirement to make a record in the case of stops that do not result in a search but require a person to account for their behaviour (Code A, para. 4.12) will suffer from the same problem of 'creative accounting' by the police. By the same token, the recent emphasis on requiring supervisors to scrutinize patrol officers' accounts more carefully (Code A, para. 5.1; Home Office 2005a) is likely to have limited effect.

Research has not found the control and accountability mechanisms in PACE to have achieved their intended effects: in 2003/04 police records showed that a black person was 6.4 times, and an Asian person 1.9 times, more likely to be stop-searched than a white person (Home Office 2005b). Some researchers argue that when statistics on recorded stops and searches are compared with the population 'available' to be stopped and searched (i.e., those who use public places when and where stops take place) no general pattern of bias against those from ethnic minorities is evident (MVA and Miller 2000; Waddington *et al.* 2004). However, findings based on *recorded* stop-searches is flawed as Bland *et al.* (2000) found evidence of substantial under-recording of both stops and searches, and one cannot assume that the level of under-recording is the same for different suspect groups, particularly in the areas where this research was carried out (Sanders and Young 2006: ch. 2 and see Home Office 2005a: 39). In addition, these studies did not examine: whether ethnic minorities suffered more often than did whites from stops and searches that were not legally justified (i.e., no reasonable suspicion); whether the use of stop-search powers resulted in an arrest (i.e., whites may have been less often drawn further into the system); and whether the use of stop-search powers was accompanied by differing degrees of respectful treatment according to the colour of the suspect's skin. Finally, and as MVA and Miller rightly acknowledge, their study does not controvert the fundamental point that black and Asian people are over-represented in the stop-search figures relative to their presence in the overall population and that this remains 'an important indicator of the actual experience of different ethnic groups within police force areas' (2000: 88). Black people, Brown concluded in a review of PACE research, are more likely to be stopped than white people or Asians, more likely to be repeatedly stopped, more likely (if stopped) to be searched, and more likely to be arrested (1997: chs 2 and 4; see also Phillips and Bowling, Chapter 14, this volume, particularly on the relationship between crime, lifestyle, and police attention).

The new requirement on senior police managers to compile and examine comprehensive statistics of stop-searches, and to investigate any apparently disproportionate use of the powers by particular officers or groups of officers in relation to specific sections of the community is thus to be welcomed (Code A, para. 5.3), as is the Race Relations (Amendment) Act 2000 which makes it unlawful for the police to discriminate on the grounds of race, colour, ethnic origin, or nationality when using their powers.

Statistics will only ever give senior officers a partial picture, however. This is not just due to the problem of under-recording but also because statistics can never convey the experience of an abusive or disrespectful stop-search. Bland *et al.* (2000: 87) confirmed that the manner in which the police exercise their powers affects whether their actions were regarded as legitimate: 'It's not what they say, it's how they say it'. Offensive and racist language was particularly resented. One Pakistani young adult described his interaction as follows: 'their exact words were, yeah (and I've got witnesses because I was with two other people, yeah) was: "Don't fuck me about right, and I won't fuck you about, where have you got your drugs?" ' (2000: 83). Black people were far less likely than Asian or white people to report any positive experiences of respectful treatment by the police. Despite (or perhaps partly because of) the strongest possible exhortations from the government for stop and search to be deployed in an 'intelligence-led' way, under which the police are meant to focus on crime 'hotspots' and 'persistent offenders', and despite its angst about racial disproportionality (Home Office 2005a), racial disparities continue to disfigure the criminal justice system. While much of this stems from indirect discrimination (arising through the targeting of young males), some is a product of naked racism (BBC 2003).

Stop and search is a crude instrument of crime control. Although more stops generally lead to more arrests, the proportion of stops that lead to arrest decreases as the number of stops rises. This predictable consequence of the crime-control approach can be observed in most years since 1986 as the number of recorded PACE stops has increased eightfold since 1986 yet the proportion leading to arrest declined from 17 per cent in 1984 to 11 per cent in 2004/5 (Ayres and Murray 2005; Sanders and Young 2006: ch. 2). In other words, it is rare for police suspicions to be borne out by evidence on which to base an arrest. Searches where there is no legal requirement of reasonable suspicion, discussed above, are even more 'inefficient', with about a 3 per cent chance that they will lead to an arrest (Ayres and Murray 2005). A low arrest rate is not inconsistent with crime-control goals, however. First, stop-and-search is increasingly used for intelligence-gathering, with the enthusiastic backing of the Home Office and ACPO (Miller *et al.* 2001: 44–45, Home Office 2005a). Second, crime control favours actuarial methods in which suspect populations are actively policed, irrespective of whether they are doing anything wrong on a particular occasion. Whether these crime control practices are effective is another matter. Overall, it has been estimated that the various types of searches conducted by the police in 1997 reduced the number of crimes susceptible to this tactic by just 0.2 per cent (Miller *et al.* 2000: 28).

McConville *et al.* (1991) identify several 'working rules' which structure police decision-making. The first is 'previous' (i.e. being known to the police). As an arresting officer told McConville *et al.*: 'When you get to know an area, and see a villain about at 2.00 a.m. in the morning, you will always stop him to see what he is about' (1991: 24). This working rule, which results in a focus on the 'usual suspects' (McAra and McVie 2005) also finds expression in police briefings (Quinton *et al.* 2000) and the government's emphasis on targeting known and persistent offenders (Home Office 2005a). The second concerns disorder and police authority. Dealing with disorder is a prime police task. The police arrest people who do not cease their disorderly behaviour even when it is trivial (Brown and Ellis 1994). This is in part because of the challenge thereby presented to police authority, even if no specific charge fits the facts or if the offence— such as cannabis possession—is trivial (Warburton *et al.* 2005). The new emphasis since the start of this century on 'reassurance policing' (i.e., providing highly visible policing to reassure 'the public' that 'law and order' is being maintained) feeds into this long-standing phenomenon, as a recent study of five police forces has highlighted:

> In a number of forces stop and search was used as a tool for public reassurance and to prevent people who were seen as creating a public nuisance from gathering in certain places, although there was no reasonable suspicion of a crime. [Home Office 2005a: 38].

Other working rules include consideration of victims and their wishes, 'information received', and workload. But perhaps the most important working rule is 'suspiciousness'. This entails the suspect being 'out of the ordinary' or 'unco-operative', or keeping the wrong company (see further McAra and McVie 2005), or it being 'just a matter of instinct' on the officer's part, 'something undefinable' (all these phrases are from officers quoted in McConville *et al.* 1991: 26–8). A study carried out in the wake of the Stephen Lawrence Inquiry (Macpherson 1999) confirmed the continuing purchase of all of these working rules (Quinton *et al.* 2000: 19–52).

Dixon *et al.* (1989) argue that non-adherence to due-process standards is not so much wilful failure by police officers as the failure of due-process standards to meet the reality of policing. Policing is about the creative use of experience in crime control. The development, and diminution, of suspicion is a dynamic process. It cannot, they argue, be reduced to compartmentalized legalistic steps dependent on precisely measured levels of evidence. This is not to say that, under certain conditions, changes in formal rules are completely ineffective. Studies of domestic violence in the 1990s and 2004 assessed the impact of Home Office policies that encouraged arrest wherever there was evidence of an offence. Arrests rose significantly as a result, although not to the extent that full compliance would have produced (Hoyle 1998; HMIC and HM CPSI 2004; Paradine and Wilkinson 2004). The perception by 'cop culture' of domestic assaults as 'rubbish' can, it seems, be *partially* overcome. As Chan (1996) argues, police culture is not independent of societal pressures and legal rules. So, Hoyle found that, in the enthusiasm of police officers to implement this new policy, many arrests took place on inadequate evidence: a classic example of legal rules being overridden by non-legal concerns. It will be harder, however, to change police practice in the direction of *less* frequent use of their power, or more frequent *compliance with safeguards* as can be seen by the minimal impact on street-level policing of the high-profile Macpherson Report (1999) on the reasons for an inadequate police response to the murder of a young black man.

STOP-SEARCH AND ARREST: INCLUSIONARY OR EXCLUSIONARY?

Arrests usually follow information from, and complaints by, victims or witnesses (Shapland and Vagg 1988; Steer 1980) although a revival of proactive policing began in the late 1990s (see Sanders and Young 2006: ch. 7 for discussion of, for example, surveillance, phone tapping, and the use of informers). If relatively few arrests are proactive, does discretion, and the patterns of bias that are reflected by it, play only a minor part in determining the shape of the official suspect population? McConville *et al.* (1991) argue that most of the studies cited above are based on indictable offences, missing out the summary offences (such as public order, prostitution, drunkenness, etc.) in which police initiative is more pronounced. Also, the issue is less who is influenced by stereotyping than whether the initiator, whoever he or she is, is so influenced. Store detectives stereotype (Cameron 1964; Murphy 1986), and doubtless 'ordinary' members of the public do too. Further, citizen initiation rarely takes the form of citizen arrest. More usually it is simply the transmission of rather sketchy and sometimes downright unreliable information to the police (Quinton *et al.* 2000: 31–33). That information has to be sifted, evaluated, and acted upon (or not) by the police. The police record, at most, three-quarters of the crime reported to them (Nicholas *et al.* 2005: 36). McConville *et al.* (1991: 2) provide several examples where, even when the police did act upon complaints (for instance, by an ex-lodger and by a restaurateur), the way in which they acted, whether or not to arrest, was decided according to the working rules discussed earlier, and Sanders *et al.* (1997) provide further examples. In other words, police discretion and the exercise of judgement are still operative even when arrests are citizen initiated. The same is true of information from informants, on which the police increasingly depend (Maguire and Norris 1992; Field and Pelser 1998; Billingsley *et al.* 2001: 5). Information from the public is one resource among many which the police use in exercising discretion on the street according to their own priorities, and so the community is harnessed by the police in an inclusionary way, but only where doing so is consistent with police working rules.

The increased formal powers of stop-search and arrest given to the police since the mid-1980s, together with the ability of the police to stop-search and arrest largely when they want to on the basis of broad intangible suspicion, have led to the increased use of this intrusive activity since PACE was enacted. Other new laws, such as section 5 of the Public Order Act 1986, provide arrest powers for trivial offences that the police use extensively to bolster their authority (Brown and Ellis 1994). Young males, especially from poor and minority sections of the community, bear the brunt of all this power (Brown 1997: chs 2 and 4; Clancy *et al.* 2001). They feel—with some justification—discriminated against, and the consequent social unrest creates a vicious spiral of yet more policing and more unrest (Scarman 1981; Keith 1993; Macpherson 1999). The police sometimes use arrest powers to stamp their authority on challengers, often without any intention of prosecuting (Choongh 1997; Warburton *et al.* 2005). In these circumstances, the poor and underprivileged are treated dismissively as part of, and in order to emphasize, their exclusion from normal standards of protection (M. Young 1991). If our 'freedom' approach underlay the criminal justice system, arrest and stop-search powers would be used very differently and with restraint. One positive development is that the police may now release suspects on 'street bail' following arrest (to seek further evidence) instead of taking them to the police station (see Hucklesby 2004). It remains to be seen how widely this measure is used to reduce the amount of coercive power used on suspects.

DETENTION IN THE POLICE STATION

We have seen that in relatively recent times the law moved in a crime-control direction by allowing interference in the liberty of the citizen without sufficient evidence to prosecute. This was initially unplanned, ad hoc, and imprecise, giving rise to legal 'fudges' like 'helping police with their enquiries'. The Royal Commission on Criminal Procedure (RCCP) (1981) was therefore urged, on the one hand, to prohibit pre-charge detention (the due-process position) and on the other to extend it (the crime-control position). The Royal Commission decided that pre-charge detention should be reduced, and allowed only when it was 'necessary'. In this and other ways the Royal Commission attempted to satisfy both due-process and crime-control lobbies, but we shall see in this section that PACE and subsequent legislation has increasingly moved the system in a crime-control direction (see Sanders and Young 2006: ch. 1 for a brief recent history).

DETENTION WITHOUT CHARGE

In line with the RCCP's recommendations, PACE provides that anyone at a police station should either be free to leave at will or be under arrest (section 29). If the latter, there are clear time limits on how long a suspect can be held: up to 36 hours; or even 96 hours with the leave of the magistrates (sections 41–4). On arrest, all suspects, except in exceptional cases, should be taken directly to a police station (section 30). It is then for the 'custody officer' (the old station sergeant, with an enhanced role and training) to decide whether or not the suspect should be detained. There are only two grounds for detention: in order to charge or caution (warn) the suspect, or, where there is insufficient evidence to charge or caution, in order to secure that extra evidence. But this is allowed only where detention is *necessary* for that purpose (section 37), and only for as long as it is necessary; senior officers are supposed periodically to review detention to ascertain this.

The aims of these provisions should be clear. Being either arrested or free to go was designed to eliminate the travesty of 'helping the police with their enquiries'. Clear time limits were designed to ensure that both suspects and police knew what their respective rights and powers were, and to ensure that suspects were not intimidated by the prospect of indefinite detention. And immediate transit to a police station where a custody officer then becomes responsible for the suspect (and then, only when detention is 'necessary') was designed to ensure that suspects did not remain in the hands of officers who might mistreat them.

However, many of the RCCP's hopes are unfulfilled. Although 'independent' custody officers have to complete 'custody sheets' on all suspects that record the particulars of their detention, and so forth, this 'evidence' is written by the police against whom this is supposed to be a protection for suspects—like records of stop and search. It is not surprising to find that 'helping with enquiries' has not been eliminated, detention is hardly ever refused, and detention is continued for as long as investigating officers wish (subject to the time limits in PACE) by custody officers in the same routinized way that it is authorized in the first place (McConville *et al.* 1991; Dixon *et al.* 1990; Phillips and Brown 1998; Britton 2000).

ACCESS TO LEGAL ADVICE

The most striking due-process aspect of PACE is the provision, under sections 58–9, of free legal advice to all suspects who request it. Information about this unambiguous right has to be provided by the custody officer to the suspect. Advice may be delayed in exceptional cases but not denied outright. Custody records state whether or not suspects were informed of their rights, whether or not suspects requested advice, and what (if anything) happened then. Request rates have risen to around 40 per cent and actual advice rates to around 34 per cent (Bucke and Brown 1997). This is a massive increase over the pre-PACE situation, but it is still lower than one might have expected. Why should nearly two out of three people reject an entirely free service? Why do over one out of ten requests fail?

First, some suspects do not request advice because they are not informed (wholly or partly) of their rights. Secondly, some suspects' requests are denied, ignored, or simply not acted upon, custody records recording only some of these malpractices. This underlines the point made earlier about police-created records. Thirdly, the police often use 'ploys' to attempt to dissuade suspects from seeking advice and to persuade them to cancel their requests. These ploys ranged from the incomprehensible reading of rights to scare stories, such as 'You'll have to wait in the cells until the solicitor gets here'.

The problem does not lie wholly with the police. Many suspects have negative attitudes towards solicitors, which is not surprising, given their level of service. Advice is frequently provided by telephone, rather than in person, in many cases solicitors do not attend interrogations, and when they do they are usually passive. Legal aid lawyers have a generally non-adversarial stance and take their lead from the police. They routinely allow the police to use overbearing tactics, such that in one notorious case the suspect's lawyer had not objected to intimidation that the Court of Appeal condemned without hesitation (the Cardiff Three case, discussed by Sanders and Young 2006: ch. 5). The net result is that the possibility of help from a solicitor is one thing among many that suspects must weigh up when detained. Belatedly, police station legal advice and assistance is now regulated more rigorously, but the effect of this is undermined by changes to the right of silence (see below and, more generally, Sanders and Young 2006: chs 4 and 5).

POLICE INTERROGATION

Interrogation has assumed ever greater importance in police investigation over the years. Nearly half of all detained suspects are interrogated. In part this is because, as we have seen, investigation now usually takes place after, rather than before, arrest. It is also a product of the *mens rea* requirements of substantive criminal law. It is usually necessary to prove that the suspect intended the offences or was reckless. Since these are features of the suspect's mental state the best evidence is a confession. Even when other ways of securing evidence are available, interrogation often serves as a 'short cut' and produces information about other offences and other offenders (Phillips and Brown 1998: 73). The PACE Code of Practice on Detention and Questioning (Code C) sets out basic standards for interrogation (the provision of proper heating, ventilation, breaks, access to solicitors and others, and so forth), but also states that the police may persist in interrogating non-cooperative or silent suspects (para. 12.5). So, police officers may attempt to persuade suspects to change their minds about speaking and hold them, subject to the time limits, for as long as that takes. Detention is experienced as *coercive* by suspects as, for example, time passes 'exceedingly slowly in the cells' (Newburn and Hayman 2002: 97). Given the importance attached by most suspects to the shortest detention possible (Brown and Larcombe 1992), and recent changes to the right of silence (see below) the pressures on suspects to speak are considerable (also see Hillyard 1993; Choongh 1997).

How is evidence of guilt secured? First, there are those many suspects who simply and speedily acquiesce, against whom there would often be plenty of evidence anyway (Moston and Williamson 1992; Evans 1993; J. Baldwin 1993). Secondly, many suspects are susceptible to 'deals' (confessions or information in exchange for favours or reduced charges). Suspects are in a relatively weak position in these negotiations—they want to strike deals because of the coercive setting in which they find themselves, and the police use this to their advantage. Dunnighan and Norris (1996) found that 84 per cent of informers either were in custody or had proceedings against them when they were recruited, and in 85 per cent of cases it was the 'handler' who initiated the discussion about becoming an informer. Then there are those who are intimidated by being held against their will in 'police territory' where the environment is deliberately denuded of psychological supports (Holdaway 1983; Walkley 1987; Cape 2003: 264), by being in fear of spending the night in the cells (Sanders *et al.* 1989), or by the employment of any number of 'tactics' against them (Evans 1993; McConville *et al.* 1994: ch. 5). Such tactics include offering inducements such as bail, claiming that there is overwhelming evidence against the suspect, using custodial conditions such as return to the cells, and so forth. The effectiveness of the latter tactic is related to the nature of the typical police cell: 'Many detainees are reluctant either to sit or lie because they feel uncomfortable about the level of cleanliness. . . . The [integral] toilets have no separate seat and the top surfaces are badly discoloured. They have no lids and the cells sometimes smell fetid. Toilet paper is provided on request, but in limited amounts because of fears that a detainee will attempt to block the system. There is no hand basin and drinking water has to be requested.' (Newburn and Hayman 2002). The fact that detainees can be observed whilst going to the toilet is a further humiliation. If a tactic does not work in the initial interrogation, 36 hours allows ample time for the suspect to be psychologically 'softened up' for further interrogation. Evans (1993: 49) found a strong statistical association between the use of tactics and confessions.

Extreme tactics (such as violence, or blatant lies about the strength of the evidence against a suspect) are now rare in formal interrogations since they are tape recorded. This gives rise to a fourth way of securing confession: through informal interrogation. The extent of this is controversial but its existence is not. Informal interrogation occurs on the way to the police station (the 'scenic route': Evans and Ferguson 1991; Maguire and Norris 1992: 5); before and after formal interrogations (Sanders *et al.* 1989; McConville *et al.* 1991: 4, 7; McConville 1992; Dixon 2005); and in the cells under the guise of 'welfare visits' (Dixon *et al.* 1990). Custody records are supposed to record the precise times at which interviews begin and end, but this does not prevent officers having 'a little chat to get things straight before I switch on the tape' (Evans and Ferguson 1991; see also Evans 1993: 36; McConville 1992). It is precisely on confessions allegedly made 'informally' (but not repeated 'formally') that so many appeals have turned. To the extent that 'tactics' are now used less frequently in formal interrogations than they were before PACE, it is likely that they are now simply being used more under 'low visibility' conditions (Maguire and Norris 1992). Brown and Larcombe (1992) and Moston and Stephenson (1993) found that officers admitted to a considerable amount of informal interviewing. The low visibility of informal interviews provides the opportunity to officers to 'gild the lily' (Holdaway 1983). As one officer told Maguire and Norris (1992: 46–7), there was nothing to prevent him from distorting the contents of informal conversations 'if I was dishonest'.

Coercion may occur too, in both informal and formal interrogations. This is inevitable under English law, for the job of the police interrogator is to elicit answers even from suspects who have declared a refusal to provide answers: in other words, to change their minds. Even interrogation practices which would be innocuous to most people are coercive to vulnerable people (Gudjonsson and MacKeith 1982; Littlechild 1995). Procedures for identifying, and making allowances for, vulnerable people in police custody are inadequate (Laing 1995, 1999; Palmer 1996; Bucke and Brown 1997; Phillips and Brown 1998; Young 2002). And even supposedly non-vulnerable people often make 'coerced-passive' confessions (McConville *et al.* 1991: 4) as a result of leading questions (defended by Walkley 1987) and legal-closure questions (Irving

1985). Thus suspects get trapped into accepting they have 'stolen' when they in fact would put it in a different, exculpatory, way (see also Sanders *et al.* 1989: 7; Evans 1993).

Finally, there are false confessions. Gudjonsson and McKeith (1988) discuss various types of false confession arising from coercion, but coercion is not always necessary. Questioning taking the form of a supported direct accusation (i.e. an accusation with details of the crime itself) can lead to internalization by suggestible suspects whose subsequent 'confessions' will contain only the details provided by the police themselves (Moston 1992; Gudjonsson 2003: 103–5). While vulnerable suspects figure particularly among cases of false confession (Littlechild 1995), many people who are apparently robust are vulnerable to police tactics and the sheer fear of being cut off and confined for a period of time beyond one's own control. As one of the authors of a false confession in the 'Kerry Babies' case put it, 'I didn't think my mind was my own' (O'Mahony 1992). Whilst false confessions arising from disorientation are doubtless rare, falsity can be a matter of interpretation and degree. McConville *et al.* (1991) argue that interrogation is a process of construction whereby facts are made and not discovered. An example is given by Maguire and Norris (1992: 4), who report a CID sergeant saying that he had been taught to induce people found carrying knives to say that they were for their own protection. This, unknown to the suspect, constitutes admission of the crime of carrying an 'offensive weapon'. This type of confession, with elements of falsity arising from the process of case construction, is doubtless far more common than 'false confessions', yet equally likely to lead to wrongful convictions.

Moston (1992) argues that police failure to verify confessions and avoid leading questions is simply a matter of technical competence, a failure of training, and the decision to adopt adversarial styles. Inquisitorial styles, going under labels such as 'investigative interviewing' or 'ethical interviewing' were advocated in the early 1990s by the Home Office and the police as well as by academics such as Moston. New guidelines were issued, training packages were devised, and, by the end of the 1990s, over two-thirds of officers had received the new training. Code C (note 11B) now calls on interviewers to pursue all lines of enquiry whether they point towards or away from the suspect in front of them. But what difference has all this made to actual police interviewing? Clarke and Milne (2001) found a decline in the use of leading questions and the more frequent provision of information such as the right to legal advice. But the training failed radically to change police behaviour. For example, listening skills were rated as poor, interviews were found to be dominated by the use of closed questions, and 10 per cent of the interviews probably breached PACE. Interviews with victims and witnesses raised even more concern, and 'damning' evidence was found of interviewers apparently looking to interviewees to confirm police suspicions rather than provide their own accounts. There was little effective supervision of interviewing and scant interest had been shown by police leaders in ensuring that their officers actually used the skills taught in training. Complacency about standards of interviewing within the police probably derives in part from police confidence that they are good at distinguishing truth from falsehood in interview, even though, according to Vrij (2000), they are quite wrong about this.

Technical solutions to problematic interviewing styles, such as better training or video-recording (Baldwin and Bedward 1991), imply a bureaucratic explanation for false confessions and coercion. They presuppose that due process is achievable in interrogation. Against this, McConville *et al.* (1991) argue that the search for 'better' or more 'objective' interrogation is naive, because the job of the police is to build a case, not to identify verifiable facts. Nothing has happened since 1991 to suggest they were wrong. While the (slow) shift towards investigative interviewing is welcome, miscarriages of justice arising from coercion and false confessions would be more effectively reduced by preventing confession evidence forming the sole basis of convictions, and by providing the defence with the same resources as are provided to the prosecution, than by trying to change interrogation practices. But that is simply not on the agenda. Instead, in the context of custodial interrogation, blatant police oppression and trickery is being replaced by latent police power and control. The attenuation of the right to silence brought about by the Criminal Justice and Public Order Act 1994 is one clear example of that (see below), and the increase in the length of police-authorized custody for all indictable offences from 24 hours to 36 hours (effected by section 7 of the Criminal Justice Act 2003 as amended by section 43(7) of, and Schedule 7 to the Serious Organised Crime and Police Act 2005) and, with limited judicial oversight, from seven to 14 days for terrorist offences (section 306, Criminal Justice Act 2003) is another. The attempt by the government in 2005 to increase the length of time terrorist suspects can be detained without charge to three months displayed such utter contempt for suspects' rights that it was bound to provoke strong, and, as it turned out, effective opposition in Parliament. But no one should mistake the overall trend towards increasing latent police power. Indeed, that 'government defeat' still resulted in the House of Commons amending the Terrorism Bill 2005 to extend the permissible detention of terrorist suspects from 14 to 28 days. Against this background of increasing police power, ethical custodial interrogation looks increasingly like a contradiction in terms.

THE RIGHT OF SILENCE

Over half of all suspects who are interrogated either confess or make incriminating statements to the police (see, for the most recent research, Bucke *et al.* 2000). We have seen that the police have various methods of securing confessions, but these do not always work, and they work with varying success according to a wide range of factors, in particular, offence severity, prior legal advice, and strength of evidence (Moston and Stephenson 1993). Evans (1993) also found age and criminal record to be significant. When suspects exercise their 'right to remain silent' are the police unjustifiably impeded? The answer turns principally on three things: what, precisely, 'silence' means in this context; what the association is between silence and outcome; and in what ways the police are obstructed by silence (although there are of course arguments of principle as well as practical policy at stake: Easton 1998). Only 2–4 per cent of suspects in the post-PACE studies exercise absolute silence although a further 5 per cent or so simply make flat denials, while 8–15 per cent answer some questions and not others, and some suspects are silent at the start but then answer questions later (or vice versa). Leng (1992) made the best estimate of a 'true' silence rate of 4.5 per cent. He found that in only a small percentage of 'no further actions' or acquittals was silence exercised, and that these outcomes rarely seemed to be a product of silence. Leng found that 'ambush' defences (not disclosed until trial) were rare. When they were used, they were unsuccessful. Most acquittals were the result of unforeseen, but not unforeseeable, defences—sometimes they mirrored exculpatory statements to which the police would not listen in interrogation.

The Royal Commission on Criminal Justice (RCCJ) therefore concluded in 1993 that the right to silence should be retained, as abolition would benefit the police in few cases, and would put pressure on innocent people instead of experienced criminals. Despite this, the government enacted the Criminal Justice and Public Order Act 1994. In line with changes made in Northern Ireland, this provides that, when someone relies in court on a fact which s/he could have been reasonably expected to mention when questioned by the police, the court can draw an adverse inference from this silence. Similarly, courts can draw adverse inferences from failures to answer questions in court. Exactly what inferences a court should draw from silence is a matter of debate. Despite Article 6 of the ECHR proclaiming that 'Everyone . . . shall be presumed innocent until proved guilty by law', the European Court of Human Rights accepted the lawfulness, with caveats, of these provisions (Sanders and Young 2006: ch. 5). As might be expected, the effect of the new provisions is to lower the use of the right of silence, probably because lawyers, who were becoming more adversarial in the early to mid-1990s, became more circumspect again about advising silence. Interestingly, abolishing the right of silence has made little difference to admission and conviction rates (Bucke *et al*. 2000: 34 and 66–7). While abolition may have greater symbolic-electoral value than instrumental use, we should not forget the broader purposes of interrogation, such as gaining general criminal intelligence, and exercising disciplinary power over suspects. That more suspects are now talking to the police is therefore of sociological significance, even if the police do typically characterize the additional information obtained as 'a pack of lies' (Bucke *et al*. 2000: pp 34–46). The conviction rate may not have increased, but the erosion of the privacy and freedom of the citizen certainly has.

A SEA CHANGE IN THE NATURE OF DETENTION?

Rather than leading to less pre-charge detention, the RCCP's scheme (enacted in PACE) led to more. The formalization of pre-charge procedures was intended to protect suspects, and it doubtless does so to some extent. But detention can still be lengthy and intimidating, access to lawyers can be obstructed and is often of little value (particularly now that the right of silence has been further restricted), and the police have learned to substitute psychological pressure for physical pressure. On the broader impact of PACE on policing, researchers have reached different conclusions. As part of a critique of *The Case for the Prosecution* (McConville *et al*. 1991) Dixon (1992) divides criminal justice researchers into two main camps: the 'sea change theorists' who argue that PACE has significantly obstructed the police and enhanced protections for suspects; and 'new left pessimists' who argue that the changes are largely cosmetic (for further debate about *The Case for the Prosecution* see Duff 1998; McConville *et al.* 1997; Smith 1997 and 1998; various articles in Noaks *et al.* 1995; also see Maguire 2002, for a similar view to that of Dixon).

It seems that PACE has changed practices, but largely by *shifting* the unwanted behaviour instead of eradicating or even reducing it. Thus there is little violence now, although deaths in custody are still scandalously high (Vogt and Wadham 2003; Sanders and Young 2006: ch. 4). But there is more use of other tactics and pressures, and of deceptive covert policing (see Sanders and Young 2006: ch. 6); and confessions purportedly given in 'informal' interrogations are still admissible. The PACE framework is like the post-*Miranda* approach in the United States, where interrogation has similarly shifted from physical to psychological strategies. As Leo puts it, 'The law has also empowered the police to create more specialised and seemingly more effective interrogation strategies . . . they can lie, they can cajole, and they can manipulate' (1994: 116). The new rules and constraints that are implicitly relied upon by Dixon are access to lawyers, tape recording of interrogation, custody records, and the general supervisory role of the custody officer. As we have seen—and as Dixon (1991) partially acknowledges himself—these developments hardly represent a 'sea change' in policing.

PACE only appears to provide a 'balance' between due process and crime control because we now unquestioningly accept the right of the police to use coercive powers. But why do suspects not want to wait for a lawyer, for instance, to come to the station? Why are so many people so vulnerable that PACE has to establish elaborate codes and protections? Why do suspects 'voluntarily' answer police questions? Only because they are in the police station against their will in the first place. So, for example, most suspects do want lawyers, but the desire to get out of the station quickly is stronger. And why is police station legal work so poor so often? Again, largely because the police have the power to create the forces that so shape it. Solicitors send unqualified staff, give telephone advice, or miss interrogations largely because of all the time they would otherwise waste. But it is the police who control the time frame. And the legal 'trading' which undermines adversarialism is forced onto lawyers—who, it has to be admitted, usually need little persuading—because the police are in control. Once the police are given the right to detain, the rule of law is jeopardized, due process is made unviable, and human rights norms are tested to their limit. Thus PACE does not merely 'balance' rights and powers poorly, but, in providing the right to detain in such broad circumstances, it cedes most practical power to the police (Sanders and Young 1994). The 'sea change', if there has been one, has been in favour of the police and subsequent legislative changes reinforced this.

Why do we put up with this? Is it because it is not 'we' who bear the brunt of these powers? Most people who are stopped, searched, arrested, detained, and interrogated are young working-class men, especially in ethnic minorities. The treatment they are given is frequently humiliating—and deliberately so (M. Young 1991; Choongh 1997). These groups are also treated worse than others when in custody, being more than twice as likely to be strip-searched, for example (Newburn, Shiner, and Hayman 2004). Opinion-formers, lawyers, and legislators, on the other hand (older middle-class white men in the main), are very rarely subjected to such exclusionary processes. It is true that over one-third of men will have been convicted of at least one non-motoring offence before they reach the age of 40, which means that many more than this will have been stopped, arrested, and/or reported for motoring offences. But the way in which police power is exercised and its frequency are as important as outcome (Tyler 1990), and this bears down far more heavily on the poor than on the wealthy. Of course some middle-class people are roughly treated and some poor people are not. But the contrast between the integrated and the excluded is as striking in the field of criminal justice as in other fields of social policy. Arguably, major advances in liberty are only ever secured in the United Kingdom when the middle classes are threatened. If so, we can expect this divided society to manifest these exclusionary processes for a long time to come and for 'freedom' in the sense we use it here to be given little weight by policy-makers and practitioners.

WHETHER OR NOT TO PROSECUTE

When the police were first established they gradually took over responsibility for prosecution in the absence of any specific or exclusive prosecution powers or controls over their discretion. As arrest turned into a tool for (rather than the culmination of) investigation, pre-charge detention increased and the police developed various non-prosecution dispositions. To secure consistency of decision-making, and to counterbalance extra police powers, the RCCP recommended establishing the Crown Prosecution Service (CPS). Apart from organizational and accountability matters with which we shall not be concerned here (on which see Sanders and Young 2006: ch. 7), the government followed the Royal Commission's recommendations in the Prosecution of Offences Act 1985. The CPS is built around the pre-existing system, and is headed by the Director of Public Prosecutions (DPP), whose office had previously been responsible for prosecutions of particular importance and for the prosecution of police officers. The police continued to charge, summons, caution, and take no further action in the same way as before, simply handing prosecutions over to the CPS. Consequently, and to 'narrow the justice gap' by increasing 'efficiency' (meaning more guilty pleas and fewer acquittals: Home Office 2002), prosecution decisions were transferred to the CPS by the 'statutory charging scheme' in the Criminal Justice Act 2003.

NO FURTHER ACTION

Around one in four suspects are released from pre-charge detention with no further action (NFA). Police officers make release decisions themselves on the basis of their own criteria and on evidence collected and evaluated by themselves.

McConville *et al.* (1991: 6) found that many arrests were a result of pressure from the public. If the police arrested reluctantly the outcome was often NFA, usually after consultation with the victim, regardless of the strength of evidence. Other reasons for NFA in cases where the police did find (or could have found) evidence include the doing of 'deals' with suspects, especially informants. And just as prosecution is sometimes used to protect the police against allegations of malpractice, so in some circumstances NFA prevents the airing in public of events about which the police prefer to keep quiet (McConville *et al.* 1991: 111). Some NFAs, of course, are simply cases in which the police would have liked to prosecute had they had more evidence. The obstacle here is rarely physical or legal, but simply one of resources. Cases are a product of police work, and so the absence of a case is also a police product. On the other hand, many NFAs are a product of purely speculative arrests (McConville *et al.* 1991: 2). Often the police accept that the suspect did not commit the offence or that there is no evidence: for instance, where the police 'trawl' local people with relevant previous convictions simply to eliminate them from a major rape enquiry; where suspects are arrested so that they can be held pending their questioning as witnesses; and where *all* inhabitants of, and visitors to, a building where there has been a drugs raid are arrested, even though the building consists of several self-contained flats (Leng 1992).

Arrest and detention are not always geared to prosecution. If the police arrest in furtherance of the 'assertion of authority' working rule, for instance, the arrestee may be detained in order to be humbled. The exercise of power is sometimes used to intimidate sections of the population such as the Irish (Hillyard 1993) or other ethnic minorities (Choongh 1997). NFAs would have been anticipated even at the moment of arrest. In these types of case, and in many of those discussed earlier, no due-process standards, substantive or procedural, are adhered to. This is all consistent with the 'new left pessimist' argument that the 'PACE regime' facilitates the 'crime-control' drift.

DIVERSION FROM PROSECUTION

The ratio of police prosecutions to police cautions is about 3 : 1 and more juveniles are cautioned than are prosecuted. This reflects a massive increase in the cautioning of both adults and juveniles since the 1970s. The RCCP (1981: Table 23.4) noted considerable variations in cautioning rates among police forces that could not be explained solely by offence variations. The Home Office responded with successive sets of guidelines in 1985, 1990, 1994, and 2005 that established clearer criteria for prosecution and caution: offence seriousness, previous convictions, dramatic mitigating circumstances, wishes of the victim, and so forth. However, both inter-force and intra-force disparities continue, partly because the guidelines are vague (how serious an offence or record? what kinds of personal circumstance should be taken into account?), manipulable (the police themselves sometimes influence the wishes of victims), and largely non-prioritized (though now offence seriousness predominates). Diversion is encouraged in many cases which would once have been prosecuted, because it is cheaper than prosecution and because it is thought to avoid stigmatizing offenders. Drawing on labelling theory (e.g. Becker 1963), it was generally accepted in the 1980s and early 1990s that prosecution and punishment can exaggerate criminal self-identity. But now the Crime and Disorder Act 1998 (which put cautioning for youths on a statutory basis) specifies that a maximum of two cautions (save in exceptional circumstances) can be offered to youths in the form of 'reprimands' for minor offences, or 'warnings' for more serious or repeat offending (see Evans and Puech 2001, and Morgan and Newburn, Chapter 30, this volume, for discussion of this punitive approach). Warnings are supposed to be accompanied by 'action plans' drawn up by the multi-agency Youth Offender Teams created under the 1998 Act and the emphasis is now on 'early intervention', 'nipping crime in the bud', and restorative justice, although cost-reduction are punitive and stigma-avoidance aims have not been entirely dispensed with (for discussion of some of the problems see Ashworth 2002; R. Young and Hoyle 2003; Gray 2005; Edwards 2006).

The various objectives of cautioning would be undermined if cautions, reprimands, and warnings were used in cases that would not otherwise be prosecuted. This 'net-widening' undoubtedly occurs, but it is difficult to assess its extent (Warburton *et al.* 2005). Preconditions for caution are that there is sufficient evidence to prosecute and that the suspect admits the offence and accepts the caution (the requirement of consent was removed in the case of youths by the 1998 Act). But these preconditions are often ignored (Evans and Puech 2001; Gillespie 2005). Indeed, some suspects are cautioned precisely *because* there is insufficient evidence to prosecute. The low-visibility nature of caution decisions, and the fact that the police should, but need not, seek CPS advice on cautioning in difficult cases, also enables the police to use cautions as bargaining tools with suspects who would normally be prosecuted (McConville *et al.* 1991: 6) and to deal inappropriately with people with learning disabilities and mental health problems (H. Young 2002). The Criminal Justice Act 2003 gave the CPS a power to 'conditionally caution'. Since, at the time of writing, this has hardly begun to operate, it remains to be seen whether more rigorous due process standards will be imposed on diversion processes.

PROSECUTION

There are now well over a million police prosecutions per year. Police and CPS decision-making should be based on the *Code for Crown Prosecutors*, the latest edition of which was published in 2004. In order to prosecute there should be a 'realistic prospect of prosecution' and it should be in the 'public interest' (otherwise the case should be diverted as discussed above). Under the statutory charging scheme, when fully implemented, prosecutors will decide whether or not to prosecute all non-trivial cases. To prevent delays and/or unnecessary time in custody, and to increase the efficiency and quality of decision-making, prosecutors are increasingly being sited in police stations and working with police officers on these decisions. Where appropriate, the police will be told they need to secure more evidence, and suspects are sometimes released on bail for this purpose. Is this likely to reduce police over-charging and CPS unwillingness to discontinue weak cases? To answer this, it is necessary to understand the pre-existing system. Currently, the police follow their working rules when making charge decisions, and use prosecutions, like stop-and-search, arrest, interrogation, and caution as a policing resource. They do this by constructing cases to appear strong, in accordance with adversarial principles. Since the system is concerned more with legal truth than with actual truth, the police are also more concerned with the former, selecting, interpreting, and sometimes even 'creating' facts which bear little relation to any reality which the suspect might recognize (McBarnet 1981). This is simply a continuation of processes revealed in studies of interrogation and other policing practices. It follows that, just as officers can often secure cautions when NFA would be more in keeping with the rules, so they can often secure charges when cautions would be more appropriate (and vice versa). The police 'overcharging' that this leads to was castigated as recently as 2003 by HM Crown Prosecution Service Inspectorate (2003).

McConville *et al.* (1991) found that the CPS rarely dropped cases that were evidentially weak (confirmed by HM CPSI 1999), and that when they did so this was usually on the initiative of the police and/or only after several court appearances. There were three main reasons for this: policy (the furtherance of police working rules, shared by both prosecutors and police officers); the chance of a freak conviction (because verdicts are so hard to predict); and guilty pleas (just because a case is evidentially weak it does not follow that the defendant will contest the case; weak cases are continued in the often correct expectation of a guilty plea). If the CPS is passive in relation to weak cases where case failure is a measure of institutional inefficiency, it is not surprising to discover that it is even more passive in relation to cautionable cases. McConville *et al.* (1991) found no cases at all being dropped on this ground alone, despite many similar cases being cautioned by the police. Again, where police working rules point to prosecution, the CPS is reluctant to stop the case. Cretney and Davis (1996) and Sanders *et al.* (1997) found, for example, that the police and CPS prosecuted weak cases with victims of domestic violence and with vulnerable victims because they believed in the guilt of the suspect, ignoring the probability that problems concerning the victims' testimony would lead to acquittal. In these and other sensitive cases, such as sexual offences, this is urged on the police and the CPS. If this leads to innovative ways of securing successful prosecutions, this is commendable, but not if the 'public interest' in such cases simply trumps the 'evidential' test (Sanders and Young 2006; ch. 7).

In recent years there has been a significant rise in discontinuances, particularly on evidential grounds, but there are still a remarkable number of Crown Court acquittals in cases that are obviously weak from the outset (Sanders and Young 2006: ch. 10). However, many 'public interest' discontinuances are of trivial cases, and are made on cost grounds.

Ethnic minority defendants have their cases disproportionately discontinued by the CPS *and* dismissed in court (Mhlanga 2000; HM CPSI 2004). This suggests that the CPS counters some of the race bias produced by the police discussed earlier in this chapter, but not all. The CPS is in a structurally weak position to carry out its ostensible aims primarily because of police case construction. The CPS reviews the quality of police cases on the basis of evidence provided solely by the police. This is like the problem of written records, where those who are being evaluated write their own reports. Cases being prosecuted are usually presented as prosecutable; the facts to support this are selected, and those that do not are ignored, hidden, or undermined. Thus weaknesses or cautionable factors, whether known by the police or not, often emerge only in or after trial (Leng 1992). This situation is exacerbated when the CPS relies on police summaries, which are very selective indeed. But the statutory charging scheme *requires* prosecutors to rely on police summaries (often oral), if only so that most suspects can be released from custody in a reasonable time. Further, the new scheme allows the police or CPS to make an initial charge based on a very low evidential threshold in serious cases. Thus the CPS remains structurally weak. Even a prosecutor argues that a major cultural change on the part of both police and CPS is needed to make the new scheme work (Brownlee 2004).

That the CPS is primarily a police prosecution agency is hardly surprising in an adversarial system, but it does suggest that suspects cannot rely on the CPS, as presently constituted, to protect them. Prosecutors could become adequate reviewers of either evidence or public interest only if placed in an entirely different structural relationship with the police. This would require fundamental changes in the adversarial system, and might well then be unsuccessful, if the evidence we have of continental systems is anything to go by (Hodgson 2001). It would be better to strengthen the position of the defence in the adversarial system, but the new 'Criminal Defence' service, including a 'Public Defender' service on US lines, is likely to take us further in the crime control direction (see Goriely 2003, on a Scottish experiment; and JUSTICE 2001 and Sanders and Young 2006: chs 7 and 9 for general discussion).

NON-POLICE AGENCIES

Many other agencies also prosecute. These include HM Revenue and Customs (HMRC), the Department of Social Security (DSS), the Health and Safety Inspectorate (HSI), and so forth. Although these agencies follow a diversity of policies and procedures they all share a propensity not to prosecute, attempting to secure compliance with the law and/or to secure financial compensation primarily through informal negotiation. Whether their approach is so different from that of the police because the offences with which they deal are viewed differently by 'society', or whether the causal effect is in the other direction, is not clear (see Nelken, Chapter 6, this volume). Hawkins entitled his study of the Health and Safety Inspectorate *Law as Last Resort* appropriately. He says, 'prosecution tends to be used in those cases which have something special about them' (2002: xii). In recent years government rhetoric has urged a more punitive response, but this has had little effect 'on the ground' (R. Baldwin 2004). Even the treatment by the police of people who are unlawfully killed is completely different to that of non-police agencies, which virtually never consider prosecuting for manslaughter in circumstances where this would be viable and, arguably, desirable (Slapper 1999).

The patterns of bias identified in street policing (race, class, and so forth) may also be evident in prosecution and diversion decisions, but the greater class bias is between police-enforced and other crime. The police overwhelmingly prosecute instead of cautioning. Both the police and other types of agency have near-absolute discretion. The police (dealing with mainly working-class crime) use it in one way, while most other agencies (dealing with mainly middle-class crime) use it in another. Indeed, non-police agencies that deal with poor people (such as the DSS) behave much more like the police than like HMRC or HSE (Walker and Wall 1997; Pantazis and Gordon 1997; McKeever 1999). It is difficult to see how this can be justified in terms of offence seriousness, previous criminality, and so forth except, perhaps, in terms of a narrowly defined 'efficiency' (R. Baldwin 2004; Middleton 2005). Thus the dispositions of both police and non-police agencies serve to further the different working rules of those different agencies. And the stigmatizing and exclusionary process of prosecution is used routinely against the poor but rarely against the wealthy. Because arrest does not necessarily lead to prosecution, prosecution need not be the normal response to suspected crime, and the specific charge prosecuted is an entirely discretionary matter. This allows completely different standards to be applied to different types of crime and criminal on the basis of unarticulated criteria (Sanders and Young 2006: ch. 7). But the drift towards crime control for the excluded is set to continue as police cautioning rates, under pressure from government, fall, and as on-the-spot-fine systems are developed.

PRE-TRIAL PROCESSES

POLICE BAIL

After charge, the custody officer decides whether to release on bail or to hold the suspect in custody pending the next magistrates' court hearing (usually the next morning). Detention is allowed only if the suspect's real name and address cannot be ascertained, if he is unlikely to appear in court to answer the charge, if he is likely to interfere with witnesses or further police investigations, or if he is likely to commit a significant crime. Whilst this is consistent with the ECHR, the case law of the European Court of Human Rights provides that refusal of bail for any of these reasons must be based on evidence, not speculation. However, like much human rights-speak this is both unrealistic and inconsistent with the crime-control elements of English law and practice: most of these provisions require custody officers to predict what might happen if the suspects were released, relying on what investigating officers say, and on what little may be known about the suspect's previous record of appearing in court, offending on bail, and so forth. Also, suspects cannot prove that they would not do something wrong if they are given the opportunity to do it. Thus decisions are taken quickly on the basis of inadequate information; although decisions are taken by theoretically independent custody officers to protect suspects from the partisanship of arresting/investigating officers, most of the information used will come from the very officers against whom protection is provided; and assessment of the quality of decision-making is almost impossible. The bail/custody decision remains entirely for the police under the statutory charging scheme, although having prosecutors in the police station much of the time at least provides an obvious opportunity for police to consult someone with legal expertise.

Bail gives the police a powerful bargaining tool in interrogation. Although they should not offer 'inducements' (of which bail is one), this is a recognized interrogation 'tactic' (Irving 1980): 'They [the police] said if I cough I'll get bail; if not then I'll be in court tomorrow' (McConville and Hodgson 1992: 79). The opportunity for informal 'chats' discussed above ensures that such negotiations need never take place in front of tape recorders, researchers, or solicitors, and most suspects know or think they know that they can make deals on these lines. For bail-bargaining is 'all part of the relationship' (detective, quoted in McConville *et al.* 1991: 63). The building of relationships is regarded as a vital working practice, and, like other working norms, cannot simply be legislated away (Maguire and Norris 1992). The power of the police to deny bail is enhanced by the suspect's fear of being held overnight and by the failure of many solicitors to attend the station and when they do, to stay long. Implicit bargaining over bail leading to 'voluntary' confessions is part of the differential power relationship between officer and suspect which leads suspects 'voluntarily' to agree to many similar things like stop-and-search, attendance at the station, search of premises, and so forth. However, victims also sometimes have an interest in whether alleged offenders secure bail or the terms on which they get bail. Victims of violence, for example, may want a 'no contact' condition. Courts have for many years been able to grant conditional, as well as unconditional, bail (see later discussion). The police were given the power to set conditions in the mid-1990s because it was believed that the police were refusing bail to some suspects in order to encourage the court to set conditions which the police (often justifiably) thought were appropriate. The result has been an increase in the percentage of defendants being granted bail (now around 80 per cent), but a reduction in the percentage of suspects given unconditional bail (Hucklesby 2001). No changes in the rate of offending while on bail are discernible as a result of this increase in bail (Bucke and Brown 1997; Raine and Willson 1997).

COURT BAIL

Court bail may or may not be opposed by the police (through the CPS), and may or may not be requested by the defendant (usually through a solicitor). While the CPS does not always oppose bail when the police ask them to, in such cases it almost invariably asks for conditions to be attached to bail (Morgan 1996). Not surprisingly, magistrates usually reach the same conclusions as the police and the CPS, for they consider similar criteria and similar information (Hucklesby 1996). This is often 'incomplete and for that and other reasons inaccurate' (Auld 2001: 428). As with police bail decisions, this is at odds with the spirit of the human rights approach to which the UK supposedly adheres, and probably the letter of the law as well (Burrow 2000).

Courts have considerable scope for the exercise of discretion and judgement, leading to disparity (Paterson and Whitaker 1994 and 1995). Overall, bail is refused in about 11–13 per cent of magistrates' cases (100,000) each year. Though a small (but rising) percentage of all cases, remand prisoners form a substantial percentage of people in prison, greatly contributing to overcrowding and the huge cost of criminal justice. Most hearings seem to take less than ten minutes (Doherty and East 1985; Dhami and Ayton 2001). This shocked Lord Woolf in his enquiry into prison disturbances (1991), and reflects the limited information that is usually provided (Hucklesby 1996). When information from more diverse sources is presented, bail is less frequently opposed by the CPS and more frequently granted. Bail information schemes, organized by local probation services, lead to the release of higher proportions of defendants than normal, demonstrating the partial (i.e. adversarial) approach of the police and the over-cautious approach of many courts. As with schemes to encourage more diversion from prosecution, this shows the potential in the CPS for more independence if independent information is provided to it.

A suspect's remand in custody can obstruct defence work (including preparation of bail applications): defendants remanded in custody are, all other things being equal, more likely to be convicted and, if convicted, to be given custodial sentences than those given bail. But since not all defendants remanded in custody are convicted and given custodial sentences, some defendants who are legally innocent are held in custody, and some whose offence or circumstances do not warrant custodial sentences, are also held in custody before sentence (this is true of nearly half of all male remand prisoners, many of whom are in custody for over three months: see Morgan and Liebling, Chapter 32, this volume). On the other hand, 10–17 per cent of all persons released on bail commit an offence while at liberty (Hucklesby and Marshall 2000; Morgan and Henderson 1998). Clearly magistrates have inadequate information on which to make confident decisions, yet the stakes are high. Offending on bail is undesirable; yet so, in a supposedly due-process-based system, is pre-trial imprisonment of innocent people and minor offenders. Magistrates seem to cope by over-using conditions when they do grant bail (Hucklesby 1994), and by developing an 'unquestioning culture' whereby information from the CPS is seen as factual but information from the defence is seen as partial. This is a problem in relation to all magistrates' decisions, such as applications for search warrants (Sanders and Young 2006: ch. 6). Magistrates even sometimes refer to prosecutors as 'our solicitor' (Hucklesby 1996: 218–19, 224). Despite all this, the three post-1997 Labour governments followed the lead of the early to mid-1990s Conservative governments in introducing ever-more draconian anti-bail laws. Although these are likely to have little practical effect, as the ECHR does provide a safety net, they further legitimize crime-control policy, practice and rhetoric.

DISCLOSURE OF EVIDENCE

The failure of the police to disclose information helpful to the defence can make cases not only appear strong to prosecutors, but actually be strong in court—often leading to wrongful convictions. The types of evidence in question are almost infinite, but include scientific tests and identification evidence that point to suspects other than the suspect, and witness evidence that suggested the suspect was somewhere else when the crime occurred or acted in self-defence. In an attempt to secure some limited balance of crime-control and due-process considerations, the Criminal Procedure and Investigations Act 1996 (CPIA 1996) created a three-stage process for disclosure, preceded by the police sending the CPS two schedules of material: 'non-sensitive' (that can, in principle, be seen by the defence) and 'sensitive' (for which a court order would have to be obtained—such as relating to state secrets, informers, or other covert methods of collecting intelligence). The three stages are: the CPS sends the defence all material that might undermine the prosecution case; the defence sends the CPS an outline of its case; the CPS then sends additional material that might assist that case. Leaving aside the issue of 'sensitive' material, the problems with this scheme include: the police often have little time, training, or inclination to do the job adequately; the CPS, as seen earlier, are adversarial and also are often disinclined to undermine their own cases; even were they more inclined to be objective, they are entirely reliant on the police for the information and how it is described in the schedules; and the system was in principle unfair in holding back material that could shed light on a claim of innocence (HM CPSI 2000; Plotnikoff and Woolfson 2001; Quirk 2006). The Criminal Cases Review Commission identified non-disclosure as the third most common reason for referring convictions to the Court of Appeal in its Annual Report for 1999–2000, and it identified this as a problem again four years later. The DPP himself accepted that this could lead to miscarriages of justice (*The Guardian*, 15 July 1999). The Criminal Justice Act 2003 attempts to deal with some of these problems by requiring disclosure of material possibly helpful to the defence at the first stage, but this leaves all the other problems unchanged (for background to the problem, see Leng 2002; for a fuller discussion see Sanders and Young 2006: ch. 7).

GUILTY PLEAS

Of those defendants whose cases proceed to a hearing, the overwhelming majority— around 60 per cent in the Crown Court and 92 per cent in the magistrates' courts— either plead guilty or fail to appear and are found guilty in their absence (Sanders and Young 2006: ch. 8) Why do so many defendants give up their right to put the prosecu-tion to proof? The nature of the legal profession is a major explanatory factor (Morison and Leith 1992; McConville *et al.* 1994; Mulcahy 1994), although the wider system and wider society shape legal attitudes and practices (McConville and Mirsky 1988 and 2005; Sanders and Young 1994). In both the United Kingdom and the United States, police and prosecutorial pre-trial practices are geared to securing guilty pleas. Confessions are particularly important, for it is difficult for suspects to contest the guilt that they admitted to the police earlier. Confessions, then, guarantee guilty pleas in most cases.

The system has increasingly encouraged overt bargaining to secure guilty pleas in recent years. Explicit plea-bargaining over sentence was banned under the *Turner*

[1970] Q.B. 321 rules, but following the decision in *Goodyear* [2005] EWCA Crim 888 Crown Court judges are now allowed at the pre-trial stage to indicate (on a request from the defendant) the maximum sentence they would impose if a guilty plea were to be entered immediately. This followed on from provisions in the Criminal Justice Act 2003 which allow a defendant in the magistrates' courts to ask whether a custodial or non-custodial penalty would be more likely were a guilty plea to be entered and the case dealt with summarily. These bargaining practices are underpinned by the systemic incentive to plead guilty provided by sentence discounts. These were first put on a statutory basis by the 1994 Criminal Justice and Public Order Act (section 48), but guilty pleas had attracted large discounts for years. A guilty plea sometimes determines not just the length, but also the type, of sentence, putting immense pressure on defendants (some of whom will be innocent) to admit guilt in order to avoid prison. However, since few offences have fixed sentences in Britain, the difference between reducing sentence for a guilty plea and raising it for a not guilty plea is largely presentational: it seems that many defendants are 'ripped off' in that they are not awarded the discounts that their guilty plea is supposed to merit (see discussion of previously unpublished research findings in Sanders and Young 2006: ch. 8). Bargaining also takes place between defence and prosecution over the seriousness of the charge and over venue, for cases that are kept in the lower courts are generally sentenced more lightly. All criminal courts now have pre-trial reviews which aim, among other things, to promote plea-bargaining.

We have seen that defence lawyers often fail to attend interrogations, sending to suspects the due process message that it is the court, not police questioning, which is important (Sanders *et al.* 1989). However, this facilitates crime-control practices at the police station, and hence confessions, leaving little for the defence lawyer to do in court other than to mitigate on a guilty plea and to bargain. J. Baldwin (1985), in a study of pre-trial reviews, showed that defence lawyers frequently provide information to the prosecution which they need not, agree not to press their case when it might succeed, and agree to 'lean on' or 'pressure' their clients or 'beat them over the head' (also see McConville *et al.* 1991, 1994). The result is a remarkably high guilty plea rate, achieved with the cooperation of the legal defence community. Inevitably, some innocent people plead guilty: over 10 per cent of guilty pleaders in the Crown Court claim to be innocent, in a similar number of cases the CPS believe there would have been a reasonable chance of acquittal, and in around half of these cases—some 1,400 each year—claims of innocence are believed by their barristers (Zander and Henderson 1993).

The RCCJ accepted the risk of the innocent sometimes pleading guilty because of 'the benefits to the system . . . of encouraging those who are in fact guilty to plead guilty' (1993: 111), although it underestimated the risks on scandalously thin grounds (McConville and Mirsky 1994). Moreover, the mass production of confessions and guilty pleas hides the absence of legal grounds in many cases for arrest, detention, and prosecution. This encourages 'fishing expeditions' by the police which impact not only on the legally guilty (whether factually so or not) but also on those held without charge (or prosecuted and acquitted) who should never have been deprived of their liberty without reasonable suspicion in the first place (McBarnet 1981; McConville *et al*. 1991; McConville and Mirsky 1992, 1995). Finally, the system has discriminatory effects: since black defendants contest their cases more often than do white defendants they get heavier sentences (Hood 1992). Yet the pressures to plead guilty are, as we have seen, increasing rather than decreasing. As a final example, less serious cases are now 'fast-tracked', which includes pressure to finish the case at the first hearing—almost inevitably, by a guilty plea. This 'Narey' reform (Narey 1997) gives little time to the police (to prepare a file, so the evidence will not always be complete), the CPS (to consider that evidence), and the defence lawyer, if there is one (to consider what plea to advise) (Bridges 1999).

The government's obsession with 'cracked trials' (last minute guilty pleas) and 'ineffective hearings' (i.e., where the case collapses or has to be adjourned) has led to a great deal of 'offender blaming'. By contrast, Bridges argues that cracked trials happen largely when the CPS agrees to reduce charges only at the last minute, and that many more relatively trivial cases go to the Crown Court because magistrates send them there (see also Herbert 2003), often at the behest of the prosecution (Cammiss 2006), than because defendants 'play the system' (Bridges *et al*. 2000; Bridges 2000). Similarly 'ineffective hearings' are largely caused by inadequate police and prosecution preparation (Lord Chancellor's Department 2001), which in turn is a product of the systemic expectation that the case will 'go guilty' anyway.

CONCLUSION

Criminal justice continually evolves in response to new ideas, new pressures, new scandals, and deeper socio-economic and political changes (Garland 2001). No system corresponds exactly with any one theoretical model, and there are always gaps between rhetoric, rules, and reality. Thus we have seen a largely due-process-based rhetoric (although in recent years crime-control rhetoric has featured prominently), rules which (often incoherently) combine both crime control and due process, and a largely crime-control reality. Even in court the presumption of innocence is compromised of the erosion of the right of silence, the guilty plea system, and bail systems whereby most decisions are made on the basis of police information.

The gap between many legal rules and the working rules of the police shows that the law appears to exert little moral force on the police. If legal rules were enforced rigorously it is not clear whether crime would be less well controlled. It depends on how successful the police (and associated agencies) are in establishing actual guilt and innocence. The infamous miscarriages of justice of the last twenty-five years raise serious doubts about this, as do the less dramatic findings of research on unsuccessful stops, NFAs in the police station, police inability to detect when suspects are telling the truth, questionable cautioning decisions, and the failure of cases in court. Just because due process is a suspect-orientated way of establishing 'truth' it does not follow that it is a less effective one. As it is, law-breaking by the police and lesser failures of due process are tolerated by a system which fails to punish and deter the police or to compensate most victims of those practices (despite a new police complaints body that, however, leaves most of the police complaints investigation system untouched: Sanders and Young 2006: ch. 12). It is argued by some (such as Maguire 2002) that changes to legal rules can radically change police practices rather than simply do so at the margin. These critics point to an apparent effect of PACE on changes in interrogations, leading to 'ethical interviewing', less informal interviewing, fewer confessions, and a drop in convictions. Early indications do suggest that there is some truth in this. However, the effect is seen, first, in the speedy response of government to erode the right of silence, thus returning to the police their reduced interrogation power; and, secondly, in the displacement of crime-control activity to another part of the system. Proactive policing—including the use of informants, surveillance, and bugging—is an increasingly important part of the police armoury. This is even less controllable and less visible than interrogation (Sanders and Young 2006: ch. 6). Patterns of bias on the street particularly concerning class and race are reproduced throughout the system, so that in the prisons black and working-class people in particular are grossly over-represented.

Suspects are not a subset of the wider criminal population; rather, criminals are a subset of the wider (official) suspect population. How closely this relates to the 'actually guilty' population must remain a matter of speculation, but any close relationship could well be coincidental. For the criminal justice system is not geared solely to detecting and punishing criminal activity. It—and its modern arm, the police—has always been at least as concerned with high-level politics and low-level disorder: that is, with the control of the less powerful. It follows that the interests of victims (especially less powerful victims) are furthered where this fits in with broader working rules, but not necessarily otherwise (Roach 1999; Garland 2001). The social integration and exclusion approach should, in future, help us to understand these processes more than any other model, for according to this approach the system prioritizes authority and control over the less powerful above justice, the Rule of Law, and the interests of victims—for victims can be the victims of exclusionary criminal justice practices as much as of criminal practices (Sanders 2002). This is especially true of ethnic minority victims (see Phillips and Bowling, Chapter 14, this volume).

Prospects for change depend in part on one's view of the reasons why criminal justice operates as it does. Bureaucratic explanations, which focus on the values of particular institutions, produce more optimistic scenarios than do societal ones. They also depend on the impact of changes to criminal justice processes, about which we know too little. There has been an explosion of criminal justice research in the last twenty-five years, but most of it is 'top-down', trying to solve the system's problems; very little has been 'bottom-up', asking what it feels like for suspects and defendants. Research should pay more attention to the experiences of suspects, to the lessons to be drawn from Northern Ireland, and to the linking of theoretical, policy, and empirical questions

(Hudson 1993) as in the few, but notable, examples of Hillyard 1993; Carlen 1996; Loader 1996; Choongh 1997; and McConville and Mirsky 2005.

Only rarely is the fundamental question 'why prosecute?' asked in relation to the police and the CPS. Prosecution often does too much and too little: in many cases it does too much by stigmatizing offenders and driving a wedge between them and their victims; and it does too little to protect victims from re-offending. In other cases it does too much by putting the victim through the ordeal of the court process and too little by allowing a plea-bargain, discontinuance, or acquittal which minimizes the harm done to the victim. For victims and defendants alike a reintegrative approach would be more effective and less alienating than the punitive dichotomous approach embodied in prosecution. Since victims are generally less punitive than the tabloid media would have us believe, this might be widely welcomed. So 'restorative' and conditional cautioning, in so far as these actually take place, are welcome, but traditional police agendas still dominate some restorative encounters, leaving offenders and victims almost as marginalized as before in some cases (R. Young and Goold 1999; R. Young 2001). This fits with our argument that prosecution processes and many diversionary processes are currently exclusionary. The question 'why prosecute?' is a question that could only be asked from an inclusionary perspective. The question is at least implicitly asked in one sphere of criminal justice: 'white-collar' law enforcement. Here, inclusionary policies are adopted by non-police agencies. They avoid prosecution and the other trappings of crime control such as arrest, detention, oppressive interrogation, and so forth. Instead they use techniques of 'compliance'. It is hardly credible that these differences are the product of bureaucratic pressures or accident. Present practice reflects processes of inclusion for 'white-collar criminals' and processes of exclusion for the poor, deprived, and powerless. This is a society in which some of the most damaging criminals are treated in the most humane ways while those who are arguably society's victims are treated as society's enemies so that, in time, they live up to their labels. The increasingly fuzzy boundary between civil and criminal processes, regarding antisocial behaviour, for example, exacerbates this problem (see Morgan and Newburn, and Downes and Morgan, Chapters 30 and 9, respectively, this volume). It remains to be seen whether the recent enthusiasm for restorative justice will result in more inclusionary freedom-enhancing ways of responding to street-level crime or will simply create new sites for unaccountable extensions of state power wielded to exclusionary ends.

■ SELECTED FURTHER READING

There are now several texts on criminal justice, many of which cover sentencing and penal policy as well as the earlier stages discussed in this chapter; the pick of the bunch is L. Zedner, *Criminal Justice* (Oxford: Oxford University Press, 2004). Most textbooks take either a 'legal' or a 'social policy' approach. Two texts which integrate legal and sociological material, and which do not discuss sentencing and penal policy, are A. Ashworth and M. Redmayne, *The*

Criminal Process, 3rd edn (Oxford: Oxford University Press, 2005) and A. Sanders and R. Young, *Criminal Justice*, 3rd edn (London: OUP, 2006). These books utilize contrasting theoretical frameworks: Ashworth and Redmayne adopt a human rights approach, while Sanders and Young use Packer's crime-control and due-process models for descriptive purposes and the freedom perspective as a prescriptive guide. For a detailed legal treatment see D. Clark, *Bevan and Lidstone's The Investigation of Crime* (London: LexisNexis, 2004).

Among the edited collections, N. Lacey (ed.), *Criminal Justice* (Oxford: Oxford University Press, 1994) provides a broad selection of previously published articles and book extracts, while T. Newburn (ed.), *Policing: Key Readings* (Cullompton, Devon: Willan, 2005) does exactly what it says on the tin. Original essays may be found in the same editor's *Handbook of Policing* (Cullompton, Devon: Willan, 2003). C. Walker and K. Starmer (eds), *Miscarriages of Justice: A Review of Justice in Error* (London: Blackstone, 1999) takes miscarriages of justice as its theme. All the chapters are written for the volume but summarize the salient issues arising from the main stages of the pre-trial and trial process. Another useful collection is M. McConville and G. Wilson (eds), *Handbook of Criminal Procedure* (Oxford: Oxford University Press, 2002).

Among the monographs in this area of work, D. McBarnet, *Conviction* (London: Macmillan, 1981) is still well worth reading for its analysis of the relationship between legal rules and the reality of the criminal justice system. Lawyers receive critical scrutiny from M. McConville, J. Hodgson, L. Bridges, and A. Pavlovic, *Standing Accused* (Oxford: Oxford University Press, 1994). High-quality monographs which blend theory with strong empirical analysis include I. Loader, *Youth, Policing and Democracy* (Basingstoke: Macmillan, 1996), C. Hoyle, *Negotiating Domestic Violence* (Oxford: Clarendon Press, 1998), S. Choongh, *Policing as Social Discipline* (Oxford: Clarendon Press, 1997) and K. Hawkins, *Law as Last Resort* (Oxford: Oxford University Press, 2002).

■ REFERENCES

ASHWORTH, A. (2002), 'Responsibilities, Rights and Restorative Justice', *British Journal of Criminology*, 42: 578.

——and REDMAYNE, M. (2005), *The Criminal Process*, 3rd edn, Oxford: Oxford University Press.

AULD, LORD JUSTICE (2001), *Review of he Criminal Courts of England and Wales*, London: TSO.

AYRES, M., and MURRAY, L. (2005), 'Arrests for Recorded Crime (Notifiable Offences) and the Operation of Certain Police Powers under PACE: England and Wales, 2004/05', Home Office Statistical Bulletin 21/05, London: Home Office.

BALDWIN, J. (1985), *Pre-Trial Justice*, Oxford: Basil Blackwell.

——(1993), 'Police Interview Techniques: Establishing Truth or Proof?' *British Journal of Criminology*, 33: 325.

——and BEDWARD, J. (1991), 'Summarising Tape Recordings of Police Interviews,' *Criminal Law Review*, 671.

——and MCCONVILLE, M. (1977), *Negotiated Justice*, Oxford: Martin Robertson.

BALDWIN, R. (2004), 'The New Punitive Regulation', *Modern Law Review* 67: 351.

BBC (2003), 'The Secret Policeman', documentary first broadcast on 21 October 2003.

BECKER, H. (1963), *Outsiders: Studies in the Sociology of Deviance*, New York: Free Press.

BILLINGSLEY R., NEMITZ T., and BEAN P. (eds) (2001), *Informers: Policing, Policy, Practice*, Cullompton, Devon: Willan.

BLAND, N., MILLER, J., and QUINTON, P. (2000), *Upping the PACE? An evaluation of the recommendations of the Stephen Lawrence Inquiry on stops and searches*, Police Research Series Paper 128, London: Home Office.

BRIDGES, L. (1999), 'False Starts and Unrealistic Expectations', *Legal Action*, 6 October: 6.

——(2000), 'Taking Liberties', *Legal Action*, 6 July: 8.

——, CHOONGH, S., and McCONVILLE, M. (2000), *Ethnic Minority Defendants and the Right to Elect Jury Trial*, London: CRE.

BRITTON, N. (2000), 'Race and Policing: A Study of Police Custody', *British Journal of Criminology*, 40: 639.

BROWN, D. (1997), *PACE Ten Years On: A Review of the Research*, Home Office Research Study No. 155. London: HMSO.

—— and ELLIS, T. (1994), *Policing Low Level Disorder*. Home Office Research Study No. 135. London: HMSO.

—— and LARCOMBE, K. (1992), *Changing the Code: Police Detention under the Revised PACE Codes of Practice*, Home Office Research Study No. 129, London: HMSO.

BROWNLEE, I. (2004), 'The Statutory Charging Scheme in England and Wales: Towards a Unified Prosecution System?, *Criminal Law Review*, 896.

BUCKE, T., and BROWN, D. (1997), *In Police Custody: Police Powers and Suspects' Rights under the Revised PACE Codes of Practice*, Home Office Research Study No. 174, London: HMSO.

——, STREET, R., and BROWN, D. (2000), *The Right of Silence: The Impact of the CJPO 1994*, Home Office Research Study No. 199, London: HMSO.

BURROW, J. (2000), 'Bail and the Human Rights Act 1998', *New Law Journal* 150: 677.

CAMERON, M. (1964), *The Booster and the Snitch*, New York: Free Press.

CAMMISS, S. (2006), '"I will in a moment give you the full history": Mode of Trial, Prosecutorial Control and Partial Accounts' *Criminal Law Review*: 38.

CAPE, E. (2003), *Defending Suspects at Police Stations*, 4th edn, London: LAG.

—— (ed.) (2004), *Reconcilable Rights? Analysing the Tension Between Victims and Defendants*, London: LAG.

CARLEN, P. (1996), *Jigsaw: A Political Criminology of Youth Homelessness*, Buckingham: Open University Press.

CHAN, J. (1996), 'Changing Police Culture', *British Journal of Criminology*, 36: 109.

CHOONGH, S. (1997), *Policing as Social Discipline*, Oxford: Clarendon Press.

CLANCY A., HOUGH M., AUST, R., and KERSHAW C. (2001), *Crime, Policing and Justice: the experience of ethnic minorities. Findings from the 2000 British Crime Survey*, Home Office Research Study No. 223, London: Home Office.

CLARKE, C., and MILNE, R. (2001), *National Evaluation of the PEACE Investigative Interviewing Scheme*, Police Research Award Scheme Report No: PRAS/149, London: Home Office.

CLARKSON, C., CRETNEY, A., DAVIES, G., and SHEPHERD, J. (1994), 'Criminalising Assault', *British Journal of Criminology*, 34: 15.

CRETNEY, A., and DAVIS, G. (1996), 'Prosecuting Domestic Assault', *Criminal Law Review*, 162.

DAMASKA, E. (1973), 'Evidentiary Barriers to Conviction and Two Models of Criminal Procedure: A Comparative Study', *University of Pennsylvania Law Review*, 121: 506–89.

DHAMI, M., and AYTON, P. (2001), 'Bailing and Jailing the Fast and Frugal Way' *Journal of Behavioural Decision Making*, 14: 141.

DIXON, D. (1991), 'Common Sense, Legal Advice, and the Right of Silence', *Public Law*, 233–54.

—— (1992), 'Legal Regulation and Policing Practice', *Social and Legal Studies*, 1: 515.

—— (2005), 'Regulating Police Interrogation', in T. Williamson, *Investigative Interviewing: Rights, research, regulation*, Cullompton, Devon: Willan.

——, BOTTOMLEY, A., COLEMAN, C., GILL, M., and WALL, D. (1989), 'Reality and Rules in the Construction and Regulation of Police Suspicion', *International Journal of the Sociology of Law*, 17: 185–206.

—— (1990), 'Safeguarding the Rights of Suspects in Police Custody', *Policing and Society*, 1: 115–40.

DOHERTY, M., and EAST, R. (1985), 'Bail Decisions in Magistrates' Courts', *British Journal of Criminology*, 25: 251–66.

DUFF, P. (1998), 'Crime Control, Due Process and "The Case for the Prosecution" ', *British Journal of Criminology*, 38: 611.

DUNNIGHAN, C., and NORRIS, C. (1996), 'A Risky Business: The Recruitment and Running of Informers by English Police Officers: *Police Studies*, 19:1.

EASTON, S. (1998), *The Case for the Right of Silence*, Aldershot: Ashgate.

EDWARDS, I. (2006), 'Restorative Justice, Sentencing and the Court of Appeal', *Criminological Law Review*, 110–23.

ERICSON, R. (1981), *Making Crime*, London: Butterworths.

EVANS, R. (1993), 'The Conduct of Police Interviews with Juveniles', Royal Commission on Criminal Justice, Research Study No. 8, London: HMSO.

—— and FERGUSON, T. (1991), *Comparing Different Juvenile Cautioning Systems in One Police Force*, London: Home Office, unpublished report.

EVANS, R., and PUECH, K. (2001), 'Reprimands and Warnings: Populist Punitiveness or Restorative Justice?', *Criminal Law Review*, 794.

FAULKNER, D. (1996), *Darkness and Light*, London: Howard League.

——(2001), *Crime, State and Citizen: A Field Full of Folk*, Winchester: Waterside Press.

FIELD, S., and PELSER, C. (1998), *Invading the Private: State Accountability and New Investigative Methods in Europe*, Aldershot: Dartmouth

——and THOMAS, P. (eds), (1994), *Justice and Efficiency?*, Oxford: Blackwell.

FITZGERALD, M. (1999), *Stop and Search: Final Report*, London: Metropolitan Police.

FOSTER, J. (2003), 'Police Cultures', in T. Newburn (ed.), *Handbook of Policing*, Cullompton, Devon: Willan.

GARLAND, D. (2001), *The Culture of Control*, Oxford: Oxford University Press.

GILLESPIE, A. (2005), 'Reprimanding Juveniles and the Right to Due Process', *Modern Law Review*, 68: 1006.

GOLDSTEIN, J. (1960), 'Police Discretion not to Invoke the Criminal Process: Low Visibility Decisions in the Administration of Justice', *Yale Law Journal*, 69: 543.

GORIELY, T. (2003), 'Evaluating the Scottish Public Defence Solicitors' Office', *Journal of Law and Society*, 30: 84.

GRAY, P. (2005), 'The Politics of Risk and Young Offenders' Experiences of Social Exclusion and Restorative Justice', *British Journal of Criminology*, 45: 938.

GUDJONSSON, G. (2003), *The Psychology of Interrogations and Confessions: A Handbook*, Chichester: Wiley.

——and MCKEITH, J. (1982), 'False Confessions', in A. Trankell (ed), *Reconstructing the Past*, Deventer: Kluwer.

——and ——(1988), 'Retracted Confessions: Legal, Psychological and Psychiatric Aspects', *Medicine, Science, and the Law*, 28: 187–94.

HAWKINS, K. (2002), *Law as Last Resort*, Oxford: Oxford University Press.

HERBERT, A. (2003), 'Mode of Trial and Magistrates' Sentencing Powers: Will increased powers inevitably lead to a reduction in the committal rate?', *Criminological Law Review*, 314.

HILLYARD, P. (1993), *Suspect Community*, London: Pluto.

HM CPSI (1999), *Review of adverse cases*, London: CPSI.

——(2000), *Thematic Review of the Disclosure of Unused Material*, London: CPSI.

——(2003), *Thematic review of attrition in the prosecution process (the Justice Gap)*, London: CPSI.

——(2004), *A follow-up review of cases with an ethnic minority dimension*, London: CPSI.

HMIC and HM CPSI (2004), *Violence at Home: The Investigation and Prosecution of Cases Involving Domestic Violence*, London.

HODGSON, J. (2001), 'The Police, the Prosecutor and the Juge d'Instruction: Judicial Supervision in France, Theory and Practice', *British Journal of Criminology*, 41: 342–61.

HOLDAWAY, S. (1983), *Inside the British Police*, Oxford: Blackwell.

HOME OFFICE (2002), *Justice for All*, ch. 1, Cm. 5563, London: Stationery Office.

——(2005a), *Stop & Search Manual*, London: Home Office.

——(2005b), *Statistics on Race and the Criminal Justice System 2004*, London: Home Office.

HOOD, R. (1992), *Race and Sentencing*, Oxford: Oxford University Press.

HOYLE, C. (1998), *Negotiating Domestic Violence*, Oxford: Clarendon Press.

HUCKLESBY, A. (1994), 'The Use and Abuse of Conditional Bail', *Howard Journal*, 33: 258.

——(1996), 'Bail or Jail', *Journal of Law and Society*, 23: 213.

——(2001), 'Police Bail and the Use of Conditions', *Criminal Justice*, 1: 441.

——(2004), 'Not necessarily a trip to the police station', *Criminal Law Review*, 803.

——and MARSHALL, E. (2000), 'Tackling Offending on Bail', *Howard Journal*, 39: 150.

HUDSON, B. (1993), *Racism and Criminology*, London: Sage.

HUTTER, B. (1988), *The Reasonable Arm of the Law? The Law Enforcement Procedures of Environmental Health Officers*, Oxford: Oxford University Press.

IRVING, B. (1980), *Police Interrogation: A Study of Current Practice*, London: HMSO.

——(1985), 'Research Into Policy Won't Go', in E. Alves and J. Shapland (eds), *Legislation for Policing Today: The PACE Act*, Leicester: Leicester University Press.

JUSTICE (2001), *Public Defenders: Learning from the US Experience*, London: JUSTICE.

KEITH, M. (1993), *Race, Riots and Policing*, London: UCL Press.

LAING, J. (1995), 'The Mentally Disordered Suspect at the Police Station', *Criminal Law Review*, 371.

—— (1999), *Care or Custody? Mentally Disordered Offenders in the Criminal Justice System*, Oxford: Oxford University Press.

LENG, R. (1992), 'The Right to Silence in Police Interrogation', RCCJ Research Study No. 10, London: HMSO.

—— (2002) 'The Exchange of Information and Disclosure', in M. McConville and G. Wilson (eds), *Handbook of the Criminal Justice Process*, Oxford: Oxford University Press.

LEO, R. (1994), 'Police Interrogation and Social Control', *Social and Legal Studies*, 3: 93.

LITTLECHILD, B. (1995), 'Re-assessing the Role of the Appropriate Adult', *Criminal Law Review*, 540.

LOADER, I. (1996), *Youth, Policing and Democracy*, Basingstoke: Macmillan.

LORD CHANCELLOR'S DEPARTMENT (2001), *Evaluation Report of the Joint Performance Management Pilot Scheme on Cracked, Ineffective and Vacated Trials*, London: Lord Chancellor's Department. Available from www.dca.gov.uk/magist/evaluation. htm.

MCARA. L., and MCVIE S. (2005), 'The Usual Suspects? Street-Life, Young People and the Police', *Criminal Justice*, 5(1): 5.

MCBARNET, D. (1981), *Conviction*, London: Macmillan.

MCCONVILLE, M. (1992), 'Videotaping Interrogations: Police Behaviour on and off Camera', *Criminal Law Review*, 522–48.

—— and BRIDGES, L. (eds) (1994), *Criminal Justice in Crisis*, Aldershot: Edward Elgar.

—— and HODGSON, J. (1992), 'Custodial Legal Advice and the Right to Silence', RCCJ Research Study No. 16, London: HMSO.

—— and MIRSKY, C. (1988), 'The State, the Legal Profession, and the Defence of the Poor', *Journal of Law and Society*, 15: 342–60.

—— and —— (1992), 'What's in the Closet: The Plea Bargaining Skeletons', *New Law Journal*, 142: 1373–81.

—— and —— (1994), 'Re-defining and Structuring Guilt in Systemic Terms', in M. McConville and L. Bridges (eds), *Criminal Justice in Crisis*, Aldershot: Edward Elgar.

—— and —— (1995), 'The Rise of Guilty Pleas', *Journal of Law and Society*, 22: 443.

—— and —— (2005), *Jury Trials and Plea Bargaining: A True History*, Oxford: Hart.

—— SANDERS, A., and LENG, R. (1991), *The Case for the Prosecution*, London: Routledge.

——, ——, and —— (1997), 'Descriptive or Critical Sociology', *British Journal of Criminology*, 37: 347.

—— HODGSON, J., BRIDGES, L., and PAVLOVIC, A. (1994), *Standing Accused*, Oxford: Oxford University Press.

MCKEEVER, G. (1999), 'Detecting, Prosecuting and Punishing Benefit Fraud: The Social Security Administration (Fraud) Act 1997', *Modern Law Review*, 62: 261.

MACPHERSON, SIR WILLIAM (1999), *The Stephen Lawrence Inquiry*, Cm 4262-I, London: Stationery Office.

MAGUIRE, M. (1992), 'Complaints against the Police: Where Now?', unpublished paper.

—— (2002), 'Regulating the police station: the case of the Police and Criminal Evidence Act 1984', in M. McConville and G. Wilson (eds), *Handbook of Criminal Procedure*, Oxford: Oxford University Press.

—— and NORRIS, C. (1992), *The Conduct and Supervision of Criminal Investigations*, RCCJ Research Study No. 5, London: HMSO.

MHLANGA, B. (2000), *Race and the CPS*, London: Stationery Office.

MIDDLETON, D. (2005), 'The Legal and Regulatory Response to Solicitors Involved in Serious Fraud: Is Regulatory Action More Effective than Criminal Prosecution?', *British Journal of Criminology*, 45: 810.

MILLER, J., BLAND, N., and QUINTON, P. (2000), *The Impact of Stops and Searches on Crime and the Community*, Police Research Series Paper 127, London: Home Office.

MORGAN, P. (1996), 'Bail in England and Wales: Understanding the Operation of Bail', in F. Paterson (ed.), *Understanding Bail in Britain*. London: HMSO.

—— and HENDERSON, P. (1998), *Remand Decisions and Offending on Bail*, Home Office Research Study No. 184, London: Home Office.

MORISON, J., and LEITH, P. (1992), *The Barrister's World*, Oxford: Oxford University Press.

MOSTON, S. (1992), 'Police Questioning Techniques in Tape Recorded Interviews with Criminal Suspects', *Policing and Society*, 3.

—— and Stephenson, G. (1993), 'The Questioning and Interviewing of Suspects outside the Police Station', Royal Commission on Criminal Justice, Research Study No. 22, London: HMSO.

—— and Williamson, T. (1992), 'The Effects of Case Characteristics on Suspect Behaviour during Police Questioning', *British Journal of Criminology*, 32: 23–40.

Mulcahy, A. (1994), 'The Justifications of Justice', *British Journal of Criminology*, 34: 411.

Murphy, D. (1986), *Customers and Thieves*, Farnborough: Gower.

MVA and Miller, J. (2000), *Profiling Populations Available for Stops and Searches*, Police Research Series Paper 131, London: Home Office.

NACRO (1997), *Policing Local Communities: The Tottenham Experiment*, London: NACRO.

Narey, M (1997), *Review of Delay in the Criminal Justice System*, London: Home Office.

Newburn, T., and Hayman, S. (2002), *Policing, Surveillance and Social Control*, Cullompton, Devon: Willan.

——, Shiner, M., and Hayman, S. (2004), 'Race, crime and injustice? Strip-search and the treatment of suspects in custody', *British Journal of Criminology*, 44: 677.

Nicholas S., Povey D., Walker A., and Kershaw C. (2005), *Crime in England and Wales 2004/2005*, Home Office Statistical Bulletin 11/05, London: Home Office.

Noaks, L., Levi, M., and Maguire, M. (eds) (1995), *Contemporary Issues in Criminology*, Cardiff: University of Wales Press.

Norris, C., *et al.* (1992), 'Black and Blue: an Analysis of the Influence of Race on Being Stopped by the Police', *British Journal of Sociology*, 43: 207.

O'Mahony, P. (1992), 'The Kerry Babies Case: Towards a Social Psychological Analysis', *Irish Journal of Psychology*, 13: 223.

Packer, H. (1968), *The Limits of the Criminal Sanction*, Stanford, Cal.: Stanford University Press.

Palmer, C. (1996), 'Still Vulnerable After All These Years', *Criminal Law Review*, 633.

Pantazis, C., and Gordon, D. (1997), 'TV Licence Evasion and the Criminalisation of Female Poverty', *Howard Journal of Criminal Justice*, 36: 170.

Paradine, K., and Wilkinson, J. (2004), *Protection and Accountability: The Reporting, Investigation and Prosecution of Domestic Violence Cases*, London: HMIC and HM CPSI.

Paterson, F., and Whitaker, C. (1994), *Operating Bail*, Edinburgh: HMSO.

—— and —— (1995), 'Criminal Justice Cultures: Negotiating Bail and Remand', in L. Noaks (ed.), *Contemporary Issues in Criminology*, Cardiff: University of Wales Press.

Phillips, C., and Brown, D. (1998), *Entry into the Criminal Justice System*, Home Office Research Studies No. 185, London: Home Office.

Plotnikoff, J., and Woolfson, R. (2001), *'A Fair Balance'? Evaluation of the Operation of Disclosure Law*, London: Home Office.

Pollard, C. (1996), 'Public Safety, Accountability and the Courts', *Criminal Law Review*, 152.

Quinton, P., Bland, N., and Miller, J. (2000), *Police Stops, Decision-making and Practice*, Police Research Series Paper 130, London: Home Office.

Quirk, H. (2006), 'The significance of culture in criminal procedure reform: why the revised disclosure scheme cannot work', *Evidence and Proof*, 10: 42.

Raine, J., and Willson, M. (1997), 'Police Bail with Conditions', *British Journal of Criminology*, 37: 593.

Reiner, R. (2000), *The Politics of the Police*, 3rd edn, Oxford: Oxford University Press

Roach, K. (1999), *Due Process and Victim's Rights*, Toronto: Toronto University Press..

Royal Commission on Criminal Justice (1993), *Report*, London: HMSO.

Royal Commission on Criminal Procedure (1981), *Report*, London: HMSO.

Sanders, A. (2002), 'Victim Participation in Criminal Justice and Social Exclusion', in C. Hoyle and R. Young (eds), *New Visions of Crime Victims*, Oxford, Hart:

—— and Young, R. (1994), 'The Rule of Law, Due Process and Pre-trial Criminal Justice', *Current Legal Problems*, 47: 125.

—— and —— (2006), *Criminal Justice*, 3rd edn, London: Oxford University Press.

——, ——, Bridges, L., Mulvaney, A., and Crozier, G. (1989), *Advice and Assistance at Police Stations and the 24 Hour Duty Solicitor Scheme*, London: Lord Chancellor's Department.

—— Creaton, J., Bird, S., and Weber, L. (1997), *Victims with Learning Disabilities: Negotiating the Criminal Justice System*, Occasional Paper No. 17, Oxford: Centre for Criminological Research.

SCARMAN, LORD (1981), *The Scarman Report: The Brixton Disorders*, London: HMSO.

SCOTT, M., and LYMAN, S. (1968), 'Accounts', *American Sociological Review*, 33: 46–62.

SHAPLAND, J., and VAGG, J. (1988), *Policing by the Public*, London: Routledge.

SLAPPER, G. (1999), *Blood in the Bank: Social and Legal Aspects of Death at Work*, Aldershot: Ashgate.

SMITH, D. (1997), 'Case Construction and the Goals of the Criminal Process', *British Journal of Criminology*, 37: 319.

—— (1998), 'Reform or Moral Outrage', *British Journal of Criminology*, 38: 616.

STEER, J. (1980), *Uncovering Crime: The Police Role*, London: HMSO.

TYLER, R. T. (1990), *Why Do People Obey the Law?*, New Haven, Conn., and London: Yale University Press.

VOGT, G., and WADHAM, J. (2003), *Deaths in Police Custody: Redress and Remedies*, London: Civil Liberties Trust.

VRIJ, A. (2000), *Detecting Lies and Deceit*, Chichester: Wiley.

WADDINGTON, P., STENSON, K., and DON, D. (2004), 'In proportion: Race, and Police Stop and Search', *British Journal of Criminology*, 44(6): 889.

WALKER, C., and WALL, D. (1997), 'Imprisoning the Poor: TV Licence Evaders and the Criminal Justice System', *Criminal Law Review*, 173.

WALKLEY, J. (1987), *Police Interrogation*, Police Review, London: HMSO.

WARBURTON, H., MAY, T., and HOUGH, M. (2005), 'Looking the Other Way: The Impact of Reclassifying Cannabis on Police Warnings, Arrests and Informal Action in England and Wales', *British Journal of Criminology*, 113.

WOOLF, LORD JUSTICE (1991), *Prison Disturbances April 1990*, Report of an Inquiry by The Rt. Hon. Lord Justice Woolf (Parts I and II) and His Honour Judge Stephen Tumim (Part II), Cm 1456, London: HMSO.

YOUNG, H. (2002), 'Securing Fair Treatment: An Examination of the Diversion of Mentally Disordered Offenders from Police Custody', unpublished PhD thesis, Birmingham University.

YOUNG, J. (1999), *The Exclusive Society*, London: Sage.

YOUNG, M. (1991), *An Inside Job*, Oxford: Oxford University Press.

YOUNG, R. (2001), 'Just Cops Doing "Shameful" Business: Police-Led Restorative Justice and the Lessons of Research', in A. Morris and G. Maxwell (eds), *Restorative Justice for Juveniles*, Oxford: Hart.

——, and GOOLD, B. (1999), 'Restorative Police Cautioning in Aylesbury: From Degrading to Reintegrative Shaming Ceremonies?', *Criminal Law Review*, 126.

—— and HOYLE, C. (2003), 'Restorative Justice and Punishment', in S. McConville (ed), *The Use of Punishment*, Cullompton, Devon: Willan.

—— and SANDERS, A. (1994), 'The Royal Commission on Criminal Justice: A confidence trick?', *Oxford Journal of Legal Studies*, 14: 435.

—— and —— (2004), 'The Ethics of Prosecution Lawyers', *Legal Ethics*, 7(2): 190.

ZANDER, M., and HENDERSON, P. (1993), 'Crown Court Study', Royal Commission on Criminal Justice, Research Study No. 19, London: HMSO.

29

SENTENCING

Andrew Ashworth

The passing of a sentence on an offender is probably the most public face of the criminal justice process. This chapter discusses several aspects of the sentencing decision. It begins by pointing to the growing politicization of sentencing policy, a trend which threatens to marginalize principled and empirically based arguments about sentencing. The chapter does not follow that trend. It turns next to examine the various rationales for sentencing. There is then detailed discussion, in turn, of sentencing procedures, of custodial sentencing, and of non-custodial sentencing. In conclusion, possible directions for the reform of sentencing are considered.

SENTENCING AND POLITICS

The 1990s witnessed a sharp rise in the politicization and in the severity of sentencing policy (for broader analysis, see Downes and Morgan, Chapter 9, this volume). Although the Criminal Justice Act 1991 was chiefly a moderating piece of legislation, the judges and some magistrates objected to the fettering of the discretion they had previously enjoyed, objections which gained some strength from the abysmal drafting of parts of the 1991 Act. Their campaign was soon taken up more widely, and in 1993, a year of heightened media interest in law and order, the government brought forward legislation which abandoned some key pillars of the 1991 Act. The appointment of Michael Howard as Home Secretary brought 'law and order' to the very centre of party politics: he proclaimed that 'prison works', and introduced a range of measures including curtailment of the right of silence and major changes to the law on disclosure of evidence. A populist sentencing policy soon came to be thought politically advantageous for both major parties, with Howard leading the way and challenging the then Opposition to disagree, at peril of being called 'soft on crime'. When Howard proposed the introduction of mandatory minimum sentences, the Labour Party did not oppose them, and it was largely left to the Lord Chief Justice, other senior judges, and some bishops to force amendments in the House of Lords (see Dunbar and Langdon 1998; Ashworth 2001; Downes and Morgan, Chapter 9, this volume).

Under New Labour there has been a bewildering mixture of policies. Crime prevention has been a priority, and this has also led to various initiatives for reducing reoffending ('accredited programmes') in the prisons and in the community. Some restorative elements have been introduced into youth justice, and in some areas into the adult system. At the same time, there is an abiding strain of severity, apparent both in the use of custody generally and in the targeting of repeat offenders. The enormous rise in the prison population (from 42,000 in early 1993 to 61,000 in 1997 to 70,000 in 2002 and to 77,000 in late 2005) cannot be justified, especially at a time of declining crime as reported by the British Crime Survey (almost a 40 per cent decline from 1995 to 2004: Dodd *et al.* 2004: Table 2.1). Although the government is 'talking up' community sentences and planning the reinvigoration of fines, the most visible aspects of its sentencing policy remain the raising of maximum sentences, escalating penalties for persistent offenders, lengthy incarceration for a widely defined category of 'dangerous' offenders, and the proliferation of preventive orders (of which the Anti-Social Behaviour Order is the most prominent) which have custody as the chief response to breach. The cumulative consequences of all these developments are reflected in the sentencing trends exhibited in Table 29.1.

Table 29.1 Percentage use of different sentences for males aged 21 and over sentenced for indictable offences at all courts, England and Wales, 1975–2004

Disposals	1975	1980	1985	1990	1995	2000	2004[1]
Absolute/conditional discharge	9	7	9	13	15	13	14
Fine	55	52	43	43	34	28	23
Community rehabilitation order[2]	6	5	7	7	11	11	11
Community punishment order[3]	1	4	7	7	11	9	9
Community punishment and rehabilitation order[4]	–	–	–	–	3	3	2
Curfew order	–	–	–	–	–	0	2
Drug treatment and testing order	–	–	–	–	–	0	3
Fully suspended imprisonment	13	12	12	10	1	1	1
Immediate imprisonment	16	17	17	17	24	30	31
Total numbers sentenced	**170,000**	**200,300**	**211,700**	**188,400**	**178,400**	**184,700**	**187,600**

Notes: (1) Figures for 2005 currently unavailable.
(2) Probation order prior to April 2001.
(3) Community service order prior to April 2001.
(4) Combination order prior to April 2001.

RATIONALES FOR SENTENCING

The events of recent years can only sharpen interest in examining the justifications for sentencing in general and for particular sentencing policies. When a court passes sentence, it authorizes the use of state coercion against a person for committing an offence. The sanction may take the form of some deprivation, restriction, or positive obligation. Deprivations and obligations are fairly widespread in social contexts—e.g., duties to pay taxes, to complete various forms, etc. But when imposed as a sentence, there is the added element of condemnation, labelling, and censure of the offender for what has been done. In view of the direct personal and indirect social effects this can have, it calls for justification.

Much writing about the rationales of sentencing has focused on one or more particular justifications. In order to unravel punishment as a social institution, however, and to understand the tensions inherent in any given 'system', there is benefit in identifying the main thrusts of the several approaches. Among the issues to be considered are the behavioural and the political premises of each approach, its empirical claims, and its practical influence.

DESERT OR RETRIBUTIVE THEORIES

Retributive theories of punishment have a long history, including in the writings of Kant and Hegel. In their modern guise as the desert approach, they came to prominence in the 1970s, to some extent propelled by the alleged excesses and failures of rehabilitative ideals (von Hirsch 1976; Bottoms and Preston 1980). Desert theorists argue that punishment is justified as the morally appropriate response to crime: those who culpably commit offences deserve disapproving censure; this censure should be conveyed through some 'hard treatment' that prompts the offender to take the censure seriously, but the amount of hard treatment should remain proportionate to the degree of wrongdoing, respecting the offender as a moral agent (see von Hirsch and Ashworth 2005). The justification for the institution of state punishment also incorporates the consequentialist element of underlying general deterrence: without the restraining effect of a system of state punishment, anarchy might well ensue. Some, notably Duff (2000), tie further consequentialist aims into a fundamentally retributivist justification, arguing that punishment ought not only to communicate justified censure but also thereby to persuade offenders to repentance, self-reform, and reconciliation. The behavioural premise of desert is that individuals are and should be treated as responsible (though occasionally fallible) moral agents. The political premise is that all individuals should be respected as moral agents: an offender deserves punishment, but does not forfeit all rights on conviction, and has a right not to be punished disproportionately to the crime committed.

Proportionality is the key concept in desert theory (cf. the critique by Bottoms 1998). Cardinal proportionality is concerned with the magnitude of the penalty, requiring that it not be out of proportion to the gravity of the conduct: five years' imprisonment for theft from a shop would clearly breach that, as would a small penalty for a very serious offence. Social conventions and cultural traditions tend to determine the 'anchoring points' of the punishment scale, i.e. the contrasting levels at which sentences are set in different national or historical contexts, although these conventions can change for various reasons. Ordinal proportionality concerns the ranking of the relative serious-ness of different offences. In practice, much depends here on the evaluation of conduct, especially by sentencers, and on social assumptions about traditional or 'real' crime (e.g. street crime) compared with new types of offence (e.g. commercial fraud, pollu-tion). In theory, ordinal proportionality requires the creation of a scale of values which can be used to assess the gravity of each type of offence: culpability, together with aggra-vating and mitigating factors, must then be assimilated into the scale. This task, which is vital to any approach in which proportionality plays a part, makes considerable demands on theory (see von Hirsch and Ashworth 2005: Appendix 3; Ashworth 2005: ch. 4); some would say that decisions on relative offence-seriousness can never be more than contingent judgements which bear the marks of the prevailing power structure.

DETERRENCE THEORIES

Deterrence theories regard the prevention of further offences through a deterrent strategy as the rationale for punishing. As an exercise of state power, sentencing can be justified only by its consequences. The quantum of the sentence depends on the type of deterrent theory. There is little modern literature on individual deterrence, which sees the deterrence of further offences by the particular offender as the measure of punish-ment. A first offender may require little or no punishment. A recidivist might be thought to require an escalation of penalties. The seriousness of the offence becomes less important than the prevention of repetition. Traces of this approach can certainly be detected in the treatment of persistent offenders and so-called 'dangerous offenders' in contemporary sentencing, as noted below.

More attention has been devoted to general deterrence, which involves calculating the penalty on the basis of what might be expected to deter others from committing a similar offence. Major utilitarian writers such as Bentham (1789; cf. Walker 1991) and economic theorists such as Posner (1985) develop the notion of setting penalties at levels sufficient to outweigh the likely benefits of offending. The behavioural premise is that of responsible and predominantly rational, calculating individuals—a premise that criminologists may call into question. The political premise is that the greatest good of the greatest number represents the supreme value, and that the individual counts only for one: it may therefore be justifiable to punish one person severely in order to deter others effectively, thereby overriding the claims of proportionality. The strength of this reasoning depends on convincing empirical evidence of the effect of deterrent sentencing on individual behaviour. This requires, among other things, demonstration that people are aware of the level of likely sentences; and that they desist from offending largely because of that sentence level and not for other reasons.

A careful analysis of the general deterrence research by von Hirsch *et al.* (1999) found that there is some evidence of a link between the *certainty* of punishment and crime rates, but considerably weaker evidence of a link between the *severity* of sentences and crime rates (see also Doob and Webster 2003). This distinction is particularly important when marginal deterrence is the issue, i.e. not whether the threat of punishment deters (which it often does), but whether the threat of greater punishment would have greater deterrent effect. The authors discuss reasons why the commonsense belief that greater punishment would deter more cannot be accepted without substantial qualifications: it is heavily dependent on the context.

REHABILITATIVE SENTENCING

Sentencing aimed at the reformation of the offender's law-breaking tendencies has a lengthy history, being evident in the early days of probation and of borstal institutions. The rationale here is to prevent further offending by the individual through the strategy of rehabilitation, which may involve therapy, counselling, intervention in the family, cognitive-behavioural programmes, skills training, etc. Still a leading rationale in many European countries, it reached its zenith in the United States in the 1960s, declined spectacularly in the 1970s, and then began to regain ground in the 1990s (see von Hirsch and Ashworth 1998: ch. 1). A humanitarian desire to provide help for those with obvious behavioural problems has ensured that various treatment programmes continue to be developed. The key issue is the effectiveness of various interventions, and there is a long-running debate about the concept and the measurement of effectiveness (e.g. Lloyd *et al.* 1994). The true position is probably that certain rehabilitative programmes are likely to work for some types of offender in some circumstances. The 'What Works?' movement has rekindled interest in various programmes for behaviour modification, with the development of 'accredited' programmes in prisons and as part of community sentences (see McGuire 2002; Harper and Chitty 2005), but a sober assessment of the available results shows that the claims made by the Home Office and other protagonists have not been translated into practice (Bottoms 2004).

The behavioural premise of rehabilitative theory is that some or many criminal offences are to a significant extent determined by social pressures, psychological difficulties, or situational problems of various kinds. Drug treatment and testing programmes are a particular example of this; more generally, the links with positivist criminology are strong. The political premise is that offenders are seen as unable to cope in certain situations and as in need of help from experts, and therefore (perhaps) as less than fully responsible individuals. The rehabilitative approach indicates that sentences should be tailored to the needs of the particular offenders: in so far as this needs-based approach places no limits on the extent of the intervention, it conflicts with the idea of a right not to be punished disproportionately. Its focus instead is upon the processes of diagnosis, treatment, and the completion of accredited programmes. 'Diagnostic' tools such as OASys and the pre-sentence report are seen as essential to this approach to sentencing (see further Raynor, Chapter 31, this volume).

INCAPACITATIVE SENTENCING

The incapacitative approach is to identify offenders or groups of offenders who are likely to do such harm in the future that special protective measures (usually in the form of lengthy incarceration) are warranted. The primary example of this, introduced by the Criminal Justice Act 2003, is IPP (imprisonment for public protection), prescribed for certain offenders classified as dangerous. The nature of this sentence is discussed below.

The incapacitative approach has no behavioural premise. It is neither linked with any particular causes of offending nor dependent on changing the behaviour of offenders: it looks chiefly to predicted risk and to the protection of potential victims. The political premise is often presented as utilitarian, justifying incapacitation by reference to the greater aggregate social benefit and therefore sacrificing the individual's right not to be punished disproportionately to the wrongdoing. It is sometimes said that in these cases the rights of potential victims are being preferred to the rights of the offenders. This notion of a conflict of rights attracted some discussion in the Floud Report, which also found that predictions of 'dangerousness' tended to be wrong more often than not (Floud and Young 1981); rather different analyses of the conflict of rights can be found in Bottoms and Brownsword (1982) and Wood (1988). The repeatedly confirmed fallibility of predictive judgments (e.g., Brody and Tarling 1981; Monahan 2004) calls into question the justification for any lengthening of sentences on grounds of public protection, and yet the political pressure to have some form(s) of incapacitative sentence available to the courts has been felt in most countries. If this is the reality of penal politics then there is surely a strong case for procedural safeguards to ensure that the predictive judgments are soundly based and open to thorough challenge, ideals not achieved in the Criminal Justice Act 2003. Various proposals for the special incarceration of certain 'dangerous' disturbed citizens, floated in the Dangerous People with Severe Personality Disorder Bill 1999 but not yet enacted, are open to many procedural and substantive objections (see McAlinden (2001); and Peay, Chapter 16, this volume).

RESTORATIVE AND REPARATIVE THEORIES

These are not regarded as theories of punishment. Rather, their argument is that sentences should move away from punishment of the offender towards restitution and reparation, aimed at restoring the harm done to the victim and to the community (see Hoyle and Zedner, Chapter 15, this volume). At the core of most restorative theories lies an emphasis on the significance of stakeholders in the offence (not just the state and the offender, but also the victim and the community), on the importance of process (bringing the stakeholders together in order to decide on the response to the offence), and on restorative goals (usually some form of reparation to the victim and 'restoration' of the community, and often extending to rehabilitation and reintegration of the offender). There are many variations of restorative justice in different countries, some established in law and others at an experimental stage, and an assessment cannot be given here (see Johnstone 2001; Dignan 2005; and Hoyle and Zedner, above). They are often based on a behavioural premise similar to rehabilitation for the offender, and also on the premise that the processes help to restore the victim; their political premise is that the response to an offence should not be dictated by the state but determined by all the interested parties, placing compensation and restoration ahead of mere punishment of the offender, and encouraging maximum participation in the processes so as to bring about social reintegration.

There are other victim-oriented initiatives which are not restorative but may be reparative in their goal. One that is widespread in both European and common law countries is to allow victims to submit a 'victim impact statement' to the court, detailing the effects of the crime from their point of view. In England and Wales a 'victim personal statement' may now be submitted to any sentencing court. It is debatable whether this change is either appropriate in principle or desirable in practice (cf. Erez 1999 with Sanders *et al.* 2001). In some countries the statement may also include the victim's opinion on the appropriate sentence, a development which raises deep questions about crimes as public and/or private wrongs (see Ashworth 2005: 352–8).

SOCIAL THEORIES

There has been a resurgence of writings which emphasize the social and political context of sentencing (see Duff and Garland 1994: ch. 1). Important in this respect are Garland's (1990) analysis of the theoretical underpinnings of historical trends in punishment, and Hudson's arguments (1987, 1993) in favour of a shift towards a more supportive social policy as the principal response to the problem of crime. Those who have been influenced by Hart's distinction (1968) between the general justifying aim of punishment (in his view, utilitarian or deterrent) and the principles for distribution of punishment (in his view, retribution or desert) should consider the challenge to this dichotomy in Lacey's work (1988). She argues that both these issues raise questions of individual autonomy and of collective welfare, and that, rather than denying it, we should address this conflict and strive to ensure that neither value is sacrificed entirely at either stage. In developing this view she explores the political values involved in state punishment and argues for a clearer view of the social function of punishing.

The political philosophy underlying the work of Braithwaite and Pettit (1990) is what they term republicanism, at the heart of which lies the concept of dominion. Its essence is liberty, not in the sense of simple freedom from constraint by others, but more in the form of a status of guaranteed protection from certain kinds of interference, based on a political compromise in which each citizen has participated. This leads them to propose that sentences should be such as to increase the dominion of victims with the least loss of dominion to the offenders punished. They gesture towards (vague) upper limits on severity, but not lower limits, and their view is that the censuring function of the criminal justice system can and should so far as possible be fulfilled by means other than punishment. Since dominion lays emphasis on reassuring citizens about the prospect of liberty, it might require long preventive sentences based on deterrence or incapacitation. There is thus no recognition of an individual's right not to be punished more than is proportionate to the seriousness of the crime: all depends on what will advance overall dominion, which might happen to be more or less in any individual case than the 'deserved' punishment (see further the debate in von Hirsch and Ashworth 1998: ch. 7).

MULTIPLE SENTENCING RATIONALES?

It will be evident from the foregoing discussion that the various rationales for sentencing point in different directions. Despite this obvious conclusion, the Government proclaimed that it was taking a significant step towards consistency in sentencing by enacting section 142 of the Criminal Justice Act 2003, which provides:

(1) Any court dealing with an offender in respect of his offence must have regard to the following purposes of sentencing—
  (a) the punishment of offenders,
  (b) the reduction of crime (including its reduction by deterrence),
  (c) the reform and rehabilitation of offenders,
  (d) the protection of the public, and
  (e) the making of reparation by offenders to persons affected by their offences.

The White Paper *Justice for All* claimed that the aim was to ensure that sentencers consider the various purposes and achieve 'the right balance' between them (Home Office 2002). The difficulty with this is not only that they are conflicting, except for (e) which can sometimes be achieved alongside another purpose, but also that, as the Halliday Report (2001) pointed out, the evidence for (b) and (d) is unpromising, and as noted above, the evidence for (c) is in practice weak. It is not clear on what evidence an individual sentencer could make a rational choice among the various purposes.

However, the 2003 Act contains other provisions that may be used to clarify the position. Section 143(1) states that:

In considering the seriousness of any offence, the court must consider the offender's culpability in committing the offence and any harm which the offence caused or was intended to cause or might foreseeably have caused.

Further, when the Act sets the threshold for community sentences and for custody, and the standard for the length of custodial sentences, it uses 'the seriousness of the offence' as the key indicator. On this basis the Sentencing Guidelines Council, whose functions are discussed below, has issued a guideline entitled *Overarching Principles—Seriousness* (2004) to the effect that the proportionality principle enshrined in section 143(1) should be used by sentencers as the touchstone. That is fully consistent with the thresholds set by the 2003 Act, but leaves the 'pick and mix' approach of section 142 somewhat in limbo.

It remains to be seen how the various rationales for sentencing will impinge on sentencing practice. In the past judges have often shown a great attachment to general deterrence, and have proclaimed that they are passing a particular sentence in order to deter others. As mentioned above, the evidence for the effectiveness of such sentences is weak, and there are objections to sacrificing one person's liberty in this way. Will the new guideline turn judges away from this habit? Parliament too has legislated for mandatory sentences—most recently the mandatory minimum of five years for possession of certain firearms, in section 287 of the Criminal Justice Act 2003—based on a deterrent rationale. Protection of the public (incapacitation) remains as an exception to the proportionality principle when dealing with so-called dangerous offenders, and those provisions of the 2003 Act are discussed below. The reform and rehabilitation of offenders is a relevant purpose once the court has decided that a community sentence of a particular level is justified by the seriousness of the offence: in those cases, therefore, the proportionality principle must be applied first, and once the threshold is passed the possibility of achieving a rehabilitative purpose enters into the equation. All these points will be taken further below. What they suggest, and as the new guideline states, is that proportionality should be the sentencer's touchstone, except in dangerousness cases, but that within the framework of a proportionate sentence it may be possible to aim for rehabilitation. A reparative measure may also be possible.

In so far as the proportionality principle holds sway, it places some limits on the use of state power over those who offend. Even approaches that are critical of desert theory, such as the republicanism of Braithwaite and Pettit (1990) and the communitarianism of Lacey (1988), argue in favour of some limits to state power at the sentencing stage, although without great detail. The argument that desert theory leads to harsh penalties is not sustainable by reference to international comparisons (von Hirsch and Ashworth 2005, ch. 6), although it does need to be combined with the principle of penal parsimony to ensure that this outcome is avoided.

THE MECHANICS OF SENTENCING

In this part of the chapter some basic elements of the law and practice of sentencing are set out. The various stages of a criminal case are discussed, together with the procedures which surround the sentencing stage itself.

THE SELECTION OF CASES FOR SENTENCE

It is a commonplace that the courts pass sentence for only a small proportion of the crimes committed in any one year. Findings from the 1997 British Crime Survey suggested that only some 45 per cent of offences committed are reported. Police recording practices reduce that figure, so that only 24 per cent of all offences are recorded as such. Since only one-fifth of these offences are 'cleared up' (i.e. traced to an offender) by the police, the figure is further reduced to just over 5 per cent of offences committed. By no means all those offences which are cleared up result in the taking of official action, perhaps because the suspected offender is too young, perhaps because the evidence is not sufficiently strong. This reduces to 3 per cent of all crimes the numbers proceeded with (Home Office 1999: 29). Overall about one-third of offenders are cautioned rather than prosecuted: that leaves 2 per cent of all offences in any one year which result in convictions and court sentences (see further Maguire, Chapter 10, this volume). This is not to suggest that sentencing is unimportant, for it may be thought to have a social or symbolic importance considerably in excess of the small proportion of crimes dealt with. But it does suggest the need for caution in assessing the crime-preventive effects of sentencing. Those theoretical rationales which look to the social consequences of sentencing may overestimate its potential for altering general patterns of behaviour.

The selection of cases for sentence is not merely a quantitative filtering process. There are also various filters of a qualitative kind, some formal, some informal. The role of the regulatory agencies is significant: the Health and Safety Executive, the Environment Agency, and various other regulatory bodies tend to regard prosecution as a last resort (see, for example, Hawkins 2003; cf. Baldwin 2004). These and other agencies, such as HM Revenue and Customs, also have various means of enforcing compliance without resort to prosecution, such as warning notices or the 'compounding' of evaded tax and duty. When an offence is reported to the police, the choice among alternative courses (whether to warn an offender informally, or to take no further action, or to administer a formal caution, or to prosecute) has relatively low visibility: see further on these issues Sanders and Young, Chapter 28, this volume). However, the Criminal Justice Act 2003 introduced the 'statutory charging scheme', whereby the Crown Prosecution Service (CPS) and the police are meant to work together in the early stages to ensure that weak cases are discarded and others are pursued appropriately. The power of decision lies with the CPS. A simple police caution remains a possibility, but the 2003 Act also introduced 'conditional cautions', which allow the CPS to decide that a person should receive a caution if certain conditions (such as making reparation) are fulfilled. The Code for Crown Prosecutors (2004) states that a prosecution should not be brought unless there is a realistic prospect of conviction on the charge, but allows the CPS not to proceed if to do so would not be in the public interest, and gives guidance on this decision and on choice of charge. At the stage of plea the system contains strong incentives to plead guilty, and there is no shortage of empirical evidence that negotiation is a familiar part of justice in magistrates' courts and in the Crown Court (see Ashworth and Redmayne 2005: ch. 10). Guidelines on 'the acceptance of pleas' have been issued (Attorney-General 2001), but it is unclear to what extent judges and advocates adhere to them.

In summary, therefore, the offences for which the courts have to pass sentence are both quantitatively and qualitatively different from what might be described as the social reality of crime. The courts see only a small percentage of cases. Even if it may be assumed that these are generally the more serious offences, how they are presented in court may be shaped as much by the working practices and priorities of the police, prosecutors, and defence lawyers as by any objective conception of 'the facts of the case' (see further Sanders and Young, Chapter 28, this volume).

CROWN COURT AND MAGISTRATES' COURTS

Of the two levels of criminal court in England and Wales, the Crown Court deals with the more serious cases and the magistrates' courts with the less serious. The Crown Court sits as a trial court with judge and jury. Some two-thirds of Crown Court cases involve a guilty plea, and these are dealt with by judge alone, since juries have no part in sentencing. The most serious Crown Court cases are taken by a High Court judge on circuit, but the majority of cases are taken by a Circuit Judge (full-time), or by a Recorder (part-time). The magistrates' courts are organized on a local basis: there are some 30,000 lay magistrates in England and Wales, and they usually sit in benches of three, advised by a justices' clerk. Typically a lay magistrate will sit in court one day a fortnight. There are also some full-time district judges (formerly known as stipendiary magistrates), together with some who sit part-time. District judges are professionally qualified appointees, and they tend to be assigned the longer or more difficult cases. They used to sit mostly in metropolitan areas, but they are now to be found more widely as their numbers have increased to some 140. From the Crown Court an offender may appeal against sentence (with leave) to the Court of Appeal; from a magistrates' court the offender may appeal against sentence to the Crown Court. If a Crown Court sentence is considered unduly lenient, the Attorney-General may refer it to the Court of Appeal and the sentence may be increased (Shute 1999).

For the purpose of deciding at which level of court a case will be heard criminal offences are divided into three categories. Indictable-only offences are the most serious group, and may be dealt with only in the Crown Court. Summary-only offences are the least serious group, and may be dealt with only in the magistrates' courts. Between them lies the category of offences triable either way. These are offences of intermediate gravity, which will generally be tried in a magistrates' court unless either the defendant elects to be committed for Crown Court trial (an absolute right), or the magistrates decide that the case should be committed to the Crown Court. Governments have repeatedly attempted to reduce the number of cases going to the Crown Court. In 1996 Parliament introduced the 'plea before venue' procedure, to ensure that defendants who intend to plead guilty at the Crown Court have the opportunity to be sentenced by magistrates if they think fit. This resulted in a fall in committals to the Crown Court for trial, but a rise in committals to the Crown Court for sentence. The Criminal Justice Act 2003 raises magistrates' sentencing powers from six to 12 months on a single charge (or a total of 65 weeks on two or more charges), and allows defendants to seek an 'indication of sentence' from the magistrates before deciding on plea. When these changes are fully in force (autumn 2006), there will be a further shift from the Crown Court to the magistrates' courts.

Hand in hand with this continued transfer of business to magistrates' courts, there has been a movement to remove from magistrates' courts many of the less serious offences. For some years the number of traffic offences for which the police may issue fixed penalty notices has been increasing. Thus in 2003 some 80,000 defendants were tried in the Crown Court, some 1.5 million people were prosecuted in the magistrates' courts, and a further 3.6 million fixed penalty notices were issued by the police (and more by local authorities for parking offences). A further development is the issue of Penalty Notices for Disorder, introduced in 2001, which accounted for some 64,000 offences in 2004 (mostly either drunk and disorderly or causing harassment, alarm, or distress). It is now possible to issue such notices for a range of offences including a first offence of theft from shops of up to £100 (or exceptionally £200), and this may remove many more cases from magistrates' courts.

MAXIMUM SENTENCES

Apart from a few common law offences which have no fixed maximum (e.g., manslaughter, conspiracy to outrage public decency), Parliament has generally provided the maximum sentence for each offence. These maxima have been set at different times, in different social circumstances, and without any overall plan, often adopting the 'seven times table' established for transportation (Radzinowicz and Hood 1990: ch. 15). Many had hoped that the Advisory Council on the Penal System would be able to improve the coherence of the system, but in its 1978 Report on *Sentences of Imprisonment: a Review of Maximum Penalties* it declined to revise the various statutory maxima, regarding the task as too controversial. Parliament has therefore continued to assign and revise maximum penalties on a piecemeal basis. Thus the Sexual Offences Act 2003 introduced new offences and higher maxima, the Criminal Justice Act 2003 abolished imprisonment for several summary offences but raised the maxima for many other summary offences, and the maximum for causing death by dangerous driving has been increased from ten to 14 years.

THE RANGE OF AVAILABLE SENTENCES

Beneath the maximum penalty for the offence, the court usually has a wide discretion to choose among alternatives. The English tradition is to create maximum penalties in terms of either a period of custody, or an amount or level of fine. Since the mid-1960s there has been a tendency to enact broadly defined offences with relatively high maximum penalties, a tradition continued in the many overlapping crimes created by the Sexual Offences Act 2003. Also, England and Wales are unusual in having a single offence of theft, with a maximum of seven years' imprisonment, compared with the grades of theft with separate (lower) maxima which are normal in other European countries. The English approach leaves sentencers with much greater discretion (see Thomas 1974).

At the lowest level, the range of available sentences begins with absolute and conditional discharges, and binding over. Fines come next, and a compensation order should be considered in every case involving death, injury, loss, or damage. At the next level comes the community sentence, with its choice of requirements (see below). Then come suspended sentences of imprisonment, intermittent custody (where available), custody plus, and imprisonment itself. All these forms of sentence are discussed further below. There are separate orders for young offenders (see Morgan and Newburn, Chapter 30, this volume) and for mentally disordered offenders (see Peay, Chapter 16, this volume). The many changes in sentencing law in the 1990s led to increasing confusion, and in 2000 Parliament consolidated most of the law in the Powers of Criminal Courts (Sentencing) Act. However, many of its provisions have now been overtaken by the Criminal Justice Act 2003, the far-reaching effects of which are discussed below.

DISCRETION IN SENTENCING

Alleged inconsistencies in sentencing have been a frequent cause for concern. This might seem an obvious consequence of the expanse of discretion left by fairly high maximum penalties and the wide range of available sentences. But there is a paradox here. Many sentencers seem to place more emphasis on the restrictions on 'their' discretion than on the choices that remain. Judges have often been critical of the various limits which Parliament places on their powers, and of the duties imposed upon them. Courts are now under an obligation to consider making a compensation order in every case of death, injury, loss, or damage; and in drug-trafficking cases a court is required to follow the prescribed statutory procedure for confiscation of the offender's assets, as stipulated by the Proceeds of Crime Act 2002.

One of the intended effects of the guideline movement (see below) is to structure the discretion of sentencers so that they have the same starting points and take account of the same aggravating and mitigating factors. Yet even before these statutory restrictions and guidelines began to appear in the 1980s, judges expressed themselves as having little choice in the sentences they passed: 'the least possible sentence I can pass . . . ', 'I have no alternative but to . . . ' (Oxford Pilot Study 1984: 53–4); the sentencers interviewed by Hough *et al.* (2003: 38) expressed themselves similarly. To some extent this terminology may reflect self-generated constraints, stemming from the attitudes and beliefs of the sentencer, or situational constraints. In magistrates' courts, where most sentencing takes place, local variations are a long-standing phenomenon. Just as Hood (1962) showed that some benches are 'probation-minded' and others are not, so Tarling (1979) demonstrated that among the 30 courts he surveyed the use of probation varied between 1 and 12 per cent, suspended sentences between 4 and 16 per cent, fines between 46 and 76 per cent, and so on. Significant elements of these variations remained after account had been taken of the different 'mix' of offences coming before the courts (Tarling *et al.* 1985). As Hood found in his study of motoring cases (1972), membership of a particular bench tends to be a major determinant of a magistrate's approach to sentencing. The influence of magistrates' clerks, who generally undertake the initial training of new magistrates, may be considerable (Darbyshire 1999). The 2004 figures show variations in the use of custody for indictable offences by magistrates' courts from 8 per cent in Warwickshire and Cleveland to 23 per cent in Essex and 21 per cent in Bedfordshire, and variations in the use of community sentences from over 40 per cent in some areas (e.g. Leicestershire and South Yorkshire) down to 29 per cent in Northamptonshire and 26 per cent in Dorset (Home Office 2005).

Variations are also to be found in the Crown Court: in their survey of sentencing in both levels of courts in the mid-1990s, Flood-Page and Mackie (1998) found that 'attempts to predict sentences on the basis of case factors were not particularly successful', indicating wide differences in the way that community sentences, in particular, were used. In 2004 the custody rate in the Crown Court varied from over 70 per cent in North Wales and Warwickshire down to barely 50 per cent in Northumbria and Greater Manchester, and the rate of community sentences varied from 39 per cent in Greater Manchester and 37 per cent in Derbyshire to under 20 per cent in Northamptonshire (Home Office 2005). Local explanations for these variations may be more convincing than differences in the mix of cases, and findings of this kind underlay the proposal in the Halliday Report (2001) for the introduction of comprehensive sentencing guidelines for all courts.

While discretion is important to enable sentencers to take account of the wide and varying range of factors that might be relevant, it does leave decision-making open to irrelevant influences (see Galligan 1986; Hawkins 1992). For example, Hood's 1992 study showed that at some courts black offenders are significantly more likely to receive custody than similarly situated white offenders. Hedderman and Gelsthorpe (1997) found detailed variations in the sentencing of men and women that cannot be explained by case factors, and show that sentencers' attitudes may explain why women are fined less frequently and given certain community sentences more frequently than men. Judges tend to argue strongly against any curtailment of 'their' discretion—an argument raised loudly against the mandatory and minimum sentences introduced in 1997—but rarely acknowledge the risks of discrimination, individual idiosyncrasy, and other irrelevant influences which accompany discretion that is not well structured or well monitored (see Hudson 1998).

INFORMATION ABOUT THE OFFENCE

Courts depend for their information on what they hear or what they are told. Since over 90 per cent of cases in magistrates' courts and around two-thirds of cases in the Crown Court are pleas of guilty, the information is usually constructed for the court by the prosecutor or others. The main source of information about the offence is likely to be the statement of facts which the prosecutor reads out. It will usually have been compiled by the police, and the way in which it describes or omits certain factors may reflect a particular view of the offence, or perhaps a 'charge-bargain' struck with the police (see Sanders and Young, Chapter 28, this volume). In addition to the prosecution statement of facts, the court may gather further information about the offence from the defence plea in mitigation, and perhaps from a pre-sentence report. Any account of 'the facts' is likely to be selective, determined to some extent by the compiler's preconceptions. It is likely that judges and magistrates will be influenced by the selections made by those who inform them, as well as by their own perspectives.

The prosecution's account of the facts may be disputed by the defence. In a trial there is usually an opportunity to resolve these matters, but this is not always so: some facts relevant to sentencing are irrelevant to criminal guilt. The greatest difficulty arises where the defendant pleads guilty but only on the basis of a more favourable version of the facts than the prosecution present. The courts have developed a procedure for resolving most such issues by means of a pre-sentence hearing, known as a '*Newton* hearing' (after the leading case of *Newton* (1982) 4 Cr. App. R. (S.) 388), at which evidence is presented and witnesses may be heard. There is now a wealth of case law on the situations in which a '*Newton* hearing' is necessary and on the procedures to be followed (Ashworth 2005: ch. 11). Since the outcome can have a considerable effect on the length of a custodial sentence, procedural fairness at this stage is important.

INFORMATION ABOUT THE OFFENDER

The court may obtain information about the offender from at least five sources: the police antecedents statement; the defence plea in mitigation; a pre-sentence report; a medical report; and the offender's own appearance in court.

The contents of the *antecedents statement* are regulated by a Practice Direction from the Lord Chief Justice reissued in 2002. They are compiled by the police from the Police National Computer, and should always contain personal details and information about previous convictions and previous cautions. The purpose of a *defence plea in mitigation* is to show the offender and offence in the best light. In practice, it appears that a realistic recognition of any aggravating factors may improve the credibility of what is said in mitigation (Shapland 1981: ch. 5).

The purpose of a *pre-sentence report* is to assist the sentencer by providing information and analysis of offence, offender, and related matters. The form of the report is regulated by National Standards for the Supervision of Offenders in the Community, a new edition of which is imminent. The 2000 version required the report to set out the basic facts, followed by an offence analysis, an offender assessment, an assessment of the risk to the public of reoffending, and conclusions that make 'a clear and realistic proposal for sentence designed to protect the public and reduce reoffending, including for custody where this is necessary'. Any proposal for a community sentence should indicate the most appropriate requirements in the light of available programmes to meet the offender's perceived needs.

A *psychiatric report* is relatively rare, but a court may decide to call for one, and is obliged to obtain one before passing a custodial sentence if the defendant is or appears to be mentally disordered (see further Peay, Chapter 16, this volume). The impact of *the offender's own appearance* and demeanour in court is difficult to gauge, but judges recognize that they take account of it and tend to feel that sentencing would be even more difficult if they did not see the offender in person (Cooke 1987: 58; Oxford Pilot

Study 1984: ch. 3). This fifth source of influence serves to demonstrate that the impact of the reports, etc., received by a court may be mediated by the attitudes of the sentencer (Shapland 1987).

REPRESENTATIONS ON SENTENCE

The English tradition is that the prosecutor plays no part in sentencing, in the sense that no sentence is 'asked for' or recommended. However, prosecutors are now encouraged to be more active at the sentencing stage. The Code for Crown Prosecutors (2004) states that the prosecutor should draw the court's attention to aggravating and mitigating factors disclosed by the prosecution case, to any statutory provisions or relevant guidelines, to any victim personal statement, and (where appropriate) to the 'impact of the offending on the community.'

Some of what is said by an advocate making a defence plea in mitigation will bear directly on the sentence, and the advocate may propose a particular course to the sentencer. However, the defence advocate also has a duty to prevent the judge from passing an unlawful sentence, and to remind the judge of any relevant sentencing guidelines. Indeed, where guidelines exist, advocates may use them as a basis for arguing in favour of a particular outcome.

SENTENCING GUIDELINES

In 1998 the Sentencing Advisory Panel was created, to formulate advice for the Court of Appeal on guidelines for sentencing particular types of offence. The Panel is required to take account of sentencing statistics and the cost and effectiveness of penal measures. It must consult both the public and an approved list of organizations, and issues a Consultation Paper for this purpose. The Panel is a part-time body with a broad membership, including three academics, three judges, three lay members with no criminal justice background, and others experienced in policing, probation, prisons, and magistrates' courts. It produced about 12 sets of draft guidelines in its first four years. Following proposals in the Halliday Report (2001), which called for comprehensive sentencing guidelines, the system was changed by the Criminal Justice Act 2003. The Panel still operates in a similar fashion, but its function now is to formulate advice for a new body called the Sentencing Guidelines Council. This body is chaired by the Lord Chief Justice and has a judicial majority (seven members), with four other members drawn from prosecutions, police, defence lawyers, and victim services. The Council receives the Panel's advice (draft guideline), discusses it, issues its own draft guideline for consideration by the Home Secretary and the Home Affairs Committee of the House of Commons, receives their comments, and then formulates what is termed a 'definitive guideline.' Courts are bound to have regard to such guidelines and to give reasons if they wish to depart from an applicable guideline (Ashworth 2005: 35–41 and 54–7).

All the guidelines mentioned above may be consulted at www.sentencing-guidelines.gov.uk, and they are also available to sentencers in a 'Guideline Judgments—

Case Compendium', which includes pre-1999 Court of Appeal guidelines too. The Council has had to tackle new and wide areas of sentencing, issuing guidelines on general principles and on sentencing under major statutes such as the Criminal Justice Act 2003 and the Sexual Offences Act 2003. The Council's obligation to consult politicians was designed to remedy an alleged 'democratic deficit' in the previous procedure, but Michael Tonry is still critical of the dominance of judges in the Council and sees that as a barrier to real change (Tonry 2004: ch. 5). Since those criticisms were written (based on the US experience), the influence of the judges has increased through the Court of Appeal's decision to begin to create guidelines again—largely to 'fill gaps' because the many consultative obligations of the Panel and the Council make them unable to respond quickly to perceived needs for guidance (see Ashworth 2005: 35–41, 2006).

ENGLISH SENTENCING PROCEDURES

From this brief review, three main themes emerge. First, it is evident that other actors, apart from judges and magistrates, exert considerable influence on the sentencing process. Not only do the police and prosecutors select and shape the cases which come to court, but they (together with probation officers and defence lawyers) provide the courts with information which they have selected and constructed. Secondly, what courts may receive in terms of information about the offence and the offender, and representations on sentence, is governed mostly by court practice and judicial decisions. Apart from pre-sentence reports, there is little legislative intervention in the field. The judges themselves have developed '*Newton* hearings'. They could equally develop or modify other practices. And thirdly, the proliferation of sentencing guidelines is designed to bring more 'rule of law' values into sentencing and to structure discretion. To what extent these guidelines are followed faithfully in practice has not yet been tested, and they may leave room for different approaches to be taken by particular judges or particular benches of magistrates. More research and analysis of the decision-making of sentencers is needed, to discover to what extent legal or other factors actually determine judicial sentencing.

CUSTODIAL SENTENCING

THE EVOLUTION OF A 'TARIFF'

Apart from the few mandatory and minimum sentences, discussed below, the general English approach is to set a fairly high maximum sentence for each offence. One consequence is that most day-to-day sentencing practices are little affected by legislative constraints. For Crown Court sentencing some normal ranges or starting points developed over the years, often termed 'the going rate' by judges and 'the tariff' by others. Historically the idea of 'normal' sentences can be traced back at least as far as the 'Memorandum of Normal Punishments' drawn up by Lord Alverstone, the Lord Chief Justice, in 1901 (Radzinowicz and Hood 1990: 755–8). Since 1907 the Court of Criminal Appeal, and since 1966 its successor the Court of Appeal (Criminal Division), has adjusted and altered aspects of the tariff. Increased reporting of Court of Appeal decisions on sentencing assisted the concretization of sentencing principles, and the publication of the first edition of Dr David Thomas's *Principles of Sentencing* (1970) was a landmark in the development of a common law of sentencing.

It remains true, however, that the bulk of Court of Appeal decisions deal with fairly severe and long sentences, and one of the tasks of the Panel and the Council has been to generate guidelines for frequent offences such as theft, burglary, fraud, and handling stolen goods. New guidelines also deal with levels of offending that attract non-custodial sentences. For lower courts the Magistrates' Association took the initiative in 1989 in promulgating its own sentencing guidelines, in an effort to fill the vacuum created by the lack of guidance from other quarters. In the 1990s other stakeholders in the magistrates' courts were brought into the process of revising the guidelines, and the name was changed to the Magistrates' Courts Sentencing Guidelines (latest edition 2003). On advice from the Panel, the Sentencing Guidelines Council is likely to issue a definitive version of these guidelines in late 2006.

MANDATORY AND MINIMUM SENTENCES

There has long been a minimum sentence of disqualification from driving for 12 months on conviction for drunk driving. The introduction of mandatory minimum prison sentences in 1997 followed a fierce battle between the Home Secretary and the senior judiciary. The government argued that such sentences would have deterrent and inca-pacitative effects. The judiciary pointed to low detection rates as undermining those effects, and also to the injustice of having to pass such sentences in inappropriate cases (see Dunbar and Langdon 1998: ch. 10; Ashworth 2001). These counter-arguments, together with the unpromising American evidence (Tonry 1996: ch. 5), had only limited effects. The Crime (Sentences) Act 1997 introduced the automatic life sentence for the second serious sexual or violent offence (abolished by the 2003 Act in favour of the new dangerousness sentence discussed below), and two other minimum sentences.

First, a court is required to impose a minimum sentence of seven years for the third Class A drug-trafficking offence, unless it would be 'unjust to do so in all the circum-stances'. In fact most such offenders would receive at least seven years anyway, and therefore this minimum prescription has impinged little on sentencing practice. Secondly, a court is required to impose a minimum sentence of three years for the third domestic burglary conviction, so long as the offender is aged at least 18 and each burglary was committed after the previous conviction for burglary. There is now a guideline judgment dealing particularly with the first and second sentences for burglary (*McInerney and Keating* [2003] 2 Cr. App. R. (S.) 240), but even on the third conviction courts have some room for manoeuvre. Where there is a guilty plea, a court may reduce the minimum by 20 per cent: the 36 months minimum thus becomes just over 28 months for most guilty pleaders. Also, a court is not bound to impose the minimum it if would be 'unjust to do so in all the circumstances'. It is not clear to which extent this minimum sentence has deflected courts from their normal approach.

The Criminal Justice Act 2003 introduced a further mandatory minimum sentence: for possession of prohibited firearms a court is required to impose at least five years' imprisonment (three years if the offender is under 18). This is a much stronger provision than the others just discussed, since it applies to a first offence and courts may depart only in 'exceptional circumstances.'

The 2003 Act also altered the sentencing approach for murder. Since 1965 a court sentencing an offender for murder has been bound to impose life imprisonment. The trial judge would propose a minimum term, reviewed by the Lord Chief Justice, but the final decision would be that of the Home Secretary. On expiry of the minimum term, the murderer would remain in prison until deemed not to present a risk to the public, and would then be released on licence (and subject to recall) for the rest of his life. Following various decisions of the European Court of Human Rights, the House of Lords decided in 2002 that fixing the minimum term for a life sentence is a sentencing decision, and must therefore be taken by an 'independent and impartial tribunal' and not by the Home Secretary (*R (Anderson)* v. *Secretary of State for the Home Department* [2003] 1 A.C. 837). Mr. Blunkett, the then Home Secretary, reacted to this decision by seeking to neutralize its effect through legislation. Section 269 of the Criminal Justice Act 2003 essentially requires a court, when setting the minimum term to be served by a person convicted of murder, to have regard to the principles set out in Schedule 21 to the Act. The Schedule indicates three starting points:

- a whole life minimum term for exceptionally serious cases, such as premeditated killings of two people, sexual or sadistic child murders, or political murders;
- 30 years for particularly serious cases such as murders of police or prison officers, murders involving firearms, sexual or sadistic killings, or murders aggravated by racial or sexual orientation;
- 15 years for other murders not falling within either of the higher categories.

However, the language in Schedule 21 is not constraining, and judges may take account of aggravating and mitigating factors when calculating the minimum term (*Sullivan* [2005] 1 Cr. App. R. (S.) 308). It remains controversial whether it is right to have a mandatory sentence for murder, in view of the considerable variations in the gravity of the offence.

STATUTORY RESTRICTIONS ON CUSTODIAL SENTENCES

The Criminal Justice Act 2003 establishes two significant principles: by section 152(2) a custodial sentence should not be imposed unless the offence is too serious for a community sentence or fine, and by section 153(2) any custodial sentence must be 'for the shortest term . . . commensurate with the seriousness of the offence'. These judgments depend on proportionality, as mentioned earlier. The Sentencing Guidelines Council has established guidelines on the application of the custody threshold, stating that its clear intention 'is to reserve prison as a punishment for the most serious offences' and that 'passing the custody threshold does not mean that a custodial sentence should be deemed inevitable', since there may be personal mitigation or 'a suitable intervention in the community which provides sufficient restriction (by way of punishment) while addressing the rehabilitation of the offender to prevent future crime' (SGC, *Overarching Principles—Seriousness* (2004)). Although this guideline has been in place since December 2004, there is little evidence of a reduction in the use of short custodial sentences. The Home Secretary has commended the greater use of community sentences, but the general political climate hardly encourages a reduction in sentence severity.

NEW FORMS OF SHORT CUSTODIAL SENTENCE

When the new sentence of custody plus comes into force (currently undecided), the penal landscape will change. The Criminal Justice Act 2003 introduced three new forms of sentence at this level. First, a refurbished form of suspended sentence becomes available, allowing the suspension of sentences of up to 51 weeks combined with one or more requirements to be imposed during the supervision period. This may be used particularly for those who have committed fairly serious offences but have not yet been to prison. Secondly, there is a new sentence of intermittent custody (where available locally) with between 14 and 90 custodial days to be served, together with a licence with one or more requirements. This should allow the offender to retain employment and/or family ties while undergoing a custodial sentence. And thirdly a new sentence of custody plus is introduced, which will be the only immediate custodial sentence of 51 weeks or less. Its essence is to combine deprivation of liberty with demanding supervision in the community: the custodial element must be between two and 13 weeks, and the supervision portion at least 26 weeks, with one or more requirements (such as unpaid work, or a prohibited activity, etc.) attached. In the past, short custodial sentences have not been followed by supervision, and the aim of custody plus is to place greater emphasis on resettlement in the community. However, much will depend on the way in which the courts use the three new measures. If they apply the statutory restrictions and follow the Council's guideline, reserving custody for the most serious cases, then the advent of custody plus will not lead to greater use of custody and might even reverse the recent trend towards more short prison sentences. But if some courts regard custody plus as a form of community sentence with a short dose of prison added, then offenders may be projected up-tariff without good reason. If some courts regard the periods of custody (2–13 weeks) as too short, they might be tempted to impose a sentence of 12 months' imprisonment rather than custody plus, another malfunction that would produce disproportionate sentences. Only if the Council's guidelines are followed faithfully will the more constructive aspects of custody plus bear fruit.

PROPORTIONALITY, THE TARIFF, AND GUIDELINES

As outlined above, a conventional tariff or 'going rate' for many offences has developed over the years, shaped and assisted by judgments of the Court of Appeal. In the early 1980s the Court of Appeal began to attempt the structuring of sentencing discretion by formulating 'guideline judgments'. Lord Lane, the then Lord Chief Justice, would occasionally take a particular case and, rather than giving a judgment on the facts alone, would construct a judgment dealing with sentencing for all the main varieties of that particular crime. The first of these was in the case of *Aramah* (1982) 4 Cr. App. R. (S.) 407, where guidance was given on sentencing levels for the whole gamut of drugs offences, from large-scale trafficking down to possession of small amounts for individual use. This judgment was subsequently revised (in *Aroyewumi* (1995) 16 Cr. App. R. (S.) 211) so that its guidance is calibrated according to weight and purity level rather than estimates of 'street value', and parallel guidance for newer drugs has been added in other judgments (e.g. for 'Ecstasy' in *Warren and Beeley* [1996] 1 Cr. App. R. (S.) 233). Guideline judgments were given on various other offences, such as rape, robbery, and causing death by dangerous driving. It appears that these judgments have been respected by judges and magistrates, probably because they were developed *by* judges *for* judges, and because the guidance is in the familiar narrative form of a judgment. Guidelines only indicate starting points or sentence ranges, however, and leave the judge to make appropriate adjustments in the light of variations in the offence, aggravating factors, and mitigating factors.

Court of Appeal guidelines have been piecemeal and based on judicial views only. The new guideline system, outlined earlier, is supposed to be working towards comprehensive sentencing guidelines. The Council began by issuing a guideline on *Overarching Principles—Seriousness*, setting out the principles to be applied throughout. Between 1999 and 2004 the Panel formulated advice for the Court of Appeal that led to guideline judgments on racially aggravated offences, opium offences, offensive weapons, handling stolen goods, domestic burglary, rape, child pornography offences, causing death by dangerous driving, and alcohol and tobacco smuggling. Some effort was made to ensure that the guidelines relate to one another, and that effort continues with the Panel's advice to the Council which has produced guidelines on robbery and on offences under the Sexual Offences Act 2003. From the viewpoint of the Crown Court judge or recorder, these guidelines and those established by the Court of Appeal now add up to a formidable body of guidance. Proportionality between them is not assured, since several of the Court of Appeal guidelines have not yet been reassessed by the Panel and the Council, but there are now several signposts in what was previously a wide area of discretion. Careful research is needed to determine what effect guidelines have on the approach to sentencing of judges and magistrates, and whether the effect has been to make sentences more or less severe overall. The opinion of judges questioned by Hough *et al.* (2003: 25) was that they do have an effect, and that the effect is to raise the sentence levels of lenient judges without bringing severe judges down, but this research needs to be replicated on a larger scale.

AGGRAVATION AND MITIGATION

When courts are determining the seriousness of an offence, they should have regard to its aggravating and mitigating features. Flood-Page and Mackie (1998: 77) found that custody is significantly more likely in Crown Court cases where there is a breach of trust, the victim is elderly, or the offender is a ringleader, or the offence was planned, or a weapon was used, and there are Court of Appeal judgments supporting all these aggravating factors (see Ashworth 2005: ch. 5.2). Among the mitigating factors recognized by the courts are various forms of reduced culpability (e.g. mental disturbance, financial pressures) and a good previous record. Courts also give mitigating effect to various factors that have no bearing on the offence or the offender's culpability—the collateral impact of the sentence on others, an act of heroism by the offender, the payment of compensation to the victim, or the giving of information to the police about other offenders (ibid.: ch. 5.4). The interplay of these factors is critical where a case is 'on the cusp' of custody: in such cases Hough *et al.* (2003: 36–8) found no difference in the offence categories of those assigned to custody or to non-custodial disposals, but in the custody cases the sentencers placed more emphasis on the nature of the offence or the criminal record, whereas in the non-custodial cases the emphasis was on factors personal to the offender.

How significant should a bad criminal record be in sentencing? The common law principle was said to be progressive loss of mitigation: a first offender received substantial mitigation, which would be lost after the second or third conviction, but it would not be right to 'sentence on the record' and to impose a penalty disproportionate to the seriousness of the offence committed (Ashworth 2005: ch. 6.2). This principle succumbed to a silent eclipse during the 1990s, and section 143(2) of the Criminal Justice Act 2003 now proclaims an entirely different approach—that a court must treat each previous conviction as an aggravating factor if its relevance to the current offence, and the time that has elapsed since that conviction, make it reasonable to do so. This section indicates a recidivist premium that chimes well with this Government's aim of targeting 'seriously persistent offenders' (Home Office 2002: para. 5.7), and may indeed represent the practice that many courts have been following for years. It remains to be seen whether the result will be the imprisonment of minor offenders for long periods.

Perhaps the most substantial mitigating factor is the plea of guilty. Well established at common law, the 'discount' was put into statutory form in 1994 and is now set out in section 144 of the 2003 Act. The Sentencing Guidelines Council has issued a guideline on *Reduction of Sentence for a Guilty Plea* (2004), which recognizes various pragmatic reasons for the discount—saving cost, avoiding trials, reducing anxiety among victims and witnesses. The guideline establishes a sliding scale, with a maximum reduction of one-third for a guilty plea indicated at the earliest opportunity, reducing to one-tenth if the guilty plea is tendered 'at the door of the court'. The guideline also states that 'the reduction principle may properly form the basis for imposing . . . an alternative to an immediate custodial sentence'. Thus the guilty plea discount may well make the difference between prison or not, and the statistics bear this out—for example, for offences of violence a custody rate of 55 per cent for guilty pleaders and 72 per cent for those convicted after trial, and for sexual offences rates of 71 and 89 per cent respectively. For those who are sent to prison, average sentences for violence were 21.6 months (guilty plea) and 34.9 months (convicted after trial), and for sexual offences 36.9 months and 52.9 months respectively (*Criminal Statistics* 2002: Table 4D). Such substantial discounts place enormous pressure on defendants to forgo the right to trial which goes with the presumption of innocence. Where defendants are advised that the discount may make the difference between a custodial and a non-custodial sentence, the risk of innocent people pleading guilty is particularly high. A further development heightens this risk. The Court of Appeal has altered its position on judges giving indications of sentence, and it is now possible for a defendant who has pleaded not guilty to ask the judge what would be the maximum sentence imposed if the defendant were to change plea to guilty at this stage (*Goodyear* [2005] Crim. L.R. 659). If the judge indicates a community sentence, and counsel suggests that it would be custody if the defendant persisted in pleading not guilty and were convicted, then the pressure on the defendant would be enormous. A similar procedure of advance indication of sentence is available in magistrates' courts.

'DANGEROUSNESS' SENTENCES

Despite the poor prospects of accurate prediction, governments in many countries regard it as politically necessary to have some kind of 'dangerousness' statute, proclaiming greater public protection from sexual and violent predators. The Criminal Justice Act 2003 adopts this approach and introduces a new three-pronged strategy against 'dangerous' offenders. Thus, where the offence is a 'serious' one (carrying imprisonment of ten years or more), the court must impose a sentence of life imprisonment if the offence has a maximum of life imprisonment, if the court finds that the current offence is serious enough to justify a life sentence, and if the offender is 'dangerous'. If the offence is 'serious' but either does not carry life or is not sufficiently serious, the court must impose a sentence of imprisonment for public protection. This new IPP sentence is hardly less constraining than life imprisonment, in the sense that the court sets a minimum term, after which release is only when the Parole Board thinks the risk to the public no longer justifies imprisonment, and release is on licence indefinitely. Then there is the third form of sentence, the extended sentence, which a court must impose if the offence is a 'specified' one and carries between two and ten years' imprisonment. This sentence is composed of the proportionate sentence for the offence, plus an extension period (on licence with conditions) of up to five years for a violent offence and up to eight years for a sexual offence.

The condition that must be fulfilled before a court imposes any of these new sentences is a finding that 'there is a significant risk to members of the public of serious harm occasioned by the commission by him of further specified offences'. The Court of Appeal has given a guideline judgment on the new 'dangerousness' provisions which identifies three separate issues here (*Last* [2006] Crim. L.R. 174). First, the 2003 Act leaves the key term 'significant risk' undefined: the choice of 'significant' rather than 'substantial' may suggest a widening of the net, but the Court of Appeal requires a risk that is 'of considerable amount or importance'. Secondly, there must be a significant risk of this offender committing further 'specified' offences. And thirdly, those offences must be such as to put members of the public at significant risk of serious harm. 'Serious harm' means 'death or serious personal injury, whether physical or psychological'. However, a court must have regard to section 229, which creates the presumption of significant risk of serious harm where an offender over 18 has been convicted of another such offence; a court should assume this unless, having considered the nature of the offences and any reports about the offender, it considers that it would be unreasonable to regard the risk as significant. Moreover, the presumption applies where there is just one previous conviction of any of more than 150 specified offences, which vary considerably in their seriousness. Thus the list of specified offences includes, for example, affray and assault occasioning actual bodily harm (with maxima of three and five years respectively). For other offenders—those under 18, and those over 18 without a relevant previous conviction—courts are required to take account of information about the offence, about a relevant pattern of behaviour, and about the offender, before deciding whether there is a significant risk to the public. The 2003 Act contains no requirement on courts to obtain relevant reports on the offender, only to consult a report if there is one. In view of the severely restrictive nature of these sentences and the well-known fallibility of judgments of dangerousness (Brown and Pratt 2000; Monahan 2004), the new provisions subject far too many offenders to lengthy detention.

CUSTODIAL SENTENCES AND EXECUTIVE RELEASE

One aspect of sentencing which is open to much public misunderstanding is the meaning of custodial sentences in terms of the time served. The system has changed several times in recent decades, and the Criminal Justice Act 2003 has altered matters again. Now, all offenders serving determinate sentences of imprisonment are released on licence after serving one-half, and are then on licence under supervision with requirements until the end of their nominal sentence. Release on Home Detention Curfew (for up to 135 days before scheduled release), used considerably in recent years, is now also available for longer-term prisoners. Although this may mean earlier release for some prisoners serving four years or longer, the impact of supervision and its requirements (with recall to prison for breach) will be felt for a much longer time, i.e. to the very end of the nominal sentence. The consequent increase in penal weight of medium and long-term sentences led the Sentencing Guidelines Council to instruct sentencers who decide on a custodial term of longer than 12 months to reduce it by around 15 per cent (*New Sentences—Criminal Justice Act 2003*, para. 2.1.9). Whether this will actually happen is another test of the effectiveness of guidelines. If it does, the result will be to reduce the use of imprisonment, at least unless and until such offenders come to be re-imprisoned for breach of requirements.

Decisions on release from sentences of imprisonment for life or IPP, imposed under the 'dangerousness' provisions of the 2003 Act, will continue to be made by the Parole Board by reference to the continuing need to protect the public. Research has shown the risk assessments made by the Parole Board to be unduly conservative in many cases (Hood and Shute 2000).

NON-CUSTODIAL SENTENCING

Thus far the focus has been on custodial sentencing, chiefly in the Crown Court. But the figures for 2004 show that some 85 per cent of sentences for indictable offences in the magistrates' courts and some 40 per cent of Crown Court sentences were non-custodial. The reforms introduced by the Criminal Justice Act 2003 left the first tier of the penal ladder untouched (absolute and conditional discharges, fines), but, as already noted, they establish thresholds for a community sentence—only to be imposed if the offence is serious enough to justify such a sentence—and for a custodial sentence—only to be imposed if neither a community sentence nor a fine is adequate. The lower levels of some sets of sentencing guidelines (such as handling stolen goods, domestic burglary, and lesser sexual offences) do now specify a community sentence or a fine as the 'starting point', and that has long been the case for the Magistrates' Courts Sentencing Guidelines.

FIRST-TIER SENTENCES

The least order a court can make on conviction is an *absolute discharge*. Such orders are usually reserved for cases of very low culpability, or where the offender is seriously ill, or where the court thinks the prosecution should not have been brought (Wasik 1985). A conviction followed by a discharge does not rank as a conviction for any other purposes. For a *conditional discharge*, the condition is that the offender is not convicted of another offence within a specified period (up to three years). If there is such a conviction, the offender is liable also to be resentenced for the original crime. Conditional discharges are used for around 10 per cent of adult male indictable offenders and over 20 per cent of adult female indictable offenders. Courts also have various powers to 'bind over' offenders, an order much used in some courts and little used in others.

Although the *fine* remains a much-used sentence, even for indictable offences, it has declined significantly in proportionate use in recent years—from 55 per cent in 1975 to 21 per cent in 2004 (Home Office 2005: 68). The decline has often been attributed to courts being reluctant to fine unemployed offenders or feeling it inappropriate to fine them 'small' amounts, i.e. amounts that seem small to people with average incomes or more. The Criminal Justice Act 1991 had attempted to tackle the issue of fairness of fines by introducing 'unit fines' into magistrates' courts. This approach, modelled on the 'day fines' much used in other European countries, requires a careful separation of the seriousness of the offence (worth x units) from the offender's ability to pay (£y per unit). Unit fines were resisted by some courts, and sections of the media attacked them for relating the size of the fine to the means of offenders rather than to the offence. This, of course, was the very purpose of unit fines—to equalize the impact of fines on people of different means. However, the unit fine system was removed from the legislation in 1993, and only a few courts continued to use this approach voluntarily in subsequent years (Charman *et al.* 1996). But the use of fines continued to decline, and it appears that courts have been deliberately choosing community sentences where in earlier years they would have imposed a fine. Not only have levels of punitiveness been thus ratcheted upwards, but the Probation Service has become 'silted up' with offenders who do not really need the level of intervention entailed by a community sentence (Morgan 2003). In 2003 the Carter Review, commissioned by the Government, accepted this analysis and proposed that 'fines should replace community sentences for low risk offenders', suggesting that some 30 per cent of community sentences ought to be replaced by fines (Carter, Review 2003: 27). The Government is expected to bring forward legislation that will reintroduce a form of unit fine, in an attempt to reinvigorate the use of financial penalties and to ensure that they are calculated fairly.

Research demonstrates that calculating the amount of a fine fairly in the first instance is the key to ensuring payment or successful enforcement of the fine later (Moore 2004; Raine *et al.* 2004). One success story in recent years has been the sharp reduction in the use of imprisonment for fine defaulters. The Crime (Sentences) Act 1997 introduced two alternatives to the use of custody for fine defaulters—short community service orders and curfew orders (with the further alternative of an attendance centre order if the offender is under 25). Since then, the use of imprisonment for fine default has declined dramatically: whereas in 1994 almost 24,000 fine defaulters were committed to prison, the number was little over 5,000 by 1998, and around 1,000 in 2002. Moreover, the Courts Act 2003 provided for the appointment of fines officers for each area, in an effort to ensure that more fine are enforced and paid.

In every case involving death, injury, loss, or damage, a court must consider making a *compensation order*. A court may use it as the sole order in a case, and courts are required to give priority to a compensation order over a fine if the offender had limited means. Notwithstanding the requirement placed on courts, the number of compensation orders is only now returning to the level of two decades ago: whereas in 1983 some 128,000 compensation orders were made by the criminal courts, that figure dropped to 97,000 in 1993 and then rose to 123,000 by 2004. The most significant change has been the decline in the use of compensation orders in the Crown Court, from 21 per cent of all cases in 1990 down to only 7 per cent of cases in recent years, a decline that is probably connected to the rising use of custodial sentences. Magistrates' courts are now imposing correspondingly more compensation orders, many for summary offences (Home Office 2005: 70). The contribution of compensation orders to greater justice for victims is important, but possibly more at a symbolic level than in terms of actual recompense for large numbers of victims (see further Hoyle and Zedner, Chapter 15, this volume). It remains to be seen whether the arrival of conditional cautions, stipulating the payment of compensation to the victim as the condition, will be effective in raising the number of victims who actually receive compensation from 'their' offender.

COMMUNITY SENTENCES

For many of the last thirty years it has been official policy that the courts should use community sentences instead of some shorter custodial sentences. In the 1980s and before, sentences such as probation and community service were officially described as 'alternatives to custody' for this purpose. The Criminal Justice Act 1991 introduced the term 'community sentence', emphasizing the demanding nature of 'punishment in the community' and the restrictions on liberty involved (see Brownlee 1998; Bottoms *et al.* 2001). The Criminal Justice Act 2003 has taken this a step further by abolishing the separate sentences of probation, community service, and their short-lived successors (community punishment orders, community rehabilitation orders), and replacing them with a single, generic community sentence. As we will see, different forms of community sentence are still available, but the emphasis now is on the 'punitive weight' of the order made. The 2003 Act retains the requirement that a court should not impose any community sentence unless satisfied that the offence is serious enough to warrant it; and also the requirement that, if the court decides that the case is serious enough, it should ensure that the community order (a) is the most suitable for the offender, and (b) imposes restrictions on liberty which are commensurate with the seriousness of the offence (Criminal Justice Act 2003, section 148(2)). In most such cases a 'pre-sentence report' (see above) will have been prepared by the Probation Service to 'assist' the court.

The theory and practice of community sentences are discussed by Raynor in this volume (Chapter 31), and the 12 possible requirements (including supervision, unpaid work, drug rehabilitation, and so on) are set out there. The legislative scheme is designed to ensure that community sentences are proportionate, while allowing some room for choices among types of community sentence so as to reflect the perceived needs of the offender (Rex 1998). What is new under the 2003 Act is that the Sentencing Guidelines Council has created a guideline that attempts to differentiate the 'punitive weight' of different requirements by reference to three community sentence ranges—low, medium, or high. Thus the court must decide whether the offence requires low, medium, or high intervention, and must then consider the purpose of the order, the risk of reoffending, the offender's ability to comply, and the availability of programmes in the local area. The Council's guideline on *New Sentences: Criminal Justice Act 2003* (2004) gives examples of what a low range may include (e.g. 40–80 hours of unpaid work, or a curfew requirement for a few weeks, etc.), and then a medium-range order (e.g. 80–150 hours of unpaid work, or an activity requirement of 20–30 days, etc.), and then a high-range order (e.g. 150–300 hours of unpaid work, curfew orders of 4–6 months, etc.). Although this is a bold step towards greater clarity and fairness, it still leaves some cloudy areas. A supervision requirement appears to be assumed to form part of all three ranges, but this is not mentioned. Combinations of requirements are not discussed in the guideline, but presumably may feature at least in high-range community orders. The onerous nature of many of the requirements leads to the issue of breach. Schedule 8 to the 2003 Act sets out strong powers for the courts on breach. The Council's guideline modifies these slightly, stating that the court's primary objective when dealing with a breach should be to ensure that 'the requirements of the sentence are finished', and that 'custody should be the last resort, reserved for those cases of deliberate and repeated breach where all reasonable efforts to ensure that the offender complies have failed' (SGC, *New Sentences: Criminal Justice Act 2003*, para. 1.1.47). However, there remains a concern that tough requirements will lead to breach and hence to prison for many people whose original offence would not have merited such a sanction.

SUSPENDED SENTENCES

As mentioned earlier, a sentence of imprisonment of between 28 and 51 weeks may be suspended for a period of up to two years. This new suspended sentence, introduced by the Criminal Justice Act 2003 as part of a package that includes custody plus, intermittent custody, and the new generic community sentence, has two particular features. First, supervision accompanies the sentence and the court may order the offender to comply with one or more requirements during the supervision period. The requirements are the same 12 requirements that may form part of the community sentence, discussed above. Secondly, there are provisions for review hearings at which the court may monitor the offender's progress on the suspended sentence. This is the first statutory example of court review of the kind that has been introduced in some American jurisdictions, as part of drug courts or domestic violence courts, whereby the sentencer is able to establish some relationship with the offender and encourage him or her to comply. Non-compliance with the supervision requirements can be dealt with at such hearings. However, if the offender breaches the suspended sentence by being convicted of another offence committed during the operational period, the court must activate the suspended sentence in addition to the sentence for the new crime, unless it is 'unjust to do so'. Suspended sentences were not always imposed appropriately after their introduction in 1967. Research showed that courts sometimes defied the law by imposing suspended sentences when immediate imprisonment would not be justifiable, and by imposing longer sentences when suspending (Bottoms 1981; Moxon 1988: 34–8). The 2003 reforms make the suspended sentence much more demanding than hitherto, because of the supervision and added requirements, and it would therefore be doubly unfortunate if these malfunctions recurred. The Sentencing Guidelines Council's guideline on *New Sentences: Criminal Justice Act 2003* attempts to forestall such malfunctions by requiring a court to satisfy itself that the custody threshold has been passed and that a custodial sentence is 'unavoidable', and by requiring courts to ensure that any added requirements are not unduly onerous. Nonetheless, the possibility remains that many of these suspended sentences will be breached and the offenders will find themselves in prison, probably for longer than they would otherwise have been.

REVIEW OF POLICY AND PRACTICE

The sharp rise in the prison population in the last decade, to over 80,000 in 2006, has already been noted (see further Morgan and Liebling, Chapter 32, this volume). The judiciary and the magistracy tend to explain this as a response to what they regard as the climate of opinion in society, fuelled largely by political and media rhetoric. Despite strong evidence of widespread public misunderstanding about sentencing levels (Hough and Roberts 1998), politicians and the media continue to press for severity. An escalating response to previous convictions and to breaches of court orders has also played a major part in the trend to severity.

The effect of full implementation of the Criminal Justice Act 2003 is difficult to predict. While there are some provisions that have the potential to reduce the prison population—notably the new community sentence, the suspended sentence, and the sentence reduction for pleading guilty—the impact of the remainder of the Act seems unlikely to avoid high levels of custody. Custody plus may be a bold attempt to introduce more supervision and more constructive elements into short sentences, but will its purpose, as underpinned by the Council's guideline, be translated effectively into sentencing practice? The new dangerousness provisions point unmistakably in the direction of greater severity, and the presumption of dangerousness is likely to skew sentencing in some cases. The provision on previous convictions seems likely to result in more small-time repeat offenders going into prison. Some mandatory or minimum sentences also exist, opposed by the judges who point to the need for discretion in sentencing. However, to follow up the earlier discussion, discretion has its disadvantages as well as its advantages. It is a good thing to avoid mechanical sentencing and rigid controls which prevent courts from taking account of particular factors in individual cases. But it is undesirable to allow different approaches that amount to discrimination on grounds of race (Hood 1992) or gender (Hedderman and Gelsthorpe 1997), or allow individual judges to pursue their own policies, or local courts to follow local traditions. Steps are now being taken to structure sentencing discretion by means of guidelines, but there is an urgent need for research to assess their practical effectiveness in shaping the decisions of the courts.

Vital to the success of the 2003 Act in moderating levels of custodial sentencing are decisions around the custody threshold. Where sentences have tended to be ratcheted up, they need to be brought down again. It is not yet known whether the Government will bring forward legislation on unit fines, as part of a strategy to revive the use of financial penalties. Both the 2003 Act and the Council's guideline makes it clear that

■ REFERENCES

ADVISORY COUNCIL ON THE PENAL SYSTEM (1978), *Sentences of Imprisonment: a Review of Maximum Penalties*, London: HMSO.

ASHWORTH, A. (2001), 'The Decline of English Sentencing', in M. Tonry and R. Frase (eds), *Sentencing and Sanctions in Western Countries*, New York: Oxford University Press.

—— (2004) 'Social Control and "Anti-Social Behaviour": the Subversion of Human Rights', *Law Quarterly Review*, 120: 263–91.

—— (2005), *Sentencing and Criminal Justice*, 4th edn, Cambridge: Cambridge University Press.

—— (2006), 'The Sentencing Guideline System in England and Wales', *South African Journal of Criminal Justice*, 19: 1–22.

—— and Redmayne, M. (2005), *The Criminal Process*, 3rd edn, Oxford: Oxford University Press.

ATTORNEY-GENERAL (2001), *Guidelines on the Acceptance of Pleas*, 1 Cr. App. R. 425.

BALDWIN, R. (2004), 'The New Punitive Regulation', *Modern Law Review*, 67: 351.

BENTHAM, J. (1789), *Principles of Morals and Legislation*, London.

BOTTOMS, A. E. (1981), 'The Suspended Sentence in England, 1967–78', *British Journal of Criminology*, 21: 1–25.

—— (1998), 'Five Puzzles in von Hirsch's Theory of Punishment', in A. Ashworth and M. Wasik (eds), *Fundamentals of Sentencing Theory*, Oxford: Oxford University Press.

—— (2004), 'Empirical Research relevant to Sentencing Frameworks', in A. Bottoms, S. Rex, and G. Robinson (eds), *Alternatives to Prison: Options for an Insecure Society*, Cullompton, Devon: Willan.

—— and BROWNSWORD, R. (1982), 'The Dangerousness Debate after the Floud Report', *British Journal of Criminology*, 22: 229.

—— and PRESTON, R. H. (eds) (1980), *The Coming Penal Crisis*, Edinburgh: Scottish Academic Press.

——, GELSTHORPE, L., and REX, S. (eds) (2001), *Community Penalties: change and challenges*, Cullompton, Devon: Willan.

BRAITHWAITE, J., and PETTIT, P. (1990), *Not Just Deserts*, Oxford: Oxford University Press.

BRODY, S. R., and TARLING, R. (1981), *Taking Offenders out of Circulation*, Home Office Research Study No. 64, London: HMSO.

BROWN, M., and PRATT, J. (eds) (2000), *Dangerous Offenders: Punishment and Social Order*, London: Routledge.

BROWNLEE, I. (1998), *Community Punishment: a Critical Introduction*, London: Longman.

BURNEY, E. (2005), *Making People Behave: Anti-social behaviour, politics and policy*, Cullompton, Devon: Willan.

CARTER REVIEW (2003), *Managing Offenders, Reducing Crime*, London: The Strategy Unit.

CHARMAN, E., GIBSON, B., HONESS, T., and MORGAN, R. (1996), *Fine Impositions and Enforcement following the Criminal Justice Act 1993*, Research Findings 36, London: Home Office.

COOKE, R. K. (1987), 'The Practical Problems of the Sentencer', in D. Pennington and S. Lloyd-Bostock (eds), *The Psychology of Sentencing*, Oxford: Centre for Socio-Legal Studies.

DARBYSHIRE, P. (1999), 'A Comment on the Powers of Magistrates' Clerks', *Criminal Law Review*, 377–86.

DIGNAN, J. (2005), *Understanding Victims and Restorative Justice*, Maidenhead: Open University Press.

DODD, T., NICHOLAS, S., POVEY, D., and WALKER, A. (2004), *Crime in England and Wales 2003/04*, Home Office Statistical Bulletin 10/04, London: Home Office.

DOOB, A., and WEBSTER, C. (2003), 'Sentence Severity and Crime: Accepting the Null Hypothesis', *Crime and Justice: a Review of Research*, 30: 143.

DUFF, R. A. (2000), *Punishment, Communication and Community*, New York: Oxford University Press.

——, and GARLAND, D. (eds) (1994), *A Reader on Punishment*, Oxford: Oxford University Press.

DUNBAR, I., and LANGDON, A. (1998), *Tough Justice: Sentencing and Penal Policies in the 1990s*, London: Blackstone Press.

EREZ, E. (1999), 'Who's Afraid of the Big, Bad Victim', *Criminal Law Review*, 545–56.

FLOOD-PAGE, C., and MACKIE, A. (1998), *Sentencing Practice: an examination of decisions in magistrates' courts and the Crown Court in the mid-1990s*, Home Office Research Study No. 180, London: Home Office.

FLOUD, J., and YOUNG, W. (1981), *Dangerousness and Criminal Justice*, London: Heinemann.

GALLIGAN, D. (1986), *Discretionary Powers*, Oxford: Oxford University Press.

GARLAND, D. (1990), *Punishment and Modern Society*, Oxford: Oxford University Press.

HALLIDAY REPORT (2001), *Making Punishments Work: Report of a Review of the Sentencing Framework*, London: Home Office.

HARPER, G., and CHITTY, C. (eds) (2005), *The Impact of Corrections on Re-offending: a review of 'what works'*, Home Office Research Study 291, London: Home Office.

HART, H. L. A. (1968), *Punishment and Responsibility*, Oxford: Oxford University Press.

HAWKINS, K. (ed.) (1992), *Discretion*, Oxford: Oxford University Press.

—— (2003), *Law as Last Resort*, Oxford: Oxford University Press .

HEDDERMAN, C., and GELSTHORPE, L. (1997), *Understanding the Sentencing of Women*, Home Office Research Study No. 170, London: Home Office.

HOME OFFICE (1999), *Digest 4: Information on the Criminal Justice System in England and Wales*, London: Home Office.

—— (2000), *National Standards for the Supervision of Offenders in the Community*, 3rd edn, London: Home Office.

—— (2002), *Justice for All*, London: Stationery Office.

—— (2005), *Sentencing Statistics 2004*, Home Office Statistical Bulletin 15/05, London: Home Office.

HOOD, R. (1962), *Sentencing in Magistrates' Courts*, London: Tavistock.

—— (1972), *Sentencing the Motoring Offender*, London: Heinemann.

—— (1992), *Race and Sentencing*, Oxford: Oxford University Press.

—— and SHUTE, S. (2000), *The Parole System at Work*, Home Office Research Study No. 202, London: Home Office.

HOUGH, M., and ROBERTS, J. V. (1998), *Attitudes to Punishment: Findings from the British Crime Survey*, Home Office Research Study No. 179, London: Home Office.

——, JACOBSON, J., and MILLIE, A. (2003), *The Decision to Imprison*, London: Prison Reform Trust.

HUDSON, B. (1987), *Justice through Punishment: a Critique of the Justice Model of Corrections*, London: Macmillan.

—— (1993), *Penal Policy and Social Justice*, London: Macmillan.

—— (1998), 'Doing Justice to Difference', in A. Ashworth and M. Wasik (eds), *Fundamentals of Sentencing Theory*, Oxford: Oxford University Press.

JOHNSTONE, G. (2001), Restorative Justice, Cullompton, Devon: Willan.

LACEY, N. (1988), *State Punishment*, London: Routledge.

LLOYD, C., MAIR, G., and HOUGH, M. (1994), *Explaining Reconviction Rates: a critical analysis*, Home Office Research Study No. 135, London: HMSO.

MCALINDEN, A. (2001), 'Indeterminate Sentences for the Severely Personality Disordered', *Criminal Law Review*, 108–23.

MCGUIRE, J. (ed.) (2002), *Offender Rehabilitation and Treatment: Effective Programmes and Policies to Reduce Re-Offending*, New York: John Wiley.

MONAHAN, J. (2004), 'The Future of Violence Risk Management', in M. Tonry (ed.), *The Future of Imprisonment*, New York: Oxford University Press.

MOORE, R. (2004), 'The Methods of Enforcing Financial Penalties: The Need for a Multi-Dimensional Approach', *Criminal Law Review*, 728–44.

MORGAN, R. (2003), 'Thinking about the Demand for Probation Services', *Probation Journal*, 50: 7–19.

MOXON, D. (1988), *Sentencing Practice in the Crown Court*, Home Office Research Study No. 103, London: HMSO.

OXFORD PILOT STUDY (1984), *Sentencing in the Crown Court*, by A. Ashworth, E. Genders, G. Mansfield, J. Peay, and E. Player. Oxford: Centre for Criminological Research.

POSNER, R. (1985), 'An Economic Theory of the Criminal Law', *Columbia Law Review*, 85: 1193–1231.

RADZINOWICZ, SIR L., and HOOD, R. (1990), *The Emergence of Penal Policy in Victorian and Edwardian England*, Oxford: Oxford University Press.

RAINE, J., DUNSTAN, E., and MACKIE, A. (2004), 'Financial Penalties: Who Pays, Who Doesn't, and Why Not', *Howard Journal of Criminal Justice*, 43: 518.

REX, S. (1998), 'Applying Desert Principles to Community Sentences: Lessons from two Criminal Justice Acts', *Criminal Law Review*: 381.

SANDERS, A., HOYLE, C., MORGAN, R., and CAPE, E. (2001), 'Victim Impact Statements: Don't Work, Can't Work', *Criminal Law Review*, 447–58.

SHAPLAND, J. (1981), *Between Conviction and Sentence*, London: Routledge.

—— (1987), 'Who Controls Sentencing? Influences on the Sentencer', in D. Pennington and S. Lloyd-Bostock (eds), *The Psychology of Sentencing*, Oxford: Centre for Socio-Legal Studies.

SHUTE, S. (1999), 'Who Passes Unduly Lenient Sentences?', *Criminal Law Review*. 603.

TARLING, R. (1979), *Sentencing Practice in Magistrates' Courts*, Home Office Research Study No. 56, London: HMSO.

——, MOXON, D., and JONES, P. (1985), 'Sentencing of Adults and Juveniles in Magistrates' Courts', in D. Moxon (ed.), *Managing Criminal Justice*, London: HMSO.

THOMAS, D. A. (1970), *Principles of Sentencing*, London: Heinemann.

—— (1974), 'The Control of Discretion in the Administration of Criminal Justice', in R. Hood (ed.), *Crime, Criminology and Public Policy*, London: Heinemann.

TONRY, M. (1996), *Sentencing Matters*, New York: Oxford University Press.

—— (2004), *Punishment and Politics*, Cullompton, Devon: Willan.

VON HIRSCH, A. (1976), *Doing Justice*, New York: Hill and Wang.

—— and ASHWORTH, A. (eds) (1998), *Principled Sentencing: Readings in Theory and Policy*, 2nd edn, Oxford: Hart.

—— and —— (2005), *Proportionate Sentencing*, Oxford: Oxford University Press.

——, BOTTOMS, A. E., BURNEY, E., and WIKSTRÖM, P.-O. (1999), *Criminal Deterrence: an Analysis of Recent Research*, Oxford: Hart.

WALKER, N. (1991), *Why Punish?*, Oxford: Oxford University Press.

WASIK, M. (1985), 'The Grant of an Absolute Discharge', *Oxford Journal of Legal Studies*, 5: 211.

WOOD, D. (1988), 'Dangerous Offenders and the Morality of Protective Sentencing', *Criminal Law Review*: 424–33.

30

YOUTH JUSTICE

Rod Morgan and Tim Newburn

In 1998 the system for dealing with the criminal offences of children and young persons in England and Wales was fundamentally reformed by the Crime and Disorder Act. This chapter is divided into two main parts. The first provides a brief sketch, increasingly detailed as the 1998 reforms are approached, of how a dedicated youth justice system emerged from its origins in the middle of the nineteenth century onwards. The second, longer, section explains what the reformed youth justice system comprises and reviews its working. We conclude with some thoughts about future directions.

THE BACKGROUND TO THE 1998 REFORMS

THE EMERGENCE OF JUVENILE JUSTICE

A separate system of juvenile justice has existed for approximately a century. Social reformers in the nineteenth century increasingly campaigned to protect children from danger and exploitation and as part of this sought to remove them from the 'adult' prison system. Reformatories for the 'dangerous classes' were introduced by the Youthful Offenders Act 1854, and within a few years industrial schools for the 'perishing classes' had also been established. Although initially they were part of the educational rather than the penal system, they housed children aged between seven and 14 who had been convicted of vagrancy.

Juvenile courts emerged at the beginning of the twentieth century. The Probation of Offenders Act 1907 provided a statutory basis for the probation service, and in 1908 the Children Act created the juvenile court. The 1908 Act barred under-14s from prison and restricted the imprisonment of 14–15-year-olds. The juvenile courts—special sittings of the magistrates' courts in the early years—were empowered to act in criminal, begging, and vagrancy cases, though they remained, in essence, criminal courts.

At the same time 'borstals' were created to cater for 16–21-year-olds (the 'juvenile-adult category') who 'by reason of his criminal habits and tendencies or associations with persons of such character, it is expedient that he should be subject to detention for such a term and such instruction and discipline as appears most conducive to his reformation and the repression of crime' (quoted in Garland 1985: 219). This 'welfare principle' was reinforced by the Children and Young Persons Act 1933 which prohibited capital punishment for those under the age of 18, and reorganized the reformatory and industrial schools. 'Approved schools' were to provide juvenile offenders with education and training. Remand homes were created to accommodate remanded juveniles apart from adult prisoners.

The use of imprisonment for juveniles was further restricted by the 1948 Criminal Justice Act, which also introduced remand centres, attendance centres, and support for probation hostels, and abolished corporal punishment. However, following pressure from the Magistrates' Association, a short-term custodial sentence—the detention centre order—was introduced. This was intended to be a short, unpleasant sentence combining hard work with the minimum of amusement—a sentence not unlike the 'short, sharp shock' experiment of the early 1980s. Detention centres were introduced in the 1950s and developed slowly. Further welfarist legislation, the Children Act 1948, sought to end the placement of neglected children in approved schools alongside offenders, and set up local authority children's departments with their own resources for residential care—'the first professional social work service exclusively for children' (Harris and Webb 1987).

According to Windelsham (1993: 69) from the early post-war period onwards, 'the twin claws of the pincer that was to hold the development of penal policy fast in its grip were the remorseless increase in the incidence of crime, and the overcrowding in the prisons'. Indeed, levels of recorded crime rose in a generally sustained and sharp way from the mid-1950s on, with an almost 100 per cent increase in the numbers of juvenile offenders per 100,000 population cautioned or convicted for indictable offences in the period 1961–85. Nevertheless a strong welfarist imperative continued to influence juvenile justice policy throughout the 1950s and most of the 1960s. At the end of the 1950s the Ingleby Committee proposed that the age of criminal responsibility be raised from eight to 14: this was not taken up but the Children and Young Persons Act 1963 did raise it to 10. The Children and Young Persons Act 1969 subsequently abolished the system of approved schools, and the remand homes or remand centres for juveniles which existed alongside them: they were replaced with community homes with residential and educational facilities. Care was preferred over criminal proceedings and the circumstances in which court proceedings were possible were narrowed. The intention was that the juvenile court should become a welfare-providing agency and 'an agency of last resort' (Rutter and Giller 1983), referral happening only in those cases in which informal and voluntary agreement had not been reached between the local authority, the juvenile and parents (Morris and McIsaac 1978). It was also intended that detention centres and borstals for juveniles be phased out and replaced by a new form of intervention—intermediate treatment. According to Rutherford (1986a: 57) this 'was less a policy of decarceration than a reiteration of the traditional welfare abhorrence of the prison system'.

The 1969 Children and Young Persons Act was arguably the high point of 'welfarism'. But the general election of 1970 and the change of government which it brought about put paid to any possibility of full implementation of the Act. The consequence was that juvenile courts continued to function largely as before: criminal proceedings for 10–14-year-olds continued, powers in relation to 14–16-year-olds were not restricted, and the minimum age for a borstal sentence was not increased. Perhaps most significantly, although care proceedings on the commission of an offence were made possible, such powers were used exceedingly sparingly, and the number of custodial sentences rose from 3,000 in 1970 to over 7,000 in 1978 (Rutter and Giller 1983).

Against this background of rapidly increasing use of custody, it is worth considering what full implementation of the 1969 Act would have meant. It would have abolished prosecution of any child under 14 for a criminal offence, with the exception of homicide. It would have restricted civil care measures for that group as well. And children would have been dealt with, wherever possible, outside court. Though 14–16-year-olds could have been prosecuted, non-criminal care proceedings would be available, and the preferred alternative in most cases. For those prosecuted, there would have been two main disposals available—the care order and the supervision order—both of which would be supervised by social workers given considerable discretion (Bottoms 1974). The intention was that the use of penal custody for offenders aged 14 to 16 be phased out (Nellis 1991). This added up to 'the most developed application of welfare principles to criminal justice ever seen in an English statute' (Bottoms and Stevenson 1992: 36).

Partial implementation, and the consequences which flowed from that, led one group of commentators at the end of the decade to argue that the 'tragedy' of the 1969 Act was that people had been led to believe that the system was becoming softer and softer, when in reality the reverse was largely the case (Thorpe *et al.* 1980). Though only partly implemented, the Act became the major scapegoat for the perceived ills of juvenile crime and justice in the 1970s, and the 'welfare' model it espoused was replaced by an expanding youth justice system in which the emphasis was increasingly on 'justice' or punishment. There was a significant backlash against welfarism across criminal justice and penal policy in the 1970s, and the criticisms came from all parts of the political spectrum. Those on the Right were critical of what they took to be the insufficiently tough approach characteristic of contemporary juvenile justice. Those on the Left felt that behind all the talk of 'treatment', restrictive and potentially punitive forms of intervention were on the increase. The 1970s witnessed a doubling in the use of custody for juveniles with a concomitant decline in the use of community-based alternatives, while at the same time the use of cautions increased substantially.

In the 1980s 'short sharp shock' detention centre regimes were experimentally introduced, and though found to fail in terms of reoffending rates, were then extended to all detention centres. Youth justice policy was now a far cry from that envisaged by the 1969 Act. Yet though Thatcherite rhetoric remained tough the juvenile justice legislation contained countervailing tendencies. The Criminal Justice Act 1982 aimed to limit the use of custody for young offenders, shortened the detention centre sentence and, via the new Youth Custody Order, signalled the end of borstals and indeterminate sentences. Against this background a significant and sustained decline in the numbers of young being processed by the courts took place in the latter half of the 1980s—a decline all the more remarkable for having occurred during a period dominated by a 'law and order' government.

THE SUCCESSFUL REVOLUTION?

The so-called 'successful revolution' in juvenile justice (Jones 1989) involved a halving of the number of 14–16-year-old youths receiving custodial penalties in England and Wales between 1984 and 1988 (see Figure 30.1), a decline in the use of custody not seen for other age groups (see also Ashworth, and Morgan and Liebling, Chapters 29 and 32, respectively, this volume).

Why did this fall occur? Several factors can be identified. First, between 1981 and 1998 there was an 18 per cent drop in the population of 14–16-year-old males. This helps explain the declining overall use of custody but not the fall in proportionate use (12 per cent of 14–16-year-old offenders received custodial sentences in 1985 compared with 7 per cent in 1990). Secondly, the Criminal Justice Act 1982 contained restrictions on the use of custody and introduced a range of non-custodial penalties. New requirements that could be added to supervision orders were also introduced and Allen (1991) argued that, though far from conclusive, the evidence suggests that supervision orders were used as an increasingly high tariff option throughout the 1980s. Thirdly, there was the increase in intensive intermediate treatment schemes which, though difficult to assess, appear to have served as an alternative to custody (though see Parker *et al.* 1989).

Fourthly, and crucially, there was diversion from court. This was central to the significant decline in the number of juveniles prosecuted in the latter half of the 1980s (Farrington 1992). Indeed, so successful was the general cautioning policy in relation to juveniles believed to be that, as early as the 1988 Green Paper, *Punishment, Custody and the Community*, the Home Office signalled its intention to transfer the lessons learned in juvenile justice to policies for offenders generally. In a statement which both captures

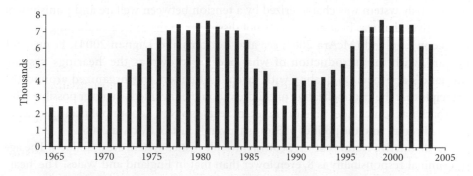

Fig. 30.1 Young offenders sentenced to immediate custody, 1965–2004

the thinking at the time and indicates just how far penal policy has travelled since, the Green Paper stated that:

> Most young offenders grow out of crime as they become more mature and responsible. They need encouragement and help to become law abiding. Even a short period of custody is quite likely to confirm them as criminals, particularly as they acquire new criminal skills from the more sophisticated offenders. They see themselves labelled as criminals and behave accordingly [Home Office 1988: paras 2.17–2.19].

Diversion from custody and from court was emphasized and, consequently, cautioning continued to have a central role in this approach. In the same period, two major new pieces of legislation affecting young offenders came into force. The Children Act 1989 finally removed all civil care proceedings from the juvenile court. and the Criminal Justice Act 1991 changed the name of the juvenile court to the youth court and extended its jurisdiction to include 17-year-olds.

The 1991 Act reduced the maximum term of detention in a young offender institution (YOI) to 12 months. YOIs had been introduced in 1988, superseding the youth custody centres that had themselves replaced borstals in 1982. Again reinforcing lessons learned from developments in practice over the previous decade, the 1991 Act signalled the importance of inter-agency and joint working. It gave chief probation officers and directors of social services joint responsibility for making local arrangements ('action plans') for dealing with young offenders, and more generally for providing services to the youth court. This represented the final nail in the coffin of the 'welfare' model, and further reinforced, though temporarily, the pre-eminence of the 'justice' model in juvenile justice. Yet by this stage at least one commentator was arguing that it no longer made sense to talk in terms of welfare *or* justice. Rather, Pratt (1989) argued, what was emerging in English juvenile justice was a form of 'corporatism'. Centralized authority and bureaucratic control over decision-making was driving a system increasingly characterized by multi-agency working, in which the aims of 'economy' and 'efficiency' were of growing importance in the management of those caught up in the system.

It is appropriate at this point briefly to consider the juvenile justice system in Scotland. The Scottish system, with its particularly strong commitment to welfarism, provides an important contrast to the approach south of the border. Prior to the 1970s the Scottish system was characterized by a tension between welfare and punishment imperatives that was in some respects not dissimilar to the pressures shaping juvenile justice in England (McAra 2002; see also Bottoms and Dignan 2004). From 1971 onward, with the introduction of what became known as the 'hearings' system, Scotland's approach to dealing with juvenile offenders was organized around the principle that the criminalization of children should be avoided wherever possible. This approach has come under pressure in recent years as a New Labour political agenda has gradually crept into the politics of Scottish juvenile justice (McAra 2006).

The distinctive features of the Scottish juvenile justice system are as follows. The age of criminal responsibility is 8, even lower than that in England and Wales. The 'hearings' system deals with children aged 8 to 15 inclusive (beyond 15 they are dealt with in the adult criminal justice system). Children's hearings and court proceedings are subject to the principle that the 'the welfare of that child throughout his childhood shall be their or its paramount consideration'—enshrined initially in the Social Work (Scotland) Act 1968 and now expressed as part of the Children (Scotland) Act 1995. The 1968 Act established the children's hearings system in which the majority of cases where offending is alleged are dealt with in a manner similar to cases where the issues at hand are primarily to do with the health and welfare of the child. Once an offence is alleged, in the vast majority of cases the referral is investigated by a 'reporter' whose task is to consider whether statutory grounds for referral have been met and whether compulsory measures of care are necessary. If so, then the case proceeds to a hearing. The child and parents must accept the grounds for the referral (i.e. there must be an admission of guilt in cases where offending is alleged): without an admission of guilt the case proceeds to the sheriff court.

Hearings are private and usually involve three members of a lay panel, the child and their parents, a lawyer or advisor, the reporter, a social worker, and, where appropriate, other professionals such as a teacher or psychologist. Apart from discharging the case there are two primary options for disposal: residential and non-residential supervision. The former involves placing the child in a residential establishment; the latter means that the child will continue to live at home, most likely under the supervision of a social worker. This approach, it will now be clear, differs markedly from the system of juvenile justice that emerged in England and Wales during the retreat from the intentions of the Children and Young Persons Act 1969. Which is not to say that the Scottish system did not suffer from many of the tensions and difficulties often associated with welfarist approaches, such as indeterminate and disproportionate interventions and the potential, at least, for 'net-widening'. Nevertheless, as Westminster politics drifted rightwards in the 1980s and 1990s the contrasting character of the Scottish system was enviously regarded by many practitioners and commentators in England. North of the border it became 'inextricably linked to a sense of Scottishness' (McAra 2006). In recent years, however, populist punitive politics have begun to reshape Scottish juvenile justice, though this process has been more recent and arguably less dramatic than the changes that have refashioned youth justice in England and Wales.

THE REBIRTH OF POPULIST PUNITIVENESS

In the early 1990s there was a dramatic change in the tenor of official comment about juvenile offending. Concerns were fuelled by a number of events, including the well-publicized urban disturbances of 1991 (Campbell 1993) and an emergent moral panic about so-called 'persistent young offenders' (Hagell and Newburn 1994). In March 1993, the government announced that it proposed introducing a new disposal, the secure training order (STO), aimed at 'that comparatively small group of very persistent juvenile offenders whose repeated offending makes them a menace to the community' (*Hansard*, 2 March 1993, col. 139). It was to apply to 12–15-year-olds (later amended to 12–14-year-olds) who had been convicted of three imprisonable offences, and who had proved 'unwilling or unable to comply with the requirements of supervision in the community while on remand or under sentence'.

Public and political concern might not have reached the pitch it did were it not for the tragic events of 12 February 1993 and their highly publicized aftermath. The abduction of 2-year-old James Bulger from a shopping centre in Bootle, Liverpool, and the protracted search that followed his disappearance, including the broadcasting of CCTV images of the toddler being led away, led to very understandable public concern. But the subsequent arrest and charging of two 10-year-old boys 'inspired a kind of national collective agony' (Young 1996: 113), and provided the strongest possible evidence to an already worried public that something new and particularly malevolent was afoot. The trial of the two youngsters accused of James Bulger's murder took place in November 1993 amidst massive national and international media interest, which continued after the verdict (Franklin and Petley 1996). The tone of most of the coverage—despite the age of the offenders—was unforgiving in its punitiveness. Leading politicians from both main parties also used the opportunity to air their tough-on-crime credentials. Tony Blair, then Shadow Home Secretary, delivered what one biographer (Sopel 1995: 155) described as a powerful 'speech-cum-sermon':

> The news bulletins of the last week have been like hammer blows struck against the sleeping conscience of the country, urging us to wake up and look unflinchingly at what we see. We hear of crimes so horrific they provoke anger and disbelief in equal proportions . . . These are the ugly manifestations of a society that is becoming unworthy of that name. A solution to this disintegration doesn't simply lie in legislation. It must come from the rediscovery of a sense of direction as a country and most of all from being unafraid to start talking again about the values and principles we believe in and what they mean for us, not just as individuals but as a community. We cannot exist in a moral vacuum. If we do not learn and then teach the value of what is right and what is wrong, then the result is simply moral chaos which engulfs us all.

The then Home Secretary, Michael Howard, also responded by embracing a 'populist punitive' (Bottoms 1995) rhetoric and introducing a package of new measures, at the heart of which was the reassertion of the centrality of custody. Most famously, he announced that previous approaches which involved attempts to limit prison numbers were henceforward to be abandoned. The new package of measures would be likely to result in an increase in prison numbers, an increase which he appeared to welcome because '*Prison works*. It ensures that we are protected from murderers, muggers and rapists—and it makes many who are tempted to commit crime think twice' (quoted in Newburn 2003: 263, emphasis added).

The Criminal Justice and Public Order Act 1994 doubled the maximum sentence in a YOI for 15–17-year-olds to two years. The Act introduced the possibility that parents of young offenders be bound over to ensure that their children carried out their community sentences, and provided for the introduction of STOs for 12–14-year-olds. Five secure training centres (STCs) were to be built, each housing approximately 40 inmates. The new sentences would be determinate, of a maximum of two years, half of which would be served in custody and half under supervision in the community. Outside Parliament, there was widespread criticism of the new provisions and Home Office-funded research cast doubt on the likely efficacy of such a policy (Hagell and Newburn 1994). But the STO met with relatively little political hostility with New Labour seeking to outflank the Conservatives over 'law and order' (see Downes and Morgan, Chapter 9, this volume). The predictable consequence was a rise in the use of youth custody. The number of 15–17-year-olds given custodial sentences rose by almost four-fifths between 1992 and 1998. The number of young people serving custodial sentences rose by 122 per cent between 1993 and 1999 (see Figure 32.3 in this volume).

THE RISE OF MANAGERIALISM

Established to promote economy, efficiency, and effectiveness in public services, the Audit Commission became increasingly influential in criminal justice during the course of the 1990s. Though its initial focus was on policing (Morgan and Newburn 1997), by the middle of the decade it had turned its attention to the youth justice system and added its voice to the growing roll-call of commentators calling for increased emphasis on 'criminality prevention' (inter alia Utting *et al.* 1993; Farrington 1996). The Opposition Home Affairs team was simultaneously preparing their proposals for youth justice reform. The parallels between New Labour's pre-election consultation document, *Tackling Youth Crime: Reforming Youth Justice* (Labour Party 1996), and the Audit Commission's hugely influential report, *Misspent Youth* (Audit Commission 1996), were striking—in terms of both the issues covered and the proposals contained.

The Audit Commission had little of a positive nature to say about the youth justice system and a number of biting criticisms. Its view was that the system in England and Wales was uneconomic, inefficient, and ineffective. The Commission was critical of the cautioning system, and particularly of 'repeat cautioning'. It argued that first-time cautions were reasonably effective, but that subsequent use became progressively less effective and ran the risk of bringing the youth justice system into disrepute. At a general level, it was critical of the lack of programmes directed at offending behaviour and was dismayed by what it saw as the absence of coordinated working within the youth justice system. The problem was that 'the agencies dealing with young offenders have different views about what they are trying to achieve . . . these different approaches need to be reconciled if agencies are to work together and fulfil their different responsibilities' (ibid. para. 21). According to the Audit Commission, it was not just the approach of youth justice teams that was problematic. The whole court system, it suggested, was becoming less and less efficient. In its most damning indictment it suggested that 'overall, less is done now than a decade ago to address offending by young people. Fewer young people are now convicted by the courts, even allowing for the fall in the number of people aged 10–17 years, and an increasing proportion of those who are found guilty are discharged' (ibid.: para. 69). The system, the Commission argued, needed to be streamlined and speeded up, and greater attention needed to be given to early preventive work. Its approach was heavily influenced by the results of longitudinal criminological research that identified the 'risk factors' associated with offending by juveniles. These factors may be used to target areas where young people are at particular risk and help identify approaches that may reduce the risks.

The Commission's analysis and proposals and the subsequent legislation—the Crime and Disorder Act 1998—were heavily managerialist in approach, emphasizing inter-agency cooperation, the necessity of an overall strategic plan, the creation of key performance indicators, and active monitoring of aggregate information about the system and its functioning. To a youth justice system that had been the site of competing philosophies, approaches, and ideologies—notably welfarism, punitiveness, and systems management—New Labour added a further dose of managerialism, together with its own potent blend of communitarianism and populism (Newburn 1998). The consequence of this blend, for some commentators, has been the emergence of a 'new youth justice' (Goldson 2000).

NEW LABOUR, NEW YOUTH JUSTICE?

THE POST-1997 ELECTION STRUCTURE FOR YOUTH JUSTICE

The first six months of New Labour in government were characterized by a frenzy of activity. In less than two months six consultation documents on the subject of youth crime were published, each of which contained considerable discussion of various proposals that had first been outlined in *Tackling Youth Crime*: *Reforming Youth Justice* (Labour Party 1996). The essence of New Labour's approach was expressed in the title of its White Paper, *No More Excuses* (Home Office 1997a). The major proposals eventually found their way, largely unchanged, into the Government's flagship legislation, the Crime and Disorder Act 1998. This Act, though followed by others, contains the key elements of Labour's 'new youth justice': the establishment of the Youth Justice Board (YJB), the creation of local authority youth offending teams (YOTs), and the restructuring of the non-custodial penalties available to the youth court. In *No More Excuses*, the Government had identified:

Confusion about the purpose of the youth justice system and the principles that should govern the way in which young people are dealt with by youth justice agencies. Concerns about the welfare of young people have too often been seen as in conflict with the aims of protecting the public, punishing offences and preventing offending . . .

The Government does not accept that there is any conflict between protecting the welfare of a young offender and preventing that individual from offending again. Preventing offending promotes the welfare of the individual young offender and protects the public [Home Office 1997a: para. 2.1–2].

The Crime and Disorder Act, section, 37, accordingly established that 'It shall be the principal aim of the youth justice system to prevent offending by children and young persons' and the Government set out five aims for the new system:

- a clear strategy to prevent offending and reoffending.
- offenders, and their parents, to face up to their offending behaviour and take responsibility for it;
- earlier, more effective intervention when young people first offend;
- faster, more efficient procedures from arrest to sentence;
- partnership between all youth justice agencies to deliver more effective interventions.

Juvenile justice has historically varied a good deal in terms of service delivery from one part of the country to another. Inspired by the excoriating criticisms of the extant system by the Audit Commission (1996), New Labour sought, as in so many aspects of its social policy, to impose order from the centre. With an enormous legislative programme envisaged, the new Home Secretary established a Youth Justice Task Force in June 1997. Its aims were to maintain the momentum developed in Opposition and to provide a continuing formal link with the major agencies involved with young offenders (Windelsham 2001). The Task Force was chaired by Norman (subsequently Lord) Warner, who had been adviser to the Home Secretary, Jack Straw, in Opposition. Its secretary was Mark Perfect, co-author of the 1996 Audit Commission report. When, following section 41 of the Crime and Disorder Act, the YJB was created a non-departmental public body sponsored by the Home Office, these two became its first Chair and Chief Executive respectively.

The YJB's principal functions are to establish appropriate performance measures, monitor the operation of the youth justice system in the light of national standards, conduct research, promulgate good practice, and advise ministers. The 1998 Act provided for the Home Secretary to expand the Board's role and, in April 2000 he did so. The YJB additionally became the commissioning body for all placements of under-18s in secure establishments on remand or sentence from a criminal court. The Comprehensive Spending Review of the secure estate had concluded that there was 'little positive to say about the current arrangements . . . Regime standards are inconsistent and often poor. Costs vary considerably. There is no effective oversight or long term planning' (Home Office 1998a). Since 2000, therefore, the YJB has had the responsibility of purchasing sufficient places from the Prison Service, from commercial contractors, and from the local authorities, to cater for all children and young persons who the courts determine shall be in custody.

If New Labour's commitment to the core elements of 'systemic managerialism' (Bottoms 1995) was reflected in the creation of the YJB, then the establishment of YOTs, the embodiment of partnership working, was arguably the most significant reform introduced by the 1998 Act. Prior to 1998, youth justice teams, comprising mainly social workers, had primary responsibility for working with young offenders subject to non-custodial penalties, and for liaising with other criminal justice and treatment agencies in connection with that work. Stimulated by a concern with efficiency and consistency on the one hand, and a pragmatic belief in multi-agency working on the other, YOTs must include representatives of both criminal justice and welfare agencies—social services, the police, probation, education, and health. Whether local authorities cooperate to form a YOT, or provide their own, is a matter for them. Arrangements, as a consequence, vary from one area to another and to some extent shift over time. There are currently 157 YOTs in England and Wales with great variation between them in size, composition, funding, and line management arrangements. YOTs are generally co-located, most have in the range of 20–60 full-time equivalent staff (though the largest, Birmingham, has 359 staff and six have fewer than 20 staff) and, though they are discrete entities, their managers are generally line managed from either within social services (or combined children's services departments) or chief executives' departments.

As Pitts (2001) notes, the constitution of the YOTs mirrors the Multi-Agency Diversion Panels of the 1980s and, in particular, the Northampton Diversion Scheme; the latter having been given a particularly good press by the Audit Commission (1996). However, whereas the diversion schemes were the product of an earlier era—the 1980s 'corporatism' in juvenile justice (Pratt 1989)—YOTs were established not to divert but to target and intervene. The two primary functions of YOTs are to coordinate the provision of youth justice services for all those in the local authority's area who need them, and to carry out such functions as are assigned to the team in the youth justice plan formulated by the local authority.

Local youth justice plans are heavily influenced by the performance framework which has over the eight years of its existence been developed by the YJB. This, in turn, has reflected the performance framework developed by the Home Office, which provides the bulk of the YJB's budget, and the interdepartmental Office for Criminal Justice Reform (OCJR), a trilateral centre (Home Office, Department for Constitutional Affairs, and Attorney General's Department), which reports monthly to a National Criminal Justice Board, which in turn oversees the 42 Local Criminal Justice Boards (LCJBs), on which all the key criminal justice agencies, including the YOTs, are represented (HM Government 2004). The nature and extent of this reporting system is an indication of just how significant the managerialist reforms to youth justice have been in the past decade.

The one specific pledge concerning crime which New Labour offered in its victorious 1997 General Election campaign concerned young offenders. The famous slogan: 'tough on crime and tough on the causes of crime', first used by Tony Blair in 1993, was illustrated with the undertaking; 'and halve the time it takes persistent juvenile crime to come to court' (Labour Party 1997). Achievement of this pledge is regularly reported in the annual reports of the YJB—the 142 days of 1996 having been reduced to 76 by the time of the 2001 Election and 66 in 2005 (YJB 2005a: 8). To this quantitative target the YJB had by 2005 added others, for example:

- to reduce the number of first-time entrants to the youth justice system by 5 per cent by March 2008 compared to the 2005 baseline;

- to reduce reoffending by young offenders by 5 per cent, relative to a 2000 baseline, by March 2006;

- to reduce, between 31 March 2005 and 31 March 2008, the number of under-18s in custody by 10 per cent (ibid.: 8–11 and YJB 2005b: 18–25).

These three targets illustrate the principal foci of the YJB and the performance management system the Board has put in place for the YOTs and the closed estate—prevention, and programmes which will reduce reoffending, delivered to the greatest extent possible without resort to custody.

POST-1998 POWERS AND PROCEDURES

New Labour promised increased, and earlier, interventions in the lives of young offenders (and those 'at risk' of becoming young offenders). One of the clearest illustrations of the influence of the Audit Commission was New Labour's critique and reform of the cautioning system. The Crime and Disorder Act scrapped the caution (informal and formal) and replaced it with a reprimand (for less serious offences) and a final warning. As the name implies, the crucial characteristic of the final warning is that, unless there is a substantial lapse of time, it may be used only once. In addition to the change of nomenclature, and the more sparing manner of usage, the new system of reprimands and final warnings also initiated other activities—such as those previously associated with 'caution plus'—more frequently, and often earlier, than had previously been the case. Under the Act, all young offenders receiving a final warning should be referred to a YOT. Offenders are then expected, 'unless they consider it inappropriate to do so', to participate in a rehabilitation programme (in which reparation is expected generally to be present). According to one informed commentator (Dignan 1999: 52) 'this new approach represents a considerable improvement on Michael Howard's much more restrictive plans simply to crack down on repeat cautioning'. Moreover, the Criminal Justice and Court Services Act 2000 removed the requirement that a police reprimand or final warning be given to a young offender only at a police station. This introduced the possibility of 'conferences' at which parents, victims, and other adults could be present—what has sometimes been referred to as 'restorative cautioning' (Young and Goold 1999)—and it is clear that some YOTs and police force areas have implemented vigorous and imaginative schemes (Holdaway and Desborough 2004). However, as we shall see, this is not everywhere the case and ironically there is now less discretion about diverting children and young offenders from court proceedings than with adults.

While the new system of 'cautioning' under the Crime and Disorder Act stipulates 'two strikes and then you're out', other measures designed to prevent up-tariff responses now operate both upstream and downstream of reprimands and final warnings. Responding to research evidence highlighting the link between early and frequent offending and later, extended criminal careers, the YJB has developed several early prevention schemes whose avowed purpose is to mitigate crime and antisocial behaviour and generally to prevent offending and criminalization. In this regard, the YJB has encouraged the development within YOTs of:

- Youth Inclusion and Support Panels (YISPs), comprising representatives of the key agencies (police, education, health, social services, and the YOT) to work with 8–13-year-olds identified as at risk of offending. The aim is to support the young people and their families in accessing mainstream services with a view to addressing the factors in their lives that put them at risk of offending.

- Youth Inclusion Programmes (YIPs) which aim to engage the 50 young people in an area who the key agencies identify as most at risk of offending. Again the aim is to address the factors in their lives that place them at risk through positive activities, offending behaviour programmes, and improved access to services, particularly education.

- Parenting programmes, mostly voluntary, often as an adjunct to YISPs and YIPs, but in a minority of cases through Parenting Contracts or Parenting Orders, the latter being provided for by section 8 of the 1998 Act.

- Safer Schools Partnerships (SSPs), whereby, on the grounds that not attending school or being engaged in education greatly increases the risk that children and young people will offend, police officers are more or less intensively attached to schools with a view to reducing crime and victimization, making the school and its environment more safe and secure and reducing truancy and exclusions.

These initiatives, none of which are without controversy on the grounds that they represent an expansion of the criminal justice orbit and risk stigmatizing environments, children, and their families, with potentially net-widening consequences, have grown rapidly in number. Most YOTs now have a number of early prevention schemes (delivery of some of them contracted out to organizations like NACRO or Crime Concern) in their most deprived neighbourhoods or schools, with further expansion planned.

If the 1998 Act provided the basis for earlier interventions in the lives of young offenders and their parents (thereby adopting the 'what works' paradigm and employing the language of 'risk—see Raynor, Chapter 31, this volume), it also moved into the even more ambiguous territory of antisocial behaviour (ASB). In doing so it became 'the first piece of criminal justice legislation in England and Wales (at least since the Vagrancy Statutes of the early 19th century) to act explicitly against legal *and* moral/social transgressions' (Muncie 2001: 146). It contained a range of orders—the child safety order, the antisocial behaviour order (ASBO), the local child curfew, and the sex offender order—where there is no necessity for either the prosecution or the commission of a criminal offence. These, together with the abolition of *doli incapax*–the rebuttable common law presumption that a child aged 10–13 does not know the difference between right and wrong and therefore cannot be convicted—represent the most controversial aspects of the 'new youth justice'.

The abolition of *doli incapax* places England and Wales further out of step with most jurisdictions in the rest of Europe, where the age of criminal responsibility is 12 to 15 (Tonry and Doob 2004). The measure, which drew sustained criticism when first mooted (*inter alia* Wilkinson 1995), has recently attracted condemnation both internationally and domestically (European Commissioner for Human Rights 2005: paras 105–6; Commission on Families and the Wellbeing of Children 2005: 33–7). During the course of the 1990s, spurred in part by the Bulger case, pressure had built up to abolish the principle, and politicians from both major parties were vocal in their criticism of it. In fact the doctrine nearly disappeared in 1996 when the Divisional Court ruled that *doli incapax* was no longer part of the criminal law. This decision was later overturned by the House of Lords (*C (A Minor)* v. *DPP* [1996] 1 A.C. 1, HL), though it took the view that the law was in need of reform. New Labour worked hard to appear a convincing party of 'law and order', and 'responsibilization', of parents and young offenders, including those below the age of full criminal responsibility, was a key part of their approach. The Home Secretary was vehemently critical of the doctrine of *doli incapax*, arguing that it was archaic, illogical, and unfair (Leng *et al.* 1998). He stated his reasons for the reform robustly: 'The presumption that children aged 10 to 13 do not know the difference between serious wrongdoing and simple naughtiness flies in the face of common-sense and is long overdue for reform' (Straw 1998). The abolition of *doli incapax* arguably had more to do with the Government's 'remoralizing' mission and its focus on individual and parental responsibility than it did with 'what works'. Furthermore, as the independent Commission on Families and the Wellbeing of Children has pointed out (2005: 29) the enforcement through Parenting Orders of 'parents' role in managing their children's behaviour, while at the same time enhancing children's agency in relation to criminal activity', has arguably created 'legitimate concerns that the contradiction between these two propositions is too severe to sustain'.

The Labour Party in Opposition had been much influenced by the 'Broken Windows' thesis (Wilson and Kelling 1982; and Crawford, Chapter 26, this volume) and introduced a range of measures enabling local agencies to tackle 'low-level disorder' or ASB. One of these new measures, the child safety order, relates to children under 10, and thus not criminally responsible. The order, made in a family proceedings court, is aimed at controlling ASB rather than protecting a child's welfare and involves placing a child under supervision usually for a period of three months, up to a maximum of 12 months. Though the child safety order was subject to criticism in some quarters (Family Policy Studies Centre 1998) it was the ASBO which drew the greatest ire. Originally termed the Community Safety Order in Labour's consultation documents, the order was renamed because of its confusion with the proposed Community Protection Order (which became the Sex Offender Order) and because the original was felt not to capture its purpose.

The order was designed specifically to tackle ASB defined as: 'a matter that caused or was likely to cause harassment, alarm or distress to one or more persons not of the same household'. Prior to the 1998 Act much of this behaviour had been dealt with, if at all, under the provisions of the Housing Act 1996, the Noise Act 1996, the Environmental Protection Act 1990, or the Protection from Harassment Act 1997. However, proceedings against juveniles were often problematic under such legislation (Nixon *et al.* 1999). The ASBO was designed, inter alia, with juvenile ASB in mind.

ASBOs have morphed, however. As a result of legislation since 1998, applications for orders can be made by social landlords as well as the police and local authorities. Orders are formally civil, requiring a civil burden of proof but, following the Police Reform Act 2002, they can also be made on conviction (colloquially known as CRASBOs) and the evidence suggests that subjects of such orders often have many and serious prior convictions. ASBOs, which are for a minimum of two years, comprise prohibitions deemed necessary to protect people within the area from further ASB. What is most controversial, however, is that non-compliance is a criminal matter, triable either way and carrying a maximum sentence, in the Crown Court, of five years' imprisonment. This led some of the most distinguished critics of the new order (Gardner *et al.* 1998) to observe that it was strange 'that a government which purports to be interested in tackling social exclusion at the same time promotes a legislative measure destined to create a whole new breed of outcasts'.

There was initially great reluctance in most parts of the country to seek ASBOs. But Prime Minister Blair and successive Home Secretaries repeatedly kickstarted the initiative with major speeches. In 2003 a unit (the ASBU) was created within the Home Office to promote local activism, and further legislation (the Criminal Justice and Court Services Act 2000, the Criminal Justice and Police Act 2001, the Police Reform Act 2002, and, in particular, the Anti-Social Behaviour Act 2003) added a raft of additional powers which the courts, police, and local authorities were encouraged vigorously to use. If the number of ASBOs, and adoption of the term as a colloquialism, are the criteria, the Government's campaign was brilliantly successful. The number of orders imposed nationally ran at around 100 per quarter until the end of 2002 but by the end of 2004 the rate was over 500 rising to 600 per quarter in 2005, juveniles being the subjects of 45 per cent of them. Great pressure from above was exerted on decision-makers in areas without ASBOs in place. Most police force plans now include targets for either the number of ASBOs to be sought or aim generally to increase their number (Morgan 2006a).

The ASB policy was also subjected to excoriating criticism from authorities international and domestic. The Council of Europe Commissioner for Human Rights observed:

> The ease of obtaining such orders, the broad range of prohibited behaviour, the publicity surrounding their imposition and the serious consequences of breach all give rise to concerns. . . . What is so striking . . . about the multiplication of civil orders in the United Kingdom, is the fact that the orders are intended to protect not just specific individuals, but entire communities. This inevitably results in a very broad, and occasionally, excessive range of behaviour falling within their scope as the determination of what constitutes anti-social behaviour becomes conditional on the subjective views of any given collective. . . . such orders look rather like personalised penal codes, where non-criminal behaviour becomes criminal for individuals who have incurred the wrath of the community. . . . I question the appropriateness of empowering local residents to take such matters into their own hands. This feature would, however, appear to be the main selling point of ASBOs in the eyes of the executive, One cannot help but wonder . . . whether their purpose is not

more to reassure the public that something is being done—and, better still, by residents themselves—than the actual prevention of anti-social behaviour itself, [European Commissioner for Human Rights 2005: paras 109–11; see also Simester and von Hirsch 2006].

An independent evaluation came to similar conclusions, pointing out that the Government's ASB campaign reinforced a 'declining standards' narrative, negatively focused on young people (Millie *et al.* 2005).

By 2005 concerns were being expressed regarding the impact of ASBOs on children and young people. First, that the minimum order was so long and the number of prohibitions imposed so often excessive, that breach was made likely. Secondly, despite guidance being issued emphasizing the need for full consultation with the relevant YOT prior to an order being sought (YJB *et al.* 2005), evidence that in some parts of the country the YOTs, and thus the partnership spirit of the 1998 reforms, were effectively being circumvented, and ASBO applications normally being heard in adult courts not covered by YOT representatives. Thirdly, that in some areas ASBOs were being sought and granted without the recommended (ibid.) lower-tier measures (home visits, warnings letters, and acceptable behaviour contracts (ABCs)) first being tried. Fourthly, that ASBOs, following breach, were dragging into custody some young people who would not previously have got there or, possibly more commonly, were providing an evidential short cut for the police to fast-track persistent young offenders into custody (see the evidence to and report of the Home Affairs Committee 2005). These criticisms led to the introduction, at the end of 2005 and in early 2006, of ASBO reviews after 12 months and a practice direction that ASBO applications relating to juveniles be heard, whenever possible, by youth court magistrates.

Opposition was also aimed at the provisions in the Crime and Disorder Act permitting local authorities to introduce 'local child curfew schemes'. The introduction of curfews in the UK had been foreshadowed by proposals in the consultation paper, *Tackling Youth Crime* (Home Office 1997b) and the White Paper, *No More Excuses* (Home Office 1997a). The former described the problem thus: 'unsupervised children gathered in public places can cause real alarm and misery to local communities and can encourage one another into anti-social and criminal habits' (1997b: para. 114). The provisions in the 1998 Act enabled local authorities, after consultation with the police and with support of the Home Secretary, to introduce a ban on children of specified ages (though under 10) in specified places for a period of up to 90 days. Children breaking the curfew were to be taken home by the police, and breach of the curfew constitutes sufficient grounds for the imposition of a child safety order. In practice, there has been remarkable reluctance to use such powers. Despite such reluctance, and sustained criticism of curfews from some quarters, the Government has remained keen on the idea. Armed with what appeared to be some positive results from an evaluation of a scheme in Hamilton, Scotland (McGallagly *et al.* 1998), new legislation was introduced to extend the reach of curfew powers. The Criminal Justice and Police Act 2001 extends the maximum age at which children can be subject to a curfew up from 10 to 'under 16', and also makes provision for a local authority or the police to make a curfew on an area and not just an individual.

Critics of the direction being taken by New Labour's youth justice policy also pointed to its perceived failure to tackle the problem of increasing use of custodial sentences for young offenders. In its first term, Labour continued with the previous administration's STC building programme—even arguing that it might be extended—and introduced a new, generic custodial sentence: the Detention and Training Order (DTO). Available to the courts from April 2000, DTOs are from six to 24 months, half the sentence being served in custody and half in the community. The DTO replaces both the Secure Training Order (for 12–14-year-olds) and detention in a YOI (for 15–17-year-olds). DTOs, available to the youth court, sit alongside continued provisions whereby grave offences—in the case of murder, mandatorily—are committed to the Crown Court and liable to 'long-term detention' (to distinguish the sentence from a DTO) for which the maximum period is the same as if the child or young person were an adult. These long-term detention cases are known as section 90 or 91 cases (Powers of the Criminal Courts (Sentencing) Act 2000, formerly section 53 of the Children and Young Persons Act 1933).

The DTO represented an increase in the powers of the youth court to impose custodial sentences. Whereas the maximum period of detention in a YOI for 15–17-year-olds had been six months for a single offence, the DTO has a maximum of two years. Further, though the STO for 12–14-year-olds already provided for a two-year maximum, New Labour replaced the strict criteria for offenders under 15 relating to 'persistence' with the provision that the sentence be available where the court 'is of the *opinion* that he is a persistent offender'. The courts, including the Court of Appeal, have interpreted this power rather broadly (see Ball *et al*. 2001).

Yet if the Government relaxed the criteria for use of custody it also gave greater emphasis to reparation and restorative justice, building on the experimental practice of restorative cautioning in Thames Valley (Young and Goold 1999). The reformed cautioning system, action plan, reparation, and, following the Youth Justice and Criminal Evidence Act 1999, referral orders all promoted the idea of reparation and, wherever possible, victim involvement (see Hoyle and Zedner, Chapter 15, this volume).

The action plan order was designed to be the first option for young offenders whose offending is serious enough to warrant a community sentence. *No More Excuses* described the order as 'a short, intensive programme of community intervention combining punishment, rehabilitation and reparation to change offending behaviour and prevent further crime' (Home Office 1997a). Reparation orders require reparation to either a specified person or persons or 'to the community at large'. New Labour made a concerted effort to make both victims' views and reparation more central aspects of youth justice than previously had been the case. However, Dignan (1999: 58) was undoubtedly correct when he argued that these 'reforms hardly amount to a 'restorative justice revolution', let alone the 'paradigm shift that some restorative justice advocates have called for'. Following the implementation of the 1998 Act, the YJB also committed considerable funds to the stimulation of restorative justice projects for young offenders and, together with Crime Concern, issued guidance on the establishment of victim-offender mediation and family group conferencing programmes. Of all New Labour's restorative youth justice initiatives, arguably the most significant, however, has been the creation of referral orders as part of the Youth Justice and Criminal Evidence Act 1999.

The referral order is available in the youth court and may be made for a minimum of three and a maximum of 12 months depending on the seriousness of the crime (as determined by the court). The order is mandatory for 10–17-year-olds pleading guilty to an imprisonable offence and convicted for the first time by the courts, unless the crime is serious enough to warrant custody or the court orders an absolute discharge. The disposal involves referring the young offender to a youth offender panel (YOP). The intention is that the panel provide a forum away from the formality of the court. As Crawford (2002) argues, the panels draw on at least three sources: the Scottish Children's Hearings system (Whyte 2000), the experience of family group conferencing (Morris and Maxwell 2000), and the experience of victim-offender mediation (Marshall and Merry 1990) and restorative cautioning (Young 2000). The order consti-tutes the entire sentence for the offence (though it can be combined with certain ancillary orders, including those for costs) and, as such, substitutes for action plan orders, reparation orders, and supervision orders.

The Act extends the statutory responsibility of YOTs to include the recruitment and training of YOP volunteers, administering panel meetings, and implementing referral orders. Panels comprise one YOT member and at least two community panel members, one of whom leads the panel. Parents of all offenders aged under 16 are expected to attend all panel meetings. The offender can also nominate an adult to support them, but it is not intended that legal representatives participate. To encourage the restorative nature of the process a variety of other people, particularly victims, may be encouraged voluntarily to attend given panel meetings. The aim of the initial panel meeting is to devise a 'contract' and, where the victim chooses to attend, for him or her to meet and talk about the offence with the offender. The contract should always include reparation to the victim or wider community and a programme of activity designed primarily to prevent further offending.

Youth justice in England and Wales, then, has undergone a series of significant changes in terms of both its organization and the instruments it uses and, to a degree, the philosophy that underpins it. Had the Scottish system been unaffected by the political tides shaping English youth justice the contrast between the two would have become greater. However, over the past decade there have also been a number of important changes in the Scottish juvenile justice system. In particular, increasing managerialism with target-setting focusing on crime reduction, and a growing focus on the problem of persistent offenders, including the development of fast-tracking proced-ures and a pilot youth court for responding to such offending, have complicated the penal philosophy underpinning the system. Although it retains many of the features, and much of the philosophy derived from the Kilbrandon Report in the 1960s, recent changes have served to reduce the contrast with English youth justice, setting in train a process that McAra (2006) refers to as the 'de-tartanisation' of the Scottish system.

THE REFORMED SYSTEM IN PRACTICE

The prevailing view within Whitehall is that the restructured youth justice system in England and Wales is one of the success stories of New Labour's 'modernising government' agenda. This much is clear from the repeated, positive references to the YJB and YOT structure and its working (for example Carter 2002; Home Office 2002: para. 1.11; HM Government 2006: para. 1.11). The two most authoritative official statements are to be found in the reviews undertaken by the Audit Commission (2004) and the National Audit Office (2004). The Audit Commission found that:

- the new arrangements were a significant improvement and represented a good model for delivering public services;

- juvenile offenders were now more likely to receive an intervention, were dealt with more quickly, and were more likely to make amends for their wrongdoing;

- magistrates were generally very satisfied with the service received from YOTs;

- reconviction rates for young offenders had fallen.

The NAO review, as is customary, was more reserved. It acknowledged that the YJB had developed the additional range of community penalties within a 'comparatively short time' and introduced 'improvements to the arrangements for assessing offenders' needs at the start of a sentence'. In addition, a raft of inspectorate reports have noted improvements in standards met and offered evidence of good joint working and improving delivery of community programmes (see, for example, HMIP 2002: 34, 2004: 44, 2005: 56–60).

These official bodies have also voiced criticisms, however. The Audit Commission, for example, found that: too many minor offenders are appearing before the courts; the amount of contact time with offenders subject to supervision orders has not increased; public confidence in the youth justice system remains low; and black, minority ethnic, and mixed-race offenders remain substantially over-represented among the stubbornly high custodial population. Further, the inspectorates have found serious fault with the performance of individual YOTs and custodial establishments and identified general shortcomings in both the delivery of community-based provision and the operation of the custodial system. For example, that the YOTs generally fail to pay sufficient attention to public protection issues (HMIP 2005: 3 and 20–1) and young offenders in custody are too often housed in unsuitably large accommodation wings and, probably related, too often feel unsafe (HMIP/YJB 2005: 11–16).

Moreover, these Whitehall criticisms chime with those from independent, penal pressure groups (see, for example, the Carlile Report (2006) on the excessive use of physical restraint and other control measures on children and young people in custody) and academic commentators, some of whom have accorded them overriding, master status. Smith, for example, has concluded:

Despite the vast array of youth justice reforms since 1997, there is little evidence of any significant impact on young people, on the outcomes administered by the courts, or on other key stakeholders such as victims . . . In some quarters, it might be felt that a greater level of activity and a greater intensity of intervention . . . (is) indicative of a more responsive and committed approach to youth justice . . . On the other hand, serious questions must be asked about the consequences of this commitment . . . there is clearly a diminution of the rights of children . . . with collateral impacts such as increasing evidence of harmful treatment in custody, and persistent inequality of treatment for particular ethnic groups . . . propagation of a much broader range of interventions, based on singling out for special treatment young people who offend (or are 'at risk' of offending) is both inefficient in the purely economic sense and inconsistent with other policy streams . . . The price of a more certain response to youth crime is both too high in human terms and, ultimately, unnecessary [Smith 2003 138: see also Pitts 2001 and Bateman and Pitts 2005].

These criticisms demand closer analysis of youth justice trends and programmes.

THE CRIMINALIZATION OF YOUTH AND OVERALL REOFFENDING RATES

Given that the statutory purpose of the reformed system is to prevent offending (including reoffending), how successful, according to the best available evidence, is it proving to be? Assuming that the incidence of youth crime is to only a limited extent determined by criminal justice and penal policy, we shall look principally to the number of children drawn into the youth justice system and, setting aside their well-known shortcomings (see Raynor, Chapter 31, this volume), the headline reconviction rates. We shall then consider the available evidence accruing from evaluations of some of the programmes which the YJB has put in place.

Various indicators suggest that volume crime has fallen by approximately one third since the mid-1990s (see Maguire, Chapter 10, this volume) and the survey evidence indicates that youth crime rates have not increased (see Newburn, Chapter 18, this volume). However, since most crime, whether committed by youth or adults, goes undetected, there is no straightforward relationship between rates of offending and criminalization. What then has been the impact of the 1998 reforms on the criminalization of children and young people?

It is apparent from Figure 30.2 and Tables 30.1 and 30.2 that the years immediately preceding and following the 1998 reforms exhibit both continuity and change. If pre-court cautions and court sentences are aggregated there has been little change in the overall number of children and young people drawn into the system, only 6 per cent more in 2004 than in 1994. However, whereas two-thirds of cases were dealt with pre-court in 1994, only around half are today. Children and young people who offend and are apprehended are now very much more likely to be prosecuted than was formerly the case. This outcome is to a large extent the logical outcome of the 1998 reforms and to that extent was intended. But it has led to the complaint that too many minor cases are now being unnecessarily brought before the youth court (Audit Commission 2004: 3). Since repeat cautions beyond two were relatively uncommon prior to 1998 (see Bottoms and Dignan 2004: 80) what other factors may have driven the process?

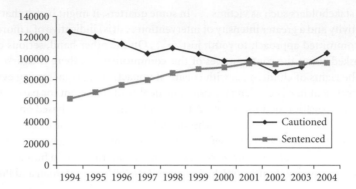

Fig. 30.2 Cautions and sentences of 10–17-year-olds, 1994–2004

Is it because pre-court interventions, despite the promise of the enhanced final warning system, have become less effective than expected? The evidence suggests not. Table 30.3 shows that the effectiveness of reprimands and final warnings was statistically better than expected in the first years of operation, and though that improvement has not been sustained, the reconviction rate remains at the expected level.

If crime has been falling and pre-court interventions are at least as effective as in the past, why then are more children and young people being drawn into the system, particularly before the courts? We can reasonably speculate that the following four characteristics of the youth justice system have contributed to this process. First, police forces have been set targets for the number of *offences brought to justice* (OBTJs). As informal warnings do not count as OBTJs more children and young people are being acted against for offences that it is relatively easy for the police to process: that is, young people, whose offending typically takes place in groups in public places and who therefore represent a relatively soft touch. Secondly, the development of inter-agency information exchange and application of the police intelligence model (see Newburn and Reiner, Chapter 27, this volume) has meant that the police have become more effective at targeting persistent young offenders, a hypothesis supported by the fact that an increased proportion of sentenced young offenders have prior convictions, often many (see Home Office 2005: ch. 6). Thirdly, the Government, as we have seen, has explicitly targeted the behaviour of young people through the ASB and 'respect' campaigns (Morgan 2006b) both of which are likely to draw young people into the justice system. Fourthly, it is widely argued that the effectiveness of informal controls (in many neighbourhoods, families, schools, care homes, etc.) has declined to such an extent that the police are now more frequently called on to intervene in settings that used typically to consume their own smoke. With the police no longer being rewarded for exercising their discretion with regard to the manner in which they deal with juvenile offenders pre-court, it is reasonable to assume that a proportion of such police work is contributing to the growing number of juveniles being formally dealt with.

Table 30.1 Sentences of 10–17-year-olds, 1994–2004

	1994	1995	1996	1997	1998	1999	2000	2001	2002	2003	2004
Discharge	21,274	23,043	24,269	25,118	26,869	27,464	22,646	17,510	14,187	14,116	12,683
Fine	13,306	14,380	16,962	18,460	21,050	20,695	21,391	22,039	15,120	13,508	15,666
Referral orders	0	0	0	0	0	0	594	2,057	19,208	25,357	26,122
Community sentence (excl. referral orders)	21,318	23,337	25,122	26,530	28,941	30,622	35,378	40,978	34,979	29,605	30,593
Custody	4,719	5,464	6,497	7,083	7,217	7,653	7,414	7,596	7,416	6,200	6,325
Other	1,375	1,575	1,746	1,910	2,217	3,725	4,057	5,481	3,638	3,755	4,799
Total sentenced	61,991	67,800	74,598	79,092	86,294	90,160	91,480	95,485	94,458	92,531	96,188

Table 30.2 Proportionate use of different sentences (%), 1994–2004

	1994	1995	1996	1997	1998	1999	2000	2001	2002	2003	2004
Discharge	34	34	32	32	31	30	25	18	15	15	13
Fine	21	21	23	23	24	23	23	23	16	15	16
Referral order	0	0	0	0	0	0	1	2	20	27	27
Community penalty (excl. referral orders)	34	34	34	34	34	34	39	43	37	32	32
Custody	8	8	9	9	8	8	8	8	8	7	7
Other	2	2	2	2	3	4	4	6	4	4	5
Total sentenced	61,991	67,800	74,598	79,092	86,294	90,160	91,480	95,485	94,458	92,531	96,188

Table 30.3 Reconviction rates by disposal (2000 baseline)

	% difference 2003	% difference 2002	% difference 2001
Pre-court disposal	+0.2	−5.3	−6.5
First tier penalty			
Discharge	−6.1	−7.2	−3.2
Fine	−7.8	−6.4	−7.1
Referral order	−6.5	−3.8	−0.4
Reparation order	−1.2	−2.0	−5.2
Community penalty			
Attendance centre order	+0.6	−4.6	−5.4
Supervision order	−0.1	−0.8	−1.3
Action plan order	+5.1	+2.5	+0.6
CRO	+0.9	+11.2	+8.2
CPO	1.8	−4.3	−4.8
Curfew order	+6.2	+11.9	+7.0
Custody	+4.4	+1.1	+3.2
All offenders	−2.4	−3.6	−4.5

Note: Figures in bold denote a significant difference between the actual and the expected rate at the 0.05 level.
Source: Home Office (2005a).

What is happening to the increased number of children brought before the courts? Tables 30.1 and 30.2 demonstrate that the changes have been considerable, even where the proportions are largely unchanged. Most notable has been the introduction of the referral order, which now accounts for more than one-quarter of all sentences and which has drawn candidates from across the complete range of alternatives, from discharges and fines (the proportionate uses of which have declined substantially), community penalties (which have likewise declined), and custody (the number of which sentences has modestly declined both absolutely and proportionately from the highpoint period of 1999–2002). When offences are imprisonable and the offender is appearing before the youth court for the first time, sentencers have no option but to impose a referral order, unless they consider the case warrants a custodial sentence. It is clear that in some instances where they would formerly have resorted to custody sentencers are imposing referral orders, which can be made onerous and where failure to comply results in the offender being returned to court for re-sentencing.

Nevertheless the pattern is clear. Young offenders are today more likely to be criminalized and subject to a greater level of intervention than before the 1998 reforms. If dealt with pre-court their warning is more likely to be accompanied by an intervention. They are more likely to be prosecuted. If convicted they are less likely to receive a discharge or fine. If subject to a community sentence it is more likely to be onerous. And last but not least, despite the relative *proportionate* decline in custodial sentences since

2002, the *number* of children and young people sentenced to custody is still 35 per cent higher than a few years before the 1998 Act (see Figure 30.1).

Has the trend towards greater intervention served to reduce reoffending rates? In 1999 the YJB was set a target by the Home Office of reducing reoffending by young offenders by 5 per cent by 2004. The initial findings were very positive and a comparison of reconviction rates in 1997 and 2000 showed significant reductions across practically all offence categories. By 2001 the Home Office estimated that there had been a reduction in overall reoffending of 22.5 per cent. The Prime Minister congratulated the YJB on the startling success of the new youth justice reforms (see YJB 2003: 2–3). However, on closer inspection the estimates were found to have excluded a large number of cases, predominantly more serious cases, and the estimated reduction in reoffending was revised down to 7 per cent. More recent figures, using 2000 as the baseline, are more modest still (see Table 30.4).

Further, consideration of the actual against the expected reconviction rates for different disposals shows (Table 30.3) that the most significant reductions have been achieved with the lower-tier penalties: reprimands and final warnings, discharges, fines, referral orders, and reparation orders. These gains, however, have been quite substantially mitigated by the less than impressive results from higher-tier penalties, including custody, the proportionate use of which has increased and where reconviction rates have, with the exception of the community punishment order (what used to be termed community service), deteriorated from an already poor baseline. All of which suggests that were the current trend reversed—that is, a higher proportion of cases dealt with pre court (albeit in a manner more risk-proportionate than at present—a topic to which we return) or by means of discharges, fines, referral, and reparation orders—the system would be just as effective, and possibly more so, in achieving its stated aim.

INTENSIFYING COMMUNITY PROGRAMMES

The YJB's stated aim is to build public, sentencer, and criminal justice agency partners' confidence in early prevention schemes designed to reduce the risk of offending and, when offending occurs, increase the use of effective pre-court and community-based measures. This stance is grounded on the accumulating evidence which indicates

Table 30.4 Juvenile reconviction rates (2000 baseline)

Year	Actual reconviction rate	Predicted reconviction rate	Difference between predicted and actual reconviction rate
2003	36.9	37.8	−2.4%
2002	36.5	37.9	−3.6%
2001	35.3	37.0	−4.5%
2000	36.8	—	—

Source: Home Office (2005b).

overwhelmingly that these approaches better reduce offending than resort to custody, provided they are combined with improved engagement by the young people concerned with mainstream services (social services, education, health including mental health, housing, youth services, etc.). Which is to say that preventing youth crime is not a project for the criminal justice system alone: it relies as much, if not more so, on such outcomes as educational engagement and attainment. If the proportion of young people leaving school ill-equipped to find a satisfying place in the labour market continues to be as high as is currently the case, the prospects for the incidence of youth crime are poor. Britain currently compares very unfavourably in all the international surveys of economic inequality, social exclusion, and high-risk youth behaviour (teenage pregnancy, smoking, use of alcohol and illegal drugs, etc.) and, despite substantial expenditure and several initiatives designed to combat absenteeism and exclusions from school, the picture in recent years has not improved (see New Philanthropy Capital 2005; and Commission on Families 2005). This is the backcloth to the YIPs, YISPs, and SSPs (see above) which the YJB is promoting by providing YOTs with limited funding to build their development.

YIPs and YISPs

There are currently 72 YIPs and 92 YISPs. The YIPs were an early subject of a YJB-commissioned evaluation (Morgan *et al.* 2003) which identified some encouraging outcomes as well as some concerns. First, 73 per cent of the targeted high-risk children (50 per scheme) were being engaged, though few (8 per cent) at the aimed-for level of 10 hours per week. Moreover the schemes, all of them in deprived neighbourhoods, were engaging over 18,000 children not identified as high risk in various activities (sport, arts projects, education-related, etc.) of which sport was the most common. There was a significant reduction in the number of arrests, and in the seriousness of the offences for which they were arrested, for those of the targeted children engaged from the beginning. The school-related data the evaluators were able to collect were seriously incomplete—itself an interesting finding. But the limited evidence suggested that though there was a modest reduction in the number of permanent school exclusions, school attendance among the participating target group marginally deteriorated. It is possible that this outcome reflects a wider concern arising from the creation of YOTs. This is that their very existence has to some extent displaced the statutory attentions of the mainstream agencies from which YOT staff were originally recruited and that, in the case of the early prevention schemes, YOT-related activities are to some extent substituting for those of other agencies, in this case the schools.

Safer School Partnerships

There are already approaching 500 Safer School Partnerships (SSPs) throughout England and Wales (only a handful of them funded by the YJB), though there is wide variation in the degree of police and youth service personnel investment in individual schools. An initial evaluation of 15 SSP schools matched with 15 schools characterized by similar truancy and educational achievement rates (Bowles *et al.* 2005), found evidence of reduced truancy, reduced authorized absenteeism, and improved exam pass rates—though the available data did not permit estimation of offending behaviour both within and in the environs of the schools. Because the number of schools in the study was small the results were not statistically significant, and thus were described as no more than 'a promising indication'. However, more recent work on a larger sample of schools has detected statistically significant results in relation to reduced authorized absence, reduced unauthorized absence, and improved educational attainment (Bowles *et al.* 2006). Given that *not* attending school is a major criminogenic risk factor, these results are important.

Mentoring

Of the community-based initiatives adopted by New Labour in the attempt to tackle youthful offending and antisocial behaviour, mentoring quickly became established as one of the most popular. The range of locations in which mentoring was adopted by New Labour was extremely broad—one of the most significant being the New Deal initiative focused on unemployed young people aged 18 and over. The YJB issued guidelines for mentoring with young offenders in the aftermath of the passage of the 1998 Act and subsequently moved quickly to use its financial muscle to stimulate considerable activity in that area. Between 2001 and 2004 the YJB was supporting at least 80 separate mentoring schemes. Recently published evidence from a substantial YJB-commissioned evaluation (St James Roberts *et al.* 2006) found relatively little evidence of improvements in behaviour, literacy, or numeracy and, even more disappointingly, found no appreciable impact on reoffending within a year of the end of the programme. However, a separate evaluation which focused on more disaffected young people in non-YJB mentoring programmes, though again finding little impact on offending behaviour, uncovered evidence of a substantial impact on the young people's engagement with education, training, and work (Newburn and Shiner 2005). Both studies indicate that mentoring continues to hold promise, but neither provide, particular support for those advocates that see mentoring as a significant method of reducing reoffending.

Referral orders and restorative justice

The referral order is arguably the emerging 'jewel in the crown' of the reformed system, though the available research data (Newburn *et al.* 2002; Crawford and Newburn 2003) are mostly derived from the introductory phase rather than contemporary practice. It already accounts, as we have seen, for more than one-quarter of all youth court sentences and is more effective in terms of reoffending than the characteristics of the offenders subject to it lead one to expect. Further, though some YOTs continue to fail to convene initial panel meetings (usually because of empanelling difficulties) within the 15 working days which the YJB has laid down as the standard, most parts of the country have now managed to recruit a healthy list of YOP volunteer members and no longer need to advertise. Further, in most YOTs the composition of the more than 5,000 YOP volunteers is increasingly diverse in terms of sex, age, and ethnicity. This achievement bears out the results from a YJB-commissioned 2004 MORI survey of the public which revealed that large numbers of people, an estimated 3.4 million aged 16 or over, would be *very* interested in undertaking voluntary work with young offenders, in particular assisting them with basic literacy and numeracy needs (YJB 2004b).

Reparation is the essence of the referral order and the independent evaluation of its introduction reported encouraging results:

> Within a relatively short period of time the panels have established themselves as constructive, deliberative and participatory forums . . . The informal setting of youth offender panels would appear to allow young people, their parents/carers, victims (where they attend), community panel members and Yot advisors opportunities to discuss the nature and consequences of a young person's offending, as well as to respond to this in ways which seek to repair the harm done and to address the causes of the young person's offending behaviour [Newburn *et al.* 2002: 62].

This early assessment has been borne out by the Home Office reconviction data (see Table 30.3 above). The evidence suggests, however, that referral order outcomes would be even more favourable were YOTs more successfully to engage victims in the process. In the pilot sites victims personally participated in only 13 per cent of referral order cases by attending one or more YOP sessions. There was considerable variation in the rate from one YOT to another, largely as a result of the skill and effort devoted to cultivating victim participation (ibid.: 41–8). The YJB evidence suggests that the direct participation of victims continues to vary greatly from one YOT to another and that the overall rate of involvement remains at a relatively low level. This may be the consequence of the fact that the YJB has hitherto measured YOT performance simply in terms of their contacting victims rather than employing the more time-consuming methods—visiting and speaking to them rather than merely writing—which experience shows encourage participation. The evidence suggests the investment would be worthwhile. Victims who participate generally, though not always, consider the referral order procedurally fair and, as with other forms of restorative justice, generally feel a greater sense of security and closure following their participation (Daly 2001).

It has been in the youth justice arena that government attempts to experiment with restorative justice-influenced initiatives have been most extensive. Referral orders represent the most significant of these changes, but the reforms to the cautioning system and the attempted inclusion of reparative elements within the terms of other orders also signal increasing government interest in this area. However, as a number of authors have noted (Dignan 1999; Crawford 2002; Fionda 2005), there are some important tensions between attempts to extend the reach of restorative justice and other aspects of New Labour's approach to youth justice. First, the apparent promotion of restorative justice exists alongside continuing increases in the number of juveniles in prison. Secondly, despite the more inclusionary tone associated with restorative justice, there remain elements of contemporary youth justice discourse which are significantly more punitive. Thirdly, there is a tension between New Labour's managerialist concern with speed, efficiency, cost reductions, and performance measurement, and broader communitarian appeals to local justice in which there is an expectation that local people will play a central role in the handling of cases in their neighbourhood (Crawford and Newburn 2003: Home Office 2006). The growing emphasis on output and outcome measurement potentially undermines restorative justice processes which place greater emphasis on providing a secure forum in which there is room for emotions to be expressed and for sometimes complex negotiations to take place. Most fundamentally, the greatest danger remains the possibility that the potential of restorative justice and the generally positive image it enjoys might be subverted by more traditional, punitive approaches to dealing with young offenders (Dignan 1999).

Intensive Supervision and Surveillance Programmes

The YJB has invested considerable resources in Intensive Supervision and Surveillance Programmes (ISSPs) as the principal alternative to custodial remands and sentences in cases where that outcome is likely. An ISSP can be used as a condition of bail or as an adjunct to a community or custodial sentence for serious offenders or persistent young offenders who at the time of appearing in court have previously been charged, warned, or convicted on four or more separate occasions in the preceding 12 months and have previously received at least one community or custodial sentence. An ISSP runs for a maximum of six months with intensive supervision (including electronic tagging or tracking) and engagement (education or vocational training, offending behaviour programmes, recreational activities, etc.) for 25 hours a week for the first three months. The ISSP was launched by the YJB in July 2001 in 80 areas and extended to all areas in October 2003. The programme has independently been evaluated, an early cohort having been followed up for two years (Moore *et al.* 2004; Gray *et al.* 2005).

The research shows that the ISSP is being targeted at relatively serious and persistent offenders (burglary and robbery being the most common index offences, with on average 12 offences in the preceding two years), a high proportion of whom would have been likely to have received a custodial sentence had the ISSP not been an option. It is nevertheless conceded that there has been some net-widening effect. Though the headline two-year reconviction rate of 91 per cent is very high, the reconviction rate for offenders with as many previous-offences released from custody is at 95 per cent (Home Office 2005a: Table 11.8) higher still. Arguably more important, however, are the gains masked by the headline reconviction rate. The frequency of reoffending is down by 40 per cent and the seriousness of those further offences down 13 per cent. Further, the research shows that substantial engagement in education and other positive activities is being achieved and offenders' multiple practical problems are being addressed. Yet the evaluation also shows that a comparison group of offenders eligible for an ISSP but not receiving it (refused bail, placed on a community order, or sentenced to a DTO) did just as well in terms of reoffending, a finding which has led some critics (Green 2004) to suggest that investment in the ISSP is not worthwhile. It is more than likely, however, that the intensity of ISSP surveillance means that the further offences of the young people subject to the programme are more likely to be detected. Furthermore, although the initial availability of ISSPs did not lead to any greater reduction in the use of custody than was true in areas without them, the fact that an ISSP is generally being targeted at offenders at high risk of custody, and given that sentencers reportedly have confidence in the programme, it is also possible that the proportionate use of custody would be greater than it is were it not for the existence of the ISSP.

DIVERSITY ISSUES: SEX AND ETHNICITY

There has been a noteworthy increase in the number of girls being drawn into the youth justice system at all levels relative to boys (see also Heidensohn and Gelsthorpe, Chapter 13, this volume). Whereas the number of boys cautioned declined by one-fifth in the period 1994–2004, the number of girls stayed roughly constant. Further, whereas the number of boys sentenced increased by a half, the number of girls doubled. Because of what remains the relatively low number of girls relative to boys (a ratio of 1. 6.5 in 2004 compared to 1 : 8.6 in 1994) this trend should not be over-stated. But it does signal either a significant shift in the offending behaviour of girls or a change of attitude towards girls on the part of the police and the courts, or most likely both. At the deepest level of the system, the change also poses a dilemma for the YJB. Though girls remain a small proportion of children and young people in custody (7 per cent) the proportionate increase in their number (272 per cent) in the last decade has greatly outstripped the increase in the number of boys (40 per cent).

As with adults in the criminal justice system generally (see Phillips and Bowling, Chapter 14, this volume) some of the minority ethnic groups, particularly the black communities, are significantly over-represented in the youth justice system, a feature commented on critically by the Audit Commission (2004: para. 73) and responded to by the YJB in 2005 by requiring all YOTs to audit their practice and develop action plans to improve equal treatment (YJB 2005b: 8). This initiative followed an in-depth study (Feilzer and Hood 2004). According to the most recent YJB statistics, 12 per cent of all the children and young people drawn into the system and whose ethnicity was recorded were from the minority ethnic groups. Half of these young people, that is 6 per cent, were black. (YJB 2005e: 55) This is consistent with the picture for adults (see Phillips and Bowling, Chapter 14, this volume).

The Feilzer and Hood study was based on a small sample of YOTs and a large number of cases dealt by them. Regression analysis was employed to explore the degree to which different ethnic groups are more or less likely to be differentially treated at different decision-making points in the system for reasons apparently not legally legitimate (seriousness of offence, prior convictions, no early plea of guilty, etc.). The results from the study were complicated. Mixed-race youths were significantly more likely to be prosecuted as opposed to being dealt with pre-court than their case characteristics suggested was justified. Black and mixed-race youths were significantly more likely to be remanded in custody and then not convicted. Further, though black and mixed-race offenders were no more likely to receive a custodial sentence, they were more likely to receive a longer sentence, either in the community or in custody. Asian

Table 30.5 Children and young persons in penal custody, June 1991–2005

	1991	1993	1995	1997	1999	2001	2003	2005
LASHs	70	70	80	95	90	258	292	238
STCs	—	—	—	—	55	118	185	248
Prison Service accommodation	1345	1304	1675	2479	2422	2415	2267	2339
Total	1415	1374	1755	2574	2567	2791	2744	2825

youths, however, were more likely to be sentenced to custody than white youths with the same characteristics, a finding which points to the fallacy of assuming that the absence of over-representation of a minority ethnic group within a particular category is the equivalent of showing that there is no differential treatment.

CHILDREN AND YOUNG PEOPLE IN CUSTODY

There are effectively three groups of providers of youth custodial services—the Prison Service or commercially managed YOIs, the commercially run STCs, and the local authority or commercially run secure homes (LASHs). Table 30.5 shows the number of children and young people in custody since 1991. Though the number has risen since the 1998 reforms, that increase has been modest compared to the very substantial rise prior to 1998 and, further, the custodial population has largely stabilized since 2000–1.

The YJB currently purchases a total of 3,293 beds in three categories of establishment: 2,784 beds for males in 13 YOIs, all but two of which are managed by the Prison Service, plus four Prison Service units for 17-year-old girls; 274 beds in four STCs, all commercially managed; and 235 beds in 15 secure homes, all but one of which are managed by local authorities. As can be seen from Table 30.6, older adolescents aged 15–17 are mostly held in the YOIs and younger children, under 15, in the LASHs. The STCs mostly accommodate adolescents aged 15–16, though both they and the LASHs house a minority of older adolescents for whom, for one reason or another, the YOIs are considered unsuitable.

All but five of the YOIs are split-site establishments (juveniles in one section and young adults in another, more or less separated and self-sufficient) and typically provide large (60–80 bed) accommodation blocks of a traditional penal design. By contrast the LASHs are typically small establishments of 10–25 beds and are further subdivided into 6–8-bed living units. The STCs are larger but, like the LASHs, are also broken down into 6–8-bed living units.

Though the YJB plans for some flexibility in the number of places it purchases (the existing infrastructure is not geographically well distributed and beds are always out of commission for repair and refurbishment), this is often offset by the fact that young offenders who become 18 during the custodial portion of their DTOs are normally not

Table 30.6 Children and young persons in penal custody by age and category of provison, 1 November 2005

Age	LASHs	STCs	YOIs	Total
10				
11	2			2
12	12	1		13
13	37	12		49
14	91	75		166
15	41	79	275	395
16	55	74	*735	864
17	3	14	*1,446	1,463
Total	241	255	2,456	2,952

* In November 2005 three 16-year-olds and four 17-year-olds were being held in high-security adult accommodation due to the extreme gravity of their charges or offences.

transferred to adult establishments. At the time of writing (March 2006) the system is close to full. This means that the YJB's aim of holding inmates within 50 miles of home is satisfied in approximately only two-thirds of cases. In these circumstances, and given the characteristics of the children and young people in custody, it is perhaps not surprising that tragedies within the system are a regular occurrence. Fourteen children and young persons have died in custody since 1997, 13 by suicide and one while being restrained, two in STCs and 12 in YOIs (see Coles and Goldson 2005).

The epidemiological data reveal how needy and troubled is the population being housed (see Morgan 2006b). Histories of self-harm are relatively common. Almost one-third have identifiable mental health problems and over half have significant or borderline learning difficulties (Harrington and Bailey 2005). It is difficult to say to what extent the latter finding reflects intrinsic learning difficulties or an absence of intellectual stimulation. Two-thirds of DTO detainees have been excluded from education, four in ten have at some stage been in the care of a local authority, and 17 per cent have been on a child protection register (Hazell *et al.* 2002; see also HMIP 2005). The result is that children in custody typically have literacy and numeracy ages some four to five years below their chronological ages. These problems are often compounded by substance abuse, with around one-third reporting that they have taken drugs not to get high but just to 'feel normal', or to 'forget everything' or 'blot everything out' (Galahad SMS Ltd 2004)—i.e. as a form of self-medication.

It is not surprising therefore that the YJB estimates that some 200–300 older boys 'require more intensive support than can currently be provided in YOIs' (YJB 2005c: para. 16). The more overcrowded the system the more likely it is that further tragedies will occur. Further, that risk will not be reduced if staff are not trained to deal with young people some of whose behaviour is extremely challenging. The Carlile Report (2006: para. 57) observed that:

> In some cases there appeared to be a culture where dissent was not tolerated and that physical restraint was used to secure conformity . . . Over-reaction, especially if capricious and sudden, can be counter-productive and even dangerous.

It is clear that though much has improved within closed institutions for young offenders there remains, as the YJB has acknowledged, 'a long way to go' (2005c: 5).

CONCLUSION: WHITHER YOUTH JUSTICE?

There have always been tensions within youth justice between differing aims, objectives, and penal philosophies. Initially that tension was primarily between the dual goals of *punishment* and *welfare*. The passage of the 1969 Children and Young Persons Act marked the high water mark of welfarism, and the next two decades or so ushered in a period of heightened managerialism together with the emergence of an unpleasant cocktail of populism and punitiveness, particularly in the aftermath of the abduction and murder of James Bulger in 1993. The arrival of New Labour in power in 1997 brought some far-reaching changes, not least to the organization, funding, and management of the youth justice system. Youth justice policy since that time is not easy to characterize. As Muncie (2001) has observed, it is an odd 'melange' of policies and practices, some of which are punitive and criminalizing (the abolition of *doli incapax*, the embracing of the antisocial behaviour agenda, and the shift away from pre-court measures), and others of which involve experimentation with more inclusionary, restorative justice-based practices at both the pre-court and post-sentencing stages of the system. What can be in little doubt though is that the so-called 'new youth justice' is significantly better funded, and is therefore *potentially* better placed to deliver necessary services, than the system it replaced.

What lies next? There seem to us to be some fairly clear priorities for youth justice in the next few years. First, it should be a, and arguably *the*, central priority to reduce the number of young people in custody, a prospect to which the YJB is committed and which appears to have been given some recent, limited encouragement by the Government, whose action plan states: 'We believe that it is important to keep children out of prison if at all possible' (HM Government 2006: para. 3.31). Secondly, at the other end of the spectrum, it is important to reverse the trend whereby the proportion and numbers of young people dealt with informally is decreasing whilst the numbers prosecuted increases. There are a number of barriers to achieving this. One is the concern that increasing pre-court disposals will lead inevitably to the re-creation of the type of problem the Audit Commission identified in relation to repeat cautioning in the mid-1990s. Another is the difficulty we highlighted earlier that, as things stand, informal action pre-court does not count toward OBTJ targets. Thus, a first and simple reform would be to change this situation. The concern relating to encouraging overuse or misuse of pre-court measures could be dealt with, at least in part, by ensuring that the performance measures introduced in relation to the new neighbourhood policing teams paid particular attention to and, indeed, rewarded, constructive and effective police preventive activity in this area.

Current evidence in relation to reconviction rates for young offenders suggests that increasing the proportion of cases dealt with pre-court would in itself be an effective measure, but might well also ensure that an increased proportion of cases brought before the courts were dealt with in a more risk-proportionate manner by way of discharges, fines, and referral and reparation orders. This, in turn, might allow greater confidence to be shown in taking a similarly risk-proportionate approach by supervising YOTs in relation to medium- and high-risk cases, thereby enabling custodial sentences to be used more sparingly. Finally, a reduced juvenile prison population would also open up the possibility that the YJB could restructure the custodial estate in order to meet its aim of making it more dedicated and child centred. On many occasions in the recent past such proposals would have felt very much out of line with government policy and rhetoric. However, the recently unveiled Home Office five-year strategy for *Protecting the Public and Reducing Re-offending* (HM Government 2006) provides at least some encouragement for criminological optimists.

■ SELECTED FURTHER READING

David Garland's *Punishment and Welfare* (Aldershot: Gower, 1985) is the best history of the emergence of a separate youth justice system in Britain. The 1998 youth justice reforms cannot be fully appreciated without a reading of the two key documents, the Audit Commission's *Misspent Youth* (London: Audit Commission, 1996) and New Labour's subsequent White Paper, *No More Excuses* (London: Home Office, 1997), which informed the Crime and Disorder Act 1998. John Muncie's *Youth and Crime* (2nd edn, London: Sage, 2004) and Roger Smith's *Youth Justice: Ideas, policy and practice* (Cullompton, Devon: Willan, 2003) are the best general introductions to the recent history of the system. Michael Tonry and Anthony Doob's edited collection of essays, *Youth Crime and Youth Justice* (Chicago: University of Chicago Press, 2004), contains authoritative accounts of juvenile justice provision in Great Britain, Canada, New Zealand, the Netherlands, Denmark, Sweden, and Germany, and provides a useful comparative overview. Finally, the Youth Justice Board website—www.yjb.gov.uk—provides access to a large array of evaluative studies of current provision as well as national youth justice statistics.

■ REFERENCES

ALLEN, R. (1991), 'Out of jail: The reduction in the use of penal custody for male juveniles 1981–88', *Howard Journal of Criminal Justice*, 30(1): 30–52.

AUDIT COMMISSION (1996), *Misspent Youth: Young people and crime*, London: Audit Commission.

—— (2004), *Youth Justice 2004: A review of the reformed youth justice system*, London: Audit Commission.

BALL, C., MCCORMAC, K., and STONE, N. (2001), *Young Offenders: Law, Policy and Practice*, 2nd edn, London: Sweet & Maxwell.

BATEMAN T., and PITTS, J. (2005), *The RHP Companion to Youth Justice*, Lyme Regis: Russell House.

BOTTOMS, A. E. (1974), 'On the decriminalisation of the English juvenile courts', in R. Hood (ed.), *Crime, Criminology and Public Policy*, London: Heinemann.

—— (1995), 'The philosophy and politics of punishment and sentencing', In C. M. V. Clarkson and R. Morgan (eds), *The Politics of Sentencing Reform*, Oxford: Oxford University Press.

—— and DIGNAN, J. (2004), 'Youth Justice in Great Britain', in M. Tonry and A. N. Doob (eds), *Youth Crime and Youth Justice: Comparative and Cross-National Perspectives*, Chicago: University of Chicago Press.

—— and STEVENSON, S. (1992), 'What went wrong? Criminal justice policy in England and Wales 1945–1970', in D. Downes (ed.), *Unravelling Criminal Justice*, Basingstoke: Macmillan.

BOWLES R., REYES, M. G., and PRADIPTYO, R. (2005), *Monitoring and Evaluating the Safer School Partnerships (SSP) Programme*, London: YJB.

——, ——, ——, and REYES, M. G. (2006), *Estimating the Impact of the Safer School Partnerships Programme*, York: Centre for Criminal Justice Economics and Psychology, University of York.

CAMPBELL, B. (1993), *Goliath: Britain's Dangerous Places*, London: Methuen.

CARLILE, LORD (2006), *An Independent Inquiry into the use of physical restraint, solitary confinement and forcible strip searching of children in prisons, secure training centres and local authority secure children's homes*, London: Howard League for Penal Reform.

CARTER, P. (2002), *Managing Offenders, Reducing Crime: A New Approach*, London: Home Office.

COLES, D., and GOLDSON, D. (2005), *In the Care of the State? Child Deaths in Penal Custody*, London: Inquest.

COMMISSION ON FAMILIES AND THE WELLBEING OF CHILDREN (2005) *Families and the State: Two-way support and responsibilities—An inquiry into the relationship between the state and the family in the upbringing of children*, Bristol: Policy Press.

CRAWFORD, A. (2002), 'The prospects of restorative justice for young offenders in England and Wales: A tale of two Acts', in K. McEvoy and T. Newburn (eds), *Criminology and Conflict Resolution*, Basingtoke: Palgrave.

—— and NEWBURN, T. (2003), *Youth Offending and Restorative Justice: Implementing reform in youth justice*, Cullompton, Devon: Willan.

DALY, K. (2001), 'Conferencing in Australia and New Zealand: Variations, research findings and prospects', in A. Morris and G. Maxwell (eds), *Restorative Justice for Juveniles: Conferencing, Mediation and Circles*, Oxford: Hart.

DIGNAN, J. (1999), 'The Crime and Disorder Act and the Prospects for Restorative Justice', *Criminal Law Review*: 48–60.

EUROPEAN COMMISSIONER FOR HUMAN RIGHTS (2005), *Report by Mr Alvaro Gil-Robles, Commissioner for Human Rights, on his Visit to the United Kingdom 4–12 November 2004*, Strasbourg: Council of Europe.

FAMILY POLICY STUDIES CENTRE (1998), *The Crime and Disorder Bill and the Family*, London: Family Policy Studies Centre.

FARRINGTON, D. P. (1992), 'Trends in English juvenile delinquency and their explanation', *International Journal of Comparative and Applied Criminal Justice*, 16(2): 151–63.

—— (1996), *Understanding and preventing youth crime*, York: Joseph Rowntree Foundation.

FEILZER, M., and HOOD, R. (2004), *Differences or Discrimination: minority ethnic young people in the youth justice system*, London: YJB.

FIONDA, J. (2005), *Devils and Angels: Youth, Policy and Crime*, Oxford: Hart.

FRANKLIN, B., and PETLEY, J. (1996), 'Killing the age of innocence: newspaper reporting of the death of James Bulger', in J. Pilcher and S. Wagg (eds), *Thatcher's Children: Politics, childhood and society in the 1980s and 1990s*, London: Falmer.

GALAHAD SMS LTD (2004), *Substance Misuse and the Juvenile Secure Estate*, London: YJB.

GARDNER, J., VON HIRSCH, A., SMITH, A. T. H., MORGAN, R., ASHWORTH, A., and WASIK, M. (1998),

'Clause 1—The Hybrid Law from Hell?', *Criminal Justice Matters*, 31 (Spring): 25–7.

GARLAND, D. (1985), *Punishment and Welfare: A history of penal strategies*, Aldershot: Gower

GOLDSON, B. (ed.), (2000) *The New Youth Justice*, Lyme Regis: Russell House.

GRAY, E., TAYLOR, E., ROBERTS, C., MERRINGTON, S., FERNANDEZ,R., and MOORE, R. (2005), *ISSP: The Final Report*, London: YJB.

GREEN, D. (2004), *The Intensive Supervision and Surveillance Programme*, London: Civitas Available at www.civitas.org.uk/pdf/issp.pdf.

HAGELL, A., and NEWBURN, T. (1994), *Persistent Young Offenders*, London: Policy Studies Institute

HARRINGTON, R., and BAILEY, S. (2005), *Mental Health Needs and Effectiveness of Provision for Young Offenders in Custody and in the Community*, London: YJB.

HARRIS, R., and WEBB, D. (1987), *Welfare, Power and Juvenile Justice*, London: Tavistock.

HAZELL, N., HAGELL, A., LIDDLE, M., ARCHER, D., GRIMSHAW, R., and KING, J. (2002), *Detention nnd Training: Assessment of the Detention and Training Order and its impact on the secure estate across England and Wales*, London: YJB.

HM GOVERNMENT (2004), *Cutting Crime, Delivering Justice: A Strategic Plan for Criminal Justice 2004–08*, Criminal Justice System, London: Stationery Office.

—— (2006), *A Five Year Strategy for Protecting the Public and Reducing Re-offending*, London: Stationery Office.

HM INSPECTORATE OF PRISONS (HMIP) (2002), *Annual Report 2001–2*, London: HMIP.

—— (2004), *Annual Report 2002–3*, London: HMIP.

—— (2005), *Annual Report 2003–4*, London: HMIP.

—— and YJB (2005), *Juveniles in Custody 2003–4: An analysis of children's experiences of prisons*, London: HMIP/YJB.

HM INSPECTORATE OF PROBATION (2004), *Joint Inspection of Youth Offending Teams: Annual Report 2003/2004*, London: HMIP.

HOLDAWAY, S., and DESBOROUGH, S. (2004), *Final Warning Schemes*, London: YJB.

HOME AFFAIRS COMMITTEE (2005), *Anti-Social Behaviour*, Fifth Report, London: Stationery Office.

HOME OFFICE (1988), *Punishment, Custody and the Community*, Cm. 424. London: HMSO.

—— (1997a), *No More Excuses—A New Approach to Tackling Youth Crime in England and Wales*, Cm. 3809, London: Home Office.

—— (1997b), *Tackling Youth Crime*, London: Home Office.

—— (1998) *Summary of the Response to the Comprehensive Spending Review of Secure Accommodation for Remanded and Sentenced Juveniles*, London: Home Office.

—— (2002), *Justice for All*, Cm. 5563, London: Stationery Office.

—— (2005a), *Offender Management Caseload Statistics 2004*, Statistical Bulletin 17/05, London: Home Office.

—— (2005b), *Juvenile Reconviction: Results from the 2003 Cohort*, Online Report 08/05, London: Home Office.

—— (2006), *Respect Action Plan*, London: Home Office/COI.

JONES, D. (1989), 'The Successful Revolution', *Community Care*, 30 March: i–ii.

LABOUR PARTY (1996), *Tackling Youth Crime: Reforming youth justice*, London: Labour Party.

—— (1997), *New Labour—Because Britain Deserves Better*, London: Labour Party.

LENG, R., TAYLOR, R., and WASIK, M. (1998), *Blackstone's Guide to the Crime and Disorder Act 1998*, London: Blackstone.

MCARA, L. (2002), 'The Scottish Juvenile Justice System: Policy and Practice', in J. Winterdyk (ed.), *Juvenile Justice Systems: International Perspectives*, Toronto: Canadian Scholars Press.

—— (2006), 'Welfare in Crisis? Key developments in Scottish Youth Justice', in J. Muncie and B. Goldson (eds), *Comparative Youth Justice*, London: Sage.

MCGALLAGLY, J., POWER, K., LITTLEWOOD, P., and MEIKLE, J. (1998), *Evaluation of the Hamilton Child Safety Initiative*, Crime and Criminal Justice Research Findings No. 24, Edinburgh: Scottish Office.

MARSHALL, T., and MERRY, S. (1990), *Crime and Accountability*, London: HMSO.

MILLIE, A., JACOBSON, J., MCDONALD, E., and HOUGH, M. (2005), *Anti-social behaviour strategies: finding a balance*, Bristol: Policy Press and Joseph Rowntree Foundation.

MOORE, R., GRAY, E., ROBERTS, C., MERRINGTON, S., WATERS, I., FERNANDEZ, R., HAYWARD, G., and ROGERS, R. (2004), *ISSP: The Initial Report*, London: YJB.

MORGAN, HARRIS, BURROWS (2003) *Youth Inclusion*, London: YJB.

MORGAN, R. (2006a), 'With Respect to Order, the Rules of the Game Have Changed: New Labour's

Dominance of the "Law and Order" Agenda', in T. Newburn and P. Rock (eds), *The Politics of Law and Order: Essays in Honour of David Downes*, Oxford: Clarendon Press.

—— (2006b), 'Improving provision for young people who offend', in *Young People and Crime: The Donald Winnicott Memorial Lecture*, London: Karnac.

—— and NEWBURN, T. (1997), *The Future of Policing*, Oxford: Oxford University Press.

MORRIS, A., and MCISAAC, M. (1978), *Juvenile Justice?*, London: Heinemann.

—— and MAXWELL, G. (2000), 'The Practice of Family Group Conferences in New Zealand: Assessing the Place, Potential and Pitfalls of Restorative Justice', in A. Crawford and J. Goodey (eds), *Integrating a Victim Prespective within Criminal Justice*, Aldershot: Avebury.

MUNCIE, J. (2001), 'A new deal for youth? Early intervention and correctionalism', in G. Hughes, J. Muncie, and E. McLaughlin (eds), *Crime Prevention and Community Safety: New Directions*, London: Sage.

—— (2004), *Youth and Crime*, 2nd edn, London: Sage.

NATIONAL AUDIT OFFICE (2004), *Youth Offending: the delivery of community and custodial sentences*, HC 190, London: NAO.

NELLIS, M. (1991), 'The last days of "juvenile" justice?', in P. Carter, T. Jeffs, and M. Smith (eds), *Social Work and Social Welfare Yearbook 3*, Milton Keynes: Open University Press.

NEW PHILANTHROPY CAPITAL (2005), *School's out?: Truancy and exclusion—A guide for donors and funders*, London: New Philanthropy Capital.

NEWBURN, T. (1998), 'Young Offenders, drugs and prevention', *Drugs, Education, Prevention and Policy*, 5(3): 233–43.

—— (2003), *Crime and Criminal Justice Policy*, 2nd edn, Harlow: Longman.

—— and SHINER, M. (2005), *Young People, Mentoring and Social Exclusion*, Cullompton, Devon: Willan.

—— CRAWFORD, A., EARLE, R., GOLDIE, S., HALE, C., MASTERS, G., NETTEN, A., SAUNDERS, R., HALLAM, A., SHARPE, K., and UGLOW, S. (2002), *The Introduction of Referral Orders into the Youth Justice System: Final Report*, Home Office Research Study No. 242, London: Home Office.

NIXON, J., HUNTER, H., and SHAYER, S. (1999), *The use of legal remedies by social landlords to deal with neighbourhood nuisance: Survey report*, Centre for Regional Economic and Social Research Paper No. H8, Sheffield: Sheffield Hallam University.

PARKER, H., SUMNER, M., and JARVIS, G. (1989), *Unmasking the Magistrates: The 'custody or not' decision in sentencing young offenders*, Milton Keynes: Open University Press.

PITTS, J. (2001), 'The new correctionalism: young people, youth justice and New Labour', in R. Matthews and J. Pitts (eds), *Crime, Disorder and Community Safety*, London: Routledge.

PRATT, J. (1989), 'Corporatism: The third model of juvenile justice', *British Journal of Criminology*, 29(3): 236–54.

RUTHERFORD, A. (1986a), *Growing Out of Crime: Society and young people in trouble*, Harmondsworth: Penguin.

—— (1986b), *Prisons and the Process of Justice*, Oxford: Oxford University Press.

RUTTER, M., and GILLER, H. (1983), *Juvenile Delinquency: Trends and perspectives*, Harmondsworth: Penguin.

ST JAMES ROBERTS, I., GREENLAW, G., SIMON, A., and HURY, J. (2006), *National Evaluation of Youth Justice Board Mentoring Schemes, 2001–2004*, London: YJB.

SIMESTER, A. P., and VON HIRSCH, A. (2006), 'Regulating Offensive Conduct through Two-Step Prohibitions', in A. von Hirsch and A. P. Simester (eds), *Incivilities: Regulating Offensive Behaviour*, Oxford: Hart.

SMITH, R. (2003), *Youth Justice: Ideas, policy, practice*, Cullompton, Devon: Willan.

SOPEL, J. (1995), *Tony Blair: The Moderniser*, London: Michael Joseph.

STRAW, J. (1998), Speech to Magistrates Association, Blackburn, 25 June.

THORPE, D., SMITH, D., GREEN, C., and PALEY, J. (1980), *Out of Care: the community support of juvenile offenders*, London: George Allen and Unwin.

TONRY, M., and DOOB, A. N. (eds) (2004), *Youth Crime and Youth Justice, Comparative and Cross-National Perspectives—Crime and Justice: A Review of Research*, Vol. 31, Chicago: University of Chicago Press.

UTTING, D., BRIGHT, J., and HENRICSON, C. (1993), *Crime and the Family*, London: Family Policy Studies Centre.

WHYTE, B. (2000), 'Between two stools: Youth justice in Scotland', *Probation Journal*, 47(2): 119–25.

WILKINSON, T. (1995), 'Doli Incapax resurrected', *Solicitors Journal*, 14 April: 338–9.

WILSON, J. Q., and KELLING, G. (1982), 'Broken Windows', *Atlantic Monthly*, March, 29–38.

WINDELSHAM, LORD (1993), *Responses to Crime (vol. 2): Penal Policy in the Making*, Oxford: Oxford University Press.

WORLD HEALTH ORGANIZATION (2004), *Young People's Health in Context: Health Behaviour in School-aged Children (HBSC) Study: international report from the 2001/2002 survey*, Copenhagen: WHO Europe.

YOUNG, A. (1996), *Imagining Crime: Textual outlaws and criminal conversations*, London: Sage.

YOUNG, R. (2000), 'Integrating a multi-victim perspective into criminal justice through restorative justice conferences', in A. Crawford and J. Goodey (eds), *Integrating a Victim Perspective Within Criminal Justice*, Aldershot: Ashgate.

—— and GOOLD, B. (1999), 'Restorative police cautioning in Aylesbury—from degrading to reintegrative shaming ceremonies?', *Criminal Law Review*, 126–38.

YOUTH JUSTICE BOARD (2003), *Annual Review 2002/2003: Gaining Ground in the Community*, London: YJB.

—— (2004a), *Sustaining the Success: Extending the guidance, Establishing Youth Offending Teams*, London: YJB.

—— (2004b), 'YJB Volunteering Strategy—Potential Public Interest in Working with Young People Who Offend', unpublished, London: YJB.

—— (2005a), *Annual Review and Accounts 2004–5*, London: YJB.

—— (2005b), *Corporate and Business Plan 2005/06 to 2007/08*, London: YJB.

—— (2005c), *Strategy for the Secure Estate for Children and Young People*, London: YJB.

—— (2005d), *Annual Report and Accounts 2004/05*, London: YJB.

—— (2005e), *Youth Justice Annual Statistics 2003/04*, London: YJB.

——, ACPO and HOME OFFICE (2005), *Anti-Social Behaviour: A guide to the role of Youth Offending Teams in dealing with anti-social behaviour*, London: YJB.

31

COMMUNITY PENALTIES: PROBATION 'WHAT WORKS', AND OFFENDER MANAGEMENT

Peter Raynor

INTRODUCTION: CATCHING THE SLIPPERY FISH

The term 'community penalty' is widely used but not always easy to define. For example, 'community penalty' is not normally used simply to describe forms of punishment imposed in the community, or outside prison. If this were its usual meaning, most discussions of community penalties would probably be about fines, since these are the most widely used non-custodial punishment. Instead, we find that most discussions of community penalties are actually about probation, a penalty which allows the offender to retain his or her liberty by complying with the requirements of a court order and being supervised by an appropriately authorized official employed by, or acting on behalf of, a probation service. In recent years such discussions have also included community service orders (a rather different kind of penalty involving indirect reparation supervised by probation services) and other forms of supervisory penalty such as electronically monitored curfew orders, which are not necessarily supervised by probation services. On the other hand, discussions of community penalties often exclude a large proportion of the offenders actually supervised by probation services (at least in Britain) because their original sentences are custodial, and they are being supervised under a form of licence or conditional release.

A further difficulty is that the term 'probation order', understood throughout the English-speaking world and beyond, has been replaced in England and Wales, first by the term 'community rehabilitation order' introduced in the Criminal Justice and Court Services Act 2000, and more recently by the generic community sentence in the Criminal Justice Act of 2003. This Act, which will be discussed in more detail later in the chapter, also blurs the concept of a community penalty by introducing a new kind of hybrid sentence which begins in prison and ends with a period of supervision in the community (known as 'custody plus'), which both resembles and differs from earlier combinations of custodial sentence with post-custodial supervised licence. These changes, together with reorganizations and reconfiguration of the service itself, are part of a much larger shift, not confined to England and Wales, in the politics of penal policy and consequent perceptions of the role of probation services. The changes will be discussed more fully below, but here they serve to illustrate the continuing fluidity of the concept of a 'community penalty', and its dependence on changing social and political environments.

The chapter concentrates mainly (though not exclusively) on developments in England and Wales, and this is less parochial than it seems. These countries have one of the world's longest histories of probation (though not the longest), and during the period of the development of welfare states in the mid-twentieth century they were routinely placed among the pioneers and world leaders of this kind of work. For example, in 1952 Max Grünhut (a German lawyer and criminologist who, like Hermann Mannheim and Leon Radzinowicz, had escaped from the Nazi regime before the war and helped to found the academic discipline of criminology in Britain) wrote: 'Probation is the great contribution of Britain and the USA to the treatment of offenders. Its strength is due to a combination of two things, conditional suspension of punishment, and personal care and supervision by a court welfare officer. With the growing use of probation, social case work has been introduced into the administration of criminal justice' (Grünhut 1952: 168). In a similar vein, in 1958 Leon Radzinowicz wrote: 'If I were asked what was the most significant contribution made by this country [i.e. England] to the new penological theory and practice which struck root in the twentieth century . . . my answer would be probation' (Radzinowicz 1958: x). In the previous year Manuel Lopez-Rey, head of the United Nations Social Defence Section, had written in the *Howard Journal*: 'If I were asked which, among the modern methods for the treatment of offenders is the most promising, without hesitation I would say: Probation' (Lopez-Rey 1957: 346), but Radzinowicz, in expressing a similar view, linked it specifically to British developments.

More recently, as we shall see later in the chapter, England and Wales have been well to the fore in embracing and implementing several profound shifts in the international theory and practice of community penalties, and have been strongly influenced in turn by temporary fashions for social casework, 'nothing works', just deserts, risk management, and the recent movement towards evidence-based probation or 'what works'. At the end of the twentieth century the investment in 'what works' was so great that England and Wales were again seen as international leaders. So massive was the claimed commitment to evidence-based practice and the accompanying organizational changes that they were watched carefully by correctional services in many countries: as one member of the Conférence Permanente Européenne de la Probation put it:

> The Probation service in England and Wales has always been in the vanguard in these developments, and many other European countries are watching it like a hawk, ready to accept that which seems to be working and to criticise that which isn't [Ploeg 2003: 8].

Overall, there are strong arguments for using England and Wales as a particularly illuminating case study of community penalties, and perhaps the paradigm case of how they have developed in response both to internal developments in the specialist world of corrections and to external pressures from the worlds of social and economic policy and politics. It is less clear whether the latest developments outlined at the end of this chapter, involving the introduction of a unified National Offender Management Service (NOMS) and commercial competition between different 'providers' of correctional services, are likely to be emulated by other countries. British probation may this time have left the mainstream to pursue an idiosyncratic path of its own, but only time will tell. (The USA, for example, has some provision of probation supervision by private-sector companies, but no equivalent of NOMS.) In the meantime, in spite of all the changes, a number of commentators (for example Vanstone 2004) still identify strong elements of continuity in the core features of community sentences, and describe them in terms not very different from those used by Grünhut above. These include giving offenders an opportunity to demonstrate that they can avoid further offending, and holding them accountable through a supervision process which combines monitoring with encouragement and assistance—the mixture of supervision and help which, as we shall see, has been probation's preferred style since very early in its evolution. Thus 'community penalties' are usually not purely punitive (like a fine), neither are they based on coercive restriction of liberty like a prison; instead they rely on the cooperation of offenders in accepting the requirements of a court order, and often on the capacity of supervisors to negotiate, motivate, and persuade.

This chapter, then, is mainly about 'community penalties', mainly but not exclusively about Britain (particularly England and Wales), and mainly about adults, though some mention will be made of some similar orders for juvenile offenders and occasionally of those aspects of post-custodial supervision which resemble community penalties. The chapter briefly describes the current variety of community penalties and their use in sentencing, and outlines the changes in the functions and perception of probation services which have led up to the current pattern of work. In particular the emergence of new evidence of effectiveness, and its adoption to support evidence-based practice or 'What Works', had a profound and controversial impact on the world of community sentencing. This chapter explores the background to these developments, their implementation, their mixed results, and their implications for the future of probation services. The final parts of the chapter are concerned with current plans for 'end-to-end' offender management and a National Offender Management Service.

CURRENT COMMUNITY PENALTIES IN ENGLAND AND WALES

Much of the history of community penalties is about probation orders (requiring an offender to be under the supervision of a probation officer) and community service orders (requiring the performance of supervised unpaid work as a form of reparation to the community), and these terms will be used frequently throughout this chapter. However, in England and Wales these familiar names were replaced in 2000 by 'community rehabilitation orders' and 'community punishment orders' respectively, together with a combination of the two known as a 'community punishment and rehabilitation order'. These cumbersome and not particularly popular redesignations are currently in their turn being replaced under the 2003 Criminal Justice Act, by a new 'generic community sentence' which can be up to three years in length, although shorter terms can be specified. To this order can be attached any of (and most combinations of) 12 different requirements relating to unpaid work, specified activities, accredited programmes, prohibited activities, curfews, exclusions from specified places, residence in specified places, mental health treatment, drug rehabilitation, alcohol treatment, supervision by a responsible officer, and attendance centres for younger offenders. With several of these, electronic monitoring can also be included. Some of these are derivatives of earlier familiar orders (for example, unpaid work is community service, and drug treatment requirements resemble the earlier drug treatment and testing orders (Turnbull *et al.* 2000)). The details of permitted time limits and combinations are too complex to expound here, and readers seeking this level of detail are referred to one of the legal guides to the Act, such as Gibson (2004). What is much less clear is how these new orders will impact on the sentencing landscape: for example, will sentencers be tempted to combine large numbers of requirements into over-demanding packages which will result in higher breach rates? Many of the same requirements are also available for use with the new hybrid or semi-custodial sentences which are described below, as well as during the non-custodial intervals of new intermittent prison sentences ('weekend prison'). Personal supervision, traditionally the core of community sentencing, becomes simply one requirement among many, although current signs are that it will remain a popular one.

For many years the Probation Service has also been responsible for supervising some young offenders on licence after their release from custodial institutions, and adult prisoners on parole and (since the 1991 Criminal Justice Act) on automatic conditional release. This increasingly prevalent pattern of a custodial sentence followed by a period of conditional liberty under supervision came during the late 1990s to be seen as a single 'seamless' sentence to be planned as one continuous process (Maguire and Raynor 1997). The Halliday report (2001) and the 2003 Criminal Justice Act then adapted this principle to address the difficult issues surrounding the inadequate provision of resettlement and post-release supervision to the relatively large numbers (currently almost 62,000 per year) of short-term prisoners sentenced to less than 12 months. What emerged was a new kind of 'hybrid' sentence, known as 'custody plus', which is intended to be a major influence on the future development of both short custodial and community sentences. To be introduced when resources allow, the arrangements are somewhat complicated. Both the length of the overall sentence and the length of the custodial period will be specified by the court. Any prison sentence up to 51 weeks in length will be served as a mixed sentence, with the custodial part lasting from two weeks (in a 28-week sentence) to 13 weeks (in a 51-week sentence), followed by a period under supervision in the community ranging from 26 weeks in a short sentence to 38 weeks at the longest end of the range (or even more if the court specifies a 51-week sentence with a custodial period of less than 13 weeks). Another variant (known as 'custody minus') suspends the prison term, creating a suspended prison sentence combined with supervision. A version of this existed under earlier legislation but was not popular with sentencers: the new arrangements seem likely to be more attractive.

The Probation Service's workload in England and Wales at the time of writing does not yet reflect most of these new developments, and considerable growth is expected. However, an idea of the current scale of the operation is obtainable from Home Office figures (Home Office RDS NOMS 2005) which show about 220,000 offenders under supervision at the end of December 2004, including about 64,000 on community rehabilitation orders, 43,000 on community punishment orders, 19,000 on community punishment and rehabilitation orders, nearly 7,000 on drug treatment and training orders, and rather less than 2,000 on money payment supervision orders (which place a fined offender under supervision until the fine is paid). Another 81,000 were subject to statutory supervision on release from prisons and other custodial establishments, but only about 22,000 of these were actually being supervised in the community. Voluntary after-care cases were counted at over 2,000, mostly in prison, with just over 400 in contact post-release.

Community penalties similar to the main options outlined above are also available in Scotland. Probation and community service orders retain their original titles there, but are not supervised by officers of a probation service, which has not existed in Scotland since 1969; instead they are normally the responsibility of criminal justice specialists working in social work departments of local authorities. Elsewhere in Europe many countries have some form of probation (van Kalmthout and Derks 2000), and the idea of community penalties is spreading to eastern European countries where the levels of imprisonment inherited from former authoritarian regimes are seen as no longer necessary or affordable (see, Jones 2001). Similar developments are under way in the developing world in an attempt to control or reverse growth in prison numbers. There the most favoured option seems sometimes to be community service, which has been successfully introduced in several African jurisdictions without the need for a large, professionalized probation service (Stern 1998). Ironically, the increasing popularity of probation and community service throughout the world has coincided with a period in Britain when they have often struggled for political approval and support. The next part of this chapter illustrates how concepts of probation and community penalties have changed over time, and how technical developments within the correctional field have interacted with wider social and political changes to produce several major shifts in the accepted view of what a community penalty is or should be.

ORIGINS: FROM RELIGIOUS MISSION TO SOCIAL CASEWORK

The history of community penalties has been shaped by changing ideas of the purposes of criminal justice and of the functions and effects of penal sanctions. Through most of their history community penalties have also been the subjects of research, but because the vast majority of such research has been funded by government it has usually been shaped by taken-for-granted policy assumptions. This section aims to trace the interaction of policy and research in community penalties up to and through the era of 'nothing works'. It illustrates how research, funded mainly by government, has often been more a product or reflection of current policy than an influence on it.

Probation had its origins in local court practices in the early nineteenth century, whereby young offenders or those guilty of minor offences could be discharged or bound over if a suitable person offered to take responsibility for supervising their future conduct. In 1876 the Church of England Temperance Society began to maintain an active presence in some city police courts in order to promote the moral reform of offenders and abstention from alcohol. Sentencers developed the practice of seeking information from the missionaries about offenders and placing some of them under informal supervision in lieu of other punishment if they seemed likely to reform. This was an opportunity to 'prove' themselves: hence the term 'probation', a proof or test.

A similar system, rooted in missionary work, charitable endeavour, and the temperance movement, had developed in parts of the United States from the 1840s, and seems first to have been formalized in the legal guise of supervision by an officer of the court in Massachusetts in 1869. Developments there were eagerly studied by penal reformers campaigning for a probation law in Britain. Their efforts bore fruit in 1907 in the Probation of Offenders Act, but several more decades were to elapse before probation services everywhere in Britain were provided by salaried public officials rather than by a mixed workforce of professionals and missionaries. This early period is described by McWilliams, in his seminal series of articles on the history of probation (McWilliams 1983, 1985, 1986, 1987), as concerned with saving souls, but it also played a part in the emergence of what Garland has called the 'penal-welfare' complex (Garland 1985). More recent historical work by Vanstone (2004) has documented other influences on some of the court-based missionaries and early probation officers, including interest in eugenics and in Lombrosian theories about the constitutional inferiority of criminals. A marked theoretical eclecticism has been a feature of the Probation Service throughout its history. However, by the time that serious research on probation began to be undertaken the emerging professional service had found itself a new theory: like the rest of social work, it had adopted a psychosocial rationale strongly influenced by psychoanalytic ideas about the unconscious and defence mechanisms (see Richmond 1917 for a pre-Freudian model of diagnostic social work, and Hollis 1964 for a more developed and psychoanalytically influenced version).

THE TREATMENT MODEL AND EARLY RESEARCH

The new theory co-opted the old term 'casework' (which in its original usage by the Charity Organization Society meant simply 'work on cases') and changed its meaning to denote a process of therapeutic work in which the offender's needs and motivations, characteristically hidden behind a 'presenting problem', could be revealed through a process of insight facilitated by a relationship with a probation officer (see, for example, Monger 1964). The fact that psychotherapeutic relationships were intended to be voluntary whereas the probation officer could prosecute his 'client' for not cooperating was an apparent inconsistency, and a source of concern for those inclined to redefine probation as psychotherapy. However, as Foren and Bailey (1968) explained, those who were helped to gain increased insight would then realize that they would have volunteered if they had understood their own needs properly, and so the relationship was really voluntary in a kind of retrospective way, even if this was not apparent at the time. This principle was concretely illustrated by Hunt (1964) in an article in the *British Journal of Delinquency* which contained a letter from a young man in borstal (a young offenders' custodial institution) thanking the probation officer who sent him there, on the grounds that it was what he really needed all along. The evident convenience of such theories kept them going for several decades, consolidating what McWilliams called probation's diagnostic era. In Harris's words, probation had moved 'from a theologically to a psychiatrically driven discourse' (Harris 1994: 34). Armed with such theories, the Probation Service could take its place alongside other useful but paternalistic agencies as a small but significant part of the post-war welfare state.

During the next five decades, from the 1950s to the 1990s, probation was to undergo at least two further periods of rethinking and reformulation, each with major implications for the questions addressed by probation research. Early British studies of the effects of probation, such as Wilkins (1958) and Radzinowicz (1958), were clearly located within what subsequently became known as the 'treatment model': in Radzinowicz's formulation, probation was 'a form of social service preventing further crime by a readjustment of the culprit' (Radzinowicz 1958: x), and the studies were designed to measure whether this readjustment had been successfully achieved. They investigated reconviction, assumed to be a surrogate measure of reoffending. The two studies were methodologically different, since Radzinowicz documented subsequent offending without comparing it with those subject to other sentences while Wilkins used a comparison group; perhaps not surprisingly, they also came to rather different conclusions about effectiveness, with more negative conclusions in Wilkins's study. However, from the point of view of this chapter it is more interesting to consider where they directed their attention and where they did not. In line with the 'treatment' model, they looked for effects on offenders' subsequent behaviour; they were not interested in criminal justice system issues such as impacts on sentencing, 'market shares' (i.e. the extent to which probation orders were preferred to other sentences by the courts), or the tariff level of those supervised ('tariff level' in this context refers to the severity of sentence an offender might expect if not on probation: prison is high in the sentencing 'tariff', fines are low; see Ashworth, Chapter 29, this volume.) They also appeared to have little interest in the methods used: probation is regarded as a method in itself, and the package is not unwrapped to see what lies inside. The research agenda was confined to the claims of the treatment model and circumscribed by contemporary assumptions about what probation was for, though Wilkins did at least raise the important question of whether probation's effects were measurably better than those of other disposals.

Soon after this the Home Office launched an ambitious programme of research aimed at classifying probationers and their problems empirically, leading to large and interesting studies such as Davies (1969) and eventually to a focus on what probation officers actually did in response to these problems (Davies 1974). A significant emerging concern was that probation as psychosocial casework aspired, at least in the textbooks, to a focus on emotional problems (particularly 'underlying' ones) while probationers clearly had many social and environmental difficulties which probation officers addressed to varying degrees. Often, according to Davies, there was not much evidence of resulting change. The agenda was still 'treatment', but anxieties were emerging about the fit between the treatment provided and actual needs. The Probation Service, of course, could claim that caseloads were too high to allow it to show what it could achieve given better resources, and the eventual response to this was a controlled experiment. The IMPACT study ('Intensive Matched Probation and After-Care Treatment') randomly allocated probationers to normal or 'intensive' caseloads, and compared both the work done and the subsequent offending in these two groups—a classic research design for testing 'treatment'.

The results of the study (Folkard *et al.* 1976) were remarkably little discussed in the Probation Service but had a significant effect on the research agenda. The probationers in the experimental small caseloads did receive more attention; the nature of the attention was left to the officers, and could mostly be summarized as more of what they would normally do. The overall results were 'small non-significant differences in reconviction in favour of the control cases', and no confirmation that more probation 'treatment' produced better (or any) effects. The one significant exception was that 'the only experimental cases that apparently do much better are those which have been rated as having low criminal tendencies and which perceive themselves as having many problems', a fairly small group and arguably rather untypical of offenders in general, but broadly resembling offenders who showed positive results in some other studies (Shaw 1974; Adams 1961; Palmer 1974). One possible interpretation is that the typical content of probation in the 'treatment' era could be helpful to those who were distressed, anxious to change, and not particularly criminal. This prefigured later findings about the limited relevance of relationship-based counselling to work with persistent offenders, but the overall conclusion had to be seen as a negative verdict on probation as a general-purpose 'treatment' for crime. Most of the 'culprits' were not being 'readjusted', and the Home Office began to turn its research attention elsewhere. As the Home Office was (and still is) the dominant player in the funding and management of research on the penal system in Britain, this was to have decisive effects on the next decade of British probation research and a significant impact on the development of the Probation Service itself.

'NOTHING WORKS' AND 'ALTERNATIVES TO CUSTODY'

By the end of the 1970s the 'treatment model' was being strongly criticized on a number of empirical and ethical grounds. Empirically, studies of the effectiveness of penal sanctions of all kinds had produced generally discouraging results, and while this was not true of all studies, the general impression that 'nothing works' was reinforced by journalistic summaries (Martinson 1974) and by the overall conclusions of wide-ranging research reviews (Lipton *et al.* 1975; Brody 1976). These findings also gained strength from what were essentially moral or philosophical arguments against 'treatment', such as that it objectified or dehumanized its subjects, or that it rested on unsubstantiated claims of superior professional wisdom (Bottoms and McWilliams 1979). Legal scholars were increasingly questioning whether unreliable predictions about future behaviour should continue to influence sentencing and argued instead for proportionate 'justice' based on the seriousness of the offence (Hood 1974; von Hirsch 1976).

DIVERSION FROM CUSTODY

Meanwhile, researchers on juvenile justice following the 'treatment'-oriented Children and Young Persons Act 1969 were beginning to document unintended adverse consequences, such as increased incarceration following the failure of community-based supervision to prevent further offending (Thorpe *et al.* 1980). It began to appear that young offenders, like their older counterparts, might actually benefit from proportionate 'tariff' sentencing which did not aim to do them good but would at least avoid the excesses of over-ambitious compulsory 'treatment'. If the emphasis of the 1970s had been on doing good, without much success in demonstrating that good was being done, the 1980s were to be about avoiding harm, in particular by reducing unnecessary incarceration. This seemed a more achievable aim, and one which might commend itself on the grounds of economy even to communities or politicians who were not in sympathy with the underlying humanitarian aim. So began the era of 'alternatives to custody': probation was to be a non-custodial penalty aiming to increase its market share and reduce imprisonment, rather than a 'treatment' aiming to change people.

Elsewhere, and particularly across the Atlantic, some similar processes were at work, but the more pluralistic research environment allowed the continuation of some research which ran counter to the received orthodoxies of the time. The 1975 research review by Lipton, Martinson, and Wilks (which prompted Martinson's headline-grabbing 'nothing works' article of 1974) did not in fact reach uniformly negative conclusions about the studies it examined, and later re-examinations of the same studies (for example by Thornton 1987) found a number of positive results. Other reviews also began to point to more encouraging conclusions: for example, Blackburn (1980) reviewed a more recent group of studies than those covered by Lipton *et al.*, and found that while few studies met rigorous methodological standards, those which did meet them showed reductions in recidivism. In Canada, Gendreau and Ross identified a number of studies with positive outcomes and reviewed them as 'bibliotherapy for cynics' (Gendreau and Ross 1980), an early example of the many positive contributions Canadian researchers were to make to the literature of effective rehabilitation. Perhaps most surprisingly, Martinson himself published a reappraisal of his earlier conclusion that 'nothing works' (Martinson 1979), arguing that this view was simply incorrect.

The debate which seemed largely closed in Britain continued in other countries, with positive findings emerging from elsewhere in Europe (for an early example, see Berntsen and Christiansen 1965) as well as from North America. Even in Britain, some earlier studies had shown positive results, but were not followed up when 'nothing works' became the orthodox view. For example, enhanced input from prison welfare officers prior to release led, in a well-designed study, to lower reconvictions than in a randomly allocated control group (Shaw 1974), and probation hostels with firm but caring wardens showed less reoffending among their residents than other hostels (Sinclair 1971). Shaw's study in particular prefigured current concerns about the 'resettlement' of prisoners. However, these results were seen as anomalous and did little, in Britain, to dent the 'nothing works' consensus.

The apparently conclusive demise of 'treatment' produced not only a major shift in policy-makers' views of what probation might realistically achieve, but also a corresponding shift in focus for the questions asked by evaluative researchers. The influence of early juvenile justice system studies (such as Thorpe *et al.* 1980) has been mentioned already. These studies paid detailed attention to patterns of decision-making in the juvenile courts in an attempt to measure how the activities of social workers were reducing or increasing incarceration, but showed little interest in the content of supervision or the subsequent behaviour of offenders: the guiding assumption seemed to be that post-custodial reconviction rates for juveniles were already so high that any likely outcome of a community-based project would be an improvement. The Home Office itself had already begun to undertake studies guided by a similar set of assumptions about what it was interesting to measure: as well as early work on police cautions, which addressed system issues such as net-widening (Ditchfield 1976), a substantial programme of evaluative work on the new community service order had been developing in parallel with the final stages of the probation research programme.

Community service, introduced by the 1972 Criminal Justice Act, was initially implemented on an experimental basis in a number of pilot areas, and the associated Home Office research was primarily concerned with whether it was feasible to implement it; whether courts were using it; and how far it was being used for offenders who would otherwise be sent to prison (Pease *et al.* 1977; Pease and McWilliams 1980). In other words, the community service research agenda was about effects on systems rather than people, and a complete departure from the 'treatment' agenda. This departure was so complete that the decision to extend community service to all probation areas was taken before effects on reoffending had been assessed, and issues such as the kinds of help needed or received by offenders and its effects on their behaviour were not addressed until a much later Scottish study (McIvor 1992). Community service was intended to influence sentencers rather than offenders, and the research conformed closely to these priorities. Other more rehabilitation-oriented innovations, such as the day training centres, received far less official research attention (Vanstone and Raynor 1981). Although activities such as social enquiry reports (reports to sentencers by probation officers about offenders prior to sentence, now known as pre-sentence reports) continued to attract interest (Thorpe 1979), government-sponsored research on the effectiveness of probation virtually ceased after IMPACT. One of the few exceptions to this was a short study of probation day centres (Mair 1988), which revealingly pointed out that 'it is difficult to assess the success of centres in preventing reoffending; there is little monitoring of the centres in this respect and the main aim of the centres is to provide an alternative to custody'.

The dominance of new post-treatment, system-centred aims was underlined by the publication in 1984 of a *Statement of National Objectives and Priorities* for probation services in England and Wales (Home Office 1984, usually known as SNOP). This document, the first attempt at a national statement of the Probation Service's purpose, was clearly informed by the intention to develop community-based supervision in such a way as to reduce custodial sentencing. Social enquiry reports were to be a high priority 'where the court may be prepared to divert an offender from what would otherwise be a custodial sentence', and probation and community service orders were desirable 'especially in cases where custodial sentences would otherwise be imposed'. After-care of prisoners, presumed to have no diversionary impact, was allocated a lower place in the order of priorities. Nothing was said about the content or methods of supervision.

This strategy was in fact quite successful. When, later on, policy moved away from a focus on diversion, this was not because diversion had failed. On the contrary, among juveniles in particular it succeeded quite well, with very substantial reductions in custodial sentencing and the almost complete disappearance of residential care for juvenile offenders during the 1980s (Smith 1995). Although concentrating too exclusively on diversion may involve doing too little about some persistent offenders, in its own terms the policy of 'alternatives to custody' for juvenile offenders succeeded until public and political opinion in the 1990s began to favour a more punitive approach and the numbers of juvenile offenders in custody began to rise again (see Morgan and Newburn, Chapter 30, this volume).

THE PROBLEM OF 'NET-WIDENING'

It has sometimes been suggested that the creation of 'alternatives to custody' is a self-defeating strategy which has the unintended effect of increasing recruitment to the custodial part of the system. Several commentators, most notably Cohen (1985), have argued that the creation of less severe sentencing options often serves simply to draw more people into the net of social control measures ('net-widening') and that this exposes them to more severe sanctions when lower-tariff measures 'fail' (a process known in youth justice circles as 'tariff escalation'). Worries of this kind accompanied, for example, the introduction of specific requirements in probation orders intended to operate as 'alternatives to custody' (Drakeford 1983). Were probationers being 'set up to fail' by over-demanding requirements which would lead to custodial sentences on breach? (Similar concerns are expressed currently about the stringent approach to enforcement of community sentences demanded by Home Office National Standards, and are discussed further near the end of this chapter.) Such concerns, particularly about net-widening, were not groundless: for example, juvenile justice researchers in the late 1970s found that virtually all custodial sentences passed on juvenile offenders were recommended by social workers (Thorpe *et al.* 1980) and that supervision orders on first offenders could, if breached, lead to a custodial sentence much earlier in the offending career than would otherwise have been expected. Much was also made of the finding that suspended prison sentences appeared to have led to an increase in the prison population rather than a reduction (Bottoms 1980). The reason seemed to be that sentencers were passing suspended prison sentences in cases where they would not otherwise have sentenced custodially, and when some offenders reoffended the resulting custodial sentence was lengthened by the addition of the suspended term, leading to a substantially longer first custodial sentence than they might otherwise have expected.

However, there was not much other evidence of a general tendency towards tariff escalation. (The case of suspended sentences is special, in that the court is *required* to sentence custodially on breach except in very narrowly defined exceptional circumstances.) Among adults, probation orders in the 1980s successfully moved 'up-tariff' to accommodate a more heavily convicted group of offenders (see Table 31.1, later in this chapter). Studies of successful 'alternative' projects emphasized appropriate targeting to ensure that only those genuinely at risk of custodial sentences became involved, and appropriate enforcement strategies, agreed with the courts, to ensure that the outcome of enforcement action would be a return to the project in as many cases as possible. For example, seven out of ten breach cases in one successful project (Raynor 1988) resulted in returns to the project rather than custodial sentences, despite the 'high-tariff 'nature of the offenders concerned. In short, the unintended outcomes identified by Cohen can happen, but can also be avoided by conscious attention to targeting, to appropriate proposals in reports to sentencers, and to influencing decision-making in local criminal justice systems.

Given such safeguards, the existence of additional sentencing options can be advantageous, and appropriate targeting is quite feasible: for instance, it appeared to be achieved in several early 'intensive probation' experiments (Mair *et al.* 1994) which recruited offenders clearly at risk of custodial sentences. Early studies of community service also found that 45–50 per cent of such orders appeared to be made instead of prison (Pease *et al.* 1977). Even in a generally punitive climate, local criminal justice systems have some relative autonomy. Unfortunately the determinism of Cohen's account may have contributed to the resistance shown by some probation officers to the inclusion and enforcement of additional requirements in probation orders. However, the evidence of the 1980s indicates that given good information and a systematic approach, community sentences can successfully be used on a considerable scale where otherwise custodial sentences would be passed.

For the Probation Service the 1980s were a period of rapid and varied development. Community service seemed to be a marketing success, but the market share of probation orders had been falling through most of the 1970s. Probation orders which could be seen as a credible disposal for more serious offenders would need to offer more demanding and, if possible, effective programmes of supervision. The 1982 Criminal Justice Act encouraged the inclusion of additional requirements in probation orders to facilitate special programmes, but new, larger packages needed more content. Juvenile justice specialists were already developing intensive Intermediate Treatment (that is, programmes of supervised activity undertaken as part of a supervision order) with often quite sophisticated programme content (e.g. Denman 1982), and probation services began to follow suit with various forms of enhanced probation, despite the reservations of some of their staff (Drakeford 1983). Occasionally these involved an almost bizarre degree of emphasis on control and discipline (Kent Probation and After-Care Service 1981), but more often they looked for content which seemed likely to be useful to offenders and was intended to reduce their offending. Among these piecemeal and usually unevaluated developments, a few projects took research more seriously and involved local academics in what became a new style of evaluative study.

Such local projects were typically concerned both with 'market shares' and with impacts on offending, and the combination of modest scale and locally based research allowed for adequate follow-up of both sentencing trends and the behaviour of offenders. Two studies in particular, carried out during the 1980s and published towards the end of the decade (Raynor 1988; Roberts 1989), were able to address some of the issues about effectiveness which had almost vanished from the national research agenda, and in both cases some diversion from custody and some impact on reconviction could be reasonably convincingly demonstrated. One of the studies (Raynor 1988) was also able to document changes in offenders' self-perceived problems and suggested a link between these and subsequent reductions in offending. However, such projects did not represent the mainstream of practice at the time and are best understood as rather isolated precursors of later developments. At the end of the 1980s the Probation Service found itself in a confusing situation, expected by the Home Office to facilitate diversion from custody but retaining, within the Service itself, a considerable measure of belief in the possibility of effective rehabilitation, without much evidence to support it. Wider policy, meanwhile, was moving in a different direction: as the next section describes, the Government was beginning to outline a new 'centre stage' role for the Service as a provider of punishments in the community.

JUST DESERTS AND 'PUNISHMENT IN THE COMMUNITY'

THE 1991 CRIMINAL JUSTICE ACT

The 1991 Criminal Justice Act was a rare attempt to move beyond pragmatism towards a philosophically coherent sentencing system and penal policy. Bringing together much of the thinking and experience of the long period of Conservative government since 1979, it reflected the 'back to justice' movement of the late 1970s (von Hirsch 1976; Hood 1974) by emphasizing the individual moral responsibility of offenders, and sentencing them for what they had done ('just deserts') rather than for their individual characteristics, their treatment needs, or their expected future behaviour. The Act was preceded by several Green and White Papers (Home Office 1988, 1990a, 1990b) and accompanied by a comprehensive training programme for sentencers and probation staff. It also aimed to bring about a significant shift in probation and related non-custodial penalties which had previously been seen as orders made 'instead of sentence'. In future, they were to be part of the sentencing tariff, 'community sentences' to be imposed if the sentence was 'serious enough', but not 'so serious' that only a custodial sentence could be justified. This redefinition of probation as a 'punishment in the community' (Home Office 1998) was initially resisted by probation staff, and some commentators (for example Rumgay 1989) warned that what was presented primarily as a change of language, intended to sell a reform package to a sceptical electorate, could eventually influence the nature of the activity to which it was applied. On the other hand, for those who had been campaigning against excessive use of imprisonment it was enormously encouraging to see a White Paper stating that imprisonment 'can be an expensive way of making bad people worse' (Home Office 1990b: 6).

At the same time, paradoxically, probation services were suddenly discouraged by Home Office officials from using the language of 'alternatives to custody': community sentences and prisons were no longer to be in competition but were targeting different levels of seriousness. The two services were meant to be cooperating in new forms of throughcare for prisoners (Maguire and Raynor 1997), which would not be helped if one service continued to define its mission as saving people from the other. In practice, the 1991 Act turned out to be genuinely decarcerative: there were very substantial reductions in the use of custodial sentences during the few months of 1992 and 1993 in which the Act was allowed to operate as intended, before politicians shifted their stance and repealed key sections of it. However, the decisive shift away from the language of 'alternatives to custody' turned out to be one of the more enduring legacies of the 1991 Act, to the extent that much of what was learned from successful diversionary research and practice in the 1980s is seldom discussed.

LAW AND ORDER POLITICS

In 1993, the policy context suddenly and dramatically changed (see Downes and Morgan, Chapter 9, this volume). As part of an unprecedented package of populist 'Law and order' initiatives, the recently appointed Conservative Home Secretary Michael Howard announced that 'prison works'. Before long he was proposing a series of changes to the Probation Service which were intended to constitute a definitive break with its former 'social work' identity. These included the abolition of training places for probation officers on university-based social work courses, a policy backed up by a remarkable campaign of media disinformation (see Aldridge and Eadie 1997) and a token review by civil servants (Dews and Watts 1994). Other proposals included threats of extensive privatization, and 'fast-track' recruitment of redundant military personnel who, it was claimed, would not require much training since they already knew about discipline and 'handling men'.

One surprising feature of Howard's ideologically motivated assault was that it had not come much earlier. Margaret Thatcher's Conservative Governments of 1979 to 1992 had shown a consistent neo-liberal hostility to the welfare state and welfare professionals, often portraying them as self-interested, expensive, and ineffective (for a representative example of the anti-social work writing of the time, see Brewer and Lait 1980); but probation officers, although mildly criticized in the build-up to the 1991 Criminal Justice Act, had on the whole been protected by the fact that they were essential to the policies of the Home Secretaries who preceded Michael Howard (for example Douglas Hurd, later president of the Prison Reform Trust). In the end it was perhaps inevitable that the next Conservative Government, headed by John Major and consistently unpopular, should seek to recover its electoral standing by taking a populist stance. Although the Government was ousted in 1997, its criminal justice policies have had profound consequences for the prison population, rising almost continuously since Michael Howard's 1993 speech, and for the Probation Service, which needed urgently to find a new mission around which to build a case for survival. The new mission became the 'What Works' movement and led to another period of major change for probation services.

COMMUNITY PENALTIES AND CRIME REDUCTION: THE REDISCOVERY OF REHABILITATION

THE RESEARCH BACKGROUND

The origins of this movement and the theories behind it have been thoroughly reviewed elsewhere (for example, Raynor and Vanstone 2002; Raynor and Robinson 2005; from a more sceptical stance Mair 2004; and see also Hollin, Chapter 2, this volume). Readers interested in the full detail and psychological background are referred to these sources. This chapter is mainly concerned with the impact of 'What Works' on community penalties and the Probation Service. In brief, the existence of a body of research pointing to effective methods of work with offenders was already entering the British probation world in the late 1980s, not from the Home Office (where such research was still paralysed by the legacy of Martinson) but largely from other countries where reputable research on effective methods had continued. Work carried out in Canada and the USA was drawn to the attention of British audiences by the early 'What Works' conferences, in which James McGuire played a leading role (McGuire 1995); by a research review funded by the Scottish Office, which had never lost its commitment to rehabilitative penal methods (McIvor 1990); and by many other contributions. Particularly influential were two large meta-analyses of service and project evaluations which supported the argument that the right kind of intervention with offenders under supervision could make a significant difference to levels of reoffending (Andrews *et al.* 1990; Lipsey 1992). These meta-analyses tended to favour methods which were based on the now familiar principles of risk, need, and responsivity (see Hollin, Chapter 2, this volume), and the use of cognitive-behavioural methods designed to help offenders to change antisocial beliefs and attitudes and acquire new skills for dealing with problems.

In addition, some local projects in Britain which used structured forms of groupwork with persistent young adult offenders had already produced small but convincing positive results in the late 1980s (for example Raynor 1988; Roberts 1989), and a carefully evaluated local pilot of the Canadian cognitive-behavioural 'Reasoning and Rehabilitation' programme (Ross *et al.* 1988) was under way in a South Wales probation area by the summer of 1991 (see Raynor and Vanstone 1996, 1997). Although the full results of this project were not published until 1996, some early results were available in 1994 and were described by Christine Knott in McGuire's influential 'What Works' edited collection (Knott 1995). This study showed that British probation officers could deliver this kind of programme, and there were indications of modest beneficial effects on programme completers, particularly in comparison with similar offenders who received custodial sentences. Programme members did not do significantly better, in terms of reconviction, than people who received 'ordinary' probation orders without a programme: the project was targeted on people who would otherwise have received a custodial sentence rather than a standard probation order, and custodial sentences were the key comparison group for the evaluation. In the 'nothing works' era these results would probably not have attracted much attention, and the widespread interest aroused by this project was itself an indicator of how the climate was beginning to change.

While this and other local experiments were proceeding, managers, practitioners, and researchers who were interested in the possibilities of effective practice were actively disseminating the new ideas. In addition to the series of 'What Works' conferences which began in 1991, an influential conference at Green College, Oxford also helped to promote the new approaches, and in 1993 the Home Office organized a conference in Bath, followed by another conference in London in 1995 on 'Managing What Works'. This was followed by a circular (Home Office 1995) encouraging (or requiring) probation services to adopt effective methods and promising a follow-up inspection by Her Majesty's Inspectorate of Probation (HMIP). This was the first of a number of attempts to transform the Service from the top down, in a fundamentally different direction from that laid down by SNOP in 1984.

Other jurisdictions and agencies took rather different routes to the implementation of the new ideas. In Scotland the chosen development strategy emphasized education and incremental development in a context where implementation was necessarily devolved and localized. The Scottish Office (later, after political devolution, the Scottish Executive) funded an advanced university course for senior practitioners and a Development Unit, and aimed to influence service providers in the right direction by using its powers to set standards and fund services. In England and Wales (the policies come from England, since criminal justice powers are not yet devolved to the Welsh Assembly Government) rather different approaches emerged for young offenders, under the auspices of the Youth Justice Board, from those which were developed for adult offenders by the probation service and the prison service. The Youth Justice Board (YJB), working through Youth Offending Teams (YOTs) in each locality, encouraged experimentation and diversity by funding a wide variety of local schemes. This was probably a good way of engaging the energies and creativity of local agencies and practitioners, although it created problems for research and for consistency of practice.

THE NATIONAL STRATEGY FOR PROBATION

The Probation Service adopted, by contrast, a highly centralized development strategy accompanied by a systematic programme of research. Instead of a simple inspection to follow up the 1995 circular, a research exercise was set up involving a detailed survey of probation areas by Andrew Underdown, a senior probation manager who was already closely involved in issues around effective practice. The results, eventually published in 1998 (Underdown 1998), after the election of a Labour government expected to be better disposed towards the Probation Service, were alarming. Of the 267 programmes which probation areas claimed they were running based on the principles of effective practice set out in the 1995 Circular, evidence of actual effectiveness based on reasonably convincing evaluation was available only for four. One of the four was the Mid-Glamorgan STOP programme; the others were in London (Wilkinson 1997, 1998). Underdown's report included an introduction by Graham Smith, at that time Her Majesty's Chief Inspector of Probation, who played a central role in the promotion of the 'What Works' agenda within the Home Office and the Probation Service. His wording clearly shows the importance he attached to 'What Works' as a survival strategy for probation: 'This is the most important foreword I have ever written . . . The report offers the probation service . . . an opportunity to renew and revitalise community penalties . . . the rewards will be immense in terms of increased confidence and public belief in and support for community sanctions' (Underdown 1998: iii).

The poor results of the Inspectorate's survey of current practice pointed to the need for a centrally managed initiative to introduce more effective forms of supervision. The

Home Office's Probation Unit worked closely with the Inspectorate to develop the 'What Works initiative'; publications were issued to provide guidance (Chapman and Hough 1998; McGuire 2000) and a number of promising programmes were identified for piloting and evaluation as 'pathfinder' programmes, with support in due course from the Government's Crime Reduction Programme (CRP). The pathfinders included several cognitive-behavioural programmes (Hollin *et al.* 2004) but also included work on basic skills (improving literacy and numeracy to improve chances of employment (McMahon *et al.* 2004; Haslewood-Pocsik *et al.* 2004)), pro-social approaches to supervision in community service (Rex and Gelsthorpe 2002; Rex *et al.* 2003), and a number of joint projects run by probation services with prisons and in some cases voluntary organizations working on the resettlement of short-term prisoners after release (Lewis *et al.* 2003; Clancy *et al.* 2006).

In the meantime a new probation service was taking shape, to come formally into existence as the National Probation Service for England and Wales in April 2001, replacing the old separate area probation services and explicitly committed to public protection and crime reduction. Instead of 54 separate probation services, each responsible to and employed by a local Probation Committee consisting largely of local magistrates, the new National Probation Service (NPS) was a single organization run by a Director with a substantial central staff located in the Home Office (the National Probation Directorate). Some local influence was still provided by the 42 area boards, each employing the staff in its own area (apart from the area's Chief Officer) but responsibility for policy moved to the centre and was implemented through a national management structure. The new areas were coterminous with police, court, and Crown Prosecution Service areas in order to facilitate multi-agency working in the criminal justice system (though they did not coincide with local authorities or with YOTS), and board members were chosen on the basis of relevant expertise, with much less representation of sentencers than on the old Committees. The new Service started with an annual budget of about £500 million (roughly 4 per cent of overall spending on the criminal justice system). By the end of 2002 this figure was reported as £693 million, with 8,000 probation officers employed (including trainees) and 9,300 other staff (Home Office 2004a). Recent statements from the Probation Boards Association (PBA) mention a staffing figure of 20,000 (PBA 2005).

The new structure had emerged from a substantial review of prison and probation services (Home Office 1998) which, among other possibilities, considered merging prisons and probation into a single correctional service, but (ironically, in view of later developments) concluded that this would be a step too far. (The review also considered new names for the probation service, which nearly became the Community Punishment and Rehabilitation Service until it was realized that only a small transposition of word order resulted in the acronym CRAPS.) The main aim of the changes was to create an organization which could be more effectively managed and directed from the centre. Detailed national policies and targets were published in a document intriguingly entitled *A New Choreography* (NPS 2001) incorporating 'stretch objectives' designed to produce change, and performance was monitored. All this represented a considerable transformation over a very short period of time, and the new organization was faced with the problem of how to maintain a sense of involvement among those groups which had less influence in the new structure than they had in the past. These groups included the magistrates who passed most of the community sentences, and some of the Service's own staff, who found their traditional autonomy reduced by a more managerial regime. At the same time, the Service's new Director chose to empha- size a decisive shift in direction by adopting the slogan 'Enforcement, rehabilitation and public protection' (NPS 2001). The priority given to enforcement was not accidental, and some of the consequences are discussed below.

WHAT WORKED AND WHAT DIDN'T?

The end of the twentieth century marked the high point of optimism for the 'What Works' movement in England and Wales—or at least its highest point to date. Promising programmes were identified and being piloted; the Joint Prisons and Probation Accreditation Panel (later the Correctional Services Accreditation Panel) was set up in 1999 to apply some independent quality control to the programmes adopted by prisons and probation services, and substantial funding was attracted from the Treasury to finance programme implementation and research (though not without strings, such as hugely ambitious target numbers for programme completions and an unrealistically short period during which evaluations were to be completed: for fuller discussion of the problems of the crime reduction programme see Hough 2004; Homel *et al.* 2005). A good example of the general optimism is provided by John Halliday in his influential review of sentencing (Halliday 2001), which provided the underpinning rationale for most of the 2003 Criminal Justice Act: 'if the programmes are developed and applied as intended . . . reconviction rates might be reduced by 5–15 percentage points (i.e. from the present level of 56% within two years, to (perhaps) 40%)' (Halliday 2001: 7). It is not clear how Halliday arrived at this remarkable example of a 'best case' scenario, but clearly he had been talking with the Home Office and probation staff who were enthusiastically pressing ahead with 'What Works'.

More difficult times lay ahead. No correctional service anywhere in the world had tried to implement 'What Works' principles on such a scale, at such a speed, and subject to such comprehensive scrutiny and evaluation. This inevitably led to a number of short cuts, sometimes running well ahead of or even contrary to the available evidence. For example, the targets for accredited programme completions set in 1999, which drove the pace of the roll-out of offending behaviour programmes, had been negotiated with Treasury officials without any systematic prior assessment of the characteristics of offenders under supervision and their suitability for programmes (Raynor 2006). After experiments with other simpler risk and need assessment instruments (Raynor *et al.* 2000), a new assessment instrument was developed known as the Offender Assessment

System (OASys). This was originally promised for August 2000, but was not available to inform the target-setting process and is still not used for all offenders in the prison and probation services at the time of writing. The targets quickly proved too high for most probation areas to achieve and were eventually reduced, but not before consuming much time and effort and causing many problems for staff and managers. The creation of the National Probation Service itself, although intended to promote effectiveness, diverted energy into new arrangements for governance and management and, in some cases, the complex and time-consuming amalgamation of areas. In some of the amalgamated areas this caused additional disruption and delay in implementing the 'What Works' agenda.

Within the pathfinder programmes themselves, researchers noted a large number of implementation difficulties: projects were often not running in a fully developed form when the evidence which would be used to measure their effectiveness was collected. The very mixed results of the pathfinder evaluations have been reviewed elsewhere (for example Raynor 2004a, 2004b; Roberts 2004a, 2004b; Harper and Chitty 2004). For the purposes of this chapter, it is sufficient to note that, for a variety of reasons, they fell short of a clear demonstration of the effectiveness of the pathfinder projects. However, they contained many lessons about the implementation of new service designs. Often, as in the resettlement study, local projects depended on small numbers of staff and were vulnerable to staff sickness or communication problems (Lewis *et al.* 2003). In all the pathfinder studies, projects tended to make a slow start and not to achieve their target numbers; in the 'basic skills' and 'employment' pathfinders (McMahon *et al.* 2004; Haslewood-Pocsik *et al.* 2004) numbers completing were so small that the evaluation could not be carried out as intended. In the 'offending behaviour' pathfinders (for example Roberts 2004a; Hollin *et al.* 2004) the high levels of attrition, due in large part to enforcement action leading to the termination of orders for non-compliance, led to difficulties in interpreting evidence. Outcomes based on programme completers, when these are only a small proportion of those who start the programme, may show effects of the programme or may show simply the effects of whatever selection or self-selection processes led to those people, rather than others, completing it.

In addition, the top-down management style which was seen as necessary to drive implementation forward within the prescribed timescale (Blumsom 2004) alienated parts of the workforce, particularly probation officers who were used to a high degree of autonomy. Staff in some areas found their workloads spiralling out of control at the same time as demands to meet targets were increasing. At one stage (luckily after most of the pathfinder data had been gathered) most probation areas were involved in industrial action over workloads, and the probation officers' union NAPO expressed its concern in conference resolutions which rejected aspects of the 'What Works' approach (NAPO 2001). In such circumstances researchers could hardly be surprised if some of the data quality was poor.

Reliance on central direction and a managerialist approach also contradicted some of the British evidence about how to engage staff in effective innovation (Raynor and Vanstone 2001): the STOP programme, like many other successful innovations, involved a substantial period of local discussion and a high level of input and ownership by local practitioners. Similar lessons are emerging from a new international interest in problems of effective implementation (Gendreau *et al.* 1999). Some warning notes might, however, have been sounded by an American study (Lipsey 1999) of differences between 'demonstration' and 'practical' interventions. The former are the special pilot projects which are often the source of the research covered in systematic reviews, and the latter are the routine implementations which follow organizational decisions to adopt new methods, as in the rapid roll-out of the Probation Service's new programmes. Better results are more commonly found among the 'demonstration' projects: in Lipsey's study the 196 'practical' programmes reviewed were on average half as effective as the 205 'demonstration' programmes. (Even this level of effectiveness depended heavily on a few programmes, as 57 per cent of the 'practical' programmes had no appreciable effect.) As he points out, 'rehabilitative programmes of a practical "real world" sort clearly can be effective; the challenge is to design and implement them so that they, in fact, are effective' (Lipsey 1999: 641).

Problems also arose from a tendency to be preoccupied with implementing programmes or 'interventions' rather than with providing an experience of supervision which would be effective as a whole. Although this had been pointed out by earlier British research (Raynor and Vanstone 1997), by Rod Morgan when, as Chief Inspector of Probation, he warned against 'programme fetishism' (Morgan 2003) and by the Correctional Services Accreditation Panel which insisted on continuity as one of its accreditation criteria (Correctional Services Accreditation Panel 2003), little attention was paid to the need for effective case management until attrition rates started to cause concern. Recent Home Office research (Partridge 2004) has examined the merits of different case management models, and found strong support for 'generic' models which aimed to keep offenders in contact with the same case manager/supervisor through the whole of their orders, as opposed to 'functional' models (favoured by managers but disliked by most staff and offenders) which broke up supervision into separate tasks carried out by different people. Meanwhile research in other countries has pointed clearly to the benefits of continuity of contact with skilled practitioners (Trotter 1993; Dowden and Andrews 2004). The pathfinder projects were not designed with this in mind, and the associated evaluations are therefore able to say little about its contribution to outcomes, which is likely to have been substantial.

The early 'What Works' years in England and Wales have also been criticized for their lack of a clear penal strategy. In other words, there does not seem to have been any clear shared vision of the pattern of sentencing which was intended to result from the initiative, or any clear policy regarding the functions and desirable levels of custodial and community sentencing. Although efforts were made, with only partial success, to ensure that programmes were not used for low-risk offenders, little else was done to eliminate the down-tariff drift of community sentences which had been going on throughout the 1990s. Table 31.1 shows how the proportion of those sentenced to community sentences who were first offenders, which fell overall during the 1980s, rose again during the 1990s, while the proportion of orders passed for less serious or summary offences also rose. These trends, noted by Raynor (1998) and Morgan (2002), occurred in spite of evidence that for first offenders a fine is much less likely to be followed by reconviction than a probation order (Walker *et al.* 1981). The down-tariff drift of probation has also coincided with increased imprisonment and a reduction in the use of fines. However, in a remarkable act of collective amnesia, probation's leaders made no connection between the 'What Works' agenda and their earlier strategy of reducing reliance on custodial sentences. There was little attempt to promote programmes as an alternative to short custodial sentences. The potential impact of the 'What Works' initiative on the wider penal system was probably diminished as a result.

During this period several other developmental issues have attracted attention by way of special projects and research, and space does not allow a full exploration of them here. The 'What Works' initiative was criticized for over-generalizing from research on white men, leading to research on minority ethnic offenders (Lewis *et al.* 2006) and to proposals for distinctive provision for women offenders (Shaw and Hannah-Moffatt 2004). The assessment and management of risk attracted two kinds of attention based on two meanings of risk, perhaps better understood as risk and danger respectively. Risk-need assessment (Raynor *et al.* 2000), based on assessing levels of criminogenic need or dynamic risk factors, became the dominant method for assessing the risk of reoffending and developing supervision plans to reduce it, while the risk of harm to the public from dangerous violent or sexual offences was assessed in other ways geared to the identification of triggers and the development of inter-agency methods of control

Table 31.1. How the main community sentences[a] were used in three decades[b]

	1981	1991	2001
People made subject to community sentences (thousands)	78	91	123
Probation Orders[c]: % without previous convictions	23	11	27
Probation Orders: % passed for summary offences	12	28	37
Probation Orders: % passed on female offenders	33	19	20
Community Service[d]: % without previous convictions	10	14	51
Community Service: % passed for summary offences	10	31	43
Community Service: % passed on female offenders	6	6	12

[a] i.e. the two most commonly used community sentences in England and Wales over the period covered by the table. In addition, from 1992 the Combination Order (later Community Punishment and Rehabilitation Order) became available. Used in much smaller numbers, it showed a similar pattern to other Orders during the 1990s: in 1993 10% of those made subject to such orders were first offenders, and in 2001 28%.

[b] From 2002 onwards, figures on the criminal histories of people subject to community penalties were not provided on the same basis, so that comparability in the time series cannot be assumed. After 2002 the series of Probation Statistics, England and Wales was superseded. This table is therefore based on the last *full* set of Home Office Probation Statistics (for 2001, published in 2002) and the corresponding figures published 10 and 20 years previously. All figures are based on numbers of persons made subject to Orders, not numbers of Orders passed.

[c] Later Community Rehabilitation Orders.

[d] Later Community Punishment Orders, and from 2003 Unpaid Work.

and surveillance to protect potential victims through multi-agency public protection arrangements (MAPPA: see Kemshall and Maguire 2001, Kemshall *et al*. 2005). The comprehensive risk assessment instrument OASys (OASys Development Team 2001) was designed to address both kinds of risk, and is now in widespread use in England and Wales, although no full evaluation of its effectiveness has been published at the time of writing. Recent high-profile cases of serious offences committed by people under supervision continue to raise questions about the adequacy of risk assessments, MAPPA arrangements, and supervision planning.

Thinking about community penalties has also been influenced by research on the process of desistance from offending (for example Zamble and Quinsey 1997; Farrall 2002; Maruna 2001; Maguire and Raynor 2006). Such research probably offers the best chance of striking an appropriate balance between attention to social conditions as causes of crime (the position favoured by many social-work-trained probation staff) and the attention to individual thinking, attitudes, beliefs, and motivation which has been the focus of many of the 'What Works' developments. For example, one attempt to combine both perspectives in a way which could be relevant to many people who serve community or hybrid sentences is provided by Zamble and Quinsey (1997: 146–7): 'factors in the social environment seem influential determinants of initial delinquency for a substantial proportion of offenders . . . but habitual offending is better predicted by looking at an individual's acquired ways of reacting to common situations'.

Overall, in spite of the hard work and undeniable achievements of many very able and dedicated staff, it is clear that the early results of the 'What Works' initiative were not impressive enough to bring about the radical change in the Probation Service's standing and prospects for which Graham Smith and others originally hoped. With hindsight, it is also clear that a three-year implementation timescale, with a major reorganization in the middle, was never likely to be long enough to show clear benefit from such a complex process of change.

AFTER 'WHAT WORKS', WHAT NEXT?
NOMS AND THE FUTURE

In the winter of 2003–4 the National Probation Service received a severe shock, in the form of a proposal to bring the prison and probation services together under the single organizational umbrella of a National Offender Management Service (NOMS). The threat which seemed to have been seen off in 1998 was suddenly revived. Briefly, this proposal arose from a review of correctional services carried out by Patrick Carter, a businessman with experience of the private health-care sector and highly regarded in Downing Street. His report (Carter 2003) offered a diagnosis of the system's problems with which few specialists would disagree, pointing to prison overcrowding, failure to help short-term prisoners, and the fact that for persistent offenders who pass repeatedly through the custodial and community systems, no one agency had the clear responsibility for managing the sentence as a whole in the way that offered the best prospect of reducing reoffending. The proposed alternative, known as 'end-to-end offender management', required, in Carter's view, a single agency to run it, namely NOMS. Under a Chief Executive and a National Offender Manager, ten Regional Offender Managers (ROMs) would 'commission' the services required, whether custodial or non-custodial, for the management of offenders in their region. (In Scotland, following a long consultation of the kind that was barely attempted in England and Wales, a proposal for a single correctional service was abandoned in favour of a strategy for better coordination of the existing services under the overall guidance of a new Community Justice Agency.) Even more controversial was Carter's proposal that the best way to improve the effectiveness of services in the community was to introduce contestability or market testing. This was already in limited use in the prison system but had not previously been a feature of probation except for an expectation during the 1990s that they should spend a small proportion of area budgets on 'partnerships' with other organizations.

It is difficult to take issue with the argument that probation services needed to work more in partnership with other organizations. The range of services needed by offenders greatly exceeds what the probation service itself is equipped to supply. The 'Reducing Re-offending Action Plan' (Home Office 2004b), based partly on work by the Social Exclusion Unit (SEU 2002) and others on the resettlement needs of prisoners, identified seven 'pathways' for the development of services to support resettlement and rehabilitation. These were accommodation; education, training, and employment; mental and physical health; drugs and alcohol; finance, benefits, and debt; children and families of offenders; and attitudes, thinking, and behaviour. Intervention in relation to almost all of these would require collaboration with other organizations. However, it is much harder to see how the core of offender management, which coordinates these other elements and provides continuity and structure for the offender, can benefit from the fragmentation implied by contestability. This aspect of the proposals has been widely criticized (see, for example, Hough *et al.* 2006). For the purposes of this chapter, it is also important to note that the Carter proposals actually constituted a significant rupture in the 'What Works' project as it developed up to 2003. Instead of a process of evidence-based change driven by piloting and evaluation, the Carter review offered the market solution of contestability as if this guaranteed better results. Commissioning, a purchaser-provider split, contestability, and a greater role for the private sector were standard ingredients in New Labour's 'reform' programme for public services. In other ways, however, the National Probation Service itself may have unwittingly paved the way for NOMS. The nationalization of a service which was formerly rooted in localities and at least to some degree in a sense of ownership by local sentencers may have made it more vulnerable to politically driven change: a single service based in London under the eye of the Home Office was arguably a more obvious focus of political awareness and target for political gestures than 54 locally based services involving hundreds of influential magistrates, particularly when the single service was being criticized as slow to meet targets and prone to overspend its budget.

At the time of writing it is not yet clear exactly how far or in what ways the Carter proposals will be implemented. Both NAPO and the Probation Boards Association (PBA) have produced powerful counter-arguments (for example, NAPO 2005; PBA 2004, 2005) and there have been some contradictory messages from the Government: for example, officials have pointed out in reassuring tones that only a tiny proportion of the prisons estate is run by the private sector, but the *NOMS Partial Regulatory Impact Assessment* (Home Office 2005b) assumed 50 per cent contracting out of probation service business within five years.

Two aspects of the Carter proposals and the NOMS 'reform' package which attracted wide-ranging support were the end-to-end offender management model, and the underpinning aim of controlling the growth of imprisonment. The importance of continuity in offender management had been strongly indicated by a series of studies of the resettlement of prisoners (Maguire *et al.* 1996; Maguire *et al.* 2000; Lewis *et al.* 2003; Clancy *et al.* 2006) and was also supported by a Home Office study of case management practice in the Probation Service (Partridge 2004; see also Robinson 2005) and in due course by a practical pilot study (PA Consulting Group 2005). What eventually emerged was the National Offender Management Model (NOMM: Home Office 2005c) which emphasized that a named 'offender manager' should be responsible for each offender throughout a sentence, including both custodial and community components, in order to ensure consistent assessment, planning, and intervention. However, the NOMM is also seen as combining three separate processes of 'management', 'supervision', and 'administration' which may be carried out by different individuals, so that the actual experience of being supervised may be less seamless than the model implies. There is also provision for four 'tiers' of cases: all offenders will undergo 'punishment', but only some will also require help. Of these, only some will also require change efforts such as programmes, and even fewer will require active measures of control to reduce risks of serious harm to the public. The four-tier model can therefore be summed up, in ascending order of resource commitment, as punishment only (Tier 1); punishment plus help (Tier 2); punishment plus help plus change (Tier 3); and punishment plus help plus change plus control (Tier 4).

The allocation of offenders to tiers will in theory depend on the levels of assessed risk and need, though inevitably the perceived seriousness of the offence and consequent severity of the sentence will also play a part. In short, the model offers a comprehensive typology of approaches to case management, but can accommodate a variety of approaches and some degree of fragmentation in practice, depending on resources and on how well it is implemented. If resource constraints dictate, as seems likely, that only the upper tiers will receive attention from trained and experienced staff, the work done with lower-tier offenders may be somewhat tokenistic. The design also raises some more basic questions: for example, about the relationship between the very different principles of need and seriousness in the allocation process; about whether all the combinations will 'work' (do all offenders who require control also seek or benefit from opportunities to change?); and about the relationship between delivering punishment and aspiring to help or effect change. In addition, it is never easy to reconcile tidy models with the unpredictable day-to-day reality of supervising people who are often disorganized, distressed, or difficult, and beset by unpredictable or at least unforeseen practical problems. If offenders had tidy and predictable lives they would not need supervision.

Carter's other central aim, to control the use of imprisonment, was to be achieved through the linked strategies of providing sentencers with guidance which no longer ignored the relative costs of different sentences, replacing short prison sentences with intermittent or hybrid custody/community sentences, and encouraging a return to the widespread use of fines. These proposals aimed to address the long-standing problem of around 60,000 offenders per year receiving short prison sentences, in which little could be done to help them, and which were followed by no adequate support for resettlement and a high reconviction rate (Social Exclusion Unit 2002; Maguire and Raynor 2006). Some commentators found these aspects of Carter's proposals sufficiently encouraging to offset doubts about the wisdom of yet another major criminal justice reorganization: they seemed to provide precisely that kind of strategic thinking about sentencing patterns and the intended shape of the penal system which had been lacking in the 'What Works' initiative. However, at the time of writing it is much less clear whether developments are still underpinned by these same principles, or whether other aspects of the package, such as contestability, are now more central.

SOME CRITICAL CHOICES FOR THE FUTURE

On several major questions which significantly affect the likely future of community penalties official guidance has been confusing or absent. Part of the reason for the continuing confusion seems to be political. We have already seen how the Carter report was seized on as the basis for policy announcements at the beginning of 2004 without a consultation period. Consultation was later offered on the details of implementation, but not the principles. The 'Correctional Services Review' which Patrick Carter led was owned by the Government's Strategy Unit and had the flavour of Downing Street rather than the Home Office; perhaps this was not unconnected with the expectation that 2005 would bring a General Election. The Labour Party manifesto for that election included a section on 'crime and security' with a conspicuous emphasis on toughness and tabloid language (such as 'exclude yobs from town centres' (Labour Party 2005: 46)). The NOMS reforms were mentioned briefly: 'voluntary organisations and the private sector will be offered greater opportunities to deliver offender services' (op. cit.: 48), but there was no mention of any attempts to contain the growth of imprisonment. Instead there was what looked like a boast that 'we have built over 16,000 more prison places than there were in 1997' (op. cit.: 47); see also Downes and Morgan, Chapter 9, this volume. Private-sector involvement was important enough to go in the manifesto, but an end to the growth of imprisonment was not. (For a useful discussion of whether NOMS really has a credible prospect of reducing growth in imprisonment, see Hedderman 2006.)

When Charles Clarke became Home Secretary later in the year, he set out some of his views on penal policy in a widely reported speech to the Prison Reform Trust, in which he emphasized the reduction of reoffending as a major goal of correctional services (Clarke 2005). However, in the same week *The Guardian*, reported that the Carter review's target of limiting prison numbers to 80,000 was being quietly abandoned, and sentencing guidelines provided for judges and magistrates would not, as previously proposed, include guidance on cost-effectiveness (*The Guardian*, 19 September 2005). A few weeks later the Home Secretary published his proposals on *Restructuring Probation to Reduce Re-offending* (Home Office 2005a). These indicated that not just 'interventions' such as programmes or drug services but also offender management services in the community would be subject to contestability, so that in principle all the functions of the Probation Service in a given geographical area could be transferred to a private or voluntary sector bidder. Probation Boards would be abolished and replaced by more business-oriented Probation Trusts, which would then be required to tender for their own former work in competition with other providers (Home Office 2005a). The new proposals provoked considerable criticism: according to NAPO (2006) less than 1 per cent of the consultation responses supported them. It remains to be seen which proposals, if any, will change.

In a nutshell, it is not yet possible to determine whether the implementation of the NOMS reforms will be guided, as the Carter report was at least partly guided, by evidence about what is effective in correctional services, or whether they will be driven by a faith in the capacity of the private sector to transform public services. The answer to this may depend on the amount and level of political interference in the implementation process. (For a review of the reasons why contestability is likely to create more problems for offender management than for 'interventions' see Raynor and Maguire 2006.)

A second unresolved question concerns the choice between continued reliance on centralized managerialism and a degree of empowerment for local decision-makers to respond to local needs and characteristics. The centralization of management and development in the National Probation Directorate in 2001 reduced the real power and influence of the Probation Boards in comparison with the old Probation Committees, and the Boards themselves were constituted in a way which reduced the number and influence of magistrates in the governance of the Service. The proposed arrangements for commissioning in NOMS appear to envisage most commissioning of services being done at a regional level, and at the time of writing it is still proposed that Probation Boards will be replaced by Trusts (Home Office 2006), with less local representation and probably coterminous with new larger Police Authorities. The Probation Boards Association has argued against this (PBA 2005), pointing to the Government's own commitment to involving local communities and local organizations in 'civil renewal': 'to empower citizens and their communities to work in partnership with public bodies to develop local solutions to local problems' (NOMS and YJB 2005). The Probation Boards, in arguing the case for their own survival, stress the importance of the local agenda and local partnerships. However, in the larger probation areas the Boards themselves are hardly local, and (if they survive) will need to develop a strategy to re-engage with the much smaller geographical units within which local responses to crime can actually be developed, at the level of petty sessional divisions, YOTs or local probation offices. For example, at the time of writing England and Wales have 42 Probation Boards and 157 YOTs.

The proposals in *Restructuring Probation to Reduce Re-offending* seem to imply some recognition of past problems of over-centralized management: we are told that the National Probation Directorate should become 'increasingly light touch' and that Chief Officers should be appointed and employed locally (as they were before 2001) rather than centrally. These measures appear to be designed to facilitate contestability at regional level rather than to empower local communities. However, some revitalization of probation's local roots could be an important part of strategies to build public support and perceived legitimacy (Raynor 2001). For example, 'community payback' schemes now allow local communities a role in identifying appropriate 'unpaid work' (formerly community service) projects to be undertaken by people serving community sentences. Further development of local influence and governance in offender management, to a level far beyond that envisaged so far in the plans for NOMS, will be needed if this approach is to be consolidated and extended. One implication of this would be that instead of rehabilitative programmes being seen primarily as a benefit to offenders, and therefore arguably unfair to those facing similar difficulties who have not offended, probation services should try to present rehabilitation as work that offenders undertake as a consequence of a crime: work which is directed to changing their own behaviour and attitudes in a more pro-social direction, to the advantage of the communities in which they live. A rehabilitative penalty can reflect the interests and values of the wider community, and perhaps equip offenders with skills to maintain themselves more effectively and to contribute more to society. The notion of rehabilitation as offenders working to rehabilitate themselves may be better aligned with community values, and more consistent with restorative principles, than the notion of offenders simply receiving help.

A third question which will require some arguably overdue clear thinking concerns how far probation services (or their successors) are or should be involved in the explicit delivery of punishment. This is a complex argument to which it is impossible to do justice in this chapter, but a few points are worth mentioning here. As outlined above, a significant obstacle to the success of the 'What Works' initiatives was the National Probation Service's commitment to rigorous enforcement and the reduction of practitioners' discretion to show flexibility even in low-risk cases, or with offenders whose lifestyles were so chaotic that the only realistic target would be improved compliance rather than full compliance. It is well known that the 2000 version of the 'National Standards' on enforcement was made significantly more punitive by the personal intervention of a Home Office minister, and the latest version (NOMS 2005) shows no relaxation: indeed the new four-tier model of offender management assumes that all people under supervision require punishment, while only some require help, change, or control.

This may mean no more than that correctional services should be seeking to ensure that all offenders meet the requirements of their various sentences and licences, but in reality punishment does not seem a sensible priority for every sentence at every stage. For example, community sentences are still sometimes imposed on people who are seen as needing help rather than punishment, or are seen as less blameworthy because of the difficulties they face. Another example can be found in the new hybrid sentences such as 'custody plus'. Is it sensible to understand the post-custodial resettlement phase as simply an extension of punishment, or is its main purpose the reintegration of people who have already served what they will undoubtedly see as the punitive part of their sentence? If we remember the important distinction between serving a sentence *as* punishment (i.e. offenders lose some freedom to use their time as they please) and serving it *for* punishment, with punitive content informed by punitive attitudes which are the direct opposites of 'What Works', then it becomes possible to think more strategically about enforcement. The main point of enforcement is surely to encourage compliance (for which it is one of several strategies, and not necessarily the most important or effective (Bottoms 2001)) and to allow review of orders which are not working and need to be revisited by sentencers. Currently nearly 9,000 people per year find themselves in prison as a result of enforcement of community sentences (Home Office RDS NOMS 2005). Implementation of the 2003 Criminal Justice Act is likely to increase this number, as courts cannot vary a requirement of a breached community sentence except by imposing a more rigorous requirement, or a custodial sentence if the failure to comply is repeated. Research has also shown that probation areas with a highly rigorous approach to enforcement do not achieve lower levels of reconviction than those with a more flexible approach (Hearnden and Millie 2003). In short, the practice of enforcement in community sentences cries out for an evidence-based review, which it has not so far received because rigorous and punitive enforcement has been seen as an inescapable political requirement.

Meanwhile, there is beginning to be more evidence that the improvements in consistency and performance that were part of the aim of the 'What Works' initiative are actually happening. The original three-year timescale was too short, but now, after roughly twice as long, targets for programme completions are being exceeded, rates of attrition (though still high) are reducing, and there is evidence of positive change during programmes in most of the areas assessed by routine psychometric testing (National Probation Service 2005). Equally important, the case management and supervision process is now taken seriously as an essential support and reinforcement for other 'interventions' and sometimes as an intervention in itself, and national training programmes have been developed to equip a wide range of staff with useful approaches such as pro-social modelling and motivational interviewing. There is some foundation for the Director of Probation's claim that the Service is delivering 'more . . . than at any time in our history' (National Probation Service 2005: 2). It is clear that the Probation Service is capable of delivering work which benefits both offenders and the community, and which is in an intelligible line of descent from the traditions and aspirations which informed its past.

It is less clear, at the time of writing, whether the latest reorganization will consolidate or threaten these achievements, but the uncertainly, contradictions, and confusion which have characterized the early implementation of NOMS suggest a very real possibility that, roughly a century after the 1907 Probation of Offenders Act, the Probation Service in England and Wales could lose much of its traditional identity and much of its traditional role. Instead of having a public responsibility for the supervision of offenders in their communities, Probation Trusts could find themselves just one of a number of bodies tendering for the provision of offender management services and interventions. At the same time, they will be clearly involved in the implementation of sentences which are officially defined as punishment, whether or not they also contain the other elements of help, change, and control. The speed and comprehensiveness of these changes can be judged from even a cursory glance at the probation literature of the recent past: little more than ten years ago it was possible to describe the purpose of probation as:

> to engage offenders in a reintegrative dialogue and offer opportunities for them to participate in constructive responses to the harm caused by offending, including efforts to find alternatives to offending in their own lives. This also involves influencing criminal justice processes towards less coercive and more participatory outcomes [Raynor and Vanstone 1994: 401].

Although such ideas are well represented in international movements to promote restorative justice, and recent commentators have pointed to strong connections between rehabilitative and restorative assumptions (Raynor and Robinson 2005), they are far removed from today's official rhetoric of offender management. Instead, a recent Inspectorate report (HMIP 2006) has proposed a new slogan for probation based on the four tiers in the National Offender Management Model: 'Punish, help, change and control'.

A FUTURE FOR PROBATION?

At the beginning of this chapter I suggested that the experience of England and Wales offers a particularly useful paradigm case through which to study the changing fortunes of probation services, their historical commitment to rehabilitation, and their transformation in response to changes generated both within and outside the field of corrections. Whether the most recent changes will also become the typical experience of probation systems around the world depends on how far they are a necessary consequence of broad social and cultural changes which affect many countries. In 1997 at the Probation Studies Unit colloquium in Oxford, David Garland argued that trends towards toughness and punitiveness in the world of probation were an example of a wider trend in the penal systems of many countries (Garland 1997). As in his influential book *The Culture of Control* (Garland 2001) he attributed this to broad social and cultural changes characteristic of late modern societies. Some of the recent changes in British probation are clearly in line with these arguments: for example, a preoccupation with risk and the technology of risk management recalls the arguments of Giddens (1990) and Beck (1992). Some of the uses of risk assessment, and in particular the re-emergence of sentencing according to risk rather than desert, are consistent with the critique developed by Feeley and Simon (1992) and Hudson (2003), although other uses are more consistent with rehabilitative aims (Raynor *et al.* 2000). The new developments in 'hybrid' sentencing which combine elements of custodial and community sentences vividly recall Cohen's arguments, over twenty years ago, about the 'blurring' of different forms and levels of control (Cohen 1985). The globalization of capital and the colonization of public life and public services by commercial business models and economic rationality (Christie 1993, 2004) define the context for privatization and 'contestability', whilst developments in information and communication technology (ICT) transform the possibilities for impersonal supervision of offenders by ever more sophisticated forms of tagging (Nellis 2004a).

The same or related developments in ICT also allow new forms of technical routinization of what used to be areas of professional discretion (Robinson 2003) and more managerialist supervision of staff. Critics of criminal justice managerialism have also suggested that managers in a changing environment will try to aim for, and be judged by, achievable targets within their sphere of control (Feeley and Simon 1992) rather than broader social or public service goals. While the recent history of targeting in the National Probation Directorate hardly demonstrates the deliberate selection of achievable targets, it does show a substitution of internal performance indicators (e.g. programme completion rates) for broader external goals (for example, reduction in avoidable custodial sentencing, which was the explicit aim set in 1984). Other influences of penal policy stem from political short-termism and the media-driven need for constant new initiatives and knee-jerk policy proposals (identified by Garland (1995) as 'signs and symbols', and by Christie (2004) as the use of criminal justice as an arena for 'self-presentation' by politicians). The New Labour Governments since 1997 have created new criminal justice policy and legislation at a rate never contemplated by previous governments. Perhaps the most pervasive form of this politicized tendency in recent British penal policy has been the rise of 'populist punitiveness' (Bottoms 1995) and the need felt by politicians of all parties to include a display of 'toughness' in every new policy pronouncement and initiative.

However, there is a risk that these arguments could lead to excessive pessimism about the future prospects of probation in general (see, for example, Nellis 2004b). England and Wales at the time of writing seem no longer to be in the mainstream of international probation development: instead, they offer the largest example of a probation service threatened with loss or blurring of identity through absorption into a general purpose 'offender management service', and possible fragmentation through 'contestability'. As noted above, one possible outcome of the current policy muddle over NOMS is that the centenary of British probation in 2007 could also mark its passing, at least as far as England and Wales are concerned. A recent article written with the centenary in mind (Robinson and Raynor 2006) suggests some promising future directions for rehabilitation with or without probation services to act as a focus: without such a focus, rehabilitation will be more fragmented and vulnerable, but probation services have never been the only organizations promoting and carrying out the rehabilitation of offenders. The article also argues, following Garland (2001), that the current populist distortions of penal policy are not inevitable, but are the product of human choices, and particularly of political choices.

A more balanced picture of the prospects for probation services, and consequently for the whole range of non-custodial rehabilitative measures of which they have been the main providers and promoters, can perhaps be formed by considering some international comparisons. In most of eastern Europe, and particularly in those countries with ambitions to joint the European Union, governments are deliberately moving away from former Soviet-style policies of mass incarceration and are trying to develop a more community-based sentencing practice. In several of them the development of an effective probation service is seen as the key to this process, and consultants from the NPD and elsewhere are helping in this development. Another example is provided by Finland, where a conscious policy of reducing reliance on imprisonment, pursued with support across the political spectrum, has led to a dramatic decrease in prison numbers without a corresponding rise in crime (Lappi-Seppälä 2005). Punitive penal policies also stimulate new forms of critical argument: for example, Hudson (2003) argues for a renewed emphasis on human rights as a protection against excessive punishment, and others (such as Rotman 1990) have argued that rehabilitation should be seen as a citizen's right and an obligation of the state. This is based on the idea of a social contract in which the citizen's duty to refrain from crime is matched by the state's duty to maintain adequate social conditions and support for crime-free living.

In conclusion, it is worth mentioning a recent positive and progressive example from what many might consider an unlikely source: the United States of America. In recent years we are more used to seeing the USA identified as the source of populist policies of 'toughness' and high incarceration (as well as the encouragement of a commercial correctional sector), which are then emulated by British politicians (see, for example, Tonry 2004). However, a recent paper at the American Society of Criminology's conference in Toronto (Cox 2005) described recent initiatives in probation in the state of Connecticut. There, politicians recently became concerned at the cost of their high prison population, and also noted that a considerable proportion of new receptions into prison were there as a consequence of violations (in UK parlance breaches) of probation or post-custodial supervision rather than for new offences. They therefore instructed the state's probation service to reduce the rate of violations by helping offenders to comply with the requirements of supervision. It became clear that it tended to be the offenders with more problems who were more likely to violate their orders, and special programmes of supervision were devised to address their criminogenic needs, including practical needs like accommodation, training, and employment, in order to help them to establish a more stable way of life and to have a better chance of complying with their supervision requirements. Officers were given training in social work methods and prisoners were introduced to a post-release supervisor several months before release, so that the last part of the sentence could be used to set up the services (health, education) or the resources (accommodation, work) which the prisoner would need on release.

The reported outcome of these and similar methods (intriguingly described as 'probation as it was always meant to be') was a striking reduction in receptions into prison for violations, without any corresponding increase in offending by people under supervision. Such examples amply illustrate the point that with enthusiasm, creativity, local support, and clear evidence, promising initiatives can be developed even against the grain of wider trends and attitudes.

■ SELECTED FURTHER READING

General texts on probation and community penalties quite quickly become dated. Among the most useful at the moment are Worrall and Hoy's *Punishment in the Community* (Cullompton, Devon: Willan, 2005), Raynor and Vanstone's *Understanding Community Penalties* (Buckingham: Open University Press, 2002) and Raynor and Robinson *Rehabilitation, Crime and Justice* (Basingstoke: Palgrave, 2005). Three good edited collections are Nollio and Chui's *Moving Probation Forward* (Harlow: Pearson Education, 2003), Burnett and Roberts's *What Works in Probation and Youth Justice* (Cullompton, Devon: Willan, 2004) and, most comprehensive of all, Bottoms, Rex, and Robinson's *Alternatives to Prison* (Cullompton, Devon: Willan, 2004). Good histories of the probation service can be found in Vanstone's *Supervising Offenders in the Community: a history of probation theory and practice* (Aldershot: Ashgate, 2004) and Whitehead and Statham's *The History of Probation* (Crayford: Shaw & Sons, 2006). A new *Probation Handbook* edited by Gelsthorpe and Morgan is in preparation for Willan. For NOMS, see Patrick Carter's original report, *Managing Offenders, Reducing Crime* (London: Home Office, 2003) and *Reshaping Probation and Prisons* edited by Hough, Allen, and Padel (Bristol: Policy Press, 2006).

Other useful texts and articles on particular aspects of probation service practice include Trotter's *Working with Involuntary Clients* (London: Sage, 1999), and Bottoms and Stelman's excellent *Social Inquiry Reports* (Aldershot: Wildwood House, 1988). Community service orders (later community punishment orders, now 'unpaid work') were well covered in their early days by texts such as Pease and McWilliams' edited collection, *Community Service by Order* (Edinburgh: Scottish Academic Press, 1980) and, more recently, by McIvor's Scottish evaluative study, *Sentenced to Serve* (Aldershot: Avebury, 1992). References to the Community Service Pathfinder research are given in the main text of this chapter.

The resettlement of prisoners is addressed in a seminal report by the Social Exclusion Unit, *Reducing Re-offending by Ex-Prisoners* (London: SEU, Office of the Deputy Prime Minister, 2002) and in several recent studies, of which the latest is Clancy *et al.*, *Getting out and Staying*

Out (Bristol: Policy Press, 2006). On risk, Kemshall's *Risk in Probation Practice* (Aldershot: Ashgate, 1998) and *Understanding Risk in Criminal Justice* (Buckingham: Open University Press, 2005) are useful, as are a number of articles (for example, Robinson (1999), 'Risk Management and Rehabilitation in the Probation Service: Collision and Collusion, *Howard Journal*, 38(4): 421–33; and Kemshall and Maguire (2001), 'Public Protection, Partnership and Risk Penality: The Multi-Agency Risk Management of Sexual and Violent Offenders', *Punishment and Society*, 3: 237–64).

Lastly, the recent literature on 'What Works' includes two excellent edited collections, one from Britain and one from America: McGuire's *Offender Rehabilitation and Treatment* (Chichester: Wiley, 2002) and Harland's *Choosing Correctional Options that Work* (Thousand Oaks, Cal.: Sage, 1996). Anyone still needing to be convinced about why probation and resettlement services are necessary and useful might try Tony Parker's *The Unknown Citizen* (London: Hutchinson, 1963).

■ REFERENCES

ADAMS, S. (1961), 'Interaction between individual interview therapy and treatment amenability in older youth authority wards', in *Inquiries Concerning Kinds of Treatment for Kinds of Offenders*, 27–44 Sacramento, Cal.: California Board of Corrections,

ALDRIDGE, M., and EADIE, C. (1997), 'Manufacturing an Issue: the Case of Probation Officer Training', *Critical Social Policy*, 17: 111–24.

ANDREWS, D. A., ZINGER, I., HOGE, R. D., BONTA, J., GENDREAU, P., and CULLEN, F. T. (1990), 'Does Correctional Treatment Work? A Clinically Relevant and Psychologically Informed Meta-Analysis', *Criminology*, 28: 369–404.

BECK, U. (1992), *Risk Society: Towards a New Modernity*, London: Sage.

BERNTSEN, K., and CHRISTIANSEN, K. (1965), 'A resocialization experiment with short-term offenders', *Scandinavian Studies in Criminology*, 1: 35–54.

BLACKBURN, R. (1980), 'Still not working? A look at recent outcomes in offender rehabilitation', Paper presented at the Scottish Branch of the British Psychological Society Conference on Deviance, University of Stirling.

BLUMSOM, M. (2004), 'First steps and beyond: the pathway to our knowledge of delivering programmes', *VISTA*, 8: 171–6.

BOTTOMS, A. E. (1980), *The Suspended Sentence after Ten Years*. Leeds: Centre for Social Work and Applied Social Studies, University of Leeds.

—— (1995), 'The philosophy and politics of punishment and sentencing', in C. Clarkson and R. Morgan (eds), *The Politics of Sentencing Reform*, Oxford: Clarendon Press.

—— (2001), 'Compliance and community penalties', in A. E. Bottoms, L. Gelsthorpe, and S. Rex (eds), *Community Penalties: Change and Challenges*. Cullompton, Devon: Willan.

—— and McWILLIAMS, W. (1979), 'A non-treatment paradigm for probation practice', *British Journal of Social Work*, 9: 159–202.

BREWER, C., and LAIT, J. (1980), *Can Social Work Survive?*, London: Temple Smith.

BRODY, S. R. (1976), *The Effectiveness of Sentencing*, Home Office Research Study 35, London: HMSO.

CARTER, P. (2003), *Managing Offenders, Reducing Crime: A New Approach*, Correctional Services Review, London: Home Office.

CHAPMAN, T., and HOUGH, M. (1998), *Evidence-Based Practice*, London: Home Office.

CHRISTIE, N. (1993), *Crime Control as Industry*, London: Routledge.

—— (2004), *A Suitable Amount of Crime*, London: Routledge.

CLANCY, A., HUDSON, K., MAGUIRE, M., PEAKE, R., RAYNOR, P., VANSTONE, M., and KYNCH, J. (2006), *Getting Out and Staying Out: results of the prisoner resettlement Pathfinders*, Bristol: Policy Press.

CLARKE, C. (2005), 'Where next for penal policy', Speech to Prison Reform Trust, 19 September.

COHEN, S. (1985), *Visions of Social Control*, Cambridge: Polity Press.

CORRECTIONAL SERVICES ACCREDITATION PANEL (2003), *Report 2002–2003*, London: CSAP.

COX, S. (2005), 'Preliminary findings of two pilot programs to reduce probation violations in Connecticut', Paper to the American Society of Criminology 57th Annual Meeting, Toronto, November.

DAVIES, M. (1969), *Probationers in their Social Environment*, Research Study 2, London: HMSO.

—— (1974), *Social Work in the Environment*, Research Study 21, London: HMSO.

DENMAN, G. (1982), *Intensive Intermediate Treatment with Juvenile Offenders: a Handbook of Assessment and Groupwork Practice*, Lancaster: Centre of Youth, Crime and Community, Lancaster University.

DEWS, V., and WATTS, J. (1994), *Review of Probation Officer Recruitment and Training*, London: Home Office.

DITCHFIELD, J. (1976), *Police Cautioning in England and Wales*, Home Office Research Study 37, London: HMSO.

DOWDEN, C., and ANDREWS, D. (2004), 'The importance of staff practice in delivering effective correctional treatment: a meta-analysis', *International Journal of Offender Therapy and Comparative Criminology*, 48: 203–14.

DRAKEFORD, M. (1983), 'Probation: containment or liberty?', *Probation Journal* 30: 7–10

FARRALL, S. (2002), *Rethinking What Works with Offenders: Probation, Social Context and Desistance from Crime*, Cullompton, Devon: Willan.

FEELEY, M., and SIMON, J. (1992), 'The new penology: notes on the emerging strategy of corrections and its implications', *Criminology*, 30, 449–74.

FOLKARD, M. S., SMITH, D. E., and SMITH, D. D. (1976), *IMPACT Volume II: The results of the experiment*, Home Office Research Study 36, London: HMSO.

FOREN, R., and BAILEY, R. (1968), *Authority in Social Casework*, Oxford: Pergamon Press.

GARLAND, D. (1985), *Punishment and Welfare: A History of Penal Strategies*, Aldershot: Gower.

—— (1995), 'Penal modernism and postmodernism', in T. G. Blomberg and S. Cohen (eds), *Punishment and Social Control*, New York: Aldine de Gruyter.

—— (1997), 'Probation and the reconfiguration of crime control', in R. Burnett (ed.), *The Probation Service: Responding to Change* (Proceedings of the Probation Studies Unit First Colloquium: Probation Studies Unit Report No. 3), Oxford: University of Oxford Centre for Criminological Research.

—— (2001), *The Culture of Control*, Oxford: Oxford University Press.

GENDREAU, P., and ROSS, R. (1980), 'Effective correctional treatment: bibliotherapy for cynics', in R. Ross and P. Gendreau (eds), *Effective Correctional Treatment*, Toronto: Butterworths.

——, GOGGIN, C., and SMITH, P. (1999), 'The forgotten issue in effective correctional treatment: program implementation', *International Journal of Offender Therapy and Comparative Criminology*, 43: 180–7.

GIBSON, B. (2004), *Criminal Justice Act 2003: a guide to the new procedures and sentencing*, Winchester: Waterside Press.

GIDDENS, A. (1990), *The Consequences of Modernity*, Cambridge: Polity Press.

GRÜNHUT, M. (1952), 'Probation in Germany', *Howard Journal*, 8: 168–74.

Guardian, The (2005), 'Clarke to scrap plan to peg prison numbers', *The Guardian*, 19 September, 4.

HALLIDAY, J. (2001), *Making Punishments Work: Report of a Review of the Sentencing Framework for England and Wales*, London: Home Office.

HARPER, G., and CHITTY, C. (2004), *The impact of corrections on re-offending: a review of 'what works'*, Home Office Research Study 291, London: Home Office.

HARRIS, R. (1994), 'Continuity and Change: Probation and Politics in Contemporary Britain', *International Journal of Offender Therapy and Comparative Criminology*, 38: 33–45.

HASLEWOOD-POCSIK, I., MERONE, L., and ROBERTS, C. (2004), *The evaluation of the Employment Pathfinder: lessons from Phase 1 and a survey for Phase 2*, Online Report 22/04. London: Home Office.

HEARNDEN, I., and MILLIE, A. (2003), *Investigating links between probation enforcement and reconviction*. Online Report 41/03. London: Home Office.

HEDDERMAN, C. (2006) 'Keeping a lid on the prison population—will it work?', in M. Hough, R. Allen, and U. Padel (eds), *Reshaping Probation and Prisons: the new offender management framework*, Bristol: Policy Press.

HER MAJESTY'S INSPECTORATE OF PROBATION (2006), *An Independent Review of a Serious Further Offence case: Damien Hanson and Elliot White*, London: HMIP.

HOLLIN, C., PALMER, E., MCGUIRE, J., HOUNSOME, J., HATCHER, R., BILBY, C., and Clark, C. (2004), *Pathfinder Programmes in the Probation Service: a retrospective analysis*, Home Office Online Report 66/04, London: Home Office.

HOLLIS, F. (1964), *Casework: a Psychosocial Therapy*, New York: Random House.

HOME OFFICE (1984), *Probation Service in England and Wales: Statement of National Objectives and Priorities*, London: Home Office.

—— (1988), *Punishment, Custody and the Community*, Cm, 424, London: HMSO.

—— (1990a), *Supervision and Punishment in the Community*, Cm. 966, London: HMSO.

—— (1990b), *Crime, Justice and Protecting the Public*, Cm. 965, London: HMSO.

—— (1995), *Managing What Works: Conference Report and Guidance on Critical Success Factors for Probation Supervision Programmes*, Probation Circular 77/1995, London: Home Office.

—— (1998), *Joining Forces to Protect the Public: Prisons-Probation*, London: Home Office.

—— (2004a), *Probation Statistics England and Wales 2002*, London: Home Office.

—— (2004b), *Reducing Re-offending National Action Plan*, London: Home Office.

—— (2005a), *Restructuring Probation to Reduce Re-offending*, London: Home Office.

—— (2005b), *NOMS Partial Regulatory Impact Assessment*, London: Home Office.

—— (2005c), *The NOMS Offender Management Model*, London: Home Office. Available at, www.noms.homeoffice.gov.uk/downloads/NOMS_Offender_Management_Model.pdf.

—— (2006), *Working with probation to protect the public and reduce re-offending*, London: Home Office.

—— RDS NOMS (2005), *Offender Management Statistics 2004*, London: Home Office.

HOMEL, P., NUTLEY, S., WEBB, B., and TILLEY, N. (2005), *Investing to Deliver: reviewing the implementation of the UK Crime Reduction Programme*, Home Office Research Study No. 281, London: Home Office.

HOOD, R. (1974), *Tolerance and the Tariff*, London: NACRO.

HOUGH, M. (ed.) (2004), *Criminal Justice* 4(3), Special Issue: *Evaluating the Crime Reduction Programme in England and Wales*.

——, ALLEN, R., and PADEL, U. (eds) (2006), *Reshaping Probation and Prisons: the new offender management framework*, Bristol: Policy Press.

HUDSON, B. (2003), *Justice in the Risk Society*, London: Sage.

HUNT, A. W. (1964), 'Enforcement in probation casework', *British Journal of Delinquency*, 4: 239–52.

JONES, K. (2001), 'Probation in Romania', *Probation Journal*, 48: 269–79.

KEMSHALL, H., and MAGUIRE, M. (2001), 'Public protection, partnership and risk penality: the multiagency risk management of sexual and violent offenders', *Punishment and Society*, 3: 237–64.

——, MACKENZIE, G., WOOD, J., BAILEY, R., and YATES, J. (2005), *Strengthening Multi-Agency Public Protection Arrangements*, Home Office Development and Practice Report 45, London: Home Office.

KENT PROBATION AND AFTER-CARE SERVICE (1981), 'Probation Control Unit: a community-based experiment in intensive supervision', in *Annual Report on the Work of the Medway Centre*, Maidstone: Kent Probation and After-Care Service.

KNOTT, C. (1995), 'The STOP programme: reasoning and rehabilitation in a British setting', in J. McGuire ed., *What Works* 115–26, Chichester: Wiley.

LABOUR PARTY (2005), *The Labour Party Manifesto*, London: The Labour Party.

LAPPI-SEPPÄLÄ, T. (2005), 'Penal Policy in Finland', *Criminology in Europe*, 4: 3–15.

LEWIS, S., RAYNOR, P., SMITH, D., and WARDAK, A. (eds) (2006), *Race and Probation*, Cullompton, Devon: Willan.

——, VENNARD, J., MAGUIRE, M., RAYNOR, P., VANSTONE, M., RAYBOULD, S., and RIX, A. (2003), *The Resettlement of Short-term Prisoners: An Evaluation of Seven Pathfinders*, RDS Occasional Paper No. 83, London: Home Office.

LIPSEY, M. (1992), 'Juvenile delinquency treatment: a meta-analytic enquiry into the variability of effects', in T. Cook, H. Cooper, D. S. Cordray, H. Hartmann, L. V. Hedges, R. L. Light, T. A. Louis, and F. Mosteller (eds), *Meta-Analysis for Explanation: a case-book*, 83–127, New York: Russell Sage.

—— (1999), 'Can rehabilitative programs reduce the recidivism of juvenile offenders? An inquiry into the effectiveness of practical programs', *Virginia Journal of Social Policy and the Law*, 6: 611–41.

LIPTON, D., MARTINSON, R., and WILKS, J. (1975), *The Effectiveness of Correctional Treatment*, New York: Praeger.

LOPEZ-REY, M. (1957), 'United Nations activities and international trends in probation', *Howard Journal*, 9: 346–53.

McGuire, J. (ed.) (1995), *What Works: Reducing Reoffending*, Chichester: Wiley.

—— (2000), *Cognitive-Behavioural Approaches*, London: Home Office.

McIvor, G. (1990), *Sanctions for Serious or Persistent Offenders*, Stirling: Social Work Research Centre.

—— (1992), *Sentenced to Serve*, Aldershot: Avebury.

McMahon, G., Hall, A., Hayward, G., Hudson, C., and Roberts, C. (2004), *Basic Skills Programmes in the Probation Service: an Evaluation of the Basic Skills Pathfinder*, Home Office Research Findings 203, London: Home Office.

McWilliams, W. (1983),'The mission to the English Police Courts 1876–1936', *Howard Journal*, 22: 129–47.

—— (1985), 'The Mission Transformed: Professionalisation of Probation Between the Wars', *Howard Journal*, 24: 257–74.

—— (1986), 'The English Probation System and the Diagnostic Ideal', *Howard Journal*, 25: 241–60.

—— (1987), 'Probation, pragmatism and policy', *Howard Journal*, 26: 97–121.

Maguire, M., and Raynor, P. (1997), 'The revival of throughcare: rhetoric and reality in Automatic Conditional Release', *British Journal of Criminology*, 37(1): 1–14.

—— and —— (2006), 'How the resettlement of prisoners promotes desistance from crime: or does it?', *Criminology and Criminal Justice*, 6: 19–38.

——, Perroud, B., and Raynor, P. (1996), *Automatic Conditional Release: the first two years*, Research Study 156, London, Home Office.

——, Raynor, P., Vanstone, M., and Kynch, J. (2000), 'Voluntary after-care and the Probation Service: a case of diminishing responsibility', *Howard Journal of Criminal Justice*, 39: 234–48.

Mair, G. (1988), *Probation Day Centres*, Home Office Research Study 100, London: HMSO.

—— (ed.) (2004), *What Matters in Probation*, Cullompton, Devon: Willan.

——, Lloyd, C., Nee, C., and Sibbitt, R. (1994), *Intensive Probation in England and Wales: an evaluation*, London: HMSO.

Martinson, J. (1974), 'What works? Questions and answers about prison reform', *The Public Interest*, 35: 22–54.

—— (1979), 'New findings, new views: a note of caution regarding sentencing reform', *Hofstra Law Review*, 7: 243–58.

Maruna, S. (2001) *Making Good*. Washington: American Psychological Association.

Monger, M. (1964), *Casework in Probation*, London: Butterworth.

Morgan, R. (2002), 'Something has got to give', *HLM—the Howard League Magazine* 20 (4): 7–8.

—— (2003), 'Foreword', *Her Majesty's Inspectorate of Probation Annual Report 2002/2003*, London: Home Office.

National Association of Probation Officers (2001), 'AGM resolutions 2001', *NAPO News*, 134: 10–15.

—— (2005), *Restructuring Probation: What Works?*, London: NAPO.

—— (2006), 'NOMS legislation pulled!', *NAPO News*, 176, February: 1.

National Probation Service (2001), *A New Choreography*, London: Home Office.

—— (2005). *Performance Report 18 and Weighted Scorecard Q2 2005/06*, London: National Probation Service.

Nellis, M. (2004a), 'The Electronic monitoring of Offenders in Britain: a critical overview', in S. Collett (ed.), *Electronic Monitoring of Offenders: Key Developments*, ICCJ Monograph 5, London: NAPO.

—— (2004b), 'Into the Field of Corrections: the end of English probation in the early 21st century?', *Cambrian Law Review* 35: 115–34

NOMS (2005), *National Standards 2005*, London: National Offender Management Service.

—— and Youth Justice Board (2005), *NOMS and YJB Approach to Communities and Civil Renewal*, London: NOMS and YJB.

OASys Development Team (2001), *Offender Assess-ment System User Manual*, London: Home Office.

PA Consulting Group (2005), *Action Research Study of the Implementation of the National Offender Management Model in the North West Pathfinder*, London: PA Consulting Group.

Palmer, T. (1974), 'The Youth Authority's Community Treatment Project', *Federal Probation*, 38: 3–14.

—— (1975), 'Martinson revisited', *Journal of Research in Crime and Delinquency*, 12: 133–52.

Partridge, S. (2004), *Examining Case Management Models for Community Sentences*, Home Office Online Report 17/04, London: Home Office.

Pease, K., and McWilliams, W. (eds) (1980), *Community Service by Order*, Edinburgh: Scottish Academic Press.

PEASE, K., BILLINGHAM, S., and EARNSHAW, I. (1977), *Community Service Assessed in 1976*, Home Office Research Study No. 39, London: HMSO.

PLOEG, G. J. (2003), 'Moving Probation Forward: a review', *Bulletin of the Conférence Permanente Européenne de la Probation*, 29: 8.

PROBATION BOARDS ASSOCIATION (2004), *Response to 'Managing Offenders: Reducing Crime' and 'Reducing Crime: Changing Lives'*, London: PBA.

—— (2005), *PBA response to restructuring probation*. London: PBA.

RADZINOWICZ, L. (ed.) (1958), *The Results of Probation*, A Report of the Cambridge Department of Criminal Science, London: Macmillan.

RAYNOR, P. (1988), *Probation as an Alternative to Custody*, Aldershot: Avebury.

—— (1998), 'Reading Probation Statistics: a Critical Comment', *VISTA*, 3: 181–5.

—— (2001), 'Community penalties and social integration: "community" as solution and as problem', in A. Bottoms, L. Gelsthorpe, and S. Rex (eds), *Community Penalties: Change and Challenges*, Cullompton, Devon: Willan.

—— (2002), 'Community penalties: probation, punishment and "what works" ', in M. Maguire, R. Morgan, and R. Reiner, (eds), *The Oxford Handbook of Criminology*, 3rd edn, Oxford: Oxford University Press.

—— (2004a), 'Rehabilitative and reintegrative approaches', in A. Bottoms, S. Rex, and G. Robinson (eds), *Alternatives to Prison*, 195–223, Cullompton, Devon: Willan.

—— (2004b), 'The probation service "pathfinders": finding the path and losing the way?', *Criminal Justice*, 4: 309–25.

—— (2006), 'Risk and need in British probation: the contribution of LSI-R', *Psychology, Crime and Law* (forthcoming).

—— and MAGUIRE, M. (2006), 'End-to-end or end in tears? Prospects for the effectiveness of the National Offender Management Model', in M. Hough, R. Allen, and U. Padel (eds), *Reshaping probation and prisons. The new offender management framework*, Bristol: Policy Press.

—— and ROBINSON, G. (2005), *Rehabilitation, Crime and Justice*, Basingstoke: Palgrave Macmillan.

—— and VANSTONE, M. (1994), 'Probation practice, effectiveness and the non-treatment paradigm', *British Journal of Social Work*, 24: 387–404.

—— and —— (1996), 'Reasoning and Rehabilitation in Britain: the results of the Straight Thinking On Probation (STOP) programme', *International Journal of Offender Therapy and Comparative Criminology*, 40: 272–84.

—— and —— (1997), *Straight Thinking On Probation (STOP): The Mid Glamorgan Experiment. Probation Studies Unit Report No. 4*, Oxford: University of Oxford Centre for Criminological Research.

—— and —— (2001), 'Straight Thinking On Probation: evidence-based practice and the culture of curiosity', in G. Bernfeld, D. Farrington, and A. Leschied (eds), *Offender rehabilitation in practice*, Chichester: Wiley.

—— and —— (2002), *Understanding Community Penalties*, Buckingham: Open University Press.

——, KYNCH, J., ROBERTS, C., and MERRINGTON, M. (2000), *Risk and Need Assessment in Probation Services: an Evaluation*, Research Study 211, London: Home Office.

REX, S., and GELSTHORPE, L. (2002), 'The role of Comm-unity Service in reducing offending: evaluating pathfinder projects in the UK', *Howard Journal*, 41: 311–25.

——, ——, ROBERTS, C., and JORDAN, P. (2003), *Crime Reduction Programme: an Evaluation of Community Service Pathfinder Projects: Final Report 2002*, RDS Occasional Paper 87, London: Home Office.

RICHMOND, M. (1917), *Social Diagnosis*, New York: Russell Sage Foundation.

ROBERTS, C. (1989), *Hereford and Worcester Probation Service Young Offender Project: first evaluation report*, Oxford: Department of Social and Administrative Studies.

—— (2004a), 'An early evaluation of a cognitive offending behaviour programme ("Think First") in probation areas', *VISTA*, 8: 137–45.

—— (2004b), 'Offending behaviour programmes: emerging evidence and implications for research', in R. Burnett and C. Roberts (eds), *What Works in Probation and Youth Justice*, 134–58, Cullompton, Devon: Willan.

ROBINSON, G. (1999), 'Risk management and rehabilitation in the probation service: collision and collusion, *Howard Journal*, 38(4): 421–33.

—— (2003), 'Technicality and indeterminacy in probation practice: a case study', *British Journal of Social Work*, 33: 593–610.

—— (2005), 'What works in offender management?', *Howard Journal*, 44: 307–18.

—— and RAYNOR, P. (2006), 'The future of rehabilitation: what role for the Probation Service?', *Probation Journal*, 53(4): 334–6.

Ross, R. R., Fabiano, E. A., and Ewles, C. D. (1988), 'Reasoning and rehabilitation', *International Journal of Offender Therapy and Comparative Criminology*, 32: 29–35.

Rotman, E. (1990), *Beyond Punishment: A New View of the Rehabilitation of Offenders*, Westport, Conn.: Greenwood Press.

Rumgay, J. (1989), 'Talking tough: empty threats in probation practice', *Howard Journal*, 28: 177–86.

Shaw, M. (1974), *Social Work in Prisons*, Home Office Research Study 22, London: HMSO.

—— and Hannah-Moffatt, K. (2004), 'How cognitive skills forgot about gender and diversity', in G. Mair (ed.) *What Matters In Probation*, Cullompton, Devon: Willan.

Sinclair, I. (1971), *Hostels for Probationers*, Home Office Reasearch Study 6, London: HMSO.

Smith, D. (1995), *Criminology for Social Work*, Basingstoke: Macmillan.

Social Exclusion Unit (2002), *Reducing Re-offending by Ex-prisoners*, London: Office of the Deputy Prime Minister.

Stern, V. (1998), *A Sin Against the Future: Imprisonment in the World*, Harmondsworth: Penguin.

Thornton, D. (1987), 'Treatment effects on recidivism: a reappraisal of the nothing works doctrine', in B. McGurk, D. Thornton, and M. Williams (eds), *Applying Psychology to Imprisonment. Theory and Practice*, London: HMSO.

Thorpe, D. H., Smith, D., Green, C. J., and Paley, J. (1980), *Out of Care*, London: Allen & Unwin.

Thorpe, J. (1979), *Social Inquiry Reports: a survey*, Home Office Research Study 48, London: HMSO.

Tonry, M. (2004), *Punishment and Politics*, Cullompton, Devon: Willan.

Trotter, C. (1993), *The Supervision of Offenders— What Works? A Study Undertaken in Community Based Corrections, Victoria*, Melbourne: Social Work Department, Monash University and Victoria Department of Justice.

Turnbull, P., McSweeney, T., Webster, R., Edmunds, M., and Hough, M. (2000), *Drug Treatment and Testing Orders: final evaluation report*, Home Office Research Study 212, London: Home Office.

Underdown, A. (1998), *Strategies for Effective Supervision: Report of the HMIP What Works Project*, London: Home Office.

van Kalmthout, A., and Derks, J. (2000), *Probation and Probation Services: a European perspective*, Nijmegen: Wolf Legal Publishers.

Vanstone, M. (2004), *Supervising Offenders in the Community: A History of Probation Theory and Practice*, Aldershot: Ashgate.

—— and Raynor, P. (1981), 'Diversion from prison— a partial success and a missed opportunity', *Probation Journal*, 28: 85–9.

von Hirsch, A. (1976), *Doing Justice: The Choice of Punishments*, Report of the Committee for the Study of Incarceration, New York: Hill and Wang.

Walker, N., Farrington, D., and Tucker, G. (1981), 'Reconviction rates of adult males after different sentences', *British Journal of Criminology*, 21: 357–60.

Wilkins, L. T. (1958), 'A small comparative study of the results of probation', *British Journal of Delinquency*, 8: 201–9.

Wilkinson, J. (1997), 'The Impact of Ilderton Motor Project on Motor Vehicle Crime and Offending', *British Journal of Criminology*, 37: 568–81.

—— (1998), 'Developing the evidence-base for probation programmes', PhD thesis, University of Surrey.

Zamble, E., and Quinsey, V. (1997), *The Criminal Recidivism Process*, Cambridge: Cambridge University Press.

32

IMPRISONMENT: AN EXPANDING SCENE

Rod Morgan and Alison Liebling

The aim of this chapter is to examine five questions. What are the social forces associated with the emergence and use of imprisonment? What are the purposes of imprisonment and what objectives should prison administrators pursue? How are prisons currently organized and made accountable? What is the character of the growing prison population? How do the changing dynamics of prison life—that is, the sociology of the prison—affect the prison experience and the stated objectives?

SETTING THE SCENE

The incarceration rate in England and Wales is the highest in Western Europe (Home Office 2005a: Figure 8.14). The Criminal Justice Act 2003 introduced several new sentences that make it likely that the heavy reliance on custody will continue (see Ashworth, Chapter 29, this volume). There are currently around 80,000 persons in prison in England and Wales, 7,000 in Scotland and 1,300 in Northern Ireland. In the case of England and Wales this is almost double the numbers imprisoned in 1991–2. Having risen modestly during the 1980s the prison population peaked at around 50,000 in 1988–9 then declined to around 45,000 during the period 1990–3. It rose dramatically to 62,000 by the time of the 1997 General Election, following a reactive turnaround by the Conservative Party and a declaration by the then Home Secretary that 'prison works'. Contrary to expectations, the prison population has risen steeply throughout Labour's tenure. (see Figure 32.1)

IMPRISONMENT 1945 TO 2006

During the period 1945–85 the prison system in England and Wales suffered escalating overcrowding. There was virtually no overcrowding in the 1950s, but it reached

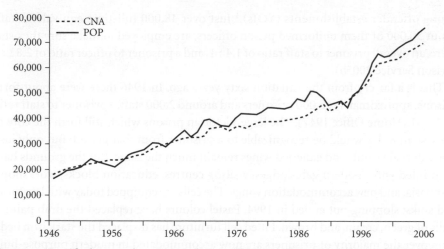

Fig. 32.1 Certified normal accommodation (CNA) and average prison population (POP), 1946–2005

Source: Annual *Prison Statistics* to 2002 and thereafter RDS/NOMS online.

10–15 per cent by the 1980s. There then began the largest prison building programme since the middle of the nineteenth century. Between 1980 and 2006 25 new prisons were opened providing 14,285 additional places (since the early 1990s all new prisons have been built and operated by the private sector, see further below). Twice this number of places has been created by developing existing prisons and inserting new accommodation or 'ready to use' units within their grounds. These additions represented a 50 per cent increase in capacity. The total number of prison places and prisoners came briefly into equilibrium during 1993. By spring 1994, however, the surge in prison numbers brought a return to overcrowding, which, despite the addition of several new prisons and the construction of extra accommodation at existing sites, has continued ever since. The average size of a prison has increased from around 400 to around 800 prisoners (with some holding over 1,300). Further, because some spare capacity must always be reserved, and because there is always a disparity between the geographical location and type of prisoners and available places, many individual prisons are seriously crowded. The London area, for example, has 13,000 prisoners but only 7,500 places. Prisoners from London are therefore exported to the south east, south west, and eastern area (and sometimes further afield). At the close of 2005, 33 of the 142 prisons were crowded above their 'certified normal accommodation' by 30 or more per cent. The term 'operational capacity' (safe level of overcrowding) has been introduced to cater for this long-term problem. An expenditure of £1.5 billion (at £110,000 per new prison place) would be required to solve the crisis, at today's population figure.

This massive expansion is costing a great deal of money, as well as making it difficult to locate prisoners close to their home areas. About £14 billion is currently spent on 'law and order' services of which 16 per cent, or £2.4 billion, goes on prisons. This translates to a cost to the taxpayer of £26,412 per prisoner per annum, or £508 per week (Prison Service 2005a: 103). About 120,000 individuals are committed annually to prison or to young offender establishments (YOIs).[1] Just over 48,000 full-time equivalent staff, about 30,000 of them uniformed prison officers, are employed to make sure they stay there, an overall prisoner to staff ratio of 1.4 : 1, and a prisoner to officer ratio of 2.82 : 1 (Prison Service 2005b).

This is a far cry from the situation sixty years ago. In 1946 there were about forty prisons, approximately 15,000 prisoners and around 2,000 staff, a prisoner to staff ratio of 7.5 : 1 (Home Office 1947). The large Victorian prisons which still form the core of the system today would be recognizable to a prisoner from that period. But only just. The external layouts and galleried wings remain much the same. But the grounds have been filled with modern gate-lodges, visiting centres, education blocks, workshops, gymnasia, and new accommodation wings. The cells are equipped today with lavatories and sinks: slopping-out ended in 1994. Pastel colours have replaced the drab painted walls of green, cream, and brown. Fitted cell furniture has displaced the stark iron beds. Moreover the majority of prisoners are now accommodated in modern purpose-built establishments constructed since the 1950s on greenfield sites, many of them replacing the converted houses and wartime camps that were taken over for use as prisons in the immediate post-war period.

Managerially, prison life has been transformed. Whereas sixty years ago prison governors were largely autonomous and well out of reach of headquarters, today performance management systems, area managers, and modern technology have made it possible for the Director General to have a 'management reach' into establishments that was unimaginable during the post-war era. Governors are described as 'looking upwards', and multiple, and specific objectives are set and closely monitored from above.

The social character of prison life has changed dramatically. There are no longer rows of convicts hand-sewing mailbags in silence. The flogging triangles and bread and water dietary punishments have been abolished and the shabby ill-fitting serge uniforms of grey and brown have gone. When they are not alone (or doubled up) locked into their better-appointed cells, or milling about in groups on the landings and in the recreational areas, prisoners are now more likely to be engaged in literacy programmes, occupational training, and a variety of offence-focused courses, including drug treatment, shod in their own trainers. Nevertheless, though prisoners now have more material comforts, may use the telephone, and can see their families more often in more civilized environments, these gains have to be set against new psychological pressures and insecurities that have not diminished the pains of imprisonment. For some prisoners these pains prove unbearable.

First, most contemporary prisoners are in custody for longer than their predecessors. Though imprisonment was used proportionately more often by the courts in the 1940s, the sentences were typically short compared to now, though there has been a dramatic

---

[1]   Custodial provisions for juveniles have since April 2000 been subject to the direction of the Youth Justice Board (YJB) which acts as the purchaser for services provided by the Prison Service (see Morgan and Newburn, Chapter 30, this volume).

increase in the number of short prison sentences in the last ten years. In 1945 only 10 per cent of offenders sentenced to immediate imprisonment were given more than 12 months, life sentences were rare, and prisoners serving determinate sentences over 10 years almost unknown. Of the daily average sentenced population fewer than 7 per cent were serving four years or more. Today one-third of all prison sentences are for one year or more, over half the average daily sentenced population are serving four years of whom over five and a half thousand are serving a life sentence (Home Office 2005a: Tables 7.1 and 8.1).

Secondly, prisoners now are subject to security measures unknown or scarcely developed sixty years ago—prison perimeters made virtually impenetrable by multiple high-tech barriers, landings and stairwells draped with wire mesh, CCTV, electronic locking systems, intensive staff surveillance, strip searches, and random compulsory drug testing. Moreover, the amount of time many prisoners now spend out of their cells is modest compared to that which was taken for granted in most training prisons thirty years ago. Communal activities, like eating in dining halls, for example, are today considered too risky an arrangement to be generally viable. Instead, prisoners collect their meals on a tray and eat in their cells.

It is difficult to assess whether prisons have become less orderly and safe. Concerted acts of prisoner indiscipline used to be rare (Fox 1952: 160) and staff industrial action unheard of. In the 1980s, culminating in the Strangeways and associated riots of 1990, prison disturbances became frequent and managing prison officers was for a period a more difficult task for prison administrators than managing prisoners. The serious industrial disputes and prisoner disorders in the 1970s and 1980s led to two major inquiries—the May Committee in 1978–9 and the judicial inquiry conducted by Lord Justice Woolf in 1990–1—the reports of which have become landmarks for analysts of prisons policy. Fear became a significant feature of prison life during the 1980s (King and McDermott 1995: ch. 3). By the early 1990s both hard and soft drugs were freely available in many prisons—a trend which the Prison Service is trying to reverse (Edgar and O'Donnell 1998; Singleton *et al.* 2005: Prison Service 2005a: 110). More than 3,000 prisoners are segregated for their own protection, either under Rule 43 or in vulnerable prisoner units (VPUs) scattered around the country. The number of recorded assaults on both staff and prisoners increased between 1989 and 1994 but has been declining slightly since. In 2004 a new category of 'serious assaults' was introduced, making longitudinal comparisons difficult. In 2005, 78 prisoners committed suicide, a substantial reduction from previous years (95 in 2004, 93 in 2003, and 95 in 2002). This reduction may reflect a renewed emphasis on suicide prevention and substantial investment in new, first night, reception, and induction procedures and facilities in high-risk (local) prisons. Two sets of escapes from maximum security prisons in 1994–5, however, led to increased internal as well as perimeter security, to greater staff vigilance, and to the use of incentives and earned privileges schemes aimed at increasing prisoner compliance.

THE POLITICS OF IMPRISONMENT

It is now several years since the last major prison riot. But robustly independent, critical Chief Inspectors of Prisons have repeatedly identified 'appalling' or 'unhealthy' prisons in which regimes are impoverished and the staff culture is antagonistic. Prisons are: costly; overcrowded, a constant management headache; apparently difficult places in which to maintain a positive regime (Laming Report 2000); a conspicuous failure in terms of the subsequent behaviour of those committed to them (about three-quarters of all young offenders and over half of all adults are reconvicted within two years of release—Home Office 2005a: ch. 11); and of marginal value in terms of public protection, because so small a proportion of those responsible for offences are caught, convicted, and imprisoned (estimated as 0.3 per cent—see Home Office 1999: 29).

All of the above means that there is perennial debate about the purpose and value of imprisonment. What constitutes a sensible rate of imprisonment? Though international comparisons are fraught with difficulty (Pease 1994), England and Wales rely on the use of imprisonment to an extent greater than practically all other countries in western Europe. In 2005 141 persons were incarcerated per 100,000 population in England and Wales, compared to 97 in Germany and Italy, 88 in France, 81 in Sweden, and 65 in Norway (ICPS January 2006, www.prisonstudies.org). There are other countries with far higher incarceration rates—the USA, China, and most countries in eastern Europe, for example. But these countries have markedly different serious crime rates, histories, or political cultures. They do not make comfortable penal bedfellows.

Should we be unconcerned about the size of our prison population and focus rather on the serious crime against which the courts have a duty to protect the public? If locking up more offenders means that conditions in prisons are less than ideal, should we conclude that this is no more than prisoners deserve? Or does the prison reflect a punitive obsession, and a largely ineffective crime-control device, the use of which we could significantly reduce without risk to anyone? Should we regard poor prison conditions as a bar to our claims to be civilized and a misuse of state power against vulnerable and disadvantaged minorities? What should prisons be like: dark deterrent statements of the consequences of committing crime; training camps in citizenship; human warehouses; or protective therapeutic communities for damaged and sometimes dangerous offenders?

THE EMERGENCE OF THE MODERN PRISON AND
THE USE OF IMPRISONMENT

Prisons, as places of confinement, have existed since time immemorial. Yet prisons as we know them today—places to which offenders are sent as a punishment, there to be changed—are a product of the industrial age. The modern prison emerged slowly in Northern Europe from the sixteenth century onwards, but it was not until the late eighteenth century that the idea came to fruition. The gaols that John Howard travelled the country visiting in the 1770s were mostly small and seldom purpose built. They were rooms in ancient city gateways, stables behind the keeper's house, or cellars within town halls. Only in the major cities were there prisons built for the purpose and here their inhabitants were typically herded together, little subject to regulation save in the exploitative interests of their custodians (Howard 1784). When opened in 1842, Pentonville Prison, dubbed the 'Model Prison', represented the scale of the transformation: over 500 identical cells in each of which a prisoner was separately to live in silence according to a routine meticulously regulated by a uniformed staff employed by the state. The modern prison, and its institutional counterpart—the workhouse for the indigent poor, the asylum for the insane, the reformatory for wayward youth, and the penitentiary for fallen women—reflected what Foucault (1967: ch. 2) termed 'the great confinement' and emerged alongside the factory (Melossi and Pavarini 1981). They were social and architectural counterparts. In the factories labour was rationalized for the purposes of more efficient production. In the new institutions of confinement those unproductive sections of the labour force were differentiated, segregated, and disciplined. John Howard's proposals for the better regulation of the insanitary and morally corrupting gaols of the eighteenth century were the corollary of the managerial revolution being wrought in Richard Arkwrights' mill at Cromford and Josiah Wedgwood's factory at Etruria. Over each of their model buildings, both actually and metaphorically, was placed a clock according to the hands of which everything was now done (McGowan 1995).

Prisons have historically had three uses: *custodial*, *coercive*, and *punitive*. Though imprisonment was used from medieval times as a punishment, it was generally for minor offences (Pugh 1970). Its primary legal function was custodial or coercive. Accused persons were held awaiting 'gaol delivery' (the arrival of travelling courts) or following conviction pending execution of sentence, generally an assault on the body or death, carried out in a public place. To this was later added imprisonment pending transportation to the colonies. The coercive function of imprisonment was almost entirely for civil debt. The modern prison emerged as its function changed from being primarily custodial-coercive to punitive (Radzinowicz and Hood 1990)—a transformation dramatically illustrated in the opening pages of Foucault's seminal study *Discipline and Punish: the Birth of the Prison* (1977), where the grotesquely brutal execution of a regicide in 1757 Paris is juxtaposed with the clockwork precision of a totally regulated daily regime at a Paris reformatory half a century later. For Foucault the modern prison, with its mechanisms of total surveillance, represented a new form of knowledge and power. Between 1750 and 1850, throughout most of Europe, imprisonment became the principal punishment for serious crime—*carceral* rather than *corporal* punishment, addressing the soul (or the mind) rather than the body (or the outward reputation). Judicial torture was formally abolished (Peters 1985), and the death penalty, henceforth carried out within prisons rather than in public, was reserved for only the most heinous crimes (Spierenburg 1984).

During the nineteenth century this transformation was mostly represented as a vital subplot in the Whig version of history as progress: the triumph of reason over superstition, civilization over barbarism. John Howard, Elizabeth Fry, and other penal reformers were depicted as Enlightenment saviours whose efforts ushered in humanity. Some Victorian observers, for example Charles Dickens, had their doubts, discovering in the reformed prisons new torments imposed in the name of the people (Collins 1962), a phenomenon which in the twentieth century became devastatingly apparent with the rise of the totalitarian state, the re-emergence of torture, and the mass incarcerations of the concentration camps, gulags, and Soviet and Chinese resocialization centres (see Stern 1998; Applebaum 2003).

Attention turned to the origins of those mechanisms which twentieth-century states were using to oppress their citizens. Rusche and Kirchheimer (1968), pioneering Marxist theorists in the realm of penal studies, argued that it was not punishment that needed to be explained but specific and concrete *forms of punishment*. Particular penalties, they argued, could be linked to particular modes of production and labour market conditions. When labour was cheap and plentiful, penalties were careless of human life and health. When labour became more valuable the penal system responded to the economic imperatives of the day: transportation was developed to serve the interests of imperialism; the Houses of Correction were designed to make productive use of the recalcitrant poor; and 'less eligibility', the utilitarian doctrine that convicted prisoners are morally less deserving than the least well-off persons enjoying their freedom in the community, and should therefore not enjoy a lifestyle and facilities superior or equal to those enjoyed outside the prisons and workhouses, was an ancillary discipline for the labour market beyond the walls.

Rusche and Kirchheimer's economic determinism was crude and their analysis did not exactly fit the facts. But their work stimulated a wealth of scholarship such that today there is a rich historical penal policy literature on which students may draw. A more nuanced account has emerged of historical and contemporary 'penality', that is, our ideas about and practices of imprisonment (Garland and Young 1983) and how it varies between countries and over time (see the collection of essays in Morris and Rothman 1995). The eighteenth-century penal reformers *were* nearly all motivated by religious faith pursuing what they perceived to be a humanitarian mission. There *was* a growing revulsion against public corporal and capital punishment which, the evidence suggests, was also counterproductive in that it often served to inflame rather than subdue the mob. Imprisonment comprised both a vivid and a subtle symbolic message. The reformed prisons, monolithically built in rusticated stone, generally sited in the new working-class districts of the expanding urban centres, represented the growing power of the state. Whereas the transaction between the public executioner and the hapless offender appeared personal and arbitrary, the mysterious prison represented impersonal regularity, orderliness, and certainty. In the age of liberty it was particularly apt that those who breached the social contract should lose their freedom. Prison sentences were meted out, proportionate to the gravity of the offence and were served, at least in theory, in a perfectly regulated environment where all were stripped of their external identities and treated equally (see Ignatieff 1978; McConville 1981).

The multifaceted appeal of the prison, then and now, emphasizes that imprisonment, like punishment generally, needs to be understood from a variety of perspectives, as: a technical means to an end; a coercive relationship; an instrument of class domination; a form of power; and an expression of collective moral feeling ritually expressed (for a review of the sociological literature, see Garland 1990). To the extent that imprisonment serves different social functions this suggests that attempts to change the degree to which imprisonment is used are unlikely to succeed simply by proclaiming the utilitarian shortcomings of the enterprise.

All developed societies, whatever their ideological pretensions, employ imprisonment as their principal penalty for serious crime. Everyone claims to support the use of imprisonment only as a last resort. Yet the rate at which imprisonment is used varies greatly over time and between jurisdictions (Rutherford 1984; Christie 1994; Cavadino and Dignan 2005). These variations cannot fully be explained by: crime rates; changing fashions in the philosophy of punishment; demographic factors; levels of economic activity; or public policy considerations; though factors subsumed by these headings— unemployment or the supply of prison places, for example—have undoubtedly influenced the rate of imprisonment in some countries in some periods (Zimring and Hawkins 1991). The use of imprisonment is a complex issue (see, for example, Downes 1988 and 1997 for examinations of penal policy in the Netherlands). Yet the rate of imprisonment is not beyond government control. It is ultimately a matter of political choice.

THE PURPOSE OF IMPRISONMENT

THE LEGAL FUNCTIONS OF IMPRISONMENT

The most fundamental way of answering the question, 'What are prisons for', is to distinguish the three legal functions, *custodial*, *coercive*, and *punitive*.

Suspects refused bail and detained before trial, or convicted but not yet sentenced, are held in custody to ensure that the course of justice proceeds to its conclusion and that everyone concerned is protected against the likelihood of harm in the interim. A small number of non-criminal prisoners—held under the Immigration Act, for example—are imprisoned pending completion of enquiries or execution of an administrative decision. There is no justification for holding such prisoners in conditions more oppressive than is warranted by the fact of custody itself, either because they are not eligible for punishment (the unconvicted are subject to the presumption of innocence) or, if convicted, because the court has not yet determined that loss of liberty is the appropriate sentence.

Offenders held coercively—nowadays almost entirely fine defaulters—are kept in prison for as long as they fail to comply with a court order that they pay a financial penalty enforced by the court. As soon as they pay, or once the custodial period in lieu of payment is served, they are released. In this case the prison, the loss of liberty, and possibly also the conditions in custody, is used to pressurize the offender into conforming.

Finally, there are persons held punitively—nowadays the great majority—as a sanction for offences of which they stand convicted. Since the abolition of the death penalty in 1965 imprisonment has been the most serious penalty the courts can impose in Britain. The punishment of imprisonment for sentenced prisoners might comprise both loss of liberty and harsh living conditions in the name of 'less eligibility' (see above) or deterrence. Today prison administrators generally disavow such purposes, reiterating Paterson's famous dictum that offenders are sent to prison 'as a punishment, not for punishment' (Ruck 1951: 23). However, it is difficult to square conditions and practices in many prisons with this disavowal and 'less eligibility' remains a potent political if not administrative imperative (Garland 1990; Sparks 1996). Remand prisoners, in spite of the presumption of innocence, tend to be viewed by prison staff as sentenced prisoners in waiting (Fox 1952: 286). Their living conditions are often among the worst to be found in the system (King and Morgan 1976; Morgan 1993; Scottish Executive 2000; HMCIP 2000a; for recent inspection reports critical of remand conditions in local prisons see HMCIP 2003b and 2005a).

A distinction needs to be drawn between sentencers' purposes and prison managers' objectives. The two should ideally be consistent and spring from the same principles. But they are not the same and, prior to the Human Rights Act 1998, sentencers were not required to spell out the rationale for their decisions. Whatever justifications sentencers have for using imprisonment (see Ashworth, Chapter 29, this volume), prison administrators have to manage prisons with regard to the welfare of staff as well as prisoners. What then inspires the daily management practice of the Prison Service?

THE LEGAL AND MANAGERIAL FRAMEWORK

The primary legislation under which the Prison Service conducts its work is the Prison Act 1952 which lays down the general duties of the prison authorities; defines what a prison is; and empowers the Minister to make rules for the management of prisons (section 47(1)). The rules are exercisable by statutory instrument and were substantially revised in 1999 (S.I. 1999/728). Further amendments were consolidated in 2004. A parallel statutory instrument relates to the management of Young Offender Institutions (YOIs). The core rules regarding purpose remain the same as those dating from 1964 (see Loucks and Plotnikoff 1993). 'The purpose of the training and treatment of convicted prisoners shall be to encourage and assist them to lead a good and useful life' (rule 3). 'Order and discipline shall be maintained with firmness, but with no more restriction than is required for safe custody and well ordered community life' (rule 6). The treatment of prisoners shall also promote 'self-respect' and the development of 'personal responsibility'. However, the rules have always been unspecific about what prisoners should be provided with in terms of conditions and access to facilities. This tendency has now been entrenched by rule 8: there shall 'be established at every prison systems of privileges . . . appropriate to the classes of prisoners there'. The privileges may include time out of cell and in association with other prisoners greater than that normally permitted (rule 8(2)). Further, the system may include arrangements whereby privileges are granted 'to prisoners only in so far as they have met, and for so long as they continue to meet, specified standards in their behaviour and their performance in work or other activities' (rule 8(3)). To emphasize the meaning of the terminology, though the arrangements for granting privileges shall include 'a requirement that the prisoner be given reasons for any decision adverse to him', nothing in rule 8 'shall be taken to confer on a prisoner any *entitlement* to any *privilege*' (emphasis added). Which is to say, the rules do not confer *rights*.

The current rules endorse the operational reality and legal position *status quo ante*. They remain ungenerous in their provisions, are seldom specific, and, even when specific, generally grant prison managers extensive discretion as to whether facilities will be provided (Richardson 1993). The rules are underpinned by an enormous array of administrative directions (manuals; Instructions to Governors (IGs); Advice to Governors (AGs), etc.) that do not have the force of law but may be described as 'plac[ing] a gloss upon the substantive law' (Cheney 1999). They make clear what the courts had previously held, namely, that breaches of the rules do not provide the basis for an action for breach of statutory duty and do not vest prisoners with any special rights (*Hague* v. *Deputy Governor of Parkhurst Prison* [1991] 3 All E.R. 733, confirming *Arbon* v. *Anderson* [1943] K.B. 252). To establish their common law rights prisoners have resorted to the courts, on a case by case basis, to determine their residual position after Lord Wilberforce's dictum in *Raymond* v. *Honey* [1983] 1 A.C. 1, 10): 'A prisoner retains all those rights that are not taken away either express or by necessary implication'.[2] The question at issue, therefore, is whether the arguments which raged in the 1980s about the relative merits of competing formulations to summarize the proper aims of prisons management—'treatment and training', 'humane containment', or 'positive custody'— have been made irrelevant as a result of subsequent managerialist initiatives (for a review of the debate, see Bottoms 1990). The official answer to that question is possibly to be found in the fact that no reference was made to the new 1999 Prison Rules in the annual reports of the Prison Service for 1998–9 and 1999–2000: the emphasis is entirely on Home Office and Prison Service management objectives and performance indicators.

The essence of imprisonment is loss of liberty. Winston Churchill maintained, in a much-quoted passage, that 'the mood and temper of the public in regard to the treatment of crime and criminals is one of the most unfailing tests of the civilisation of any country' (*HC Debates*, col. 1354, 20 July 1910). To ensure that prisoners are not ill-treated, we have to know what is done to them in our collective name.

Since 1878, when prisons were brought wholly under central government control, prisons in England and Wales have been the financial and administrative responsibility of the Home Secretary. Until 1962 the Prison Service was managed by a Prison

---

[2] For detailed reviews of the degree to which the domestic and European courts have intervened in prison life, see Creighton and King 2000; Feldman 2002; Livingstone *et al.* 2003.

Commission, and subsequently a Prison Department, within the Home Office. In 1993 the Prison Service briefly became a government executive agency, but this independence was never achievable in practice and it was formally returned to the Home Office in 2004. Her Majesty's Prison Service is now part of the National Offender Management Service (NOMS) within the Home Office, and is responsible for the management of public-sector prisons. Privately managed prisons constitute a separate strand of NOMS and are currently coordinated through the Office of Contracted Prisons (OCP). Transfer of responsibility to Regional Offender Managers is under way, however. NOMS was established with a Chief Executive in 2004 in order to 'transform the management of offenders and provide clear accountability for reducing reoffending' (Home Office 2005b). One of the key mechanisms is the use of *contestability* or competition between and within the public, private, and voluntary sectors, to ensure the effective implementation of sentences.

The public-sector Prison Service receives its budget from the Chief Executive of NOMS. It is responsible for 131 prisons and is headed by a Director General who is accountable to the Chief Executive of NOMS. Its formal role is to contribute to Home Office Objective 2: to ensure that 'More offenders are caught, punished and stop offending and victims are better supported'. It also contributes to Objectives 1 ('People are and feel more secure in their homes and daily lives') and 3 ('Fewer people's lives are ruined by drugs and alcohol'). It contributes to these objectives by 'holding prisoners securely' and 'reducing the risk of prisoners reoffending' (Prison Service 2005a: 13). Private-sector prisons are also accountable to the Chief Executive of NOMS. There are currently 11 private prisons, operated by four companies. Prisons are organized into geographical areas, and are overseen by Area Managers. Regional Offender Managers (ROMS) are likely to replace Area Managers, however, as they have the criminal justice budget for their regions, and are expected to buy prison places, and other sentence places, from the best providers in their area. These new arrangements are intended to bring about better inter-agency planning and partnership working for such issues as the resettlement of prisoners (but see Hough *et al.* 2006 on the uncertainty generated).

There has always been considerable tension between ministers and senior prison executives, and between individual prisons and headquarters. Both tensions have been the subject of frequent organizational changes intended to clarify responsibilities between 'operations' and 'policy'. In 1995, in the wake of high-profile escapes, the Director General, Derek Lewis, was sacked. The report of the inquiry into the escapes (Learmont 1995) and Lewis's autobiographical account of the period (Lewis 1997) show the extent of day-to-day interference by the Minister. Despite the importance given by Woolf (1991: Section 12) to these matters, they have never been satisfactorily resolved. The current management arrangement acknowledges that ministers wish to be involved in setting strategic policy and should also ensure that the aims and objectives of the Service are integrated with those of the criminal justice system generally. But the emergence of NOMS has introduced ambiguity regarding the division of responsibility between NOMS and Prison Service senior managers.

The Prison Service is required to produce an annual report for the Minister to lay before Parliament, and this is supplemented by an annual statistical account produced by the Home Office. The Service publishes an *Annual Report and Accounts* and a *Corporate and Business Plan*. These and other documents are available on the Prison Service website (details at the end of the chapter). There has been progress in the accountability of the Service as a result of these developments. Until recently, for example, no Service publication provided details about facilities and arrangements (about such matters as visits, for example), a gap which an ex-prisoner remedied by independently producing *The Prisons Handbook* (Leech 2006).

Today there is an informative entry for each prison on the Service website. However, the greater information provided about some aspects of policy and performance in the increasingly glossy *Annual Report* —better financial accounts, performance data by establishment, etc.—is offset by the provision of less or inadequate information about other matters.

Posted at the entrance of all Prison Service establishments is a *Statement of Purpose*:

> Her Majesty's Prison Service serves the public by keeping in custody those convicted by the courts. Our duty is to look after them with humanity and to help them lead law abiding and useful lives in custody and after release.

This *Statement*, with its references to security, basic standards, and rehabilitation, is backed up by an increasingly complex set of interrelated Home Office, Criminal Justice Service, and Prison Service 'aims', 'objectives', 'targets', and 'key performance indicators' (KPIs).

The problems associated with management frameworks of this kind include: paying attention to those aspects of performance that are not easily measured; paying too much attention to that which is easily measured; focusing on *outputs* rather than *outcomes*; stifling professionalism and local initiative by exerting excessively centralized control; and sapping staff morale with too great a burden of bureaucratic compliance and formal inspection processes. Considerable energy has been spent on finding meaningful ways of measuring prison quality and comparing performance, particularly in the light of increased emphasis on competition (see Liebling 2004).

In his report on the 1990 disturbances Lord Woolf found merit in the Prison Service's *Statement of Purpose*, but he added two caveats. He was critical of the absence of any reference to justice and he did not consider the *Statement* adequately covered the unconvicted and unsentenced (Woolf 1991: paras 10.16–64).

Woolf maintained that when the Prison Service says it 'serves the public' it does so by preventing crime. That means, *inter alia:* looking after prisoners with humanity; safeguarding prisoners' 'civil rights which are not taken away expressly or by necessary implication' (*Raymond* v. *Honey* [1982] 1 All E.R. 756 quoted in Woolf: para. 10.22); minimizing 'the negative effects of imprisonment which make re-offending more likely'; ensuring 'that life in prisons . . . [is] as close to life outside as the demands of imprisonment permit'; as well as providing opportunities for training and rehabilitation (para. 10.29). This did not mean 'a return to . . . the treatment model' (para. 10.34) because imprisonment is not justified for reformative purposes, nor is 'being a criminal . . . a creative condition'. But if prisoners are released 'in an embittered and disaffected state' then the criminal justice objective of preventing reoffending is undone (paras. 14.8–9).

> If the Prison Service contains [the] prisoner in conditions which are inhumane or degrading . . . then a punishment of imprisonment which was justly imposed will result in injustice . . . it is the Prison Service's duty to look after prisoners with humanity. If it fulfils this duty, the Prison Service is partly achieving what the Court must be taken to have intended when it passed a sentence of imprisonment [para. 10.19].

Woolf assumed that Paterson's dictum (see above) had come into its own as a statement of what sentencers use prisons for. He was also endorsing the Prison Department view that: 'Imprisonment itself . . . is the punishment inflicted by law and no further available hardship should be imposed on a prisoner except by way of formal disciplinary action' (Home Office 1984: para. 108).

In order that basic living conditions be addressed Woolf favoured an interlocking hierarchy of 'contracts' or 'compacts'—between the Chief Executive of the Service and the Minister, between area managers and governors, between governors and officers, and between governors and prisoners—setting out resources and facilities to be provided for a stated prison population. This would permit, in the case of prisoners, 'legitimate expectations' to be generated (Woolf Report 1991: para. 12.129), which 'could provide a platform for an application for judicial review' were those expectations unreasonably not met (ibid.: para. 12.123). The contracts should not be drawn up in such a way that they would give prisoners private rights leading to awards of damages if breached. But the contracts might lead, Woolf hoped, to the promulgation of aspirational standards, to a system of accrediting prisons for having achieved those standards (as happens in the USA), and, eventually, to the incorporation of those standards in a new set of Prison Rules. Furthermore, Woolf recommended that prisoners be given reasons, in writing if they reasonably request it, 'for any decision which materially and adversely affects them' (ibid.: paras. 14.300, 14.307).

Woolf's recommendation is hazily reflected in prison rule 8(4) which requires that reasons be given to prisoners having privileges withdrawn. However, this is some distance from the proposition that prisoners have 'legitimate expectations' capable of judicial review, a prospect which some critics (Richardson 1993) considered a 'notoriously flexible' doctrine. It is certainly a far cry from the aspirations of earlier critics seeking legally enforceable minimum standards (Casale 1984; Gostin and Staunton 1985; Casale and Plotnikoff 1989, 1990).

The Prison Service has taken several steps in the direction of securing performance standards, and increasing prisoners' perceptions of justice, albeit with certain deviations along the way. Woolf's 'contracts' have been turned, through the 'national framework for incentives and earned privileges' (IEPs) (Prison Service 1996: 26–7), and as some commentators warned was likely (Casale 1993), into mechanisms for exerting greater control *over* prisoners rather than establishing minimum standards and rights for *their* protection (for an evaluation of the IEP scheme see Liebling *et al*. 1997, 1999). These are the arrangements legitimated by rule 8. Secondly, the Prison Service has developed a set of 61 Performance Standards which: 'conform to current legislation'; are 'achievable and affordable across the Service'; are 'measurable and auditable'; and which 'communicate clearly and succinctly what the Prison Service *aims* to deliver and why' (emphasis added); they keep 'prescriptive elements to the minimum required to achieve consistent delivery of Service' and they 'do not change the legal rights of individuals nor do they imply additional rights or entitlements' (Prison Service 2000). The current Standards do not incorporate any minimum standards for untried and unsentenced prisoners beyond those meagre provisions in the Prison Rules (HMCIP 2000a: 22).

Thus prisoners can still be transferred in large numbers, without explanation, to prisons relatively distant from their homes in order better to distribute prisoner numbers within the prison estate, or as an administrative control measure. Prisoners still have no entitlement to be given reasons for either their initial or subsequent security classification, a decision which critically affects the quality of their lives. And Woolf's key proposal to prevent overcrowding and thereby safeguard basic living conditions—that there be introduced a prison rule that no prison hold more prisoners than 3 per cent above its certified normal accommodation (CNA), except temporarily, or following the laying by the Minister of an authorizing certificate before both Houses of Parliament (Woolf Report: paras. 11.141–11.142)—was initially rejected (Home Office 1991: para 6.13) and has not subsequently been resurrected. On the other hand, adjudications likely to involve the awarding of additional days must now be heard by a district judge, and all adjudication decisions are reviewed at Area Manager level.

The case for having legally enforceable, detailed standards remains as strong as ever. The process of contracting out the management of prisons, and the performance-testing of existing public-sector prisons, is keeping the question of what custodial standards should apply to the fore.

PRIVATIZATION AND PERFORMANCE TESTING

Privatization was arguably the most controversial prisons development of the 1990s (for reviews of competing arguments see Logan 1990; Shichor 1995). The privatized management of prisons has been vigorously opposed in principle on the grounds that the administration of state punishment is fundamentally a state responsibility and because it is wrong to derive financial profit from it. A pragmatic long-term objection is that the growth of privatized prisons represents an investment stake by the shrinking military-industrial complex in the burgeoning crime-control industry, an investment which will create a vested commercial interest in the expanded use of imprisonment. The huge growth of the prison and gaol population in the United States, which is now well in excess of two million or 724 per 1,000,000 population (almost six times the rate in the UK—see KCPS 2006), is taken by some to be the spectre to which privatization might contribute (Christie 1994; Donziger 1995). However, most of the argument about privatization has concerned day-to-day accountability and standards.

The Criminal Justice Act 1991 provided that for every contracted-out prison a 'controller', a Crown servant, should be appointed to oversee the running of the prison and ensure compliance with the Prison Rules and the specific terms of the contract. The 'prison custody officers' and the 'director' appointed by the contractor must be approved and though they have the power to search prisoners and their visitors they do not yet have formal disciplinary powers. These are vested in the controller, who in practice is a governor-grade employee of the Prison Service with an office within the contracted-out prison. Thus, it has been argued by some, contracted-out prisons are *more accountable* than state-run prisons (Harding 1997), although discussions are under way (and provisions drafted in the delayed Management of Offenders and Sentencing Bill) to allow private prison directors to take over the disciplinary function. In addition to the general legal framework, the contract is regarded as a means of delivering the higher standards which are only slowly being enforced in state-run establishments via competition and performance-testing. Moreover, the contracting out of particular services within prisons—employment, education, and training, the provision of food, laundry, medical services, and so on—arguably represents the 'normalization' of prison regimes for which many critics have long pressed. It is doubtful whether privatization in the UK reflects the demise of the rehabilitative ideal and acceptance that prisoners can as easily be warehoused by the private sector as the state (Beyens and Snacken 1996: 241). The early English evidence, which may not be replicated in other jurisdictions, is that contracts have been used to attempt to breathe life back into the rehabilitative ideal and stimulate cross-fertilization of practice between state and privately managed institutions.

The deeply felt antagonisms over privatization—not least among the prison staff associations who have vigorously opposed it, but from whose senior ranks the security industry has easily recruited its directors—has stimulated a process of selective reporting which has made objective appraisal difficult. The Government pursued privatization primarily to tackle restrictive staff practices, and thus high costs, in a state-run system not reputed for its innovative or effective management. By this test the success of the initiative does not rest on the relative unit costs of contracted-out compared to state-run institutions—costs that for various reasons are difficult to compare—but rather in the degree to which practices in state-run prisons are transformed by the threat of privatization and the need to tender against contractor-competitors. What is clear is that the small contracted-out sector is setting some high standards—as the House of Commons Home Affairs Committee (1997) and successive inspection reports from the Chief Inspector testify (see, for example, HMCIP 1999b, 2001b)—though not always (see James *et al.* 1997; Park 2000; National Audit Office 2003; HMCIP 2002, 2003a). Poorly performing public-sector prisons (and more recently, even highly performing prisons) are increasingly being required to bid against the private sector to retain management of their establishments. So far the public sector has been successful in these competitions. Those prisons that have been through such performance-testing processes also operate on a contract or 'Service Level Agreement' (SLA), to which they are held.

INSPECTION AND COMPLAINTS

Every prison in England and Wales is served by an Independent Monitoring Board (IMB, formerly boards of visitors (BoV)), a body of lay volunteers appointed by the Secretary of State. IMB members are independent and unpaid, appointed by Home Office Ministers to monitor the day-to-day life in their local prison and ensure that proper standards of care and decency are maintained. The boards have four functions: to monitor the fair treatment and welfare of prisoners and deal with any complaints or requests they make; to monitor the regimes, state, and administration of the prison; to listen to the concerns of staff; and to report matters of concern to the Governor or Director and, if necessary, the Secretary of State. Until April 1992 they undertook disciplinary hearings of more serious charges. The latter duty was long held by critics to be incompatible with the others and the principal reason why the boards' 'watchdog' role was so poorly developed (Prior Report 1985; Woolf Report 1991: paras. 14.363–435). A review of boards found that they had no real existence in the general management structure of the Prison Service ('no duty is laid on governors to deal with them; no obligation on Area Managers to respond to matters they raise'); members feel that nobody listens to them; and many prison staff feel that board members need to 'get real' in interpreting their role (Lloyd 2001: 13–14). The review led to several changes, including a change of title, relocation to the same building as the Prisons Ombudsman, and publication of their reports. It is not clear that their credibility has greatly improved in the light of these changes.

There has been a prisons inspectorate, outwith the Prison Service, though part of the Home Office, since 1981. The establishment of HMCIP was recommended by the May Committee (1979: 92–6) and represents that Committee's only lasting achievement (see Morgan 1985). The Inspectorate's reports are published and, under the leadership of successive Chief Inspectors (Judge Stephen Tumin 1987–1995, Sir David (now Lord) 'Rambo' Ramsbotham 1995–2001, and Anne Owers 2001–), HMCIP has established a reputation for conspicuous independence. HMCIP is charged with reporting to the Minister 'on the treatment of prisoners and conditions in prison' (Prison Act 1952, section 5A(3)), and does so by undertaking: regular inspections of prisons (each is fully inspected every five years, though the Youth Justice Board requires that YOIs housing juveniles be inspected annually); thematic reviews of aspects of policy (these have recently included reports on resettlement (HMCIP/Probation 2001)) and race (HMCIP 2005b); and by occasionally investigating major incidents. The Chief Inspector's critiques invariably attract publicity, but they have sometimes lacked policy impact because it was not always clear by what standards they concluded that provisions were 'impoverished', 'degrading', 'unacceptable', and so on. Further, by falling out with Home Office Ministers or senior Prison Service administrators, Chief Inspectors have sometimes lost the cooperation of policy-makers (see Ramsbotham 2003).

In July 2001, as his last act, Sir David Ramsbotham published in an annexe to his *Annual Report* more than 100 pages of 'Expectations: criteria for assessing the treatment and conditions for prisoners'. These standards are designed to guide inspectors when assessing the quality of what the Prison Service provides and ensure they make 'accurate and consistent judgements'. The majority of the criteria—and the terminology is significant, for seldom are the criteria expressed as specific standards —are said to be in 'harmony with existing Prison Service policies' (HMCIP 2001c: Annex 7, 1). The current Chief Inspector, Anne Owers, deploys less purple prose than her predecessors and her reports are now structured according to the inspectorate's revised 'expectations' (HMCIP 2004). Government plans to absorb the prisons inspectorate within a general criminal justice inspectorate have, as we write (autumn 2006), been abandoned; but there remains a suggestion that they are to be resurrected, administratively, by the back door.

It was partly lack of precision, and thus accountability, which robbed the prisoner complaints system of credibility with prisoners and which, inter alia, led Woolf to conclude that there was an absence of justice in prisons. Prisoners have always been able to complain about any aspect of their custody to their IMB/BoV, to their Governor, or to the Secretary of State, by way of petition. But the system lacked the straightforwardness, expedition, effectiveness, and independence which Woolf argued any satisfactory grievance ventilation system should have (para. 14.309). A new integrated grievance system was already being introduced when Woolf conducted his inquiry but he, like previous commentators, considered there should be an independent 'complaints adjudicator' at the apex of the internal system (paras 14.326–362). This independent element was introduced in the form of a Prisons Ombudsman, the first of whom was appointed and began receiving complaints in 1994, though the position still lacks a statutory basis. The Prisons Ombudsman reports to the Home Secretary.

The Prisons Ombudsman is not restricted, as the title implies, to matters of maladministration, but may consider the merits of decisions, including all disciplinary findings and punishments save those imposed by District Judges, and the remit of the office-holder covers both state-run and contracted-out prisons. As the current Ombudsman, Stephen Shaw, says in his 2004–5 annual report: 'we exist to promote decency, justice and openness in the penal system, to resolve problems and promote good practice' (PPO 2005). He also conducts ad hoc inquiries (such as the investigation into the disturbance and fire at Yarl's Wood immigration detention centre). The role of the post has been expanded twice, to Prisons and Probation Ombudsman (PPO) in 2001, and to include investigations into deaths in custody in 2004. The number of complaints received by the Ombudsman has increased significantly in recent years. Prisoners must first exhaust the internal complaints avenues, and the efficiency of these has recently been improved. The largest category of investigated prisoner complaints is about alleged damage to or loss of property, followed by adjudications, Home Detention Curfew decisions, security categorization decisions, links with families, complaints about living conditions, and transfers, etc. Young prisoners are much less likely to complain to the Ombudsman than adults, women are slightly under-represented compared to men, and long-term high-security prisoners are much more likely to complain than their short-term, low-security counterparts. This pattern is to some extent unavoidable: adults have more confidence and long-termers will not be deterred by delay. But the Ombudsman has pursued a number of initiatives (surgeries and more user-friendly publicity for use in YOIs) to make his services more accessible to less advantaged or motivated prisoners. The Ombudsman aims to resolve complaints in an informal, restorative manner wherever possible. Around one-third of the cases he takes up result in an outcome in some way favourable to the prisoner. Where the Ombudsman issues a formal report and recommendations, only very rarely are his findings and recommendations *not* accepted by the Director General, in the case of public-sector prisons, or the Office for Contracted Prisons, in the case of private-sector prisons. The Management of Offenders and Sentencing Bill (introduced in January 2005 but which fell because of the 2005 General Election and likely to be reintroduced in 2006) contained provisions to put the PPO on a statutory footing and formally equip him with enhanced powers of investigation.

THE PRISON ESTATE

There are two main types of institutions. First are the local prisons and remand centres. Their primary task is to receive prisoners from and deliver prisoners to the courts and to assess and allocate those serving sentences. Second are the prisons to which sentenced prisoners are allocated, the YOIs and the adult *training* prisons. The latter are further subdivided into closed and open institutions. This subdivision reflects a prisoner security classification and the level of security. Prisoners are security classified A, B, C, or D according to a basic scheme adopted in 1966 on the recommendation of Lord Mountbatten (1966; see also King and Elliott 1977; King and Morgan 1980; ACPS 1968). There are currently four high-security prisons and several local prisons designated as able to hold Category A prisoners on remand. Around 50 prisoners are accommodated in Close Supervision Centres—small units for difficult prisoners (see further Clare and Bottomley 2001; HMCIP 1999a; and historically, Bottomley and Hay 1991). These establishments together comprise the 'high security estate' (see further Liebling 2001).

The unintended consequence of capital investment in training prisons up to the 1990s was that those prisoners who should be given the least oppressive conditions typically experience the most impoverished regimes, and vice versa. In successive reports the Chief Inspector of Prisons chronicled: the 'degrading' and 'insanitary' accommodation; the 'enforced idleness'; the prolonged daily cellular confinement; the miserable visiting rooms; and the general absence of facilities (for graphic examples see HMCIP 1988, 1990a, 1993). The untried were the 'forgotten people' (HMCIP 1989; para. 4.30), held in 'completely insupportable' conditions (House of Commons Home Affairs Committee 1981: para. 54). The Council of Europe Committee for the Prevention of Torture concluded in 1990 that conditions in Brixton, Leeds, and Wandsworth Prisons—all three Victorian local prisons—amounted to 'inhuman and degrading' treatment (Council of Europe 1991; for commentary see Morgan and Evans 1994; Evans and Morgan 1998: 243–5). The phrase suggested that the conditions might be held to breach Article 3 of the European Convention for the Protection of Fundamental Human Rights, and certainly not to comply with Prison Rule requirements regarding the encouragement of useful lives, self-respect, and a sense of personal responsibility. It was in response to these conditions that the pressure for minimum standards in the 1980s was mounted. Many of the newly built and privately managed prisons since the early 1990s have been local prisons, and they tend to (but do not invariably) have better regimes and facilities than 'traditional locals'. This means there is something of a two-tier local prison system in operation, for recent inspectorate reports (for example HMCIP 2003b, 2005a) suggest that the old local prisons continue to bear the brunt of overcrowding and reduced regimes. However, not all of the differences in regime quality and culture are related to inadequate buildings (see, e.g., Liebling 2004 on prison differences).

WHO ARE THE PRISONERS?

Prisoners are overwhelmingly young, male, socially and economically disadvantaged, repetitive property offenders. Most prisoners are transient, even if a high proportion return again and again: the staff, typically, spend much more of their lives in prison than their charges. A growing minority of prisoners, however, are forced to make the prison their long-term home. Indeed, a few seem destined to remain incarcerated until they die.

THE GROWTH IN THE LONG-TERM PRISON POPULATION

It is important to distinguish prison 'receptions' and the 'average daily population' (ADP). The overwhelming majority of prisoners are in prison for a matter of days, weeks, or months rather than years. Remand prisoners are in custody for on average less than two months. Eighty per cent of sentenced prisoners are released within 12 months.[3] The ADP figures tell a different story, however. At any one time 30 per cent of remand prisoners have been in custody for more than three months and long-term adult prisoners dominate prisons both numerically and, more importantly, culturally: 47 per cent of the ADP are serving sentences of four or more years.

The contrast between prison receptions and the ADP has progessively become more marked as 'bifurcation' has been pursued at all decision-making levels. First are the changes in sentencing. In spite of the increase in recorded crime, the proportionate use

---

[3] All figures, unless otherwise stated, are taken from the annual *Prison Statistics* (since 2004 the *Offender Management Caseload Statistics*), the most recent of which were published in 2005 (Home Office 2005a). For a general review of prison statistics see Morgan (1995).

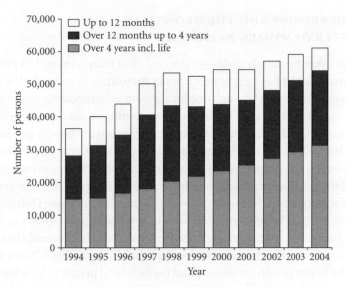

Fig. 32.2 Sentenced population by length of sentence, 1990–2004
Source: Annual *Prison Statistics* to 2002 and thereafter RDS/NOM online.

of custody gradually declined until the 1980s, then fluctuated and, since the early 1990s, has increased markedly: despite the fact that since the mid-1990s recorded crime has fallen by approximately one-third. The greater part of this recent increase has comprised very short sentences: the number of sentences of six months or less has more than doubled (see Home Office 2005a: Tables 2.1 and 2.2). There has also been a dramatic increase in the number of prisoners sentenced to very long sentences. In 1965, the year that the death penalty was abolished, 88 prisoners were received with sentences of 10 years or more, including life: 979 such prisoners were received in 2004. The increase in the number of long-term prison receptions has been matched by an increase in the proportion of their sentences served in prison. In 1985 the average time served by life-sentence prisoners released on licence was 10.7 years: in 2004 it was 14 years. Both murderers (for whom the life sentence is mandatory) and discretionary life-sentence prisoners are generally now required to remain longer in prison before being conditionally released. Moreover, bifurcation has characterized executive release policy across the whole range of sentences. The shorter the sentence, the smaller the proportion of the sentence the prisoner is required to serve in prison, and vice versa (see Home Office 2005a: Table 10.1).[4]

These trends have transformed the character of the ADP. Long-term prisoners now preoccupy prison administrators because long-term prisoners dominate life in most training prisons (see Figure 32.2).

---

[4] After a cautious beginning, when parole was seen very much as a privilege to be earned by prisoners who had reached a 'recognisable peak in their training' (Home Office 1965), executive release has been gradually liberalized for short-sentence prisoners, but made harder to achieve for long-term and especially discretionary life-sentence prisoners (see Hood and Shute 2000; Padfield 2002).

GENDERED PRISONS AND THE GROWTH IN
THE NUMBER OF WOMEN PRISONERS

Prisoners are overwhelmingly male—91 per cent of all receptions and 94 per cent of the ADP. Moreover, since it has long been the policy for women to be housed in institutions used exclusively for women (though one local prison accommodates males and females in separate wings), and because, until relatively recently, prison officers were employed exclusively to work with prisoners of the same sex, prisons are heavily gendered institutions. This has influenced the differential regimes thought appropriate for male and female prisoners, the nature of the relationships between prisoners and staff, the character of the activities provided, and the relative use of drugs, disciplinary measures, and so on (for accounts of the history of women's imprisonment see Dobash *et al.* 1986; Zedner 1994, 1995). The tendency has been to label women prisoners as mad or sad rather than bad and the activities organized for them have traditionally been geared to the roles of mother and homemaker rather than the labour market (Carlen 1983). Thus Holloway, the largest prison for women and the only local prison to have been rebuilt in recent times—was redesigned to operate on medically oriented therapeutic lines (Rock 1996), an approach considered particularly appropriate for women, but marginalized for men, as evidenced by the failure, until 2001, to replicate, despite its evident success, the experimental therapeutic prison at Grendon Underwood (Genders and Player 1994; Marshall 1997). The most recent survey evidence suggests that most work provided for women prisoners continues to comprise menial, unskilled maintenance tasks little integrated with their training (Hamlyn and Lewis 2000). The staffing gender profile of prisons is changing, however. By 2005 25 per cent of prison officers were female and in all prisons a growing proportion of officers were of the opposite sex to their charges.

The female prison population is in several respects different from that of the male population. It is not clear that women, all other things being equal, are more likely to receive a custodial sentence, but the differences between the men and women in custody nevertheless raise important questions of justice. First, 21 per cent of the female ADP comprises remands compared to 16 per cent for men, this in spite of the fact that the average remand period for women is significantly shorter (40 compared to 53 days in 2004). The principal explanation for the disparity is that a far lower proportion of female than male custodial remands—36 compared to 48 per cent—do not subsequently receive a custodial sentence.[5] This prompts the question as to whether so many women need be remanded in custody.

Sentenced women prisoners also differ from men. They are typically: older; serving shorter sentences; less recidivist; and less likely to have committed sexual, violent, or robbery offences. They are also less likely to be reconvicted, a consideration reflected in their higher release rate under the Home Detention Curfew scheme (see HMCIP/ Probation 2001: para. 7.12). They are more likely to be addicted to drugs, and to have

---

[5] After 2002 the Home Office ceased publishing data on time spent on remand and whether periods on remand were followed by conviction and a custodial sentence. On the latter issue see Prison Reform Trust 2004.

experienced repeated emotional, sexual, and physical abuse. Some writers, notably Carlen (1990; Carlen and Tchaikovsky 1996), argue that these differences in the male and female prison populations mean that the imprisonment of women is *different* from that of men and indicate that, despite their relatively small number, there is a powerful case for there being substantially fewer. In fact the opposite is occurring, and the rate of increase has been dramatic. At the end of 2005 there were over 4,000 women in prison, a 150 per cent increase over ten years compared to a 40 per cent increase for men. Precisely why the female prison population has risen so dramatically is not well understood, though one factor is the growth in the number of female foreign nationals convicted of drug-trafficking (see below).

Nineteen out of the 142 Prison Service establishments currently house women. Most of these accommodate women only. Approximately two-thirds of women prisoners have at least one child below the age of 18, but whereas the children of male prisoners are mostly looked after by wives or partners (Dodd and Hunter 1992), those of women prisoners tend to be cared for by grandmothers or friends (Caddle and Crisp 1997). A high priority for many women prisoners is not surprisingly to be in a prison close to home so as to be able to see their children and other family members regularly (HMCIP 1997: 12–15). Because there are relatively few prisons for women they tend to be a greater average distance from prisoners' homes. The Prisons Inspectorate has concluded that the sharing of sites with men does not benefit women. *Equality* of provision for women should not mean the *same* provision as for men. Their needs are different.

ETHNICITY, NATIONALITY, RELIGION, AND IMPRISONMENT

Approximately one in ten of the population in Britain today is made up of minority ethnic groups. Yet a quarter of all remands in custody, 18 per cent of all sentenced receptions, and a quarter of the ADP is drawn from the ethnic minorities. The difference is starker when sex is taken into account: 31 per cent of the female ADP comprises ethnic minorities compared to 24 per cent of the male. Closer scrutiny reveals that nationality is a major part of the explanation. A growing proportion of the prison population comprises foreign nationals—12 per cent in 2004 (21 per cent of women)—and just over three-quarters of the foreign nationals are non-white, the overwhelming majority of them black This reflects a rising tide throughout Europe (Tomashevski 1994). Many of these foreign nationals are not normally resident in Britain, a large proportion of them sentenced for drugs offences: these are the drug 'mules' apprehended at ports of entry (Green 1991).

If foreign nationals and children under 16 years are excluded from the analysis, black residents are imprisoned at roughly eight times the rate of white residents—a difference greater than in the USA—whereas persons of South Asian origin are incarcerated at roughly the same rate as whites. Further, within these groups there are significant differences, persons of Caribbean origin being incarcerated at a rate much higher than persons of African origin, and people of Pakistani origin being incarcerated at a rate approaching two or three times as high as persons of Bangladeshi and Indian origin respectively (Home Office 2001: Figure 6.6). Over-representation of the ethnic minorities compared to the white population is partly a matter of their youth: thus the over-representation is greatest among young adult prisoners. Finally, the ethnic minorities are most over-represented among the remand population—a feature which has attracted much critical attention (see Hood 1992; Fitzgerald and Marshall 1996)— and among sentenced prisoners their offence and sentence profile is different from that of the white population. Within all the ethnic minority groups, male and female, foreign nationals and British, the proportion of drug offenders is significantly higher than that of whites. Drug offences, particularly trafficking, attract longer than average sentences, and this explains part of the general over-representation in the ADP.

Religion is an increasingly important, complex feature of prison life. Whereas a rapidly growing proportion of prisoners, now almost one in three, record having 'no religion', what have previously been considered minority faiths have more and more prisoner adherents. Moreover, faith is often as important an aspect of self-identity as race. Today almost one in ten prisoners, for example, is Muslim (Home Office 2005a: Table 8.6; Ali 2005: 5)

THE YOUNG BUT AGEING PRISON POPULATION

Imprisonment is experienced largely by the young. Twenty per cent of sentenced receptions, are under 21 years of age and prisoners in their twenties dominate life in most prisons. This is not surprising. Crime, or at least the sort of crime that leads to conviction, is largely the activity of adolescents and young adults, and sentences of imprisonment are generally imposed on repeat offenders: more than two-thirds of the offenders sentenced to immediate custody have three or more previous convictions, over a quarter have 11 or more. The modal age of prisoners, male and female, is in the late twenties. Yet the prison population is ageing. The long-term trend, substantially reversed in the 1990s, has been a reduction in the number of very young prisoners and growth in the number of middle-aged and even elderly prisoners. Younger prisoners tend to have shorter sentences. In 1989 some 41 per cent of the sentenced ADP was under 25 years and approximately 15 per cent was aged 40 years or more; in 2004 the proportions were 30 and 22 per cent. There are now over 1,500 prisoners at any one time over 60 years of age, many of them serving long sentences.

The period since 1945 has witnessed the use of several differently titled custodial sentences for prisoners under 21—immediate imprisonment, borstal training, detention in a detention centre, and youth custody—but all were replaced by detention in a YOI by the Criminal Justice Act 1988, for which sentence the minimum age was raised in 1991 from 14 to 15 years. This simplification was thrown into reverse by the Crime and Disorder Act 1998 which introduced the Detention and Training Order (DTO) for juveniles, a sentence which can be served in a Prison Service YOI or one of the four contracted-out Secure Training Centres (STCs) or local authority secure homes. The latter two categories of establishment cater mostly for younger juveniles (see Morgan and Newburn, Chapter 30, this volume). The overwhelming majority of juveniles and young persons in custody, almost all the 15–17-year-old boys and 17-year-old girls, are accommodated in what continue to be called the YOIs, most of which are occupied, in separate wings, by *both* juveniles serving DTOs *and* young adults (18–20-year-olds). It is the YJB's ambition that juveniles eventually be held separately in dedicated establishments (YJB 2005) and on the basis that the transition to full adult male independence extends beyond the age of 20 there are advocates (NACRO 2001) of male prisoners, aged 18–24, being housed and provided for separately from older prisoners.

The number of juveniles and young adults received into custody rose sharply during the 1990s, thereby tracking the upward trend in the use of custody for adults. In the new millennium, however, the number has stabilized, bucking the adult trend. Nevertheless the number of offenders under 21 sentenced to an immediate custodial sentence remains only three-fifths of what it was in the early 1980s and is now at about the same level it was thirty years ago (see Figure 32.3).

The number of juveniles held on remand has also risen in recent years, though remanding in custody of 14-year-old boys ceased in 1992. The Government has said it is committed to ending remands in prison of 15- and 16-year-old boys (girls of this age are already excluded), a commitment prompted by the furore over the suicide of two 15-year-old boys in local prisons in 1990 and 1991. Since then all sense of urgency appears to have evaporated: at the time of writing there are more than 600 juveniles on remand in Prison Service establishments (information provided by the YJB). The Prisons Inspectorate has found that a 'significant minority of these young people are even more isolated, victimised and disturbed' than their adult counterparts (HMCIP 2000a: 25; see also Goldson 2000).

PRISONERS' SOCIO-ECONOMIC CHARACTERISTICS

The prison population is socially and economically disadvantaged relative to the population generally. Prisoners are disproportionately working class (83 per cent of male prisoners are from manual, partly skilled, or unskilled groups, compared to 55 per cent of the population generally—see Walmsley *et al.* 1992) and exhibit telling indicators of social stress, a fact well summarized by the Social Exclusion Unit (2002: ch. 2). They are much more likely than the population at large to:

- have a family member convicted of a criminal offence (43 compared to 16 per cent); 35 per cent have a family member who has been in prison;
- have been in care as a child (27 compared to 2 per cent);
- be unmarried (81 compared to 39 per cent, 85 per cent since their imprisonment); divorced (9 compared to 4 per cent); young fathers (25 per cent of young offenders compared to 4 per cent); or lone parents (21 per cent of women prisoners compared to 9 per cent); all of which suggests that many children of prisoners are destined to suffer the same disadvantaged start in life (see Shaw 1992);
- be, prior to their imprisonment, unemployed (67 compared to 5 per cent of the general population); have no qualifications (52 per cent of men and 71 per cent of

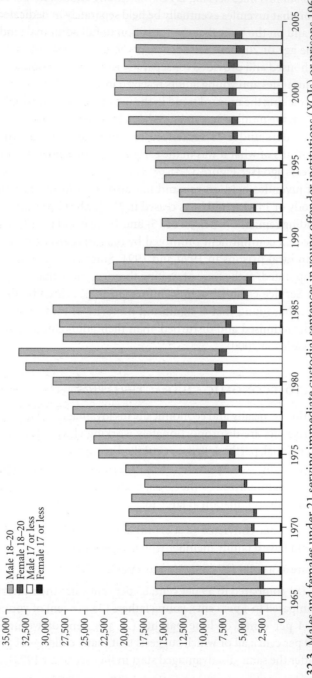

Fig. 32.3 Males and females under 21 serving immediate custodial sentences in young offender institutions (YOIs) or prisons 1965–2004

Source: Annual Prison Statistics to 2002 and thereafter RDS/NOMS online.

women compared to 15 per cent of the population generally); and have literacy and numeracy ages below that of an 11-year-old (48 and 65 per cent compared to 22 and 23 per cent respectively);

- be, prior to their imprisonment, sleeping rough (4.7 compared to 0.001 per cent) or lacking permanent accommodation (32 compared to 0.9 per cent);

- be smokers (77 of men and 82 per cent of women compared to 28 and 27 per cent respectively) or have a long-standing illness of disability (46 compared to 29 per cent);

- be, prior to their imprisonment, in receipt of benefits (72 compared to 14 per cent) or be indebted (48 compared to 10 per cent).

PRISONERS' MENTAL HEALTH

The mental health of prisoners has been a perennial cause for concern. Several epidemiological studies (Gunn *et al.* 1991; Dell *et al.* 1991) have been undertaken to assess levels of morbidity. The most recent data (Singleton *et al.* 1998) indicate that 10 per cent of male and 20 per cent of female prisoners have been mental hospital patients at some point prior to their incarceration and that very high proportions of all prisoner groups—78 per cent of male remands, 64 per cent of sentenced males, and 50 per cent of sentenced females—have some form of personality disorder. Whereas an estimated 0.4 per cent of the general population are psychotic, 7 per cent of the male sentenced population are. At 10 and 14 per cent respectively, the figures for male remand and female prisoners are even higher.

Proportionately three times as many male prisoners display high scores for neurotic symptoms as in the population generally. The figures for women are worse. The most severe of the neurotic conditions measured is the *depressive episode*. It is found in 2.1 per cent of the general population. Among prisoners the proportions are: 17 and 21 per cent of male and females remands; and 8 and 15 per cent of male and female sentenced prisoners. Thoughts of suicide among prisoners are relatively commonplace, particularly among remand prisoners. Forty-six per cent of male remands report having thought of suicide at some stage of their lives, 35 per cent in the last year, and 12 per cent in the week prior to interview. Twenty-seven per cent report that they have attempted to kill themselves at some point, 2 per cent in the week prior to interview. Again the figures for women are even higher: a quarter of women remand prisoners report having tried to kill themselves in the year prior to interview.

Very high proportions of prisoners are abusers of all categories of drugs. Fifty-eight per cent of male remands, 63 per cent of sentenced males, and more than one-third of all female prisoners have engaged in hazardous drinking prior to their imprisonment. The overwhelming majority of all prisoners have used cannabis at some stage. However, whereas use of cannabis is also widespread in the general population, use of heroin is not. Between one-third and one-half of prisoners in different categories have used heroin and/or crack cocaine (May 2005). Two-fifths of all women prisoners have injected drugs at some stage in their lives and between two-fifths and one-half of prisoners in all categories report having been dependent on one drug or another during the year prior to their incarceration. Prisoners convicted of property offences have above-average rates of drug dependence.

The overall picture of the prison population is one of multiple deprivation, social stress, and co-morbidity. Prisoners are seriously disadvantaged before their imprisonment and their social marginality is heightened by their incarceration.

THE SOCIOLOGY OF PRISONS

Prisons represent the power of the state to coerce. Order within prisons may in the last resort depend on the use of force by staff. Yet disorder is not the norm of prison life. As in any other social setting, order in prisons is negotiated (McDermott and King 1988; Liebling and Price 2001). The negotiation is not between equals. But it is for the most part achieved with the more or less grudging consent of prisoners who invariably far outnumber the prison officers who guard them. The 108,000 offences against the prison disciplinary code formally punished in 2004 (35 per cent fewer than ten years previously—Home Office 2005a: para. 9.2) belies the fact that staff and prisoners generally coexist harmoniously: frictions are for the most part resolved through more subtle accommodations. What counts as order within prisons?

The sociological literature on prisons suggests the existence of a prison culture—a set of attitudes and a way of doing things—in which both prisoners and prison officers have roles. To the extent that prisons exhibit a specific culture there has been a long-standing debate as to whether it is of primarily *indigenous* or *imported* origin. The indigenous approach is represented by Sykes's classic account of the *Society of Captives* (1958) and Goffman's seminal discussion of *Asylums* (1968). Both writers stress the distinctiveness of prison life. Prisons are 'total institutions' and prisoners are relatively shut off from the world at large. The prison has been seen as a more or less closed social system in which it is the task of one group of persons, the prison officers, to manage or process another group, the prisoners. Sykes's focus is on the 'pains of imprisonment'— the various deprivations that living in prisons involves—while Goffman stresses the dynamics of mortification—the transformation of the self—that results from entering a 'people-processing' institution. In both accounts the prisoner is described as being under psychological assault, with the usual supports for and expressions of personal identity—possessions, control over personal appearance, autonomy of movement, personal privacy, security, and so on—being greatly diminished (for a contemporary review of these arguments and recent empirical evidence, see Liebling and Maruna 2005). Prisoners may develop individualistic responses to these stresses, responses ranging from escape attempts or playing the role of the barrack-room lawyer to psychological withdrawal or intensive auto-didacticism. However, for Sykes the distinctive aspect of the prison culture—largely, though not entirely, its emphasis on prisoner solidarity against staff—represents a functional response to these social and psychological assaults: a means by which the rejected can reject their rejectors (McCorkle and Korn 1954) and thus maintain a degree of self-esteem. According to this view, the more that prisoners adopt a cohesive stance, the more the pains of imprisonment can be mitigated for everyone.

This process points to a paradox. Some of the relative deprivations of prison life are the result of staff attempts to maintain external security and internal order. Yet the pains of imprisonment can stimulate a solidaristic counter-culture subversive of official objectives. Thus the apparently total power of staff is compromised by their need to reach an accommodation with their charges in order that routine tasks be accomplished. In this way, whatever purposes prisons officially pursue are in practice undermined by the daily reality of the negotiated settlements which take place between officers and prisoners. This suggests that in reality prisons are unlikely to be about the pursuit of noble missions: they are ultimately more about practical survival in settings which, because inherently coercive, have an ever-present potential for instability and disorder. In the case of the uniformed staff the essence of a good day is one in which the routines are accomplished professionally without trouble, including the need to use unnecessary force (see Liebling and Price 2001: chs 5 and 6).

The problem with indigenous accounts of prison culture is that they fail to provide an explanation of change, other than the sort of minor shifts from crisis to equilibrium which might occur within a closed system. They do not explain the more fundamental changes in operational policy and prisoner response which have taken place in British prisons since 1945 or, more dramatically, which occurred in American prison systems in the wake of the black civil rights movement in the 1960s. Thus, by contrast, importation theorists stress the connection between relationships within prisons and those outside—for example, changes in political expectations, the legitimacy of authority, and legal culture (see Jacobs' (1977) classic study of *Stateville* Prison, Illinois). Importationists also highlight the degree to which the cultural norms to which prisoners subscribe, and the individual roles they adopt in prison, are extensions of subcultures of which they are a part before being incarcerated (Irwin and Cressey 1962; Irwin 1970). According to this approach the prison culture is not peculiar to prison: it is both a microcosm of the wider society and a sort of career continuation of the criminal culture of the streets from which a high proportion of prisoners are drawn. Thus Irwin and Cressey identify a 'thief subculture' outside prison which stresses group loyalty and toughness. To the extent that there is group solidarity between *some* prisoners within prison, then this 'convict' or 'prisoner' subculture is both an extension of that street culture *and* an adaption in response to the contingencies of life inside.

Indigenous and importationist perspectives are nowadays generally seen as complementary (Jacobs 1979). Moreover, whatever is to be learned from the American literature, British (and, indeed, most western European) prisons are unlikely to exhibit the same cultural patterns as in the USA. There has hitherto not, for example, been sophisticated organized crime in Britain as found in the USA; nor, with one or two notable exceptions, have criminal street gangs regularly employing life-threatening violence been a prominent feature of British crime, and thus their influence has not been greatly felt in prisons. Further, maximum-security prisons of the kind widely employed for the mainstream prison population in some US states (King 1999), have only relatively recently become part of the English system, and even today only a tiny minority of the prison population is housed in such conditions. Finally, though British society is riven by deeply ingrained class differences and racial divides, Britain is nevertheless culturally a relatively homogeneous society. With the exception of Northern Ireland (McEvoy 2001), there are not the deep cleavages which in the USA have historically separated the African American from the white population and in more recent times, the Hispanic from the English-speaking community. These cleavages have fatally dominated parts of the American prison scene (Colvin 1992; Wacquant 2001) to an extent largely unknown in Britain, and indeed, most of western Europe. Mathieson's (1965) classic study of a Norwegian prison failed to reveal much in the way of prisoner solidarity. Prisoners were relatively weak and isolated: they were vulnerable to the discretionary favours which the staff were in a position to distribute. Recent research suggests that power has shifted upwards in British prisons, and that prisoners are preoccupied with individual incentives (for example, to get home leave or early release) rather than collective politics (Liebling 2004; Crewe 2006).

The British 'sociology of prisons' literature has emphasized the complexity and varied quality of prison communities. The regime which different groups of prisoners experience differs considerably within prisons (King and Morgan 1976: ch. 3; Sparks *et al*. 1996). Thus, while prisoners' responses to custody may owe much to their previous institutional, criminal careers, and political affiliations (McEvoy 2001) they are also shaped by the length of their sentences (see, for example, Sapsford 1983, on life-sentence prisoners), the physical restrictions to which they are subject (see Cohen and Taylor 1972, on a high-security unit), whatever opportunities and facilities (or lack of them) are provided (King and Elliott 1977; Sparks *et al*. 1996; Liebling *et al*. 1999), and on the moral or emotional climate generated by staff working within them (Liebling 2004).

It is also evident from the literature on prison staff that the background characteristics of prison officers have changed a good deal in recent years, as have their working conditions. Officers now, as in the past, generally join the Service in their late twenties or thirties, after a spell in other occupations. But whereas the majority used to be recruited from the regular armed forces (Morris and Morris 1963: ch. 4; Jones and Cornes 1977: ch. 7), this is seldom the case today. Forty years ago few prison officers had any educational qualifications. Today the indelibly working-class culture of the majority, shaped now by previous experience of manual and clerical work rather than military discipline, is blended with a sizeable minority of recruits with A levels or degrees (26 per cent in 1985—see Marsh *et al*. 1985: Table 3.6) seeking advancement within an integrated career structure (Liebling and Price 2001: ch. 2). Moreover, the simple world of the 'gentleman' governors and prison 'screws' of the 1940s and 1950s has been complicated by the employment of women in all institutions and at all levels, and the importation of specialists who, in the 1960s and 1970s at least, took on the majority of the plum 'treatment and training' tasks—education, social work, and the various therapies with which the Service flirted (Thomas 1972: ch. 9). Prison officers typically spend a far higher proportion of their lives in prison than do their charges. They also have a culture, shaped by their previous experience and the increasingly complicated managerial (and emotional) context within which they operate (Liebling and Price 2001: ch. 8; Crawley 2004). The living conditions of prisoners are the working conditions of prison officers.

In criminal career terms, indigenous and importationist factors may reinforce each other. Clemmer (1940), a pioneer American analyst of the prison community, wrote of the process of 'prisonization', the gradual destructive socialization of prisoners into the norms of prison life which make it difficult for them successfully to adapt to a law-abiding life outside, thereby possibly deepening criminality. The idea of prisonization, which most researchers have rejected on the grounds that it posits too mechanical and linear a process, bears a close resemblance to the idea of institutionalization, a syndrome which analysts of mental hospitals have employed to describe the adjustment, with pathological consequences, of patients to stultifying regimes. Most prison studies identify a minority of prisoners whose reaction to custody is one of extreme social withdrawal, prisoners who know how to 'do time' passively 'behind their doors', typically 'old lags' imprisoned on many previous occasions and resistant to more open regimes and extended association (see Morris and Morris 1963: 172–3; King and Elliott 1977: 241–4).

To the extent that there is a prisoner culture it is plausible to see it as the product of utilitarian responses which different groups of prisoners, depending on their background, reputation, offence, and length of sentence, make to the pressures and opportunities arising out of captivity. There may be an informal code of not 'grassing' to staff, but there is also as much rivalry and enmity in prisons as there is camaraderie (Morris and Morris 1963: 168; Crewe 2005). Moreover, there are plenty of ways in which prisoners can inform staff about those prisoners whose behaviour they may wish to control, either for reasons of power play or simply to prevent a breakdown in the orderliness which most prisoners and staff have a vested interest in preserving. Many British studies emphasize with Sykes that one of the worst aspects of prison life is having to live with other prisoners. This may be because fellow prisoners are 'dirty in their personal habits or socially unpleasant or guilty of crimes which other prisoners regard as revolting' (Morris and Morris 1963: 168–9); or because of a lack of privacy within a highly restricted physical space (Cohen and Taylor 1972: 80–1); or because of the discomforting strategies which colleagues adopt to cope with whatever time they have to serve (King and Elliott 1977: ch. 8); or for reasons of racial prejudice (Genders and Player 1989) or political attachment (McEvoy 2001).

There are moral and power hierarchies within prisons. One of the reasons why most prisoners are keen that order, however tenuous, should be maintained is that disturbances provide opportunities to settle scores and confirm moral hierarchies (see Woolf 1991: section 3). It is doubtful that British prisoner communities can be characterized in class analogy terms in which the gangsters constitute a ruling class and the sex offenders (or 'nonces') a lumpenproletariat (Genders and Player 1994). The categories 'gangster' and 'sex offender' are problematic and subject to subtle qualifications relating to the nature of a prisoner's original offence and the reputation he or she establishes within prison (Cohen and Taylor 1972: ch. 3). Nevertheless, it is clear that certain categories of sex offenders, particularly those who have committed offences against children, are anathematized, and that established professional criminals who have experienced prison before, are older, and are doing longer than average sentences, tend within training prisons to be the 'top men' (King and Elliott 1977: 254–6). But social prominence within prisons is a complex matter (for a contemporary study, see Crewe 2005). Whereas Irwin's (1970) professional Californian thieves were allegedly orientated to the outside world, King and Elliott's 'top men' had as few outside contacts as their 'retreatists'. Nor were they heavily involved in power cliques and the culture of barter in contraband goods. On the contrary, their reputation enabled them to secure good positions (attractive cell locations and valued jobs) and non-interference from prisoners and staff alike. They were able to do their 'bird' in relative peace and security. The prisoners prominent in 'jailing' activities—regarded by the 'top men' as 'hotheads', 'tearaways', and 'borstal boys'—were on the whole younger, shorter-sentence prisoners whose criminal careers were disorganized (King and Elliott 1977: 250–2).

Power structures within prisons vary a good deal according to the nature of the prison (there has, for example, been virtually no research attention given to the predatory behaviour which, according to HMCIP, dominates many young-offender and low-security adult institutions—see HMCIP 2000b and 2001a for two recent examples) and depend less on a rigid class structure and rather more on a fluid pattern of competing groups based on ethnic and regional affinities as well as prior friendships and 'business' interests (Sparks *et al.* 1996: ch. 5). There is not one prisoner world, but many (Rock 1996: 39–41) and it is a shifting world. Ditchfield's review (1990) of the literature on disturbances and control in prisons found little evidence that the likelihood of incidents could straightforwardly be related to such factors as overcrowding, architectural design, or prisoner facilities, though changes, both positive and negative, which destabilized power structures and relationships increased the likelihood of disorder (see also Adams 1992: chs 5–7). However, order in prison can be linked to *legitimacy*, or perceptions of fairness and staff-prisoner relationships (Sparks *et al.* 1996; Liebling 2004). Attempts by prison psychologists to identify prisoners likely to be control problems, or to find common features among those prisoners identified by governors as control problems and transferred to special units, have not been conspicuously successful (see Williams and Longley 1987; and a critical review by King and McDermott 1990). Nor, despite references by senior prison administrators to disorder-prone 'toxic mixes' in their reviews of some prison disorders (see HMCIP 1987 on disturbances at Wymott and Northeye in 1986; also Ditchfield 1990: ch. 4), was the Woolf Inquiry able to identify a pattern among the *prisoners* prominent in the 1990 disturbances. His diagnosis of the disturbances was the widespread sense of injustice prevailing in dilapidated and outdated local prisons. The fact 'that a prisoner who creates control problems in one prison, may behave with complete propriety in another' (para. 9.48) suggested that more attention needed to be paid to the quality of relationships between prisoners and staff, to the nature of regimes, to procedural justice, and to day-to-day fairness (ibid.: section 9; see Sparks *et al.* 1996; Liebling 2004).

There are three lessons to be drawn from this research. First, though there are undoubtedly a few prisoners whose response to most penal situation is so disruptive or aggressive—the extreme case being prisoners who have killed within prison—that they must for a time be placed in special units, attention needs most to be paid to trouble-generating *situations* and *procedures* rather than to the relatively illusive 'disruptive' population. Removal of 'troublesome' prisoners is seldom a solution. Such labelled prisoners often go on to confirm their labels (Boyle's autobiographical accounts (1977, 1984) are object lessons in this process) and the situation within which their trouble-some behaviour was first identified typically generates further trouble. Secondly, the regime experienced by the 'mainstream' population has to be got right. It is there that trouble sporadically occurs and the proliferation of special units disrupts the ladder of incentives and disincentives on which the stability and fairness of the whole system ultimately rests. Thirdly, relationships between prisoners and prison officers are critical to the quality of prisoners' lives. This suggests, to take the crime-preventative analogy adopted by Sparks *et al.* (1996), that benefits are likely to flow from adopting a 'social' rather than 'situational' control strategy, in effect what Dunbar (1985) termed 'dynamic security'. This involves devising 'active' regimes for 'healthy' prisons for prisoners in which prison officers are positively involved *with* prisoners in the delivery of programmes, services, and facilities between which prisoners may exercise a degree of responsible choice. The same lessons are implicit in the developing literature on suicide prevention in prison (Liebling *et al.* 2005a; Dear 2006). There are a few prisoners who recognizably feel so suicidal that they can be identified and focused measures can be taken to prevent their taking their own lives (Prison Service 1992; Liebling 1992). A high proportion of prison suicides are not predictable, although research suggests they may occur disproportionately in disorganized prisons with poor cultures, where levels of distress among prisoners are found to be highest. The solution is to enhance the quality of life for *all* prisoners, to focus regimes on future well-being, and to increase mental health in-reach provision and training for staff (HMCIP 1990b; Liebling *et al.* 2005b).

■ SELECTED FURTHER READING

Discussions of imprisonment ideally take place within the broader context of the debate on the philosophy and sociology of punishment: Nigel Walker's *Why Punish?* (Oxford: Oxford University Press, 1991) is an excellent introduction to the former and David Garland's *Punishment and Modern Society* (Oxford: Oxford University Press, 1990) is a masterly overview of the major theorists who have explored the latter.

The current organization of imprisonment is heavily influenced by past practice. Michael Ignatieff's *A Just Measure of Pain* (London: Macmillan, 1978) provides an inspirational account of the emergence of imprisonment as the principal penalty for serious crime at the end of the eighteenth century and *The Oxford History of the Prison* (edited by Norval Morris and David Rothman, New York: Oxford University Press, 1995) comprises a fine collection of essays by leading historians on the international origins and use of imprisonment.

As far as the contemporary use and organization of imprisonment is concerned, there is no substitute for becoming familiar with the annual reports of the Prison Service and NOMS, the Home Office Research Development and Statistics Directorate's Research Findings (for example, Nos 262 and 260 on CARAT drug services and basic skills training), and the annual *Offender Management Caseload Statistics* (formerly the *Prison Statistics*). To access these and many other documents (the reports of the Prisons Inspectorate, the Prisons and Probation Ombudsman, and the Parole Board, for example), the Home Office website (www. homeoffice.gov.uk) is essential. The websites of the Prison Reform Trust (www. prisonreformtrust.org.uk), NACRO (www.nacro.org.uk), and the Kings College Centre of Criminal Justice Studies (www.kcl.ac.uk/depsta/rel/ccjs) are also very useful.

As far as introductory texts are concerned Michael Cavadino and James Dignan's *The Penal System: An Introduction* (3rd edn, London: Sage, 2002) is the best available, although *The Prisons Handbook* (edited by Yvonne Jewkes, Willan) should become available in early 2007. A thorough analysis of recent attempts to modernize and improve prison life, and their effects on prisoners and staff can be found in Alison Liebling's *Prisons and their Moral Performance* (Oxford: Oxford University Press, 2004). A scholarly analysis of the important history of imprisonment in Northern Ireland is provided by Kieran McEvoy's *Paramilitary Imprisonment in Northern Ireland: Resistance, Management and Release* (Oxford: Oxford University Press, 2001).

Imprisonment is ultimately an experience which only those who have been incarcerated can adequately relate. Victor Serge's *Men in Prison* (London: Gollancz, 1970), Rod Caird's *A Good and Useful Life* (London: Hart-Davies, 1977), Jimmy Boyle's *A Sense of Freedom* (London: Canongate, 1977), Audrey Peckham's *A Woman in Custody* (London: Fontana, 1985) and Erwin James' *A Life Inside* (London: Atlantic Books, 2003), are among the best accounts.

■ REFERENCES

ADAMS, R. (1992), *Prison Riots in Britain and the USA*, New York: St Martins Press.

ADVISORY COUNCIL ON THE PENAL SYSTEM (1968), *The Regime for Long-Term Prisoners in Conditions of Maximum Security* (Radzinowicz Report), London: HMSO.

ALI A. (2005), *Muslim Youth in Britain: A Ticking Time Bomb?*, London: British Muslim Research Centre.

APPLEBAUM, A. (2003), *Gulag: A History*, London: Allen Lane.

BEYENS, K, and SNACKEN, S. (1996), 'Prison privatization: an international perspective', in R. Matthews and P. Francis (eds), *Prisons 2000: an International Perspective on the Current State of and Future of Imprisonment*, Basingstoke: Macmillan.

BOTTOMLEY, K. (1995), *CRC Special Units: A General Assessment*, London: Home Office Research and Planning Unit.

—— and HAY, W. (eds) (1991), *Special Units for Difficult Prisoners*, Hull: Centre for Criminology and Criminal Justice.

——, JAMES, A., CLARE, E., and LIEBLING, A. (1997), *Monitoring and Evaluation of Wolds Remand Prison*, Home Office Research and Planning Unit, London: Home Office.

BOTTOMS, A. E. (1990), 'The Aims of Imprisonment', in D. Garland (ed.), *Justice, Guilt and Forgiveness in the Penal System*, University of Edinburgh, Centre for Theology and Public Issues, Occasional Paper No. 18.

BOYLE, J. (1977), *A Sense of Freedom*, Edinburgh: Canongate.

—— (1984), *The Pain of Confinement: Prison Diaries*, Edinburgh: Canongate.

CADDLE, D., and CRISP, D. (1997), *Mothers in Prison*, Research Findings 38., London: Home Office.

CARLEN, P. (1983), *Women's Imprisonment*, London: Routledge.

—— (1990), *Alternatives to Women's Imprisonment*, Milton Keynes: Open University Press.

—— and TCHAIKOVSKY, C. (1996), 'Women's imprisonment in England and Wales at the end of the twentieth century, realities and utopias', in R. Matthews and P. Francis (eds) *Prisons 2000: an International Perspective on the Current State and Future of Imprisonment*, Basingstoke: Macmillan.

CASALE, S. (1984), *Minimum Standards for Prison Establishments*, London: NACRO.

—— (1993), 'Conditions and standards', in E. Player and M. Jenkins (eds), *Prisons After Woolf: reform through riot*, London: Routledge.

—— and PLOTNIKOFF, J. (1989), *Minimum Standards for Prisons: A Programme of Change*. London: NACRO.

—— (1990), *Regimes for Remand Prisoners*, London: Prison Reform Trust.

CAVADINO, M., and DIGNAN, J. (2005), *Penal Systems: A Comparative Approach*, London: Sage.

CHENEY, D. (1999), *Criminal Justice and the Human Rights Act 1998*, Bristol: Jordans.

CHRISTIE, N. (1994), *Crime Control as Industry: Towards Gulags, Western Style*, London: Routledge.

CLARE, E., and BOTTOMLEY, K. (2001), *Evaluation of Close Supervision Centres*, Research Study 219, London: Home Office.

CLEMMER, D. (1940), *The Prison Community*, New York: Holt, Rinehart and Winston.

COHEN, S., and TAYLOR, L. (1972), *Psychological Survival*, Harmondsworth: Penguin.

COLLINS, P. (1962), *Dickens and Crime*, Basingstoke: Macmillan.

COLVIN, M. (1992), *The Penitentiary in Crisis: from Accommodation to Riot in New Mexico*, Albany, N.Y.: State University of New York Press.

COUNCIL OF EUROPE (1991), *Report to the United Kingdom Government on the Visit to the United Kingdom Carried Out by the European Committee for the Prevention of Torture and Inhuman or Degrading Treatment or Punishment from 29 June 1990 to 10 August 1990*, Strasbourg: Council of Europe.

CRAWLEY, E. (2004), *The Public and Private Lives of Prison Officers*, Cullompton, Devon: Willan.

CREIGHTON, S., and KING, V. (2000), *Prisoners and the Law*, 2nd edn, London: Butterworths.

CREWE, B. (2005), 'The Prisoner Society in the Era of Hard Drugs', *Punishment and Society*, 7(4): 457–81.

—— (2006), 'Power, Resistance and Adaptation in the Late-Modern Prison', *British Journal of Criminology* (forthcoming).

DEAR, G. E. (ed.) (2006), *Preventing Suicide and Other Self-Harm in Prison*, London: Palgrave-Macmillan.

DELL, S., GROUNDS, A., JAMES, K., and ROBERTSON, G. (1991), *Mentally Disordered Remanded Prisoners: Report to the Home Office*, Cambridge: University of Cambridge.

DITCHFIELD, J. (1990), *Control in Prisons: A Review of the Literature*, Home Office Research Study No. 118, London: HMSO.

DOBASH, R., DOBASH, R., and GUTTERIDGE, S. (1986), *The Imprisonment of Women*, Oxford: Blackwell.

DODD, T., and HUNTER, P. (1992), *The National Prisoner Survey 1991: A Report to the Home Office of a Study of Prisoners in England and Wales carried out by the Social Survey Division of OCPS*, London: HMSO.

DONZIGER, S. R. (1995), *The Real War on Crime: the Report of the National Criminal Justice Commission*, New York: Harper Collins.

DOWNES, D. (1988), *Contrasts in Tolerance: Post-War Penal Policy in the Netherlands and England and Wales*, Oxford: Oxford University Press.

—— (1997), 'The buckling of the shields: Dutch penal policy 1985–1995', in N. South and R. Weiss (eds), *International Prison Systems*, Reading: Gordon and Breach.

DUNBAR, I. (1985), *A Sense of Direction*, London: Prison Service.

EDGAR, K., and O'DONNELL, I. (1998), *Mandatory drug testing in prisons: the relationship between MDT and the level and nature of drug misuse*, Research Study No. 189, London: Home Office.

EVANS, M., and MORGAN, R. (1998), *Preventing Torture: A Study of the European Convention for the Prevention of Torture and Inhuman or*

Degrading Treatment or Punishment, Oxford: Oxford University Press.

FELDMAN, D. (2002), *Civil Liberties and Human Rights in England and Wales*, 2nd edn, Oxford: Oxford University Press.

FITZGERALD, M., and MARSHALL, P. (1996), 'Ethnic minorities in British prisons: some research implications', in R. Matthews and P. Francis (eds), *Prisons 2000: An International Perspective on the Current State and Future of Imprisonment*, Basingstoke: Macmillan.

FOUCAULT, M. (1967), *Madness and Civilisation*, London: Tavistock.

—— (1977) *Discipline and Punish: The Birth of the Prison*, London: Allen Lane.

FOX, L. (1952), *The English Prison and Borstal System*, London: Routledge.

GARLAND, D. (1990), *Punishment and Modern Society: A Study in Social Theory*, Oxford: Oxford University Press.

—— and YOUNG, P. (1983), 'Towards a Social Analysis of Penality', in D. Garland and P. Young (eds), *The Power to Punish*, London: Heinemann.

GENDERS, E., and PLAYER, E. (1989), *Race Relations in Prison*, Oxford: Clarendon Press.

—— (1994), *Grendon: A Study of a Therapeutic Prison*, Oxford: Clarendon Press.

GOFFMAN, E. (1968), 'The Characteristics of Total Institutions', in *Asylums*, Harmondsworth: Penguin.

GOLDSON, B. (ed.) (2000), *The New Youth Justice*, Lyme Regis: Russell House.

GOSTIN, L., and STAUNTON, M. (1985), 'The Case for Prison Standards: Conditions of Confinement, Segregation and Medical Treatment', in M. Maguire, J. Vagg, and R. Morgan (eds), *Accountability and Prisons: Opening Up a Closed World*, London: Tavistock.

GREEN, P. (1991), *Drug Couriers*, London: Prison Reform Trust.

GUNN, J., MADEN, A., and SWINTON, M. (1991), *Mentally Disordered Prisoners*, London: Institute of Psychiatry.

HAMLYN, B., and LEWIS, D. (2000), *Women Prisoners: a survey of their work and training experiences in custody and on release*, Research Study No. 208, London: Home Office.

HARDING, R. W. (1997), *Private Prisons and Public Accountability*, Buckingham: Open University Press.

HER MAJESTY'S CHIEF INSPECTOR OF PRISONS (1987), *Report of an Inquiry into the Disturbances in Prison Service Establishments in England between 29 April and 2 May 1986*, HC 42, London: HMSO.

—— (1988), *HM Remand Centre Risley*, London: Home Office.

—— (1989), *Prison Sanitation*, London: Home Office.

—— (1990a), *HM Prison Brixton*, London: Home Office.

—— (1990b), *Suicide and Self-Harm in Prison Service Establishments in England and Wales*, Cm. 1383, London: HMSO.

—— (1993), *HM Prison Cardiff*, London: Home Office.

—— (1997), *Women in Prison: A Thematic Review*, London: Home Office.

—— (1999a), *Suicide is Everyone's Concern: A Thematic Review*, London: Home Office.

—— (1999b), *HM Altcourse*, London: Home Office.

—— (2000a), *Unjust Deserts: A Thematic Review of the Treatment and Conditions for Unsentenced Prisoners in England and Wales*, London: Home Office.

—— (2000b), *YOI Brinsford*, London: HMIP.

—— (2001a), *YOI Stoke Heath*, London: HMIP.

—— (2001b), *HMP The Wolds*, London: HMIP.

—— (2001c), *Annual Report 1999–2000*, London: Home Office.

—— (2002), *HMP Forest Bank*, London: HMIP.

—— (2003a), *HMP Rye Hill*, London: HMIP.

—— (2003b), *HMP Brixton*, London: HMIP.

—— (2004), *Expectations: Criteria for assessing the conditions in prisons and the treatment of prisoners*, London: HMIP.

—— (2005a), *HMP Leeds*, London HMIP.

—— (2005b), *Race*, London: HMIP.

HMCIP/PROBATION (2001), *Through the Prison Gate: A Joint Thematic Review by HM Inspectorates of Prison and Probation*, London: Home Office.

HOME OFFICE (1947), *Report of the Commissioners of Prison and Directors of Convict Prisons for the Year 1946*, Cmd. 7271, London: HMSO.

—— (1965), *The Adult Offender*, Cmnd. 2852, London: HMSO.

—— (1984), *Managing the Long-Term Prison System: The Report of the Control Review Committee*, London: HMSO.

—— (1991), *Custody, Care and Justice: The Way Ahead for the Prison Service in England and Wales*, Cmnd. 1647, London: HMSO.

—— (1999), *Digest 4: Information on the Criminal Justice System in England and Wales*, London: Home Office.

—— (2001), *Prison Statistics England and Wales 1999*, Cmnd 5250, London: Home Office.

—— (2005a), *Offender Management Caseload Statistics 2004*, Statistical Bulletin 17/05, London: Home Office.

—— (2005b), *Restructuring Probation to Reduce Re-Offending*, London: Home Office.

HOOD, R. (1992), *Race and Sentencing: A Study in the Crown Court*, Oxford: Clarendon Press.

—— and SHUTE, S. (2000), *The Parole System at Work: a study of risk based decision-making*, Research Study 202, London: Home Office.

HOUGH, M., ALLEN, R., and PADEL, U. (eds) (2006), *Reshaping Probation and Prisons: the new offender management framework*, Bristol: Policy Press.

HOUSE OF COMMONS HOME AFFAIRS COMMITTEE (1981), *The Prison Service*, vol. 1, HC 412, 1980/1, London: HMSO.

—— (1997) *The Management of the Prison Service (Public and Private)*. London: HMSO.

HOWARD, J. (1784), *The State of the Prisons in England and Wales with Preliminary Observations, and an Account of some Foreign Prisons and Hospitals*, 3rd edn, Warrington.

IGNATIEFF, M. (1978), *A Just Measure of Pain*, London: Macmillan.

IRWIN, J. (1970), *The Felon*, Englewood Cliffs, N.J.: Prentice-Hall.

—— and CRESSEY, D. (1962), 'Thieves, Convicts and the Inmate Culture', *Social Problems*, 10(92): 145–55.

JACOBS, J. (1977), *Stateville: The Penitentiary in Mass Society*, Chicago: University of Chicago Press.

—— (1979), 'Race Relations and the Prisoner Sub-Culture', in N. Morris and M.Tonry (eds), *Crime and Justice: An Annual Review of Research*, vol. 1, Chicago: University of Chicago Press.

—— (1980), 'The Prisoners' Rights Movement and its Impacts, 1960–1980', in N. Morris and M. Tonry (eds), *Crime and Justice: An Annual Review of Research*, vol. 2, Chicago: University of Chicago Press.

JAMES, A. L., BOTTOMLEY, A. K., CLARE, E., and LIEBLING, A. (1997), *Privatizing Prisons: Rhetoric and Reality*, London: Sage.

JAMES, E. (2003), *A Life Inside: A Prisoner's Notebook*, London: Atlantic.

JONES, H., and CORNES, P. (1977), *Open Prisons*, London: Routledge.

KCPS (2006), *World Prison Population List*, London: Kings College Centre for Prison Studies. Available at www.kcl.ac.uk/depsta/rel/icps/home.html.

KING, R. D. (1999), 'The rise and rise of supermax: an American solution in search of a problem', *Punishment and Society*, 1(2): 163–86.

—— and ELLIOTT, K. (1977), *Albany: Birth of a Prison—End of an Era*, London: Routledge.

—— and MCDERMOTT, K. (1990), 'My Geranium is Subversive: Some Notes on the Management of Trouble in Prisons', *British Journal of Sociology*, 41: 445–71.

—— and —— (1995), *The State of Our Prisons*, Oxford: Clarendon Press.

—— and MORGAN, R. (1976), *A Taste of Prison: Custodial Conditions for Trial and Remand Prisoners*, London: Routledge.

—— and —— (1980), *The Future of the Prison System*, Aldershot: Gower.

LAMING, LORD (2000), *Modernising the Management of the Prison Service: An independent report by the Targeted Performance Initiative Working Group* (Laming Report), London: Home Office

LEARMONT REPORT (1995), *Review of Prison Service Security in England and Wales and the Escape from from Parkhurst Prison on Tuesday 3rd January 1995*, Cm. 3020, London: HMSO.

LEECH, M., and CHENEY, D. (ed.) (2002), *The Prisons Handbook*, Winchester: Waterside Press.

LEWIS, D. (1997), *Hidden Agendas*, Hamish Hamilton: London.

LIEBLING, A. (1992), *Suicides in Prison*, London: Routledge.

—— (2001), 'A "liberal regime within a secure perimeter?": Dispersal prisons and penal practice in the late 20th century', Paper delivered at a Radzinowicz Commemorative Symposium, Institute of Criminology, University of Cambridge, March.

—— (2004) *Prisons and their Moral Performance: A Study of Values, Quality and Prison Life*, Oxford: Oxford University Press.

—— and MARUNA, S. (eds) (2005), *The Effects of Imprisonment*, Cullompton, Devon: Willan.

—— and PRICE, D. (2001), *The Prison Officer*, London: Prison Service Journal.

——, MUIR, G., ROSE, G., and BOTTOMS, A. (1997), *An Evaluation of Incentives and Earned Privileges: Report for the Home Office*, Cambridge: Insitute of Criminology.

LIEBLING, A., MUIR, G., ROSE, G., and BOTTOMS, A. (1999), *Incentives and earned privileges—an evaluation*, Research Findings 87, London: Home Office.

—— TAIT, S., DURIE, L., STILES, A. (2005a), 'Revisiting suicides in prison: the role of fairness and distress', in A. Liebling and S. Maruna (eds), *The Effects of Imprisonment*, Cullompton, Devon: Willan.

——, ——, ——, and HARVEY, J. (2005b), 'Safer Locals Evaluation', *Prison Service Journal*, 162: 8–12.

LIVINGSTONE, S., OWEN, T., and MACDONALD, A. (2003), *Prison Law*, 3d edn, Oxford: Oxford University Press.

LLOYD, SIR P. (2001), *Review of the Boards of Visitors: A Report of the Working Group*, London: Home Office.

LOGAN, C. H. (1990), *Private Prisons: Pros and Cons*, New York: Oxford University Press.

LOUCKS, N., and PLOTNIKOFF, J. (1993), *Prison Rules: A Working Guide*, London: Prison Reform Trust.

MCCONVILLE, S. (1981), *A History of English Prison Administration*, vol. 1: 1750–1877. London: Routledge.

MCCORKLE, L., and KORN., R. (1954), 'Resocialisation within the Walls', *Annals of the American Academy of Political and Social Science*, 293: 88–98.

MCDERMOTT, C., and KING, R. D. (1988), 'Mind Games: Where the Action is in Prisons', *British Journal of Criminology*, 28 (3): 357–77.

MCEVOY, K. (2001), *Paramilitary Imprisonment in Northern Ireland: Resistance, Management and Release*, Oxford: Oxford University Press.

MCGOWAN, R. (1995), 'The Well-Ordered Prison: England 1780–1865' in N. Morris and D. Rothman (eds), *The Oxford History of the Prison*, New York: Oxford University Press.

MARSH, A., DOBBS, J., MONT, J., and WHITE, A. (1985), *Staff Attitudes in the Prison Service*, London: HMSO.

MARSHALL, P. (1997), *A Reconviction Study of HMP Grendon Therapeutic Community*, Research Findings 53, London: Home Office.

MATHIESON, T. (1965), *The Defences of the Weak*, London: Tavistock.

MAY, C. (1999), *Explaining Reconviction following a Community Sentence: the role of social factors*, Research Study 192, London: Home Office.

—— (2005), *The CARAT drug service in prisons: findings from the research database*, Research Findings, No. 262, London: Home Office.

MAY COMMITTEE (1979), *Report of the Committee of Inquiry into the United Kingdom Prison Services*, Cmnd. 7673. London: HMSO.

MELOSSI, D., and PAVARINI, M. (1981), *The Prison and the Factory: The Origins of the Penitentiary*, Basingstoke: Macmillan.

MORGAN, R. (1985), 'Her Majesty's Inspectorate of Prisons', in M. Maguire, J. Vagg, and R. Morgan (eds), *Accountability and Prisons: Opening Up a Closed World*, 106–23, London: Tavistock.

—— (1993), 'An Awkward Anomaly: Remand Prisoners', in E. Player and M. Jenkins, (eds), *Prisons After Woolf: reform through riot*, London: Routledge.

—— (1995), 'Prison', in M. Walker (ed.), *Interpreting Crime Statistics*, Oxford: Clarendon Press.

—— and EVANS, M. (1994), 'Inspecting Prisons: the view from Strasbourg', in R. D. King and M. Maguire (eds), *Prisons in Context*, Oxford: Clarendon Press.

MORRIS, N., and ROTHMAN, D. J. (eds) (1995), *The Oxford History of the Prison*, New York: Oxford University Press.

MORRIS, T., and MORRIS, P. (1963), *Pentonville: A Sociological Study of an English Prison*, London: Routledge.

MOUNTBATTEN REPORT (1966), *Report of the Inquiry into Prison Escapes and Security*, Cmnd. 3175, London: HMSO.

NACRO (2001), *Young Adult Offenders: a period of transition*, London: NACRO.

NATIONAL AUDIT OFFICE (2003), *The Operational Performance of PFI Prisons Report by the Comptroller and Auditor General*, HC Session 2002–2003, London: The Stationery Office.

PADFIELD, N. (2002), *Beyond the Tariff: Human Rights and the Life Sentence Prisoner*, Cullompton, Devon: Willan.

—— and LIEBLING, A. (2000), *An Exploration of Decision-Making at Discretionary Lifer panels*, Research Study 213, London: Home Office.

PARK, I. (2000), *Review of Comparative Costs and Performance of Privately and Publicly Operated Prisons 1998–99*, Statistical Bulletin 6/00, London: Home Office.

PEASE, K. (1994), 'Cross-national imprisonment rates: limitations of method and possible conclusions', in R. D. King and M. Maguire (eds), *Prisons in Context*, Oxford: Clarendon Press.

PETERS, E. (1985), *Torture*, Philadelphia: University of Philadelphia Press.

PRIOR REPORT (1985), *Report on the Departmental Committee on the Prison Disciplinary System*, London: HMSO.

PRISON REFORM TRUST (2004), *Lacking Conviction: The rise of the women's remand population*, London: Prison Reform Trust.

PRISON SERVICE (1992), *Caring for Prisoners at Risk of Suicide or Self-Injury: The Way Forward*, London: Prison Service

—— (1996), *Corporate Plan 1996–9*, London: Prison Service.

—— (2000), *HM Prison Service Performance Standards Manual*, London: Prison Service.

—— (2005a), *Annual Report and Accounts 2004–2005*, HC 193, London: Prison Service.

—— (2005b), *Staff Profiles and Projections 2005*, Internal Report.

PRISONS AND PROBATION OMBUDSMAN (2005), *Annual Report 2005*, London: PPO.

PUGH, R. B. (1970), *Imprisonment in Mediaeval England*, Cambridge: Cambridge University Press.

RADZINOWICZ, L., and HOOD, R. (1990), *The Emergence of Penal Policy in Victorian and Edwardian England*, Oxford: Clarendon Press.

RAMSBOTHAM, D. (2003), *Prison-Gate: The Shocking State of Britain's Prisons and the Need for Visionary Change*, London: Free Press.

RICHARDSON, G. (1993), 'From Rights to Expectations', in E. Player and M. Jenkins (eds), *Prisons After Woolf*, London: Routledge.

ROCK, P. (1996), *Reconstructing a Women's Prison: The Holloway Redeveopment Project*, Oxford: Clarendon Press.

RUCK, S. K. (ed.) (1951), *Paterson on Prisons: Prisoners and Patients*, London: Hodder and Stoughton.

RUSCHE, G., and KIRCHHEIMER, O. (1968), *Punishment and Social Structure*, New York: Columbia University Press.

RUTHERFORD, A. (1984), *Prisons and the Process of Justice*, Oxford: Oxford University Press.

SAPSFORD, R. (1983), *Life Sentence Prisoners*, Milton Keynes: Open University Press.

SCOTTISH EXECUTIVE (2000), *A Review of Conditions for Remand Prisoners in Scotland at the End of the 20th Century* (HM Chief Inspector of Prisons, Scotland, thematic report), Edinburgh: Scottish Executive.

SHAW, R. (ed.) (1992), *Prisoners' Children: What are the Issues?*, London: Routledge.

SHICHOR, D. (1995), *Punishment for Profit: Private Prisons—Public Concerns*, Thousand Oaks, Cal.: Sage.

SINGLETON, N., MELTZER, H., and GATWARD, R. (1998), *Psychiatric Morbidity among Prisoners in England and Wales*, London: Stationery Office.

——, PENDRY, E., SIMPSON, T., GODDARD, E., FARRELL, M., MARSDON, J., and TAYLOR, C. (2005), *The impact and effectiveness of mandatory drug testing in prisons*, Findings 223, London: Home Office.

SOCIAL EXCLUSION UNIT (2002), *Reducing re-offending by ex-prisoners*, London: ODPM.

SPARKS, R. (1996), 'Penal "Austerity": The Doctrine of Less Eligibility Reborn?', in R. Matthews and P. Francis (eds), *Prisons 2000: An International Perspective on the Current State and Future of Imprisonment*, Basingstoke: Macmillan.

—— BOTTOMS, A. E., and HAY, W. (1996), *Prisons and the Problem of Order*, Oxford: Clarendon Press.

SPIERENBERG, P. (1984), *The Spectacle of Suffering: Executions and the Evolution of Repression, from a Pre-industrial Metropolis to the European Experience*, Cambridge: Cambridge University Press.

STERN, V. (1998), *A Sin Against the Future: Imprisonment in the World*, Harmondsworth: Penguin.

SYKES, G. (1958), *The Society of Captives*, Princeton: Princeton University Press.

THOMAS, J. E. (1972), *The English Prison Officer since 1850*, London: Routledge.

TOMASHEVSKI, K. (1994), *Foreigners in Prison*, Helsinki: European Institute for Crime Prevention and Control.

WALMESLEY, R. (1989), *Special Security Units*, Research Unit Study No. 109, London: HMSO.

——, HOWARD, L., and WHITE, S. (1992), *The National Prison Survey 1991: Main Findings*, Research Study 128, London: HMSO.

WACQUANT, L. (2001), 'Deadly Symbiosis: when ghetto and prison meet and merge', *Punishment and Society*, 3 (1): 95–133.

WILLIAMS, M., and LONGLEY, D. (1987), 'Identifying Control—Problem Prisoners in Dispersal Prisons', in A. E. Bottoms and R. Light (eds), *Problems of Long-Term Imprisonment*, Aldershot: Gower.

Woolf Report (1991), *Prison Disturbances April 1990: Report of an Inquiry by the Rt. Hon. Lord Justice Woolf (part I and II) and His Honour Judge Stephen Tumin (Part II)*, Cm. 1456, London: HMSO.

Youth Justice Board (2005), *Strategy for the Secure Estate for Children and Young People*, London: YJB.

Zedner, L. (1994), *Women, Crime and Custody in Victorian England*, Oxford: Clarendon Press.

—— (1995), 'Wayward sisters', in N. Morris and D. Rothman (eds), *The Oxford History of the Prison*, New York: Oxford University Press.

Zimring, F. E., and Hawkins, G. (1991), *The Scale of Imprisonment*, Chicago: Chicago University Press.

INDEX